American
Slang
Dictionary

American Slang Dictionary

The Ultimate Reference to Nonstandard Usage, Colloquialisms, Popular Jargon, and Vulgarisms

Richard A. Spears

McGraw·Hill

New York   Chicago   San Francisco   Lisbon   London   Madrid   Mexico City
Milan   New Delhi   San Juan   Seoul   Singapore   Sydney   Toronto

A hardcover version of this book was published as *McGraw-Hill's Dictionary of American Slang and Colloquial Expressions*.

2 3 4 5 6 7 8 9 10 11 12 13 14 15 16 17 18   FGR/FGR   0 9 8 7

ISBN-13: 978-0-07-146108-5
ISBN-10:   0-07-146108-6

Interior design by Terry Stone

McGraw-Hill books are available at special quantity discounts to use as premiums and sales promotions, or for use in corporate training programs. For more information, please write to the Director of Special Sales, Professional Publishing, McGraw-Hill, Two Penn Plaza, New York, NY 10121-2298. Or contact your local bookstore.

This book is printed on acid-free paper.

Contents

How to Use This Dictionary

- The dictionary is alphabetized word by word, rather than letter by letter.
- The entry words or phrases are not altered from their normal state. That is, you will find **have an ace up one's sleeve**, and not **ace up one's sleeve, have an**.
- When looking up a phrase, try to find it first in the body of the dictionary. If it is not found, look for a key word in the phrase in the **Index of Hidden Key Words**.
- Definitions of the terms and abbreviations used can be found on page xxv.
- A key to the International Phonetic Alphabet symbols used in the pronunciations can be found on page xxix.
- Each entry has at least one example sentence. Most of the examples show the entry word in a slang context. Some examples show the entry words in quotation marks, indicating that they are being used in a Standard English context. Both types are considered accurate portrayals of the use of individual slang terms.
- When looking for a slang word with a particular meaning, use the **Thematic Index**. It serves as a reverse index for slang and colloquial expressions.
- For a list of all the phrases containing a specific slang word, look up that word in the **Index of Hidden Key Words**.
- Because most racial matters in American slang relate to skin color, the vague terms *black* and *white* are used here. Only a very small number of terms relate to descendants of pre-Colombian native Americans, and the traditional term *American Indian* is used. *East Asian*, though inexact for the Pacific Rim peoples, is used in preference to *Asian*, which is far too broad.
- Slang words that appear in standard dictionaries can be considered to have standard spelling. There are many variations in the way that slang is spelled and hyphenated. There is no authority in this matter.

Introduction

What Is Slang?

The word *slang* is not a technical term. Although it is defined in dictionaries, it really does not have a definition that always makes it possible to distinguish a slang expression from other types of expressions. It is, in fact, an umbrella term that covers many kinds of informal expressions that people employ when they are not involved in producing edited writing in the world of formal communication. *Slang* is used in dictionary entries as a convenient label covering many kinds of words that one might not wish to include in the most serious and formal English, spoken or written. Other such labels, with other meanings, include *dialect*, *obsolete*, *substandard*, *vernacular*, and *vulgar*. Words bearing these labels, and others, are thought not to be as widely known or understood as the standard vocabulary being taught in schools. These labels are included in dictionaries of Standard English and are there to help people with *diction* or word choice.

The term *slang* has been used to refer to specialized vocabularies (*cant*, *jargon*, or *patter*) used among criminals, drug users, students, street people, hip-hoppers, video game players, surfboarders, bodybuilders, gamblers, journalists, aviators, food service workers, medical workers, military personnel, and on and on. Some of the expressions used by these groups get carried out of the group into wider use into what is called general or popular slang. These "escaped" expressions may broaden in meaning and become the basis for further development of even more general slang terms. For instance, going *cold turkey* in early drug slang referred to suddenly and totally stopping drugs. The term is now used in general slang with the broader meaning of stopping any habit or practice suddenly.

By the way, it should not be assumed that slang and Standard English are complete opposites. There are many slang terms that are as widely known and as long lasting as words in the standard vocabulary. Slang terms like **chicken** (coward), **beaucoup** (many), **breadbasket** (belly), **cabbage** (money), **canary** (informer), **mouthpiece** (lawyer), and **smashed** (drunk) are widely known slang terms, each of which has substantially the same meaning nationwide. All of them are at least half a century old, and each appears in *Merriam-Webster's Collegiate Dictionary, Tenth Edition*. In choosing vocabulary for use in formal Standard English, except for effect, slang is rarely the first choice.

Characteristics of Slang Meaning and Function

There are a number of observations that can be made about the types of words that have been called slang. Rather than being squeezed into a single long and complex definition, they appear in the following list. These observations have been made by dictionary compilers, teachers, writers, and scholars. These are the kinds of expressions found under the umbrella of *general slang*.

- Much of the general slang vocabulary is viewed as fun to hear and fun to use.
- Many slang expressions are synonyms of, or nicknames for, widely known, standard words and expressions. For instance, **crockery** for *teeth* or **magpie** for *chatterer*.
- Many of the slang and colloquial expressions for sexual and scatological matters are euphemistic for more direct terms. For instance, **poop** is less offensive than *shit* or *dung*. Many of the cute names for sexual parts, such as **blouse bunnies** and **melons** = breasts, are euphemistic in the sense that they can be used to lighten the mention of these parts.
- Other slang expressions are called dysphemisms. A neutral or good term is replaced by one with some degree of negativity. For example, **frog slicing** replaces *biology class*. "Food dirtying," such as *shit on a shingle*, represents another class of dysphemisms.
- Many slang terms are conundrums in that they can be understood by a clever person using context, setting, and native intelligence. Like riddles or word puzzles, they often contain enough information to allow a clever person to figure them out. For instance, when you hear "This coffee is bitter. Pass me the sand, will you?" you will probably

pass the sugar because it looks more like sand than anything else in the vicinity and will counteract bitterness. You will be right, **sand** = sugar.

- Some slang terms, often called *cant*, were not intended to be understood by the general public. Some in-group jargon and patter, such as with drug users, pickpockets, carnival workers, and middle school students, is meant to disguise what is being said so outsiders cannot understand it. A few examples are **merchandise** = contraband, **away** = in prison, **big fish** = crime boss.

- Many general slang terms are simply paraphrases of other slang terms with the same meaning. Typical of these thematic groupings are **cop, gaffle, glom, nick, pinch**. The words in the set each have the same (two in this case) meanings, here *steal* and *arrest*. Similar cases are **bacon, pig, pork, lard**, which are related in their standard meaning and also share the same single slang meaning, *police officer*.

- Many slang expressions involve some kind of word play and seem to entertain people, at least on first hearing. Some people enjoy seeing and hearing new slang just for fun, whether they ever intend to use it or not.

- Some slang is ephemeral within some of the groups that originate it (such as youth slang) but tends to live longer if it "escapes" and becomes general slang. Many terms for marijuana were originally devious terms of this type. **Grass, pot, ganjah, broc(coli), herb, hemp**, and many others fall into this category.

- Slang, informal sexual terms, and scatology all seem to obey the same exclusionary rules, that is, they tend to be avoided in polite and formal English to the same extent.

- Some slang can be described as *verbal weapons* because it is meant to insult or demean people.

- Slang appearing in a major newspaper is often in quotes and explained to the reader. Much general slang first meets the public eye showcased in this manner. For instance, *The youth described his car as "the bomb," meaning it is the best.*

- Slang is avoided in formal writing, academic writing, and writing intended to appear serious of purpose and reflect intellectual authority. It is less likely to be spoken on the speaker's platform (pulpit, etc.) than on the streets and in classroom hallways.

- Many slang expressions are typically used with an "attitude" and are created to raise eyebrows and provoke censure. They act as a foil to both the standard language and standards of behavior.

Characteristics of Slang Formation and Origins

In general slang there are often clues that help the hearer figure out what is being said. Understanding the patterns of slang formation can allow the pleasurable "figuring out" of slang terms. Given information about the setting, context, and cultural details, many slang and colloquial expressions can be understood even on first hearing. Here are some of the types of slang formation.

- Raw coinages, such as **moolah** (money). A completely new word is made up without reference to any part of an existing word. It is difficult to guess the meaning of a raw coinage.
- Rhyming compounds, such as **anchor-clanker** (sailor). The first and second words rhyme.
- Alliterative compounds, such as **bed-bunny** (easy woman). The initial letters of the two words are the same.
- Front clippings, such as **roni**. The front part or first syllable of a word is left off, in this case, *pepper*.
- Reinterpretations, such as **bumper sticker**. The existing term (meaning an adhesive sign for a car bumper) is applied to a new situation where it fits just as well, in this case to a *tailgater* = someone who follows a car too closely.
- Back clippings, such as **hydro**. The back part of a word is left off, in this case, *ponic*.
- Initialisms, such as **AWHFY**. The letters constitute an abbreviation that is not pronounced as one word but sounded out one by one. This one is an abbreviation of *Are we having fun yet?*
- Acronyms, such as **FISHMO**. The letters constitute an abbreviation that is pronounced as if it were an English word. This one is an

abbreviation of *Fuck it, shit happens, move on!* Most acronyms are not slang, however.

- Elaborations, such as **Kentucky fried**. The well-known brand of fried chicken is used as an elaboration of *fried*, meaning drunk or drug intoxicated.
- Suffixations, as with *tunage*. The suffix, *age*, is attached to the end of a word that retains its basic meaning, in this case *tune + age.*
- Spelling disguises, such as **phat**. An alternative spelling of a word is used. The respellings follow the English spelling patterns and are very easy to decode when seen in print. This is an unusual phenomenon for a spoken expression.
- Numerals and letters as words, such as **L8**, **CU**, and **CU2**. Letters or numbers that sound like words are used as words or parts of words: *late, see you, see you too.*
- Borrowings from a foreign word, such as **plonk**. This is from French [*vin*] *blanc.*
- Phonetic alphabets, such as **Adam Henry**. The words of the NATO "Phonetic Alphabet" are used to stand for an initialism that has a slang meaning. *Adam Henry > A.H. > asshole.* This is a word alphabet, not a phonetic alphabet.
- *Izzle*-words, such as **shizzle, hizzle, mizzle**. The initial letter of a standard word has the suffix *izzle* added. The process is attributed to Snoop Dogg, a hip-hop performer.
- Borrowings from Standard English, such as **heinous**. The entire standard term is used with the same meaning in a slang context. Its overuse and misuse make it seem like slang.
- Blends, such as **fantabulous**. Parts of two words are combined to make a new one.
- Extensions and exaggerations, such as **bambi, annihilated, animal**. The basic standard meaning is extended or exaggerated for effect. These examples mean *any deer, devastatingly drunk*, and *a crude and rude male.*

Many of us enjoy "presenting" a new slang term to a listener by slipping it into conversation. As listeners, many of us enjoy hearing a new slang term and figuring out what it means, using context, setting, and our own brain power. This element of social word play is primarily what attracts word-wise people to slang and what makes a dictionary of this type interesting reading as well as a reference work.

What Is Included in This Dictionary?

For an informal expression to be included in this dictionary, it should exemplify some of the characteristics in the previous list. Some slang dictionary compilers stipulate a rigid definition of slang and then exclude all the words that do not fit the definition. This compiler takes the somewhat more relaxed and less "scientific" position that expressions that are analogous to slang should be included if people are likely to look up such expressions in a slang and colloquial dictionary. Considerable pains have been taken to avoid including expressions that appear to have been created only for membership in lists of terms, although evidence of widespread (i.e., nationwide) use is not a requirement for inclusion. There are also some common colloquial expressions included that function similarly to slang. Some of the taboo terminology (sex and scatology) falls into this area. The average person is more likely to encounter general slang than the many additional slang terms belonging to the jargon and patter of specialized groups. This dictionary is about general slang, because that is what the reader is likely to hear or read in lunchrooms, bars, movies, streets, hallways, newspapers, books, radio, etc.

All slang dictionaries include expressions that are not considered to be slang by some people, and all these dictionaries also lack expressions that some people think should be included. This is the nature of trying to capture vocabulary that represents many kinds of social functions and many uneven patterns of dissemination.

What Is Meant by *Colloquial*?

Colloquial refers to conversation, particularly informal conversation. *Slang* and *colloquial* are similar in that they are thought of as more indicative of spoken language than formal, written language. In fact, some people might consider *slang* to be a special variety of *colloquial* speech. Colloquial expressions tend not to arise from in-group jargon or patter, and they are rarely entertaining conundrums, unlike *slang*. A word or expression could be excluded from use in Standard English because it sounds too informal and would therefore be called colloquial. This dictionary includes some of the colloquial expressions that are typically used side by side with slang.

Both slang and Standard English have received attention from scholars and chroniclers over the years, but there are many commonplace colloquial phrases that have fallen through the cracks. The availability of old movies opens up a new area for slang and colloquial research. Even more promising is the restoration of tens of thousands of radio programs dating from the mid-1930s. Imagine a lexicologist's excitement at hearing "You're the man!" in a 1937 episode of *Calling All Cars*, with exactly the same meaning and intonation that this very common phrase has in today's colloquial English. Of course, the street version, "You da man!" is better known to some.

Previous slang chroniclers have puzzled over deciding what the boundary between slang and colloquial is, if, in fact, there is one. In the past, they have devised titles that include words that hedge the issue, as in Farmer and Henley's *Slang and Its Analogues*, Eric Partridge's *A Dictionary of Slang and Unconventional English*, or Barrère and Leland's *A Dictionary of Slang, Jargon, and Cant*. This dictionary follows the tradition of naming a "gray area" that allows for the inclusion of expressions that look like slang but might not meet the compiler's personal definition of slang. There are dictionaries that deal with colloquial English without regard to whether it is slang or standard. For general conversational English, examine *Common American Phrases*, and for colloquial English in specific contexts, examine *NTC's Dictionary of Everyday American English Expressions*.

What Is Meant by *Idiom*?

Slang is not the same as *idiom*. *Idioms* are phrases in which the meaning of the phrase is not the same as the expected literal meaning of the sequence of individual words in the phrase, such as with *sitting on a gold mine*. This idiom is interesting because its literal meaning leads to a mental picture of someone seated atop a mine entrance labeled "gold." As an idiom, it means to be in control of a valuable asset. It is simply a phrase that must be interpreted nonliterally. Whereas figuring out the metaphor involved in an idiomatic expression may give the hearer the same kind of "reward" as figuring out that the slang **bacon** and **pig** mean "police officer," the idiom *sitting on a gold mine* is not slang. Other non-slang idioms are: *change one's tune, lead a dog's life, raised in a barn,* and *steaming mad.* Idioms that are also slang include: *spew one's guts out, dead from the neck up, do a job on someone,* and *ream someone out.*

Many slang phrases are also idiomatic, but *slang* and *idiom* refer to different aspects of words and expressions. *Slang* focuses on informality and the characteristics bulleted previously, whereas *idiomatic* refers to the nonliteral interpretation of a phrase. Some slang phrases are idioms, but all idioms are not slang. Only a small percentage of idiomatic expressions, such as *open a can of worms,* also have literal (mis)interpretations that could be considered entertaining. A good reference work for increasing understanding of American idioms is *McGraw-Hill's Dictionary of American Idioms and Phrasal Verbs.*

Who Is This Book For?

1. This book is for those who need to know what slang expressions mean. This includes students of English as a second language and foreign travelers in the U.S. or those planning to come to the U.S. An effort has been made to include additional cultural information for persons who are not steeped in American culture. It is for this reader that colloquial expressions have been included, especially vulgarisms that are used alongside slang in the examples. Another group that needs to know a slang word occasionally is the older American. Generally, seniors are excellent repositories of established slang, but they are baffled by the current crop of terms. This dictionary will help.
2. It is for those who read for curiosity or enjoyment and those who wish to look up a specific word they have heard somewhere. It is for

this group that a few devilishly clever but less common expressions have been included. The enjoyment of the linguistic creativity is encouraged here.

3. It is for writers and editors. This includes journalists and various other writers who are looking for confirmation of the meaning of a slang term or who are seeking a slang expression to liven up their writing. Toward serving this audience, this dictionary has a **Thematic Index** that allows the user to look up a Standard English word or phrase that leads to the slang expression for that standard meaning.

Point of View

The dictionary is compiled from general, popular sources (observation, video, and print) and not from within the groups that created the expressions. That means that the compiler did not spend a year in a middle school lunchroom or a year on the streets of L.A. or a year pacing the halls of a brothel—notebook in hand—or a year playing video games in the arcade or a year repeatedly falling off a skateboard somewhere. The search has been for generally available words that students, foreigners, and readers are likely to want to know about. The words listed here will not equip you with the vocabulary you need to become a hip-hop star, succeed as a popular teenager, or allow you to survive until dawn on the streets of a major U.S. city.

Usage cautions, such as "Usually objectionable" are made from the point of view of polite adults wishing to avoid offending people. Of course, these usage suggestions could not possibly apply to all people in all situations. The usage comments are suggestions for readers who recognize that some people object to scatology as well as racial and sexual epithets and appreciate having these matters pointed out. These usage comments are also intended to give guidance to persons learning about American language and culture. On the other hand, readers who use slang and colloquial terms exclusively and do not recognize these restrictions will view the usage comments as old-fashioned and stuffy.

Concerns About "Taboo"

"Taboo" as used here refers only to restrictions against using offensive words in polite company. It does not refer to a general, cultural taboo. Taboo words are words that many people avoid using in general audiences because they are, or can be interpreted as, offensive. Taboo words are not necessarily slang, but they are often treated as such. The rigorous study of words of this nature is a field in itself and is beyond the scope of a general slang dictionary. The subject matter of this dictionary includes both topics and words that many groups of people find objectionable for a variety of reasons. Personal sexual and excremental matters have long been considered private and not the subject of public discussion. Parallel to that are references to race, women, and a growing list of human types. There are nicknames and insults for all of these groups. It is not possible to list and define slang terms without dwelling on matters that are offensive to various groups of people.

The objection to so-called taboo words is not only to the harshness of the words themselves but to the fact that their very use represents a violation of etiquette. A search for the four-letter words in the **Hidden Key Word Index** will bring up lists of negative, insulting, and deliberately offensive terms and nicknames for people, in addition to the simple words themselves. These words represent effective "verbal weapons" that are far more important as such than their actual, basic negative references. Some of the terms were *meant* to hurt and offend. There is no reason for the reader to take any of these terms personally.

The word list of this dictionary includes the most common offensive terms, and they are defined as thoughtfully as possible. The example sentences, however, do display attitude, arrogance, and whatever rudeness is necessary for the purpose of showing how an expression can be used.

In general, the meaning of an expression will tell a lot about its appropriateness in a particular situation. If the guidance given is not up to the task, **avoid using the expression**. In the instances that a term has obvious malicious intent, that is noted in the entry. It should be pointed out that unfamiliar terms referring to women and minorities may be **assumed** to have malicious intent even though the term may only be teasing or humorous in the mind of the user.

Creation, Dispersion, and Life Cycle

Most of us have heard that language is always changing. Most of the change that we are aware of, however, is the addition of vocabulary items. Whereas the standard, literary form of the language is fairly resistant to change, slang and colloquial have no rules, goals, stylebooks, teachers, editors, or traditions that discourage innovation and word play. In fact, the remarkable thing about Standard English is the relative **lack** of change other than the admission of needed new vocabulary. People seem happy and eager, however, to take up new expressions and use them the way that other people seem to be using them. It is reminiscent of the middle school students who eagerly embrace any slang terms that they hear, simply to be accepted by their peers.

Some vocabulary changes are prescribed, such as *African-American* (for black or Negro), *Native American* (for Indian or American Indian), *Asian* (for Oriental), *he or she* (for the indeterminate [grammatical] gender he), and *chairperson* (for chairman). Other new or expanded uses of existing expressions seem to become popular as a matter of style, similar to the way that slang spreads. For instance, *gender* (for sex), *mentor* (for tutor, advisor, sponsor, advocate), *change out* (for exchange), *graphic* (for explicit violence or sex), *build-out* (for project completion), and *issue* (for problem). Whether these will continue to be used this way or simply fade away, as with the frequent use of *redux* in the 1990s, remains to be seen.

Slang expressions often spread in waves into wider use as with the word **issue** mentioned earlier, but they can get a boost from media and entertainment sources, which allow them to leapfrog through the country. Other innovative terms may drift around for decades before either dying out or suddenly breaking into more general use. Some slang terms are used only locally and may stay at home for their entire lives. Some, like *cool*, may be used for decades, take a decade off, and come back as strong as ever for another decade or so. How does a newly invented expression move into wider usage and even become general slang? Almost any answer one can conceive of will be correct for at least one slang expression. There is anecdotal evidence about how a word is faring in one place, but there is no similar information about how the same word is faring in all other places. No human being is in a position to observe all words at all locations over time.

Slang is normal and natural human linguistic creativity. It is mostly word play and the intelligent manipulation of sound and meaning for all sorts of social purposes, both worthy and unworthy. There are no stabilizing influences, such as grammars and stylebooks, to stifle creativity, limit expansion, or prevent the making of errors. There are dictionaries, of course, but no one is encouraged to consult them or to obey them if they do consult them. Users are free to innovate, make errors, and repeat misinterpretations that become new slang.

Slang is typically thought of as being a spoken phenomenon, although a few expressions are probably the product of the imaginations of writers. Slang is often described as ephemeral, meaning that it disappears almost as quickly as it is created. That is a gross overgeneralization. Much "contemporary" slang was created decades ago. The fastest changing slang is found among the young. Some youths use what can be called fad slang. The rapid replacement of one slang expression with another is typical of an age when children are developing socially. The need to be like others in the group and do what the others are doing is evidenced in their clothing and hairstyles and their informal language also. It would be impossible to write a useful dictionary of *only* fad slang or just the expressions in style in one place at the present time. It would change before the book was printed. In addition, a given word won't necessarily be at its peak with every group at the same time. It is possible, however, to compile a dictionary of the slang in general and popular use over the past few decades, and that is what has been done here.

General slang is not here today and gone tomorrow, however. Once a word has spread into general usage, it may be around for years. When it is recorded in movies that will be watched for decades, novels that will be read for years to come, newspaper archives, and the common usage of the population, it is assured a long life. Many of the slang terms known today have long histories of use and many records of use in print. A slang term is not dead until nobody uses it or encounters it any longer. Old-time radio and old movies, as well as printed sources, make slang expressions available to the general public. Much of it resides in the memories of people, available for an appropriate insertion into an utterance for special effect. It may live well over a century before it dies, buried with the memories of its last users.

History and Origins

We can describe words in terms of their origin, or etymology, and the history of their use through time. A typical dictionary etymology of a Standard English word shows the word's historical forms, including the forms that the word may have had in an earlier stage of the language or in some ancient language. Changes in meaning are also shown by giving examples of use of the word as found in print through the ages. Related words in other languages are also often shown. The history of a word is shown in a Standard English dictionary by showing dated examples of its appearance in print from its beginning to the present. The major dictionary of this type is the *Oxford English Dictionary*. Most slang follows a path of origin far different from the core vocabulary of Standard English.

There is very little English slang currently in use that comes from an older form of English. Slang terms almost always originate through a specific act of creation (or multiple acts of creation) and not through derivation from an earlier state of the language. The identity of the originator or instant of origin is rarely known. The "etymology" of a slang word is a statement of its allusions, form and meaning components, formation patterns, and domain of creation and use.

The history of a slang word would be a record of its use through time—when and where it was created, when it was first recorded, and when and *if* it became widespread and well known—and a record of its progression through the country. All we have of the distant past is what can be found in print. This means that the early use and the time of creation may be completely undocumented. Since slang and colloquial expressions are primarily spoken phenomena, even the earliest published examples of a slang word may or may not be close to the actual act originating the word. Even before a slang term is widespread and seen frequently in readily available printed material, the term may appear much earlier in an obscure source. Finding that source is hit or miss. Nonetheless, a very large amount of slang has appeared in print. There is a dictionary that shows the record of use of many American slang words that have been used in print. This detailed and exhaustive work, *Random House Historical Dictionary of American Slang*, shows dated citations of an amazing amount of slang used in print (and some film). The multivolume set (completed through volume two and the letter O) demonstrates that there has been abundant use of slang in print, although not as formal Standard English. This rigorous project shows that there are a large number of slang terms that have the same qualities of uniformity of meaning across the nation and through time as the vocabulary of Standard English. The reader also gets the idea that much of what we consider contemporary slang is much older than we thought.

Although *American Slang Dictionary* is about meaning, not dating usage, the origin of an expression is given where it is recognized. Most etymologies consist of spelling out how the expression was formed and listing the component forms or meanings.

New in the Fourth Edition

This completely revised and enlarged edition features more than 12,000 contemporary slang and colloquial senses in 9,400 entries. With approximately 900 new main entries, this fourth edition includes street slang, hip-hop terms, college terms, the usual scatology, sexual expressions, and the terms and abbreviations peculiar to the Internet. Arranged alphabetically, entries include additional usage information, slang type, source, allusions, meaning components, formation patterns, and other information about whether the term is, for example, objectionable, derogatory, or provocative. Pronunciation information is included for words that are not pronounced according to ordinary spelling-to-speech rules. The alphabetic arrangement is augmented by an **Index of Hidden Key Words**, making it possible for the user to find noninitial key words hidden within entry phrases. A new **Thematic Index** serves as a reverse English dictionary, allowing users to find a slang expression that matches a standard word or meaning. The body of the dictionary has many new cross-references to various entries with similar or same meanings.

References Mentioned in the Introduction

Barrère, Albert, and Charles G. Leland. *A Dictionary of Slang, Jargon, and Cant.* 1889–90. Two volumes. London: Ballantyne.

Farmer, John S., and W. E. Henley. *Slang and Its Analogues.* 1890–1904. Seven volumes. Published for subscribers at London and Edinburgh.

Lighter, J. E., et al. *Random House Historical Dictionary of American Slang, Volume I, A–G.* 1994. New York: Random House.

———. *Random House Historical Dictionary of American Slang, Volume II, H–O.* 1997. New York: Random House.

Mish, Frederick C., ed. *Merriam-Webster's Collegiate Dictionary, Tenth Edition.* 1998. Springfield, Massachusetts: Merriam-Webster.

Partridge, Eric. *A Dictionary of Slang and Unconventional English.* 8th ed. Paul Beale, ed. 1984. New York: Macmillan.

Simpson, J. A., and Weiner, Edmund S., eds. *The Oxford English Dictionary, Second Edition.* 1989. Twenty volumes. Clarendon: Oxford University Press.

Spears, Richard A. *Common American Phrases in Everyday Contexts.* 2nd ed. 2002. New York: McGraw-Hill.

———. *McGraw-Hill's Dictionary of American Idioms and Phrasal Verbs.* 2004. New York: McGraw-Hill.

———. *NTC's Dictionary of Everyday American English Expressions.* 1995. New York: McGraw-Hill.

Terms, Symbols, and Abbreviations

♦ marks the beginning of an example in the main dictionary and serves as a separator in the indexes.

[ ] enclose parts of a definition that aid in its understanding but are not represented in the entry head.

abb. abbreviation, referring to both acronyms and initialisms.

acronym a kind of abbreviation where the initial letters or syllables of the words of a phrase are combined into a pronounceable word, such as GIGO = garbage in, garbage out.

AND indicates that additional variants follow.

black people of African descent and other dark-skinned people.

cliché an overly-familiar and trite phrase.

comp. abb. computer abbreviation, the initialisms and acronyms used in computer communication, such as email and instant messaging.

digitus impudicus the Latin term for the raised middle finger, the *rude finger* or simply "the finger."

East Asian a person who is Chinese, Japanese, Korean, or a citizen of a Southeast Asian country or the Pacific islands.

exclam. an exclamation.

Go to indicates that the information you want is at the entry listed after **Go to**. Leave this entry and go to the one indicated.

in. an intransitive verb or a phrase containing a intransitive verb.

initialism a kind of abbreviation where the initial letters of the words in a phrase are pronounced one by one, such as BCNU = Be seein' you.

interj. an interjection.

interrog. an interrogative.

jargon the specialized vocabulary, including phrases, belonging to a particular occupation or to the a group of workers engaged in a particular occupation.

mod. a modifier of some type, such as an adjective or adverb.

n. noun or noun phrase.

NATO Phonetic Alphabet is a kind of verbal spelling where a complete word is used rather than the letter name. The letter being spelled is the first letter of the word uttered. Thus Bravo, Alfa, Delta is BAD. The complete list is Alfa, Bravo, Charlie, Delta, Echo, Foxtrot, Golf, Hotel, India, Juliet, Kilo, Lima, Mike, November, Oscar, Papa, Quebec, Romeo, Sierra, Tango, Uniform, Victor, Whiskey, X-ray, Yankee, Zulu. This is not really a phonetic alphabet but is rather a *letter alphabet*. It is NATO because it has been adopted by the military of each member country of NATO.

patter the slang and colloquial expressions used constantly by a particular group, including the young, thieves, and barkers. Similar to jargon, except that the latter focuses more on vocabulary.

phr. a phrase.

pro. a pronoun.

See also indicates that there is additional information at the entry listed after **See also**. Consult or consider the entry indicated. It is not required that you visit the indicated entry to understand the current entry. **See also** does not mean "synonymous with" the entry indicated.

sent. a sentence.

so someone.

sth something.

streets slang associated with street gangs and the popular "gangsta" culture. Many elements are taken from the rap or hip-hop music scene.

taboo avoided in polite, formal, dignified, older, or refined settings.

term of address a word that can be used to address a person directly.

try AND **try also** suggests that you study the *index entry* listed to see if it is what you are looking for.

tv. a transitive verb or a phrase containing a transitive verb.

underworld slang from criminal and organized crime. Overlaps with **streets**.

white people of European descent and other light-skinned people.

Pronunciation Guide

Some expressions in the dictionary are followed by a phonetic transcription in International Phonetic Alphabet (IPA) symbols. These expressions include words whose pronunciations are not predictable from their spellings, difficult or unfamiliar words, and words where the stress placement is contrastive or unique. The style of pronunciation reflected here is informal and tends to fit the register in which the expression would normally be used. A [d] is used for the alveolar flap typical in American pronunciations such as [wɑdɚ] "water" and [ə'naɪələdəd] "annihilated." The transcriptions distinguish between [ɑ] and [ɔ] and between [w] and [ʍ] even though not all Americans do so. In strict IPA fashion, [j] rather than the [y] substitute is used for the initial sound in "yellow." The most prominent syllable in a multisyllabic word is *preceded* by a [']. The use of AND or OR in a phonetic transcription echoes the use of AND or OR in the preceding entry phrase. The use of "..." in a transcription indicates that easy-to-pronounce words have been omitted. Parentheses used in a transcription either correspond to parentheses in the preceding entry phrase or indicate optional elements in the transcription. For instance, in ['ɑrtsi 'kræf(t)si] "artsy-craftsy," the "t" may or may not be pronounced. The following chart shows the American English values for each of the IPA symbols used in the phonetic transcriptions. To use the chart, first find the large phonetic symbol whose value you want to determine. The two English words to the right of the symbol contain examples of the sound for which the phonetic symbol stands. The letters in **boldface** type indicate where the sound in question is found in the English word.

[ɑ]	stop top	[ɚ]	bird turtle	[n]	new funny	[tʃ]	cheese pitcher
[æ]	sat track	[f]	feel if	[n̩]	button kitten	[θ]	thin faith
[ɑu]	cow now	[g]	get frog	[ŋ]	bring thing	[u]	food blue
[ɑɪ]	bite my	[h]	hat who	[o]	coat wrote	[ʊ]	put look
[b]	beet bubble	[i]	feet leak	[oɪ]	spoil boy	[v]	save van
[d]	dead body	[ɪ]	bit hiss	[ɔ]	caught yawn	[w]	well wind
[ð]	that those	[j]	yellow you	[p]	tip pat	[ʍ]	wheel while
[dʒ]	jail judge	[k]	can keep	[r]	rat berry	[z]	fuzzy zoo
[e]	date sail	[l]	lawn yellow	[s]	sun fast	[ʒ]	pleasure treasure
[ɛ]	get set	[l̩]	bottle puddle	[ʃ]	fish sure	[']	'water ho'tel
[ə]	but nut	[m]	family slam	[t]	top pot		

Numerical Entries

10-4 Go to ten-four.™

20/20 hindsight Go to twenty-twenty hindsight.

24-7 Go to twenty-four, seven.

4 real *mod.* for real. ◆ *R U 4 real?*

404 Go to four-oh-four.

411 Go to four-one-one.

4-banger *n.* a four-cycle engine. (See also banger.) ◆ *Your 4-banger shouldn't be so loud. How's the muffler?*

5-O Go to five-oh.

773H Go to seven-seven-three-aitch.

86 Go to eighty-six.

A-1 AND **A number 1** *mod.* of the highest rating. ♦ *This steak is really A-1!*

A2O Go to apples to oranges.

AAMOF Go to as a matter of fact.

abandominiums *n.* abandoned apartments used by drug addicts to take crack. (Contrived and forced.) ♦ *Row after row of abandominiums lined the once proper middle-class neighborhood.*

abbreviated piece of nothing *n.* an insignificant person or thing. ♦ *Tell that abbreviated piece of nothing to get his tail over here, but fast.*

abe *n.* a five-dollar bill. (From the picture of Abraham Lincoln on the bill.) ♦ *This wine cost three abes. It had better be good.*

able to cut sth *tv.* able to manage or execute something. (Often negative.) ♦ *Do you think you're able to cut it?* ♦ *He's just not able to cut it.*

abolic *n.* anabolic steroids as used by veterinarians and abused by humans. ♦ *You keep taking in that abolic, and you'll swell up and die!*

(a)bout it *mod.* ready; knowledgeable; cool. (Black.) ♦ *Sam is smart. He's really about it.*

abs [æbz] *n.* the abdominal muscles. (Bodybuilding. See also six-pack; washboard abs.) ♦ *Look at the abs on that guy. Like a crossword puzzle!*

abso-bloody-lutely ['æbsobladi'lutli] *mod.* absolutely; emphatically. ♦ *We are abso-bloody-lutely sick to death of your wishy-washy attitude.*

absotively (posilutely) ['æbsə'tɪvli 'pazə'lutli] *mod.* absolutely; decidedly. ♦ *I will be there at ten, absotively posilutely.*

accidentally-on-purpose *mod.* deliberate, but meant to look like an accident. ♦ *Then I accidentally-on-purpose spilled water on him.*

AC-DC AND **AC/DC** *mod.* bisexual. (Older. Initialism.) ♦ *I didn't realize at first that we were in an AC-DC bar!* ♦ *He was reported to be "AC/DC" by a member of the press.*

ace 1. *mod.* [of persons] best; top-rated. ♦ *She is an ace reporter with the newspaper.* **2.** *n.* one dollar. ♦ *It only costs an ace. Buy two.* **3.** *tv.* to pass a test easily, with an A grade. (See also ace out.) ♦ *I knew I wouldn't ace it, but I never thought I'd flunk it!* **4.** *n.* a nickname for a foolish and ineffectual person. (Sarcastic. Usually a term of address.) ♦ *Hey, ace, hand me that monkey wrench—if you know what one is.* **5.** *tv.* to surpass someone or something; to beat someone or something; to ace so out. ♦ *The Japanese firm aced the Americans by getting the device onto the shelves first.*

ace boom-boom AND **ace boon-coon** *n.* one's good and loyal friend. (Black. Ace boon-coon is not as common as the first entry and is objected to because of *coon*.) ♦ *Hey girlfriend, you are my ace boom-boom.* ♦ *Where is my old ace boon-coon, bro?*

ace boon-coon Go to ace boom-boom.

ace in the hole *n.* something important held in reserve. ♦ *Mary's beautiful singing voice was her ace in the hole in case everything else failed.*

ace in(to sth) *in.* to happen onto something good; to manage to get into something. ♦ *I hope I can ace into the afternoon physics class.*

ace out *in.* to be fortunate or lucky. ♦ *I really aced out on that test in English.*

ace so **out** *tv.* to maneuver someone out; to win out over someone. (See also **aced**; **ace**.) ♦ *Martha aced out Rebecca to win the first-place trophy.*

aced 1. *mod.* outmaneuvered; outscored. ♦ *"You are aced, sucker!" shouted Rebecca as she passed Martha in the 100-yard sprint.* **2.** *mod.* alcohol intoxicated. ♦ *How can anybody be so aced on three beers?*

acid *n.* lysergic acid diethylamide (LSD). (Drugs.) ♦ *Freddy got hold of some bad acid and freaked out.*

action 1. *n.* excitement; activity in general; whatever is happening. ♦ *This place is dull. I want some action!* **2.** *n.* a share of something; a share of the winnings or of the booty. (See also **piece (of the action)**.) ♦ *I did my share of the work, and I want my share of the action.* **3.** *n.* sex; copulation. ♦ *All those guys are just trying for a little action.* **4.** *n.* illegal activity; commerce in drugs; acts of crime. (Underworld.) ♦ *Things have been a little slow here, but there's some action on the East Coast.*

activated *mod.* tipsy; alcohol intoxicated. ♦ *All four of them went out and got a little activated.*

Adam *n.* MDMA (3-4 methylenedioxymethamphetamine), Ecstasy. (Drugs. See also the unrelated **up an' Adam**.) ♦ *She spent the early part of the evening trying to score some Adam.*

Adam Henry *n.* an AH = asshole, = jerk. Treated as a name. ♦ *Why don't you get some smarts, Adam Henry?*

addict *n.* someone showing a strong preference for something or someone. (Not related to drug addiction.) ♦ *Sam is a real opera addict. He just loves the stuff.*

addy *n.* address. ♦ *What's your addy so I can send you an invitation?*

adios muchachos [ɑdi'os mu'tʃɑtʃos] *tv.* good-bye everyone, it's the end for you. (Spanish.) ♦ *If you step out in front of a car like that again, it's adios muchachos.*

adobe dollar [ə'dobi 'dɑlɚ] *n.* a Mexican peso. ♦ *How many of these adobe dollars does it take to buy a can of pop here?*

AFAIK *phr.* as far as I know. (Acronym. Computers and the Internet.) ♦ *Everything is okay with the server, AFAIK.*

African golf ball AND **African grape** *n.* a watermelon. (Alludes to an early stereotype of Americans of African descent being very fond of watermelon. Forced, contrived, and demeaning.) ♦ *When he said we were having African grapes for dessert, I though he meant sherbet.* ♦ *Look at the size of that African golf ball!*

African grape Go to African golf ball.

Afro AND **fro** *n.* a hairdo, sometimes worn by American blacks, where the hair appears to be a large puffy ball. (From *African*.) ♦ *Man, I thought Afros went out in the sixties!* ♦ *This rain's gonna ruin my fro!*

After while(, crocodile). *phr.* Good-bye till later.; See you later. (*Crocodile* is used only for the sake of the rhyme. This is the response to See you later, alligator.) ♦ MARY: *See you later.* BILL: *After while, crocodile.*

ag AND **aggro** *mod.* aggrivated = irritated: annoyed. ♦ *Hey, man. Don't get yourself so aggro!* ♦ *She said she was too "ag" to help with the dishes.*

aggie ['ægi] **1.** *mod.* agricultural. ♦ *She spent a year at some aggie college, but didn't like it.* **2.** *n.* a student of an agricultural (college) training program. (Specifically, Texas A&M) ♦ *More and more aggies are going back for their MBAs.* **3.** *n.* an agricultural futures contract. (Securities markets. Usually plural.) ♦ *The March aggies are looking good right now.* **4.** *n.* an agate marble or a glass imitation of one. ♦ *I found the old aggies I played with when I was a kid.*

AH *n.* an asshole; a really wretched person. (A euphemistic disguise. Also a term of address. Rude and derogatory.) ♦ *Look here, you goddamn AH! Who the hell do you think you are?*

A-hole *n.* an asshole, a very stupid or annoying person. (Usually refers to a male. Rude and derogatory.) ♦ *Tom can be an A-hole before he's had his coffee.*

AI Go to **As if!**

aight *mod.* all right. (Streets.) ♦ *Aight, my bruva, aight, aight.*

AIIC Go to **As if I care!**

aim for the sky AND **reach for the sky; shoot for the sky** *in.* to aspire to something; to set one's goals high. (See a different sense at **reach for the sky.**) ♦ *Shoot for the sky, son. Don't settle for second best.* ♦ *Don't settle for less. Reach for the sky!*

ain't 1. *in.* is not. (Colloquial. Stigmatized, jocular, mock undereducated, as well as undereducated use. Its use is widespread and sometimes deliberate in educated spoken use and when writing for effect. Properly an old contraction of *am not* or *are not.* The battle against *ain't* was lost at least two centuries ago but is still fought in isolated areas. See also **If it ain't broke don't fix it.; If it ain't broke, fix it till it is.; That ain't hay!; There ain't no such thing as a free lunch.**) ♦ *Saying "Ain't ain't in the dictionary" ain't so.*

ain't long enough *phr.* of a sum of money that isn't adequate; without adequate funds. (Streets.) ♦ *I can't go with you. I ain't long enough.*

air ball *n.* a basketball throw that misses everything, especially the basket. ♦ *Old Fred has become a master with the air ball. The net will never get worn out.*

air biscuit *n.* a breaking of wind; a fart. (See also **cut a muffin.**) ♦ *Who is responsible for that air biscuit?*

air guitar *n.* an imaginary guitar, played along with real music. ♦ *Jed, who sees himself as some sort of rock star, plays air guitar when he's happy or sad.*

air hose *n.* invisible socks; no socks. ♦ *How do you like my new air hose? One size fits all.*

air kiss *n.* a kiss that is placed on the inside of the fingers of one's hand then "blown" to the recipient who is likely to be some distance away. ♦ *A mass of air kisses drifted down to the wharf from the passengers departing on the huge* Titanic.

air one's belly *tv.* to empty one's stomach; to vomit. ♦ *That must have been some party. I heard you airing your belly for most of the night, after you got home.*

air one's pores *tv.* to undress oneself; to become naked. ♦ *I'm fixing to air my pores and take a shower.*

air-bags *n.* the lungs. ♦ *Fill those air-bags with good Colorado air!*

airbrain Go to **airhead.**

airhead AND **airbrain** *n.* a stupid person. (Someone with air where there should be brains.) ♦ *Some airbrain put mustard in the ketchup dispenser.* ♦ *Bart seems like such an airhead, but he's all heart.*

airheaded *mod.* stupid; giddy. (A head full of air.) ♦ *You are the most airheaded twit I have ever met!*

airish *mod.* [of the weather] chilly or briskly cool. ♦ *It's airish enough to freeze the brass off a bald monkey!*

airy-fairy *mod.* insubstantial; of wishful thinking. ♦ *I don't care to hear any more of your airy-fairy ideas.*

ak AND **ok** [ɑk] *n.* October. (Securities markets: options and futures trading.) ♦ *When the oks expire on Friday, we'll start looking at the dec index.* ♦ *I told him to buy the "aks," or Octobers, and he looked at me like I was crazy!*

alchy AND **alkie; alky** ['ælki] **1.** *n.* alcohol; an alcoholic beverage. ♦ *The crooks stole most of the alchy from the bar at the club.* ♦ *My great-grandfather made his own "alky" during prohibition.* **2.** *n.* a drunkard. ♦ *You see alchy after alchy all up and down Maxwell Street.*

alike as (two) peas in a pod Go to **(as) alike as (two) peas in a pod.**

alkie Go to **alchy.**

alkied (up) *mod.* alcohol intoxicated. ♦ *That old bum looks completely alkied up.*

alky Go to **alchy.**

all meat and no potatoes Go to all (that) meat and no potatoes.

All options stink. AND **AOS** *phr. & comp. abb.* All options stink.; There is no good solution. ♦ *I don't know what to do. All options stink.* ♦ *Since AOS, I'll do nothing at all.*

all over so **like a cheap suit** *phr.* pawing and clinging; seductive. (A cheap suit might *cling* to its wearer.) ♦ *She must have liked him. She was all over him like a cheap suit.*

all over sth *mod.* very fond of something. ♦ *Dave is all over old bikes.*

all right 1. *interj.* yes; okay. ♦ *All right. I'll do it.* **2.** *mod.* for sure; for certain. ♦ *He's the one who said it, all right.* **3.** *mod.* okay. (This is hyphenated before a nominal. Slang when used before a nominal.) ♦ *Willy is an all-right guy.* **4.** *exclam.* That's good!; Keep it up! (A general expression of approval, often cried out from the audience during a performance or at applause time. Usually **All right!** The *right* is drawn out and falling in pitch.) ♦ *"All right!" cried the crowd when they heard the announcement about the pay increase.*

All right already! AND **All righty already!** *phr.* All right!; Okay. (The second version is more comical than rude.) ♦ *All right already! Stop pushing me!*

all sharped up *mod.* dressed up; looking sharp. ♦ *Chuckie, my man, you are totally sharped up.*

(all) shook up *mod.* excited; disturbed; upset. ♦ *They were pretty shook up after the accident.*

all show and no go *phr.* equipped with good looks but lacking action or energy. (Used to describe someone or something that looks good but does not perform as promised.) ♦ *That shiny car of Jim's is all show and no go.*

All systems are go. *sent.* Everything is ready or things are going along as planned. (Borrowed from the jargon used during America's early space exploration.) ♦ BILL: *Can we leave now? Is the car gassed up and ready?* TOM: *All systems are go. Let's get going.*

all that and then some *phr.* everything mentioned and even more. ♦ Q: *Did she say all those terrible things so that everyone could hear her?* A: *All that and then some.*

all that jazz *n.* all that stuff; all that nonsense. ♦ *She told me I was selfish, hateful, rude, ugly, and all that jazz.*

all (that) meat and no potatoes *phr.* said of a tremendously fat person. (Rude.) ♦ *Look at that guy—all meat and no potatoes.*

all the way *mod.* with everything on it, as with a hamburger. (See also go all the way.) ♦ *I'd like one double cheeseburger—all the way.*

all the way live *mod.* very exciting; excellent. ♦ *Oh, Tiffany is just, like, all the way live!*

all wet *mod.* completely wrong. ♦ *Wrong! Wrong! You're all wet!*

alley apple 1. *n.* a piece of horse manure. (See also road apple.) ♦ *The route of the parade was littered with alley apples after about twenty minutes.* **2.** *n.* a brick or stone found in the rubble of the streets. ♦ *Kelly kicked an alley apple so that it struck a garbage can with a crash.*

alligator AND **gator** *n.* a long, heavy, black segment of the outside of a tire, usually a truck tire, found on the highway. ♦ *We dodged off onto the shoulder to avoid running over an alligator.* ♦ *A gator bashed in the bottom of my gas tank.*

all-nighter 1. *n.* something that lasts all night, like a party or study session. ♦ *After an all-nighter studying, I couldn't keep my eyes open for the test.* **2.** *n.* a place of business that is open all night. ♦ *We stopped at an all-nighter for a cup of coffee.* **3.** *n.* a person who often stays up all night. ♦ *I'm no all-nighter. I need my beauty sleep, for sure.*

Alpha Charlie *n.* a bawling out; a severe scolding. (Based on *AC* = **ass-chewing**. NATO Phonetic Alphabet.) ♦ *The cop* *stopped me and gave me a real Alpha Charlie for speeding.*

alphabet soup *n.* initialisms and acronyms in general. ♦ *Just look at the telephone book! You can't find anything because it's filled with alphabet soup.*

Am I right? *interrog.* Isn't that so?; Right? (A way of demanding a response and stimulating further conversation.) ♦ *You want to make something of yourself. Am I right?*

ambulance chaser AND **chaser 1.** *n.* a lawyer or entrepreneur who hurries to the scene of an accident to try to get the business of any injured persons. ♦ *The insurance companies are cracking down on ambulance chasers.* ♦ *A chaser got here before the ambulance, even.* **2.** *n.* a derogatory term for any lawyer. (Also a rude term of address.) ♦ *That ambulance chaser is trying to charge me for reaching his office when I called a wrong number!* ♦ *Three-hundred dollars an hour for what? You two-bit chaser!*

Ameche *n.* telephone. (Very old slang. From the name of actor Don Ameche, who starred in the film *The Story of Alexander Graham Bell*, 1939.) ♦ *Won't somebody please answer the Ameche?*

amigo [ə'migo] *n.* a friend. (Spanish. Also a term of address.) ♦ *Hey, amigo, let's go somewhere for a drink.*

ammo ['æmo] **1.** *n.* ammunition. ♦ *There they were, trapped in a foxhole with no ammo, enemy all over the place. What do you think happened?* **2.** *n.* information or evidence that can be used to support an argument or a charge. ♦ *I want to get some ammo on the mayor. I think he's a crook.*

ammunition 1. *n.* toilet tissue. ♦ *Could somebody help me? We're out of ammunition in here!* **2.** *n.* liquor. (See also **shot.**) ♦ *He's had about all the ammunition he can hold.*

amped 1. *mod.* high on methamphetamine. ♦ *She is so amped that she could fly!* **2.** *mod.* excited. ♦ *Don't get so amped! Chill!* **3.** *mod.* angry. ♦ *I got so amped, I nearly hit him.*

amps *n.* amphetamines. (Drugs.) ♦ *I never do any drugs except maybe a few amps now and then, and the odd downer, and maybe a little grass on weekends, but nothing really hard.*

anal applause *n.* the release of intestinal gas. (Jocular.) ♦ *Who is responsible for this pungent anal applause?*

anchor-clanker *n.* a sailor. (Army.) ♦ *How can you anchor-clankers stand being cooped up on those cans?*

ancient history *n.* someone or something completely forgotten, especially past romances. (See also **history.**) ♦ *That business about joining the army is ancient history.*

and a half *n.* someone or something greater, more severe, or more intense than normal. ♦ *This computer problem is a mess and a half!*

and change *phr.* plus a few cents; plus a few hundredths. (Used in citing a price or other decimal figure to indicate an additional fraction of a full unit.) ♦ *The New York Stock Exchange was up seven points and change for the third broken record this week.*

And how! *exclam.* I agree! ♦ BILL: *I am pleased you are here.* BOB: *Me, too! And how!*

and stuff like that (there) *n.* and other things similar to what was just mentioned. ♦ *Please gather up all the empty bottles, the picnic things, and stuff like that there.*

And your point is? AND **AYPI** *sent. & comp. abb.* Please get to the point.; What is your point? ♦ *I read all that stuff, AYPI?* ♦ *Yada, yada, yada! And your point is?*

angel 1. *n.* a secret financier. ♦ *I was hoping for an angel to see this project through, but all the fat-cats seem to have disappeared.* **2.** *n.* a sweetheart. (Also a term of address.) ♦ *Okay, angel, let's get in the car.* **3.** *n.* a sniper hiding in a high place, such as on the roof of a building. ♦ *The guards looked upward, watching for angels.* **4.** *n.* 1,000 feet of altitude, in flight. ♦ *At about eighteen angels, we began to level out.*

angel dust AND **angel hair; dust of angels** *n.* the common name for phencyclidine (PCP). (Originally drugs.) ♦ *I thought that angel hair and stuff like that was a problem of the sixties.* ♦ *He had a bit of a problem with some "dust of angels." It almost killed him.*

angel hair Go to angel dust.

angle 1. *n.* a person's understanding of something; someone's unique perspective on an event or happening. ♦ *What Bob says is interesting. What's your angle on this, Molly?* **2.** *n.* a scheme or deception; a pivotal or critical feature of a scheme; the gimmick in a scheme or plot. ♦ *I got a new angle to use in a con job on the old guy.*

animal *n.* a male who acts like a beast in terms of manners, cleanliness, or sexual aggressiveness. (Also a term of address. See also party animal, study animal.) ♦ *Stop picking your nose, animal.*

ankle 1. *n.* an attractive woman or girl. (Typically with *some*.) ♦ *Now, there's some ankle I've never seen around here before.* **2.** *in.* to walk [somewhere]. ♦ *I have to ankle down to the drugstore.* **3.** *in.* to walk away from one's employment; to leave. (See also walk.) ♦ *I didn't fire her. I told her she could ankle if she wanted.*

ankle biter Go to rug rat.

annihilated *mod.* very drunk; intoxicated with a drug. ♦ *Pete and Gary went out and got annihilated.*

another peep (out of you) *n.* another complaint, word, or sound from someone. (Usually in the negative.) ♦ *I don't want to hear another peep out of you!*

ante ['ænti] **1.** *n.* an amount of money that must be contributed before playing certain card games such as poker. (See also penny-ante.) ♦ *That's a pretty high ante. Forget it!* **2.** *n.* the charge or cost. ♦ *What's the ante for a used 1985 four-door?*

anti ['ænti OR 'æntɑɪ] **1.** *n.* someone who is against someone or something. ♦ *All the antis are going to vote for it this time.* **2.** *mod.* against someone or something. (Sometimes with the force of a preposi-tion.) ♦ *I'm not anti the proposal, I just have some questions.*

anticipointment *n.* a disappointment about something that has been anticipated. (Contrived.) ♦ *The fans really suffered a severe anticipointment when the knuckleheads came up with nada after four quarters of lackluster play.*

antifreeze *n.* liquor; any legal or illegal alcohol. ♦ *With enough antifreeze, I can stand the cold.*

antifreezed *mod.* alcohol intoxicated. ♦ *He appears to be frozen even though he's antifreezed.*

antsy ['æntsi] *mod.* nervous; restless. (See also have ants in one's pants.) ♦ *She gets antsy before a test.*

Anytime. *interj.* You are welcome.; Happy to oblige. (Sometimes said in response to *Thank you*.) ♦ MARY: *Thanks for the ride.* PAUL: *Anytime. Think nothing of it.*

A-OK *mod.* in the best of condition. ♦ *I really feel A-OK.*

AOS Go to All options stink.

ape *n.* a hoodlum or strong-arm man, especially if big and strong. (Underworld.) ♦ *Tell your ape to let me go!*

ape hangers *n.* long steering handles on a bicycle or motorcycle. ♦ *Who is that guy riding the bike with ape hangers?*

aped [ept] *mod.* alcohol intoxicated. ♦ *I've never seen my brother so totally aped before.*

apeshit 1. *mod.* excited; freaked out. (See also go apeshit over so/sth. Usually objectionable.) ♦ *He was so apeshit about that dame!* **2.** *mod.* drunk. (Acting as strangely or comically as an ape.) ♦ *The guy was really apeshit. Couldn't even stand up.*

app *n.* an application; a computer software application. ♦ *Ted's killer app can run circles around your old WordSun program.*

apple 1. *n.* a baseball. ♦ *Jim slammed the apple over the plate, but the ump called it a ball.* **2.** *n.* an American Indian who behaves more like a European than an Indian. (Like the apple, the person is red on the outside and white on the inside. Patterned on oreo. See also banana. Rude and derogatory.) ♦ *Stop acting like an apple all the time!* **3.** *n.* a breast. (Usually plural. Usually objectionable.) ♦ *Look at the firm little apples on that girl!*

apple-polisher *n.* a flatterer. ♦ *Everybody at the office seems to be an apple-polisher but me.*

apples to oranges AND **A2O** *phr. & comp. abb.* [but that's comparing] apples to oranges; [You are] making an unfair comparison. ♦ *Chevvies and Beemers! That's apples to oranges! They're not even in the same class!* ♦ *It's A2O! What can I say?*

applesauce *n.* nonsense. ♦ *That's just applesauce!*

arb [ɑrb] *n.* an arbitrageur; a market speculator. (Securities markets.) ♦ *I wanted to be an arb, but it takes about forty million to get in the door.*

Are we away? *interrog.* Shall we go?; Let's go. (Really a command to depart expressed as a question.) ♦ *The car's warmed up. Are we away?*

Are we having fun yet? AND **AWHFY** *sent. & comp. abb.* This isn't the fun that you stated or implied it would be, is it? ♦ *Are we having fun yet? This is really dull.* ♦ *Gr8t d8t! AWHFY?*

(Are you) ready for this? *interrog.* Are you prepared to hear this news? (A way of presenting a piece of news or information that is expected to excite or surprise the person spoken to.) ♦ *Boy, do I have something to tell you! Are you ready for this?*

areous *n.* [an] area. (Streets.) ♦ *Keep that baby gangsta outa ma areous!*

ark [ɑrk] *n.* an old car. ♦ *Why don't you get rid of that old ark and get something that's easier to park?*

arm *n.* a police officer. (Underworld. See also long arm of the law.) ♦ *What'll you do if the arms come in while you're sawing the bars of your cell?*

armpit *n.* any undesirable place. (A nickname for an undesirable town or city.) ♦

The town should be called the armpit of the nation.

arm-twister *n.* someone who uses strong persuasion. ♦ *I hate to seem like an arm-twister, but I really need your help on this project.*

arm-twisting *n.* powerful persuasion. ♦ *If nice talk won't work, try a little arm-twisting.*

army brat *n.* a child born to a parent in the army. (Such a child will live in many different places.) ♦ *I was an army brat and went to seven different schools before I got out of high school.*

(a)round the bend 1. *mod.* crazy; beyond sanity. ♦ *I think I'm going around the bend.* **2.** *mod.* alcohol or drug intoxicated. ♦ *From the look in her eye, I'd say she is completely round the bend now.*

artillery 1. *n.* handguns; grenades. (Underworld.) ♦ *Where does Frank stash the artillery?* **2.** *n.* flatware; cutlery. ♦ *Who put out the artillery? I didn't get a fork.*

artist *n.* a combining form meaning *specialist.* For specific meanings go to booze artist; bullshit artist; burn artist; castor oil artist; con artist; flimflam artist; hype artist; make-out artist; off artist; (rip-)off artist; take-off artist.

artsy (fartsy) *mod.* obviously or overly artistic; effete. (Mildly offensive.) ♦ *The decorations were sort of artsy fartsy, but the overall effect was quite nice.*

artsy-craftsy *mod.* dabbling in arts and crafts; artistic. ♦ *The artsy-craftsy crowd held a show in the library parking lot last Sunday.*

as a matter of fact AND **AAMOF** *phr. & comp. abb.* actually; in fact. ♦ *AAMOF, Bob just came in.* ♦ *As a matter of fact, he's right here. You want to talk to him?*

(as) alike as (two) peas in a pod *phr.* very similar. (The peas in a pod are essentially identical.) ♦ *The twins are as alike as two peas in a pod.*

(as) clear as mud *mod.* not understandable at all. ♦ *All of this is clear as mud to me.*

(as) clear as vodka 1. *mod.* very clear. ♦ *The river wasn't exactly as clear as vodka because it had just rained.* **2.** *mod.* very understandable. (Often used sarcastically.) ♦ *Everything he said is as clear as vodka.*

(as) close as stink on shit *phr.* very close; intimate; inseparable. ♦ *In love? He's as close to her as stink on shit.*

(as) dull as dishwater *mod.* very dull. ♦ *Life can be as dull as dishwater.*

(as) fat as a beached whale *phr.* very, very fat. ♦ *That dame is as fat as a beached whale.*

(as) fresh as a daisy *mod.* someone who is always alert and ready to go. ♦ *How can you be fresh as a daisy so early in the morning?*

(as) gay as pink ink *mod.* having to do with an obviously homosexual person, usually a male. ♦ *These two guys—as gay as pink ink—came in together.*

As if! AND **AI** *exclam.* an expression said when someone says something that is not true but wishes that it were. (Also, and perhaps usually, sarcastic.) ♦ *A: I've got a whole lot of good qualities. B: AI!* ♦ *My hair should look like a pile of wet thatch? As if!*

As if I care! AND **AIIC** *exclam. & comp. abb.* What has led you to believe that I care at all? (See also **As if!**) ♦ *So he left you. AIIC!* ♦ *So, some hairdresser jerk dyed your hair orange! As if I care!*

(as) jober as a sudge [ˈdʒobɚ æz ə ˈsədʒ] *mod.* sober. (A deliberate spoonerism on (as) sober as a judge.) ♦ *Me? I'm as jober as a sudge.*

(as) nutty as a fruitcake *mod.* very silly or stupid. ♦ *The whole idea is as nutty as a fruitcake.*

(as) phony as a three-dollar bill AND **(as) queer as a three-dollar bill** *mod.* phony; bogus. ♦ *The whole deal stinks. It's as queer as a three-dollar bill.* ♦ *Stay away from him. He's phony as a three-dollar bill.*

(as) queer as a three-dollar bill 1. Go to (as) phony as a three-dollar bill. **2.** *mod.* definitely or obviously homosexual. (Usually objectionable.) ♦ *That guy is as queer as a three-dollar bill.*

(as) right as rain *mod.* completely correct. ♦ *She was right as rain about the score.*

(as) sober as a judge *mod.* as sober (free from alcohol) as it is possible to be. ♦ *Kelly—who was starched as could be—claimed to be sober as a judge.*

(as) sure as hell *mod.* absolutely certain. ♦ *I'm sure as hell he's the one.*

as the white on rice Go to like the white on rice.

(as) tight as a tick 1. *mod.* very tight. ♦ *The windows were closed—tight as a tick—to keep the cold out.* **2.** *mod.* alcohol intoxicated. (An elaboration of **tight**.) ♦ *The host got tight as a tick and fell in the pool.*

(as) ugly as sin *mod.* very ugly. ♦ *This car's as ugly as sin, but it's cheap and dependable.*

asleep at the switch *mod.* inattentive to duty. (Not literal.) ♦ *Donald was asleep at the switch when the call came in.*

asphalt jungle *n.* the paved landscape of the city; the city viewed as a savage place. ♦ *I don't look forward to spending the rest of my days in an asphalt jungle.*

ass 1. *n.* the buttocks. (Usually objectionable.) ♦ *This big monster of a guy threatened to kick me in the ass if I didn't get out of the way.* **2.** *n.* women considered as sexual gratification. (Rude and derogatory.) ♦ *All he could think about was getting some ass.* **3.** *n.* one's whole body; oneself. (Usually objectionable.) ♦ *Your ass is really in trouble!*

ass is grass, so's Go to so's ass is grass.

ass out *mod.* broke. (Usually objectionable.) ♦ *I ain't got a cent. I'm ass out, man.*

ass over tit *mod.* [of someone falling] rolling and bounding over. (Usually objectionable.) ♦ *He fell, ass over tit, down the stairs.*

ass-chewing *n.* a bawling out. (See also Alpha Charlie. From chew so's ass out.) ♦ *If* he does it again, I'm going to give him one hell of an ass-chewing.

asshat 1. *n.* the imaginary garment worn by one with one's head up one's ass. (Offensive.) **2.** *n.* a person said to be wearing an **asshat** (sense 1). ◆ *Wake up you stupid asshat!*

asshole 1. *n.* the opening at the lower end of the large bowel; the anus. (Usually objectionable.) ◆ *I was so mad I could have kicked him in the asshole.* **2.** *n.* a worthless and annoying person. (Also a term of address. Rude and derogatory.) ◆ *Somebody get this asshole outa here before I bust in his face!*

ass-kicker Go to butt-kicker.

ass-kisser AND **ass-licker** *n.* a flatterer; an apple polisher; someone who would do absolutely anything to please someone. (Rude and derogatory.) ◆ *Sally is such an ass-kisser. The teacher must have figured her out by now.* ◆ *The rest of the guys thought he was an ass-licker for what he told the boss.*

ass-kissing AND **ass-licking 1.** *n.* the act of fawning over and flattering people. (Rude and derogatory.) ◆ *After his show of ass-kissing, Fred thought the judge would let him off with a light fine.* **2.** *n.* pertaining to the act of fawning over and flattering people. (Rude and derogatory.) ◆ *Shut your ass-licking mouth and start talking straight, or I'm gonna bust you one.* ◆ *Get your ass-kissing butt out of here!*

ass-licker Go to ass-kisser.

ass-licking Go to ass-kissing.

ass-wipe AND **butt-wipe 1.** *n.* a useless and annoying person. (Rude and derogatory.) ◆ *Get outa here, you ass-wipe!* ◆ *Who's the butt-wipe with that pile of wet thatch for a haircut?* **2.** *n.* toilet paper. (Usually objectionable.) ◆ *There's no goddamn ass-wipe left in here!* ◆ *What am I supposed to use for butt-wipe?*

at a snail's gallop Go to at a snail's pace.

at a snail's pace AND **at a snail's gallop** *mod.* very slowly. ◆ *Poor old Willy is creeping at a snail's gallop because his car has* a flat tire. ◆ *The building project is coming along at a snail's pace.*

at loose ends *mod.* nervous and anxious; bored with nothing to do; unemployed. ◆ *Tom usually works puzzles whenever he's at loose ends.*

ate up with so/sth *mod.* consumed with someone or something; intrigued by someone or something. ◆ *Bob is really ate up with his new girlfriend.*

atomic wedgie *n.* an instance of pulling someone's underpants up very tightly—from the rear—so that the cloth is pulled between the victim's buttocks; a severe **wedgie** or **melvin**. ◆ *I'm going to sneak up behind Bob and give him an atomic wedgie.*

A-town *n.* Atlanta, Georgia. ◆ *We do everything possible to avoid driving through A-town.*

attic *n.* the head, thought of as the location of one's intellect. ◆ *She's just got nothing in the attic. That's what's wrong with her.*

attitude-adjuster *n.* a police officer's nightstick; any club. ◆ *Andy had a black attitude-adjuster hanging from his belt, and I wasn't going to argue with him.*

Aunt Flo *n.* a woman's menstrual period. (Used especially in expressions. See also **visit from Flo**. Refers to the menstrual flow.) ◆ *I am sorry to announce that Aunt Flo has come for a visit.*

avenue tank *n.* a bus. ◆ *Watch out for them avenue tanks when you cross the street.*

the **avs** [ævz] *n.* the law of averages. (Streets.) ◆ *The avs say that I ought to be dead by now.*

(Aw) shucks! *exclam.* a mild oath. (Colloquial.) ◆ *Aw shucks, I ain't never been this close to a woman before.*

away *mod.* in prison. (Underworld. See also **Are we away?**) ◆ *My cousin is away for a year.*

awesome 1. *exclam.* Great!; Excellent! (Usually **Awesome!** Standard English, but used often in slang.) ◆ *You own that gorgeous hog? Awesome!* **2.** *mod.* impressive. ◆ *That thing is so awesome!*

AWHFY Go to Are we having fun yet?

AWOL [e ˈdəbˌlju ˈo ˈɛl OR ˈewɑl] *mod.* absent without leave; escaped from prison or from the military. (Acronym or initialism.) ♦ *If I don't get back to the base, they're going to think I'm AWOL.*

axe *n.* a musical instrument. (Originally a saxophone.) ♦ *Get out your axe and let's jam.*

AYPI Go to And your point is?

Aztec two-step *n.* diarrhea, specifically that contracted in Mexico or South America by tourists; Montezuma's revenge. ♦ *I was there for only two days before I was struck down with the Aztec two-step.*

B

B. and B. *mod.* breast and buttock, having to do with entertainment featuring female nudity. ◆ *Many movies add a little B. and B. just to get an R-rating.*

BA *n.* bare ass; the naked buttocks. (See also hang a BA (at SO).) ◆ *The guy was running around with his BA showing.*

babe 1. AND **babes** *n.* a term of endearment for a woman or a man. (Also a term of address. See also baby.) ◆ *Look, babe, get in there and tackle that guy! We're losing!* ◆ *Hey, babes, let's us two get this done and head on home.* **2.** *n.* a good-looking woman. ◆ *Who is that babe standing on the corner over there?* ◆ *I saw you with that orange haired babe last night. What's the story?*

babe magnet AND **chick magnet 1.** *n.* a male who seems to attract good looking females easily. ◆ *Keep your woman away from Chuck. He's a babe magnet.* ◆ *Wilfred thinks he's a chick magnet, but he only snags the dogs.* **2.** *n.* something, such as a car, that attracts good-looking females to a male. ◆ *Man, I like your new chick magnet. Get any yet?* ◆ *He thought of a new car as a "babe magnet," but all it drew was the repo man.*

baboon *n.* a jerk; a stupid person. (Also a rude term of address.) ◆ *Tell that ugly baboon to get out of here.*

baby 1. *n.* a lover; one's sweetheart. (Also a term of address.) ◆ *Come over here and kiss me, baby.* **2.** *n.* a term of address for a friend or pal of either sex. ◆ *Come on, baby, push this thing—hard!* **3.** *n.* a thing; a gadget; a machine, such as a car. (Similar to sucker.) ◆ *Hand me that baby with the sharp point, will you?* **4.** *n.* a project thought of as an offspring. (Always with a possessor.) ◆ *Whose baby is the Johnson account?*

baby bear *n.* a beginning highway patrol officer; a rookie cop. (Citizens band radio. See also Smokey (the Bear).) ◆ *Some baby bear tried to arrest me for speeding, but I conned him out of it.*

(baby) boomer *n.* someone born during the baby boom—from the last years of World War II until the early 1960s. ◆ *When the baby boomers get around to saving up for retirement, you're going to see a lot of investment scams.*

baby gangsta AND **BG** *n.* a baby gangster; a fake gangster. (Streets.) ◆ *He's just a baby gangsta. Got a lot of growing to do.* ◆ *Little "BGs" grow up to be real ones.*

Baby it's cold outside. AND **BICO** *sent. & comp. abb.* It's cold. (From a popular, midcentury song.) ◆ *Temp's about 20. BICO!* ◆ *Zip up your overcoat, baby it's cold outside.*

The **baby needs shoes.** *sent.* Give me luck. (Said in games of chance, such as dice or bingo.) ◆ *He shook the bones, saying, "The baby needs shoes."*

babycakes AND **honeycakes** *n.* a term of endearment; sweetie; dear. (Also a term of address.) ◆ *Look, honeycakes, I found some lipstick on your collar.* ◆ *Gee, babycakes, it must be yours!*

baby-kisser *n.* a politician. ◆ *There were lots of promises at the town square today when four local baby-kissers tried to rally interest in the upcoming election.*

bach (it) Go to ba(t)ch (it).

back *n.* one's support or second in a fight. (From *back-up*.) ◆ *I need a back I can depend on.*

back number *n.* an old-fashioned person. (Like an out-of-print issue of a magazine.) ♦ *Some old back number wearing gaiters wants to have a word with you.*

back room *mod.* secret; concealed. ♦ *All the candidates were selected in back room meetings.*

back room boys Go to boys in the back room.

back to square one *phr.* back to the beginning. (Often with *go*.) ♦ *We've got to get this done without going back to square one.*

back to the salt mines *phr.* back to the workplace. ♦ *Well, it's Monday morning. Back to the salt mines.*

back up *in.* to refuse to go through with something; to back out (of something). ♦ *Fred backed up at the last minute, leaving me with twenty pounds of hot dogs.*

backassed *mod.* pertaining to a manner that is backward, awkward, or roundabout. (Old and widely known. Usually objectionable.) ♦ *Of all the backassed schemes I've ever seen, this one is tops.*

backbone *n.* courage; integrity. (Colloquial.) ♦ *If you had any backbone, you would be able to deal with this.*

backdoor trot(s) *n.* a case of diarrhea. (From the time when people had to go out the back door to the outhouse.) ♦ *I can't go out tonight. I got a case of the backdoor trots.*

backed up *mod.* drug intoxicated. ♦ *Old Benny's really backed up.*

back-ender Go to rear-ender.

backer *n.* a supporter; a financier of a play, political campaign, etc. ♦ *I was hoping for a backer, but the project was too chancy.*

backfire *in.* to release intestinal gas anally and audibly. (Usually objectionable.) ♦ *Whew! Somebody backfired!*

backfire (on so**)** *in.* [for a scheme meant to cause harm to someone or something] to harm the person who runs the scheme. ♦ *I hope this plan doesn't backfire on me.*

backhander *n.* a backhand slap in the face. ♦ *Yes, officer, a perfectly strange woman came up and clobbered me with a backhander that loosened a tooth.*

backseat driver *n.* an annoying passenger who tells the driver how to drive; someone who tells others how to do things. ♦ *I don't need any backseat driver on this project.*

backside *n.* the buttocks; one's rear. ♦ *There is some mustard or something on your backside.*

backslapper *n.* someone who is overly friendly and outgoing. ♦ *At election time, city hall is filled with backslappers and baby-kissers.*

bacon *n.* the police; a police officer. (See also pig.) ♦ *Keep an eye out for the bacon.*

bad 1. *mod.* powerful; intense. ♦ *This grass is bad!* **2.** *mod.* suitable; excellent; good. ♦ *I got some new silks that are really bad.*

bad egg *n.* a repellent person. ♦ *You're not such a bad egg after all.*

bad hair day *n.* a bad day in general. (Also used literally when one's inability to do anything with one's hair seems to color the events of the day.) ♦ *I'm sorry I am so glum. This has been a real bad hair day.*

bad news 1. *n.* the bill for something. ♦ *Here comes the bad news.* **2.** *mod.* unpleasant; unfortunate; repellent. ♦ *That poor guy is really bad news.*

bad paper *n.* bad checks; a bad check. ♦ *She got six months for passing bad paper.*

bad rap 1. *n.* a false criminal charge. (Underworld. The same as bum rap.) ♦ *Freddy got stuck with a bad rap.* **2.** *n.* unjustified criticism. ♦ *Butter has been getting sort of a bad rap lately.*

bad shit 1. *n.* a bad event; bad luck; evil practices. (Usually objectionable.) ♦ *I had to put up with a lot of bad shit at my last job. Is this one gonna be the same?* **2.** *n.* bad drugs; adulterated drugs. (Usually objectionable.) ♦ *Freddy got hold of some bad shit, and he's really sick.*

bad trip 1. *n.* a bad experience with a drug. (Drugs.) ♦ *My first trip was a bad trip, and*

I never took another. **2.** *n.* any bad experience or person. ♦ *Harry can be such a bad trip.*

badass 1. *mod.* tough; bad; belligerent. (Usually objectionable.) ♦ *Stop acting like such a badass punk!* **2.** *n.* a tough guy; a belligerent and arrogant person, usually a male. ♦ *Don't be such a badass all the time.*

baddy AND **baddie** ['bædi] *n.* a bad thing or person. ♦ *Using butter is supposed to be a real "baddy."* ♦ *Don't be such a baddie. Tell me you just love my hair!*

bad-mouth 1. *tv.* to speak ill of someone or something. (See also dirty mouth; poor-mouth.) ♦ *I wish you would stop bad-mouthing my car.* **2.** *n.* someone who speaks ill of someone or something. ♦ *Harry is such a bad-mouth!*

bag 1. *tv.* to capture and arrest someone. (See also bagged. Underworld.) ♦ *They bagged the robber with the loot still on him.* **2.** *n.* an ugly woman. (Rude and derogatory.) ♦ *Tell the old bag to mind her own business.* **3.** *n.* one's preference; something suited to one's preference. ♦ *That kind of stuff is so not my bag!* **4.** *tv.* to obtain something. ♦ *I'll try to bag a couple of tickets for you.* **5.** *n.* a container of drugs. (Drugs. Not necessarily a real bag.) ♦ *Two bags of H. for two dimes?* **6.** *in.* to die. ♦ *The guy was coughing so hard that I thought he was going to bag right there.* **7.** *tv.* to apply a respirator to someone. (Medical. The respirator has a bag attached to hold air.) ♦ *Quick, bag him before he boxes.*

one's **bag** *n.* one's preferences; one's talents. ♦ *Hey, Tom, what's your bag? What do you like to do?*

bag ass (out of somewhere**)** AND **barrel ass (out of** somewhere**); bust ass (out of** somewhere**); cut ass (out of** somewhere**); drag ass (out of** somewhere**); haul ass (out of** somewhere**); shag ass (out of** somewhere**)** *tv.* to hurry away from some place; to get oneself out of a place in a hurry. (Usually objectionable.) ♦ *I gotta shag ass, Fred. Catch you later.* ♦ *Let's haul*

ass out of here and go get a beer. ♦ *It's late, you twits. Time to go. Let's drag ass!*

Bag it! 1. *exclam.* Drop dead! (California. See also Bag your face!; Bag that!) ♦ *You are not rad, and you are not awesome, so, like, bag it!* **2.** *exclam.* Shut up! ♦ *Bag it! I'm reading.*

bag of wind Go to windbag.

bag on so **1.** *in.* to criticize someone. ♦ *Stop bagging on me! I'm tired of all your complaining.* **2.** *n.* to tease someone. ♦ *He is always bagging on his little sister.*

bag some rays Go to catch some rays.

bag so *tv.* to put someone on a respirator. (To apply a medical device, part of which is a rubber bag, used to help someone breathe.) ♦ *Bag this guy quick. He is struggling to get his breath.*

Bag that! *tv.* Forget that! ♦ *There are four—no, bag that!—six red ones and three blue ones.*

Bag your face! *exclam.* Go away! (See also Bag it!) ♦ *You are so in the way! Bag your face!*

bagged 1. *mod.* alcohol intoxicated. ♦ *How can anybody be so bagged on four beers?* **2.** *mod.* arrested. ♦ *"You are bagged," said the officer, clapping a hand on the suspect's shoulder.*

bagman ['bægmæn] **1.** *n.* a tramp. ♦ *Two old bagmen wandered slowly down the lane.* **2.** *n.* a drug dealer. (Drugs.) ♦ *Sam was a bagman for a well-known dealer for a while.* **3.** *n.* any racketeer. ♦ *Some bagman from the mob was pulled out of the river yesterday.*

bail on so *in.* to walk out on someone; to leave someone. ♦ *She bailed on me after all we had been through together.*

bail (out) *in.* to resign or leave; to get free of someone or something. ♦ *Albert bailed just before he got fired.*

bail out on so *in.* to depart and leave someone behind; to abandon someone. ♦ *Bob bailed out on me and left me to take all the blame.*

bake the tube steak *tv.* to copulate. ♦ *Bobby was set to bake the tube steak last night, but he failed to preheat the oven.*

baked 1. *mod.* sunburned. ♦ *I was out in the sun until I got totally baked.* **2.** *mod.* alcohol or drug intoxicated. ♦ *I've never seen anybody so baked.*

bald-headed hermit AND **bald-headed mouse; one-eyed pants mouse** *n.* the penis. (Usually objectionable.) ♦ *Somebody said something about the attack of the one-eyed pants mouse, and all the boys howled with laughter.* ♦ *Although "bald-headed hermit" gave her mental images of Ghandi on vacation, she soon figured out the riddle.*

bald-headed mouse Go to bald-headed hermit.

baldwin *n.* a good-looking male. (As in Alec Baldwin.) ♦ *Who is that Baldwin I saw you with last night?*

baldy AND **baldie** ['bɔldi] *n.* a bald-headed man. ♦ *I'm getting to be an old baldie.* ♦ *I'd rather be a baldy than a skinny kid with a pile of wet thatch sticking out of my head.*

ball 1. *n.* a wild time at a party; a good time. ♦ *We really had a ball. See ya!* **2.** *n.* a testicle. (Usually plural. Usually objectionable. See also balls.) ♦ *The teacher preferred "testicles" to "balls," if they had to be mentioned at all.* **3.** *in.* to enjoy oneself. (Ambiguous with the next sense.) ♦ *The whole crowd was balling and having a fine time.* **4.** *in.* to depart; to leave. ♦ *It's late. Let's ball.* **5.** *tv. & in.* to copulate [with] someone. (Usually objectionable.) ♦ *Isn't there anything more to you than balling?* **6.** *in.* to play a ball game. (Probably a deliberate pun on sense 5.) ♦ *Bob's out balling with the guys.*

one's **ball and chain** *n.* a wife; a girlfriend. (Mostly jocular.) ♦ *I've got to get home to my ball and chain.*

The **ball is in** so's **court.** *phr.* to be someone else's move, play, or turn. ♦ *I can't do anything as long as the ball is in John's court.*

ball of fire AND **fireball** *n.* an energetic and ambitious person; a go-getter. ♦ *That guy is a real ball of fire when it comes to sales.* ♦ *Wilfred ain't no fireball, but he gets his stuff in on time.*

ball off Go to beat off.

ball so/sth **up** *tv.* to mess someone or something up; to put someone or something into a state of confusion. ♦ *When you interrupted, you balled me up and I lost my place.*

ball up *in.* to mess up; to make a mess of things. ♦ *Take your time at this. Go slow and you won't ball up.*

ball-breaker AND **ball-buster 1.** *n.* a difficult task; a difficult or trying situation requiring extremely hard work or effort. (Usually objectionable.) ♦ *That whole construction job was a real ball-breaker.* ♦ *Why should moving furniture end up being such a ball-buster?* **2.** *n.* a hard taskmaster; a hard-to-please boss. (Usually objectionable.) ♦ *Tom gets a day's work for a day's pay out of his men, but he's no ball-breaker.* ♦ *My boss is a ball-buster, but he pays well.* **3.** *n.* a female who is threatening to males. (Usually objectionable.) ♦ *Mrs. Samuels has a terrible reputation as a "ball-breaker." Wholly deserved, I might add.*

ball-buster Go to ball-breaker.

ball-busting 1. *mod.* very difficult or challenging. (Usually objectionable.) ♦ *Man, that was a real ball-busting job. I hope I never have to do that again.* **2.** *mod.* very obnoxious and threatening. (Usually objectionable.) ♦ *Who is that ball-busting bitch?* **3.** *mod.* very industrious. (Usually objectionable.) ♦ *That's a real ball-busting crew working on that job.*

balled up *mod.* confused; mixed up. (This is hyphenated before a nominal.) ♦ *That dame is so balled up she doesn't know anything.*

baller *n.* an athlete. (One who plays with footballs, basketballs, baseballs, etc.) ♦ *You will make a lot of money as a professional baller.*

ballhead *n.* an athlete; someone obsessed with ball games. (Perhaps a stupid one.) ♦ *If you want to be a ballhead, you have to have talent and stamina.*

balloon knot *n.* the anus (From its appearance.) ♦ *Yeeeouch! Right in the balloon knot!*

balloons *n.* a woman's breasts, especially large ones. (Usually objectionable.) ♦ *What fine balloons on Jim's girl!*

balls 1. *n.* the testicles. (Usually objectionable.) ♦ *He got hit in the balls in the football game.* **2.** *exclam.* of disbelief. (Usually an exclamation: **Balls!** Usually objectionable.) ♦ *Out of gas! Balls! I just filled it up!* **3.** *n.* courage; bravado. (Usually refers to a male, but occasionally refers to female. Usually objectionable.) ♦ *He doesn't have enough balls to do that!*

ballsy 1. *mod.* courageous; daring; foolhardy. (Usually said of a male. Usually objectionable.) ♦ *Who is that ballsy jerk climbing the side of the building?* **2.** *mod.* aggressive; masculine. (Said of a female, especially a masculine female. Usually objectionable.) ♦ *You act too ballsy, Lillian. You put people off.*

balmed *mod.* alcohol intoxicated. (See also **bombed (out)**; **embalmed**.) ♦ *Tom was totally balmed and went to bed.*

balmy 1. *mod.* crazy; giddy. ♦ *You are totally balmy if you think I will put up with that stuff.* **2.** *mod.* alcohol intoxicated. ♦ *She's not just drunk, she's a little balmy.*

baloney AND **bologna** [bə'loni] *n.* nonsense. (Also as an *exclam.*) ♦ *Don't give me all that baloney!*

baloney pony *n.* the penis. (Contrived for the sake of the rhyme.) ♦ *All he could think about was riding the old baloney pony.*

baltic *mod.* cold; very cold. ♦ *It really looks baltic out there today.*

bam and scram *n.* a hit and run accident. ♦ *The sirens were blaring and a dozen black and white headed to a bam and scram over on Maple.*

bambi *n.* a deer, especially one that suddenly appears on the highway. ♦ *We just missed a bambi on the road last night.*

bamboozle [bæm'buzl] **1.** *tv.* to deceive someone; to confuse someone. (See also **bamboozled**.) ♦ *Don't try to bamboozle me! I know what I want!* **2.** *tv.* to steal something. ♦ *The crooks bamboozled the old man's life savings.*

bamboozled [bæm'buzld] **1.** *mod.* confused. ♦ *This stuff sure has me bamboozled.* **2.** *mod.* alcohol intoxicated. (Collegiate.) ♦ *She's not just drunk, she's totally bamboozled.*

bamma *n.* a rural person, such as someone from Alabama; a hick. (Rude and derogatory.) ♦ *Some bamma in a pickup truck nearly ran me off the road.*

banana *n.* an American of East Asian descent who acts too much like a Caucasian. (The person is yellow on the outside and white on the inside. Patterned on **oreo**. See also **apple**. Rude and derogatory.) ♦ *Stop acting like such a banana!*

banana hammock *n.* a bikini for a male. (See also **grape smugglers**.) ♦ *He was wearing a little yellow banana hammock that drew a lot of stares.*

banana oil *n.* nonsense. ♦ *I refuse to listen to any more of your childish banana oil.*

banana-head *n.* a stupid person. (Usually objectionable.) ♦ *Ask that banana-head why she is wearing a coat like that in July.*

bananas 1. *mod.* crazy. (Often with *go*, see also **go bananas**.) ♦ *You were bananas before I ever showed up on the scene.* **2.** *mod.* enthusiastic. ♦ *The audience was bananas over the new star.*

bang 1. *n.* a bit of excitement; a thrill; some amusement. ♦ *We got a bang out of your letter.* **2.** *n.* the degree of potency of the alcohol in liquor. ♦ *This stuff has quite a bang!* **3.** *n.* an injection of a drug; any dose of a drug. (Drugs.) ♦ *If Albert doesn't have a bang by noon, he gets desperate.* **4.** *tv. & in.* to inject a drug. (Drugs.) ♦ *They were in the back room banging away.* **5.** *n.* a drug rush. (Drugs.) ♦ *One snort and the bang will knock you over.* **6.** *tv.*

to copulate [with] someone. (Usually objectionable.) ♦ *Did you bang her? Huh? Tell me!* **7.** *n.* an act of copulation. (Usually objectionable.) ♦ *One bang was never enough for Wallace T. Jones. He was never satisfied.*

(bang) dead to rights *mod.* in the act; [guilty] without question. ♦ *We caught her dead to rights with the loot still on her.*

bang for the buck *n.* value for the money spent; excitement for the money spent; the cost-to-benefit ratio. ♦ *How much bang for the buck did you really think you would get from a twelve-year-old car—at any price?*

bang in (sick) *in.* to call in sick. ♦ *Two more people just banged in sick!*

bang in the arm *n.* an injection of narcotics. (Drugs. See also **bang**. Compare this with **shot in the arm**.) ♦ *One good bang in the arm leads to another, they always say.*

banger 1. *n.* the front bumper of a vehicle. (See also **4-banger**.) ♦ *Other than a dent or two in the banger, this buggy's okay.* **2.** *n.* a hypodermic syringe. (Drugs.) ♦ *Jed dropped his banger and really panicked when it broke.*

banging 1. *mod.* good; exciting. ♦ *We had a banging good time at the concert.* **2.** *mod.* good looking; attractive. ♦ *Who was that banging chick I saw you with last night?* **3.** *mod.* [of music] loud. ♦ *That band is really banging. I think I am deaf!*

bang-up *mod.* really excellent. ♦ *I like to throw a bang-up party once or twice a year.*

banjaxed ['bændʒækst] **1.** *mod.* demolished; ruined. ♦ *My car is totally banjaxed. What a mess!* **2.** *mod.* alcohol intoxicated. ♦ *All four of them went out and got banjaxed.*

bank 1. *n.* money; ready cash. (From **bankroll**.) ♦ *I can't go out with you. No bank.* **2.** *n.* a toilet. (Where one makes a deposit.) ♦ *Man, where's the bank around here?* **3.** *tv.* to gang up on and beat someone. (An intransitive version is **bank on**

so.) ♦ *They banked the kid and left him moaning.*

bank on so *in.* to beat up on someone. (The transitive version is **bank**.) ♦ *Freddy was banking on Last Card Louie and almost killed him.*

banker's hours *n.* short work hours: 10:00 A.M. to 2:00 P.M. ♦ *When did you start keeping banker's hours?*

bankroll 1. *n.* a roll or wad of currency; one's cash assets. ♦ *Don't show that bankroll around here!* **2.** *tv.* to finance something. ♦ *We were hoping to find somebody who would bankroll the project.*

barb *n.* a barbiturate; a barbiturate capsule. (Drugs.) ♦ *Joey is so hooked on barbs!*

Barbie doll *n.* a pretty, giddy girl or woman. ♦ *Ask that little Barbie doll if she wants a drink.*

bare-ass(ed) *mod.* with a naked posterior exposed; totally naked. (Usually objectionable.) ♦ *He ran right through the room—totally bare-assed—looking scared as hell.*

bareback *mod.* [copulating] without a condom. ♦ *I couldn't find a raincoat, and she wouldn't let me do it bareback.*

barf [barf] **1.** *in.* to empty one's stomach; to vomit. ♦ *I think I'm going to barf!* **2.** *n.* vomit. ♦ *Is that barf on your shoe?* **3.** *in.* [for a computer] to fail to function. ♦ *My little computer barfs about once a day. Something is wrong.* **4.** AND **barfola** [barf'olə] *interj.* dammit; Good grief! (Often **Barfola!**) ♦ *Barfola! You're out of your mind!* ♦ *When he said "Barf!" I felt wow, so vintage!*

barf bag *n.* a bag available on an airplane for persons who are nauseated. ♦ *I hope I never even have to see anyone use a barf bag.*

Barf City *n.* someone or something disgusting or undesirable. (Barf = vomit.) ♦ *The guy is so gross! Just plain Barf City!*

Barf out! *exclam.* This is awful! (California.) ♦ *Barf out! Get a life!*

barf out *in.* to become very upset; to freak out; to psych out. ♦ *I nearly barfed out when I heard he was coming.*

barf so out *tv.* to totally disgust someone. ♦ *God! That kind of music just barfs me out! Who can stand all that slow stuff?*

barfly 1. *n.* a person who frequents bars. ♦ *Who will trust the word of an old barfly like Willy?* **2.** *n.* a drunkard. ♦ *Some barfly staggered out of the tavern straight into the side of a car.*

barfola Go to barf.

barf-out *n.* an unpleasant person or thing. ♦ *That guy is a real barf-out.*

bari AND **bary** ['bæri] *n.* a baritone saxophone, the saxophone with a pitch range approximating that of the human baritone voice. (Musicians.) ♦ *Willy played the bari when he was in college.* ♦ *He pawned his bary and made everybody happy.*

barking spider AND **trumpet spider** *n.* the imaginary source of the sound of an audible release of intestinal gas. (With reference to the image of a anus.) ♦ *Heidi, do you know anything about the trumpet spider I keep hearing?* ♦ *Although Dr. Waddlington-Stowe had never heard "barking spider" with reference to the affected part, he caught the connection immediately.*

Barney 1. *n.* the penis, especially if erect. (Usually a nickname. Alludes to color.) ♦ *Now, put Barney away and let's talk about our relationship.* **2.** *n.* a nerd; a wimp; an unattractive male. (From the Flintstones character or the children's dinosaur character.) ♦ *If you weren't such a Barney, you'd stick up for your own rights.* **3.** *n.* a good-looking guy. ♦ *Man she's really found herself a Barney!*

barnstorm 1. *tv. & in.* [for an entertainer] to perform in small towns for short engagements. ♦ *My great-uncle used to barnstorm Kansas and Oklahoma with his medicine show.* **2.** *in.* to perform stunts in a biplane in small towns. (Presumably swooping around barns.) ♦ *The old biplane we used to barnstorm with is the safest plane ever built.*

barracuda *n.* a predatory person, especially a predatory woman. ♦ *She's a barracuda. Better watch out!*

barrel 1. *tv. & in.* to drink liquor to excess. ♦ *Stop barreling beer and let's go home.* **2.** *n.* a drunkard. ♦ *The old barrel was full up and through for the evening.* **3.** *in.* to go fast; to speed while driving. ♦ *She barreled out of here like a bat out of hell.*

barrel ass *in.* to move or drive carelessly and rapidly. (Usually objectionable.) ♦ *He was barrel assing along at nearly ninety.*

barrel ass (out of somewhere**)** Go to bag ass (out of somewhere).

barrel fever 1. *n.* drunkenness. ♦ *She seems to get barrel fever about once a week.* **2.** *n.* a hangover. ♦ *Man, have I ever got barrel fever.* **3.** *n.* the delirium tremens. ♦ *The old man is down with barrel fever again.*

barrel of fun 1. *n.* a tremendous amount of fun. ♦ *We have a barrel of fun at the zoo.* **2.** *n.* a person who is a lot of fun. ♦ *Taylor is just a barrel of fun on dates.*

barreled (up) *mod.* alcohol intoxicated. ♦ *She spends a lot of time barreled.*

bary Go to bari.

base *mod.* rude; gross. (California.) ♦ *You are so, like, base!*

bash [bæʃ] **1.** *n.* a wild party; a night on the town. ♦ *What a bash! I'm exhausted!* **2.** *in.* to party; to celebrate. ♦ *Let's go out and bash, how 'bout it?* **3.** *tv.* to criticize; to join in the destructive criticism of someone or something. ♦ *A bunch of old Jonathan Computer fans love to bash Macrosoft whenever they can.*

bashed [bæʃt] **1.** *mod.* crushed; struck. ♦ *Give me that bashed one, and I'll straighten it out.* **2.** *mod.* alcohol intoxicated. ♦ *All four of them went out and got bashed.*

bashing *n.* criticizing; defaming. (A combining form that follows the name of the person or thing being criticized.) ♦ *On TV they had a long session of candidate bashing, and then they read the sports news.*

basket *n.* the stomach. (See also breadbasket.) ♦ *You've got a lot of guts in the basket. It's huge.*

basket case *n.* a person who is a nervous wreck. (Formerly referred to a person who is totally physically disabled.) ♦ *After that meeting, I was practically a basket case.*

Basra belly ['bɑsrə 'bɛli] *n.* diarrhea; a case of diarrhea. ♦ *The Basra belly hit me while I was on the bus.*

basted ['bestəd] **1.** *mod.* beaten; harmed. ♦ *The team got basted three games in a row.* **2.** *mod.* alcohol intoxicated. ♦ *I got so basted I vowed never to touch another drop.*

bat 1. *n.* a drinking bout. ♦ *She was on a bat that lasted over a week.* **2.** *n.* a drunkard; a person on a drinking spree. ♦ *A tired old bat—still waving a bottle—met me on the stairs.*

ba(t)ch (it) [bætʃ...] *tv. & in.* to live alone like a bachelor. ♦ *I tried to bach it for a while, but I got too lonely.*

bathtub crank *n.* homemade amphetamine. (From *bathtub gin.*) ♦ *Somehow she got hold of some bathtub crank and had a really bad trip.*

bathtub scum *n.* a totally despised person. (See also pond scum; shower scum. Also a term of address.) ♦ *Look out, bathtub scum, outa my way!*

bats 1. AND **batty** *mod.* crazy. ♦ *You are driving me batty!* ♦ *You are bats if you think I would ever wear a haircut like that.* **2.** AND **batty** *mod.* alcohol intoxicated; confused and drunk. ♦ *The guy was bats—stewed to his ears.* ♦ *He was a bit batty, but he'd been drinking since noon, so no one was surprised.* **3.** the **bats** *n.* the delirium tremens. (Always with *the.*) ♦ *My buddy is shaking because of a slight case of the bats.*

batted 1. *mod.* alcohol intoxicated. ♦ *She spends a lot of time completely batted.* **2.** AND **batted out** *mod.* arrested. (Underworld.) ♦ *This gal got batted twice last year on the same rap.* ♦ *He was batted out three times in January for theft.*

batted out Go to batted.

battered *mod.* alcohol intoxicated. ♦ *Man, was I battered. I will never drink another drop.*

battle of the bulge *n.* the attempt to keep one's waistline normal. (Named for a World War II battle.) ♦ *She appears to have lost the battle of the bulge.*

battleships Go to gunboats.

batty Go to bats.

bawangos Go to bazoongies.

bay window *n.* a belly; an abdomen. ♦ *You are going to have to do something about that bay window.*

bazillion [bə'zɪljən] *n.* an indefinite, enormous number. ♦ *Ernie gave me a bazillion good reasons why he shouldn't do it.*

bazoo AND **wazoo 1.** *n.* the human mouth. ♦ *You want me to punch you in the wazoo?* ♦ *Shut your damn wazoo!* **2.** *n.* the stomach or belly. ♦ *His great wazoo hung poised, out over his belt, like it might dive down to the floor and bounce off across the room.* ♦ *Pow, right in the wazoo!* **3.** *n.* the anus; the buttocks. (Jocular and euphemistic.) ♦ *One more word like that and I'll give you a kick in the wazoo that you'll remember for a long time.* ♦ *She fell so down! Right on her skinny bazoo.*

bazoom(s) *n.* a woman's breasts; the female bosom. (Usually objectionable.) ♦ *I don't know how it happened, but a whole bowl of jello went down this lady's, uh, bazoom, and we haven't the slightest idea what to do about it!*

bazoongies AND **bawangos** *n.* a woman's breasts. (Usually objectionable.) ♦ *Every time she moved forward, even just a little, her bazoongies tended to stay behind, for just a second.* ♦ *With bawangos like that, she could be in the movies.*

BB brain *n.* a stupid person; a person seemingly with a brain the size of buckshot. (Also a rude term of address.) ♦ *What BB brain left the door open?*

B-ball *n.* basketball; a basketball. (See also hoops; V-ball.) ♦ *Let's go play some B-ball.*

BBFN Go to Bye-bye, for now.

BBL *in.* be back later. (Used in electronic mail and computer forum or news group messages. Not pronounced aloud.) ♦ *Bye. BBL.*

BCNU [ˈbiˈsiˈənˈju] *tv.* Be seeing you. (An initialism. Appears in informal written contexts.) ♦ *Todd always closes his notes with "BCNU."*

be on the look out AND **BOLO** *phr. & comp. abb.* establish and maintain surveillance [for someone]. (A police notation.) ♦ *BOLO for a 65-year-old woman with tattoos on her upper arms.* ♦ *We'll be on the look out for your stolen car.*

be right back AND **BRB** *phr. & comp. abb.* I will return to communicating shortly. ♦ *Excuse me, BRB.* ♦ *He's out of pocket, but he'll be right back.*

Be there or be square. *sent.* Attend or be at some event or place or be considered uncooperative or not "with it." ♦ *There's a bunch of people going to be at John's on Saturday. Be there or be square.*

Be there with bells on. AND **BTWBO** *sent. & comp. abb.* [I will] be there happily.; I am eager to come there. (Said in response to an invitation.) ♦ *Thanks for the invitation. I'll be there with bells on.* ♦ *Don't B L8T. BTWBO.*

beach bum *n.* a young man who frequents beaches. ♦ *A bronzed beach bum helped me find my lotion.*

beach bunny *n.* a young woman who frequents beaches. ♦ *This little beach bunny bounced up and offered to put lotion on me.*

beak 1. *n.* a nose. ♦ *What a beak on that guy!* **2.** *in.* to gossip; to chatter. ♦ *Stop beaking and get to work.*

beam Go to (I-)beam.

Beam me up, Scotty! *sent.* Get me out of here!; Take me away from this mess! (From the television program *Star Trek*.) ♦ *This place is really crazy! Beam me up, Scotty!*

beam up *in.* to die. (From the television program *Star Trek*.) ♦ *Pete Dead? I didn't think he was old enough to beam up.*

beamer *n.* a user of IBM computers; one who is knowledgeable about IBM computers. (See also **beemer**.) ♦ *I'm no beamer! I'm a Mac fan.*

beaming Go to on the beam.

bean 1. *n.* the head. ♦ *I got a bump right here on my bean.* **2.** *tv.* to hit someone on the head. (See also **beanball**.) ♦ *The lady beaned me with her umbrella.* **3.** Go to beans. **4.** *n.* a human nipple, especially as seen through clothing. (From the shape.) ♦ *Gee, I can see her beans, even when it's not cold!*

bean head 1. *n.* an oaf. (Also as one word.) ♦ *You are such a bean head!* **2.** *n.* a drug user who uses pills habitually. (Drugs.) ♦ *You bean heads are just as much junkies as the jerks who shoot.*

bean time *n.* dinnertime. ♦ *I'm hungry. When's bean time around here?*

Bean Town *n.* Boston, Massachusetts. (From *Boston baked beans*.) ♦ *I plan to hit Bean Town about noon.*

beanball *n.* a pitched baseball that strikes the batter on the head, usually by accident. (Baseball.) ♦ *He got hit by a beanball and went after the pitcher with a bat.*

bean-counter *n.* a statistician; an accountant. ♦ *When the bean-counters get finished with the numbers, you won't recognize them.*

beaned up *mod.* high on amphetamines. (Drugs.) ♦ *Two students were beaned up and were sent home.*

beanery *n.* a cheap eating establishment. (Where baked beans might be served.) ♦ *I stopped in for a cup of brew at a little all-night beanery on Thirty-fourth. Marlowe was waiting.*

beanpole *n.* a skinny person. ♦ *I'm getting to be such a beanpole.*

beans 1. *n.* nothing. ♦ *I have nothing I can give you. Nothing, zotz, beans!* **2.** *n.* nonsense. (Refers to beans that produce gas, which is hot air or nonsense.) ♦ *Stop feeding me beans.* **3.** *n.* soybean futures contracts. (Securities markets. Usually with the.) ♦ *Buy the jan beans and sell puts on* the bellies. **4.** *n.* money; dollars. ♦ *Gimme some beans. I gotta get some gas.*

bear 1. *n.* a difficult task. ♦ *This problem is a real bear.* **2.** *n.* an ugly woman. (Derogatory.) ♦ *Tell the old bear to hold her tongue.* **3.** *n.* a highway patrol officer. (See also **Smokey (the Bear).**) ♦ *There's a bear hiding under that bridge.*

bear cage *n.* a police station. (Citizens band radio.) ♦ *Have you ever been in a country bear cage?*

bear in the air *n.* a police officer in an airplane or a helicopter. (Citizens band radio.) ♦ *They've got a bear in the air on duty in northern Indiana.*

bear trap *n.* a hidden speed trap, one set by a bear. (Citizens band radio.) ♦ *That whole town is a glorified bear trap.*

beast 1. *n.* an ugly person. ♦ *That beast should give the monkey back its face before the poor creature bumps into something.* **2.** *n.* a crude, violent, or sexually aggressive male; an **animal.** ♦ *Oh, Martin, you're such a beast!* **3.** *n.* liquor. ♦ *Pour me some more of that beast.*

beasty *mod.* [of a person] undesirable; yucky. (California.) ♦ *You are like, so like, beasty!*

beat 1. *mod.* exhausted; worn-out. ♦ *The whole family was beat after the game.* **2.** *mod.* down and out; ruined. ♦ *This thing is beat. I don't want it.* **3.** *n.* the area that a worker, a police officer, reporter, etc., is assigned to cover. ♦ *That's not on my beat. You'll have to talk to someone else.* **4.** *n.* [in music] the rhythm, especially the bass. ♦ *Man, that is just the kind of beat I like.* **5.** *mod.* having to do with the Bohemian youths of the 1950s. ♦ *My brother looked sort of beat, but I was neat as a pin.* **6.** *mod.* broke. ♦ *Man, I'm beat. I got no copper, no bread.* **7.** *tv.* to get free from a specific criminal charge or rap. ♦ *I beat it twice, but there is no third time.* **8.** *mod.* having to do with counterfeit or bogus drugs. (Drugs.) ♦ *This stuff is beat. Ditch it!* **9.** *mod.* having to do with marijuana after the smokable substance is exhausted; **cashed.** ♦ *Who sold you this beat*

dope? **10.** *mod.* lousy; unfortunate. (Collegiate.) ♦ *What a beat deal you got!*

beat box *n.* the person who provides the (verbal) rhythmic beat in a rap song. ♦ *What makes him sound so good is his beat box.*

Beat it! *exclam.* Get out!; Go away! ♦ *Beat it! I've had it with you.*

beat off AND **ball off; jack off; jag off; jerk off; pull** oneself **off; toss off; wack off; wank off; whack off; whank off; whip off 1.** *in.* to masturbate. (Usually objectionable.) ♦ *They say if you beat off too much, you'll get pimples.* **2.** *in.* to waste time; to waste one's efforts; to do something inefficiently. ♦ *The whole lot of them were jacking off rather than sticking to business.* ♦ *Stop whanking off and get on with your work!*

beat one's **brains out (to do** sth) *tv.* to work hard at a task. ♦ *I'm tired of beating my brains out to do what you want.*

beat one's **gums** *tv.* to waste time talking a great deal without results. ♦ *I'm tired of beating my gums about this stuff.*

beat one's **meat** Go to beat the dummy.

beat so/sth **out** *tv.* to outdistance someone or some group; to perform better than someone or some group. ♦ *We have to beat the other company out, and then we'll have the contract.*

beat so's **brains out 1.** *tv.* to beat someone severely. ♦ *She threatened to beat my brains out.* **2.** *tv.* to drive oneself hard (to accomplish something). ♦ *I beat my brains out all day to clean this house, and you come in and track up the carpet!*

beat sth **out** *tv.* to type something or play something on the piano. ♦ *He beat out a cheery song on the old ivories.*

beat the drum for so/sth *tv.* to promote or support someone or something. ♦ *I spent a lot of time beating the drum for our plans for the future.*

beat the dummy AND **beat the meat; beat** one's **meat; beat the pup; choke the chicken; pound** one's **meat; pull** one's **pud; pull** one's **wire; whip** one's **wire; whip the dummy; yank** one's

strap *tv.* to masturbate. (Usually objectionable.) ♦ *Are you going to sit around all day pulling your pud?* ♦ *We heard him in there "choking the chicken," as the street crowd says.*

beat the meat Go to beat the dummy.

beat the pup Go to beat the dummy.

beat the rap *tv.* to evade conviction and punishment (for a crime). ♦ *The police hauled Tom in and charged him with a crime. His lawyer helped him beat the rap.*

beat the shit out of so AND **kick the shit out of** so, **knock the shit out of** so *tv.* to beat someone very hard. (Usually objectionable.) ♦ *Shut up, or I'll beat the shit out of you!* ♦ *The teacher wanted to kick the shit out of the little felon but wisely restrained himself.*

beat up *mod.* visibly worn; shabby. (This is hyphenated before a nominal.) ♦ *Get your beat-up car painted or something!*

beater *n.* a junky old car. ♦ *I like my old beater even if it has no bumpers.*

beats me *tv.* [the answer is] not known to me. (The emphasis is on *me*.) ♦ *I don't know the answer. Beats me!*

beauhunk *n.* a good-looking male. (Based on bohunk. A play on *beau* = boyfriend, and hunk.) ♦ *Who is that gorgeous beauhunk over there?*

beaut [bjut] *n.* someone or something excellent, not necessarily beautiful. ♦ *This is a beaut of a day!*

beautiful *mod.* very satisfying; excellent. ♦ *Man, this place is beautiful! You got your own sink and toilet right in the room and good strong bars to keep the riffraff out.*

beauty sleep *n.* sleep; the sleep one requires. (Usually mentioned by nonbeautiful men as a joke.) ♦ *You really need some beauty sleep. Why don't you try a week of it and see if that works?*

beaver 1. *n.* the female genitals. (Usually objectionable.) ♦ *He thought he could see her beaver through her swimming suit.* **2.** *n.* women considered as receptacles for the penis. (Rude and derogatory.) ♦ *He*

devoted most of his teen years to dreaming about beaver.

beaver-cleaver *n.* the penis. (See also beaver. Also a play on *Beaver Cleaver* the lead character in the old television show, *Leave It to Beaver*.) ♦ *He seemed proud of his beaver-cleaver, as he called it. No one knew why.*

bed of roses *n.* a luxurious situation; an easy life. ♦ *Who said life would be a bed of roses?*

bed-bunny 1. *n.* a young female who will copulate with any male. ♦ *Willy says he's looking for a nice warm bed-bunny.* **2.** *n.* a female who enjoys sex immensely. ♦ *Wanda turned out to be a hot bed-bunny even though she had seemed sort of dull.*

bedrock 1. *n.* fundamentals; solid facts. ♦ *Let's get down to bedrock and quit wasting time.* **2.** *mod.* fundamental. ♦ *You've been avoiding the bedrock issues all your life.*

bedroom eyes *n.* seductive eyes. ♦ *Beware of bedroom eyes. They mean trouble.*

bedtime story Go to fairy tale.

beef 1. *n.* a complaint; a quarrel. ♦ *I gotta beef against you.* **2.** *n.* a criminal charge or complaint. ♦ *The beef is that you appear to have left the bank Monday with about seventy-five grand that isn't yours. That's the beef!* **3.** *n.* a large and muscular male. ♦ *Let's get one of those beefs in here to help.* **4.** *in.* to complain. ♦ *What's he beefing about now?* **5.** *in.* to break wind; to release intestinal gas audibly. (Usually objectionable.) ♦ *Willy warned everybody that he was going to beef.* **6.** *n.* an act of breaking wind. (Usually objectionable.) ♦ *All right! Who's beef was that?* **7.** *in.* to crack up and get injured as in a skateboard accident. ♦ *Chuck beefed and wrecked his elbow.*

beef about so/sth *in.* to complain about someone or something. ♦ *He is always beefing about his working conditions.*

beef sth **up** *tv.* to add strength or substance to something. ♦ *They beefed up the offer with another thousand dollars.*

beefcake 1. *n.* a display of the male physique. (See also cheesecake.) ♦ *There* *was one calendar showing beefcake rather than the usual cheesecake.* **2.** *n.* a muscularly handsome male. ♦ *She's been going out with a real beefcake.*

beef-head *n.* an oaf; a meathead. ♦ *Look you beef-head, lay off!*

beef-hearts *n.* audible releases of intestinal gas through the anus. (Rhyming slang for *farts.* Usually objectionable.) ♦ *No more of these beef-hearts!*

beema *n.* a beemer; a BMW automobile. (Pop gangsta.) ♦ *Who's holding the kizzle to my beema?*

beemer ['bimɚ] *n.* a BMW automobile. (See also beamer.) ♦ *I had to sell my beemer when the stock market crashed.*

been and gone and done it *phr.* have actually done something. ♦ *You shot him! You really been and gone and done it!*

been around (the block) *phr.* sexually experienced. ♦ *He's just a kid. He hasn't been around the block yet.*

been bobbing for fries *phr.* [has] a really ugly face. (As if badly burned.) ♦ *Look at that face. Been bobbing for fries, I guess.*

been had AND **was had 1.** *phr.* been copulated with; been made pregnant. ♦ *I've been had, and I'm going to have the baby.* ♦ *I was so had! Twins!* **2.** *phr.* been mistreated, cheated, or dealt with badly. (See also taken.) ♦ *Look at this shirt! I was had!*

Been there, done that (got the T-shirt). AND **BTDT(GTS)** *phr. & comp. abb.* I've been through all this before. ♦ *BTDTGTS. I need some other suggestions.*

been to hell and back *phr.* to have survived a great deal of trouble. ♦ *What a terrible day! I feel like I have been to hell and back.*

beeper *n.* a portable electronic pager (signal). ♦ *I have somebody call me during a meeting so my beeper will go off and get me out of it.*

beer 1. *in.* to drink beer. ♦ *Fred and Tom sat in there watching the game and beering and belching like two old whales.* **2.** *tv.* to get oneself drunk on beer. ♦ *I beered myself, but good.*

beer and skittles [...'skɪdlz] *n.* something very easy to do; an easy time of it. ♦ *Did you think life was all beer and skittles?*

beer belly AND **beer gut** *n.* a large belly. ♦ *You're going to end up with a real beer belly hanging over your belt if you don't let up on that stuff.* ♦ *How long does it take to grow a beer gut like that?*

beer blast AND **beer bust** *n.* a beer-drinking party; a beer binge. ♦ *Kelly's having a beer blast at his place, starting tonight.* ♦ *Dad, I think your "beer bust" is called something else now.*

beer bust Go to beer blast.

beer goggles [...'gɑglz] *n.* imaginary lenses (associated with too much beer) worn by someone for whom all persons of the opposite sex look very attractive. (Usually said about the eyes of males. See also male blindness.) ♦ *See how Willy is looking at that dog? He's got his beer goggles on!*

beer gut Go to beer belly.

beer up *in.* to drink a lot of beer. ♦ *Those guys are out there beering up like mad.*

beerbong ['birbɔŋ] **1.** *n.* a can of beer prepared for drinking in one gulp. (An opening is made in the bottom of a can of beer. The can, with the opening placed in the mouth, is turned upright, and the tab opener is pulled, releasing all the beer directly into the mouth. In another version, the beer is poured into a funnel attached to a plastic tube that leads to the drinker's mouth.) ♦ *A beerbong is a great way to liven up a party.* **2.** *in.* to drink beer as described in sense 1. ♦ *Those guys who were beerbonging all barfed after it was over.*

beeswax ['bizwæks] *n.* business; concern. (See also mind your own beeswax; none of so's beeswax.) ♦ *Tend to your own beeswax.*

beetle *n.* the original Volkswagen automobile. ♦ *I remember when people used to put big windup keys on their beetles to make them look like windup toys.*

beetlebrain ['bidlbren] *n.* a stupid person. ♦ *Why are you such a beetlebrain when it comes to math?*

beeveedees Go to BVDs.

beezer ['bizɚ] *n.* the nose. ♦ *I've got a zit on my beezer.*

begathon *n.* a televised appeal for contributions, especially as conducted by U.S. public television stations. ♦ *It seems like this station is one long begathon all year long.*

behind *n.* the posterior; the buttocks. (This euphemism is losing out to plain old *ass* and *butt* on TV and elsewhere.) ♦ *She needs some jeans that will flatter her behind.*

behind bars *mod.* in jail; in prison. ♦ *You belong behind bars, you creep!*

behind the eight ball 1. *mod.* in trouble; in a weak or losing position. ♦ *I'm behind the eight ball again.* **2.** *mod.* broke. ♦ *I was behind the eight ball again and couldn't make my car payment.*

Behind you! *phr.* Look behind you!; There is danger behind you! (See also **check your six**; **on your six**.) ♦ *"Behind you!" shouted Tom just as a car raced past and nearly knocked Mary over.*

beige [beʒ] *mod.* boring; insipid. (California. See also **vanilla**.) ♦ *This day is way beige! Bag it!*

bejeer *n.* an act of fellatio. (From B.J.) ♦ *Sometimes, a beejer just won't do the job.*

belch [bɛltʃ] *n.* beer, especially bad beer. ♦ *Pass the belch. Anything's good on a hot day.*

belcher ['bɛltʃɚ] **1.** *n.* a beer drinker. ♦ *Look at the belly on that belcher!* **2.** *n.* a hard drinker; a drunkard. ♦ *A couple of belchers wandered in about midnight. Other than that, the night is dead.*

Believe it or not. AND **BION** *sent. & comp. abb.* That's the story; you can choose to believe it or not believe it. ♦ *That's what really happened, Believe it or not.* ♦ *I'm l8t! BION.*

Believe you me! *sent.* You really should believe me!; You'd better take my word for it! ♦ *Believe you me, this is the best cake I've ever eaten!*

bellies *n.* pork bellies; pork belly futures. (Securities markets. Often with *the*.) ♦ *Buy the bellies and sell the beans.*

bells and whistles *n.* extra, fancy gadgets. ♦ *All those bells and whistles add to the cost.*

belly button *n.* the navel. ♦ *Is your belly button an insy or an outsy?*

belly fiddle *n.* a guitar. ♦ *Listen to that guy play that belly fiddle!*

belly laugh *n.* a loud, deep, uninhibited laugh. ♦ *I don't want to hear giggles when I tell a joke. I want long belly laughs.*

belly up 1. *mod.* alcohol intoxicated. ♦ *Sylvia was boiled—belly up—glassy-eyed.* **2.** *mod.* dead. ♦ *That's the end. This company is belly up.* (See also **turn belly up**.) ♦ *After the fire the firm went belly up.* **3.** Go to **belly up (to sth)**.

belly up (to sth) *in.* to move up to something, often a bar. (See also **belly up**.) ♦ *The man swaggered in and bellied up to the counter and demanded my immediate attention.*

bellyache ['bɛli ek] **1.** *n.* a stomachache. ♦ *Oh, mama, do I have a bellyache!* **2.** *in.* to complain. ♦ *You are always bellyaching!*

bellyful *n.* more than enough; more than one needs. ♦ *I've had a bellyful of your excuses.*

belt 1. *n.* a blow with the fist or hand. ♦ *Quiet or I'll give you a belt in the chops.* **2.** *tv.* to strike someone. ♦ *Quiet or I'll belt you one!* **3.** *n.* a kick or a thrill. ♦ *We all got quite a belt from your jokes.* **4.** *n.* the rush or jolt from an injection of a drug. (Drugs.) ♦ *This stuff has one hell of a belt.* **5.** *n.* an injection of a drug. (Drugs.) ♦ *I could use a belt of smack to hold off the pain.* **6.** *n.* a swallow of liquor. ♦ *Three more quick belts and he was ready to sit down and talk.* **7.** *tv.* to drink (something). (See also **belt the grape**.) ♦ *He belted his drink and asked for another.*

belt the grape *tv.* to drink wine or liquor heavily and become intoxicated. ♦ *He has a tendency to belt the grape—twenty-four hours a day.*

belted *mod.* alcohol or drug intoxicated. ♦ *We were belted out of our minds.*

bench 1. *tv.* to take someone out of a ball game. ♦ *The coach benched Jim, who injured his arm.* **2.** *tv.* to retire someone; to withdraw someone from something. ♦ *The manager benched the entire sales staff for cheating on their expense reports.*

bench jockey *n.* a player who sits on the bench and calls out advice. ♦ *The coach told all the bench jockeys to shut up.*

bench warmer *n.* a ballplayer who spends most of the game on the bench waiting to play; a second-rate player. ♦ *You'll never be anything but a bench warmer.*

bend one's **elbow** AND **bend the elbow; lift** one's **elbow** *tv.* to take a drink of an alcoholic beverage; to drink alcohol to excess. ♦ *He's down at the tavern, bending his elbow.* ♦ *If you didn't spend so much time lifting your elbow, you'd get more done.*

Bend over, here it comes again. AND **BO-HICA** *sent. & comp. abb.* Trouble isn't over yet, there is more on the way. ♦ *It snowed ten inches yesterday. BOHICA. They forecast another foot!*

bend the law *tv.* to cheat a little bit without breaking the law. (Jocular.) ♦ *I didn't break the law. I just bent the law a little.*

benda *n.* a bender; a girl who copulates without much fuss. (Streets.) ♦ *He's always got a bunch of bendas following his ass around.*

bender 1. *n.* a drinking binge. (See also twister.) ♦ *Her benders usually last about ten days.* **2.** *n.* a heavy drinker; a drunkard. ♦ *This bender comes up to me and nearly kills me with his breath, asking for a match.* **3.** *n.* a girl who copulates without much fuss. (Her legs bend easily. The same as benda.) ♦ *Maydene is a bender and everybody knows it!* **4.** *n.* a release of intestinal gas when someone bends over. ♦ *I stooped over and let a bender that rocked the room.*

benies *n.* employment benefits. (See also benny.) ♦ *The salary is good, but the benies are almost nonexistent.*

Benjamin AND **Benji** *n.* a one hundred dollar bill. (Bearing a picture of Benjanin Franklin.) ♦ *You owe me two Benjamins!* ♦ *Here's the Benji I owe you.*

benny AND **bennie** *n.* a Benzedrine capsule or tablet. ♦ *You got a benny or two you could spare a poor man?* ♦ *Aren't bennies sort of out of style?*

bent 1. *mod.* alcohol or drug intoxicated. ♦ *I've never seen two guys so bent.* **2.** *mod.* dishonest; crooked. ♦ *I'm afraid that Paul is a little bent. He cheats on his taxes.* **3.** *mod.* angry. ♦ *He was so bent there was steam coming out of his ears.*

bent out of shape 1. *mod.* angry; insulted. ♦ *Man, there is no reason to get so bent out of shape. I didn't mean any harm.* **2.** *n.* alcohol or drug intoxicated. ♦ *I was so bent out of shape I thought I'd never recover.*

benz [bɛnz] **1.** *n.* Benzedrine. (Drugs.) ♦ *Stay off the benz. Coffee is enough to perk anybody up.* ♦ *He had some benz in an inhaler, but there's much better medication available.* **2.** AND **Benz** *n.* a Mercedes Benz automobile. ♦ *My uncle had a Benz that he took back to Germany every two years for service.*

beotch Go to bitch.

berp AND **burp 1.** *in.* to bring up stomach gas. (See also belch.) ♦ *She burped quietly behind her hanky, so no one would notice.* **2.** *n.* an upward release of stomach gas. ♦ *The burp did not go unnoticed.*

berps AND **burps** *n.* liquor; beer. (See also belch.) ♦ *Did you bring the berps for the party?*

berpwater *n.* beer; ale; champagne. ♦ *I don't care for all that berpwater. Give me some whiskey.*

berries AND **1.** the **berries** *n.* the best; the finest. (Always with *the*. A noun with the force of an adjective.) ♦ *Man, this stuff is the berries!* **2.** *n.* wine. (Originally black. See also grape(s).) ♦ *Lemme stop at the liquor store for some berries.*

best bud *n.* a best buddy; a best friend. ♦ *Isn't Bill your best bud? Why are you so mad at him?*

best buy *n.* a sexually loose woman. (Punning on the electronics store.) ♦ *That chick is a best buy.*

one's **best shot** *n.* one's best attempt (at something). ♦ *That was his best shot, but it wasn't good enough.*

bet one's **bottom dollar** *tv.* to be very certain of something; to bet in complete certainty of winning. (Need not refer to an actual bet.) ♦ *I bet my bottom dollar you never ever went to Alaska!*

bet so **dollars to doughnuts** *tv.* to bet something of value against something worth considerably less. ♦ *I bet you dollars to doughnuts that she is on time.*

better get used to it AND **BGUTI** *phr. & comp. abb.* It may be bad, but you should get used to it. ♦ *Sorry you don't like it. BGUTI.* ♦ *A: I am so not used to it! B: Better get used to it.*

one's **better half** *n.* one's wife, and occasionally, one's husband. ♦ *My better half disapproved of the movie.*

Better luck next time. *sent.* I wish you luck when you try again. ♦ *You blew it, you stupid twit. Better luck next time.*

betty 1. *n.* some fake drugs; a bad drug buy. ♦ *John's supplier slipped him some betty.* **2.** *n.* a good-looking girl or woman. (Usually **Betty.**) ♦ *Who's your new Betty, Bob?*

between a rock and a hard place *mod.* in a very difficult position; facing a hard decision. ♦ *I'm between a rock and a hard place. I don't know what to do.*

between you, me, and the bedpost Go to between you, me, and the lamppost.

between you, me, and the lamppost AND **between you, me, and the bedpost** *phr.* just between you and me. ♦ *Between you, me, and the lamppost, things are going to get worse before they get better.* ♦ *It's supposed to be a secret, but between you, me, and the bedpost, he quit his job.*

bewottled *mod.* alcohol intoxicated; tipsy. ♦ *Sam was so bewottled that he could hardly walk.*

bezongas *n.* a woman's breasts. (Usually objectionable.) ♦ *I've never seen so many definitely fine bezongas all in one place at the same time.*

BF 1. *n.* BF = best friend. (Initialism. Collegiate.) ♦ *Sharon is my BF.* **2.** *n.* BF = boyfriend. ♦ *Who's your BF?*

BFD *exclam.* Big fucking deal!; So what? (Usually objectionable.) ♦ *So, you've got serious money problems. BFD!*

BFE Go to butt-fucking Egypt.

BFG Go to big fat grin.

BG 1. *interj.* big grin. (An initialism used in computer forum or news groups to show that the writer is joking or happy. Not pronounced. Often enclosed, **<BG>**.) ♦ *I haven't seen you on the board. I thought you had run away from home. <BG>* **2.** Go to baby gangsta.

BGUTI Go to better get used to it.

bhang [bæŋ OR baŋ] **1.** *n.* the marijuana plant. (Drugs. From Hindi.) ♦ *Martha grows bhang in a pot in her room.* **2.** *n.* a marijuana cigarette; the smoking of a marijuana cigarette. ♦ *The kids found an old bhang in Fred's car.*

bhang ganjah [bæŋ 'gændʒə OR baŋ 'gɑndʒə] *n.* marijuana; marijuana resin. (Drugs.) ♦ *It's the bhang ganjah that gives the stuff its kick.*

bhong Go to bong.

bi 1. *n.* one of the biceps. (Bodybuilding. Typically **BI.** Usually plural.) ♦ *I have to work on my BIs and then build up my thighs.* **2.** *mod.* bisexual. ♦ *Suddenly she suspected that she was getting involved in some sort of strange bi activities.* **3.** *n.* a bisexual person. ♦ *This information of interest only to bis and gays.*

biatch Go to bitch.

BICO Go to Baby it's cold outside.

biff [bɪf] **1.** *tv.* to hit someone. ♦ *Tom biffed Fred on the snoot.* **2.** *n.* a blow. ♦ *The biff on the nose gave Fred a nosebleed.* **3.** *in.* to fall; to fail; to crash. ♦ *His bike hit a bump and he biffed.*

biffy [ˈbɪfi] *n.* a toilet. ♦ *The house we toured has a pink biffy. Can you believe it?*

the **Big Apple** *n.* New York City. ♦ *The Big Apple is filled with young kids trying to get into show biz.*

big blue *n.* the stock of International Business Machines or the company itself. (Securities markets. See also (I-)beam.) ♦ *Big blue led the market lower again today.*

big board *n.* the New York Stock Exchange. (Securities markets.) ♦ *On the big board, stocks were down again today, bringing the loss this week on the Dow to nearly 175 points.*

big brother 1. *n.* a personification of the totalitarian state. (From George Orwell's *1984*.) ♦ *Big brother has changed the tax laws again.* **2.** *n.* someone who personifies the totalitarian state: the police, parents, teachers. ♦ *Big brother says the paper is due tomorrow, or else.*

big bucks *n.* a lot of money. (See also megabucks.) ♦ *She gets paid big bucks to worry about stuff like that.*

big cheese *n.* the boss; the key figure; the leader. ♦ *Here's a note from the big cheese telling me to come in for a chat.*

big deal 1. *n.* something really important. ♦ *Don't make such a big deal out of it!* **2.** *exclam.* So what!; What does it matter? (Usually **Big deal!**) ♦ *So he snores! Big deal! Snore back!*

big Dick *n.* a ten rolled with the dice in craps. (Likely a veiled, punning reference to phallic length.) ♦ *Come, on! I want a big Dick! Baby needs shoes!*

Big Dig *n.* the extensive, underground interstate highway (and commuter route) tunneled under Boston, MA. ♦ *The Big Dig has about 300 water leaks raining down inside.*

big drink *n.* the Atlantic Ocean; an ocean. ♦ *We flew over the big drink in an hour or two.*

big drink of water 1. *n.* a very tall person. (Folksy.) ♦ *Tim is sure a big drink of water.* **2.** *n.* a boring person or thing. (A

pun on *hard to take*.) ♦ *The lecture was a big drink of water.*

big enchilada [...ɛntʃəˈlɑdə] *n.* the boss; the leader. (See also big cheese.) ♦ *The big enchilada has sent word that it's safe to return.*

big fat grin AND **BFG** *phr. & comp. abb.* I'm smiling while I write this. ♦ *Just kidding! BFG.*

big fish *n.* the boss; the leader. (Underworld.) ♦ *We took in the little guys, but the big fish got away.*

big gun *n.* an important and powerful person, such as an officer of a company. (Often with *bring in* as in the example.) ♦ *I knew they would bring in the big guns at the last minute.*

the **big house** *n.* a state or federal penitentiary. ♦ *Two years in the big house is like two years in a custom-made hell.*

big iron *n.* a large, mainframe computer. (Computers. See also iron.) ♦ *We'll have to run this job on the big iron over at the university.*

big jab *n.* a lethal injection used to carry out a death sentence. (Journalistic.) ♦ *Nearly 59 prisoners got the big jab in Texas this year.*

big John *n.* the police; a police officer. ♦ *Big John took her in and hit her with a vice rap.*

big juice *n.* a big-time crook. (See also juice.) ♦ *So, you're the big juice around here.*

big kahuna *n.* the important person; the knowledgeable authority on some matter. (From the Hawai'ian word for "priest." Sometimes capitalized.) ♦ *Joe is the big kahuna around here when it comes to predicting stock market prices.*

big league 1. *n.* a situation where competition is keen and a high level of performance is expected. (Usually plural. Referred originally to major league sports.) ♦ *You're in the big leagues now—no more penny-ante stuff.* **2.** AND **big-league** *mod.* professional; big time. (From baseball.) ♦ *When I'm a big-league star, I'll send you free tickets.*

Big Mac attack *n.* a sudden and desperate need for a Big Mac sandwich, a product of the McDonald's restaurant chain. (*Big Mac* is a protected trade name of McDonald's.) ♦ *I feel a Big Mac attack coming on!*

big man on campus *n.* an important male college student. (See more examples at BMOC.) ♦ *Hank acts like such a big man on campus!*

big mouth 1. *n.* a person who talks too much or too loudly; someone who tells secrets. (Also a term of address.) ♦ *Okay, big mouth! Shut up!* **2.** *tv.* to spread secrets around. ♦ *Why do you always have to big mouth everything around?*

big name 1. *n.* a famous and important person. ♦ *Lots of big names were there lending their support to the cause.* **2.** AND **big-name** *mod.* famous; important. ♦ *Some big-name star I've never heard of was there pretending to serve dinner.*

big noise 1. *n.* an important person. ♦ *If you're such a big noise, why don't you get this line moving?* **2.** *n.* the important current news; the current scandal. ♦ *There's a big noise up on Capitol Hill. Something about budget cuts.*

big of SO **1.** *mod.* magnanimous of someone. ♦ *It was big of Tom to come back and apólogize.* **2.** *mod.* nice of someone. (Often sarcastic.) ♦ *A whole pound. Wow, that is really big of you!*

big shot AND **bigshot 1.** *n.* a very important person. ♦ *I'm no big shot, but I do have a little power around here.* **2.** *mod.* mighty; overbearing; overly important. ♦ *If you think that a big shot title impresses me, you're wrong.*

big stink *n.* a major issue; a scandal; a big argument. ♦ *Don't make such a big stink about it.*

big time 1. *n.* the high level of success. ♦ *I've finally reached the big time!* **2.** AND **big-time** *mod.* outstanding; extravagant. ♦ *This is one of your real big-time stars.* **3.** AND **big-time** *mod.* felonious. (Un-derworld.) ♦ *Frank is into big-time stuff now.*

big top 1. *n.* a circus tent; the circus, in general. ♦ *And now, one of the greatest acts under the big top.* **2.** *mod.* having to do with the circus. ♦ *One big top experience is enough to last me a lifetime.*

big wheel *n.* a very important person. ♦ *Some big wheel wrote the order. Don't blame me.*

big with SO *mod.* preferred by someone. ♦ *Soup is big with everybody in cold weather.*

big woman on campus *n.* an important female college student. (See more examples at BWOC.) ♦ *Helen acts like such a big woman on campus!*

big Zs *n.* sleep. ♦ *I need me some of them big Zs.*

bigass 1. *n.* a person with very large buttocks. (Usually objectionable.) ♦ *Some bigass came in and broke the chair when he sat down.* **2.** *mod.* pertaining to someone who has very large buttocks. (Usually objectionable.) ♦ *Tell that bigass jerk to get out!* **3.** *mod.* pertaining to a person who is self-important, overbearing, or arrogant; pertaining to anything having to do with arrogance. (Usually objectionable.) ♦ *Take your bigass ideas and go back where you came from.* **4.** *mod.* really big. ♦ *Did you see that bigass SUV hit the little Honda?*

big-C. 1. *n.* cancer. (Usually with *the*.) ♦ *She was struck with the big-C.* **2.** *n.* cocaine. (Drugs.) ♦ *When she started taking big-C., she was only eight.*

big-D. *n.* Dallas, Texas. ♦ *Kelly is from big-D.*

bigface *n.* the newer version of the $20 bill bearing a larger portrait on the front. (Streets. Additional bills now carry the larger portraits.) ♦ *We only accept the big-face on twenties right now. The others just don't look right.*

biggie 1. *n.* something or someone important. ♦ *As problems go, this one's a biggie.* **2.** *n.* copulation. (Usually with *the*.) ♦ *But I don't think I'm ready for the biggie.*

biggity ['bɪgədi] *mod.* haughty; aloof. ♦ *Kelly is too biggity for my taste.*

big-H. *n.* heroin. (Drugs.) ♦ *She's started on big-H. Soon she'll be so hooked!*

bighead *n.* a headache and other ill effects from drinking. ♦ *I got a case of the big-head. Too much soda in my drinks, I guess.*

bigheaded 1. *mod.* conceited. ♦ *What a bigheaded jerk!* **2.** *mod.* having a hang-over. ♦ *I feel sort of bigheaded. Too much beer, I guess.*

big-O. *n.* opium. ♦ *The big-O. is making a comeback, I hear.*

big-ticket *mod.* having to do with something expensive. ♦ *In a survey taken last month, heads of families said they were unwilling to put big-ticket items at the bottom of their shopping lists.*

big-time operator AND **BTO 1.** *n.* someone who does business in a big way. (The abbreviation is an initialism.) ♦ *If you're such a BTO, why are we standing here in the rain?* **2.** *n.* a man who chases women. ♦ *That twit thinks he's a big-time operator. A stud he's not.* ♦ *A big-time operator needs a big-time car!*

big-time spender *n.* someone who spends a lot of money. ♦ *A big-time spender does-n't look at the prices on the menu.*

bigwig *n.* an important person; a self-important person. ♦ *Some bigwig in a pin-stripe suit waltzed through and asked me to leave.*

bike *n.* a motorcycle; a bicycle. ♦ *You have to wear a helmet with a bike that size, don't you?*

bike boys *n.* cops; the police. ♦ *Look out! Here come the bike boys.*

biker *n.* a motorcycle rider. ♦ *Four bikers roared by and woke up the baby.*

bill and coo *in.* to kiss and cuddle. (In the manner of love birds.) ♦ *Keep an eye on those kids. They aren't going to be satisfied with billing and cooing forever, you know.*

billie AND **bill(y)** ['bɪli] *n.* paper money; a bill. ♦ *Do you have any billies on you?* ♦ *Lend me a billy or two.*

bim *n.* a shortening of bimbo. ♦ *Yo ho's a bim!*

bimbo ['bɪmbo] **1.** *n.* a clownlike person. ♦ *If that bimbo doesn't keep quiet, I'll bop him.* **2.** *n.* a giddy woman; a sexually loose woman. (See also bim.) ♦ *Now that bimbo is a star in the movies!*

bind *n.* a problem; a wrinkle. ♦ *Unfortu-nately, a new bind has slowed down the project.*

bindle 1. *n.* a packet or bundle; a hobo's pack. ♦ *Throw your bindle over yonder, and plunk your butt on that empty crate.* **2.** *n.* a packet of drugs. (Drugs.) ♦ *She had a bindle of H. in her purse.*

binge [bɪndʒ] **1.** *n.* a drinking or drugging spree. ♦ *Larry is the type who likes a good binge every now and then.* **2.** *n.* any spree of self-indulgence: emotional, glutton-ous, etc. ♦ *About Thanksgiving time I start a monthlong eating binge.* **3.** *in.* to drink heavily. ♦ *She binges about once a month and is stone-cold sober the rest of the time.*

binged ['bɪndʒd] *mod.* alcohol intoxicated. ♦ *She sat there, binged out of her mind.*

Bingo! ['bɪŋgo] *exclam.* Yes!; That's right! (From the game Bingo.) ♦ *Bingo! I've got the answer!*

bio break *n.* a toilet break. (Contrived and euphemistic.) ♦ *She out of pocket for a bio break.*

BION Go to Believe it or not.

bird 1. *n.* a woman; a girl. ♦ *I like the bird you were with last night.* **2.** *n.* a derisive noise made with the lips; a raspberry. ♦ *The third time he fumbled, he was greeted by two thousand mouths making the bird.* **3.** *n.* an odd person. ♦ *Some old bird came up to me and tried to sell me a cookbook.* **4.** *n.* a rude gesture made with the mid-dle finger. (Usually with *the*. See com-ments at finger wave.) ♦ *A lot of little kids give people the bird all the time because they see it on television.* **5.** *n.* an airplane. ♦ *I like this bird. She's a dream to fly.* **6.** *n.* one hundred dollars. ♦ *This thing cost three birds! Bull!*

bird watcher *n.* a girl watcher; someone, usually a man, who enjoys watching women go by. ♦ *You bird watchers should just mind your own business!*

birdbrain 1. *n.* a stupid-acting person. ♦ *I'm such a birdbrain. I forgot my driver's license, officer.* **2.** AND **birdbrained** *mod.* stupid. ♦ *Look, you birdbrained idiot, you are dead wrong!*

birdbrained Go to birdbrain.

bird-dog 1. *tv.* to take away another man's girlfriend. ♦ *Why'd you have to go and bird-dog me, your best buddy?* **2.** *tv.* to supervise someone; to tail someone. ♦ *Marlowe knew somebody was bird-dogging him, but he was too smart to show it.*

birds of a feather AND **BOF** *phr. & comp. abb.* people who share an interest or proclivity. ♦ *Those guys are really birds of a feather. They are always together.* ♦ *We're BOF and love to hike and enjoy nature.*

birdseed 1. *n.* a small amount of money. (See also chicken feed.) ♦ *Forty billion is birdseed to a government with a 600 billion dollar budget.* **2.** *n.* nonsense. (Based on BS.) ♦ *I've heard enough birdseed here to last for a lifetime.*

birdturd 1. *n.* an obnoxious person. (Rude and derogatory.) ♦ *You silly birdturd. Wake up!* **2.** *mod.* stupid; obnoxious; lousy; worthless. (Usually objectionable.) ♦ *Of all the stupid, underhanded, birdturd tricks—this takes the cake!* **3.** *n.* bird dung, especially if dried. (Usually objectionable.) ♦ *There's birdturd on your shoe.*

birdy AND **birdie** *mod.* crazy; strange. ♦ *She acts a little birdy from time to time.*

biscuit ['bɪskət] *n.* the head. (See also float an air-biscuit.) ♦ *She got a nasty little bump on the biscuit.*

bison *in.* to vomit. (Probably a play on yak.) ♦ *He stepped aside to bison in the bushes.*

bit 1. *n.* a jail sentence. (Underworld.) ♦ *Mooshoo did a two-year bit in Sing Sing.* **2.** *n.* a small theatrical part. (From *bit part*.) ♦ *It was just a bit, but I needed the money.* **3.** *n.* any part of an act; any isolated activity or presentation. ♦ *I didn't like that bit concerning penalties.*

a **bit much** *mod.* more than enough; more than good taste allows. ♦ *That was a bit much, Paul. After all there is such a thing as good taste.*

bit of the action Go to piece (of the action).

bit-bucket *n.* the imaginary place where lost computer data goes. (Computers.) ♦ *I guess my data went into the bit-bucket.*

bitch 1. *n.* an unpleasant or irritating female. (Rude and derogatory. See the complete list of all entries with bitch in the **Index of Hidden Key Words**.) ♦ *How can anyone be expected to deal with a bitch like that?* **2.** *in.* to complain. (Usually objectionable.) ♦ *Oh, stop bitching! I'm sick of hearing your noise.* **3.** *n.* a complaint. (Usually objectionable.) ♦ *I've got a bitch about this new foreman.* **4.** *n.* a difficult thing or person. (Usually objectionable.) ♦ *This algebra problem is a real bitch.* **5.** *tv.* to ruin something. (Usually objectionable. See also bitch sth up.) ♦ *You really bitched this coil of wire.* **6.** *n.* one's girlfriend. (Black. Usually objectionable.) ♦ *Me and my bitch really like this kind of stuff.* **7.** AND **biatch; beotch** *n.* buddy; cohort. (Streets. Also additional spellings.) ♦ *Good, man, ma biatch.*

bitch box *n.* a public-address system loudspeaker. (Military. Because it is always nagging.) ♦ *I'm sick of listening to that bitch box day and night.*

bitch of a so/sth *n.* a very difficult or unpleasant person or thing. (Usually objectionable.) ♦ *This is a bitch of a math problem!*

bitch out *in.* to complain. (Usually objectionable.) ♦ *You are always bitching out no matter how well off you are.*

bitch session *n.* a session of complaining; an informal gripe session. (See also bitch. Usually objectionable.) ♦ *We were just having a bitch session. Come on in.*

bitch slammer *n.* a women's prison. (Streets.) ♦ *They threw her in the bitch slammer for three years.*

bitch so **off** *tv.* to make someone very angry. (See also piss so off. Usually objectionable.) ♦ *You know what bitches me off? Soggy French fries, that's what!*

bitch sth **up** *tv.* to mess something up; to ruin or spoil something. (Usually objectionable.) ♦ *The rain so bitched up our picnic!*

bitch tits *n.* gynecomastia; the development of breast tissue in the male. (From bodybuilding, in reference to breast development caused by steroids. Usually objectionable.) ♦ *If you don't let up on the gorilla juice, you'll get bitch tits.*

bitchen Go to bitchin'.

bitchin' AND **bitchen; bitching 1.** *mod.* excellent; great; classy. (Usually objectionable.) ♦ *This is a totally bitchin' pair of jeans!* **2.** *exclam.* Terrific! (Usually **Bitchin'!**) ♦ *Four of them? Bitchen!*

bitchy *mod.* irritable; complaining. (Usually objectionable.) ♦ *Why are you so bitchy today?*

bite 1. *in.* to accept a deception; to fall for something; to respond to a come-on. ♦ *We put up a sign advertising free pop, but nobody bit.* **2.** *in.* [for someone or something] to be bad or threatening. ♦ *My dad bites, but don't worry, he's in a good mood.* **3.** *in.* to be irritating. (More severe than to suck, as in It sucks.) ♦ *This party bites. Sko.* **4.** *tv.* to copy something without permission; to steal something. ♦ *Sue bit a copy of my term paper, and I almost got in trouble.*

bite on so *in.* to copy something that someone else has done; to dress the same way someone else does. ♦ *Jennifer is always biting on Anne, who is a careful dresser.*

bite the big one *tv.* to die. ♦ *I was so tired that I thought I was going to bite the big one.*

bite the bullet *tv.* to accept something difficult and try to live with it. ♦ *You are just going to have to bite the bullet and make the best of it.*

bite the dust 1. *tv.* to die. ♦ *A shot rang out, and another cowboy bit the dust.* **2.** *tv.* to break; to fail; to give out. ♦ *My car finally bit the dust.*

Bite the ice! *exclam.* Go to hell! ♦ *If that's what you think, you can just bite the ice!*

biter 1. *n.* a thief. (See also bite.) ♦ *Some biter made off with my algebra book.* **2.** *n.* someone who copies someone else. (From the first sense.) ♦ *That's my steelo, you biter!*

biters *n.* the teeth. ♦ *I gotta get my biters to the dentist while there are still a few left.*

biz [bɪz] **1.** *n.* a business; business. ♦ *I'm in the plumbing biz.* **2.** *n.* apparatus for injecting drugs. (Drugs.) ♦ *The biz is right there in the towel on top of the stack.* **3.** *mod.* busy. ♦ *Get out! I'm biz!*

bizatch AND **biznitch** *n.* bitch (sense 7). (Streets.) ♦ *Fo sho, ma bizatch!*

biznitch Go to bizatch.

bizzle a wild card word for words beginning with B, such as bitch, bong, or bowl (of marijuana). (Streets. Also for other words with initial B.) ♦ *Shut up, my bizzle!* ♦ *The teacher had no idea what "bizzle" meant, but she didn't like being called one.*

B.J. *n.* a blow job; an act of fellatio. ♦ *She offered him a blow job when he stopped at a traffic light.*

blab [blæb] **1.** *n.* talk; chatter; meaningless talk. ♦ *I never pay any attention to blab like that.* **2.** *tv.* to tell a secret; to reveal something private in public. ♦ *Tiffany blabbed the whole thing.*

blabbermouth 1. *n.* someone who talks too much and tells secrets. ♦ *You are such a blabbermouth!* **2.** *tv.* to tell secrets in public. ♦ *Don't blabbermouth this to everybody.*

black *mod.* without cream or milk. (Said of coffee.) ♦ *Black coffee, good and hot, please.*

black and blue *mod.* bruised, physically or emotionally. ♦ *I'm still black and blue from my divorce.*

black and white *n.* the police; a black and white police patrol car; any police car. ♦ *Call the black and whites. We got trouble here.*

black eye *n.* a moral blemish; an injury to the prestige of someone or something. ♦ *That kind of behavior can give us all a black eye.*

blackball *tv.* to vote against someone in a secret ballot. ♦ *Someone blackballed the prospective member.*

black-collar workers *n.* people, usually affected, who wear black all the time. (Contrived. A play on *white-collar* and *blue-collar* workers.) ♦ *I hate to go over to the gallery. It's filled with black-collar workers. Reminds me of the Adams Family.*

blacklist 1. *n.* a list of the names of banned people; a list of people undesirable to some group. ♦ *I hear they keep a blacklist of all the people they disagree with.* **2.** *tv.* to put someone's name on a list of undesirables. ♦ *They blacklisted me for not belonging to the right organizations.*

bladdered *mod.* drunk, especially with a full bladder. ♦ *I'm really bladdered! Somebody drive me home?*

blade 1. *n.* a knife. ♦ *Bring your blade over here and cut this loose.* **2.** *n.* a young man, witty and worldly. ♦ *A couple of blades from the international jet set ordered vintage wine for everyone.* **3.** *n.* a homosexual man. (From *gay blade*.) ♦ *Some blade came over and offered to buy me a drink.*

blah [blɑ] **1.** *mod.* bland; dull. ♦ *After a blah day like this I need something really exciting like a hot bath.* **2.** *mod.* depressed; worn out. ♦ *I'm really blah. Would you mind awfully if I just went home?* **3.** *mod.* alcohol intoxicated; very drunk. ♦ *We are going to get totally blah tonight.*

blah-blah ['blɑ'blɑ] *phr.* a phrase echoic of gibberish or incessant chattering. (It can be repeated many times.) ♦ *Why all this blah-blah-blah?*

the **blahs** [blɑz] *n.* a state of mental depression; the blues. ♦ *You look like you've got the blahs.*

blame shifting *n.* a process in business and government wherein the blame for something bad is shifted from person to person. (A coinage that has appeal because it fills the need to express the concept succinctly.) ♦ *Can't we have a decent argument without your constant blame shifting?*

blanco *n.* a white person; a Caucasian. (From Spanish. Potentially derogatory.) ♦ *The blancos arrived in droves to enjoy our beaches.*

blanket drill *n.* a night's sleep; sleep. (Military.) ♦ *Fred is still on blanket drill. He's in for it.*

blast 1. *n.* an exciting party. ♦ *What a blast we had!* **2.** *n.* a thrill; a kick. ♦ *The roller coaster was a blast.* **3.** *tv.* to shoot someone with a gun. ♦ *The speeding car drove by, and somebody tried to blast him with a machine gun.* **4.** *tv.* to attack or criticize someone or something verbally. ♦ *He blasted his brother until we all left in embarrassment.* **5.** *n.* a verbal attack. ♦ *The senator leveled a blast at the administration.* **6.** *n.* the kick or rush from taking or injecting a drug. (Drugs.) ♦ *With a blast like that, somebody's gonna get hooked fast.*

blast off (for somewhere) *in.* [for someone] to leave for a destination quickly. ♦ *I've got to blast off. It's late.*

blasted 1. *mod.* alcohol or drug intoxicated. ♦ *I got so blasted I swore never to blow another joint.* **2.** *mod.* damned. ♦ *Shut your blasted mouth!*

blaster Go to (ghetto) blaster.

blaze *in.* to smoke marijuana. ♦ *The teacher caught two of them blazing in the john.*

blazes *n.* hell. (Especially with blue.) Just go to blue blazes.

blazing *mod.* really good; really good looking; really hot. (See also blaze.) ♦ *We had a blazing time at Jane and Bob's wedding reception.*

bleed *tv.* to drain someone of money through extortion or continuous demands for payment. ♦ *I'm going to bleed you till I get what I deserve.*

bleed for so *in.* to sympathize with someone. ♦ *I really bleed for you, but there's nothing I can do.*

bleed so **dry** Go to bleed so white.

bleed so **white** AND **bleed** so **dry** *tv.* to take all of someone's money; to extort money from someone. (See also bleed.) ♦ *The creeps tried to bleed me white.* ♦ *These taxes are going to bleed me dry!*

blimp *n.* a nickname for an obese person. ♦ *This enormous blimp managed to get on the plane but couldn't get into a seat.*

blimp out *in.* to overeat. ♦ *I love to buy a bag of chips and just blimp out.*

blimped *mod.* alcohol intoxicated; swollen with drinking. ♦ *I am still a little blimped from our party last night.*

blind drunk *mod.* heavily alcohol intoxicated. ♦ *They drank till they were blind drunk.*

blind(ed) *mod.* alcohol or drug intoxicated. ♦ *I guess she was blinded. She couldn't stand up.*

blindside *tv.* [for someone or something] to surprise someone, as if sneaking up on the blind side of a one-eyed person (or animal). ♦ *The new tax law blindsided about half the population.*

bling-bling 1. *n.* fancy jewelry, especially chains and the like that sparkle or tinkle when in motion. (Streets.) ♦ *All that bling-bling's gonna give you a sore neck!* **2.** *mod.* fancy or sparkly, from the glimmer of light. (Streets.) ♦ *Tiff! Your chains are so bling-bling!*

blinkers *n.* the eyes. ♦ *As I opened my blinkers, guess who I saw?*

blinky AND **winky** ['blɪŋki AND 'wɪŋki] *n.* a device for smoking crack, a form of cocaine. (Drugs.) ♦ *Hold the blinky here and wait till I tell you.* ♦ *His winky blew up, and he's in the hospital.*

blip [blɪp] **1.** *n.* an intermittently appearing light on a radar screen. ♦ *A blip caught the controller's eye for an instant.* **2.** *n.* anything quick and insignificant; a one-time thing of little importance. ♦ *It was nothing, just a blip. The press blew it out of proportion.*

bliss ninny ['blɪs 'nɪni] *n.* a giddy and disoriented person; a blissed-out person.

(See also bliss out.) ♦ *You silly bliss ninny! Who watches over you, anyway?*

bliss out *in.* to become euphoric. (See also blissed (out).) ♦ *I always bliss out from talk like that, but I still love Willy.*

bliss so **out** *tv.* to cause someone to be overcome with happiness. ♦ *This kind of sunny weather just blisses me out.*

blissed (out) AND **blissed-out** [blɪst...] **1.** *mod.* in a state of emotional bliss. ♦ *After the second movement, I was totally blissed out.* **2.** *mod.* alcohol or drug intoxicated. ♦ *She is more than blissed. She is stoned.*

blisterfoot *n.* someone who walks a lot: a police patrol officer, a soldier, etc. ♦ *This blisterfoot puts his hand on my shoulder and says, "What's the rush, chum?"*

blitz [blɪts] **1.** *n.* a devastating attack. ♦ *After that blitz from the boss, you must feel sort of shaken.* **2.** *tv.* to attack and defeat someone or demolish something. ♦ *The team from downstate blitzed our local team for the third year in a row.*

blitz so **out** *tv.* to shock or disorient someone. ♦ *The accident blitzed her out for a moment.*

blitzed (out) [blɪtst...] *mod.* alcohol or drug intoxicated. ♦ *I want to go out and get totally blitzed. I'll show her who's in charge!*

blivit ['blɪvət] *n.* someone or something annoying and unnecessary. ♦ *Don't be a blivit. Just calm down.*

blix *tv.* to look at something; to glance at something. ♦ *She blixed my face and saw that I was so out of control!*

blixed [blɪkst] *mod.* mildly drug intoxicated. (Drugs.) ♦ *He was a little blixed when I last saw him.*

blizzy *n.* a marijuana cigarette. ♦ *Lemme have a toke of that blizzy.*

blob [blɑb] **1.** *n.* a fool; an oaf. ♦ *Don't be a blob. Get up and get going.* **2.** *n.* a useless dishrag of a person; a wimp. ♦ *I'm amazed that blob can tie his own shoes.* **3.** *n.* a very fat person. ♦ *What a blob!*

Must have been kicked out of Fat Watchers.

block 1. *n.* the head. ♦ *Try to get this stuff through your block before the test.* **2.** *n.* the auction block. ♦ *The painting went on the block and sold for nearly fifty-three million dollars.* **3.** *n.* a stupid person. (Possibly a back formation on blockhead.) ♦ *You silly block! Get out of the way.*

blockbuster 1. *n.* something enormous, especially a movie or book that attracts a large audience. ♦ *That blockbuster should make about twenty million.* **2.** *mod.* exciting and successful. ♦ *With a blockbuster novel like that in print, you should make quite a bundle.*

blocked *mod.* alcohol or drug intoxicated. ♦ *Man, he is really blocked. Don't let him drive.*

blockhead *n.* a stupid person. (See also block.) ♦ *Without a blockhead like you to remind me of the perils of stupidity, I might be less efficient than I am.*

blog Go to weblog.

blogging *n.* making an entry into a weblog or blog = online diary. ♦ *When John said he was busy blogging, Sally said he should get a life!*

blond moment *n.* a lapse in thinking, something like a *senior moment.* ♦ *Sorry. I was having a blond moment. And that's hard for a redhead.*

blood 1. *n.* catsup. ♦ *Somebody pass the blood.* **2.** Go to blood (brother). **3.** *n.* a black buddy or fellow gang member. (Streets. Also a term of address.) ♦ *My bloods aren't going to like this.*

blood and guts 1. *n.* strife; acrimony. ♦ *Cut out the blood and guts and grow up!* **2.** *mod.* acrimonious. (This is hyphenated before a nominal.) ♦ *There are too many blood-and-guts arguments around here. Cool it!*

blood (brother) *n.* a fellow black male. (See also blood.) ♦ *One of the bloods came up to say hello.*

blooey [ˈblui] **1.** *mod.* gone; destroyed. ♦ *Everything is finished, blooey!* **2.** *mod.* al-

cohol intoxicated. ♦ *Man, I'm blooey. I'm stoned to the bones.*

blooper [ˈblupɚ] **1.** *n.* an embarrassing broadcasting error that must be bleeped or blooped out of the program. ♦ *There is a record you can buy that lets you hear the famous bloopers of the past.* **2.** *n.* an error. ♦ *That was a real blooper. Did you get fired?*

blot so out *tv.* to kill someone. (Underworld.) ♦ *They blotted out the witness before the trial.*

blotter 1. *n.* a drunkard. (See also sponge.) ♦ *The guy's a blotter. He'll drink anything and lots of it.* **2.** *n.* the drug LSD, sold on bits of blotting paper. (Drugs.) ♦ *Blotter can bring one to five dollars a pop.* **3.** *n.* a police station log of arrests; a police blotter. ♦ *The blotter is full of the names of petty criminals and drunks.*

blotto [ˈblɑdo] **1.** *n.* strong liquor. ♦ *Let's go get a little of that blotto.* **2.** *mod.* alcohol intoxicated; dead drunk. ♦ *Let's get some smash and get blotto.*

blouse bunnies *n.* the (covered) female breasts. ♦ *He couldn't keep his eyes off her busy little blouse bunnies.*

blow 1. *tv. & in.* to leave (someplace) in a hurry. (See also blow town; blow the joint.) ♦ *It's late. I gotta blow.* **2.** *tv.* to ruin something; to ruin an opportunity. ♦ *It was my last chance, and I blew it.* **3.** *n.* a setback; an attack. ♦ *Acme Systems Industries suffered a blow to its plans to acquire ABC Steel Widgets.* **4.** *tv.* to waste money; to spend money. ♦ *Mary blew forty bucks on a secondhand radio.* **5.** *in.* to become very angry; to lose one's temper. (See also blow a fuse.) ♦ *Finally I had had enough, and I blew.* **6.** *in.* to play a musical instrument, not necessarily a wind instrument. ♦ *He blows, and everybody listens.* **7.** AND **blow-out** *n.* a drinking party. ♦ *What a blow over at Joe's. I'll never get sober.* ♦ *We blew out of the blow-out at about midnight.* **8.** *tv.* to snort any powdered drug; to take snuff. (Drugs.) ♦ *Those guys spend all their time blowing coke.* **9.** *in.* to smoke marijuana. (Drugs.) ♦ *He sits there blowing by the hour. How* *can he afford it?* **10.** *n.* cocaine. (Drugs.) ♦ *You can get some good blow over at that crack house.* **11.** *tv.* to perform an act of oral sex on someone, especially males. (Usually objectionable.) ♦ *Tom was looking for some bone addict who would blow him for nothing.*

blow a fuse AND **blow** one's **fuse; blow a gasket; blow** one's **cork; blow** one's **lid; blow** one's **top; blow** one's **stack** *tv.* to explode with anger; to lose one's temper. ♦ *Go ahead, blow a gasket! What good will that do?* ♦ *Crunk! I so blew my top!*

blow a gasket Go to blow a fuse.

blow a hype *tv.* to overreact; to spaz out. ♦ *I was afraid she would blow a hype about the broken window.*

blow a snot rocket Go to blow snot rockets.

blow beets *tv.* to empty one's stomach; to vomit. ♦ *What was in that stew? I feel like I gotta blow beets.*

blow chow Go to blow chunks.

blow chunks AND **blow chow; blow grits; blow lunch** *tv.* to vomit. ♦ *She drank too much and left the room to blow chunks.* ♦ *Oh my God! She's blowing grits on my sofa!*

blow cold *in.* [for a person] to display disinterest. ♦ *The committee blew cold as my plan unfolded.*

blow grits Go to blow chunks.

blow in *in.* to arrive. ♦ *I just blew in last night. Where can I find a room?*

Blow it out your ear! Go to (Go) blow it out your ear!

blow jive *tv.* to smoke marijuana. (See also jive.) ♦ *Man, let's go out and blow some jive!*

blow job *n.* an act of fellatio. (Usually objectionable.) ♦ *The hustler knew very well what the expression "blow job" meant.*

blow lunch Go to blow chunks.

blow off 1. *in.* to goof off; to waste time; to procrastinate. ♦ *You blow off too much.* **2.** *n.* a time-waster; a goof-off. (Usually **blow-off.**) ♦ *Get busy. I don't pay blow-offs around here.* **3.** *n.* something that can be done easily or without much effort. (Usually **blow-off.**) ♦ *The test was a blow-off.* **4.** *n.* the final insult; an event that causes a dispute. (Usually **blow-off.**) ♦ *The blow-off was a call from some dame named Monica who asked for Snookums.* **5.** *n.* a dispute; an argument. (Usually **blow-off.** See also blow up.) ♦ *After a blow-off like that, we need a breather.*

blow off (some) steam AND **let off (some) steam** *tv.* to release emotional tension by talking or getting angry. ♦ *Let off some steam. Get it out of your system.* ♦ *The kids run around and let off some steam.*

Blow on it! *exclam.* Cool it!; Take it easy! ♦ *It's all right, Tom. Blow on it!*

blow (one's) cookies *tv.* to empty one's stomach; to vomit. ♦ *Okay, if any of you guys gotta blow your cookies or something, do it here, not inside!*

blow one's **cool** *tv.* to become angry. ♦ *I almost blew my cool when the dog wet my pants leg.*

blow one's **cork** Go to blow a fuse.

blow one's **doughnuts** AND **lose** one's **doughnuts** [...'donəts] *tv.* to empty one's stomach; to vomit. ♦ *The stuff was so vile, I thought I would blow my doughnuts.* ♦ *I felt better after I lost my doughnuts.*

blow one's **fuse** Go to blow a fuse.

blow one's **groceries** *tv.* to empty one's stomach; to vomit. ♦ *She blew her groceries all over the front seat.*

blow one's **lid** Go to blow a fuse.

blow one's **lines** *tv.* to forget one's lines in a play; to speak one's lines incorrectly in a play. ♦ *There I was in my first major role, and I blow my lines!*

blow (one's) lunch AND **lose** one's **lunch** *tv.* to empty one's stomach; to vomit. ♦ *I almost lost my lunch, I ran so hard.* ♦ *I blew my lunch just watching her run.*

blow one's **own horn** AND **toot** one's **own horn** *tv.* to brag. ♦ *Gary sure likes to toot his own horn.* ♦ *Say something nice. I'm not one to blow my own horn.*

blow one's **stack** Go to blow a fuse.

blow one's **top** Go to blow a fuse.

blow smoke 1. *tv.* to state something in a way that conceals the truth. (See also smoke and mirrors.) ♦ *She is a master at blowing smoke. She belongs in government.* **2.** *tv.* to smoke marijuana. (Drugs.) ♦ *Frank sits around blowing smoke when he's not selling.*

blow snot rockets AND **blow a snot rocket** *tv.* to blow gobs of nasal mucus from one nostril at a time by blocking off the other nostril with a thumb. ♦ *Bob is always blowing snot rockets! How crude!* ♦ *He tried to blow a snot rocket at the dog, but it kept right on barking.*

blow so **away 1.** *tv.* to kill someone; to shoot someone. (Underworld.) ♦ *The boss said we was to blow you away if you gives us any trouble.* **2.** *tv.* to overwhelm someone; to amaze someone. ♦ *The whole idea just blew her away.*

blow so/sth **off 1.** *tv.* to neglect or ignore someone or something. ♦ *Get it done now. Don't blow it off!* **2.** *tv.* to cheat someone or a group; to deceive someone or a group. ♦ *Don't try to blow me off! I know what's what.*

blow so **out** *tv.* to kill someone, especially with gunshots. ♦ *Lefty set out to blow Harry the Horse out once and for all.*

blow so **out of the water** *tv.* to utterly destroy someone. (As a ship is blown up by a torpedo.) ♦ *This is too much. I'm gonna blow that guy out of the water.*

blow so's **brains out** *tv.* to kill someone with a gun. ♦ *Harry the Horse was so depressed that he wanted to blow out his brains.*

blow so's **cover** *tv.* to reveal someone's true identity; to ruin someone's scheme for concealment. ♦ *The dog recognized me and blew my cover.*

blow so's **doors off** *tv.* to defeat someone; to surpass someone. (As if someone were going by another vehicle on the highway at such a high speed that the doors would be blown off in passing.) ♦ *We're gonna really blow your doors off in the next game.*

blow so's **mind 1.** *tv.* to impress someone; to overwhelm someone. ♦ *This whole business just blows my mind.* **2.** *tv.* [for a drug] to intoxicate someone. ♦ *This stuff will blow your mind.*

blow so **to** sth *tv.* to treat someone to something, such as a meal, a movie, a drink, etc. ♦ *I think I'll blow myself to a fancy dessert.*

blow sth *tv.* to ruin or waste something. ♦ *I had a chance to do it, but I blew it.*

blow sth **wide open** AND **bust** sth **wide open** *tv.* to expose corrupt practices or a scheme; to put an end to corruption. ♦ *The press is trying to blow the town wide open, and the feebies are trying to hush them up so they can move about in secret.* ♦ *We'll blow this gang wide open!*

blow the joint *tv.* to get out of a place, probably in a hurry. (Underworld. See also joint.) ♦ *Come on, let's blow the joint before there's trouble.*

blow the lid off sth *tv.* to expose a scandal or corrupt practice; to expose political dishonesty. ♦ *I'm going to blow the lid off another phony candidate.*

blow town *tv.* to get out of town, probably in a hurry. (Underworld.) ♦ *I gotta pack and blow town. The cops are onto me.*

blow up 1. *in.* to burst into anger. ♦ *So she blew up. Why should that affect you so much?* **2.** *n.* an angry outburst; a fight. (Usually **blowup**.) ♦ *After the third blowup, she left him.* **3.** *n.* an enlarged version of a photograph, map, chart, etc. (Usually **blowup**.) ♦ *Kelly sent a blowup of their wedding picture to all her relatives.* **4.** *n.* the ruination of something; the collapse of something. (Usually **blowup**.) ♦ *The blowup in the financial world has ruined my chances for early retirement.*

blow Zs [...ziz] *tv.* to sleep. ♦ *I got to blow Zs for a while; then we'll talk.*

blowed (away) *mod.* alcohol or drug intoxicated. (See also blown away.) ♦ *I was so blowed away I couldn't see straight.*

blower 1. *n.* a cocaine user. (Drugs.) ✦ *Max is a blower, among other things.* **2.** *n.* cocaine. (Drugs.) ✦ *What's the best quality blower around here?* **3.** *n.* a cigarette. ✦ *You got a blower I can bum?* **4.** *n.* a handkerchief. ✦ *He pulled a crusty blower from his back pocket.*

blowhard ['bloˈhɑrd] *n.* a braggart; a big talker. ✦ *When and if this blowhard finishes, let's go.*

blown Go to blown away.

blown away 1. *mod.* dead; killed. (Underworld.) ✦ *Four of the mob were already blown away when the cops got there.* **2.** AND **blown** *mod.* alcohol or drug intoxicated. ✦ *Whatever that pill was, Cecilia is totally blown away.* ✦ *She's blown and alone and making a groan.* **3.** *mod.* overwhelmed; greatly impressed. (Often with with or by.) ✦ *We were just blown away by your good words.*

blown (out) *mod.* alcohol or drug intoxicated. ✦ *Fred stood at the door and told us he was blown—something that was totally obvious anyway.*

blown (up) *mod.* alcohol intoxicated. (See also blown away; blown (out).) ✦ *You are blown as blazes, you twit!*

blow-out Go to blow.

blubber gut(s) ['bləbɚ 'gət(s)] *n.* a fat person. (Also a rude term of address.) ✦ *Why doesn't that blubber gut do something about all that weight?*

blue 1. *mod.* depressed; melancholy. ✦ *That music always makes me blue.* **2.** *mod.* obscene; vulgar; dirty. ✦ *Those blue jokes don't go over very well around here.* **3.** *n.* the sky; the heavens. ✦ *The idea came to me right out of the blue.* **4.** *mod.* alcohol intoxicated. ✦ *You might say I'm blue. Others might note that I am stoned.* **5.** *n.* an amphetamine tablet or capsule, especially a blue one. (Drugs.) ✦ *How are blues different from reds and yellows?* **6.** *n.* a police officer; the police. ✦ *The blues will be here in a minute.* **7.** *n.* a 10-mg tablet of Valium. (Drugs.) ✦ *In treatment they kept giving me blues to calm me down. Now I can't live without them.*

blue and white *n.* a police car; the police. (Patterned on black and white and used in cities where the police cars are painted blue and white.) ✦ *A blue and white suddenly appeared, and I knew we were finished.*

blue around the gills AND **green around the gills 1.** *mod.* ill; nauseated. ✦ *How about a little air? I feel a little green around the gills.* **2.** *mod.* alcohol intoxicated. ✦ *Marty—now thoroughly green around the gills—slid neatly under the table, and everyone pretended not to notice.*

blue balls AND **hot-rocks** *n.* a painful condition of the testicles caused by unrelieved sexual need. (Usually objectionable.) ✦ *She always gives me hot-rocks.* ✦ *It may sound funny, but the "blue balls" are neither blue nor funny.*

blue boys AND **blue coats** *n.* the police. (See also men in blue.) ✦ *Four blue boys held me while a fifth slipped the cuffs on me. I ain't no pushover.* ✦ *The blue coats are at the door, sounding sort of mad.*

blue chip 1. *n.* stock shares of a large company that has a high value. (Securities markets.) ✦ *The blue chips took another nose dive in today's trading.* **2.** *mod.* having to do with the stock of large, valuable companies. (Securities markets.) ✦ *The blue chip rally ran for a third day.*

blue coats Go to blue boys.

blue devils 1. *n.* melancholia; depression. ✦ *Hank is down with the blue devils again.* **2.** *n.* the delirium tremens. ✦ *The shakes, or the blue devils, are a sure sign of a serious drinking problem.* **3.** *n.* capsules of Amytal, a barbiturate. ✦ *How much for a little box of blue devils?*

blue flu 1. *n.* an imaginary disease afflicting police officers who call in sick during a work stoppage or slowdown. (Journalistic. Occurs where strikes are illegal.) ✦ *Another epidemic of the blue flu struck the city's police officers early today.* **2.** *n.* a hangover. ✦ *He was out late last night and has the blue flu.*

blue funk [ˈblu ˈfəŋk] *n.* a state of depression. ◆ *You've got to get out of your blue funk and get back to work.*

blue in the face *mod.* pale from exhaustion or exertion. ◆ *I laughed until I was blue in the face.*

blue screen of death AND **BSOD** *phr. & comp. abb.* the blue computer screen that appears in early versions of Windows when Windows discovers a programming or operational error. ◆ *Every time I run that program I get the BSOD.* ◆ *No matter what program causes the blue screen of death, Bill Gates gets the blame.*

blue suit *n.* a police officer. (Usually plural.) ◆ *Watch out for the blue suits if you are going to drive this fast!*

blue-eyed *mod.* innocent. ◆ *He's sure his blue-eyed wonder couldn't have hit my child.*

bluehair *n.* an old lady, especially one whose hair is tinted blue. ◆ *The cruise was nice but sort of dull because of all the bluehairs aboard.*

bluh *n.* a buddy; a **blood** (sense 2). (Streets.) ◆ *Yo, ma bluh!*

BM 1. *n.* a bowel movement; an act of defecation. (Mostly a euphemism used with children.) ◆ *If I don't have a BM soon, I'm gonna die.* **2.** *n.* a disgusting and annoying person. (Also a term of address. A humorous way of calling someone a **shit**. Usually objectionable.) ◆ *The new guy has to be the world's worst BM.*

BMOC *n.* big man on campus, an important or self-important male college student. (Initialism. Collegiate. See also **BWOC**.) ◆ *Who's the BMOC who keeps trying to get elected class president?*

BO 1. *n.* (bad) body odor. (Initialism.) ◆ *Man, do you have BO!* **2.** *n.* box office, where tickets to some event are sold. ◆ *If you want your money back, you'll have to go to the BO.* **3.** *n.* HBO, Home Box Office, the cable television channel. (Initialism and dysphemism based on sense 1.) ◆ *There is boxing on BO but no movie.*

BO juice *n.* a deodorant; an underarm deodorant. (Collegiate. See also **BO**.) ◆ *Help*

this man find his BO juice, fast! He really needs it.

boag *in.* to vomit. ◆ *I think I'm gonna boag!*

boat 1. *n.* a big shoe. (See also **gunboats**.) ◆ *Those boats are special made, in fact.* **2.** *n.* a big car; a full-size car. ◆ *I don't want to drive a big boat like that.*

boat anchor *n.* a useless computer; anything heavy and useless. ◆ *Why don't you replace that boat anchor with a new model?*

bobo *mod.* drunk. ◆ *I think he's bobo. Get him out of here before he barfs.*

bod [bad] **1.** *n.* a body, especially a nice body. (See also **odd-bod**.) ◆ *You got a nice bod, Tom.* **2.** *n.* a person. ◆ *Who's the bod with the tight slacks?*

bodacious [boˈdeʃəs] *mod.* assertive; audacious. ◆ *That is a bodacious plan, for sure.*

bodacious tatas *n.* excellent, well-formed, female breasts. (See also **bodacious** and **tatas**.) ◆ *She is afflicted with the most bodacious tatas ever molded!*

bodega *n.* a corner store; a local shop. (From a Spanish term for a wineshop, or simply borrowed from Hispanic speakers in the U.S.) ◆ *I picked this little thing up at my local bodega.*

body count 1. *n.* the total of dead bodies after a battle. ◆ *The body count at Hill 49 was three.* **2.** *n.* the total number of casualties after some kind of shake-up. ◆ *The pink slips are coming out every day. The body count on Monday was twenty-three.* **3.** *n.* a count of people present. ◆ *The body count was about forty-five at the meeting.*

body shake *n.* a shakedown of the body; a skin-search. (Underworld. See also **shakedown**.) ◆ *They give everybody who passes through these doors a body shake.*

BOF Go to **birds of a feather**; **boring old fart**.

boff [baf] **1.** *tv.* to punch someone. ◆ *Ted boffed Harry playfully.* **2.** *in.* to empty one's stomach; to vomit. (See also **barf**.) ◆ *She boffed and boffed, until she was exhausted.* **3.** *tv. & in.* to copulate [with] someone. (Usually objectionable.) ♦ *They were boffing in the faculty lounge and the principal caught them.*

boffo ['bɑfo] **1.** *n.* a box-office hit; a successful play, musical, movie, etc. ♦ *The last one was a tremendous boffo, but we only broke even.* **2.** *mod.* successful; tremendous. ♦ *Another boffo success for Willy!*

bogard Go to bogart.

bogart AND **bogard** ['bogɑrt AND 'bogɑrd] **1.** *in.* to monopolize a communal marijuana cigarette; to hold a communal marijuana cigarette so long—Bogart style—that one drools on it. (From *Humphrey Bogart,* the screen actor.) ♦ *Stop bogarding and take a hit!* **2.** *in.* to stall. ♦ *The lawyer for the other side is bogarding, and it will take weeks to get it settled.* **3.** *in.* to act in a tough manner like Humphrey Bogart. ♦ *There's nothing funnier than a wimp trying to bogard around.*

bogue [bog] *mod.* bogus; fake. ♦ *Keep your bogue gold watch. I don't want it!*

bogus ['bogəs] **1.** *mod.* phony; false; undesirable. ♦ *This class is really bogus.* **2.** *mod.* great; excellent. ♦ *Man, this place is really bogus!*

bogus beef AND **bum beef** *n.* a false complaint or charge. (See also beef.) ♦ *The cops took them in on a bogus beef.* ♦ *It's a bogus beef. I'll be back on the street in twenty minutes.*

boheme [bo'him] *n.* a (feminine) personal style consisting of no makeup, large baggy clothing, long skirts, and comfortable shoes. (Collegiate.) ♦ *Boheme is not you.*

BOHICA Go to Bend over, here it comes again.

bohunk 1. *n.* a resident of or an immigrant from an Eastern European country, such as Poland, Hungary, etc. (A nickname. Can be perceived as derogatory. Usually objectionable.) ♦ *The bohunks can really cook up some fine food.* **2.** *n.* an oafish person. (Usually refers to a male. Usually objectionable.) ♦ *Get outa here, you stupid bohunk!* **3.** *n.* a term of endearment

for a close friend or child. ♦ *Okay, you bohunks, come to dinner now.*

boil the ocean *tv.* to waste one's time attempting to do the impossible. (See also plowing water.) ♦ *You're wasting my time. You might as well be boiling the ocean.*

boiled 1. *mod.* angry. ♦ *Now, don't get boiled. It was only a joke.* **2.** *mod.* alcohol intoxicated. ♦ *How can you get so boiled on wine?*

boiling (mad) *mod.* very mad. ♦ *Mad, I'm not mad. I'm just boiling.*

boink *tv. & in.* to copulate [with] someone. (Usually objectionable.) ♦ *He said he boinked her twice.*

boinkable *mod.* suitable and agreeable for copulation. ♦ *See that babe? Wow, is she boinkable!*

bojangling *n.* acting stupid; acting like a stupid black. ♦ *Stop bojangling and settle down to work.*

bokoo AND **boku** ['bo'ku] *mod.* many. (A play on French *beaucoup.*) ♦ *There are already boku people invited.*

boku Go to bokoo.

bold *mod.* great; outstanding. ♦ *Bold move, Charles. You outfoxed them.*

BOLO Go to be on the look out.

bologna Go to baloney.

bolt *in.* to leave; to go away. (Not necessarily fast.) ♦ *Time to go, man. Let's bolt.*

bolt-on *mod.* [of a woman's breasts] surgically augmented. ♦ *That's a bolt-on job if I ever saw one.*

bolus ['boləs] *n.* a physician. (From the Latin name for a pill.) ♦ *The bolus kept trying to get me to lose weight.*

bomb 1. *n.* a bad performance or an inherently bad show. ♦ *They tried as hard as they could, but the thing was a bomb from Act One on.* **2.** *in.* to fail. ♦ *My first try bombed, but things got better.* **3.** Go to bomb(shell).

the **bomb** AND **da bomb** *n.* something really great. ♦ *This tingle is really da bomb.*

♦ *She described our car as "the bomb" and our house as a "joint."*

bomb (out) *in.* [for a computer or computer program] to fail. ♦ *The whole thing bombed out at just the wrong time.*

bomb out (of sth**)** *in.* to flunk out of or fail at something, especially school or a job. ♦ *She was afraid she would bomb out of school.*

bombed (out) *mod.* alcohol or drug intoxicated. (Possibly from **embalmed**.) ♦ *How can I drive when I'm bombed out?*

bomb(shell) *n.* a stunning piece of news that is dropped without warning. (See also bomb.) ♦ *I am still recovering from your bombshell of last evening.*

bone 1. *n.* a trombone. (Musicians. See also bones.) ♦ *She plays the bone like nobody's business.* **2.** Go to boner.

bone factory 1. *n.* a hospital. ♦ *After about two months in the bone factory, I was back on the job.* **2.** *n.* a cemetery. ♦ *I know I'll end up in the bone factory just like everyone else.*

bone out *in.* to leave. ♦ *It's time we boned out and got home.*

bonehead 1. *n.* a stupid or stubborn person. ♦ *You are such a bonehead when it comes to buying cars.* **2.** AND **boneheaded** *mod.* stupid; stubborn. ♦ *Of all the boneheaded things to do!* ♦ *You are a bonehead jerk!*

boneheaded Go to bonehead.

boner 1. *n.* a silly error; a gaffe. (See also pull a boner.) ♦ *What a boner! You must be embarrassed.* **2.** AND **bone** *n.* an erection. ♦ *He always gets a boner when he doesn't need it and never when he does.*

bones 1. *n.* dice. (See additional forms at bone.) ♦ *Toss me the bones and get out your checkbooks.* **2.** *n.* a nickname for a ship's physician. (From **sawbones**. Also the nickname of the doctor on the starship *Enterprise* of *Star Trek* fame.) ♦ *This fat bones actually wanted me to lose weight.* **3.** *n.* a nickname for a skinny person. (Also a term of address.) ♦ *Ask bones there what he wants to drink.* **4.** *n.* dollars;

money; cash. ♦ *The tickets only cost a few bones, but the play was lousy and I want my money back.*

boneyard 1. *n.* a cemetery. ♦ *I'd like to be planted in a boneyard like that.* **2.** *n.* a junkyard. (From sense 1) ♦ *This old car's ready for the boneyard.*

bong AND **bhong** [bɔŋ] **1.** *n.* a marijuana smoking device that cools the smoke by passing it through water. (Drugs.) ♦ *This bong is really getting sort of nasty.* **2.** *tv. & in.* to smoke marijuana or other drugs with a bong or other device. (Drugs.) ♦ *Wanna go bong a bowl?* **3.** *n.* a puff or hit of marijuana taken through a bong. (Drugs.) ♦ *I'll take two bongs, and then I gotta go.* **4.** *tv. & in.* to drink keg beer through a hose. (California. See also beerbong.) ♦ *Everybody bonged till the keg was empty.*

bonged (out) [bɔŋd...] *mod.* exhausted from too much marijuana. (Drugs.) ♦ *I was bonged all through the holidays.*

bonk [bɔŋk] **1.** *tv.* to strike one's head. ♦ *He bonked his head on the shelf.* **2.** *tv.* to strike someone on the head. ♦ *I bonked John on the head.* **3.** *tv. & in.* to copulate [with] someone. (Usually objectionable.) ♦ *She bonked him all night. At least that's what he said.*

bonkers ['bɔŋkɚz] **1.** AND **crackers** *mod.* insane; crazy. ♦ *I think I am going crackers.* **2.** *mod.* slightly intoxicated. ♦ *She's too bonkers to drive.*

Bonus! ['bonəs] *exclam.* That's great!; That's good enough to earn a bonus! ♦ *Bonus! That's the best news I've heard in a long time!*

bonzo ['banzo] *mod.* crazy. ♦ *You are completely bonzo!*

boob [bub] **1.** *n.* a stupid person; a rural oaf. ♦ *Why did I marry a boob like you?* **2.** AND **booby** ['bubi] *n.* a breast. (Usually plural. Usually objectionable.) ♦ *With boobs like that, she can go anywhere she likes.*

boobage *n.* a woman's breasts; breasts in general. ♦ *Fantastic boobage! Know what I mean? Know what I mean?*

boo-bird ['bu'bɚd] *n.* a person who boos frequently at games or other public events. ♦ *The catcher turned and stared right at the loudmouthed boo-bird. Everybody knew what he was thinking.*

boo-boo ['bubu] **1.** *n.* an error. (See also make a boo-boo.) ♦ *It's only a small boo-boo. Don't stress yourself.* **2.** *n.* a hurt; a cut; a bruise. ♦ *She has a little boo-boo on her knee.*

boob-tube ['bub'tub] *n.* a television set. (Something for a boob to watch.) ♦ *You spend too much time in front of the boob-tube.*

booby Go to boob.

booby hatch ['bubi...] *n.* a mental hospital. ♦ *I was afraid they would send me to the booby hatch.*

boodle ['budl̩] *n.* loot; the proceeds from a crime. (Underworld.) ♦ *All of the boodle was recovered in a suitcase.*

boody AND **boodie; bootie; booty 1.** *n.* the buttocks. (Potentially offensive. Usually objectionable.) ♦ *Look at the nice little boody on that guy.* **2.** *n.* someone or something disliked. (From sense 1.) ♦ *Why don't you clean up all this boody? This place is a mess.* ♦ *Don't be such a bootie!* **3.** *n.* the female genitals; the vulva and vagina. (Usually objectionable.) ♦ *He wants to get into her boody.* **4.** *n.* women considered as a receptacle for the penis. (Rude and derogatory.) ♦ *He likes boody better than anything.*

booger 1. *n.* a blob of nasal mucus, moist or dry. (Usually objectionable.) ♦ *Keep your boogers to yourself!* **2.** Go to boogie.

boogie ['bugi OR 'bʊgi] **1.** *n.* a kind of rock dance. ♦ *I didn't like the boogie until I learned how to do it right.* **2.** *in.* to dance rock-style. ♦ *I'm too old to boogie.* **3.** *n.* a party where the boogie is danced. ♦ *There's a boogie over at Steve's tonight.* **4.** *in.* to get down to work; to get down to business. ♦ *All right, it's time to boogie. Cool it!* **5.** AND **booger** *n.* a piece of nasal mucus. (Usually objectionable.) ♦ *Is that a boogie on your lip, or what?* ♦ *There's a booger on his collar.* **6.** *in.* to leave. ♦ *Come on, man. Let's boogie.* **7.** *n.* a tumor.

(Medical slang. See also guber.) ♦ *Looks like a little boogie down in the lung.* **8.** *in.* to copulate; to have sex. (Usually objectionable.) ♦ *Let's go boogie.*

boogie down (to somewhere**)** *in.* to hurry (to somewhere); to go (somewhere). ♦ *So, why don't you boogie down to the store and load up with bud and berries for the weekend?*

boogie-board ['bugibord OR 'bʊgibord] **1.** *n.* a surfboard. (California.) ♦ *Get your boogie-board out there in that tube.* **2.** *n.* a skateboard. (Teens.) ♦ *Can you imagine a boogie-board costing 600 dollars?*

boogieman ['bugimæn OR 'bʊgimæn] *n.* an imaginary man who is said to frighten people; a false threat of any kind. ♦ *Don't turn me into a boogieman. Spank the child yourself.*

book (on) out *in.* to leave in a hurry; to depart very suddenly and rapidly. ♦ *Let's book on out of this place as soon as we can.*

bookie *n.* a bookmaker for betting. ♦ *My bookie wants his money on the spot.*

bookmark *tv.* to make a note of something, mental or written. (From the concept of bookmarking web pages.) ♦ *That's a good thought. I'll bookmark that.*

boom *in.* to listen to music, as with a boom box. ♦ *If you're going to boom all the time, why don't you get some headphones?*

boom box *n.* a portable stereo radio. (See also box, thunderbox.) ♦ *Turn down that damn boom box, or I'll kick it in.*

boom sticks *n.* drumsticks. (Musicians.) ♦ *He always carries his boom sticks in his back pocket, and he beats on walls, radiators, desks—you name it.*

boomer 1. *n.* a laborer who moves from one economic boom to another. ♦ *Fred's great uncle was a boomer in the days of the Oklahoma oil rush.* **2.** Go to (baby) boomer.

boon *in.* to leave the road in a car for the boondocks. ♦ *Tom has a four-wheel-drive so we can really boon!*

boonies *n.* a remote and undeveloped place. (From boondocks.) ♦ *He lives out there in the boonies.*

boosiasm(s) *n.* a woman's breasts. (A blend of *bosom* and *enthusiasm*. Occurs both as a count and a noncount noun. Old but recurrent. Usually objectionable.) ♦ *Did you see the boosiasms on that dame?*

boost 1. *tv. & in.* to steal or shoplift something. (Underworld.) ♦ *He specializes in boosting meat for resale.* **2.** *tv.* to praise or hype someone or something; to support someone or something. ♦ *She is always boosting some cause.*

booster 1. *n.* a shoplifter. ♦ *The cops hauled in two boosters by noon.* **2.** *n.* a supporter (of someone or some cause). ♦ *I'm a booster of lots of good causes.*

boot 1. *n.* a thrill; a charge. ♦ *I get a real boot out of my grandchildren.* **2.** *tv.* to dismiss or eject someone. ♦ *I booted him myself.* **3.** *n.* a dismissal or ejection. ♦ *I got the boot even though I had worked there for a decade.* **4.** *tv. & in.* to start the operating system of a computer. ♦ *When I booted, all I got was a feep.* **5.** *in.* to empty one's stomach; to vomit. ♦ *The kid booted and booted and will probably never smoke another cigar.*

boot so **out** *tv.* to throw someone out; to kick someone out. ♦ *Are you going to boot me out?*

bootie Go to boody.

bootleg 1. *mod.* unauthorized or illegal [copy or something]; illegally obtained. (See also buttlegging.) ♦ *He crossed the state line to buy cigarettes and then returned by a back road with his bootleg smokes.* **2.** *n.* to sell unauthorized or illegal copies; to sell contraband. ♦ *They arrested the guy for bootlegging current movies on DVDs.*

booty Go to boody.

booty call 1. *n.* sexual arousal. (Usually objectionable.) ♦ *Sam said he was feeling the booty call and needed to find his woman.* **2.** *n.* calling someone up for sex. (Usually objectionable.) ♦ *Reg stopped at a phone booth in the bar to make a booty call.*

booty check *n.* a search of the rectum, as when police look for drugs. ♦ *Willie got arrested and had a booty check since he was walking funny.*

booty-cheddar *n.* nonsense; bullshit. ♦ *I'm tired of listening to all your booty-cheddar.*

booze [buz] **1.** *n.* beverage alcohol. (Slang since the 1500s.) ♦ *I don't care for booze. It makes me sneeze.* **2.** AND **booze up** *in.* to drink alcohol to excess; to go on a bash. ♦ *Stop boozing for a minute and listen up, guys.* ♦ *Let's booze up and watch TV.*

booze artist *n.* a drunken person; a drunkard. ♦ *A wobbly booze artist sat musing on the stool in the corner.*

booze it (up) *tv.* to drink excessively; to drink to intoxication. ♦ *You come home every night and booze it up. How can you keep on this way?*

booze up Go to booze.

boozed *mod.* alcohol intoxicated. ♦ *Wow, is he ever boozed!*

boozy-woozy ['buzi'wuzi] *mod.* alcohol intoxicated. ♦ *I think I am just an itty-bitty boozy-woozy.*

bop [bɑp] **1.** *tv.* to strike someone or something. ♦ *You wanna get bopped in the beezer?* **2.** *n.* a style of jazz popular in the 1940s. ♦ *We heard some bop in an old movie.* **3.** *n.* a drug in pill form; a dose of a drug. (See also hit.) ♦ *You gonna drop both of them bops?*

boring old fart AND **BOF** *phr. & comp. abb.* a very boring older person. (See also birds of a feather.) ♦ *Bob's dad is a vintage BOF. But all old guys are.* ♦ *Don't be a boring old fart. Let's go out tonight.*

bosom chums AND **bosom friends** *n.* lice. ♦ *The old guy sat there scratching at his bosom chums.* ♦ *My bosom friends keep me awake all night.*

bosom friends Go to bosom chums.

boss *mod.* excellent; powerful; superior. ♦ *That is a boss tune.*

boss dick *n.* a cop; a police officer. (Streets. See also dick = detective.) ♦ *The boss dick slugged me in the face and said I should be more careful.*

boss lady *n.* the woman in charge. ♦ *You'll have to ask the boss lady.*

boss man *n.* the man in charge. ♦ *I guess the boss man is about ready to retire.*

both sheets in the wind *mod.* alcohol intoxicated. (See also three sheets in the wind.) ♦ *She's both sheets in the wind at the moment.*

bottle 1. *n.* a drunkard. ♦ *The bar was empty save an old bottle propped against the side of a booth.* **2.** the **bottle** *n.* liquor. (Always with *the* in this sense.) ♦ *Her only true love is the bottle.* **3.** *in.* to drink liquor to excess. ♦ *Let's go out and bottle into oblivion.*

bottle baby *n.* an alcoholic. ♦ *The bottle babies sat there, waiting to be thrown out at closing time.*

bottleache ['bɑdḷek] *n.* a hangover; the delirium tremens. ♦ *I got a touch of the bottleache this morning.*

bottom 1. *n.* the buttocks. ♦ *My bottom is sore from sitting too long.* **2.** *n.* the second half of a baseball inning. ♦ *Wilbur hit a double-bagger in the bottom of the second.* **3.** *tv.* to drink something to the bottom. ♦ *He bottomed the beer and ordered another one.*

one's **bottom dollar** *n.* one's last dollar. (See also bet one's bottom dollar.) ♦ *I'm down to my bottom dollar. How about a little loan?*

bottom fishing *n.* seeking something at its lowest price; seeking something at a low cost and willing to accept inferior quality. ♦ *I don't think bottom fishing for stocks is always wise. There is always a good reason why the price is low.*

the **bottom line 1.** *n.* the grand total; the final figure on a balance sheet. (Securities markets.) ♦ *The company's bottom line is in bad shape.* **2.** *n.* the result; the nitty-gritty; the score. ♦ *The bottom line is that you really don't care.*

bottom of the barrel AND **bottom of the heap** *n.* the location of persons or things of the very lowest quality. (Usually with *from*. See also scrape the bottom of the barrel.) ♦ *That last secretary you sent me was really from the bottom of the barrel.* ♦ *If you drop out of school, you stay at the bottom of the heap.*

bottom of the heap Go to bottom of the barrel.

bottom out *in.* to reach the lowest or worst point of something. ♦ *All my problems seem to be bottoming out. They can't get much worse.*

bottomless pit 1. *n.* a very hungry person. ♦ *The guy is a bottomless pit. There isn't enough food in town to fill him up.* **2.** *n.* an endless source of something, usually something troublesome. ♦ *Our problems come from a bottomless pit. There is just no end to them.*

Bottoms up. *sent.* Let us drink up! (A drinking toast.) ♦ *They all raised their glasses, and the host said, "Bottoms up!"*

bounce 1. *in.* [for a check] to be returned from the bank because of insufficient funds. (See also rubber (check).) ♦ *The check bounced, and I had to pay a penalty fee.* **2.** *tv.* to write a bad check. ♦ *He bounced another one, and this time the bank called him up to warn him about what would happen if he did it again.* **3.** *in.* to leave; to depart. ♦ *It's late. Let's bounce.* **4.** *tv.* [for a bank] to refuse to honor a check. ♦ *They bounced another of my checks today.* **5.** *tv.* to throw someone out. ♦ *Willie bounced me, and I ran to my car and beat it.* **6.** *n.* pep; energy. ♦ *I never have any bounce when I wake up early.*

bounce for sth Go to spring for sth.

bounce sth **off (of)** so *tv.* to try out an idea on someone; to get someone's opinion of an idea. ♦ *Let me bounce this off of you.*

bouncer *n.* a strong man hired to eject unruly people from a bar or similar place. (People supposedly bounce when thrown out.) ♦ *I saw the bouncer looking at me, and I got out of there fast.*

bouquet of assholes *n.* an annoying or disgusting person or thing. (Rude and derogatory.) ♦ *Don't pay any attention to him. He's just another one of the bouquet of assholes you find around here.*

bousta *phr.* about to [do something]. (Streets.) ♦ *He's bousta go.*

bout it Go to (a)bout it.

bow to the porcelain altar *in.* to empty one's stomach; to vomit. (The *porcelain altar* is the toilet bowl.) ♦ *He spent the whole night bowing to the porcelain altar.*

bowl *n.* a pipe or other device for smoking cannabis. (Drugs.) ♦ *There's somebody's bowl out in the hall. Go get it before the neighbors call the fuzz.*

bowser ['bɑʊzɚ] *n.* a person with a dog face or ugly face. (Typically applied to females.) ♦ *Fred went out with a real bowser but said he had a good time anyway.*

bow-wow ['bɑʊwɑʊ] **1.** *n.* a dog. (Juvenile.) ♦ *We're going to get you a bow-wow!* **2.** *n.* an ugly woman; a dog. (Derogatory.) ♦ *I would have chosen a better nose if I had been given a chance, but—all in all—I'm not such a bow-wow.*

box 1. *n.* the genitals of the male, especially as contained within a garment, such as underwear. (Usually objectionable.) ♦ *God, did you see the box on him?* **2.** *n.* the genitals of a female; the vagina considered as a container for the penis. (Usually objectionable.) ♦ *He wants to get in her box.* **3.** *n.* a coffin. ♦ *Put him in a box and put the box in a hole. Then the matter is closed.* **4.** *n.* a phonograph player. ♦ *Yours is old! My box still has tubes!* **5.** *n.* a portable stereo radio. ♦ *Does that damn box have to be so loud?* **6.** *n.* a piano. ♦ *She sure can pound the devil out of that box!* **7.** *in.* to die. ♦ *The old man looks like he's going to box at any minute.* **8.** Go to (ghetto) box. **9.** Go to (squeeze-)box.

box on the table *mod.* die on the (operating) table. (Medical. See also boxed.) ♦ *The surgeon did the best job possible, but the patient boxed on the table.*

box so in *tv.* to put someone into a bind; to reduce the number of someone's alternatives. (See also boxed in.) ♦ *I don't want to box you in, but you are running out of options.*

boxed *mod.* dead; died. (The box is possibly a coffin.) ♦ *He's boxed. There's nothing that can be done.*

boxed in *mod.* in a bind; having few alternatives. ♦ *I got him boxed in. He'll have to do it our way.*

boxed (up) 1. *mod.* alcohol or drug intoxicated. ♦ *I am way boxed, and I feel sick.* **2.** *mod.* in jail. ♦ *Pat was boxed up for two days till we got bond money.*

Boy! AND **Boy, oh boy!** *phr.* a sentence opener expressing surprise or emphasis. (This is not a term of address and can be used with either sex, although it is quite informal.) ♦ *Boy! Am I glad to see you, Molly!*

Boy howdy! *phr.* an exclamation of excited surprise. (Colloquial and folksy.) ♦ *Boy howdy! Am I glad to see you!*

boy-beater *n.* a sleeveless shirt or undershirt allegedly for women or homosexuals. (From the wife-beater.) ♦ *They sat there looking macho in their tints and boy-beater.*

boys in blue Go to men in blue.

boys in the back room AND **back room boys** *n.* any private male group making decisions, usually politicians. ♦ *The boys in the back room picked the last presidential candidate.* ♦ *Who picks out the back room boys? Who's really in charge?*

bozo ['bozo] *n.* a clown; a jerk; a fool. (Also a term of address.) ♦ *Look, you bozo, I've had enough of your jabber.*

bozo filter *n.* a setting on an internet email reader that will filter out selected annoying people. (Refers to bozo, a jerk.) ♦ *Welcome to my bozo filter, jerk!*

bra-burner *n.* a nickname for a woman who supported the women's liberation movements of the 1960s and 1970s. (Derogatory.) ♦ *Didn't the bra-burners give way to whale-savers in the seventies?*

bracelets *n.* handcuffs. ♦ *The cops put the bracelets on Jane and led her away.*

brack-brain ['brækbren] *n.* a fool. ♦ *The brack-brains in Washington have done it again!*

brain 1. *n.* a good student; a very intelligent person. (See also brains.) ♦ *I'm no brain, but I get good grades.* **2.** *tv.* to hit someone (in the head). ♦ *I ought to brain you for that!*

brain bucket *n.* a bike or motorcycle helmet. (See also skid-lid.) ♦ *He refuses to wear a brain bucket when he rides.*

brain-burned AND **brain-fried** *mod.* brain-damaged from drugs. (Drugs. See also burnout.) ♦ *Man, you're gonna get brain-burned from this stuff.* ♦ *When he finally got totally brain-fried, he asked for help.*

brainchild 1. *n.* someone's good idea viewed as an offspring of the brain. ♦ *Is this your brainchild? It won't work.* **2.** *n.* a person who has good ideas. ♦ *The boss's new brainchild seems to have gone dry.*

brain-dead *mod.* stupid. ♦ *I don't know why he's so dull. He's seems brain-dead half the time.*

brain-drain *n.* the movement of intellectuals from one country to another where the pay and job opportunities are better. ♦ *Where there is a good education system, there will always be a brain-drain.*

brain-fried Go to brain-burned.

brains *n.* the person(s) in charge of thinking something through. ♦ *John is not what I would call the brains of the gang.*

brainstorm 1. *n.* a good idea; an idea that enters one's head suddenly. ♦ *I had a sudden brainstorm and got out of bed to write it down.* **2.** *in.* to try to think up good ideas, especially as a group. ♦ *Let's brainstorm on this for a little while.*

brain-teaser Go to brain-twister.

brain-twister AND **brain-teaser** *n.* a puzzle, especially one that requires thinking. ♦ *Can you help me with this brain-teaser?* ♦ *I can spend my whole vacation doing brain-twisters.*

(brand) spanking new *mod.* completely new; brand new. ♦ *Look at that brand spanking new car!*

brass *n.* high-ranking military or civilian officers. (See also top brass.) ♦ *We'll see what the brass has to say first.*

brass hat *n.* a member of the brass. ♦ *A brass hat came up to me and asked me where I was going.*

brass SO **off** *tv.* to make someone angry. (Primarily military. As angry as the "brass," or officers, might get about something.) ♦ *You really brass me off.*

brass tacks *n.* essential business. (Usually in get down to brass tacks.) ♦ *Now that we are talking brass tacks, how much do you really want for this watch?*

brassed (off) *mod.* angry; disgusted. ♦ *You look so brassed off at the world. Smile!*

Bravo Sierra *n.* nonsense; bullshit. (NATO Phonetic Alphabet.) ♦ *Sure, you're rich! What Bravo Sierra!*

BRB Go to be right back.

bread *n.* money. ♦ *I need to get some bread to live on.*

bread and butter *n.* one's livelihood. ♦ *It's bread and butter to me. I have to do it.*

breadbasket AND **dinner basket** *n.* the belly; the stomach. ♦ *I hit him, pow, right in the breadbasket.* ♦ *I have a little pain in the dinner basket.*

break 1. *n.* a chance; an opportunity. ♦ *Come on, give me a break!* **2.** *n.* an escape from prison; a prison breakout. ♦ *I hear there's a break planned for tonight.* **3.** *in.* [for a news story] to unfold rapidly. (Journalism.) ♦ *As the story continues to break, we will bring you the latest.* **4.** *n.* a solo played when the rest of the band stops. ♦ *This is your break, Andy. Let's hear it, man.*

Break a leg! *exclam.* Good luck! (A special theatrical way of wishing a performer good luck. Saying *good luck* is considered to be a jinx.) ♦ *"Break a leg!" shouted the stage manager to the heroine.*

Break it up! *exclam.* Stop it! (An order to two or more people to stop doing something, such as fighting.) ♦ *All right you two, break it up!*

break one's **balls to do** sth Go to bust (one's) ass (to do sth).

break out *in.* to leave. ♦ *It's late, man. Time to break out.*

break so's **balls** *tv.* to wreck or ruin someone; to overwork someone; to overwhelm someone. (Usually objectionable.) ♦ *I'm gonna break your balls. You understand me?*

break the ice 1. *tv.* to be the first one to do something. ♦ *No one wants to break the ice. I guess I will be first.* **2.** *tv.* to attempt to become friends with someone. ♦ *A nice smile does a lot to break the ice.*

breaker 1. *n.* a break dancer. (Break dancing is a rhythmic and energetic impromptu performance usually done by untrained urban youths.) ♦ *He is one of the best breakers in the city.* **2.** *n.* someone attempting to use a citizens band radio channel. ♦ *There's a breaker trying to use this channel. Let's drop down to eleven.*

breakfast of champions *n.* a first alcoholic drink of the day, taken in the morning, instead of breakfast. (Collegiate.) ♦ *He calls it the breakfast of champions. I call it a bad sign of something out of hand.*

breather *n.* a rest period; a lull. (A chance to catch one's breath.) ♦ *As soon as we've had a breather, it's back to work.*

breeder *n.* a nonhomosexual. (In a homosexual context.) ♦ *Don't invite Willy. He's a breeder.*

breeze *n.* an easy task. ♦ *Nothing to it. It was a breeze.*

brew 1. *n.* coffee; occasionally, tea. ♦ *This is my kind of brew, hot, black, and aromatic.* **2.** *n.* beer; a can, bottle, or glass of beer. ♦ *Hey, give me a cold brew, will ya?*

brewed *mod.* alcohol intoxicated. ♦ *He tries to get brewed as soon as he can after work.*

brew-ha ['bruhɑ] *n.* brew; a beer. ♦ *One brew-ha over here, innkeeper!*

brew-out *n.* a beer blast; a beer blow-out. ♦ *Were you at Tom's brew-out? I was too bombed to see who was there.*

brews brothers *n.* (male) beer-drinking college students. (A play on *The Blues Brothers*, a popular movie released in 1980.) ♦ *You guys look like the devil and you smell like the brews brothers.*

brewski AND **brewsky** ['bruski] *n.* beer; a beer. ♦ *Hey, how 'bout a brewski?* ♦ *This is only my third brewsky, but the night is young.*

brewsky Go to brewski.

brewster ['brustɚ] **1.** *n* a beer drinker; a beer drunkard. ♦ *Fred has become a committed brewster. He pounds one beer after another.* **2.** *n.* beer; a can of beer. ♦ *Toss me a cold brewster, will you?*

brick 1. *n.* a failed shot (in basketball) that bounces off the rim or backboard. ♦ *Chalk up another brick for Michael.* **2.** *n.* any failure. ♦ *This whole thing is a mess. Whose brick is this anyway?* **3.** *in.* to fail. (From sense 1.) ♦ *The whole project bricked because we sat on the contract too long.* **4.** *tv.* to strike or punch someone. (Streets.) ♦ *That dude just bricked a cop!* **5.** *n.* a block of marijuana; a kilo of cocaine. (Drugs.) ♦ *Man, I can't afford a brick! Gimme a bag.* ♦ *The police said he was carrying a "brick" of cannabis when arrested.* **6.** *n.* a large, brick-shaped, handheld mobile telephone that is a precursor to the modern cellphone. ♦ *I still have my old "brick," but I'd be embarrassed to use it, even if it did still work.*

brickhouse *n.* a large-breasted woman. (A confused or euphemistic reference to built like a brick shithouse. Usually objectionable.) ♦ *Clara's a real brickhouse. I don't see how she stands up.*

brig [brɪg] *n.* jail. (From the term for a naval prison or a shipboard jail.) ♦ *Throw this jerk in the brig.*

bright-eyed and bushy-tailed *mod.* alert and ready to do something; as alert and as active as a squirrel. ♦ *You look all bright-eyed and bushy-tailed this morning.*

brights *n.* the eyes. (From *bright eyes.*) ♦ *Don't you close your brights and look bored when I'm talking to you!*

brim *n.* a hat. ♦ *Man, that is one fine brim you got.*

bring so **down 1.** *tv.* to terminate one's own or someone else's drug experience. (Drugs.) ♦ *It took a lot to bring her down.* **2.** *tv.* to depress someone. ♦ *The news really brought me down.*

bring so **on** *tv.* to arouse someone sexually. ♦ *Look at her! She's doing her best to bring him on! Why are men so stupid?*

bring sth **up 1.** *tv.* to mention something. (Standard English.) ♦ *Why did you have to bring that up?* **2.** *tv.* to vomit something up; to cough something up. ♦ *I did, and he brought up a nickel instead!*

bring-down 1. *n.* something that depresses someone. ♦ *The news was a terrible bring-down.* **2.** *n.* something that brings someone back to reality. ♦ *I have had one bring-down after another today.*

broad *n.* a woman. (Originally underworld slang. Often jocular. Usually considered rude and derogatory.) ♦ *When is that broad gonna show up?*

broccoli Go to coli.

Bronx cheer ['brɑŋks 'tʃir] *n.* a rude noise made with the lips; a raspberry. ♦ *The little air compressor in the corner of the parking lot made a noise like a Bronx cheer.*

brother Go to (soul) brother.

brown bag it 1. *tv.* to carry one's lunch from home, as in a brown paper bag; to eat a lunch brought from home rather than go out to eat. ♦ *I'm broke, so I'll have to brown bag it today.* **2.** *tv.* to copulate with a very ugly person (woman). (A play on sense 1. The person receiving the action is so ugly as to require a paper bag covering over the face to make the process less odious.) ♦ *He hated to date and was too proud to brown bag it. So he suffered.*

brown bottle flu *n.* a hangover or sickness from drinking. (Probably from beer, which is often sold in brown bottles.) ♦ *Wayne had a case of the brown bottle flu and didn't make the meeting.*

brown hole 1. *n.* the anus. (Usually objectionable.) ♦ *Sam Spade tried to kick Joel Cairo in the brown hole but missed.* **2.** *n.* to poke someone in the anus; to goose someone. (Usually objectionable.) ♦ *Fred brown-holed Tom on the stairway, and they had quite a fight.*

brown out 1. *in.* [for the electricity] to fade and dim down. (Something less than a blackout.) ♦ *The power kept browning out.* **2.** AND **brown out** *n.* a period of dimming or fading of the electricity. ♦ *They keep building all these expensive power stations, and then we still have brown outs.*

brown so **off** *tv.* to make someone angry. (See also browned (off).) ♦ *I'm afraid I'm going to brown off everyone but here goes anyway.*

brown-bag 1. *n.* a bag lunch. ♦ *Bring a brown-bag, and we'll talk and eat at the same time.* **2.** *in.* to carry a bag lunch. ♦ *He's back to brown-bagging while he saves up for his vacation.* **3.** *mod.* having to do with an event during which people eat their own bag lunches. ♦ *These brown-bag affairs seem so tacky.*

browned (off) *mod.* angry. ♦ *I am really browned off at you!*

brownie Go to brown-nose.

brownie points *n.* imaginary credit for doing something well. (Originally "demerits" in railroading.) ♦ *How many brownie points do I get for not frowning when you take my picture?*

brown-nose 1. AND **brownie; brown-noser** *n.* a sycophant; one who flatters for self-serving motives. ♦ *You are just a plain old brown-nose.* ♦ *Will some brown-noser please try to get the teacher to put off the test?* **2.** *tv. & in.* to curry favor with someone; to be a sycophant. ♦ *Don keeps brown-nosing, and the professor pretends not to notice.*

brown-noser Go to brown-nose.

browse Go to graze.

bruised [bruzd] *mod.* alcohol intoxicated. ♦ *I am bruised. My head hurts, and my gut feels yucky.*

bruiser ['bruzɚ] *n.* a large, rough male. ♦ *That bruiser must weigh a ton.*

brush *n.* an encounter; a close shave. ♦ *My brush with the bear was so close I could smell its breath—which was vile, I might add.*

brushoff ['brəʃɔf] *n.* a dismissal; an act of ignoring someone. (See also give so the brushoff.) ♦ *I got the brushoff, but I can take it.*

brutal *mod.* excellent; powerful. ♦ *Man, what a brutal tune!*

bruva *n.* a brother; my brother; my (black) buddy. (Black. Streets. May be social dialect only.) ♦ *Yo, bruva! Fo shizzle.*

BS 1. *n.* bullshit; nonsense; deception. (Partly euphemistic. Usually objectionable.) ♦ *Don't feed me that BS! I know the score!* **2.** *tv.* to deceive or attempt to deceive someone with lies or flattery. (Usually objectionable.) ♦ *Don't try to BS me with your sweet talk!*

BSOD Go to blue screen of death.

BTDT(GTS) Go to Been there, done that (got the T-shirt).

BTO Go to big-time operator.

BTW *interj.* By the way. (Used in electronic mail and computer forum or news group messages. Not pronounced aloud.) ♦ *I am, BTW, very interested in what you said about the high cost of software.*

BTWBO Go to Be there with bells on.

bubble water AND **bubbles** *n.* champagne. ♦ *More bubble water, or do you want something stronger?* ♦ *I just love the way bubbles tickles my little old nose.*

bubblehead 1. *n.* a fool; a giddy person. ♦ *If you can't say anything without coming off like a bubblehead, keep your mouth shut.* **2.** *n.* a heavy drinker of champagne. ♦ *It takes a pretty good bankroll to be a real high-class bubblehead.*

bubbles Go to bubble water.

bubbly *n.* champagne. (Often with *the.*) ♦ *I'd like a big glass of bubbly, if you don't mind.*

buck 1. *n.* a dollar. ♦ *Gimme a buck for a bottle of wine, will you mister?* **2.** *tv.* to resist something. ♦ *He enjoys bucking the system.* **3.** *n.* a buckskin (leather) shoe. (Usually plural.) ♦ *Look at my new white bucks!*

buck for sth *in.* to work ambitiously for something, such as a promotion. ♦ *You can tell she's bucking for promotion.*

buck up *in.* to cheer up; to perk up. ♦ *Come on, now, buck up. Things can't be all that bad.*

buckage *n.* money. (See also buck.) ♦ *Can you spare a little buckage until payday?*

bucket 1. *n.* the goal (hoop and net) in basketball. (Sports.) ♦ *Freddy arced one at the bucket and missed.* **2.** *n.* a hoop or basket in basketball. (Sports.) ♦ *Four buckets in two minutes. Is that a record, or what?* **3.** *n.* the buttocks. (See also can.) ♦ *Sam's getting a real fat bucket, isn't he?* **4.** *n.* an old car. (From bucket of bolts.) ♦ *How much did you pay for that old bucket?*

bucket of bolts *n.* a machine, such as a car or a motorcycle, that is old, run-down, or worn-out. ♦ *My old bucket of bolts wouldn't start this morning.*

bucko ['bəko] *n.* friend; pal. (Also a term of address. Can also be used with a sneer to convey contempt.) ♦ *Hey, bucko, come here a minute.*

buckpasser *n.* someone who cannot accept the responsibility for something. (See also pass the buck.) ♦ *When something really goes wrong, everybody suddenly becomes a buckpasser.*

bud [bəd] *n.* a Budweiser beer; any beer. (See also budhead.) ♦ *How 'bout one of them buds in a green bottle?*

buddage *n.* marijuana buds. ♦ *I'm out of buddage. Where's the man?*

buddy up to so *in.* to become very friendly toward someone. ♦ *Why are you buddying up to me? I don't even know you.*

buddy up (with SO) *in.* to share living space with someone; to share something with someone. ♦ *Let's buddy up, okay?*

buddy-buddy ['bədi'bədi] *mod.* friendly; too friendly. ♦ *Why is that guy so buddy-buddy with me?*

budget *mod.* [of something] of low quality or cheap. ♦ *Don't you dare bring back any of that budget pizza!*

budget crunch Go to budget squeeze.

budget dust *n.* a minor amount of money considering the size of the entire budget; money left over at the end of the budget year. ♦ *The amount is just budget dust, chump change! What's the big deal?*

budget squeeze AND **budget crunch** *n.* a situation where there is not enough money in the budget. ♦ *Facing another budget squeeze, the legislators were forced to put off their pay increase.* ♦ *If it wasn't for the budget crunch, I'd get a good raise this year.*

budhead ['bədhɛd] *n.* a beer drinker. (See also bud.) ♦ *Here comes Charlie, my favorite budhead. How about a brew, Charlie?*

buffaloed ['bəfəlod] *mod.* confused; stumped. ♦ *These tax forms really have me buffaloed.*

buff(ed) [bəft] *mod.* strong; muscular. ♦ *He has such buff legs! Does he have a job or does he just work out?*

bug 1. *n.* a flaw in a computer program. ♦ *As soon as I get the bugs out, I can run my program.* **2.** *n.* someone who is enthusiastic about something. (A combining form.) ♦ *Mary is a camera bug.* **3.** *n.* an obsession or urge. ♦ *I've got this bug about making money.* **4.** *n.* a spy device for listening to someone's conversation. ♦ *I found a little bug taped under my chair.* **5.** *tv.* to conceal a microphone somewhere. ♦ *We will have to bug the bookie joint to get the goods on those guys.* **6.** *tv.* to annoy someone. ♦ *This kind of thing really bugs me.*

bug nut *n.* a wire nut; a twist-on wire connector used to connect the ends of wires to complete a circuit. ♦ *Charlie, hand me*

a couple bug nuts, will ya? ♦ *Hold them together, twist, and screw on the bug nut, See?*

Bug off! *exclam.* Get out!; Go away! ♦ *Bug off! Get out of here!*

bug out 1. *in.* to pack up and retreat. (Military, Korean War.) ♦ *Orders are to bug out by oh-nine-hundred.* **2.** *in.* to get out of somewhere fast. ♦ *I gotta find a way to bug out of here without getting caught.*

bug-fucker 1. *n.* a male with a small penis. (Rude and derogatory.) ♦ *Tell the little bug-fucker he doesn't get a discount, no matter what he's got!* **2.** *n.* a small penis. (Usually objectionable.) ♦ *Well, a bug-fucker is better than no fucker at all.* **3.** *n.* an insignificant and worthless male. (Rude and derogatory.) ♦ *Listen to me, you stupid bug-fucker! Get your things and get outa here!*

buggy ['bəgi] *n.* an automobile. ♦ *Other than a dent in the front bumper, this buggy is in A-1 condition.*

bugly ['bəg li] *mod.* butt-ugly; really ugly. ♦ *I have never seen such a bugly guy in my life!*

buick *in.* to vomit. (Onomatopoetic. Based on the automobile name.) ♦ *Dave buicked on the lawn and then stumbled into the house.*

built like a brick shithouse 1. *mod.* pertaining to a very strong and well-built person. (Usually refers to a male. Refers to the sturdiness of an outhouse [outdoor toilet] built of brick rather than the traditional wooden outhouse. Usually objectionable.) ♦ *Chuck is built like a brick shithouse. The only fat on him is where his brain ought to be.* **2.** *mod.* pertaining to a beautiful and curvaceous woman. (Refers to the imagined curving and uneven walls of an outhouse built hastily and carelessly of brick. This sense is a misinterpretation of the first sense. Usually objectionable.) ♦ *Look at that dame! She's really built like a brick shithouse.*

bull 1. *n.* nonsense; bullshit. ♦ *Don't give me that bull! I won't buy it.* **2.** *tv. & in.* to lie to or deceive someone. ♦ *Stop bulling me!*

3. *n.* a police officer; a private detective or guard. ♦ *Here come the bulls. Get out.*

bull bitch *n.* a strong and masculine woman. (Rude and derogatory.) ♦ *So, this bull bitch walks up to me and says, "Hey, buddy, got a match?"*

bull session *n.* a session of casual conversation. ♦ *The gals were sitting around enjoying a bull session.*

bull-dagger Go to bulldiker.

bulldiker AND **bull-dagger; bulldyker** *n.* a lesbian, especially if aggressive or masculine. (Rude and derogatory.) ♦ *Some old bulldiker strutted in and ordered a beer and a chaser.* ♦ *She was described by her friends as a "bull-dagger," and I can't imagine what her enemies called her.*

bulldog edition *n.* the first edition of a newspaper edition to hit the streets. ♦ *The story appeared in the bulldog edition, but it was all wrong.*

bulldoze *tv.* to apply pressure or force to get someone to do something. ♦ *You think you can bulldoze people into doing what you want!*

bulldyker Go to bulldiker.

bullets *n.* nipples. ♦ *Nice boobage. Nice bullets.*

bullet-stopper *n.* a U.S. Marine. (From the Persian Gulf War.) ♦ *About a dozen bullet-stoppers came into the bar and the army guys tried to start a fight.*

bullheaded *mod.* stubborn. ♦ *You are the most bullheaded man I've ever known.*

bull-pucky ['bʊlpəki] **1.** *n.* bull dung. ♦ *Why didn't you watch where you were going? Didn't you expect to find bull-pucky in a barnyard?* **2.** *n.* nonsense; bullshit. ♦ *That's all just bull-pucky. Don't believe a word of it.*

bullshit 1. *n.* lies; deception; hype; nonsense. (Also an exclamation: **Bullshit!** Widely known and used by both sexes. Usually objectionable.) ♦ *That's just a lot of bullshit!* **2.** *tv.* to deceive someone verbally. (Usually objectionable.) ♦ *Are you trying to bullshit me?* **3.** *in.* to tell lies; to hype and promote. (Usually objection-

able.) ♦ *Can't you stop bullshitting about how good you are?* **4.** *mod.* false; deceptive. (Usually objectionable.) ♦ *I'm sick of those bullshit ads on TV.*

bullshit artist AND **bullshitter** *n.* a person expert at lies, deception, and hype. (See also bullshit. Usually objectionable.) ♦ *What can you expect from a bullshit artist? The truth?* ♦ *Listen to me. Don't ever try to bullshit a bullshitter!*

bullshitter Go to bullshit artist.

bullyrag ['bʊliræg] *tv. & in.* to harass someone. ♦ *Don't bullyrag me just because you're upset.*

bum 1. *n.* a vagrant; a good-for-nothing. ♦ *You had better get your finances in order unless you want to become a bum.* **2.** *mod.* bad; faulty. ♦ *This is a bum fuse. No wonder it won't run.* **3.** Go to bum sth (off so).

bum about so/sth *in.* to be depressed about someone or something. ♦ *She's really bum about her grades. They suck.*

bum around *in.* to wander around; to kick around. ♦ *I thought I'd bum around for a few years before I settled down.*

bum beef Go to bogus beef.

bum check *n.* a bad check; a forged check. (See also paper.) ♦ *I never wrote a bum check in my life.*

bum out 1. *in.* to have a bad experience with drugs. (Drugs.) ♦ *I bummed out on angel dust.* **2.** *in.* to have any bad experience. ♦ *The test was horrible. I bummed out, for sure.*

bum rap 1. *n.* a false criminal charge. (Underworld. The same as bad rap.) ♦ *This is a bum rap, and you know it.* **2.** AND **bum-rap** *tv.* to talk ill about someone; to accuse someone of something falsely. ♦ *You're always bum-rapping your car!*

bum's rush *n.* the ejection of a person from a place. ♦ *Give this dame the bum's rush. She can't pay for nothin'.*

bum so out *tv.* to discourage someone. (See also bummed (out).) ♦ *The failure of his tires bummed out the race driver.*

bum steer ['bəm 'stir] *n.* a false lead; false information. ♦ *You sure gave me a bum steer when you told me who he was.*

bum sth **(off** so**)** *tv.* to beg or borrow something (from someone). ♦ *Can I bum two quarters for a phone call?*

bum trip Go to bummer.

Bumblefuck Go to Bumfuck.

Bumfuck AND **Bumblefuck** *n.* an imaginary place where everyone is a rural oaf. (Usually objectionable.) ♦ *I have to drive my cousin home. He lives out in West Bumfuck or something.* ♦ *There we were, twenty miles from Bumblefuck, and no food, water, or money!*

bummage *n.* despair. (As in bummed (out).) ♦ *I got a load of bummage today. I'll get over it.*

bummed (out) *mod.* discouraged; depressed. ♦ *I feel so bummed. I think I need a nice hot bath.*

bummer 1. AND **bum trip** *n.* a bad drug experience. (Drugs.) ♦ *She almost didn't get back from a bum trip.* ♦ *I had a real bummer on that stuff. I may quit yet.* **2.** *n.* a disagreeable thing or person. ♦ *The game was a bummer you wouldn't believe.* **3.** *mod.* disappointing; unpleasant. ♦ *I had a real bummer day.*

bumming *mod.* down; depressed; suffering from something disagreeable. (Collegiate.) ♦ *I'm really bumming. I think I need somebody to talk to.*

bump *tv.* to remove someone from an airplane flight, usually involuntarily, because of overbooking. ♦ *They bumped me but gave me something to make up for it.*

bump so **off** *tv.* to kill someone. (Originally underworld.) ♦ *What am I supposed to do, bump her off?*

Bump that! *tv.* Forget that! ♦ *Bump that! I was wrong.*

bump uglies *tv.* [for two people] to copulate. ♦ *You been bumpin' uglies with Joannie again?*

bumper sticker *n.* a car or other vehicle following too closely on one's bumper. (A reapplication of the term for a kind of adhesive sign stuck on a car bumber.) ♦ *I can't talk now, I've got a bumper sticker that's taking all my attention.*

bumping 1. *mod.* [of music] having a good beat. ♦ *Man, this music is bumping. I can feel the beat.* **2.** *mod.* crowded and busy. ♦ *This place is bumping. Let's sit in the corner, out of the way.* **3.** *mod.* really good; cool. ♦ *We had a bumping time at Tiff's last night.*

bumping fuzzies *n.* copulation. (The *fuzzies* refer to the participants' pelvic regions.) ♦ *She caught them bumping fuzzies in the pantry.*

bunch of fives *n.* the fist. ♦ *How would you like a bunch of fives right in the kisser?*

bunch-punch 1. *n.* an act of serial copulation with one female and a group of males. ♦ *Sam always dreamed about being involved in a bunch-punch.* **2.** *n.* an act of group rape of a woman. ♦ *There was a bunch-punch in this neighborhood last night, and the night before, and the night before that. Where are the police?*

buncombe Go to bunkum.

bundle *n.* a large amount of money. (See also lose a bundle; make a bundle; package.) ♦ *He still has a bundle from the sale of his house.*

bundle from heaven Go to bundle of joy.

bundle of joy AND **bundle from heaven** *n.* a baby. ♦ *We are expecting a bundle of joy next September.* ♦ *Robert, your little bundle from heaven smells like a saddle bag from the other place.*

bundle of nerves *n.* a very nervous person. ♦ *I'm just a bundle of nerves. I wish this were over.*

bunghole 1. *n.* the mouth. ♦ *I've heard enough out of you! Shut your bunghole!* **2.** *n.* the anus. (Usually objectionable.) ♦ *She tripped and fell down on her bunghole.*

bunked *mod.* drunk. ♦ *That's enough. You're bunked.*

bunkie ['bəŋki] *n.* a roommate. ♦ *My bunkie is from Iowa.*

bunkum AND **buncombe** ['bəŋkəm] *n.* nonsense. ♦ *That's just plain bunkum!* ♦

Your Honor, counselor's airbrained bun-combe is an insult to the court. I object!

buns *n.* the buttocks. ♦ *Look at the buns on that guy!*

burb [bɝb] *n.* a suburb. (Usually plural.) ♦ *I've lived in the burbs all my life.*

burbed out [bɝbd...] *mod.* looking very middle-class and suburban; decked out like a suburban citizen. ♦ *She's all burbed out with new clothes and a fancy car.*

burg [bɝg] *n.* a small town. (Disdainful.) ♦ *I can't stand another day in this burg.*

burger *n.* a hamburger sandwich; a hamburger patty. ♦ *You ready for another burger?*

burger-flipper *n.* a lowly hamburger cook in a fast-food restaurant. (See also hole digger.) ♦ *If you drop out of school now, you'll end up being a burger-flipper for the rest of your life.*

burn 1. *n.* a cigarette. ♦ *Fred just stood there with a burn on his lower lip and his hands in his pockets.* **2.** *tv.* to smoke a cigarette. ♦ *I need to burn a fag. Just a minute.* **3.** *tv.* to smoke cannabis. (Drugs.) ♦ *The two of them sat there burning reefers for hours on end.* **4.** *tv.* to execute someone in the electric chair. (Underworld.) ♦ *I'll see that they burn you for this!* **5.** *in.* to die by electrocution in the electric chair. (Underworld.) ♦ *I ain't afraid I'll burn, copper!* **6.** *tv.* to cheat or rob someone. ♦ *Tom tried to burn me by selling me a bum watch, but I'm too clever.* **7.** *tv.* to shoot someone. (Underworld. See also burner = gun.) ♦ *He burned the guy with a pistol, but it didn't stop him.* **8.** *n.* a deception; an instance of being cheated. ♦ *Man, that was a burn. That guy was really mad.* **9.** *n.* the charge or rush after the injection of a drug into a vein. (Drugs.) ♦ *I don't want a big burn; just drag it out for about an hour.* **10.** *tv.* to cook food. ♦ *Why don't you burn some chow for me?*

burn artist *n.* someone who cheats or harms someone else; an informer. (Underworld.) ♦ *Never trust a known burn artist.*

burn rubber *tv.* to run a car engine so fast that one spins the tires so that rubber is left on the street. (See also lay (some) rubber.) ♦ *When George was at the age when the greatest thrill was burning rubber, he began to shave once a week.*

burn so down *tv.* to humiliate someone. ♦ *You just want to burn down everybody to make yourself seem better.*

burn so up *tv.* to make someone very angry. ♦ *That kind of thing just burns me up.*

burn with a low blue flame 1. *in.* to be heavily alcohol intoxicated. ♦ *Yeah, he's burning with a low blue flame.* **2.** *in.* to be quietly and intensely angry. ♦ *She just sat there with her steak in her lap, burning with a low blue flame.*

burned 1. *mod.* cheated; betrayed. ♦ *Man, did I get burned in that place!* **2.** *mod.* disappointed; humiliated; put down. ♦ *Ha! You're burned!* **3.** AND **burned up** *mod.* very angry. ♦ *I've never been so burned up at anyone.* ♦ *I am really burned! Totally burned!*

burned out AND **burnt out 1.** *mod.* tired; bored. ♦ *I'm burned out after all that partying.* **2.** *mod.* having to do with the ruined veins of an addict. (Drugs.) ♦ *My veins are burnt out so I shoot in the jug.* **3.** *mod.* ruined by marijuana smoking. (Drugs. See also burnout.) ♦ *What's left for these burned out kids?* **4.** *mod.* no longer affected by a particular drug. (Drugs.) ♦ *It's no good. I'm just burned out. The stuff doesn't affect me at all.*

burned up Go to burned.

burner *n.* a gun; a pistol. (See also burn = to kill.) ♦ *You got your burner on you?*

burnout ['bɝnaʊt] **1.** *n.* a person who is ruined by drugs. ♦ *Two burnouts sat on the school steps and stared at their feet.* **2.** *n.* someone no longer effective on the job. ♦ *We try to find some other employment for the burnouts.*

burnt out Go to burned out.

burp Go to berp.

burps Go to berps.

burrnips *mod.* cold. (Cold enough to make nipples harden.) ♦ *It's really cold, burrnips cold.*

bury the hatchet 1. *tv.* to make peace. (From an alleged American Indian practice.) ♦ *I'm sorry. Let's stop arguing and bury the hatchet.* **2.** *tv.* to leave surgical instruments in the patient. (Medical.) ♦ *The idea that a doctor would bury the hatchet is a very old joke.*

bush 1. *n.* the pubic hair. (Usually objectionable.) ♦ *How old were you when you started growing a bush?* **2.** *n.* a woman considered as a receptacle for the penis. (Rude and derogatory.) ♦ *Bubba says he gotta have some bush.*

bush bitch AND **bush pig** *n.* an ugly or unpleasant female. (Derogatory.) ♦ *Tom's been dating some bush pig from Adamsville.* ♦ *Shut your shitty mouth, you skanky bush bitch!*

bush patrol 1. *n.* a session of necking and petting. (Here *patrol* has the military meaning of assignment.) ♦ *Martha and Paul spent the evening on bush patrol.* **2.** *n.* an imaginary search through campus shrubbery to flush out the necking couples. ♦ *Bush patrol starts at midnight, so be in by then.*

bush pig Go to bush bitch.

bushed [buʃt] *mod.* exhausted. ♦ *Another hard day! I am more bushed than ever.*

business end (of sth**)** *n.* the dangerous end of something; the part of something that does something as opposed to the part one holds on to. ♦ *Harry burned himself on the business end of a soldering iron.*

bust 1. *n.* a failure. ♦ *The whole project was a bust from the beginning.* **2.** *tv.* to reduce someone's rank. (Originally military, now also in civilian use as with the police.) ♦ *The brass busted her on the spot.* **3.** *n.* a riotous drinking party. ♦ *There was a big bust in the park until two in the morning.* **4.** *n.* a raid by the police. ♦ *I knew it was a bust the minute they broke in the door.* **5.** *tv.* [for the police] to raid a place. ♦ *The bacon busted Bill's bar and put Bill in the slammer.* **6.** *tv.* to arrest someone. ♦ *The feds finally busted Frank*

on a tax rap. **7.** *n.* an arrest. ♦ *The bust was carried off without much stress.* **8.** *tv.* to inform on someone, leading to an arrest. ♦ *Tom busted Sam because there's bad blood between them.* **9.** *n.* the police. ♦ *Here comes the bust. Beat it!* **10.** Go to busted.

bust a grub *tv.* to eat a meal. ♦ *Man, I'm starved. Let's go bust a grub.*

bust a gut (to do sth**)** *tv.* to make a great effort (to do something). (Usually objectionable.) ♦ *I busted a gut trying to get just the thing you wanted!*

bust a move *tv.* to leave (a place). ♦ *Let's bust a move. Lots to do tomorrow.*

bust a nut 1. *tv.* to ejaculate. ♦ *I almost busted a nut when I saw her bend over.* **2.** *tv.* to work hard to accomplish something. ♦ *I busted a nut to get it done on time.*

bust ass (out of somewhere**)** Go to bag ass (out of somewhere).

bust on so/sth *n.* to attack someone or a group. ♦ *These three guys busted on Bubba and broke his arm.*

bust (one's) ass (to do sth**)** AND **break (one's) balls (to do** sth**); bust (one's) butt (to do** sth**); bust (one's) nuts (to do** sth**)** *tv.* to work very hard to do something; to work very hard at something. (Usually objectionable.) ♦ *You get down there and bust your ass to get the job done right! You hear me?* ♦ *I busted my butt to please her, and what do I get?*

bust (one's) butt to do sth Go to bust (one's) ass (to do sth).

bust (one's) nuts to do sth Go to bust (one's) ass (to do sth).

bust out (of some place**)** *in.* to break out of some place, especially a prison. (*Bust* is a nonstandard form of *burst* meaning "break" here.) ♦ *Somehow the gangsters busted out of prison and left the country.*

bust (some) suds 1. *tv.* to drink some beer. ♦ *Let's go out and bust some suds.* **2.** *tv.* to wash dishes. ♦ *You get into that kitchen and bust some suds to pay for your meal!*

bust so **one** *tv.* to punch someone; to give someone a punch, probably in the face. ♦ *You better shut up, or I'll bust you one!*

bust so **out of** somewhere **1.** *tv.* to help someone escape from prison. (*Bust* is a nonstandard form of *burst* meaning "break" here.) ♦ *Lefty did not manage to bust Max out of prison.* **2.** *tv.* to expel or force someone to withdraw from school. (*Bust* is a nonstandard form of *burst* meaning "break" here.) ♦ *The dean finally busted Bill out of school.*

bust so **up 1.** *tv.* to cause lovers to separate; to break up a pair of lovers, including married persons. (*Bust* is a nonstandard form of *burst* meaning "break (apart)" here.) ♦ *Mary busted up Terri and John.* **2.** *tv.* to beat someone up; to batter someone. ♦ *You want me to bust you up?*

bust so **wide open** *tv.* to beat someone severely. ♦ *If you ever take a step onto my property, I'll bust you wide open.*

bust sth **up** *tv.* to ruin a marriage by coming between the married people. ♦ *He busted their marriage up by starting rumors about Maggie.*

bust sth **wide open** Go to blow sth wide open.

bust up *in.* [for lovers] to separate or break up. ♦ *Tom and Alice busted up for good.*

busta *n.* a young kid trying to act tough; *buster.* (Streets. From or supported by Buster, the nickname.) ♦ *Sammy's just a busta. He won't get nowhere.*

bust-ass Go to kick-ass.

busted 1. AND **bust** *mod.* arrested. ♦ *Harry the Horse is bust again. The third time this month.* ♦ *How many times you been busted for speeding?* **2.** *mod.* alcohol intoxicated. ♦ *I went to a beer bust and got busted.*

But, hey *phr.* a sentence opener used often to get attention and perhaps contradict a previous remark. ♦ A: *Please don't track sand all over the restaurant carpet!* B: *But, hey, it's my vacation!*

but-boy *n.* someone, usually a male, who raises objections frequently. (The opposite of a *yes-man*.) ♦ *I wish you wouldn't be such a but-boy, Higgins. Can't you ever agree with anyone?*

butch [bʊtʃ] **1.** *n.* a physician. (Derogatory. From *butcher*.) ♦ *The butch at the infirmary was no help at all.* **2.** *mod.* virile and masculine. (In a homosexual context.) ♦ *Really, Clare. How butch!*

butt [bət] **1.** *n.* the buttocks. (Colloquial. Potentially offensive, although heard almost everywhere. See the complete list of all entries with butt in the **Index of Hidden Key Words**.) ♦ *She fell right on her butt.* **2.** *n.* a cigarette butt. ♦ *Don't leave your butts in the houseplants!* **3.** *n.* a cigarette of any kind. ♦ *You got a butt I can bum?* **4.** *n.* someone or something that is disliked. (Rude and derogatory. See also boody.) ♦ *The guy's a real butt. A real squid.*

butt floss Go to butt thong.

butt naked *mod.* totally nude. (Mildly objectionable.) ♦ *I was butt naked in the shower and couldn't get the phone.*

Butt out! *exclam.* Get out of my affairs!; Mind your own business! ♦ *Go away! Butt out!*

butt thong AND **butt floss** *n.* a thong bathing costume. (Mildly objectionable.) ♦ *You're not going to wear that butt thong in public are you?* ♦ *My mother called my bathing suit "butt-floss!"*

butter *mod.* good; really fine. ♦ *This guy Walter, he's butter, totally butter.*

butter face *n.* a very ugly woman; a woman with everything just right *but her face.* ♦ *Nice shape, but she's a butterface.*

butt-fucking Egypt AND **BFE** *n.* a place that is very far away. (Usually objectionable.) ♦ *My brother lives out in butt-fucking Egypt somewhere.* ♦ *Gotta be somewhere in BFE at noon, and I ain't even left yet.*

butthead *n.* a stupid or obnoxious person of either sex. (Also a term of address. Rude and derogatory.) ♦ *Don't be such a butthead!*

butthole *n.* the anus; the asshole. (Usually objectionable.) ♦ *Why are you always scratching your butthole?*

buttinsky AND **buttinski** [bə'tɪnski] *n.* someone who interrupts; someone who gets involved in other people's business. ♦ *I hate to be a buttinski, but what are you talking about?*

butt-kicker AND **ass-kicker** *n.* someone or something capable of defeating or surpassing all others. ♦ *That idea is a real butt-kicker.* ♦ *He is an ass-kicker, but he at least rewards us for putting up with him.*

buttlegging ['bətlɛgɪŋ] *n.* the transportation of untaxed or undertaxed cigarettes across a state line. (Patterned on *bootlegging.* See also bootleg.) ♦ *Most of the guys at the plant do buttlegging on the way home from work.*

buttload AND **shitload** *mod.* a lot; a large amount. (Usually objectionable.) ♦ *I know we can sell a buttload of these recordings—if we can only get a shipment of them in time.* ♦ *I've got a shitload of problems and no idea how to work through them.*

butt-munch *n.* a despised male. (Usually objectionable.) ♦ *You dumb butt-munch! Why did you do that?*

button 1. *n.* the termination of a recitation; the punch line of a joke; a zinger. (The equivalent of a button punched to signal a response.) ♦ *When I got to the button, I realized that I had told the whole joke wrong.* **2.** *n.* a police officer's badge or shield. ♦ *The guy flashed his button, so I let him in.*

Button your lip! *imperative* Shut up!; Be quiet! ♦ *I've heard enough outa you! Button your lip!*

buttonhole *tv.* to accost someone; to make someone listen to one. (As if grabbing someone by the coat lapel to keep them from getting away.) ♦ *The guy buttonholed me on my way out, and started asking me a lot of questions.*

butt-ugly *mod.* very ugly. (Usually objectionable.) ♦ *That is the most butt-ugly car I've ever seen.*

butt-wipe Go to ass-wipe.

buy 1. *n.* a purchase. ♦ *Man, this is a great buy.* **2.** *tv.* to believe something. ♦ *It sounds good to me, but will your wife buy it?*

buy it *tv.* to die. (See also buy the farm; buy the big one.) ♦ *He lay there coughing for a few minutes, and then he bought it.*

buy SO's **woof ticket** *tv.* to challenge someone's boast or taunt. (Also spelled *wolf.*) ♦ *He's such a fighter. He'll buy anybody's woof ticket.*

buy the big one *tv.* to die. ♦ *She conked out for good—you know, bought the big one.*

buy the farm *tv.* to die; to get killed. (The farm may be a grave site. No one knows the origin.) ♦ *I'm too young to buy the farm.*

buzhie ['buʒi] **1.** *n.* a middle-class person. (From *bourgeoisie.*) ♦ *I live in a neighborhood of buzhies.* **2.** *mod.* middle-class. ♦ *I live in a buzhie house and drive a buzhie car.*

buzz 1. *n.* a call on the telephone. (Usually with *give.* See also jingle.) ♦ *I'll give you a buzz tomorrow.* **2.** *tv.* to call someone on the telephone. ♦ *Buzz me about noon.* **3.** *tv.* to signal someone with a buzzer. ♦ *I'll buzz my secretary.* **4.** *n.* a thrill. ♦ *I got a real buzz out of that.* **5.** *n.* a chuckle. ♦ *Here's a little joke that'll give you a buzz.* **6.** *n.* the initial effects of drinking alcohol or taking certain drugs. ♦ *Sam got a little buzz from the wine, but he still needed something stronger.*

buzz along 1. *in.* to depart. ♦ *Well, I must buzz along.* **2.** *in.* to drive or move along rapidly. ♦ *"You were buzzing along at eighty-two miles per hour," said the cop.*

buzzard *n.* an old man; a mean old man. (Especially with *old.*) ♦ *Some old buzzard is at the door asking for Mary Wilson.*

buzzard meat *n.* someone or something that is dead or outdated. ♦ *If you don't watch out, you're going to become buzzard meat!*

buzzing *mod.* drunk. ♦ *Sally was buzzing after only a few drinks.*

buzzkill *n.* someone or something that ruins enjoyment or pleasure; someone or something that ruins a buzz sense 4. ♦ *Oh, Willy! You're such a buzzkill!*

BVDs AND **beeveedees** *n.* underwear; men's underwear. (The first entry is an initialism. From *Bradley, Voorhies, and Day*, the manufacturers. Always plural.) ♦ *He stood there in his BVDs, freezing.*

BWOC *n.* big woman on campus, an important or self-important female college student. (Initialism. Collegiate. See also BMOC.) ♦ *It's always the same BWOCs you see in the paper.*

Bye-bye, for now. AND **BBFN** *phr. & comp. abb.* Good-bye until next time. ♦ *Gotta go. BBFN.* ♦ *See you on the flip side. Bye-bye, for now.*

BYO(B) *mod.* bring your own (booze or bottle). (Initialism.) ♦ *A note on the invitation says that the party is BYOB.*

C. *n.* the sum of one hundred dollars, as in C-note. (Underworld. The *C* is the Roman numeral 100.) ♦ *Four C.s for an old junker like that? You're crazy!*

C4N Go to Ciao, for now.

cabbage *n.* money. (Originally underworld. See also **green**; **spinach**.) ♦ *How much cabbage you want for this heater?*

cabbagehead *n.* a fool; a stupid person. ♦ *What cabbagehead put this thing on upside down?*

caboose [kə'bus] *n.* the buttocks. (From the name of the car at the end of a railroad train.) ♦ *You just plunk your caboose over there on the settee and listen up to what I have to tell you.*

caca AND **kaka** ['kɑkɑ] **1.** *n.* dung; feces. (Juvenile. From Spanish. Usually objectionable.) ♦ *There's fresh caca in the front yard.* **2.** *in.* to defecate. (Juvenile. Usually objectionable.) ♦ *Jimmy kakad in his diaper!*

cack [kæk] **1.** *n.* dung; feces. (Usually objectionable. See also **caca**.) ♦ *Wipe that cack off your shoes before you come in here!* **2.** *in.* to defecate. (Usually objectionable.) ♦ *The dog cacked right there on Fifth Avenue.* **3.** AND **kack; kak** *in.* to empty one's stomach; to puke; to vomit. (Onomatopeotic.) ♦ *I cacked all night with the flu.* **4.** AND **kack; kak** *tv.* to kill someone. ♦ *Frank threatened to cack Veronica if she didn't straighten up.* **5.** *tv.* to deceive someone; to **shit** (sense 7) someone. ♦ *That didn't happen! You're just cacking me.*

cackleberry *n.* an egg. ♦ *You want cackleberries for breakfast?*

cactus (buttons) *n.* peyote cactus containing mescaline. (Drugs.) ♦ *Gert came back from vacation with a bag of cactus buttons.*

cactus juice *n.* tequila. (A Mexican liquor.) ♦ *Ernie brought back a big jug of cactus juice from Mexico.*

caddy ['kædi] *n.* a Cadillac automobile. ♦ *What I really want is a caddy. Keep your yuppie beemer.*

cadge sth **from** so AND **cadge** sth **off** so *tv.* to beg or borrow something from someone. ♦ *I cadged this jacket off a friendly guy I met.* ♦ *He tried to cadge a ten-spot from me.*

Cadillac ['kædlæk] **1.** *n.* the name of something powerful or superior. (From the name of the automobile.) ♦ *Acme is the Cadillac of monochrome closed-circuit retail surveillance equipment.* **2.** *n.* a powerful drug, especially cocaine. (Drugs.) ♦ *Just a pinch of Cadillac in my junk seems to keep me a little more lively.*

the **cage of anger** *n.* a prison. (Streets.) ♦ *The judge put JoJo into the cage of anger for a three-year stretch.*

cagey ['kedʒi] *mod.* sneaky; shrewd. ♦ *John is pretty cagey. You have to keep an eye on him.*

caine Go to cane.

cake 1. *n.* money. (From bread, dough.) ♦ *I can't scrape together enough cake to do the job.* **2.** Go to cakes.

cake hole Go to word hole.

cakes *n.* the buttocks. (Like buns.) ♦ *You behave yourself or I'll blister your cakes.*

cakewalk *n.* something very easy. (See also sleepwalk.) ♦ *Nothing to it. It's a cakewalk.*

calaboose ['kæləbus] *n.* jail. (From a Spanish word.) ♦ *Are we going to tell what happened, or are we going to spend the night in the calaboose?*

calendar *tv.* to set a date for something; to put something on one's calendar or in one's diary. ♦ *I will calendar the date and try to be there on time.*

call 1. *n.* a decision; a prediction. ♦ *The market behaved just as you said it would. Good call.* **2.** *tv.* to challenge someone. ♦ *I called him, but he ignored me.* **3.** *n.* the early effects of a drug; the beginning of a rush; a rush. (Drugs.) ♦ *You may not get the call on this stuff for twenty minutes or more.*

call (all) the shots *tv.* to decide on the course of action; to be in charge. ♦ *Why do you have to call all the shots?*

call earl Go to call hughie.

call hogs *tv.* to snore really loudly. ♦ *Mike was calling hogs all night long and I got hardly a wink of sleep.*

call house *n.* a brothel. ♦ *The cops busted a call house on Fourth Street last week.*

call hughie AND **call earl** [...'hyui AND ...'ɚl] *tv.* to vomit. (Onomatopoetic from the sound of retching.) ♦ *Fred spent an hour in the john calling hughie.* ♦ *He stepped aside and began calling earl, right there on Maple Street!*

Call my service. *sent.* Please call me through my answering service. (Not a friendly or encouraging invitation.) ♦ *Good to talk to ya, babe. Call my service. Love ya!*

call of nature Go to nature's call.

call ralph Go to cry ruth.

call ruth Go to cry ruth.

call shotgun *phr.* to call out and claim the seat beside the driver in an automobile. ♦ *Bob called shotgun so he could sit next to the driver.*

call so out *tv.* to challenge someone to a fight. ♦ *Max wanted to call him out but thought better of it.*

call-girl *n.* a woman who is *on call* as a prostitute. (Possibly refers to a prostitute who can be contacted by a telephone call.) ♦ *The cops dragged in a whole flock of call-girls after the convention.*

cam (red) *n.* Cambodian red marijuana. ♦ *He claims he scored some cam.*

camel toes *n.* a woman's vulva as it appears through blue jeans, especially jeans that have been pulled up too tight. ♦ *There's nothing attractive about camel toes.*

camp 1. *n.* something cute and out of fashion; something of such an anachronistic style as to be intriguing. ♦ *Nobody really knows what style camp really is, and very few even care.* **2.** AND **campy** *mod.* overdone; out of fashion and intriguing. ♦ *Most camp entertainment is pretentious and overdrawn.* **3.** *mod.* having to do with homosexual persons and matters. ♦ *She is so camp, I could scream!*

camp it up 1. *tv.* to overact. ♦ *Can you make it a little more lively without camping it up?* **2.** *tv.* to overdo effeminacy; [for a homosexual male] to act too effeminate in public. ♦ *John just loves to burst into the most sedate hotel in town and camp it up in the lobby.*

campi ['kæmpaɪ] *n.* campuses. (The Latin plural of *campus* = field.) ♦ *I'll see you about the campi. Ciao!*

campy Go to camp.

can 1. *n.* the head. ♦ *Jerry landed one on Frank's can. Frank crumpled.* **2.** *n.* toilet. ♦ *Restroom? Hell, I ain't tired! Where's the can?* **3.** *n.* the buttocks. (Usually objectionable. See also bucket.) ♦ *The guy slipped on the ice and fell on his can.* **4.** *n.* jail. (Usually with the.) ♦ *I had to spend the night in the can, but it wasn't too bad.* **5.** *tv.* to dismiss someone from employment. ♦ *The jerk canned everybody who played a part in the gag.* **6.** *n.* a car. ♦ *That's a good-looking can he's driving.* **7.** Go to cans. **8.** *n.* a breast. (Usually objectionable. Usually plural.) ♦ *Man, look at the cans on that dame!* **9.** *n.* a measurement of marijuana. (Drugs.) ♦ *How much do you want for a can?*

Can it! *exclam.* Shut up! ♦ *That's enough out of you! Can it!*

can of corn 1. *n.* a baseball that drops straight down into the glove of a waiting player (for an out). (Since the 1940s.) ♦ *It's a can of corn! Right into Sammy's mitt.* **2.** *n.* something that is really easy [to do], as in *easy as catching a can of corn.* (From the image of an old-time grocery store clerk who would grasp a can from the top shelf with the special long tool, and then drop it straight down into his hand.) ♦ *Nothing to it. A can of corn.*

can of worms *n.* an intertwined set of problems; an array of difficulties. (Often with *open.*) ♦ *When you brought that up, you opened a whole new can of worms.*

canary [kəˈnɛri] **1.** *n.* a female singer. ♦ *The band had a cute canary who could really sing.* **2.** *n.* a capsule of Nembutal, a barbiturate. (Drugs. The capsule is yellow.) ♦ *There are a couple of blues, which ought to do the same as canaries.* **3.** *n.* a police informer who *sings* to the police. (See also **stool (pigeon).**) ♦ *Spike is no canary. He would never squeal on us.*

cancel so **out of** sth *tv.* to eliminate someone; to kill someone. ♦ *The drug lord threatened to cancel out his former partner for testifying against him.*

cancel so's **Christmas** *tv.* to kill someone; to destroy someone. (Underworld. The dead person will miss Christmas.) ♦ *If he keeps bugging me, I'm gonna cancel his Christmas.*

cancer stick *n.* a tobacco cigarette. (From the notion that cigarette smoking is a major cause of lung cancer. Old but recurrent.) ♦ *Kelly pulled out his ninth cancer stick and lit it up.*

candied [ˈkændid] *mod.* addicted to cocaine. (Drugs. See also **nose (candy).**) ♦ *Unfortunately, Paul is candied, and he lost his job so he can't buy toot.*

candlelight *n.* dusk; dawn. ♦ *I'll see you along about candlelight.*

candy *n.* drugs in general. (Drugs. See also **nose (candy).**) ♦ *I gotta go get some candy from the candy man.*

candy man *n.* a drug dealer. (Drugs.) ♦ *Lefty said he had to go meet with the candy man.*

candy store *n.* a liquor store. ♦ *Let's stop at this candy store and get some bubbles.*

candy-ass 1. *n.* a coward; a timid person. (Mildly objectionable.) ♦ *Sue is such a candy-ass when it comes to dealing with her children.* **2.** Go to **candy-ass(ed).**

candy-ass(ed) *mod.* timid; frightened; cowardly. (Mildly objectionable.) ♦ *What a candy-assed twit you are!*

cane AND **caine** *n.* cocaine. (Drugs.) ♦ *Even the kids can afford to buy cane now. The social problems of the twenty-first century are starting right here.*

canned 1. *mod.* alcohol intoxicated. ♦ *I'll drive. I'm too canned to walk.* **2.** *mod.* having to do with prerecorded laughter or applause that is added to the sound track of a television program. ♦ *The dialogue was funny enough that they didn't need to have the laughter canned.*

cannon *n.* a gun; a revolver. (Underworld.) ♦ *Rocko pulled out his cannon and aimed it at Marlowe's throat.*

cannot see (any) further than the end of (one's**) nose** Go to **see no further than the end of** one's **nose.**

cans *n.* earphones. ♦ *The guy with the cans on his head is the radio operator.*

can-shaker *n.* a fund-raiser. (As if a person were holding a can for the solicitation of coins from passersby.) ♦ *Fred was a professional can-shaker for a museum. Maybe he has some ideas as to how we can raise some money.*

can't find one's **butt with both hands (in broad daylight)** *tv.* is stupid or incompetent. (Mildly objectionable.) ♦ *Why did they put Jim in charge? He can't find his butt with both hands!*

can't hit the (broad) side of a barn *tv.* cannot aim something accurately. ♦ *You're way off. You couldn't hit the broad side of a barn.*

can't remember a fucking thing AND **CRAFT** *phr. & comp. abb.* a phrase said when one's memory fails. (Usually objectionable.) ♦ *Gee, I'm getting old. CRAFT.* ♦ *What's your name, again? I can't remember a fucking thing!*

can't remember shit AND **CRS** *phr. & comp. abb.* can't remember anything. (Usually objectionable.) ♦ *Tom can't remember shit. He has to write everything down.* ♦ *I was diagnosed with CRS. It comes with age!*

can't win (th)em all *tv.* (one should) expect to lose every now and then. ♦ *It doesn't really matter. You can't win them all.*

cap 1. *n.* a capsule of a drug. ♦ *Do you want it in caps or elixir?* **2.** *tv.* to exceed something; to surpass something. ♦ *I know I can't cap that. That's just super!* **3.** *tv.* to make a capsule. ♦ *I must have capped 300 placebos today.* **4.** *tv.* to kill someone. ♦ *The kid capped his friend for dissing him.*

caper ['kepɚ] **1.** *n.* any stunt or event; a trick or a scam. ♦ *That little caper the kids did with the statue from the town square was a dandy.* **2.** *n.* a criminal job: theft, kidnapping, blackmail, etc. (Underworld.) ♦ *The black and whites pulled up right in the middle of the caper.*

capish [kə'piʃ] *in.* to understand. (Usually as a question. From an Italian dialect.) ♦ *The matter is settled. No more talk. Capish?*

capital *n.* cash; money. ♦ *I'm a little short of capital right now.*

capper ['kæpɚ] *n.* the climax or clincher of something. ♦ *The capper of the evening was when the hostess got lathered before midnight and couldn't celebrate the New Year.*

carb [kɑrb] *n.* an engine carburetor. ♦ *This can needs a new carb.*

carb(o)s ['kɑrb(o)z] *n.* carbohydrates. (Bodybuilding and dieting. *Carbs* is displacing *carbos*.) ♦ *You need more protein and less carbs.*

carburetor *n.* a device for smoking cannabis that mixes the smoke with air. (Drugs.) ♦ *I have a carburetor with the rest of my stash.*

carcass ['kɑrkəs] *n.* one's body; a large or heavy body. ♦ *Put your carcass on a chair, and let's chew the fat.*

card 1. *n.* a funny person. ♦ *Britney is such a card. She cracks me up.* **2.** *tv.* to check people's ID cards for age or other eligibility. (See also **carded**.) ♦ *They card everybody at the football games, even the parents.* **3.** Go to **phish**.

carded AND **proofed** *mod.* [of an ID card] examined to determine whether one has reached the legal drinking age. ♦ *Dave got carded at the party even though he is thirty and looks it.* ♦ *As soon as we were proofed, we got in and got some brews.*

carding Go to **spoofing**.

carebear *n.* a nice person who is against violence and disputes. (Especially in the domain of computer games. From the name of a set of lovable children's characters.) ♦ *These carebears don't want us to play the really good games!*

carrier *n.* a narcotics seller or transporter. (Drugs. See also **courier**.) ♦ *The carrier has the most dangerous job of all.*

carry 1. *in.* to carry drugs on one's person. (Drugs.) ♦ *If you get busted while you're carrying, you are in big trouble with the man.* **2.** *n.* drugs carried on the person as an emergency supply in case of arrest. (Underworld.) ♦ *The cops found my carry, and I spent three days in the clink climbing the walls.*

carry (an amount of) weight *tv.* to have a degree of influence. ♦ *Tom carries a lot of weight with the mayor. Ask him.*

carry the stick *tv.* to live as a hobo, on the streets. (Streets. From the stick that supports the hobo's bundle.) ♦ *I was afraid I'd be carrying the stick if I got laid off.*

carrying a (heavy) load *mod.* alcohol intoxicated. ♦ *Marty is carrying a heavy load.*

cas [kæz] *mod.* okay; fine. (From *casual*. See also **cazh**.) ♦ *That's cas, man. Good to hear it.*

case of the shorts Go to **short**.

case so/sth **out** *tv.* to look someone or something over carefully, with a view to additional activity at a later time. ♦ *He cased out the fixtures to see which ones to replace.*

case the joint 1. *tv.* to look over some place to figure out how to break in, what to steal, etc. (Underworld. See also joint.) ♦ *First of all you gotta case the joint to see where things are.* **2.** *tv.* to look a place over. (No criminal intent. From sense 1.) ♦ *The dog came in and cased the joint, sniffing out friends and foes.*

cash cow *n.* a dependable source of money; a good investment. ♦ *Mr. Wilson turned out to be the cash cow we needed to start our repertoire company.*

cash flow *n.* cash; ready money. ♦ *When I get a little cash flow at the end of the week, I'll treat you to a hamburger.*

cash in (one's**) checks** Go to cash in one's chips.

cash in (one's**) chips** AND **cash in (**one's**) checks** *tv.* to die; to finish the game (of life). ♦ *He opened his eyes, said good-bye, and cashed in his chips.* ♦ *The cowboy sighed softly and cashed in his checks.*

Cash is king. *sent.* It is best to keep one's investment money in cash. (Said when the prices in the securities market are too high. It is better to build up cash and wait for a break in the market.) ♦ *Things look a little pricey now. I'd say that cash is king for the moment.*

Cash is trash. *sent.* It is unwise to keep one's investment money in cash. (Said when there are good opportunities in securities and it is foolish to stay on the sidelines in cash.) ♦ *Cash is trash. Get into the market or you stand to lose a bundle.*

cash so **out** *tv.* to pay someone (off). ♦ *Come on, cash me out. I did the job. I want to go home.*

cashed 1. *mod.* expired; depleted; burnt out. (From *cashed in.*) ♦ *My pen is cashed. Where can I get a new one?* **2.** *mod.* tired. ♦ *Man, I'm cashed. Can we rest here for a while?*

casper *med.* gone; departed. (In the manner of Casper, the friendly ghost—a cartoon character.) ♦ *I'm casper. See you later.*

casting couch *n.* a legendary couch found in the offices of casting directors for use in seducing young people by offering them roles. ♦ *They say the director got his job on the casting couch, too.*

castor oil artist *n.* a medical doctor. ♦ *This two-bit castor oil artist tried to get me to lose weight.*

cat 1. *n.* a fellow; a guy; a dude. ♦ *Now, this cat wants to borrow some money from me. What should I do?* **2.** *in.* to empty one's stomach; to vomit. ♦ *Looks like somebody catted in the bushes.* **3.** *n.* a gossipy woman. ♦ *Mary can be such a cat, you know.*

catch 1. *n.* a drawback. ♦ *Okay, that sounds good, but what's the catch?* **2.** *tv.* to view something; to attend something; to hear something. ♦ *Did you catch* Gone with the Wind *on TV?*

catch some rays AND **bag some rays** *tv.* to get some sunshine; to tan in the sun. ♦ *We wanted to catch some rays, but the sun never came out the whole time we were there.* ♦ *I want to get out on that beach and bag some rays.*

catch some Zs AND **cop some Zs; cut some Zs** *tv.* to get some sleep. ♦ *Why don't you stop a little bit and try to cop some Zs?* ♦ *Max pulled over to the side of the road to catch some Zs.*

catch sth *tv.* to see or listen to something. (More specific than the colloquial sense, to *manage to hear something.*) ♦ *Did you catch that radio program about cancer last night?*

catch up *in.* to break the drug habit; to withdraw from drugs. (Drugs.) ♦ *I just know I can catch up, if I can just get through the first week.*

Catch you later. *sent.* I will talk to you again when I next see you. ♦ *Sorry, gotta rush. Catch you later.*

catch-22 *n.* a directive that is impossible to obey without violating some other, equally important, directive. ♦ *There was nothing I could do. It was a classic catch-22.*

catholic bagel *n.* a nontraditional bagel made or flavored with cinnamon, blueberries, strawberries, etc. (Jocular.) ♦ *At breakfast, they had catholic bagels and sweet rolls.*

cats and dogs *n.* slow-selling or undesirable merchandise. ♦ *During the Christmas season, the merchants try to get rid of all their cats and dogs.*

cat-soup ['kætsup] *n.* catsup; ketchup. ♦ *Do you want some cat-soup on your burger?*

cattle-rustler *n.* a thief who steals meat from supermarkets for resale. (Underworld.) ♦ *Marty is a cattle-rustler, and she's got some stuff for sale.*

caucasian waste *n.* worthless white people. (A play on *(poor) white trash.* Contrived.) ♦ *I'm not caucasian waste! I wouldn't ever live there!*

caveman *n.* a strong, virile man. ♦ *He's sort of a caveman, big and hairy.*

cazh [kæʒ] *mod.* casual. (From *casual.* See also **cas.**) ♦ *Tom showed up dressed cazh, and all the other guys were in tuxes.*

celeb [sə'lɛb] *n.* a celebrity. ♦ *There were celebs all over the place, but nobody I recognized.*

celestial transfer *n.* death. (Hospital, cruel, jocular word play.) ♦ *He's circling the drain. Almost ready for a celestial transfer.*

cellular Macarena *n.* the activity seen when a cell phone rings in public. ♦ *Beethoven's Fifth rang out and seven people started playing cellular Macarena.*

cement city *n.* a cemetery. ♦ *I'm too young to end up in cement city.*

cent *n.* one dollar. (Underworld.) ♦ *One cent for one joint? Not bad.*

century note *n.* a one-hundred-dollar bill. (Underworld. The *C* is the Roman numeral for *100.* See also **C-note.**) ♦ *I got a couple of century notes for driving these guys home from the bank.*

CF Go to **cluster fuck.**

chain(saw) *tv.* to destroy something; to cut something up severely. ♦ *The senatorial committee tried to chainsaw the nominee, but the full senate voted for confirmation.*

chain(-smoke) *in.* to smoke cigarette after cigarette. (As if each cigarette were a link in a chain.) ♦ *I never wanted to chain-smoke, but I got addicted.*

chain-smoker *n.* someone who smokes cigarette after cigarette. ♦ *She was a chain-smoker for thirty years, and then suddenly, boom. She's gone.*

the chair *n.* the electric chair, as used in the execution of the death penalty. (Underworld.) ♦ *You'll fry in the chair for this, Lefty!*

cham AND **chammy; sham; shammy** [ʃæm(i)] *n.* champagne. ♦ *Would you like a little more shammy?* ♦ *I want the biggest bottle of cham you got!*

chamber of commerce *n.* toilet; restroom. ♦ Q: *Where's Bob?* A: *Oh, Bob's in the chamber of commerce.*

chammy Go to **cham.**

champ [tʃæmp] **1.** *n.* a champion. (Also a term of address.) ♦ *Mark is a real champ—always there to help.* **2.** *n.* a dependable member of the underworld. (Underworld. See also **thoroughbred.**) ♦ *Lefty is a champ. He stood by me the whole time.*

champers AND **shampers** ['ʃæmpɚz] *n.* champagne. (Older.) ♦ *My dad sent us a bottle of French champers.* ♦ *Shampers tickles my nose.*

change *n.* money. (See also **and change.**) ♦ *It takes a lot of change to buy a car like that.*

change the channel *tv.* to switch to some other topic of conversation. ♦ *Let's change the channel here before there is a fight.*

changes *n.* an alteration in one's mental state. (See also **go through the changes.**) ♦ *I'm forty and I'm finished with the changes, and if there's anything I don't want it's to be young again.*

chank *n.* a fat, ugly woman. (From chunky skank. Contrived and forced.) ♦ *What a chank! A real butterface.*

channel hopping AND **channel surfing; channel zapping** *n.* using a remote control to move quickly from one television channel to another, pausing only a short time on each channel. ♦ *I wish you would stop channel hopping!* ♦ *He spends more time channel zapping than actually watching.*

channel surfer *n.* a person who practices channel hopping. ♦ *My husband is a confirmed channel surfer. I can't understand why he does it.*

channel surfing Go to channel hopping.

channel zapping Go to channel hopping.

chap *tv.* to anger or annoy someone. (See also chapped.) ♦ *That whole business really chapped me.*

chapped *mod.* angry; annoyed. ♦ *I was chapped. There was no way to get around it.*

chapter and verse *mod.* in the finest detail. (From the *chapter and verse* organization of the Bible.) ♦ *He could recite the law concerning state-funded libraries, chapter and verse.*

charge 1. *n.* a dose or portion of a drug. (Drugs.) ♦ *Just a little charge till I can get to my candy man.* **2.** *n.* a drug's rush. (Drugs.) ♦ *What kind of charge do you expect out of half-cashed weed?* **3.** *n.* a thrill. ♦ *I got a tremendous charge out of your last letter.*

charged (up) 1. *mod.* slightly overdosed with drugs. (Drugs.) ♦ *He was talking fast and nodding his head back and forth. I think he was charged.* **2.** *mod.* drug intoxicated. (Drugs.) ♦ *Paul was one charged up guy after the session.* **3.** *mod.* excited. ♦ *The audience was charged up and ready for the star to come out.*

Charles 1. *n.* cocaine. (Drugs.) ♦ *Is there a house where I can buy some Charles somewhere close?* **2.** *n.* a Caucasian. (Black. Not necessarily derogatory.) ♦ *And what is Charles gonna say about what you did to his car?*

Charley *n.* the Viet Cong in Vietnam. (Military. From *Victor Charley,* which is from *VC.*) ♦ *How come Charley never gets bit to death by those snakes?*

Charlie Foxtrot AND **CF** (The CF is from the so-called NATO Phonetic Alphabet.) **1.** Go to **cluster fuck** (sense 1). **2.** Go to **cluster fuck** (sense 2).

Charlie Irvine *n.* a police officer. (Streets. See also Irv.) ♦ *Look smart, dude, here comes Charlie Irvine.*

chart *n.* a musical score. (Musicians. See also map.) ♦ *Come on, man! Look at the chart! You're making clinkers like hot cakes.*

charts *n.* the trade magazine rankings of current pop music. ♦ *The big one is back on the charts this week. Give it a listen.*

chas AND **chez** [tʃæz AND tʃɛz] *n.* matches. (Collegiate. A clipping of *matches.*) ♦ *You got a couple of chez?*

chase the dragon *tv.* to inhale opium fumes through a straw, or similarly with other drugs. (Drugs.) ♦ *Harry thinks that chasing the dragon sounds like real fun.*

chaser 1. *n.* an alcoholic drink taken after a nonalcoholic one; beer, water, or some similar liquid drunk after a shot of hard liquor. (See also wash.) ♦ *I could use a little chaser with this soda.* **2.** Go to ambulance chaser.

chassis *n.* a woman's body. (See also classy-chassis.) ♦ *She a fine chassis! Like to see more of it.*

C-head 1. *n.* a cocaine user. (Drugs.) ♦ *How much money does a C-head need to get through the day?* **2.** *n.* an LSD user who takes LSD on sugar cubes. (Drugs.) ♦ *Why don't you C-heads grow up?*

cheap shot *n.* a remark that takes advantage of someone else's vulnerability. ♦ *It's easy to get a laugh with a cheap shot at cats.*

cheapie *n.* a cheaply made article. (See also el cheapo.) ♦ *It broke. I guess it was a cheapie.*

cheapskate ['tʃipsket] *n.* a miserly person; a very cheap person. (See also **piker**.) ♦ *A 5 percent tip! What a cheapskate!*

cheaters *n.* sunglasses. (Formerly referred to all spectacles. See also **shades**; **sunshades**.) ♦ *Get your cheaters on. The sun's really bright.*

check 1. *n.* a dose of a drug in a capsule or folded in a paper. (Drugs.) ♦ *How much you want for a check?* **2.** *interj.* okay; yes; yes, it is on the list. ♦ BILL: *Four quarts of oil.* TOM: *Check.*

check out the plumbing AND **visit the plumbing** *tv.* to go to the bathroom. ♦ *I think I'd better check out the plumbing before we go.* ♦ *Excuse me. I need to visit the plumbing.*

check sth **out** *tv.* to examine something; to think about something. ♦ *It's something we all have to be concerned with. Check it out.*

check that *tv.* cancel that; ignore that (last remark). ♦ *At four, no, check that, at three o'clock this afternoon, a bomb exploded at the riverside.*

check your six *tv.* look behind you (where there may be danger). (See also **on your six**. Refers to six o'clock as being behind one, as if one were facing twelve o'clock.) ♦ *Check your six, bud. Some gangsta's getting close to your wallet.*

chedda Go to **cheddar**.

cheddar AND **chedda** *n.* money; cash. (Streets. From *cheddar*. See also **cheese** = money.) ♦ *Shizzle! I'm out of chedda.* ♦ *I'm totally out of cheddar. Can you loan me a Benji?*

cheese 1. *n.* vomit. ♦ *There's cheese on the sidewalk. Look out!* **2.** *in.* to empty one's stomach; to vomit. ♦ *Somebody cheesed on the sidewalk.* **3.** *in.* to smile, as for a photographer who asks you to say *cheese* when a picture is taken. ♦ *Why are you cheesing? Did something good happen.* **4.** *n.* money. (See also **cheddar**.) ♦ *I don't have the cheese to buy a new car.*

Cheese it (the cops)! *exclam.* Run away, the cops are coming! ♦ *If you see the fuzz coming, you're supposed to yell, "Cheese it,*

the cops!" But I don't know why. Then they know we're doing something wrong.

cheese so **off** *tv.* to make someone very angry. ♦ *Bobby cheesed off every person in the club.*

cheesecake 1. *n.* a display of the female form, probably wearing little clothing, often in photographs. (See also **beefcake**.) ♦ *Women don't like to see all that cheesecake on the walls when they bring their cars in here to be fixed.* **2.** *n.* a good-looking woman; good-looking women. ♦ *Who's the cheesecake in that low-cut job?*

cheesed off *mod.* angry; disgusted. ♦ *Clare was really cheesed off at the butler.*

cheese-eater *n.* an informer; a **rat fink**. (Rats eat cheese.) ♦ *Some cheese-eater called the clerk and warned her we were coming.*

cheesehead 1. *n.* a stupid-acting person. ♦ *Is this cheesehead bothering you?* **2.** *n.* someone from the state of Wisconsin. (Much cheese is made is Wisconsin. Not usually derogatory.) ♦ *I moved to Wisconsin and became a cheesehead.*

cheesing *mod.* smiling. (From the practice of forcing people to smile by saying *cheese* when attempting to photograph them.) ♦ *Don't stand there cheezing. What do you want?*

cheesy *mod.* cheap; **tacky**. ♦ *I wouldn't live in a cheesy place like this if I could afford better.*

cheezer *n.* a very bad smelling release of intestinal gas; a foul-smelling **fart**. ♦ *God, who let the cheezer?*

cherry 1. *n.* an inexperienced person; a novice. ♦ *He's just a cherry. He don't know from nothing.* **2.** *n.* the hymen. (Usually objectionable.) ♦ *You jerk! All you care about is scoring cherries!*

chevrolegs *n.* the human legs, as used for transportation, instead of a car. (From the trade name, Chevrolet.) ♦ *I'll be late, because I only have my chevrolegs to get there—unless you want to give me a ride.*

chew *in.* to eat. ♦ *Man, I'm hungry. It's time to chew!*

chew face *tv.* to kiss. (More jocular than crude.) ♦ *A couple of kids were in a doorway chewin' face.*

chew so **out** *tv.* to scold someone. ♦ *I knew my dad was going to chew me out.*

chew so's **ass out** *tv.* to scold someone severely. (Usually objectionable.) ♦ *The cop was really mad and chewed Bob's ass out.*

chew sth **over 1.** *tv.* to talk something over. ♦ *Why don't we do lunch sometime and chew this over?* **2.** *tv.* to think something over. ♦ *I'll have to chew it over for a while. I'm not sure now.*

chew the cheese *tv.* to vomit. ♦ *Fred's out in the bushes, chewing the cheese.*

chew the fat AND **chew the rag** *tv.* to chat or gossip. ♦ *Put your carcass over on the chair, and let's chew the fat for a while.* ♦ *We chewed the rag for a while and then went out to eat.*

chew the rag Go to chew the fat.

chewed *mod.* abused. ♦ *After that argument at the office yesterday, I really felt chewed.*

chez Go to chas.

chi-chi ['ʃiʃi] *mod.* elegant. ♦ *Her living room is so chi-chi that you are afraid to go in.*

chick *n.* a girl or woman. ♦ *We're gonna take some chicks to dinner and then catch a flick.*

chick magnet Go to babe magnet.

chicken *n.* a coward. ♦ *Come on, let's go. Don't be a chicken.*

chicken feed *n.* a small amount of money. (See also peanuts.) ♦ *It may be chicken feed to you, but that's a month's rent to me.*

chicken out (of sth) *in.* to manage to get out of something, usually because of fear or cowardice. ♦ *Freddy chickened out of the plan at the last minute.*

chicken powder *n.* powdered amphetamine. (Drugs.) ♦ *Those kids seem to be satisfied with chicken powder.*

chicken shit 1. *n.* virtually nothing. (From chicken feed. Usually objectionable.) ♦ *Fifty bucks! That's just chicken shit!* **2.** *mod.* cowardly. (Usually objectionable.) ♦ *You are such a chicken shit coward! Stand up and fight!* **3.** *mod.* worthless. (Usually objectionable.) ♦ *I don't want this chicken shit pizza! Get me one with pepperoni on it, not dead fish.*

chicken-hearted *mod.* cowardly. ♦ *He's chicken-hearted, but I still love him.*

chick-flick *n.* a movie intended for women and female interests. ♦ *I hate chick-flicks. It's a guy thing.*

chickster *n.* a cool and good looking woman or chick. ♦ *She's one fine chickster.*

chief *n.* the person in charge. (Also a term of address.) ♦ *You got a couple of clams to pay the toll with, chief?*

chief cook and bottle washer Go to head cook and bottle washer.

chill 1. AND **chilly** *n.* a cold can of beer. ♦ *Hey, toss me a chill, would ya, buddy?* ♦ *How 'bout a chilly, Billy?* **2.** *tv.* to kill someone. (Underworld.) ♦ *I'll chill you with one blast from my cannon, you creep!* **3.** *tv.* to frighten someone. (Standard English.) ♦ *The prospect of having to go in there alone chilled Willy, but he went in anyway.* **4.** *tv.* to reject someone. ♦ *She chilled me once too often. I won't take that from a dame.* **5.** Go to chill (out). **6.** *tv. & in.* to relax; to cause someone to relax; to hang out [with someone]. (See also chill (out).) ♦ *They are chilling now. For a while they were real rowdy.*

chill (out) *in.* to calm down; to be cool; to get cool; to relax. ♦ *Before we can debate this matter, you're all gonna have to chill out.*

chill so's **action** *tv.* to squelch someone; to prevent someone from accomplishing something. ♦ *Just wait! I'll chill his action—just you wait.*

chillaxin' *n.* a period of relaxing and chilling. (Contrived. See also chill (sense 6).) ♦ *What do you mean, I'm chillaxin'? I'm just taking it easy.*

chillin' *mod.* great; excellent. ♦ *Everybody there was chillin'.*

chillum ['tʃɪləm] *n.* a pipe or device used for the smoking of marijuana. (Drugs.) ♦ *He keeps a chillum in his stash.*

chilly Go to chill.

China *n.* the teeth. (See also ivories.) ♦ *I spent a damn fortune trying to get this China fixed up.*

Ching! AND **Ka-ching!** *exclam.* the sound of a cash register, said to indicate money or imply a financial motive or success. ♦ *Just got another big order. Ka-ching!* ♦ *Tell, me what's important, dude. Ching! Right?*

chinmusic *n.* talk; chatter. ♦ *I've heard about enough of your chinmusic! Hush!*

chip *n.* a bargaining chip. ♦ *He used his inside info as a chip.*

chippy around *in.* to be sexually promiscuous. ♦ *She has been known to chippy around, but not with just anyone and never for money!*

chips 1. *n.* money. (See also chip.) ♦ *She saved some chips over the years and bought herself a little place on the beach.* **2.** *n.* a carpenter. (Also a term of address.) ♦ *Tell me, Chips, how fast can you build a coffin?*

chisel in (on so/sth**)** *in.* to use deception to get a share of something. ♦ *I won't chisel in on your deal.*

chism Go to jism.

chit [tʃɪt] **1.** *n.* a bill or tabulation of charges that one signs rather than paying. ♦ *I don't have any cash. Can I sign a chit for it?* **2.** *n.* a check. ♦ *She wrote out a chit for the balance due.*

chitchat ['tʃɪt tʃæt] **1.** *n.* talk; idle talk. ♦ *That's enough chitchat. Please get to work.* **2.** *n.* a short, friendly conversation. ♦ *I'd like to have a little chitchat with you when you have time.*

Chi(town) ['ʃaɪtaʊn OR 'tʃaɪtaʊn] *n.* Chicago, Illinois. ♦ *I can't wait to get back to old Chitown.*

chiv Go to shiv.

chiz [tʃɪz] *in.* to relax. (Collegiate.) ♦ *I gotta get back to my room and chiz a while.*

chizzle a wild card word for words beginning with *C*, such as chill. (Streets. Also for other words with initial *C*.) ♦ *Chizzle, ma bruva. Chizzle.*

choad AND **chode 1.** *n.* the penis. (There are numerous ideas about the origin of this (these). They may not have the same origin. One possibility is French *chaud* = hot.) ♦ *Quit scratching your chode.* **2.** *n.* a real or imaginary penis that is short and squat. ♦ *You wimp! Get out and take your chode with you!* **3.** *n.* a jerk or oafish male. (Similar to prick, etc. This is probably the most common, current use.) ♦ *You stupid chode!* **4.** *n.* the perineum; the flesh between the genitals region and the anus. (See also gooch.) ♦ *A mountain bike team called the "Choad Chafers" won the championship.*

chocoholic *n.* a person who craves chocolate. (Patterned on *alcoholic.*) ♦ *Cake, ice cream, pie—make it chocolate. I'm a chocoholic and I'm glad.*

choice *mod.* nice; cool. ♦ *We had a choice time at Tom's party.*

choke 1. *in.* [for a computer] to fail to take in information being fed to it. (Computers.) ♦ *If you don't have your modem and your software set the same way as the host, your machine will choke.* **2.** *in.* to panic before or during a test. (From *choke up.*) ♦ *She always chokes during a test.*

choke the chicken Go to beat the dummy.

choked *mod.* having to do with overly diluted drugs. ♦ *Why is this stuff so stepped on—you know, choked?*

choker 1. *n.* a cigarette; a cigarette butt. ♦ *Put that damn choker out in my house!* **2.** *n.* a necktie. ♦ *Hey, Tom! That's a classy new choker you're wearing!*

chones 1. *n.* the testicles. (From Spanish *cojones.* Usually objectionable.) ♦ *You look at me that way again, and you will be saying good-bye to your chones.* **2.** *n.* bravado. (See also balls; ballsy. Usually objectionable.) ♦ *Man, has he got chones!*

chooms *n.* the testicles. (Usually objectionable.) ♦ *He got hit in the chooms in the football game.*

chop *n.* a rude remark; a cutting remark. ♦ *That was a rotten chop! Take it back!*

chopped liver *n.* someone or something worthless. ♦ *And who am I? Chopped liver?*

chopper *n.* a helicopter. ♦ *The chopper that monitors the traffic goes over my house every morning at 6:00.*

choppers *n.* the teeth. ♦ *I may be on my last legs, but my choppers are still my own.*

chop-shop *n.* a place where stolen cars are cut or broken up into car parts for resale. ♦ *The state is cracking down on these chop-shops.*

chotchke Go to tchotchke.

chow 1. *n.* food. ♦ *What time is chow served around here?* **2.** *tv. & in.* to eat (something). (See also chow down.) ♦ *I've been chowing canned tuna and stale bagels to save money.* **3.** Go to ciao.

chow down *in.* to eat; to take a meal. ♦ *Over there is where we chow down.*

chow hound *n.* someone who loves to eat; a heavy eater. ♦ *Okay, listen up all you chow hounds. There's extra beans tonight!*

chow sth **down** *tv.* to eat something, probably quickly or without good manners. ♦ *I found a box of cookies and chowed it down before anybody knew what I was doing.*

chowderhead *n.* a stupid person. ♦ *Look, chowderhead, do what I told you!*

Christmas tree *n.* a drunkard. (From being lit like a Christmas tree.) ♦ *A well-dressed Christmas tree sat in the corner—lit up, of course.*

chrome-dome *n.* a shiny, bald head; a man with a bald head. (Also a rude term of address.) ♦ *The guy with the chrome-dome suddenly grasped his chest and made a face.*

chronic *n.* very high quality marijuana containing lots of THC. (Probably from the association of THC with the use of marijuana in cases of chronic pain.) ♦ *Where can I get some genuine chronic.*

chub Go to chub(by).

chubbo ['tʃəbo] *n.* a fat person. (From chubby.) ♦ *Look at those chubbos gobbling all those French fries.*

chub(by) *n.* an erection. (Usually objectionable.) ♦ *He always gets a chubby when he doesn't need it and never when he does.*

Chuch! *interrog. & exclam.* a general emphatic question tag meaning, roughly, *Right?*, and calls for the response Chuch! = Right! (Streets. Possibly derived from church implying truth.) ♦ *We're going to settle this now! Chuch?*

chuck 1. AND **chuck up** *in.* to empty one's stomach; to vomit. (See also upchuck.) ♦ *I think I gotta chuck!* ♦ *Mommy, I'm going to chuck up.* **2.** *tv.* to throw something away. ♦ *Chuck this thing! It's no good.* **3.** *in.* to eat voraciously. ♦ *The two guys sat guzzling and chucking till they were full.* **4.** *n.* food. ♦ *Who cooked this chuck, man? It's garbage!* **5.** *n.* a white male. (Usually capitalized. Often a term of address or a generic for all white males. Black.) ♦ *Hey, Chuck. Where do you think you are?*

chuck a dummy *tv.* to empty one's stomach; to vomit. ♦ *Somebody chucked a dummy on the patio.*

chuck it in *tv.* to quit; to give up. (See also throw in the towel.) ♦ *If I didn't have to keep the job to live, I'd have chucked it in long ago.*

chuck sth **down** *tv.* to eat something very quickly. ♦ *Don't just chuck your food down. Enjoy it!*

chuck up Go to chuck.

chucked *mod.* alcohol intoxicated. ♦ *I'm too chucked to drive.*

chuckers AND **chucks** *n.* a great hunger; an enormous appetite. (Usually with *the*.) ♦ *We've got three impatient young boys with the chuckers! Feed 'em!* ♦ *Oh, man, I really got the chucks. What time is chow?*

chucks Go to chuckers.

chug *in. & tv.* [for one person] to drink something, usually beer, quickly and in large volumes. ♦ *He chugged three in a row, and they came right back up again.*

chum *n.* a pal; a good friend. ♦ *We've been chums for years. Went to college together.*

chummy *mod.* friendly. ♦ *Don't get too chummy with me. I'm a real son of a bitch.*

chump *n.* a stupid person; a gullible person. ♦ *See if that chump will loan you some money.*

chump change *n.* a small amount of money; the kind of salary or amount of money a chump would work for. ♦ *I refuse to work for chump change! I want a real job.*

chumphead *n.* a stupid person. ♦ *What a chumphead! You painted over the windows!*

chunk 1. *in.* to empty one's stomach; to vomit. (Collegiate.) ♦ *The cat chunked all over the carpet.* **2.** *in.* to do badly; to blunder. ♦ *Sorry. I really chunked on that last deal.* **3.** *n.* a gun considered as a chunk of iron. (Underworld.) ♦ *You carrying a chunk?* **4.** *n.* a fat or stout person. ♦ *Billie's getting to be such a chunk!*

chunk so *tv.* to beat someone up. ♦ *Maurice threatened to chunk me.*

chunky *mod.* stout; fat. ♦ *Harry—the chow hound—is getting a little chunky.* ♦ *It's not all fat! He's always been a chunky brute.*

church key *n.* a beer can opener designed to puncture a can, leaving a triangular hole; a bottle opener. (Older. No longer widely known, but still in use. One type of bottle opener is formed from metal following the outline of a large keyhole. This may have contributed to the origin of this term.) ♦ *Where is the church key when I need it?*

churn *tv.* [for a stockbroker] to cause a heavy turnover in the portfolio of an investor. (The broker collects commissions on each transaction.) ♦ *I reported my broker for churning my account.*

ciao AND **chow** [tʃɑʊ] Good-bye. (Italian.) ♦ *Ciao! See you soon.* ♦ *Chow, baby. Call my service.*

Ciao, for now. AND **C4N** *phr. & comp. abb.* Good-bye for the present. (*Ciao* is Italian. Phrase is current English.) ♦ *See U L8R. C4N.* ♦ *That's all for the moment. Ciao, for now.*

CICO Go to coffee in, coffee out.

cig [sɪg] *n.* a cigarette; a cigar. ♦ *Toss me my pack of cigs, will ya?*

cigarette with no name AND **no brand cigarette; no name cigarette** *n.* a marijuana cigarette. (Drugs.) ♦ *You got one of them cigarettes with no name?* ♦ *Bud's been smoking no name cigarettes again.*

ciggy AND **ciggie** ['sɪgi] *n.* a cigarette. ♦ *How 'bout a ciggy before we take off?*

cinch [sɪntʃ] **1.** *n.* something very easy. ♦ *No sweat! It was a cinch!* **2.** *tv.* to have something settled and secured. ♦ *It only took a handshake to cinch the deal.*

cinched [sɪntʃt] *mod.* settled; secured; sealed (up). (As one tightens the saddle girth on a horse.) ♦ *I've got it cinched! No sweat!*

circle-jerk 1. *n.* a gathering of males performing mutual masturbation. (Partly jocular. Usually objectionable.) ♦ *There were twelve boys involved in a circle-jerk, and the principal caught them.* **2.** *n.* a boring or time-wasting meeting. (From sense 1.) ♦ *That board meeting was the typical circle-jerk that it always is.*

circling (the drain) *tv. & in.* to be in the final process of dying; to be in extremis. (Jocular but crude hospital jargon.) ♦ *Get Mrs. Smith's son on the phone. She's circling the drain.*

circular file AND **round file** *n.* a wastebasket. (See also file thirteen.) ♦ *Most of the junk mail sits here until I can put it into the circular file.* ♦ *Oh, that letter? It went straight to the round file.*

civil serpent *n.* a civil servant. ♦ *You have no idea the kinds of things "civil serpents" have to put up with.*

civvies ['sɪviz] *n.* civilian clothes rather than a uniform. (Originally military.) ♦ *I re-upped because I couldn't stand the thought of civvies and stuff like that.*

clam 1. *n.* a dollar. (Underworld.) ♦ *You got a couple of clams I can bum for a little bottle?* **2.** *n.* a tight-lipped person. ♦ *Suddenly, she became a clam and wouldn't talk anymore.*

clam up *in.* to get quiet. (See also dummy up.) ♦ *The minute they got him inside the cop-shop, he clammed up.*

clanked *mod.* exhausted; pooped. ♦ *I'm really clanked, man. Gotta take a rest.*

clap *n.* a case of gonorrhea. (Very old and still in use.) ♦ *He thinks he got the clap from her.*

class 1. *n.* high style; elegance. ♦ *The dame's got class, but no brains.* **2.** *mod.* first-rate; high-class. ♦ *This was a class suburb just a few years ago.*

class act *n.* a high-quality act; a high-quality way of doing things. ♦ *The prof puts on a real class act, but he grades very hard.*

classy *mod.* elegant; dandy. ♦ *How much does a classy car like this cost?*

classy-chassis [... 'tʃæs i] *n.* a really fine and stimulating woman's body. (See also chassis.) ♦ *She has one fine, classy-classis.*

clay *n.* good-quality hashish. (Drugs.) ♦ *Ask John where you can dig up some clay.*

clay pigeon *n.* a gullible person; a pigeon. (Underworld.) ♦ *We need a clay pigeon to divert attention from the snatch.*

clean 1. *mod.* not using drugs; not involved with drugs. ♦ *I've been clean for more than a month now.* **2.** *mod.* sober; not intoxicated with drugs at the moment. (Almost the same as sense 1.) ♦ *Just being clean for a day is an accomplishment.* **3.** *mod.* not breaking any law. (Police and underworld.) ♦ *I'm clean, officer. You can't charge me with anything.* **4.** *mod.* not carrying a weapon. (Police and underworld.) ♦ *I frisked him. He's clean.* **5.** *mod.* well-dressed. ♦ *Now there's a clean dude!*

clean one's **act up** *tv.* to reform one's conduct; to improve one's performance. ♦ *We were told to clean our act up or move out.*

clean so **out 1.** *tv.* to get all of someone's money. (See also cleaned out.) ♦ *The bill for supper cleaned me out, and we couldn't go to the flick.* **2.** *tv.* to empty someone's bowels. (See also cleaned out.) ♦ *That medicine I took really cleaned me out.*

clean sweep *n.* a broad movement clearing or affecting everything in the pathway. (Usually figurative.) ♦ *Everybody got a raise. It was a clean sweep.*

clean up (on sth**)** *in.* to make a lot of money on something. ♦ *If we advertise, we can clean up.*

cleaned out 1. *mod.* broke; with no money. ♦ *Tom's cleaned out. He's broke. He'll have to go home.* **2.** *mod.* with one's digestive tract emptied. ♦ *That medicine really left me cleaned out.*

clear 1. *mod.* alcohol intoxicated. ♦ *He was clear. You know, polluted.* **2.** *mod.* [of liquor] undiluted; neat. ♦ *I like mine clear with just one ice cube.* **3.** *tv.* to earn a specific net amount of money. ♦ *We just want to clear a decent profit. Nothing greedy.*

clear as mud Go to (as) clear as mud.

clear as vodka Go to (as) clear as vodka.

clear out *in.* to leave; to depart. ♦ *The boss gave me till next week to clear out. I'm fired—canned.*

clear sailing *mod.* easy; easy going. ♦ *It'll be clear sailing from now on.*

click (with so**)** *in.* to catch on with someone; to intrigue someone; to become popular with someone. ♦ *Sam and Mary are getting along fine. I knew they'd click.*

climb 1. *n.* a marijuana cigarette. (Drugs. The means to a high.) ♦ *I need a climb to set me straight.* **2.** *tv.* to scold someone. ♦ *The boss climbed Harry for being late.*

climb the wall(s) *tv.* to do something desperate when one is anxious, bored, or excited. ♦ *I was climbing the walls to get back to work.*

clinch [klɪntʃ] *tv.* to settle something; to make something final. ♦ *I was able to clinch the deal, and I got a raise for it.*

clincher ['klɪntʃɚ] *n.* the final element; the straw that broke the camel's back. (See also capper.) ♦ *The clincher was when the clerk turned up the volume.*

cling like shit to a shovel AND **stick like shit to a shovel 1.** *in.* to stick or adhere [to someone or something] tightly. (Usually objectionable.) ♦ *That oily stuff* sticks like shit to a shovel. **2.** *in.* to be very dependent on someone; to follow someone around. (Often with an indirect object. Usually objectionable.) ♦ *She's so dependent. She clings to him like shit to a shovel.* ♦ *He hates her, but he sticks like shit to a shovel.*

clink *n.* jail. ♦ *We'll throw you in the clink if you don't talk.*

clinker 1. *n.* a mistake; (in music) a misplayed note. ♦ *Look at the score, man! That series of clinkers just isn't there.* **2.** *n.* a worthless person or thing. (From the term for a cinder.) ♦ *Ralph has turned out to be a real clinker. We'll have to pink slip him.*

clip 1. *tv.* to cheat someone. (See also clipped; clip joint.) ♦ *That guy in there clipped me for a fiver.* **2.** *tv.* to kill someone. ♦ *Frank and John had set out to clip Rocko first.* **3.** *n.* a holder for a marijuana cigarette butt. (Drugs. See also roach clip.) ♦ *My clip's at home in my stash.* **4.** *n.* a music video; a short film. ♦ *This next clip is something you'll all recognize.* **5.** *n.* a fast rate of speed. ♦ *You were moving at a pretty good clip when you ran into the truck.* **6.** *tv.* to sock someone. ♦ *Max clipped Lefty on the jaw, and Lefty drew his gun.*

clip a butt *tv.* to pinch out a cigarette for later smoking. (Also with *the.*) ♦ *Like an old soldier, Willy took a puff and then clipped the butt for later.*

clip joint *n.* a business establishment that cheats customers. ♦ *The clip joint on Fourth Street was busted last night.*

clip so's wings *tv.* to restrain someone; to reduce or put an end to a teenager's privileges. ♦ *One more stunt like that and I'm going to clip your wings for a couple of weeks.*

clipped 1. *mod.* cheated. ♦ *You weren't clipped by me. I just made a mistake.* **2.** *mod.* arrested. ♦ *Frank got clipped as he got out of his car.* **3.** *mod.* circumcised. ♦ *Fred couldn't imagine what not being clipped would be like.*

clit AND **clitty** *n.* the clitoris. (Usually objectionable.) ♦ *Have I got a present for you and your clitty!*

clobbered *mod.* alcohol intoxicated. ♦ *He's the kind of guy who goes home and gets clobbered after work.*

clock *tv.* to earn, score, or total up someone or something. (As if the person or thing gained were being metered or clocked.) ♦ *Sam clocked a date with Sally, and is he ever proud!*

clock in *in.* to record one's arrival at a set time. ♦ *He clocked in three minutes late.*

clock watcher *n.* someone—a worker or a student—who is always looking at the clock. ♦ *People who don't like their jobs can turn into clock watchers.*

clod *n.* a stupid and oafish person. (Usually refers to a male. Widely known. Usually objectionable.) ♦ *Don't be such a clod! Put on your tie, and let's go.*

clodhopper 1. *n.* a big shoe. ♦ *Wipe the mud off those clodhoppers before you come in here.* **2.** *n.* a stupid person; a rural oaf. ♦ *You don't know it, but that clodhopper is worth about two million bucks.*

close as stink on shit Go to (as) close as stink on shit.

Close, but no cigar. [klos…] *phr.* Close, but not close enough to win a prize! ♦ *Close, but no cigar! Give it another try.*

close call Go to close shave.

close combat sock *n.* a condom. ♦ *I'm all equipped with money and close combat socks.*

close shave AND **close call** *n.* a narrow escape. ♦ *The car passed this close to us—a real close call.* ♦ *Man, that was a close call!*

closet *mod.* secret; concealed. (Alludes to something being hidden in a closet. See also come out of the closet.) ♦ *Marty is a closet chocolate fiend.*

clotheshorse ['klozhors] *n.* someone who is obsessed with clothing and looking good in it. ♦ *Her brother is the real clotheshorse.*

clouted *mod.* arrested. ♦ *They do things like that to get clouted so they can have a warm place to stay overnight.*

clown *n.* a fool. ♦ *Tell that clown in the front row to shut up.*

clown around *in.* to act silly; to mess around. ♦ *We were just clowning around. We didn't mean to break anything.*

cluck AND **kluck** [klək] *n.* a stupid person; a person as stupid as a chicken. ♦ *Why did they send me a dumb cluck to do this work?* ♦ *You silly kluck! Why'd you do that?*

cluckhead *n.* a stupid oaf. ♦ *Wrong again! I'm getting to be such a cluckhead!*

clucky *mod.* stupid; oafish. ♦ *The plan you submitted to this office was rejected by the policy committee. They noted that it was the cluckiest idea they had ever seen.*

clue so **in** *tv.* to set someone straight (about something); to inform someone of the facts. ♦ *What's going on? Clue me in.*

clueless *mod.* unaware. ♦ *I have never seen anyone so totally clueless. What a dunce!*

cluelessness *n.* total stupidity. (See also totally clueless.) ♦ *I just shake my head in wonder at the cluelessness of my fellow humans.*

clunk 1. *tv.* to strike someone or something. ♦ *The branch clunked the roof as it fell.* **2.** *n.* a hit; the sound of a hit. ♦ *I heard a clunk on the roof. Must be reindeer.*

clunker 1. *n.* an old car. ♦ *He drives an old clunker and doesn't have any insurance.* **2.** *n.* someone or something worthless; a clinker. ♦ *We have to get the clunkers off the payroll.*

clunkhead *n.* an oaf; a stupid dolt. ♦ *My brother can be such a clunkhead! Can't do nothing right!*

clunky *mod.* ponderous and inefficient. ♦ *I got rid of all the clunky stuff. Now it's lean and mean.*

cluster fuck 1. *n.* an act of group rape. (Also Charlie Foxtrot from the initials CF. Usually objectionable.) ♦ *Look at her! She's just asking for a cluster fuck.* **2.** *n.* any event as riotous as an act of group rape. (Figurative on sense 1. The same allusion as sense 1.) ♦ *This goddamn day has been one long cluster fuck!*

clutch (up) *in.* to become very tense and anxious; to freeze with anxiety. ♦ *I have been known to clutch up before a race.*

clutched *mod.* nervous. ♦ *I get so clutched before a test.*

Clyde [klaɪd] *n.* an oaf; a square, usually a male. (See also Zelda. Also a term of address.) ♦ *Well, Clyde, I think you're way off base.*

C-note AND **C-spot** *n.* a one-hundred-dollar bill. (The *C* is the Roman numeral for *100*. See also century note.) ♦ *You owe me three C-notes!* ♦ *That guy wanted a C-spot to fix my muffler!*

coaster *n.* someone who lives near the ocean on the coast. (California.) ♦ *Tiffany is a coaster now, but she was born, like, somewhere else.*

cob 1. *n.* a sharp poke or goose in the anus. ♦ *Ouch! That cob hurt!* **2.** *tv.* to give someone a sharp poke in the anus. ♦ *Tom cobbed Fred when he passed by.*

cock 1. *n.* the penis. (Taboo. Usually objectionable. Mainly in parts of the South, this refers instead to the female genitals.) ♦ *He made some joke about a cock, but nobody laughed.* **2.** *n.* the female genitals. (In southern parts of the U.S.) ♦ *The doctor heard her say something about her "cock" and had no idea what to expect during the examination.*

cockamamie ['kɑkəmemi] *mod.* ridiculous; inconceivable. ♦ *That is the most cockamamie thing I ever heard of.*

cock-blocking *mod.* [someone or something] interfering with a man's activities with a woman. ♦ *You're just a cock-blocking playa-hata.*

cock-cheese Go to crotch-cheese.

cocked *mod.* drunk. ♦ *She's too cocked to drive. You drive her home.*

cockeyed ['kɑkaɪd] *mod.* crazy. ♦ *Who came up with this cockeyed idea, anyway?*

cocksocket *n.* the vagina. ♦ *My little puck bunny has the sweetest cocksocket.*

cocksucker 1. *n.* a male who performs fellatio (licking and sucking of the penis). (See also dick-sucker. Also a provocative term of address. Rude and derogatory.) ♦ *There is one question I've always wanted to ask a cocksucker, but I have never had the chance.* **2.** *n.* a low and despicable male; a male who is despicable enough to perform fellatio. (Rude, provocative, and derogatory.) ♦ *You rotten cocksucker! I ought to punch you in the face.* **3.** *n.* a male who performs oral sex on a woman. (In southern parts of the country, cock = female genitals.) ♦ *I don't care if he's a cocksucker, as long as he loves his mother.* **4.** *n.* an obsequious and flattering male; a male sycophant. (Rude and derogatory.) ♦ *Why doesn't that stupid cocksucker talk straight. He's always trying to butter somebody up.*

cocksucking *mod.* despicable; contemptible. (Usually objectionable.) ♦ *Get your goddamn cocksucking foot outa my doorway!*

code brown *n.* a fecal accident. (Jocular word play based on a hospital's PA announcements of various color codes.) ♦ *Code brown on third floor east.*

code yellow a urinary accident. (Jocular word play based on a hospital's PA announcements of various color codes.) ♦ *Whoops. Code yellow. Change the sheets and the mattress.*

coffee and *n.* coffee and a doughnut or a pastry. ♦ *We stopped at a little shop for coffee and.*

coffee in, coffee out AND **CICO** *phr. & comp. abb.* a phrase relating to drinking coffee and then urinating. (A play on FIFO, GIGO, etc.) ♦ *Yikes! I really got to go! CICO.* ♦ *Let's stop again at the next rest area. Coffee in, coffee out, you know.*

coffin nail 1. AND **coffin tack** *n.* a cigarette. (Coffin nail is very old.) ♦ *You still smoking them coffin nails?* ♦ *Every coffin tack you smoke takes a little off the end of your life.* **2.** *n.* a drink of liquor. ♦ *How about another coffin nail?*

coffin tack Go to coffin nail.

coffin varnish *n.* inferior liquor. ♦ *You want some more of this coffin varnish?*

coffin-dodger [ˈkɔfn̩ dɑdʒɚ] *n.* a heavy smoker. ♦ *I just hate these damn coffin-dodgers who smoke right outside the door!*

coin *n.* money. (See also hard coin; do some fine coin.) ♦ *He made a lot of coin on the last picture.*

coincidink AND **coinkidink** *n.* a coincidence. (Old collegiate.) ♦ *I didn't plan it. It was just a coincidink.*

cojones *n.* the testicles. (Spanish. Usually objectionable.) ♦ *He kicked that old cat right in the cojones and sent it flying.*

cokeaholic [kokəˈhɑlɪk] *n.* a cocaine addict. (Drugs.) ♦ *When I realized I was a cokeaholic, I decided to stop, but I couldn't.*

cokehead *n.* a heavy cocaine user; a cocaine addict. (Drugs.) ♦ *We get a few depressed cokeheads in the emergency room who have tried suicide.*

cokespoon AND **(flake) spoon** *n.* a small spoon used to carry powdered cocaine to a nostril. (Drugs.) ♦ *The principal wrote a letter to Mrs. Simpson telling her that Jimmy had brought a cokespoon to school.* ♦ *She used an old-fashioned flake spoon right until she died.*

cold 1. *mod.* [stopping something] suddenly and totally. ♦ *I stopped cold—afraid to move further.* **2.** *mod.* dead. ♦ *This parrot is cold—pifted!* **3.** *mod.* not good. ♦ *The lecture was cold and dull.* **4.** *mod.* excellent. (Very cool.) ♦ *That last pitch was cold, man.*

cold blood AND **cold coffee** *n.* beer. ♦ *How would you like a little cold blood to start things off?*

cold call *tv.* to call a sales prospect from a list of persons one has never met. ♦ *Things have to be pretty bad when the senior brokers at a major house have to cold call people to get business.*

cold coffee Go to cold blood.

cold feet *n.* a wave of timidity or fearfulness. ♦ *Suddenly I had cold feet and couldn't sing a note.*

cold fish *n.* a dull and unresponsive person. ♦ *I hate to shake hands with a cold fish like that. He didn't even smile.*

a **cold piece of work** *n.* a person who is difficult to deal with. ♦ *Buddy, you are a cold piece of work.*

cold sober *mod.* sober; completely sober. (See also **sold cober**.) ♦ *He had a fine head on and wanted more than anything to be cold sober and alert.*

cold turkey *mod.* [stopping something] suddenly, without tapering off. (Said especially of stopping an addictive drug intake. Originally drugs.) ♦ *Martha stopped cold turkey and survived.*

coldcock *tv.* to knock someone out. ♦ *The clerk coldcocked the would-be robber with a champagne bottle.*

coli AND **broccoli** ['bɑk ə li, 'kɑli] *n.* marijuana. (Drugs. From *broccoli*.) ♦ *Who got into my stash and took the coli?* ♦ *Don't forget your broccoli! Love them vegetables!*

collar 1. *tv.* to arrest someone. (See also collared.) ♦ *The cops collared her as she was leaving the hotel.* **2.** *n.* an arrest. ♦ *It was a tough collar, with all the screaming and yelling.*

collared *mod.* arrested. ♦ *Got collared during a routine traffic stop.*

Columbian (gold) *n.* Light-colored Columbian marijuana. ♦ *He claimed he scored some Columbian.*

combo ['kɑmbo] **1.** *n.* a small group of musicians; a small band. (From *combination*.) ♦ *Andy started his own combo and made money from day one.* **2.** *n.* a combination of people or things. ♦ *The dish was a combo of fish, garlic, and cream.* **3.** *n.* a bisexual person. ♦ *Nobody would have thought that Fred's a combo.*

comboozelated [kəm'buzəledəd] *mod.* alcohol intoxicated. (Collegiate.) ♦ *I believe I am just a little comboozelated.*

come AND **cum 1.** *in.* to experience an orgasm. (There is no other single word for this meaning. Usually objectionable.) ♦ *God, I thought she'd never cum.* **2.** *n.* se-

men. (Usually objectionable.) ♦ *Do you think cum is alive?*

come across (with sth) *in.* to give or deliver something; to tell information. ♦ *You guys had better come across with what you owe me!*

come clean (with so) **(about** sth) *in.* to admit (something) to someone. ♦ *You're gonna have to come clean eventually.*

come down 1. *in.* to happen. ♦ *Hey, man! What's coming down?* **2.** *n.* a letdown; a disappointment. (Usually **comedown**.) ♦ *The loss of the race was a real comedown for Willard.* **3.** *in.* to begin to recover from the effects of alcohol or drug intoxication. ♦ *She came down slow, which was good.*

come down hard *in.* to come out of a drug use session badly. (Drugs.) ♦ *Mike came down hard, and it took them a long time to calm him down.*

come down hard on so *in.* to scold someone; to punish someone severely. ♦ *Joe's parents came down hard on him when they learned he had been suspended from school.*

Come off it! 1. AND **Get off it!** *exclam.* Stop acting arrogantly! ♦ *Come off it, Tiff. You're not the Queen of England.* ♦ *Get off it, you conceited slob!* **2.** *exclam.* Give up your incorrect point of view! ♦ *You are arguing from a foolish position. You're dead wrong. Get off it!*

come on 1. *n.* a lure; bait. (Usually **come-on**.) ♦ *It's just a come on. Nobody is giving away a decent color TV just for listening to a sales pitch.* **2.** *n.* an invitation; a sexual invitation. (Usually **come-on**.) ♦ *She stared at him with her bedroom eyes, giving him that age-old come-on.* **3.** *in.* to begin to perform well. ♦ *In the second scene, the entire cast came on, and the audience loved it.* **4.** *in.* to feel the effects of a drug; for a drug to take effect. (Drugs.) ♦ *After what seemed a long time, I began to come on to the stuff.* **5.** *exclam.* You are wrong! (Usually **Come on!**) ♦ *Come on! Wasteful spending occurs at all levels of all governments! Nobody is innocent!*

come on like gangbusters Go to come on strong.

come on strong AND **come on like gangbusters** *in.* to seem aggressive; to impress people initially as very aggressive and assertive. (See explanation at like gangbusters.) ♦ *She has a tendency to come on strong, but she's really a softie.* ♦ *Bob comes on like gangbusters and gets meaner the more he drinks.*

come on to SO **1.** *in.* to make advances to a person. ♦ *She didn't even know he was coming on to her, till they got to his place.* **2.** *in.* to try to get someone to respond romantically or sexually. ♦ *She was just starting to come on to me when her parents came home.* **3.** *in.* to begin to become friendly. ♦ *After a few minutes, they began to come on to each other.*

come out ahead *in.* to end up with a profit; to end up with some benefit. ♦ *I never seem to come out ahead at the end of the month.*

come out in the wash *in.* to be dealt with in the normal chain of events. (As if someone were counseling someone who had caused a clothing stain.) ♦ *Whatever it is, it'll come out in the wash. Don't worry.*

come out of the closet *in.* to appear publicly as a homosexual; to cease concealing one's homosexuality. (The phrase has many nonsexual metaphorical meanings.) ♦ *They say he came out of the closet when he was eight years old.*

come out on top *in.* to end up to the better; to win. ♦ *Tim always has to come out on top—a classic poor loser.*

come up for air *in.* to pause for a break. ♦ *The kissers—being only human—had to come up for air eventually.* ♦ *They were taking in money so fast at the box office that there wasn't a minute to come up for air.*

come-hither look [kəmˈhɪðɚ lʊk] *n.* an alluring or seductive look or glance, usually done by a woman. ♦ *She blinked her bedroom eyes and gave him a come-hither look.*

comer [ˈkəmɚ] *n.* someone with a bright future. ♦ *Fred is a real comer. You'll be hearing a lot about him.*

comfort station 1. *n.* a restroom; toilet facilities available to the public. (Euphemistic.) ♦ *We need to stop and find a comfort station in the next town.* **2.** *n.* an establishment that sells liquor. ♦ *Let's get some belch at a comfort station along here somewhere.*

coming out of one's **ears** *mod.* in great abundance. (As if full of a liquid. Often said of money.) ♦ *Mr. Wilson has money coming out of his ears.*

comma-counter *n.* a pedantic person; a pedantic copy editor. ♦ *When you need a proofreader, you need a comma-counter.*

commode-hugging drunk *mod.* heavily alcohol intoxicated; drunk and vomiting. ♦ *I could tell by the sounds coming from the bathroom that Ernie had come home commode-hugging drunk again.*

comp 1. *tv.* to accompany someone [musically]. ♦ *I have to sing a solo at a wedding and need someone to comp me.* **2.** *tv.* to give something to someone free. (Either as *compensation* for difficulties endured or as a *complimentary* gift.) ♦ *The movie patron was angry and demanded his money back. The manager comped him with a few free passes and he was happy.* **3.** *n.* a complimentary gift. ♦ *I expect comps when I spend a lot of money in a casino.*

company bull *n.* a detective or guard who works for a private firm. ♦ *Pete is a company bull for Acme Systems. He works nights.*

company man *n.* a man who always sides with his employers. ♦ *Ken's a company man—he'll always take management's side.*

con 1. *n.* a convict. ♦ *Is that guy in the gray pajamas one of the escaped cons?* **2.** *n.* a confidence scheme. ♦ *They pulled a real con on the old lady.* **3.** *tv.* to swindle or deceive someone. ♦ *Don't try to con me. I know the score.*

con artist Go to con man.

con job *n.* an act of deception. ♦ *This is not an annual report! It's a con job!*

con man AND **con artist** *n.* someone who makes a living by swindling people. ♦ *Gary is a con artist, but at least he's not on the dole.* ♦ *I was taken by a real con man!*

conehead 1. *n.* a fool; an oaf. ♦ *You can be pretty much of a conehead yourself sometimes, you know.* **2.** *n.* an intellectual; a pointy-head. ♦ *They build fences around universities to keep the coneheads in.*

cones *n.* the breasts; female breasts. ♦ *She ain't much in the cones department.*

confuckulated *mod.* confused and messed up. (Usually objectionable.) ♦ *I'm so confuckulated! Let me think this through.*

conk AND **konk** *n.* the head. ♦ *Where'd you get that nasty bump on your konk?*

conk off *in.* to fall asleep. ♦ *I conked off about midnight.*

conk out 1. *in.* [for someone] to collapse, and perhaps fall asleep. ♦ *I was so tired I just went home and conked out.* **2.** *in.* [for something] to break down; to quit running. ♦ *I hope my computer doesn't conk out.*

conk-buster AND **konk-buster** ['kɔŋkbəstɚ] **1.** *n.* inferior liquor. ♦ *Jed kept a jar of conk-buster under his bed against night sweats.* **2.** *n.* a hard-to-answer question or problem. ♦ *Man, what you're asking is really a conk-buster.*

connect (with so**)** *in.* to meet someone; to talk to someone on the telephone. ♦ *We connected over a drink and discussed the matter fully.*

connect (with sth**)** *in.* [for a batter] to hit a ball. ♦ *He swung but didn't connect with the ball.*

connection *n.* a seller of drugs; someone who is a source for drugs. (Originally drugs.) ♦ *This connection you keep talking about—is he dependable?*

conniption (fit) [kə'nɪpʃən…] *n.* a burst of anger; a **spaz**. ♦ *He had a conniption fit over the question of my marriage to Fred.*

constitutional *n.* the first drink or dose of drugs of the day. (See also **breakfast of** champions.) ♦ *He downed a constitutional and made ready to set out for the office.*

cooch 1. *n.* the female genitals; the vulva and vagina. (Usually objectionable.) ♦ *He thought he could see her cooch through her swimming suit.* **2.** *n.* women considered as a receptacle for the penis. (Rude and derogatory.) ♦ *Q: Don't you ever think about anything except getting some cooch? A: No.*

coo-coo AND **cuckoo 1.** *mod.* unconscious. ♦ *I socked him on the snoot and knocked him coo-coo.* **2.** *mod.* insane. ♦ *How did I ever get involved in this cuckoo scheme, anyway?*

cooked *mod.* alcohol or drug intoxicated. ♦ *Pete is cooked, fried, boiled, baked—drunk.*

cooked up *mod.* contrived. (This is hyphenated before a nominal.) ♦ *The whole thing seems so cooked up.*

cookie pusher 1. *n.* a bootlicker; someone who flatters other people for self-serving motives. ♦ *When you've got a whole office full of cookie pushers, there's always someone to take you to lunch.* **2.** *n.* a lazy do-nothing. ♦ *I'm just looking for a cookie pusher to fire today.*

cooking with gas *in.* doing exactly right. (Always with *-ing*.) ♦ *That's great! Now you're cooking with gas!*

cool 1. *mod.* unabashed; unruffled; relaxed. (See also **keep** one's **cool**; **lose** one's **cool**.) ♦ *She is totally cool and easygoing.* **2.** *mod.* good; excellent. ♦ *This is a really cool setup!* **3.** *mod.* [of music] mellow; smooth. ♦ *This stuff is so cool, I'm just floating.* **4.** *mod.* no less than [some amount of money]. ♦ *She cleared a cool forty thousand on the Wilson deal.* **5.** *in.* to die; to become cold after death. (Medical euphemism.) ♦ *We were afraid that he would cool.*

Cool bananas! Go to **Cool beans!**

Cool beans! AND **Cool bananas!** *exclam.* Wow! ♦ *Cool beans, man. That's great!* ♦ *I won again! Cool bananas!*

cool, calm, and collected *mod.* cool; unabashed. ♦ *Albert is almost always cool, calm, and collected.*

cool cat *n.* someone who is cool, usually a male. ♦ *Monty is a cool cat. I really like him.*

cool down *in.* to calm down. ♦ *Now, just cool down. Chill, chill. Everything's gonna be real cool.*

Cool it! *exclam.* Calm down! ♦ *Come on, cool it, man!*

cool off *in.* to calm down. ♦ *I knew things would cool off eventually.*

cool out *in.* to calm down; to relax. (See also cooled out.) ♦ *Now, just cool out, man. This will pass.*

cool so **out** *tv.* to calm someone; to appease someone. ♦ *The manager appeared and tried to cool out everybody, but that was a waste of time.*

cooled out *mod.* calm; unabashed. ♦ *Ted is a really cooled out kind of guy.*

cooler *n.* jail. (Usually with the.) ♦ *Do you want to talk, or do you want to spend a little time in the cooler?*

coolth *mod.* coolness. (Old. The mate to warmth.) ♦ *Close the door! You're letting all the coolth out of the fridge.*

cop 1. *tv.* to take or steal something. (Originally underworld.) ♦ *Somebody copped the statue from the town square.* **2.** *n.* a theft. (Underworld.) ♦ *They pulled the cop in broad daylight.* **3.** *n.* a police officer. (From sense 1.) ♦ *The cop wasn't in any mood to put up with any monkey business.* **4.** *tv.* to arrest someone. (See also copped.) ♦ *They copped Sam with the evidence right on him.* **5.** *n.* an arrest. ♦ *It was a smooth cop. No muss, no fuss.*

cop a drag *tv.* to smoke a cigarette. (See also drag.) ♦ *Smokers who have to leave the office to cop a drag must cost this nation billions each year.*

cop a fix *tv.* to obtain a dose of drugs. ♦ *She was gonna, like, die if she didn't cop a fix pretty soon.*

cop a head *tv.* to become alcohol or drug intoxicated. ♦ *He was mad and depressed and went home having decided to cop a head.*

cop a heel *tv.* get out; start walking; leave (here). ♦ *If you're finished you can cop a heel.*

cop a plea *tv.* to plead guilty to a lesser charge. ♦ *Rocko copped a plea and got off with a week in the slammer.*

cop a squat *tv.* to sit down. ♦ *Cop a squat and crack a tube.*

cop a tube *tv.* to catch a perfect tubular wave. (Surfers.) ♦ *Mark—as drunk as all get out—said he was gonna go out and cop a tube.*

cop an attitude *tv.* to take a negative or opposite attitude about something. (See also tude.) ♦ *I think you're copping an attitude. Not advised, dude. Not advised.*

cop onto sth *in.* to understand or become aware of something. ♦ *I think I'm copping onto the significance of this at last.*

cop out 1. *in.* to plead guilty (to a lesser charge). (Underworld. See also cop a plea.) ♦ *I decided not to cop out and got a mouthpiece instead.* **2.** *in.* to give up and quit; to chicken out (of sth). ♦ *Why do you want to cop out just when things are going great?* **3.** *n.* a poor excuse to get out of something. (Usually **cop-out** or **copout**.) ♦ *That's not a good reason. That's just a cop-out.*

cop some Zs Go to catch some Zs.

copasetic [kopə'sɛdɪk] *mod.* agreeable; satisfactory. (Originally black. Probably from French.) ♦ *Everything is copasetic. Couldn't be better.*

copped *mod.* arrested. ♦ *I was copped for doing absolutely nothing at all.*

copper 1. *n.* a police officer. (Originally underworld. Because the copper *cops, pinches, nabs* or *takes* = arrests. See also cop.) ♦ *See that copper over there? He busted me once.* **2.** *n.* money. (From copper penny. See also rivets.) ♦ *How much copper you got on you?*

cop-shop *n.* a police station. ♦ *The pigs down at the cop-shop tried to act like they didn't know who Frank was.*

a **copy** *n.* a piece, as with an item produced. ♦ *We sell the toy at $14 a copy.*

cords *n.* a basketball net. ♦ *They cut the cords down after the game.*

corked (up) AND **corky** *mod.* alcohol intoxicated. ♦ *You'd be corked up, too, if you'd drunk as much as I have.* ♦ *Willie's acting sort of corky.*

corker *n.* someone or something good, funny, or entertaining. ♦ *That was a real corker. I thought I'd die laughing.*

corkscrewed (up) *mod.* courageous because of alcohol; with one's courage screwed by alcohol. ♦ *After getting himself corkscrewed up, he went into the boss's office for a word.*

corky Go to corked (up).

corn *n.* money. ♦ *I need some corn to pay the rent.*

corn squabble *n.* a fight. (Perhaps referring to chickens fighting over corn.) ♦ *Stop this silly corn squabble and let's try to talk this through.*

cornball 1. *n.* a stupid or corny person, especially if rural. ♦ *Who invited this cornball to my party?* **2.** *mod.* stupid or corny. ♦ *What a cornball idea!*

corned *mod.* alcohol intoxicated. ♦ *Let's go out and get corned!*

cornfed *mod.* rural; backward; unsophisticated. ♦ *I enjoy her honest, cornfed humor.*

cornhole 1. *n.* the anus. (Usually objectionable.) ♦ *Well, doc, I got this terrible itch in the cornhole, you know.* **2.** *n.* a sharp poke or goose in the anus. (Usually objectionable.) ♦ *They delivered a painful cornhole to the bully and then ran off.* **3.** *tv.* to poke someone in the anus. (Usually objectionable.) ♦ *Let's sneak up and cornhole that guy!*

corny 1. *mod.* having to do with simpleminded, overdrawn humor. (Alludes to rural or folksy style.) ♦ *This corny dialogue has to be revised before I'll act in this play.* **2.** *mod.* having to do with overdone sentiment. ♦ *The love scenes were your corny hands-off-the-naughty-parts events, but nobody laughed.*

corpse 1. *n.* an empty liquor or beer bottle. (See also dead soldier.) ♦ *Throw your corpses in the trash can, you jerk!* **2.** *n.* a cigarette butt. ♦ *The wino picked up the corpse and put it in a little box of them he carried with him.*

corral dust *n.* nonsense, lies, and exaggeration. (A euphemism for bullshit.) ♦ *The way Judy handles the corral dust, she must be running for political office.*

cosmic *mod.* excellent; powerful. ♦ *This pizza is absolutely cosmic!*

cotton-picking AND **cotton-pickin'** *mod.* worthless; damned. (Folksy.) ♦ *Who is this cotton-picking bigwig pushing us around?*

couch potato *n.* a lazy, do-nothing television watcher. (See also sofa spud.) ♦ *If there was a prize for the best couch potato, my husband would win it.*

couch-doctor AND **couch-turkey** *n.* a psychiatrist; a psychoanalyst. ♦ *I finally walked out on my couch-doctor. Now I'm getting it all together.* ♦ *I bought three new cars for that couch-turkey! Now I'm paying for his kid's college!*

couch-turkey Go to couch-doctor.

Cough it up! *tv.* to give something—typically money—to someone, especially if done unwillingly. ♦ *You owe me twenty bucks. Cough it up!*

cough sth **up** *tv.* to produce something (which someone has requested), usually money. ♦ *Cough up what you owe me!*

country drunk *mod.* alcohol intoxicated; drunk and disorganized. (Folksy.) ♦ *Them good old boys know how to get country drunk.*

county-mounty *n.* a highway patrol officer. (Citizens band radio.) ♦ *There's a county-mounty waiting under that bridge ahead of you.*

courier *n.* a small-time drug seller; a drug runner; a carrier of contraband. (Drugs.) ♦ *The cops can catch the couriers whenever they want. It's the big guys they're after.*

Cover your ass. AND **CYA** *sent. & comp. abb.* Do what is necessary to protect yourself from discovery or criticism.

(Usually objectionable.) ♦ *CYA when the shit hits the fan.*

cover-up *n.* an act of concealing something. ♦ *The candidate accused her opponent of a cover-up.*

cow *n.* a fat or ugly woman. (Cruel.) ♦ *Wouldn't you think a cow like that would go on a diet?*

cow chips *n.* dried cow dung. ♦ *There's a whole field of cow chips out there! Why do you want to buy a bag of the stuff at a nursery?*

cow flop AND **cow plop** *n.* a mass of cow dung. ♦ *Mrs. Wilson is out in the pasture gathering cow flops for her garden.* ♦ *When walking out on the range land, we try to avoid "cow plops," as the wranglers call them.*

cow juice Go to moo juice.

cow plop Go to cow flop.

cowboy *n.* a reckless and independent man; a reckless driver. (Also a term of address.) ♦ *Come on, cowboy, finish your coffee and get moving.*

cow-doots [...'duts] *n.* cow dung; masses of cow dung. ♦ *Don was walking through the pasture gathering cow-doots to use as fertilizer.*

coyote-ugly ['kɑɪot 'əgli OR 'kɑɪoti 'əgli] *mod.* extremely ugly. (Crude, cruel, and potentially offensive. Said of people. See also double-bagger; triple-bagger. Supposedly, if one woke up and found one's arm around a coyote-ugly person, one would chew off one's arm—in the manner of a coyote escaping from a steel-jaw trap—rather than pull it back away from this person.) ♦ *Is that your pet monkey, or is your date just coyote-ugly?*

cozy up (to so) *in.* to become overly friendly with someone in hope of gaining special favors. ♦ *Taylor cozied up to the prof, hoping for a good grade at least.*

crab *n.* a louse. (Usually plural.) ♦ *He's scratching like he's got crabs.*

crack 1. *n.* the gap between the buttocks. ♦ *You wanna get kicked in the crack?* **2.** *n.* the gap between the lips of the vulva.

(Usually objectionable. See also crack-rack.) ♦ *He screamed something rude about her crack and slapped her.* **3.** *n.* women considered as the object of copulation and male sexual release. (Usually with *some*. Rude and derogatory.) ♦ *Jed said he had to have some crack soon or he would die.* **4.** *n.* a joke; a smart-aleck remark. ♦ *Another crack like that and your nose will be so reshaped.* **5.** *n.* a try (that may or may not succeed). ♦ *Have another crack at it.* **6.** *n.* a unit of something (for a particular price); a use (of something). ♦ *You would think twice, too, if you remembered that it's seven dollars a crack.* **7.** *n.* crystalline, smokable cocaine. (Drugs.) ♦ *This crack seems to have become the drug of choice for punks of all ages.* **8.** *in.* to break down and talk under pressure. (Underworld.) ♦ *They kept at her till she finally cracked and talked.* **9.** *mod.* [of a person] excellent; top-flight. ♦ *The dealer's crack salesman was no help at all.* **10.** *tv.* to break into something. (Underworld.) ♦ *We almost cracked the safe before the alarm went off.*

crack a book *tv.* to open a book to study. (Usually in the negative.) ♦ *I never cracked a book and still passed the course.*

crack a tube *tv.* to open a can of beer. (See also tube.) ♦ *Why don't you drop over this evening, and we'll crack a few tubes?*

crack house *n.* a house or dwelling where crack (sense 7) is sold and used. (Drugs.) ♦ *In one dilapidated neighborhood, there is a crack house on every block.*

crack open a bottle *tv.* to open a bottle of liquor. (Also with *the*.) ♦ *He cracked the bottle open and poured a little for everyone to try.*

crack so up *tv.* to make someone laugh. ♦ *The lecturer would talk along sort of boring like, and then all of a sudden he would crack up everybody with a joke.*

crack some suds *tv.* to drink some beer. ♦ *Let's go out tonight and crack some suds.*

crack up 1. *in.* to have a wreck. ♦ *The plane cracked up and killed two of the passengers.* **2.** *in.* to break out in laughter. ♦ *I knew I would crack up during the love* scene. **3.** *in.* to have a nervous break-down. ♦ *The poor guy cracked up. It was too much for him.* **4.** *n.* an accident; a wreck. (Usually **crack-up**.) ♦ *There was a terrible crack-up on the expressway.*

crackbrain *n.* a fool; a stupid oaf. ♦ *Did you hear about the crackbrain who said he found part of the sky floating in the lake?*

crackbrained *mod.* stupid; ridiculous. ♦ *I've heard enough of your crackbrained schemes.*

cracked *mod.* crazy. ♦ *You're cracked if you think I'll agree to that.*

cracked up to be *mod.* supposed to be. ♦ *This pizza isn't what it's cracked up to be.*

crackerjack *mod.* excellent; industrious. ♦ *Fred is a crackerjack stockbroker, but his personal life is a mess.*

crackers Go to bonkers.

crackhead *n.* a user of crack. (Drugs.) ♦ *They brought an eight-year-old crackhead in for treatment.*

crackpot 1. *n.* a fake; a person with strange or crazy plans. ♦ *Some crackpot called to tell us that the sky is falling in.* **2.** *mod.* having to do with crazy things, mainly ideas. ♦ *We need a crackpot idea around here just so we'll have something to compare your ideas to.*

crack-rack *n.* a extra seat on a motorcycle, behind the driver. (Refers either to the anatomy of the buttocks placed thereon, or to the genital anatomy of a female passenger. See also **pussy-pad**.) ♦ *Get on the crack-rack, and I'll give you a ride.*

CRAFT Go to can't remember a fucking thing.

cram *in.* to study hard at the last minute for a test. ♦ *If you would study all the time, you wouldn't need to cram.*

crank 1. *n.* a crackpot; a bothersome person with a bogus message. ♦ *A crank called with a bomb threat.* **2.** *mod.* bogus; false; phony. ♦ *We had four crank calls threatening to blow up the Eiffel tower.* **3.** *n.* a crabby person. (Collegiate.) ♦ *Why are you such a crank? Is something wrong in your life?*

crank bugs *n.* a drug-induced hallucination that insects are crawling under one's skin. (Drugs.) ♦ *There's no such thing as crank bugs, so stop scratching them.*

crank sth **out** *tv.* to produce something; to make a lot of something. ♦ *She can crank mystery novels out like fury. They're all good, too.*

crank sth **up 1.** *tv.* to start something up. (Probably alludes to the old style car that had to be started with a crank.) ♦ *I'll go out and crank the car up so it can warm up.* **2.** *tv.* to increase the volume of an electronic device. ♦ *Kelly cranked up his stereo until we were nearly deafened.*

cranking *mod.* exciting; excellent. ♦ *We had a massively cranking time at your place.*

cranky *mod.* irritable; fretful. ♦ *Don't be cranky. We're almost there.*

crap 1. *n.* dung; feces. (Often used as a milder replacement for shit. Usually objectionable.) ♦ *There's dog crap on my lawn!* **2.** *in.* to defecate. (Usually objectionable.) ♦ *Your dog crapped on my lawn!* **3.** *n.* nonsense; lies. (See also BS.) ♦ *Stop talking crap and get serious!* **4.** *n.* junk; shoddy merchandise. ♦ *Send this crap back. I won't pay for it!*

crap out 1. *in.* to evade something; to chicken out (of sth). (From dice, meaning to roll a seven when trying to make a point.) ♦ *Now, don't crap out on me at the last minute.* **2.** *n.* to fail; to break down. ♦ *Great! My TV crapped out just when the game came on.*

craphouse *n.* a privy. (Usually objectionable.) ♦ *Willy's out in the craphouse reading, I guess.*

crap-list Go to shit-list.

crapped (out) *mod.* dead; finished. (Not prenominal. From dice, not from the other senses of crap.) ♦ *After a serious encounter with a rattlesnake, my two dogs were crapped by dawn.*

crapper 1. *n.* a toilet, privy, or restroom. (Usually objectionable. See also crap.) ♦ *Old Jed never passes up a chance to use an indoor crapper.* **2.** *n.* a braggart. (Usually objectionable.) ♦ *The guy is a crapper and can't be trusted at all.*

crapper dick *n.* a police officer or detective who patrols public toilets. ♦ *When he flubbed up the Wilson case, they made him a crapper dick in the central business district.*

crappy 1. *mod.* messed up with dung; dungy. ♦ *Clean off your crappy shoes before you go in there!* **2.** *mod.* lousy; junky; bad; inferior. ♦ *This has been a real crappy day for me.*

crapshoot *n.* a gamble; a matter of chance. (Like a crap [dice] game.) ♦ *The stock market isn't concerned with value anymore. It's just a crapshoot.*

crash 1. *tv. & in.* to attend a party or other event uninvited. (See also crasher.) ♦ *The boys who tried to crash also broke a window.* **2.** *in.* to spend the night. ♦ *I crashed at a friend's place in the city.* **3.** *in.* to sleep. ♦ *If I don't crash pretty soon, I'm going to die!* **4.** *n.* a place to sleep. ♦ *I think I know of a crash for tonight.* **5.** *in.* [for a computer] to stop working. ♦ *This thing crashes every time I hit a certain key.* **6.** *n.* a total failure of a computer. ♦ *Crashes are to teach you to back up your data.* **7.** *in.* [for any electronic device] to fail. ♦ *My stereo crashed, so I've been watching TV.* **8.** *in.* [for a securities market] to lose a significant portion of its value in a short time. ♦ *The market crashed and scared the stuffing out of everybody.* **9.** *n.* a collapse of a securities market. ♦ *After the crash, a lot of people swore off the market for good.* **10.** *in.* to pass out from drinking alcohol to excess. ♦ *Let's get Wilbur home before he crashes for good.*

crash and burn 1. *in.* [for a young man] to fail brilliantly with a romance. (Collegiate. See also go down in flames.) ♦ *It stands to reason that if Carole hadn't shot me down, I wouldn't have crashed and burned.* **2.** *in.* to fail spectacularly. ♦ *I have to be prepared. I don't want to crash and burn if I don't have to.*

crash cart *n.* a nickname for the hospital cart that carries equipment used to attempt to restore a heartbeat, such as a defibrilator. ♦ *Get the crash cart to third west.*

crashed 1. *mod.* alcohol intoxicated. ♦ *There were two crashed freshmen asleep on the lawn.* **2.** *mod.* raided by the police. (See also bust.) ♦ *Our pad got crashed, and a lot of kids were arrested.*

crasher *n.* a person who attends a party uninvited. (See also crash.) ♦ *The crashers ruined the party, and my dad called the cops.*

crate *n.* a dilapidated vehicle. ♦ *This crate gets me to work and back. That's good enough.*

crater 1. *n.* an acne scar. ♦ *Walter was always sort of embarrassed about his craters.* **2.** *in.* to collapse and go down as with a falling stock price. ♦ *The stock cratered and probably won't recover for a year or two.*

crater-face AND **pizza-face; pizza-puss; zit-face** *n.* a person with acne or many acne scars. (Intended as jocular. Rude and derogatory.) ♦ *I gotta get some kind of medicine for these pimples. I'm getting to be a regular crater-face.* ♦ *I don't want to end up a zit-face, but I love chocolate!*

crawling with so/sth *mod.* covered with someone or something; alive with someone or something. ♦ *The place was crawling with police and FBI agents.*

crazy 1. *n.* a crazy person. ♦ *The guy's a crazy, and he keeps coming in here asking for money.* **2.** *mod.* cool. ♦ *This stuff is really crazy, man. I love it!*

crazy bone *n.* the elbow. ♦ *Ouch! I hit my crazy bone!*

cream 1. *tv.* to beat someone; to outscore someone. ♦ *The other team creamed us, but we had better team spirit.* **2.** semen. (Usually objectionable.) ♦ *His father found some cream in the john and went into a purple rage.* **3.** *in. & tv.* to ejaculate [semen]. (See **cream (in)** one's **pants**.) ♦ *He creamed right on the floor.* **4.** vaginal secretions. ♦ *Now, that ought to bring on the cream!* **5.** to copulate [with] someone, usually a female. (Usually objectionable.) ♦ *He acted like he wanted to cream her.*

cream (in) one's **pants** AND **cream** one's **jeans** *in.* [for a male] to ejaculate in his pants from excessive sexual excitement. (Usually objectionable.) ♦ *She makes me want to cream my pants.* ♦ *The kid creamed his jeans in the nudie movie.*

cream one's **jeans** Go to cream (in) one's pants.

cream puff 1. *n.* a weakling; a wimp. ♦ *Don't be a cream puff all your life! Join a health club!* **2.** *n.* a used car that is in very good condition. ♦ *This one is a real cream puff. Only driven to church by a little old lady.*

creamed 1. *mod.* beaten; outscored. ♦ *We were really creamed in that last game, and the coach is steamed.* **2.** *mod.* alcohol intoxicated. (Based on sense 1.) ♦ *I got myself creamed last night, didn't I?*

creamed foreskins *n.* creamed chipped beef (served on toast). (Military. Usually objectionable.) ♦ *Oh, boy! It's creamed foreskins again tonight!*

creased *mod.* exhausted. ♦ *What a day. I am totally creased.*

cred *n.* credibility; believability. (See also street cred.) ♦ *They got no cred with me.*

credenzaware *n.* reports that sit on an executive's credenza, primarily for show. (Contrived.) ♦ *Everything I send her ends up as credenza ware.*

creep *n.* a weird person; an eerie person. ♦ *Charlie is such a creep when he's stoned.*

creep dive Go to creep joint.

creep joint AND **creep dive** *n.* an unpleasant place populated by creeps. ♦ *You shouldn't go into a creep joint like that alone.* ♦ *What's a nice girl like you doing in a creep dive like this?*

creeping-crud 1. *n.* any unidentified disease. ♦ *There is some kind of creeping-crud between my toes.* **2.** *n.* a repellent person. ♦ *Willy has become such a creeping-crud since he inherited all that money.* **3.** *n.* any nasty, slimy substance. ♦ *That's not creeping-crud! That's pecan pie!*

the **creeps** *n.* the jitters; a case of nerves. ♦ *These movies always give me the creeps.*

creepy *mod.* eerie; frightening. ♦ *I have this creepy feeling that someone is just this very moment reading something that I wrote.*

crib 1. *n.* a location where thieves gather to plot; a dwelling for thieves, prostitutes, etc. (Underworld.) ♦ *The police busted a crib over on Fourth Street.* **2.** *n.* a dwelling; home. ♦ *My good threads are all back at my crib.*

cricket *mod.* acceptable. (See negative examples at not cricket.) ♦ *Is it really cricket to play under two different names?*

crips *n.* marijuana. ♦ *This ain't crips; it's alfalfa.*

crisco ['krɪsko] *n.* a fat person. (Cruel. Also a rude term of address. The brand name of a baking shortening.) ♦ *Some crisco came in and ordered ten large fries.*

crisp *mod.* drug intoxicated. (Akin to fried. Compare to toasted.) ♦ *Man, is he crisp!*

crispy-critter *n.* a person under the effects of marijuana. (From the brand name of a breakfast cereal.) ♦ *He's fried all right. A real crispy-critter.*

croak 1. *in.* to die; to expire; to succumb. ♦ *The parrot croaked before I got it home.* **2.** *tv.* to kill someone or something. ♦ *The car croaked the cat just like that.*

croaker *n.* a doctor. ♦ *The croaker said my tonsils have to come out.*

crock 1. *n.* nonsense. (From crock (of shit).) ♦ *What a crock! You don't know what you are talking about!* **2.** *n.* a drunkard. ♦ *Give the old crock some money, anything to get him outa here before he barfs or something.*

crock (of shit) 1. *n.* a mass of lies and deception worth no more than dung. (Usually objectionable.) ♦ *That's nothing but a crock of shit! I don't believe a word of it.* **2.** *n.* a person who tells lies. (Rude and derogatory.) ♦ *He's just a crock of shit. He never tells the truth.* **3.** *n.* a braggart. (Rude and derogatory.) ♦ *He's such a crock. He makes everything he has done sound ten times better than it really is.*

crock so/sth **up** *tv.* to damage or harm someone or something. ♦ *I really crocked up my car last night.*

crocked [krɑkt] *mod.* alcohol intoxicated. ♦ *Oh, my God! You're crocked again!*

crockery *n.* the teeth. (See also China.) ♦ *I gotta go to the dentist for some work on my crockery.*

cromagnon [kro'mægnən] *n.* an ugly male. (Collegiate. Essentially *caveman.* From *Cro-Magnon,* the ancestor of the current human species. See also neanderthal, which is a variety of man presumed to be uglier and less like modern man.) ♦ *Who is that cromagnon you were with last night?*

cros *n.* Velcro. (A protected trade name for hook and loop fasteners.) ♦ *His pants pocket has cros, and I get to his wallet.*

cross so **(up)** AND **cross up** so *tv.* to go against someone; to thwart someone. ♦ *Don't cross me up if you know what's good for you.*

cross up so Go to cross so (up).

cross-eyed (drunk) *mod.* alcohol intoxicated. ♦ *He sat on the bar stool, cross-eyed and crying.*

crotch rocketeer *n.* a motorcycle driver; one who drives a crotch-rocket. ♦ *None of these crotch rocketeers is wearing a helmet.*

crotch-cheese AND **cock-cheese** *n.* smegma; any nasty, smelly substance—real or imagined—that accumulates around the genitals, especially in athletes. (Usually objectionable.) ♦ *Man, this stuff is vile. It smells like crotch-cheese.*

crotch-cobra *n.* the penis. (Usually objectionable.) ♦ *He held his hands over his crotch-cobra and ran for the bedroom.*

crotch-monkey Go to crotch-pheasant.

crotch-pheasant AND **crotch-monkey** *n.* a louse. (Usually in the plural.) ♦ *He appears to be afflicted with what you might call "crotch-pheasants."* ♦ *Stop scratching your crotch-monkeys, Zeke.*

crotch-rocket *n.* a motorcycle. (For some, only foreign motorcycles are so called.)

♦ *I can buy a nice car for less than you paid for that crotch-rocket.*

crotch-rot *n.* a skin irritation or disease characterized by itching in the genital area, usually said of males. (See also grunge.) ♦ *What will get rid of crotch-rot?*

crowd 1. *tv.* to pressure or threaten someone. ♦ *Frank began to crowd Sam, which was the wrong thing to do.* **2.** *tv.* to gang up on someone. ♦ *They moved in from all sides, carrying clubs, and began to crowd us.*

crown *tv.* to hit someone on the head. ♦ *The clerk crowned the robber with a champagne bottle.*

CRS Go to can't remember shit.

crud 1. *n.* any nasty substance. (An old form of the word *curd.*) ♦ *There's some crud on your left shoe.* **2.** *n.* junk; stuff; personal possessions. ♦ *Get your crud outa my way, will you!* **3.** *n.* a repellent person. (Rude and derogatory.) ♦ *Don't be such a crud!*

cruddie Go to cruddy.

cruddy AND **crudy; cruddie** ['krədi] *mod.* nasty; awful. ♦ *What is this cruddy stuff on my plate?*

cruise 1. *in.* to travel at top speed. ♦ *This old caddy can really cruise.* **2.** *in.* to drive around looking for friends or social activity. ♦ *We went out cruising but didn't see anybody.* **3.** *tv.* to pursue a member of the opposite sex. ♦ *Tom was cruising Tiffany, but she got rid of him.* **4.** *in.* to move on; to leave. ♦ *Time to cruise. Monty Python's on in ten minutes.* **5.** *in.* to move through life at a comfortable pace. ♦ *I'm cruising just the way I want now.* **6.** *tv.* to pass a course easily. ♦ *I'm gonna cruise that math course.*

cruiser *n.* a car; a fast car. ♦ *This old hog is a real cruiser.*

cruising for a bruising AND **cruisin' for a bruisin'** *in.* asking for trouble. ♦ *You are cruising for a bruising, you know that?*

crum sth **up** AND **crumb** sth **up** *tv.* to mess something up; to louse something up.

(See comments at crumb.) ♦ *Now, don't crum up this deal.*

crumb [krəm] *n.* a repellent person. (From an old slang word for a *body louse.* Most of the *crum(b)* entries refer to *lice* or *lousy.*) ♦ *The old man was a real crumb and tried to cheat us.*

crumb sth **up** Go to crum sth up.

crumb-cruncher AND **crumb-crusher** *n.* a child. ♦ *How many crumb-crunchers do you have at home.*

crumb-crusher Go to crumb-cruncher.

crumbum AND **crumbbum** ['krəmbəm] **1.** *n.* a repellent person; a bum or hobo. (A *crumb(y) bum.* See note at crumb. The *hobo* may be infected with lice.) ♦ *A skid row crumbum asked us for a buck.* **2.** *mod.* inferior; lousy. ♦ *I sent the crumbum food back to the kitchen. There was a bug in it.*

crumby Go to crummy.

crummy AND **crumby** ['krəmi] *mod.* lousy; bad; inferior. (See comments at crumb.) ♦ *You know, this stuff is pretty crummy.*

crumped (out) 1. *mod.* alcohol intoxicated. ♦ *She was too crumped out to drive herself home.* **2.** *mod.* dead. ♦ *Our old dog crumped out at age fourteen.*

crunch *n.* a crisis; a time of pressure or tightness, especially of a budget. ♦ *The budget crunch meant that we couldn't take trips to Europe anymore.*

crunchers *n.* the feet. ♦ *New shoes can be hard on your crunchers.*

crunchie *n.* a soldier; a marching infantry soldier. (Military. See also crunchers.) ♦ *Crunchies have a pretty hard life.*

crunchy *mod.* [of someone] loving nature, plants, and animals. (The type of person who lives on granola.) ♦ *He's such a crunchy guy, always saving whales and trees.*

crunk AND **krunk 1.** *mod.* wild; crazy; out of control. (The word itself has many uses, each freshly misunderstood or derived earlier senses. It could be a blend of *crud + junk, crazy + drunk,* or other words, such as being a pseudo past participle of **crank** cocaine. There is an "en-

ergy drink" called crunk, and it claimed that the whole phenomenon is related to an extremely energetic Atlanta hip-hop star.) ♦ *He's acting crunk. Don't let him drive!* **2.** *mod.* drunk. ♦ *They went out and got totally crunk to celebrate.* **3.** *mod.* hip; cool; totally excellent. ♦ *Man, this CD is crunk!* **4.** *in.* to get excited or hyped up. ♦ *This brother is really crunking.*

crush *n.* the person on whom one has a crush; one's main squeeze; one's boyfriend or girlfriend. ♦ *I'm gonna go study with my crush tonight.*

crust *n.* nerve; gall. ♦ *She's got a lot of crust—coming in here like that.*

crusty *mod.* feisty; gruff. (Very old, 1500s.) ♦ *Unlike most crusty, old men, Jed hasn't a single redeeming quality.*

crutch 1. *n.* a car. (Streets.) ♦ *That's one fine crutch you got here, Bud.* **2.** *n.* a device to hold a marijuana cigarette butt. ♦ *Here's a crutch so you can finish your smoke.*

cry hughie ['kraɪ 'hjui] *tv.* to empty one's stomach; to vomit. ♦ *He is in the john crying hughie.*

cry ralph Go to cry ruth.

cry ruth AND **call ruth; call ralph; cry ralph** *tv.* to empty one's stomach; to vomit. (See also ruth. Also with capital *r.*) ♦ *I think I have to cry ruth! Stop the car!* ♦ *Don't you dare call ralph in my car!*

crying drunk *mod.* alcohol intoxicated and weeping. ♦ *I really hate it when they come in here crying drunk.*

crying towel *n.* someone or something used to comfort someone. ♦ *It's so sad. I guess I really need a crying towel today.*

crying weed *n.* marijuana. ♦ *I must have got hold of some crying weed. This stuff leaves me cold.*

crystal 1. *n.* crystallized cocaine. (Drugs. See also crack.) ♦ *Crystal—an older name for crack—was a favorite many years ago.* **2.** *n.* liquid Methedrine in glass ampoules. (Drugs.) ♦ *I hear that Willy's shooting crystal. Is that true?*

crystals *n.* the testicles. (From *crystal balls*.) ♦ *He got hit right in the crystals. It was real embarrassing, as well as painful.*

C-spot Go to C-note.

CU *tv.* see you (later). (Used in electronic mail and computer forum or news group messages.) ♦ *Bye. CU L8R.*

CU2 Go to See you, too.

cube [kjub] **1.** *n.* a very square person. ♦ *This nerd was the most unbelievable cube you have ever seen.* **2.** *n.* a die, one of a pair of dice. (Usually in the plural.) ♦ *She shook the cubes, saying, "Baby needs shoes!"* **3.** *n.* a sugar cube impregnated with LSD. (Drugs. Often in the plural.) ♦ *First they took it on cubes. Then on little bits of paper.*

cuckoo Go to coo-coo.

cuddie AND **cuddy** *n.* homie; buddy. (Pop gansta.) ♦ *Tsup, cuddy?*

cuddle bunny *n.* a female lover. ♦ *All you want is a cuddle bunny with big tits! Grow up, Maxwell Wilson!*

cuff *tv.* to put a charge on one's bill. ♦ *Would you cuff this for me, please?*

cuff quote *n.* an off-the-cuff quote of a financial instrument price. (Securities markets.) ♦ *This is just a cuff quote, but I would say it's about ninety-four.*

cuffs *n.* handcuffs. ♦ *I felt the cuffs tighten and snap shut on my wrists.*

CUIAL Go to See you in another life.

CUIC Go to See you in church.

CUL8R Go to See you later.

cull *n.* a socially unacceptable person. ♦ *This place is so filled with culls! Let's split.*

culture-vulture 1. *n.* an avid supporter of the arts. ♦ *Many culture-vultures seem to be long on enthusiasm and short on taste.* **2.** *n.* someone who exploits the arts for monetary gain. ♦ *Some culture-vultures are throwing a wine and cheese party on behalf of some of the young dolts they have grubstaked.*

cum ['kəm] **1.** *n.* semen; come. (Usually objectionable. See other related senses at come.) ♦ *I would never say "cum" to a doctor or nurse!* **2.** *in.* to experience orgasm; to ejaculate. ♦ *I think I'm going to cum!* **3.** AND **cume** [kjum] *n.* a cumulative average, such as a grade-point average. ♦ *My cume is not high enough to get into law school.*

cunt 1. *n.* the female genitals; the vulva and vagina. (One of the oldest English four-letter words. Usually objectionable.) ♦ *He thought he could see her cunt through her swimming suit.* **2.** women considered as nothing more than a receptacle for the penis; a wretched and despised woman. (Rude and derogatory.) ♦ *Jed announced that he really needed some cunt, bad.* **3.** *n.* a wretched and disgusting male. (Rude and derogatory.) ♦ *Don't act like such a cunt, you twit!*

cunt fart AND **pussy fart** *n.* a vaginal fart, the sudden release of air—from the vagina—trapped on insertion of the penis during copulation. (Usually objectionable.) ♦ *He heard a little cunt fart and started laughing so hard, he had to stop.*

cunt hound *n.* a lecher. (Rude and derogatory.) ♦ *Tod is such a cunt hound. All he thinks about is dames.*

cunt-hooks AND **shit-hooks** *n.* the fingers; the hands. (Crude and objectionable.) ♦ *Put your shit-hooks around those oars and row!* ♦ *Go wash your cunt-hooks, you slob.*

cup of tea *n.* something preferred or desired. (Often negative.) ♦ *Driving children around all afternoon is not my cup of tea.*

cupcake *n.* an attractive woman. (Also a term of address.) ♦ *Who is that cupcake driving the beemer?*

curl up and die Go to (just) curl up and die.

curly *n.* a bald person, almost always a male. (Also a jocular term of address.) ♦ *Well, Curly, looks like you got your dome sunburned!*

the **curse** *n.* the menses. ♦ *The curse struck this morning.*

curtains *n.* death. (Underworld.) ♦ *Okay, Marlowe, this time it's curtains.*

cushy ['kʊʃi] *mod.* soft; easy. (From *cushion*.) ♦ *That's a cushy kind of life to lead.*

cut 1. *mod.* alcohol intoxicated. ♦ *He got cut on beer, which is unusual for him.* **2.** *tv.* to dilute something. ♦ *She always cuts her eggnog with cola. Yuck!* **3.** *n.* a share of the loot or the profits. (Originally underworld.) ♦ *You'll get your cut when everybody else does.* **4.** *n.* a single song or section of music on a record. ♦ *This next cut is one everybody likes.* **5.** *tv.* to eliminate something; to stop (doing something). ♦ *Okay, chum, cut the clowning.* **6.** *mod.* muscular; with well-defined muscles, especially in reference to the abdominal muscles. ♦ *He works out and he's really cut!* **7.** *mod.* circumcised. (Not usually prenominal.) ♦ *I'm not cut and neither is my brother.*

cut a check *tv.* to write a check. ♦ *We'll cut the check tonight and send it out in tomorrow's mail.*

cut a deal *tv.* to arrange a deal; to seal a bargain. ♦ *Maybe we can cut a deal. Let's talk.*

cut a fart AND **cut one; let a fart; let one** *tv.* to release intestinal gas through the anus. (Usually objectionable.) ♦ *Fred cut a fart right in the middle of English class, and nobody moved a muscle.* ♦ *He let one that echoed through the whole auditorium!*

cut a muffin Go to cut the cheese.

cut and run *in.* to stop what one is doing and flee. ♦ *The cops were coming, so we cut and run.*

cut ass (out of somewhere**)** Go to bag ass (out of somewhere).

cut corners *tv.* to do something more easily; to take shortcuts; to save money by finding cheaper ways to do something. (As if one were speeding somewhere and took the shortest way possible through intersections, i.e., by making left turns that cut across oncoming traffic lanes.) ♦ *I won't cut corners just to save money. I put quality first.*

cut loose *in.* to let go; to become independent; to grow up and leave home. ♦ *It was hard to cut loose from home.*

cut no ice (with so**)** *tv.* to have no influence on someone; to fail to convince someone. ♦ *I don't care who you are. It cuts no ice with me.*

cut one Go to cut a fart.

cut one's **losses** *tv.* to do something to stop a loss of something. ♦ *I knew I had to do something to cut my losses, but it was almost too late.*

cut one's **own throat** *tv.* to do something that harms oneself. ♦ *He's just cutting his own throat, and he knows it.*

cut one's **wolf loose** *tv.* to go on a drinking bout; to get drunk. ♦ *I'm gonna go out and cut my wolf loose tonight.*

cut out *in.* to leave; to run away. ♦ *It's late. I think I'll cut out.*

cut so **a break** AND **cut** so **some slack** *tv.* to give someone a break; to allow someone a reprieve from the consequences of an action. ♦ *Come on! Cut me a break! I won't do it again!* ♦ *Cut me some slack and I'll be sure to pay you all I owe in a month.*

cut so **in (on** sth**)** *tv.* to permit someone to share something. ♦ *We can't cut you in. There's not enough.*

cut so **some slack** Go to cut so a break.

cut some Zs Go to catch some Zs.

cut the cheese AND **cut the mustard; cut a muffin** *tv.* to release intestinal gas. (Usually objectionable.) ♦ *People who cut the mustard in the car have to get out and walk!* ♦ *Somebody cut a muffin!*

Cut the comedy! *exclam.* Get serious!; Stop acting silly! ♦ *That's enough, you guys. Cut the comedy!*

Cut the crap! *exclam.* Stop the nonsense! (Usually objectionable.) ♦ *Cut the crap. Talk straight or get out.*

cut the dust *tv.* to take a drink of liquor. ♦ *I think I'll stop in this joint here and cut the dust.*

cut the mustard 1. *tv.* to be able to do something requiring youth or vigor. (Usually in the expression **too old to cut the mustard**.) ♦ *Do you really think he* *can cut the mustard?* **2.** Go to cut the cheese.

cut to the chase *in.* to focus on what is important; to abandon the preliminaries and deal with the major points. ♦ *After a few introductory comments, we cut to the chase and began negotiating.*

cut (up) *mod.* having well-defined abdominal muscles. ♦ *Andy works hard to try to get a gut that's cut.*

cut up (about so/sth**)** *mod.* emotionally upset about someone or something. ♦ *She was all cut up about her divorce.*

cutie *n.* a cute thing or person. (Also a term of address.) ♦ *Come here, cutie, let me fix your collar.*

cutie pie *n.* a cute person, typically a woman or a baby. (Also a term of address.) ♦ *What's your name, cutie pie?*

cut-rate *mod.* cheap; low-priced. ♦ *Where are your cut-rate sweaters?*

cuts *n.* sharply defined musculature, especially in the abdominal area. ♦ *Look at the cuts on that guy! What great abs!*

cuz [kəz] *n.* cousin. (Old colloquial. The spelling is eye-dialect. *Cous* probably would not be recognized as *cousin*.) ♦ *I've got to go to Denver to visit my cuz.*

CYA Go to Cover your ass.

da bomb Go to the bomb.

daddy (of them all) Go to (grand)daddy (of them all).

daffy ['dæfi] *mod.* silly; crazy. ♦ *Kelly was acting daffy because she was so happy.*

dagwood (sandwich) ['dægwʊd...] *n.* a tall sandwich with many layers of food. (From the comic strip character Dagwood by Chick Young.) ♦ *I really like to make an old-fashioned dagwood sandwich every now and then.*

daily dozen *n.* a short set of daily exercises. ♦ *I need to do my daily dozen before breakfast.*

daily grind *n.* the tedious pattern of daily work. (See also rat race.) ♦ *Well, it's Monday. Time to start another week of the daily grind.*

dairies *n.* the breasts. ♦ *Fine dairies on that one!*

daisy *n.* an excellent thing. (See also doosie.) ♦ *I want a daisy of a haircut. Something unusual with bangs or something.*

damage *n.* the cost; the amount of the bill (for something). (See also bad news.) ♦ *As soon as I pay the damage, we can go.*

damaged *mod.* drunk. ♦ *Them guys went out and really got damaged.*

Damn straight! *exclam.* You are absolutely right!; Yes!; Right on! ♦ *Am I mad? Damn straight!*

Damned if I know. AND **DIIN; DIIK** *phr. & comp. abb.* I don't know.; I have no idea. (DIIN is for poor spellers.) ♦ *Don't ask me! DIIK.*

dank [dæŋk] **1.** *mod.* very good. ♦ *We stopped for a while in this real dank little bistro on the main boulevard.* **2.** *mod.* very bad. ♦ *Class was so dank today. I thought I would die of terminal boredom.* **3.** *n.* potent, moist marijuana. (Said to be stored away from light.) ♦ *I'll take dank any day.*

dap [dæp] *mod.* well-dressed. (From dapper.) ♦ *Man, you look so dap!*

darb [dɑrb] *n.* an excellent person or thing. ♦ *Carl is a real darb. I'm glad to know him.*

dark horse 1. *n.* an unknown entrant into a contest; a surprise candidate for political office. ♦ *The party is hoping that a dark horse will appear before the election.* **2.** *mod.* previously unknown. ♦ *A dark horse player can win if all the others are creeps.*

data miner Go to spyware.

dawg Go to dog.

day one *n.* the first day. (Often with since.) ♦ *You haven't done anything right since day one! You're fired!*

day person *n.* a person who prefers to be active during the daytime. (Compare this with night person.) ♦ *I am strictly a day person. Have to be in bed early.*

day the eagle flies Go to when the eagle flies.

day the eagle shits *n.* payday. (Military. Usually objectionable.) ♦ *Tomorrow is the day the eagle shits, and do I ever need it.*

day-tripper *n.* a tourist who makes one-day trips. ♦ *At about 4:00 P.M. the day-trippers start thinning out.* ♦ *Being a day-tripper is hard on your feet sometimes.*

dead 1. *mod.* quiet and uneventful; boring. ♦ *The day was totally dead.* **2.** *mod.* very tired. ♦ *I went home from the office, dead as usual.* **3.** *mod.* dull; lifeless; flat. ♦ *This meal is sort of dead because I am out of onions.* **4.** *mod.* no longer effective; no longer of any consequence. ♦ *That guy is dead—out of power.* **5.** *mod.* [of an issue] no longer germane; no longer of any importance. ♦ *Forget it! It's a dead issue.*

dead and gone 1. *mod.* [of a person] long dead. ♦ *Old Gert's been dead and gone for quite a spell.* **2.** *mod.* [of a thing] gone long ago. ♦ *That kind of thinking is dead and gone.*

dead broke *mod.* completely broke; without any money. ♦ *I'm dead broke—not a nickel to my name.*

dead cinch *n.* an absolute certainty; an easy thing to do. ♦ *It's a dead cinch. I foresee no problems.*

dead drunk *mod.* alcohol intoxicated; totally inebriated. ♦ *They were both dead drunk. They could only lie there and snore.*

dead duck *n.* a person or thing doomed to failure or disaster. ♦ *This whole plan was a dead duck from the beginning.*

dead easy *mod.* very easy. ♦ *This whole job is dead easy.*

dead from the neck up 1. *mod.* stupid. (With a *dead* head.) ♦ *She acts like she is dead from the neck up.* **2.** *mod.* no longer open to new ideas. ♦ *Everyone on the board of directors is dead from the neck up.*

dead horse *n.* a dead issue, especially one that is referred to continually. (Often with *beat, whip.*) ♦ *Forget it! Don't waste time whipping a dead horse.*

dead in the water *mod.* stalled; immobile. (Originally nautical.) ♦ *The project is dead in the water for the time being.*

dead issue *n.* an issue that doesn't matter anymore. ♦ *It's a dead issue. Forget it.*

dead letter 1. *n.* a letter that cannot move through the post office because the addressee does not exist or because the address is wrong or illegible. (Standard English.) ♦ *Every now and then they open the dead letters to see if they can figure out who they were meant for.* **2.** *n.* an issue

that does not matter anymore. ♦ *This contract is a dead letter. Forget it!*

dead man Go to dead soldier.

dead marine Go to dead soldier.

dead on *mod.* exactly right; on target. ♦ *That's a good observation, Tiffany. You are dead on.*

dead one Go to dead soldier.

dead president *n.* a piece of U.S. paper money. (Refers to the pictures of presidents on the bills.) ♦ *This silly magazine costs three dead presidents!*

(dead) ringer (for so) *n.* someone who is an exact duplicate of someone else. (Here *dead* means *absolute*. See also ringer.) ♦ *You are sure a dead ringer for my brother.*

dead soldier AND **dead man; dead marine; dead one 1.** *n.* an empty liquor or beer bottle. ♦ *Toss your dead soldiers in the garbage, please.* ♦ *There's a dead one under the bed and another in the fireplace!* **2.** *n.* a cigarette butt. (Less common than sense 1.) ♦ *The bum found a dead soldier on the ground and picked it up.*

dead to rights Go to (bang) dead to rights.

dead to the world 1. *mod.* sound asleep. ♦ *After all that exercise, he's dead to the world.* **2.** *mod.* alcohol intoxicated. ♦ *By midnight almost everybody was dead to the world.*

deadbeat *n.* someone who doesn't pay debts or bills. ♦ *Some deadbeat with the same name as mine is ruining my credit rating.*

deadcat bounce *n.* a small, knee-jerk rally in one of the financial markets. (A dead cat—or any other animal—will bounce only slightly after being dropped. Refers to a stock index or security price that bounces up only slightly after a precipitous fall. Securities market.) ♦ *The whole market gave only a deadcat bounce after the string of losses this last week.*

dead-catty *mod.* with only a slight bounce. (See the explanation at deadcat bounce. Securities markets.) ♦ *We expected the stock to go up a lot today, but the increase was no better than dead-catty.*

deaded 1. *mod.* spent; used up; done for; cashed. ♦ *All my goodwill is gone. Cashed. Deaded.* **2.** *tv.* to kill someone. ♦ *The gang deaded him with a deuce-deuce.*

dead-end kid *n.* a youth with no future, usually a male. ♦ *Frank was a dead-end kid from the day he was born.*

deadhead 1. *n.* a stupid person. ♦ *Wow, are you a deadhead!* **2.** *tv. & in.* [for someone] to return an empty truck, train, airplane, etc., to where it came from. ♦ *I deadheaded back to Los Angeles.* **3.** *n.* a follower of the rock group the Grateful Dead. ♦ *My son is a deadhead and travels all over listening to these guys.*

deadly (dull) *mod.* very dull. ♦ *The lecture was deadly dull, and I went to sleep.*

deadneck *n.* a stupid person. ♦ *Who's the deadneck who painted the fence purple?*

deadpan 1. *n.* an expressionless face. (See also pan = face.) ♦ *This guy has a super deadpan.* **2.** *n.* a person with an expressionless face. ♦ *When you come on stage, look like a deadpan.* **3.** *mod.* dull and lifeless. (Usually said of a face, expression, etc.) ♦ *He has such a deadpan approach to everything.*

deadwood *n.* nonproductive or nonfunctional persons. ♦ *We'll have to cut costs by getting rid of the deadwood.*

deal stock *n.* a stock that is a takeover candidate. (Securities markets.) ♦ *I try to spot the deal stocks early and buy them before others do.*

deal with so *in.* to kill someone. (From the milder expression meaning to cope with or tend to someone.) ♦ *The agent planned how best to deal with the rebel leader without getting caught.*

Dear John letter *n.* a letter a woman writes to her boyfriend in the military service telling him that she does not love him anymore. ♦ *Sally sends a Dear John letter about once a month.*

death on so/sth *n.* causing the death or destruction of someone or something. (See also death on sth.) ♦ *This kind of road is just death on tires.*

death on sth *n.* moving very fast or skillfully on something, such as wheels. ♦ *He is way fast—just death on wheels.*

deathly *mod.* excellent. ♦ *Did you see Kelly's deathly new convertible?*

dec Go to des.

decent *mod.* good; very good. ♦ *This is some pretty decent jazz.*

deck 1. *tv.* to knock someone to the ground. ♦ *Fred decked Bob with one blow.* **2.** *n.* a pack of cigarettes. ♦ *Can you toss me a deck of fags, please?*

deduck ['didək] **1.** *n.* a tax deduction. (From *deduct*.) ♦ *I need a few more deducks this year.* **2.** AND **duck** *n.* a deduction from one's paycheck. ♦ *More of my pay goes to deducks than I get myself.* ♦ *What's this duck for?*

deduction *n.* a child. (Actually a child is an exemption on the U.S. income tax return. See also expense.) ♦ *How many little deductions do you have running around your home?*

deejay Go to disk jockey.

deep *mod.* intense; profound. ♦ *She gave this really deep speech to us about how we should stay off drugs.*

deep pockets 1. *n.* a good source of money. ♦ *Deep pockets are hard to find since the stock market crashed.* **2.** *n.* a rich person. ♦ *The lawyer went after the doctor who was the deep pockets of the organization.*

deep six 1. *tv.* to jettison something, including a corpse, from a ship at sea. (Usually **deep-six** as a verb.) ♦ *They deep-sixed the body of the first mate, who had died of the shakes.* **2.** the **deep six** *n.* burial at sea. (Always with *the* in this sense.) ♦ *I think I'd want the deep six, but I'll probably kick off on dry land.* **3.** *tv.* to kill or dispose of someone. (Underworld. Usually **deep-six** as a verb.) ♦ *The thugs tried to deep-six the witness, but failed.* **4.** *tv.* to throw something away. (Usually **deep-six** as a verb.) ♦ *Take this old thing out and deep-six it.* **5.** the **deep six** *n.* a grave. (Always with *the* in this sense. Graves are usually six feet deep.) ♦ *When* *you know the deep six is at the end of the line no matter who you are, it makes you take life less seriously.*

def [dɛf] **1.** *mod.* better; cool. (Originally black. From *definitive*.) ♦ *Man, that yogurt is def!* **2.** *mod.* definitely. ♦ *This is def the best there is.*

defrosted *mod.* even with someone who has insulted, embarrassed, or angered oneself. (See also chill; ice.) ♦ *He yelled at her till he was defrosted, and then things settled down.*

déjà moo *n.* [tired] old bullshit. (Based on *déjà vu*, and the *moo* brings in the bovine aspect. Contrived, but admirable nonetheless.) ♦ *Are you still peddling that nonsense. Nothing but déjà moo, all over again.*

Delhi belly ['dɛli bɛli] *n.* diarrhea, as suffered by tourists in India. (Contrived for the sake of the rhyme.) ♦ *I've got something you can take for Delhi belly.*

delish [də'lɪʃ] *mod.* delicious. ♦ *Oh, this cake is just delish.*

delts [dɛlts] *n.* the deltoid muscles. (Bodybuilding.) ♦ *Look at the delts on that dame!*

dem Go to demo.

demo ['dɛmo] **1.** AND **dem** [dɛm] *n.* a member of the Democratic Party. ♦ *A couple of dems are running for the caucus, but no other party is represented.* **2.** *n.* a demonstration (of something). ♦ *Hey, Chuck, give this man a demo.* **3.** *n.* an automobile or other machine or device that has been used by a dealer for demonstration purposes. ♦ *I can give you a demo for half price.* **4.** *tv.* to demonstrate something (to someone). ♦ *Let me demo this for you so you can see how it works.* **5.** *tv.* to demonstrate (something) to someone. ♦ *I've got to go demo these people on this software.*

des AND **dec** [dis] *n.* December. (Securities markets. Futures and options trading.) ♦ *The bean futures for des fell out of bed yesterday.* ♦ *Sell the aks and buy the des.*

desert cherry *n.* a new soldier in a desert war; a soldier new to the desert in war-time. (From the Persian Gulf War. See also cherry.) ♦ *About 5,000 desert cherries arrived last week. Something is going to happen soon.*

desk jockey *n.* someone who works at a desk in an office. (Patterned on disk jockey.) ♦ *I couldn't stand being a cooped-up desk jockey.*

destroyed *mod.* drug intoxicated. ♦ *The kid who took angel dust is destroyed most of the time.*

deuce [dus] **1.** *n.* the devil. (Always with the.) ♦ *I'll knock the deuce out of you if you come around here again.* **2.** *n.* the two in playing cards. ♦ *If I could only get a deuce.* **3.** *n.* two dollars. ♦ *Can you loan me a deuce till payday?* **4.** *n.* a two-year prison sentence. (Underworld.) ♦ *The DA made sure that Mooshoo got more than a deuce.* **5.** *n.* a table for two. ♦ *Give the next couple the deuce over in the corner.*

deuce-deuce *n.* a .22-caliber pistol. (Streets.) ♦ *My buddy popped his uncle with a deuce-deuce.*

a devil of a time AND **the devil of a time.** *n.* a very difficult time. ♦ *I had a devil of a time with my taxes.*

the devil's own time *n.* a very difficult time; a hellish time. ♦ *I had the devil's own time with these tax forms.*

dew Go to (mountain) dew.

dialog *tv.* to attempt to deceive someone; to attempt to seduce someone. ♦ *Ron was dialoging this dame when her brother came in.*

diamond in the rough *n.* a person who is wonderful despite a rough exterior; a person with great potential. ♦ *He's a diamond in the rough—a little hard to take at times, but okay mostly.*

diarrhea of the jawbone Go to diarrhea of the mouth.

diarrhea of the mouth AND **diarrhea of the jawbone** *n.* an imaginary disease involving constant talking. ♦ *Wow, does he ever have diarrhea of the mouth!* ♦ *Sorry. I seem to get diarrhea of the jawbone whenever I get in front of an audience.*

dibs on sth *phr.* a claim on something. ♦ *Dibs on the front seat!*

dicey ['daɪsi] *mod.* touchy; chancy; touch and go. ♦ *Things are just a little dicey right now.*

dick 1. *n.* a detective; a police officer. (Underworld. From *detective*.) ♦ *Marlowe is a private dick who has to keep one step ahead of the cops.* **2.** *n.* the penis. (Usually objectionable. Currently the most publicly used word for this organ.) ♦ *She told some dirty joke about a dick, but everybody just sat there and looked straight ahead.* **3.** *n.* a stupid person, usually a male. (Rude and derogatory.) ♦ *What stupid dick put this thing here in the way?* **4.** *n.* nothing. (Usually objectionable.) ♦ *The whole idea isn't worth dick.* **5.** *tv. & in.* to copulate [with] a woman. (Usually objectionable.) ♦ *If you think I'm going out with a guy who only wants to get me dicked, you're crazy.* **6.** *tv.* to cheat or deceive someone. (Usually objectionable. See also **fuck, hose, screw**.) ♦ *That salesman dicked me for ten extra bucks.*

dick around *in.* to waste time; to goof off. (Usually objectionable.) ♦ *Stop dicking around and get to work!*

dick for *n.* a person dumb enough to ask "What's a dick for?" (Jocular and contrived. Usually objectionable.) ♦ *The guy's a real dick for.*

dick smack *n.* a moron; a stupid jerk. (Possibly a reference to masturbation.) ♦ *You loony dick smack! Get out of my face!*

dickens 1. the **dickens** *n.* the devil. (Always with *the* in this sense.) ♦ *I felt as bad as the dickens, but what could I do?* **2.** *n.* a devilish or impish child. (Also a term of address. Usually with *little*.) ♦ *You are such a cute little dickens!*

dickhead 1. *n.* a stupid person, usually a male. (Rude and derogatory.) ♦ *See if you can get that dickhead to do it right this time.* **2.** *n.* the head of the penis. (Usually objectionable.) ♦ *If you like your dickhead attached, you had better do just exactly as you are told.*

dick-sucker 1. *n.* a male who performs fellatio. (Rude and derogatory.) ♦ *In the bar, this dick-sucker came up and wanted to know my sign.* **2.** *n.* a low and despicable male; a male who is despicable enough to perform fellatio. (Rude and derogatory.) ♦ *You slimy dick-sucker. I'll get you for this.*

dickwad *n.* a stupid and ineffective male. (Possibly a reference to semen, see **wad** (sense 2).) ♦ *What a dickwad! Beat it!*

dickweed *n.* a stupid and ineffective male. ♦ *He's nothing but a pathetic dickweed!*

dicky-licker *n.* someone who performs oral sex on the penis, usually a homosexual male. (Rude and derogatory.) ♦ *One of the dicky-lickers started staring at me.*

dicty ['dɪkti] *mod.* snobbish. (Black.) ♦ *That dicty lady told me I could come to the back to get a tip if I wanted.*

diddle 1. *tv.* to feel someone sexually. (See also **feel** so **up**. Usually objectionable.) ♦ *She moved her hand over, like she was going to diddle him, then she jabbed him in the crystals.* **2.** *in.* to masturbate [oneself]. (Usually objectionable.) ♦ *Have you been diddling again?* **3.** *tv.* to masturbate someone else. (Akin to sense 1. Usually objectionable.) ♦ *She diddled him since it was his birthday.* **4.** *tv.* to cheat someone. ♦ *The shop owner diddled me out of ten bucks.* **5.** *tv. & in.* to copulate [with] someone. (Usually objectionable.) ♦ *I'm tired of hearing who has diddled whom in Hollywood.*

diddle sth **out of** so *tv.* to get something from someone by deception. ♦ *We diddled about forty bucks out of the old lady who runs the candy shop.*

diddle with sth *in.* to play with something; to toy with something. ♦ *Here, don't diddle with that watch.*

diddly-shit AND **doodly-shit 1.** *n.* anything at all. (Usually in the negative. Usually objectionable.) ♦ *I don't give a diddly-shit what you do!* **2.** *mod.* virtually worthless; useless. (Usually objectionable.) ♦ *I'm gonna take this diddly-shit watch back to the store and get my money back.*

diddly-squat AND **(doodly-)squat** ['dɪdliskwɑt AND 'dudliskwɑt] *n.* nothing.

(Folksy. Originally black or southern.) ♦ *This contract isn't worth diddly-squat.*

DIDO *phr.* dreck in, dreck out; garbage in, garbage out. (Computers. Acronym. See also **dreck**. If you get **dreck** out of a computer, it's because you put **dreck** in. See also **GIGO**.) ♦ *Look at this stuff that the printer put out. What is it? Oh, well. DIDO.*

die *in.* to "perish" (figuratively) from laughter or some other emotionally intense response. ♦ *The whole audience died laughing.*

die of throat trouble *in.* to be hanged. (Old.) ♦ *He died of throat trouble after the posse caught up with him.*

die on so 1. *in.* [for a patient] to die under the care of someone. ♦ *Get that medicine over here fast, or this guy's gonna die on me.* **2.** *in.* [for something] to quit running for someone. ♦ *My stereo died on me, and I had to listen to the radio.*

diesel ['dizl] *mod.* really good. ♦ *I am set for a diesel evening and I intend to enjoy it.*

diff [dɪf] *n.* difference. ♦ *Aw, come on! What's the diff?*

different strokes for different folks *phr.* different things please different people. ♦ *Do whatever you like. Different strokes for different folks.*

differential *n.* the buttocks; the rear (end). (From the name of the device that joins the axle to the driveshaft in motorized vehicles.) ♦ *You're walking like there's something wrong with your differential.*

dig 1. *tv. & in.* to understand something. ♦ *I just don't dig what you are saying.* **2.** *tv.* to appreciate something; to like something. ♦ *He really digs classical music.*

Dig up! *exclam.* Listen up!; Pay attention! ♦ *Dig up, man! This is important.*

digits *n.* [someone's] telephone number. ♦ *Give me your digits, and I'll call you.*

digs *n.* a dwelling; a dwelling and its furnishings. ♦ *You got some pretty swell digs, here.*

DIIK Go to Damned if I know.

DIIN Go to Damned if I know.

dike AND **dyke** *n.* a lesbian; a bulldiker. (Rude and derogatory.) ♦ *Who's the dike in the cowboy boots?*

dikey AND **dykey** *mod.* in the manner of a lesbian; pertaining to lesbians. (Usually objectionable.) ♦ *She walks kinda dikey, doesn't she?*

dildo ['dɪldo] *n.* a stupid person, usually a male. (Rude and derogatory. The term refers to an artificial penis.) ♦ *Hank can be such a dildo sometimes.*

dilly *n.* something excellent. ♦ *This little car is a real dilly.*

dim *n.* the evening; the night. (Streets.) ♦ *Where'll you be this dim?*

dim bulb *n.* a dull person; a stupid person. ♦ *George seems to be a dim bulb, but he's a straight-A student.*

dime store *n.* an establishment that is chaotic because of its small scale. ♦ *I can't stand this dime store anymore. This is no way to run a law firm.*

dime-dropper *n.* an informer. (Underworld. Because an informer at one time could drop a dime in a public telephone and call the police or drop a dime on the sidewalk as a signal for the police to move in and make an arrest. See also **drop a dime**.) ♦ *I think that Taylor is the dime-dropper who caused the roust.*

dimwit ['dɪmwɪt] *n.* an oaf; a dullard. (Also a rude term of address.) ♦ *Oh, Dave, you can be such a dimwit!*

dinero [dɪ'nɛro] *n.* money. (Spanish.) ♦ *I don't have as much dinero as I need, but other than that, I'm doing okay.*

ding 1. *tv.* to shoot, dent, or knock something. ♦ *The rock dinged my left fender.* **2.** *tv.* to negate; to cast out; to blemish. ♦ *The reviewer dinged the book, but it sold well anyway.* **3.** *n.* a dent or blemish. ♦ *The hail put a lot of dings in the hood of my car.*

ding-a-ling ['dɪŋəlɪŋ] *n.* a stupid person; a giddy person who hears bells. ♦ *This ding-a-ling comes up and asks me for a dollar* for the orphans. I tell her I got all the orphans I can use at any price.

dingbat 1. *n.* a name for a gadget. ♦ *Isn't there supposed to be a little red dingbat that goes in this hole?* **2.** *n.* a stupid person. ♦ *Who is the dingbat with Bob?* **3.** *n.* any undesirable person. (Also a rude term of address.) ♦ *I'm tired of reading about that dingbat in the paper every day.*

ding-dong 1. *n.* the penis. (Usually objectionable.) ♦ *He held his hands over his ding-dong and ran for the bedroom.* **2.** *n.* a stupid person of either sex. ♦ *You silly ding-dong! Try again.* **3.** *mod.* damned. (A euphemism.) ♦ *Get your ding-dong junk outa my way!*

dinged out *mod.* alcohol intoxicated. ♦ *Gary is dinged out and can't drive.*

dinghead *n.* a stupid person. ♦ *Shut up, you stupid dinghead.*

dingleberry 1. *n.* a blob of fecal matter clinging to the hairs around the anus. (Usually objectionable.) ♦ *Is there no permanent cure for the heartbreak of dingleberries?* **2.** *n.* a stupid-acting person of either sex. ♦ *You are such a dumb dingleberry! Wise up!*

dingle(-dangle) *n.* the penis. (Usually objectionable.) ♦ *Come on, Billy. Shake your dingle and put it away.*

dingus 1. *n.* a thing or gadget. ♦ *I have a little dingus that helps me clean venetian blinds.* **2.** AND **dingy** *n.* the penis; the male *thing.* (Usually objectionable.) ♦ *Jimmy, shake your dingus and put it away!*

dingy ['dɪŋi] **1.** *mod.* loony; giddy. ♦ *That friend of yours sure does act dingy sometimes.* **2.** Go to dingus.

dink 1. *n.* a person of East Asian (including Japanese) nationality or decent; originally a person of Chinese nationality or descent. (Much used during the Vietnam War for the Vietnamese. Rude and derogatory.) ♦ *He said he fought against dinks in the war.* **2.** *n.* *n.* the penis, especially a small one. (Usually objectionable.) ♦ *God, Fred, you really got a dink. Is it full grown yet?* **3.** AND **DINK** *n.* double income, no kids; a (young) married

couple with two incomes and no children. (Acronym.) ♦ *The whole neighborhood is populated by dinks. Not a single child on the block.*

dink SO **off** *tv.* to make someone angry. ♦ *Why did you have to start out your speech by dinking off the entire audience?*

dinky ['dɪŋki] *mod.* small; undersized. ♦ *I'll take the dinky piece. I'm on a diet.*

dinner basket Go to breadbasket.

dip 1. *n.* a drunkard. (From *dipsomaniac.*) ♦ *Buy the dip a drink. That'll shut him up for a while.* **2.** AND **dipper** *n.* a pickpocket. (Underworld.) ♦ *The dip tried a snatch, but the dupe turned around at the wrong time.* ♦ *The cops picked up three dippers, working as a group, at the fairgrounds.* **3.** *n.* a pinch or helping of snuff. ♦ *He took a dip just before he picked up the bat.* **4.** *n.* a wad of chewing tobacco. ♦ *You could see he had a big dip in his cheek.* **5.** *n.* an oaf; a jerk. (Probably from dipshit.) ♦ *Why are you acting like such a dip?*

diphead Go to dipshit.

dipper Go to dip.

dippy *mod.* crazy; loony. ♦ *Who is that dippy chick with the lamp shade on her head?*

dipshit 1. AND **diphead; dipstick** *n.* an oaf; a jerk. (Rude and derogatory. See also dip.) ♦ *Look, dipstick, I'm in a hurry.* ♦ *Don't be such a diphead!* **2.** *mod.* pertaining to someone or something obnoxious, stupid, or offensive. (Usually objectionable.) ♦ *Here's another one of his dipshit ideas.*

dipso ['dɪpso] *n.* a drunkard; an alcoholic. (From *dipsomaniac.* See also dip.) ♦ *She's sort of a closet dipso.*

dipstick 1. *n.* the penis. (From the name of the metal stick used to measure the amount of oil in an automobile engine. Usually objectionable.) ♦ *He held his hands over his dipstick and ran for the bedroom.* **2.** Go to dipshit.

dipsy ['dɪpsi] *mod.* tipsy; alcohol intoxicated. (See also dipso.) ♦ *The cop pulled the dipsy dame over and arrested her.*

dipwad ['dɪpwɑd] *n.* a jerk; a nerd. (Euphemistic for dipshit.) ♦ *If you weren't a big dipwad, you would give me a hand with this.*

dirt 1. *n.* low, worthless people. (Singular with the force of plural.) ♦ *I am not dirt. I'm just temporarily financially embarrassed.* **2.** *n.* gossip; scandal; incriminating secrets; dirty linen. ♦ *What's the dirt on Taylor?*

dirt cheap *mod.* very cheap. ♦ *Get one of these while they're dirt cheap.*

dirtbag *n.* a low, worthless person. ♦ *Spike is a slimy dirtbag, and I want him put away for good.*

dirty 1. *mod.* obscene. ♦ *The movie was too dirty for me.* **2.** *mod.* low and sneaky. ♦ *What a dirty thing to do!* **3.** *mod.* illegal; on the wrong side of the law. (Compare this with clean.) ♦ *The cops knew that Last Card Louie was dirty, and they searched his car until they found something they could use against him.*

dirty crack *n.* a rude remark. ♦ *Another dirty crack like that and I'll leave.*

dirty deal *n.* an unfair deal. ♦ *I got a dirty deal at that shop, and I won't go back.*

dirty dog *n.* a low and sneaky person. ♦ *That dirty dog tried to get fresh with me!*

the **(dirty) dozens** *n.* a game of trading insulting remarks about relatives. (Originally black.) ♦ *Freddy is out giving the dozens to Marty.*

dirty joke 1. *n.* an obscene joke. ♦ *No dirty jokes around here. We get enough of that on television.* **2.** *n.* a very ugly or very stupid person. ♦ *Look at that face. That's a dirty joke.*

dirty laundry Go to dirty linen.

dirty linen AND **dirty laundry** *n.* scandal; unpleasant private matters. ♦ *I wish you wouldn't put our dirty linen out for everyone to see.* ♦ *She seems always to drag out her dirty linen whenever possible.*

dirty look *n.* a frown meant to show displeasure with something that has been said or done. ♦ *I gave him a dirty look, and he took his arm off my shoulder.*

dirty old man *n.* a lecherous old man. (Usually jocular.) ♦ *What a terrible joke. You are a dirty old man!*

dirty pool *n.* activities conducted using unfair or sneaky tactics. ♦ *When they start playing dirty pool, it's time to get mean.*

dirty word *n.* a curse word; an informal word concerned with sex or excrement. ♦ *Some kid got the microphone and yelled a dirty word into it.*

dirty work 1. *n.* menial work; hard work. ♦ *Why do I always get stuck with the dirty work?* **2.** *n.* sneaky activities. ♦ *I hear that Sam is up to his old dirty work again.*

dirty-minded *mod.* having a tendency to see the lewd or obscene aspects of anything; having a tendency to place an obscene interpretation on the words and actions of others. ♦ *Sam is sort of dirty-minded, but he wouldn't do anything really vile.*

dirty-mouth 1. *n.* a person who talks dirty. (See also bad-mouth.) ♦ *Some dirty-mouth yelled out the most obscene things during the meeting.* **2.** *tv.* to speak ill of someone or something. (See also bad-mouth.) ♦ *Please stop dirty-mouthing my friends.*

disc jockey Go to disk jockey.

discipline *n.* drugs. ♦ *She smokes this stuff she calls discipline. Smells like pot to me.*

discombobulate [dɪskəm'bɑbjəlet] *tv.* to confuse or perplex someone. ♦ *That kind of discussion discombobulates me something awful.*

discombobulated AND **discomboobulated** [dɪskəm'bɑbjəledəd AND dɪskəm'bubjəledəd] **1.** *mod.* confused. ♦ *I get completely discombobulated when I think of figures that big.* **2.** *mod.* alcohol intoxicated. ♦ *From the way she is walking, I'd say she is discombobulated.*

discomboobulated Go to discombobulated.

dish 1. *n.* a good-looking woman. ♦ *Now there's a good-looking dish.* **2.** *tv.* to criticize someone or something; to spread gossip about someone or something. (Probably short for dish the dirt. See also dis(s).) ♦ *The critics all dished the opening of the play mercilessly.*

dish sth **out 1.** *tv.* to serve up food to people. (Standard English.) ♦ *I'll dish it out, and you take it to the table.* **2.** *tv.* to distribute information, news, etc. ♦ *The press secretaries were dishing reports out as fast as they could write them.* **3.** *tv.* to give out trouble, scoldings, criticism, etc. ♦ *The boss was dishing criticism out this morning, and I really got it.*

dish the dirt *tv.* to spread gossip; to gossip. ♦ *Let's sit down, have a drink, and dish the dirt.*

dishrag Go to (limp) dishrag.

disk jockey AND **deejay; disc jockey; DJ** *n.* a radio announcer who introduces music from phonograph records. (The abbreviations are initialisms. Compare this with desk jockey. See also veejay.) ♦ *The disk jockey couldn't pronounce the name of the singing group.*

dispose of SO *in.* to kill someone. ♦ *The boss ordered Max to dispose of Lefty.*

dis(s) *tv.* to belittle someone; to show disrespect for someone. (From *disrespect*.) ♦ *Please stop dissing my little sister. She didn't do any of those things.*

dis(s) (on SO**)** ['dɪs...] *in.* to belittle [someone]; to show disrespect [for someone]. (From *disrespect*.) ♦ *Gary is such a complainer. All he does is diss.*

ditch 1. *tv.* to dispose of someone or something; to abandon someone or something. ♦ *The crooks ditched the car and continued on foot.* **2.** *tv. & in.* to skip or evade someone or something. ♦ *Pete ditched class today.*

dither ['dɪðɚ] *n.* a state of confusion. (See also in a dither.) ♦ *He can't seem to get out of this dither he's in.*

ditsy Go to ditzy.

ditz AND **ditzo** [dɪts(o)] *n.* a giddy, absent-minded person. ♦ *I'm getting to be such a ditz!* ♦ *What a ditzo!*

ditzo Go to ditz.

ditzy AND **ditsy** ['dɪtsi] *mod.* giddy; unaware; flighty. ♦ *You are such a ditzy geek!*

♦ *She's not the ditsy blonde she appears to be.*

dive *n.* a low drinking establishment; a cheap saloon. ♦ *I don't think I want to spend the whole evening in this dive.*

dive a muff *tv.* to perform oral sex on a woman. (Usually objectionable.) ♦ *Tod likes to dive a muff every now and then.*

divot ['dɪvət] *n.* a toupee; a partial toupee. (See also rug.) ♦ *His divot slipped, but no one laughed.*

divvy ['dɪvi] *n.* a share of something. (See also divvy sth up.) ♦ *How much is my divvy?*

divvy sth **up** *tv.* to divide something up. ♦ *They divvied up the fish and drove back to the city.*

dizzle a wild card word for words beginning with *D*, such as dawg. (Streets. Also for other words with initial *D*.) ♦ *Come on in, dizzle.*

dizzy *mod.* stupid; scatterbrained. ♦ *Who is that dizzy dame?*

DJ Go to disk jockey.

DL Go to the down low.

DNK [dɪŋk] did not keep (a medical appointment). (Medical.) ♦ *When that DNK calls for another appointment, make sure she knows when it is.*

do 1. *n.* a party; a social event. ♦ *I'm having a do for a friend this weekend. Would you like to come?* **2.** *tv. & in.* to use a drug or drugs in general. (See also do a line; do drugs.) ♦ *Taylor never stopped doing. She just switched from dust to splash.* **3.** AND **doo** *n.* a hairdo. ♦ *I can't go out in this rain and get my doo wet!* **4.** Go to (must) do. **5.** *in.* to serve (a purpose) well. (Usually with will or won't.) ♦ *This will do quite nicely.* **6.** Go to doo-doo. **7.** *tv.* to copulate [with] someone. (Usually objectionable.) ♦ *He did Martha, then he did Sue, then he did Gloria.*

do a bean count *tv.* to stare at female breasts, looking for hard nipples. (A play on bean-counter.) ♦ *He thinks that early spring is a great time for a bean count. No jackets and cool breezes!*

do a dump on so/sth AND **dump all over** so/sth; **dump on** so/sth *tv.* to criticize someone or something; to destroy someone or something. (From take a dump, to defecate.) ♦ *That rotten jerk really did a dump on my car. Look at that fender!* ♦ *She did a dump all over my report. Why do I bother.*

do a fade *tv.* to leave; to sneak away. ♦ *It's time for me to do a fade.*

do a job on so/sth **1.** *tv.* to ruin someone or something; to give someone or something a thorough working over. ♦ *The cops did a job on Rocko, but he still wouldn't talk.* **2.** Go to do a number on so.

do a line *tv.* to snort a dose of a powdered drug, usually cocaine. (Drugs.) ♦ *Ernie has to do a line about every four hours—night and day.*

do a number on so AND **do a job on** so (From do a number on sth.) *tv.* to harm or deceive someone. ♦ *The prof did a number on me because of my term paper.* ♦ *My local friendly plumber did a job on me cleaning out my drain.*

do a number on sth **1.** *tv.* to urinate or defecate on something. ♦ *Billy did a number on the bathroom floor.* **2.** *tv.* to damage or ruin something; to destroy something. ♦ *The truck really did a number on my car.*

do a slow burn *tv.* to be quietly angry. (See also slow burn.) ♦ *I did a slow burn while I was getting my money back.*

do a snow job on so *tv.* to deceive or confuse someone. ♦ *She thought she did a snow job on the teacher, but it backfired.*

do dope Go to do drugs.

do drugs AND **do dope** *tv.* to take drugs; to use drugs habitually. (Drugs and now general.) ♦ *Is she still doing dope?* ♦ *Rocko doesn't do drugs, and he doesn't drink.*

Do I have to draw (you) a picture? Go to Do I have to paint (you) a picture?

Do I have to paint (you) a picture? AND **Do I have to draw (you) a picture?** *interrog.* Do you understand yet?; How simple do I have to make it for you? ♦ *This is supposed to be easy. Do I have to paint a picture?* ♦ *Do I have to draw a picture? It's really simple if you pay attention!*

do one's (own) thing *tv.* to do what one wants; to do what pleases oneself no matter what others think. ♦ *I've always done my thing, and I don't see a great amount of benefit from it.*

do or die *mod.* having to try as hard as one can. ♦ *He has the obsessive do or die attitude.*

do's and don'ts *n.* the rules; the things that should be done and those that should not be done. ♦ *I must admit that a lot of the do's and don'ts don't make much sense to me either.*

do some bongs *tv.* to smoke some marijuana, usually with a water pipe. (Drugs. See also bong.) ♦ *All the kids think that doing bongs is the greatest thing on earth.*

do some fine coin *tv.* to make a large sum of money. ♦ *When I get my big break, I'm going to do some fine coin.*

do so **dirt** *tv.* to do ill to someone; to harm someone's reputation. ♦ *It seemed that the lawyer was determined to do me dirt right there in the courtroom.*

do so **in 1.** *tv.* to make someone tired. ♦ *That tennis game really did me in.* **2.** *tv.* to cheat someone; to take so in. ♦ *The scam artists did the widow in by talking her into giving them all the money in her bank account.* **3.** *tv.* to kill someone. ♦ *The crooks did the bank guard in.*

Do tell. *sent.* Is that so? (A disinterested way of holding up one end of a conversation.) ♦ *So, you're a dentist. Do tell.*

do the drink thing *tv.* to drink alcohol heavily. ♦ *He's been doing the drink thing quite a lot lately.*

do the drug thing *tv.* to be involved with drugs; to take drugs. ♦ *Man, you gotta stop doing the drug thing.*

do the trick *tv.* to do exactly what is needed. ♦ *Does this little tool do the trick?*

do time *tv.* to serve a sentence in prison; to serve a specific amount of time in prison. (Underworld. See also hard time.) ♦ *You'd* *better talk and talk fast if you don't want to do time.*

(Do) you eat with that mouth? AND **(Do) you kiss your momma with that mouth?** *interrog.* Do you actually eat with the mouth you use to talk that filth?; Do you actually use that filthy mouth to kiss your mother? (Said to someone who talks dirty all the time.) ♦ *That's a lot of foul talk. Do you eat with that mouth?* ♦ *What did you say? You kiss your mama with that mouth?*

(Do you) get my drift? *interrog.* Do you understand me? ♦ *Get my drift? Should I explain it again?*

(Do) you kiss your momma with that mouth? Go to (Do) you eat with that mouth?

DOA 1. *mod.* dead on arrival. (Hospitals. Initialism.) ♦ *The kid was DOA, and there was nothing anybody could do.* **2.** *n.* a person who is dead on arrival at a hospital. ♦ *They brought in two DOAs Saturday night.* **3.** *n.* phencyclidine (PCP). (Because it is deadly.) ♦ *Stay away from DOA. There's a good reason why it's called that.*

doc(s)-in-a-box *n.* a walk-in emergency health care center, as found in shopping centers. (See also McDoctor(s).) ♦ *I was cut and went immediately to the docs-in-a-box in the mall.*

dode [dod] *n.* a nerd; a simpleton. ♦ *My roommate is a loser. I was afraid I'd end up with a dode.*

dodge [dɑdʒ] *n.* a swindle; a scam; a deception. ♦ *What sort of dodge did you get flimflammed with?*

dodja *n.* marijuana. ♦ *Where can I score some dodja?*

dog 1. *n.* a foot. (Usually plural.) ♦ *I gotta get home and soak my dogs.* **2.** *n.* an ugly girl. (Rude and derogatory.) ♦ *I'm no dog, but I could wish for some changes.* **3.** *n.* something undesirable or worthless; merchandise that no one wants to buy. ♦ *Put the dogs out on the sale table so people will see them.* **4.** *n.* dog dung. (See also dog-doo.) ♦ *There's some dog on the lawn.* **5.** *tv.* to follow someone. ♦ *The cop dogged Lefty*

for a week. **6.** *tv.* to stay with one and haunt one. ♦ *Will this memory dog me all the days of my life?* **7.** *tv.* to eat something; to eat something as a dog eats. ♦ *He dogged his hamburger and ran out the door to catch the bus.* **8.** *tv.* to criticize someone or something. ♦ *Stop dogging me about every little thing!* **9.** AND **dawg; dogg.** *n.* buddy; friend. (Originally black. Also a term of address. The spelling variations do not affect pronunciation.) ♦ *Hey, dog! Tsup?* ♦ *Word, dog.*

dog and pony show *n.* a demonstration; a speech, skit, or other presentation that is presented often. ♦ *Willy was there with his dog and pony show about water safety.*

dog collar *n.* the collar worn by priests and some other clerics. ♦ *The man in the dog collar prayed for a while, then we ate dinner.*

dog meat *n.* a dead person. (Typically in a threat.) ♦ *Make one move, and you're dog meat.*

dog's mother *n.* a bitch; a bitchy person. (Euphemistic.) ♦ *If Sally insists on being a dog's mother on this matter, I'll tell her what I think of her.*

dog-dew Go to dog-doo.

dog-do Go to dog-doo.

dog-doo AND **dog-dew; dog-do** ['dɔgdu] *n.* dog dung. ♦ *When the snow melts, the sidewalks are covered with dog-doo.*

dog-eat-dog *mod.* cruel; highly competitive. ♦ *This is a dog-eat-dog world.*

dogface *n.* an infantry soldier. (World War II. Also a term of address.) ♦ *Get those dogfaces over here on the double.*

dog-fashion Go to dog-ways.

dogg Go to dog (sense 9).

doggo ['dɔgo] *mod.* hidden away; quiet and waiting. (See also lie doggo.) ♦ *This error was there, doggo, for nearly thirty years.*

doggone(d) ['dɔ'gɔn(d)] *mod.* darn(ed); damn(ed). ♦ *I sort of wish my hooter wasn't so doggone big.*

doggy bag ['dɔgibæg] *n.* a bag—supplied by a restaurant—in which uneaten food can be carried home. ♦ *We do not have doggy bags, but I can give you a styrofoam box. You must fill it yourself.*

dog-log *n.* a section of dog feces. (Contrived.) ♦ *I think I stepped in a a pile of dog-logs. Yuck!*

dognutz *n.* a friend; a buddy. (Streets. See also dog and nuts (sense 3).) ♦ *Come on, dognutz. Let's get moving.*

do-gooder [ˈdugʊdɚ] *n.* a person who is always trying to help others. (Often derogatory.) ♦ *I don't consider myself a do-gooder, but I try to help people.*

dog-style Go to dog-ways.

dog-ways AND **dog-fashion; dog-style** *mod.* [copulation] in the manner of dogs, that is, with the male approaching from the rear. ♦ *They did it dog-style, so they could both watch television.* ♦ *Dog-ways, mish, it's all good!*

doink *tv.* to steal something. ♦ *We doinked a few apples from the cart.*

doje *n.* the penis. (Probably from one of the many vague words for *thing*, such as *doogie*.) ♦ *Stop scratching your doje.*

doll 1. *n.* a pretty girl or woman. ♦ *Who's the doll I saw you with last night?* **2.** *n.* a pill. (Drugs. Usually plural.) ♦ *Taking dolls is different from shooting up.*

dome *n.* the head, especially if bald. ♦ *I need a new hat for my shiny dome.*

domed *mod.* hit on the head. (See also dome.) ♦ *I domed him accidentally with the ladder.*

dome-doctor *n.* a psychologist or psychiatrist. ♦ *The dome-doctor lets me talk while he keeps score.*

domino *n.* a one-hundred-dollar bill. ♦ *How many dominos is that going to cost?*

done and done *mod.* completed and finalized; signed, sealed, and delivered. ♦ *Sure I finished. It's done and done.*

done by mirrors AND **done with mirrors** *mod.* illusory; accomplished in a way that is purposefully deceptive. ♦ *He's not really smart. It's all done by mirrors.* ♦ *The whole budgetary process is done with mirrors.*

done deal *n.* a completed deal; something that is settled. ♦ *The sale of the property is a done deal. There is nothing that can be changed now.*

done for *mod.* lost; dead; doomed. ♦ *I'm sorry, this whole scheme is done for.*

done over *mod.* beat; outscored. ♦ *Bruno felt that Frank would get the idea if he was done over a little.*

done to a turn 1. *mod.* well-cooked; nicely cooked. ♦ *The entire meal was done to a turn.* **2.** *mod.* beaten. ♦ *When Wilbur's opponent was done to a turn, Wilbur was declared the winner.*

done with mirrors Go to done by mirrors.

dong *n.* the penis. (Usually objectionable.) ♦ *He held his hands over his dong and ran for the bedroom.*

donkey's breakfast *n.* something made of straw: a straw hat, a straw mattress, etc. ♦ *The tourist was wearing a red dress and had a donkey's breakfast on her head.*

donkey's years *n.* a long time. (From British colloquial.) ♦ *I haven't seen you in donkey's years.*

donnybrook *n.* a big argument; a brawl. ♦ *There was a big donnybrook at the concert, and the police were called.*

donorcycle *n.* a motorcycle. (Refers to the availability of donor organs after a motorcycle accident.) ♦ *Guess what happens when you ride a donorcycle without a helmet?*

Don't ask. *sent.* The answer is so depressing, you don't even want to hear it. ♦ *This has been a horrible day. How horrible, you say? Don't ask.*

Don't call us, we'll call you. *sent.* a formulaic expression given to job applicants who have just interviewed or auditioned for a job. ♦ *Stupendous, Gloria, just stupendous. What glamour and radiance! Don't call us, we'll call you.*

Don't get your bowels in an uproar! *exclam.* Don't get so excited! ♦ *Now, now, don't get your bowels in an uproar. Everything will be all right.*

don't give a hoot *tv.* don't care at all. (Folksy.) ♦ *She doesn't give a hoot if you go into town without her.*

don't give a rip *tv.* don't really care at all. ♦ *Go ahead! Ruin your life! I don't give a rip.*

Don't have a cow! *exclam.* Calm down!; Don't get so excited! (An utterance made famous in the television show, *The Simpsons*.) ♦ *Chill out, man! Don't have a cow!*

Don't I know it! *exclam.* That is really true! ♦ *Late? Don't I know it. I'm yawning like hot cakes.*

Don't make a federal case out of it! *sent.* Don't make such a fuss!; This isn't as important as you are making it. ♦ *So, I dropped a whole dozen eggs! I'll clean it up. Don't make a federal case out of it!*

Don't make me laugh! *exclam.* That is a stupid suggestion! ♦ *Don't make me laugh. Tom could never do that.*

Don't sweat it! *exclam.* Don't worry about it! ♦ *Don't sweat it! We'll take care of it.*

(Don't) you wish! *exclam.* I'm sure you wish it were true. ♦ *There's no school tomorrow? You wish!*

doo Go to do.

doobage Go to dubage.

doobie AND **dooby; duby** ['dubi] *n.* a marijuana cigarette; a fat marijuana cigarette. (Drugs.) ♦ *Frank sells doobies like they were candy.* ♦ *Can you spare me a dooby, brother?*

doodad ['dudæd] *n.* a name for a gadget. ♦ *I don't know what they're called. If they had names, they wouldn't be doodads, now would they?*

doodle 1. *n.* the penis. (Usually objectionable.) ♦ *Put your doodle away, Jimmy, and flush the toilet.* **2.** *n.* feces, especially a baby's feces. (Baby talk.) ♦ *Billy's got doodle in his diapers.* **3.** *in.* to defecate. (See also doo-doo. Baby talk.) ♦ *The dog doodled on the back porch.*

doodly-shit Go to diddly-shit.

(doodly-)squat Go to diddly-squat.

doo-doo 1. *n.* dung; fecal material. ♦ *There's dog doo-doo on your shoe.* **2.** *in.* to defecate. ♦ *Mommy, the cat's doo-dooing in the kitchen!*

doofer AND **dufer** ['dufɚ] *n.* a (found or borrowed) cigarette saved for smoking at another time. (It will *do for* later.) ♦ *He takes two fags, one to smoke and a dufer.*

doofus AND **duffis** ['dufəs] *n.* a jerk; a nerd. ♦ *Get out, doofus!* ♦ *My roommate is a duffis and I'm tired of putting up with her.*

doohickey Go to doojigger.

doojigger AND **doohickey; doohickie** ['dudʒɪgɚ AND 'duhɪki] *n.* a name for a gadget. ♦ *Toss me that little red doohickey, will you?*

dook AND **duke** [duk] **1.** *mod.* really bad. (Probably related to duky. See also the entry for duke.) ♦ *This day was really dook!* **2.** *in.* to defecate. ♦ *Mom, I gotta dook.* **3.** to perform anal sex. (Offensive if understood.) ♦ *The dude wanted to dook me!*

doorag *n.* a headcap that covers and protects a hairdo. ♦ *He caught his doorag on a branch.*

doormat *n.* a weak-willed person who is abused by others. ♦ *Why do people treat me like a doormat?*

doosie AND **doozie; doozy** ['duzi] *n.* something extraordinary, good or bad. ♦ *The trade show was a real doozy this year.*

doowacky ['dumæki] **1.** *n.* a thing; a nameless gadget. ♦ *Is this your doowacky? I was going to throw it away.* **2.** *n.* money. ♦ *You got some doowacky I can borrow?*

doozie Go to doosie.

doozy Go to doosie.

dope 1. *n.* a stupid person. ♦ *That dope has done it again!* **2.** *n.* drugs in general; marijuana. ♦ *How much dope do you do in a week anyway?* **3.** *n.* news; information; scuttlebutt. ♦ *I got some dope on the tavern fire if you want to hear it.* **4.** *mod.* best; most excellent. ♦ *We had a great time there. It was dope and dudical.*

dope fiend *n.* a dope addict; someone heavily addicted to a drug who will do anything to get it. ♦ *Some dope fiend broke into the shop and stole the cash register.*

dope sth **out** *tv.* to figure out something from the dope (information) available. ♦ *I think I can dope this thing out from the evidence available.*

dope up 1. *in.* to inject drugs; to take a dose of a narcotic. (Drugs.) ♦ *I'm hurting, man, I gotta dope up, now!* **2.** *in.* to purchase a supply of drugs. (Drugs.) ♦ *Frank is doping up, himself. He doesn't grow it himself, you know.*

dopey 1. *mod.* stupid. ♦ *That was a dopey thing to do.* **2.** *mod.* sleepy. ♦ *The soft music made him dopey.* **3.** *mod.* drug intoxicated. ♦ *The chick is too dopey to drive. See that she gets home, Ralphy, huh?*

do-re-me Go to do-re-mi.

do-re-mi AND **do-re-me** ['do're'mi] *n.* money. (From dough.) ♦ *It takes too much do-re-mi to live in this part of town.*

dorf [dorf] *n.* a stupid person; a weird person. ♦ *You are a prize-winning dorf.*

dork [dork] **1.** *n.* the penis. (Usually objectionable.) ♦ *Paul told a joke about a dork, but everybody just sat there and looked straight ahead.* **2.** *n.* a jerk; a strange person. (See also megadork.) ♦ *Ye gods, Sally! You are a dork!*

dork off *in.* to waste time; to goof off. ♦ *The whole class was dorking off and the teacher got furious.*

dorkmeier AND **dorkmunder** ['dorkmaɪr AND 'dorkməndɚ] *n.* a total jerk; a simpleton. (An elaboration of dork sense 2.) ♦ *Ellen, stop acting like such a dorkmeier!* ♦ *Where did you get that haircut? You look like a dorkmunder!*

dorkmunder Go to dorkmeier.

dorkus maximus ['dorkəs 'mæksɪməs] *n.* a simpleton or fool; a great fool. ♦ *Tim is now the dorkus maximus of our dorm since he broke the dorm's television set.*

dorky *mod.* tacky, stupid, or awkward. (From dork.) ♦ *I don't want any of this dorky food!*

dorm *n.* a dormitory. ♦ *Fred lives in a co-ed dorm.*

dosia *n.* marijuana. ♦ *He's got some good dosia in his knapsack.*

doss down (for some time**)** *in.* to lie down to sleep for a period of time. ♦ *Chuck dossed down for a few hours before the evening performance.*

double 1. *n.* a drink consisting of two servings of liquor. ♦ *Sam usually has two doubles on the way home.* **2.** Go to double saw(buck).

double buffalo Go to double nickels.

double cross 1. *tv.* to betray someone. (Originally a more complicated switching of sides in a conspiracy wherein the double-crosser sides with the victim of the conspiracy—against the original conspirator.) ♦ *Don't even think about double crossing me!* **2.** *n.* a betrayal. (See comments with sense 1.) ♦ *It's one double cross Frank is sorry about.*

double digits *n.* the range of numerals from 10 though 99. ♦ *When Billy moved into the double digits, he had some behavior problems, but when he was nineteen he sort of straightened out.*

double nickels AND **double buffalo** *n.* the number fifty-five; the fifty-five-mile-per-hour speed limit. (Originally citizens band radio. The buffalo is on one side of the nickel.) ♦ *You'd better travel right on those double nickels in through here. The bears are hungry.* ♦ *Double buffalo is for trucks. You can go seventy.*

double saw(buck) AND **double; dub** *n.* a twenty-dollar bill. (See also sawbuck.) ♦ *This whole thing only cost a double sawbuck.* ♦ *Can you loan me a dub?*

double six *n.* a year; a pair of six-month periods. (Streets.) ♦ *Johnny spent a double six in the slammer.*

double take *n.* a surprised second look at something. ♦ *Fred did a double take, then recognized Britney.*

double whammy ['dəbl̩ 'ʍæmi] *n.* a double portion of something, especially something troublesome. (From *Li'l Abner*, a comic strip by Al Capp.) ♦ *This morning was bad, but this afternoon the boss gave us a double whammy.*

double-bagger 1. *n.* a hit good for two bases in baseball. ♦ *Wilbur hit a nice double-bagger in the top of the fourth.* **2.** *n.* a very ugly person. (Cruel. With a face so ugly that it takes two paper bags to conceal it. See also Bag your face!; brown bag it; triple-bagger; coyote-ugly.) ♦ *Fred is what I would call a double-bagger. What a mug!*

double-barreled slingshot *n.* a brassiere. ♦ *Did you see the size of that double-barreled slingshot hanging on that clothesline?*

double-crosser *n.* a person who betrays someone. (Often with *dirty.* See comments at double cross.) ♦ *You dirty, low-down double-crosser, you!*

double-decker 1. *n.* a two-level bus. ♦ *Some double-deckers don't have tops.* **2.** *n.* a sandwich of two layers. ♦ *He put away a giant double-decker and a glass of milk.*

double-deuces *n.* the number twenty-two. ♦ *The National Weather Service says it's going down to the double-deuces tonight.*

double-dipper 1. *n.* a person who collects two salaries; a federal employee who collects a federal pension and Social Security. ♦ *The double-dippers say they weren't doing anything wrong.* **2.** *n.* a person who dips a chip or veggie into a dip or sauce after having taken a bite of the chip or veggie, thus risking the introduction of germs into the dip. ♦ *I always watch the snack table to make sure there are no double-dippers.*

double-dome 1. *n.* an intellectual. ♦ *It's not that what the double-domes say is wrong, it's that they are so sure that they are right that scares me.* **2.** *mod.* intellectual. ♦ *Most kids need to be exposed to double-dome profs at college for a while.*

double-gaited *mod.* weird; eccentric. ♦ *Carl is a little double-gaited at times. Tries too hard for a laugh.*

double-trouble *n.* a very troublesome thing or person. ♦ *Oh, oh. Here comes double-trouble.*

douche bag 1. *n.* a wretched and disgusting person. (Rude and derogatory.) ♦ *Don't be a douche bag. Pick up your things and go home, Chuck.* **2.** *n.* an ugly girl or woman. (Rude and derogatory.) ♦ *Look at that face! What a douche bag!*

dough [do] *n.* money. (See also bread.) ♦ *I got a lot of dough for that ring I found.*

dough head *n.* a nerd; a simpleton. ♦ *Tom, don't be such a dough head. Read the instructions and do it right.*

doughboys *n.* the female breasts. ♦ *What a nice pair of doughboys!*

dove [dəv] *n.* someone who supports a peace-seeking U.S. defense policy. (Compare this with hawk.) ♦ *The doves want to sell the tanks and distribute the money to the poor.*

down 1. *mod.* depressed; melancholy. (See also down with sth.) ♦ *I feel sort of down today.* **2.** *mod.* [of a machine] inoperative. (Originally said of a computer.) ♦ *The system is down. Come back later.* **3.** *tv.* to eat or drink something down quickly. ♦ *She downed her sandwich in record time.* **4.** *tv.* to throw someone down, as in wrestling; to knock someone down as in a fight. ♦ *Wilbur downed his opponent and won the match.* **5.** *mod.* behind in a score. ♦ *They're twenty points down, and it looks like the Adamsville team has won.* **6.** *mod.* finished; completed; behind one. ♦ *One down and three to go.* **7.** *mod.* learned; memorized. (From sense 6.) ♦ *I've got the dates down, but not the names.* **8.** *mod.* okay; satisfactory; cool; in agreement. (See also down (with so).) ♦ *We had a fight, but we're down now.* **9.** *mod.* prepared; knowledgeable. (From senses 7 and 8.) ♦ *Are you down for the test tomorrow?* **10.** *mod.* alcohol intoxicated. ♦ *Five beers and he was down.* **11.** Go to downer.

down for the count *mod.* inactive for the duration (of something). (From boxing.) ♦ *I've got a terrible cold, and I think I'm down for the count.*

the down low AND **the DL** the information or explanation; the lowdown. (Streets.) ♦ *Give me the haps. What the down low?*

down the drain *mod.* gone; wasted. ♦ *A lot of money went down the drain in that Wilson deal.*

Down the hatch! *exclam.* Let's drink it! (A drinking toast. See also hatch.) ♦ *Down the hatch! Have another?*

down time *n.* the time when a computer is not operating. (Compare this with up time.) ♦ *I can't afford a lot of down time in the system I buy.*

down to the wire *mod.* until the very last minute. ♦ *We went right down to the wire on that one.*

down trip *n.* any bad experience. (See also downer.) ♦ *My vacation was a down trip.*

down under *n.* the area of Australia; Australia. ♦ *I've always wanted to visit down under.*

down (with so) *mod.* friends with someone; to be okay or on good terms with someone. (*Down* = okay.) ♦ *It's okay. I'm down with Chuck.*

down with sth 1. *mod.* comfortable with something; comfortable. (Usually with get.) ♦ *Let's get down with some good music.* **2.** *mod.* ill with something; sick in bed with something. ♦ *I was down with the flu for two weeks.*

down with the haps *mod.* knowing what's happening; comfortable with what's happening. (Streets.) ♦ *Tell me what's going on! I gotta be down with the haps.*

downbeat *mod.* cool; easygoing. (Compare this with upbeat.) ♦ *He is sort of a downbeat character—no stress.*

downer AND **down; downie 1.** *n.* a barbiturate or a tranquilizer. (Drugs.) ♦ *Too much booze with those downers, and you're dead.* **2.** *n.* a bad drug experience; a down trip. (Drugs.) ♦ *That stuff you gave me was a real downer.* **3.** *n.* a depressing event; a bad situation; a down trip. ♦ *These cloudy days are always downers.*

downie Go to downer.

doxy ['dɑksi] *n.* a gangster's woman. (Underworld.) ♦ *Lefty's good-looking doxy dropped off this package. It's ticking.*

dozens Go to the (dirty) dozens.

DQ *n.* Dairy Queen, a trade name for a franchise fast-food store specializing in frozen desserts. (Initialism. Teens and collegiate.) ♦ *Let's go to DQ, okay?*

draft board *n.* a tavern; a saloon. (Alludes to draft beer.) ♦ *Let's stop in the local draft board and toss a couple.*

drafty *n.* a draft beer; beer. ♦ *How about a cold drafty?*

drag 1. *n.* something dull and boring. ♦ *What a drag. Let's go someplace interesting.* **2.** *n.* an annoying person; a burdensome person. (See also schlep.) ♦ *Gert could sure be a drag when she wanted.* **3.** *n.* a (female) date. ♦ *You got a drag for the dance yet?* **4.** *n.* a puff of a cigarette. ♦ *One more drag and he coughed for a while and stubbed out the fag.* **5.** *tv.* to pull or puff on a cigarette. ♦ *She dragged a couple and sat in the funk for a while.* **6.** *tv.* to race a car against someone; to race someone in a car. ♦ *I'm planning to drag you at the fairgrounds next Saturday. Better be there.*

drag ass around *in.* to go around looking very sad and depressed. (Usually objectionable.) ♦ *Why do you drag ass around all the time, Tom?*

drag ass (out of somewhere**)** Go to bag ass (out of somewhere).

a **drag (on so)** *n.* a burden (to someone). ♦ *I wish you wouldn't be such a drag on your friends.*

a **drag (on sth)** *in.* a puff or any kind of cigarette. ♦ *She had a drag on her cigarette and crushed it out on the sidewalk.*

dragged *mod.* anxious or frightened after smoking marijuana. (Drugs.) ♦ *The kid was dragged. You could tell he didn't have much experience with the real world.*

dragged out *mod.* exhausted; worn-out. ♦ *I feel so dragged out. I think I need some iron.*

draggin'-wagon *n.* a fast car; a car customized for racing. ♦ *Your draggin'-wagon can't be driven in town, can it?*

dragon *n.* the penis. (See also drain the dragon = urinate.) ♦ *I think he's in love with his dragon.*

drain the bilge *tv.* to empty one's stomach; to vomit. ♦ *Fred left quickly to drain the bilge.*

drain the dragon *tv.* [for a male] to urinate. (See also dragon = penis.) ♦ *Bobby? He went to drain the dragon.*

Drat! [dræt] *exclam.* Damn! ♦ *Oh, drat! Another broken nail!*

dreamboat *n.* just the kind of lover one has always dreamed of. (Also a term of address.) ♦ *Oh, Pete is my dreamboat.*

dreck [drɛk] *n.* dirt; garbage; feces. (From German via Yiddish.) ♦ *I've had enough of this dreck around here. Clean it up, or I'm leaving.*

dressed to kill *mod.* dressed in fancy or stylish clothes to impress someone. ♦ *I'm never dressed to kill. I just try to be neat.*

dressed to the nines AND **dressed to the teeth** *mod.* dressed very stylishly with nothing overlooked. (See also the whole nine yards for the *nine*.) ♦ *She always goes out dressed to the nines.* ♦ *Clare is usually dressed to the teeth in order to impress people.*

dressed to the teeth Go to dressed to the nines.

the **drink** *n.* the water of the ocean, lake, pond, etc. ♦ *Stay away from the edge of the boat unless you want to fall in the drink.*

Drink up! *exclam.* Finish your drink!; Finish that drink, and we'll have another! ♦ *Okay, drink up! It's closing time.*

drinkage *n.* drinking; drinks. ♦ *The school tried to outlaw drinkage on campus but failed.*

drinkies *n.* drinks; liquor. ♦ *Okay, kids, it's drinkies all around.*

drinkypoo ['drɪŋkipu] *n.* a little drink of liquor. ♦ *Wouldn't you like just one more drinkypoo of Madeira?*

drip *n.* an oaf; a nerd. ♦ *Bob is a drip, I guess, but he's harmless.*

drippy *mod.* weak; ineffective; undesirable. ♦ *Bob can be so drippy without even trying.*

drive so **around the bend** *tv.* to drive someone crazy. (See also (a)round the bend.) ♦ *This tax stuff is about to drive me around the bend.*

drive so **bonkers** AND **drive** so **nuts** *tv.* to drive someone crazy. (See also bonkers; nuts.) ♦ *Shat up! You're driving me bonkers.* ♦ *These tax forms are driving me nuts.*

drive so **nuts** Go to drive so bonkers.

drive so **up the wall** *tv.* to frustrate someone; to drive someone to distraction. ♦ *These days of waiting drive me up the wall.*

drive the big bus AND **drive the porcelain bus; ride the porcelain bus** *tv.* to vomit into the toilet. ♦ *Harry's in the john driving the big bus.* ♦ *I guess that "drive the porcelain bus" refers to holding onto the toilet seat while you vomit.*

drive the porcelain bus Go to drive the big bus.

dro AND **hydro** *n.* hydroponically grown marijuana. ♦ *He raises hydro in his basement.* ♦ *He's got some kickin' dro. Want a piece?*

droid [drɔɪd] *n.* a robot-like person; a nerd. (From *android*.) ♦ *Beavis is as close to a droid as we'll ever see.*

droob AND **drube** [drub] *n.* a dullard; an oaf. ♦ *Who's the droob standing by the punch bowl?*

drool (all) over so/sth *in.* to show enormous desire for someone or something. ♦ *Sam was drooling over Martha like a lovesick calf.*

drool-proof *mod.* can withstand idiots who drool. (Of well-written software that even droolings idiots can operate without crashing.) ♦ *This software package is drool-proof. Even my grandmother could use it.*

droopy-drawers *n.* someone—usually a child—whose pants are falling down. (Also a term of address.) ♦ *Hey, droopy-drawers, pull up your pants.*

drop 1. *tv.* to kill someone or something. ♦ *Lefty tried to drop the leader of the gang.* **2.** *in.* to get arrested. (Underworld.) ♦ *Sam dropped, but Mr. Gutman got him off.* **3.** *tv.* to knock someone down. ♦ *Jim dropped Willard with a punch to the shoulder.* **4.** *n.* a small drink of liquor; a small serving of liquor. ♦ *I'll take just another drop of that dew, if you don't mind.* **5.** *n.* a place at which drugs, alcohol, or other contraband is left to be claimed by the recipient. ♦ *They switched drops constantly just in case of discovery.* **6.** *tv.* to take a drug, specifically acid. (Drugs.) ♦ *Ted dropped some stuff and went on a trip.*

drop a bomb(shell) Go to drop a brick.

drop a bop *tv.* to take a drug in pill form. (See also bop.) ♦ *Wanna come over and drop a bop or two?*

drop a brick AND **drop a bomb(shell)** *tv.* to reveal startling information. ♦ *Britney came in and dropped a brick that scared us all.* ♦ *She dropped a bombshell when she told us she was married again.*

drop a bundle (on so) *tv.* to spend a lot of money pleasing or entertaining someone. ♦ *I dropped a bundle on the candidate, and it didn't help me at all.*

drop a bundle (on sth) *tv.* to pay a lot of money for something. ♦ *Pete dropped a bundle on this car.*

drop a dime *tv.* to inform the police of criminal activity. (Underworld. See explanation at dime-dropper.) ♦ *No, almost anybody will drop a dime these days.*

Drop dead! *exclam.* No!; Beat it!; Go away and don't bother me! ♦ *I don't care. Just drop dead!*

Drop it! *exclam.* Forget it!; Never mind! ♦ *Drop it! I should never have brought it up.*

drop one's cookies *tv.* to empty one's stomach; to vomit. (See also toss one's cookies.) ♦ *If you feel like you're going to drop your cookies, don't do it on the carpet.*

drop one's teeth *tv.* to react with great surprise. ♦ *I almost dropped my teeth when she told me her news.*

drop out 1. *in.* to withdraw from a conventional lifestyle. ♦ *Sometimes I just want to drop out and raise pigs or something.* **2.** *in.* to drop out of school or some organization. ♦ *Don't drop out of school. You'll regret it.* **3.** AND **dropout** *n.* someone who has dropped out of school. ♦ *Dropouts may find it very hard to get a job.*

drop so *tv.* to knock someone down; to punch and knock down a person. ♦ *Fred dropped Mooshoo with one punch to the jaw.*

drop so/sth like a hot potato *tv.* to disassociate oneself with someone or something instantly. ♦ *When we learned of the conviction, we dropped him like a hot potato.*

drop so some knowledge *tv.* to give someone some information. ♦ *Come on, What's the 411. Drop some knowledge on me.*

drop the ball *tv.* to fail at something; to allow something to fail. ♦ *I didn't want to be the one who dropped the ball, but I knew that someone would flub up.*

Drop you! *exclam.* Fuck you! (The obvious euphemism used in *West Side Story,* set in the mid-1900s.) ♦ *Gee, Officer Krupke, drop you!*

drop-dead 1. *mod.* stunning enough to make one drop dead. (Not literal.) ♦ *I had my living room done in a bright drop-dead red that makes your blood run cold!* **2.** *mod.* rude, as if telling someone to drop dead. ♦ *I couldn't stand the boss's drop-dead attitude, so I quit.*

drop-dead gorgeous *mod.* very good looking. ♦ *Perry's girlfriend is drop-dead gorgeous. How can a twit like him hold onto a looker like that?*

drop-dead list *n.* an imaginary list of annoying people whom one could live happily without. ♦ *You are right at the top of my drop-dead list.*

dropped *mod.* arrested. ♦ *Harry the Horse was dropped only once last year.*

drube Go to droob.

drug 1. *in.* to use drugs. (Drugs.) ♦ *There is no way that she will stop drugging by herself.* **2.** AND **drug out** *mod.* down; depressed. ♦ *We are all drug out after that meeting.*

drug lord *n.* a drug dealer high up in the distribution chain. ♦ *The drug lords like Mr. Big seem never to get arrested.*

drug out Go to drug.

druggie AND **druggy** *n.* a drug addict or user. ♦ *There are too many druggies in this neighborhood.*

drughead *n.* a heavy drug user; an addict. (Drugs.) ♦ *They find a drughead in the river about once a month.*

drugola [drəg'olə] *n.* a bribe paid by drug dealers to the police for protection. (Patterned on payola.) ♦ *Frank pays a little drugola, but mostly the cops never come into this area anyway.*

drugstore cowboy *n.* a male who hangs around drugstores and other public places trying to impress women. ♦ *You don't see the old drugstore cowboys around this part of town anymore.*

drunk *n.* [of baseball bases] loaded. (See also loaded (sense 1).) ♦ *We're at the bottom of the fifth and the bases are drunk.*

drunk back *mod.* alcohol intoxicated; very drunk. ♦ *Larry was drunk back and couldn't drive us home.*

drunk tank *n.* a jail cell where drunks are kept. (See also junk tank.) ♦ *They hose down the drunk tank every hour on Friday and Saturday nights.*

dry 1. *mod.* sober; no longer alcohol intoxicated. ♦ *How long will Ernie stay dry, do you think?* **2.** *n.* a prohibitionist; an abstainer from alcohol. ♦ *The drys are in an increasing majority.* **3.** *mod.* having to do with a region where alcoholic beverages cannot be purchased. (Compare this with wet.) ♦ *Some small towns are dry, but not many.*

Dry up! *exclam.* Shut up!; Go away and don't bother me! ♦ *Aw, dry up! I've heard enough.*

dry-as-dust *mod.* dull; lifeless. ♦ *I can't take another one of his dry-as-dust lectures.*

dub [dəb] **1.** *tv. & in.* to duplicate something; to copy something. ♦ *Dub this and keep a copy yourself.* **2.** *n.* a duplicate; a copy. ♦ *The dub was so poor we couldn't understand the dialogue.* **3.** Go to double saw(buck).

dubage AND **doobage** ['dubɪdʒ] *n.* drugs; marijuana. (See also doobie.) ♦ *I detect the smell of dubage in the hallway!*

dub-dub-dub AND **dubya-dubya-dubya** *n.* double-u, double-u, double-u, the letters WWW found in World Wide Web addresses. (The second version is merely a colloquial pronunciation of double-u, and neither is commonly written or printed.) ♦ *Our address is dub-dub-dub dot reindeer dot com.*

duby Go to doobie.

dubya-dubya-dubya Go to dub-dub-dub.

ducats AND **duc-ducs** ['dəkəts AND 'dəkdəks] *n.* money. (See also gold.) ♦ *Who's got enough ducats to pay for the tickets?* ♦ *I don't have enough duc-ducs to buy the ducks.*

duc-ducs Go to ducats.

duck 1. *n.* a male urinal bedpan. (Hospitals.) ♦ *Somebody in room 212 needs a duck.* **2.** *tv.* to avoid someone or something. ♦ *Clare is ducking her responsibility.* **3.** Go to deduck. **4.** *n.* a ticket. (Probably akin to ducats.) ♦ *Did you buy the ducks early, or do we have to stand in line?*

duck-butt 1. *n.* a very large pair of buttocks. (Use with caution.) ♦ *What an enormous duck-butt!* **2.** AND **dusty butt** *n.* a short person, especially someone with large buttocks. (Rude and derogatory.) ♦ *The duck-butt who just came in reminds me of somebody I once knew.*

duck-squeezer *n.* someone with strong concerns about the environment and conservation, especially rescuing oil-covered ducks. (See also eagle freak.) ♦ *Some duck-squeezers were complaining about what the new dam might do.*

ducky *mod.* okay; good. (Often used sarcastically.) ♦ *Now, isn't that just ducky?*

dud [dəd] *n.* a failure; something that fails to perform as intended. (See also duds.) ♦ *The whole idea turned out to be a dud.*

dude [dud] **1.** *n.* a male friend; a guy. (Also a term of address. There is no evidence as to the origin of this term. The earliest uses refer to a male who is carefully and meticulously dressed. Some people derive dude from *dud.* See also dude up.) ♦ *Who's the dude with the cowboy boots?* **2.** *mod.* excellent. (See also dudical.) ♦ *The game was severely dude! We won!*

dude (oneself) up *tv.* to dress in fancy or stylish clothing. ♦ *Why don't you dude yourself up so we can go out tonight?*

dude up *in.* to dress up. (Possibly as in *dood-ed up.*) ♦ *Let's get all duded up and go out.*

duded up *mod.* dressed up. ♦ *He hates fancy clothes. He didn't even get duded up for his own wedding.*

dudette ['dudɛt] *n.* a young woman; the feminine of dude. ♦ *The place was filled with good-looking dudettes, just waiting for the right guy to come along.*

dudical ['dudɪkl̩] *mod.* really good. (Derived from dude.) ♦ *It is truly dudical to see you here, Dave.*

duds [dədz] *n.* clothes. (Always plural.) ♦ *Are those new duds?*

dufer Go to doofer.

duff [dəf] *n.* the buttocks. ♦ *Don't you get tired of sitting around on your duff?*

duffer ['dəfɚ] **1.** *n.* a foolish oaf; a bumbler. ♦ *Pete's just a duffer—he's not really serious at it.* **2.** *n.* an unskilled golfer. ♦ *Those duffers up ahead are holding up the game.*

duffis Go to doofus.

duke 1. *in.* to empty one's stomach; to vomit. (Collegiate. Rhymes with puke. See also dukes.) ♦ *She's in the john, duking like a goat.* **2.** Go to dook.

duke it out *phr.* to have a fistfight. ♦ *John told George to meet him in the alley so they could duke it out.*

duke so out *tv.* to knock someone out. (See also dukes.) ♦ *Wilbur tried to duke the guy out first.*

dukes 1. *n.* the fists. ♦ *Okay, brother, put your dukes up.* **2.** *n.* the knees. ♦ *He went down on his dukes and prayed for all sorts of good stuff.*

duky ['duki] *n.* feces. (Originally black and primarily juvenile. Possibly from the juvenile euphemism *duty* = job = bowel movement.) ♦ *Mommy, there's duky in Jimmy's diaper.*

dull as dishwater Go to (as) dull as dishwater.

dull roar *n.* a relatively quiet degree of noisiness. ♦ *Try to keep it at a dull roar if you can.*

dullsville ['dəlzvɪl] **1.** *n.* a dull place. ♦ *This place is just dullsville!* **2.** *n.* something dull. ♦ *When each movie I see turns into dullsville, I want to give up seeing them.*

dumb bunny *n.* a stupid person; an oaf. ♦ *Who's the dumb bunny in the double-knits?*

dumb cluck *n.* a stupid oaf; a person as stupid as a chicken. ♦ *Sally is not a dumb cluck, but she is sort of slow.*

dumb Dora *n.* a stupid woman; a giddy woman. ♦ *Who's the dumb Dora with the blonde hair and long fingernails?*

dumb ox *n.* a large and stupid person, usually a man. ♦ *Do you think I'm going to argue with that big dumb ox?*

dumb-ass AND **stupid-ass 1.** *mod.* stupid; dumb. (Usually derogatory.) ♦ *That was a real dumb-ass thing to do.* ♦ *That is so stupid-ass!* **2.** *n.* a stupid person. (Rude and derogatory.) ♦ *Don't be such a dumb-ass! You know what I mean!*

dumbbell *n.* a stupid oaf. (Also a rude term of address.) ♦ *I'm afraid I come on like a dumbbell sometimes.*

dumb-dodo ['dəm'dodo] *n.* a very stupid person. ♦ *What a dumb-dodo you are!*

dumb-dumb AND **dum-dum** *n.* a stupid oaf; a dullard. ♦ *Marvin is no dum-dum. He just looks that way.*

dumbhead *n.* a stupid person. ♦ *Bob is no dumbhead, but he sure is strange.*

dumbo ['dəmbo] **1.** *n.* a stupid oaf. (Also a rude term of address.) ♦ *Say, dumbo, could you move out of the way?* **2.** *n.* someone with large ears. (Also a rude term of address. The name of a cartoon character elephant whose ears were large enough to fly with.) ♦ *Wow, look at that dumbo with size twenty ears!*

dumbshit 1. *n.* a very stupid person. (Rude and derogatory.) ♦ *He's a dumbshit. He can't do any better than that.* **2.** *mod.* stupid; dumb. (Usually objectionable.) ♦ *That was really a dumbshit thing to do.*

dumbski ['dəmski] **1.** *n.* a stupid person. ♦ *He's not the dumbski he seems to be.* **2.** *mod.* stupid; dumb. ♦ *It is not a dumbski idea!*

dum-dum Go to dumb-dumb.

dummy 1. *n.* an empty liquor or beer bottle. ♦ *Toss your dummies over here, and I'll put them in the bin.* **2.** *n.* a cigarette butt. ♦ *The guy tossed a dummy out the window of his car.* **3.** *n.* a stupid person. (Rude and derogatory.) ♦ *Don't be such a dummy.* **4.** *n.* the penis. (Usually objectionable.) ♦ *He held his hands over his little dummy and ran for the bedroom.*

dummy up *in.* to refuse to talk. (Underworld. See also clam up.) ♦ *Rocko dummied up right away. He's a real thoroughbred.*

dump 1. *tv. & in.* to empty one's stomach; to vomit. ♦ *She turned green, and I knew she was going to dump.* **2.** *in.* to defecate. (Usually objectionable. See also dump one's load.) ♦ *He dumped and then came back.* **3.** *n.* an act of defecation. (Usually objectionable.) ♦ *He had a dump and then came back.* **4.** *n.* a low or cheap establishment; a joint. ♦ *My mama didn't raise me to spend the rest of my days in a run-down dump like this.*

dump all over so/sth Go to do a dump on so/sth.

Dump it. *tv.* throw it away. ♦ *We don't need it. Get rid of it! Dump it!*

dump on so **1.** *in.* to scold someone severely. ♦ *Please, don't dump on me. I've had a hard day.* **2.** *in.* to place a large burden of guilt or grief on someone; to give someone all of one's troubles. ♦ *She had had a bad day, so she dumped on me for about an hour.*

dump on so/sth **1.** *in.* to snow on someone or something. ♦ *Well, it dumped on us again last night.* **2.** Go to do a dump on so/sth.

dump one's **load 1.** *tv.* to empty one's stomach; to vomit. ♦ *He's in the john dumping his load.* **2.** *tv.* to defecate. (Usually objectionable. Also with a load.) ♦ *He had to go dump a load.*

dumped on 1. *mod.* maligned; abused. (From take a dump = defecate.) ♦ *I really feel dumped on.* **2.** *mod.* snowed on. ♦ *The entire Midwest was dumped on with about ten inches of snow.*

dupe 1. *n.* a potential victim of a confidence trick; a patsy. ♦ *The crooks found a good dupe and started their scheme.* **2.** *tv.* to trick someone; to swindle someone. ♦ *I did not try to dupe you. It was an honest mistake.* **3.** *n.* a duplicate; a copy. ♦ *I've got a dupe in the files.* **4.** *tv.* to duplicate something; to copy something. ♦ *Just a minute, I have to dupe a contract for the boss.*

durge *n.* a moron; a jerk. ♦ *You incredible durge! What were you thinking?*

dust 1. *in.* to leave; to depart. ♦ *They dusted out of there at about midnight.* **2.** *tv.* to defeat someone; to win out over someone. ♦ *We dusted the other team, eighty-seven to fifty-four.* **3.** *tv.* to kill someone. (Underworld.) ♦ *The gang set out to dust the witnesses but got only one of them.* **4.** *n.* fine tobacco for rolling cigarettes. (Prisons.) ♦ *How about trading a little dust for this candy bar?* **5.** *n.* a powdered drug: heroin, phencyclidine (PCP), cocaine; fine cannabis. (Drugs.) ♦ *It's the dust that can really do you damage.* **6.** *tv.* to add a powdered drug to the end of a (tobacco or cannabis) cigarette. (Drugs.) ♦ *Pete dusted one, then lit it up.* **7.** *n.* worthless matter. ♦ *John said that Frank was going* to be dust if Mr. Gutman ever heard about what happened.

dust of angels Go to angel dust.

dust so **off** *tv.* to give someone a good pounding or beating. ♦ *Bob dusted off Larry; then he started for Tom.*

dust so's **pants** *tv.* to spank someone, usually a child. ♦ *My dad will dust my pants if he hears about this.*

duster *n.* the buttocks. (See also rusty-dusty.) ♦ *She fell down right on her duster.*

dust-up *n.* a fight. ♦ *There was a dust-up at the party that ruined the evening for everyone.*

dusty butt Go to duck-butt.

the **Dutch act** AND the **Dutch cure** *n.* suicide. ♦ *Well, Ken took the Dutch cure last week. So sad.* ♦ *It was the Dutch act. He ate his gun.*

Dutch courage 1. *n.* liquor; false courage from drinking liquor. ♦ *A couple of shots of Dutch courage, and he was ready to face* anything. **2.** *n.* drugs. ♦ *Max deals in Dutch courage, as he calls it.*

Dutch cure Go to Dutch act.

dweeb [dwib] **1.** *n.* an earnest student. (Collegiate.) ♦ *Don't call Bob a dweeb! Even if he is one.* **2.** *n.* a strange or eccentric person; a nerd. ♦ *This place is filled with dweebs of all sizes.*

dyke Go to dike.

dykey Go to dikey.

dynamic duo [daɪ'næmɪk 'duo] *n.* a very special pair of people or things. (From the *Batman* television program. Used mostly for humor.) ♦ *The dynamic duo, Beavis and Fred, showed up late and without the beer.*

dynamite 1. *n.* anything potentially powerful: a drug, news, a person. ♦ *The story about the scandal was dynamite and kept selling papers for a month.* **2.** *mod.* excellent; powerful. ♦ *I want some more of your dynamite enchiladas, please.*

E

eager-beaver *n.* a person who is very eager to do something. ♦ *Rocko is an eager-beaver when it comes to collecting money for Mr. Big.*

eagle *n.* a dollar bill. (From the picture of the eagle on the back.) ♦ *This thing ain't worth four eagles!*

eagle freak *n.* someone with strong concerns about the environment and conservation, especially the preservation of the eagle. (A play on eco freak.) ♦ *The eagle freaks oppose building the dam.*

eagle-eye 1. *n.* a busybody; a person who watches or monitors other people's actions: a floorwalker, a detective, a hall-monitor. ♦ *Some old eagle-eye across the street saw me standing in the cold and called my wife who came down and let me in.* **2.** *n.* an eye or eyes with very keen vision. ♦ *Keep your eagle-eye trained on the entrance.*

ear candy *n.* soft and pleasant popular music; music that is sweet to the ear. (See also elevator music.) ♦ *I find that kind of ear candy more annoying than heavy metal.*

ear hustle *in.* to eavesdrop. ♦ *I was ear hustling while you were talking, and felt I had to correct something you said about me.*

ear hustler *n.* someone who gossips. ♦ *You cowardly ear hustler! Can't you mind your own business?*

ear hustling *n.* eavesdropping. ♦ *Your ear hustling will get you in trouble, especially when people are talking about you.*

ear-duster *n.* a gossipy person. ♦ *Sally is sort of an "ear-duster," but she's all heart.*

earful ['irful] **1.** *n.* a tremendous amount of gossip. ♦ *I can give you an earful about*

the mayor. **2.** *n.* a scolding. ♦ *Her mother gave her an earful when she finally got home.*

earl [ɚl] *in.* to vomit. (Onomatopoetic. Possibly from hurl.) ♦ *Who's earling in the john?*

early beam(s) *n.* dawn; early morning. (Streets.) ♦ *He was away every day, early black to early beam.*

early bird 1. *n.* a person who gets up early. ♦ *The early birds saw the corpse on the street and called the cops.* **2.** *n.* a person who arrives early. ♦ *There were some early birds who arrived before the tea things were laid.* **3.** *mod.* having to do with early arrival. ♦ *Early bird arrivals will be given a free cup of coffee.*

early black *n.* dusk; early evening. (Streets.) ♦ *He was away every day, early black to early beams.*

earp AND **urp 1.** *in.* to vomit. ♦ *She went over by the bushes and earped and earped.* **2.** *n.* vomit. ♦ *God, there's earp right there on the sidewalk.* ♦ *That's not urp! That's tuna salad.*

Earp slop, bring the mop. *tv.* Someone has vomited. (Juvenile.) ♦ *See what's in the hall? Earp slop, bring the mop.*

earth pads *n.* shoes. (Streets.) ♦ *Where are your earth pads, girlfriend? You can't go to town with nekkid feet!*

Earth to *so.* *phr.* Hello *someone*, are you listening? (A means of getting the attention of someone who is ignoring you or who is daydreaming. As if one were on the earth, trying to contact someone in a spaceship. The implication is that the person being addressed is spacy.) ♦ *Earth* to Mom! Earth to Mom! What's for dinner?

easy *mod.* easy to please; flexible. ♦ *Don't worry about me. I'm easy.*

Easy does it. 1. *phr.* Calm down.; Relax. ♦ *Easy does it! Relax and go slow!* **2.** *phr.* Be gentle.; Handle with care. ♦ *Easy does it. Two people can handle this heavy old thing if they go slow.*

easy make *n.* someone who can be copulated with without much trouble. ♦ *She's got a reputation as an easy make.*

easy mark *n.* a likely victim. ♦ *Mary is an easy mark because she is so unsuspecting.*

easy money *n.* money earned or gained with little or no difficulty. ♦ *All you guys want easy money. Don't you want to work for it?*

easy street *n.* a place or position in life where living is easy. (See also fat city; on easy street.) ♦ *Easy street is no place for an active guy like Sam.*

eat 1. *tv.* [for something] to bother or worry someone. ♦ *Nothing's eating me. I'm just the nervous type.* **2.** *tv.* to absorb the cost or expense of something. ♦ *We'll eat the costs on this one. It's the least we can do.* **3.** *tv.* to perform oral sex on someone. (Usually objectionable.) ♦ *She said she wanted to eat me!*

eat at the Y *in.* to perform oral sex on a woman. (Usually objectionable.) ♦ *Hey, sailor, you wanna eat at the Y?*

eat crow *tv.* to display total humility, especially when shown to be wrong. ♦ *Well, it looks like I was wrong, and I'm going to have to eat crow.*

eat face *tv.* to kiss [someone] deeply. (See also suck face.) ♦ *There were some kids eating face over in the corner.*

Eat me! *tv.* an expression meaning roughly *suck my genitals.* (Usually objectionable.) ♦ *Eat me, you creep!*

Eat my shorts! *sent.* Leave me alone!; Nonsense!; Drop dead! ♦ *You think I'm going to clean up after you? Eat my shorts!*

eat nails *tv.* to do something extreme in extreme anger. (Probably refers to construction nail, buy may also be conceived of as finger nails. See also mad enough to eat nails.) ♦ *Sam was ready to eat nails.*

eat one's **gun** *tv.* to commit suicide by firing one's gun into one's mouth. ♦ *The cop was very depressed and ended up eating his gun.*

eat one's **hat** *tv.* to do something extraordinary. (Always with *if.*) ♦ *I'll eat my hat if our advertisement actually brings us a president.*

eat one's **heart out 1.** *tv.* to suffer from sorrow or grief. ♦ *Don't eat your heart out. You really didn't like him that much, did you?* **2.** *tv.* to suffer from envy or jealousy. (Usually a command.) ♦ *Yeah, this one's all mine. Eat your heart out!*

Eat shit! *tv.* Drop dead! (Usually objectionable.) ♦ *Eat shit, mother-fucker!*

eat so's **lunch** *tv.* to best someone; to defeat, outwit, or win against someone. (In the way that a school bully takes away children's lunches and eats them at recess.) ♦ *The upstart ABC Computer Company is eating IBM's lunch.*

eat sth **up 1.** *tv.* to consume something rapidly, such as food or money. ♦ *Running this household eats my income up.* **2.** *tv.* to believe something. ♦ *Those people really eat that stuff up about tax reduction.* **3.** *tv.* to appreciate something. ♦ *The stuff about the federal budget went over well. They really ate up the whole story.*

eat up *in.* to eat in enjoyment. (Usually a command.) ♦ *Eat up! There's plenty more where this came from.*

eco freak AND **eco nut** ['iko frik AND 'iko nət] *n.* someone with strong concerns about the environment and conservation. (Mildly derogatory. From *ecology.*) ♦ *They call me an eco freak, which is okay by me.* ♦ *The eco freaks are protesting the tree trimming.*

eco nut Go to eco freak.

Ecstasy ['ɛkstəsi] *n.* a hallucinogen similar to LSD. (Drugs.) ♦ *Chemicals with names like "Ecstasy" are being put on the streets every day.*

eddress *n.* an electronic address. ♦ *Please tell me your eddress so I can send you some email.*

edge *n.* drunkenness; the early stage of intoxication from alcohol or drugs. (See also **have an edge on.**) ♦ *She was beginning to show a little edge, but she obviously still could drive.*

edged *mod.* alcohol or drug intoxicated. ♦ *We were edged and full of rich food. We needed only to sleep.*

effing AND **F-ing** *mod.* fucking. (Usually objectionable.) ♦ *What an effing stupid idea!* ♦ *Who is that F-ing idiot.*

effing around AND **F-ing around** *in.* fucking around; messing around. (See also **fuck around.** Usually objectionable.) ♦ *They were F-ing around with the switch and turned it on accidentally.*

EGBOK Go to Everything's going to be okay.

egg-beater 1. *n.* an outboard boat motor. ♦ *My egg-beater has been acting up, so I didn't go out on the lake today.* **2.** *n.* a helicopter. (See also **rotorhead.**) ♦ *The egg-beater landed on the hospital roof.*

egghead *n.* an intellectual person. ♦ *The eggheads aren't exactly taking over the world.*

egg-sucker *n.* a flatterer; a sycophant. ♦ *The guy is a chronic egg-sucker. Ignore him.*

ego trip *n.* a public expression of one's feelings of importance or superiority. ♦ *The guy is on another ego trip. Pay no attention.*

ego tripper *n.* a person who habitually goes on an **ego trip**. ♦ *Not another ego tripper running for public office!*

eighteen-wheeler *n.* a large trailer truck. (There are a total of eighteen wheels on the cab and trailer.) ♦ *An eighteen-wheeler almost ran me off the road.*

the **eighty-eight** *n.* a piano. (Pianos have eighty-eight keys.) ♦ *Sam can really beat the eighty-eight.*

eighty-six AND **86** *tv.* to dispose of someone or something; to nix someone or something. ♦ *He wants $400? Eighty-six that! We can't afford it.*

el cheapo [ɛl 'tʃipo] **1.** *n.* the cheap one; the cheapest one. (Mock Spanish.) ♦ *I don't want one of those el cheapos.* **2.** *mod.* cheap. ♦ *This is el cheapo. I don't want it.*

(el) primo [(ɛl) 'primo] *mod.* [of something] top quality. (From Spanish for *the first.*) ♦ *I want some more of that el primo C.*

elbow-bending *n.* drinking liquor; drinking liquor to excess. ♦ *She spends quite a bit of time at elbow-bending.*

elbow-grease *n.* effort. ♦ *All this job needs is a little more elbow-grease.*

electrified *mod.* alcohol intoxicated. ♦ *Her eyes were staring straight ahead, and I knew she was electrified.*

elevated *mod.* alcohol intoxicated; tipsy. ♦ *Sam was elevated from the drinking he did.*

elevator music *n.* dull, uninteresting music of the type that can be heard in elevators or shops. (As compared to exciting jazz or rock. See also **ear candy.**) ♦ *Elevator music is better than listening to someone chewing food.*

eliminated 1. *mod.* killed. ♦ *When Frank is eliminated, there will be no competition.* **2.** *mod.* alcohol intoxicated. ♦ *How can anybody get eliminated on four beers?*

em AND **emm** [ɛm] *n.* an empty liquor bottle. (See also **knock** so's **block off.**) ♦ *Put your ems in the garbage, not on the floor.*

embalmed *mod.* alcohol intoxicated. ♦ *By morning they were all embalmed.*

embalming fluid *n.* strong liquor; raw whiskey. ♦ *Bartender, pour out this embalming fluid and get me your best.*

empty *n.* an empty beer or liquor bottle. ♦ *Whose empties are these, and how many are there?*

empty-nesters *n.* parents whose children have grown and moved out. ♦ *There are a few adjustments that empty-nesters have to make.*

the **end** *n.* the final insult; too much; the last straw. ♦ *When she poured her drink down my back, that was the end.*

end of the ball game *n.* the end of everything. ♦ *It looked like the end of the ball game as we sped too fast around the curve.*

ends 1. *n.* money. (Streets.) ♦ *You got enough ends to get you through the week?* **2.** *n.* shoes. (Streets.) ♦ *You even got holes in your ends.*

enforcer *n.* a bully; a thug or bodyguard. ♦ *Sam is the perfect enforcer. Meaner than all get out.*

enhanced *mod.* high on marijuana. (Drugs.) ♦ *Fred's demeanor is completely enhanced by dinnertime each day.*

Enough, already! *exclam.* That is enough! Stop! ♦ *Please stop! Enough, already!*

equalizer *n.* a gun; a pistol. (Underworld.) ♦ *Rocko carried an equalizer but wouldn't dream of using it.*

erase *tv.* to kill someone. ♦ *Mr. Gutman decided who was gonna erase who.*

erb Go to herb.

erotic dancer *n.* a dancer, typically female, who performs teasing and sexually stimulating dances, usually on a stage. ♦ *She was a school teacher by day and an erotic dancer by night.*

Ervine Go to Irv.

ESAD! *tv.* Eat shit and die!; take what's coming to you. (Usually objectionable.) ♦ *All right, you bastard, ESAD!*

the eternal checkout *n.* death. ♦ *Hank knew the eternal checkout was just around the corner, and he suddenly got religion.*

eternity-box *n.* a coffin. ♦ *When I'm in my eternity-box, then you can have my stereo.*

euchre ['jukɚ] *tv.* to cheat or deceive someone. ♦ *Those guys'll try to euchre you, so watch out.*

evened out *mod.* back to normal; restored to sanity. ♦ *Finally, at about age thirty, you could say that Sam was evened out.*

even-Steven 1. *mod.* evenly divided. ♦ *He made the two piles of diamonds even-Steven and then let me choose which one I wanted.* **2.** *mod.* even; balanced. ♦ *Now that we've given each other black eyes, are we even-Steven?*

everything but the kitchen sink Go to everything from soup to nuts.

everything from A to Z Go to everything from soup to nuts.

everything from soup to nuts AND **everything from A to Z; everything but the kitchen sink** *n.* everything imaginable. (Colloquial.) ♦ *I have everything from soup to nuts in my briefcase.* ♦ *He brought everything but the kitchen sink.*

Everything's going to be okay. AND **EGBOK** *sent. & comp. abb.* Don't worry, everything will be fine. ♦ *EGBOK. Stop fretting.*

evidence *n.* liquor. (Usually with *the*. Incorporated into a suggestion that the evidence be destroyed by drinking it.) ♦ *There is only one thing to do with evidence like this, and that's drink it.*

evil *mod.* excellent. (See also wicked.) ♦ *This wine is really evil!*

evil twin *n.* an illegal duplicate of an internet sign-in page into which people enter passwords and credit card numbers, thinking they are signing up for the real thing. ♦ *There was an evil twin operating at the coffee shop, and I gave out my credit card number before I knew what was going on.*

evilware Go to malware.

ex [ɛks] *n.* a former spouse or lover. ♦ *My ex is in town, but we don't talk much anymore.*

Excellent! *exclam.* Fine! (Like awesome, this expression is a Standard English overused in slang contexts.) ♦ *A new stereo? Excellent!*

Excuse me for breathing! Go to (Well,) pardon me for living!

Excuse me for living! Go to (Well,) pardon me for living!

Excuse my French. Go to Pardon my French.

exec [ɛg'zɛk] *n.* an executive. ♦ *The execs are well treated around here.*

expense *n.* a baby; a child. (See also **deduction**.) ♦ *The little expense just cries, craps, and chows.*

eye candy *n.* someone or something worth looking at. (Compare to **ear candy**.) ♦ *The dame is just eye candy! Her brain is occupied with hair and nails appointments, and strained to do even that!*

eyeball *tv.* to look hard at someone or something. ♦ *The two eyeballed each other and walked on.*

eyeball to eyeball *mod.* face to face. ♦ *Let's talk more when we are eyeball to eyeball.*

eyeful *n.* the sight of something that one was not meant to see. ♦ *I got an eyeful of that contract. Yikes! What a giveaway!*

eye-in-the-sky *n.* an overhead surveillance camera, usually in a dome; a traffic police helicopter. ♦ *The cops used an eye-in-the-sky to get the evidence and make the arrest.*

eye-opener 1. *n.* a real surprise. ♦ *This day has been an eye-opener for me.* **2.** *n.* a wake-up drink of liquor; a strong drink any time. ♦ *He knocked back a quick eye-opener and finished dressing.*

eye-popper 1. *n.* something astonishing. (Alludes to the comical view of eyes bulging outward in surprise or amazement.) ♦ *What an eye-popper of a story!* **2.** *n.* a very good-looking woman or girl. ♦ *Isn't that foxy lady an eye-popper?*

eyewash 1. *n.* nonsense; deception. ♦ *It's not eyewash! It's true!* **2.** *n.* liquor. ♦ *You've been putting away a lot of that eyewash, haven't you?*

F

F2F Go to face to face.

fab [fæb] *mod.* fabulous. (Also part of the nickname of a popular British television comedy seen in the U.S., Ab Fab = *Absolutely Fabulous*.) ♦ *Your pad is not what I'd call fab. Just okay.*

face card *n.* an important person; a self-important person. (As with the royal characters in playing cards.) ♦ *Who's the face card getting out of the benz?*

(face) fungus *n.* whiskers; a beard. ♦ *If John would shave off that face fungus, he'd look a lot better.*

face man *n.* a good-looking young man with no personality. (Collegiate.) ♦ *Harry is just a face man and as dull as dishwater.*

face the music *tv.* to receive the rebuke that is due one. (This *music* is a reprimand. See also chinmusic.) ♦ *You have to face the music eventually.*

face time *n.* time spent face to face with someone. (As opposed to over the telephone or by email, etc.) ♦ *I need to have more face time with my children.*

face to face AND **F2F** *phr. & comp. abb.* in person; speakers and listeners facing each other. (The full form is Standard English.) ♦ *I need to CU F2F.* ♦ *She spoke to us face to face, and we felt better.*

faced 1. *mod.* alcohol intoxicated. (From shit-faced.) ♦ *Lord, is he faced!* **2.** *mod.* rejected by a member of the opposite sex. (Collegiate. Probably also from shit-faced.) ♦ *I've been faced again, and I hate it!*

face-off *n.* a confrontation. (From hockey.) ♦ *The face-off continued for a few moments till both of them realized that there was no point in fighting.*

fack [fæk] *in.* to state the facts; to tell (someone) the truth. (Streets.) ♦ *Now is the time to start facking. Where were you?*

facts of life 1. *n.* an explanation of human reproduction, especially as presented to a child. ♦ *No one ever explained the facts of life to me. I read books about it.* **2.** *n.* the truth about life's difficulties. ♦ *You had better face up to the facts of life and get a job.*

fade 1. *in.* to leave. ♦ *I think that the time has come for me to fade. See ya.* **2.** *in.* [for someone] to lose power; [for someone] to lose influence. ♦ *Ralph is fading, and someone else will have to take over.*

faded *mod.* drunk; drug intoxicated. ♦ *Man, is that guy ever faded! Look at him weave from one lane to another.*

fadoodle [fə'dudl] *n.* something ridiculous; nonsense. ♦ *Oh, stop your silly fadoodle!*

fag [fæg] **1.** *n.* a cigarette. ♦ *Hey, pal, gimme a fag.* **2.** AND **faggot** *n.* a homosexual. (Derogatory.) ♦ *Who's the fag with the fancy hat?* ♦ *Who're you calling a faggot?* **3.** *n.* a repellent male. (Rude and derogatory.) ♦ *You creepy fag. Stop it!*

fag SO **out** *tv.* to tire someone out. ♦ *All that work really fagged me out.*

fag-bashing Go to fag-busting.

fag-busting AND **fag-bashing** *n.* doing violence to homosexuals. (Usually objectionable.) ♦ *He was involved in a fag-busting incident that got him kicked out of school.* ♦ *What's this strange need you have for fag-bashing? What's your problem?*

fagged out *mod.* exhausted. ♦ *I'm really fagged out after all that running.*

faggot Go to fag.

fair shake *n.* a fair chance. (From shaking dice.) ♦ *I want to give you both a fair shake.*

fair-haired boy *n.* a promising young man; a young man who receives favoritism. ♦ *Ted is the boss's fair-haired boy now, but he'll be just like the rest of us in a month.*

fair-weather *mod.* temporary; insincere. (From *fair-weather sailor.*) ♦ *I need something more than a fair-weather friend to help me through all this.*

fairy *n.* a male homosexual. (Rude and derogatory.) ♦ *Bob got fired for calling Bill a fairy.*

fairy tale AND **bedtime story** *n.* a simplistic and condescending explanation for something; a lie. ♦ *I don't want to hear a fairy tale, just the facts, ma'am.* ♦ *I've already heard your little bedtime story. You'll have to do better than that!*

fake it *tv.* to pretend (to do something). ♦ *If you don't know the right notes, just fake it.*

fake off *in.* to waste time; to goof off. ♦ *Hey, you guys, quit faking off! Get to work!*

fake on so *in.* to deceive someone; to lie to someone; to stand someone up. ♦ *If you fake on me again, we're through.*

fake so **out** *tv.* to deceive someone, as with a football pass. ♦ *They faked me out, and then I stumbled over my own feet. The coach was fuming.*

fake the funk *tv.* to pretend to be in the know; to pretend to be fly; to fake being stylish. (Black.) ♦ *He's only faking the funk to survive in the hood. He gets an A in every class in school.*

fakus ['fekəs] *n.* a gadget; something with no name or a forgotten name. ♦ *This little fakus goes right in here.*

falderal AND **folderol** ['fɑldə·ɑl] *n.* wasted effort; nonsense. ♦ *I had about enough of your falderal.*

fall 1. *in.* to be arrested; to be charged with a crime. (Underworld. See also **fall guy.**) ♦ *I heard that Mooshoo fell. Is that right?* **2.** *n.* one's arrest; being arrested and charged. (Underworld.) ♦ *Who took the fall for the bank job?*

fall guy *n.* a victim; a **dupe**; the guy who takes the **fall**. (Originally underworld.) ♦ *I didn't want to be the fall guy, so I sat out the last job.*

fall off the wagon 1. *in.* to resume drinking after having stopped. (The wagon is presumed to be the *water wagon.*) ♦ *It looks to me like he wanted nothing more than to fall off the wagon.* **2.** *in.* to resume any previously stopped behavior including smoking, drug use, overeating, or any other disavowed behavior. ♦ *He's back to watching TV again. Fell off the wagon I guess.*

fall out *in.* to depart. (Probably from the military command meaning *disperse.*) ♦ *Let's fall out. I have to get up early in the morning.*

fall out of bed *in.* to fall far down, as with the drop in some measurement. ♦ *The temperature really fell out of bed last night! It was twenty-three below!*

falling-down drunk 1. *mod.* alcohol intoxicated; very drunk. ♦ *Poor Fred is falling-down drunk and has no way to get home.* **2.** *n.* a drunken person who falls down. ♦ *One more falling-down drunk in this neighborhood will not be anything new.*

falling-out *n.* a disagreement. ♦ *Tom and Bill had a little falling-out.*

fallout *n.* the results of something; the flack from something. ♦ *The fallout from this afternoon's meeting was not as serious as some expected.*

falsies *n.* artificial breasts; stuffing for making the breasts appear larger and more shapely. ♦ *I don't care if she is wearing falsies. She's got a beautiful smile.*

family jewels *n.* the testicles. (Jocular and euphemistic. They are necessary to produce a family.) ♦ *Hey, careful of the family jewels!*

fan *tv.* to ignore someone or something; to cut a class; to **blow** so/sth **off.** (Fan = *blow* as in **blow** so **off.** *Fan*, from *fanatic* meaning "devotee" or "admirer" is very old and is Standard English.) ♦ *You have to meet with your teacher? Oh, fan that. It doesn't matter.*

fan the breeze *tv.* to chat or gossip. ♦ *We're just fanning the breeze, so you didn't interrupt anything.*

fancy footwork AND **fast footwork** *n.* artful maneuvering; fast and clever thinking. ♦ *Ken did a lot of fancy footwork to get out of that one.*

Fancy that! *exclam.* Imagine that! ♦ *Fancy that! There's a piece of pie left in the fridge.*

fancy-schmancy ['fæntsi'ʃmæntsi] *mod.* fancy; very fancy. ♦ *This one is just too fancy-schmancy for Heidi.*

fanigle Go to finagle.

fanny *n.* the buttocks. (Euphemistic in the U.S. The term has taboo implications in the U.K.) ♦ *He fell down right on his fanny.*

fanny-bumper *n.* an event that draws so many people that they bump into one another. ♦ *There was a typically dull fanny-bumper in the village last night.*

fanny-dipper *n.* a swimmer, as opposed to a surfer. (California.) ♦ *The fanny-dippers are not supposed to go out that far.*

Fantabulous! *exclam.* Great! (A blend of *fantastic* and *fabulous*.) ♦ *You're here at last. Fantabulous!* ♦ *Where did you get that fantabulous haircut. There's no two hairs that are going in the same direction! Fab! Fab! Fab!*

fantods Go to screaming fantods.

FAQ *n.* a list of frequently asked questions. (Particularly in the domain of computer use.) ♦ *Is there a FAQ for this newsgroup.*

far gone 1. *mod.* in an extreme state. ♦ *Wow, that chick is far gone. Listen to her rave.* **2.** *mod.* alcohol intoxicated. ♦ *Larry's far gone and looking sick.*

far out 1. *mod.* cool; great; extraordinary. ♦ *This jazz is really far out!* **2.** *mod.* very hard to understand; arcane; highly theoretical. ♦ *This stuff is too far out for me.*

3. *mod.* alcohol or drug intoxicated. ♦ *Three beers and Willy was really far out.*

fart 1. *in.* to release intestinal gas through the anus. (Often objectionable. One of the classic four-letter words. It should be noted that English does not have a single, "polite" word, noun or verb, for this matter. *Break wind* is common, but there is no parallel noun. See the complete list of all entries with **fart** in the **Index of Hidden Key Words.**) ♦ *Okay, who farted?* **2.** *n.* the sound or odor of the release of intestinal gas. (Often objectionable.) ♦ *Who made that smelly fart?* **3.** *n.* a stupid, despicable, and annoying person. (Usually objectionable.) ♦ *The guy's nothing but a fart. Just forget him.*

fart around *in.* to waste time; to do something ineffectually or inefficiently. (Usually objectionable.) ♦ *Stop farting around and get to work!*

fart hole *n.* a wretched and worthless person; an **asshole.** (Rude and derogatory.) ♦ *Stop acting like such a fart hole!*

fart off *in.* to waste time; to goof off. (Usually objectionable.) ♦ *Why are you farting off when there's work to be done?*

fart sack *n.* one's bed. (Military. Apparently a place where one can break wind at will. Usually objectionable.) ♦ *Come on! Get out of the fart sack and get moving!*

farts *n.* fine arts. (Dysphemism.) ♦ *Ted is studying over in the farts department.*

fast buck Go to quick buck.

fast footwork Go to fancy footwork.

fast one 1. *n* a fast act of sex; a quickie; a quick one. ♦ *I think we've got time for a fast one!* **2.** *n.* a fast or quickly performed activity, such as eating or drinking something. ♦ *Here's a tavern. You got time for a fast one?* **3.** *n.* a clever and devious trick. (See also pull a fast one.) ♦ *That was a fast one. I didn't know you were so devious.*

faster than a speeding bullet AND **FTASB** *phr. & comp. abb.* Very fast. (From the introduction to the old radio program, *The Adventures of Superman.* Superman was faster than a speeding bullet.) ♦ *I'll be there FTASB.* ♦ *I ordered it on Wednesday,* *and it was on my doorstep, faster than a speeding bullet, the next day.*

fat 1. *mod.* great; excellent. (See also the spelling variant **phat**.) ♦ *Mary thought the rally was fat, but she left early anyway.* **2.** *mod.* well supplied with something; having an overabundance of something. ♦ *We're fat with paper, but there's not a toner cartridge in sight.* **3.** *mod.* sexy. ♦ *You are truly fat, Wendy.*

fat as a beached whale Go to (as) fat as a beached whale.

fat chance *n.* a very poor chance. (Sarcastic.) ♦ *Fat chance I'll ever get a new car.*

fat city 1. *n.* a state of wealth and comfort; easy street. ♦ *She's living in fat city ever since she inherited her fortune.* **2.** *n.* fatness (expressed as a place). ♦ *I've had it with fat city. I'm going on a diet.*

fat lip Go to lip.

fat skrill *n.* lots of money (See also skrilla.) ♦ *The car cost some real fat skrill.*

fat-ass(ed) *mod.* having large buttocks. (Usually objectionable.) ♦ *Get your fat-ass self outa my car!*

fat-cat 1. *n.* someone with great wealth and the accompanying success. ♦ *I like to watch the fat-cats go by in their beemers.* **2.** *mod.* having to do with wealth or a wealthy person. ♦ *You'll never see me driving any of those fat-cat cars.*

fathead *n.* a stupid person; someone who has fat where brains ought to be. ♦ *You can be such a fathead!*

fatheaded *mod.* stupid. ♦ *Let's not come up with another fatheaded plan. This one has to make sense.*

fatso ['fætso] *n.* a fat person. (Cruel. Also a rude term of address.) ♦ *Some fatso tried to get on the plane and couldn't even get through restroom the door!*

fatty *n.* a derogatory nickname for a fat person. (Cruel. Also a rude term of address.) ♦ *Okay, fatty, you get the biggest piece of cake because you deserve it.*

fattygews ['fætigjuz] *n.* fatigues. (Originally military.) ♦ *I'll slip into some fattygews and be right with you.*

faulty 1. *mod.* fake. ♦ *Faulty leather on this chair. Gimme the real stuff.* **2.** *mod.* wrong. ♦ *No. You are just faulty about the number.*

FB Go to fuck bunny.

feather brain *n.* a stupid person. (Also a rude term of address.) ♦ *Hey, feather brain. Wake up and get busy!*

fed 1. AND the **feds** *n.* a federal agent concerned with narcotics, tax collection, customs, etc. ♦ *Some fed was prowling around asking questions about you.* **2. The Fed** *n.* the Federal Reserve Board. (Colloquial. Usually **Fed**. Always with *the* in this sense.) ♦ *The Fed is not likely to raise interest rates very soon again.*

federal diploma *n.* a U.S. bank note. ♦ *I could use a few extra of those federal diplomas.*

federal jug *n.* a federal prison. (Underworld. See also jug.) ♦ *Lefty is fresh and sweet—just out of the federal jug.*

the **feds** Go to fed.

feeb [fib] *n.* an oaf; a stupid person. (From feebleminded.) ♦ *Don't be a feeb. Wake up!*

feebee Go to feeby.

feeby AND **feebee** ['fibi] *n.* the FBI, the Federal Bureau of Investigation. ♦ *The locals were going to call in the feebies, but the DA said to wait.*

feed one's **face** *tv.* to put food in one's mouth; to eat (something). ♦ *You're always feeding your face. You're going to get fat.*

feel a draft *tv.* to sense that one is being rejected; to sense that someone is cool toward one, possibly for racial reasons. ♦ *Oh, man, I feel a draft in here. Let's leave.*

feel groovy 1. *in.* to feel really good and mellow. ♦ *It's a beautiful day, and I really feel groovy.* **2.** *in.* to be alcohol or drug intoxicated. ♦ *Looks like Kelly is feeling groovy on gin again.*

feel so *tv.* to understand someone. ♦ *Do you feel me? If not, I'll say it again and again till you do!*

feel so **up** *tv.* to feel someone sexually. ♦ *He tried to feel her up, but she wasn't that drunk.*

feeling no pain 1. *mod.* numbed by alcohol and feeling nothing; alcohol intoxicated. ♦ *He drank the whole thing, and he's feeling no pain.* **2.** *mod.* feeling nothing; dead. ♦ *Your aunt is feeling no pain now. She slipped away before dawn.*

feen for sth *in.* to desire something habitually; to be a fiend for something. (From *fiend*, meaning addict, as in **dope fiend**.) ♦ *Billy Bob's feening for some grub.*

feep [fip] **1.** *n.* the beep made by a computer. ♦ *This thing only makes a feep when I try to run my program.* **2.** *in.* [for a computer] to make a little beep. ♦ *It just feeps to get your attention.*

fella ['fɛlə] *n.* a fellow; a guy. (Also a term of address.) ♦ *Hey, fella. Got a match?*

fence hanger *n.* someone who cannot decide which side to be on. ♦ *We need to find a way to persuade the fence hangers to come over to our side.*

fenced *mod.* angry. (California.) ♦ *Boy, was that old man fenced!*

fender-bender 1. *n.* a minor accident. (See also **rear-ender**.) ♦ *There are a couple of fender-benders on the expressway this morning, so be careful.* **2.** *n.* a reckless driver (who causes minor accidents). ♦ *I can't get insurance on my seventeen-year-old, who is a hopeless fender-bender.*

fer shur [fɚ 'ʃɚ] *phr.* for sure; absolutely. (Eye-dialect. Used in writing only for effect. See also **for sure**.) ♦ *I'll be there. Fer shur!*

feshnushkied [fɛ'ʃnuʃkid] *mod.* alcohol intoxicated. ♦ *Wow, is that guy ever feshnushkied!*

festy *mod.* nasty. (From *festered*.) ♦ *That scratch is looking sort of festy.*

fetch up *in.* to empty one's stomach; to vomit. ♦ *I really felt like I was going to fetch up.*

fettie *n.* money. (Streets. Possibly akin to *confetti*.) ♦ *How much fettie you got with you?*

a **few ticks** *n.* a few minutes; a few seconds. ♦ *Just wait. I'll be there in a few ticks.*

fib [fɪb] **1.** *n.* a small lie. ♦ *It was just a little fib. I'm sorry.* **2.** *in.* to tell a small lie. ♦ *Did you fib to the teacher?*

fibber *n.* a liar. ♦ *Harry can be a fibber sometimes. You got to watch him.*

fiddle-fart Go to **monkey-fart**.

field grounders *tv.* to look downward for cigarette or cigar butts. ♦ *Stink in school unless you want to end up flipping burgers and fielding grounders.*

fierce *mod.* really good. ♦ *This is some fierce coffee!*

FIFO. *phr.* first in, first out; the first items placed in the stack are the first items to be retrieved. (Computers. Acronym. See also **GIGO**; **LIFO**.) ♦ *Oh, I thought this thing was FIFO, and I put the stuff in the wrong order.*

fifth wheel *n.* an extra and unneeded person. ♦ *I feel like such a fifth wheel around here.*

filch sth **(from** so/sth**)** *tv.* to grab or steal something from someone. ♦ *Who filched my wallet from me?*

file Go to **(pro)file**.

file thirteen *n.* the wastebasket. (See also **circular file**.) ♦ *I'm afraid that the papers you want went into file thirteen two days ago.*

fill one's **face** AND **stuff** one's **face** *tv.* to eat food fast; to stuff food into one's face. ♦ *Slow down. Stop filling your face and talk to me.* ♦ *Everytime I see you, you are stuffing your face. No wonder you're overweight!*

fill or kill AND **FOK** *phr.* a broker's notation advising the stock exchange to fill a stock order or kill it. (The abbreviation is an initialism. Securities markets.) ♦ *Get rid of this order. It was fill or kill, and it should have been killed yesterday.*

fill so **full of lead** *tv.* to shoot someone. ♦ *Don't move, or I'll fill you full of lead.*

filling station *n.* a liquor store. (From an old name for an automobile service station.) ♦ *Please stop at the filling station and get some suds on your way home.*

fill-mill *n.* a tavern. ♦ *She stopped off at the fill-mill again this evening.*

filthy lucre [...'lukɚ] *n.* money. ♦ *I sure could use a little of that filthy lucre.*

filthy rich 1. *mod.* very wealthy. ♦ *I wouldn't mind being filthy rich.* **2.** *n.* people who are very wealthy. ♦ *The filthy rich can afford that kind of thing, but I can't.*

fin AND **finn** [fɪn] *n.* a five-dollar bill. (Germanic via Yiddish. As in German *funf* = five.) ♦ *I gave the old guy a finn, and he nearly passed out.*

finagle AND **fanigle** [fɪ'negl AND fə'nɪgl] **1.** *in.* to plot and plan; to conspire; to arrange (something). ♦ *He's pretty good at finagling.* **2.** *tv.* to acquire something through conniving. ♦ *Can I finagle a buck from you?*

fine and dandy *mod.* nice; good; well. (Often sarcastic.) ♦ *Well, that's just fine and dandy. Couldn't be better!*

fine wolf *n.* a sexy or desirable man. (Streets.) ♦ *Who is that fine wolf I seen you with last night?*

finer than frog hair *n.* fine; good. (Pseudo folksy. Note the interpretation of *fine*.) ♦ *This chair is just fine...finer than frog hair in fact.*

F-ing Go to effing.

F-ing around Go to effing around.

finger 1. *tv.* to point someone out; to identify someone (as having done something, been somewhere, etc.). ♦ *Pete fingered Marty as being the one who arrived first.* **2.** *n.* someone who identifies criminals for the police; a police informer. (Underworld.) ♦ *Taylor has become a finger for the cops.* **3.** *n.* an amount of liquor poured into a glass equal to the width of a finger. ♦ *Britney said she only drank one finger, but the glass was five inches in diameter!*

finger so as so *tv.* to identify someone as a certain person. (As if one were pointing a finger at someone.) ♦ *Last Card Louie fingered his partner as the gunman.*

finger wave *n.* the act of giving someone the finger; displaying the middle finger upright as a sign of derision. (The gesture is taboo. See also give so the finger.) ♦ *The salute turned into a finger wave when the Major turned away.*

fink [fɪŋk] **1.** *n.* an informer; a stool (pigeon). (From *Pinkerton*. See also rat fink.) ♦ *Taylor has turned into a fink. She can't be trusted.* **2.** Go to fink (on so). **3.** *n.* any strange or undesirable person. ♦ *You are being such a fink. Stop it!*

fink (on so) *in.* to inform on someone. ♦ *Rocko never finks on his friends.*

fink out (on so/sth) *in.* to decide not to cooperate with someone or something (after all). ♦ *Come on, don't fink out on us now.*

finn Go to fin.

fire a line *tv.* to snort a line of cocaine. (Drugs.) ♦ *Rocko has never fired a line in his life.*

fire away *in.* to start asking questions; to start talking; to start doing something. ♦ *The cops fired away at him for an hour.*

fire so up *tv.* to motivate someone; to make someone enthusiastic. (See also fired up.) ♦ *See if you can fire John up and get him to paint the house.*

fire sth up *tv.* to start something such as an engine; to light something. ♦ *Fire this thing up, and let's get going.*

fire up *in.* to light a marijuana cigarette. ♦ *Frank fires up at every chance.*

fireball Go to ball of fire.

fired up *mod.* excited; enthusiastic. ♦ *How can you be so fired up at this time of the morning?*

firewater *n.* whiskey. (From cowboy and Indian talk.) ♦ *This firewater leaves a lot to be desired.*

fireworks 1. *n.* excitement. ♦ *When the fireworks are over, come in and we'll talk.* **2.** *n.* trouble; a display of temper. ♦ *Cut out the fireworks, Sally. Calm down and get back to work.*

the **firstest with the mostest** *mod.* the earliest and in the largest numbers; the earliest with more of what's needed. ♦ *Pete got the prize for being the firstest with the mostest.*

fish *n.* a stupid and inept person. (Derogatory.) ♦ *The guy's a fish. He can't do anything right.*

Fish or cut bait. *sent.* Do something or get out of the way. ♦ *Decide whether you're going to watch or help. Fish or cut bait.*

fish story AND **fish tale** *n.* a great big lie. (Like the fisherman who exaggerates the size of the fish that got away.) ♦ *All we got was a fish story about his luck with the girls. What a liar!* ♦ *He's a master at the fish tale. Maybe he should be a politician.*

fish tale Go to fish story.

FISHDO Go to Fuck it, shit happens, drive on.

fish-fight *n.* a fight between females. ♦ *There's a "fish-fight" over by the biology building.*

fishing expedition *n.* an exploratory search for facts. (This involves asking questions with no preconceived notion of what the answers might reveal.) ♦ *The lawyer was on a fishing expedition. There was no real wrong committed to justify a lawsuit.*

fish-kiss 1. *tv. & in.* to kiss (someone) with puckered up lips. (Collegiate.) ♦ *He fish-kissed me, then ran back to his car.* **2.** *n.* a kiss made with puckered up lips. (Collegiate.) ♦ *The actor planted a big fish-kiss right on her lips and frightened her.*

FISHMO Go to Fuck it, shit happens, drive on.

fishtail *in.* [for the rear of a car] to whip back and forth like a fish moving its tail. ♦ *The caddy fishtailed on the curb and almost spun around.*

fishy *mod.* dubious; questionable; likely to be improper or illegal. (See also smell fishy.) ♦ *That was a pretty fishy story you told us.*

fitshaced *mod.* drunk. ♦ *He goes out and get really fitshaced almost every night.*

fitted *mod.* well dressed. (Outfitted.) ♦ *Man you are really fitted! Iced out and looking really fine!*

five it Go to take the fifth.

a **five-alarm fire** Go to a three-alarm fire.

five-finger discount *n.* the acquisition of something by shoplifting. ♦ *Mooshoo used his five-finger discount to get the kind of ring Britney wanted.*

five-oh AND **5-O** *n.* the police. (From a television program, *Hawaii Five-O.*) ♦ *If you hit me again, I'll call the five-oh!*

fiver ['faɪvɚ] *n.* a five-dollar bill. (See also tenner.) ♦ *Give him a fiver, and let's get outa here.*

fix 1. AND **fix-up** *n.* a dose of a drug, especially for an addict who is in need of drugs. (Drugs. It fixes the suffering of withdrawal.) ♦ *It was clear that the prisoner needed a fix, but there was nothing the cops would do for him.* **2.** *in.* to buy a dose of drugs; to take drugs. (See also fixed. Drugs.) ♦ *Frank had to fix before he could even talk to me.* **3.** *tv.* to castrate or spay an animal, especially a pet. (See also fixed. Jocularly of people.) ♦ *Sally suggested that someone ought to fix Beavis— if he isn't already.* **4.** *n.* a bribe. (See also fixed.) ♦ *Rocko never took a fix in his life.* **5.** *tv.* to influence the outcome of a contest or an election. (See also fixed.) ♦ *Sam knows what it takes to fix an election— cash.* **6.** *n.* a scheme to influence the outcome of a contest or an election. ♦ *Something is wrong with this game. I smell a fix.* **7.** *n.* a repair made to a computer program. (Computers.) ♦ *This little fix should make the whole program run faster.* **8.** *n.* a cure for a social ill. (See also quick fix.) ♦ *There is no easy fix for a problem like this.*

fixed 1. *mod.* doped; intoxicated. ♦ *Frank is comfortable now that he's fixed.* **2.** *mod.* bribed. ♦ *The cop is fixed and won't give you guys any trouble.* **3.** *mod.* having the outcome prearranged. (Said of a contest, race, or election.) ♦ *The election was fixed, and we are going to protest.* **4.** *mod.* neutered. ♦ *I wouldn't buy anything but an already-fixed dog.*

fixed up *mod.* provided with a date. ♦ *Okay, Sam is fixed up with a date for Saturday.*

fixer *n.* a lawyer. (Underworld.) ♦ *Mooshoo's fixer didn't show up in court.*

fixing to die AND **FTD** preparing to die. (Hospital jocular, cruel word play.) ♦ *Yes, he's going. FTD. Circling the drain.* ♦ *Bed 205 is fixin' to die. Call the family.*

fix-up Go to fix.

FIZZBO Go to for sale by owner.

fizzle ['fɪzl̩] **1.** *n.* a failure; something that sputters away. ♦ *The whole project was a fizzle.* **2.** *in.* to fail; to peter out. ♦ *The whole plan fizzled, and we had to start over.* **3.** a wild card word for words beginning with *F*, such as fuck, fool. (Streets. Also for other words with initial *F*.) ♦ *That dude is such a fizzle!*

flack Go to flak.

flack (out) *in.* to collapse in exhaustion; to go to sleep. ♦ *Betsy flacked out at nine every night.*

flackery ['flækɚi] *n.* an advertising agency. ♦ *Ted works for a flackery over on Maple Street.*

flag **1.** *tv.* to fail a course. ♦ *Pat flagged English again.* **2.** *n.* the grade of F. ♦ *I'll get a flag on algebra for the semester.* **3.** *tv.* to arrest someone. (See also flagged.) ♦ *They flagged Bob for speeding even though he was a judge.* **4.** *n.* a headcloth or bandana, especially one that shows gang identity. (Streets.) ♦ *The kid wore a "flag" that alerted the officers to the fact that he was a gang member.*

flagged *mod.* arrested. ♦ *Sally was flagged, and she called her fixer to come get her out.*

flak AND **flack** [flæk] **1.** *n.* complaints; criticism; negative feedback. (Originally referred to antiaircraft guns and the explosions and damage they caused. The first form is an initialism from German *Fliegerabwehrkanonen* = flyer defense cannons. I.e., the initial *fl* plus the first *a* plus the *k*.) ♦ *Why do I have to get all the flak for what you did?* **2.** *n.* publicity; hype. ♦ *Who is going to believe this flack about being first-rate?* **3.** *n.* a public relations agent or officer. ♦ *The flak made an announcement and then disappeared.*

flake **1.** *n.* a person who acts silly or giddy. ♦ *Sally is such a flake!* **2.** *n.* a medicinal form of crystallized cocaine. (Drugs. Similar to crack.) ♦ *Where can I get some flake around here?* **3.** *tv.* [for the police] to place drugs or traces of drugs on a person during an arrest. (Underworld. The person is then charged with possession of drugs.) ♦ *That's not mine! You flaked me!* **4.** AND **flakes** *n.* phencyclidine (PCP), an animal tranquilizer. ♦ *Even Shorty won't sell flake, and he's not what I would call a concerned citizen.*

flake down *in.* to go to bed; to go to sleep. ♦ *After I flake down for about three days, I'll tell you about my trip.*

flake (out) **1.** *in.* to pass out from exhaustion; to fall asleep. (See also flack (out).) ♦ *After jogging, I usually flake for a while.* **2.** *in.* to fall asleep after drug use. (Drugs.) ♦ *An hour after she took the stuff, she just flaked.*

(flake) spoon Go to cokespoon.

flaked Go to flaked out.

flaked out **1.** *mod.* alcohol intoxicated. ♦ *You are too flaked out to drive home. Give me your keys.* **2.** AND **flaked** *mod.* passed out because of drugs. (Drugs.) ♦ *Jerry took the stuff and ended up flaked.* **3.** *mod.* unconscious; exhausted; tired out. ♦ *There are too many flaked out people working at dangerous machines.*

flakes Go to flake.

flako Go to flaky.

flaky ['fleki] **1.** *mod.* unreliable. ♦ *I'm getting so flaky. Must be old age.* **2.** *mod.* habituated to the use of cocaine. (Drugs.) ♦ *He looks a little flaky. Look at his eyes and nose.* **3.** AND **flako** ['fleko] *mod.* alcohol intoxicated. ♦ *Paul was flaky and couldn't drive.* ♦ *Man is he flako!*

flamage ['fleimɪdʒ] *n.* a flame sense 2; a series of flames and their content; writing or participating in a series of flames. ♦ *The moderator has some warnings about all the flamage of late.*

flamdoodle Go to flapdoodle.

flame 1. *in.* to write an excited and angry note in a computer forum or news group. (See also flamage.) ♦ *Stop flaming a minute and try to explain your position calmly.* **2.** *n.* a verbal attack as in sense 1. ♦ *My email is full of flames this morning!* **3.** *in.* to appear obviously homosexual. ♦ *Man, she's flaming today!*

flamer 1. *n.* a blatantly obvious homosexual person. (Primarily and originally for males.) ♦ *He tries not to be a flamer, but what can he do?* **2.** *n.* a person who writes excited and angry notes on a computer forum or news group. ♦ *There are too many flamers on this board to make it interesting and entertaining.*

flame-war *n.* an angry and excited exchange of notes on a computer forum or news group. ♦ *A flame-war erupted on the board last night and a lot of people*

flap *n.* an argument; a minor scandal. ♦ *I'm sorry about that flap we had yesterday, but it was all your fault.*

flapdoodle AND **flamdoodle** ['flæpdudl̩ AND 'flæmdudl̩] *n.* nonsense. ♦ *I've heard enough of this flapdoodle.* ♦ *That's all a lot of flamdoodle!*

flapjaw ['flæpdʒɔ] **1.** *n.* a talkative person. ♦ *Martin is anything but a flapjaw. I bet he doesn't say a dozen words per hour.* **2.** *n.* chatter; gossip. ♦ *Too much flapjaw for me to concentrate in here.*

flash 1. *n.* something suddenly remembered; something suddenly thought of. ♦ *I had a flash and quickly wrote it down.* **2.** *n.* a very short period of time; an instant. (See also in a flash.) ♦ *I'll be there in a flash.* **3.** *tv.* to display something briefly. ♦ *You'd better not flash a wad like that around here. You won't have it long.* **4.** *in.* to display one's private parts briefly. ♦ *She flashed briefly, providing the show that people came to see, and left the stage.* **5.** *n.* a drink of liquor. ♦ *Here, have a little flash, and let's chat a little longer.*

flash on so *in.* to get angry at someone. ♦ *Don't flash on me like that! I didn't do it!*

flash on sth *in.* to remember something suddenly and vividly. ♦ *I was trying to flash on it, but I couldn't bring it to mind.*

flash the hash *tv.* to empty one's stomach; to vomit. ♦ *Dave left quickly to go out and flash the hash, I think.*

flashback *n.* a memory of the past; a portrayal of the past in a story. ♦ *Suddenly, Fred had a wonderful flashback to his childhood.*

flasher *n.* a male exhibitionist; a male who shows his penis to women. ♦ *The cops hauled in a couple of flashers from the public library.*

flat broke *mod.* having no money at all. ♦ *Sorry, I'm flat broke. Not a cent on me.*

(flat) on one's **ass 1.** *mod.* completely exhausted. (Usually objectionable.) ♦ *I'm just flat on my ass. I need some rest.* **2.** *mod.* broke; financially destroyed. (Usually objectionable. An elaboration of flat broke.) ♦ *Sorry, I can't help you. I'm broke—flat on my ass.*

flat out 1. *mod.* totally. ♦ *We were all flat out disgusted.* **2.** *mod.* at top speed. ♦ *If we run flat out, we can get there before dusk.*

flat-ass *mod.* absolutely; totally. (From a general slang term flat-out.) ♦ *She opened it up as flat-ass fast as it would go.*

flat-chested *mod.* with little or no female breast development. ♦ *I wish I wasn't so flat-chested!*

flatfoot AND **flatty** *n.* a police officer, especially a foot patrol officer. (Older.) ♦ *Think about how the flatfoot on the beat is affected by this cold.* ♦ *There's a flatty on the corner. Go ask him for some help.*

flat-hatting *n.* flying an airplane low and recklessly. (As if flying low enough that only people wearing flat hats could escape being struck.) ♦ *Some of the air force pilots were flat-hatting over the desert when one of them crashed.*

flathead *n.* a stupid person. ♦ *Carl, don't act like such a flathead.*

flatheaded *mod.* stupid. ♦ *Martin seems flatheaded, but he's quite brilliant.*

flatline *in.* to die. (From the flatness of the line on an EEG monitor when the heart stops.) ♦ *It appeared that the patient flatlined during the night.*

flatten *tv.* to knock someone down with a blow. ♦ *Shorty flattened the kid with a jab to the nose.*

flatty Go to flatfoot.

fleabag ['flibæg] *n.* a cheap hotel; a flophouse. ♦ *Rocko never stays in fleabags. He's too proud. Sam doesn't care.*

fleabite *n.* a small chip off something. ♦ *This cup has a little fleabite, but it doesn't really harm its value.*

fleece *tv.* to cheat someone; to steal everything from someone. (Underworld.) ♦ *Sam fleeced the kids for a lot of money.*

flesh-presser AND **palm-presser** *n.* a politician. ♦ *Being a flesh-presser is risky during flu season.* ♦ *A palm-presser came to our door to ask us what we thought about his issues.*

flexed out of shape *mod.* very angry; bent out of shape. ♦ *The boss was completely flexed out of shape.*

flick *n.* a movie. ♦ *That was a pretty good flick, right?*

flimflam ['flɪmflæm] **1.** *n.* a confidence trick or deception. ♦ *The whole business sounds like a bit of flimflam to me.* **2.** *n.* nonsense; deception. ♦ *Beware of the flimflam they will try to pull on you.* **3.** *tv. & in.* to cheat or deceive (someone). ♦ *Don't try to flimflam me. I wasn't born yesterday, you know.*

flimflam artist *n.* someone who practices confidence tricks or deceptions on someone else. ♦ *I don't trust that flimflam artist at all.*

fling up *in.* to empty one's stomach; to vomit. ♦ *I was afraid I was going to fling up.*

fling-wing *n.* a helicopter. ♦ *The fling-wing from the radio station is hovering over the traffic jam.*

flip *in.* to go crazy. ♦ *Wow, I've got so much to do, I may just flip.*

flip one's **lid** Go to flip one's wig.

flip one's **wig** AND **flip** one's **lid** *tv.* to go crazy; to lose control. ♦ *I so flipped my lid when I got the news.* ♦ *I nearly flipped my wig when I heard.*

flip (out) *in.* to lose control of oneself; to go crazy. ♦ *Wow, I almost flipped out when I heard about it.*

flip over so/sth *in.* to become very excited about someone or something; to lose control because of someone or something. ♦ *The guests really flipped over the Beef Wellington!*

flip side 1. *n.* the "other" side of a phonograph record. ♦ *On the flip side, we have another version of "Love Me Tender" sung by Beverly Mills.* **2.** *n.* the "other" side of something, such as an argument. ♦ *I want to hear the flip side of this before I make a judgment.* **3.** *n.* the return trip of a long journey. (Citizens band radio.) ♦ *See ya. Catch you on the flip side, maybe.*

flip so **off** AND **flip** so **out** *tv.* to give so the finger. (Collegiate.) ♦ *Did you flip me off? You better not have.* ♦ *Ernie flipped Tom out, and Tom flattened Ernie. Ah, life in the big city.*

flip so **out** Go to flip so off.

flip so **the bird** *tv.* to give so the finger; to display the *digitus impudicus* to someone. ♦ *Max flipped the cop the bird—and that was just the wrong thing to do.*

flip the script 1. *tv.* to lie; to change one's story. ♦ *The guy flips the script depending on whose listening.* **2.** *tv.* to reverse positions in a situation; to turn the tables on someone. ♦ *Now he's the one who's in trouble! That's really flipping the script!*

flip-flop 1. *n.* a reversal. ♦ *The president denied making a flip-flop. He said he simply forgot his earlier position.* **2.** *n.* the return trip of a long journey. (Citizens band radio. See also flip side.) ♦ *Didn't we chat on the flip-flop last week?* **3.** *in.* to change direction or intensity. ♦ *Jed flip-flopped twice in the evening, leaving us where we started.* **4.** *in.* to waver in one's decisions. ♦ *Well, you just flip-flop all you want. I know what I want.*

flipping *mod.* damnable. (Euphemistic for fucking. Usually objectionable.) ♦ *Get this flipping dog out of here!*

flipping burgers *tv.* cooking hamburger patties in a fast food restaurant as an occupation that school drop outs end up doing. (An occupation that offers practically no opportunities for advancement.) ♦ *Do you want to spend the rest of your life flipping burgers! Do your damn homework!*

flivver ['flɪvɚ] *n.* an old car. (Once a nickname for the Model-T Ford.) ♦ *Whose flivver is that parked out in the street?*

FLK ['ɛf 'ɛl 'ke] *n.* funny looking kid. (Initialism. A strange looking child, especially one being treated for social or physical problems.) ♦ *When the mother came in with an FLK in tow, Jane knew her afternoon would be busy.*

float an air biscuit *tv.* to break wind; to fart. (See also cut a muffin.) ♦ *Who floated the air biscuit? P.U.*

flog [flɑg] *tv.* to promote, hype, or support something; to try to sell something aggressively. ♦ *Fred was flogging this car so hard, I figured he was trying to get rid of it.*

flooey ['flui] *mod.* alcohol intoxicated. ♦ *You're flooey again. That's every night this week.*

floored 1. *mod.* surprised. ♦ *You looked floored when I came in. Wasn't I invited?* **2.** *mod.* knocked to the floor by a blow. ♦ *The guy was floored and didn't move a muscle—ever again.* **3.** *mod.* alcohol intoxicated. ♦ *He's totally floored. Can't see a hole in a ladder.*

floozie ['fluzi] *n.* a promiscuous woman. ♦ *Britney was enraged when Rocko called her a floozie.*

flop 1. *n.* a failure. ♦ *The play was a flop. The entire audience left during the second act.* **2.** *n.* a place to sleep for the night; a bed in a flophouse. ♦ *The old man was looking for a flop for the night.*

flophouse *n.* a very cheap hotel offering only rows of beds. ♦ *This place is a flophouse! I won't stay here for a moment.*

flopper-stopper *n.* a brassiere. ♦ *She's very shy. She won't even hang her flopper-stoppers out on the line to dry.*

flow *in.* to menstruate. ♦ *She's flowing and could go swimming.*

flub sth **up** *tv.* to do something incorrectly; to mess up a procedure. ♦ *Now don't flub this up.*

flub the dub *tv.* to fail to do the right thing. ♦ *Martin is flubbing the dub with the fund-raising campaign.*

flub (up) 1. AND **flub-up** *n.* an error; a blunder. ♦ *Who is responsible for this flub-up?* **2.** *in.* to mess up; to foul up. ♦ *You are flubbing up again, aren't you?*

fluff [fləf] **1.** *n.* nonsense; irrelevant stuff; hype. ♦ *Cut out the fluff and talk straight.* **2.** *tv. & in.* to make an error; to do something incorrectly. ♦ *Todd fluffs his lines in the same place every night.*

fluff-stuff *n.* snow. ♦ *There is supposed to be an inch of fluff-stuff tonight.*

flush *mod.* wealthy; with plenty of money. ♦ *Today I am flush. By tomorrow, I'll be broke.*

flusher *n.* a toilet. (Compared to an outhouse.) ♦ *I hear they put in a flusher over at the Babbits'.*

fly 1. *mod.* knowledgeable; alert and in the know. ♦ *This dude is fly; there's no question about it.* **2.** *mod.* nice-looking; stylish. ♦ *I like your fly shoes, Sam.*

fly kites *tv.* to distribute or pass bad checks. (Underworld. See also kite.) ♦ *Marty was picked up for flying kites in three different cities.*

fly light *in.* to skip a meal or eating. ♦ *Nothing for me, thanks. I'm flying light today.*

fly mink *n.* a fine woman; a sexually attractive woman. (Black. See also mink.) ♦ *Who was that fly mink I saw you with last night?*

fly the coop *tv.* to escape from somewhere; to get away. ♦ *I was afraid he would fly the coop if I didn't tie him up.*

fly trap *n.* the mouth. ♦ *Close your fly trap. You talk too much.*

flyboy *n.* a pilot. (Military.) ♦ *Rocko was a flyboy in Korea.*

fly-by-night *mod.* undependable; dishonest. ♦ *Sam seems like such a fly-by-night character.*

flying-fuck 1. *n.* a real or imaginary act of copulation where the male leaps or dives onto and into the female. (Usually objectionable.) ♦ *The movie showed some jerk allegedly performing a flying-fuck, just for laughs.* **2.** AND **french-fried-fuck** *n.* something totally worthless. (Usually objectionable.) ♦ *Who gives a flying-fuck anyway?* ♦ *I wouldn't give you a french-fried-fuck for all the crummy cars like that in the world.*

fo shizzle AND **fo sho** *phr.* for sure. (Streets. See also shizzle. *Sho* is just dialectal for *sure.*) ♦ *I'm ready! Fo shizzle!*

Fo shizzle, ma nizzle! *phr.* For sure, my nigga! (Streets.) ♦ *Am I here? Fo shizzle, ma nizzle.*

fo sho Go to fo shizzle.

foam *n.* beer. ♦ *All the guy thinks about is foam.*

FOB *mod.* fresh off the boat; as gullible and trusting as a new immigrant. (Initialism. A play on the initials of *Free on Board.*) ♦ *Where did you get those FOB shoes? Blue suede is back?*

FOBlish *n.* rudimentary English; English spoken by someone who is FOB = fresh off the boat. ♦ *I can't understand your FOBlish! Let me speak to your supervisor.*

fo-fo *n.* a .44-caliber pistol. (See also deuce-deuce.) ♦ *He traded up his deuce-deuce for a fo-fo.*

the **foggiest (idea)** *n.* (even) a hazy idea. (Usually in the negative.) ♦ *I'm sorry I don't know. I haven't the foggiest.*

FOK Go to fill or kill.

fold 1. *in.* to fail; to close. ♦ *I was afraid my business would fold because of the recession.* **2.** *in.* to collapse from drinking. ♦ *Dave had just one more drink, and then he folded.*

folded *mod.* alcohol intoxicated. ♦ *Pete is folded. That's the third time this week.*

folderol Go to falderal.

folding money AND **folding stuff** *n.* U.S. paper bank notes, as opposed to coins. ♦ *All I got is change—no folding stuff.* ♦ *Sorry, I don't have any folding money with me. Can you pick up the bill?*

folding stuff Go to folding money.

folks *n.* one's parents. (Always with the possessive.) ♦ *I'll have to ask my folks if I can go.*

fomp [famp] *in.* to play around sexually. (Collegiate.) ♦ *Jerry wanted to fomp, and I wanted to get him out of my sight.*

foodaholic *n.* a glutton. ♦ *Kelly is a foodaholic and has a real eating problem.*

foodie *n.* someone who is interested in foods, cooking, and the latest food and restaurant fads. ♦ *The foodies are all clamoring for fried sweet potatoes with salmon.*

fooey Go to phooey.

foo-foo water ['fufuwadɚ] *n.* aftershave lotion; cologne. ♦ *Don't use so much of that foo-foo water.*

foot it *tv.* to go somewhere by foot; to walk or run. (See also ankle; shank it. Compare to hook it.) ♦ *I have to foot it over to the drugstore for some medicine.*

foot-in-mouth disease *n.* the tendency to say the wrong thing at the wrong time. ♦ *Well, Ralph has foot-in-mouth disease again.*

foozle ['fuzl] **1.** *n.* an error; a messed up task. ♦ *What a stupid foozle!* **2.** *tv.* to mess something up; to bungle something. (See also foozlified.) ♦ *Who foozled the copying machine?*

foozlified ['fuzlɪfaɪd] **1.** *mod.* bungled. ♦ *I've never seen such a foozlified mess in my life!* **2.** *mod.* alcohol intoxicated. ♦ *Why do you always come home foozlified?*

FOP Go to fucking old person.

for all I know *phr.* as far as I know; I really don't know. ♦ *She came in late because she had an accident, for all I know.*

for (all) one's trouble *phr.* in spite of one's efforts; in very poor payment for one's efforts. ♦ *He got a punch in the jaw for all his trouble.*

for chicken feed Go to for peanuts.

for free *mod.* free from monetary charge; gratis. ♦ *Is all this really mine for free?*

for keeps *mod.* forever. ♦ *Does that mean I'm going to have this scar for keeps?*

for kicks *mod.* for fun; for a thrill. ♦ *We just did it for kicks. We didn't mean to hurt anyone.*

for peanuts AND **for chicken feed** *mod.* for practically no money at all. (See also chicken feed.) ♦ *I won't work for peanuts!* ♦ *They expect me to do all that for chicken feed.*

For Pete's sake! AND **For pity's sake!; For the love of Mike!** *exclam.* Good grief! ♦ *For Pete's sake! Is that you Charlie?* ♦ *For pity's sake! Ask the man in out of the cold!*

For pity's sake! Go to For Pete's sake!

for real *mod.* genuine; not imaginary. ♦ *Ken is really strange. Is he for real?*

for sale by owner AND **FIZZBO** for sale by owner. ♦ *One computer. FIZZBO. $100.*

for sure *phr.* absolutely. (The same as fer shur.) ♦ *I'll be there, for sure.*

for the birds *mod.* undesirable. ♦ *I don't like this kind of life. It's for the birds.*

for the devil of it AND **for the heck of it; for the hell of it** *mod.* because it is slightly evil; for no good reason. (Use caution with hell.) ♦ *The kids broke the window just for the devil of it.* ♦ *I painted the garage blue, just for the heck of it.*

for the heck of it Go to for the devil of it.

for the hell of it Go to for the devil of it.

For the love of Mike! Go to For Pete's sake!

Forget it! 1. *exclam.* Never mind, it wasn't important! ♦ *I had an objection, but just forget it!* **2.** *exclam.* Never mind, it was no trouble at all! ♦ *No trouble at all. Forget it!*

Forget you! *exclam.* Drop dead!; Beat it! (Possibly euphemistic for *Fuck you!*) ♦ *Forget you! Get a life!*

fork sth **over** *tv.* to hand something over (to someone). ♦ *Okay, fork over the dough and be quick about it!*

Fork you! *exclam.* Fuck you! (A partial disguise. Rude and derogatory.) ♦ *Fork you, you stupid twit!*

forty winks *n.* a nap; sleep. (Usually with a quantifier. Either *forty* or *some, a few, a bunch of,* etc.) ♦ *I could use forty winks before I have to get to work.*

fosho *mod.* for sure. (Streets.) ♦ *I'll be there on time fosho.*

fossil 1. *n.* an old-fashioned person. ♦ *Some old fossil called the police about the noise.* **2.** *n.* a parent. ♦ *My fossils would never agree to anything like that.*

foul mouth *n.* a person who uses obscene language habitually. ♦ *Sally is turning into a real foul mouth.*

foul up 1. *in.* to blunder; to mess up. ♦ *The quarterback fouled up in the first quarter, and that lost us the game.* **2.** *n.* a blunder; an error. (Usually **foul-up.**) ♦ *That was a fine foul-up! Is that your specialty?*

fouled up *mod.* messed up; ruined; tangled up. ♦ *You sure are fouled up, you know.*

four sheets in the wind AND **four sheets (to the wind)** *mod.* alcohol intoxicated. (See comments at three sheets in the wind.) ♦ *He can't talk straight because he's four sheets in the wind.* ♦ *After only three beers, Gary was four sheets to the wind.*

four sheets (to the wind) Go to four sheets in the wind.

four wheels *n.* a car; transportation. (See also wheels.) ♦ *I need four wheels to get me around town.*

four-bagger *n.* a home run in baseball. ♦ *Wilbur hit his third four-bagger of the season.*

four-bits *n.* fifty cents. (A bit is equal to twelve and one-half cents.) ♦ *Here's four-bits. Keep the change.*

four-eyes *n.* someone who wears glasses. (Also a rude term of address.) ♦ *Hey, four-eyes, betcha you can't see this!*

four-flusher *n.* a cheater. ♦ *Bruno is a lousy four-flusher, among other unpleasant things.*

four-oh-four AND **404** *phr.* the answer to your question is unknown; the location you seek is unknown. (From the internet message: *Error - 404* that is received when the internet cannot find the address you are seeking.) ♦ Q: *Where's the kitchen?* A: *404. You'll have to find it yourself.*

four-one-one AND **411** *n.* information; the details about something or someone. (In the U.S., the telephone number of directory assistance or information is 411.) ♦ *What's the 411 on the new guy in the front office?*

four-topper *n.* a restaurant table that will seat four people. (Restaurant jargon.) ♦ *Please seat these two couples at the four-topper in the corner.*

fox *n.* an attractive girl or young woman. ♦ *Man, who was that fox I saw you with?*

fox trap *n.* an automobile customized and fixed up in a way that will attract women. ♦ *I put every cent I earned into my fox trap, but I still repelled women.*

foxy 1. *mod.* sexy, especially having to do with a woman. ♦ *What a foxy dame!* **2.** *mod.* smelly with perspiration odor. ♦ *Subway cars can sure get foxy in the summer.* **3.** *mod.* alcohol or drug intoxicated. (On the stinking drunk theme.) ♦ *He's worse than foxy—he's stinking drunk.*

foxy lady *n.* a sexually attractive woman or girl. ♦ *A couple of foxy ladies stopped us on the street.*

fracture *tv.* to cause someone to laugh very hard. ♦ *Now, this joke'll fracture you.*

fractured 1. *mod.* alcohol intoxicated. ♦ *This is the third night this week that Pete has rolled in fractured.* **2.** *mod.* demolished by laughter. ♦ *The whole audience was fractured by the time my ten minutes were up.*

frag [fræg] *tv.* to assassinate an unpopular military officer in Vietnam. (Military.) ♦ *The guy was so certain that nobody was going to frag him that he got careless and Charlie got him.*

fragged [frægd] *mod.* destroyed; ruined. (As if destroyed by a fragmentary bomb.) ♦ *My clothes are fragged, and I need a haircut.*

fraidy cat ['fredi...] *n.* a coward; a person who is frightened of everything. (Used in children's taunts.) ♦ *Don't be a fraidy cat. Go ahead, jump!*

frail Go to twist.

frame 1. *tv.* to cause an innocent person to be blamed for a crime; to contrive evidence so that someone appears to be guilty. (Originally underworld.) ♦ *Jimmy tried to frame his sister for painting the cat yellow.* **2.** AND **frame-up; frameup** *n.* a scheme where an innocent person is made to take the blame for something; incrimination caused by contrived evidence. (Underworld.) ♦ *The frame-up would have worked if it weren't for one little thing.*

frame-up Go to frame.

frantic *mod.* great; wild. ♦ *We had a frantic time at Chez Freddy.*

frat [fræt] **1.** *n.* a fraternity. (Collegiate.) ♦ *Are you going to join a frat?* **2.** *mod.* having to do with fraternities and their members. (Collegiate.) ♦ *Is there a frat party tonight?*

frat-rat *n.* a college fraternity member. (Derogatory.) ♦ *The frat rats had a kegger that ended up a brawl.*

freak mommy *n.* a good-looking female. ♦ *Sally is such a freak mommy. My eyes just water!*

freak (out) 1. *in.* to panic; to lose control. ♦ *I was so frightened, I thought I would freak.* **2.** *n.* a bad drug experience; a psychotic reaction to the drug LSD. (Drugs. Usually **freak-out** or **freakout**.) ♦ *Some of them get turned off to drugs by a really good freakout.* **3.** *n.* a wild party of any type; any exciting happening. (Usually **freak-out** or **freakout**.) ♦ *There is a big freak-out at Freddy's joint tonight.* **4.** *n.* a freaked (out) person. (Usually **freak-out** or **freakout**.) ♦ *Some poor freak-out sat in the corner and rocked.*

freak so **out** *tv.* to shock or disorient someone. ♦ *The whole business freaked me out.*

freaked (out) 1. *mod.* shocked; disoriented. (Perhaps from drugs or alcohol.) ♦ *I was too freaked out to reply.* **2.** *mod.* tired out; exhausted. ♦ *I'm too freaked out to go on without some rest.*

freaker 1. *n.* an incident that causes someone to freak (out). (Collegiate.) ♦ *Wasn't that weird? A real freaker.* **2.** *n.* a freaked (out) person. (Collegiate.) ♦ *Some poor freaker sat in the corner and rocked.*

freaking *mod.* damned. (Euphemistic for fucking. Usually objectionable.) ♦ *Get your freaking socks off my bed!*

freaky *mod.* strange; eccentric. ♦ *I get a freaky feeling whenever I hear that music.*

free lunch *n.* something free. (Often negative.) ♦ *There is no such thing as a free lunch.*

free ride *n.* an easy time; participation without contributing anything. ♦ *You've had a free ride long enough. You have to do your share of the work now.*

free show *n.* a peek at a private part of someone's body, usually a woman. ♦ *Martin looked like the type who was always waiting for a free show that was never to be.*

free trip *n.* an echo or a flashback of an LSD experience. (Drugs.) ♦ *The kid got a free trip, and it scared her to death.*

freeball *in.* [for a male] not to wear underpants. (See also go commando.) ♦ *Geesh! It's to cold out to freeball.*

freebee Go to freebie.

freebie AND **freebee; freeby** ['fribi] *n.* something given away free. ♦ *They gave me a freebie with my purchase.*

freeload *in.* to live off someone else; to eat and drink at someone else's expense; to live off someone else. ♦ *Don't come around here and expect to freeload.*

freeloader *n.* someone who eats and drinks at someone else's expense; a parasitic person. ♦ *Ken is sort of a freeloader, but he's a lot of fun anyway.*

free-wheeling *mod.* lacking restraint; flamboyant and uncontrolled. ♦ *These high-spending, free-wheeling palm-pressers appear out of nowhere at election time.*

freeze 1. *n.* the act of ignoring someone; the cold shoulder. ♦ *Everybody seems to be giving me the freeze.* **2.** *tv.* to ignore someone; to give someone the cold shoulder. ♦ *Don't freeze me, gang! I use a mouth wash!* **3.** *in.* to hold perfectly still. (Also a command given by a police officer that implies there is a gun pointed at a suspect.) ♦ *The fuzz shouted, "Freeze, or you're dead meat!"*

freeze so **out 1.** *tv.* to make it too cold for someone, usually by opening windows or through the use of air conditioning. (See also play freeze-out.) ♦ *Are you trying to freeze out everybody? Close the door.* **2.** *tv.* to lock someone out socially. ♦ *They froze out the newcomers.*

freezer burn *n.* an imaginary reaction to seeing brightly sparkling jewelry, especially diamonds. ♦ *He's really iced out! I got freezer burn just looking at him.*

freezing cold *mod.* very cold. ♦ *It's freezing cold out there.*

French 1. *n.* an act of oral sex. (Usually objectionable.) ♦ *How much is a French at a cathouse like that?* **2.** *mod.* referring to oral sex. (Usually objectionable.) ♦ *He tried some French stuff on her, and she nearly killed him.* **3.** *tv.* to perform oral sex on someone. (Usually objectionable.) ♦ *He wanted her to French him.* **4.** *tv. & in.* to kiss someone using the tongue; to French kiss. ♦ *We were French kissing when the teacher came in.*

French kiss 1. *n.* kissing using the tongue; open-mouth kissing. ♦ *I didn't know whether I was going to get a French kiss or a fish-kiss.* **2.** *tv.* to kiss someone using the tongue. ♦ *He tried to French kiss me, but I stopped him.*

french-fried-fuck Go to flying-fuck.

fresh 1. *mod.* cheeky; impudent. ♦ *Ken sure is fresh sometimes.* **2.** *mod.* a little aggressive sexually; prone to caress too eagerly. ♦ *Hey, buster! Don't get fresh with* *me!* **3.** *mod.* cool; okay. ♦ *That stuff's really fresh. It's a winner.* **4.** *mod.* good-looking. ♦ *Tom is fresh and buff.*

fresh and sweet *mod.* just out of jail. (Streets.) ♦ *Hey, Lefty, you look all fresh and sweet.*

fresh as a daisy Go to (as) fresh as a daisy.

fricking *mod.* lousy; damn. (A euphemism for fucking.) ♦ *What a fricking mess you've made of this!*

fridge [frɪdʒ] *n.* a refrigerator. ♦ *Put this in the fridge so it won't spoil.*

fried 1. *mod.* alcohol or drug intoxicated. (See also brain-burned; crisp; southern-fried.) ♦ *How the hell did you get so fried?* **2.** *mod.* sunburned. ♦ *Man, is that babe fried!*

frig 1. *tr & in.* to copulate [with] someone. (Usually objectionable.) ♦ *Bob and Mary were in the back room frigging.* **2.** *tv.* to ruin something; to fuck sth up. ♦ *Somebody frigged my rear bumper.*

frigging 1. *mod.* damnable. (A euphemism for fucking.) ♦ *Who made this frigging mess?* **2.** *mod.* damnably. ♦ *What a frigging stupid thing to do!*

Frisco ['frɪsko] *n.* San Francisco, California. (Said to be objected to by residents of that city. Still in use despite the claim.) ♦ *My cousin lives in Frisco.*

friz [frɪz] *n.* a Frisbee. ♦ *Whose friz is that in the tree?*

fro Go to Afro.

frog face *n.* a nerd; a geek. (Especially as a rude term of address.) ♦ *Look here, frog face, what makes you think you can talk to me that way?*

frog slicing *n.* biology class; a biology course. (A dysphemism.) ♦ *Dave dreaded going to frog slicing. The smell got to him.*

from A to Z *mod.* of a complete and wide variety. (See also everything from A to Z.) ♦ *We have just about everything from A to Z.*

from hell, so/sth Go to so/sth **from hell**

from hunger Go to (strictly) from hunger.

from the bottom of my heart AND **FT-BOMH** *phr. & comp. abb.* very sincerely. ♦ *Thanks FTBOMH.*

from (the) git-go *mod.* from the very start. (See also git-go; jump (street).) ♦ *This kind of thing has been a problem from the git-go.*

front 1. *in.* to pay out money in advance of receiving goods; to pay up front. (See also front money.) ♦ *I fronted about $550 for the new computer.* **2.** *n.* a respectable appearance. ♦ *Jan can put up a good front, but most of us know the real Jan.* **3.** *in.* to pretend; to lie. ♦ *Stop fronting and be yourself.* **4.** *tv.* to challenge someone; to confront someone, perhaps in anger. ♦ *Don't front me unless you are ready for a fight.*

front man *n.* a respectable and well-known man who represents a less respectable person or organization. ♦ *The former advisor now serves as a front man for a large foundation.*

front money *n.* money paid in advance; earnest money. ♦ *I put up a lot of front money and have nothing to show for it.*

front off about sth *in.* to complain about something; to be brash and resentful about something; to be confrontational about something. (See also front sense 4.) ♦ *Todd was fronting off about his assignment and got a detention for it.*

front runner *n.* the leader; the person or thing most likely to win. ♦ *The press found out some juicy secrets about the front runner and made them all public.*

fronts *n.* clothing; a sports jacket. ♦ *You got some good-looking fronts there.*

froody ['frudi] *mod.* grand; wonderful; cool. (From Douglas Adams' *The Hitchhiker's Guide to the Galaxy.*) ♦ *The curtains parted to the most froody, funky set I've ever seen.*

frosh [frɔʃ] **1.** *n.* a freshman. ♦ *Ken is just a frosh, but he looks older.* **2.** *mod.* having to do with freshmen. ♦ *The frosh dorm is full again this year.*

frost *tv.* to make someone angry. (See also frosted (over).) ♦ *The little car frosted me by zooming into my parking place.*

frosted (over) *mod.* angry; annoyed. ♦ *The clerk was really frosted over when I asked for a better one.*

frosty 1. AND **frosty one** *n.* a beer; a cold beer. ♦ *I need a frosty one after all that work.* ♦ *Hey, dude! How bout a frosty?* **2.** *mod.* cool; really cool and mellow. ♦ *That music is really frosty.*

frosty one Go to frosty.

froth *n.* a beer. ♦ *How about another pitcher of frost, innkeeper?*

froyo *n.* frozen yogurt. ♦ *Let's stop at the store and get some froyo.*

fruit 1. *n.* a strange person. (Now overwhelmed by sense 2.) ♦ *Ted is such a fruit.* **2.** AND **fruiter** *n.* a homosexual male. (Usually rude and derogatory.) ♦ *Bob thinks that you-know-who is a fruit.*

fruit loop Go to fruitcake.

fruitcake 1. *n.* a silly-acting person. (Also a term of address.) ♦ *You can be such a silly fruitcake sometimes.* **2.** *n.* a male homosexual. (Rude and derogatory. An elaboration of fruit.) ♦ *We went into this bar, but it was filled with fruitcakes, so we left.* **3.** AND **fruit loop** *n.* a foolish oaf. (Someone who is as nutty as a fruitcake. Fruit loop is borrowed from the cereal of the same [protected trade] name.) ♦ *What a fruitcake! Doesn't even know where his head is at.* ♦ *Out of the way, fruit loop.*

fruiter Go to fruit.

fruity 1. *mod.* silly-acting. ♦ *Why are you acting so fruity? Not get enough sleep?* **2.** *mod.* in the style or manner of a male homosexual. (Usually objectionable.) ♦ *The entertainers were sort of fruity, but other than that, the show was okay.*

fry 1. *in.* to die in the electric chair. (Underworld.) ♦ *The DA is determined that you will fry.* **2.** *tv.* to execute someone in the electric chair. (Underworld.) ♦ *They're gonna fry you for this.*

FTASB Go to faster than a speeding bullet.

FTBOMH Go to from the bottom of my heart.

FTD Go to fixing to die.

fuck 1. *tv. & in.* to copulate [with] someone. (Taboo. Usually objectionable. It should be noted that English does not have a one-word, standard, transitive verb for this act. All expressions with the same meaning are phrases, slang, or colloquial. See the complete list of all entries with fuck in the **Index of Hidden Key Words**.) ♦ *They want to fuck all night.* **2.** *n.* an act of copulation. (Taboo. Usually objectionable.) ♦ *I need a fuck.* **3.** *n.* a person with whom one can copulate. (Taboo. Usually objectionable.) ♦ *Man, he's a good fuck if I ever saw one.* **4.** *n.* semen. (Taboo. Usually objectionable.) ♦ *Clean up that fuck before somebody sees it!* **5.** *exclam.* an exclamation of anger or exasperation. (Usually **(Oh,) fuck!** Taboo. Usually objectionable.) ♦ *Oh, fuck! I'm outa beer.*

Fuck a dog! Go to Fuck a duck!

Fuck a duck! AND **Fuck a dog!** *exclam.* Oh, hell!, an expression of anger or distress. (Taboo. Usually objectionable.) ♦ *Fuck a duck! I won't do it!* ♦ *Get up at 6:00 A.M.? Fuck a dog!*

fuck around *in.* to waste time; to mess around. (Taboo. Usually objectionable.) ♦ *Stop fucking around and get busy!*

fuck around with SO **1.** AND **fuck** SO **around** *tv. & in.* to harass or intimidate someone; to give someone a hard time. (Taboo. Usually objectionable.) ♦ *Don't fuck around with me all the time! Give me a break.* ♦ *Stop fucking me around!* **2.** *in.* to fiddle or toy with someone or something. (Taboo. Usually objectionable.) ♦ *Please, don't fuck around with my stuff.*

fuck buddy AND **fuck puppet** *n.* a sexual partner with whom one has no romantic or nonsexual interests. (Usually objectionable.) ♦ *Bob an Barb are just fuck buddies. They really don't care a thing about each other.* ♦ *She showed up about midnight with her cheap fuck puppet in tow.*

fuck bunny AND **FB** *n.* someone who just loves to copulate. (Usually a female. Taboo. Usually objectionable.) ♦ *She's a real fuck bunny, isn't she?*

Fuck it (all)! *exclam.* Damn! (Taboo. Usually objectionable.) ♦ *Oh, fuck it all! I don't care what you do!*

Fuck it, shit happens, drive on. AND **Fuck it, shit happens, move on.; FISHDO; FISHMO** *sent. & comp. abb.* Sorry about your trouble, forget it and get on with your life. (Usually objectionable.) ♦ *Stop going on and on about your problem. FISHMO.* ♦ *Grow up, chum. Fuck it, shit happens, drive on.*

Fuck it! *tv.* To hell with it!; Forget it! (Taboo. Usually objectionable.) ♦ *Your idea is stupid. Fuck it! Try something else.*

fuck nut *n.* an idiot. (A fucking nutcase. Usually objectionable.) ♦ *Bob is such a fuck nut. If his head wasn't screwed on, he'd leave it at home!*

fuck off 1. *in.* to masturbate. (Taboo. Usually objectionable.) ♦ *Stop fucking off! You wanna get pimples?* **2.** *in.* to waste time. (Taboo. Usually objectionable.) ♦ *Stop fucking off and get to work.* **3.** *in.* to go away; to get out of a place; to beat it. (Taboo. Usually objectionable.) ♦ *I told him to fuck off, but he still keeps hanging around.*

fuck puppet Go to fuck buddy.

fuck SO **around** Go to fuck around with SO.

fuck so/sth **up** *tv.* to mess someone or something up; to damage or ruin someone or something. (Taboo. Usually objectionable.) ♦ *You fuck up everything you get your hands on!*

fuck SO **over** *tv.* to give someone a very hard time; to abuse someone physically or mentally; to cheat, deceive, or trick someone. (Taboo. Usually objectionable.) ♦ *The big guys fucked him over for a while and then let him go.*

fuck SO's **mind (up)** *tv.* to confuse or disorient someone; [for a drug] to affect or destroy someone's mind. (Taboo. Usually objectionable.) ♦ *She's really fucked your mind up. I'd stay away from her if I were you.*

fuck sth **up** *tv.* to mess something up; to wreck something. (Usually objectionable.) ♦ *Who fucked up my file cabinet?*

fuck up *in.* to mess up; to fail. (Taboo. Usually objectionable.) ♦ *Don't fuck up this time or you're fired.*

fuck with SO *in.* to cause trouble for someone; to threaten someone. (Taboo. Usually objectionable.) ♦ *Don't fuck with me if you know what's good for you!*

fuck with sth *in.* to meddle with something. (Taboo. Usually objectionable.) ♦ *Stop fucking with the radio!*

Fuck you! *tv.* Go to hell! (A very insulting curse. Taboo. Usually objectionable.) ♦ *Fuck you, you shit!*

fuckable 1. *mod.* readily agreeable to copulation. (Taboo. Usually objectionable.) ♦ *About midnight, she got sorta fuckable, and then she fell asleep.* **2.** *mod.* highly desirable for copulation; suitable or acceptable for copulation. (Taboo. Usually objectionable.) ♦ *Isn't he about the most fuckable hunk you've ever seen?*

fuckathon *n.* serial copulation or sexual activity; an orgy. (Taboo. Usually objectionable.) ♦ *It was no honeymoon. It was a first-class fuckathon!*

fuck-brained 1. *mod.* stupid; mindless. (Taboo. Usually objectionable.) ♦ *What a stupid, fuck-brained idea!* **2.** *mod.* obsessed with sex. (Taboo. Usually objectionable.) ♦ *All he thinks about is dames. He is totally fuck-brained.*

fucked out 1. *mod.* exhausted from copulation. (Taboo. Usually objectionable.) ♦ *They went at it until they were both fucked out.* **2.** *mod.* totally exhausted from doing anything. (As exhausted as if one had been copulating excessively. Taboo. Usually objectionable.) ♦ *Some fucked-out dude was lying on the floor, and another was collapsed on the chair.*

fucked up *mod.* messed up; confused; ruined. (Taboo. Usually objectionable.) ♦ *This whole project is so fucked up, it'll take months to straighten out.*

fucker 1. *n.* a male who copulates frequently or well. (Taboo. Usually objectionable.) ♦ *Tod thinks he's a big fucker. I think he's a big faker.* 2. *n.* any male; a buddy. (Low. Taboo. Usually objectionable.) ♦ *Tell that goddamn fucker to get the hell out of here!* 3. *n.* the penis; the erect penis. (Taboo. Usually objectionable.) ♦ *He held his hands over his little fucker and ran for the bedroom.* 4. *n.* a female who is known to agree to copulate readily. (Taboo. Usually objectionable.) ♦ *I'm out to find me a real first-class fucker tonight.*

fuckery AND **fuck-house** *n.* a brothel; a house of prostitution. (Taboo. Usually objectionable.) ♦ *This street is just one fuckery after another.* ♦ *The suspect referred to the brothel as a "fuck-house," if you'll pardon my French.*

fuckface *n.* a despised person. (Also a term of address.) ♦ *Look, fuckface! Who the hell do you think you are?*

fuck-freak *n.* someone who is obsessed with copulation. (Taboo. Usually objectionable.) ♦ *She is a hot little fuck-freak, and she'll wear out any dude that takes her on.*

fuckhead *n.* a stupid and obnoxious person. (Taboo. Usually objectionable.) ♦ *Don't be such a fuckhead! Go back there and stand up for yourself!*

Fuckheaded *mod.* stupid; senseless. (Taboo. Usually objectionable.) ♦ *You idiot! What a fuckheaded thing to do!*

fuck-house Go to fuckery.

fucking *mod.* damnable; lousy; cursed. (Taboo. Usually objectionable.) ♦ *Get that fucking idiot out of here!*

Fucking A! *exclam.* absolutely; totally absolutely. (Usually objectionable.) ♦ *Q: Will you be at the concert? A: Fucking A!*

fucking old person AND **FOP** *n.* an old person. (Usually objectionable.) ♦ *I know who's slowing traffic up ahead. A FOP, that's who.*

fuck-me boots *n.* knee-high women's boots that signal that the wearer is willing to copulate. ♦ *Eveline! You simply can't go to the prom in those fuck-me boots!*

fuck-shit *n.* a truly wretched and obnoxious person. (Taboo. Usually objectionable.) ♦ *Get out of here you slimy fuck-shit!*

fuck-up 1. *n.* a mess; a hopeless hodgepodge. (Taboo. Usually objectionable.) ♦ *When you went home yesterday, you left behind a first-class fuck-up. Now you can clean it up.* 2. *n.* someone who does everything wrong; someone who messes everything up. (Taboo. Usually objectionable.) ♦ *Poor Willie is such a fuck-up. What a mess he has made.*

fud Go to fuddy-duddy.

fuddy-duddy AND **fud** ['fədidədi AND fəd] *n.* a stuffy person; an old-fashioned person, especially a male. ♦ *There seems to be a convention of fuddy-duddies in the park today.* ♦ *I woke up some old fud sleeping on a park bench. He was mad.*

fudge [fədʒ] 1. *in.* to cheat; to deceive (someone). (Disguise of fuck.) ♦ *Bill, you're fudging. Wait till the starting gun fires.* 2. *n.* nonsense; deception. ♦ *I've heard enough of your fudge. Let's get honest, okay?*

fudge factor *n.* a margin of error. ♦ *I never use a fudge factor. I measure correctly, and I cut the material exactly the way I measured it.*

fugly ['fəgli] *mod.* fat and ugly; fucking ugly. ♦ *Man, is that dog of yours ever fugly! What or who did it eat?*

full blast *mod.* as strongly as possible. ♦ *He honked the horn full blast for a long time.*

full of beans *mod.* full of nonsense; full of hot air. ♦ *Oh, be quiet. You're just full of beans.*

full of bull Go to full of hot air.

full of hops *mod.* full of nonsense. (As if one were full of beer, which contains hops.) ♦ *The guy was full of hops. Nothing he said made any sense.*

full of hot air AND **full of bull; full of it** *mod.* full of nonsense. ♦ *You're so full of hot air. I don't believe you.* ♦ *Go on! You're full of bull!* ♦ *You're full of it, not me!*

full of it Go to full of hot air; full of shit.

full of Old Nick Go to full of the devil.

full of prunes *mod.* full of nonsense. (See also full of beans. Prunes can cause gas = hot air = nonsense.) ♦ *You're just silly. Completely full of prunes.*

full of shit AND **full of it** *mod.* full of lies; stupid. (Usually objectionable.) ♦ *You're full of shit, you liar!* ♦ *You are so full of it!*

full of shizzle *phr.* full of shit. (See also shizzle.) ♦ *Dude. You full of shizzle.*

full of the devil AND **full of Old Nick** *mod.* always making mischief. ♦ *Little Chucky is sure full of the devil.* ♦ *All those kids are full of Old Nick.*

full sesh ['fʊl 'sɛʃ] *mod.* totally; completely. (California.) ♦ *It was a great game. They went at it full sesh the whole time.*

fun *mod.* pleasant; entertaining. ♦ *We had a real fun time.*

fun and games *n.* nonsense; a waste of time. ♦ *I've had enough fun and games. Let's get on with the business.*

fungus Go to (face) fungus.

fungus-face *n.* a bearded man. (See also (face) fungus. See also fuzz-face.) ♦ *Hey, fungus-face! Who is that behind all the fuzz?*

funk [fəŋk] **1.** *n.* a bad odor; a stench. ♦ *What is that ghastly funk in here?* **2.** *n.* tobacco smoke. ♦ *Most of those important decisions are made by party hacks in funk-filled back rooms.* **3.** *n.* a depressed state. ♦ *I've been in such a funk that I can't get my work done.* **4.** *n.* cowardice; terror. ♦ *She suffers this terrible funk whenever she has to give a talk.* **5.** *n.* a kind of blues rock; jazz based on gospel music. ♦ *Man, groove on that funk, would ya?*

funked out *mod.* alcohol or drug intoxicated. ♦ *Do you think you can go through life funked out all the time?*

funking *mod.* damnable. (Euphemistic for fucking. Usually objectionable.) ♦ *Who put this funking milk crate in the hall?*

funky AND **phunky 1.** *mod.* strange; far out. ♦ *I like your funky hat.* **2.** *mod.* basic and simple; earthy. ♦ *I like to be around funky people.* **3.** *mod.* smelly; obnoxious. ♦ *This place is really funky. Open some windows.* **4.** *mod.* unkempt. ♦ *Your hair is sort of funky. Comb it.*

funky-drunk *mod.* alcohol intoxicated; stinking drunk. ♦ *The guy is funky-drunk, and I think he's going to be sick.*

funky-fresh *mod.* very good. (See also fresh.) ♦ *Mary is funky-fresh when she works out, but a real slow runner when she's been lazy.*

funny business Go to monkey business.

funny farm *n.* an insane asylum; a psychiatric hospital. ♦ *He's really weird. They're going to send him to the funny farm.*

funny money 1. *n.* counterfeit money. ♦ *The bank teller spotted the funny money in the man's deposit almost immediately.* **2.** *n.* military script; temporary or substitute money, good only in certain places. ♦ *What am I going to do with all this funny money when I leave here? It's no good anywhere else.* **3.** *n.* foreign currency. (Jocular.) ♦ *We had better buy some gifts and get rid of some of this funny money before our flight.*

fur *n.* the police. (A play on the fuzz.) ♦ *I think the fur is onto you, Rocko.*

furball Go to hairball.

furphy ['fɚfi] *n.* news; gossip; a groundless rumor; scuttlebutt. (Old. From the proper name of an Australian firm that appeared on water wagons in WWI. This source of water was used as a gathering place where gossip was exchanged. Compare to the origin of scuttlebutt. See also latrine rumor.) ♦ *I heard a furphy about you yesterday.*

fuse box *n.* the head; the brain. ♦ *I'm afraid she's missing a little something in the fuse box.*

futz Go to phutz.

futz around Go to putz around.

futz sth up *tv.* to mess something up. ♦ *I don't want to futz up the deal, so I will be quiet.*

fuzz [fəz] **1.** AND **fuzz man; fuzzy (tail)** *n.* the police; a jail keeper; a detective. ♦ *The fuzz is onto you.* ♦ *Tell the fuzz man I was out of town when the job was pulled.*

2. AND **fuzzle** *in.* to get drunk. ♦ *They were just sitting there fuzzling away the day.* ♦ *He fuzzled and fuzzled like booze was going out of style.*

fuzz man Go to fuzz.

fuzz station *n.* a police station. ♦ *He had to spend about an hour at the fuzz station, but nothing happened to him.*

fuzzed AND **fuzzled; fuzzy** *mod.* alcohol intoxicated. ♦ *You are too fuzzed all the time to hold the job. Pack!*

fuzz-face *n.* a man with a beard. (See also fungus-face.) ♦ *A couple of fuzz-faces came in and asked for mustache wax.*

fuzzle Go to fuzz.

fuzzled Go to fuzzed.

fuzzword *n.* a confusing term usually meant to obscure meaning. (See also buzzword.) ♦ *The current crop of fuzzwords contains a few that have come back from the twenties.*

fuzzy Go to fuzzed.

fuzzy (tail) Go to fuzz.

FWIW *interj.* for what it's worth. (Used in electronic mail and computer forum or news group messages. Not pronounced aloud.) ♦ *I think you are just too sensitive, FWIW.*

F-word *n.* the word fuck. (A euphemism that can be used to refer to the word alone without reference to the various meanings of the word.) ♦ *They said the F-word seven times in the movie we saw last night.*

G

G 1. *n.* guy. ♦ *What's up G?* **2.** *interj.* grin. (An initialism used on computer forum or news groups to show that the writer is grinning or happy. Usually, **<G>**. Not pronounced.) ♦ *When are you going to learn to spell? <G>* **3.** Go to **grand**.

gab [gæb] **1.** *in.* to chatter; to gossip. ♦ *Can you stop gabbing just for a minute?* **2.** *n.* mindless chatter; gossip. ♦ *Enough of this gab—on with the show!*

gab room *n.* a women's restroom where women are said to chatter. ♦ *She went to the gab room to powder her nose.*

gabfest ['gæbfɛst] *n.* an event where much chattering or gossip takes place. ♦ *There's a gabfest going on in Clare's room.*

gabmeister *n.* a talk show host or hostess. ♦ *There are so many of these "gabmeisters" that I can hardly keep them straight.*

gack sth *tv.* to steal something. (The same as **gank**.) ♦ *He gacked some skates off that little kid.*

gaffer ['gæfɚ] *n.* an old man; a rustic old man. (From *grandfather*.) ♦ *Nobody out there but some old gaffer with a cane.*

gaffle 1. *tv.* to steal something. ♦ *Somebody gaffled my bike!* **2.** *tv.* to arrest someone. ♦ *The copper gaffled Fred Monday.*

gaffled ['gæfld] *mod.* arrested. ♦ *Fred got himself gaffled for speeding.*

gag [gæg] *n.* a joke; a trick. ♦ *What a great gag! Everybody will love it.*

gaga ['gɑgɑ] **1.** *mod.* crazy; eccentric. ♦ *Sometimes you are so gaga!* **2.** *mod.* dazzled. ♦ *Tom was totally gaga after he got promoted.*

gagger *n.* an obnoxious person or thing. (Something that make one want to gag.) ♦ *Her fit is a gagger!*

galloping dandruff Go to **walking dandruff**.

galumph (around) [gə'lʌmpf...] *in.* to walk around; to **schlep** around. ♦ *I spent all day galumphing around, looking for a present for Ted.*

game *mod.* willing to do something. ♦ *Is anybody game for some pizza?*

game plan *n.* a plan of action; a scheme. (From sports.) ♦ *The game plan for the election was beginning to shape up.*

game time *n.* time to go do what has to be done; time to go to work. (From sports. See also **(It's) showtime!**) ♦ *Okay, gang, let's get going. It's game time.*

gams *n.* legs; a woman's legs. (From Ital. *gamba* = leg.) ♦ *Look at the gams on that dame.*

GAMMD Go to **Go ahead, make my day.**

gander *n.* a look. (As if the looker's neck is stretching to get a better look. See also **rubberneck**.) ♦ *Let me take a gander at it and see if it's done right.*

gang-bang 1. AND **gang-shag** *n.* an act of serial copulation, with one female and a group of males. ♦ *It was nothing but a gang-bang, and a drunken one at that.* **2.** AND **gang-shag** *n.* group rape of a woman. ♦ *There was another gang-bang in the park last week.* **3.** *in. & in.* to perform an act of serial copulation, as in senses 1 or 2. ♦ *A bunch of guys gang-banged Sally, for a fee, of course.* **4.** *tv. & in.* to gang up on someone or something. ♦ *They're always gang-banging. The punks!*

gangbanger *n.* a member of a street gang. ◆ *The gangbangers threatened the old lady too often, and finally she pulled out a can of mace and gave them a little lesson in good manners.*

gangbusters ['gæŋbəstɚz] *n.* a wild, busy, and successful event. (See also like gangbusters.) ◆ *Our party was truly gangbusters, for sure.*

gang-shag Go to gang-bang.

gank sth *tv.* to steal something. ◆ *Who ganked my bike!*

GAPO ['gæpo] *n.* giant armpit odor; a bad underarm odor. ◆ *That cab driver really has the GAPO.*

garbage 1. *n.* nonsense; gibberish. ◆ *He's just talking garbage.* **2.** *n.* jumbled computer code. ◆ *All I get is garbage on the screen.*

garbage freak AND **garbagehead** *n.* an addict who will take any drug. (Drugs.) ◆ *They're only teenagers and already they're garbageheads.* ◆ *The garbageheads will take beans or anything else.*

garbage mouth *n.* someone who uses obscene language. ◆ *Who's the garbage mouth making all the noise?*

garbage sth **down** *tv.* to gobble something up; to bolt something down. ◆ *That guy will garbage down almost anything.*

garbagehead Go to garbage freak.

garbanzos *n.* a woman's breasts. (Usually objectionable.) ◆ *Look at the splendid garbanzos on that chick!*

garden tool *n.* a whore; a hoe. (Contrived word play.) ◆ *She's nothing more than a garden tool.*

gargle 1. *in.* to drink liquor. ◆ *They sat and gargled for an hour or two.* **2.** *n.* liquor; a drink of liquor. ◆ *You want some more gargle?*

gargle factory *n.* a saloon; a tavern. ◆ *Gary spends a lot of time at the gargle factory.*

gargler *n.* a drinker; a drunkard. ◆ *You are going to turn into a gargler if you don't let up on your drinking.*

gas 1. *n.* intestinal gas. ◆ *The baby has gas and will cry for a while longer.* **2.** *n.* nonsense. ◆ *Hey, that's about enough of your gas.* **3.** *in.* to talk nonsense; to brag. (See also gasbag.) ◆ *Stop gassing for a minute and listen.* **4.** *in.* to have a good time. ◆ *We gassed all evening.* **5.** AND **gasser** *n.* a joke; a prank; a wild time. ◆ *What a gas! I had a great time.* **6.** *n.* liquor, especially inferior liquor. ◆ *Pour me a little more of that gas, will you?* **7.** AND **gas up** *in.* to drink excessively; to get drunk. ◆ *I come home every night and find that you've been gassing all day.* ◆ *He gassed up for a couple of hours while waiting for the plane.*

gas up Go to gas.

gasbag *n.* a braggart. ◆ *What's the old gasbag going on about now?*

gas-guzzler *n.* a large automobile that uses much gasoline. ◆ *The old gas-guzzlers were certainly comfortable.*

gash *n.* the female genitals; the vulva. (Usually objectionable.) ◆ *He thought he could see her gash through her swimming suit.*

gash bucket *n.* a refuse bucket; a bucket used as a urinal. (Underworld and military.) ◆ *Don't kick over the gash bucket over there!*

gashawk *n.* an airplane. (A play on goshawk, a species of hawk. From the point of view of a bird watcher.) ◆ *All we saw this morning were two sparrows and a gashawk.*

gas-passer *n.* a jocular nickname for an anesthetist. (Hospitals.) ◆ *My gosh! The gas-passer charged almost as much as the surgeon.*

gassed (up) *mod.* alcohol or drug intoxicated. ◆ *Fred is gassed up and very wobbly.*

gasser Go to gas.

gat *n.* a handgun; a revolver. ◆ *Willie kept his gat in his pocket when the cops walked up.*

the **gate** *n.* a forced exit; sending (someone) away. (See also give so the gate.) ◆ *I could see in his eyes that it was the gate for me.*

gator Go to alligator.

gaucho [ˈɡɑʊtʃo] *tv. & in.* to expose the buttocks (at someone), usually through a car window; to moon. ♦ *Victor gauchoed the cops as they went by.*

gay as pink ink Go to (as) gay as pink ink.

gaydar *n.* the remarkable sense that allows someone to spot gay people. (Word play.) ♦ *Looks like he picked up somebody on his gaydar.*

gazinkus AND **gazunkus** [ɡəˈzɪŋkəs AND ɡəˈzəŋkəs] *n.* a gadget. ♦ *Is this the little gazunkus you were looking for?*

gazizzey AND **gazob** [ɡəˈzɪzi AND ɡəˈzɑb] *n.* a fool. ♦ *What gazizzey put the sugar in the salt shaker?* ♦ *You stupid gazob! Wake up!*

gazob Go to gazizzey.

gazoo [ɡəˈzu] *n.* the buttocks; the anus. ♦ *He fell down flat, smack on his gazoo.*

gazoony [ɡəˈzuni] *n.* a bully or strong-arm man. (Underworld.) ♦ *Bruno didn't like being called a gazoony, although that is what he is.*

gazumph [ɡəˈzʊmpf] **1.** *tv.* to raise the price of a house after it is sold. ♦ *They tried to gazumph the price at the closing.* **2.** *tv.* to subject someone to the raising of the price of a house after it is sold. ♦ *If they try to gazumph you, tell them to forget the deal.*

gazunkus Go to gazinkus.

GBed [ˈdʒiˈbid] *mod.* goofballed; drug intoxicated. (Initialism. Drugs.) ♦ *Gert got GBed fairly often before the accident.*

GBG *interj.* a great big grin. (An initialism used on computer forum or news groups to show that the writer is grinning, joking, or happy. Not pronounced. Often enclosed, **<GBG>**.) ♦ *I think you are just talking nonsense.* <GBG>

gear **1.** *mod.* excellent. ♦ *This jazz is really gear!* **2.** *n.* an asterisk (*). ♦ *The gear stands for anything you want it to stand for.*

g'ed up *mod.* well dressed; *gangstered* up. (Streets.) ♦ *He's fitted. You know, iced up and g'ed up.*

gee [dʒi] **1.** *n.* a portion of liquor, a gallon or a single drink. ♦ *You want another gee of this booze?* **2.** *exclam.* Wow! (An abbreviation of *Jesus!*, although not always recognized as such. Usually **Gee!**) ♦ *Golly gee, do I have to?* **3.** *mod.* gross; disgusting. (The initial letter of *gross*.) ♦ *Tiffany is acting way gee lately.* **4.** Go to grand.

geedunk [ɡiˈdəŋk OR ˈɡidəŋk] *n.* ice cream. ♦ *Let's go out and get some geedunk for dessert.*

geedus Go to geetis.

geegaw AND **gewgaw; googaw** [ˈɡiɡɔ AND ˈɡuɡɔ] *n.* a gadget; a bauble. ♦ *What do you do with these gewgaws? Hang them on a tree?*

geek AND **geke** **1.** *n.* a disgusting and repellent person; a creep. (Rude and derogatory.) ♦ *The convention was a seething morass of pushy sales geeks and gladhanders.* **2.** *n.* an earnest student; a hardworking student. (Usually objectionable.) ♦ *It looks like the geeks are taking over this campus. How gross!* **3.** *n.* a person, soldier, or civilian of an East Asian country, especially in wartime. (Rude and derogatory.) ♦ *Willy is tired of geeks and the way they talk.*

geek out *in.* to study hard. (See also geek.) ♦ *Big test tomorrow. I've got to get home and geek out.*

geekazoid [ˈɡikəzoɪd] *n.* a social outcast; a nerd. ♦ *If you weren't such a geekazoid, I'd be surprised at the dumb things you do!*

geek-chic [ˈɡikˈʃik] *mod.* stylish or fashionable only for social outcasts. (See also geek.) ♦ *Why do you have to buy all this geek-chic stuff? Don't they give it away somewhere?*

geekdom *n.* the realm of the hard-studying students or geeks. ♦ *This dorm is not exactly geekdom. Almost all the guys here are on academic probation.*

Geesh! [ɡiʃ] *exclam.* Good grief! (Shows shock and disgust.) ♦ *Geesh! I love my work but hate my job!*

geetis AND **geedus; geetus** ['gidəs] *n.* money. ♦ *I don't have the geetis to throw around on something like that.*

geetus Go to geetis.

geezer ['gizɚ] **1.** *n.* a strange old man; a buzzard. ♦ *He is a nice geezer, but a little talkative.* **2.** *n.* a drink of liquor. ♦ *Toss down a geezer of this stuff and see how you like it.*

geke Go to geek.

gel [dʒɛl] *in.* to relax and let one's hair down. ♦ *I've got to go home and gel for a while. Things are too stressful just now.*

gender-bender 1. *n.* a device that changes electrical plugs or sockets to the opposite gender—male to female, female to male. ♦ *You need what's called a gender-bender to match those plugs.* **2.** *mod.* having to do with something that obscures male/female distinctions. ♦ *Those gender-bender hairstyles can be confusing.*

generic [dʒə'nɛrɪk] *mod.* cheap; plain; undesirable. ♦ *I don't want any old generic car, I want something with power and good looks.*

genuine article ['dʒɛnjəwən 'ɑrtɪkl̩ OR 'dʒɛn'juwɑin 'ɑrtɪkl̩] *n.* the real thing rather than a substitute. ♦ *Is this the genuine article or some cheap made substitute?*

george 1. *tv. & in.* to copulate [with] a woman. (Usually objectionable.) ♦ *He was in the back room georging some dame.* **2.** *in.* to defecate. (Usually objectionable.) ♦ *Man, I gotta george!*

geri *n.* an old person. (From *geriatric.*) ♦ *Some geri slowed down the cafeteria line to a standstill.*

GERK AND **gerk** [gɚk] *n.* an elderly simpleton; an old nerd. (Acronym. From *geriatric* and *jerk*.) ♦ *A couple of "gerks" sat on the park bench, snoozing.*

German goiter Go to Milwaukee goiter.

Geronimo! [dʒə'rɑnəmo] *exclam.* Here I go! (Originally said by parachutists leaving a plane. From Spanish for *Jerome*.) ♦ *There's my cue. Geronimo!*

get a bang out of so/sth AND **get a kick out of** so/sth *tv.* to get a thrill from someone or something. ♦ *I always get a bang out of her jokes.* ♦ *We got a kick out of him and the way he just sat there.*

get a buzz out of so/sth *tv.* to get some humor from someone or something. (See also give so a buzz.) ♦ *I thought you'd get a buzz out of that gag.*

get a can on *tv.* to get drunk. (See also tie one on.) ♦ *The entire office staff got a can on to celebrate the contract.*

get a fix AND **get a gift** *tv.* to buy drugs; to take a dose of drugs. (Drugs.) ♦ *Gert had to get home and get a fix.*

get a gift Go to get a fix.

get a kick out of so/sth Go to get a bang out of so/sth.

Get a life! *exclam.* Change your life radically! (See also Get real!) ♦ *You are such a twit! Get a life!*

get a load of sth or so *tv.* to look at someone or something. ♦ *Get a load of the chrome on that set of wheels!*

get a load off one's **feet** AND **take a load off** one's **feet** *tv.* to sit down and relax. ♦ *Sit down and get a load off your feet.* ♦ *I need to relax somewhere and take a load off my feet.*

get a load off one's **mind** *tv.* to say what one is thinking; to speak one's mind; to talk something out. ♦ *I'm sorry, but I just had to get a load off my mind.*

get a toehold *tv.* to work one's way into some association or relationship. ♦ *As soon as I get a toehold in the company, I'll be more relaxed.*

Get a wiggle on! *exclam.* to hurry up. ♦ *Hey, you guys! Get a wiggle on! We gotta finish before nightfall.*

get an eyeball on so/sth *tv.* to manage to spot someone or something; to catch sight of someone or something. ♦ *When I finally got an eyeball on the speeding car, it was too far away for me to read the license plate.*

Get away! ['gɛt ə'we] *exclam.* Stop being a pest!; I don't believe you! ♦ *Get away! Nobody is that stupid!*

get behind so/sth *in.* to support someone or something. ♦ *Let's all get behind the party in the next election.*

get behind sth *in.* to enjoy something, such as a drug or music. (Originally drugs.) ♦ *I'm really getting behind heavy metal.*

get brain *tv.* to receive an act of fellatio. ♦ *I can get brain any day. I want pussy!*

Get cracking! *imperative* Get moving!; Get started!; Hurry up! ♦ *Hurry up! Get cracking!*

get down 1. *in.* to lay one's money on the table. (Gambling.) ♦ *Get down, and let's get going!* **2.** *in.* to concentrate; to do something well. ♦ *Come on, Sam, pay attention. Get down and learn this stuff.* **3.** *in.* to copulate. ♦ *All Steve wants to do is get down all the time.* **4.** *in.* to dance. ♦ *Whenever I hear that band, I really want to get down.*

get down on so *in.* to be critical of someone; to **get on** so's **case.** ♦ *Don't get down on me. I didn't do it!*

get down to some serious drinking *in.* to settle down to a long session of drinking. ♦ *Well, now we can get down to some serious drinking.*

get down to the nitty-gritty *in.* to get down to the basic facts. (See also nitty-gritty.) ♦ *If we could only get down to the nitty-gritty and stop wasting time.*

get face *tv.* to gain respect; to increase one's status. (The opposite of *lose face.*) ♦ *He's doing his best in life to get face.*

get hot 1. *in.* to begin to get lucky, as in gambling. ♦ *I knew I was getting hot when I got all the right cards.* **2.** *in.* to become busy or hectic. ♦ *Things always get hot around here toward the end of the month.*

get in bad (with so) *in.* to get into trouble with someone. ♦ *We got in bad with each other from the start.*

get in on the act *in.* to become involved in something with someone else. (The involvement is not necessarily welcome.) ♦ *Everybody wants to get in on the act.*

get in so's **face** *in.* to provoke someone; to move one's face close and become argumentative. ♦ *I know you are angry, but don't get in my face. I had nothing to do with it.*

get in the groove *in.* to become attuned to something. (See also in the groove.) ♦ *I was uncomfortable at first, but now I'm beginning to get in the groove.*

get in(to) so's **pants** *in.* to manage to copulate with a certain female; to seduce a female. (Usually objectionable.) ♦ *Are you sure you don't just want to get into my pants?*

get into sth *in.* to become deeply involved with something. ♦ *I got into computers when I was in junior high school.*

get it 1. *tv.* to understand a joke; to understand a point of information. ♦ *Sorry. I don't get it.* **2.** *tv.* to get punished. ♦ *I just know I'm going to get it when I get home.*

get it (all) together *tv.* to get oneself organized; to get mentally adjusted. ♦ *When I get it together, I'll try to go back to school.*

get it in the neck *tv.* to receive something bad, such as punishment or criticism. (See also pain in the neck.) ♦ *Jimmy was afraid he'd get it in the neck for being late.*

get it off *tv.* to ejaculate; to achieve sexual release; to copulate. (Usually objectionable.) ♦ *The entire crew of the yacht came ashore to get it off.*

get it on 1. *tv.* to begin something. ♦ *Get it on, you guys! Time to start your engines.* **2.** *tv.* to begin dancing. ♦ *He wanted to get it on, but my feet hurt.* **3.** *tv.* [for people] to copulate. (Usually objectionable.) ♦ *Come on, baby, let's get it on.* **4.** *tv.* to undertake to enjoy oneself. ♦ *Let's go listen to some new age and get it on.* **5.** *tv.* to get an erection; to become sexually aroused. (Usually objectionable.) ♦ *He's too tired to get it on.*

get it out *tv.* to tell (someone) about a problem; to pour out one's grief. ♦ *He would feel better if he could get it out.*

get it up 1. *tv.* to get an erection of the penis. (Usually objectionable.) ♦ *He's so drunk all the time, he can hardly get it up.* **2.** *tv.* to get excited about something. ♦ *I just couldn't get it up about going off to college.*

get lip *tv.* to get some kissing; to neck. (Teens.) ♦ *Jim's been out getting lip again. Look at the lipstick.*

Get lost! *exclam.* Go away!; Beat it! ♦ *Get lost, you're bothering me!*

get mad (at sth**)** *in.* to muster great physical strength and determination in order to do something. ♦ *You're gonna have to get mad at it if you want to move it.*

Get my drift? Go to (Do you) get my drift?

get naked *in.* to enjoy oneself thoroughly; to relax and enjoy oneself. ♦ *Let's all go out and get naked tonight.*

get narkied [...'nɑrkid] *in.* to inject drugs; to become addicted. (Drugs.) ♦ *Rocko only got narkied once in his life.*

get nowhere fast *in.* to make very poor progress. ♦ *We are getting nowhere fast around here.*

Get off it! Go to Come off it!

Get off my ass! AND **Get off my tail!; Get off my back!** *exclam.* Leave me alone!; Stop following me!; Stop dogging me! (Usually objectionable.) ♦ *Stop pestering me! Get off my ass!* ♦ *Get off my back! Go bug somebody else.*

Get off my back! Go to Get off my ass!

Get off my bumper! 1. *exclam.* Stop following my car so closely! ♦ *Don't follow me so close! Get off my bumper!* **2.** *exclam.* Stop monitoring me!; Get off my back! ♦ *Look, man. I can take care of myself. Get off my bumper!*

Get off my tail! Go to Get off my ass!

get off (on sth**) 1.** *in.* to get pleasure from something; to become sexually aroused by something. ♦ *I don't get off on music anymore.* **2.** *in.* to take a drug and experience a rush. (Drugs.) ♦ *Max likes to get off, but he's got his business to run.* **3.** *in.* to do well on something. ♦ *Wayne is get-*

ting off on history, much to everyone's surprise.

get off one's **rear** *in.* to get up and get busy. (Euphemistic for Get off my ass!) ♦ *It's time to get off your rear and get to work.*

get off so's **back** AND **get off** so's **case** *in.* to stop annoying someone. (Compare this with get on so's case.) ♦ *I've had enough of you. Get off my back!* ♦ *Get off my case! You aren't my mother.*

get off so's **case** Go to get off so's back.

get off the dime *in.* [for something or someone] to start moving. (To get off the dime that one stopped on in *stop on a dime.*) ♦ *If this project gets off the dime, we'll be okay.*

get on one's **horse** *in.* to prepare to leave. ♦ *It's late. I have to get on my horse.*

get on so's **case** *in.* to start harassing someone about a personal problem; to annoy someone. (Compare this with get off so's case.) ♦ *I'll get on Tom's case about being late so much.*

get on the stick *in.* to get organized and get busy. ♦ *Get on the stick and get this job done!*

get one's **act together** AND **get** one's **shit together; get** one's **stuff together 1.** *tv.* to organize oneself; to get one's possessions organized. (Usually objectionable.) ♦ *Let me get my act together, and I'll be right with you.* ♦ *As soon as I get my shit together and put it away, I be with you.* **2.** AND **get** one's **head together** *tv.* to calm down and get mentally organized. (Usually objectionable.) ♦ *As soon as I get my head together, I can be of more help.*

get one's **ass in gear** AND **get** one's **tail in gear** *exclam.* to get moving; to get organized and get started. (Usually objectionable.) ♦ *Come on, you guys. Get moving. Get your ass in gear!* ♦ *Get moving, guys. Get your tail in gear and keep moving!*

get one's **bowels in an uproar** *tv.* to become overly anxious or excited. ♦ *Fred's always getting his bowels in an uproar about nothing.*

get one's **head together** Go to get one's act together.

get one's **hooks into** so *tv.* [for a woman] to succeed in "capturing" a specific man. ♦ *When she got her hooks into him, she decided he wasn't so great after all.*

get one's **hooks into** sth *tv.* to get a hold of something; to gain control of something. ♦ *If I could get my hooks into the control of the company, I would change things for the better.*

get one's **kicks (from** so/sth**)** *tv.* to get pleasure from someone or something. ♦ *I get my kicks from Billy Simpson. What a great entertainer!*

get one's **knob polished** *tv.* to copulate or otherwise have sex. (Refers to a male. Usually objectionable.) ♦ *Man, if you want to get your knob polished, just let me know. I got girls! I got girls you wouldn't believe!*

get one's **lumps** *tv.* to get the result or punishment one deserves. (See also take one's lumps.) ♦ *If she keeps acting that way, she'll get her lumps.*

get one's **nose cold** *tv.* to snort cocaine. (Drugs.) ♦ *Shorty is always ready to get his nose cold.*

get one's **nose out of joint** *tv.* to feel slighted by something someone has done; to take offense at something. (See also put so's nose out of joint.) ♦ *You get your nose out of joint too easily about stuff like that.*

get one's **nuts off** Go to get one's rocks off.

get one's **rocks off** AND **get** one's **nuts off** *tv.* [for a male] to copulate or ejaculate. (Usually objectionable.) ♦ *His idea of a good time was getting his rocks off.* ♦ *He went into town to get his nuts off.*

get one's **rocks off (on** sth**)** *tv.* to enjoy something. (See also get one's rocks off.) ♦ *I've listened to the stuff, but I sure don't get my rocks off on it.*

get one's **shit together** Go to get one's act together.

get one's **stuff together** Go to get one's act together.

get one's **tail** somewhere **fast!** AND **get** one's **tail** somewhere **now!**; **get** one's **tail** somewhere **immediately!** *tv.* to move oneself to a particular place fast. ♦ *You get your tail over here immediately!* ♦ *I'll tell you one more time. Get your tail into my office immediately!*

get one's **tail** somewhere **immediately!** Go to get one's tail somewhere **fast!**

get one's **tail** somewhere **now!** Go to get one's tail somewhere **fast!**

get one's **teeth into** sth AND **sink** one's **teeth into** sth *tv.* to undertake to do something. ♦ *She'll do better as soon as she gets her teeth into the task.* ♦ *I can't wait to sink my teeth into that Wallace job.*

get one's **ticket punched** *tv.* to die; to be killed. (Literally, to be canceled.) ♦ *Poor Chuck got his ticket punched while he was waiting for a bus.*

get one's **wings** *tv.* to use heavy drugs for the first time; to succeed in becoming a drug addict. (Drugs.) ♦ *Gert got her wings after fiddling around with stuff for a long time.*

get out of Dodge *in.* to leave a place. (Refers to Dodge City, Kansas, and a cliché from Western entertainment adventures about this town.) ♦ *Things are looking bad here. It's time to get out of Dodge.*

Get out of here! *exclam.* You are just kidding me!; You are making that up! ♦ *See you tomorrow. I'm out of here!*

Get out of my face! *exclam.* Stop arguing with me!; Stand back! Don't confront me with your arguments and challenges! (See also get in so's face.) ♦ *Get outa my face if you know what's good for you.*

Get out of town! *exclam.* Beat it!; Get out of here! ♦ *You'd better get out of town, my friend. You are a pest.*

get (out) while the gettin(g)'s good AND **get (out) while the goin's good** *in.* to leave while it is still safe or possible to do so. ♦ *I can tell that it's time for me to get while the gettin's good.* ♦ *I think we should go. Let's get while the going's good.*

get (out) while the goin's good Go to get (out) while the gettin(g)'s good.

get pasted 1. *mod.* alcohol or drug intoxicated. (From paste.) ♦ *Bart got pasted on beer.* **2.** *mod.* beaten; outscored. ♦ *Our team really got pasted.*

Get real! *exclam.* Start acting realistically! (See also Get a life!) ♦ *Hey, chum! You are way off base! Get real!*

get right Go to get straight.

get smart (with so) *in.* to become fresh with someone; to talk back to someone. ♦ *If you get smart again, I'll bop you.*

get some shut-eye *tv.* to get some sleep. ♦ *We all could use some shut-eye.*

get some yokes on *tv.* to build up one's muscles. (Bodybuilding.) ♦ *If I keep working at this, I know I can get some yokes on.*

get so going *tv.* to get someone excited; to get someone talking excitedly. ♦ *The whole business really makes me mad. Don't get me going.*

get so's goat *tv.* to irritate someone. ♦ *Don't let Mary get your goat. She's just irritable today.*

get so's motor running 1. *tv.* to get someone excited. ♦ *I've got some news that'll really get your motor running.* **2.** *tv.* to get someone sexually aroused. ♦ *She knows how to get his motor running.*

get sth going (with so) *tv.* to start a romance with someone. ♦ *Mary and Sam got something going.*

get spun *in.* to get drunk. ♦ *Let's go out and get spun.*

get straight AND **get right** *in.* to take a dose of a drug to end drug craving. (Drugs.) ♦ *You'll never get straight if you keep smoking that stuff.* ♦ *I need to get right before anything else.*

get stupid *in.* to become intoxicated; to make oneself alcohol or drug intoxicated. ♦ *It's been one totally screwed up week. I think I'll just stay home tonight and get stupid.*

get the ax Go to get the sack.

get the drop on so 1. *tv.* to succeed in getting an advantage over someone. ♦ *I got the drop on almost everybody by sending in my registration by mail.* **2.** *tv.* [for person A] to manage to get a gun aimed at person B before person B can aim back at person A. (The gun is then dropped by person B.) ♦ *Rocko got the drop on Shorty in a flash.*

get the goods on so *tv.* to uncover incriminating evidence against someone. ♦ *The IRS tried to get the goods on Rocko, but Rocko knows all the angles.*

Get the lead out! *exclam.* Get moving!; Hurry up! (Crude. It is assumed that one has bowels full of lead.) ♦ *Come on, you turkeys. Get the lead out!*

Get the message? AND **Get the picture?** *interrog.* Do you understand?; Are you able to figure out what is meant? ♦ *How many times do I have to tell you? Do you get the message?* ♦ *Things are tough around here, and we need everyone's cooperation. Get the picture?*

get the nod *tv.* to be chosen. (See also give so the nod.) ♦ *Fred got the nod for class treasurer.*

Get the picture? Go to Get the message?

get the sack AND **get the ax** *tv.* to be dismissed from one's employment. ♦ *Poor Tom got the sack today. He's always late.* ♦ *If I miss another day, I'll get the ax.*

get the show on the road *tv.* to get (something) started. ♦ *Let's get started! Get the show on the road!*

get there *in.* to get drunk. ♦ *Another hour of drinking and Pete knew he was going to get there.*

get to first (base) (with so) *in.* to achieve a basic or initial level of intimacy with someone, such as getting some attention or even getting kissed. ♦ *I'm too shy. I just know I can't get to first base with her.*

get to so 1. *in.* [for someone or something] to annoy someone after a period of exposure to the annoyance. ♦ *The whole business began to get to me after a while.* **2.** *in.* [for someone or something] to please or entice someone. ♦ *Sad music gets to me and makes me cry.*

get with it 1. *in.* to modernize one's attitudes and behavior. ♦ *Get with it, Martin. Get real!* **2.** *in.* to hurry up and get busy; to be more industrious with something. ♦ *Let's get with it. There's a lot of work to be done.*

get with so *in.* to find out about someone; to get to know someone. ♦ *I'd really like to get with her, but she's so distant.*

get with the program *in.* follow the rules; do what you are supposed to do. ♦ *Jane just can't seem to get with the program. She has to do everything her way, right or wrong.*

Get your ass over here! AND **Get your buns over here!; Get your butt over here!** *imperative* Get yourself over here, now! (Usually objectionable.) ♦ *Get your ass over here and clean this up.* ♦ *Get your butt over here and help me move this trunk.*

Get your nose out of my business! AND **Keep your nose out of my business!** *exclam.* Mind your own business and leave me alone. ♦ *Get your nose out of my business! This is not your affair.* ♦ *I'll thank you to keep your nose out of my business!*

getaway ['getəwe] **1.** *n.* an escape from the law. (Originally underworld.) ♦ *There was no time to make a getaway, so we had to talk to Mrs. Wilson.* **2.** *n.* a place to escape to; a hideaway. ♦ *The lover had a little hideaway in a small town on the state line.* **3.** *n.* a quick vacation. ♦ *What you need is a weekend getaway.*

gets one **right here** *tv.* to affect one deeply in a specific way. (Usually accompanied with a hand gesture showing exactly where one is affected: the heart = lovingly, the stomach or bowels = sickeningly.) ♦ *Pete clasped his hand to his chest and said, "That sort of thing gets me right here."*

Getting any? *interrog.* Have you been having any sexual activity? (An inquiry or greeting between some males. Usually objectionable.) ♦ *Hey, Tom! Getting any?*

gewgaw Go to geegaw.

ghetto *mod.* super; cool. (Streets.) ♦ *He called the iced out pimp 100 percent ghetto.*

ghetto bird 1. *n.* someone who hangs around the [black] neighborhood. ♦ *Sam is just a ghetto bird who has lots of skills but no job.* **2.** *n.* a police helicopter. ♦ *I see the light. Some ghetto bird is headed this way.*

(ghetto) blaster AND **(ghetto) box** ['gɛdo blæstɚ AND 'gɛdo baks] *n.* a huge portable stereo, often carried on the shoulder. (Associated with blacks.) ♦ *Hey, turn down that ghetto blaster in here!*

ghetto booty *n.* big buttocks on a black woman. ♦ *Look at that ghetto booty on that mama.*

(ghetto) box Go to (ghetto) blaster.

ghetto sled *n.* a junky car. ♦ *He stood in front of some old ghetto sled, and said "Kizzle?"*

ghost so *tv.* to kill someone. ♦ *Mooshoo threatened to ghost the guy.*

ghost turd *n.* a wad of lint, as found under a bed. (Use caution with **turd.**) ♦ *There's a lot of ghost turds under the bed.*

GIB *mod.* good in bed; good as a sexual partner. (Usually objectionable. Initialism.) ♦ *How does he know if he's GIB?*

gibber-gabber ['dʒɪbɚdʒæbɚ] *n.* nonsense; gossip and chatter. ♦ *There sure is a lot of gibber-gabber coming from your room, Jimmy.*

Giddy up! ['gɪdi...] *exclam.* Move faster! (Properly said to a horse to start it moving. Also said to people or things as a joke.) ♦ *Giddy up, Charlie! It's time to start moving.*

gidget *n.* a silly-acting female; a ditzy dame. ♦ *Sally is just a blonde gidget without a care in the world.*

giffed [gɪft] *mod.* alcohol intoxicated. (From TGIF Thank God it's Friday. Said of people who celebrate the end of the workweek with liquor.) ♦ *He left the tavern pretty giffed.*

the gift of gab *n.* the ability to speak well in public; the ability to persuade people verbally; the ability to speak well extemporaneously. ♦ *I wish I had the gift of gab. I'm just so shy.*

gig 1. *n.* a onetime job; an engagement. (Musicians.) ♦ *I had a gig out on the west side, but I couldn't get there.* **2.** *in.* to play or perform. (Musicians.) ♦ *I didn't gig at all last week. I'm getting hungry for a job.* **3.** *n.* any job of an assignment nature; a onetime job such as when a newspaper reporter is assigned to write a particular story.* ♦ *I didn't want that election gig, but I got it anyway.* **4.** *n.* a bother; an annoyance; a job. ♦ *Man, this paperwork is such a gig.* **5.** *n.* a giggle; a bit of laughter. ♦ *Her little story gave us all a good gig.*

giggle goo [ˈgɪgl̩ gu] *n.* liquor. ♦ *Can I pour you a little of that giggle goo?*

giggling *n.* going to clubs and bars. ♦ *We spent the whole night giggling, but never got really, totally drunk.*

GIGO *phr.* garbage in, garbage out. (Computers. Acronym. If you get garbage out of a computer, it's because you put garbage in. See also **DIDO**.) ♦ *The program failed, and I know it's my fault. You know, GIGO.*

gimme [ˈgɪmi] *phr.* give me. (Eye-dialect. Typical spoken English. Used in writing only for effect. Used in the examples of this dictionary.) ♦ *Do you wanna gimme the thingy and lemme go ahead with my work?*

Gimme a break! Go to **Give me a break!**

gimp [gɪmp] **1.** *n.* a lame person. (Originally underworld. Rude and derogatory.) ♦ *Lefty tried to mug an old gimp with a cane.* **2.** *in.* to limp about. ♦ *I'll gimp over there as soon as I can. It'll take a while on these crutches.*

gimpy [ˈgɪmpi] **1.** *mod.* crippled; lame. ♦ *I got a gimpy leg. I'll catch up in a minute.* **2.** *n.* a police officer. (Also a rude term of address. A pun on **lame**, an inept person.) ♦ *Here comes gimpy, swinging his stick.*

gin dive Go to **gin mill**.

gin mill AND **gin dive; gin palace** *n.* a saloon; a low liquor establishment. (Older.) ♦ *Fred hit every gin mill on the way home.* ♦ *The joint looks like a gin dive. I'm not going in there!*

gin palace Go to **gin mill**.

ginhead *n.* a drunkard. ♦ *Gert could have ended up a ginhead, but she went another route instead.*

girked *mod.* intoxicated with heroin. ♦ *He shot himself up and was girked in no time.*

girl 1. *n.* a woman; a young woman. (Objectionable to some as demeaning to women.) ♦ *A bunch of us girls got together for coffee today.* **2.** *n.* the queen of playing cards. (See also **bitch**.) ♦ *What I needed in that last hand was the girl.*

girl thing *n.* something that women do; something that appeals to women. ♦ *You wouldn't understand. It's a girl thing.*

girlfriend *n.* one's female friend. (This sense in addition to the Standard English meaning that includes steady date, female lover, etc. A term of address primarily between females.) ♦ *Look, girlfriend, you can't let him treat you like that!*

girlie magazine *n.* a magazine featuring pictures of nude women. ♦ *The girlie magazines were hidden under the counter.*

girlie show *n.* a performance featuring nude women. ♦ *This movie has turned out to be nothing but a girlie show.*

gism Go to **jism**.

git-go [ˈgɪtgo] *n.* the very beginning. (See also **from (the) git-go**.) ♦ *He's been gritching ever since git-go.*

give a fuck (about so/sth**)** Go to **give a shit (about** so/sth**)**.

give a shit (about so/sth**)** AND **give a fuck (about** so/sth**)** *tv.* to care about someone or something. (Usually objectionable. Often negative.) ♦ *If you think I give a shit about you or anyone else, you're full of shit.* ♦ *Do you think I give a fuck about what you do?*

give head *tv.* to perform oral sex on someone, usually a male. (Usually objectionable.) ♦ *Does she give head?*

Give it a rest! *exclam.* Shut up! (The *it* is a mouth. See also Give me a rest!) ♦ *Give it a rest! You talk too much.*

give it the gun *tv.* to gun an engine; to rev an engine up. ♦ *I gave it the gun, and it backfired.*

Give it up! *exclam.* Quit now!; Enough is enough! ♦ *Give it up! You can't pitch!*

Give me a break! AND **Gimme a break!** **1.** *exclam.* That is enough!; Stop it! ♦ *Do you have to go on and on? Give me a break!* **2.** *exclam.* Don't be so harsh!; Give me a chance! ♦ *I'm sorry! I'll do better! Give me a break!* **3.** AND **GMAB** *exclam. & comp. abb.* I don't believe it!; You don't really think I believe that! ♦ *Come on, GMAB! How dumb do you think I am!*

Give me a rest! *exclam.* Lay off!; That is enough! (See also Give it a rest!) ♦ *Haven't I told you everything you need to know? Give me a rest.*

Give me five! Go to Give me (some) skin!

Give me (some) skin! AND **Give me five!; Slip me five!** *exclam.* Shake my hand! (A request for some form of hand touching in greeting. See also give so five; high five.) ♦ *Hey, man! Give me some skin!* ♦ *Give me five, dude!*

give one one's pounds *tv.* thumping a buddy with the fist out of respect and brotherhood. ♦ *All his buds gave Willy his pounds.*

give (out) with sth *in.* to give out information. ♦ *Come on, give out with the facts, man.*

give so a buzz 1. *tv.* to give someone a telephone call. ♦ *Give me a buzz sometime.* **2.** *tv.* to give someone a chuckle or a bit of enjoyment. ♦ *It always gives me a buzz to watch Sally do her act.*

give so a dig *tv.* to insult someone; to say something which will irritate a person. ♦ *Jane gave Bob a dig about his carelessness with money.*

give so a (good) talking to *tv.* to scold someone; to lecture someone sternly. ♦ *The teacher gave Jimmy a talking to.*

give so a (good) working over *tv.* to scold or beat someone. ♦ *The boss gave me a good working over before firing me.*

give so a melvin *tv.* to jerk up someone's pants or underwear, drawing the fabric up sharply between the buttocks. (It is assumed that some **geek** named Melvin goes about with his underwear in this uncomfortable position.) ♦ *Tom came up behind Fred and, with a deft motion, gave Fred a melvin that he would never forget.*

give so a pain *tv.* to annoy or bother someone. ♦ *You give me a pain!*

give so an earful 1. *tv.* to scold someone. ♦ *Sally gave Sam an earful for the way he treated Mary.* **2.** *tv.* to tell someone surprising secrets. ♦ *Willy gave Sally an earful about Todd's tax problems.*

give so five 1. *tv.* to give someone a helping hand. ♦ *I gotta give this guy five with the crate. Be right with you.* **2.** *tv.* to slap hands in greeting. (See also high five; Give me five!) ♦ *Jerry gave John five as they passed in the corridor.*

give so hell 1. *tv.* to bawl someone out; to scold someone severely. (Use caution with hell.) ♦ *The boss just gave me hell about it.* **2.** *tv.* to trouble someone. (Use caution with hell.) ♦ *This problem is giving us hell at the office.*

give so the ax 1. *tv.* to dismiss someone from employment. ♦ *I was afraid they would give me the ax.* **2.** *tv.* to divorce someone. ♦ *She gave him the ax because he wouldn't stop smoking like he promised.*

give so the brushoff *tv.* to repel someone; to ignore someone. (See also brushoff.) ♦ *The manager gave her the brushoff when she asked for a raise.*

give so the business 1. *tv.* to harass someone; to scold someone. ♦ *The guys have been giving me the business about my haircut.* **2.** *tv.* to kill someone. (Underworld.) ♦ *Lefty wanted to give Rocko the business for being so damn perfect.*

give so the finger 1. *tv.* to display the middle finger upright as a sign of derision. (The gesture is taboo.) ♦ *Somebody gave the cop the finger.* **2.** *tv.* to mistreat someone; to insult someone. ♦ *You've been giving me the finger ever since I started working here. What's wrong?*

give so **the gate** *tv.* to get rid of someone. ♦ *The chick was a pest, so I gave her the gate.*

give so **the go-by** *tv.* to bypass someone; to ignore someone. (See also go-by.) ♦ *I didn't mean to give you the go-by. I'm preoccupied, that's all.*

give so **the nod 1.** *tv.* to signal someone by nodding. (Not slang.) ♦ *I gave Pete the nod, and he started the procedure.* **2.** *tv.* to choose someone. (See also get the nod.) ♦ *The committee gave Frank the nod for the job.*

give so **the raspberry** *tv.* to make a rude noise with the lips at someone. (See also Bronx cheer; raspberry.) ♦ *The audience gave him the raspberry, which gave him some second thoughts about his choice of career.*

give so **the shaft** *tv.* to cheat or deceive someone; to mistreat someone. (See also shaft.) ♦ *The boss really gave Willy the shaft.*

give so **the slip** *tv.* to escape from a pursuer. ♦ *We were on his tail until he gave us the slip.*

give so **up** *tv.* to betray someone; to turn someone in to the authorities. ♦ *No, I didn't give Mooshoo up!*

giveaway *n.* something that reveals a fact that was meant to be concealed. (Often with *dead*.) ♦ *The way he was walking was a giveaway to the fact that he was the one who was injured.*

gizmo ['gɪzmo] *n.* a gadget. ♦ *What is this silly little gizmo on the bottom for?*

gizzle a wild card word for words beginning with *G*, such as **gangsta** (Streets. Also for other words with initial *G*.) ♦ *You are my gizzle bizzle.*

gizzum Go to jism.

gizzy ['gɪzi] *n.* marijuana. (Drugs.) ♦ *The cops found a little gizzy in the guy's pocket.*

glad *mod.* alcohol intoxicated. ♦ *After a few beers she was a mite glad.*

glad rags *n.* fancy clothes; best clothing. (See also rag.) ♦ *I'll get on my glad rags, and we'll go out tonight.*

glad-hand *tv.* to greet someone effusively. (The *hand* is the hand that is offered to quickly to each person who is greeted.) ♦ *The senator was glad-handing everyone in sight.*

glad-hander *n.* someone who displays effusive friendship, typically a politician. (See comment at glad-hand.) ♦ *The glad-handers were out in full force at the Independence Day parade.*

glam *mod.* glamorous. ♦ *Wow! Isn't she glam!*

glamour puss *n.* a person with a beautiful face. ♦ *I'm no glamour puss, but I'm no dog either.*

Gland Canyon *n.* the cleavage (between the breasts). (Punning on *Grand Canyon*. See also Mammary Lane.) ♦ *I'd like nothing better than being lost in Gland Canyon.*

glass gun *n.* a hypodermic syringe. (Drugs.) ♦ *A lot of those gangsters don't even use a glass gun.*

glass(y)-eyed *mod.* alcohol or drug intoxicated; drugged or suffering from an illness. ♦ *Mary is looking sort of glassy-eyed, and it's only midnight.*

glazed (drunk) AND **glazed (over)** *mod.* alcohol intoxicated. ♦ *She has had too much. She's glazed drunk.*

glazed (over) Go to glazed (drunk).

gleep [glip] *n.* a fool; an oaf. ♦ *What a gleep! Does he know what's what?*

glick [glɪk] a strange person; a nerd. ♦ *Fred seems to be a classic glick, but he is really an all-right guy.*

glitch [glɪtʃ] *n.* a defect; a bug. ♦ *There is a glitch in the computer program somewhere.*

glitz [glɪts] *n.* flashiness and glamour. ♦ *The place was a morass of eager sales geeks and phony glitz.*

glitzy ['glɪtsi] *mod.* fashionable; glamorous. ♦ *Some glitzy blonde sang a couple of songs, and then the band played again.*

glock *n.* a gun; a revolver. (Generalized from Glock, the name of an Austrian manufacturer of semiautomatic pistols. Generic and inexact in this sense.) ♦ *Sam was carrying a glock and threatened to end the argument his own way.*

glom [glɑm] **1.** *tv.* to steal something. (Underworld.) ♦ *He gloms just about everything he needs.* **2.** *tv.* to take a look at someone or something. (Underworld.) ♦ *Come over here and glom the view of the bank from this window.* **3.** *tv.* to arrest someone. ♦ *The copper glommed Fred on Tuesday.*

glommed [glɑmd] *mod.* arrested. (Underworld.) ♦ *Wilmer got glommed on a speeding charge. I didn't even know he could drive.*

glop [glɑp] **1.** *n.* unappetizing food; gunk; anything undesirable. ♦ *Do we have the same old glop again tonight?* **2.** *tv.* to slop or plop something (onto something). ♦ *She glopped something horrible onto my plate.*

glorified *mod.* overblown; overhyped; phony. ♦ *Why, this is just a glorified potato chip!*

glow *n.* a mild state of drug or alcohol intoxication. ♦ *What was supposed to be a nice glow turned out to be a terrifying hallucination.*

glow worm *n.* a drunkard; an alcoholic. (From glow.) ♦ *Gary came out of the bar and tripped over a napping glow worm near the entrance to the alley.*

glue factory *n.* the place where old horses are sent so their bones can be made into glue; a similar, imaginary place for people. ♦ *I'm not as young as I used to be, but I'm not ready for the glue factory yet.*

glued 1. *mod.* arrested. (Underworld.) ♦ *Shorty goes to great extremes to keep from getting glued.* **2.** *mod.* alcohol intoxicated. ♦ *About three more beers and I'll be glued.*

gluer Go to gluey.

gluey AND **gluer** *n.* a person, usually a teenager, who sniffs glue. (Drugs.) ♦ *Teddy is a gluey. That's why he's failing in school.*

glug [glǝg] *n.* a gulp or shot of liquor. ♦ *I took one glug and spit it out.*

glutes *n.* the gluteus maximus muscles. (Bodybuilding.) ♦ *I need to exercise to tighten up my glutes.*

glutz [glǝts] *n.* a slut; a woman of low morals. ♦ *I didn't say she is a glutz!*

GMAB Go to Give me a break!

G-man ['dʒimæn] *n.* a government investigative agent; an FBI agent. ♦ *The G-men busted in and started shooting.*

(g)narly ['nɑrli] *mod.* extreme; excellent; great; superior. (California.) ♦ *This pizza is too gnarly for words!*

go 1. *n.* a try (at something). ♦ *I'd like to have another go at it, if I can.* **2.** *in.* to urinate. ♦ *Jimmy's gonna go in his pants!* **3.** *tv.* to say or utter something. (Mostly teens. Used in writing only for effect.) ♦ *Then she goes, "Like . . . ," and just stops talking.*

Go ahead, make my day. AND **GAMMD** *sent. & comp. abb.* I'll be happy if you do something that will cause me to harm you. ♦ *So, you're gonna do it anyway! Go ahead, make my day!*

go all the way *in.* to copulate; to carry necking all the way to copulation. (Euphemistic. Usually objectionable.) ♦ *He keeps wanting me to go all the way.*

go ape (over so/sth**)** *in.* to become very excited over someone or something. ♦ *I just go ape over chocolate.*

go apeshit over so/sth *in.* to get very excited about someone or something. (Usually objectionable.) ♦ *She really went apeshit over the ice cream.*

go bananas *in.* to go mildly crazy. (See also bananas.) ♦ *I thought he was going to go bananas.*

go belly up Go to turn belly up.

go bitchcakes *in.* to go wild or crazy. (Usually objectionable.) ♦ *All this rude talk just makes me go bitchcakes.*

go blooey AND **go flooey** [go 'blui AND go 'flui] *in.* to fall apart; to go out of order. All my plans went blooey because of the rain. ♦ *I just hope everything doesn't go flooey at the last minute.*

(Go) blow it out your ear! *tv.* Go away and stop bothering me with your nonsense. ♦ *You are not way rad, you're just way out, twit! Blow it out your ear!*

Go chase your tail! Go to Go chase yourself!

Go chase yourself! AND **Go chase your tail!; Go climb a tree!; Go fly a kite!; Go fry an egg!; Go jump in the lake!; Go soak your head!; Go soak yourself!** *exclam.* Beat it!; Go away! ♦ *Oh, go chase yourself!* ♦ *Go soak your head! You're a pain in the neck.*

Go climb a tree! Go to Go chase yourself!

go commando AND **go freeball(ing)** *in.* [for a male] to go about not wearing underpants. (The same as freeball.) ♦ *Bobby is always going commando. Even when it's cold.*

go down 1. *in.* to happen; [for a process or sequence] to unfold. ♦ *Something strange is going down around here.* **2.** *in.* to be accepted. (See also swallow.) ♦ *We'll just have to wait a while to see how all this goes down.* **3.** *in.* to be arrested. (Underworld.) ♦ *Mr. Gutman said that somebody had to go down for it, and he didn't care who.*

go down in flames *in.* to fail spectacularly. (See also shoot so down in flames; crash and burn.) ♦ *The whole team went down in flames.*

go down on SO *in.* to perform oral sex on someone. (Usually objectionable. Formerly also had the meaning to eat food. See also eat.) ♦ *She was just gonna go down on him when the camera panned over to the window.*

go down the chute Go to go down the tube(s).

go down the line *in.* to snort a line of cocaine. (Drugs.) ♦ *They found her in the john, going down the line.*

go down the tube(s) AND **go down the chute** *in.* to fail totally; to be ruined. ♦ *I*

tried, but it all went down the tube. ♦ *All my plans just went down the chute.*

go downhill *in.* to decline. ♦ *Things began to go downhill when the county cut the maintenance budget.*

go Dutch *in.* [for two people] to split the cost of something, such as a meal. (See also Dutch treat.) ♦ *How about dinner tonight? We'll go Dutch, okay?*

Go figure. *interj.* Try to figure it out.; Just try to explain that! ♦ *They heat the water to make the tea hot, then they put ice in it to make it cold, then they put lemon in it to make it sour, and then they put sugar in it to make it sweet. Go figure.*

go flooey Go to go blooey.

Go fly a kite! Go to Go chase yourself!

go for broke *in.* to choose to risk everything; to try to succeed against great odds. ♦ *We decided to go for broke, and that is exactly how we ended up.*

Go for it! *exclam.* Do it!; Try it! ♦ *It looked like something I wanted to do, so I decided to go for it.*

go for the fences *in.* to set extremely high goals and do whatever is needed to meet them. (Alludes to attempting to hit a home run against the fences of a baseball stadium.) ♦ *We are going to go for the fences on this one. Don't hold back on anything.*

go freeball(ing) Go to go commando.

Go fry an egg! Go to Go chase yourself!

Go fuck yourself! *tv.* Go to hell!; Get out of here! (Taboo. Usually objectionable.) ♦ *You worthless mungshit! Go fuck yourself!*

go great guns *in.* to do very well; to go very fast. ♦ *The project is finally going great guns, just as we planned.*

go green on SO *in.* to turn against someone; to move against someone; to get angry at someone; to rage at someone. ♦ *Don't go green on me! You know I'm your best bud!*

go haywire 1. *in.* [for a person] to go berserk. ♦ *Sorry, I guess I just went haywire for a minute.* **2.** *in.* [for something] to go out of order; to break down. ♦ *I'm afraid my car's gone haywire. It won't start.*

go home in a box *in.* to be shipped home dead. ♦ *You had better be careful on this camping trip, or you'll go home in a box.*

go into orbit *in.* to become very excited. ♦ *The entire staff went into orbit when they got the news.*

Go jump in the lake! Go to Go chase yourself!

go mental *in.* go crazy; to act stupid. ♦ *Another day in that history class and I know I will go mental.*

go off half-cocked *in.* to proceed without knowing all the facts. ♦ *The boss went off half-cocked and exploded into a rage about the mess.*

go off on *so in.* to berate someone. ♦ *Don't go off on me! I'm not the cause of your problems!*

go off the deep end *in.* to do or experience something in the extreme: to fall madly in love, to go crazy, to commit suicide, to fly into a rage, etc. ♦ *I saw what he had done, and I just went off the deep end. I was in a blind rage and didn't know what I was doing.*

Go on! *exclam.* I don't believe you!; I deny it! ♦ *Go on! You weren't even there.*

go on (and on) about *so/sth in.* to rave about someone or something endlessly. ♦ *Why do you have to go on about your sister so?*

go over big *in.* to be appreciated as a success. ♦ *Well, it didn't go over very big with the boss.*

go over like a lead balloon *in.* [for something meant to be good] to fail to be good. (See also go over big.) ♦ *I'm afraid your plan went over like a lead balloon.*

go over the hill *in.* to escape from a prison or from the military service. (See also over the hill; go over the wall.) ♦ *Jed and Tom planned to go over the hill last night. What happened?*

go over the wall *in.* to escape from a prison. ♦ *Lefty tried to go over the wall, but the warden got wind of it.*

go overboard *in.* to do far more than is necessary. ♦ *Now don't go overboard for us. We're just folks.*

go peddle your papers *phr.* [get out of my face and] stop annoying me like an aggressive paper boy. ♦ *Get out of here and go peddle your papers!*

go postal *in.* to become wild; to go berserk. ♦ *He made me so mad I thought I would go postal.*

go public 1. *in.* to sell to the public shares of a privately owned company. (Securities markets.) ♦ *We'll go public at a later time.* **2.** *in.* to reveal something to the public. (Especially with *with,* as in the examples.) ♦ *Just let me know when we can go public with this.*

go Rinso [...'rɪnso] *in.* to fail; to collapse in price. (A play on to go **down the drain.** *Rinso* is a laundry soap that goes down the drain after it is used. Used in the context of the securities markets or other financial setting.) ♦ *I knew my bank account would go Rinso after last month's bills came in.*

Go soak your head! Go to Go chase yourself!

Go soak yourself! Go to Go chase yourself!

go sour *in.* to turn bad or unpleasant. ♦ *My whole life is going sour right now.*

go South AND **head South 1.** *in.* to fall; to go down. (Securities markets. This is a way of saying *down.* South is usually "down" on a map.) ♦ *The market headed South today at the opening bell.* **2.** *in.* to quit; to drop out of sight. ♦ *After pulling the bank job, Shorty went South for a few months.* **3.** *in.* to make an escape; to disappear. ♦ *The mugger went South just after the crime.*

go straight 1. *in.* to stop breaking the law. ♦ *I think I'll give all this up and go straight—some day.* **2.** *in.* to get off drugs. (Drugs.) ♦ *I'll go straight one of these days.*

go the limit *in.* to do as much as possible; to get as much as possible. ♦ *We'll go the limit. To heck with the cost.*

go through so **like a dose of (the) salts** *in.* to move through someone's digestive tract like a strong laxative. ♦ *That stuff they served last night went through me like a dose of salts.*

go through the changes 1. *in.* to experience life's changes. ♦ *A good day, a bad day—it's all part of going through the changes.* **2.** *in.* to go through a reconstruction of one's life. ♦ *I've been going through the changes lately. It's tough to grow up at this age.*

go Titanic *in.* to fail; to sink. (Refers to the sinking of the passenger ship *Titanic*.) ♦ *The whole project went Titanic. We're out of a job.*

go tits up *in.* to die; to go to ruin; to fall apart. (A play on *go belly up* which has the same meaning. Refers to an animal like a goldfish that turns belly up when it dies.) ♦ *Her firm went tits up after the stock market crash.*

Go to! *exclam.* Go to hell! ♦ *Oh, you're terrible. Just go to!*

Go to blazes! AND **Go to the devil!** *exclam.* Go to hell! ♦ *Go to blazes! Stop pestering me!* ♦ *You can just go to the devil!*

Go to the devil! Go to Go to blazes!

go to town *in.* to do something with gusto; to do something with great speed and energy. ♦ *The main office is really going to town on collecting overdue payments.*

Go to your room! Go to On your bike!

go underground *in.* to go into hiding; to begin to operate in secret. ♦ *The entire operation went underground, and we heard no more about it.*

go up *in.* to start to feel the effects of a drug. (Drugs.) ♦ *Gert started to go up and suddenly fell asleep.*

go West *in.* to die. ♦ *When I go West, I want flowers, hired mourners, and an enormous performance of Mozart's "Requiem."*

go with it Go to go with the flow.

go with the flow AND **go with it** *in.* to cope with adversity; to accept one's lot. ♦ *No, just relax and go with the flow.*

go zonkers *in.* to go slightly crazy. ♦ *I went a little zonkers there for a minute. Sorry.*

go-ahead *n.* permission to proceed; the signal to go ahead. (See also say-so.) ♦ *I gave him the go-ahead, and the tanks started moving in.*

goat *n.* a fast and powerful car; a Pontiac GTO. ♦ *His goat conked out on him.*

gob [gɑb] **1.** *n.* a blob or mass of something. ♦ *Take that horrid gob of gum out of your mouth!* **2.** *n.* a large amount of something. (Often in the plural.) ♦ *I need gobs of money to get through school.* **3.** *n.* the mouth. (Chiefly British.) ♦ *Pop that in your gob and see if you like it!*

gobbledygook ['gɑbl̩digʊk] **1.** *n.* nonsense; officialese or government gibberish. ♦ *They must have a full time staff to dream up all this gobbledygook.* **2.** *n.* any mess, especially of food. ♦ *Do we have the same old gobbledygook tonight?*

go-by ['gobaɪ] *n.* an instance of ignoring or passing by (someone). (See also give so the go-by.) ♦ *I got the go-by from her every time I saw her.*

God's acre *n.* a cemetery. ♦ *When I end up in God's acre, I want everything to go on without me.*

God willing and the creek don't rise AND **GWATCDR** *phr. & comp. abb.* If we are lucky. ♦ *I'll be there, GWATCDR.*

gofer Go to gopher.

go-getter *n.* an energetic person. ♦ *Willy is a real go-getter. He'll go places.*

goggle-eyed AND **googly-eyed** ['gɑglaɪd AND 'gugliaɪd] *mod.* alcohol intoxicated and staring. ♦ *Willy was goggle-eyed and couldn't stand up.*

go-go ['gogo] **1.** *mod.* having to do with fast-dancing young women on display in a nightclub. ♦ *Those go-go places have mostly changed their style.* **2.** *mod.* vigorous; energetic; frantically moving. (Extended from sense 1.) ♦ *I bought some silly go-go stock, and it collapsed immediately.*

going high *n.* a long-lasting type of drug high. (Drugs.) ♦ *Gert was always after a real going high.*

going over 1. *n.* an examination. ♦ *I gave your car a good going over, and I fixed a lot of little things.* **2.** *n.* a beating. ♦ *After a going over like that, the guy spent two weeks in the hospital.*

goings-on *n.* happenings; events. ♦ *Some big goings-on downtown tied up the traffic.*

gold *n.* money. (See also ducats.) ♦ *Do you have enough gold to pay the bill?*

gold digger *n.* a woman who pays attention to a man solely because of his wealth. (Certainly also applicable to men as well.) ♦ *Sam called Sally a "gold digger," and she was devastated.*

goldbrick 1. *n.* a lazy person. ♦ *Pete is just a lazy goldbrick.* **2.** *in.* to be lazy; to shirk one's duty. ♦ *Whoever is goldbricking when I come back gets a real talking to.*

goldbricker *n.* a loafer. (Also a term of address.) ♦ *Get moving, you goldbrickers.*

golden *mod.* excellent; really cool. ♦ *Look at the guy she is with. He is golden.*

golden handcuffs *n.* monetary inducements to stay on the job. (Usually for highly paid executives in large corporations. See also golden parachute.) ♦ *The company provided a variety of golden handcuffs to keep its execs happy through a takeover.*

golden parachute *n.* a special kind of severance pay for persons who may be forced to leave a job. (Usually for highly paid executives in large corporations. If the company is taken over and the executives are fired, they are very well provided for. See also golden handcuffs.) ♦ *If all the golden parachutes were used at the same time, it would bankrupt the company.*

golden-ager *n.* an old person; a senior citizen. ♦ *When I'm a golden-ager, I'm going to have a part-time job.*

goldie locks *n.* a policewoman. (Citizens band radio.) ♦ *There was a goldie locks waiting under the bridge to spring on poor unsuspecting people like me.*

golf-clap *n.* a quiet kind of "patting" applause like that made in golf tournaments. (One had quietly claps against the back of the other hand.) ♦ *The audience sat there throughout. Not even a little golf clap. I think our act is washed up.*

gomer ['gomɚ] **1.** *n.* a stupid oaf; a social reject. (From the television character Gomer Pyle.) ♦ *Who's that gomer in the overalls?* **2.** AND **goomer** ['gumɚ] *n.* a person unwelcome in a hospital. (Supposedly an acronym for *Get out of my emergency room.*) ♦ *I don't want that goomer back in the emergency room.*

gone 1. AND **gone under** *mod.* unconscious. ♦ *He's gone under. You can begin the procedure now.* **2.** AND **gone under** *mod.* alcohol or drug intoxicated. ♦ *Those chicks are gone—too much to drink.* ♦ *Wow, he's really gone.* **3.** *mod.* cool; out of this world. (Typically real gone.) ♦ *This ice cream is gone, man, gone!*

gone goose *n.* someone or something finished or done for. (A play on dead duck.) ♦ *I'm afraid that your old car is a gone goose.*

gone under Go to gone.

goner ['gonɚ] *n.* someone or something finished or nearly finished. ♦ *The horse was a goner, so it had to be destroyed.*

gonged [gɔŋd] *mod.* drug intoxicated. (Drugs. Originally on opium.) ♦ *Mooshoo found himself in the alley, gonged.*

gonna ['gɔnə OR 'gʊnə] *phr.* going to. (Eye-dialect. Used in writing only for effect. Used in the examples of this dictionary.) ♦ *I'm gonna get you, you little dickens!*

gonzo ['gɑnzo] **1.** *n.* a silly or foolish person. ♦ *Some gonzo is on the phone asking for the president of the universe.* **2.** *mod.* crazy. ♦ *Who drew this gonzo picture of me?*

goo [gu] *n.* some sticky substance; gunk. ♦ *There is some sort of goo on my plate. Is that meant to be my dinner?*

goob [gub] **1.** *n.* a pimple. (Short for gu-ber.) ◆ *I have the world's greatest goob right on the end of my nose.* **2.** *n.* a nerd; a simpleton. (See also guber.) ◆ *Gary is such a goob. Why can't he do anything right?*

goober Go to guber.

goober-grabber ['gubɚgræbɚ] *n.* someone who picks peanuts. (Typically someone native to Georgia where peanuts are grown. From guber. Forced and contrived.) ◆ *One of the local goober-grabbers took us to a peanut boil.*

goober-grease ['gubɚgris] *n.* peanut butter. ◆ *Pass me some of that goober-grease, will ya?*

goobrain ['gubren] *n.* a fool; a stupid person. (Also a rude term of address.) ◆ *Look, goobrain, think about it a while. You'll catch on.*

gooch AND **grundle; taint** *n.* the perineum. (Crude. See also choad. The taint reflects that this area is not [it ain't = 'taint] genital nor anus.) ◆ *I got a horrible itch in the gooch!* ◆ *She did what to your taint?*

good and sth *mod.* thoroughly something. (Where *something* is an adjective.) ◆ *I am really good and mad at you for that.*

good buddy *n.* a friend; a partner. (Citizens band radio. Also a term of address.) ◆ *John's my good buddy.*

Good call! *exclam.* That was a good decision! ◆ *Good call, Walter! You picked the right company to deal with.*

Good deal! *exclam.* That is good! (Old, but still heard.) ◆ *Everyone is here on time! Good deal!*

Good golly, Miss Molly! *exclam.* Good grief!; Wow! ◆ *Good golly, Miss Molly! This place is a mess!*

(Good) gravy! *exclam.* Good! ◆ *Good gravy! Are you still here?*

Good heavens! *exclam.* My goodness! (A mild exclamation of amazement, shock, etc.) ◆ *Good heavens! I didn't expect you to be here.*

good Joe *n.* a good fellow. ◆ *Fred's a little slow on the uptake, but he's a good Joe.*

(good) looker *n.* a good-looking person. ◆ *Fred is not exactly a good looker, but he is pleasant enough.*

good old boy AND **good ole boy** *n.* a good guy; a dependable companion. (Folksy.) ◆ *Old Tom is a good old boy. He'll help.*

good trip 1. *n.* a good session with LSD or some other drug. (Drugs.) ◆ *Paul said he had a good trip, but he looks like the devil.* **2.** *n.* any good time. ◆ *Compared to the last class, this one is a good trip.*

good-for-nothing 1. *mod.* worthless. (Usually having to do with a person.) ◆ *Let's get rid of this good-for-nothing car right now.* **2.** *n.* a worthless person. (Also a rude term of address.) ◆ *Tell the good-for-nothing to leave.*

good-time Charley *n.* a man who is always trying to have a good experience; an optimist. ◆ *Willy is such a good-time Charley. Who would believe the trouble he's had?*

good-time it *tv.* to party; to spend money and have a good time. ◆ *You're always good-timing it. Don't you ever study?*

good-time man *n.* a man who sells drugs. (Drugs.) ◆ *The fuzz wants to see all the good-time men behind bars.*

good-to-go *phr.* ready to go; prepared. ◆ *I'm set. We're good-to-go.*

goody two-shoes *n.* someone who tries to behave better than anyone else. (Also a term of address.) ◆ *I'm no goody two-shoes. I just like to keep my nose clean.*

gooey AND **GUI** *n.* a graphical user interface. (A type of computer control system that uses an orderly layout on the screen with icons and menus that are controlled by a computer mouse. Gooey is slang; GUI is a technical acronym. See also WIMP.) ◆ *Some of the older programs that lack a gooey require a lot less memory to run.*

goof [guf] **1.** *n.* a foolish oaf; a goofy person. ◆ *Don't be a goof. Get with it.* **2.** *in.* to use heroin or some other addictive drugs without intending to become addicted; to play around (with heroin). (Drugs.) ◆ *Gert spent the first few years just goofing.* **3.** *in.* to scratch, nod, and slobber after an injection of heroin. (Drugs.) ♦ *She has been goofing for an hour.* **4.** AND **goof up** *in.* to make a blunder. ♦ *This time, you goofed.* ♦ *I'm afraid I goofed up.* **5.** *n.* a blunder; an error. ♦ *This goof is yours, not mine.*

goof around Go to goof off.

goof off 1. AND **goof around** *in.* to waste time. ♦ *You guys are goofing off again!* ♦ *Get busy. Stop goofing around.* **2.** *n.* a time-waster; a jerk. (Usually **goof-off.**) ♦ *I'm no goof-off, but I am no scholar either.*

goof on so *in.* to play a prank on someone; to involve someone in a deception. ♦ *Hey, don't goof on me. I'm your buddy!*

goof sth **up** *tv.* to mess something up. ♦ *I hope I don't goof up the report again.*

goof up Go to goof.

goofball 1. AND **goofer** *n.* a stupid person; a fool. ♦ *You are such a silly goofball.* ♦ *What a clumsy goofer!* **2.** *n.* a barbiturate tablet. (Drugs.) ♦ *How many goofballs did you take to get like this?*

goofed (up) 1. *mod.* messed up; out of order. ♦ *All my papers are goofed up.* **2.** *mod.* confused; distraught. ♦ *I was up too late last night, and now I'm all goofed up.* **3.** *mod.* high on drugs. ♦ *Bob's a little goofed up after partying too much.*

goofer Go to goofball.

goof-proof 1. *mod.* foolproof; not subject to misuse. ♦ *This scheme is not goof-proof, but it's pretty sound.* **2.** *tv.* to make something foolproof; to take action to see that something cannot be misused. ♦ *See if this can be goof-proofed by Monday evening.*

goofus ['gufəs] **1.** *n.* a gadget. ♦ *Where is that little goofus I use to pry open these cans?* **2.** AND **goopus** *n.* a foolish oaf. (Also a term of address.) ♦ *You're just acting like a goofus. Be serious!* ♦ *Hey, goopus! What's up?*

goofy ['gufi] **1.** *mod.* silly. ♦ *Stop acting so goofy! What will the neighbors say?* **2.** *mod.* alcohol intoxicated. ♦ *They went out and got themselves good and goofy.*

googaw Go to geegaw.

google *in. & tv.* to search (for) something on the internet, using Google.com. ♦ *Why don't you just go to your computer and google for it yourself?*

googly-eyed Go to goggle-eyed.

goo-goo eyes ['gugu 'aɪz] *n.* flirtatious eyes. (Often with *make*.) ♦ *Who's the chick over there with the goo-goo eyes?*

gook [guk OR gʊk] **1.** *n.* a slimy substance; a sediment or residue. ♦ *Too much of that gook will ruin your engine.* **2.** *n.* a foolish oaf. ♦ *Wow, Chuck is turning into a real gook!* **3.** *n.* a tramp. ♦ *Give the gook some food and wish him well.* **4.** *n.* a prostitute. ♦ *There are a lot of gooks around here in the center of town.* **5.** *n.* a derogatory nickname for various East Asians. (Crude.) ♦ *Let the gooks fight it out amongst themselves.*

goombah ['gumbɑ] *n.* a buddy; a trusted friend. (Also a term of address. Ultimately from Italian.) ♦ *He's my goombah. I can trust him.*

goomer Go to gomer.

goon [gun] **1.** *n.* a stupid person; a fool. ♦ *Todd is a silly goon, but he's a lot of fun at parties.* **2.** *n.* a hooligan; a thug or bodyguard. (Underworld.) ♦ *Call off your goons!*

goon squad 1. *n.* an organized group of thugs; a gang of toughs. (Underworld.) ♦ *The goon squad Mr. Big sent around scared the devil out of Wilmer.* **2.** *n.* the police. ♦ *My old buddy on the goon squad tells me there'll be some action over on Maple Street tonight.*

gooned [gund] *mod.* drunk. (As though beat up by a **goon**.) ♦ *His date was gooned by ten, and he had to take her home.*

gooner ['gunɚ] *n.* a term for an East Asian. (Derogatory and demeaning. Military.) ♦ *See if one of the gooners will show you how to do it.*

goon-platoon *n.* a platoon of misfits; a platoon that is noted for its errors. (Military.) ♦ *Well, the goon-platoon's done it again!*

goop AND **goup** [gup] *n.* slop; gunk; bad food. ♦ *You get used to this goup after a while.*

goophead ['guphɛd] *n.* an inflamed pimple. (Patterned on *blackhead*.) ♦ *You ought to see the goophead on your nose.*

goopus Go to goofus.

goopy ['gupi] *mod.* gummy; syrupy. ♦ *I just love goopy desserts.*

goose 1. *n.* a silly oaf; an oaf. ♦ *Oh, I'm such a silly goose!* **2.** *tv.* to (attempt to) poke something, such as a finger, in someone's anus. ♦ *Freddy tried to goose me!* **3.** *n.* an attempt to goose someone. (As in sense 2.) ♦ *He tried to give me a goose.* **4.** *tv.* to rev up an engine; to press down hard on the accelerator of a car. ♦ *Why don't you goose the thing and see how fast it'll go?* **5.** *n.* an act of suddenly pressing down the accelerator of a car. ♦ *Give it a good goose and see what happens.*

goose egg 1. *n.* a score of zero. ♦ *We got a goose egg in the second inning.* **2.** *n.* a bump on the head. ♦ *I walked into a door and got a big goose egg on my forehead.* **3.** *n.* a failure; a zero. (Similar to sense 1.) ♦ *The result of three weeks' planning is one big goose egg.*

goosed *mod.* wearing bullet proof vest containing goose down. ♦ *He's goosed and ready for whatever bullets come his way.*

goozlum ['guzləm] *n.* any gummy, sticky substance: syrup, gravy, soup, etc. ♦ *Do you want some of this wonderful goozlum on your ice cream?*

gopher AND **gofer** ['gofɚ] **1.** *n.* someone who goes for things and brings them back. (From go for.) ♦ *You got a gopher who can go get some coffee?* **2.** *n.* a dupe; a pawn; an underling. ♦ *The guy's just a gofer. He has no say in anything.*

gopher ball *n.* a baseball pitch that is hit as a home run. (When it is hit, the batter will *go for* home.) ♦ *The center fielder did a dive over the fence trying to get the gopher ball.*

go-pills *n.* amphetamines. (Drugs.) ♦ *After a while, these go-pills just demand to be taken.*

gorilla biscuits AND **gorilla pills** *n.* amphetamines. (Drugs.) ♦ *Stay away from gorilla biscuits.* ♦ *He's high on gorilla pills.*

gorilla juice *n.* steroids. (Bodybuilding. Steroids build muscle tissue rapidly.) ♦ *Do all those muscle-bound creatures take gorilla juice?*

gorilla pills Go to gorilla biscuits.

gork [gork] **1.** *n.* a fool; a dupe. ♦ *Martin acts like such a gork sometimes.* **2.** AND **GORK** *in.* an alleged hospital chart notation of the diagnosis *God only really knows.* (Hospitals.) ♦ *I see old Mr. Kelly is in again with a hundred complaints. His chart says GORK.* **3.** *tv.* to give a patient sedation. (Hospitals.) ♦ *Dr. Wilson says to gork the patient in 226.*

gorked (out) [gorkt…] *mod.* heavily sedated; knocked out. (Hospitals.) ♦ *The guy in 226 is totally gorked out now.*

gospel (truth) *n.* the honest truth. ♦ *You gotta believe me. It's the gospel truth!*

gotcha ['gɑtʃə] **1.** *tv.* I got you!; I've caught you! (Usually **Gotcha!**) ♦ *Ha, ha! Gotcha! Come here, you little dickens.* **2.** *n.* an arrest. (Underworld.) ♦ *It was a fair gotcha. Sam was nabbed, and he went along quietly.* **3.** *tv.* I understand you. ♦ *Seven pounds, four ounces? Gotcha! I'll tell everybody.*

gouch off [gautʃ…] *in.* to pass out under the influence of drugs. (Drugs.) ♦ *After taking the stuff, Gary gouched off.*

goup Go to goop.

gourd [gord] *n.* the head. ♦ *I raised up and got a nasty blow on the gourd.*

goy [gɔɪ] **1.** *n.* a gentile. (From Hebrew. Not necessarily derogatory.) ♦ *But the goys can't do anything they want on Sunday!* **2.** *mod.* gentile; non-Jewish. ♦ *Goy pickles are sort of blah.*

GR&D *interj.* Grinning, running, and ducking. (Describes what one might be doing after having written a mischievous message on an electronic forum or news group. Used in electronic mail and computer forum or news group messages. Sometimes enclosed, <GR&D>. Not pronounced aloud.) ♦ *I guess that you got just the kind of answer that you deserve.* <GR&D>

grab some bench *tv.* go to the bench, during a game. ♦ *The coach told Freddy to go grab some bench.*

grabbers *n.* the hands. ♦ *Wash your grubby little grabbers before coming to the table.*

grade-grubber 1. *n.* an earnest, hard-working student. (In the way a pig roots or grubs around for food.) ♦ *If there are too many grade-grubbers in a class, it will really throw off the grading scale.* **2.** *n.* a student who flatters the teacher in hopes of a higher grade. ♦ *A few grade-grubbers help assure old professors that the world is not really changing at all.*

grade-grubbing 1. *n.* working hard at one's studies in hopes of a high grade. ♦ *If all you're here for is grade-grubbing, you're going to miss a lot.* **2.** *n.* flattering a teacher in hopes of a higher grade. ♦ *Some teachers don't mind a lot of grade-grubbing.* **3.** *mod.* having to do with students who are only concerned with getting high grades. ♦ *Two grade-grubbing seniors came in and begged me to change their grades.*

graduate ['grædʒuət] **1.** *n.* a person experienced in life, especially sexually experienced. ♦ *Britney is a graduate. Nothing is new to her.* **2.** ['grædʒuet] *in.* to move from casual drug use to addiction. (Drugs.) ♦ *Gert graduated to smack after only a year of skin-popping.*

grand AND **G; gee; large** *n.* one thousand dollars. ♦ *That car probably cost about twenty grand.* ♦ *You owe me three gees!* ♦ *He won three large on the slots!*

Grand Central Station *n.* any busy and hectic place. (From Grand Central Station in New York City—a very busy place.) ♦ *At just about closing time, this place becomes Grand Central Station.*

granddad *n.* an old-fashioned person; an out-of-date person. ♦ *Don't be such a granddad. Live a little.*

(grand)daddy (of them all) *n.* the biggest or oldest of all; the patriarch. ♦ *This old fish is the granddaddy of them all.*

grandstand *in.* to make oneself conspicuous. ♦ *Don't you just hate the way that Pat grandstands all the time?*

grandstand play *n.* something done exceedingly well to impress an audience or a group of spectators. ♦ *The grandstand play caught the attention of the crowd just as they were leaving.*

granny flat *n.* an apartment built into a garage or house for an elderly parent to live in. ♦ *The garage has a granny flat including all utilities.*

grape shot *mod.* alcohol intoxicated; drunk on wine. ♦ *After the reception, Hank found himself a little grape shot.*

grape smugglers *n.* tight swimming briefs. (As if the wearer had stuffed some grapes into the crotch in order to smuggle them somewhere.) ♦ *He owned a pair of grape smugglers, but never wore them in public.*

grape(s) *n.* champagne; wine. (See also berries.) ♦ *No more of the grapes for me. It tickles my nose.*

grapes of wrath *n.* wine. ♦ *Fred had taken a little too much of the grapes of wrath.*

grapevine *n.* an informal communications network. ♦ *I heard on the grapevine that Sam is moving to the east.*

grass 1. *n.* marijuana. (Drugs and now widely known.) ♦ *These kids manage to find this grass somewhere.* **2.** *n.* lettuce; salad greens. (See also rabbit food.) ♦ *I could use a little more grass in my diet.*

grass party *n.* a marijuana-smoking party. (Drugs.) ♦ *The goon squad raided Pete's grass party without any warning.*

grasser Go to grasshead.

grasshead AND **grasser; grasshopper** *n.* a marijuana smoker. (Drugs.) ♦ *The grassheads are taking over this neighborhood.* ♦ *The principle called the "grassers" in and gave them hell.*

grasshopper Go to grasshead.

grassroots 1. *n.* the common people, especially rural people. ♦ *We really haven't heard anything from the grassroots yet.* **2.** *mod.* having to do with or originating with the common people. ♦ *A grassroots movement pushed Senator Del Monte toward the nomination.*

grave-dancer *n.* someone who profits from or takes advantage of someone else's misfortune. (From *dance on* so's *grave*, seemingly in celebration of someone else's misfortune.) ♦ *I don't want to seem like a grave-dancer, but his defeat places me in line for a promotion.*

gravel-pounder *n.* an infantry soldier. (Military.) ♦ *Do you really want to join the Army and be a gravel-pounder?*

graveyard shift *n.* the night shift of work in a factory, usually starting at about midnight. (See also swing shift.) ♦ *The pay is pretty good on the graveyard shift.*

gravity check *n.* a fall as from a surfboard, bike, etc. ♦ *She rounded the turn and had a sudden gravity check, resulting in a scraped elbow.*

gravy 1. *n.* extra or easy money; easy profit. ♦ *After I pay expenses, the rest is pure gravy.* **2.** *mod.* good. ♦ *Man, her shape is gravy!* **3.** Go to (Good) gravy!

gravy train *n.* a job that brings in a steady supply of easy money or **gravy**. ♦ *This kind of job is a real gravy train.*

gravycakes *mod.* fine; super. ♦ *This little car is truly gravycakes.*

Graybar Hotel AND **Graystone College** *n.* a jail; a prison. ♦ *The two cops had to spend two years in Graybar Hotel with some of the inmates they had caught over the past few years.* ♦ *How long were you at the old Graystone College?*

grayhound *in.* [for a black] to date whites. ♦ *Somebody said you were grayhounding. Is that so?*

Graystone College Go to Graybar Hotel.

graze AND **browse** *in.* to eat a bit of everything at parties. ♦ *We will just graze on party snacks rather than eat a full meal.* ♦ *I think I'll just browse here and skip going out to dinner.*

grease *n.* protection money; bribery money. (See also grease so's palm.) ♦ *See that the commissioner of the park district gets a little grease to help us get the contract.*

grease monkey *n.* a mechanic. ♦ *I took my car to my favorite grease monkey who says I need a new something or other.*

grease so's **palm** *tv.* to pay someone a bribe. ♦ *I had to grease the clerk's palm in order to get the job done.*

grease the skids *tv.* to help prepare for the success or failure of someone or something. (See also put the skids under so/sth.) ♦ *Ray set out to grease the skids for the right things to happen.*

greased [grizd OR grist] *mod.* alcohol intoxicated. ♦ *He went out and got himself greased, even though he knew it would probably kill him.*

greased lightning 1. *n.* strong liquor. ♦ *This greased lightning of yours nearly blew my head off.* **2.** *n.* something fast or powerful. ♦ *That kid can run like greased lightning.*

greaser ['grizɚ OR 'grisɚ] *n.* a rough and aggressive male, usually with long greased down hair. ♦ *Donna has been going out with a real greaser.*

greasy spoon *n.* an untidy and unappetizing diner or restaurant. ♦ *Let's eat at the greasy spoon over on Maple. The food is gross, but the people-watching is good.*

great divide *n.* a divorce. ♦ *How did Sam survive the great divide?*

the **great unwashed** *n.* most of the common people; the hoi polloi. ♦ *I usually find myself more in agreement with the great unwashed than with the elite.*

greefo AND **griefo** ['grifo] *n.* marijuana or a marijuana cigarette. (Drugs. Mexican Spanish for weed. See also reefer.) ♦ *Max had a soggy greefo in his mouth.*

Greek to so *n.* something incomprehensible to someone; something as mysterious as Greek writing. ♦ *I don't understand this. It's all Greek to me.*

green AND **green folding; green paper; green stuff** *n.* money; paper money. (See also long bread.) ♦ *I have so much green stuff, I don't know what to do with it.* ♦ *What is need is more green! Not promises!*

green apple quickstep *n.* diarrhea. ♦ *He was stricken with the green apple quickstep on the first day of their vacation.*

green around the gills Go to blue around the gills.

green folding Go to green.

green light *n.* the signal to go ahead with something; the okay. (See also go-ahead; high sign.) ♦ *When we get the green light, we'll start.*

green paper Go to green.

green stamps *n.* money. (From *S&H Green Stamps* given as an incentive to purchase other goods.) ♦ *How many green stamps does this take?*

green stuff Go to green.

greenback ['grinbæk] *n.* a dollar bill. ♦ *It's only ten greenbacks. Anybody can afford that.*

greenie ['grini] *n.* a Heineken (brand) beer. (It comes in a green bottle.) ♦ *Tom ordered a greenie and had it put on his tab.*

greenwash *tv.* to launder money; to obliterate the illegal sources of money by moving it through a variety of financial institutions. (Underworld.) ♦ *It was shown in court that the mayor had been involved in greenwashing some of the bribe money.*

greldge [grɛldʒ] **1.** *n.* something nasty or yucky. ♦ *That's not greldge, that's just plain mud.* **2.** *exclam.* Nuts!; Darn! (Usually **Greldge!**) ♦ *Oh, greldge! I'm late!*

griefo Go to greefo.

grill *n.* face; front teeth. ♦ *Ain't you getting your grill a little close to my grill?*

grind *in.* to sell drugs. ♦ *He told the cops he wasn't grinding, but they found his junk.*

grindage *n.* food. (From the grinding of teeth, but see also grinder.) ♦ *Hear my belly? It's crying for some grindage.*

grinder Go to submarine.

gripe one's **ass** AND **gripes** one's **butt** *tv.* to annoy someone; to bother or irritate someone. (Usually objectionable.) ♦ *You really gripe my ass when you act like that!* ♦ *That jerk really gripes my butt!*

gripe one's **butt** Go to gripe one's ass.

gripe one's **soul** *tv.* to annoy someone. ♦ *That kind of thing really gripes my soul!*

grit *n.* courage; nerve. ♦ *It takes a lot of grit to do something like that.*

gritch [grɪtʃ] **1.** *in.* to complain. (A blend of *gripe* and *bitch.*) ♦ *Stop gritching all the time.* **2.** *n.* a complainer; a griper. ♦ *You are getting to be such a gritch.*

gritchy ['grɪtʃi] *mod.* complaining; irritable. ♦ *I don't feel as gritchy today as I did yesterday.*

groan box *n.* an accordion. (See also (squeeze-)box.) ♦ *Clare is pretty good on the groan box.*

groaty Go to grody.

grod AND **groddess** ['grad(əs)] *n.* an especially sloppy man or woman. (Patterned on *god* and *goddess* + grody.) ♦ *Hello, grods and groddesses, what's new?*

groddess Go to grod.

grody AND **groaty** ['grodi] *mod.* disgusting. (From *grotesque.* See also grotty.) ♦ *What a grody view of the street from this window.*

grody to the max ['grodi tu ðə 'mæks] *mod.* totally disgusting. (California. From *grotesque.* See also grody.) ♦ *This pizza is, like, grody to the max!*

grog [grag] *n.* liquor. ♦ *Here, have some more of this grog.*

grogan *n.* a bowel movement. ♦ *He's in the john, fighting with a grogan.*

groggery ['gragɚi] *n.* a tavern; a place to buy liquor. ♦ *All the groggeries are closed on Sundays.*

groggified Go to groggy.

groggy 1. *mod.* tired; in a stupor. (Standard but having a slangy history. From a term for rum as drunk aboard ship, derived from the nickname *grog*, belonging to Admiral Edward Vernon.) ♦ *I'm still groggy by ten in the morning.* **2.** AND **groggified** ['grɔgifaɪd] *mod.* alcohol intoxicated. ♦ *He was too groggified to drive.*

groghound *n.* a drunkard. ♦ *I'm afraid that Ernie is getting to be a groghound.*

grok [grɔk] *tv.* to "drink" in a concept or knowledge and assimilate it; to understand something; to appreciate someone or something; to relate to someone or something. ♦ *I don't quite grok that. Run it by again, would you?*

gronk [grɔŋk] **1.** *n.* a nasty substance, such as dirt that collects between the toes. ♦ *I don't want to hear any more at all about your gronk.* **2.** *mod.* worthless. ♦ *I don't care about your old gronk car. I'd rather take the bus.*

gronk (out) *in.* to conk out; to crash, as with a car or a computer. ♦ *The program gronks every time I start to run it.*

groove *n.* something pleasant or cool. (See also in the groove.) ♦ *This day has been a real groove.*

groove on so/sth *in.* to show interest in someone or something; to relate to someone or something. ♦ *Fred was beginning to groove on new age music when he met Phil.*

grooved [gruvd] *mod.* pleased. ♦ *I am so grooved. I'll just kick back and meditate.*

grooving *mod.* enjoying; being cool and laid back. ♦ *Look at those guys grooving in front of the television set.*

groovy 1. *mod.* cool; pleasant. ♦ *Man, this music is groovy.* **2.** *mod.* drug intoxicated. (Drugs.) ♦ *Three beers and he was a little groovy.* **3.** *mod.* out-of-date; passé. (California.) ♦ *Oh, how groovy!*

gross [gros] *mod.* crude; vulgar; disgusting. (Slang only when overused.) ♦ *What a gross thing to even suggest.*

gross so **out** *tv.* to disgust someone. ♦ *Jim's story totally grossed out Sally.*

gross-out 1. *n.* something disgusting. ♦ *That horror movie was a real gross-out.* **2.** *mod.* disgusting; gross. ♦ *What a gross-out day this has been!*

grotty ['grɑdi] *mod.* highly undesirable. (Originally British. From *grotesque*. See also grody.) ♦ *What is this grotty stuff they serve here?*

ground-pounder *n.* an infantry soldier. (Military.) ♦ *If you join the army, it means a lot of your life spent as a ground-pounder.*

group-grope *n.* a real or imagined group of people engaged in sexual activities. ♦ *That party turned into a hopeless group-grope.*

groupie *n.* a young woman who follows a band seeking romance with the band members. ♦ *Would you believe that Sally was a groupie when she was nineteen?*

grouse [graʊs] **1.** *in.* to complain. ♦ *Paul is always grousing about something.* **2.** *n.* a woman; women considered sexually. ♦ *Who's the grouse I saw you with last night?* **3.** *in.* to neck; to pet and kiss. ♦ *They were grousing in the backseat the whole trip.*

grovel ['grɑvl̩] *in.* to fondle or pet. ♦ *They spent the whole time in the backseat groveling.*

grower *n.* a small flaccid penis that can become quite large. (Compare to shower.) ♦ *He said his friend was a grower.*

growler *n.* a toilet. ♦ *Where's the growler around here?*

grub [grəb] **1.** *n.* food. ♦ *Hey, this grub's pretty good.* **2.** AND **grub up** *in.* to eat [a meal]. ♦ *Let's grub up and get going.* **3.** *tv.* to eat something; to eat a meal. ♦ *Are you going to grub that whole pizza?* **4.** *n.* an earnest student. (Collegiate. See also grade-grubber.) ♦ *The test was so hard, even the grubs did poorly.* **5.** *n.* a sloppy person. (From *grub worm*.) ♦ *Don is such a grub all the time.* **6.** Go to grubbies.

grub on sth *in.* to eat something. ♦ *What are you grubbing on? It looks horrible.*

grub up Go to grub.

grubbers Go to grubbies.

grubbies AND **grubbers; grubs** [ˈgrəbiz AND ˈgrəbɚz, grəbz] *n.* worn-out clothing; clothing one wears for the occasional dirty job. ♦ *There I was, running around in my grubs when the senator stops by to say hello!* ♦ *It's time to wash these grubbies.*

grubby [ˈgrəbi] *mod.* unclean; untidy; unshaven. ♦ *Who's that grubby guy?*

gruesome-twosome [ˈgrusəmˈtusəm] *n.* two people or things. (Jocular. Neither the things nor the people have to be *gruesome*.) ♦ *Well, it's the gruesome-twosome. Come in and join the party.*

grunch Go to grunge.

grundle Go to gooch.

grunge AND **grunch** [grəndʒ AND grəntʃ] **1.** *n.* any nasty substance; dirt; gunk. ♦ *There's some gritty grunge on the kitchen floor.* **2.** *n.* an ugly or nasty person; a repellent person. ♦ *Some grunch came by and dropped off this strange package for you.*

grungy [ˈgrəndʒi] **1.** *mod.* dirty and smelly; yucky. ♦ *Get your grungy feet off the table!* **2.** Go to gungy.

grunt [grənt] **1.** *n.* an infantry soldier. (Military. From the gutteral sound made by a pig, and anyone doing very heavy labor.) ♦ *Get those grunts out on the field at sunrise!* **2.** *n.* a low-ranking or subservient person. (Someone who is likely to utter a grunt because of the discomforts of menial labor.) ♦ *Let's hire a grunt to do this kind of work.* **3.** *n.* a belch. ♦ *Does that grunt mean you like my cooking?* **4.** *n.* a hardworking student. ♦ *The grunts got Bs on the test. It was that hard!* **5.** *n.* a wrestler. (Possibly in reference to a grunting pig.) ♦ *Two big grunts wearing outlandish costumes performed for the television cameras.*

grunt work AND **shit work** *n.* hard, menial labor; tedious work. (Work that a lesser person ought to be doing.) ♦ *Who is supposed to do the grunt work around here? Not me!* ♦ *Why am I always doing the shit work?*

gubb *n.* semen. ♦ *Clan up that gubb before somebody sees it!*

gubbish *n.* nonsense; useless information. (Computers. A combination of *garbage* and *rubbish*.) ♦ *I can't make any sense out of this gubbish.*

guber AND **goober** [ˈgubɚ] **1.** *n.* a facial pimple. (See also goob.) ♦ *How does anybody get rid of goobers?* **2.** *n.* a tumor. (Jocular medical slang. Possibly because it grows beneath the surface like the goober—the peanut. See also boogie.) ♦ *The patient with the abdominal guber is going into surgery now.*

guck [gək] *n.* a thick, sticky substance; yuck. ♦ *The doctor painted some nasty guck on my throat and told me not to swallow for a while.*

gucky [ˈgəki] *mod.* thick and sticky; yucky. ♦ *There is a lot of gucky oil and grease on the garage floor.*

guff [gəf] **1.** *n.* nonsense; bunkum. ♦ *No more guff outa you, okay?* **2.** *n.* back talk; complaining. ♦ *That's enough of your guff!* **3.** *n.* a strange person; a nerd. (Possibly related to goof.) ♦ *Willy acts like a guff when we go out. I am going to break up with him.*

gug [gəg] *n.* a repellent person. ♦ *Rocko is not a gug!*

GUI Go to gooey.

gulf *n.* heroin from the Persian Gulf region. (Drugs.) ♦ *Those pushers can call anything gulf. How does anybody know where it's from?*

gumby [ˈgəmbi] *n.* a tall, squared-off and slanting haircut that looks like the Gumby character's head. ♦ *Ted got sent to the principal's office because of his gumby.*

gumbyhead [ˈgəmbihɛd] *n.* someone who does stupid things like the character, Gumby. ♦ *Don't be a gumbyhead. Don't drink and drive.*

gump [gəmp] *n.* a fool; an oaf. (Like the rural and not too smart Andy Gump of comic strip fame in the early 1900s, later reinforced by Forrest Gump of movie fame.) ♦ *Don't act like such a gump!*

gumshoe [ˈgəmʃu] *n.* a policeman or a detective. (Underworld. Also a term of address. So named for wearing silent, gum-rubber soles.) ♦ *Has that gumshoe been around asking questions again?*

gun 1. *n.* a hired gunman; a bodyguard, an assassin, or a member of a gang of criminals. (Underworld and Western.) ♦ *Willie and his guns came by to remind Gary of what he owed Mr. Gutman.* **2.** *n.* a leader; the key member of a group. ♦ *Who's the gun around here?* **3.** *tv.* to race an engine; to rev up an engine. ♦ *See how loud it is when I gun it?* **4.** Go to guns.

gun for so *in.* to be looking for someone, not necessarily with a gun. ♦ *Sam is gunning for Wilmer.*

gunboats AND **battleships** *n.* big feet; big shoes. ♦ *Get those battleships off my sofa!* ♦ *Hasn't he got the biggest gunboats you ever saw?*

gunge [gənʤ] *n.* a skin irritation in the groin. (See also crotch-rot. Said of males.) ♦ *The sawbones'll give you something for the gunge.*

gungeon ['gənʤən] *n.* a potent type of marijuana from Africa or Jamaica; a cigarette made of this marijuana. ♦ *Is this gungeon really from Africa?*

gung-ho ['gəŋ'ho] *mod.* zealous; enthusiastic. ♦ *We're really gung-ho about the possibilities of this product.*

gungy AND **grungy** ['gənʤi AND 'grənʤi] *mod.* messy; nasty; worn-out. (See also grunge.) ♦ *Get your grungy feet off the sofa.*

gunk [gəŋk] **1.** *n.* any nasty, messy stuff. ♦ *Get this gunk up off the floor before it dries.* **2.** *n.* glue sniffed as a drug. (Drugs.) ♦ *I thought that it was illegal to sell gunk.*

gunner *n.* an earnest student. (Collegiate.) ♦ *The gunners in my algebra class always get the As.*

gunny ['gəni] *n.* a potent marijuana from Jamaica or Africa. (Drugs.) ♦ *This gunny is just junk, plain old junk.*

guns *n.* the biceps; large muscular arms. (See also pythons.) ♦ *He lifts weights to build up his guns.*

gunzel-butt ['gənzl̩bət] *n.* a strange-looking person, usually a male. (Underworld.) ♦ *Mooshoo told the gunzel-butt where to get off.*

guppy *n.* a gay yuppy. ♦ *They called themselves guppies, because they were young and urban and gay.*

guru ['guru] **1.** *n.* an experienced LSD user who guides someone else on a trip. ♦ *Wilmer volunteered to serve as a guru, but he never showed up.* **2.** *n.* a stockbroker or other financial advisor. (Securities markets.) ♦ *My guru says to sell all my bonds.* **3.** *n.* a psychiatrist; a psychotherapist. ♦ *I've started using my mirror for a guru. It's cheaper.*

gussied up ['gəsid…] *mod.* dressed up in one's best clothing. (Folksy.) ♦ *I like to get gussied up and go out on the town.*

gusto ['gəsto] **1.** *n.* beer. ♦ *Can you stop at the filling station and get some gusto?* **2.** *in.* to drink beer. ♦ *Don't you ever do anything but gusto?*

gut [gət] **1.** *n.* the belly; the intestines. ♦ *Tom poked Bill right in the gut.* **2.** *mod.* basic; fundamental. ♦ *We are not dealing with what I would call one of the gut matters of the day.* **3.** *mod.* [of a college or high school course] easy. ♦ *I won't take anymore gut economics courses. Even those are hard.* **4.** *n.* an easy course in school. ♦ *That course is a gut.*

gut reaction (to sth**)** *n.* a basic and immediate response to something. ♦ *Her gut reaction to the plan is basically a good one.*

gutbucket ['gətbəkɪt] **1.** *n.* a chamber pot, especially one used in a prison cell. (See also gash bucket.) ♦ *You got something around here I can use as a gutbucket?* **2.** *n.* a toilet; a makeshift toilet. ♦ *Where's the gutbucket around here?* **3.** *n.* the stomach. ♦ *Sam poked Pete right in the gutbucket.* **4.** *n.* a fat person, usually a man. ♦ *Look at the gutbucket waddling down the street.* **5.** *n.* a cheap saloon; a low tavern. his head off. ♦ *The pinstriper needed a drink so bad he stopped at one of those gutbuckets on Maple Street.* **6.** *n.* an earthy style of music. ♦ *You don't hear much gutbucket in public places these days.*

gutless wonder *n.* a totally spineless person. ♦ *George, don't be such a gutless wonder! Stand up for your rights!*

guts [gəts] **1.** *n.* courage; bravado. ♦ *It takes guts to do something like that.* **2.** *n.* the belly; the intestines. ♦ *I've got some kind of pain in the guts.* **3.** *n.* the inner workings of anything. ♦ *There's something wrong in the guts of this clock.* **4.** *n.* the essence of something. ♦ *Let's discuss the real guts of this issue.*

gutsy ['gətsi] *mod.* courageous; feisty. ♦ *Ernie's acting sort of gutsy today. What happened?*

guy *n.* a fellow; a man or boy. (Colloquial. Very old. Not necessarily male in the plural.) ♦ *When you guys finish getting your makeup on, we can go back to the guys.*

guy thing *n.* something that appeals to men; something that men do. ♦ *We just do it. We don't know why. It's a guy thing.*

guzzery Go to guzzlery.

guzzle ['gəzl] **1.** *tv. & in.* to drink alcohol in great quantities. (Very old.) ♦ *Stop guzzling for a while and pay attention.* **2.** *n.* a drinking spree. ♦ *Fred's out on another of his guzzles.*

guzzled ['gəzld] **1.** *mod.* arrested. (Underworld.) ♦ *Rocko got himself guzzled on a* speeding rap. **2.** *mod.* alcohol intoxicated. ♦ *Todd was too guzzled to drive home.*

guzzle-guts *n.* a drunkard; a heavy drinker. ♦ *Old guzzle-guts here would like another drink.*

guzzler *n.* a heavy drinker. ♦ *A couple of guzzlers at the bar were carrying on a low conversation when Marlowe came in.*

guzzlery AND **guzzery** ['gəzləi AND 'gəzəi] *n.* a bar; a liquor store. ♦ *Sam hit every guzzlery on Maple Street on the way home.*

GWATCDR Go to God willing and the creek don't rise.

gweeb [gwib] *n.* a studious student. (Collegiate. A variant of dweeb.) ♦ *I'm in a physics class full of gweebs.*

gweebo ['gwibo] *mod.* feeble; despicable; in the manner of a gweeb. ♦ *I'm not gweebo. I'm just eccentric.*

gym shoe *n.* a disliked person. ♦ *Who is the gym shoe who comes to class in a sport coat?*

gynie ['gaini] *n.* a gynecologist. ♦ *My gynie says I'm fine.*

gyve [dʒaɪv] *n.* marijuana; a marijuana cigarette. (Drugs. See also jive.) ♦ *Why are you always smoking gyve?*

gyvestick Go to jivestick.

H. *n.* heroin. (Drugs.) ♦ *First it was M.; now it's H.*

habit *n.* an addiction to a drug. ♦ *There are many treatment programs to help with drug habits.*

hack 1. *n.* a taxi. ♦ *Go out to the street and see if you can get a hack.* **2.** *n.* a cough. ♦ *That's a nasty hack you've got there.* **3.** *n.* a professional writer who writes mediocre material to order. ♦ *This novel shows that even a hack can get something published* **4.** *n.* a reporter. ♦ *Newspaper hacks have to know a little of everything.* **5.** *tv.* to write clumsy or inefficient computer programs. ♦ *I can hack a program for you, but it won't be what you want.* **6.** *tv.* to break into a computer electronically to steal data or corrupt it or for the challenge of breaking in. ♦ *I'm gonna hack the bank's computer because they bounced a check of mine.* **7.** *tv.* to annoy someone. (See also hacked (off).) ♦ *That kind of behavior hacks her a lot.* **8.** *n.* anyone who does poor or undesirable work. ♦ *Oh, he's just a hack. What can you expect?* **9.** *n.* a prison guard. ♦ *Watch out, man. The hacks are looking.* **10.** *in.* to play with hackysack. ♦ *They spent all their spare time hacking.*

hack around *in.* to waste time. ♦ *I wanted to hack around for a year after college, but my finances disagreed.*

hack it *tv.* to stand up to something; to endure something. ♦ *I'm afraid you can't hack it. It just isn't working out.*

hacked [hækt] *mod.* worn-out; ready to quit. ♦ *What a day! I'm hacked.*

hacked (off) *mod.* angry; annoyed. ♦ *Willy was really hacked off about the accident.*

hacker 1. *n.* a taxi driver. ♦ *You wonder how some of these hackers keep their licenses.* **2.** *n.* a sloppy or inefficient computer programmer. ♦ *This program was written by a real hacker. It's a mess, but it works.* **3.** *n.* a generally unsuccessful person. ♦ *Poor Pete is just a hacker. He'll never go any place.* **4.** *n.* someone who breaks into a computer electronically. ♦ *Some hacker broke into our computer!*

had Go to taken.

hail damage *n.* cellulite. ♦ *Man, look at that hail damage on her hips!*

hairball 1. AND **furball** *n.* an obnoxious person. ♦ *I wish that the guys I date didn't always turn out to be hairballs.* ♦ *Shut up, you skanky furball!* **2.** *exclam.* How awful! (Usually **Hairball!** An exclamation of disgust. From the name of the undigested mass of fur vomited by a cat.) ♦ *Hairball! I did it wrong again!* **3.** *n.* a mess; something difficult or unpleasant. ♦ *My life has become a hairball. I can't go on.*

hairy *mod.* hazardous; difficult. ♦ *That was a hairy experience!*

hairy-ass(ed) 1. *mod.* wild; exciting. ♦ *We had a real hairy-ass time on the roller coaster.* **2.** *mod.* strong and virile. (Usually objectionable.) ♦ *This big hairy-ass guy started to push us around.*

hakspeak Go to leetspeak.

half a bubble off plumb *phr.* giddy; crazy. ♦ *Tom is just half a bubble off plumb, but he is all heart.*

half in the bag *mod.* alcohol intoxicated. ♦ *Jerry was half in the bag when we found him.*

half up the pole *mod.* alcohol intoxicated; tipsy. ♦ *She drank till she was half up the pole.*

half-ass(ed) *mod.* clumsy; awkward and ineffectual. (Usually objectionable.) ♦ *She only made a half-ass try at passing the test.*

half-baked 1. *mod.* badly thought out. ♦ *It would have been approved if it weren't so half-baked.* **2.** *mod.* alcohol intoxicated. ♦ *Fred got himself sort of half-baked every Saturday night.*

half-blind *mod.* alcohol intoxicated. ♦ *Four cans of beer and she was half-blind.*

half-canned *mod.* alcohol intoxicated; tipsy. ♦ *He's half-canned and will be no help at all.*

half-cocked 1. *mod.* unprepared. (See also go off half-cocked.) ♦ *So he's half-cocked. So what?* **2.** *mod.* alcohol intoxicated. ♦ *He just sat there, half-cocked and singing.*

half-crocked *mod.* alcohol intoxicated. ♦ *Sam and John set out to get half-crocked.*

half-lit *mod.* alcohol intoxicated. ♦ *John was half-lit in no time at all.*

half-sprung *mod.* tipsy; alcohol intoxicated. ♦ *Ted was half-sprung and could hardly stand up.*

half-stewed *mod.* tipsy; alcohol intoxicated. ♦ *Poor Fred was half-stewed and still had to give a speech.*

half-under 1. *mod.* semiconscious. ♦ *I was half-under and could hear what the doctor was saying.* **2.** *mod.* alcohol intoxicated; tipsy. ♦ *He was half-under and could barely stand up.*

halvsies ['hævziz] *mod.* with each (of two) paying half. (See also go Dutch.) ♦ *Let's make it halvsies, and I pay for the parking, too.*

ham 1. *n.* an actor; a bad actor. (See also hams.) ♦ *What a ham! A real showoff.* **2.** *n.* an amateur radio operator. (A nickname.) ♦ *My brother is a ham, and he helped a lot during the emergency.*

hamburg *n.* a hamburger. (See also burger.) ♦ *I'd like a couple of hamburgs and a shake.*

hamburger *n.* a stupid and worthless person—meat. ♦ *The guy is just hamburger. You can't teach him anything.*

hamburgers *n.* shares in the McDonald's corporation. (Securities markets. New York Stock Exchange jargon.) ♦ *I want 400 shares of hamburgers.*

ham-handed *mod.* lacking dexterity; clumsy. ♦ *If I wasn't so ham-handed, I could probably fix the thing myself.*

hammer *n.* the accelerator of a vehicle. ♦ *She pressed down the hammer, and off they went.*

hammer a beer Go to pound a beer.

hammer some beers Go to pound a beer.

hammered *mod.* alcohol intoxicated. ♦ *Man, old Fred was really hammered.*

hammerhead 1. *n.* a stupid person; a person whose head seems to be as solid as a hammer. ♦ *You can be such a hammerhead!* **2.** *n.* a drunkard or a drug user. ♦ *These hammerheads can't even hold a simple job for the most part.*

hams 1. *n.* legs; hips. ♦ *Her great hams extended over the sides of the chair.* **2.** *n.* the hamstring muscles. (Bodybuilding.) ♦ *Can you think of any exercises that would be good for my hams?*

HAND Go to Have a nice day.

hand it to so *tv.* to acknowledge someone's excellence (at something). ♦ *Well, I have to hand it to you. That was great!*

hand job *n.* the act of masturbating someone else. (Usually applies to males.) ♦ *She offered him a hand job.*

hand over fist *mod.* repeatedly and energetically, especially as with taking in money in a great volume. ♦ *We were taking in fees hand over fist, and the people were lined up for blocks.*

hand so sth *tv.* to tell someone something; to tell someone nonsense. ♦ *She handed me a line about being a famous author.*

handful *n.* a difficult thing or person. ♦ *Little Jimmy is a handful.*

hand-in-glove *mod.* suiting one another naturally. ♦ *These two go hand-in-glove.*

handle 1. *n.* a person's name or nickname. (Western jargon and then citizens band radio.) ♦ *My handle is Goober. You can call me Goob.* **2.** *n.* a way of dealing with something; a grasp of a problem. ♦ *As soon as I get a handle on this Wilson matter, I'll give you a buzz.*

handles Go to (love) handles.

handout 1. *n.* a gift of money, food, or other goods to a needy person. (Often in the negative, as in the examples.) ♦ *Give him a handout and send him on his way.* **2.** *n.* an informational sheet of paper "handed out" to people. ♦ *As you can see on your handout, 40 percent of those who started never finished.*

hands down *mod.* easily; unquestionably. ♦ *She won the contest hands down.*

Hands up! AND **Stick 'em up!** *exclam.* Raise your hands in the air; this is a robbery! (Underworld and Western.) ♦ *Hands up! Don't anybody move a muscle. This is a heist.* ♦ *Stick 'em up, cowboy!*

hands-on 1. *mod.* having to do with an instructional session where the learners are able to handle the device they are being trained to operate. ♦ *Please plan to attend a hands-on seminar on computers next Thursday.* **2.** *mod.* having to do with an executive or manager who participates directly in operations. ♦ *We expect that he will be the kind of hands-on president we have been looking for.*

hang *in.* to hang around; to spend time aimlessly. ♦ *My mom yelled at me because I spent all day hanging with the guys.*

hang a BA (at so) *tv.* to display one's buttocks to someone in derision. (A BA is a bare ass.) ♦ *He went to the window and hung a BA—just for the hell of it.*

hang a few on *tv.* to take a few drinks; to have a few beers. ♦ *Let's hang on a few and then go on to the meeting.*

hang a huey ['hæŋ ə '(h)jui] *tv.* to make a U-turn. (The first pronunciation of *Huey* with no *hj* is probably the original version.) ♦ *Right here! Hang a huey!*

hang a left *tv.* to turn left. ♦ *He hung a left at the wrong corner.*

hang a louie ['hæŋ ə 'lui] *tv.* to turn left. ♦ *You have to hang a louie at the stop sign.*

hang a ralph ['hæŋ ə 'rælf] *tv.* to turn right. ♦ *He skied down the easy slope and hung a ralph near a fir tree.*

hang a right *tv.* to turn right. ♦ *I told him to hang a right at the next corner, but he went on.*

hang (around) *in.* to loiter; to waste away time doing nothing. ♦ *Don't just hang around. Get busy with something.*

hang five AND **hang ten** *tv.* to stand toward the front of a surfboard or diving board and hang the toes of one or both feet over the edge. (Teens and collegiate.) ♦ *Get out there and hang five. You can swim. Nothing can go wrong.*

hang in there *in.* to keep trying; to persevere. ♦ *I'll just hang in there. Maybe things will get better.*

hang it up *tv.* to quit something. ♦ *I finally had enough and decided to hang it up.*

hang loose AND **stay loose** *in.* to relax and stay cool. ♦ *Just hang loose, man. Everything'll be all right.* ♦ *Stay loose, bud.*

hang one on *tv.* to get drunk. ♦ *Fred was hacked and went out to hang one on.*

hang sth on so *tv.* to blame something on someone; to frame someone for something. ♦ *Don't try to hang the blame on me!*

hang ten Go to hang five.

hang tough (on sth) *in.* to stick to one's position (on something). ♦ *I decided I'd hang tough on it. I tend to give in too easy.*

hang up 1. *n.* a problem or concern; an obsession. (Usually **hang-up**.) ♦ *She's got some serious hang-ups about cats.* **2.** *in.* to say no; to cancel out of something. ♦ *If you don't want to do it, just hang up. I'll understand.*

hang with so *in.* to hang around with someone. ♦ *I'm going down to the corner and hang with the guys.*

hangout ['hæŋɑʊt] *n.* a place to loaf or hang (around). ♦ *I dropped by one of his favorite hangouts, but he wasn't there.*

hanky AND **hankie** ['hæŋki] *n.* a handkerchief, especially if lacy and feminine. ♦ *Do you have a hanky I can borrow?*

hanky-panky ['hæŋki'pæŋki] **1.** *n.* funny business; deceitfulness. ♦ *There's some hanky-panky going on in the treasurer's office.* **2.** *n.* sexual play; sexual misconduct. (See also mifky-pifky (in the bushes).) ♦ *There's some hanky-panky going on in the storeroom.*

happening 1. *mod.* fashionable; trendy; positive. (Collegiate.) ♦ *Wow, that's happening!* **2.** *n.* an event. ♦ *The concert was a real happening.*

happy 1. *mod.* alcohol intoxicated; tipsy. ♦ *She seems a little happy. Must have had a few already.* **2.** *mod.* obsessed with something. (A combining form showing a strong interest in the thing that is named before **happy**.) ♦ *Pete's car-happy right now. That's all he thinks about.*

happy camper *n.* a happy person. (Often in the negative.) ♦ *I am not a happy camper. I am tired, hungry, and I need a shower.*

happy juice *n.* liquor, beer, and wine. ♦ *A little more happy juice, John?*

happy pills *n.* tranquilizers. ♦ *She asked the doctor for some "happy pills."*

happy shop *n.* a liquor store. ♦ *I need something from the happy shop.*

haps *n.* things that are happening; events. (Streets.) ♦ *Come in and tell me the haps.*

hard 1. *mod.* fermented, as with cider. (See also hard liquor.) ♦ *This juice got hard. What shall I do with it?* **2.** *mod.* having to do with an addictive drug. (Compare this with soft.) ♦ *Hard drugs are easier to get than ever before.* **3.** *mod.* tough. (Akin to *hardhearted; hard as nails.*) ♦ *Only the hard guys get through basic training.*

hard case 1. *n.* a case of liquor. ♦ *Pete wanted a hard case delivered to his house.* **2.** *n.* a person who is a real problem. ♦ *Jed has turned into a hard case. He's fighting us at every turn.*

hard coin *n.* lots of money. (See also coin.) ♦ *Old Freddie is earning some hard coin these days.*

hard head *n.* a stubborn person. ♦ *I'm not really a hard head. You bring out the worst in me.*

hard liquor *n.* potent liquor such as whiskey, gin, rum, etc. ♦ *Stay off of hard liquor until your stomach feels better.*

hard off *n.* a dull and undersexed male. (The opposite of hard-on.) ♦ *Willy is a silly hard off. He seems asleep half the time.*

hard sell *n.* a high-pressure attempt to sell something. ♦ *I'm afraid I'm very susceptible to the hard sell.*

hard time 1. *n.* a difficult experience. ♦ *I had a hard time at the doctor's office.* **2.** *n.* a prison sentence. (Underworld.) ♦ *How much hard time does he have behind him?*

hard to swallow *mod.* difficult to believe. ♦ *Your story is pretty hard to swallow, but I am beginning to believe it.*

hard up 1. *mod.* alcohol intoxicated. ♦ *After a couple of six packs, Willy found himself a little hard up.* **2.** *mod.* in need of drugs or alcohol. ♦ *The old hobo was hard up for a drink.* **3.** *mod.* desperate for companionship. ♦ *Mary must be hard up to date a jerk like that.*

hardboiled *mod.* tough; heartless. ♦ *Do you have to act so hardboiled?*

hard-core 1. *mod.* sexually explicit; pornographic. ♦ *You can't sell that hard-core stuff in a store like this!* **2.** *mod.* extreme; entrenched. ♦ *There are too many hard-core cases of poverty there.* **3.** *mod.* very good; stunning; great. ♦ *I'd like a really hard-core pizza with at least five kinds of cheese.* **4.** *mod.* extreme; quintessential. ♦ *She thinks of herself as a hard-core leftist.*

hardhat 1. *n.* a protective helmet worn around construction sites. (Standard English.) ♦ *You'll need a hardhat to come into this area.* **2.** *n.* a construction worker. (Usually derogatory.) ♦ *The hardhats didn't care much for the actress's politics.*

hardheaded *mod.* stubborn. ♦ *Anybody that hardheaded is going to have trouble with everybody.*

hardliner *n.* a person who takes a strict position (on something). ♦ *Tom is sort of a hardliner when it comes to spending public money.*

hard-nosed *mod.* stern and businesslike; unsympathetic. ♦ *It takes a hard-nosed manager to run a place like this.*

hard-on *n.* an erection of the penis. (Usually objectionable.) ♦ *He must have had his last hard-on years ago.*

hardware 1. *n.* whiskey; potent liquor. ♦ *This hardware is enough to knock your socks off.* **2.** *n.* hard drugs or hard liquor. ♦ *No wine for me. Give me the hardware.* **3.** *n.* a weapon; a gun. (Underworld and Western.) ♦ *I think I see your hardware showing.* **4.** *n.* computer parts, as opposed to computer programs. ♦ *The software is okay, so it must be the hardware that's off.*

harsh *mod.* bad; rude. ♦ *She's a harsh lady and doesn't care how you feel.*

harsh toke 1. *n.* an irritating puff of a marijuana cigarette. (Drugs.) ♦ *Wow, that was a harsh toke. Yuck!* **2.** *n.* anything or anyone unpleasant. ♦ *Sally can sure be a harsh toke when she wants.*

has more money than God *phr.* is fabulously wealthy. ♦ *He has more money than God, so I guess he can throw it around any way he wants.*

has-been ['hæzbɪn] **1.** *n.* someone who used to be important; a person whose career has ended. ♦ *Marty is just a has-been. There's no future for him.* **2.** *mod.* former; burnt-out. ♦ *Some has-been singer croaked through "The Star-Spangled Banner."*

hash [hæʃ] *n.* hashish; cannabis in general. (Drugs.) ♦ *The amount of hash that moves into this city in a single day would astound you.*

hash cannon *n.* a device used in the smoking of cannabis. (Drugs. See also shotgun.) ♦ *Don had a hash cannon in his office as a sample of a device for smoking pot.*

hash pipe *n.* a small pipe for smoking cannabis. (Drugs.) ♦ *John kept a hash pipe on the shelf just for show.*

hash-head *n.* a smoker of cannabis. (Drugs.) ♦ *You can't stay a hash-head all your life.*

hash-house 1. *n.* a cheap diner. (Where hash might be on the menu.) ♦ *Tom worked for two days as a hash-slinger in a hash-house.* **2.** *n.* a place where hashish is sold and used. (Drugs.) ♦ *This hash-house is due for a raid. Let's hit it.*

hash-slinger *n.* a cook, waiter, or waitress in a hash-house. ♦ *I worked as a hash-slinger in an all-night diner.*

hat trick *n.* three successes in a row. (Typically, three hockey goals by one player, and other scoring in threes in other sports. Extended use covers three same or different sexual "scores" (see score) by a person in a period of time.) ♦ *Walter pulled a hat trick, and the fans roared.*

hatch *n.* the mouth. (See also Down the hatch!) ♦ *Pop this in your hatch.*

hate so's **guts** *tv.* to hate someone very much. ♦ *You're horrible. I hate your guts!*

haul 1. *n.* the proceeds from a theft; loot. (Underworld.) ♦ *The cops thought they must have got a pretty good haul.* **2.** *n.* the proceeds from any activity: a performance, a fishing trip, a collection of goods or money for charity, etc. ♦ *They surveyed the haul of cans and packages and decided they had done a pretty fair job.*

haul ass (out of somewhere**)** Go to bag ass (out of somewhere).

have a ball *tv.* to have an exciting time. (See also ball.) ♦ *Come on, everybody! Let's have a ball!*

have a (big) head *tv.* to have a hangover. (*Have got* can replace *have*.) ♦ *Oh, man, do I have a head!*

have a big mouth *tv.* to speak loudly and openly in public; to tell secrets. (*Have got* can replace *have*.) ♦ *He has a big mouth.*

Don't tell him anything you don't want everybody else to know.

Have a blimp! *exclam.* Have a good year! (A play on *Goodyear Tire and Rubber Company,* which operates the Goodyear blimp.) ♦ *Have a blimp! See you next summer.*

have a blowout *in.* to have a big, wild party; to enjoy oneself at a big party. ♦ *Fred and Tom had quite a blowout last night.*

have a bone on *tv.* to have an erection. (See also **bone** at **boner.** Usually objectionable.) ♦ *Look, friend, you can't do anything with me till you have a bone on. Get it up or get out. I got other customers waiting.*

have a buzz on *tv.* to be tipsy or alcohol intoxicated. (*Have got* can replace *have.*) ♦ *Both of them had a buzz on by the end of the celebration.*

have a crack at sth Go to **take a crack at** sth.

have a glow on *tv.* to be alcohol intoxicated; to be tipsy. (*Have got* can replace *have.*) ♦ *Since you already have a glow on, I guess you won't want another drink.*

Have a good one. AND **Have a nice one.** *sent.* Have a good morning, afternoon, or evening, as appropriate. (A general formulaic expression used at any time of the day or night.) ♦ *Have a good one, cowboy.* ♦ *See you tomorrow, Todd. Have a nice one.*

have a hard-on *tv.* to have an erect penis. (The most common colloquial expression for this state. See also **hard-on.** Usually objectionable.) ♦ *I had a hard-on through the whole movie.*

have a hard-on for so *tv.* to wish to do someone physical damage; to seek revenge on someone. (The aggressor and victim are usually males. Usually objectionable.) ♦ *The punk thinks he has a hard-on for Mr. Gutman.*

have a leg up on so *tv.* to have an advantage over someone; to be ahead of someone. (*Have got* can replace *have.*) ♦ *Pete has a leg up on Wilbur because of his physical strength.*

have a little visitor *tv.* to have received the menses. (*Have got* can replace *have.*) ♦ *Mary said she has a little visitor.*

have a load on *tv.* to be alcohol intoxicated. (*Have got* can replace *have.*) ♦ *Fred has a load on and is finished for the evening.*

have a loose screw Go to **have a screw loose.**

have a lot on the ball *phr.* [for someone] to have ability and knowledge and be attentive and useful. ♦ *She can do it. She's got a lot on the ball.*

have a man by the balls *tv.* to have a man in a position where he has little choice but to do what one says. (Usually objectionable.) ♦ *She's really got him by the balls. He will go along with whatever she wants.*

have a monkey on one's **back** *tv.* to have a drug addiction. (Drugs. *Have got* can replace *have.*) ♦ *Gert has a monkey on her back.*

Have a nice day. AND **HAND** *sent. & comp. abb.* Good-bye and good luck. (See also **Have a good one.**) ♦ *Thank you. Have a nice day.*

Have a nice one. Go to **Have a good one.**

have a run-in (with so/sth**)** *tv.* to have trouble with someone or something. ♦ *I had a run-in with Mrs. Wilson. She's a hard case.*

have a screw loose AND **have a loose screw** *tv.* to be silly or eccentric. (*Have got* can replace *have.*) ♦ *He's sort of strange. I think he's got a loose screw.* ♦ *You're talking like you've got a screw loose or something.*

have a shit-fit *tv.* to have a fit; to throw a temper tantrum. (Usually objectionable.) ♦ *If I'm not home on time, my father'll have a shit-fit.*

have a short fuse *tv.* to be easy to anger. (*Have got* can replace *have.*) ♦ *He's got a short fuse, so watch out.*

have a skinful *tv.* [for someone] to contain too much alcohol; to be alcohol intoxicated. (See also **skinful.** *Have got* can replace *have*.) ♦ *Pete had a skinful and just sat there quietly.*

have a spaz [...spæz] *tv.* to get angry or hysterical; to have a **conniption** (**fit**). (Teens and collegiate.) ♦ *If my dad hears about this, he'll have a spaz.*

have a tiger by the tail *tv.* to have become associated with something powerful and potentially dangerous. (*Have got* can replace *have*.) ♦ *You have a tiger by the tail. You bit off more than you could chew.*

have a whale of a time *tv.* to have an exciting time; to have a big time. ♦ *We had a whale of a time at your party.*

have a wild hair up one's **ass 1.** *tv.* to act in a hyperactive and energetic manner. (Usually objectionable.) ♦ *She has a wild hair up her ass about something. I don't know what.* **2.** *tv.* to be obsessed with some strange or offbeat idea. (Usually objectionable.) ♦ *You're acting like you've got a wild hair up your ass. Calm down.*

have a yellow streak down one's **back** *tv.* to be cowardly. (*Have got* can replace *have*.) *wrong.* ♦ *If you have a yellow streak down your back, you don't take many risks.*

have all one's **marbles** *tv.* to have all one's mental faculties; to be mentally sound. (See also **lose (all)** one's **marbles**. *Have got* can replace *have*.) ♦ *I don't think he has all his marbles.*

have an ace up one's **sleeve** *tv.* to have something useful in reserve; to have a special trick available. (*Have got* can replace *have*.) ♦ *I still have an ace up my sleeve that you don't know about.*

have an edge on *tv.* to be alcohol intoxicated. (See also **edge**. *Have got* can replace *have*.) ♦ *Bob has an edge on even though he hardly drank anything.*

have an itch for sth *tv.* to have a desire for something. (*Have got* can replace *have*.) ♦ *We had an itch for a good movie, so we went.*

have ants in one's **pants** *tv.* to be nervous and anxious. (See also **antsy**. *Have got* can replace *have*.) ♦ *All kids've got ants in their pants all the time at that age.*

have bats in one's **belfry** [...'belfri] *tv.* to be crazy. (See also **bats**. *Have got* can replace *have*.) ♦ *Pay no attention to her. She has bats in her belfry.*

have egg on one's **face** *tv.* to be embarrassed by something one has done. (As if one went out in public with a dirty face. *Have got* can replace *have*.) ♦ *She's really got egg on her face!*

have game *in.* to have skill; to have spirit or willingness to get involved in the action. ♦ *Man, I still have game! I can do this!*

have good vibes [...vaibz] *tv.* to have good feelings (about someone or something). (*Have got* can replace *have*.) ♦ *I've got good vibes about Heidi.*

have gravy on one's **grits** *tv.* to be rich. ♦ *He got himself a good job and has gravy on his grits while I'm still eating taters.*

have hot pants (for so**)** AND **have the hots (for** so**)** *tv.* to be sexually aroused over someone in particular; to lust after someone. (Also with *got* as in the examples.) ♦ *She really has hot pants for him.* ♦ *Yup, she's got the hots, all right.*

have it all together *tv.* to be mentally and physically organized; to be of sound mind. (*Have got* can replace *have*.) ♦ *Try me again later when I have it all together.*

have it made *tv.* to have succeeded; to be set for life. (*Have got* can replace *have*.) ♦ *I have a good job and a nice little family. I have it made.*

have it made in the shade *tv.* to have succeeded; to be set for life. (*Have got* can replace *have*.) ♦ *Wow, is he lucky! He has it made in the shade.*

have kittens 1. *tv.* to become enraged. ♦ *When I heard the news, I had kittens. I was hacked!* **2.** *tv.* to laugh very hard; to enjoy something enormously. ♦ *It was so funny, I had kittens laughing.* **3.** *tv.* to be surprised. ♦ *She had kittens when she heard about the wedding.*

have lead in one's **pencil 1.** *tv.* to be vigorous and active. (Widely known phrase. Not taboo.) ♦ *Your problem, Tom, is that you should have more lead in your pencil.*

You just don't have the stamina. **2.** *tv.* to have an erection of the penis. (Usually objectionable.) ♦ *Due to his drinking habits, he never has any lead in his pencil.*

have one foot in the grave *tv.* to be near death. (*Have got* can replace *have.*) ♦ *I feel like I've got one foot in the grave.*

have one's **ass in a crack** *tv.* to be stranded in a very difficult or uncomfortable state of affairs. (Usually objectionable. *Have got* can replace *have.*) ♦ *He's got his ass in a crack and needs all the help he can get.*

have one's **ass in a sling** *tv.* to be dejected or hurt; to be pouting; to be in trouble. (Usually objectionable. *Have got* can replace *have.*) ♦ *She's got her ass in a sling because she got stood up.*

have one's **brain on a leash** *tv.* to be drunk. ♦ *Wayne had his brain on a leash before he even got to the party.*

have one's **mind in the gutter** *tv.* to think or suggest something obscene. (*Have got* can replace *have.*) ♦ *Tiffany has her mind in the gutter. That's why she laughs at all that dirty stuff.*

have one's **nose wide open** *tv.* to be in love. ♦ *Sam's not dense. He's got his nose wide open. It's that Sally.*

have rocks in one's **head** *tv.* to be silly or crazy. (*Have got* can replace *have.*) ♦ *She's got rocks in her head if she thinks that.*

have shit for brains *tv.* to be exceedingly stupid. (Usually objectionable.) ♦ *You have shit for brains if you think you can get away with it.*

have snow on the roof *phr.* to have white or much gray hair. ♦ *Come on, judge, you've had hair on the roof for years!*

have so **by the short hairs** *tv.* to have someone in an awkward position; to have dominated someone. (This refers to the shorter pubic hairs. Sometime euphemized to *neck hairs.*) ♦ *They've got me by the short hairs. There's nothing I can do.*

have so **dead to rights** *tv.* to have caught someone red-handed; to have irrefutable evidence about someone's misdeed. (*Have got* can replace *have.* See also

(bang) dead to rights.) ♦ *The cops had him dead to rights.*

have sth **cinched** *tv.* to have something settled; to have the results of some act assured. (See also cinched. *Have got* can replace *have.*) ♦ *You just think you've got it cinched.*

have sth **on the brain** *tv.* to be obsessed with something. (*Have got* can replace *have.*) ♦ *I have money on the brain, I guess.*

have the hots (for so**)** Go to have hot pants (for so).

have the wrong number 1. *tv.* to be wrong. (*Have got* can replace *have.*) ♦ *You have missed the boat again. You have the wrong number!* **2.** *tv.* to be addressing the wrong person. (This use is in addition to the same expression used for a wrong telephone number. *Have got* can replace *have.*) ♦ *No, I'm Sally. You have the wrong number.*

have what it takes *tv.* to have the skills, power, intelligence, etc., to do something. (*Have got* can replace *have.*) ♦ *I guess I don't have what it takes to be a composer.*

the **have-nots** *n.* the poor; those who have little or nothing. (Compare this with the haves.) ♦ *The have-nots seem never to be able to get ahead.*

the **haves** *n.* the wealthy; those who have money. (Compare this with the have-nots.) ♦ *The haves seem to be able to take care of themselves.*

hawk 1. *n.* someone who supports a war-like U.S. defense policy. (Compare this with dove.) ♦ *The hawks want to raise taxes and buy tanks.* **2.** *in.* to cough mightily; to cough something up. ♦ *The cold has had me hawking for a week.* **3.** the **hawk** *n.* the cold winter wind. (Originally black. Always with *the* in this sense. See also Mr. Hawkins.) ♦ *Man, just feel the hawk cut through you!*

hay burner 1. *n.* a worthless racehorse; any old and worn-out horse. ♦ *I went to a dude ranch, and they gave me an old hay burner to ride.* **2.** AND **hay head** *n.* a marijuana smoker. (Drugs.) ♦ *Some hay* head was around trying to sell raffle tickets that looked handmade.

hay head Go to hay burner.

hayseed *n.* a farmer; a rustic character, usually a male. ♦ *I'm not just some hayseed fresh off the farm.*

haywire ['hewaɪr] **1.** *mod.* out of order. (Folksy.) ♦ *This telephone has gone haywire.* **2.** *mod.* disoriented. (Often from marijuana.) ♦ *Willy is sort of haywire from the grass.*

hazel ['hezl] *n.* heroin. (Drugs. A variety of H.) ♦ *She wants to spend the evening with hazel.*

head 1. *n.* a headache. ♦ *Music that loud gives me a head.* **2.** a **head** *n.* a hangover. (Always with *a* in this sense.) ♦ *How do you get rid of a head so you can go to work?* **3.** *n.* a toilet; a restroom. (Originally nautical. Usually with *the*.) ♦ *Ralph is in the head. He'll be back in a minute.* **4.** *n.* a member of the drug culture; a hippie or a person who drops out of mainstream society because of drug use. (From the 1960s and 1970s.) ♦ *You still see a few heads around, even today.* **5.** *n.* a smart person; an intellectual person. ♦ *I'm no head, but I am sure you made a mistake in your addition.*

head cook and bottle washer AND **chief cook and bottle washer** *n.* someone who is in charge of trivial things as well as the important things. ♦ *Ten years I'm here, and I'm just the head cook and bottle washer.* ♦ *The chief cook and bottle washer ends up doing everything that has to be done.*

head drug *n.* a drug that affects the mind rather than the body; a psychoactive drug. ♦ *It's these head drugs that get the kids into so much trouble.*

head hunt *tv. & in.* to recruit someone (for a job). ♦ *He went to the conference to head hunt a new employee.*

head South Go to go South.

head trip 1. *n.* a session with a head drug. (Drugs.) ♦ *Bob had his first head trip last night.* **2.** *n.* an ego trip. ♦ *Come down from your head trip and see if you can get along with the rest of us.*

headache 1. *n.* an annoying person or thing. ♦ *Cars can be such a headache.* **2.** *n.* liquor. ♦ *Pour me some more of that headache, will you?*

headache department 1. *n.* a central source of unnecessary problems; a person who habitually causes problems. ♦ *Here's another memo from the headache department.* **2.** AND **headache house** *n.* a liquor store or department. ♦ *I stopped in at the headache house for some supplies.*

headache house Go to headache department.

headache man *n.* a male law enforcement agent. ♦ *The headache man was here to see you, Ernie.*

headbone *n.* the skull. ♦ *Do you want I should conk your headbone, or will you be coming along politely?*

headfucker *n.* a person, situation, or a drug that confuses someone or disorients someone mentally. (Taboo. Usually objectionable.) ♦ *Why did you have to lay this headfucker on me?*

headhunter *n.* someone who recruits executives for employment. (*Head* means *boss* here.) ♦ *The board of directors hired a headhunter to get a new manager.*

head-job *n.* an act of fellatio. (Usually objectionable.) ♦ *The hooker asked him if he wanted a head-job.*

Heads up! *exclam.* Look out! ♦ *Heads up! Watch out for the swinging bucket!*

heads will roll *in.* someone will be punished. ♦ *When I find out who did this, heads will roll.*

Headstone City *n.* a cemetery. ♦ *Our house is just one block after the large Headstone City on the left.*

heap 1. *n.* an old car. (See also load.) ♦ *I've got to get my heap fixed up.* **2.** *n.* any dilapidated thing or person. ♦ *We have to fix up this heap if we're really going to live in it.* **3.** AND **heaps** *n.* lots (of something). ♦ *Mr. Wilson has heaps of money.*

heaps Go to heap.

heart *tv.* to love someone or something. (Teens.) ♦ *She's hearting him more every day.*

hearts and flowers *n.* sentimentality. ♦ *I didn't care for the hearts and flowers part.*

heart-to-heart (talk) *n.* a serious and intimate discussion. ♦ *We sat down and had a nice heart-to-heart for about an hour.*

heat 1. the **heat** *n.* the police. (Underworld.) ♦ *The heat is gonna catch up with you, Ernie.* **2.** *n.* pressure. ♦ *The boss put some heat on Willy, and things are moving faster now.* **3.** *n.* a gun; armaments. (Underworld. See also **heater**.) ♦ *Lefty has his heat on him at all times.*

heater *n.* a pistol. (Underworld.) ♦ *Put your heaters away, boys. This is a job for reason.*

heave [hiv] *in.* to empty one's stomach; to vomit. ♦ *He heaved and heaved and sounded like he was dying.*

heaven dust *n.* cocaine. (Drugs.) ♦ *A little heaven dust and Pat was as good as new.*

heavy 1. *n.* a villain. (Especially in movies, etc.) ♦ *He is well known for playing heavies in the movies.* **2.** *mod.* important; profound; serious. ♦ *I have some heavy things to talk over with you, Sam.* **3.** *mod.* really fine. ♦ *This is a real heavy thing you're doing for me.*

heavy artillery *n.* powerful or persuasive persons or things. (The same as **big gun**.) ♦ *Finally, the mayor brought out the heavy artillery and quieted things down.*

heavy bread AND **heavy money** *n.* a great deal of money. ♦ *Man, that car cost some heavy bread.* ♦ *He can afford it. He pulls down some heavy bread.*

heavy date *n.* an important date with someone; a date with someone important. ♦ *Mary has a heavy date with Sam tonight.*

heavy hash *n.* potent cannabis. (Drugs.) ♦ *This is heavy hash, and it will cost you.*

heavy into so/sth *mod.* much concerned with someone or something; obsessed with someone or something. ♦ *Freddie was heavy into auto racing and always went to the races.*

heavy joint *n.* a marijuana cigarette tipped with phencyclidine (PCP). (Drugs.) ♦ *He said something about smoking a heavy joint just before he passed out.*

heavy money Go to heavy bread.

heavy scene *n.* a serious state of affairs; an emotionally charged situation. ♦ *Man, that meeting was really a heavy scene.*

heavy soul *n.* heroin. (Streets.) ♦ *Your heavy soul will be on your back forever.*

heavy-handed *mod.* tactless; forceful; unfair. ♦ *Paul is a little heavy-handed at times, but mostly he's reasonable.*

heavyweight 1. *n.* an important person; a successful person; a leader. ♦ *Mr. Wilson is a heavyweight in local government.* **2.** *mod.* important; successful. ♦ *Vince is one of the heavyweight operators in this business.*

hecka *mod.* a less intense version of **hella**; heck of a. (Streets.) ♦ *Dude, that's one hecka mess!*

H-E-double-toothpicks *n.* hell. (A jocular euphemism. It is not usually written and can be spelled a number of different ways.) ♦ *Oh, H-E-double-toothpicks! I did it wrong again!*

heebie-jeebies AND **heeby-jeebies** ['hibi'dʒibiz] *n.* an extreme case of anxiety or fear. ♦ *I have the heebie-jeebies whenever I go to the dentist.*

heel *n.* a low and despicable man. ♦ *The guy is a heel, and he seems to work at it, too.*

heeled 1. *mod.* alcohol intoxicated. ♦ *Man, were those guys heeled!* **2.** *mod.* carrying drugs. (Drugs.) ♦ *Shorty is heeled and ready to deal.*

heesh [hiʃ] *n.* hashish; cannabis. (Drugs.) ♦ *Ernie started out on heesh and moved on from there.*

heinie *n.* the buttocks. ♦ *He fell down flat on his heinie.*

heinous *n.* bad; bad-looking; horrible, as in *heinous crime*. (A standard English word, used in a slangy context.) ♦ *Where on earth did you get hat heinous outfit?*

Heinz 57 (variety) [haɪnz...] **1.** *n.* a mongrel breed of dog. (From the trade name of a condiment company.) ♦ *We have one pedigreed dog and one Heinz 57 variety.* **2.** *n.* any mixture or mixed variety; any composition variable or undetermined parts. ♦ *Our old house was sort of Heinz 57. A little bit of a lot of styles.*

heist [haɪst] **1.** *n.* a theft; a robbery. (Underworld. See also lift.) ♦ *Lefty just had to pull one last heist.* **2.** *tv.* to steal something; to rob a person or place; to lift something. (Underworld.) ♦ *The thugs heisted her and took her purse and watch.*

heister ['haɪstɚ] *n.* a drunkard, who lifts or heists drinks. ♦ *Two old heisters were lifting drink after drink and tossing them down.*

helium head ['hiliəm 'hɛd] *n.* a fool; an airhead. ♦ *Well, what's that helium head done now?*

hell 1. *n.* trouble. (Use caution with hell. Common colloquial, but with a few restrictions. One would not expect middle-class children to use this at home. See the complete list of all entries with hell in the **Index of Hidden Key Words**. Hell as a destination is not considered slang or colloquial. Hell as a curse is colloquial.) ♦ *I went through all sorts of hell to get this done on time.* **2.** *exclam.* Damn! (Usually **Hell!** Use caution with hell.) ♦ *Oh, hell. I'm late.*

hell around *in.* to go around making trouble or noise. ♦ *Who are those kids who are out there helling around every night?*

hell of a mess *n.* a terrible mess. (See also mell of a hess. Use caution with hell.) ♦ *This is really a hell of a mess you've gotten us into.*

hell of a note *n.* a surprising or amazing piece of news. (Use caution with hell.) ♦ *You forgot it. That's a hell of a note.*

hell of a so/sth AND **helluva** so/sth **1.** *n.* a very bad person or thing. (Use caution with hell.) ♦ *That's a hell of a way to treat someone.* **2.** *n.* a very good person or thing. (Use caution with hell.) ♦ *He is one helluva guy. We really like him.*

hell raiser Go to heller.

Hell's bells (and buckets of blood)! *exclam.* Dammit! (Use caution with hell.) ♦ *Oh, hell's bells and buckets of blood! I forgot my keys.*

hella *mod.* (a) hell of (a).... (Streets.) ♦ *That's a hella long way to Vegas.*

hellacious [hɛl'eʃəs] **1.** *mod.* terrible. ♦ *The heat was hellacious, and the mosquitoes wouldn't leave us alone.* **2.** *mod.* wild; excellent. (Use caution with hell.) ♦ *What a hellacious good time we had!*

hellbender ['hɛlbɛndɚ] **1.** *n.* a drinking bout. (Use caution with hell. *Hellbender* is also the name of a large salamander.) ♦ *Jed is off on another of his hellbenders.* **2.** *n.* a heavy drinker; a drunkard. (The *bender* refers to bending the elbow with a drink in hand. Use caution with hell.) ♦ *Willy is a hellbender from way back.*

heller AND **hell raiser** *n.* a rowdy person; a hell-raising person. (Use caution with hell.) ♦ *Jimmy is turning out to be a real hell raiser.* ♦ *A bunch of hell raisers kept me up late last night.*

hellhole *n.* a hot and crowded place; any unpleasant place. (Use caution with hell.) ♦ *The theater was an overcrowded hellhole. Lucky there was no fire.*

Hello? *exclam.* Did you hear me?; Are you aware that I am talking to you? ♦ *A: I don't want any of that. B: Here, have some. A: Hello? No, I don't want any.*

hell-on-wheels *n.* a very impressive person or thing; an extreme type of person or thing. (Use caution with hell.) ♦ *This little machine is hell-on-wheels for general woodworking purposes.*

hellpig *n.* a fat and ugly girl or woman. (Derogatory.) ♦ *Comb your hair. You look like some hellpig!*

helluva so/sth Go to hell of a so/sth.

helmet 1. *n.* the foreskin of the penis. ♦ *He's at the doctor's, asking about getting his helmet clipped off.* **2.** *n.* the glans penis; the end of the penis. ♦ *The helmet's the sensitive part.* **3.** an ineffective and oafish male. ♦ *You stupid helmet!* **4.** *n.* a hairdo. ♦ *Her helmet looks like it's a wig.*

hemp 1. *n.* a smelly cigar. ♦ *Get that vile hemp out of here!* **2.** *n.* cannabis. (Drugs.) ♦ *The guy sort of smells like hemp.*

hen fruit *n.* (chicken) eggs. ♦ *There's nothing like hen fruit and bacon.*

hen party *n.* a gossipy party attended by women. ♦ *I have a hen party every few weeks. We love to get together.*

hep [hɛp] *mod.* aware; informed; savvy. ♦ *The chick is simply not hep.*

hepped (up) *mod.* alcohol intoxicated. ♦ *Willy is a little too hepped up to drive home.*

herb AND **erb** *n.* marijuana. (Drugs.) ♦ *Carl has found a way to synthesize the erb.*

Herb and Al *n.* marijuana and alcohol. ♦ *I'm afraid that Tom's best friends are Herb and Al.*

Here's looking at you. *sent.* I salute you. (A polite drinking toast.) ♦ *Here's looking at you. Bottoms up!*

Here's mud in your eye. *sent.* I salute you. (A jocular drinking toast.) ♦ *Here's mud in your eye. Bottoms up!*

Here's the deal. *tv.* This is the plan, scheme, or proposition. ♦ *Okay, here's the deal. You pass the ball to Bob, and I'll run in the opposite direction.*

hero Go to submarine.

hero (of the underworld) *n.* heroin. ♦ *Don says he knows the hero of the underworld well.*

herped up *mod.* infected with the *herpes simplex* virus. ♦ *Why do all the boys treat me like I was herped up or something?*

herpie AND **herp** *n.* someone who is infected with herpies. ♦ *How would you like to find out you've been going out with a herp?*

heteroflexible *mod.* bisexual. (Contrived. A blend of *heterosexual* + *flexible*.) ♦ *He has preferences, but basically, he's heteroflexible.*

Hey! *interj.* hello. (Colloquial. A standard greeting in much of the South, and now heard everywhere.) ♦ *Hey, Walter. How are you?*

Hey, bum! *interj.* hello. ♦ *Hey, bum! So good to see your smiling face.*

hickey AND **hicky** ['hɪki] **1.** *n.* a love bite; a mark on the skin caused by biting or sucking. (See also monkey bite.) ♦ *She wore a high collar to cover up a hickey.* **2.** *n.* a pimple, especially if infected. ♦ *Wouldn't you know I'd get a hickey like this right when I have to have my picture taken!*

hiddy AND **hidi** ['hɪdi] **1.** *mod.* hideous. ♦ *That skirt is just hiddy! Get a life!* **2.** *mod.* hideously drunk; very drunk. ♦ *Fred was totally hidi. He fell asleep under the table.*

hide *n.* the skin. ♦ *I need to get some rays on my hide.*

hides *n.* drums. (See also skins.) ♦ *They say his hides are worth about 4,000 clams.*

hidi Go to hiddy.

high 1. *mod.* alcohol or drug intoxicated. ♦ *They went out for the evening to get high, and for no other reason.* **2.** *n.* a state of euphoria caused by drugs or alcohol. ♦ *His life is nothing but one high after another.*

high and dry *mod.* abandoned; unsupported. (Like a ship beached or stranded ashore.) ♦ *Here I sit high and dry—no food, no money, no nothing.*

high five 1. *n.* a greeting where the palm of the hand is raised and slapped against another person's palm similarly raised. (Compare this with low five.) ♦ *They exchanged a high five and went on with the show.* **2.** *tv.* & *in.* to greet someone as described in sense 1. ♦ *They high fived and went off together.*

high mucky-muck [...'məkimək] *n.* an important person; the person in charge. ♦ *When the high mucky-mucks meet, they will decide what to do about the problem.*

high on sth *mod.* excited or enthusiastic about something. ♦ *Tom is really high on the idea of going to Yellowstone this summer.*

high roller *n.* a big gambler who risks much money; anyone who takes risks. (Refers to rolling dice.) ♦ *Rocko is a high roller and isn't afraid to lose some money.*

high sign *n.* a hand signal meaning *okay.* (The tip of the index or middle finger touches the tip of the thumb, and the hand is raised into the air.) ♦ *Give me a "high sign" when you want me to start.*

high ups AND **higher ups** *n.* the people in charge. ♦ *One of the higher ups is coming down to talk to you.*

high, wide, and handsome *mod.* happy; carefree. ♦ *Willy is high, wide, and handsome after his great triumph.*

highbrow 1. *n.* an intellectual person; a person with refined tastes. (Compare this with **lowbrow.** See also **longhair.**) ♦ *The highbrows usually congregate in there.* **2.** *mod.* having to do with an intellectual or a person with refined tastes. ♦ *Pete is sort of highbrow, but he's an okay guy.*

higher ups Go to high ups.

high-maintenance *mod.* [of a person] requiring much care and coddling. ♦ *He's sort of a high-maintenance guy. He requires lots of reassurance.*

high-res AND **hi-res** ['haɪ'rɛz] *mod.* good; satisfying. (From *high-resolution,* referring to the picture quality of a computer monitor. Compare this with **low-res.**) ♦ *I sure feel hi-res today.*

hike 1. *n.* a monetary increase. ♦ *Another hike in the electric rates takes place this spring.* **2.** *tv.* to increase an amount of money. ♦ *I wanted them to hike my salary, but they refused.*

The **Hill** *n.* the U.S. Congress; the U.S. capitol building located on Capitol Hill in Washington, D.C. ♦ *I really can't tell what's happening up on the Hill.*

hincty ['hɪŋkti] *mod.* snobbish; fussy; aloof. (Black.) ♦ *Some of those people are so hincty!*

hip 1. *mod.* informed; aware. (See also **hep.**) ♦ *The guy is just not hip. He's a nerd.* **2.** *tv.* to tell someone; to inform someone.

♦ *What's happening? Take a minute and hip me!*

hipe Go to hype.

hippie Go to hippy.

hippy AND **hippie** ['hɪpi] *n.* a long-haired, drug-using youth of the 1960s and 1970s. ♦ *That guy looks like a hippy left over from the sixties.*

hip-shooter *n.* someone who talks without thinking; someone who speaks very frankly. (See also **shoot from the hip.**) ♦ *He's just a loudmouthed hip-shooter. Pay no attention.*

hipster ['hɪpstɚ] *n.* a youth of the 1950s, characterized by an interest in jazz and cool things. ♦ *Were the hipsters the ones with the big shoulder pads?*

hired gun *n.* a paid assassin. (Underworld.) ♦ *The cops are holding a well-known hired gun until they can prepare charges.*

hi-res Go to high-res.

history *n.* someone or something in the past. (See also **ancient history; I'm history.**) ♦ *Don't make a move! If this gun goes off, you're history.*

hit 1. *n.* a success; something that meets with approval. (Often with *with.*) ♦ *The fudge with nuts in it was a great hit at the sale.* **2.** *n.* a successful result; something that is exactly as intended. ♦ *Your idea was right on target—a hit for sure.* **3.** *n.* a drink of liquor; a dose of a drug. (See also **bop.**) ♦ *He had a hit of sauce and went out to finish his work.* **4.** *tv.* to reach something; to achieve something. ♦ *I hit sixty next month, and I'm going to retire.* **5.** *tv.* to kill someone; to assassinate someone. (Underworld.) ♦ *The thug set out to hit the mayor, but got nabbed first.* **6.** *tv.* to attack or rob someone or something. (Underworld.) ♦ *Can you believe that they tried to hit a block party on Fourth Street?* **7.** *n.* a robbery; an assassination. (Underworld.) ♦ *There was a hit at the bank on Maple Street last night.*

hit by the stupid stick *mod.* made to act really stupid. ♦ *Nobody can be that dumb. You must have been hit by the stupid stick.*

hit by the ugly stick *mod.* made to be very ugly. ♦ *She is so lame. Looks like she was hit by the ugly stick till it broke!*

hit it with so *tv.* to copulate with someone. ♦ *Did she hit it with him, or what?*

hit list *n.* a list of people to whom something is going to happen. ♦ *Ralph is on my hit list for contributing money for the orphans.*

hit man 1. *n.* a hired killer. (Underworld.) ♦ *Sam was the perfect hit man. Hardly any brains or conscience.* **2.** *n.* a man hired by a helpless addict to inject drugs. (Drugs. See also pinch hitter.) ♦ *Harry the Horse refuses to be a hit man. He says that's not what he does best.*

Hit me. 1. AND **hit me again** *tv.* [in gambling] Deal me a card. ♦ *Hit me again, dealer!* **2.** *tv.* Give me the high five. ♦ *Hit me! Where you been? Hit me again!* **3.** AND **hit me again** *tv.* Serve me (another) drink. ♦ *Hit me again, bartender.*

hit me again Go to Hit me.

hit me on the hip *tv.* call me on my pager. (Pagers are usually worn attached one's belt or in a pants packet.) ♦ *When you need me, just hit me on the hip.*

hit on so *in.* to flirt with someone; to make a pass at someone. ♦ *The women were all hitting on George, but he didn't complain.*

hit on sth *in.* to discover something; to think up or invent something. ♦ *She hit on a new scheme for removing the impurities from drinking water.*

hit pay dirt AND **strike pay dirt 1.** *tv.* to discover something of value. ♦ *When we opened the last trunk, we knew we had hit pay dirt.* **2.** *tv.* to get to the basic facts of something. ♦ *When we figured out the code, we really struck pay dirt.*

hit so **below the belt** *tv.* to deal with someone unfairly; to exploit someone's vulnerabilities unfairly. (From boxing.) ♦ *You were hitting Tom below the belt when you said that.*

hit so **(up) for** sth *tv.* to ask someone for something. ♦ *I hit Fred up for some help with the committee.*

hit so **with** sth *tv.* to present someone with an idea, plan, or proposal. ♦ *Fred hit his boss with a plan to save a bundle in the front office.*

hit the books AND **pound the books** *tv.* to study hard. ♦ *I spent the weekend pounding the books.* ♦ *I gotta go home and hit the books.*

hit the booze Go to hit the bottle.

hit the bottle AND **hit the booze** *tv.* to go on a drinking bout; to get drunk. ♦ *She got caught hitting the bottle in the office.* ♦ *He's been hitting the booze for a week now.*

hit the bricks AND **hit the pavement 1.** *tv.* to start walking; to go into the streets. ♦ *I have a long way to go. I'd better hit the bricks.* **2.** *tv.* to go out on strike. ♦ *The workers hit the pavement on Friday and haven't been back on the job since.*

hit the bull's-eye Go to hit the spot.

hit the ceiling AND **hit the roof** *tv.* to get very angry. ♦ *She really hit the ceiling when she found out what happened.*

hit the deck 1. *tv.* to get out of bed. ♦ *Come on, hit the deck! It's morning.* **2.** *tv.* to fall down; to drop down. ♦ *I hit the deck the minute I heard the shots.*

hit the fan *tv.* to become publicly known; to become a scandal. (From the phrase *when the shit hit the fan.*) ♦ *It hit the fan, and within ten minutes the press had spread it all over the world.*

hit the hay AND **hit the sack** *tv.* to go to bed. ♦ *Time to go home and hit the hay!* ♦ *Let's hit the sack. We have to get an early start in the morning.*

hit the jackpot 1. *tv.* to win a large amount of money. ♦ *Sally hit the jackpot in the lottery.* **2.** *tv.* to be exactly right; to find exactly what was sought. ♦ *I wanted a small house with a fireplace, and I really hit the jackpot with this one.*

hit the panic button AND **press the panic button; push the panic button** *tv.* to panic. ♦ *She hit the panic button and just went to pieces.* ♦ *Don't press the panic button until you think it through.*

hit the pavement Go to hit the bricks.

hit the road *tv.* to leave; to begin to travel on a road. (See also smack the road.) ♦ *Let's hit the road. We have a long way to go.*

hit the roof Go to hit the ceiling.

hit the sack Go to hit the hay.

hit the skids *tv.* to decline; to decrease in value or status; to go downhill (figuratively). ♦ *Jed hit the skids when he started drinking.*

hit the spot 1. AND **hit the bull's-eye** *tv.* to be exactly right. (See also ring the bell.) ♦ *You really hit the spot with that prediction.* **2.** *tv.* to be refreshing. ♦ *I want something hot—some coffee would really hit the bull's-eye.*

hit the trail *tv.* to leave. (As if one were riding a horse.) ♦ *I have to hit the trail before sunset.*

hit under the wing *mod.* alcohol intoxicated. (See also shot. In the way that a bird is struck by shot.) ♦ *Sally was a little hit under the wing, but she wasn't bad off at all.*

hitched *mod.* married. (Folksy.) ♦ *Sam and Mary decided to get hitched.*

hizzle a wild card word for words beginning with *H*, such as *hell*, *hall*, or *house*. (Streets. Also for other words with initial *H*.) ♦ *What the hizzle!*

ho Go to hoe.

ho stro *n.* a location where prostitutes look for customers, a *whore stroll*. ♦ *What're you doing on this ho stro? It's mine.*

hoagy Go to submarine.

hobeast ['ho bist] *n.* a whore beast; a promiscuous woman. ♦ *I try to avoid that hobeast.*

hock 1. *tv.* to pawn something. ♦ *I tried to hock my watch to get some money.* **2.** *n.* a foot. ♦ *My hocks are sore from all that walking.*

hock a luggie ['hɑk ɑ 'lugi] *tv.* to cough up and spit out phlegm. ♦ *Tom suppressed the urge to hock a luggie over the bridge railing.*

hockey AND **hocky** ['hɑki] *mod.* dung. (See also horse hockey.) ♦ *Watch out for that hocky there in the gutter.*

hockey-whore AND **puck bunny** *n.* a kind of groupie that follows hockey players. (Puck bunny is a play on fuck bunny.) ♦ *She doesn't like the game, she's just a hockey-whore.* ♦ *Just a cheap, skanky puck bunny, that's her!*

hockshop *n.* a pawnshop. ♦ *We took the watch to a hockshop, but couldn't get enough money for it.*

hocky Go to hockey.

hocus *tv.* to falsify something; to adulterate something. (Part of *hocus-pocus* = magic, deception.) ♦ *Somebody has hocused the booze.*

hodad AND **hodaddy** ['hodæd(i)] **1.** *n.* someone, usually a male, who poses (badly) as a surfer. (California. Possibly a blend of ho = whore and *dad(dy)* = male.) ♦ *Who's that hodaddy with the crumby looking board?* **2.** *n.* an obnoxious person; a repellent person. (California.) ♦ *Ted is a total hodad.*

hodaddy Go to hodad.

hoe AND **ho** *n.* a prostitute; a whore. (Originally black. Streets.) ♦ *Get them hoes outa here!*

hog 1. AND **hog cadillac** *n.* a large car; a souped up car. (See also road hog.) ♦ *How do you like my new hog?* ♦ *Where are you going to park that hog cadillac.* **2.** *n.* a police officer; a pig. ♦ *The hogs are on to you.* **3.** *n.* an addict who requires very large doses to sustain the habit. (Drugs.) ♦ *Ernie is turning into a hog. He just can't get enough.* **4.** *n.* phencyclidine (PCP), an animal tranquilizer. (Drugs.) ♦ *We're glad to learn that the demand for hog is tapering off.*

hog cadillac Go to hog.

hogwash 1. *n.* bad food or drink. ♦ *This stuff is hogwash. Take it away.* **2.** *n.* nonsense. ♦ *Hogwash! That's about enough of your lies!*

hog-wild *mod.* wild; boisterous. ♦ *All the kids were completely hog-wild by the time I got there.*

ho-hum ['ho'həm] *mod.* dull; causing yawns of boredom. (Ho-hum is a representation of the sound of a yawn.) ♦ *Clare played another ho-hum concert at the music hall last night.*

hoist one *tv.* to have a drink. ♦ *Let's go out and hoist one sometime.*

ho-jo('s) ['hodʒo(z)] *n.* a Howard Johnson's restaurant or hotel. (Collegiate. Often with *the.*) ♦ *We're going to meet the others at the ho-jo.*

hokey ['hoki] *mod.* contrived; phony; ill conceived. (Probably related to *hocus-pocus.* See also **hocus.**) ♦ *That's a pretty hokey idea, but it may work.*

hokum ['hokəm] *n.* nonsense. (Probably related to *hocus-pocus.* See also **hocus.** Possibly a blend of **hocus** + **bunkum.** Possibly a pseudo Latin form of **hocus.**) ♦ *No more hokum. I want the truth.*

hold *tv. & in.* to possess drugs. (Drugs.) ♦ *Gert was holding coke when she was arrested.*

hold all the aces *tv.* to be in control of everything. ♦ *The boss holds all the aces on this deal.*

Hold everything! *exclam.* Stop everything! ♦ *Hold everything! I forgot my wallet.*

Hold it! *exclam.* Stop right there! ♦ *Hold it! Stop!*

hold one's **high** *tv.* to behave reasonably well under the influence of drugs. (Similar to **hold** one's **liquor.**) ♦ *Ernie can't hold his high. What a creep!*

hold one's **horses** *tv.* to wait up; to relax and slow down; to be patient. (Usually a command.) ♦ *Now, just hold your horses and let me explain.*

hold one's **liquor** *tv.* to be able to drink alcohol in quantity without ill effects. ♦ *Old Jed can sure hold his liquor—and a lot of it, too.*

Hold some, fold some. *sent.* to hold some of your stocks and sell some. (Securities markets.) ♦ *My best advice right now is to hold some, fold some. There is no real trend to the market.*

hold the fort *tv.* to remain behind and take care of things. ♦ *I left John there to hold the fort.*

Hold the phone! *exclam.* Wait just a minute! ♦ *Just a minute! Hold the phone!*

hold water *tv.* [for an idea, plan, etc.] to survive evaluation or scrutiny. ♦ *Nothing you've said so far holds water.*

hole *n.* a despised person; an **asshole.** (Usually objectionable. Also a term of address.) ♦ *Sam is such a hole. He needs human being lessons.*

hole digger *n.* a lowly ditch digger; a common laborer. (As disparaging as **burger-flipper.**) ♦ *Yo want to spend the rest of your life as a drunken hole digger?*

hole in the wall *n.* a tiny shop, not much wider than its doorway. ♦ *I went into this little hole in the wall where they had the nicest little gifts.*

hole up *in.* to hide (somewhere). ♦ *I just want to hole up until the whole matter is settled.*

holier-than-thou *mod.* superior in piety; condescending. ♦ *She has such a holier-than-thou attitude.*

Hollywood 1. *mod.* having phony glitter. ♦ *Who is this Hollywood dame who just came in?* **2.** *n.* a gaudily dressed person in sunglasses. (Also a term of address.) ♦ *Ask Hollywood over there to take off his shades and make himself known.*

holmes [homz] *n.* one's pal or friend. (A variant of **homes.** See also **Sherlock.** Usually a term of address.) ♦ *What do you think about that, holmes?*

Holy cow! *exclam.* Wow! ♦ *Give me a chance! Holy cow, don't rush me!*

holy Joe 1. *n.* a chaplain; a cleric; a clergyman. ♦ *Old holy Joe wants to see all of us at services.* **2.** *n.* a very pious person. ♦ *Don't let that holy Joe hear about what you've done.*

Holy mackerel! ['holi 'mækrəl] *exclam.* Wow! ♦ *Holy mackerel! What a day!*

Holy moley! ['holi 'moli] *exclam.* Wow! (The exclamation used by the comic book character Captain Marvel.) ♦ *Holy moley! A whole quarter! Shazam!*

holy stink *n.* anything repellent; a real mess; a great argument or debate; a major issue. ♦ *You really created a holy stink with that silly remark.*

holy terror *n.* a devilish person; a badly behaving child. ♦ *Why is the boss such a holy terror today?*

hombre ['ambre] *n.* a man. (From Spanish.) ♦ *Who's that hombre who just came in?*

home skillet Go to homeslice.

homeboy AND **homegirl** *n.* a buddy; a pal. (Originally between blacks. Also a term of address. Homeboy is for males and homegirl is for females.) ♦ *Come on, homeboy. Help out a friend.* ♦ *Tsup, homegirl?*

home-brew *n.* homemade liquor or beer. ♦ *My uncle makes his own home-brew.*

homegirl Go to homeboy.

homegrown 1. *mod.* local; folksy; amateur. ♦ *The homegrown talent at the fair was just as entertaining as anything could have been.* **2.** *n.* marijuana grown domestically or locally. (Drugs.) ♦ *She'd rather use homegrown than have to deal with Shorty.*

homer ['homɚ] **1.** *n.* a home run in baseball. ♦ *Wilbur hit one homer after another.* **2.** *tv. & in.* to hit a home run. ♦ *Wilbur homered another one and brought in two runs with him.*

homes AND **homey; homie** *n.* a buddy; a pal. (Originally between blacks. Also a term of address. See also holmes.) ♦ *Me and my homie want to go with you.*

homeslice AND **home skillet** *n.* a homeboy; a homegirl. ♦ *Ask my homeslice over there if he wants to go with you.* ♦ *Sure I know Davy. He's my home skillet.*

homespun *n.* homemade liquor or beer. ♦ *Jed offered a little of his homespun round the table.*

homey Go to homes.

homie Go to homes.

homo 1. *n.* a homosexual. (Usually a male. Rude and derogatory.) ♦ *Bob got fired for calling Bill a homo.* **2.** *adj.* homosexual. (Usually objectionable.) ♦ *Have you ever been to a homo bar?*

honcho ['hantʃo] **1.** *n.* the head man; the boss. (Useable for either sex.) ♦ *The marketing honcho couldn't say when the product would be on the shelves.* **2.** *tv.* to manage or boss something. ♦ *I'll honcho it until Larry gets here.*

honey ['həni] *n.* beer. ♦ *Let's stop at the happy shop and get some honey.*

honey cart Go to honey wagon.

honey fuck *n.* a gentle and loving act of sexual intercourse. (Taboo. Usually objectionable.) ♦ *I told him I'd prefer a honey fuck to a bunny fuck any day.*

honey of a sth *n.* a very special something; an excellent example of something. ♦ *This is a honey of a car. Wanna drive it?*

honey wagon 1. AND **honey cart** *n.* any vehicle used for or designed for carrying excrement: a farm manure wagon; a tank truck used to pump out septic tanks; a tank truck used to pump out airplane toilets; a portable latrine truck used in movie making. ♦ *I drove a honey cart in Hollywood for a year. How's that for glamour?* **2.** *n.* a beer truck. ♦ *What time does the honey wagon bring in new supplies?*

honeybunch *n.* a sweetheart. (Also a term of address.) ♦ *Look, honeybunch, let's hurry up. We're late.*

honeycakes Go to babycakes.

honeymoon (period) AND **honeymoon stage** *n.* an early stage in any activity, before problems set in. ♦ *You'll know the honeymoon period is over when everything seems to go wrong at once.* ♦ *Of course, this is still the honeymoon stage, but everything seems to be going all right.*

honeymoon stage Go to honeymoon (period).

Hong Kong dog ['hɔŋ 'kɔŋ 'dɔg] *n.* diarrhea; a case of diarrhea. ♦ *Andy has a* *touch of the Hong Kong dog and needs some medicine.*

honk 1. *n.* a drinking spree; a toot. ♦ *Jed's last honk lasted nearly a week.* **2.** *n.* a white male; a honky. (Black. Not necessarily derogatory.) ♦ *There are mainly honks where I work.* **3.** *in.* to vomit. (Onomatopoetic.) ♦ *I can hear someone in the john honking like mad.* **4.** *tv.* to vomit something. ♦ *He honked up his whole pizza.*

honked AND **honkers** *mod.* alcohol intoxicated. ♦ *Willy was too honked to stand up.* ♦ *Man, is he honkers!*

honker 1. *n.* a goose. (Juvenile.) ♦ *A whole flock of honkers settled on our pond.* **2.** *n.* a strange or eccentric person. ♦ *Clare is a real honker these days. Is she all right?* **3.** *n.* the nose. ♦ *Look at the honker on that guy. How can he see around it?*

honkers 1. *n.* a woman's breasts. (Jocular. See also hooters. Usually objectionable.) ♦ *Look at the honkers on that dame!* **2.** Go to honked.

honking *mod.* huge. ♦ *She showed up with this great, honking jock who keep eating with his hands!*

honky AND **honkey; honkie; hunky 1.** *n.* a white male; a Caucasian. (Black. Not necessarily derogatory. A pronunciation variant of hunky. Compare to jonx = junks.) ♦ *Some honky was around asking for you.* **2.** *mod.* in the manner of a Caucasian; white-like. ♦ *That's honky music. I want to hear soul.*

honyock ['hɑnjɑk] *n.* someone, usually a male, who acts like a peasant; a crude or unsophisticated person; a rustic oaf. (Also a rude or playful term of address.) ♦ *Steve seems like such a honyock until you get to know him.*

hoo-ah AND **hoo-rah** *exclam.* Yes! ♦ *Are we ready? Hoo-ah!* ♦ *Hoo-rah, hoo-rah, hoo-rah.*

hooch AND **hootch** [hutʃ] *n.* hard liquor; any alcoholic beverage, especially if illicitly obtained. ♦ *Let's go guzzle some hooch.*

hooch head Go to hooch hound.

hooch hound AND **hooch head** *n.* a drunkard. ♦ *Jed is a classic hooch hound. He lives for the stuff.* ♦ *Hooch heads unite! You have nothing to lose but your brains!*

hooched (up) *mod.* alcohol intoxicated. ♦ *She got herself hooched up and couldn't give her talk.*

hoocher AND **hootcher** *n.* a drunkard. ♦ *A hootcher staggered in and staggered right out again.*

hood 1. *n.* a hoodlum. ♦ *A couple of hoods hassled us on the street.* **2.** *n.* the neighborhood; the ghetto; any neighborhood. ♦ *Back in the hood, Bob's considered an important guy.*

hood rat *n.* someone who hangs around the [black] neighborhood. ♦ *Sam's just a wimpy hood rat. He never sees any action.*

hoodie *n.* a hooded sweatshirt. ♦ *It's chilly. Better grab a hoody.*

hooey ['hui] *n.* nonsense. ♦ *The whole newspaper is nothing but hooey today.*

hoof it 1. *tv.* to run away. ♦ *I saw them coming and hoofed it home.* **2.** *in.* to walk instead of ride. ♦ *My car's broken down, so I had to hoof it to work today.*

hoofer *n.* a (professional) dancer. ♦ *Clare was a hoofer when she was younger and lighter.*

hoofing *n.* walking; running. ♦ *My car's in the shop, so I'm hoofing for a few days.*

hoo-ha ['huhɑ] **1.** *n.* a commotion. ♦ *A deer created quite a hoo-ha by running frantically through the department store.* **2.** *n.* nonsense. ♦ *What is all this hoo-ha about your leaving the company?*

hook 1. *tv.* to cheat someone. ♦ *Watch the clerk in that store. He might try to hook you.* **2.** *tv.* to steal something. ♦ *Lefty hooked a couple of candy bars just for the hell of it.* **3.** *tv.* to addict someone (to something). (Not necessarily drugs.) ♦ *The constant use of bicarb hooked him to the stuff.* **4.** *n.* the grade of C. ♦ *I didn't study at all and I still got a hook!* **5.** *tv.* to earn or pull the grade of C on something in school. ♦ *History? I hooked it without any trouble.*

hook it *tv.* to get a ride by hitchhiking. (The hook is the thumb. Compare to **foot it**.) ♦ *My car broke down and I had to hook it home.*

hook, line, and sinker *mod.* totally. ♦ *They believed every word hook, line, and sinker.*

hook shop *n.* a brothel. (See also **hooker**.) ♦ *There is a secret hook shop over on Maple Street.*

hook sth **down** *tv.* to swallow something down. ♦ *Hook down one of these cookies and see what you think about them.*

hooked (on so/sth**)** *mod.* preferring someone or something; enamored of someone or something. ♦ *I'm really hooked on chocolate anything.*

hooked (on sth**)** **1.** *mod.* cheated. ♦ *I really got hooked on this travel deal.* **2.** *mod.* addicted (to a drug). ♦ *Gert is hooked on horse.*

hooker *n.* a prostitute. (Usually a female, but of either sex. This has to do with *hooking* men into a situation where they can be exploited sexually or robbed. It has nothing to do with a certain *General Hooker*.) ♦ *This neighborhood has a few hookers who hang around on the street corners.*

hooks *n.* the hands. (See also **meathooks**. Probably a shortening of **shit hooks**.) ♦ *Don't stand there with your hooks in your pocket. Get busy!*

hoopla [ˈhuplɑ OR ˈhuplə] *n.* hype; an outcry; a fuss or a **to-do**. ♦ *What's all this hoopla about?*

hoops *n.* the game of basketball. ♦ *Welcome to another evening of college hoops, brought to you by the Nova Motor Company.*

hoosegow [ˈhusgɑʊ] *n.* a jail. ♦ *The judge threw the punk in the hoosegow for a few days.*

hoot **1.** *in.* to laugh loudly. ♦ *The audience screamed and hooted with their appreciation.* **2.** *n.* a joke; something laughable. ♦ *The whole business was a terrific hoot.* **3.** *in.* to boo at someone's performance.

♦ *The audience hooted until the performer fled the stage in disgrace.*

hootch Go to **hooch**.

hootcher Go to **hoocher**.

hoo(t)chfest *n.* a drinking bout; a drinking party. ♦ *We stopped by Sally's to join in the hoochfest for a while.*

hooted *mod.* alcohol intoxicated. ♦ *Jed got himself good and hooted.*

hooter **1.** *n.* a nose; a big nose. ♦ *I sort of wish my hooter wasn't so doggoned big.* **2.** *n.* a drink of liquor. ♦ *He tossed back a big hooter of booze and stood there a minute.* **3.** *n.* cocaine. (Drugs. A drug taken through the **hooter** sense 1.) ♦ *Albert is known for his high-quality hooter.* **4.** Go to **hooters**.

hootered *mod.* drunk. ♦ *He's to hootered to drive home.*

hooters *n.* a woman's breasts. (Jocular. Usually objectionable.) ♦ *Look at the hooters on that dame!*

hoover *tv.* to perform oral sex on the penis. (Usually objectionable. From the name of the vacuum cleaner manufacturer, in reference to suction. See also a **hoovering**.) ♦ *She hoovered him twice and then left.*

hoovering **1.** *n.* an abortion. (From the suction used, referring to the vacuum cleaner.) ♦ *She said she thought a hoovering would make things right.* **2.** *n.* an act of sucking up to someone. (See also **suck up to** so.) ♦ *More of your hoovering! You are a sycophantic pain in the butt!*

hop **1.** *n.* beer. ♦ *How about some hop with your hamburger?* **2.** *n.* a dancing party for young people. ♦ *The kids are out at some school-sponsored hop.* **3.** *tv.* to get aboard a plane or train. ♦ *I'll hop a plane and be there in a couple of hours.*

hop sth **up** *tv.* to make a machine, especially a car, run extra fast or give it extra power. ♦ *He will take that junk heap home and hop it up.*

hopfest *n.* a beer-drinking party. ♦ *We went to a big hopfest over at Willy's, but it broke up early.*

hophead 1. *n.* an alcoholic or a drunkard. ♦ *Ernie is a well-established and incurable hophead.* **2.** *n.* a drug user; someone under the effects of drugs. (Drugs.) ♦ *The hopheads are taking over this part of town.*

hopped up 1. *mod.* stimulated by drugs. (Drugs.) ♦ *Two hopped up kids were hunkered down in the alley.* **2.** *mod.* [of a car] customized and speeded up. ♦ *As soon as I get this hog hopped up, you'll see some real speed.* **3.** *mod.* excited. ♦ *Paul is certainly hopped up about something.*

hopping mad *mod.* very angry; angry and jumping up and down. ♦ *I was hopping mad about the broken window.*

horizontal *mod.* alcohol intoxicated. ♦ *Stewed? No, he's totally horizontal!*

horizontal hula *n.* copulation. (Contrived.) ♦ *She wanted to do some of that horizontal hula.*

hork 1. *in.* to vomit. ♦ *God! I think I'm going to hork!* **2.** *in.* to spit. ♦ *Don't you hork on my driveway, you slob!*

horn 1. *n.* the nose. ♦ *He scratched his horn with his pencil and opened his mouth to speak.* **2.** *n.* the telephone. ♦ *She's on the horn now. What'll I tell her?* **3.** *tv.* to sniff or **snort** a narcotic. (Drugs.) ♦ *Ernie horned a line and paused for a minute.*

horner 1. *n.* a heavy drinker; a drunkard. ♦ *Willy is a real horner. He has an enormous capacity.* **2.** *n.* a cocaine user. (Drugs. Cocaine is taken through the **horn** sense 1.) ♦ *Sure, Bart is a horner. He sells the stuff to support his own habit.*

horny *mod.* sexually aroused; in need of sexual release. (Refers to the horns of the goat, not a car horn. The goat is a symbol of lust. Usually objectionable.) ♦ *He said he was so horny he could honk. What did he mean?*

horrors 1. *n.* the delirium tremens. ♦ *The old wino had the horrors all the time.* **2.** *n.* frightening hallucinations from drugs. (Drugs.) ♦ *Once he had gone through the horrors, he swore off for good.*

horse 1. *n.* heroin. (Drugs. Because it begins with H.) ♦ *Horse is still very popular in the big cities.* **2.** *n.* horse dung. ♦ *I got a job shoveling horse out of the stables.*

horse around *in.* to work inefficiently; to goof around. ♦ *You guys are always horsing around.*

horse cock *n.* a large sausage. (Usually objectionable. Military.) ♦ *Whack me off a piece of that horse cock, would ya, Clyde?*

horse doctor *n.* a doctor. (Derogatory. Originally referred to a veterinarian.) ♦ *That horse doctor says there's nothing wrong with me.*

horse hockey 1. *n.* horse dung. ♦ *You don't see horse hockey in the streets anymore.* **2.** *n.* nonsense. ♦ *I've heard enough of your horse hockey.*

horse laugh *n.* a mocking and sarcastic laugh. ♦ *He came out with a horse laugh that caused some eyebrows to raise.*

horse opera *n.* a Western movie. (See also oater.) ♦ *They're showing a series of old horse operas at the theater tonight.*

horse's ass *n.* a fool; a despised person. (Rude and derogatory.) ♦ *My ex-husband was a real horse's ass.*

horsed AND **on the horse** *mod.* under the effects of heroin; addicted to heroin. (Drugs.) ♦ *How long have you been on the horse?* ♦ *Look at those tracks on his arms. He's horsed all right.*

Horsefeathers! *exclam.* Phooey!; Nonsense! ♦ *Horsefeathers! I did no such thing!*

horseradish *n.* heroin. (Because it begins with H. See also horse.) ♦ *Bart can get you some horseradish.*

horses *n.* horse power, as in an engine. ♦ *How many horses does this thing have?*

horseshit 1. *n.* the dung of the horse. (Usually objectionable.) ♦ *After the parade, the street was littered with horseshit.* **2.** *n.* nonsense; bullshit. (Usually objectionable.) ♦ *I've heard enough of your horseshit!*

hose 1. *n.* the penis. (Usually objectionable.) ♦ *He held his hands over his hose and ran for the bedroom.* **2.** *tv. & in.* to copulate [with] a woman. (Usually objectionable.) ♦ *You don't like her, you just* *want to hose her!* **3.** *tv.* to cheat or deceive someone; to lie to someone. ♦ *Don't try to hose me! I'm onto you!*

hose so **down** *tv.* to kill someone. (Underworld. From the image of spraying someone with bullets.) ♦ *The thugs tried to hose down the witness.*

hoser 1. *n.* a good guy or buddy. (Probably the same allusion as fucker.) ♦ *Old Fred is a good hoser. He'll help.* **2.** *n.* a cheater or deceiver. ♦ *You dirty lying hoser!* **3.** *n.* a moron; a stupid acting person. (Rude and derogatory.) ♦ *Come here, you hoser. I'll show you how to do it.*

hoska Go to (ma)hoska.

hot 1. AND **hot under the collar** *mod.* angry. ♦ *Gee, that guy is really hot under the collar. What did I do?* **2.** *mod.* wanted by the police. (Underworld.) ♦ *Lefty is hot because of his part in the bank job.* **3.** *mod.* stolen. ♦ *Rocko won't touch a hot watch or anything else hot.* **4.** *mod.* carrying contraband and subject to arrest if caught. ♦ *Lefty was hot and needed a place to stay.* **5.** *mod.* having a run of good luck in gambling. ♦ *I was hot when I started. I'm broke now.* **6.** *mod.* of great renown; doing quite well for the time being. ♦ *The opera tenor was hot, and even the lowbrows would pay to hear him.* **7.** *mod.* alcohol intoxicated. (Old.) ♦ *Willy was too hot to stand up.* **8.** *mod.* selling well. ♦ *These things are really hot this season.* **9.** *mod.* sexy; sexually arousing. ♦ *Wow, who was that hot hunk you were with?*

hot air *n.* boasting; lying; nonsense. ♦ *That's just a lot of hot air. Ignore it.*

hot check *n.* a bad check. ♦ *The crook got picked up after passing a hot check.*

Hot diggety (dog)! ['hɑt 'dɪgədi ('dɔg)] *exclam.* Wow! ♦ *I made it on time. Hot diggety!*

Hot dog! *exclam.* Wow! ♦ *Hot dog! It's my turn.*

hot head *n.* a person with a bad or quick temper. ♦ *Don't be such a hot head, Chuck.*

hot item 1. *n.* an item that sells well. ♦ *This little thing is a hot item this season.* **2.** *n.*

a romantically serious couple. ♦ *Sam and Mary are quite a hot item lately.*

hot number 1. *n.* an exciting piece of music. ♦ *Now here's a hot number by the Wanderers.* **2.** *n.* an attractive or sexy girl or woman. ♦ *Who's that hot number I saw you with last night?*

hot paper *n.* bad checks; a bad check. (Underworld. See also hot check.) ♦ *That teller can spot hot paper a mile away.*

hot potato *n.* a difficult problem. ♦ *I sure don't want to have to deal with that hot potato.*

(hot) rod *n.* a car that has been customized for power and speed by the owner. ♦ *My rod'll outrun yours any day.*

hot seat *n.* the electric chair. (Underworld. See also in the hot seat.) ♦ *The hot seat is just waiting for you, Lefty.*

hot shit *n.* a male who thinks he is the greatest person alive; a conceited male. (Probably also used for females. Used with or without *a.* Usually objectionable.) ♦ *The jerk thinks he is real hot shit.*

(hot) skinny *n.* inside information. ♦ *I've got the hot skinny on Mary and her boyfriend.*

hot stuff *n.* a person who acts superior (to others). (Also a term of address.) ♦ *What makes you think you're such hot stuff?*

hot under the collar Go to hot.

hot wire *tv.* to start a car without a key. (By using a wire to carry current around the ignition switch.) ♦ *Lefty hot wired the car and used it for an hour or two.*

Hot ziggety! ['hɑt 'zɪgədi] *exclam.* Wow! ♦ *Hot ziggety! I made it!*

hotbed of sth *n.* a nest of something; a gathering place of something. ♦ *This office is a hotbed of lazy people.*

hotbox *tv.* to fill a small area with marijuana smoke. ♦ *He "hotboxed" the closet and they both sat there and drifted.*

hotdog *in.* to show off. ♦ *The coach said, "Stop hotdogging and play ball, you guys."*

hotkey *n.* one or more keys on a computer keyboard that will bring forth a special computer applications program; a short-cut key. (Computers.) ♦ *The hotkeys for my thesaurus are* control *and* F2. ♦ *Press the hotkey to bring up a calendar.*

hotshot 1. *n.* an important and energetic person. (Often used sarcastically. Also a term of address.) ♦ *If you're such a hot-shot, why not straighten out the whole thing?* **2.** AND **hot-shot** *mod.* brilliant; great. ♦ *So, you're the hot-shot guy who's going to straighten this place out?*

hotsy-totsy [ˈhɑtsiˈtɑtsi] *mod.* fine; great. ♦ *I don't feel so hotsy-totsy.*

hottie *n.* a sexually attractive person. ♦ *He's a real hottie! I wonder if he's taken.*

house moss *n.* little blobs of lint. (See also ghost turd.) ♦ *There is some house moss under the sofa.*

house of many doors *n.* a prison. ♦ *Sam just got out of the house of many doors and is looking for somebody to pull a job with.*

How does that grab you? *interrog.* What do you think of that? ♦ *Looks good, okay? How does that grab you?*

How goes it? *interrog.* How are you?; How are things going? ♦ *Nice to see you. How goes it?*

how the other half lives *n.* how poorer people live; how richer people live. ♦ *Now I am beginning to understand how the other half lives.*

How ya living? *interrog.* How are you do-ing? (The response is Living large.) ♦ *How ya living, man?*

howdy *interj.* hello. (Western, particularly the Southwest, and rural.) ♦ *Well, howdy. Long time, no see.*

howl 1. *n.* something funny. ♦ *What a howl the surprise party turned out to be when the guest of honor didn't show up.* **2.** *in.* to laugh very hard. ♦ *Everybody howled at my mistake.*

howler *n.* a serious and obvious mistake; a funny error. ♦ *Who is responsible for this howler on the Wilson account?*

howling (drunk) *mod.* alcohol intoxicated; loudly drunk. ♦ *Willy got howling drunk and ran in the streets with his coat off.*

(howling) fantods Go to screaming fan-tods.

How('re) they hanging? AND **How's it hanging?** *interrog.* an inquiry calling for a report on (1) *they,* the state of a male's testicles, (2) *it* the state of a male's penis. ♦ *You're looking okay. How're they hang-ing?* ♦ *Hey, dude! How's it hanging?*

How's it hanging? Go to How('re) they hanging?

How's tricks? *interrog.* a greeting inquiry. ♦ *What's up? How's tricks?*

HTH *n.* hometown honey, a sweetheart from home or still at home. (Initialism. Collegiate.) ♦ *Willy is my HTH, but I think I've outgrown him.*

hubbas *n.* crystallized cocaine; crack. (Drugs.) ♦ *They arrested an eight-year-old for selling hubbas.*

hubby [ˈhəbi] *n.* a husband. (A very old de-rivation of *husband.*) ♦ *My hubby will be late tonight.*

huffer [ˈhəfɚ] *n.* a person (teenager) who inhales glue vapors or some other solvent for a high. (Drugs.) ♦ *The age of the huf-fers has come to an end. Now they start out on crack.*

huffy *mod.* angry; haughty. ♦ *Now, don't get huffy. I said I was sorry, didn't I?*

hug the porcelain god(dess) AND **hug the throne** *tv.* to vomit; to vomit while holding on to the toilet seat. ♦ *By "hug the porcelain god" I assume you are referring to vomiting into the toilet bowl?* ♦ *The girls drank a lot of beer and two of them spent the night hugging the porcelain god.*

hug the throne Go to hug the porcelain god(dess).

hughie [ˈhjui] *in.* to empty one's stomach; to vomit. (See also cry hughie.) ♦ *I gotta go hughie! Outa my way!*

hum job AND **hummer** *n.* a sexual act in-volving holding the penis in the mouth while humming. (Usually objectionable. See also humdinger.) ♦ *He asked for a hum job, so she hummed him a lullaby.*

humdinger AND **hummer** [ˈhəm(ˈdɪŋɚ)] *n.* someone or something excellent. (Caution with hummer. See also hum job.) ♦ *Now, this one is a real humdinger.* ♦ *Man, that's a hummer!*

hummer 1. Go to humdinger. **2.** Go to hum job.

humongous [hju'maŋɡəs] *mod.* huge. (See also mongo.) ♦ *She lives in a humongous house on the hill.*

hump 1. *tv. & in.* to copulate [with] someone. (Refers to male arching his back in copulation, as in *fornicate*. Usually objectionable.) ♦ *The sailor spent his entire leave drinking and humping.* **2.** *n.* an act of copulation. (Usually objectionable.) ♦ *The sailor said he needed a hump and left the ship for the port.* **3.** *n.* a person who will copulate without much persuasion. (Usually objectionable.) ♦ *He's okay as a hump, but he can't dance.*

hump (along) *in.* to move along in a hurry. ♦ *Come on, move it! Hump to the main office and be fast about it!*

hump it (to somewhere**)** *tv.* to move rapidly (to somewhere). ♦ *I have to hump it over to Kate's place right now.*

humpy *mod.* sexually aroused; horny. (See also hump. Usually objectionable.) ♦ *I'm so humpy, I could screw a cow.*

hundo *n.* hundred. ♦ *How much? A hondo! Geeesh!*

hung 1. *mod.* hungover. ♦ *John is really hung this morning.* **2.** *mod.* annoyed. ♦ *Fred is hung and looking for somebody to take it out on.* **3.** Go to well-hung.

hung like a bull *mod.* having large testicles or genitals in general, like a bull. (Said of a male. Usually objectionable.) ♦ *Well, he's not exactly hung like a bull, or anything else for that matter.*

hungarian *mod.* hungry. ♦ *Man, I'm hungarian!*

the **hungries** *n.* hunger. ♦ *I get the hungries about this time every day.*

hungry 1. *mod.* eager to make money. ♦ *When he gets hungry for wealth, he'll get busy.* **2.** *mod.* ambitious. ♦ *He gets ahead because he's hungry.*

hunk *n.* a strong and sexually attractive male. ♦ *Who was that hot hunk I saw you with?*

hunk of ass Go to piece of ass.

hunk of tail Go to piece of ass.

hunky Go to honky.

hunky-dory ['həŋki'dori] *mod.* fine; okay. ♦ *As a matter of fact, everything is just hunky-dory.*

hurl 1. *in.* to empty one's stomach; to vomit. (Like the *throw* in *throw up*. See also earl.) ♦ *I think I gotta go hurl.* **2.** *n.* vomit. ♦ *There's hurl all over the bathroom floor!*

hurry up and wait *in.* to be alternately rushed and delayed in a hectic situation. (Often with the force of a modifier.) ♦ *It's always hurry up and wait around here.*

hurt 1. *mod.* very ugly; damaged and ugly. (Streets. Similar to hurting.) ♦ *That poor girl is really bad hurt.* **2.** *mod.* drug intoxicated. (Streets.) ♦ *Gert was really hurt and nodding and drooling.*

hurt for so/sth *in.* to long after someone or something; to need someone or something. ♦ *I sure am hurting for a nice big steak.*

hurting 1. *mod.* very ugly; in pain from ugliness. (Similar to hurt.) ♦ *That dog of yours is something to behold. It's really hurting.* **2.** *mod.* seriously in need of something, such as a dose of drugs. (Drugs.) ♦ *Gert is hurting. She needs something soon.*

hush money *n.* money paid to buy someone's silence. ♦ *There was some hush money paid to someone in city hall.*

hush so **up 1.** *tv.* to make someone be quiet. ♦ *Please hush your baby up!* **2.** *tv.* to kill someone. ♦ *Nobody knew how to get to Mr. Gutman to hush him up.*

hush sth **up** *tv.* to keep something a secret; to try to stop a rumor from spreading. ♦ *We wanted to hush up the story, but there was no way to do it.*

hush-hush ['həʃ'həʃ] **1.** *mod.* secret; undercover. ♦ *The matter is so hush-hush I can't talk about it over the phone.* **2.** *mod.*

secretly. ♦ *They did it so hush-hush that no one knew for a long time.*

husky ['həski] *n.* a strong man; a thug. ♦ *A couple of huskies helped me get my car unstuck.*

hustle ['həsl̩] **1.** *in.* to move rapidly; to hurry. ♦ *It's late. I've got to hustle.* **2.** *n.* hurried movement; confusion. ♦ *I can't work when there is all this hustle around me.* **3.** *n.* a scheme to make money; a special technique for making money. (Underworld. This includes drug dealing, prostitution, and other vice activities.) ♦ *Each of these punks has a hustle—a specialty in crime.* ♦ *We all know what Shorty's hustle is.* **4.** *in.* to use one's special technique for making money. ♦ *He's out there on the streets hustling all the time.* **5.** *tv.* to use a scheme on a person to try to make money; to con someone. ♦ *Don't try to hustle me, sister. I know which end is up.* **6.** *tv.* to attempt to seduce someone. ♦ *I think that Britney's hustling Max.*

hustler ['həslɚ] **1.** *n.* a gambler in a pool hall. ♦ *He made a lot of money as a hustler.* **2.** *n.* a swindler; a con artist. ♦ *The chick is a real hustler. I wouldn't trust her at all.* **3.** *n.* a prostitute. ♦ *A lot of hustlers are hooked on horse.* **4.** *n.* a stud; a man who is notoriously good with women. ♦ *He thinks he's a hustler. The chicks think he's a wimp.*

hut *n.* a house. ♦ *I've got to go to my hut and pick up some bills.*

hydro Go to dro.

hype [haɪp] **1.** *n.* publicity; sales propaganda; promotion, especially if blatant and aggressive. ♦ *There was so much hype* before the picture was released that the picture itself was a letdown. **2.** *tv.* to publicize or promote someone or something aggressively; to overpraise someone or something. ♦ *Let's hype it until everyone in the country has heard about it.* **3.** AND **hipe** *n.* a hypodermic syringe and needle. (Drugs.) ♦ *She forgot to clean the hype.* **4.** *n.* an injection of drugs. (Drugs.) ♦ *Ernie needed a hype real bad.* **5.** *n.* a drug addict who injects drugs. (Drugs.) ♦ *The hypes have a rough time in prison.* **6.** *mod.* really good; excellent. ♦ *Now this is a truly hype pizza!*

hype artist *n.* someone who produces aggressive promotional material for a living. ♦ *She is a hype artist for a public relations firm.*

hype sth **up** *tv.* to overpraise something; to propagandize something. ♦ *They hyped it up too much.*

hyped (up) 1. *mod.* excited; stimulated. ♦ *She said she had to get hyped before the tennis match.* **2.** *mod.* contrived; heavily promoted; falsely advertised. ♦ *I just won't pay good money to see these hyped up movies.* **3.** *mod.* drug intoxicated. (Drugs.) ♦ *Here comes another hyped up musician.*

hyper ['haɪpɚ] **1.** *mod.* excited; overreacting. ♦ *I'm a little hyper because of the doctor's report.* **2.** *n.* a person who praises or promotes someone or something. ♦ *She's a hyper, and she doesn't always tell things the way they are.* **3.** *n.* a person who is always overly excited or hyperactive. ♦ *Pat is such a hyper. Just can't seem to relax.* **4.** *n.* a drug user who injects drugs with a hypodermic syringe. (Drugs.) ♦ *How long have you been a hyper, Gert?*

I am so sure! *exclam.* I am right! (California.) ◆ *You are way rad! I am so sure!*

I could tell you but then I'd have to kill you. AND **ICTYBTIHTKY** *sent. & comp. abb.* a phrase said in answer to a question that one does not want to answer. ◆ *Don't ask. ICTYBTIHTKY.*

I could(n't) care less. *sent.* I don't care!; I don't care to the maximum amount, and it is, therefore, impossible to care any less. (The affirmative version does not make sense, but is widely used, nonetheless.) ◆ *So you're late. I couldn't care less.*

I don't believe this! *exclam.* What is happening right now is unbelievable! ◆ *I don't believe this! It can't be happening.*

I don't mean maybe! *exclam.* I am not kidding! ◆ *You get over here right now, and I don't mean maybe!*

I hear what you are saying. 1. AND **I hear you.** *sent.* I know what you are trying to say. ◆ *Yes, yes. I hear what you are saying, and I'm with you.* **2.** *sent.* I understand your position, but I am under no obligation to agree. (Can be used to avoid disagreeing and the resulting argument.) ◆ *I hear you, but it doesn't matter.*

I hear you. Go to I hear what you are saying.

I kid you not. *sent.* I am not kidding. (Attributed to the entertainer Jack Paar.) ◆ *She is a great singer. I kid you not.*

(I) love it! *exclam.* That is wonderful! ◆ *It's wonderful, Ted. I love it!*

I smell you. *sent.* I understand you. ◆ *I smell you. No need to go on and on.*

IAC Go to IAE.

IAE AND **IAC** *interj.* in any event; in any case. (Initialisms. Used in electronic mail and computer forum or news group messages. Not pronounced aloud.) ◆ *I will be there IAC.*

(I-)beam [ˈ(aɪ)bim] *n.* IBM, International Business Machines stock shares. (Securities markets. See also big blue.) ◆ *How much beam do you own?*

IC *in.* I see; I understand. (Used in electronic mail and computer forum or news group messages. Not pronounced aloud.) ◆ *IC, but I can't help you.*

ice 1. *n.* diamonds; jewels. (Underworld.) ◆ *That old dame has tons of ice in her hotel room.* **2.** *n.* cocaine; crystalline cocaine. (Drugs.) ◆ *Max deals mostly in ice but can get you almost anything.* **3.** *tv.* to kill someone; to kill an informer. (Underworld. See also chill.) ◆ *Mr. Big ordered Sam to ice you-know-who.* **4.** *tv.* to ignore someone. (Underworld. See also chill.) ◆ *Bart iced Sam for obvious reasons.* **5.** *tv.* to embarrass someone; to make someone look foolish. ◆ *Don't ice me in front of my friends.* **6.** *n.* money given as a bribe, especially to the police. (Underworld.) ◆ *A lot of those cops take ice.* **7.** *mod.* excellent; very cool. ◆ *Her answer was ice, and she really put down that guy.*

ice palace *n.* a jewelry store. (From ice.) ◆ *What do they sell in that ice palace that you could afford to buy?*

ice queen *n.* a cold and haughty woman. ◆ *Britney is not exactly an ice queen, but she comes close.*

iceberg *n.* a cold and unemotional person. (See also iceberg slim.) ◆ *What an insensitive iceberg!*

iceberg slim 1. *n.* a pimp. ♦ *When iceberg slim came by in his pimpmobile, Jed made a rude sign at him.* **2.** *n.* a person who exploits others; a cold, heartless person. ♦ *The guy's a regular iceberg slim.*

iced *mod.* settled once and for all; done easily. ♦ *I've got it iced. Nothing to it.*

iced out *mod.* wearing lots of diamonds (See also ice (sense 1).) ♦ *That dude is really iced out!*

iceman *n.* a killer. (Underworld. See also ice.) ♦ *It's hard to believe that Rocko is a professional iceman.*

icicles ['aɪs sɪk̩z] *n.* pure cocaine in a crystallized form. (Drugs.) ♦ *Are icicles the same as crack?*

icing on the cake *n.* an extra enhancement. ♦ *Oh, wow! A tank full of gas in my new car. That's icing on the cake!*

ick [ɪk] **1.** *n.* any nasty substance. ♦ *What is this ick on my shoe?* **2.** *exclam.* Nasty! (Usually **Ick!**) ♦ *Oh, ick! What now?* **3.** *n.* a disliked person. ♦ *Tell that ick to leave. He's polluting the place.*

icky ['ɪki] *mod.* distasteful; nasty. ♦ *This was an icky day.*

icky-poo ['ɪkipu] **1.** *mod.* disgusting. ♦ *I don't like all this icky-poo talk.* **2.** *exclam.* Nasty! (Usually **Icky-poo!**) ♦ *Oh, icky-poo! I missed my bus!*

ICTYBTIHTKY Go to I could tell you but then I'd have to kill you.

ID 1. *n.* some kind of identification card. (Initialism.) ♦ *Can you show me an ID?* **2.** *tv.* to determine the identity of someone; to check someone for a valid identification card. ♦ *The cops IDed the driver in less than thirty minutes.*

idea box *n.* the head; the brain. ♦ *You got a good solution up there in your idea box by any chance?*

idiot box *n.* a television set. ♦ *You spend too much time watching the idiot box.*

idiot card *n.* a large card that shows people on television what to say. ♦ *The floor director held up an idiot card so I could read out the telephone number.*

idiot juice AND **idiotic** ['ɪdiət dʒus AND ɪdi'ɑdɪk] *n.* a mixture of ground nutmeg and water. (Prisons.) ♦ *Somehow a bunch of these guys got hold of some idiot juice.*

idiot light *n.* a light (instead of a meter) on a car's dashboard that indicates the state of various things concerning the operation of the car. (Alludes to these lights' elimination of the knowledge required to interpret a meter reading, making them suitable for idiots.) ♦ *I don't want idiot lights. I want meters!*

idiot oil *n.* liquor; alcohol. ♦ *She drinks too much of that idiot oil.*

idiot pills *n.* barbiturates. (Drugs.) ♦ *Lay off those idiot pills, why don't you?*

idiotic Go to idiot juice.

If it ain't broke don't fix it. AND **IIABDFI** *sent. & comp. abb.* Leave well enough alone.; Don't tamper with something that is all right as it is. ♦ *It's fine. Leave it alone. If it ain't broke, don't fix it!*

If it ain't broke, fix it till it is. AND **IIABFITII** *sent. & comp. abb.* Don't leave well enough alone.; Just keep tampering. (A play on If it ain't broke, don't fix it.) ♦ *Does it work too well or something. You must say if it ain't broke, fix it till it is. Leave well enough alone.*

if I've told you once, I've told you a thousand times *phr.* I know I have told you many, many times. ♦ *If I've told you once, I've told you a thousand times, don't lean back in that chair.*

if one knows what's good for one *phr.* one had better do what is expected of one. ♦ *You'd better be on time if you know what's good for you.*

if one's a day *phr.* a phrase attached to an expression of someone's age. ♦ *I'm sure he's forty-five if he's a day.*

if push comes to shove Go to when push comes to shove.

If that don't fuck all! *exclam.* an exclamation of surprise. (An elaboration of the colloquial If that don't beat all! See also Fuck it all! Taboo. Usually objectionable.) ♦ *If that don't fuck all! You broke it, and it's my last one!*

If the shoe fits, wear it. AND **ITSFWI** *sent. & comp. abb.* If this applies to you, do something about it. ♦ *Maybe this applies to you. ITSFWI.*

If you can't stand the heat, keep out of the kitchen. *sent.* If you cannot accept the problems of involvement, do not get involved. ♦ *Yes, it's difficult to be a candidate. If you can't stand the heat, keep out of the kitchen.*

if you'll pardon the expression *phr.* excuse the expression I am about to say. ♦ *This thing is—if you'll pardon the expression—loused up.* ♦ *I'm really jacked, if you'll pardon the expression.*

iffy ['ɪfi] *mod.* marginally uncertain. ♦ *Things are still sort of iffy, but we'll know for sure in a few days.*

IIABDFI Go to If it ain't broke, don't fix it.

IIABFITII Go to If it ain't broke, fix it till it is.

ill 1. *mod.* lame; dull; bad. ♦ *That broad is truly ill and has a face that would stop a clock.* **2.** AND **illing; illin'** *mod.* excellent; cool. ♦ *We had an ill time at your party. Loved it!*

I'll bite. *sent.* You want me to ask what or why, so, what or why? ♦ *I'll bite. Why did the chicken cross the road?*

illin' ['ɪlən] **1.** *mod.* being ill; being sick. ♦ *She was illin' big time and could not come to class.* **2.** *mod.* ill-behaved. ♦ *You are most illin' and you are bugging me, Kim. Stop it!* **3.** *in.* behaving badly. ♦ *Stop illin' and pay attention.* **4.** *mod.* upset. ♦ *What are you illin' about? Everything is ice.* **5.** Go to ill.

illuminated *mod.* alcohol intoxicated. (A play on lit.) ♦ *Paul is a bit illuminated.*

I'm all ears. *sent.* I am listening carefully to what you are going to say. ♦ *You said you would tell me. Well, I'm all ears.*

I'm gone. *sent.* I'm getting ready to leave. (See also I'm out of here.) ♦ *Well, that's all. I'm gone.*

I'm history. *sent.* Good-bye, I am leaving. (See also history.) ♦ *I'm history. See you tomorrow.*

I'm listening. *sent.* Keep talking.; Make your explanation now. ♦ *I'm sure there's an explanation. Well, I'm listening.*

I'm not kidding. *sent.* I am telling the truth. ♦ *Get over here now! I'm not kidding.*

I'm out of here. AND **I'm outa here.; I'm outie.** *sent.* I am leaving this minute. ♦ *In three minutes I'm outa here.*

I'm outa here. Go to I'm out of here.

I'm outie. Go to I'm out of here.

I'm shaking (in fear). *sent.* You don't really frighten me at all. (A mocking response to a threat.) ♦ *Your threats really scare me. I'm shaking in fear.*

I'm there! *sent.* I will accept your invitation and I will be there. ♦ *If you and Tom are going to get together and watch the game, I'm there!*

IM(H)O *interj.* in my (humble) opinion. (Initialism. Used in electronic mail and computer forum or news group messages. Not pronounced aloud. See also IYHO.) ♦ *She is the person to choose, IMO.*

IMO Go to IM(H)O.

impaired *mod.* alcohol intoxicated. (Euphemistic.) ♦ *He was so impaired he couldn't see his hand in front of his face.*

in 1. *mod.* current; fashionable. ♦ *What's in around here in the way of clothing?* **2.** *mod.* private. ♦ *If it's in or something, I'm sure they won't spread it around.* **3.** *n.* someone in a special position; someone who is serving in an elective office. ♦ *When Ralph is one of the ins, he'll throw the crooks out.* **4.** *n.* a ticket or means of getting in (someplace). ♦ *I lost my in. Can I still see the show?*

in a bad way Go to in bad shape.

in a big way *mod.* very much; urgently. ♦ *He plays to win—in a big way.*

in a blue funk *mod.* sad; depressed. ♦ *Don't be in a blue funk. Things'll get better.*

in a cold sweat *mod.* in a state of fear. ♦ *He stood there in a cold sweat, waiting for something to happen.*

in a dither *mod.* confused; undecided. ♦ *Don't get yourself in a dither.*

in a familiar way *mod.* pregnant. (Euphemistic for in a family way.) ♦ *Britney is in a familiar way, have you heard?*

in a family way AND **in the family way** *mod.* pregnant. ♦ *I hear that Britney is in a family way.*

in a flash *mod.* right away; immediately. (See also flash.) ♦ *Get over here in a flash, or else.*

in a heap *mod.* alcohol intoxicated. ♦ *The guys were all in a heap after the blast.*

in a jam *mod.* in a difficult situation. ♦ *I think I'm sort of in a jam.*

in a jiff(y) *mod.* right away; immediately. (See also jiffy.) ♦ *The clerk'll be with you in a jiff.*

in a lip lock *mod.* kissing. (Contrived.) ♦ *They were rhapsodizing in a lip lock when we came in.*

in a New York minute AND **INYM** *phr. & comp. abb.* almost instantly. ♦ *I'd do it INYM.*

in a snit *mod.* in a fit of anger or irritation. ♦ *Mary is in a snit because they didn't ask her to come to the shindig.*

in a tizzy *mod.* in a state of mental disorder. ♦ *Fred is all in a tizzy.*

in a twit *mod.* upset; frantic. ♦ *She's all in a twit because she lost her keys.*

in a twitter *mod.* in a giddy state; silly. ♦ *We were all in a twitter over the upcoming event.*

in action 1. *mod.* healthy and getting around. ♦ *After I got well, I was in action again immediately.* **2.** *mod.* selling or using drugs. (Drugs.) ♦ *In this neighborhood, somebody is in action twenty-four hours a day.*

in bad shape AND **in a bad way 1.** *mod.* injured or debilitated in any manner. ♦ *Tom needs exercise. He's in bad shape.*

2. *mod.* pregnant. ♦ *Yup, she's in bad shape all right—about three months in bad shape.* **3.** *mod.* alcohol intoxicated. ♦ *Two glasses of that stuff and I'm really in a bad way.*

in business *mod.* operating; equipped to operate. ♦ *Now it works. Now we're in business.*

in cold blood *mod.* without feeling; with cruel intent. ♦ *Rocko kills in cold blood and never gives it a thought.*

in cold storage *mod.* dead; in a state of death. ♦ *Rocko gets paid for putting his subjects in cold storage.*

in deep 1. *mod.* deeply involved (with someone or something). ♦ *Bart is in deep with the mob.* **2.** *mod.* deeply in debt. (Often with *with* or *to.*) ♦ *Sam is in deep with his bookie.*

in deep doo-doo *mod.* in real trouble. (Doo-doo = dung.) ♦ *See what you've done. Now you are in deep doo-doo.*

in drag *mod.* wearing the clothing of the opposite sex. (Usually refers to women's clothing.) ♦ *Two actors in drag did a skit about life on the farm.*

in dribs and drabs *mod.* in small portions; bit by bit. ♦ *I'll have to pay you what I owe you in dribs and drabs.*

in Dutch *mod.* in trouble. ♦ *I didn't want to get in Dutch with you.*

in fine feather 1. *mod.* well dressed; of an excellent appearance. (As a healthy bird might be.) ♦ *Well, you are certainly in fine feather today.* **2.** *mod.* in good form; in good spirits. ♦ *Mary is really in fine feather tonight.*

in hock *mod.* pawned. ♦ *My watch is already in hock.*

in like Flynn 1. *mod.* successful, in a variety of contexts, sex being the major one. (The *in* can be construed to be the *in of in coitu*. Not to be confused with the James Coburn movie, *In Like Flint*. This Flynn is associated with Errol Flynn, the late film actor, but appears to have occurred earlier.) ♦ *A few nice words, a bit of bubble, and you're in like Flynn.* **2.** *mod.*

an elaboration of *in*, in any of its senses. ♦ *You got the role! You're in! You're in like Flynn!*

in nothing flat *mod.* immediately. ♦ *She changed the tire in nothing flat.*

in one's **blood** *mod.* inborn; part of one's genetic makeup. ♦ *Running is in his blood. He loves it.*

in one's sth **mode** *phr.* behaving in a specified mode. (The *something* can be replaced by *work, sleep, hungry, angry*, etc.) ♦ *Todd is always in his play mode when he should be working.*

in orbit 1. *mod.* ecstatic; euphoric. ♦ *She was just in orbit when she got the letter.* **2.** *mod.* alcohol or drug intoxicated. ♦ *Gary is in orbit and can't see a hole in a ladder.*

in play 1. *mod.* being played; inbounds. (Said of a ball in a game.) ♦ *The ball's in play, so you made the wrong move.* **2.** *mod.* having to do with a company (or its stock) that is a candidate for acquisition by another company. (Securities markets.) ♦ *These deal stocks—which are in play right now—offer excellent buying opportunities.*

in rare form 1. *mod.* well-tuned for a good performance; at one's best. ♦ *We are not exactly in rare form on Monday mornings.* **2.** *mod.* alcohol intoxicated. ♦ *Gert is in rare form, but she'll have time to sleep it off.*

in so's **face** *mod.* irritating someone. (See also **get in** so's **face; Get out of my face!;** in-your-face.) ♦ *I wish that the coach wasn't always in my face about something.*

in spades *mod.* in the best way possible; extravagantly. ♦ *He flunked the test in spades.*

in tall cotton *mod.* successful; on easy street. (Folksy.) ♦ *I won some money at the track, and I'm really in tall cotton.*

in the bag 1. *mod.* cinched; achieved. ♦ *It's in the bag—as good as done.* ♦ *The election is in the bag unless the voters find out about my past.* **2.** *mod.* alcohol intoxi-

cated. (See also **bagged.**) ♦ *Kelly looks like he is in the bag.*

in the black *mod.* financially solvent; profitable; not in debt. (From a practice of listing expenses in red and income in black.) ♦ *Now that the company is in the black, there's a good chance it will become a deal stock.*

in the buff *mod.* naked. ♦ *You can save hundreds of dollars in a lifetime by not buying pajamas and sleeping in the buff instead.*

in the catbird seat *mod.* in a dominant or controlling position. ♦ *I hold all the aces. I'm in the catbird seat.*

in the chips *mod.* wealthy; with lots of money. ♦ *I'm in the chips this month. Let's go squander it.*

in the driver's seat *mod.* in control. ♦ *I'm in the driver's seat now, and I get to decide who gets raises.*

in the family way Go to **in a family way.**

in the grip of the grape *mod.* drunk on wine; drunk. ♦ *Wayne was in the grip of the grape and couldn't talk straight.*

in the groove *mod.* cool; groovy; pleasant and delightful. (See also **get in the groove.**) ♦ *Man, is that combo in the groove tonight!*

in the gun *mod.* alcohol intoxicated. (See also **shot.**) ♦ *When Fred is in the gun, he's mean.*

in the hole *mod.* in debt; running a deficit. ♦ *Looks like we are in the hole again this month.*

in the (home) stretch *mod.* in the last stage of the process. (From horse racing.) ♦ *We're in the homestretch with this project and can't change it now.*

in the hopper *mod.* in process; in line to be processed. (A hopper is an *in-basket* for incoming work.) ♦ *Your job is in the hopper, and your turn is next.*

in the know *mod.* knowledgeable (about something); having inside knowledge (about something). ♦ *Sure I'm in the know. But I'm not telling.*

in the O-zone *mod.* dead; on the verge of death; showing the O-sign. (With the mouth hanging open, like the letter O.) ♦ *This patient is in the O-zone. Ready to go at any minute.*

in the ozone *mod.* alcohol or drug intoxicated. ♦ *We were in the ozone, but we still made a lot of sense.*

in the pink 1. *mod.* feeling quite well; feeling on top of the world. ♦ *When she's in the pink again, she'll give you a ring.* **2.** *mod.* alcohol intoxicated. ♦ *Pete is in the pink and singing at the top of his lungs.*

in the pipeline *mod.* backed up somewhere in a process; in process; in a queue. ♦ *There are a lot of goods still in the pipeline. That means no more orders for a while.*

in the Q-zone *mod.* dead; on the verge of death; with the mouth showing the Q-sign. ♦ *Look at that tongue hanging out. This guy's in the Q-zone.*

in the soup *mod.* in trouble. ♦ *I'm in the soup with the boss.*

in the suds *mod.* alcohol intoxicated. ♦ *When Bob is in the suds, he's mean.*

in the tube 1. *mod.* in the "tube" or arch of a large wave. (Surfing.) ♦ *On a day like today, I want to be out there in the tube.* **2.** *mod.* at risk. ♦ *He's in the tube now, but things should straighten out soon.*

in there *mod.* sincere; likeable. ♦ *I like a guy who's in there—who thinks about other people.*

the **in thing to do** *n.* the fashionable or orthodox thing to do. (See also in.) ♦ *Cutting your hair short on the sides is the in thing to do.*

incense *n.* marijuana. (Drugs.) ♦ *Hank likes to burn a little incense every now and then.*

incentive *n.* cocaine. (Drugs. See also initiative.) ♦ *Maybe a little of that incentive would make me work harder.*

incy-wincy ['ɪntsi'wɪntsi] *mod.* tiny. (See also itty-bitty; itsy-bitsy.) ♦ *Well, maybe an incy-wincy bit more wouldn't hurt.*

indo *n.* marijuana. ♦ *Is this indo? I asked for indo.*

initiative *n.* cocaine. (Drugs. See also incentive.) ♦ *Maybe I need some more of that initiative to get me going.*

ink 1. *n.* cheap red wine. ♦ *The old wino prefers ink to anything else.* **2.** *n.* publicity; print media coverage of someone or something. ♦ *The movie star's divorce got a lot of ink for a few days.* (The same as paint.) **3.** *n.* a tattoo. ♦ *When dya get the new ink?* **4.** *n.* tattoos in general; the amount of tattooing on someone's body. (The same as paint.) ♦ *He's got ink covering his back.*

ink slinger *n.* a professional writer; a newspaper reporter. ♦ *The ink slingers have been at the candidates again.*

innie Go to insy.

the **ins and outs** *n.* the fine points (of something); the details; the intricacies. ♦ *I'm learning the ins and outs of this business.*

inside dope *n.* the inside story; special or privileged information. (See also (hot) skinny.) ♦ *What's the inside dope on the candidate's drug addiction?*

an **inside job** *n.* a crime perpetrated against an establishment by someone associated with the victimized establishment. (Underworld.) ♦ *It was an inside job all right. The butler did it.*

inside out *mod.* drunk. ♦ *Wayne spends every weekend inside out.*

insource *tv.* to assign a task or an order to an internal department, rather than an outside vendor. (The opposite of outsource.) ♦ *The manager decided to in source the project so he could retain control.*

insy AND **innie** ['ɪnzi] *n.* a navel that recedes and does not protrude. (Compare this with outsy.) ♦ *Is yours an insy or an outsy?*

intense *mod.* serious; heavy. ♦ *Oh, wow! Now that's what I call intense!*

internut *n.* someone devoted to or addicted to using the internet. ♦ *He sits in front of the screen for hours. A real internut.*

involuntary dismount *n.* falling off a bike or motorcycle. ♦ *He impacted a monolith and suffered an involuntary dismount.*

INYM Go to in a New York minute.

in-your-face *mod.* confrontational. ♦ *Fred is just an in-your-face kind of guy. He means no harm.*

IOW *interj.* in other words. (Initialism. Used in electronic mail and computer forum or news group messages. Not pronounced aloud.) ♦ *I have heard enough on this point. IOW, shut up.*

Iraqnophobia *n.* fear of or distress about Iraq. (A play on *arachnophobia*, the fear of spiders.) ♦ *A nation, suffering from Iraqnophobia, watched the debates with interest.*

iron 1. *n.* a gun; a revolver. (Underworld.) ♦ *Rocko never carries iron unless he's going to use it.* **2.** *n.* computer hardware. (See also big iron.) ♦ *What kind of iron are you people running over there?*

Irv AND **Ervine; Irvine** *n.* a police officer. (Streets. See also Charlie Irvine.) ♦ *Tsup, Irv?* ♦ *Tell Ervine to go catch a speeder or something.*

Irvine Go to Irv.

issue *n.* problem. (In colloquial use, issue has virtually replaced the word *problem*. It is even heard in a few idioms such as *Do you have an issue with that?*) ♦ *I had an issue with my car this morning. It wouldn't start.* ♦ *You are late again! Do you have an issue with our office hours?*

It cuts both ways. Go to It cuts two ways.

It cuts two ways. AND **It cuts both ways.** *sent.* There are two sides, you know.; There are two people involved.; You are being selfish and one-sided. ♦ *It cuts two ways, you know. It can't always all be my fault.* ♦ *You do your share! It cuts both ways, you know.*

It don't make (me) no nevermind. *phr.* It doesn't matter to me. ♦ *Go ahead! Do it! It don't make me no nevermind.*

It sucks. Go to That sucks.

It will be your ass! *sent.* It will cost you your ass!; You will pay dearly! (Usually objectionable.) ♦ *It will be your ass if it isn't done right this time.*

(It) works for me. AND **WFM** *sent. & comp. abb.* It works for me.; This proposal works well enough for me and I see no reason to try anything else. (With stress on *works* and *me*.) ♦ *WFM. YMMV.*

It's been. *phr.* a phrase said on leaving a party or some other gathering. (A shortening of *It's been lovely* or some similar expression.) ♦ *Well, it's been. We really have to go, though.*

It's been a slice! *sent.* It's been good. ♦ *Good-bye and thank you. It's been a slice!*

(It's) not my dog. *phr.* It's not my problem. ♦ *So what! It doesn't matter! Not my dog.*

(It's) showtime! *exclam.* (It's) time to start! (Said of beginning anything exciting or challenging.) ♦ *Are you ready for action? Okay. It's showtime!*

It's your funeral! *exclam.* If you do it, you will suffer all the consequences! ♦ *Go if you want. It's your funeral!*

ITSFWI Go to If the shoe fits, wear it.

itsy-bitsy Go to itty-bitty.

itty-bitty AND **itsy-bitsy** ['ɪdi'bɪdi AND 'ɪtsi'bɪtsi] *mod.* tiny. ♦ *Give me an itsy-bitsy piece. I'm on a diet.*

I've been there. *sent.* I know from experience what you are talking about. ♦ *I've been there. You don't need to spell it out for me.*

I've got to fly. AND **I('ve) gotta fly.** *sent.* I have to leave right now. ♦ *I've gotta fly. See you later.*

I've got to split. *sent.* I have to leave now. ♦ *I've got to split. Call my service.*

I('ve) gotta fly. Go to I've got to fly.

ivories ['aɪvriz] **1.** *n.* the teeth. (See also China.) ♦ *I gotta go brush my ivories.*

2. *n.* piano keys. (From when piano keys were made from real elephant ivory.) ♦ *She can really bang those ivories.* **3.** *n.* dice. ♦ *Hand me those ivories. The baby needs shoes!*

ivory tower *n.* an imaginary location where aloof academics are said to reside and work. ♦ *Why don't you come out of your ivory tower and see what the world is really like?*

IYHO *interj.* in your humble opinion. (Initialism. Used in electronic mail and computer forum or news group messages. Not pronounced aloud. See also IM(H)O.) ♦ *Things are in bad shape IYHO, but I think they are great.*

J. AND **jay** *n.* a marijuana cigarette; marijuana. (Drugs. From the initial letter of joint.) ♦ *A jay will cost you two clams.*

J. Edgar (Hoover) ['dʒe 'ɛdgɚ ('huvɚ)] *n.* the police; federal officers. (Underworld.) ♦ *Max got out of town when he heard that the J. Edgars were on his tail.*

jab pop ['dʒæb'pɑp] *in.* to inject (drugs). (Drugs.) ♦ *Jab popping is a ticket to cement city.*

jabber ['dʒæbɚ] **1.** *n.* mindless chatter. ♦ *I've heard enough of your jabber.* **2.** *in.* to chatter. ♦ *Come over and we'll jabber about things over coffee.* **3.** *n.* a drug addict who injects drugs. (Drugs.) ♦ *These scars show that the victim was a jabber.*

jack 1. *n.* money. ♦ *I don't have the jack for a deal like that.* **2.** *n.* tobacco for rolling cigarettes. ♦ *You got some jack I can bum?* **3.** *n.* nothing. (Probably from jack-shit.) ♦ *Your last idea wasn't worth jack. Do I pay you to come up with stuff that bad?* **4.** *n.* a strange person; an annoying person. (Possibly from *jackass* or jack-shit.) ♦ *Willy, stop acting like such a jack!* **5.** *tv.* to steal something. ♦ *I didn't buy it, I jacked it!*

jack around *in.* to waste time; to mess around. (Akin to jack off.) ♦ *Stop jacking around and get busy.*

jack off Go to beat off.

jack so around *tv.* to hassle someone; to harass someone. (See also jerk so around.) ♦ *The IRS is jacking my brother around.*

jack so up 1. *tv.* to motivate someone; to stimulate someone to do something. ♦ *I'll jack him up and try to get some action out of him.* **2.** *tv.* to beat or stab someone.

(Underworld.) ♦ *They really jacked up Bobby. He almost died.*

jack sth up 1. *tv.* to raise the price of something. ♦ *They kept jacking the price up with various charges, so I walked.* **2.** *tv.* to mess something up. ♦ *Who jacked up the papers on my desk?*

jackal *n.* a low and devious person. ♦ *What does that jackal want here?*

jacked Go to jacked up.

jacked (out) *mod.* angry; annoyed. ♦ *Boy was that old guy jacked out at you.*

jacked up 1. AND **jacked** *mod.* excited. ♦ *I was so jacked I almost passed out.* ♦ *Don was really jacked up about the election.* **2.** *mod.* arrested. (Underworld.) ♦ *What time did Sam get himself jacked up?* **3.** *mod.* upset; stressed. ♦ *I was really jacked up by the bad news.* **4.** *mod.* high on drugs. ♦ *He's jacked up, and he may have ODed.*

jack-shit 1. *n.* a stupid and worthless person. (Usually refers to a male. Usually objectionable.) ♦ *What a jack-shit! Not a brain in his head!* **2.** *n.* anything; anything at all. (Always in a negative expression.) ♦ *This whole thing isn't worth jack-shit!*

jack-ups *n.* capsules of a barbiturate drug. (Drugs.) ♦ *Walter took a few jack-ups and went on to work.*

JAFDIP *acronym.* just another fucking day in paradise. (A sarcastic expression for a bad day or a day in an unhappy situation. Usually objectionable.) ♦ *Everything is going wrong. What do you expect. JAFDIP!*

jag 1. *n.* a Jaguar automobile. ♦ *What I really want is a jag.* **2.** *n.* a drinking bout; a prolonged state of alcohol or drug intoxication. ♦ *Is he off on another jag, or is* this the same one? **3.** *n.* a prolonged state of emotional excess, especially crying. ♦ *I've been on a jag and can't get my work done.* ♦ *Is she still on her crying jag?* **4.** *n.* a drug rush. (Drugs.) ♦ *This stuff has no jag at all.*

jag off Go to beat off.

jagged *mod.* alcohol intoxicated. ♦ *Man, is that chick jagged!*

jagster *n.* someone on a drinking spree; a heavy drinker. ♦ *Gary is a typical jagster. Drunk for a week and sober for three.*

jake **1.** *n.* a toilet; a men's restroom. ♦ *The jake is just around the corner.* **2.** *n.* a stupid person, usually a male. ♦ *Some loony jake told me we are going the wrong way.* **3.** *mod.* okay; satisfactory. ♦ *If you get here by nine, it'll be just jake.* **4.** *n.* illegal liquor. (Prohibition.) ♦ *Why, there's no jake around here. There's a law against it, you know.* **5.** *n.* a police officer. (Possibly from sense 2.) ♦ *The jakes are coming. I can hear the sirens.*

jam **1.** *n.* a problem; trouble. ♦ *I hear you're in a bad jam.* **2.** *in.* [for musicians] to play together, improvising. ♦ *They jammed until the neighbors complained.* **3.** *tv. & in.* to force a basketball into the basket; to slam dunk a basketball. ♦ *He tried to jam it, but blew it.* **4.** *n.* an act of forcing a basketball into the basket; a slam dunk. ♦ *The jam didn't work, and Fred's team rebounded the ball.* **5.** *in.* to depart. ♦ *It's time to jam. Let's go.*

jambled ['dʒæmbl̩d] *mod.* alcohol intoxicated. ♦ *Jerry was too jambled to stand up.*

jammed ['dʒæmd] **1.** *mod.* arrested. (Underworld.) ♦ *Willie got jammed for speeding.* **2.** *mod.* alcohol intoxicated. ♦ *I'm a little jammed, but I think I can still drive.* **3.** Go to jammed up. **4.** *mod.* upset; annoyed. ♦ *He's really jammed because he flunked the test.*

jammed up 1. AND **jammed** *mod.* in trouble. (From in a jam.) ♦ *He got himself jammed up with the law.* **2.** *mod.* glutted; full of food or drink. ♦ *I'm jammed up. I can't eat another bite.*

jamming *mod.* excellent. ♦ *This music is really jamming.*

jampacked AND **jam-packed** *mod.* full. ♦ *This day has been jampacked with surprises.*

jan [dʒæn] *n.* January in the financial futures markets. (Securities markets.) ♦ *The bean futures for jan fell out of bed yesterday.*

jane **1.** *n.* marijuana. (Drugs.) ♦ *Wilmer has jane coming out of his ears.* **2.** *n.* a women's restroom; the ruth. (As a counter to john.) ♦ *The jane is upstairs.*

Jane Doe Go to John Doe.

janky *n.* messed up; bad; inferior. ♦ *Sorry that my room is so janky.*

jarhead *n.* a U.S. Marine. (Attributed to the shape of a cap and to the haircut.) ♦ *Do you want to spend a few years as a gravel-pounder or a jarhead? You get free clothes with both jobs.*

java ['dʒɑvə] *n.* coffee. ♦ *How about a cup of java?*

jaw **1.** *n.* a chat. ♦ *I could use a good jaw with my old friend.* **2.** *in.* to chat. ♦ *Stop jawing and get to work.* **3.** Go to jaw(bone).

jaw so **down** *tv.* to talk someone down; to wear someone down talking. ♦ *We'll try to jaw him down. If that doesn't work, I don't know what we will do.*

jaw(bone) *tv.* to try to persuade someone verbally; to apply verbal pressure to someone. ♦ *They tried to jawbone me into doing it.*

jay Go to J.

jazz so/sth **up** *tv.* to make someone or something more exciting or sexy; to make someone or something appeal more to contemporary and youthful tastes. ♦ *They jazzed up the old girl till she looked like a teenager.*

jazzed (up) 1. *mod.* alert; having a positive state of mind. ♦ *Those guys were jazzed and ready for the game.* **2.** *mod.* alcohol or drug intoxicated. ♦ *Dave was a bit jazzed up, but not terribly.* **3.** *mod.* enhanced; with something added; having been made more enticing. ♦ *It was jazzed* enough to have the police chief around asking questions. **4.** *mod.* forged or altered. (Underworld. See also **tinseled**.) ♦ *Better not try to cash a jazzed up check at this bank.*

jazzy ['dʒæzi] *mod.* stimulating; appealing. ♦ *That's a jazzy sweater you got.*

JCL Go to Johnnie-come-lately.

JD 1. *n.* Jack Daniels whiskey. (Initialism. *Jack Daniels* is a protected trade name for a brand of whiskey.) ♦ *He poured a little JD into a glass, set it aside, and drank all of what was in the bottle.* **2.** *n.* a young kid; a young male; a *juvenile delinquent.* (Colloquial when used as an exaggeration.) ♦ *The JDs are taking over the neighborhood.*

JDLR *n.* a notation on a person's written records indicating that the person "just doesn't look right." ♦ *His record says JDLR, and that meant a lot of close scrutiny about his activities.*

Jeepers(-creepers)! ['dʒipɚz'kripɚz] *exclam.* Wow! ♦ *Jeepers-creepers! I'm sorry!*

Jeez! *exclam.* Jesus! (Uttered as a euphemistic oath.) ♦ *Jeez! I did it again!*

jeff [dʒɛf] **1.** *n.* a Caucasian; a white person. (All senses originally black. From *Jefferson Davis.* Potentially derogatory.) ♦ *The jeffs are coming around more often. What's up?* **2.** *n.* a boring or **square** person. ♦ *Don't be a jeff, man!* **3.** *tv.* to persuade or deceive someone. ♦ *You're just jeffing us!* **4.** *in.* to gentrify; to take on the ways of whites. ♦ *Cool it man; stop your jeffing.*

jel [dʒɛl] *n.* a stupid person. (Someone who has gelatin where brains ought to be.) ♦ *Oh, Wallace, don't act like such a jel.*

jellies *n.* jelly sandals; colorful shoes made from soft, flexible plastic. (From *jelly bean.*) ♦ *Jellies will crack in this weather.*

jelly babies *n.* an amphetamine tablet or capsule. (Drugs.) ♦ *Are there any jelly babies in this neighborhood?*

jerk *n.* a stupid or worthless person. (Now both males and females.) ♦ *You are such a classic jerk!*

jerk around *in.* to waste time. ♦ *All you do is jerk around. Get a move on!*

jerk off *in.* to masturbate. (See also **beat off**. Usually objectionable.) ♦ *That kid spends all his time jerking off.*

jerk SO **around** AND **jerk** SO **over** *tv.* to hassle someone; to waste someone's time. ♦ *Stop jerking me around and give me my money back!* ♦ *We jerked him over for a while, but he still wouldn't come across.*

jerk SO **over** Go to jerk SO **around**.

jerker 1. *n.* a drunkard; an alcoholic. (Because of visible shaking.) ♦ *Some of the jerkers have the DTs.* **2.** *n.* a heavy user of cocaine. (Drugs. Refers to tremors and nervous activity caused by too much cocaine.) ♦ *The jerkers who need immediate treatment are sent from ER up to detox.* **3.** *n.* a male who masturbates habitually. (Usually objectionable.) ♦ *He's s jerker. He doesn't need women.*

jerks *n.* the delirium tremens. ♦ *The old guy has the jerks.*

jerkwater *mod.* rural; backwoodsy; insignificant. (See also **one-horse town**.) ♦ *I'm from a little jerkwater town in the Midwest.*

jerry-built *mod.* carelessly and awkwardly built. ♦ *The lawyer's case was jerry-built, but the jury bought it anyway.*

Jesus boots *n.* sandals. (Use caution with *Jesus* in profane senses.) ♦ *Jesus boots are okay in the summer.*

jet *in.* to leave a place rapidly; to go somewhere fast. ♦ *Let's jet. It's late.*

jet-set(ters) *n.* young and wealthy people who fly by jet from resort to resort. ♦ *The jet-set doesn't come here anymore.*

jibe [dʒaɪb] *in.* to agree; to be in harmony. (See also **track**.) ♦ *Your story just doesn't jibe with the facts.*

jiffy ['dʒɪfi] *n.* a very short time. (See also **in a jiff(y)**.) ♦ *Just a jiffy, I'll be there.*

jig [dʒɪg] *tv. & in.* to copulate [with] someone. (Usually objectionable.) ♦ *She's claiming they jigged twice.*

The **jig is up.** *phr.* the game is ended; the scheme has been found out. ♦ *Okay, you kids. The jig's up!*

jigger 1. *n.* a drink of whiskey. (The standard term for a small container used for measuring the right amount of liquor for a drink.) ♦ *How about another jigger of that shine?* **2.** *n.* a cigarette. ♦ *You got a jigger I can bum?* **3.** *n.* a gadget. ♦ *Toss me one of those copper jiggers there in the box.*

jiggered 1. *mod.* damned. ♦ *Well, I'll be jiggered!* **2.** *mod.* alcohol intoxicated. (See also jigger.) ♦ *Todd was more than just a little jiggered.*

jillion ['dʒɪljən] *n.* an enormous, indefinite number. ♦ *I've got a jillion things to tell you.*

jimmy *n.* the penis. (From the proper name *Jimmy* or from the name for a short crowbar.) ♦ *The streaker covered his jimmy and ran across the field.*

jimmy cap *n.* a condom. (Streets. See also jimmy.) ♦ *You better get a jimmy cap on that.*

jingle 1. *n.* a buzz or tingle from alcohol. ♦ *This stuff gives me a little jingle, but that's all.* **2.** *n.* a drinking bout. ♦ *The guys planned a big jingle for Friday.* **3.** *n.* a call on the telephone. (See also buzz.) ♦ *Give me a jingle when you get into town.*

jingled *mod.* alcohol intoxicated. ♦ *She was a little jingled, but not worse than that.*

jingler *mod.* a drunkard; an alcoholic. ♦ *The jinglers have taken over the streets.*

jism AND **chism; gism; gizzum; jizz; jizzum** *n.* semen. (Usually objectionable.) ♦ *This weird doctor took a sample of my gizzum and put it on a microscope slide.*

the **jitters** ['dʒɪdɚz] *n.* the nervous shakes. ♦ *I get the jitters when I have to talk in public.*

jive [dʒaɪv] **1.** *n.* drugs; marijuana. (Drugs. See also gyve.) ♦ *That jive is gonna be the end of you.* **2.** *n.* back talk. ♦ *Don't you give me any of that jive!* **3.** *n.* lies; deception; nonsense. ♦ *No more of your jive. Talk straight or don't talk.* **4.** *mod.* de-ceptive; insincere. ♦ *I listened to her little jive speech and then fired her.*

jive talk *n.* slang; contemporary fad words. ♦ *I like to hear jive talk. It's like trying to work a puzzle.*

jive turkey *n.* a stupid person. ♦ *What jive turkey made this mess?*

jive-ass *mod.* foolish. (Usually objectionable.) ♦ *You can tell that jive-ass jerk to forget it.*

jivestick AND **gyvestick** *n.* a marijuana cigarette. (Drugs.) ♦ *Wilmer flipped a jivestick to Mooshoo and smiled.* ♦ *When my dad found it, he called it a "gyvestick" or something like that.*

jizz Go to jism.

jizzle a wild card word for words beginning with *J*, such as joint. (Streets. Also for other words with initial *J*.) ♦ *I want that dude out of this jizzle!*

jizzum Go to jism.

job 1. *n.* a drunkard. ♦ *Give the job a drink and make somebody happy today.* **2.** *n.* a theft; a criminal act. (Police and underworld. See also pull a job.) ♦ *Who did that job at the old mansion last week?*

jobber AND **jobby** ['dʒɑbɚ AND 'dʒɑbi] **1.** *n.* a gadget. ♦ *Where is the little jobber I use to tighten this?* **2.** *n.* a bowel movement. (Juvenile.) ♦ *Don't forget to jobber, Jimmy.*

jobby Go to jobber.

jober as a sudge Go to (as) jober as a sudge.

jock 1. *n.* an athlete. (See also strap; jockstrap. Now of either sex.) ♦ *The jocks are all at practice now.* **2.** *n.* an athletic supporter (garment). ♦ *Somebody dropped a jock in the hall.*

jock(e)y *n.* an addictive drug. (Drugs. Because such a drug rides one like a jockey rides a horse.) ♦ *That jockey rode her for years.*

jockstrap 1. AND **jockstrapper** *n.* an athlete. (From the name of the supporting garment worn by male athletes.) ♦ *The jockstrappers are all at practice now.* **2.** *in.*

to work as a professional athlete. ♦ *I jock-strapped for a few years and then lost my interest in it.*

jockstrapper Go to jockstrap.

joe 1. *n.* coffee. ♦ *Yeah, a cup of black joe would be great.* **2.** *n.* an ordinary man. ♦ *What does the everyday joe make of all this nonsense?*

Joe Blow AND **Joe Doakes** [ˈdʒo ˈblo AND ˈdʒo ˈdoks] *n.* a typical or average male American citizen. ♦ *What do you think Joe Blow really thinks about all this?* ♦ *Joe Doakes thinks the government ought to pay for all medical care.*

Joe Citizen [ˈdʒo ˈsɪtəsn̩] *n.* a general term for a male representative of the public. ♦ *Joe Citizen hasn't spoken yet! Watch the results of the election.*

Joe College *n.* a typical or average male college student. ♦ *Joe College never had a computer or a laser-powered record player in the good old days.*

Joe Doakes Go to Joe Blow.

Joe Schmo [ˈdʒo ˈʃmo] *n.* a jerk. ♦ *Let's say Joe Schmo wants a new car. What does he do?*

Joe Six-pack *n.* the average guy who sits around drinking beer by the six-pack. ♦ *Joe Six-pack likes that kind of television program.*

john 1. *n.* a toilet; a bathroom. ♦ *Is there another john around here?* **2.** *n.* a man. ♦ *This john came up and asked if I had seen the girl in a picture he had.* **3.** *n.* a prostitute's customer. ♦ *She led the john into an alley where Lefty robbed him.* **4.** *n.* a victim of a crime or deception; a sucker. ♦ *The john went straight to the cops and told the whole thing.*

John Doe AND **Jane Doe** [ˈdʒɑn ˈdo] *n.* a name used for a person whose real name is unknown. ♦ *The tag on the corpse said Jane Doe, since no one had identified her.* ♦ *John Doe was the name at the bottom of the check.*

John Hancock *n.* one's signature. (Refers to the signature of John Hancock, one of the signers of the Declaration of Inde-pendence.) ♦ *Put your John Hancock right here, if you don't mind.*

Johnnie-come-lately AND **JCL** *n.* someone new to a situation or status. ♦ *This Johnnie-come-lately doesn't know what it was like in the old days.*

John(ny) Law *n.* a law officer. ♦ *John Law showed up with a piece of paper that says you are in trouble.*

Johnny-be-good *n.* a police officer. ♦ *Here comes Johnny-be-good, so be good.*

johnson 1. *n.* a thing. (A general or generic name for an unknown person or thing. See also jones.) ♦ *Hand me that little johnson.* **2.** *n.* a penis. (Again, a *thing.* Usually objectionable.) ♦ *Zip up, or your johnson'll get out.*

Join the club. Go to Welcome to the club.

joined at the hip *mod.* closely connected; as thick as thieves. (As Siamese twins are joined.) ♦ *Those two are joined at the hip. They are always together.*

joint 1. *n.* a tavern; a speakeasy. (Prohibition.) ♦ *I wanted to open a joint, but I don't have the cash.* **2.** *n.* a low-class establishment; a dive. ♦ *Let's get out of this crummy joint.* **3.** *n.* a tobacco cigarette. ♦ *Why are beggars being choosers about their joints all of a sudden?* **4.** *n.* a marijuana cigarette. ♦ *The joint wasn't enough to carry him very long.* **5.** *n.* a penis. (Usually objectionable.) ♦ *He covered his joint and ran for the dressing room.* **6.** *n.* a jail; a prison. (Underworld.) ♦ *Lefty just got out of the joint.* **7.** *n.* a toilet. ♦ *I gotta get to the joint fast!*

joke *tv.* to tease someone; to make fun of someone. ♦ *Everybody was joking my roommate because of her accent.*

joker *n.* a man; a guy. ♦ *Who was that joker I saw you with last night?*

jollies *n.* a charge or thrill; a sexual thrill; kick. ♦ *He got his jollies from skin flicks.*

jollop [ˈdʒɑləp] *n.* a drink of liquor ♦ *She poured a big jollop into each of the glasses and then drank them one by one.*

jolly *mod.* alcohol intoxicated; tipsy. ♦ *Kelly was a little too jolly, and her sister told her to slow down.*

jolly-well *mod.* certainly. ♦ *You jolly-well better be there on time.*

jolt 1. *n.* the degree of potency of the alcohol in liquor. ♦ *It doesn't have much of a jolt.* **2.** *n.* a drink of strong liquor. ♦ *He knocked back a jolt and asked for another.* **3.** *n.* a portion or dose of a drug. (Drugs.) ♦ *How about a little jolt as a taste?* **4.** *n.* the rush from an injection of drugs. (Drugs.) ♦ *This stuff doesn't have much jolt.*

jones 1. *n.* a thing; a problem. (A generic name for an unknown person or thing.) ♦ *This get-rich-quick jones will land you in the joint, Lefty.* **2.** *n.* a drug habit; drug addiction. (Drugs. See also skag jones.) ♦ *That jones is really riding that guy.* **3.** *n.* a desire for someone or something; a craving. ♦ *He has a real jones for chocolate.* **4.** *tv.* to crave something. ♦ *He's jonesing chocolate pretty bad.*

jonx *n.* possessions; belongings. (A respelling of *junks*. Probably includes junk (sense 3).) ♦ *I got to get my jonx. Then I'll be right with you.*

joog [dʒug] *tv.* to stab someone. (Prisons.) ♦ *Lefty jooged the screw.*

jork *n.* a worthless person; a combination jerk and dork. ♦ *What a jork! How stupid can you get?*

josh [dʒɑʃ] *tv. & in.* to tease someone; to kid someone. ♦ *Stop joshing. Be serious.*

joy dust Go to joy flakes.

joy flakes AND **joy dust** *n.* powdered or crystallized cocaine. (Drugs. See also crack.) ♦ *She said what she wanted was some joy flakes, and I guess that's cocaine.* ♦ *"Joy dust" is sort of crack without the press coverage.*

joy juice *n.* liquor; beer. ♦ *Can I pour some more of this joy juice?*

joy ride 1. *n.* a drinking bout or party. ♦ *There's a little joy ride over at Tom's.* **2.** *n.* a state of euphoria from drug use. (Drugs.) ♦ *Ernie's on a little joy ride right now and can't come to the phone.* **3.** *n.* a ride where the passenger does not return alive. (Underworld.) ♦ *Mr. Big wanted Sam to take Harry the Horse on a joy ride.*

joy water *n.* liquor; strong liquor. ♦ *How about some more joy water?*

joybox *n.* a piano. (See also tinklebox.) ♦ *Can you play this joybox at all?*

joystick 1. *n.* the vertical lever used to control smaller aircraft. ♦ *She pulled back on the joystick and the plane took off.* **2.** *n.* an electronic control device for computer games and other program control. (From sense 1.) ♦ *The ship's first officer used a tiny joystick to control the computer program that guided the ship the next port.* **3.** *n.* the erect penis. (Usually objectionable.) ♦ *He couldn't seem to stop playing pocket pool with his joystick.*

jug 1. *n.* jail. (Usually with *the*.) ♦ *Take it easy. I don't want to end up in the jug.* **2.** *n.* a jug of liquor; a jar of moonshine; a can of beer. ♦ *Where's my jug? I need a swig.* **3.** AND **jug up** *in.* to drink heavily. (See also jugger.) ♦ *We jugged up till noon and then went to sleep.* ♦ *Let's get down to some serious jugging.* **4.** *n.* a glass vial of liquid amphetamine intended for injection. (Drugs.) ♦ *His mother found a jug and took it to a drugstore to find out what it was.* **5.** *n.* the jugular vein, used for the injection of narcotics. (Drugs.) ♦ *He's even got scars on his jugs.* **6.** *n.* a breast. (Usually plural. Usually objectionable.) ♦ *Look at the jugs on that babe!*

jug up Go to jug.

jug wine *n.* cheap wine that is sold in volume, usually in gallon jugs. ♦ *We're having a little do tomorrow—nothing special. A little jug wine and chips.*

jugged (up) *mod.* alcohol intoxicated. ♦ *I'm not jugged up. I'm not even tipsy.*

jugger *n.* an alcoholic; a drunkard. ♦ *A couple of old juggers sat in the alley, trying to figure out how to get some more.*

jughead 1. *n.* a stupid person. ♦ *I guess I'm sort of a jughead lately.* **2.** *n.* a drunkard. ♦ *Buy the jughead a drink. That'll shut him up.*

juice 1. *n.* liquor; wine. ♦ *Let's go get some juice and get stewed.* **2.** *in.* to drink heavily. ♦ *Both of them were really juicing.* **3.** *n.* electricity. ♦ *Turn on the juice, and let's see if it runs.* **4.** *n.* energy; power; political influence. ♦ *Dave left the president's staff because he just didn't have the juice anymore to be useful.* **5.** *n.* orange juice futures market. (Securities markets. Usually with *the.*) ♦ *The juice opened a little high today, but fell quickly under profit taking.* **6.** *n.* anabolic steroids. ♦ *Fred used too much juice and is growing witch tits.*

juice freak *n.* someone who prefers alcohol to drugs. (Drugs.) ♦ *Freddy is a juice freak. He won't touch dolls.*

juice house *n.* a liquor store. ♦ *Would you stop by the juice house for some foam?*

juice joint *n.* a liquor establishment; a speakeasy. (Prohibition.) ♦ *His grandfather ran a juice joint during prohibition.*

juice racket *n.* a racket where exorbitant interest is charged on loans. (Underworld.) ♦ *The cops got one of the leaders of the juice racket.*

juice sth **back** *tv.* to drink alcohol. ♦ *He's been juicing it back since noon.*

juice sth **up 1.** *tv.* to make something more powerful. ♦ *How much did it cost to juice this thing up?* **2.** *tv.* to turn on the electricity to something. ♦ *It's time to juice the stage lights up.*

juice up *in.* to drink one or more alcoholic drinks. ♦ *Hey, man, let's go out and juice up tonight.*

juicehead AND **juicer** *n.* a heavy drinker; a drunkard. ♦ *The tavern is always filled with juicers on Friday night.*

juicer Go to juicehead.

juicy *mod.* alcohol intoxicated. ♦ *Mary is just a little bit juicy, I'm afraid.*

jump 1. *tv.* to attack someone. (General slang.) ♦ *The dope addicts will jump anybody for a few bucks to buy drugs.* **2.** *tv.* to copulate [with] someone. (Usually objectionable.) ♦ *He was so horny, I just knew he was gonna try to jump me.*

jump bail *tv.* to fail to show up in court and forfeit bail. ♦ *Lefty jumped bail, and now he's a fugitive.*

jump smooth *in.* to give up illegal activities; to become **straight**. (Underworld.) ♦ *After a night in the junk tank, I knew I had to jump smooth.*

jump so's **bones** *tv.* to copulate [with] someone. ♦ *Just one look and he was ready to jump her bones.*

jump (street) *n.* the beginning; the start (of something). (Prisons and streets.) ♦ *Way back at jump street, I spotted you as a troublemaker.*

jump the gun *tv.* to start too soon; to start before the starting signal. ♦ *The secretary jumped the gun and gave out the letters too soon.*

jump-start 1. *n.* the act of starting a car by getting power—through jumper cables—from another car. ♦ *Who can give me a jump-start?* **2.** *tv.* to start a car by getting power from another car. ♦ *I can't jump-start your car. My battery is low.*

jump-start so *tv.* to get someone going or functioning. ♦ *I need to jump-start Bill early in the morning to get him going in time to get on the road by a decent hour.*

jumpy *mod.* nervous. ♦ *Now, don't be jumpy. Everything will be all right.*

jungle *n.* a vicious area of confusion; the real world. ♦ *The place is a jungle out there. You'll grow up fast out there.*

jungle juice *n.* homemade liquor; any strong liquor. ♦ *This jungle juice will knock you for a loop.*

jungle mouth *n.* a case of very bad breath; breath like the rotting jungle floor. ♦ *My husband woke up with jungle mouth, and I could hardly stand to be around him.*

jungled *mod.* alcohol intoxicated; affected by jungle juice. ♦ *He was jungled before he came here.*

juniper juice *n.* gin. (From the juniper berry flavoring of gin.) ♦ *Britney used to like juniper juice before she went on the dust.*

junk 1. *n.* herion; drugs. ♦ *Is Sam still on junk? It will kill him.* **2.** *n.* a Caucasian. (Rude and derogatory.) ♦ *Those cops are junk and they hate my guts.* **3.** AND **the junk.** *n.* the genitals. (See also jonx.) ♦ *Stop itching your junk, you freak.* **3.** *n.* possessions. ♦ *I'll be ready to go as soon as I get my junk together.*

junk bond *n.* a low-rated corporate bond that pays higher interest because of greater risk. (Parallel to junk food.) ♦ *Don't put all your money into junk bonds.*

junk fax *n.* an unwanted and irritating fax message. ♦ *We got nothing but a whole pile of junk faxes today.*

junk food *n.* food that is typically high in fats and salt and low in nutritional value; food from a fast-food restaurant. ♦ *Junk food tastes good no matter how greasy it is.*

junk heap *n.* a dilapidated old car; a dilapidated house or other structure. ♦ *They lived in that junk heap for thirty years and never painted it.*

Junk it! *imperative* Throw it away! ♦ *This is taking up too much space. Junk it!*

junk squad *n.* police who enforce the narcotics laws. (Underworld.) ♦ *The junk squad has more than it can handle trying to keep up with the hard stuff.*

junk tank *n.* a jail cell where addicts are kept. (See also drunk tank.) ♦ *That junk tank is a very dangerous place.*

junkie AND **junky** ['dʒəŋki] **1.** *n.* a drug dealer. (Drugs.) ♦ *Junkies should be put into the jug.* **2.** *n.* a drug user; an addict. (Drugs.) ♦ *Junkies have to steal to support their habits.*

(just) curl up and die 1. *in.* to retreat and die. ♦ *I was so embarrassed, I thought I would curl up and die.* **2.** *in.* to retreat; to withdraw. ♦ *Don't just curl up and die! Get in there and fight!*

just off the boat *mod.* freshly immigrated and perhaps gullible and naive. (See also FOB.) ♦ *I'm not just off the boat. I know what's going on.*

just the ticket *n.* just the perfect thing. ♦ *A nice cup of tea will be just the ticket.*

just what the doctor ordered *n.* exactly what is needed. ♦ *This nice cool beer is just what the doctor ordered.*

juvie ['dʒuvi] **1.** *n.* a police officer concerned with juveniles. (Underworld.) ♦ *The juvies have to know juvenile law cold.* **2.** *n.* a youth; a teenager under age eighteen. (Underworld.) ♦ *I work with juvies a lot. I try to get them back on the track.* **3.** *mod.* juvenile. ♦ *She still has a lot of juvie attitudes.*

K

K. [ke] **1.** AND **kee; key; ki** [ki] *n.* a kilogram of cannabis. (Drugs.) ♦ *Well, how much is a ki?* **2.** *n.* ketamine hydrochloride, a drug similar to LSD. (Drugs.) ♦ *You want to try this K. stuff?* **3.** *n.* a thousand (of anything, such as dollars, bytes, etc.). ♦ *This car is worth at least twenty K.*

Ka-ching! Go to Ching!

kack Go to cack.

kafooster [kə'fustɚ] *n.* nonsense. ♦ *This kafooster about me being a cheater is too much.*

kak Go to cack.

kaka Go to caca.

kayo Go to KO.

kee Go to K.

keep cool *in.* to keep calm. ♦ *Now, keep cool. It's going to be all right.*

Keep in touch. *sent.* Good-bye. (Sometimes a sarcastic way of saying good-bye to someone one doesn't care about.) ♦ *Sorry, we can't use you anymore. Keep in touch.*

Keep it real! *exclam.* Be serious! ♦ *Come on! Stop that jive! Keep it real!*

Keep on trucking. *sent.* Keep doing what you are doing.; Keep taking care of business. ♦ *Keep on trucking. Things'll get better.*

keep one's **cool** *tv.* to remain calm and in control. (See also **keep cool.** Compare this with **lose** one's **cool.**) ♦ *It's hard to keep your cool when you've been cheated.*

keep one's **head right** *tv.* to maintain control of oneself. ♦ *Chill, man, chill. You've got to keep your head right.*

keep one's **nose clean** *tv.* to keep out of trouble, especially trouble with the law. ♦ *I can keep my nose clean. Don't worry.*

Keep out of this! *exclam.* Mind your own business! ♦ *This is not your affair. Keep out of this!*

Keep the faith (baby)! *exclam.* a statement of general encouragement or solidarity. ♦ *You said it! Keep the faith, baby!*

Keep your hands to yourself. 1. *sent.* Do not touch things that are not yours.; Do not touch breakable things. (Said to a child.) ♦ *You can look, but don't touch. Keep your hands to yourself.* **2.** *sent.* Don't poke or hit other children. (Said to a child.) ♦ *Jimmy! Leave him alone and keep your hands to yourself.* **3.** *sent.* No intimate caressing is allowed. (Said to an adult, usually a male.) ♦ *Just keep your hands to yourself or take me home.*

Keep your nose out of my business! Go to Get your nose out of my business!

Keep your pants on! Go to Keep your shirt on!

Keep your shirt on! AND **Keep your pants on!** *exclam.* Just wait a minute!; Don't be in a rush. (Possibly said as if to avoid a fight, for which one removes one's shirt. That is, Let's not rush into a big argument or fight; wait a minute. The expressions are old and in very wide use, too wide to suggest a reference to sexual urgency.) ♦ *I'll be right with you. Keep your shirt on!* ♦ *We'll be there in a minute! Keep your pants on!*

keepage *n.* stuff that you want to keep. (The opposite of *garbage.*) ♦ *The stuff in that pile is garbage. This stack is keepage.*

keeper *n.* something that can be kept; something that qualifies. ♦ *This fish is a keeper. Throw the others out.*

keester AND **keyster; kiester** ['kistɚ] **1.** *n.* a chest; a suitcase. ♦ *The old lady was hauling the most enormous keester.* **2.** *n.* the buttocks; the anus. ♦ *Get your keester over here!*

keg *n.* a beer belly. ♦ *If you didn't drink so much beer, you wouldn't have such a keg.*

keg party *n.* a party where liquor, especially beer, is served. ♦ *The keg party ended early owing to the arrival of uninvited nabs.*

kegger 1. *n.* a party where beer is served from a keg. (Teens and collegiate.) ♦ *Tiffany is having a kegger, and a few of her intimates are invited.* **2.** AND **keggers** *n.* a keg of beer. (Collegiate.) ♦ *We came here because somebody said there was keggers.*

keggers Go to kegger.

Kentucky fried *mod.* alcohol intoxicated. (An elaboration of fried. Based on the trade name *Kentucky Fried Chicken,* now known as KFC.) ♦ *Man, is that guy really Kentucky fried!*

kevork *tv.* to kill someone. (Based on the name of *Dr. Jack Kevorkian,* the physician who advocates, and has practiced, assisted suicide.) ♦ *This guy looked mean— like he was gonna kevork me.*

kewl *mod.* an alternate spelling of *cool.*; excellent, neat, and good. ♦ *Man this is really kewl, I mean truly phat!*

key Go to K.

key figure *n.* an important person in an event; a person central to an event. ♦ *Sam is not exactly a key figure, but he can lead us to Mr. Big.*

key grip *n.* the head laborer on a movie set. (Filmmaking.) ♦ *The key grip has a complaint that could hold up production.*

keyed (up) 1. *mod.* nervous; anxious. ♦ *Sally was a little keyed up before the meet.* **2.** AND **keyed up to the roof** *mod.* alcohol or drug intoxicated. ♦ *He was a mite keyed, but still technically sober.* ♦ *Tipsy, hell! I'd say keyed up to the roof!*

keyed up to the roof Go to keyed (up).

keyster Go to keester.

ki Go to K.

KIBO Go to knowledge in, bullshit out.

kibosh ['kaɪbaʃ OR kə'baʃ] **1.** *tv.* to end something; to squelch something. ♦ *Please don't try to kibosh the scheme this time.* **2.** *n.* the end; the final blow; the thing that terminates something. (Usually with the. See also put the kibosh on sth.) ♦ *They thought the kibosh was overdone.*

kick 1. *n.* a charge or good feeling (from something); pleasure or enjoyment from something. (See also get a kick out of so/sth.) ♦ *That song really gives me a kick. I love it!* **2.** *n.* the jolt from a drug or a drink of strong liquor. ♦ *The kick nearly knocked Harry over.* **3.** *tv.* to break a drug addiction voluntarily. (Drugs.) ♦ *I knew I had the guts in me somewhere to kick juice.* **4.** *n.* a complaint. ♦ *You got another kick, troublemaker?* **5.** *in.* to complain. ♦ *Why are you always kicking?* **6.** Go to kicks.

kick around Go to knock around.

kick ass AND **kick butt** *tv.* to actively motivate people to do something. (Usually objectionable.) ♦ *It looks like I'm going to have to kick ass to get people moving around here.* ♦ *Do I need to get you guys down here and kick butt to get you to play ball like the team you are supposed to be?*

kick back 1. *in.* to relax (and enjoy something). ♦ *I like to kick back and listen to a few tunes.* **2.** *n.* money received in return for a favor. (Usually **kickback.**) ♦ *The kickback the cop got wasn't enough, as it turned out.* **3.** *in.* [for an addict] to return to addiction after having been detoxified and withdrawn. (Drugs.) ♦ *They may kick back a dozen times before it takes.*

kick butt Go to kick ass.

kick cold (turkey) *in.* to stop taking drugs without tapering off. (Drugs.) ♦ *Britney tried to kick cold turkey, but it was just too much.*

kick down with sth *in.* to give forth with something; to dole out a portion of something. ♦ *Hey, man. Kick down with my share of the brewsters!*

kick freak *n.* a nonaddicted drug user. (Drugs.) ♦ *Ernie used to be a kick freak, but all that has changed.*

kick in the ass Go to kick in the (seat of the) pants.

kick in the butt Go to kick in the (seat of the) pants.

kick in the guts *n.* a severe blow to one's body or spirit. ♦ *The news was a kick in the guts, and I haven't recovered yet.*

kick in the rear Go to kick in the (seat of the) pants.

kick in the (seat of the) pants AND **kick in the ass; kick in the butt; kick in the teeth; kick in the rear** *n.* a strong message of encouragement or a demand. (Usually objectionable.) ♦ *All he needs is a kick in the seat of the pants to get him going.* ♦ *A kick in the teeth ought to wake them up and get them moving.*

kick in the teeth Go to kick in the (seat of the) pants.

kick in the wrist *n.* a drink of liquor. ♦ *You want another kick in the wrist?*

kick it *tv.* to relax. ♦ *I need a few minutes to kick it, then I'll get back in the game.*

kick (off) *in.* to die. ♦ *We've been waiting for years for that cat to kick off.*

kick party *n.* a party where some drug is used. (Drugs.) ♦ *There was a kick party at one of the crack houses, and even little children went in.*

kick some ass (around) AND **kick some butt** *tv.* to act aggressively, directly, and as physically as necessary; to take over and start giving orders; to raise hell. (Usually objectionable.) ♦ *Do I have to come over there and kick some ass around?* ♦ *Let's go out there and kick some butt.*

kick some butt Go to kick some ass (around).

kick the bucket *tv.* to die. ♦ *I'm too young to kick the bucket!*

kick the habit *tv.* to voluntarily end any habit or custom, especially a drug habit. (See also knock the habit.) ♦ *She tried and tried to kick the habit.*

kick the shit out of so Go to beat the shit out of so.

kick up a storm *tv.* to create a disturbance; to put on an angry display. ♦ *My dad will just kick up a storm when he finds out.*

kick-ass AND **bust-ass 1.** *mod.* powerful and vigorous. (Usually objectionable.) ♦ *The guy's a real bust-ass bastard!* **2.** *mod.* really fine; excellent; cool. (Usually objectionable.) ♦ *That was a real kick-ass party you had the other night!*

kick-ass on so *in.* to give someone a hard time; to try to dominate or overwhelm someone. (Usually objectionable.) ♦ *Don't kick-ass on me! I'm not the one you're after.*

kicken Go to kickin'.

kicker *n.* a clever but stinging remark; a sharp criticism; a zinger. ♦ *I waited for the kicker, and finally it came.*

kickin' AND **kicken** *mod.* wild; super; excellent. ♦ *I don't know where you get your clothes, but that jacket's kickin'.*

kicks *n.* cleats or shoes; gym shoes. (Collegiate. See also kick.) ♦ *Don't you dare wear those kicks in here!*

kicky *mod.* exciting and energetic. ♦ *Man, what a kicky idea!*

kid stuff *n.* marijuana, a drug for *beginners.* (Drugs.) ♦ *He's still using kid stuff.*

kidney-buster 1. *n.* a rough ride; a rough road. ♦ *This road is a kidney-buster. I wish they'd fix it.* **2.** *n.* an uncomfortable or poorly built seat in a vehicle. ♦ *This kidney-buster is going to ruin my back.*

kid-vid ['kɪdvɪd] *n.* children's television; television programming aimed at children. ♦ *Kid-vid isn't good for anything other than selling cereal.*

kiester Go to keester.

kill 1. *tv.* to be very successful with an audience; to perform very well for an audience. ♦ *She really killed them with that* last joke. **2.** *tv.* to eat all of something; to drink all (of a bottle) of something. ♦ *We finally killed the last of the turkey.* **3.** *tv.* to douse a light. ♦ *Would you kill the light so they can't see we're home?* **4.** *tv.* to stop or terminate something; to quash a story; to stop a story from being printed in a newspaper. ♦ *Kill that story. It's got too many errors.*

kill for sth *in.* to be willing to go to extremes to get something that one really wants or needs. (An exaggeration.) ♦ *I could kill for a cold beer.*

killed (off) *mod.* alcohol or drug intoxicated. (Drugs.) ♦ *The team went out drinking and came home killed off.*

killer 1. *n.* a marijuana cigarette. ♦ *How about a killer, Wilmer?* **2.** *n.* a very funny joke. ♦ *She told a killer about a red-nosed juicer.* **3.** *n.* something extraordinary. ♦ *That car is a killer. I like it!* **4.** *mod.* extraordinary; great. ♦ *What a killer jacket you're wearing!*

killer weed 1. *n.* very potent marijuana. (Drugs.) ♦ *Wow, this stuff is killer weed!* **2.** *n.* phencyclidine (PCP), an animal tranquilizer. (Drugs.) ♦ *Killer weed seems to be a favorite around here just now.*

killer-diller *n.* an excellent thing or person. ♦ *She is just a real killer-diller.*

killing *n.* a great financial success. ♦ *Sally made a real killing in the stock market.*

killjoy *n.* a person who takes the fun out of things for other people; a **party-pooper**. ♦ *Don't be such a killjoy!*

kilobucks *n.* a tremendous sum of money. (See also **megabucks**.) ♦ *How many kilobucks does a set of wheels like that cost?*

King Grod [...grɑd] *n.* a very repellent male. (California.) ♦ *You are just King Grod! So gross!*

King Kong pills AND **King Kong specials** *n.* barbiturates. (Drugs. See also **gorilla biscuits**.) ♦ *Watch out for those King Kong pills.* ♦ *She's a bit numb from "King Kong specials."*

King Kong specials Go to King Kong pills.

kingpin 1. *n.* a major figure in organized crime. (Underworld. From the term for the front bowling pin in a triangular array of pins.) ♦ *The drug kingpins are well protected.* **2.** *n.* a boss. ♦ *My uncle is the kingpin in this organization.*

kink 1. *n.* a strange person; a kinky person. ♦ *The guy's a kink. Watch out for him.* **2.** *n.* a sexually deviant person. ♦ *The kinks congregate two streets over.*

kinky AND **bent; twisted 1.** *mod.* having to do with someone or something strange or weird. ♦ *The guy is so kinky that everyone avoids him.* **2.** *mod.* having to do with unconventional sexual acts or people who perform them. ♦ *She seems to have a morbid interest in kinky stuff.*

kip *in.* to sleep. ♦ *He's upstairs kipping. Can he call you back?*

kipe *tv.* to steal something. ♦ *The punk kiped a newspaper just for the heck of it.*

kiper ['kaɪpɚ] *n.* a thief; someone who steals. ♦ *The punk is a two-bit kiper and needs to be taught a lesson.*

Kiss my ass! *tv.* Drop dead!; Go to hell! (Usually objectionable.) ♦ *You can just kiss my ass!*

kiss of death *n.* the direct cause of the end of someone or something. ♦ *Your attitude was the kiss of death for your employment here.*

kiss off *n.* the dismissal of someone or something. (Usually **kiss-off**.) ♦ *The kiss-off was when I lost the Wilson contract.* **2.** *n.* death. (Usually **kiss-off**.) ♦ *When the time comes for the kiss-off, I hope I'm asleep.* **3.** *in.* to die. ♦ *The cat is going to have to kiss off one of these days soon.*

kiss so/sth **off** *tv.* to kill someone; to get rid of someone or something. ♦ *John had instructions to kiss Bart off.*

kiss so's **ass** *tv.* to fawn over someone; to flatter and curry favor with someone. (Usually objectionable.) ♦ *What does he expect me to do? Kiss his ass?*

kiss so's **hind tit** Go to suck so's hind tit.

kiss sth **good-bye** *tv.* to face and accept the loss of something. ♦ *Well, you can kiss that 100 bucks good-bye.*

kiss sth **off** *tv.* to forget about something; to ignore something. ♦ *Just kiss off any idea you might have had about running for office.*

kiss the dust *tv.* to fall to the earth, because of death or because of being struck. (Western movies. See also bite the dust.) ♦ *I'll see that you kiss the dust before sunset, cowboy!*

kiss the porcelain god *tv.* to empty one's stomach; to vomit. ♦ *He fled the room to kiss the porcelain god, I guess.*

kiss up to so *in.* to flatter someone; to make over someone. ♦ *I'm not going to kiss up to anybody to get what's rightfully mine.*

kiss-ass 1. *n.* someone who is servile and obsequious. (Rude and derogatory.) ♦ *I'm fed up with that kiss-ass!* **2.** *mod.* servile and obsequious. (Usually objectionable.) ♦ *He can be so kiss-ass. It makes me sick.* **3.** *in.* to act subservient (to someone). (Usually objectionable.) ♦ *Stop kiss-assing around and stand up to your employer.*

kisser *n.* the face; the mouth. (See also right in the kisser.) ♦ *I poked him right in the kisser.*

kissyface ['kɪsifes] **1.** *n.* kissing. ♦ *There was a lot of kissyface going on in the backseat.* **2.** *mod.* feeling the need to kiss and be kissed. ♦ *I feel all kissyface.*

kit and caboodle ['kɪt n̩ kə'budl̩] *n.* everything; all parts and property. (Often with whole.) ♦ *I want you out of here—kit and caboodle—by noon.* ♦ *She moved in to stay, kit and caboodle.*

kite 1. *n.* a drug user who is always high. (Drugs.) ♦ *The guy's a kite. He won't make any sense no matter what you ask him.* **2.** *tv.* to write worthless checks; to raise the amount on a check. (Underworld. See also fly kites.) ♦ *Chuck made a fortune kiting checks.* **3.** *n.* a worthless check. (Underworld.) ♦ *He finally wrote one kite too many, and they nabbed him.*

kited *mod.* alcohol intoxicated. (From *high as a kite.*) ♦ *Britney was too kited to see her hand in front of her.*

kitsch [kɪtʃ] *n.* any form of entertainment—movies, books, plays—with enormous popular appeal. ♦ *This kitsch sells like mad in the big city.*

kitschy ['kɪtʃi] *mod.* trivial in spite of enormous popular appeal. ♦ *A lot of people like kitschy art.*

kizzle a wild card word for words beginning with *K,* such as *kill, key(s), kilo.* (Streets. Also for other words with initial *K.*) ♦ *He stood in front of his car, patted his pockets, and said "Kizzle?"*

klepto ['klɛpto] *n.* a kleptomaniac; one who steals small things obsessively. ♦ *The cops thought Gert was a klepto until she showed them her receipts.*

klotz Go to klutz.

kluck Go to cluck.

kludge AND **kluge** [klədʒ OR kludʒ] **1.** *n.* a patch or a fix in a computer program or circuit. ♦ *This is a messy kludge, but it will do the job.* **2.** *tv.* to patch or fix a computer program circuit. ♦ *I only have time to kludge this problem.*

kludgy ['klədʒi OR 'kludʒi] *mod.* having to do with an inefficient or sloppily written computer program. ♦ *I don't care if it's kludgy. Does it work?*

kluge Go to kludge.

klutz AND **klotz** [kləts AND klats] *n.* a stupid and clumsy person. ♦ *Don't be a klutz!*

klutzy ['klətsi] *mod.* foolish; stupid. ♦ *That was really a klutzy thing to do.*

knee-deep in sth *mod.* having lots of something. (See also up to one's knees.) ♦ *We are knee-deep in orders and loving it.*

knee-deep navy *n.* the U.S. Coast Guard. (Jocular and derogatory.) ♦ *Join the knee-deep navy and see the beach!*

knee-high to a grasshopper *mod.* of very short stature. (Folksy.) ♦ *I knew you when you were knee-high to a grasshopper.*

knee-jerk *mod.* automatic; quick and without thought. ◆ *That was only a knee-jerk response. Pay no attention.*

knee-mail *n.* prayer. (A message delivered on one's knees.) ◆ *You'd better be sending some knee-mail on this problem.*

knock *tv.* to criticize someone or something. ◆ *Don't knock it if you haven't tried it.*

knock around 1. *in.* to waste time. ◆ *Stop knocking around and get to work!* **2.** AND **kick around** *in.* to wander around; to bum around. ◆ *I think I'll kick around a few months before looking for another job.*

knock back a drink AND **knock one back; knock one over** *tv.* to swallow a drink of an alcoholic beverage. ◆ *Todd knocked back one drink, and then had another.* ◆ *The cowboy swaggered in, knocked one over, and swaggered out again.*

knock boots *tv.* to copulate. ◆ *He said he wanted to knock boots with her.*

Knock it off! *exclam.* Be Quiet!; Shut up! ◆ *Hey, you guys! Knock it off!*

knock off (work) *in.* to quit work, for the day or for a break. ◆ *What time do you knock off work?*

knock one back Go to knock back a drink.

knock one over Go to knock back a drink.

knock over sth **1.** *tv.* to steal something. (The *over* is usually before the object in this expression.) ◆ *The gang knocked over an armored car.* **2.** *tv.* to rob a place. (The *over* is usually before the object in this expression.) ◆ *Max knocked over two banks in one week.*

knock some heads together *tv.* to scold some people; to get some people to do what they are supposed to be doing. ◆ *Do I have to come in there and knock some heads together, or will you kids settle down?*

knock so **dead** *tv.* to put on a stunning performance or display for someone. ◆ *She knocked us dead with her stunning performance.*

knock so **off** *tv.* to kill someone. (Underworld. See also bump so off.) ◆ *The mob knocked the witnesses off.*

knock so **out** *tv.* to surprise someone. ◆ *Her stunning beauty knocked us all out.*

knock so's **block off** *tv.* to hit someone hard in the head. (See also block.) ◆ *Wilbur almost knocked Tom's block off by accident.*

knock so's **socks off** *tv.* to surprise or startle someone; to overwhelm someone. ◆ *Wow, that explosion nearly knocked my socks off.*

knock so **some skin** *tv.* to shake hands with someone. ◆ *Hey, man, knock me some skin!*

knock so **up** *tv.* to make a woman pregnant. (See also knocked up. Crude.) ◆ *They say it was Sam who knocked her up.*

knock sth **back** *tv.* to drink down a drink of something, especially something alcoholic. (See also knock back a drink.) ◆ *John knocked back two beers in ten minutes.*

knock sth **down 1.** *tv.* to drink a portion of liquor. ◆ *He knocked down a bottle of beer and called for another.* **2.** *tv.* to earn a certain amount of money. ◆ *She must knock down about twenty thou a year.*

knock sth **into a cocked hat** *tv.* to demolish a plan, a story, etc. ◆ *You've knocked everything into a cocked hat.*

knock sth **off 1.** *tv.* to manufacture or make something, especially in haste. (See also knock sth together.) ◆ *I'll see if I can knock another one off before lunch.* **2.** *tv.* to lower the price of something; to knock off some dollars or cents from the price of something. ◆ *The store manager knocked 30 percent off the price of the coat.*

knock sth **out** AND **knock** sth **off** *tv.* to write something quickly. ◆ *Would you please knock a speech out for the senator?* ◆ *I knocked this little tune off, just for you, sweetie.*

knock sth **together** AND **throw** sth **together** *tv.* to assemble something—such as a meal—at the last moment. ◆ *Bob knocked together some lemon chicken and* *rice in only a few minutes.* ♦ *I'll see if I can throw something together.*

knock the dew off the lily AND **shake the dew off the lily** *phr.* [for a male] to urinate, especially first thing in the morning. (The *dew* is urine.) ♦ *He's up and into the bathroom, knocking the dew off the lily long before I even get my eyes open.* ♦ *I gotta go shake the dew off the lily before I explode.*

knock the habit *tv.* to stop using drugs; to break a drug addiction. (Drugs. See also kick the habit.) ♦ *I just can't knock the habit.*

knock the shit out of so Go to beat the shit out of so.

knockdown drag-out fight *n.* a prolonged and hard fight. ♦ *Trying to get my proposal accepted was a knockdown drag-out fight.*

knocked in *mod.* arrested. (Underworld.) ♦ *Would you believe that Rocko has never been knocked in?*

knocked out 1. *mod.* exhausted. ♦ *We were all knocked out at the end of the day.* **2.** *mod.* overwhelmed. ♦ *We were just knocked out when we heard your news.* **3.** *mod.* alcohol or drug intoxicated. ♦ *They were all knocked out by midnight.*

knocked up 1. *mod.* battered; beaten. ♦ *Sally was a little knocked up by the accident.* **2.** *mod.* alcohol intoxicated. ♦ *Bill was knocked up and didn't want to drive.* **3.** *mod.* pregnant. ♦ *Taylor got knocked up again.*

knockers 1. *n.* the breasts. (Usually objectionable.) ♦ *Nice knockers, huh?* **2.** *n.* the testicles. (Usually objectionable.) ♦ *Pow, right in the knockers. Ye gods, it hurt!*

knockout 1. *n.* something that is quite stunning. ♦ *Your new car is a knockout.* **2.** *n.* a good-looking man or woman. ♦ *Your date is a real knockout.* **3.** *mod.* very exciting. ♦ *It was a real knockout evening.*

knothead *n.* a stupid person. ♦ *Don't be such a knothead!*

know all the angles *tv.* to know all the tricks and artifices of dealing with some-one or something. ♦ *Ask my mouthpiece about taxes. He knows all the angles.*

know from sth *in.* to know about something. (Colloquial. Northeast U.S. See also not know from nothing.) ♦ *Do you know from timers, I mean how timers work?*

know one's **ass from a hole in the ground** *tv.* to be knowledgeable; to be alert and effective. (Usually objectionable.) ♦ *That stupid son of a bitch doesn't know his ass from a hole in the ground.*

know shit from Shinola AND **tell shit from Shinola** [...ʃɑɪˈnolə] *tv.* to know what's what; to be intelligent and aware. (Always in the negative. Shinola is a brand of shoe polish. A person who doesn't know shit from Shinola is very stupid. See also No Shinola!) ♦ *Poor Tom doesn't know shit from Shinola.*

know the score *tv.* to know the way things work in the hard, cruel world. ♦ *Don't try to con me. I know the score.*

know what's what *tv.* to be aware of what is going on in the world. ♦ *We don't know what's what around here yet.*

know where it's at *tv.* to know the way things really are. ♦ *I know where it's at. I don't need to be told.*

know where so **is coming from** *tv.* to understand someone's motivation; to understand and relate to someone's position. ♦ *I know where you're coming from. I've been there.*

know which end is up *tv.* to be alert and knowledgeable. ♦ *Don't try to hustle me, sister. I know which end is up.*

know-how *n.* the knowledge of how to do something. ♦ *I don't have the know-how to do this job.*

know-it-all *n.* someone who gives the impression of knowing everything. ♦ *Pete is such a know-it-all!*

knowledge in, bullshit out AND **KIBO** *phr. & comp. abb.* a phrase expressing distress over stupidity. (Based on FIFO.) ♦ *My head is just plain KIBO. I get everything* *confused.* ♦ *College is supposed to be knowledge in, bullshit out.*

knowledge-box *n.* the head. ♦ *Now, I want to get this into your knowledge-box once and for all.*

knuckle bones *n.* dice. (An elaboration of bones.) ♦ *Roll them knuckle bones and tell me that your expense needs earth pads.*

knuckle down (to sth) *in.* to get busy doing something. ♦ *Please knuckle down to your studies.*

knuckle sandwich *n.* a blow struck in the teeth or mouth. ♦ *How would you like a knuckle sandwich?*

knuckle under (to so/sth) *in.* to give in to or accept someone or something. ♦ *She always refused to knuckle under to anyone.*

knuckle-dragger *n.* a strong and stupid man. (Like an ape.) ♦ *Call off your knuckle-draggers. I'll pay you whatever you want.*

knucklehead *n.* a stupid person. ♦ *Oh, I feel like such a knucklehead!*

KO AND **kayo** ['ke'o] **1.** *n.* a knockout. (The abbreviation is an initialism. Boxing.) ♦ *It was a quick KO, and Wilbur was the new champ.* **2.** *tv.* to knock someone out. (See also **KOed**. Boxing.) ♦ *Wilbur planned to KO Wallace in the third round.*

KOed ['ke'od] **1.** *mod.* knocked out. (Initialism. Originally from boxing.) ♦ *Wilbur was KOed and got a cut over his eye.* **2.** *mod.* alcohol or drug intoxicated. (Initialism.) ♦ *Both guys were KOed and spent the night.*

Kojak ['kodʒæk] *n.* a police officer. (From the television character of the same name.) ♦ *Ask Kojak in for a cup of coffee.*

kong [kɔŋ] *n.* strong whiskey; illicit whiskey. (From the movie ape King Kong.) ♦ *How about a big swallow of that kong?*

konk Go to conk.

konk-buster Go to conk-buster.

kook [kuk] *n.* a strange person. ♦ *She seems like a kook, but she is just grand, really.*

kookish ['kukɪʃ] *mod.* strange; eccentric. ♦ *Who is the kookish one over there with the purple shades?*

koshe Go to kosher.

kosher ['koʃɚ OR 'koʒɚ] **1.** AND **koshe** *mod.* acceptable; cricket. (From Hebrew *kasher*, "proper," via Yiddish. Koshe is a slang clipping.) ♦ *Is it kosher to do this?* **2.** *tv.* to make something acceptable. ♦ *Do you want me to kosher it with the boss for you?* **3.** *mod.* having to do with undiluted alcohol. ♦ *I'll take mine kosher with a little ice.*

krudzu *n.* creeping stupidity. (A play on *kudzu*, an invasive, creeping vine.) ♦ *Your brain is overcome with krudzu. You're getting dumber and dumber.*

krunk Go to crunk.

kvetch AND **quetch** [kvɛtʃ AND kʌɛtʃ] **1.** *in.* to complain. (From German *quetschen*, "to squeeze," via Yiddish.) ♦ *Quit your kvetching!* **2.** *n.* a complainer. ♦ *What a kvetch you are!*

L7 [ˈɛl ˈsɛvn̩] **1.** *n.* a **square**; a dull person. (From the square formed when a capital *L* comes before an uncrossed 7.) ♦ *That guy is an L7.* **2.** *mod.* dull; **square.** ♦ *This guy was real, like, you know, L7.*

L8R *mod.* good-bye; later. (L + eight + R. Used in electronic mail and computer forum or news group messages. Not pronounced aloud.) ♦ *Bye, CU L8R.*

L8R G8R Go to **Later, gator.**

label mate *n.* someone who records on the same label (as the speaker). (Record industry.) ♦ *Frank Duke is my label mate, and we like to get together and gossip about the record industry.*

labonza [ləˈbɑnzə] **1.** *n.* the buttocks. ♦ *Good grief, what a gross labonza!* **2.** *n.* the pit of the stomach. ♦ *That kind of beautiful singing really gets you right in the labonza.* **3.** *n.* the belly. ♦ *I feel the effects of last night's celebration in my wallet and in my labonza.*

LABTYD Go to **Life's a bitch, then you die.**

lace 1. *tv.* to add alcohol to coffee or tea; to add alcohol to any food or drink. ♦ *Who laced the punch?* **2.** *tv.* to add a bit of one drug to another; to add drugs to any food or drink. (Drugs.) ♦ *Somebody laced the ice cubes with acid.* **3.** *n.* money. (Underworld.) ♦ *You got any lace in those pockets?*

lacy *mod.* feminine; effeminate. ♦ *The hotel lobby is a little lacy, but it's clean.*

ladies' room *n.* the women's restroom. ♦ *Is there a ladies' room somewhere close?*

lady bear *n.* a female officer of the law. (See also **Smokey (the Bear); mama bear.**) ♦ *This lady bear asks me if I'm going to a fire.*

Lady Snow *n.* cocaine. (Drugs.) ♦ *I spent the afternoon with Lady Snow.*

ladyfinger *n.* a marijuana cigarette. (Drugs.) ♦ *Sam knows how to roll a ladyfinger.*

lady-killer *n.* a man who is very successful with women. ♦ *Bruno is anything but a lady killer.*

lah-di-dah [ˈlɑˈdiˈdɑ] **1.** *mod.* casual; relaxed and uncaring. ♦ *She's not all that calm about her possessions, but she is very lah-di-dah with men.* **2.** *interj.* a jeer; a mocking response. ♦ *So you have a new car! Well, lah-di-dah.*

laid 1. AND **layed** *mod.* drug intoxicated. (See also **laid out.**) ♦ *Man, did I get myself laid.* **2.** *mod.* copulated with. (Usually objectionable.) ♦ *If you come home laid, don't say I didn't warn you.*

laid back 1. *mod.* calm and relaxed. ♦ *Sam is not what I would call laid back.* **2.** *mod.* alcohol or drug intoxicated. ♦ *He's a little laid back and can't come to the phone.*

laid out 1. *mod.* alcohol or drug intoxicated. ♦ *I'm too laid out to go to work today.* **2.** *mod.* well-dressed. ♦ *Look at those silks! Man are you laid out!* **3.** *mod.* knocked down (by a punch). ♦ *He was down, laid out, and the cowboy just stood there panting.*

laid to the bone 1. *mod.* alcohol intoxicated. ♦ *He got himself laid to the bone.* **2.** AND **silked to the bone** *mod.* naked. ♦ *She was laid to the bone and screaming bloody murder when he opened the door.* ♦ *I was all silked to the bone, getting ready for a shower, when the phone rings.*

laine Go to lame.

lambasted *n.* drunk. ♦ *He went out and got himself lambasted, and then he wrecked his car.*

lame AND **laine; lane 1.** *mod.* inept; inadequate; undesirable. ♦ *That guy's so lame, it's pitiful.* **2.** *n.* a **square** person. (Streets. Underworld.) ♦ *Let's see if that lame over there has anything we want in his pockets.* **3.** *n.* an inept person. ♦ *The guy turned out to be a lame, and we had to fire him.*

lame duck 1. *n.* someone who is in the last period of a term in an elective office. ♦ *You can't expect much from a lame duck.* **2.** *mod.* having to do with someone in the last period of a term in an elective office. ♦ *You don't expect much from a lame duck president.*

lamebrain AND **lame-brain 1.** *n.* a fool. ♦ *Please don't call me a lamebrain. I do my best.* **2.** AND **lamebrained** *mod.* foolish. ♦ *No more of your lamebrained ideas!*

lamebrained Go to lamebrain.

lamp *tv.* to look at someone or something. (The "lamps" are the eyes.) ♦ *Here, lamp this tire for a minute. It's low isn't it?*

lamps *n.* the eyes. (Crude.) ♦ *His lamps are closed. He's asleep or dead.*

land a blow 1. *tv.* to strike someone. ♦ *He kept moving, and I found it almost impossible to land a blow.* **2.** *tv.* to make a point. ♦ *I think I really landed a blow with that remark about extortion.*

land a job *tv.* to find a job and be hired. ♦ *As soon as I land a job and start to bring in some money, I'm going to get a stereo.*

landowner ['lændonɚ] *n.* a corpse; a dead person. (See also buy the farm.) ♦ *Now old Mr. Carlson was a landowner for real.*

lane Go to lame.

lap dancer *n.* an exotic dancer who writhes and rubs her posterior on the lap of a seated customer. ♦ *Most of us lap dancers follow rules about no touching.*

lap dancing *n.* sexually stimulating erotic writhing and rubbing of a woman's posterior against the lap of a seated, male customer. ♦ *Our town has outlawed lap dancing.*

lapper *n.* a drunkard. (Alludes to lapping up liquor.) ♦ *The street was empty except for an old lapper staggering home.*

lard *n.* the police. (Streets. Derogatory. See also bacon; pig; pork.) ♦ *If the lard catches you violating your parole, you're through.*

lard ass 1. *n.* someone with very fat buttocks. (Rude and derogatory. See also crisco.) ♦ *Here comes that lard ass again.* **2.** *n.* very large buttocks. (Rude and derogatory.) ♦ *I'm gonna have to do something about this lard ass of mine.*

lardhead 1. *n.* a stupid person. ♦ *What a lardhead! Where are your brains?* **2.** *mod.* foolish. ♦ *Now here's something from the lardhead department.*

large Go to grand.

last roundup *n.* death. (Western.) ♦ *To everyone's surprise, he clutched the wound and faced the last roundup with a smile.*

last straw *n.* the final act or insult; the act that finally calls for a response. ♦ *This is the last straw. I'm calling the police.*

Later. AND **Late.; Laters.** *interj.* Good-bye. ♦ *It's time to cruise. Later.* ♦ *CU. Laters.*

Later, gator. AND **L8R G8R** *phr. & comp. abb.* See you later, alligator. ♦ *C U L8R G8R.*

Laters. *phr.* Good-bye.; See you later. ♦ *See you, Fred. Laters, Henry.*

lathered ['læðɚd] *mod.* alcohol intoxicated. ♦ *The two brothers sat there and got lathered.*

latrine lips [lə'trin 'lɪps] *n.* a person who uses dirty language. ♦ *Hey, latrine lips! Cool it!*

latrine rumor [lə'trin 'rumɚ] *n.* any rumor, especially one that is alleged to spread at the latrine [general toilet facilities]. (Military. See also furphy, scuttlebutt.) ♦ *Somebody started spreading a latrine rumor about the colonel's wife.*

latrine wireless [lə'trin 'waɪɚləs] *n.* the free exchange of information and gossip at the general toilet facilities. (See also grapevine; latrine rumor. This *wireless* alludes to the older term for a radio, not to modern wireless telephony.) ♦ *It came over the latrine wireless this morning. We're all shipping out.*

latrino(gram) [ləˈtrino(græm)] *n.* a latrine rumor. ♦ *There was a latrino yesterday about the colonel and his golf game.*

lats [læts] *n.* the *latissimus dorsi*; the muscles of the back. (Bodybuilding.) ♦ *Your lats are coming along fine. Now let's start working on your delts.*

laugh at the carpet *in.* to vomit; to vomit on a carpet. ♦ *Tom bent over and laughed at the carpet, much to the embarrassment of the entire group.*

laughing academy *n.* a mental hospital; an insane asylum. ♦ *About four years in the laughing academy would get you straightened out.*

laughing soup AND **laughing water** *n.* liquor; champagne. ♦ *This laughing water tickles my nose.* ♦ *Laughing soup flowed like fury at the reception.*

laughing water Go to laughing soup.

launch (one's **lunch**) *tv. & in.* to empty one's stomach; to vomit. ♦ *When I saw that mess, I almost launched my lunch.*

launder *tv.* to conceal the source and nature of stolen or illicitly gotten money by moving it in and out of different financial institutions. (Underworld. See also greenwash.) ♦ *The woman's sole function was to launder the money from drug deals.*

the **law** *n.* the police. ♦ *She is in a little trouble with the law.*

lawn *n.* poor quality marijuana. (Drugs.) ♦ *This isn't good grass; it's lawn.*

lay 1. *tv.* to copulate [with] someone. (Crude. Usually objectionable.) ♦ *She laid him on the spot.* **2.** *n.* a sexual act. (Crude. Usually objectionable.) ♦ *I could use a good lay about now.* **3.** *n.* a person considered as a potential sex partner. (Crude. Usually objectionable.) ♦ *He actually said that she was a good lay.*

lay a guilt trip on SO Go to lay a (heavy) trip on SO.

lay a (heavy) trip on SO **1.** *tv.* to criticize someone. ♦ *There's no need to lay a trip on me. I agree with you.* **2.** *tv.* to confuse or astonish someone. ♦ *After he laid a heavy trip on me about how the company is almost broke, I cleaned out my desk and left.* **3.** AND **lay a guilt trip on someone** *tv.* to attempt to make someone feel very guilty. ♦ *Why do you have to lay a guilt trip on me? Why don't you go to a shrink?* ♦ *Keep your problems to yourself. Don't lay a trip on me!*

lay an egg 1. *tv.* [for someone] to do something bad or poorly. ♦ *I guess I really laid an egg, huh?* **2.** *tv.* [for something] to fail. ♦ *The community theater laid an egg last night with the opening performance of Death of a Salesman.* ♦ *The film was fun to make, but it laid an egg at the box office.* **3.** *tv.* to laugh very hard; to cackle long and loudly. (As if one were a chicken.) ♦ *Half the audience laid an egg when I told this one.*

lay down *in.* to give up. ♦ *Do you expect me to just lay down?*

lay it on the line *tv.* to speak very frankly and directly. ♦ *I'm going to have to lay it on the line with you, I guess.*

lay off (SO/STH) *in.* to stop bothering or harming someone or something; to stop being concerned about someone or something. ♦ *Lay off the booze for a while, why don't ya?*

lay one on Go to tie one on.

lay (some) rubber *tv.* to spin one's car tires when accelerating, leaving black marks on the street. (See also burn rubber.) ♦ *At that age all they want to do is get in the car and lay some rubber.*

lay some sweet lines on SO AND **put some sweet lines on** SO *tv.* to speak kindly to someone; to soft soap someone. ♦ *I just laid some sweet lines on her, and she let me use her car.* ♦ *Don't you put your sweet lines on me, you liar!*

lay SO **out 1.** *tv.* to scold someone severely. (See also laid out.) ♦ *She really laid out the* guy but good. What did he do, rob a bank? **2.** *tv.* to knock someone down with a punch. ♦ *The boxer laid out his opponent with a blow to the head.* **3.** *tv.* to prepare someone for burial. (See also laid out. Not slang.) ♦ *The undertaker did not lay Aunt Fanny out to my satisfaction.*

lay so **out in lavender** *tv.* to scold or rebuke someone severely. ♦ *She really laid him out in lavender for that.*

lay sth **on** so **1.** *tv.* to present a plan or an idea to someone. ♦ *Here is this century's greatest idea. Let me lay it on you.* **2.** *tv.* to attempt to make someone feel guilty about something. ♦ *Don't lay that stuff on me. Face your own problem.*

lay sth **out 1.** *tv.* to spend some amount of money. ♦ *I can't lay that kind of money out every day!* **2.** *tv.* to explain a plan of action or a sequence of events. ♦ *Let me lay it out for you.*

layed Go to laid.

layout 1. *n.* a place; a place to live. (See also setup.) ♦ *How much does a layout like this set you back a month?* **2.** *n.* a floor plan. ♦ *Let's see if the layout is what we want.* **3.** *n.* a scheme. (Underworld.) ♦ *Now here's the layout. Lefty goes in this side, and Ratface comes in the other way.*

lazybones *n.* a lazy person. ♦ *I'm just a lazybones, but I don't eat much.*

lead poisoning *n.* death caused by being shot with a lead bullet. (Underworld.) ♦ *He pifted because of a case of lead poisoning.*

leadfoot *n.* a speeder in an automobile. ♦ *There is a leadfoot driving behind me and wanting to pass.*

leaf *n.* cocaine. (Sometimes with *the*. Cocaine is extracted from the leaves of the *coca* plant.) ♦ *The entire shipment of leaf was seized by the feds.*

lean and mean *mod.* capable and ready for hard, efficient work. ♦ *Ron got himself lean and mean and is ready to play in Saturday's game.*

leapers *n.* amphetamines. (Drugs.) ♦ *You can tell Sam's on leapers. He's wired as hell.*

leather or feather *n.* a choice of beef or chicken for a meal on an airplane. (Contrived.) ♦ *What do the victims get today? Oh, yes, it's leather or feather.*

leave so **cold** *tv.* to leave someone unaffected. ♦ *He said it was dull, and it left him cold.*

leeky store ['liki stor] *n.* a liquor store. (Black. From *liquor*. See also take a leak.) ♦ *Get me some grapes at the leeky store.*

leerics ['lirɪks] *n.* sexually suggestive song lyrics. (From *leer*. Contrived.) ♦ *For those of you out there who go in for leerics, listen carefully to this tune.*

leetspeak AND **hakspeak** *n.* a way of writing or typing on the internet where letters are replaced by number or other symbols. (From *elite speak.*) ♦ *The word is spelled p1$t01, rather than pistol in "leetspeak."*

left coast *n.* the west coast of the U.S. ♦ *There is some weird stuff going on out on the left coast.*

left-handed monkey wrench *n.* a nonexistent tool. (New workers are sometimes sent to fetch nonexistent tools. See also sky hook.) ♦ *Hand me the left-handed monkey wrench, huh?*

leg work *n.* the physical work accompanying a task. ♦ *I don't mind making the phone calls if you do the leg work.*

legal-beagle AND **legal-eagle** ['ligl'bigl] AND 'ligl'igl] *n.* a lawyer. ♦ *I've got a legal-beagle who can get me out of this scrape.*

legal-eagle Go to legal-beagle.

legit [lə'dʒɪt] *mod.* honest; legal. (From *legitimate*.) ♦ *If she's not legit, I won't work with her.*

lemme ['lɛmi] *phr.* let me. (Eye-dialect. Typical spoken English. Used in writing only for effect. Used in the examples of this dictionary.) ♦ *Do you wanna gimme the thingy and lemme go ahead with my work?*

let a fart Go to cut a fart.

Let her rip! AND **Let it roll!** *exclam.* Let it go!; Let it start! ♦ *Time to start. Let her rip!* ♦ *Let's go. Let it roll!*

let it all hang out *tv.* to be yourself, assuming that you generally are not. (What is hanging out has never been clear, but something involving nudity has been suggested.) ♦ *Come on. Relax! Let it all hang out.*

Let it roll! Go to Let her rip!

let off (some) steam Go to blow off (some) steam.

let one Go to cut a fart.

Let's bump this place! *tv.* Let's get out of this place!; Let's leave! ♦ *Time to go. Let's bump this place!*

Let's do lunch (sometime). AND **Let's do the lunch thing.** *sent.* Let us have lunch together sometime. ♦ *Great seeing you, Martin, absolutely great. Let's do lunch.* ♦ *Let's do the lunch thing some time. Right, baby?*

Let's do the lunch thing. Go to Let's do lunch (sometime).

Let's dump. *interj.* Let's go. ♦ *Let's dump. I've still got a lot to do at home tonight.*

Let's have it! *exclam.* Please tell (us) the news! ♦ *What's happened? Let's have it!*

let sth **ride** *tv.* to let something remain as is; to ignore something (for a while). ♦ *Don't bother with it now. Let it ride for a day or two.*

lettuce *n.* money. ♦ *How much lettuce do you have left?*

level best *n.* one's very best effort. ♦ *I will do my level best to find your husband.*

level one's **locks** Go to level the locks.

level the locks AND **level** one's **locks** *tv.* to comb one's hair. (Streets.) ♦ *Just give me a minute to level my locks.*

level with so *in.* to speak truly and honestly with someone. ♦ *Okay, I'm gonna level with you. This thing is a steal at this price!*

Lex *n.* a Lexus automobile. ♦ *This dude's Lex ain't no ghetto sled.*

libber ['lɪbɚ] *n.* a woman who advocates woman's liberation movements; a feminist. (Usually derogatory.) ♦ *She sure sounds like a libber.*

liberate *tv.* to steal something. (Originally military.) ♦ *We liberated a few reams of paper and a box of pens.*

library *n.* a bathroom; an outhouse. (Not a public restroom.) ♦ *John is in the library at the moment.*

a **lick and a promise** *n.* a very casual treatment. ♦ *A lick and a promise isn't enough. Take some time and do it right.*

lick sth **into shape** AND **whip** sth **into shape** *tv.* to put something into good condition, possibly with considerable effort. ♦ *I've got about two days more to lick this place into shape so I can sell it.* ♦ *Whip this manuscript into shape, then we'll talk about publishing it.*

licker *n.* a tongue. (Streets.) ♦ *Yeouchh! I bit my licker.*

lickety-split [lɪkɪdi'splɪt] *mod.* very fast. ♦ *They ran across the field lickety-split.*

licorice pizza *n.* a 33.3 (speed) vinyl record. (Contrived.) ♦ *Why don't you replace all these silly licorice pizzas with real CDs?*

licorice stick ['lɪkrɪʃ stɪk] *n.* a clarinet. (Jazz musicians.) ♦ *Man, can he play the licorice stick.*

lid 1. *n.* an eyelid. ♦ *Her lids began to close, and the professor raised his voice to a roar.* **2.** *n.* one half to one ounce of marijuana. (Drugs. An amount that will fill a Prince Albert tobacco can lid. Often plural.) ♦ *It looks like a matchbox to me. Why do they call it a lid?* **3.** *n.* a hat. ♦ *Where did you get that silly lid?*

lid poppers Go to lid proppers.

lid proppers AND **lid poppers** *n.* amphetamine tablets or capsules. (Drugs. Refers to the eyelids.) ♦ *Kelly has to have a couple of lid proppers each morning.*

lie doggo ['laɪ 'dɔgo] *in.* to remain unrecognized (for a long time). (See also doggo. Old, but Standard English.) ♦ *If* *you don't find the typos now, they will lie doggo until the next edition.*

lie like a rug *in.* to tell lies shamelessly. ♦ *He says he didn't take the money, but he's lying like a rug.*

Life's a bitch, then you die. AND **LABTYD** *sent. & comp. abb.* Life is tough, a general lament. ♦ *LABTYD. How depressing.* ♦ *God, I hate this disease. Life's a bitch, then you die.*

lifejacket *n.* a condom. ♦ *Be sure and take a lifejacket with you!*

lifer ['laɪfɚ] *n.* someone who is attached to an institution for life, such as a lifetime soldier or a prisoner serving a life sentence. (Prisons and military.) ♦ *Most of the lifers are kept in this cell block.*

LIFO *phr.* last in, first out. (Computers. Acronym. Refers to the order of data put in and returned from the processor.) ♦ *I can't remember whether the stack is LIFO or FIFO.*

lift 1. *n.* the potency of alcohol in liquor. ♦ *Now, this imported stuff has enough lift to raise the dead.* **2.** *n.* a brief spiritual or ego-lifting occurrence. ♦ *Your kind words have given me quite a lift.* **3.** AND **lift-up** *n.* drug euphoria; a rush. (Drugs.) ♦ *The lift-up from the shot jarred her bones.* **4.** *tv.* to steal something. ♦ *She had lifted this ring. We found it on her when we arrested her.* **5.** *tv.* to take something away. ♦ *It was his third offense, so they lifted his license.* **6.** *n.* a tall heel on shoes that makes someone seem taller. (Usually plural.) ♦ *I feel better in my lifts.* **7.** *n.* a surgical face-lift. ♦ *He had a lift on his vacation, but his face still looked two sizes too big.* **8.** *n.* a device—worn under the hair at the temples—that provides some of the effects of a surgical face-lift. ♦ *Do you think she's wearing a lift?* **9.** *n.* a ride; transportation. ♦ *Would you like a lift over to your apartment?*

lift one's **elbow** Go to bend one's elbow.

lifted *mod.* drunk; high. ♦ *He was acting a little lifted. He only had twelve beers.*

lift-up Go to lift.

light 1. *mod.* alcohol intoxicated. ♦ *I began to feel a little light along about the fourth beer.* **2.** *n.* an eye. (Crude. Usually plural.) ♦ *You want I should poke your lights out?* **3.** *n.* a police car. ♦ *A couple of lights turned the corner just as the robbers were pulling away.*

light bulb *n.* a pregnant woman. (Jocular. Refers to the shape of a pregnant woman.) ♦ *Who's the light bulb on the sofa?*

light into so Go to sail into so.

light stuff 1. *n.* low-proof liquor. ♦ *Poor Sam is trying to cut down by drinking the light stuff. He drinks twice as much, though.* **2.** *n.* marijuana and nonaddictive drugs. ♦ *Sure, it's innocent. Sure, they're just kids. Do you know what kids do when they get through with the light stuff? They do coke, they shoot H., and they do the big one somewhere in an alley!*

lightning rod *n.* someone, something, or an issue that is certain to draw criticism. ♦ *Why write such a boastful introduction to your book. I will just be a lightning rod for criticism.*

lights Go to light (sense 2).

lights out 1. *n.* bedtime. ♦ *It's lights out, kids. Radios off, too!* **2.** *n.* death; time to die. (Underworld.) ♦ *It's lights out for you, chum.*

lightweight 1. *mod.* inconsequential. ♦ *This is a fairly lightweight matter.* **2.** *n.* an inconsequential person; someone who accomplishes very little. ♦ *Don't worry about her. She's just a lightweight.*

like 1. *interj.* an emphatic or meaningless word that, when said frequently, marks the speaker as speaking in a very casual or slangy mode. (See also like, you know. Used in writing only for effect.) ♦ *This is, like, so silly!* **2.** *interj.* a particle meaning roughly *saying.* (Always with some form of *be.* Never used in formal writing.) ♦ *And I'm like, "Well, you should have put your hat on!"*

like a bat out of hell *mod.* very fast or sudden. (Use caution with hell.) ♦ *The cat took off like a bat out of hell.*

like a million (dollars) *mod.* very good or well. (Usually with *feel.*) ♦ *This old buggy runs like a million dollars.*

like a ton of bricks *mod.* like something very ponderous and heavy. ♦ *Hitting the back end of that truck was like hitting a ton of bricks.*

like crazy AND **like mad** *mod.* furiously; very much, fast, many, or actively. ♦ *Look at those people on the bank. They're catching fish like mad!* ♦ *I'm running like mad and still can't catch up.*

like death warmed over *mod.* horrible; deathlike. ♦ *A tall, black-garbed gentleman lay there, looking like death warmed over.*

like gangbusters *mod.* with great excitement and fury. (From the phrase *Come on like gangbusters*, a radio show that *came on* with lots of sirens and gunshots.) ♦ *She works like gangbusters and gets the job done.*

Like hell! *exclam.* That is not true!; I do not believe you! (Use caution with *hell.*) ♦ *You're going to a Dead concert! Like hell!*

Like I care. *phr.* You are telling me this news like it matters to me. (Nonchalant and sarcastic.) ♦ *So, there's problems in South America. Like I care.*

Like I really give a shit! AND **LIRGAS** *exclam. & comp. abb.* I really don't care. (Usually objectionable.) ♦ *You are telling me this why? LIRGAS!*

Like it or lump it! *exclam.* Give up!; Shut up!; Accept it or go away! (See also **Lump it!**) ♦ *If you don't want to do it my way, like it or lump it!*

Like it's such a big deal. *phr.* You are making an incredible fuss over some minor issue. ♦ *So I broke the table. Like it's such a big deal.*

like mad Go to **like crazy**.

like nobody's business *mod.* very well; very much; very fast. ♦ *She can sing like nobody's business. What a set of pipes!*

like stink *mod.* rapidly. (As fast as a smell spreads.) ♦ *Those kids moved through the whole test like stink. Real eager-beavers.*

like the white on rice AND **as the white on rice** *phr.* as close as anything can be. ♦ *Those two are really close—like the white on rice.*

like there was no tomorrow *mod.* as if there would never be another opportunity. ♦ *She was drinking booze like there was no tomorrow.*

like, you know *interj.* a combining of the expressions like and you know. (Never used in formal writing.) ♦ *She is, well, like, you know, PG.*

lily-livered *mod.* cowardly. ♦ *That lily-livered guy is up hiding under his bed till this blows over.*

limbo Go to **lumbo**.

limejuicer AND **limey** *n.* a British sailor; and British citizen, typically a male. (The first one is old. Both are a little derogatory.) ♦ *Some limey answered the telephone and I could hardly understand what she was saying.*

limey Go to **limejuicer**.

(limp) dishrag *n.* a totally helpless person; a cowardly and spineless person. ♦ *He's sweet, but he's a dishrag.*

limpdick *n.* a weak or ineffective male. ♦ *Stand up for yourself. Don't be such a limpdick.*

line 1. *n.* a story or argument; a story intended to seduce someone. (See also **lines**.) ♦ *Don't feed me that line. Do you think I was born yesterday?* **2.** AND **rail** *n.* a dose of finely cut cocaine arranged in a line, ready for insufflation or snorting. ♦ *Let's you and me go do some lines, okay?* ♦ *The addict usually "snorts" one or two of these "rails" with some sort of a tube.*

line one's **own pocket(s)** *tv.* to make money for oneself in a greedy or dishonest fashion. ♦ *They are interested in lining their pockets first and serving the people second.*

lines *n.* words; conversation. (See also **line**.) ♦ *We tossed some lines back and forth for a while and then split.*

lineup *n.* a row of suspects arranged at a police station so that a witness can identify one of them. (Underworld.) ♦ *When they round up all the likely suspects and put them in the lineup, they always stick in a desk sergeant to spy on the rest.*

lingo *n.* language; special vocabulary. ♦ *When you catch on to the lingo, everything becomes clear.*

linkrot *n.* the gradual fading away of URL links in a web page. (The URLs are replaced by newer addresses or simply are deleted.) ♦ *After a month or two, linkrot sets in and your links become deadends, one by one.*

lion's share *n.* the largest portion. ♦ *I earn a lot, but the lion's share goes for taxes.*

lip 1. *tv. & in.* to kiss someone intimately. ♦ *The two of them were in the corner, lipping intently.* **2.** *n.* a lawyer. (Underworld. See also mouth.) ♦ *So I brought in my lip, and he got me off the rap.* **3.** AND **fat lip** *n.* back talk; impudent talk. ♦ *Don't give me any more of your lip!* ♦ *I've had enough of your fat lip!*

lip gloss *n.* lies; deception; exaggeration; BS. (From the name of a lipstick-like cosmetic.) ♦ *Everything he says is just lip gloss. He is a liar at heart.*

LIQ *n.* a liquor store. (Initialism or acronym.) ♦ *Let's stop at the LIQ and get some berries.*

liquefied *mod.* alcohol intoxicated. ♦ *Ten beers and I am absolutely liquefied!*

liquid cork *n.* a medicine that stops diarrhea. ♦ *This liquid cork isn't so bad if you get it good and cold before you take it.*

liquid laugh *n.* vomit. ♦ *If you drink much more, you're gonna come out with a liquid laugh.*

liquid lunch *n.* a lunch consisting of alcoholic drinks. ♦ *Sounds like the boss had another liquid lunch again today.*

liquidate *tv.* to kill someone. (Underworld.) ♦ *They used a machine gun to liquidate a few troublesome characters.*

LIRGAS Go to Like I really give a shit!

listen up *in.* to listen carefully. (Usually a command.) ♦ *Now, listen up! This is important.*

lit 1. *n.* literature, as a school subject. ♦ *I'm flunking English lit again.* **2.** AND **lit up** *mod.* drunk. ♦ *Todd was lit up like a Christmas tree at our office party.* ♦ *He's lit and can't drive home.*

lit up Go to lit.

literally *mod.* figuratively; absolutely. (Literally is frequently used colloquially for emphasis and not with its literal meaning.) ♦ *When I saw him I literally died!* ♦ *There were literally thousands at our house for the Super Bowl.* ♦ *The flu was so bad that I literally coughed my head off.*

little black book *n.* a book containing the names and addresses of acquaintances who are potential dates, usually put together by men. ♦ *Am I in your little black book, or can you already tell that I wouldn't go out with you?*

little boy blue *n.* a (male) police officer. ♦ *Little boy blue is coming this way, and he's mad.*

little boys' room *n.* the boys' restroom; the men's restroom. ♦ *Can you tell me where the little boys' room is?*

little girls' room *n.* the girls' restroom; the women's restroom. ♦ *Can you please tell me where the little girls' room is?*

(little) pinkie AND **(little) pinky** *n.* the littlest finger on either hand. ♦ *Ouch! I smashed my pinky.*

little shit *n.* a stupid and insignificant person. (Rude and derogatory. Usually refers to a male.) ♦ *What's a little shit like him doing running a big company like this one?*

live *mod.* cool; great. ♦ *Everything's live! No problem!*

(live) wire *n.* an energetic and vivacious person. ♦ *With a wire like Taylor in charge, things will get done, that's for sure.*

liveware ['laɪvwer] *n.* the human component of computer use. (Patterned on *software* and *hardware*.) ♦ *If I don't get some sleep, you're going to see a liveware crash.*

living chilly *in.* living well with lots of diamonds. (Refers to ice, diamonds.) ♦ *That dude's livin' chilly, fo shizzle. He's so iced out!*

Living large. *phr.* Doing okay. (The response to How ya living?) ♦ *I'm living large. How you doing?*

lizzle a wild card word for words beginning with *L*, such as *lad, like, lighter.* (Streets. Also for other words with initial *L*.) ♦ *Well, my lizzle, you ready to go?*

load 1. *n.* as much liquor as one can hold. (See also loaded.) ♦ *Harry had quite a load of booze.* **2.** *n.* a drink of liquor. ♦ *Can I have a load from your bottle?* **3.** *n.* a dose of drugs; an injection of drugs. (See also loaded. Drugs.) ♦ *She shoots a load every day or two.* **4.** *n.* a drug supply; a stash. (Drugs.) ♦ *If his load dwindles, he gets more easily.* **5.** *n.* a large purchase of heroin. (Drugs.) ♦ *I've scored a load that'll last me a few days.* **6.** *n.* an (old) car. (See also heap.) ♦ *Whose junky old load is that parked in front of the house?*

loaded 1. *mod.* alcohol or drug intoxicated. ♦ *If you're loaded, don't drive.* **2.** *mod.* spiked with liquor; containing much alcohol. ♦ *There's a little rum in the eggnog, but it's certainly not what I would call loaded.* **3.** *mod.* having all available accessories. (Said of a car.) ♦ *Did you want to see a car that's loaded, or is this to be a budget car?* **4.** *mod.* wealthy; loaded with money. ♦ *Mr. Wilson is loaded, but he is also generous with his money.*

loaded for bear 1. *mod.* alcohol intoxicated. ♦ *He's been drinking mule since dawn, and he's loaded for bear.* **2.** *mod.* ready for the hardest problems. ♦ *I'm loaded for bear, and that's good because this is going to be a rough day.* **3.** *mod.* very angry. ♦ *I had been loaded for bear when I came into the room, and I left as meek as a lamb.*

loaded to the barrel Go to loaded to the gills.

loaded to the gills AND **loaded to the barrel** *mod.* alcohol intoxicated. ♦ *He's loaded to the gills. Couldn't see a hole in*

a ladder. ♦ *Those guys are loaded to the barrel and are getting mean.*

loady AND **loadie** ['lodi] *n.* a drinker or drug user. (Teens and collegiate. One who gets loaded frequently.) ♦ *I hear that Willy is a loady. Is that true?*

local yokel ['lokl 'jokl] *n.* a local resident of a rural place. (Mildly derogatory.) ♦ *One of the local yokels helped me change the tire.*

locked down *mod.* [of a person] in jail. ♦ *Mooshoo got himself locked down.*

loco ['loko] *mod.* crazy. (From Spanish.) ♦ *Who is that loco kid jumping up and down in the front seat?*

log *in.* to defecate. (See also dog-log.) ♦ *Bubba's in the crapper, logging.*

LOK *comp. abb.* (a) lack of knowledge. ♦ *You're not stupid, just suffering from LOK.*

LOL *interj.* laughing out loud. (Indicates that one is laughing in response to a previous remark. Used in electronic mail and computer forum or news group messages. Not pronounced aloud.) ♦ *I'm LOL about the last remark you made.*

lollapalooza [lɑləpə'luzə] **1.** *n.* something very big; something wondrous. ♦ *Look at that bump on your head. That's a lollapalooza!* **2.** *n.* a big lie. ♦ *What a lollapalooza! You expect me to believe that?*

lommix Go to lummox.

lone wolf *n.* a man who stays to himself. ♦ *Fred is sort of a lone wolf until he has a few drinks.*

long arm of the law *n.* the police; the law. (See also arm.) ♦ *The long arm of the law is going to tap you on the shoulder some day, Lefty.*

long bread AND **long green** *n.* money; much money. ♦ *Man, that must have cost you some long bread!* ♦ *How much long green I gotta lay down for that car?*

long dozen *n.* thirteen; a baker's dozen. ♦ *They used to give you a long dozen in that bakery.*

long green Go to long bread.

long knife 1. *n.* an assassin. (Underworld.) ♦ *Some long knife showed up, but Marty took him out before he made his move.* **2.** *n.* a destroyer; a hatchet man. ♦ *One of his long knives came over to pressure us into cooperating.*

long shot *n.* a wild guess; an attempt at something that has little chance of succeeding. ♦ *You shouldn't expect a long shot to pay off.*

long story short *phr.* to make a long story short. ♦ *Then the guy comes over, and—long story short—"You got a match?"*

Long time no see. *phr.* I haven't seen you in a long time. ♦ *Hey, John! Long time no see!*

longhair 1. *n.* a highbrow with long hair; especially a musician. ♦ *There were a few longhairs at the bar, but none of the regulars.* **2.** *mod.* highbrow; [of music] classical. ♦ *Longhair stuff like symphonies and art galleries bores me to tears.* **3.** *n.* a hippy; a long-haired youth of the 1960s. (Usually derogatory.) ♦ *There are fewer longhairs around here than there were in the sixties.*

long-tall-Sally *n.* a tall girl or woman. ♦ *Isn't she a gorgeous long-tall-Sally?*

loo *n.* toilet. (Originally and primarily British.) ♦ *I gotta use the loo. Be with you in a minute.*

look after number one *in.* to take care of oneself first. (See also **number one.**) ♦ *It's a good idea to look after number one. Who else will?*

Look alive! *exclam.* Move faster!; Look and act alert! ♦ *There's work to be done! Look alive!*

Look (at) what the cat dragged in! *imperative* Well, look who has just arrived! ♦ *Look what the cat dragged in! I thought you would never get here.*

Look who's talking! *exclam.* You are just as guilty!; You are just as much at fault! ♦ *Look who's talking. You were there before I was.*

looker Go to **(good) looker.**

a **look-see** *n.* a look; a visual examination. ♦ *Take a look-see at this one and see if you like it.*

loony AND **looney; loonie 1.** *n.* a crazy person. (From *lunatic.*) ♦ *I'm beginning to feel like a loonie the longer I stay around here.* **2.** *mod.* crazy. ♦ *That is a loony idea. Forget it.* **3.** *mod.* alcohol intoxicated. ♦ *She's acting a little loonie. Let's get her home before she's sick.*

loony bin *n.* an insane asylum; a mental hospital. ♦ *Today's loony bins are far different from those of just a few decades ago.*

looped AND **loopy** *mod.* alcohol intoxicated. ♦ *She got loopy very quickly and had to be helped to a chair.*

loop-legged *mod.* alcohol intoxicated. ♦ *She has this strange tendency to get a little loop-legged when she has four or five drinks.*

loopy Go to **looped.**

loose *mod.* very drunk. ♦ *Mary was a little loose and had to be driven home.*

loose cannon *n.* a loudmouth; a braggart. ♦ *As it turned out, he's not just a loose cannon. He makes sense.*

loot 1. *n.* stolen goods; stolen money. ♦ *Where's the loot? I want my piece.* **2.** *n.* money in general. ♦ *It takes too much loot to eat at that restaurant.*

Lord love a duck! *exclam.* Wow! ♦ *Lord love a duck, I'm tired!*

lo-res Go to **low-res.**

lorg [lorg] *n.* a stupid person. ♦ *Why is Frank such a lorg? Can't he get with it?*

lose a bundle *tv.* to lose a lot of money. (See also **bundle.** Compare this with **make a bundle.**) ♦ *Don lost a bundle on that land purchase.*

lose (all) one's marbles *tv.* to become crazy. (See also **have all one's marbles.**) ♦ *Have you lost all your marbles?*

lose it 1. *tv.* to empty one's stomach; to vomit. (Collegiate.) ♦ *Oh, God! I think I'm going to lose it!* **2.** *tv.* to get angry; to lose one's temper; lose control. ♦ *I sat there calmly, biting my lip to keep from losing it.*

lose one's **cool** *tv.* to lose control; to lose one's temper. (Compare this with **keep** one's **cool**.) ♦ *Now, don't lose your cool. Relax.*

lose one's **doughnuts** Go to blow one's doughnuts.

lose one's **grip** AND **lose** one's **hold** *tv.* to lose one's control over something. ♦ *When I begin to lose my grip, I will just quit.* ♦ *The old man is clearly losing his hold.*

lose one's **hold** Go to lose one's grip.

lose one's **lunch** Go to blow (one's) lunch.

lose one's **shirt** *tv.* to go broke; to lose everything of value, even one's shirt. ♦ *I lost my shirt on that bank deal.*

loser ['luzɚ] *n.* an inept person; an undesirable or annoying person; a social failure. ♦ *Those guys are all losers. They'll never amount to anything.*

lost cause *n.* a hopeless or worthless thing or person. ♦ *The whole play began to wash out during the second act. It was a lost cause by the third.*

lost in the sauce *mod.* alcohol intoxicated and bewildered. ♦ *Sally got lost in the sauce at the party and made quite a spectacle of herself.*

lost-and-found badge *n.* a military identification tag; a military dog tag. (From the Persian Gulf War.) ♦ *My father still keeps his lost-and-found badge from the Korean War.*

Lots of luck! 1. *exclam.* Good luck! ♦ *Lots of luck in your new job!* **2.** *exclam.* You don't have a chance!; Good luck, you'll need it! (Sarcastic.) ♦ *Think you stand a chance? Lots of luck!*

loudmouth *n.* a person who talks too much or too loudly. ♦ *I try not to be a loudmouth, but I sometimes get carried away.*

louse [laʊs] *n.* a thoroughly repellent person, usually a male. ♦ *You can be such a louse!*

louse sth **up** *tv.* to botch something up. ♦ *Please don't louse the typewriter ribbon up this time.*

lousy ['laʊzi] *mod.* rotten; poor; bad. ♦ *This mushy stuff is lousy. Do I have to eat it?*

lousy with so/sth *mod.* having lots of someone or something. (Like an infestation of lice.) ♦ *Tiffany is lousy with jewels and furs, but she's got bad teeth.*

love bombs *n.* affirmations of affection. ♦ *These two were dropping love bombs on each other, even though they hate each other's guts.*

(love) handles *n.* rolls of fat around the waist that can be held on to during lovemaking. ♦ *Ted worked out daily, trying to get rid of his love handles.*

Love it! Go to (I) love it!

Love you! *exclam.* You are great! (Almost meaningless patter.) ♦ *See ya around, Martin. Let's do lunch! Love ya! Bye-bye.*

love-in 1. *n.* an event during the 1960s where one or more couples made love in a public place. ♦ *My uncle was at one of those love-ins, and he said if anything was going on, it was going on under blankets.* **2.** *n.* an event in the 1960s where everyone became euphoric—with the help of marijuana—about love and respect for their fellow humans. ♦ *Everyone at the annual company love-in was throwing love bombs around at each other.*

low blow *n.* an unfair blow. (See also hit (so) below the belt.) ♦ *Coming in like that unannounced was a pretty low blow.*

low five *n.* the slapping of hands at waist level as a greeting. (Compare this with high five.) ♦ *The two eight-year-olds tried to give each other a low five, but they both hurt their hands.*

low rent 1. *n.* a low person; someone without grace or spirit. (Also a rude term of address.) ♦ *Look, low rent, where is what you owe me?* **2.** *mod.* cheap; unfashionable. ♦ *This place is strictly low rent.*

lowbrow ['lobraʊ] **1.** *n.* a nonintellectual person; an anti-intellectual person. ♦ *Some lowbrow came in and made a stink about not being able to find any Gene Autry records.* **2.** *mod.* nonintellectual; anti-intellectual. ♦ *I like my lowbrow music and my lowbrow friends!*

lowdown 1. *mod.* rotten; bad. ♦ *What a dirty, lowdown thing to do.* **2.** *n.* the facts on something; the scuttlebutt about something. ♦ *What's the lowdown on that funny statue in the park?*

low-key *mod.* not obvious; not hyped. ♦ *Let's try to keep this low-key so as not to upset the family.*

low-life 1. *n.* a low person; a repellent person. ♦ *This low-life smells like bacon.* **2.** *mod.* mean; belligerent. ♦ *We don't need any low-life characters around here.*

low-res AND **lo-res** ['lo'rɛz] *mod.* poor; unpleasant. (From *low resolution* in a computer terminal. Compare this with **high-res.**) ♦ *The party is lo-res. Let's cruise.*

LSD *n.* lysergic acid diethylamide, a hallucinogenic drug. (Initialism. Drugs. A mainstay of the 1960s and 1970s drug culture.) ♦ *LSD isn't the problem it used to be, but it's far from gone.*

LT *in.* living together. (Initialism and euphemism.) ♦ *They have been LT for some time.*

lube *n.* butter. ♦ *Pass the lube, will ya, huh?*

lubricated *mod.* alcohol intoxicated. ♦ *He's not fit to talk to until he's lubricated a bit.*

lubrication *n.* liquor. ♦ *Willy has had a little too much lubrication.*

lucci *n.* money. (Possibly from *lucre,* "money, reward" as in filthy lucre.) ♦ *Can you loan me some of that lucci?*

luck of the draw *n.* the results of chance; the lack of any choice. ♦ *The team was assembled by chance. It was just the luck of the draw that we could work so well together.*

luck out *in.* to be fortunate; to strike it lucky. ♦ *I really lucked out when I ordered the duck. It's excellent.*

lucky dog *n.* a lucky person, perhaps undeserving. (Also a term of address. Older than the more recent use of **dogg** = buddy, guy.) ♦ *Bart was a lucky dog because he won the football pool.*

lude *n.* a capsule of Quaalude, a tranquilizer. (Drugs.) ♦ *I don't know what he gave me. Mary said it was a "lude" or something.*

lug [ləg] *n.* a stupid male. (Possibly akin to the sense of "pull" = one who pulls or drags something as a laborer.) ♦ *Is this lug bothering you, lady?*

lughead *n.* a stupid person. (Also a term of address.) ♦ *Hey, lughead! Watch where you are going.*

a lulu *n.* someone or something extraordinary. ♦ *Man, that car's a lulu!*

lumbo AND **limbo** ['ləmbo AND 'lɪmbo] *n.* Colombian marijuana. (Drugs. See also **lum(s).**) ♦ *He showed up with a bag of lumbo.*

lummox AND **lommix; lummux** ['ləmaks AND 'ləməks] *n.* a heavy, awkward, stupid person, usually a male. ♦ *Sam is what you would call a lummox—but not to his face, of course.*

lummux Go to lummox.

lump *n.* a stupid clod of a person. ♦ *I am not a lump! I am just sedate and pensive.*

Lump it! *exclam.* Forget it!; Go away! (See also Like it or lump it!) ♦ *Well, you can just lump it!*

lumpus ['ləmpəs] *n.* a stupid oaf. ♦ *Is this lumpus giving you any trouble, ma'am?*

lum(s) [ləm(z)] *n.* cannabis from Colombia. (The *lum* is based on the misspelling *Columbia.*) ♦ *Mooshoo preferred lums, but he would take what he could get.*

lunching *mod.* absent minded; giddy; out to lunch. ♦ *What a giddy twit. He's so lunching!*

lung-butter *n.* vomit. ♦ *God, you got lung-butter on my shoe!*

lunger *n.* a large and nasty mass of phlegm coughed up from the lungs and spat out. (See also **nose-lunger.**) ♦ *Wayne loved to pretend that he was going to plant a lunger on somebody's shoe.*

lurk *in.* to read computer newsgroups or forums without ever making a comment. ♦ *I've been lurking for a few weeks but just have to get in a few comments.*

lurker *n.* someone who reads the messages in an Internet new group without out responding or participating. (Sometimes considered derogatory.) ♦ *These lurkers read everything but never contribute.*

lush 1. *n.* liquor. ♦ *Who's bringing the lush to the party?* **2.** AND **lush up** *in.* to drink alcohol to excess. ♦ *We sat lushing up for an hour waiting for the plane.* ♦ *I just want to get my feet up and lush for a while.* **3.** *n.* a drunkard. ♦ *There were four confirmed lushes at the party, but they all passed out and didn't bother us much.*

lush up Go to lush.

M

M. and M.s *n.* capsules of Seconal, a barbiturate. (From the brand name of a type of brightly colored candy pellets.) ♦ *Is there somewhere around here I can get some M. and M.s?*

Ma Bell *n.* AT&T, the American Telephone and Telegraph Company; any telephone company. (Formerly, AT&T was the only provider of local telephone service. See also **Baby Bell**.) ♦ *Ma Bell is still one of the largest firms in the nation.*

mañana [məˈnjɑnə] *mod.* tomorrow; in the future, not now. (Spanish.) ♦ *It's always mañana with you. Isn't there any "today" or "now" in your vocabulary?* ♦ *He's a mañana kind of guy. You know—real laid back.*

mac out *in.* to overeat, especially the type of food served at McDonald's fast-food restaurants. (From the Big Mac sandwich. See also **Big Mac attack**. See also **blimp out; pig out; pork out; scarf out**.) ♦ *I've been in Europe for a month, and I just want to get home and mac out.*

mace SO's **face** [mes…] *tv.* to do something drastic to someone, such as spraying mace in the face. (Chemical Mace is a brand of tear gas sold in pressurized cans for personal protection.) ♦ *I look at him, and suddenly I just want to mace his face or something.*

macho [ˈmɑtʃo] **1.** *mod.* masculine; virile. (From Spanish. Used as a derogation by feminists.) ♦ *Does the world really need one more macho man?* **2.** *n.* a masculine or virile male. ♦ *He's such a macho. He even chews tobacco.*

Mac(k) [mæk] *n.* a generic name for a man. (Also a term of address.) ♦ *Look, Mac, you want to make some big money?*

mack *n.* a pimp. (From *mackerel*, a form of which once had the meaning "broker.") ♦ *This gal's mack was slapping her silly when the police came.*

mack daddy *n.* a man who is popular with the ladies. ♦ *Sam is a real mack daddy. Sure knows how to treat the ladies.*

mack on SO **1.** *in.* to make a sexual proposition to someone. ♦ *You try to mack on anything that wears a skirt!* **2.** *in.* to make out with someone. ♦ *Sam is in the back room macking on Mary.*

mad enough to eat nails *mod.* (See also **eat nails**.) ♦ *After we got home, she was mad enough to eat nails.*

mad money *n.* money to be spent in a frivolous fashion. ♦ *This is my mad money, and I'll do with it as I please.*

madam *n.* the female keeper of a brothel. ♦ *The cops led the madam away, followed by a parade of you-know-whats.*

Madison Avenue 1. *n.* the style or image of the major U.S. center for advertising agencies. (The agencies are located on Madison Avenue in New York City.) ♦ *It's too much like Madison Avenue. We want a calm, sincere mood.* **2.** *mod.* in the manner of intense promotion; propaganda like. ♦ *More and more people simply do not respond to Madison Avenue hype.*

mag *n.* magazine. ♦ *I gotta stop and get a computer mag.*

maggot 1. *n.* a cigarette. (Probably a play on **faggot**.) ♦ *Can I bum a maggot off of you?* **2.** *n.* a low and wretched person; a vile person. ♦ *You maggot! Take your hands off me!*

maggot(t)y *mod.* alcohol intoxicated; very drunk. (A play on rotten.) ♦ *Rotten, hell. They were absolutely maggotty!*

magic bullet Go to silver bullet.

magic mushrooms AND **sacred mushrooms** *n.* mushrooms of the genus *Psilocybe*, which cause visions or hallucinations when eaten. (Drugs.) ♦ *Magic mushrooms are okay because they are natural, or something like that.* ♦ *They sometimes call peyote cactus buds, the "sacred mushrooms."*

magpie *n.* a person who chatters; a person who annoys others by chattering. ♦ *Why do those horrendous magpies all go to the same movies I go to?*

(ma)hoska [məˈhɑskə] **1.** *n.* narcotics; any contraband. (Underworld.) ♦ *The tall pinstriper asked where he could get some mahoska.* **2.** *n.* energy; strength; moxie. ♦ *The guy's got mahoska and guts!*

mail *n.* money. ♦ *The bills are due. I need some mail.*

main drag *n.* the main street. ♦ *The main drag is solid with traffic on Saturday nights.*

main squeeze 1. *n.* one's boss; the person in charge. ♦ *The main squeeze has a lot of responsibility.* **2.** *n.* one's steady girlfriend or boyfriend. (Possibly related to crush.) ♦ *My main squeeze is coming over to talk tonight.*

main stash *n.* the home of a drug user described in terms of where one's major store of drugs is kept. (Drugs. See also stash.) ♦ *My main stash is on Maple, but I'm usually not there.*

major *mod.* excellent; serious; severe. (Collegiate.) ♦ *This rally is, like, major!* ♦ *Nick is a major dweeb.*

majorly *mod.* very. ♦ *He got majorly toasted and ended up staying in the park all night.*

make 1. *tv.* to identify someone. (Underworld.) ♦ *We tried to make him down at the station but came up with nothing.* **2.** *n.* an identification. (Underworld.) ♦ *We ran a make on her. She's got two priors.* **3.** *tv.* to arrive at a place; to cover a distance. ♦ *We made forty miles in thirty minutes.* **4.** *tv.* to achieve a specific speed. ♦ *This buggy will make twice the speed of the old one.*

make a boo-boo *tv.* to make an error. (See also boo-boo.) ♦ *Everybody makes a boo-boo every now and then.*

make a bundle AND **make a pile** *tv.* to make a lot of money. (See also bundle.) ♦ *She made a bundle on a website investment.* ♦ *I want to buy a few stocks and make a pile in a few years.*

make a federal case out of sth *tv.* to exaggerate the importance of an error; to overdo something. ♦ *Do you have to make a federal case out of everything?*

make a killing *tv.* to make an enormous profit; to become an enormous success. ♦ *I wanted to make a killing as a banker, but it didn't work out.*

Make a lap! *exclam.* to sit down. ♦ *Hey, make a lap and get out of the way!*

make a mountain AND **pitch a tent** *n.* to have a morning erection that raises the covers; to have an erection that makes a bulge in one's clothing; to get an erection. ♦ *Bobby makes a mountain almost every morning.* ♦ *When I was in the hospital, I was afraid I would pitch a tent in the morning.*

make a pig of oneself *tv.* to overeat; to take more of something than anyone else gets; to be selfish. ♦ *I have a tendency to make a pig of myself at affairs like this.*

make a pile Go to make a bundle.

make a score *tv.* to do a criminal act: to buy or sell drugs, to rob someone, to perform a scam. (Underworld.) ♦ *We made a score with that bank job in Adamsville, didn't we?*

make a stink (about so/sth**)** Go to raise a stink (about so/sth).

make book on sth *tv.* to make or accept bets on something. ♦ *Well, she might. But I wouldn't make book on it.*

make drain babies *n.* to masturbate (male). (The genetic material goes down the drain. Clever but contrived.) ♦ *My so-*

cial life stinks. I'm limited to making drain babies.

make for somewhere *in.* to set out for somewhere; to run or travel to somewhere. ♦ *Marlowe made for the stairs, but two shots rang out, and he knew it was all over for Mary.*

make hamburger out of so/sth AND **make mincemeat out of** so/sth *tv.* to beat someone or something to a pulp; to destroy someone or something. ♦ *The puppy made mincemeat out of my paper.* ♦ *Say that again and I'll make hamburger out of you!*

make it 1. *tv.* to achieve one's goals. (See also make (it) big.) ♦ *I can see by looking around this room that you have really made it.* **2.** *tv.* to copulate [with] someone. ♦ *There was no doubt in his mind that those bedroom eyes were telling him their owner wanted to make it.*

make (it) big *tv. & in.* to become successful, especially financially. ♦ *I always knew that someday I would make it big.*

make it hot for so *tv.* to make things difficult for someone; to put someone under pressure. (Note the variation in the examples.) ♦ *The cops were making it hot for him, so he blew town.*

Make it snappy! *exclam.* Hurry up!; Make it fast! ♦ *Make it snappy, Fred. The cops are headed up the walk now.*

make like a tree and leave *in.* to leave; to depart. (A pun on the *leaf* of a tree.) ♦ *Hey, Jane. Don't you have an appointment somewhere? Why don't you make like a tree and leave?*

make like so/sth *in.* to act like someone or something. ♦ *Why don't you make like a bunny and run away? Beat it!*

make mincemeat out of so/sth Go to make hamburger out of so/sth.

Make my day! *exclam.* Go ahead, do what you are going to do, and I will be very happy to do what I have to do! (A cliché said typically by a movie police officer who has a gun pointed at a criminal. The police officer wants the criminal to do something that will justify pulling the

trigger, which the police officer will do with pleasure. Used in real life in any context, and especially in sarcasm.) ♦ *Move a muscle! Go for your gun! Go ahead, make my day!*

Make no mistake (about it)! *sent.* an expression signifying the sincerity of the speaker's previous statements. ♦ *Make no mistake! This is the real thing.*

make one's **bed** *tv.* to be the cause of one's own misery. ♦ *Well, I guess I made my own bed. Now I have to lie in it.*

make oneself **scarce** *tv.* to leave; to be in a place less frequently; to be less in evidence. ♦ *Here come the boys in blue. I'd better make myself scarce.*

make out 1. *in.* to neck and pet. ♦ *He started making out when he was twelve.* **2.** *in.* to succeed. ♦ *How did you make out?*

make so *tv.* to identify someone. ♦ *The cop stared at Bart and tried to make him, but failed to identify him and let him go.*

make the scene 1. *tv.* to attend an event. (See also scene.) ♦ *I hope everybody can make the scene.* **2.** *tv.* to understand a situation; to appreciate the situation. (Underworld. See also make.) ♦ *I can't quite make the scene, but it looks like Sam punched the guy over here. Then he moved to the window over here, and that's when the old dame across the street saw him.*

make tracks *tv.* to move out of a place fast. ♦ *Let's make tracks. We gotta hit Adamsville before noon.*

make waves *tv.* to cause difficulty. (Often in the negative.) ♦ *If you make waves too much around here, you won't last long.*

make with the sth *in.* to make something visible; to use something; to apply something. ♦ *I want to know. Come on, make with the answers!*

make-out artist *n.* a seducer; a lecher, usually a male. (See also lady-killer.) ♦ *He might have been a make-out artist in his youth, but I doubt it.*

malark(e)y [məˈlɑrki] *n.* nonsense; flattery. ♦ *Don't give me that malarkey!*

male blindness *n.* the imagined failure on the part of a male to see approaching dangers owing to the male's eyes being focused on a some well-proportioned female attribute. ♦ *After an attack of male blindness, he walked into a lamppost.*

male chauvinist pig Go to MCP.

mallet *n.* a police officer. ♦ *Sam was struck by a mallet this noon.*

malware AND **evilware** *n.* malicious software; software that intentionally harms normal computer software. (Includes viruses, spyware, data miners, trojan horses, and other programs designed to damage or destroy a computer.) ♦ *The industry is concerned about the increase in "malware" but leaders don't know what to do at this point.* ♦ *I used all sorts of stuff to get rid of the evilware, but it's still there somewhere.*

mama bear *n.* a policewoman. (See also lady bear.) ♦ *As we came under the bridge, we saw a mama bear sitting in a pigmobile.*

Mammary Lane *n.* cleavage. (See also Gland Canyon.) ♦ *Let you finger do the walking down Mammary Lane.*

man 1. *n.* one's friend; a buddy, not necessarily male. (Also a term of address.) ♦ *Look, man, take it easy!* **2.** *exclam.* Wow! (Usually **Man!**) ♦ *Man, what a bundle!* **3.** AND the **man** *n.* a drug seller or pusher. (Drugs.) ♦ *The man won't give you credit, you numskull!* **4.** AND the **man** *n.* a police officer; the police; the establishment. ♦ *You better check with the man before you get seen with me.*

the **man** Go to man.

manhood *n.* penis. ♦ *His reflexes automatically protect his manhood.*

manicure 1. *tv.* to trim and clean marijuana for smoking. (Drugs.) ♦ *Sam never would manicure the stuff. Some people would buy it anyway.* **2.** *n.* good-quality, cleaned marijuana. ♦ *Ah, this manicure should bring some good coin.*

map 1. *n.* one's face. ♦ *With a map like that, she could really go somewhere.* **2.** *n.* sheet music. (Jazz musicians. See also chart.) ♦ *I left the map at home. Can I look at yours?*

Marble City Go to marble orchard.

marble dome *n.* a stupid person. (Someone who has marble where brains should be.) ♦ *The guy's a marble dome. He has no knowledge of what's going on around him.*

marble orchard AND **Marble City** *n.* a cemetery. ♦ *I already bought a little plot in a marble orchard.* ♦ *There is a huge Marble City south of town.*

marinate *n.* to wait calmly for something to happen. ♦ *I'll just sit here and marinate until you figure out what you want us to do.*

marine officer Go to marine (recruit).

marine (recruit) AND **marine officer** *n.* an empty beer or liquor bottle. (See also dead soldier; dead marine. These expressions are probably meant as derogatory to either marines or officer.) ♦ *Every now and then the gentle muttering of the customers was accented by the breaking of a marine as it hit the floor.* ♦ *There's a marine officer laying in the fireplace.*

mark *n.* a dupe; a victim selected for a theft or a swindle. (Underworld.) ♦ *I bumped the mark on the shoulder, and he put his hand on his wallet just like always.*

mark time *tv.* to wait; to do nothing but wait. ♦ *Do you expect me to just stand here and mark time?*

marker *n.* a personal promissory note; an IOU. ♦ *Bart signed a marker for $3,000 and handed it to Sam.*

marksman *n.* a serious college student who works hard to get good marks (grades). ♦ *Bill kept saying that Todd was a geek and a marksman, until Todd flunked algebra.*

marvy *mod.* marvelous. ♦ *It's just grand! Marvy!*

Mary J. Go to Mary Jane.

Mary Jane 1. AND **Mary J.; Maryjane** *n.* marijuana. (Drugs. See also jane.) ♦ *I can't live another day without Mary Jane!* **2.** *n.* a plain-looking girl. ♦ *She's just a Mary Jane and will never be a glamour girl.*

mash *in.* to neck and pet. (Collegiate.) ♦ *Who are those two mashing in the corner?*

mashed *mod.* alcohol intoxicated. ♦ *Both guys were so mashed. I called my brother, who came and rescued me.*

massive *mod.* excellent. (California.) ♦ *That was a totally massive party, Tiff.*

massively *mod.* excellently; totally. ♦ *Max showed up for the meeting massively stoned and singing at the top of his lungs.*

mattress mambo *n.* an act of copulation. (Contrived.) ♦ *I get my exercise doing the mattress mambo.*

maven AND **mavin** ['mevṇ] **1.** *n.* an expert; a self-proclaimed expert. (From Hebrew *mevin* via Yiddish.) ♦ *A maven in the stock market you are not.* **2.** *in.* to act as a maven (sense 1). ♦ *She's always mavening about something.*

mavin Go to maven.

maw [mɔ] *tv. & in.* to kiss and pet; to smooch. (Probably from *maul.*) ♦ *Come on, don't maw me. You've been watching too many movies—or two few.* ♦ *Let's go out somewhere and maw.*

max *n.* the maximum. (See also to the max.) ♦ *I want the max. I'm hungry.*

max out *in.* to reach one's maximum in something, such as weight in weight lifting or credit on a credit card. ♦ *Andy finally maxed out at 300 pounds.*

maxed out 1. *mod.* exhausted; tired. ♦ *I am just maxed out. I haven't been getting enough sleep.* **2.** *mod.* alcohol intoxicated. ♦ *I hadn't seen Marlowe so maxed out in years. He was nearly paralyzed.*

maxin' *in.* relaxing. ♦ *I spent Saturday just maxin' around the house and doing some tunage.*

mayo ['meo] *n.* mayonnaise. ♦ *I'll take both mayo and mustard, thank you.*

mazulla Go to mazuma.

mazuma AND **mazulla** [mə'zumə AND mə'zulə] *n.* money. (From Hebrew *mezu* via Yiddish.) ♦ *She's got more mazuma than she knows what to do with.* ♦ *I won some mazulla on the horses and lost it all playing poker.*

MBWA *abb.* management by walking around. (A "theory" of management that includes having managers being visible and observant.) ♦ *The boss just left my cubicle. She's one of those NBWA types.*

McCoy Go to (real) McCoy.

McD's AND **McDuck's** *n.* McDonald's, the franchised fast-food restaurant. (Teens and collegiate. The *duck* is a play on the Walt Disney character *Donald Duck.*) ♦ *Can you take McD's tonight, or do you want some slow food?*

McDoc(s) Go to McDoctor(s).

McDoctor(s) AND **McDoc(s)** *n.* a jocular term for a walk-in, emergency medical clinic as found in shopping malls. (See also doc(s)-in-a-box.) ♦ *They took the kid to McDoctors, or whatever it is, over in the mall.*

McDuck's Go to McD's.

McFly ['mɪk'flaɪ] **1.** *n.* a stupid person; a simpleton. (Also a term of address.) ♦ *Hey, McFly. What do you think you are doing?* **2.** *mod.* stupid; simple-minded. ♦ *That was a McFly thing to do.*

MCP AND **male chauvinist pig** *n.* a male who acts superior to and aggressively toward women. (From the woman's liberation movements of the 1970s.) ♦ *The guy is just a male chauvinist pig, and he'll never change.* ♦ *That's you! Walter L. Waddington, MCP.*

meadow muffin *n.* a mass of cow dung. ♦ *Jill stepped in a meadow muffin while she was bird-watching.*

meals rejected by Ethiopians *n.* military rations, **MRE** = meal ready to eat. (Cruelly designated at a time when Ethiopians where starving to death. Implying that not even starving humans would eat MREs. That said, it is also known that such rations have been rejected by hungry people who desire more familiar food.) ♦ *The reporter was embarrassed to describe the MREs as "meals rejected by Ethiopians."*

meals rejected by the enemy Go to MRE.

mean *mod.* having to do with someone or something that is very good; **cool.** ♦ *This music is mean, man, mean. What a great sound!*

mean business *tv.* to be very, very serious. ♦ *Stop laughing! I mean business.*

a **mean** sth *mod.* having to do with an excellent example of the art of doing something well habitually. ♦ *John plays the piano quite well. Fred says that John plays a mean piano.*

meany AND **meanie** *n.* a mean or grouchy person. ♦ *Come on! Don't be such a meany.*

meat 1. *n.* the penis. ♦ *He held his hands over his meat and ran for the bedroom.* **2.** *n.* the genitals of either sex; the sexual parts of either sex. ♦ *I don't want to see your meat! What kind of creep do you think I am?* **3.** *n.* a person of either sex considered sexually. ♦ *If she doesn't manage to wrap her legs around that big hunk of meat within the next twenty minutes, I'd lose my bet.*

meat puppet 1. *n.* the penis. ♦ *Stop scratching your meat puppet!* **2.** *n.* a TV announcer; a **talking head** on television. ♦ *These documentaries are just one meat puppet after another.*

meat wagon *n.* an ambulance. ♦ *The meat wagon showed up just as they were pulling what was left of Marty out of what was left of her car.*

meat whistle *n.* the penis. ♦ *Stop scratching your meat whistle.*

meathead *n.* a stupid oaf. ♦ *Is this meathead bothering you, miss?*

meatheaded *mod.* stupid; simple-minded. ♦ *Of all the meatheaded ideas. This one takes the cake!*

meathooks *n.* the hands. (See also **hooks.** These are hooks made of meat, i.e., flesh and bone.) ♦ *Get your meathooks off my car!*

meatloaf *n.* unwelcome email messages, jokes, etc., "homemade spam." ♦ *My so-called friends filled up my mailbox with meatloaf while I was gone.*

medico ['mɛdiko] *n.* a doctor. (From Spanish.) ♦ *It's hard to take it seriously when a fat medico tells you to shed a few pounds.*

meet *n.* a meeting or an appointment. (Mostly underworld.) ♦ *If this meet works out, we could score a cool million.*

mega ['mɛgə] *mod.* large; serious. ♦ *Some mega beast boogied down to the front of the auditorium and started screaming.*

megabitch *n.* a truly obnoxious **bitch.** ♦ *Anne called herself a megabitch and said she didn't care what people thought of her.*

megabucks *n.* a lot of money; **big bucks.** (See also **kilobucks.**) ♦ *A stereo that size must cost megabucks.*

megadork ['mɛgədork] *n.* a very stupid person. (See also **dork.**) ♦ *Tiffany, you are, like, such a megadork!*

megillah [mə'gɪlə] *n.* a long and complicated story. (From Hebrew *megillah* via Yiddish.) ♦ *Here you come in here with this megillah about a flat tire and how your brother-in-law stole your jack and how your arthritis is kicking up—what do you think I am, some sort of shoulder to cry on?*

mell of a hess *n.* hell of a mess. (A deliberate spoonerism.) ♦ *What a mell of a hess you've gotten us into this time.*

mellow 1. *mod.* relaxed; untroubled; laid back. ♦ *She is the mellowest fox I know.* **2.** *mod.* slightly alcohol or drug intoxicated. ♦ *I got mellow and stopped drinking right there.*

mellow out 1. *in.* to calm down; to get less angry. ♦ *When you mellow out, maybe we can talk.* **2.** *in.* to become generally more relaxed; to grow less contentious. ♦ *After his illness, he mellowed out and seemed more glad to be alive.*

melons *n.* large breasts. (Usually objectionable.) ♦ *Look at the melons on that babe!*

melvin ['mɛlvən] **1.** *n.* a studious or unattractive male. (Teens and collegiate.) ♦ *Do you think I would go out with that melvin?* **2.** *n.* a situation where one's underpants ride up high between the buttocks. (Named for a person so stupid and unaware that he is comfortable with this arrangement. See also give so a melvin.) ♦ *How could anybody go around all day with a melvin like that?*

men in blue AND **boys in blue** *n.* the police; policemen. (See also blue boys.) ♦ *The men in blue are hammering at my door. I'm going out the back way.* ♦ *You can depend on the boys in blue to clean things up in this town.*

mensch [mɛntʃ] *n.* a mature and responsible person. (From German via Yiddish.) ♦ *Now there goes a real mensch!*

mental 1. *mod.* mentally retarded. (Usually objectionable. Derogatory.) ♦ *The girl's mental. Leave her alone.* **2.** *n.* a mentally retarded person. (Usually objectionable. Derogatory.) ♦ *He's a mental. He'll need some help.* **3.** *n.* a stupid person. ♦ *You're such a mental lately.*

mental giant *n.* a genius. ♦ *I'm no mental giant, but I do know trouble when I see it.*

mental midget *n.* a stupid person. ♦ *I hate to seem like a mental midget, but what's so great about that?*

merchandise *n.* any contraband. (Underworld.) ♦ *How much of the merchandise can you deliver by midnight?*

merger-mania *n.* an apparent need for companies to merge with one another. (Securities markets and journalism.) ♦ *The market meltdown put an end to merger-mania.*

mesc [mɛsk] *n.* mescaline, a hallucinatory substance. (Drugs.) ♦ *Tiffany is totally hooked on mesc. I don't know where she gets it.*

mesh *n.* a crosshatch or octothorpe, #. (See also pigpen.) ♦ *What does the mesh stand for in this equation?*

meshuga AND **meshugah** [məˈʃʊgə] *mod.* crazy. (From Hebrew *meshuggah* via Yiddish.) ♦ *This guy is meshugah!*

mess 1. *n.* a hopeless, stupid person. ♦ *The guy's a mess!* **2.** *n.* dung. (Usually with *a*.) ♦ *There's a mess in Jimmy's diapers, Mom.*

mess about (with so) Go to mess around (with so).

mess about (with sth) Go to mess around (with sth).

mess around (with so) AND **mess about (with** so); **monkey around (with** so) **1.** *in.* to play with someone sexually. ♦ *Those two have been messing around.* ♦ *He started monkeying around, so I got out of the car.* **2.** *in.* to waste someone's time. ♦ *Don't mess around with me. Just answer the question, if you please.* **3.** *in.* to waste time with someone else. ♦ *I was messing around with John.*

mess around (with sth) **mess about (with** sth); AND **monkey around (with** sth) *in.* to play with or fiddle with something. ♦ *You'll break it if you don't stop monkeying around with it.*

mess so **over** *tv.* to treat someone badly; to beat or harm someone. ♦ *Harry the Horse messed Lefty over and sent him to the hospital.*

mess so's **face up** *tv.* to beat someone around the face. (Underworld.) ♦ *I had to mess his face up a little, boss, but he's been real cooperative since then.*

mess so **up** *tv.* to beat someone up. (Underworld.) ♦ *The boss says me and the boys is supposed to mess you up a little.*

mess up *in.* to make an error; to do something wrong; to flub (up). ♦ *I hope I don't mess up on the quiz.*

mess with so/sth AND **monkey with** so/sth *in.* to bother or interfere with someone or something. ♦ *Don't mess with me unless you want trouble.* ♦ *Don't monkey with the TV. It's out of kilter.*

messed up 1. *mod.* confused. ♦ *I'm sort of messed up since my divorce.* **2.** *mod.* alcohol or drug intoxicated. ♦ *Somehow I must have got messed up. What caused it, do you think?*

meth 1. *n.* denatured alcohol; methyl alcohol. (Streets and underworld.) ♦ *Meth used to be pink. Now they put something in it to make you vomit.* **2.** *n.* methamphetamine. (Drugs.) ♦ *Usually meth is injected, having almost an immediate effect.* **3.** *n.* methadone. (Drugs.) ♦ *Sometimes* *meth means methadone, a drug used in drug treatment.*

meth monster *n.* a habitual user of methamphetamine. ♦ *These teenage meth monsters can be a real menace when they need juice.*

metric shitload *n.* a whole lot (of something). (Usually objectionable.) ♦ *He is one metric shitload of trouble.*

metros ['mɛtroz] *n.* the police; the metropolitan police. (Not used in all metropolitan areas.) ♦ *The metros took ten minutes to get to the scene of the crime, and the entire city is enraged.*

Mexican breakfast *n.* a cigarette and a cup of coffee or a glass of water. ♦ *After a Mexican breakfast, I went to Marlowe's hotel hoping to catch him before he went out.*

MF Go to motherfucker.

mick Go to mickey (sense 5).

mickey AND **micky 1.** *n.* a hip flask for liquor. ♦ *He took a little swig out of a mickey he carries in his pocket.* **2.** Go to Mickey (Finn). **3.** *n.* a small bottle of wine. ♦ *See if you can get a mickey of something for a buck.* **4.** *n.* a tranquilizer. (Drugs.) ♦ *Whatever that mickey was you gave me, it helped.* **5.** AND **mick** an easy or trivial college course. (From mickey mouse sense 2.) ♦ *I've got a light load this quarter. Three micks and two education courses.*

Mickey D's *n.* McDonald's fast-food restaurant. (Teens and collegiate.) ♦ *Let's hit Mickey D's for chow this noon.*

Mickey finished *mod.* alcohol intoxicated; totally drunk. (A play on Mickey (Finn).) ♦ *I guess the old guy is about Mickey finished. He's plootered!*

Mickey (Finn) 1. *n.* a drink containing chloral hydrate; a drink containing a fast-acting laxative. ♦ *He slipped her a Mickey Finn, but she switched glasses.* **2.** *n.* chloral hydrate as put in drinks to knock people out. ♦ *There was a Mickey Finn in this drink, wasn't there?*

mickey mouse 1. *n.* nonsense; something trivial. (From the world-famous mouse character by the same name, owned by The Walt Disney Company.) ♦ *This is just a lot of mickey mouse.* **2.** *mod.* trivial; time wasting; lousy. ♦ *I want out of this mickey mouse place.* **3.** *n.* a police officer. (Streets.) ♦ *Mickey mouse is hanging around asking about you.* **4.** *n.* a bit of blotter impregnated with LSD with a picture of The Walt Disney Company's Mickey Mouse on it. (Drugs.) ♦ *How much is the mickey mouse?*

mickey mouse ears *n.* the two lights found on top of a police car. (This is the older form of emergency lights. A bar of lights with varying functions is now the norm in towns and cities.) ♦ *There were no mickey mouse ears, but the jerk inside looked like your average ossifer.*

mickey mouse habit *n.* a trivial drug habit. (Drugs.) ♦ *Nothing to it. Just a little mickey mouse habit. I can stop any time I want.*

micky Go to mickey.

middle of nowhere *n.* an isolated place. ♦ *I don't want to stay out here in the middle of nowhere.*

middlebrow *mod.* middle-class; average or mediocre. (Between highbrow and lowbrow.) ♦ *She has average middlebrow tastes and drives a midsized Chevrolet.*

midi ['mɪdi] **1.** *n.* a mid-length woman's garment. ♦ *Shall I wear my midi, or is it too hot?* **2.** *mod.* having to do with a mid-length woman's garment. ♦ *This midi style is out, and the mini is back in.*

miffed *mod.* angry. ♦ *She was a little miffed when I failed to show up, but she calmed down after a while.*

mifky-pifky (in the bushes) *n.* illicit sex; hanky-panky. ♦ *Jeff got caught again. Mifky-pifky in the bushes seems to be his style.*

mil *n.* a million; a million dollars. ♦ *The government spent forty mil on this building.*

milk 1. *tv.* to attempt to persuade an audience to laugh or applaud. ♦ *She went on milking the crowd for adulation long after they had demonstrated their appreciation.* **2.** *tv.* to attempt to get recognition from an audience. ♦ *His performance was marred by an amateurish attempt to milk applause.*

milk a duck *tv.* to do [or not do] something totally impossible. ♦ *She can't do that. That's harder than milking a duck.*

milled *mod.* alcohol intoxicated. (See also cut.) ♦ *She was cut up with all that booze—milled, I guess.*

milquetoast ['mɪlktost] *n.* an ineffectual man; a shy coward; an effeminate male. ♦ *This little milquetoast goes up to the biker, looks at him sort of sad like, and then karate chops him into a quivering pulp.*

Milwaukee goiter AND **German goiter** [mɪl'wɔki 'gɔɪdɚ AND 'dʒɚmən 'gɔɪdɚ] *n.* a beer belly. (Refers to Milwaukee, Wisconsin, a major beer-brewing city, and to Germany.) ♦ *By the time he was twenty-six, he was balding and had a Milwaukee goiter that would tip him over if he turned too fast.* ♦ *If you want to get rid of that German goiter, stop drinking beer!*

mind *n.* [one's] head. ♦ *Quiet or I'll clout your mind!*

mind your own beeswax […'bizwæks] *tv.* to mind one's own business. (Juvenile.) ♦ *Lay off! Mind your own beeswax!*

mind-bender AND **mind-blower** *n.* a hallucinogenic drug, typically LSD. (Drugs.) ♦ *That mind-bender takes a long time to wear off.* ♦ *This stuff is a real mind-blower.*

mind-blower Go to mind-bender.

mingy ['mɪndʒi] *mod.* mean and stingy. ♦ *Why can't you borrow it? I'm just mingy, that's all.*

mini ['mɪni] **1.** *mod.* small; miniature. ♦ *I have a mini problem you can maybe help me with.* **2.** *n.* a miniskirt. ♦ *I look pretty good in a mini.*

mink *n.* a woman. (Black.) ♦ *Take this home to your mink. She'll like it.*

Minnehaha [mɪni'hɑhɑ] *n.* champagne. (From Longfellow's *Song of Hiawatha*. *Minnehaha* means "laughing waters.") ♦ *Minnehaha tickles my nose.*

mint 1. *n.* a lot of money. ♦ *He makes a mint. He can afford a little generosity.* **2.** *mod.* good-looking; superior. (As *in mint condition.*) ♦ *These tunes are mint, all right!*

mish *n.* the so-called missionary sexual position. ♦ *Mish, mish, mish! No imagination.*

mish-mash AND **mish-mosh** ['mɪʃmæʃ AND 'mɪʃmɑʃ] *n.* a mixture; a disorderly conglomeration. ♦ *There's no theme or focus. It's just a mish-mash.*

mish-mosh Go to mish-mash.

miss the boat *tv.* to have made an error; to be wrong. ♦ *If you think you can do that, you have just missed the boat.*

mitt *n.* a hand. ♦ *The kid's got mitts on him like a gorilla.*

mix it up (with SO**)** *tv.* to fight with someone; to quarrel with someone. ♦ *Max came out of the shop and began to mix it up with Mooshoo.*

mixed (up) 1. *mod.* confused; mentally troubled. (This is hyphenated before a nominal.) ♦ *I was a little mixed up after the accident.* **2.** *mod.* alcohol intoxicated. ♦ *I'm just a little mixed-up, nothing serious. No reason you should be swaying around like that.*

mizzle a wild card word for words beginning with M, such as *muff* = female genitals. (Streets. Also for other words with initial *M*.) ♦ *He is thinking about her mizzle.*

mob [mɑb] *n.* the crime syndicate. (Underworld and journalistic.) ♦ *One of the biggest fish in the mob was pulled from the river yesterday.*

moby ['mobi] **1.** *mod.* enormous; unwieldy. (Like Herman Melville's great white whale, *Moby Dick*.) ♦ *This is a very moby old car.* **2.** *n.* a megabyte, a measurement of computer memory size. (A megabyte is whale-sized compared to a kilobyte.) ♦ *My fixed disks give me a capacity of over two thousand mobies.*

mod [mɑd] *mod.* contemporary and fashionable in clothing and ideas. ♦ *Your* clothes are mod, but you're just a plain, old-fashioned prude.

mod poser ['mɑd 'pozɚ] *n.* someone who looks mod in dress only. (Collegiate.) ♦ *Tiffany is such a mod poser. At home it's jeans and a T-shirt.*

modulate *n.* to relax; to chill. ♦ *Cool it man. Modulate. Relax.*

moist around the edges *mod.* alcohol intoxicated. ♦ *Charlie is more than moist around the edges. He is soused.*

mojo ['modʒo] **1.** *n.* magic or spells. (Assumed to originate with African slaves. Very old.) ♦ *The old lady was said to possess powerful "mojo" which the others feared her for.* **2.** *n.* power; charisma. ♦ *She seemed to radiate a penetrating mojo that made her easy to deal with.* **3.** *n.* sex appeal; sex drive. ♦ *Man, does he have mojo to spare!* **4.** *n.* heroin; morphine; cannabis. (Drugs. See also on the mojo.) ♦ *Why don't you try to kick the mojo?* **5.** *n.* a narcotics addict. (Drugs.) ♦ *These mojos will rob you blind if you don't keep an eye on them.*

moldy fig *n.* an old-fashioned person; a square. ♦ *Don't be a moldy fig! Lighten up!*

Molly whop so *tv.* to beat someone up; to slap someone hard. ♦ *Quiet or I'll Molly whop you.*

mondo ['mɑndo] *mod.* totally; very much. (California.) ♦ *This place is like, so, like, mondo beige.*

mondo bizarro *mod.* very weird. ♦ *You are one mondo bizarro dude!*

monet *mod.* good-looking from a distance. (From the works of the painter, Monet.) ♦ *He's sort of monet. Okay from a distance, but up close: yuck. But that's just my impression.*

money from home 1. *n.* easily gotten money. (Underworld.) ♦ *This job is like taking candy from a kid. It's money from home.* **2.** *n.* something as welcome as long-awaited money from home. ♦ *Having you visit like this is like getting money from home, Taylor.*

money grubber *n.* a stingy person. ♦ *The boss is such a money grubber. He still has his first paper clip.*

money talks *in.* money can buy cooperation; having money makes one influential. ♦ *Like they say, money talks, but don't try making it talk to a cop.*

moneybags *n.* a nickname for a wealthy person. ♦ *When you get to be a big moneybags, don't forget those you left behind.*

mongo *mod.* great; very; huge. (Probably akin to humongous.) ♦ *When I get some cash, I'm gonna buy me one mongo car with leather seats.*

moniker AND **monniker** ['mɑnəkɚ] *n.* a nickname. ♦ *With a moniker like that, you must get in a lot of fights.*

monkey 1. *n.* a playful child. (Also a term of address.) ♦ *Come here, you little monkey!* **2.** *n.* a drug addiction. (Drugs. See also have a monkey on one's back.) ♦ *That monkey of mine is getting hungry again.*

monkey around (with so**)** Go to mess around (with so).

monkey around (with sth**)** Go to mess around (with sth).

monkey bite *n.* a kiss that leaves a blotch or mark. (See also hickey.) ♦ *Who gave you that monkey bite?*

monkey business AND **funny business** *n.* silliness; dishonest tricks. ♦ *That's enough monkey business. Now, settle down.* ♦ *Stop the funny business and get to work!*

monkey swill *n.* inferior liquor; strong liquor. ♦ *Where did you get this monkey swill? This would kill a monkey anyway.*

monkey talk *n.* distorted speech, as uttered while drug intoxicated. (Drugs.) ♦ *Their pupils are pinpoint-sized, and they talk monkey talk. That's how you can tell they're on H.*

monkey wagon *n.* drug addiction. (Drugs.) ♦ *Some of these treatment centers won't get you off the monkey wagon unless you have insurance.*

monkey wards *n.* Montgomery Wards, a department store chain. (The first mail-order house, it operated through the entire twentieth century. It now operates online.) ♦ *I get that kind of stuff at monkey wards.*

monkey with so/sth Go to **mess with** so/sth.

monkey-fart AND **fiddle-fart** *in.* to waste time; to do something ineffectually or inefficiently. (A blend of *monkey around* and *fart around*.) ♦ *Stop monkey-farting and get over here and get to work.* ♦ *He wasted his time fiddle-farting, and never got the job done.*

monkeyshines *n.* tricks; small acts of mischief. ♦ *These kids are a lot of fun despite their monkeyshines.*

monniker Go to moniker.

monolithic [manə'lɪθɪk] *mod.* heavily drug intoxicated. (Drugs. A play on stoned.) ♦ *She's not just stoned, she's monolithic!*

monster 1. *n.* any powerful drug affecting the central nervous system. (Drugs.) ♦ *This PCP is a monster. Why don't the cops put a stop to it?* **2.** *mod.* having to do with a powerful or addictive drug. (Drugs.) ♦ *Where the devil did you get that monster dust?*

monster weed *n.* cannabis; powerful marijuana. (Drugs.) ♦ *This is what they call monster weed. Stay away from it. It may have angel dust on it.*

Montezuma's revenge [mantə'zuməz rɪ'vɛndʒ] *n.* diarrhea; tourist diarrhea. (Refers to tourists in Mexico.) ♦ *I had a little touch of Montezuma's revenge the second day, but other than that we had a wonderful time.*

monthlies *n.* the period of menstruation. ♦ *It's her monthlies. You know how she feels then.*

moo juice AND **cow juice** *n.* milk. ♦ *Some good, cold moo juice would be good about now.* ♦ *While you're at the store, get some more cow juice.*

mooch [mutʃ] **1.** *tv. & in.* to beg for money, liquor, or drugs in public places. ♦ *No mooching around here! Move along!* **2.** *n.* a beggar. ♦ *I don't want to be a mooch, but could I borrow your lawn mower?* **3.** *n.* narcotics. (Drugs. See also hooch.) ♦ *He's*

gonna have to work hard to get off the mooch.

moocher 1. *n.* a beggar. ♦ *I try to give every moocher a little change.* **2.** *n.* a drug addict. (Drugs.) ♦ *These moochers will do anything to get a few bucks for a load.*

moolah ['mulɑ] *n.* money. (Originally underworld.) ♦ *That is a whole lot of moolah!*

moon 1. *n.* the buttocks. ♦ *He rubbed his plump moon where he had been kicked, but said no more.* **2.** *tv. & in.* to show (someone) one's nude posterior through a window (usually of an automobile). (See also mooner; gaucho.) ♦ *When the plane flew over Cuba, this guy named Victor actually mooned a Russian MIG that flew by.*

mooner 1. *n.* a drunkard. (From moonshine.) ♦ *This old mooner from up in the hills wandered into town last Friday and died in the town square.* **2.** *n.* an idler who does nothing better than stare at the moon. ♦ *He's sort of a mooner. No direction and no goals in life.*

moonlight 1. *n.* illicit liquor; moonshine. ♦ *Where's that bottle of moonlight you used to keep under the counter?* **2.** *in.* to traffic in illicit liquor. (Best done under the cover of darkness.) ♦ *He moonlighted during prohibition.* **3.** *in.* to work at a second job. ♦ *Larry had to moonlight to earn enough to feed his family.*

moonlight requisition *n.* a nighttime theft. (Military. See also liberate.) ♦ *It took a moonlight requisition to get the medicine we needed.*

moonlit *mod.* alcohol intoxicated, with moonshine. ♦ *He's on the jug again. See, he's all moonlit.*

moonrock *n.* a form of crack that contains heroin. ♦ *Max was caught with a supply of moonrock on him.*

moonshine 1. *n.* nonsense; humbug. ♦ *That's just moonshine! I don't believe a word.* **2.** *n.* homemade whiskey; any cheap or inferior liquor. ♦ *Moonshine is supposed to be strong, not good.* **3.** *in.* to distill or traffic in illicit liquor. (See also moonshiner.) ♦ *You would be amazed at* *how much people moonshine back in the hills.*

moonshiner *n.* a maker of moonshine. ♦ *Moonshiners in the Georgia hills are using sophisticated electronic warning systems to keep one step ahead of the feds.*

moose *n.* a Korean girlfriend (in Korea); any girlfriend. (Crude. Military. More specifically, a Korean girl slave, bought by a G.I. from her parents.) ♦ *She's one fine moose, if you ask me.*

mop [mɑp] **1.** *n.* a drinking bout. ♦ *She is off somewhere on another mop.* **2.** *n.* a heavy drinker; a drunkard. ♦ *The guy's a mop. There is nothing you can do till he decides he's had enough.* **3.** *n.* hair; a hairdo. ♦ *How do you like my new mop?*

mop the floor up with SO AND **wipe the floor up with** SO *tv.* to beat someone to a pulp. (Also with other verbs: *clean, dust,* etc.) ♦ *Max whacked Bruno one and then mopped up the floor with him.* ♦ *One more crack like that, and I'll have Sam wipe the floor up with you.*

mope [mop] **1.** *n.* a tired and ineffectual person. ♦ *I can't afford to pay mopes around here. Get to work or get out!* **2.** AND **mope around** *in.* to move around slowly and sadly. ♦ *He just mopes around all day and won't eat anything.* ♦ *Stop moping and get moving.*

mope around Go to mope.

mopped AND **moppy** *mod.* alcohol intoxicated. ♦ *Jack was a little moppy to be driving.*

mopping-up operation *n.* a clean-up operation; the final stages in a project where the loose ends are taken care of. ♦ *It's all over except a small mopping-up operation.*

moppy Go to mopped.

more than one **bargained for** *n.* [getting] more than one expected. ♦ *This is certainly more than I bargained for!*

the **morning after (the night before)** *n.* a hangover. ♦ *Do worries about the morning after keep you from having a good time at parties?*

morning glory AND **morning missile** *n.* a morning erection. ♦ *Always happy to see the morning glory.* ♦ *Bobby has a morning missile instead of an alarm clock.*

morning missile Go to morning glory.

mos def *mod.* most definitely. ♦ *Am I mad. Mos def!*

mossback [ˈmɔsbæk] *n.* an old square; a stick in the mud. ♦ *Walter, you are such an old mossback.*

the **most** *n.* something that is the best. ♦ *This noodle stuff is the most, Mom!*

mother 1. *n.* marijuana. (Drugs. See also mother nature('s).) ♦ *She grows her own mother in a pot in her room.* **2.** *n.* a drug dealer; one's own drug dealer upon whom one depends. (Drugs.) ♦ *If you can't trust your mother, who can you trust?* **3.** Go to motherfucker (sense 3).

mother nature('s) *n.* marijuana. (Drugs.) ♦ *No chemicals for me. I find that mother nature is everything I need.*

motherfucker AND **MF 1.** *n.* a despicable adversary; a moronic jerk. (Also a dangerous, derogatory, and provocative term of address. Taboo.) ♦ *You stupid motherfucker! You're gonna die for that!* **2.** *n.* a gadget; a part or thing. (Taboo.) ♦ *This little motherfucker fits in right here.* **3.** AND **mother** *n.* a problem or difficulty. (Taboo.) ♦ *This test is a real mother.*

motherfucking *mod.* despicable; worthless; frustrating. (Powerful and provocative. Taboo.) ♦ *Get that motherfucking idiot out of here before I kill him!*

motion-lotion *n.* gasoline; motor fuel. (Citizens band radio.) ♦ *Let's stop up ahead for some motion-lotion.*

motor *in.* to depart. ♦ *Well, let's motor, you guys. It's getting late.*

motorized rice *n.* maggots. ♦ *This dead squirrel stinks and it's alive with motorized rice!*

motor-mouth Go to ratchet-mouth.

Motown [ˈmotɑʊn] *n.* motor town, Detroit, Michigan. ♦ *We went to Motown to buy a car once.*

(mountain) dew 1. *n.* Scotch whiskey. ♦ *The real mountain dew is smoky-tasting and amber.* **2.** *n.* illicit liquor; any liquor. ♦ *Mountain dew is what I want. As long as it's not store bought.*

mouse potato *n.* someone who spends a great amount of time using a computer. (Based on **couch potato.**) ♦ *Every since we go the new computer, Jane has turned into a regular mouse potato.*

a **mouth 1.** *n.* a hangover. ♦ *I've got quite a mouth this morning. I guess I overdid it.* **2.** Go to mouth(piece).

a **mouth full of South** *n.* a southern accent. ♦ *I just love to hear a man with a mouth full of South.*

mouth off *in.* to give (someone) back talk. ♦ *If you mouth off, I will ground you for three weeks.*

mouth-breather *n.* a stupid-acting person. ♦ *I always end up with a mouth-breather on a blind date.*

mouthful 1. *n.* a true statement. ♦ *You said a mouthful, and I agree.* **2.** *n.* a tirade. ♦ *Paul really gave me a mouthful. I didn't know I hurt his feelings.*

mouth(piece) *n.* a lawyer specializing in criminal cases. (Underworld.) ♦ *I won't answer anything without my mouth right here by me.*

mouthwash *n.* liquor; a drink of liquor. ♦ *I could use a shot of that mouthwash.*

move on so *in.* to attempt to pick up someone; to attempt to seduce someone. (Collegiate.) ♦ *Don't try to move on my date, old chum.*

movers and shakers *n.* people who get things done; organizers and managers. ♦ *The movers and shakers in this firm haven't exactly been working overtime.*

movies *n.* a case of diarrhea. (Because it keeps you on the move, going to the john.) ♦ *A case of the movies kept me going all night.*

mow, blow, and go *n.* the lawn service that quickly mows the grass, blows the pavements clean, and leaves. ♦ *Now you see them and now you don't. It's mow, blow, and go time.*

mow one's **lawn** Go to mow the lawn.

mow the lawn AND **mow** one's **lawn** *tv.* to comb one's hair. ♦ *I'll be with you as soon as I mow the lawn.* ♦ *Don't you think you better mow your lawn?*

moxie ['mɑksi] *n.* energy; spunk; spirit. ♦ *Now here's a gal with real moxie.*

Mr. Big 1. *n.* an important man; the boss man. (Also the name of a character in HBO's *Sex and the City.*) ♦ *So you're Mr. Big. I thought you'd be taller.* **2.** *n.* a nickname for the head of a group of criminals, especially one who wants to remain anonymous. ♦ *Lefty was asked to pay a visit to Mr. Big, and Lefty was scared.*

Mr. Hawkins *n.* the winter wind. (Originally black. See also hawk.) ♦ *Put something on your head, or Mr. Hawkins will cut you down.*

Mr. Nice Guy *n.* a friendly, forgiving fellow. ♦ *Oh, my boss is Mr. Nice Guy. He'll let me off, I'm sure.*

Mr. Right *n.* the one man who is right for a woman. ♦ *Some day Mr. Right will come along and sweep you off your feet.*

Mr. Whiskers AND **Uncle Whiskers; whiskers (man)** *n.* a federal agent. (Underworld. From the whiskers of Uncle Sam.) ♦ *Mr. Whiskers is trying to get me to pay tax on those few bucks.* ♦ *If Uncle Whiskers finds out what you're doing, you're done for.*

MRE *n.* meals ready to eat, prepackaged food used by the armed forces in combat. (Also reinterpreted as **meals rejected by Ethiopians; meals rejected by the enemy.**) ♦ *Where is my MRE? I'm tired of living.*

Mrs. Murphy *n.* a bathroom. ♦ *Whose turn is it at Mrs. Murphy's?*

MT *n.* an empty bottle. (Initialism.) ♦ *Put your MTs in the garbage.*

mu *n.* marijuana. (Drugs.) ♦ *This mu is stale.*

mucho ['mutʃo] *mod.* very. (Spanish.) ♦ *This is a mucho happy young man.*

muck sth **up** *tv.* to mess something up; to ruin something. ♦ *Try not to muck it up this time.*

mud duck *n.* an ugly person. ♦ *She's a mud duck, but she's got a sense of humor.*

mudbud *n.* homegrown marijuana. (Drugs.) ♦ *Mudbud, hell! It's garbage.*

muddled (up) *mod.* alcohol intoxicated. ♦ *I've had a little too much muddler, I think. Anyway, I'm muddled.*

muddler *n.* liquor. ♦ *I've had a little too much muddler, I think. Anyway, I'm muddled.*

mug 1. *n.* the face. (Crude.) ♦ *Wipe that smile off your mug!* **2.** *n.* a thug; a goon. (Underworld.) ♦ *Call off your mugs. I'll come peacefully.* **3.** *tv.* to attack and rob someone. ♦ *Somebody jumped out of an alley and tried to mug me.*

mug shot *n.* a photograph of one's face taken for police records. (Underworld.) ♦ *I'm going to have to ask you to come down to the station and go through some mug shots.*

mugger *n.* someone, usually a male, who attacks and robs people. ♦ *I clobbered the mugger with a tire iron I carry just for such occasions.*

muggle *n.* someone ignorant about computers, programming, or hacking. (From the name for nonsorcerers in the Harry Potter series of books.) ♦ *This software is great for muggles. It's also drool-proof.*

muggles *n.* marijuana. (From the early twentieth century. Long before Harry Potter.) ♦ *Where can I score some of that muggles?*

muggy ['məgi] *mod.* alcohol intoxicated. ♦ *George is just a little muggy. It doesn't take much anymore.*

mule *n.* someone who delivers or smuggles drugs for a drug dealer. (Drugs.) ♦ *The jerks use a twelve-year-old kid for a mule!*

mullet *n.* a hair style or cut that is short on the top and sides and long in the back. (The longer hair may also be uncombed.) ♦ *I'm letting my hair grow out for a mullet.*

munch out *in.* to eat ravenously. (Drugs. See also **pig out**.) ♦ *I had to munch out after the party. I can't imagine why.*

munchies 1. *n.* the need to eat after using marijuana. ♦ *He came in late with the minchies, and we knew what he had been up to.* **2.** *n.* snacks, such as potato chips; any casual food. ♦ *What kind of munchies are we going to have?*

munchkin ['məntʃkən] *n.* a small or insignificant person. ♦ *You're not going to let that munchkin push you around, are you?*

mung 1. AND **MUNG** [məŋ] *n.* something that is *mashed until no good*; anything nasty or gloppy. (An acronym, but possibly a coinage before it became an acronym.) ♦ *This mung is cruel and unusual punishment. I demand to see the warden.* **2.** *tv.* to ruin something. ♦ *Look at it! You munged it!*

mung sth **up** *tv.* to mess something up. ♦ *The team munged up the play, and the coach blasted them but good.*

mungy ['məŋi] **1.** *mod.* gloppy; messy. ♦ *The spaghetti was cold and mungy by the time it was served.* **2.** *mod.* having to do with an oily feeling of the face of a person who has taken **LSD**. (Drugs.) ♦ *I feel so mungy after I take the stuff. Yuck!*

murder AND **slaughter** *tv.* to overwhelm; to beat someone in a sports contest. ♦ *We went out on the field prepared to slaughter them. The murdered us in the second half.*

murphy ['məˈfi] **1.** *n.* a potato. ♦ *I spent half my tour of duty peeling murphies.* **2.** *n.* a breast. (Crude. Usually plural. Usually objectionable.) ♦ *She stood about six feet tall and was turned in the light so her murphies stood out in silhouette.*

musclehead *n.* a stupid man; a man who has muscle where there should be brains. (Also a rude term of address.) ♦ *Look, musclehead, do exactly what I tell you!*

muscleman 1. *n.* a strong bully; a goon. (Underworld.) ♦ *Mooshoo is a muscleman for the kingpin of a local drug ring.* **2.** *n.* a man who builds muscles through bodybuilding exercises. ♦ *That muscleman doesn't have a single ounce of fat on him.*

mush 1. *n.* nonsense. ♦ *What mush! Come on, talk straight!* **2.** *n.* romance; love-making; kissing. ♦ *I can't stand movies with lots of mush in them.* **3.** *n.* one's face. (Crude.) ♦ *Put some paint on your mush, and let's get going.*

mushhead *n.* a stupid person. ♦ *Oh, good grief, I'm such a mushhead!*

mushmouth *n.* a person who does not or cannot speak clearly. ♦ *How can a mushmouth like that get a job reading news on network television?*

musical beds *n.* acts of sexual promiscuity; sleeping with many people. (From the name of the game *musical chairs*.) ♦ *Mary has been playing musical beds for about a year.*

must Go to must (do).

a **must (do)** AND **must** *n.* something that someone ought to do. ♦ *Seeing the Eiffel tower is a must do in Paris.* ♦ *Tell me some of the "musts" in southern Utah.*

mutant *n.* a total jerk; a social outcast. (Also a term of address.) ♦ *Sam, you act like such a mutant!*

My bad. *phr.* It's my fault and I'm sorry. ♦ *My bad. It won't happen again.*

my dawg Go to my dog.

my dog AND **my dawg; my dogg** *n.* my friend; my "pet" and companion. ♦ *Jane's my dawg. We cruise together.*

My foot! *exclam.* I do not believe it!; Like hell! (An exclamation of contradiction.) ♦ *You're the best in town, my foot!*

My mama didn't raise no dummy. *sent.* I'm not stupid. ♦ *Sure I know the difference between good and bad. My mama didn't raise no dummy.*

my man *n.* my brother or buddy. (Originally black.) ♦ *This is my man Sam who's gonna show you how to boogie.*

my tenda *n.* my sweetheart; my lover. (Streets. *My tender one*.) ♦ *Come here, my tenda. I want some kissing.*

MYOB. *tv.* Mind your own business. ♦ *This doesn't concern you. MYOB.*

mystery meat *n.* any unidentified meat. (Collegiate.) ♦ *There are no hints as to what this mystery meat is—except its strange pinkish color.*

mystic biscuit *n.* a chunk of peyote cactus. (Drugs.) ♦ *Willy thought he got a piece of mystic biscuit, but it was just a moldy raisin.*

nab [næb] **1.** *tv.* to arrest someone. (See also **nabbed**.) ♦ *I knew they would nab him sooner or later.* **2.** AND **nabber** *n.* a police officer; a cop. ♦ *There's a nabber at the door who wants to talk to you.*

nabbed *mod.* caught by the police; arrested. ♦ *She's down at the police station. She's nabbed.*

nabber Go to **nab**.

nabe [neb] **1.** *n.* a neighborhood; one's own neighborhood. ♦ *Hey, man, welcome back to the old nabe!* **2.** *n.* a neighborhood theater. ♦ *Do I have to go downtown to see that movie, or is it playing at the nabes yet?*

nada ['nɑdɑ] *n.* nothing; none. (Spanish.) ♦ *I asked him, but he didn't say nada.*

nads *n.* the testicles. (From *gonads*. See also **nards**.) ♦ *He got hit in the nads in the football game.*

nag 1. *tv.* to pester someone constantly. (From a centuries-old word meaning *gnaw*.) ♦ *Stop nagging me!* **2.** *n.* a worn-out horse. (Probably from a centuries-old word for *horse*.) ♦ *I bet a week's pay on that nag. Look what happened!*

nail 1. *tv.* to arrest someone. (See also **nailed**.) ♦ *The cops nailed him right in his own doorway.* **2.** Go to **coffin nail**. **3.** *tv.* to identify someone. ♦ *The officer nailed Freddy, thanks to the description the victim provided.*

nail Jell-O to a cross Go to **nail Jell-O to the wall**.

nail Jell-O to a tree Go to **nail Jell-O to the wall**.

nail Jell-O to the wall AND **nail Jell-O to a cross; nail Jell-O to a tree** *phr.* to do something that is totally futile. (*Jell-O* is a protected trade name.) ♦ *You're wasting your time. Trying to get him to do that is like nailing Jell-O to the wall.*

nail so('s hide) to the wall Go to **nail so to a cross**.

nail so to a cross AND **nail so('s hide) to the wall** *tv.* to punish or scold someone severely. (Literally, to crucify someone or to nail someone's skin to the wall like that of a captured animal.) ♦ *No reason to nail me to a cross. I didn't do it!* ♦ *She must hate your guts. She sure nailed your hide to the wall.*

nailed 1. *mod.* correctly identified. ♦ *The thugs sure got nailed fast.* **2.** *mod.* arrested. (See also **nail**.) ♦ *Why am I nailed? I didn't do anything.*

nail-em-and-jail-em AND **nailer** *n.* the police in general; a police officer. ♦ *Old nail-em-and-jail-em is going to be knocking at your door any day now.* ♦ *Victor mooned a nailer and almost got nailed.*

nailer Go to **nail-em-and-jail-em**.

naked *mod.* undiluted; having to do with neat liquor, especially gin. (See also **raw**.) ♦ *No ice, please. I want mine naked.*

naked truth *n.* the complete, unembellished truth. ♦ *Sorry to put it to you like this, but it's the naked truth.*

Nam *n.* Vietnam. ♦ *How long were you in Nam?*

namby-pamby ['næmbi'pæmbi] *mod.* overly nice; effeminate and weak, when said of a male. ♦ *Fred is too namby-pamby when it comes to making up his mind.*

the **name of the game** *n.* the way things are; the way things can be expected to be. ♦ *The name of the game is money, money, money.*

Name your poison. *sent.* State what you want to drink. (Refers to alcoholic drinks only.) ♦ *Okay, friend, name your poison.*

narc Go to nark.

narc(o) ['nɑrk(o)] **1.** *n.* a narcotic. (See also nark.) ♦ *She's been taking narcs.* **2.** *mod.* having to do with narcotics. ♦ *Does he have a narc problem?* **3.** *n.* a federal narcotics agent; any narcotics enforcement officer. ♦ *The narcs caught him.*

nard guard *n.* a male genital protector. (See also nads, nards.) ♦ *There was a nard guard attached to the center of the handlebars.*

nards 1. *n.* the testicles; the (male) genitals. (See also nads. Probably from *gonads*.) ♦ *Yeouch! Right in the nards!* **2.** *n.* courage; bravado; balls. ♦ *That guy has nards!*

nark AND **narc** [nɑrk] **1.** *n.* a police informer. ♦ *Fred is a nark. He squealed.* **2.** *in.* to inform (on someone) to the police; to squeal. (Often with *on*.) ♦ *Don't nark on me!* **3.** *tv.* to annoy someone. (See also narked.) ♦ *Stop narking me!* **4.** *n.* any unpleasant person. ♦ *Tell that narc to get lost.*

narked [nɑrkt] *mod.* annoyed. (Usually with *at* or *with*.) ♦ *He's really narked at us.*

narky ['nɑrki] *n.* a narcotic drug. ♦ *They caught him with a lot of narky in his pockets.*

narly Go to (g)narly.

narrow squeak *n.* a success almost not achieved; a lucky or marginal success; a problem almost not surmounted. ♦ *That was a narrow squeak. I don't know how I survived.*

natch [nætʃ] *interj.* yes; naturally. ♦ *Natch, you can borrow my car.*

natural *n.* someone with obvious natural talent. ♦ *Can she ever dance! What a natural!*

natural-born *mod.* born with talent or skill. ♦ *She is really a natural-born dancer.*

nature's call AND **call of nature** *n.* the feeling of a need to go to the toilet. ♦ *I think I feel nature's call coming on.*

nature stop *n.* a stop to use the toilet, especially during road travel. (Euphemistic.) ♦ *I think I need a nature stop when it's convenient.*

naughty bits *n.* genitals; breasts. (From a skit on *Monty Python's Flying Circus*, a popular late 1960–1970s BBC comedy series still seen worldwide in reruns.) ♦ *Those grape smugglers don't do much for the naughty bits.*

nause SO **out** *tv.* to nauseate someone. ♦ *That horrible smell really nauses me out.*

naw *interj.* no. ♦ *Naw, I didn't do that.*

nay *mod.* ugly; unfavorable. (From *nasty*.) ♦ *What a nay thing to say.*

NBD *interj.* no big deal. (Initialism.) ♦ *So you're a little late. NBD.*

NBT *n.* no big thing. (Initialism.) ♦ *Hey, man! Don't make a fuss! It's NBT.*

neanderthal [ni'ændɚθal] *n.* a large and ugly male. (See also caveman; cromagnon.) ♦ *Tell that neanderthal to get out of here.*

near-beer *n.* beer with less than 1/2 percent alcohol content. (Originally from the Prohibition era.) ♦ *You can drink a lot of near-beer without getting drunk.*

neat 1. *mod.* great; cool; fine. ♦ *That was not a very neat thing to do.* **2.** *exclam.* Wow! (Usually **Neat!**) ♦ *Neat! I'm glad you came.*

neato (canito) ['nito (kə'nito)] *exclam.* really fine. (HHH) ♦ *Look at this! Neato canito!*

neb(bish) ['nɛb(ɪʃ)] *n.* a dull person; a jerk. (From Yiddish.) ♦ *Taylor is such a nebbish. Why doesn't she just give up?*

Nebraska sign *n.* a flat EEG indicating the death of the patient being monitored. (From the flatness of the state of Nebraska. See also flatline. Medical.) ♦ *I saw* *the Nebraska sign on my monitor and knew it must not be hooked up right.*

the **necessary** *n.* money; an income. (Also a really old term for a toilet or bathroom.) ♦ *I can always use more of the necessary.*

neck *in.* to cuddle and kiss. (Always in reference to lovers or boy-girl relationships.) ♦ *There are some teenagers in the back room, necking.*

neck and neck *mod.* almost even. (See also **nip and tuck**. Refers to horse's necks being at the same place with regard to the finish line.) ♦ *The horses were neck and neck at the finish line.*

needle *tv.* to annoy someone. ♦ *Tom is always needling Frank.*

needle candy *n.* narcotics that are taken by injection. (Drugs. See also **nose (candy)**.) ♦ *Max likes needle candy best of all.*

negative *n.* any drawback or bad thing about someone or something. ♦ *There are too many negatives associated with your plan.*

negatory *mod.* no; negative. ♦ *Q: Are you going to leave now? A: Negatory.*

nerd AND **nurd** [nɚd] *n.* a dull and bookish person, usually a male. ♦ *That whole gang of boys is just a bunch of nurds.*

nerd magnet *n.* a girl or woman who attracts dull males. ♦ *Sally is weary of dating total drips. She is a classic nerd magnet.*

nerd mobile *n.* a full-sized, uninteresting car; a family car. ♦ *My father always buys some kind of stupid nerd mobile.*

nerd pack *n.* a plastic sheath for holding pens in a pocket, protecting the cloth from ink. (This is the classic symbol of a bookish nerd.) ♦ *A real nerd wears a nerd pack in the pocket of a dirty shirt.*

nerts Go to **nurts**.

nervous Nellie *n.* any nervous person, male or female. ♦ *Sue is such a nervous Nellie. She should calm down.*

nervy 1. *mod.* nervous. ♦ *Mary is so nervy. Anything will set her off.* **2.** *mod.* daring; courageous. ♦ *Don't get nervy with me!*

nest egg *n.* money saved for some important purpose, such as retirement. ♦ *I lost most of my nest egg in the market crash.*

net result *n.* the final result after all the assets and liabilities have balanced out. ♦ *I don't care about the little things. What is the net result?*

never mind *phr.* Forget it.; It doesn't matter anymore. ♦ *Never mind. I forget what I was going to say.*

New York's finest *n.* a New York City police officer. ♦ *Three of New York's finest were standing there at my door with my lost dog.*

newbie AND **noob** *n.* someone who is new to a group, place, activity, etc. (The opposite of **oldbie**.) ♦ *I'm just a newbie, but I do have a question for the group.* ♦ *Will you noobs ever learn to read the FAQ?*

newshound *n.* a newspaper reporter who pursues a story with the same diligence used by a bloodhound. ♦ *Tell that newshound that I'll sue her if she prints that!*

newt *n.* a stupid person; a dull and uninteresting person. ♦ *Don't act like such a newt.*

nibble 1. *n.* a cautious or preliminary response to something. (See also **nybble**.) ♦ *My advertisement got three nibbles this morning.* **2.** *in.* to reply cautiously or tentatively to something. ♦ *I hope someone who wants to buy my car nibbles at the description I posted on the Internet.*

nicca Go to **nigga**.

nice meeting you *tv.* it is nice to have met you. (Said when leaving someone whose acquaintance you have just made.) ♦ *I must go now, Fred. Nice meeting you.*

nice talking to you *in.* it's been pleasant, good-bye. (A leave-taking formula, sometimes with an air of dismissal.) ♦ *Nice talking to you. Call my service.*

nick 1. *tv.* to arrest someone. (See also **nicked**.) ♦ *The cops nicked Paul outside his* house. **2.** *tv.* to steal something. ♦ *The thugs nicked a couple of apples from the fruit stand.* **3.** *tv.* to get or take something. ♦ *Tom nicked a copy of the test for Sam, who also needed one.* **4.** *n.* nicotine. ♦ *I'm craving some nick.*

nicked *mod.* arrested. ♦ *"Now I'm nicked," he said.*

nickel and dime so **(to death)** *tv.* to make numerous small monetary charges that add up to a substantial sum. ♦ *Just give me the whole bill at one time. Don't nickel and dime me for days on end.*

nifty 1. *mod.* neat; smart. ♦ *That is a pretty nifty car you have there.* **2.** *n.* a fifty-dollar bill. (From *nifty-fifty*.) ♦ *He paid me with a nifty and a domino.*

nigga AND **nicca** *n.* nigger; Negro. (Streets. *Nicca* is pronunciation and/or spelling variant. Restricted to black to black use. White to black use is provocative.) ♦ *Hey, my nigga!*

night person *n.* a person who prefers to be active in the nighttime. (The plural is with *people*. Compare this with **day person**.) ♦ *I can't function in the morning. I'm strictly a night person.*

NIMBY Go to Not in my backyard!

nimrod ['nɪmrɑd] *n.* a simpleton; a nerd. ♦ *What stupid nimrod left the lid off the cottage cheese?*

nineteenth hole *n.* a place to buy an alcoholic beverage after a golf game. (Likely to be filled with golfers who have played eighteen holes of golf.) ♦ *I hit a hole-in-one on the first hole and went straight to the nineteenth hole to celebrate.*

nine-to-five *mod.* typical in terms of working hours; structured and scheduled, starting and ending at set times. (From the expression *from nine to five*, normal working hours.) ♦ *I really wanted a nine-to-five job until I finally got one.*

nip 1. *n.* a small, quick drink of liquor. ♦ *Here, have a nip of this stuff.* **2.** *in.* to take small drinks of liquor periodically. (See also **nipped**.) ♦ *After nipping all day, Fred was pretty well stewed by dinnertime.*

3. *tv.* to steal something. ♦ *The punk kid nipped two candy bars from the drugstore.*

nip and tuck *mod.* so close as to be almost the same; neck and neck. ♦ *They ran nip and tuck all the way to the finish line, but Tom won the race.*

nipped *mod.* alcohol intoxicated. (See also **nip**.) ♦ *All four of them went out and got nipped.*

nippers *n.* handcuffs; leg fetters. ♦ *No, not the nippers. They hurt my arms.*

nipply *mod.* [of weather] cold. (A play on *nippy [weather]* and what such weather may do to the human nipples.) ♦ *It's a little nipply out this morning.*

nitery ['naɪtə·i] *n.* a nightclub. ♦ *There is a cheap nitery over on Twelfth Street where Chuck has a job.*

nit-picker *n.* a person who is hypercritical. ♦ *Mary is such a nit-picker!*

nit-picking *n.* too much minor criticism; overly particular criticism; nagging. ♦ *Enough nit-picking! What are the major problems?*

nitty-gritty ['nɪdi 'grɪdi] *n.* the essence; the essential points. (Usually in **get down to the nitty-gritty**.) ♦ *Once we are down to the nitty-gritty, we can begin to sort things out.*

nitwit *n.* someone who behaves stupidly. (Also a term of address.) ♦ *Please stop acting like a nitwit all the time.*

nix [nɪks] (All senses from German *nichts*.) **1.** *interj.* no. ♦ *The man said nix, and he means nix.* **2.** *exclam.* No!; Stop it!; I disagree! (Usually **Nix!**) ♦ *"Nix," said Paul. "I can't permit that."* **3.** *n.* nothing. ♦ *I got nix for a tip. And after I was so helpful!* **4.** *tv.* to put a stop to something; to say no to something; to ban something; to turn something down. ♦ *I wanted to say a certain word in my speech, but the management nixed it.*

nizzle *n.* fellow black; nigga. (See also **Fo shizzle, ma nizzle!** Restricted to black to black use. White to black use is provocative. Streets. Also for other words with initial *N*.) ♦ *Tsup, nizzle?*

no bargain *n.* not an especially good person or thing. ♦ *This car gets me to work and back, but it's no bargain.*

no big deal AND **no biggie; no big whoop** *n.* (something) not difficult or troublesome. (See also NBT.) ♦ *Don't worry. It's no big deal.* ♦ *No biggie; no prob.*

no big whoop Go to no big deal.

no biggie Go to no big deal.

no brand cigarette Go to cigarette with no name.

No can do! *sent.* It can't be done.; I can't do it. ♦ *Lend you $200? No can do!*

no dice *interj.* no; not possible. ♦ *When I asked about a loan, he said, No dice.*

no earthly reason *n.* no conceivable reason. ♦ *I can think of no earthly reason why the repairs should cost so much.*

no end of sth *n.* an endless supply of something. ♦ *I've had no end of trouble ever since I bought this car.*

No fair! *exclam.* That's not fair! ♦ *That's no fair! We paid full price to see this movie.*

no go ['no 'go] *mod.* negative; inopportune. (This is hyphenated before a nominal.) ♦ *We're in a no-go situation.*

no great shakes *phr.* someone or something not very good. (There is no affirmative version of this.) ♦ *Your idea is no great shakes, but we'll try it anyway.*

no holds barred *mod.* without restriction. (There is no affirmative version of this.) ♦ *I want you to get that contract. Do anything—no holds barred.*

No kidding! *exclam.* I am not kidding.; You are not kidding (are you)? ♦ *No kidding! I never thought she would do that.*

No lie! *exclam.* Honest!; No kidding! ♦ *I was there on time. No lie! Ask my sister.*

no name cigarette Go to cigarette with no name.

No nukes! ['no 'nuks OR 'no 'njuks] *exclam.* a cry against nuclear energy, weapons, submarines, etc. ♦ *No nukes! Make my electricity the old-fashioned way.*

No problem 1. AND **No prob; NP** *phr.* All is well.; There is no problem, so don't worry or fret. (Often said after someone else says *I'm sorry.*) ♦ *No problem. I can do it easily.* ♦ *A: Gee! I'm sorry! B: No prob.* **2.** *phr.* you are welcome. (Sometimes said after someone else says *thank you.*) ♦ *A: Thanks a lot. B: No problem.*

no sale *interj.* no. ♦ *I wanted to go to Florida for the holidays, but my father said, "No sale."*

No Shinola! [...ʃaɪ'nolə] *exclam.* You are kidding!; No shit! (A play on the expression indicating that a stupid person doesn't know shit from Shinola. Shinola is a brand of shoe polish.) ♦ *So taxes are too high? No Shinola!*

No shit! *exclam.* You are kidding me, aren't you! (Usually objectionable. Akin to bullshit.) ♦ *You're really gonna do it? No shit!*

No shit, Sherlock! AND **NSS** *exclam. & comp. abb.* a phrase said when someone has stated the obvious. (Refers to Sherlock Holmes, the world's greatest fictional "Consulting Detective." See also Sherlock.) ♦ *No shit, Sherlock. Everybody knows that!*

no show AND **no-show** *n.* someone who doesn't show up for something, such as an airline flight. ♦ *The flight was canceled because there were too many no-shows.*

no soap *interj.* no. ♦ *No soap, I don't lend anyone money.*

no stress *interj.* no problem; no bother. ♦ *Relax. No stress. It doesn't bother me at all.*

no sweat *interj.* no problem; Don't worry; it is no problem. ♦ *It's no big deal. No sweat.*

No way! *exclam.* No! (Compare this with Way!) ♦ *She can't do that. No way!*

No way, José! *phr.* No! (An elaboration of *No. José* is pronounced with an initial *H*.) ♦ *Sorry. No can do. No way, José!*

a **nobody** *n.* an insignificant person. (Compare this with somebody.) ♦ *Don't pay any attention to him. He's just a nobody.*

no-brainer *n.* an easy question that takes no thinking to answer; a simple problem that requires no intellect to solve; a dilemma that requires no pondering to resolve. ♦ *His proposal of marriage was a no-brainer. She turned him down flat on the spot.*

no-brow *n.* a stupid person. (Patterned on lowbrow.) ♦ *Sam is a complete no-brow. No culture, no sense of style, and no money.*

nodded out *mod.* in heroin euphoria; under the influence of heroin. (Drugs.) ♦ *Max nodded out after his fix.*

no-good 1. *n.* a worthless person. ♦ *Tell that no-good to leave.* **2.** *mod.* worthless; bad. ♦ *I have never heard of such a no-good car dealership before.*

no-goodnik [no'gʊdnɪk] *n.* someone who is no good. (The *nik* is from Russian via Yiddish.) ♦ *Tell the no-goodnik to leave quietly, or I will call the police.*

noid *n.* a paranoid person. ♦ *Some of those noids write hilarious letters to the editor.*

noise 1. *n.* empty talk; nonsense. ♦ *I've had enough of your noise. Shut up!* **2.** *n.* heroin. (Drugs.) ♦ *Man, I need some noise now! I hurt!*

non compos ['nɑn 'kɑmpos] **1.** *mod.* out of one's mind; *non compos mentis.* ♦ *She is strictly non compos!* **2.** AND **non compos poopoo** *mod.* alcohol intoxicated. ♦ *That gal isn't just drunk. She's non compos poopoo.*

non compos poopoo Go to non compos.

none of SO's **beeswax** [...'bizwæks] *n.* none of someone's business. ♦ *It's none of your beeswax. I'm not telling.*

no-no ['nono] *n.* something that is not (to be) done. (Essentially juvenile.) ♦ *She seems to delight in doing all the no-nos.*

noob Go to newbie.

noodge Go to nudge.

noodle *n.* (one's) head. ♦ *Put your hat on your noodle, and let's go.*

noogie *n.* a painful rubbing of someone's scalp with the knuckles. ♦ *Bob gave Bill a noogie and Bill punched him in the gut.*

nookie Go to pussy.

nooky Go to pussy.

nope *interj.* no. ♦ *She asked him to do it, but he said, "Nope."*

nose (candy) *n.* powdered drugs that are inhaled, primarily cocaine, sometimes heroin. (Drugs. See also needle candy.) ♦ *Bart has some nose candy for sale.*

nose habit *n.* an addiction to sniffed drugs, usually heroin or cocaine. (Drugs.) ♦ *One sniff of that white powder and she'll get a nose habit, for sure.*

nose hit *n.* marijuana smoke taken through the nose from the burning end of the cigarette. (Drugs.) ♦ *Wilmer likes to take nose hits.*

nose job *n.* a plastic surgery operation to change the appearance of one's nose. ♦ *I don't want a nose job. What I got is good enough.*

nosebleed seats *n.* seats high up in an arena, theater, or opera house. ♦ *We could only afford the nosebleed seats for the opera.*

nose-burner AND **nose-warmer** *n.* a marijuana cigarette stub; a roach. (Drugs.) ♦ *Hey, man! Can I have a hit of that little nose-burner?* ♦ *He quickly stubbed out a little nose-burner when he heard the garage door open.*

nosedive *n.* a great drop; a great decline. (As with a bird or an airplane diving—nose first—toward the ground. See also take a nosedive.) ♦ *This year our profits have taken a nosedive.*

nose-lunger ['nozləŋɚ] *n.* a mass of nasal mucus. (See also lunger.) ♦ *Beavis thought the funniest thing in the world was having a nose-lunger dangling from his chin.*

243

nose-warmer 1. *n.* a short tobacco pipe. ♦ *Fred smokes a nose-warmer, especially in the winter.* **2.** Go to nose-burner.

nosh [nɑʃ] **1.** *n.* a snack. (From German via Yiddish.) ♦ *I don't want a nosh. I need a whole meal.* **2.** *in.* to snack. ♦ *Every time I see you, you're noshing.*

nosh on sth ['nɑʃ...] *in.* to make a snack of something. ♦ *After Thanksgiving, we noshed on turkey for three days.*

nosher ['nɑʃɚ] *n.* someone who is always eating snacks. (See also nosh.) ♦ *I don't know of a single nosher who's not fat.*

nosy parker AND **nosey Parker** ['nozi 'parkɚ] *n.* a nosy person. (Also a term of address. No one really knows who or what parker is or was. It is an old expression, used in British and American English, at least. Some would like to derive it from *nose-poker*, but there is no record of the latter aver having been said.) ♦ *Look, you nosy parker, mind your own business.*

Not! *interj.* Not really so! (A tag phrase added to the end of a statement, changing it from affirmative to negative. There is usually a pause before Not!, which is said on a level pitch somewhat higher than the sentence that comes before.) ♦ *Of course I'm going to pay $100 a ticket to see a rock concert. Not!*

not a chance *interj.* no. ♦ *Me lend you money? Not a chance!*

not all that *phr.* not all that much. (Streets.) ♦ *A: She can run like the wind. B: She can run fast but not all that.*

not all there *mod.* crazy; stupid acting. ♦ *You can't depend on Paul for much help. He's really not all there.*

not cricket *mod.* unfair; illegitimate; unorthodox. (See affirmative examples at cricket.) ♦ *What do you mean it's not cricket? You do it.*

not enough room to swing a cat *tv.* very crowded or cramped; [of a room] small, ♦ *It's really crowded in here. Not enough room to swing a cat.*

not grow on trees *in.* not to be abundant; not to be wasted. (Usually said about money.) ♦ *Don't waste the glue. That stuff doesn't grow on trees, you know.*

Not in my backyard! AND **NIMBY** *exclam. & comp. abb.* Don't locate something undesirable close to me. (Describes an attitude that people express about having noisy or dirty facilities installed close to where they live.) ♦ *When you say, build the new incinerator here, I say NIMBY.*

not just whistling Dixie [...'dɪksi] *tv.* not talking nonsense. (Folksy. Refers to a song titled *Dixie*.) ♦ *Man, you are right! You're not just whistling Dixie.*

not know beans (about sth**)** *tv.* to know nothing about something. ♦ *Don't pay any attention to her. She doesn't know beans.*

not know from nothing *in.* to be stupid, innocent, and naive. (Usually with *don't*, as in the example. Always in the negative. See also know from sth.) ♦ *Tom don't know from nothing. He is really dense.*

not know one's ass from a hole in the ground *tv.* not to be knowledgeable; not to be alert and effective. (Usually objectionable.) ♦ *That stupid son of a bitch doesn't know his ass from a hole in the ground.*

not know shit about sth *tv.* not to know anything about something. (Usually objectionable.) ♦ *You've worked here for a month, and you don't know shit about this job!*

not know shit from shinola *tv.* to know what's what; to be knowledgeable in the ways of the world. (See also No shinola! Usually objectionable.) ♦ *That jerk doesn't know shit from shinola! Don't even ask him about it!*

Not my dog. Go to (It's) not my dog.

Not to worry. *phr.* Don't worry. ♦ *You lost your ticket? Not to worry. I'll give you mine.*

not too shabby 1. *mod.* [with emphasis on *shabby*] nice; well done. ♦ *Is that your car? Not too shabby!* **2.** *mod.* [with emphasis on *too*] very shabby; very poor indeed.

(Sarcastic.) ♦ *What a way to treat someone. Not too shabby!*

not worth a damn *mod.* worthless. ♦ *When it comes to keeping score, she's not worth a damn.*

not worth a plugged nickel *mod.* worth little or nothing. ♦ *This new battery is not worth a plugged nickel.*

not worth beans *mod.* worthless. ♦ *This paint is not worth beans. I'll have to buy another can.*

notch *tv.* to count up something; to add up or score something. ♦ *Well, it looks like we notched another victory.*

Nothing doing! *exclam.* No!; I refused to do it! ♦ *Me, go to the opera? Nothing doing!*

Nothing to it! *exclam.* It is very easy! ♦ *Look, anybody can do it! Nothing to it!*

nothing to sneeze at *n.* no small amount of money; something not inconsequential. ♦ *It's not a lot of money, but it's nothing to sneeze at.*

nothing to write home about *n.* something small or inconsequential. ♦ *I got a little bit of a raise this year, but it was nothing to write home about.*

nothing upstairs *phr.* no brains; stupid. ♦ *Tom is sort of stupid acting. You know—nothing upstairs.* ♦ *I know what's wrong with you. Nothing upstairs.*

now generation *n.* the (once current) generation of young people who seemed to want only instant gratification. ♦ *All those people in the now generation want to start out with fancy cars and nice houses.*

Now what? *interrog.* What is wrong now? ♦ *I ran into the room and stopped in front of Tom. "Now what?" asked Tom.*

Now you're talking! *exclam.* What you are saying is making sense! ♦ *Now you're talking! You've got a great idea!*

nowhere *mod.* bad; no good; dull. ♦ *This place is really nowhere. Let's go.*

no-win situation *n.* a situation in which there is no hope of success. ♦ *I find myself in a no-win situation again.*

NP Go to No problem.

NSS Go to No shit, Sherlock!

nudge AND **noodge** [nʊdʒ] **1.** *n.* someone who nags. ♦ *Sally can be such a nudge!* **2.** *in.* to nag. ♦ *Don't noodge all the time.* **3.** *tv.* to nag someone. ♦ *Stop nudging me about that.*

nudie ['nudi] *n.* a movie featuring nudes. (See also skin flick.) ♦ *There is a nudie playing over at the Roxie Theater.*

nudnik ['nʊdnɪk] *n.* a bore; a pest; a crank. (From Russian via Yiddish. Also a term of address.) ♦ *Tell that nudnik to stay away from here. He is such a pest.*

nuggets *n.* the testicles. ♦ *Man, my nuggets are cold! Let's hurry up and get back in the car.*

nuke 1. *n.* a nuclear weapon. ♦ *Are there nukes aboard that ship?* **2.** *tv.* to destroy someone or something. (As with a nuclear weapon.) ♦ *Your cat ran through my garden and totally nuked my flowers!* **3.** *tv.* to microwave something. ♦ *I have to nuke my dinner and then I will be right over.*

Nuke it! *tv.* Throw it away! ♦ *You don't need this thing. Nuke it!*

nuke oneself [n(j)uk...] *tv.* to tan oneself at a tanning salon. ♦ *I nuke myself once a week in the spring so I will be ready for the summer bikini season.*

nuker ['n(j)ukɚ] *n.* a microwave oven. ♦ *I tried to do a turkey in the nuker once and made a real mess of it.*

numbed out *mod.* nearly paralyzed by phencyclidine (PCP). (Drugs.) ♦ *The teenager was nearly numbed out when they brought her in.*

number 1. *n.* a girl or woman; a sexually attractive girl. ♦ *Who is that cute little number I saw you with?* **2.** *n.* a marijuana cigarette. (Drugs.) ♦ *Shorty lit up a number just as the boss came in.* **3.** *n.* any person or thing. ♦ *This is an interesting little number. You attach it to your bicycle handlebars.* **4.** *n.* an act or performance; a performance specialty. ♦ *Ann did her number and left the stage.*

A number 1 Go to A-1.

number crunching *n.* using a computer to solve enormously complicated or complex mathematical problems. ♦ *I don't do a lot of number crunching, so I don't need a terribly fast machine.*

number one 1. *mod.* top rate; best. (See also numero uno.) ♦ *We heard the number one high school band in the whole state last night.* **2.** *n.* oneself. ♦ *I don't know who will pay for the broken window, but old number one isn't!* **3.** *n.* urination; an act of urination. ♦ *Jimmy made a mess in his pants. But don't worry. It's just number one.*

number two *n.* defecation; an act of defecation. ♦ *Mommy! I gotta do a number two.*

number-cruncher 1. *n.* someone who works with figures; an accountant. ♦ *The number-crunchers are trying to get the annual report ready.* **2.** *n.* a large and powerful computer. (Computers.) ♦ *They traded in the old computer for a powerful number-cruncher.*

numbnuts *n.* a jerk; a worthless person. (Usually a male.) ♦ *Hey, numbnuts! What did you do that for?*

numero uno ['numɚo 'uno] **1.** *n.* number one; the best. (Spanish. See also number one.) ♦ *This coffee is numero uno in my book.* **2.** *n.* oneself; number one. ♦ *I always look out for numero uno.*

nummy ['nəmi] tasty; yummy. (Also juvenile or baby talk.) ♦ *Here, Jimmy, don't you want a spoon of this nummy food?*

nunya ['nən jə] *phr.* none of your [business]. ♦ *Nunya. Why do you want to know?*

nurd Go to nerd.

nurts AND **nerts** [nɚts] **1.** *n.* nonsense. ♦ *Oh, that's just nerts. I don't believe a word of it.* **2.** *interj.* a mild expression of distress or dismay. (Usually **Nerts!; Nurts!**.) ♦ *Oh, nerts! I forgot my wallet.*

nut 1. *n.* an odd or strange person; a crazy person. ♦ *Some nut is going to try to fly from the top of one building to another.*

2. *n.* [one's] head. ♦ *The baseball came in fast. Clonk! Right on the nut!* **3.** *n.* an enthusiast (about something). ♦ *Paul is a nut about chocolate cake.*

nut factory Go to nuthouse.

nut up 1. *in.* to go crazy; to go nuts. ♦ *I've got to have a vacation soon, or I'm going to nut up.* **2.** AND **sack up** *in.* get courage; to grow some balls. ♦ *Come on, man! Nut up! Stand up for yourself!* ♦ *Sack up and let's go win this game.*

nutcake *n.* a stupid person. (See also fruitcake.) ♦ *Stop acting like such a nutcake all the time.*

nutcase *n.* a crazy person. ♦ *She's a nutcase! Always doing silly things.*

nut-foundry Go to nuthouse.

nuthatch Go to nuthouse.

nuthouse AND **nut factory; nut-foundry; nuthatch** *n.* an insane asylum. ♦ *The teacher spent three years in the nuthouse.* ♦ *When did you get out of the nut factory?*

nutpick *n.* a psychoanalyst. ♦ *Bill pays a nutpick about $100 an hour just to listen.*

nuts AND **nutz 1.** *mod.* crazy. (There is no difference in pronunciation between nuts and nutz.) ♦ *That whole idea is just nuts!* **2.** *exclam.* No!; I don't believe you!; I don't care! (Usually **Nuts!**) ♦ *Oh, nuts! I forgot my wallet.* **3.** *n.* the testicles. (Usually objectionable.) ♦ *Chuck got kneed in the nuts in a football game.*

nuts and bolts 1. *n.* the mundane workings of something; the basics of something. ♦ *She's got a lot of good, general ideas, but when it comes to the nuts and bolts of getting something done, she's no good.* **2.** *n.* the subject of psychology in college. ♦ *Tom is flunking nuts and bolts because he won't participate in the required "experiments."*

Nuts to you! *exclam.* Go away!; Drop dead! ♦ *Nuts to you! I will not lend you money!*

nutsack *n.* the scrotum. ♦ *He's got an itch on the nutsack.*

nutter *n.* a nutty person. ♦ *That guy is a real nutter. Thinks he can get a cab at this hour.*

nuttery *n.* an insane asylum; the place where nuts are kept. (See also nut.) ♦ *If you keep acting so odd, we'll have to put you in a nuttery.*

nutty *mod.* silly; giddy; stupid. ♦ *What a nutty idea!*

nutty as a fruitcake Go to (as) nutty as a fruitcake.

nutz Go to nuts.

nybble ['nɪbl̩] *n.* four bits of computer memory. (Literally, one half of a *bite*, i.e., a *byte*.) ♦ *My program wouldn't work just because I had one silly little nybble wrong!*

oak(s) [oks] *mod.* OK; satisfactory; worthy. (Prisons.) ♦ *That dude's oaks.*

oasis [o'esəs] *n.* a place to buy liquor. ♦ *Let's go into this oasis here and pick up a few bottles.*

oater ['odə˞] *n.* a Western movie. (From the oats that the horses eat. See also **horse opera**.) ♦ *Let's go out and see a good old-fashioned oater.*

ob [ɑb] *mod.* obvious. ♦ *It's pretty ob that you are just trying to start something.*

obliterated *mod.* drunk. ♦ *Fred was obliterated and couldn't walk to his car, let alone drive it.*

obno(c) ['ɑb'nɑk AND 'ɑbno] *mod.* obnoxious; disgusting. ♦ *I wish you weren't so obnoc all the time!*

obtanium 1. *n.* a substance or thing that can be obtained. ♦ *I need some kind of very strong glue. I don't know if it's obtanium.* **2.** *mod.* obtainable. ♦ *She's a beaut! Is she obtanium?*

occifer Go to **ossifer**.

OD 1. *n.* an overdose of a drug. (Initialism. Drugs.) ♦ *If you take an OD and no one is around, you may end up dead.* **2.** *in.* to purposely or accidentally give oneself a fatal dose of drugs. (Drugs.) ♦ *I knew he would OD someday.* **3.** *in.* to die from an overdose of drugs. (Drugs.) ♦ *Two kids at my school ODed last weekend.* **4.** *n.* a person who has taken an overdose of drugs. (Hospitals.) ♦ *How many ODs did you get in here last weekend?*

odd bird AND **strange bird** *n.* a strange or eccentric person. ♦ *Mr. Wilson certainly is an odd bird.* ♦ *You're a strange bird, but you're fun.*

oddball 1. *n.* an eccentric person. ♦ *Tom is sure an oddball. He ordered a pineapple and strawberry milkshake.* **2.** *mod.* strange; peculiar. ♦ *Your oddball ideas have cost us too much money.*

odd-bod ['ɑdbɑd] **1.** *n.* a strange person. ♦ *Who is that odd-bod over in the corner?* **2.** *n.* a person with a strange body. ♦ *I am such an odd-bod that it's hard to find clothes that fit.* **3.** *n.* a peculiar body. ♦ *I have such an odd-bod that it's hard to find clothes.*

odds-on *mod.* having to do with the thing or person favored to win. ♦ *My horse is an odds-on favorite to win.*

Of all the nerve! *exclam.* I am shocked by your domineering and high-handed behavior. ♦ *Of all the nerve! Asking me to do a thing like that!*

off 1. *mod.* alcohol or drug intoxicated. ♦ *She is truly off.* **2.** *tv.* to dispose of someone or something; to kill someone. ♦ *The crooks offed the witness before the trial.* **3.** *in.* to die. (See also **outed**.) ♦ *The guy just falls down and offs, right there on Main Street.*

off artist Go to **(rip-)off artist**.

off color *mod.* dirty or smutty; raunchy. (Usually hyphenated before a nominal.) ♦ *That joke was sort of off color.*

off one's **chump** *mod.* crazy; nuts. ♦ *Am I off my chump, or did that car suddenly disappear?*

off one's **meds** *phr.* acting strangely. ♦ *Man, what a temper! Must be off her meds.*

off one's **nut 1.** *mod.* crazy; out of one's head. ♦ *Don't pay any attention to her. She's off her nut.* **2.** *mod.* alcohol intoxicated. ♦ *Those guys are so off their nuts!*

off one's **rocker** *mod.* silly; giddy; crazy. (See also rocker.) ♦ *That silly dame is off her rocker.*

off one's **trolley** *mod.* silly; eccentric. ♦ *Don't mind Uncle Charles. He's a bit off his trolley.*

off the hook 1. *mod.* no longer in jeopardy; no longer obligated. ♦ *I'll let you off the hook this time, but never again.* **2.** *mod.* crazy. (Referring to the telephone—disconnected.) ♦ *She's so ditzy—really off the hook.*

off the track *mod.* not on a productive course; following the wrong lead. ♦ *You are off the track just a little. Let me help you.*

off the wagon 1. *mod.* drinking liquor after a period of abstinence. ♦ *Poor John fell off the wagon again. Drunk as a skunk.* **2.** *mod.* back on drugs after a period of abstinence. ♦ *Harry the Horse is off the wagon and shooting up again.*

off-brand cigarette *n.* a marijuana cigarette. (Drugs.) ♦ *Shorty smokes nothing but those off-brand cigarettes.*

offed Go to outed.

off-the-shelf *mod.* readily available; purchasable without any special difficulties or delays. ♦ *This is just plain old off-the-shelf hand lotion. Isn't it great?*

off-the-wall *mod.* strange; improbable; nonsensical. ♦ *Your ideas are generally off-the-wall, but this one makes sense.*

OFS Go to one-finger salute.

Oh, boy! *exclam.* Wow! ♦ *Oh, boy! What a mess!*

Oh, yeah? ['o 'jæə] *exclam.* Is that what you think?; Are you trying to start a fight? ♦ *Oh, yeah? What makes you think so?*

OIC *phr.* Oh, I see. (Initialism.) ♦ *OIC! So that's how it's done.*

oil it *tv.* to study all night. (Literally, *burn the midnight oil.*) ♦ *I have a test tomorrow, and I really have to oil it tonight.*

oiled *mod.* alcohol or drug intoxicated. ♦ *She's not just drunk; she's totally oiled.*

oilhead *n.* a drunkard; an alcoholic. ♦ *Paul gave the oilhead a quarter, knowing it would be spent on cheap wine.*

oink [oɪŋk] *n.* a police officer. (A play on pig.) ♦ *There is an oink following us on a motorcycle!*

oink out *in.* to overeat. ♦ *This Thursday starts a four-day weekend, and I plan to oink out every day.*

oinker *n.* a very fat person. (Refers to the fatness of a pig.) ♦ *Who is that oinker who just came into the cafeteria? There won't be any food left for the rest of us.*

OJ 1. *n.* orange juice. (Initialism.) ♦ *I like to have a big glass of fresh OJ every morning.* **2.** Go to overjolt.

OJ so *tv.* to stab someone. (Refers to the O. J. Simpson stabbing case.) ♦ *Don't worry. I would never OJ my buddy.*

OK AND **okay 1.** *interj.* accepted; agreed. (Initialism. From a jocular, mispelled abbreviation *Oll Kerrect.*) ♦ *So, he said, like, "okay," and, like, I go "okay." So we both go "Okay." Okay?* **2.** *mod.* acceptable. ♦ *This cake is okay, but not what I would call first rate.* **3.** *mod.* acceptably. ♦ *She ran okay—nothing spectacular.* **4.** *n.* (someone's) acceptance. ♦ *I won't give the final okay until I see the plans.* **5.** *tv.* to approve something. ♦ *She refused to okay our plans.* **6.** Go to ak.

okay Go to OK.

okey-dokey ['oki'doki] *interj.* yes; OK. (Folksy.) ♦ *Okey-dokey, I'll be there at noon.*

old flame *n.* a former sweetheart or lover. ♦ *It is best to forget an old flame.*

old fogey *n.* an old-fashioned person; an old man. ♦ *My uncle is an old fogey. He must be the most old-fashioned man in the world.*

old girl *n.* an old lady; a lively old lady. ♦ *What makes an old girl like that so feisty?*

old hand (at sth**)** *n.* someone experienced at doing something. ♦ *I'm an old hand at fixing cars.*

old hat *n.* an old-fashioned thing or person; an outmoded thing or person. ♦

That's just old hat. This is the modern world!

old heave-ho ['old 'hiv'ho] *n.* a dismissal; a physical removal of someone from a place. ♦ *I thought my job was secure, but today I got the old heave-ho.*

old lady AND **old woman 1.** *n.* (one's) mother. (Mildly derogatory.) ♦ *What time does your old lady get home?* **2.** *n.* (one's) wife. ♦ *My old woman doesn't like for me to go out without her.* **3.** *n.* (one's) girlfriend. ♦ *My old lady and I are getting married next week.*

old man 1. *n.* (one's) father. ♦ *What time does your old man get home?* **2.** *n.* (one's) husband. ♦ *My old man is sick and can't come with me.* **3.** *n.* (one's) boyfriend. ♦ *I got my old man to take me to see that movie I told you about.* **4.** the **old man** *n.* the boss; a high-ranking officer. (Always with *the* in this sense.) ♦ *The old man says do it, so you had better do it.*

the **old one-two 1.** *n.* a series of two punches delivered quickly, one after another. ♦ *Tom gave Bill the old one-two, and the argument was ended right there.* **2.** *n.* any destructive assault on an idea, thing, or person. ♦ *I gave his proposal the old one-two. Next time he will be better prepared.*

old school AND **old skool** *mod.* vintage; from an earlier time; retro. (Generally positive. As in the well-established expression from the old school.) ♦ *His way of dealing with people is strictly old school.*

old skool Go to old school.

old soldier 1. *n.* a cigarette or cigar butt; a hunk of tobacco. ♦ *The tramp bent over to pick up an old soldier off the pavement.* **2.** *n.* an empty liquor bottle; an empty beer bottle or can. ♦ *Larry hid all his old soldiers under the bed.*

old woman Go to old lady.

oldbie *n.* someone who is not a newbie; someone who is not new to a group, place, activity, etc. ♦ *Speaking as an oldbie, I wish you newbies would RTFF!*

oldie but goodie *n.* something (or even someone) that is old but still likable. ♦

Mary is an oldie but goodie. I'm glad she's still around.

old-timer *n.* an old person; an old man. (Also a term of address.) ♦ *Ask that old-timer over there if it has always been this bad around here.*

OMDB Go to Over my dead body!

on a roll *mod.* in the midst of a series of successes. (See also roll.) ♦ *Things are going great for Larry. He's on a roll now.*

on a shoestring *mod.* on practically no money; on a very tight budget. (See also shoestring.) ♦ *I run my business on a shoestring. I never know from day to day whether I will survive.*

on a tank Go to on the tank.

on a tight leash 1. *mod.* under very careful control. ♦ *We can't do much around here. The boss has us all on a tight leash.* **2.** *mod.* addicted to some drug. ♦ *Wilmer is on a tight leash. He has to have the stuff regularly.*

on easy street *mod.* in a state of financial independence and comfort. (See also easy street.) ♦ *When I get this contract signed, I'll be on easy street.*

on fire 1. *mod.* very attractive or sexy. ♦ *Look at those jet-set people! Each one of them is just on fire.* **2.** *mod.* doing very well; very enthusiastic. ♦ *Fred is on fire in his new job. He'll get promoted in no time.*

on ice *mod.* in reserve. ♦ *That's a great idea, but we'll have to put it on ice until we can afford to put it into action.*

on it *mod.* really good. ♦ *Man, Weasel is really on it! What a rad lad!*

on one's **ass** Go to (flat) on one's ass.

on one's **high horse** *mod.* in a haughty manner or mood; bossy. ♦ *Larry is on his high horse again, bossing people around.*

on one's **last legs** AND **on its last legs** *mod.* about to expire or become nonfunctional. ♦ *This car is on its last legs. We have to get a new one.*

on one's **own hook** *mod.* all by oneself. ♦ *I don't need any help. I can do it on my own hook.*

on so's **tail** *mod.* following someone closely. ♦ *There is a huge truck on my tail. What should I do?*

on so's **watch** *mod.* while someone is on duty. ♦ *I guess I have to bear the blame since it happened on my watch.*

on tap 1. *mod.* having to do with beer sold from a barrel or keg. ♦ *Do you have any imported beers on tap here?* **2.** *mod.* immediately available. ♦ *I have just the kind of person you're talking about on tap.*

on task *mod.* paying attention to the job at hand. ♦ *I find it hard to stay on task with all those babes going by.*

on the back burner *mod.* out of the way; aside and out of consideration. (See also on the shelf.) ♦ *We will have to put this on the back burner for a while.*

on the ball *mod.* knowledgeable; competent; attentive. (See also have a lot on the ball.) ♦ *If you were on the ball, this wouldn't have happened.*

on the bandwagon *mod.* with the majority; following the latest fad. (Often with *hop, get, climb,* or *jump.*) ♦ *Tom always has to climb on the bandwagon. He does no independent thinking.*

on the beam 1. *mod.* homing in on an aviation radio beam. (No longer a major navigational device.) ♦ *The plane was on the beam and landed safely in the fog.* **2.** *mod.* on the right course or track. (From sense 1.) ♦ *That is exactly right. You are right on the beam.* **3.** AND **beaming** *mod.* under the effects of marijuana. (Drugs.) ♦ *Walter is on the beam again. How can he hold a job?* **4.** *mod.* smart; clever. ♦ *That was well done, Tom. You're on the beam.*

on the bean Go to on the button.

on the bird *mod.* available on the TV satellite channels. ♦ *There is a whole lot of good stuff on the bird, but you need a receiving dish to get it.*

on the bleeding edge *phr.* having the most advanced technology; knowing about the most advanced technology. (Jocular. More advanced than *on the cutting edge.*) ♦ *Tom is on the bleeding edge*

when it comes to optical storage technology.

on the blink 1. *mod.* out of order; ill. (See also on the fritz.) ♦ *My refrigerator is on the blink again.* **2.** *mod.* alcohol intoxicated; on a drinking spree. ♦ *They all went out and got on the blink.*

on the button AND **on the bean** *mod.* exactly the right time or place; exactly the right amount. ♦ *He was there on time, right on the button.* ♦ *That's the correct total. You hit it right on the bean.*

on the chopping block *mod.* in serious and threatening straits. ♦ *Until this is resolved, our necks are on the chopping block.*

on the DL *mod.* as a secret; secretly; on the QT. (From *down low.*) ♦ *She'll get in trouble because they did it on the DL.*

on the double *mod.* very fast; twice as fast. (Originally military. Refers to *double time* in marching.) ♦ *Get over here right now— on the double!* ♦ *She wants to see you in her office on the double.*

on the fly *mod.* while something or someone is operating or moving. ♦ *I'll try to capture the data on the fly.*

on the fritz 1. *mod.* not functioning properly. ♦ *My watch is on the fritz.* **2.** *mod.* alcohol intoxicated. ♦ *She drank till she was totally on the fritz.*

on the gooch *mod.* true. ♦ *What I'm telling you is on the gooch, for sure.*

on the horse Go to horsed.

on the hot seat *phr.* in a situation where one is being scrutinized or asked questions. (See also hot seat.) ♦ *I was on the hot seat for about an hour, but they didn't learn anything from me.*

on the juice *mod.* drinking heavily; on a drinking bout. (See also juice.) ♦ *Fred spent the whole week on the juice.*

on the junk *mod.* on drugs; addicted to drugs. (See also junk.) ♦ *Max has been on the junk for all of his adult life.*

on the lam [...læm] *mod.* running from the police. (Underworld.) ♦ *When the boss found out you was on the lam, he got real mad.*

on the level *mod.* honest; straightforward. ♦ *Come on now. Be on the level with me.*

on the make *mod.* ambitious; attempting to be great. ♦ *That young lawyer is sure on the make.*

on the mojo [...'moʤo] *mod.* addicted to morphine; using morphine. (Drugs. See also mojo.) ♦ *How long you been on the mojo?*

on the money *mod.* exactly as desired; at the right amount of money. ♦ *Your new idea is right on the money.*

on the natch [...nætʃ] *mod.* free of drugs; natural and straight. ♦ *I have been on the natch for almost a year.*

on the needle *mod.* addicted to injectable drugs. (Drugs.) ♦ *My sister's on the needle, and I want to help her.*

on the nose *mod.* exactly on time; exactly as planned. ♦ *All three of them were at the appointed place right on the nose.*

on the one hand AND **OT1H** *phr. & comp. abb.* one thing to consider is.... ♦ *OT1H, U R on time, but you forgot to sign in.*

on the outs (with so) *mod.* in a mild dispute with someone; sharing ill will with someone. ♦ *Tom has been on the outs with Bill before. They'll work it out.*

on the pill *mod.* taking birth control pills. ♦ *Is it true that Mary is on the pill?*

on the prowl *mod.* looking for someone for sexual purposes, in the manner of a prowling cat. ♦ *Tom looks like he is on the prowl again tonight.*

on the QT *mod.* in secret; secretly. (From QuieT.) ♦ *He said it on the QT so no one else knows except you and me.*

on the rag 1. *mod.* menstruating. (Usually objectionable.) ♦ *Kim's on the rag and in a bad mood.* **2.** *mod.* ill-tempered. (Usually objectionable.) ♦ *Bill is on the rag and making trouble for everyone.*

on the reezie *mod.* right; true. ♦ *What I'm telling you is on the rezzie, for sure.*

on the rilla *mod.* truly; true. (Possibly related to *really*.) ♦ *On the rilla, he really did it!*

on the road *mod.* traveling from place to place, not necessarily on the highways. (See also get the show on the road.) ♦ *I was on the road with the circus for six months.*

on the rocks 1. *mod.* (of an alcoholic drink) with ice cubes. (See also rocks.) ♦ *I'd like mine on the rocks, please.* **2.** *mod.* in a state of ruin or bankruptcy. (Like a ship that has gone aground on the rocks and cannot be moved.) ♦ *That bank is on the rocks. Don't put your money in it.*

on the run 1. *mod.* while one is moving from place to place. ♦ *I will try to get some aspirin today on the run.* **2.** *mod.* running from the police. ♦ *Shorty is on the run from the cops.*

on the safe side *mod.* taking the risk-free path. ♦ *Let's be on the safe side and call first.*

on the same page *mod.* have the same understanding or amount of knowledge. (As if people were reading from the same page.) ♦ *We're not on the same page. Listen carefully to what I am telling you.*

on the same wavelength *mod.* thinking in the same pattern. ♦ *We're not on the same wavelength. Let's try again.*

on the sauce *mod.* drinking regularly; alcohol intoxicated. ♦ *Poor old Ron is on the sauce again.*

on the shelf 1. *mod.* not active socially; left to oneself in social matters. ♦ *I've been on the shelf long enough. I'm going to make some friends.* **2.** *mod.* postponed. (See also on the back burner.) ♦ *We'll have to put this matter on the shelf for a while.*

on the side 1. *mod.* extra, such as with a job or a side order of food. ♦ *I would like an order of eggs with toast on the side, please.* **2.** *mod.* extramarital; in addition to one's spouse. ♦ *He is married, but also has a woman on the side.*

on the skids *mod.* on the decline. (See also put the skids under so/sth.) ♦ *Her health is really on the skids, but she stays cheery anyway.*

on the sly *mod.* secretly and deceptively. ♦ *She was stealing little bits of money on the sly.*

on the squiff [...skwɪf] *mod.* on a drinking bout. (See also **squiff**.) ♦ *Shorty is always on the squiff, except when he's shooting dope.*

on the street 1. *mod.* using drugs; selling drugs; looking for drugs. (Drugs.) ♦ *Fred spent a year on the street before he was arrested.* **2.** *mod.* engaged in prostitution. ♦ *Mary said, "What am I supposed to do—go on the street?"* ♦ *All three of them went on the street to earn enough money to live.* **3.** *mod.* widely known. ♦ *It's on the street. There isn't anyone who hasn't heard it.* **4.** *mod.* on Wall Street or elsewhere in the New York City financial districts. (Similar to sense 3, except that it refers to a specific street. Usually with a capital S.) ♦ *I heard on the Street today that Apple is buying IBM.* **5.** *mod.* at discount prices; as available from discounters. (As if some item were being sold on the street by a peddler.) ♦ *It lists at $2,200 and can be got for about $1,650 on the street.*

on the take *mod.* taking bribes. (Underworld.) ♦ *Everyone in city hall is on the take.*

on the tank AND **on a tank** *mod.* on a drinking bout. ♦ *All the guys were on the tank last Saturday.*

on the throne *mod.* seated on the toilet. ♦ *I can't come to the phone. I'm on the throne.*

on the up-and-up *mod.* legitimate; open and aboveboard. ♦ *Everything I do is on the up-and-up. I am totally honest.*

on the wagon *mod.* not now drinking alcoholic liquor. ♦ *How long has John been on the wagon this time?*

on the warpath *mod.* very angry. ♦ *I am on the warpath about setting goals and standards again.*

on the wires *mod.* using the telephone. (Landline or cellphone.) ♦ *She can't talk to you now. She's on the wires.*

On your bike! AND **Go to your room!** *imperative* Get out of here!; Go away and stop bothing me. (Neither is to be taken literally.) ♦ *What a bad joke! No puns allowed here! On your bike!* ♦ *Nasty mouth! Such talk! Go to your room!*

on your six *phr.* [look] behind you. (At one's *six o'clock.* See also **Behind you!**)) ♦ *Look out! On your six!*

once in a blue moon *mod.* rarely. ♦ *Once in a blue moon I have a little wine with dinner.*

once over lightly 1. *mod.* quickly and superficially; carelessly; cursorily. (This is hyphenated before a nominal.) ♦ *He looked at it once over lightly and agreed to do it.* **2.** *n.* a perfunctory examination; a quick glance. ♦ *Once over lightly is not enough.*

the **once-over** *n.* a visual examination, especially of a person of the opposite sex. ♦ *The way she was giving him the once-over, I knew she would say something to him.*

one *mod.* having to do with something unique or special. (Similar to a definite article.) ♦ *Hank? Now there is one ugly son of a gun for you.*

one and one *mod.* having to do with the use of both nostrils in snorting a drug, usually cocaine. (Drugs.) ♦ *He does it one and one because it hits him faster that way.*

one brick shy of a load *mod.* stupid; dense. ♦ *Joyce has done some stupid things. Sometimes I think she is one brick shy of a load.*

one for the road AND **1FTR** *n.* a drink; a drink before a journey. ♦ *Let's have one for the road.*

one jump ahead of so/sth *n.* in advance of someone or something; a step ahead of someone or something. ♦ *I try to be one jump ahead of the problems.*

one of the faithful *n.* a drunkard. ♦ *Here comes Mr. Franklin—one of the faithful—staggering down the street.* ♦ *I saw one of the faithful standing at the bar.*

one smart apple *n.* a smart or clever person. ♦ *That Sue is one smart apple.*

one too many *n.* one drink of liquor too many, implying drunkenness. ♦ *I think I've had one too many. It's time to stop drinking.*

one-eyed pants mouse Go to bald-headed hermit.

one-finger salute AND **OFS** *phr. & comp. abb.* the finger; the *digitus impudicus.* ♦ *And an OFS to you, sir.*

one-horse town *n.* a very small town; a small and backward town. ♦ *I refuse to spend a whole week in that one-horse town!*

one-man show 1. *n.* a performance put on by one person. ♦ *It was a one-man show, but it was very entertaining.* **2.** *n.* an exhibition of the artistic works of one person. ♦ *She is having a one-man show at the Northside Gallery.*

one-night stand 1. *n.* a performance lasting only one night. ♦ *The band did a series of one-night stands down the East Coast.* **2.** *n.* a romance or sexual relationship that lasts only one night. ♦ *It looked like something that would last longer than a one-night stand.*

one-track mind *n.* a (person's) mind obsessed with only one thing. ♦ *When it comes to food, Tom has a one-track mind.*

only way to go *n.* the best way to do something; the best choice to make. ♦ *Get a four-wheel drive car. It's the only way to go.*

on-target *mod.* timely; exact; incisive. ♦ *Your criticism is exactly on-target.*

onto a good thing *mod.* having found something that is to one's advantage, such as something easy, profitable, inexpensive, etc. ♦ *I think that Bill got onto a good thing when he opened his own store.*

onto so/sth *mod.* alerted to or aware of a deceitful plan or person. ♦ *Wilmer thought he was safe, but the fuzz was onto him from the beginning.*

oodles ['udlz] *n.* lots (of something). ♦ *I don't have oodles, but I have enough to keep me happy.*

oof [uf] **1.** *exclam.* the sound one makes when one is struck in the abdomen. (Usually **Oof!**) ♦ *"Oof!" cried Tom. He couldn't talk any more after that.* **2.** *n.* the potency of the alcohol in liquor; the effect of potent alcohol. ♦ *This stuff really has oof. How old is it?*

oomph [umpf] **1.** *n.* energy; drive and vitality. ♦ *Come on, you guys. Let's get some oomph behind it. Push!* **2.** *n.* sex appeal. (Euphemistic.) ♦ *She had a lot of oomph, but didn't wish to become a movie star.*

OOSOOM Go to out of sight, out of mind.

OP's ['o'piz] *n.* other people's cigarettes; begged or borrowed cigarettes. (Initialism.) ♦ *My favorite kind of cigarettes is OP's. They're the cheapest, too.*

open (up) one's **kimono** *in.* to reveal what one is planning. (From the computer industry, referring especially to the involvement of the Japanese in this field.) ♦ *Even if Tom appears to open up his kimono on this deal, don't put much stock in what he says.*

OPP *n.* other people's property. ♦ *You ain't got respect for OPP.*

or what? *phr.* or what else can it be? (Part of a special formula that asks if something is a good example or specimen of something. The expected answer is yes. The question "Is this an X or what?" means "If this isn't a really great X, what is it then?") ♦ *Look at what I am wearing! Is that a great jacket or what?*

oreo *n.* an American of African descent who behaves more white than black. (Like the Oreo brand cookie, the person is black on the outside and white on the inside. Rude and derogatory.) ♦ *They called Sam an oreo because he wears a suit and works downtown.*

org [org] **1.** *n.* the rush caused by potent drugs. (Drugs. From *orgasm.*) ♦ *Bart hated the vomiting when he first took it, but he loved the org.* **2.** *n.* an organization. (Also the internet domain ".org" often assigned to nonprofit organizations.) ♦ *She's a member of the org and can't be expected to use independent judgment.*

organic *mod.* great. ♦ *This is one fine, organic rally! I'm glad I stopped by.*

ork-orks ['orkorks] *n.* the delirium tremens. ♦ *Whenever he gets the ork-orks, he gets himself arrested and put in jail where he can sober up.*

oscar *n.* the penis. ♦ *Stop scratching your oscar in public!*

O-sign *n.* the rounded, open mouth of a dead person. (A semijocular usage. Hospitals. See also **Q-sign**.) ♦ *The guy in room 226 is giving the O-sign.*

ossifer AND **occifer** ['asəfɚ] *n.* a police officer. (Also an ill-advised term of address.) ♦ *Ask the occifer there if he wants to step outside and discuss it.*

ossified ['asəfaɪd] *mod.* alcohol or drug intoxicated. (From **stoned (out)**.) ♦ *How can anybody be so ossified on four beers?*

OT1H Go to **on the one hand**.

Otis ['otɪs] **1.** *n.* a drunkard. (From the name of a television character who is the town drunk. Also a term of address.) ♦ *Look at Otis over there, propped up against the wall.* **2.** *mod.* drunk. ♦ *Fred was Otis by midnight and began looking like he was going to barf.*

OTL ['o'ti'ɛl] *phr.* out to lunch; spacy; giddy. (An initialism.) ♦ *Sue is OTL. She seems witless all the time.*

OTOH *phr.* on the other hand. (An initialism. A computer abbreviation, not pronounced.) ♦ *That's one good idea. OTOH, there must be many other satisfactory procedures.*

out 1. *mod.* alcohol or drug intoxicated. (Probably from **far out**.) ♦ *Those guys are really out!* **2.** *mod.* out of fashion. (The opposite of **in**.) ♦ *That kind of clothing is strictly out.* **3.** *tv.* to make someone's homosexuality public. (Can be reflexive.) ♦ *He outed himself at the party last Friday.*

out cold 1. *mod.* unconscious. ♦ *Paul was out cold when we found him.* **2.** *mod.* alcohol intoxicated. ♦ *He sat in his chair at the table, out cold.*

out in left field *mod.* wrong; off base; loony. ♦ *Don't pay any attention to her. She's out in left field as usual.*

out like a light 1. *mod.* unconscious or sleeping soundly. ♦ *I fell and hit my head. I was out like a light for two minutes, they tell me.* **2.** *mod.* heavily alcohol intoxicated. ♦ *All four of them drank till they were out like a light.*

out of it 1. *mod.* not in with the real world. ♦ *You never pay attention to what's going on. You're really out of it.* **2.** *mod.* alcohol or drug intoxicated. ♦ *When they are out of it, they are quite dangerous.*

out of kilter 1. *mod.* not functioning properly; on the fritz; out of w(h)ack. ♦ *My car's engine is out of kilter and needs some repair work.* **2.** *mod.* out of square. ♦ *That corner is not square, and the wall even looks out of kilter.*

out of left field *mod.* suddenly; from an unexpected source or direction. ♦ *All of his paintings are right out of left field.*

out of line *mod.* not in accord with what is appropriate or expected, especially in price or behavior. ♦ *Your behavior is quite out of line. I shall report you.*

out of luck *mod.* unfortunate; in a hopeless position. ♦ *If you think you are going to get any sympathy from me, you're just out of luck.*

out of one's **skull** *mod.* alcohol intoxicated. ♦ *Oh, man, I drank till I was out of my skull.*

out of pocket 1. *mod.* out from under someone's control; not manageable. ♦ *The guy is wild. Completely out of pocket.* **2.** *mod.* [of expenses] small, incidental, not charged on a credit card. ♦ *I was not able to get my out of pocket expenses reimbursed.* **3.** *mod.* out of the office; away from one's desk; unavailable. (Alluding to a pager or cell phone being out of the user's pocket, making the user unavailable.) ♦ *Sorry. I was out of pocket when you called.*

out of sight 1. *mod.* heavily alcohol or drug intoxicated; high. ♦ *They've been drinking since noon, and they're out of*

sight. 2. *mod.* very expensive; high in price. ♦ *Prices at that restaurant are out of sight.*

out of sight, out of mind AND **OOSOOM** *phr. & comp. abb.* I don't pay attention to what I can't see. ♦ *I completely forgot about it. OOSOOM!*

out of sync [...sɪŋk] *mod.* uncoordinated; unsynchronized. ♦ *My watch and your watch are out of sync.*

out of the picture *mod.* no longer relevant to a situation; departed; dead. ♦ *Now that Tom is out of the picture, we needn't concern ourselves about his objections.*

out of the way 1. *mod.* dead; killed. ♦ *Now that her husband was out of the way, she began to get out and about more.* **2.** *mod.* alcohol intoxicated. ♦ *After a few more drinks, Bill will be out of the way.*

out of the woods *mod.* freed from a previous state of uncertainty or danger; no longer critical. ♦ *As soon as her temperature is down, she'll be out of the woods.*

out of this world 1. *mod.* wonderful and exciting. ♦ *My boyfriend is just out of this world.* **2.** *mod.* drug intoxicated. ♦ *Man, is she ever out of this world! What did she drink?*

out of w(h)ack *mod.* out of adjustment; inoperative. (See also **out of kilter**.) ♦ *I think my left eye is out of wack a little. Maybe I need glasses.*

out the gazoo [...gə'zu] *phr.* in great plenty; everywhere. (**Gazoo** = anus. Usually objectionable.) ♦ *We have old magazines out the gazoo here. Can't we throw some of them away?*

out the window *mod.* gone; wasted. ♦ *My forty dollars—out the window. Why didn't I save my money?*

out to lunch *mod.* absentminded; giddy; stupid acting. (See also **OTL**.) ♦ *Old Ted is so out to lunch these days. Seems to be losing his mind.*

outa ['aʊdə] *phr.* out of. (Eye-dialect. Used in writing only for effect. Used in the examples of this dictionary.) ♦ *In two minutes I'm outa here!*

out-and-out *mod.* complete or total; blatant. ♦ *Don't be such an out-and-out stinker!*

outed 1. AND **offed** *mod.* dead; killed. ♦ *The witness was offed before a subpoena could be issued.* **2.** *mod.* having had one's homosexual identity made public. (Not prenominal.) ♦ *Yes, he's outed, but he hasn't told his parents.*

outfit 1. *n.* a group of people; a company. ♦ *That outfit cheated me out of my money.* **2.** *n.* a set of clothing. ♦ *You look lovely in that outfit.* **3.** *n.* a set of things; the items needed for some task. ♦ *My tool kit has everything I need. It's the whole outfit.*

outsy AND **outy** ['aʊtsi, 'aʊti] *n.* a navel that protrudes. (Compare this with **insy**.) ♦ *Is yours an insy or an outsy?*

outy Go to **outsy**.

Over my dead body! AND **OMDB** *exclam. & comp. abb.* [You won't do it] if I can stop you from doing it! ♦ *You'll do it OMDB.*

over one's **head** *mod.* confusing; too difficult to understand. ♦ *This stuff is too hard. It's over my head.*

over the hill 1. *mod.* escaped from prison or the military. (See also **AWOL**.) ♦ *Two privates went over the hill last night.* **2.** *mod.* too old (for something). ♦ *You're only fifty! You're not over the hill yet.*

over the hump 1. *mod.* drug intoxicated. ♦ *Things should be easy from now on. We are over the hump.*

overamped *mod.* high on amphetamines; overdosed with amphetamines. (Drugs.) ♦ *Two students were overamped and got sent to the counselor.*

overjolt AND **OJ 1.** *n.* an overdose of drugs, especially of heroin. (The abbreviation is an initialism. Drugs.) ♦ *Ted is suffering from a serious OJ.* **2.** *in.* to take an overdose of drugs, especially of heroin. (Drugs.) ♦ *She overjolted once too often.*

overkill *n.* too much. ♦ *That is enough. Any more is just overkill.*

overserved *mod.* having to do with a drunken person in a bar; alcohol intoxicated. (Euphemistic.) ♦ *The overserved guy there in the corner is going to be sick.*

owl-prowl *n.* a nighttime session of owl watching. (Bird watchers humor.) ♦ *We went on an owl-prowl last night and spotted a spotted owl. It was a barn owl, but we spotted it.*

ownage *n.* an instance of owning something; an instance of dominating something; the acquisition of control over something. ♦ *This whole idea was mine and I am still in control. This is an extreme case of ownage.*

P

pack of lies *n.* a whole collection or series of lies. ♦ *I've heard you talk about this before, and it's all a pack of lies.*

package 1. *n.* a combination of a variety of related things; a unified set of things. ♦ *The first college I applied to offered me a good aid package, so I went.* **2.** *n.* a lot of money; a bundle. ♦ *She made quite a package on that bank deal.* **3.** *n.* someone who is cute or sexually attractive. (Primarily refers to females as bundles of sexual charms. Similar in meaning to sense 1.) ♦ *How do you like that little package who just came in?* **4.** *tv.* to position or display someone or something, as in marketing, to good advantage. ♦ *The agent packaged the actress so that everyone thought she only did dramatic roles.*

packaged *mod.* alcohol intoxicated. ♦ *Man, Bart was really packaged last night!*

packing a gun *tv.* carrying a gun. ♦ *The crook was packing a gun and carrying a knife in his hand.*

pad 1. *n.* a place to live; one's room or dwelling. ♦ *Why don't you come over to my pad for a while?* **2.** *tv.* to lengthen a piece of writing with unnecessary material. (See also **padded**.) ♦ *This story would be better if you hadn't padded it with so much chitchat.*

pad down (somewhere) *in.* to make one's bed somewhere, usually a casual or temporary bed. ♦ *Do you mind if I pad down at your place for the night?*

pad out *in.* to go to bed or to sleep. (See also **pad**.) ♦ *Man, if I don't pad out by midnight, I'm a zombie.*

padded *mod.* plump or fat. ♦ *He didn't hurt himself when he fell down. He's well padded there.*

paddy *n.* a police officer, especially an Irish police officer. (Usually derogatory. Also an ill-advised term of address.) ♦ *Tell that paddy to go catch a crook or something.*

paddy wagon *n.* a police van used to take suspected criminals to the police station. ♦ *The cop put the woman in handcuffs and then called the paddy wagon.*

padre ['padre] *n.* any male religious cleric: priest, monk, or chaplain. (From Spanish. Typically military. Also a term of address.) ♦ *Hey, padre, anything new on the religion front?*

pafisticated [pə'fɪstəkedəd] *mod.* alcohol intoxicated. (A corruption of *sophisticated*.) ♦ *Look at her drive. She is a real pafisticated lady.*

paid *mod.* alcohol intoxicated. ♦ *I think I'll go out and get paid tonight.*

pain *n.* a bother; an irritating thing or person. ♦ *Those long meetings are a real pain.*

pain in the ass AND **pain in the butt; pain in the rear** *n.* a very annoying thing or person. (Usually objectionable. An elaboration of **pain**. *Rear* is euphemistic.) ♦ *You are a pain in the ass!* ♦ *Things like that give me a pain in the butt.*

pain in the butt Go to **pain in the ass**.

pain in the neck *n.* a difficult or annoying thing or person. (See also **pain in the ass**.) ♦ *My boss is a pain in the neck.*

pain in the rear Go to **pain in the ass**.

painkiller *n.* liquor. (See also **feeling no pain**.) ♦ *Pass that bottle of painkiller over here. My throat hurts.*

paint 1. *n.* a tattoo. (The same as ink sense 3.) ♦ *When dya get the new paint?* **2.** *n.* tattoos in general; the amount of tattooing on someone's body. (The same as ink sense 4.) ♦ *He's got paint covering his back!*

paint remover *n.* strong or inferior whiskey or other spirits. ♦ *What do you call that paint remover anyway? It sure is powerful.*

paint the town (red) *tv.* to go out and celebrate; to go on a drinking bout; to get drunk. ♦ *They were out painting the town red last night.*

pal [pæl] **1.** *n.* a close, male friend or buddy. ♦ *Be nice to him. He's my pal.* **2.** *n.* a term of address for a stranger, usually a male. ♦ *Look, pal, I was in line in front of you!*

pal around (with so**)** *in.* to be friends with someone; to move about socially with someone. ♦ *Tom and Heidi have palled around for years.*

palimony ['pæləmoni] *n.* alimony—living expenses—paid to a common-law wife or to a former girlfriend. ♦ *He left her, and she took him to court to try to get him to pay palimony.*

pally (with so**)** *mod.* friendly or overly friendly with someone. ♦ *I don't know why Sue acts so pally. I hardly know her.*

palm *tv.* to conceal something in the hand as in a theft or the performance of a magic trick; to receive and conceal a tip or a bribe. ♦ *The kid palmed the candy bar and walked right out of the store.*

palm so/sth **off (on** so**)** *tv.* to transfer some unwanted person or thing to another person. ♦ *Don't palm her off on me. I don't want her.*

palm sth **off (on** so**)** *tv.* to succeed in spending counterfeit money; to succeed in cashing a bad check. (Underworld.) ♦ *Max palmed four phony twenties off in less than an hour.*

palm-oil *n.* a bribe; a tip. ♦ *How much palm-oil does it take to get this deed recorded in reasonable time?*

palm-presser Go to flesh-presser.

palooka AND **paluka** [pə'lukə] *n.* a stupid person; an unskilled prizefighter; any mediocre person. (Also a term of address. From the name of the comic-strip prizefighter Joe Palooka.) ♦ *Tell that stupid palooka to sit down and shut up.*

palsy-walsy ['pælzi'wælzi] **1.** *n.* a good friend, pal, or buddy. (Also a term of address.) ♦ *Meet my old palsy-walsy, John. We've known each other since we were kids.* **2.** *mod.* friendly; overly friendly. (Often with *with*.) ♦ *Why is Tom so palsy-walsy with everyone?*

paluka Go to palooka.

pan *n.* the face. (See also deadpan.) ♦ *Look at that guy! I've never seen such an ugly pan in my life.*

pan out *in.* [for something] to work out or turn out all right. ♦ *Don't worry. Everything will pan out okay.*

panic *n.* a very funny or exciting person or thing. ♦ *Paul is a panic. He tells a joke a minute.*

pants rabbits *n.* lice. (See also seam-squirrels. Contrived.) ♦ *Bart is sure scratching a lot. Do you think he's got pants rabbits?*

paper 1. *n.* a written document; written evidence supporting something. (Often with *some*.) ♦ *Send me some paper. Let's make this official.* **2.** *n.* a forged check. (See also paper-pusher; paper-hanger.) ♦ *She was arrested for passing paper.* **3.** *n.* money. ♦ *You don't get the goods till I get the paper.*

paper over sth *tv.* to try to conceal something unpleasant; to try to cover up a misdeed. ♦ *This is a severe social problem. Don't try to paper over it.*

paper-hanger *n.* someone who tries to pass bad checks. (Underworld. See also paper; paper-pusher.) ♦ *He's wanted as a paper-hanger in four states.*

paperhanging *n.* writing and spending bad checks. (Underworld.) ♦ *She was accused of paperhanging and didn't even know what the cops were talking about, so they let her go.*

paper-pusher 1. *n.* a bureaucrat; a clerk in the military services; any office worker. (See also pencil-pusher.) ♦ *If those paper-pushers can't get their work done on time, make them stay late.* **2.** *n.* someone who passes bad checks. (See also paper; paper-hanger.) ♦ *The bank teller spotted a well-known paper-pusher and called the cops.*

paperweight *n.* a serious student; a hard-working student. ♦ *What a jerk! Nothing but a paperweight.*

parboiled *mod.* alcohol intoxicated. (See also boiled.) ♦ *Sally stayed at the bar just long enough to get parboiled.*

pard *n.* partner; friend. (From *pardner.* Also a term of address.) ♦ *Come on, pard, let's go find some action.*

Pardon me for living! Go to (Well,) pardon me for living!

Pardon my French. AND **Excuse my French.** *sent.* Excuse my use of swear words or taboo words.; Excuse my choice of vocabulary. (Does not refer to real French.) ♦ *What she needs is a kick in the butt, if you'll excuse my French.*

(parental) units *n.* parents. (Teens. Also a term of address. See also rent(al)s.) ♦ *Hey, units! I need to talk to you about something really important.*

park *in.* to neck or to make love, especially in a parked car. ♦ *They still park, but they don't have a name for it anymore.*

park it (somewhere) *tv.* sit down somewhere; sit down and get out of the way. ♦ *Bart, park it over there in the corner. Stop pacing around. You make me nervous.*

park the pink Plymouth *n.* to copulate. ♦ *He set out to park the pink plymouth but ended up in a train wreck.*

partay ['pɑr 'teɪ] *in.* to party; to celebrate. ♦ *Time to partay!*

parting shot *n.* the last word; a final comment before departing. ♦ *His parting shot concerned some comments about my ability to do simple math.*

party 1. *n.* a combining form used in expressions to refer to certain kinds of activity carried on in groups or in pairs.

(For examples, see coke party, grass party, hen party, keg party, kick party, pot party, stag-party, tailgate party, tea party.) **2.** *in.* to drink alcohol, smoke marijuana, or use other drugs. (May also include sexual activity.) ♦ *Come on, man! Let's party!*

party animal *n.* someone who loves parties. ♦ *My boyfriend and I are real party animals. Let's party!*

party bowl *n.* a marijuana pipe large enough to serve a number of smokers. (Drugs.) ♦ *The cops thought the party bowl was a flower vase!*

party down Go to party hearty.

party hearty AND **party down** *in.* to have a great time; to celebrate. (Also as an exclamation: **Party down!**) ♦ *The whole class decided to celebrate and party hearty.* ♦ *Let's party down, dudes!*

Party on! *exclam.* That's right! ♦ *Party on, Beavis! You are totally right!*

party-pooper *n.* the first person to leave a party; someone who ruins a party because of dullness or by leaving early. ♦ *Don't invite Martha. She's such a party-pooper.*

pass 1. *n.* a passing grade or mark on a test. (Compare this with *fail.*) ♦ *This is my third pass this semester.* **2.** *in.* to decline something; to decline to participate in something. ♦ *I'll have to pass. I am not prepared.* **3.** *n.* an act of declining something. ♦ *Can I have a pass on that one? There is nothing I can do.* **4.** *n.* a sexual advance or invitation. (Usually with *make.*) ♦ *When he made a pass at me, he got a pass right back.* **5.** *tv.* to succeed in spending counterfeit money; to succeed in cashing a bad check. ♦ *He was arrested for passing bad checks.*

pass for sth *in.* to pay for something; to treat someone by paying for something. ♦ *Come on. Let's go out. I'll pass for dinner.*

pass go *tv.* to complete a difficult or dangerous task successfully. (From *pass go and collect $200* in the game Monopoly.) ♦ *You had better pass go with this job, or you've had it.*

pass the buck *tv.* to shift the responsibility for something to someone else; to evade responsibility. (See also buck-passer.) ♦ *Don't pass the buck. Stand up and admit you were wrong.*

passion-pit *n.* a drive-in movie theater; any place where young people go to neck, such as an area where teenagers park. (Dated but still heard.) ♦ *She wanted me to drive down to the passion-pit, but I said I had a headache.*

passy *n.* a baby's pacifier. (Baby talk.) ♦ *Does little Johnnie want his passy?*

paste 1. *tv.* to strike someone, especially in the face. (See also paste so one.) ♦ *I hauled off and pasted him right in the face.* **2.** *tv.* to defeat a person or a team, usually in a game of some type. (See also pasting; get pasted.) ♦ *The Warriors pasted the Rockets, 70–49.*

paste so one *tv.* to land a blow on someone. (See also paste.) ♦ *Next time you do that, I'll paste you one!*

paste sth on so 1. *tv.* to charge someone with a crime. ♦ *You can't paste that charge on me! Max did it!* **2.** *tv.* to land a blow on someone. (See also paste so one.) ♦ *If you do that again, I'll paste one on you.*

pasting *n.* a beating; a defeat in a game. (See also paste.) ♦ *Our team took quite a pasting last weekend.*

pathetic Go to sorry.

patsy ['pætsi] *n.* a victim of a scam. (Underworld. See also dupe.) ♦ *That guy over there looks like a perfect patsy.*

patter of tiny feet *n.* the sound of young children; having children in the household. ♦ *Darling, I think we're going to be hearing the patter of tiny feet soon.*

paw 1. *n.* someone's hand. (Jocular.) ♦ *Get your paws off me!* **2.** *tv.* to feel someone or handle someone sexually. ♦ *If you paw me again, I'll slap you!* **3.** *tv.* to touch someone more than is necessary or desired, without any sexual intent. ♦ *I don't like for people to paw me while they're shaking hands. There is no reason to shake my shoulder, too.*

PAX *n.* passenger(s). (Travel industry abbreviation.) ♦ *How many PAX will that ship hold?*

pay a call *tv.* to go to the toilet; to leave to go to the toilet. (See also call of nature; nature's call.) ♦ *Excuse me. I have to pay a call.*

pay one's dues *tv.* to serve one's time in a menial role. (See also pay one's dues (to society).) ♦ *I spent some time as a bus boy, so I've paid my dues in the serving business.*

pay one's dues (to society) *tv.* to serve a prison or jail sentence. ♦ *I served ten years in prison. I've paid my dues to society. The matter is settled.*

pay the water bill *tv.* to urinate. ♦ *I'll be with you as soon as I pay the water bill.*

payback *n.* retribution. ♦ *You hit me, I hit you. That's your payback.*

payola [pe'olə] *n.* a bribe. (Originally a bribe paid to a disk jockey by record producers to get extra attention for their records.) ♦ *The announcer was fired for taking payola.*

p-crutch *n.* a police car. (Streets. See also crutch = car.) ♦ *Hey, bro, there's a p-crutch behind you.*

PDQ *mod.* pretty damn quick; very fast; very soon. (Initialism.) ♦ *They had better get this mess straightened out PDQ if they know what's good for them.*

peace out *in.* to depart; to leave. ♦ *Let's peace out. It's too hot in here.*

peach *n.* someone or something excellent. (Usually a person.) ♦ *That guy's a real peach.*

peachy (keen) *mod.* fine; excellent. ♦ *Your idea is really peachy!*

peanut head *n.* an oaf; a nerd. ♦ *You are so silly, Kim. You're a real peanut head!*

peanuts *n.* practically no money at all; chicken feed. ♦ *They want me to do everything, but they only pay peanuts.*

pecker 1. *n.* the penis. (Usually objectionable.) ♦ *He held his hands over his pecker and ran for the bedroom.* **2.** *n.* a stupid or obnoxious male. (Usually objectionable.) ◆ *You stupid pecker! Get out of here!*

pecker slap 1. *n.* an act of striking a male in the genitals. ◆ *She pecker slapped him and watched him writhe in pain.* **2.** *tv.* to strike a make in the genitals. ◆ *We'll pecker slap those guys with every dodge ball we throw.*

peckerhead 1. *n.* the head or end of the penis. (Usually objectionable.) ◆ *He said he had a little red sore on his peckerhead.* **2.** *n.* a stupid and ignorant male. (Rude and derogatory.) ◆ *You stupid peckerhead! Why'd you do that?*

peckerwood AND **wood** *n.* a poor white person. (Very old southern term for a woodpecker.) ◆ *What's that peckerwood want in this hood?*

peckish *mod.* hungry. ◆ *I'm just a little peckish right now. I need a bite to eat.*

pecks AND **pecs; pects** [pɛk(t)s] *n.* the pectoral muscles. (From weightlifting and bodybuilding.) ◆ *Look at the pecks on that guy!*

pecs Go to pecks.

pects Go to pecks.

pee'd *mod.* alcohol intoxicated. (Euphemistic for pissed.) ◆ *His old lady gets pee'd after a few beers.*

pee'd off *mod.* extremely angry. (Euphemistic for pissed (off).) ◆ *I've never been so pee'd off in my life!*

peel *in.* to strip off one's clothing. ◆ *I had to peel for my physical examination.*

peep 1. *n.* a noise; an utterance. ◆ *I don't want to hear another peep out of you.* **2.** *n.* people. (Often plural, *peeps.*) ◆ *How many peeps were there?*

peepers *n.* the eyes. ◆ *Come on, use your peepers. Take a good look.*

peg out *in.* to die. ◆ *I was so scared, I thought I would peg out for sure.*

peg so *tv.* to gossip about someone. ◆ *Kim is always pegging Jill. What's her problem?*

peg-leg *n.* a rude nickname for someone with a wooden peg for a leg. (Now used primarily in reference to theatrical pirates.) ◆ *Hey, peg-leg. Race you to the bar!*

pen *n.* a penitentiary; prison. (Underworld.) ◆ *Bart got sent to the pen for fifteen years.*

pencil-pusher *n.* a bureaucrat; a clerk; an office worker. (See also paper-pusher.) ◆ *Look here, you lousy pencil-pusher, I want to talk to your boss!*

penis wrinkle *n.* a despised person, usually a male. (Also a term of address.) ◆ *Get out of here, penis wrinkle.*

Pennsy *n.* Pennsylvania. ◆ *I went to a conference in Pennsy last year.*

penny *n.* a police officer. (A play on copper. See the note at copper.) ◆ *The penny over on the corner told the boys to get moving.*

penny-ante *mod.* trivial; cheap. (See also ante.) ◆ *I'm sick of this penny-ante stuff. Let's get serious.*

penny-pincher *n.* someone who is very miserly; someone who objects to the expenditure of every penny. ◆ *If you weren't such a penny-pincher, you'd have some decent clothes.*

peonied *mod.* alcohol intoxicated. (A play on pee'd and pissed.) ◆ *Man, was she peonied! Really stoned.*

people processor *n.* a nickname for an airplane propeller. (Used by people who have an occasion to get near one while it is spinning.) ◆ *Watch out for the people process or at the front end.*

pep pill *n.* a stimulant pill or capsule, such as an amphetamine. ◆ *The doctor prescribed some kind of pep pills, but I refused to take them.*

pep talk *n.* an informal speech of encouragement. ◆ *The coach gave the team a good pep talk, but they lost anyway.*

pepped (up) AND **peppy** *mod.* alcohol intoxicated. (A euphemism. See also perked (up).) ◆ *That guy looks a little pepped up. Don't give him any more booze.*

pepper-upper *n.* an amphetamine tablet or capsule; a pep pill. ◆ *I need me a little pepper-upper. Can I have a prescription?*

peppy 1. *mod.* vigorous; energetic. (See also **perky**.) ♦ *I sure don't feel very peppy right now.* **2.** Go to **pepped (up)**.

Period! *exclam.* . . . and that's final! (A way of indicating that there will be no more discussion or negotiation.) ♦ *My final offer is $30. Period!*

perk *n.* an extra financial benefit; a monetary inducement or reward. (From *perquisite*. See also **benies**.) ♦ *I don't get paid much, but the perks are good.*

perked (up) *mod.* alcohol intoxicated. (See also **pepped (up)**.) ♦ *No more. She's done. She's perked up for good.*

perking *mod.* drunk; drug intoxicated. ♦ *After a few drinks, he was really perking!*

perky *mod.* energetic; alert. (See also **peppy**.) ♦ *A perky hostess keeps parties alive.*

perma-fried *mod.* very drunk or drug intoxicated; very **fried**. ♦ *She got herself perma-fried and couldn't drive home.*

perp [pɚp] *n.* a perpetrator; someone who does something, such as committing a crime. ♦ *The perp left a good set of prints on the doorknob.*

perpetrate ['pɚpətret] *in.* to pose; to pretend. ♦ *Look at her clothes. Have you ever seen anyone perpetrate like that?*

persuader *n.* a gun or other weapon used to threaten someone. (Underworld.) ♦ *He pulls out this persuader, see, and aims it right at me, see.*

perve on so *in.* to leer at someone. ♦ *Make that jerk stop perving on me.*

pet peeve *n.* a major or principal annoyance or complaint. ♦ *Dirty dishes in restaurants are my pet peeve.*

peter *n.* the penis. ♦ *Stop scratching your peter in public!*

Peter Jay *n.* a nickname for a police officer. ♦ *You walk straight, or Peter Jay is going to bust you.*

peter out *in.* to give out; to wear out. ♦ *What'll we do when the money peters out?*

petrified *mod.* alcohol intoxicated. (Literally, turned into stone. Another way of saying **stoned**.) ♦ *She's not drunk; she's petrified.*

petting-party *n.* a session of kissing and caressing. ♦ *I just want to watch the movie. I didn't come here for some teenage petting-party!*

PFD *n.* a potential formal date; someone who looks good enough to be a date to a formal affair. (Initialism. Collegiate.) ♦ *Mike is no PFD, but he is a great friend anyway.*

PFM *n.* pure fucking magic, absolutely astounding. ♦ *The whole evening was PFM! I had a great time!*

PG *mod.* pregnant. (Initialism.) ♦ *I think I'm "PG." You know, pregnant.*

phased Go to **phazed**.

phat AND **PHAT** *mod.* good; excellent. (This is essentially a respelling of **fat** and can have all the senses that **fat** has. This is not an acronym, although there are a number of proposed acronymic origins.) ♦ *His new car is really phat.*

phat blunt *n.* a fat marijuana cigarette. (*Phat* is *fat*.) ♦ *Man, that's a phat blunt!*

phat-phree *mod.* not cool; not PHAT. (A play on *fat-free*.) ♦ *We had to read some stupid, phat-phree play by some old homie called Jakespeer.*

phazed AND **phased** [fezd] *mod.* intoxicated with marijuana. ♦ *How much booze does it take you to get really phased?*

phedinkus [fɪ'dɪŋkəs] *n.* nonsense. ♦ *That's just phedinkus. No one will believe you.*

phfft [ffft] **1.** *mod.* finished; done for; dead. (See also **piffed**.) ♦ *There is my cat, and zoom comes a car. My cat is phfft.* **2.** *mod.* alcohol intoxicated. ♦ *Three beers and she's phfft, for sure.*

Philly *n.* Philadelphia, Pennsylvania. ♦ *We left Philly for the Big Apple at noon.*

phish AND **spoof; card** *in.* to "fish" for passwords and personal information by trickery, on internet. (Sometimes by setting up a phony URL which people sign in to by giving their passwords or credit card numbers.) ♦ *They must have been* *phishing to get my credit card number while I placed an order online.*

phishing Go to spoofing.

phony 1. *mod.* bogus; fake. ♦ *This money looks phony to me.* **2.** *n.* someone or something bogus. ♦ *Look here, you phony, get out of my office!* **3.** *n.* a phone call where the caller hangs up the minute the telephone is answered. ♦ *No one was on the telephone. It was just a phony.*

phony as a three-dollar bill Go to (as) phony as a three-dollar bill.

phooey AND **fooey 1.** *n.* nonsense. ♦ *I've heard enough fooey. Let's get out of here.* **2.** *exclam.* an expression of disgust, disagreement, or resignation. (Usually **Phooey!** or **Fooey!** Used typically when something smells or tastes bad.) ♦ *Who died in here? Phooey!*

phreak *n.* a respelling of *freak*. ♦ *You stupid freak! Why'd you do that?*

phumfed ['fəm(p)ft] *mod.* drug intoxicated. ♦ *You can't get your work done when you are totally phumfed.*

phunky Go to funky.

phutz AND **futz** [fəts] *tv.* to rob, swindle, or cheat someone. ♦ *Don't futz me! Tell the truth!*

piccie *n.* a little picture; a thumbnail picture. ♦ *Put some piccies on your web page. That'll brighten it up.*

pick up on sth *in.* to become alert to something; to take notice of something; to learn or catch on to something. ♦ *She's real sharp. She picks up on everything.*

pickled *mod.* alcohol intoxicated. (Very common.) ♦ *It only takes a few drinks to get him pickled.*

picklepuss *n.* a person who has a puckered up mouth; a child who is about to cry. ♦ *She is such a picklepuss. Nothing seems to please her.*

pickler *n.* a drunkard; an alcoholic. (See also pickled.) ♦ *The cops brought in about thirty picklers last night.*

pick-me-up *n.* any food or drink that boosts energy, such as a drink of liquor,

candy, soda pop. ♦ *I can't finish the day without a little pick-me-up at lunch.*

pickup 1. *n.* something eaten or drunk to boost energy; a pick-me-up. ♦ *Bartender, I need a little pickup.* **2.** *n.* a sudden increase in something, such as speed or tempo in music. ♦ *There will be a pickup in sales during the Christmas season.* **3.** *mod.* spontaneous; unplanned. (Especially with ball games where the members of the team are *picked up* from whoever is available. See also scratch.) ♦ *A pickup game can be fun if the sides are evenly matched.* **4.** *n.* an arrest. (Underworld.) ♦ *Send Sergeant Townsend out to make the pickup.* **5.** *n.* someone whose acquaintance is made solely for sexual purposes. ♦ *She's no date. She's just a pickup.* **6.** *n.* the power of a car's engine as reflected in the car's ability to reach a high speed quickly. ♦ *Little cars hardly ever have enough pickup.*

picky 1. *mod.* choosy. ♦ *Red, blue, green! What's the difference? You are too picky.* **2.** *mod.* overly critical. ♦ *I have to do it exactly right. My boss is very picky.*

picnic *n.* a good time; an easy time. ♦ *Nothing to it. A real picnic.*

piddle 1. *in.* to urinate. (Said of children and pets.) ♦ *Please, Jimmy, don't piddle on the floor.* **2.** *n.* urine. ♦ *Don't step in the puppy's piddle.* **3.** Go to piddle (around).

piddle (around) *in.* to waste time; to work aimlessly or inefficiently. ♦ *Can't you get serious and stop piddling?*

piddler *n.* someone who wastes time. ♦ *That piddler will never get anywhere in life.*

piddling *mod.* inadequate; meager; tiny. (See also piss-poor; piddle.) ♦ *That is a piddling steak. I want a big one.*

pie hole Go to word hole.

pie in the sky 1. *n.* a reward; a special heavenly reward. ♦ *If he didn't hope for some heavenly pie in the sky, he would probably be a real crook.* **2.** *mod.* having to do with a hope for a special reward. (This is hyphenated before a nominal.) ♦ *Get rid of your pie-in-the-sky ideas!*

piece 1. *n.* a sexually attractive (young) woman. (Crude.) ♦ *Who's that piece I saw you with last night?* **2.** *n.* a gun, especially a revolver. (Underworld.) ♦ *Okay, this gun is aimed at your head. Drop your piece.* **3.** *n.* a tiny ponytail worn by males. ♦ *Even the little boys—six and seven years old—want to wear a piece.* ♦ *Tony pointed out that lots of pirates wore pieces.* **4.** *n.* a piece of shit; POS; something worthless. ♦ *This car is a piece. Couldn't you gank something better?*

piece of ass AND **hunk of ass; hunk of tail; piece of snatch; piece of tail 1.** *n.* someone considered as a partner in copulation. (Usually a female. Usually objectionable.) ♦ *Man, isn't he a fine looking piece of snatch?* **2.** *n.* an act of copulation; copulation with someone. (Usually objectionable.) ♦ *If Todd doesn't get a hunk of tail once a day, he's real grouchy.*

piece of cake 1. *n.* something easy to do. ♦ *No problem. When you know what you're doing, it's a piece of cake.* **2.** *exclam.* It's a piece of cake!; It's easy! (Usually **Piece of cake!**) ♦ *Rescuing drowning cats is my specialty. Piece of cake!*

piece of snatch Go to piece of ass.

piece of tail Go to piece of ass.

piece (of the action) AND **bit of the action; slice of the action** *n.* a share in the activity or the profits. (Especially gambling activity.) ♦ *Don't be selfish. Give me a slice of the action.* ♦ *I helped! I want a bit of the action.*

pie-eyed 1. *mod.* wide-eyed with amazement. ♦ *He didn't cry out. He just stood there pie-eyed.* **2.** *mod.* alcohol intoxicated. ♦ *We've got a pie-eyed bus driver. I want to get off!*

piffed [pɪft] **1.** AND **pifted** ['pɪftəd] *tv.* killed. (Past tense only. See also phfft.) ♦ *He piffed his goldfish by mistake.* **2.** AND **pifted** ['pɪftəd] *mod.* dead. ♦ *What will I do with a pifted cat?* **3.** *mod.* alcohol intoxicated. (See also piffled.) ♦ *How can anybody get so piffed on four beers?*

piffle ['pɪfl] **1.** *n.* nonsense. ♦ *What utter piffle!* **2.** *exclam.* a mild exclamation or expression of distress. (Usually **Piffle!**)

♦ *She finished her story, and I looked her straight in the eye and said, "Piffle!"*

piffled ['pɪfld] *mod.* alcohol intoxicated. ♦ *Three glasses of booze and she was totally piffled.*

piff(l)icated ['pɪf(l)əkedəd] *mod.* alcohol intoxicated. ♦ *How can anybody drink so much and not get totally pifflicated?*

pifted Go to piffed.

pig 1. *n.* someone who eats too much; a glutton. ♦ *I try to cut down on calories, but whenever I see red meat I make a pig of myself.* **2.** *n.* an ugly and fat woman or man. ♦ *Clare is a pig. Why doesn't she lose a ton or two?* **3.** *n.* a dirty or slovenly person. ♦ *Jimmy, change your clothes. Look at that mud, you little pig!* **4.** *n.* an officer; a police officer or a military officer. (Used mostly for a police officer. Widely known since the 1960s.) ♦ *The pigs who aren't in pig heaven are driving around in pigmobiles busting innocent people like me.* **5.** *n.* a Caucasian. (Black.) ♦ *Why do those pigs think they can walk in here like that?*

pig heaven *n.* a police station. (Chiefly black.) ♦ *All the bacon eventually goes home to pig heaven.*

pig out *in.* to overeat; to overindulge in food or drink. (See also blimp out; mac out; pork out; scarf out.) ♦ *I can't help myself when I see ice cream. I have to pig out.*

pigeon 1. *n.* a dupe; a sucker; someone singled out to be cheated. (See also patsy.) ♦ *There's our pigeon now. Don't let him see us sizing him up.* **2.** *n.* a good-looking girl or woman. ♦ *Who was the dreamy little pigeon I saw you with last night?* **3.** Go to stool (pigeon).

pigeon-eyed *mod.* alcohol intoxicated. ♦ *Who is that pigeon-eyed guy over there who is having such a hard time standing up?*

pighead *n.* someone who is both stupid and stubborn. (See also pigheaded.) ♦ *She'll never change her mind. She's a real pighead.*

pigheaded *mod.* stupidly stubborn. (From the notion that pigs are immovable and seemingly stubborn.) ♦ *You are unbelievably pigheaded!*

pigmobile *n.* a police car. (See also pig = police officer.) ♦ *Look out, here comes the pigmobile!*

pigpen *n.* a crosshatch or the number sign: #. (Computers. See also **mesh**.) ♦ *There is nothing on my printout but a whole string of pigpens.*

pigskin *n.* a football. (Alludes to the covering on an American football.) ♦ *Fred kicked the pigskin through the goal posts and won the game.*

piker ['pɑɪkɚ] **1.** *n.* a miser; a cheapskate. (Also a term of address.) ♦ *A 5 percent tip? You piker!* **2.** *n.* a lazy person; a shirker. ♦ *Come on, you lazy piker. There's plenty left for you to do.*

pile *n.* a large amount of money. ♦ *That old lady has a pile stashed in the bank.*

pile of shit 1. *n.* a mass of lies. (Refers to bullshit. Usually objectionable.) ♦ *He came in and told me this great pile of shit about how his alarm clock was in the shop.* **2.** *n.* any worthless structure or device. (Usually objectionable.) ♦ *Take this pile of shit back where you bought it and get your money back.* **3.** *n.* a totally worthless person. (Rude and derogatory.) ♦ *Todd, you are the biggest pile of shit I've ever seen.*

pileup *n.* a wreck; a vehicular crash where more than one vehicle is heavily damaged. ♦ *There is a serious pileup on the expressway.*

pilfered ['pɪlfɚd] *mod.* alcohol intoxicated. ♦ *I've had too much. I'm beginning to feel pilfered.*

pill 1. the **pill** *n.* a birth control pill. (Always with *the* in this sense.) ♦ *The pill has really changed my life.* **2.** *n.* a tobacco cigarette; a marijuana cigarette. ♦ *I'll trade you a pill for a match.* **3.** *n.* a drug in capsule form. ♦ *The doctor prescribed these pills.* **4.** *n.* a football. ♦ *Fred kicked the pill through the goal and won the game.*

pill freak Go to pillhead.

pillage *tv.* to eat a meal, perhaps by raiding a refrigerator. (Perhaps voraciously.) ♦ *Let's go pillage Tom's fridge. I'm hungarian.*

pill-dropper Go to pill-popper.

pillhead AND **pill freak** *n.* a drug user who prefers drugs in pill or capsule form. (Drugs.) ♦ *The police turned the juvenile "pillheads" over to their parents.* ♦ *You pill freaks should try some of this stuff.*

pillowed *mod.* pregnant. (Refers to the swelling in a pregnant woman's abdomen.) ♦ *She does look a bit pillowed, doesn't she?*

pill-peddler Go to pill-pusher.

pill-popper AND **popper; pill-dropper** *n.* anyone who takes pills frequently or habitually. ♦ *I knew she was always ill, but I didn't know she was a pill-dropper.* ♦ *He's not a hypochondriac, just a pill-dropper.*

pill-pusher AND **pill-roller; pill-peddler** *n.* a nickname for a physician. ♦ *I went to the infirmary, but the pill-pusher wasn't in.* ♦ *The lousy pill-roller just gave me some aspirin.*

pill-roller Go to pill-pusher.

pimp *n.* a man who solicits business for a prostitute. (Use caution with pimp and the topic.) ♦ *The guy with the diamond rings looks like a pimp.*

pimp steak *n.* a hot dog; a wiener. (See also tube steak.) ♦ *Oh, no! Not pimp steak again tonight.*

pimpish ['pɪmpɪʃ] *mod.* flamboyant in dress and manner, as with a pimp. (Use caution with pimp and the topic.) ♦ *Take the feathers off it, and it won't look quite so pimpish.*

pimpmobile *n.* a gaudy automobile, as might be driven by a pimp. (Use caution with pimp.) ♦ *He drove up in a pimpmobile and shocked all the neighbors.*

pimpstick *n.* a typical cigarette made by mass production. (Use caution with pimp. From an earlier time when pimps were likely to smoke machine-made cigarettes rather than the rugged roll-your-own type.) ♦ *Hey, chum. Why do you smoke those pimpsticks? Can't you roll one yourself?*

pin 1. *n.* someone's leg. (Usually plural.) ♦ *Stand up on your pins and speak your mind.* **2.** *n.* an important criminal leader. (From kingpin.) ♦ *The mob's getting careless. The cops think they caught the pin this time.*

pin so's **ears back 1.** *tv.* to scold someone severely. ♦ *The teacher pinned the kids' ears back for chewing gum.* **2.** *tv.* to beat someone, especially about the head. ♦ *You do something like that again, and I'll pin your ears back.*

pinch 1. *n.* a small amount of a powdered substance, such as salt, snuff, a spice, etc. (Not slang.) ♦ *He put a pinch under his lips and walked up to home plate.* **2.** *tv.* to arrest someone. ♦ *The police captain pinched her for passing bad checks.* **3.** *n.* the arrest of someone. ♦ *They made the pinch in front of her house.* **4.** *tv.* to steal something. (See also cop.) ♦ *The kid pinched a candy bar right off the counter.*

pinch hitter 1. *n.* a substitute batter in the game of baseball. ♦ *Sam is a pinch hitter for Ralph, who broke his wrist.* **2.** *n.* any substitute person. ♦ *In school today we had a pinch hitter. Our teacher was sick.*

pinched *mod.* arrested. (See also cop; pinch.) ♦ *Sam got pinched for a parole violation.*

ping so *tv.* to get someone's attention, via computer or otherwise. ♦ *I saw her on the other side of the room and pinged her.*

pink elephants AND **pink spiders 1.** *n.* the delirium tremens. ♦ *He was shaking something awful from the pink spiders.* **2.** *n.* hallucinatory creatures seen during the delirium tremens. (See also seeing pink elephants.) ♦ *He said pink elephants were trying to kill him. He's really drunk.*

pink slip 1. *n.* a piece of paper giving notice of dismissal from employment; any dismissal from employment. ♦ *I got a pink slip today. I guess I had it coming.* **2.** *tv.* to dismiss someone from employment. (See also pink-slipped.) ♦ *They pink slipped the whole office force today.* **3.** *n.* a learner's permit for driving an automobile. (In some U.S. states.) ♦ *You can't even*

drive in your own driveway without a pink slip.

pink spiders Go to pink elephants.

pinked *mod.* alcohol intoxicated; tipsy. ♦ *She's sitting there looking a bit pinked.*

pinkie Go to (little) pinkie.

pinko 1. *n.* a communist. (Popular during the 1950s.) ♦ *Get out of here, you pinko!* **2.** *mod.* having communist tendencies; in the manner of a communist. ♦ *Get that pinko jerk out of here!*

pink-slipped *mod.* fired; dismissed from employment. ♦ *I guess I've done it. I'm pink-slipped.*

pinky Go to (little) pinkie.

pinned *mod.* arrested. (Underworld.) ♦ *The boys in blue pinned him and took him away.*

pinstriper *n.* a businessman or businesswoman wearing a pinstriped suit. (See also suit; vest. From men's pinstripe business suits.) ♦ *Who's the pinstriper driving the beemer?*

pip 1. *n.* a pimple; a zit. ♦ *Good grief, I've got ear-to-ear pips!* **2.** *n.* postindustrial person. (Usually **PIP**. Acronym. A cynical reference to a person as a member of a group that has become useless because of technological change.) ♦ *The world really doesn't really need more PIPs, except as consumers, of course.* **3.** *n.* illness; a mild, nonspecific disorder. (Old colloquial.) ♦ *Grandpa's complaining again. Says it's the pip.*

pipe *n.* an easy course in school. ♦ *I don't want a full load of pipes. I want to learn something.*

pipe down *in.* to become quiet; to cease making noise; to shut up. (Especially as a rude command.) ♦ *Pipe down! I'm trying to sleep.*

pipped (up) *mod.* alcohol intoxicated. ♦ *I'm not drunk. Just a little pipped up.*

pipsqueak *n.* a small or timid man or boy. (Also a term of address.) ♦ *Shut up, you little pipsqueak, or I'll hit you.*

piss 1. *in.* to urinate. (Colloquial. Usually objectionable. Some expressions, such as pissed off, are common colloquial with wide but not universal use or acceptance. Other expressions with piss are more restricted in some circles. See the complete list of all entries with piss in the Index of Hidden Key Words.) ♦ *Who pissed on the floor of the john?* **2.** *n.* urine. (Usually objectionable.) ♦ *You got piss on your pants leg.* **3.** *n.* bad beer; bad liquor; any bad-tasting or poor-quality liquid. (Usually objectionable.) ♦ *How about another can of that piss you serve here?*

piss around *in.* to waste time; to be inefficient at something. (Usually objectionable.) ♦ *She's just pissing around. She'll never finish.*

piss blood 1. *tv.* to experience great anxiety. (Usually objectionable. See also sweat blood.) ♦ *He made me piss blood before he agreed.* **2.** *tv.* to expend an enormous amount of energy. (Usually objectionable. See also sweat blood.) ♦ *I pissed blood to come in first in the race.*

piss elegant *mod.* very pretentious; overly elegant. (Usually objectionable.) ♦ *Man, this place is piss elegant. Look at them lamp shades!*

piss factory *n.* a bar, tavern, or saloon. (Usually objectionable.) ♦ *I stopped in at the piss factory for a round or two.*

piss in the wind *in.* to do something that is futile and counterproductive; to waste one's time doing something. (Usually objectionable.) ♦ *Shut up! You're just pissing in the wind!*

piss off AND **PO** *in.* to depart; to go away. (Objectionable to many people.) ♦ *Piss off, you jerk! Get out!*

Piss on it! *in.* To hell with it! (Usually objectionable.) ♦ *Oh, piss on it! I've had enough!*

piss on so/sth **1.** *in.* to urinate on someone or something. (Usually objectionable.) ♦ *That dog pissed on my shoe!* **2.** *in.* to degrade or denigrate someone or something. (Usually objectionable.) ♦ *He spent three paragraphs pissing on the play, then he said to go see it.*

piss quiz *n.* a urine test for drugs. (Usually objectionable.) ♦ *They told me I had to take a piss quiz to work there.*

piss so **off** *tv.* to make someone angry. (Potentially offensive, even though it is widely used. See also pissed (off).) ♦ *She really pissed me off!*

piss sth **away** *tv.* to waste all of something, such as time or money. (Usually objectionable.) ♦ *He pissed away the best possible chances.*

pissant AND **piss-ant 1.** *n.* a wretched and worthless person. (Often objectionable.) ♦ *Look, you silly pissant, beat it!* **2.** *mod.* worthless. (Often objectionable.) ♦ *I don't want this little pissant piece of pie. Give me a real piece.*

piss-cutter AND **piss-whiz** *n.* an extraordinary person; someone who can do the impossible. (Usually objectionable.) ♦ *Sam is a real piss-cutter when it comes to running.* ♦ *I ain't no piss-whiz, just your average guy.*

pissed 1. *mod.* alcohol intoxicated. (Usually objectionable.) ♦ *He was so pissed he could hardly stand up.* **2.** *mod.* angry. (Potentially offensive, even though it is heard widely. See also piss so off.) ♦ *I was so pissed I could have screamed.*

pissed off about so/sth Go to pissed (off) (at so/sth).

pissed (off) (at so/sth**)** AND **pissed off about** so/sth *mod.* very angry with or about someone or something. (Objectionable to many people, but heard in all popular entertainment, schools, and the workplace.) ♦ *She's always so pissed off about something.* ♦ *He always seems pissed off at somebody.*

pisser 1. *n.* a urinal; a place [room, restroom] to urinate. (Usually objectionable.) ♦ *Who keeps missing the pisser?* **2.** *n.* a remarkable thing or person. (Usually objectionable.) ♦ *Man, isn't he a real pisser! Have you ever seen anybody bat like that?* **3.** *n.* a terribly funny joke. (You laugh so hard you wet your pants. Jocular. Usually objectionable.) ♦ *He told a real pisser and broke up the entire class.*

pisshead 1. *n.* a wretched and disgusting person. (Rude and derogatory.) ♦ *How can you even think of going out with a pisshead like Sam?* **2.** *n.* a drunkard; a drunken person. (Rude and derogatory.) ♦ *Some old pisshead in the gutter must have given you that hat.*

pissing *mod.* worthless; minimal. (Usually objectionable.) ♦ *I got a pissing amount of coffee for a buck and a quarter.*

pissing-match *n.* an argument; a pointless competition. (Usually objectionable.) ♦ *Let's call a halt to this pissing-match and get to work.*

pissovers *n.* briefs with no fly. (Usually objectionable.) ♦ *Charlie always wears pissovers. He hates boxers.*

piss-poor 1. *mod.* of very poor quality. (Usually objectionable.) ♦ *This is piss-poor coffee. Pay the bill and let's go.* **2.** *mod.* without any money; broke. (Usually objectionable.) ♦ *Tell those piss-poor jerks to go beg somewhere else.*

piss-whiz Go to piss-cutter.

pistol *n.* a person who is bright, quick, or energetic. (Implying *hot as a pistol* or *quick as a pistol*.) ♦ *Ask that pistol to step over here for a minute, would you?*

pit stop 1. *n.* a pause in a journey (usually by car) to urinate. (From the name of a service stop in automobile racing.) ♦ *I think we'll pull in at the next rest area. I need a pit stop.* **2.** *n.* an underarm deodorant. (Because it *stops* arm*pit* odor.) ♦ *Can I borrow your pit stop? I need it bad.*

PITA *n.* [a] pain in the ass. (Initialism. A computer abbreviation, not pronounced.) ♦ *The SYSOP here is a real PITA. I wish he would leave us alone.*

PITBY Go to Put it in their back yard.

pitch a bitch *tv.* to make a complaint. (Crude.) ♦ *You really love to pitch a bitch, don't you? What makes you happy?*

pitch a tent Go to make a mountain.

pitch in (and help) *in.* to volunteer to help; to join in completing a task. ♦ *If more people would pitch in and help, we could get this job done in no time at all.*

pitch it *tv.* throw it away. ♦ *We don't need it. Let's pitch it.*

pitch (the) woo *tv.* to kiss and caress; to woo (someone). (Old but still heard.) ♦ *Old Ted can hardly see any more, but he can still pitch the woo.*

pitchcharacter *n.* a person, animal, or cartoon character who delivers the major selling message in an advertisement. ♦ *You can't use a frog for a pitchcharacter in a beer commercial!*

pits 1. *n.* the armpits. (Usually crude.) ♦ *Man, you have a problem in your pits.* **2.** the **pits** *n.* anything really bad. (Always with *the* in this sense.) ♦ *This whole day was the pits from beginning to end.* **3.** the **pits** *n.* the depths of despair. (Always with *the* in this sense. Often with *in* as in the example.) ♦ *It's always in the pits with him.*

pix [pɪks] *n.* pictures; photographs. ♦ *Hold still and let me get your pix taken. Then you can jump around.*

pixilated AND **pixolated 1.** *mod.* bewildered. ♦ *That little old lady is pixilated.* **2.** *mod.* alcohol intoxicated; tipsy. ♦ *She seems a bit pixolated. She's probably been drinking.*

pixolated Go to pixilated.

pizza-face Go to crater-face.

pizza-puss Go to crater-face.

pizzazz [pəˈzæz] *n.* punch; glitter and excitement. ♦ *Listen to the way she put pizzazz into that song!*

pizzle a wild card word for words beginning with *P*, such as piss, pee. (Streets. Also for other words with initial *P*.) ♦ *I gotta pizzle.*

PJs *n.* pajamas. (Initialism. Usually juvenile.) ♦ *Get your PJs on and get into bed right now.*

plant 1. *tv.* to strike a blow (to a particular place on someone). ♦ *The boxer planted a good blow on his opponent's shoulder.* **2.** *n.* a spy who secretly participates in criminal activities in order to inform on the criminals. ♦ *Don't tell every-*

thing you know. You don't know who's a plant and who isn't.

plant sth **on** so **1.** *tv.* to hide incriminating evidence on a person for later discovery and use in prosecution. (Drugs. Allegedly a police practice used to entrap drug offenders. See also flake.) ♦ *The cops planted snow on Bart and then arrested him for carrying it.* **2.** *tv.* to conceal narcotics or other contraband on an unsuspecting person for the purpose of smuggling. (This person will bear the risk of discovery and arrest.) ♦ *The crooks planted the stuff on a passenger but couldn't find him when the plane landed.*

plastered *mod.* alcohol intoxicated. ♦ *She's so plastered she can't see.*

plastered to the wall *mod.* heavily alcohol intoxicated. (An elaboration of plastered.) ♦ *How can anybody get plastered to the wall on just four beers?*

plastic 1. *mod.* phony; false. ♦ *She wears too much makeup and looks totally plastic.* **2.** *n.* a plastic credit card. ♦ *I don't carry any cash, just plastic.* **3.** *mod.* having to do with credit cards and their use. ♦ *There is too much plastic debt in most households.*

plastic punk *n.* falsely stylish. ♦ *Isn't all punk really plastic punk?*

plate Go to platter.

platter 1. AND **plate** *n.* home base or home plate in baseball. (Usually with *the.*) ♦ *The batter stepped up to the platter.* **2.** *n.* a phonograph record. (Old but still heard.) ♦ *They call it a "platter" because it looks like a serving platter.*

play 1. *n.* a strategy; a plan of action. ♦ *That was a bad play, Bill. We lost the account.* **2.** *n.* an attractive investment; a way to make some money in the securities markets. ♦ *I just heard about a good play in the options market.*

play around (with so**) 1.** *in.* to waste time; to waste someone's time. ♦ *Stop playing around and get to work.* **2.** *in.* to flirt or have an affair with someone. ♦ *Those two have been playing around for months.* **3.** *in.* to tease, deceive, or try to trick

someone. ♦ *You're playing around with me. Leave me alone.*

play ball (with so**)** *tv.* to cooperate with someone. ♦ *Are you going to play ball, or do I have to report you to the boss?*

play fast and loose (with so/sth**)** *in.* to treat someone or something carelessly or unfairly. ♦ *The broker played fast and loose with our money. Now we are nearly broke.*

play for keeps *in.* to take serious and permanent actions. (Refers to playing a game where the money won is not returned at the end of the game.) ♦ *I always play for keeps.*

play freeze-out *tv.* to open windows and doors, or turn down a thermostat, making someone cold. (See also freeze so out.) ♦ *Wow, it's cold in here! Who's playing freeze-out?*

play hardball (with so**)** *tv.* to act strong and aggressive about an issue with someone. ♦ *Things are getting a little tough. The president has decided to play hardball on this issue.*

play hell with so/sth AND **play the devil with** so/sth *tv.* to cause difficulty for someone or something. ♦ *You know that this cake is going to play hell with my diet.* ♦ *Your driving is playing the devil with my upset stomach.*

play hide the sausage *tv.* to perform an act of copulation. (Jocular. Usually objectionable.) ♦ *Then he said he wanted to play hide the sausage.*

play hooky [...ˈhʊki] *tv.* to not go to school; to not keep an appointment. ♦ *I played hooky today and did not go to work.*

play in the big leagues *in.* to become involved in something of large or important proportions. ♦ *The conductor shouted at the oboist, "You're playing in the big leagues now. Tune up or ship out."*

play it cool 1. *tv.* to do something while not revealing insecurities or incompetence. (See also cool.) ♦ *If the boss walks in, just play it cool.* **2.** *tv.* to hold one's temper. ♦ *Come on now. Let it pass. Play it cool.*

play so **for a fool** *tv.* to treat someone like a fool; to act as if someone were a fool. ♦ *I know what you're trying to do! Don't try to play me for a fool!*

play the devil with so/sth Go to play hell with so/sth.

play the dozens AND **shoot the dozens** *tv.* to trade insulting remarks concerning relatives with another person. (Chiefly black. See also (dirty) dozens.) ♦ *They're out playing the dozens.* ♦ *There's a bunch of kids out there messing around shooting the dozens.*

play tonsil hockey *tv.* to kiss deeply, using the tongue. ♦ *Kids sit around in cars, playing tonsil hockey all evening.*

play with a full deck *in.* to operate as if one were mentally sound. (Usually in the negative. One cannot play cards with a partial deck.) ♦ *Look sharp, you dummies! Pretend you are playing with a full deck.*

play with fire *in.* to do something dangerous or risky. ♦ *Going out at night in a neighborhood like that is playing with fire.*

playa **1.** *n.* an active and popular man or woman. ♦ *She's dressed to be a playa.* **2.** *n.* someone who is skilled and respected as a successful street con; pimp; dealer; womanizer, etc. ♦ *Sam is a real playa and already has eight kids.*

playa hata *n.* someone who does not respect or is jealous of a playa. ♦ *The dude is just a playa hata. Has something against success.*

pleasantly plastered *mod.* mildly alcohol intoxicated; mellow with drink. (An elaboration of plastered.) ♦ *He wasn't really stoned. Just pleasantly plastered.*

Please! Go to Puh-leez!

plonk *n.* white wine; cheap wine; any liquor. (From French *blanc*.) ♦ *That plonk is really hard on the gut.*

plonked (up) *mod.* alcohol intoxicated. (See also plonk; blank.) ♦ *He sure is plonked up.*

plonko *n.* a drunkard. (See also plonk.) ♦ *Get that smelly plonko out of here!*

plootered ['pludɚd] *mod.* alcohol intoxicated. ♦ *We went out and got totally plootered.*

plop **1.** *n.* the sound of dropping something soft and bulky, such as a hunk of meat. ♦ *When the roast fell on the floor, it made a nasty plop.* **2.** *tv.* to put or place something (somewhere). ♦ *I don't mind cooking a turkey. You only have to plop it in the oven and forget about it.* **3.** *tv.* to sit oneself down somewhere; to place one's buttocks somewhere. (The *it* in the examples is the buttocks.) ♦ *Come in, Fred. Just plop it anywhere you see a chair. This place is a mess.*

plotzed ['platst] *mod.* alcohol intoxicated; really drunk. ♦ *They all came home so plotzed!*

plowed (under) *mod.* alcohol or drug intoxicated. ♦ *They went out and got plowed.*

plowing water *n.* wasting time doing something futile. ♦ *You're wasting your time. You're plowing water.*

pluck AND **plug** *n.* wine; cheap wine. (Originally black.) ♦ *He buys pluck by the box, yes the box!* ♦ *You spilled your plug all over my car seat!*

plug **1.** *n.* a bite-sized, pressed mass of chewing tobacco. ♦ *He put a plug in his cheek and walked away.* **2.** *n.* a drink of beer; a slug of beer. ♦ *Let me have a plug out of that bottle.* **3.** *n.* a free advertisement or a commercial boost from someone for a product. (See also plugola.) ♦ *I managed to get a plug on the Mike Michael show.* **4.** *tv.* to give an advertisement or commercial boost for something without having to pay for it. ♦ *I want to get on that TV program and plug my new book.* **5.** Go to pluck.

plugged in *mod.* excited by drugs; having to do with the drug culture; turned on. (Drugs.) ♦ *That punker is plugged in, for sure.*

plugola [pləg'olə] *n.* a bribe paid to get a free advertising plug (worth far more than the amount of the bribe). ♦ *The announcer was charged with accepting plugola.*

plug-ugly *mod.* very ugly. (See also pug-ugly.) ♦ *Your dog is just plug-ugly!*

plum *n.* a prize or reward; something that can be considered the spoils of a political office. ♦ *My plum for getting elected was a big new office.*

plumb loco ['pləm 'loko] *mod.* completely crazy. (Folksy. *Loco* is from a Spanish word meaning "mad.") ♦ *You're plumb loco if you think I'll go along with that.*

plumber's smile AND **working man's smile** *n.* the upper part of the gluteal cleft (**crack** sense 1) visible above the beltline of a man, bent over at work. *I came into the kitchen and was greeted by a plumber's smile owned by some guy working under the sink.* ♦ *She referred to the overexposure of his rear end over his belt as the "working man's smile."*

PMJI *interj.* Pardon me for jumping in. (This indicates that someone is responding to a message directed to someone else. Used in electronic mail and computer forum or news group messages. Not pronounced aloud.) ♦ *PMJI, but I have some information that would help you with your problem.*

PO Go to piss off.

pocket of time *n.* a period of available time, as might be found between appointments. ♦ *I had a pocket of time between stops that I used to get myself one of those incredibly expensive cups of coffee.*

pocket pool *n.* the act of a male playing with his genitals with his hand in his pants pocket. (Usually objectionable.) ♦ *Stop playing pocket pool and get to work.*

pocket-rocket *n.* the penis. (Usually objectionable.) ♦ *He held his hands over his pocket-rocket and ran for the bedroom.*

Podunk ['podəŋk] **1.** *n.* an imaginary rural town where everything and everyone is backward, old-fashioned, and inferior. ♦ *This is the big city, not Podunk.* **2.** *mod.* rural and backward. (Usually **podunk**.) ♦ *I want out of this podunk town.*

POed *mod.* pissed off. ♦ *The teacher was POed at the whole class.*

poindexter ['poɪndɛkstɚ] *n.* a bookish person; a well-mannered good student, usually male. (Also a term of address.) ♦ *I'm no poindexter. In fact, my grades are pretty low.*

point man 1. *n.* a ballplayer who habitually scores points. ♦ *Fred is supposed to be point man for our team, but tonight he is not doing so well.* **2.** *n.* anyone whose job it is to score successes against the opposition. ♦ *The president expects the secretary of defense to be point man for this new legislation.*

pointy end *n.* [of a ship] the bow. (Jocular term heard on cruise ships.) ♦ *The dining room is up at the pointy end.*

pointy-head *n.* a studious thinker; an intellectual. (See also conehead.) ♦ *The pointy-heads seem to be living in a world of their own.*

poison 1. *mod.* wicked; evil. ♦ *Stay away from her. She's poison.* **2.** *n.* an alcoholic drink. ♦ *Name your poison.*

poison pill *n.* an element introduced into the restructuring of a corporation so that it becomes undesirable for another corporation to take over. ♦ *Acme Corporation approved a poison pill to prevent a hostile takeover.*

poke 1. *n.* a puff of a marijuana cigarette or pipe. (Drugs. See also toke.) ♦ *Can I have a poke of that?* **2.** *tv.* [for a male] to copulate (with a female). (Crude. Usually objectionable.) ♦ *Your dog poked my dog, then ran away.*

pokey Go to poky.

poky AND **pokey 1.** *n.* jail; a jail cell. (Usually with *the*.) ♦ *She spent a day in the poky.* **2.** *mod.* slow; lagging and inefficient. ♦ *Hurry up! Don't be so poky.*

pol [pɑl] *n.* a politician. ♦ *The pols are spending my taxes like mad again.*

pole dancer *n.* a woman, thought of as a stripper, who performs erotic dances around a metal pole, onstage, exploiting the pole's phallic form. ♦ *Jed swears that he has never seen an inept pole dancer.*

pole dancing *n.* sexually stimulating erotic dancing and writhing around a metal pole, onstage, before a largely male audience. ♦ *I didn't have the body for a career in pole dancing, so I became a house painter.*

polecat *n.* a mean and deceitful person, usually male. (Folksy. *Polecat* is another U.S. word for skunk. See also skunk; stinker.) ♦ *Tell that polecat I want to talk to him.*

polished (up) *mod.* alcohol intoxicated. (See also waxed.) ♦ *How much of that do I have to drink to get good and polished?*

polluted *mod.* alcohol or drug intoxicated. ♦ *Those guys are really polluted.*

pond scum *n.* a mean and wretched person; a worthless male. (Collegiate. An elaboration of scum, less crude than scumbag. Also a rude term of address.) ♦ *Get your hands off me, you pond scum!*

poo 1. AND **poo-poo** *n.* fecal material. (See also poop. Mostly juvenile. Usually objectionable.) ♦ *Don't step in that dog poo!* **2.** *in.* to defecate. (Usually objectionable.) ♦ *That old dog pooed on our lawn.* **3.** *n.* nonsense. (From sense 1. See also poo(h)-poo(h).) ♦ *I've heard enough of your poo.* **4.** *n.* champagne. (From shampoo.) ♦ *How about another glass of poo?* **5.** Go to poo(h)-poo(h).

pooch *n.* a dog. (Also a term of address to a friendly dog.) ♦ *Hello, pooch. My goodness, you're friendly.*

poohead *n.* an obnoxious person. ♦ *What poohead left the window open?*

poo(h)-poo(h) ['pu'pu] *tv.* to belittle someone or something. ♦ *He tends to poohpooh things he doesn't understand.*

pool-hopping *n.* sneaking into private or public swimming pools at night or during the off-hours. ♦ *The kids went pool-hopping, and one of them nearly drowned.*

poop 1. *n.* information; the detailed knowledge of something. ♦ *What's the poop on the broken glass in the hall?* **2.** *n.* fecal matter. (Usually objectionable. See also poo.) ♦ *There's poop on the sidewalk.* **3.** *in.* to defecate. ♦ *Your dog pooped on my lawn!*

poop chute *n.* the rectum and anus. ♦ *The doctor actually stuck his finger up my poop chute.*

poop out *in.* to quit; to wear out and stop. (See also pooped (out).) ♦ *He pooped out after about an hour.*

poop sheet *n.* a sheet containing information. ♦ *Where is the poop sheet on today's meeting?*

pooped (out) 1. *mod.* exhausted; worn-out. (Said of a person or an animal.) ♦ *The horse looked sort of pooped in the final stretch.* **2.** *mod.* alcohol intoxicated. ♦ *He's been drinking all night and is totally pooped out.*

pooper *n.* the buttocks. ♦ *How is she going to get that humongous pooper into the chair?*

pooper-scooper *n.* a device used to pick up and carry away dog feces from public places. ♦ *Taylor actually got a ticket for walking her dog without a pooper-scooper in sight!*

poophead *n.* a person who acts very stupidly. (Also a term of address.) ♦ *Look here, poophead, you're making a fool of yourself.*

poopied *mod.* alcohol intoxicated. (A euphemism for shit-faced.) ♦ *She was so poopied that she giggled all the way home.*

poo-poo Go to poo; poo(h)-poo(h).

poor boy Go to submarine.

poor-mouth 1. *tv.* to speak ill of someone. (See also bad-mouth.) ♦ *Please don't poor-mouth my brother.* **2.** *in.* to speak repeatedly of how little money one has; to plead poverty. ♦ *Spend more time looking for a job and less time poor-mouthing.*

poot *in.* to break wind; to fart. ♦ *Who pooted?*

pop 1. *tv.* to hit or strike someone. ♦ *She popped him lightly on the shoulder.* **2.** *mod.* popular. ♦ *This style is very pop.* **3.** *n.* popular music. ♦ *I like most pop, but not if it's too loud.* **4.** a **pop** *n.* a time; a try; a piece. (Always with *a* in this sense.)

♦ *Twenty dollars a pop is too much.* **5.** *tv.* to take or swallow a pill, tablet, or capsule. ♦ *Here, pop a couple of these.*

pop for sth *in.* to pay for a treat (for someone). (See also spring for sth.) ♦ *Let's have some ice cream. I'll pop for it.*

pop off 1. *in.* to make an unnecessary remark; to interrupt with a remark; to sound off. ♦ *Bob keeps popping off when he should be listening.* **2.** *in.* to lose one's temper. (See also pop one's cork.) ♦ *I don't know why she popped off at me. All I did was say hello.* **3.** *in.* to die. ♦ *I hope I'm asleep when I pop off.* **4.** *in.* to leave; to depart in haste. ♦ *Got to pop off. I'm late.*

pop one's **cork** *tv.* to release one's anger; to blow one's top. ♦ *She tried to hold it back, but suddenly she popped her cork.*

pop (some) tops *tv.* to drink beer. ♦ *We are going to pop tops and watch the B-ball game.*

pop the question *tv.* [for a man] to ask a woman to marry him. (Could also be used by a woman asking a man.) ♦ *She waited for years for him to pop the question.*

pop wine *n.* a cheap, flavorful, sparkling wine drink. ♦ *Even if you don't like fine wines, you'll like pop wine.*

popcorn pimp *n.* a pimp who runs a small operation. (Streets. *Popcorn* here means small; as in *popcorn shrimp.*) ♦ *Reggie is nothing but a popcorn pimp. He'll never amount to much.*

pop-eyed *mod.* alcohol intoxicated, with bulging eyes. ♦ *What's he been drinking? He's pop-eyed as hell.*

popo *n.* (Streets.) the police. ♦ *The popo just picked up that stewed dude.*

popped 1. *mod.* arrested. (Similar to busted.) ♦ *He was popped for hardly anything at all.* **2.** *mod.* alcohol or drug intoxicated. ♦ *She looks glassy-eyed because she's popped.*

popper 1. AND **popsie** *n.* an ampoule of amyl nitrite, a drug that is inhaled when the ampoule is broken. (Drugs. Often plural.) ♦ *You got any popsies I can have?*

2. Go to pill-popper. **3.** *n.* a handgun. (Underworld. From the sound of a gunshot.) ♦ *He carries his popper under his coat.* **4.** *n.* a can of beer (in a pop-top can). ♦ *You ready for another popper, Tom?*

popping *in.* happening. ♦ *Things are always popping at the gym.*

poppycock *n.* nonsense. (From Dutch.) ♦ *That's nothing but poppycock.*

pops *n.* one's father; any older man. (Also a term of address.) ♦ *Hey, pops! How you doing?*

popsie Go to popper.

popskull *n.* fiery liquor; inferior whiskey; moonshine. ♦ *This popskull will burn a hole in you.*

pork 1. *n.* the police in general; a pig. (Underworld.) ♦ *Keep an eye out for the pork.* **2.** *tv. & in.* to copulate [with] someone. (Usually objectionable.) ♦ *They pork all the time, just like bunnies.*

pork hammer *n.* the penis. ♦ *Stop scratching your pork hammer, bro.*

pork out *in.* to overindulge in food and drink. (A play on pig out.) ♦ *Whenever I see french fries, I know I'm going to pork out.*

porked *mod.* copulated with; [of a female] deflowered. (Usually objectionable.) ♦ *Well, have you been porked?*

porker *n.* a fat person. ♦ *Sally is not exactly a porker, but she is not skinny either.*

porky *mod.* fat; obese; pig-like. ♦ *You are beginning to look a little porky.*

POS *n.* a piece of shit; someone or something completely worthless. (See also piece (sense 4).) ♦ *This old thing's a POS. Get rid of it.*

poser *n.* someone who pretends to belong to a group only by affecting the attributes of the group. (See also mod poser.) ♦ *What's he doing here? He's just a poser, looking for dates.*

pository *mod.* yes; positive. ♦ Q: *Is this the right one?* A: *Pository.*

posse ['pɑsi] *n.* the group of teenagers or children that someone plays with or hangs out with. ♦ *Hank and his posse are in the backyard playing.*

pot 1. *n.* a toilet. (Usually with *the.*) ♦ *Jimmy's on the pot, Mommy.* **2.** *n.* a drinking vessel. (Old but still heard.) ♦ *How about a pot of beer?* **3.** *in.* to drink heavily; to use a **pot** (sense 2) to excess. ♦ *Let's sit here and pot for a while.* **4.** *n.* a vessel, hat, basket, etc., used to collect or receive contributions. ♦ *Please pass the pot.* **5.** *n.* a sum of money collected; a pool of money. ♦ *How large is the pot this month?* **6.** *n.* cannabis; marijuana. (Originally drugs, now widely known.) ♦ *The cops found pot growing next to city hall.*

pot boiler *n.* a book or other literary work of no value except for the money it earns. ♦ *I can write one pot boiler every six months or so.*

pot hound AND **pot sniffer** *n.* a dog trained to sniff out cannabis. (Drugs.) ♦ *The pot hound at the airport is always busy finding marijuana.* ♦ *A cute beagle named sparky greeted me as today's "pot sniffer" in the baggage claim area.*

pot party *n.* a communal marijuana smoking session; a party where marijuana is smoked. (Drugs.) ♦ *I didn't know you were taking me to a pot party!*

pot sniffer Go to pot hound.

potato *n.* the head. ♦ *Put your hat on your potato, and let's get out of here.*

potato soup *n.* vodka. (This liquor is typically made from potatoes.) ♦ *Have a bit of this potato soup, why don't you?*

potatohead *n.* a stupid person. (See also potato.) ♦ *Stop acting like a potatohead.*

potbelly *n.* a big belly. ♦ *He got a potbelly from eating fried chicken.*

POTS *n.* plain old telephone service [for a computer connection to the Internet]. (As opposed to connection through a TV cable or high-speed telephone line.) ♦ *Even in five years, most people will still rely on POTS to get connected to the Internet.*

potshot *n.* a sharp criticism; a wild shot of criticism. (Usually with *take.*) ♦ *Please stop taking potshots at me!*

potted *mod.* drunk. ♦ *He's not sleepy! He's totally potted!*

potty 1. *n.* a small toilet. (Usually juvenile.) ♦ *Mommy, I've got to go to the potty.* **2.** *in.* to use the toilet. (Always juvenile.) ♦ *Be sure to potty before we leave.* **3.** *mod.* crazy. ♦ *He got more potty as he grew older.*

potty mouth AND **toilet mouth** *n.* someone who uses obscene or profane language in most social settings. (Also a term of address.) ♦ *That potty mouth is offending people again.* ♦ *Hey, toilet mouth! Watch your language!*

pound 1. *tv.* to drink something quickly. (See also pound a beer.) ♦ *Dan said he could pound the cup of coffee in thirty seconds.* **2.** *tv.* to copulate [with] someone. ♦ *He claims he pounded her all night. She says he snores.*

pound a beer AND **pound some beers; hammer a beer; hammer some beers; slam a beer; slam some beers** *tv.* to drink a beer; to drink a beer fast. ♦ *Let's go down to the tavern and pound some beers.*

pound one's **ear** *tv.* to sleep. ♦ *She went home to pound her ear an hour or two before work.*

pound one's **meat** Go to beat the dummy.

pound some beers Go to pound a beer.

pound so's **head in** *tv.* to beat someone. ♦ *Talk nice to him, or he'll pound your head in.*

pound sth **out 1.** *tv.* to play something loudly on the piano, perhaps with difficulty. ♦ *Here, pound this one out. A little softer, please.* **2.** *tv.* to type something on a typewriter. ♦ *I have finished writing it. Can I borrow your typewriter so I can pound it out?*

pound the books Go to hit the books.

pounder *n.* a police officer; a cop on the beat. ♦ *The pounder gave me a parking ticket.*

pounds *n.* dollars; money. (See also give one one's pounds.) ♦ *How many pounds does this thing cost?*

pour cold water on sth *tv.* to put an end to something; to dampen something. ♦ *I wanted to go to the party, but my brother poured cold water on that by taking the car.*

powder monkey *n.* a specialist in the use of dynamite. (See also **grease monkey**.) ♦ *How long do powder monkeys usually live?*

powder one's face Go to powder one's nose.

powder one's **nose 1.** AND **powder** one's **face** *tv.* to depart to the bathroom. (Usually said by women, or jocularly by men.) ♦ *She just went out to powder her face.* **2.** *tv.* to use cocaine. ♦ *John is in the bedroom powdering his nose. What a habit!*

powder room 1. *n.* a small bathroom without bathing facilities in a private home, usually located for the convenience of guests. ♦ *Excuse me, where is the powder room?* **2.** *n.* the ladies' restroom in a public place, especially a restaurant; the place women go to powder their noses. (The emphasis is on comforts other than toilet facilities, such as mirrors, places to rest, and even a maid to help with emergency repairs of makeup or clothing.) ♦ *The ladies went to the powder room. They'll be back in a minute.*

powder up *in.* to drink heavily; to get drunk. ♦ *He's at the tavern powdering up.*

powdered (up) *mod.* alcohol intoxicated. ♦ *Most of the bums in the gutter are really powdered.*

power hitter *n.* a batter in the game of baseball who can hit the ball great distances. ♦ *Ted is a real power hitter. They'll try to walk him.*

power tool *n.* a student who studies most of the time. (An elaboration of **tool**.) ♦ *Willard is a power tool if there ever was one. Studies most of the night.*

powerhouse *n.* a very big strong person, usually a male. ♦ *Ted is a real powerhouse. I'd hate to have him mad at me.*

powerstudy *n.* to study hard. ♦ *I've got to powerstudy for the exam. I haven't cracked a book all semester.*

pow-wow 1. *n.* a meeting; a conference. (From an American Indian word.) ♦ *Let's have a pow-wow on that issue.* **2.** *in.* to hold a meeting or a conference. ♦ *Let's pow-wow on that tomorrow.*

poz *mod.* HIV positive. ♦ *He was afraid he would turn up poz.*

prairie dog *in.* [for people in office cubicles] to pop up to see what's going on in the rest of the office. ♦ *Everybody was prairie dogging to see what was going on.*

pratfall *n.* a fall on the buttocks; a fall on the buttocks done as part of a comedy act. ♦ *If you want to be in musical comedy, you should learn to take a pratfall.*

prat(t) *n.* the buttocks. ♦ *Get out before I kick you in the pratt.*

pray to the enamel god Go to pray to the porcelain god.

pray to the porcelain god AND **pray to the enamel god** *in.* to empty one's stomach; to vomit. (Refers to being on one's knees [praying] in front of a porcelain toilet bowl.) ♦ *Wayne was in the john, praying to the enamel god.*

prayerbones *n.* the knees. ♦ *He pushed one of his prayerbones into my gut.*

preemie *n.* a premature baby. (Medical.) ♦ *There were two preemies born today.*

preg *mod.* pregnant. ♦ *Doesn't Sally look a little preg?*

prelims *n.* preliminary examinations. (Collegiate.) ♦ *What do you have to do to get the degree after you pass your prelims?*

preppie AND **preppy 1.** *mod.* in the manner or style of a student at a preparatory school. ♦ *I just love your preppy coat.* **2.** *n.* a young person who dresses and acts like a student at a preparatory school. ♦ *Those preppies are having fun now, but how will they support themselves?*

presenteeism *n.* the affliction of failing to take time off from work, even when it is available. (A jocular and contrived opposite of *absenteeism*.) ♦ *The office suffered from bouts of presenteeism during the winter when the workload was light.*

preserved *mod.* alcohol intoxicated. (See also pickled.) ♦ *He drank a quart of vodka and is totally preserved.*

President Wilson *n.* an erection. (Punning on *Woodrow* = woody Wilson.) ♦ *I am always happy to see President Wilson come round.*

press (the) flesh *tv.* to shake hands. (See also flesh-presser.) ♦ *He wanted to press the flesh, but I refused even to touch him.*

press the panic button Go to hit the panic button.

pretty *mod.* very. ♦ *I'm pretty busy at the moment.*

pretty penny *n.* a sizable amount of money. ♦ *This watch cost me a pretty penny, and I intend to take care of it.*

prexy *n.* a president. ♦ *This year's prexy will retire in March.*

pric(e)y *mod.* expensive. ♦ *Do you have anything less pricy?*

prick 1. *n.* the penis. (Usually objectionable.) ♦ *He held his hands over his prick and ran for the bedroom.* **2.** *n.* a stupid or obnoxious male. (Usually objectionable.) ♦ *You stupid prick! Get out of here!*

primed *mod.* alcohol or drug intoxicated. ♦ *The whole college was primed by midnight.*

primo ['primo] **1.** *mod.* great; first-class. ♦ *This pizza is really primo.* **2.** Go to (el) primo.

Prince Albert *n.* cannabis in general, especially marijuana sold or transported in a Prince Albert pipe tobacco can. (From the 1960s, but still heard.) ♦ *Where can I get a can of Prince Albert?*

prior *n.* a prior arrest. (Underworld.) ♦ *This guy has about fifteen priors.*

private eye *n.* a detective who is licensed to work privately rather than for a police department. ♦ *I worked for a while as a private eye.*

privy *n.* an outdoor toilet; any toilet. ♦ *Uncle Paul was out in the privy.*

pro 1. *n.* a professional (at anything); someone as good as a professional. ♦ *When it comes to typing, he's a pro.* **2.** *mod.* professional. ♦ *I hope to play pro ball next year.* **3.** *n.* a prostitute. ♦ *Do you think she's a pro or just overly friendly?*

prob *mod.* problem. ♦ *No prob!*

Probablee. *mod.* probably. (As an answer to a question. The last syllable is accented and drawn out.) ♦ Q: *Will you be there when I get home?* A: *Probablee.*

prod 1. *n.* a reminder. ♦ *She gave me a little prod about the report that is due Monday.* **2.** *tv.* to remind someone (about something). ♦ *Stop prodding me about these minor matters.*

prof *n.* a professor. (Collegiate.) ♦ *The prof was dull, the room was hot, and I kept closing my eyes.*

(pro)file *in.* to walk about and show something off; to walk carefully in a way that gets attention. (As if showing one's profile.) ♦ *Look at Albert profiling along! What a nerd.*

pronto *mod.* fast; immediately. (From Spanish. Common in Western movies.) ♦ *I want to see you in my office, pronto.*

proofed Go to carded.

props *n.* evidence of respect; one's proper respect. ♦ *You gotta give me my props.*

prosty AND **prostie** *n.* a prostitute. ♦ *The cops haul in about forty prosties a night from that one neighborhood alone.*

pseudo ['sudo] **1.** *mod.* false; bogus. ♦ *This is a very pseudo position that you are taking.* **2.** *n.* a phony person. ♦ *Randy is such a pseudo! What a fake!*

psych out *in.* to have a nervous or emotional trauma; to go mad for a brief time. (See also freak (out).) ♦ *Another day like this one and I'll psych out for sure.*

psych SO **out** *tv.* to try to figure out what someone is likely to do. ♦ *The batter tried to psych out the pitcher, but it didn't work.*

psych SO **up** *tv.* to get someone excited or mentally prepared for something. (See also psyched (up).) ♦ *I psyched myself up to sing in front of all those people.*

psyched (out) 1. *mod.* excited; overwhelmed; thrilled. ♦ *She's really psyched out.* **2.** *mod.* alcohol or drug intoxicated. (Drugs.) ♦ *She's just lying there, so psyched out.*

psyched (up) *mod.* completely mentally ready (for something). ♦ *I'm really psyched for this test.*

psycho *n.* a psychopathic person; a crazy person. ♦ *Pat is turning into a real psycho.*

ptomaine-domain AND **ptomaine-palace** ['to'men...] *n.* any institutional dining facility; a mess hall; a cafeteria. ♦ *Welcome to the ptomaine-domain. Help yourself to some mystery meat.* ♦ *Time to go over to the ptomaine-palace and eat—if you can call it that.*

ptomaine-palace Go to ptomaine-domain.

puck bunny Go to hockey-whore.

pud *n.* the penis. ♦ *Stop scratching your pud in public!*

pudding ring *n.* a mustache and goatee, grown together to form a circle. *He worked and worked to get his "pudding ring" just right, then got a huge zit that ruined the whole thing.*

puddinghead *n.* someone, usually a male, who acts very stupid. ♦ *That puddinghead sold my antique table for junk!*

puddle jumper *n.* a small airplane. ♦ *I'm not going to fly 200 miles in that puddle jumper!*

puff *in.* to get drunk. ♦ *Those guys go out and puff every Friday night.*

puffer *n.* a cigar. ♦ *Can you imagine anyone smoking a puffer like that in a restaurant?*

puggled 1. *mod.* exhausted; bewildered. ♦ *I have had a long day, and I'm really puggled.* **2.** *mod.* alcohol intoxicated. ♦ *When he started pouring his drink down his collar, I knew he was puggled.*

pug-ugly 1. *mod.* having to do with a very ugly person. ♦ *What a pug-ugly cat you have there!* **2.** *n.* a very ugly person. (Also a rude term of address.) ♦ *Hey, pug-ugly, try plastic surgery!*

Puh-leez! [pəə 'liiiz] *exclam.* Please!; That is enough! You can't expect me to accept that! (A long, drawn-out way of saying *Please!* The tone of voice shows exasperation and disgust. The spelling is highly variable.) ♦ *I am the one who's at fault? Puuuleeeze!*

puke 1. *in.* to vomit. ♦ *I thought I would puke when I smelled it.* **2.** *n.* vomit. ♦ *Tod put a big hunk of fake plastic puke on the teacher's desk.* **3.** *n.* a totally disgusting and obnoxious person. (Rude and derogatory.) ♦ *What an ugly puke. Make him leave! Make him handsome!*

puke hole ['pjuk...] **1.** *n.* a tavern. ♦ *Carl spends almost every evening at the local puke hole.* **2.** *n.* a toilet. ♦ *Bart tried to flush the dope down the puke hole, but the cops caught him.* **3.** *n.* a mouth. (Rude.) ♦ *Shut your puke hole and listen to what I am telling you!*

the pukes *n.* the feeling of nausea; the feeling of impending vomiting. (Especially with *have, get.*) ♦ *Oh my God, I've got the pukes.*

pukey AND **pukoid** *mod.* disgusting; repellent. ♦ *Who is that pukey looking guy?* ♦ *I won't eat that pukoid stuff!*

pukish *mod.* nauseated. (Folksy.) ♦ *That old pukish feeling came over me, and I just let go.*

pukoid Go to pukey.

pull 1. *n.* a drink; a swig; a drink from a flask. ♦ *He took another pull and kept on talking.* **2.** *tv.* to take a drink or a mouthful of liquor from a bottle or other container. ♦ *He pulled a slug from the bottle.* **3.** *n.* a mouthful of smoke from a cigarette; a **drag** on a cigarette. ♦ *A couple of pulls and she crushed out the cigarette.* **4.** *tv.* to smoke a cigarette. ♦ *He pulled a long filter job and then went back to work.* **5.** *in.* to pull one's **punches**. (Martial arts.) ♦ *If you pull during a fight, you're through as a fighter.*

pull a boner *tv.* to make a silly error. ♦ *That was dumb. You really pulled a boner.*

pull a fast one *tv.* to outwit or outsmart someone by a clever and timely maneuver. ♦ *Don't try to pull a fast one on me.*

pull a job *tv.* to carry out a crime, especially a robbery. (Police and underworld. Note the variations in the examples.) ♦ *Bart decided that it was not a good time to pull a bank job.*

pull an attitude *tv.* to be haughty; to put on airs. ♦ *Don't pull an attitude with me, chum!*

pull chocks AND **pull up stakes** *tv.* to leave a place. (*Chocks* refer to blocks that keep wheels from rolling, and *stakes* refers to tent stakes. See also up stakes.) ♦ *Time to pull chocks and get out of here.* ♦ *We pulled up stakes and moved on.*

pull down an amount of money *tv.* to earn a stated amount of money. (*An amount of money* is expressed as a figure or other indication of an actual amount.) ♦ *She pulls down about $80,000 a year.*

pull jive *tv.* to drink liquor. (See also jive.) ♦ *Let's go pull jive for a while.*

pull one's **belt in (a notch)** Go to take one's belt in (a notch).

pull one's **pud** Go to beat the dummy.

pull one's **punches 1.** *tv.* to pull back during a boxing punch just before the full force of a blow is felt; to land lighter blows than normal upon an opponent. (Boxing and related sports.) ♦ *The boxer started pulling his punches, and the ref ended the fight.* **2.** *tv.* to hold back in one's criticism; to attenuate the intensity of one's remarks. (Also with *any* in the negative.) ♦ *I won't pull my punches with you. This is lousy.*

pull one's **wire** Go to beat the dummy.

pull oneself **off** Go to beat off.

pull out all the stops *tv.* to use everything available; to not hold back. (Refers to pulling out all of the stops on an organ so that it will sound as loud as possible.) ♦ *Don't pull out all the stops in the first round. Wait till he's tired in the third and clobber him good.*

pull so's **chain** Go to yank so's chain.

pull so's **leg** *tv.* to kid someone; to tease someone. ♦ *They're just pulling your leg. Relax!*

pull sth **off** *tv.* to make something happen. ♦ *It takes a lot of skill to pull off something like that.*

pull the plug (on so/sth**)** *tv.* to put an end to someone or something as a problem; to defuse a problem caused by someone or something. (As if one were disconnecting an electrical appliance.) ♦ *I've heard enough from Mr. Jones. It's time to pull the plug on him.*

pummelled *mod.* alcohol intoxicated. (Collegiate.) ♦ *Can you imagine getting pummeled on peppermint schnapps?*

pump 1. *tv.* to press someone for an answer or information. ♦ *Don't pump me! I will tell you nothing!* **2.** *n.* the heart. (See also ticker.) ♦ *He has the pump of a forty-year-old.* **3.** *n.* a pumped-up muscle. (Bodybuilding.) ♦ *He's tired and can't quite make a pump.*

pump iron Go to pump (some) iron.

pump ship 1. *tv.* to urinate. (Crude. From an expression meaning to pump the bilge water from a ship.) ♦ *He stopped and pumped ship right in the alley.* **2.** *tv.* to empty one's stomach; to vomit. (Crude. Less well known than the previous sense.) ♦ *After I pumped ship, I felt better.*

pump (some) iron *tv.* to lift weights. ♦ *Andy went down to the gym to pump some iron.*

pump (so) up *tv. & in.* to excite someone; to make someone enthusiastic. ♦ *The coach gave a pep talk to pump the players up for the big game.*

pump sth **up** *tv.* to flex and tense a muscle until it is expanded to its fullest size, as with thighs and forearms. (Bodybuilding.) ♦ *She pumped up her thighs and struck a pose.*

pump up Go to pump (so) up.

pumped 1. *mod.* pregnant; impregnated. (Crude.) ♦ *Look at her! She's pumped and looks due any minute.* **2.** Go to pumped (up).

pumped (up) *mod.* excited; physically and mentally ready. (Sports.) ♦ *The team is really pumped up for Friday's game.*

punch so out *tv.* to knock someone out. (See also punch so's lights out.) ♦ *The thug punched out the cop and ran down an alley.*

punch so's lights out *tv.* to knock someone out; to close someone's eyes with a hard blow. ♦ *Shut up, or I'll punch your lights out.*

punch-drunk AND **punchy** *mod.* unstable; stupid acting; bewildered. (From a term describing a boxer suffering from brain damage.) ♦ *I feel sort of punch-drunk after a roller coaster ride.*

punchy Go to punch-drunk.

punk 1. AND **punk kid** *n.* an inexperienced boy or youth. (Derogatory. Also a term of address.) ♦ *Ask that punk kid to come over here.* **2.** *n.* a petty (male) hoodlum; a (male) juvenile delinquent. ♦ *The jails are packed with crooks who were just punks a few years ago.* **3.** *mod.* poor; dull and inferior. ♦ *The party turned punk, and we left.* **4.** *mod.* having to do with punkers or their music. ♦ *This music sounds too punk for me.*

punk kid Go to punk.

punk out 1. *in.* to chicken out. ♦ *He was supposed to ask her out, but he punked out at the last minute.* **2.** *in.* to become a punker. ♦ *If my kids ever punked out and looked like that, I think I'd clobber them.*

punker *n.* a punk rocker; a young person who dresses in the style of punk rockers. ♦ *It's not safe to walk on the street with all those weird punkers out there.*

punt [pənt] *in.* to do something different in a pinch; to improvise. (From the act of kicking the ball in order to gain ground in football.) ♦ *Everyone expected me to lose my temper, so I punted. I cried instead of getting mad.*

puppy 1. *n.* a wimp; a softie. ♦ *That silly puppy is still waiting outside your door.* **2.** *n.* a thing; a piece or part of something. ♦ *Put this little puppy right here.*

puppy love *n.* mild infatuation; infatuation as in a crush. ♦ *Look at them together. It may be puppy love, but it looks wonderful.*

pure and simple *mod.* basically; essentially. ♦ *Bart is a crook, pure and simple.*

purple kush *n.* marijuana. ♦ *He's high on purple kush.*

purr (like a cat) *in.* [for an engine] to run well and smoothly. ♦ *New spark plugs and this old heap will really purr like a cat.*

push 1. *tv.* to approach a particular age (in years). ♦ *He's only pushing thirty, but he looks much older.* **2.** *in.* to recruit new drug users and sell drugs to them; to deal in drugs. ♦ *He was pushing for two years before the cops got him.* **3.** *tv.* to hype something or someone; to pressure something or someone. ♦ *The clerk was pushing one brand so hard that I finally bought it.*

push money *n.* extra money paid to a salesperson to sell certain merchandise aggressively. (See also spiff.) ♦ *The manufacturer supplied a little push money that even the store manager didn't know about.*

push the panic button Go to hit the panic button.

pushed 1. *mod.* pressured; hurried; under pressure from someone or something. ♦ *Excuse my abruptness. I'm really pushed at the moment.* **2.** *mod.* alcohol intoxicated. ♦ *Tom is a little pushed and can't walk very straight.* **3.** *mod.* addicted to a drug. (Drugs. Probably from sense 1. See also push.) ♦ *He used H. for years before he really got pushed.*

pusher *n.* a drug dealer who works hard to establish new addicts and customers. (Drugs. See also push.) ♦ *That pusher over on Eighth Street was just mobbed by a group of angry parents.*

pushing up daisies *mod.* dead and buried. (Folksy. Usually in the future tense.) ♦ *I'll be pushing up daisies before this problem is solved.*

pushy *mod.* very aggressive in dealing with other people. ♦ *Stop being so pushy! Who do you think you are?*

puss [pʊs] *n.* the face. ♦ *I ought to poke you right in the puss!*

pussy AND **nookie; nooky 1.** *n.* the female genitals; the vulva and vagina. (Usually objectionable.) ♦ *He said he wanted to get into her pussy.* **2.** *n.* women considered as a receptacle for the penis. (Rude and derogatory.) ♦ *Man, I gotta get me some nookie.*

pussy fart Go to cunt fart.

pussy pad *n.* a extra seat on a motorcycle, behind the driver. (Refers to the genital anatomy of a female passenger. See also crack-rack.) ♦ *Most expensive crotch-rockets have a pussy pad.*

pussycat 1. *n.* a woman or young woman; one's girlfriend. (Also a term of address.) ♦ *Hi, pussycat. Don't I know you from somewhere?* **2.** *n.* a timid male; a mild-mannered and passive male. ♦ *That guy is a wimp, a real pussycat.*

pussyfoot (around) *in.* to behave in a very cautious manner; to (metaphorically) tread softly; to hedge or equivocate. ♦ *Come on and say what you mean! Stop pussyfooting.*

pussy-whipped *mod.* [of a male] dominated or controlled by a woman. ♦ *Your trouble is that you're pussy-whipped, Casper.*

put a con on so *tv.* to attempt to deceive someone; to attempt to swindle someone. (Underworld.) ♦ *Don't try to put a con on me, Buster! I've been around too long.*

Put a cork in it! Go to Stuff a sock in it!

put a damper on sth *tv.* to reduce the intensity of something, such as a problem. ♦ *The death of the chief put a damper on the ceremony.*

put a smile on so's **face** *tv.* to please someone; to make someone happy. ♦ *We are going to give Andy a pretty good raise, and I know that'll put a smile on his face.*

Put a sock in it! Go to Stuff a sock in it!

put balls on sth *tv.* to make something more masculine or powerful; to give something authority and strength. (Usu-ally objectionable.) ♦ *Come on, sing louder. Put some balls on it.*

Put it in their back yard! AND **PITBY** *sent. & comp. abb.* Locate something undesirable close to the people who complain about having it close by. (A parody of NIMBY, Not in my back yard!) ♦ *To all those NIMBYs, I say PITBY.*

put on the dog AND **put on the ritz** *tv.* to make things extra special for a special event. ♦ *Frank's really putting on the dog for the big party Friday night.* ♦ *We're going out tonight, and we're really gonna put on the ritz.*

put on the feedbag AND **put on the nosebag; tie on the nosebag** *tv.* to prepare to eat; to eat a meal. (Refers to a bag of feed tied under a horse's mouth.) ♦ *I'm starved. Must be time to put on the feedbag.* ♦ *Let's go to Mickey D's and tie on the feedbag.*

put on the nosebag Go to put on the feedbag.

put on the ritz Go to put on the dog.

put one's **nose in (where it's not wanted)** AND **stick** one's **nose in (where it's not wanted)** *tv.* to interfere in someone else's business. ♦ *Why do you always have to stick your nose in?* ♦ *Stop putting your nose in where it's not wanted!*

put oneself **straight** *tv.* to take a needed dose of drugs. (Drugs. See also straight.) ♦ *I gotta get some stuff and put myself straight.*

put some distance between so **and** so/sth *tv.* to lengthen the distance or time between oneself and someone or something (including a place). ♦ *She needed enough money to put some distance between herself and her hometown.*

put some sweet lines on so Go to lay some sweet lines on so.

put so **away 1.** *tv.* to put someone in prison for a long time. (Underworld.) ♦ *They put Bart away for fifteen years.* **2.** *tv.* to knock someone unconscious. ♦ *One tap on the head and I put him away.* **3.** *tv.* to kill someone. (Underworld.) ♦ *The gangster* *threatened to put me away if I told the police.*

put so **on 1.** *tv.* to tease or deceive someone innocently and in fun. ♦ *Come on! You're just putting me on!* **2.** *tv.* to introduce someone to cannabis use, usually smoking. (Drugs.) ♦ *Where did you get that stuff? Who put you on?*

put so/sth **out of the way** *tv.* to remove someone or something as a barrier. ♦ *Yes, she is a problem, but you'll just have to put her out of the way and concentrate on this issue.*

put so **out of the way** *tv.* to kill someone. ♦ *Sorry, my friend, we no longer need you. Spike is going to have to put you out of the way.*

put so's **nose out of joint** *tv.* to cause someone to feel slighted; to cause someone to take offense. (See also get one's nose out of joint.) ♦ *I'm sorry we didn't invite you. We didn't mean to put your nose out of joint.*

put so **to bed with a shovel** *tv.* to bury someone; to kill and bury someone. (See also put to bed with a shovel.) ♦ *The leader of the gang was getting sort of tired and old, so one of the younger thugs put him to bed with a shovel.*

put so **up** *tv.* to provide someone with temporary shelter; to let someone stay the night. ♦ *Can you put me up for a few days?*

put sth **away** *tv.* to eat something. ♦ *Did you put away that whole pizza?*

put sth **on the street** *tv.* to make something known publicly; to tell everyone one's troubles. ♦ *She gets a little problem, and she puts it on the street right away!*

Put that in your pipe and smoke it! *exclam.* Take that!; See how you like that! ♦ *You are the one who made the error, and we all know it. Put that in your pipe and smoke it!*

put the arm on so **1.** *tv.* to demand something of someone, especially money. ♦ *I know Tom wants some money. He put the arm on me, but I said no.* **2.** *tv.* to arrest someone. (Underworld.) ♦ *They put the arm on Bart for pushing pills.*

put the bite on so *tv.* to try to get money out of someone. ♦ *You're always putting the bite on me for a few bucks. Go away.*

put the chill on so AND **put the freeze on** so *tv.* to ignore someone. ♦ *She was pretty snooty till we all put the chill on her.* ♦ *Why are you guys putting the freeze on me? What I do?*

put the clamps on so/sth AND **put the clamps on** *tv.* to impede or block someone or something; to restrain or restrict someone. ♦ *Fred had to put the clamps on Tony, who was rushing his work too much.*

put the finger on so *tv.* to identify someone (for someone else, such as the police). (Underworld.) ♦ *Tyrone put the finger on the killer, then got out of town fast.*

put the freeze on so Go to put the chill on so.

put the heat on so Go to put the screws on so.

put the kibosh on sth *tv.* to squelch something. ♦ *The mayor put the kibosh on the whole deal.*

put the make on so AND **put the moves on** so; **put the hard word on** so *tv.* to attempt to seduce or proposition someone. ♦ *I think he was beginning to put the make on me. I'm glad I left.* ♦ *I put the hard word on her and she clobbered me!*

put the moves on so *tv.* to attempt to seduce someone. (With *any* in the negative.) ♦ *If somebody doesn't try to put the moves on her, she thinks she's a failure.*

put the pedal to the metal *tv.* to press a car's accelerator to the floor; to floor it. ♦ *Put the pedal to the metal, and we're out of here.*

put the screws on so AND **put the heat on** so; **put the squeeze on** so *tv.* to pressure someone; to threaten someone to achieve something. ♦ *He told everything about the plan when they put the screws on him.* ♦ *The cops put the heat on him to try to make him talk.*

put the skids under so/sth *tv.* to cause someone or something to fail. (See also on the skids.) ♦ *The mayor put the skids under my plan.*

put the squeeze on so Go to put the screws on so.

put them together for so Go to put your hands together for so.

put to bed with a shovel 1. *mod.* dead and buried. (From put so to bed with a shovel.) ♦ *You wanna be put to bed with a shovel? Just keep talking that way.* **2.** *mod.* alcohol intoxicated. (From sense 1.) ♦ *He wasn't just tipsy. He was put to bed with a shovel!*

put to it *mod.* in trouble or difficulty; hard up (for something such as money). (As if one's back were put to the wall.) ♦ *Sorry, I can't lend you anything. I'm a bit put to it this month.*

put too much on it *tv.* to make too much fuss over something. ♦ *Come on, man. Lighten up. Don't put too much on it.*

Put up or shut up! *exclam.* Speak now or remain silent for good! ♦ *Now is your chance. Put up or shut up!*

put your hands together for so AND **put them together for** so *tv.* to applaud someone. (To put hands together clapping.) ♦ *Please put your hands together for Ronald and his great musicians!*

Put your money where your mouth is! *exclam.* Stop talking big and make a bet! (From gambling. Can also be said to someone giving investment advice.) ♦ *You want me to bet on that horse? Did you? Why don't you put your money where your mouth is?*

put-down *n.* an insult; an intentionally cruel and deflating insult. ♦ *Another put-down like that and I'm going home.*

putrid *mod.* alcohol intoxicated. (See also rotten.) ♦ *That guy is stinking drunk. Putrid, in fact.*

putt-putt *n.* a small motorized vehicle, especially a small car. ♦ *That's not a motorcycle; it's just a little putt-putt.*

puttyhead *n.* a stupid person. (As if the person's head were soft as putty. Also a term of address.) ♦ *Look, you silly puttyhead, shut up!*

put-up job *n.* a deception; a deceptive event. ♦ *That's really phony. A put-up job if I ever saw one.*

putz 1. *n.* the penis. (Usually objectionable.) ♦ *He held his hands over his putz and ran for the bedroom.* **2.** *n.* a stupid or obnoxious male; a stupid person. (Usually objectionable.) ♦ *What a stupid putz!*

putz around AND **futz around** *in.* to waste time; to do something ineffectually. (Putz is probably putz (sense 1).) ♦ *Get busy and stop putzing around.*

pythons *n.* large, muscular biceps. (See also guns.) ♦ *Look at the pythons on that guy! He could lift a piano!*

Q. *n.* a quart bottle of liquor. (An abbreviation.) ♦ *She can knock off a Q. a day.*

qizzle [ˈkwɪz l] a wild card word for words beginning with *Q*, such as *question* (Streets. Also for other words with initial *Q*.) ♦ *I got a qizzle for you.*

Q-sign *n.* the rounded, open mouth of a dead person with the tongue hanging out like the tail of a capital *Q*. (A semijocular usage. Hospitals. See also **O-sign**; in the **Q-zone**.) ♦ *The old lady in the corner room is giving the Q-sign.*

quack *n.* a fraudulent physician; a derogatory term for a physician. ♦ *I won't go back to that quack ever again!*

quads *n.* the quadriceps, large muscles in the upper legs. (Bodybuilding.) ♦ *I found some great new exercises to strengthen my quads.*

quaff a brew [ˈkwɑf ə ˈbru] *tv.* to drink a beer. (See also **brew**.) ♦ *I went down to the bar to quaff a brew.*

quail *n.* any girl or woman, especially considered sexually. (Crude.) ♦ *Look at that cute little quail over there.*

qual [kwɑl] *n.* qualitative analysis. (Scientific.) ♦ *We'll have to turn to qual for that answer.*

quality Joe *n.* an innocent or straight (male) person. (Underworld.) ♦ *Lefty is not what I would call your average quality Joe.*

quan Go to **quant**.

quant 1. AND **quan** *n.* quantitative analysis. (Scientific and collegiate.) ♦ *I didn't study enough for my quant test.* **2.** *n.* a technician who works in securities market analysis. ♦ *He was a quant on Wall Street for two years.*

quarterback *tv.* to manage, lead, or direct someone or something. ♦ *I quarterbacked the whole company for more years than I care to remember.*

quartzed *mod.* alcohol intoxicated. (Related to **stoned (out)**.) ♦ *How can anybody get so quartzed on a bottle of wine?*

Que pasa? [ke ˈpɑsə] *interrog.* Hello, what's going on? (Spanish.) ♦ *Hey, man! Que pasa?*

queen *n.* a homosexual male. ♦ *Tom is getting to be such a queen.*

queer 1. *mod.* counterfeit. ♦ *I don't want any queer money.* **2.** *n.* illicit liquor, especially whiskey. (Prohibition era.) ♦ *This isn't queer; it's left over from before prohibition.* **3.** *mod.* alcohol intoxicated. ♦ *After a glass or two, he got a little queer.* **4.** *tv.* to spoil something. ♦ *Please don't queer the deal.* **5.** *mod.* homosexual. (Rude and derogatory. But now in wider use in a positive sense.) ♦ *She doesn't like being called queer.* **6.** *n.* a homosexual male, occasionally a female. (Rude and derogatory. But now in wider use in a positive sense.) ♦ *Tell that queer to stop following me.*

queer as a three-dollar bill Go to **(as) queer as a three-dollar bill.**

queer fish *n.* a strange person; an aloof person. ♦ *She's a bit odd. Sort of a queer fish.*

queer for sth *mod.* in the mood for something; desiring something. ♦ *She's queer for him because of his money.*

queer-beer 1. *n.* bad beer; beer of low alcohol content. ♦ *I hate this queer-beer.*

Get out the good stuff. **2.** *n.* any strange person. (Also a term of address.) ♦ *What does that queer-beer think he's doing?* **3.** *mod.* having to do with homosexuals; homosexual. (Usually derogatory. Resented by homosexuals.) ♦ *I won't wear that queer-beer outfit!* **4.** *n.* a homosexual male, possibly a female. (See sense 3.) ♦ *They say she's a queer-beer.*

queered *mod.* alcohol intoxicated. (In the sense *made bogus.*) ♦ *How can anybody get so queered on two beers?*

quencher ['kwɛntʃɚ] *n.* a drink of liquor or beer. ♦ *I could really use a quencher about now.*

quetch Go to kvetch.

quick buck AND **fast buck** *n.* a quickly or easily earned profit. ♦ *I want some kind of scam where I can make a quick buck.* ♦ *I'm always on the lookout to make a fast buck.*

quick fix 1. *n.* a quick and probably none too permanent or satisfactory solution to a problem. ♦ *The quick fix isn't good enough in this case.* **2.** *mod.* having to do with a temporary or unsatisfactory solution or repair. (Usually **quick-fix.**) ♦ *Frank is a master of the quick-fix solution.*

quick one AND **quickie 1.** *n.* a quick drink of booze; a single beer consumed rapidly.

♦ *I could use a quickie about now.* **2.** *n.* a quick sex act. (Usually objectionable.) ♦ *They're in the bedroom having a quick one.*

quick-and-dirty *mod.* rapidly and carelessly done. ♦ *I'm selling this car, so all I want is a quick-and-dirty repair job.*

quicker than hell *mod.* very fast. ♦ *Be careful in the stock market. You can lose all your money quicker than hell.*

quickie Go to quick one.

quimp [kʌmɪmp] *n.* a total jerk; a social outcast. (Also a term of address.) ♦ *I don't want to live in a dorm full of quimps.*

quit while one **is ahead** *in.* to stop doing something while one is successful. ♦ *Get into the market. Make some money and get out. Quit while you're ahead.*

Quit your bellyaching! *imperative* Stop complaining! ♦ *You've been bitching all day! Quit your bellyaching!*

quitter *n.* someone who gives up easily. ♦ *Don't be a quitter. Get in there and finish the job.*

quote, unquote *phr.* a parenthetical expression said before a word or short phrase indicating that the word or phrase would be in quotation marks if used in writing. ♦ *So I said to her, quote, unquote, it's time we had a little talk.*

R

R. & R. *n.* rest and recuperation; rest and relaxation; rest and recreation. (Originally military.) ♦ *I'll need a lot of R. & R. to recover from that stuff they fed us.*

rabbit food *n.* lettuce; salad greens. ♦ *Rabbit food tends to have a lot of vitamin C.*

rabbit punch *n.* a quick little punch. (Boxing and general slang.) ♦ *She battered him with about forty rabbit punches on the arm. Boy, is he ever sore!*

rack 1. *n.* a bed. ♦ *You don't get to see the rack very much in the army.* **2.** Go to rack (out). **3.** *n.* a pair of [female] breasts. (Usually objectionable.) ♦ *Look at the rack on that dame! How can she stand upright?*

rack duty Go to rack time.

rack face *n.* one's face after sleeping in a bed or rack. ♦ *In the mirror, I saw an old man with "rack face" and a scraggly beard.*

rack (out) *in.* to go to sleep or to bed. (See also rack.) ♦ *What time do you rack out?*

rack sth **up 1.** *tv.* to accumulate something; to collect or acquire something. ♦ *We racked up twenty points in the game last Saturday.* **2.** *tv.* to wreck something. ♦ *He racked up his arm in the football game.*

rack time AND **rack duty** *n.* time spent in bed. (Military.) ♦ *Gee, I need some more rack time.* ♦ *I was on rack duty for my entire leave.*

rack up *in.* to become alcohol intoxicated. (See also racked (up).) ♦ *Let's go down to the tavern and rack up.*

rackage *n.* the female bosom; a set of breasts; a rack. ♦ *He stood there admiring all the boss rackage on the beach.*

racked *mod.* struck in the testicles. (Usually objectionable.) ♦ *The quarterback got racked and didn't play the rest of the quarter.*

racked (up) *mod.* alcohol or drug intoxicated. (See also rack up.) ♦ *They drank till they were good and racked.*

racket 1. *n.* noise. ♦ *Cut out that racket! Shut up!* **2.** *n.* a deception; a scam. ♦ *This is not a service station; it's a real racket!* **3.** *n.* any job. ♦ *I've been in this racket for twenty years and never made any money.*

rad [ræd] **1.** *n.* a radical person. (California.) ♦ *My brother is a rad, but he's a good guy.* **2.** *mod.* great; wonderful; excellent; exciting. (California. From radical.) ♦ *Oh my God, that's, like, really rad!*

radical *mod.* great; excellent. (California.) ♦ *My boyfriend, he's, like, so radical!*

radioland *n.* an imaginary place where radio listeners dwell. ♦ *All you folks in radioland who enjoy country music will like this next one.*

rag 1. *n.* a newspaper. ♦ *What a rag! It's only good for putting in the bottom of bird cages!* **2.** *n.* ugly or badly styled clothing; an ugly garment. ♦ *I can't wear that rag!* **3.** *n.* any clothing, even the best. (Always plural.) ♦ *Man, I got some new rags that will knock your eyes out!* **4.** *n.* a sanitary napkin; a tampon. (For use in the menstrual cycle. Usually objectionable.) ♦ *God, I've got to change this rag!*

rag on SO AND **rake on** SO *in.* to bother someone; to irritate someone; to criticize and humiliate someone. ♦ *The kids all raked on Jed because of his intelligence.* ♦ *I wish you would stop ragging on me. I don't know why you are so annoyed at me.*

rag out *in.* to dress up. ♦ *I hate to rag out. I like comfortable clothes.*

the **rage** *n.* the current fad; an irresistible fad. (Often with *all the.* Old but current.) ♦ *One rage after another. Can't I find something that will stay the same for a while?*

rage *in.* to party; to celebrate. (Collegiate.) ♦ *Fred and Mary were raging over at the frat house last weekend.*

ragtop *n.* a convertible car. ♦ *I wanted a ragtop, but they cost nearly $3,000 more.*

ragweed *n.* inferior marijuana. (Drugs.) ♦ *Bart just sells ragweed except to his friends.*

rah-rah ['rɑ'rɑ] *mod.* having to do with college and college enthusiasm. ♦ *It was sort of a rah-rah party.*

rail Go to line (sense 2).

railroad tracks 1. *n.* dental braces. ♦ *I can't smile because of these railroad tracks.* **2.** *n.* rows of needle scars on the veins of the arms. ♦ *Look at those railroad tracks on his arm. That means he shoots drugs.*

rails *n.* powdered cocaine arranged into lines. (Drugs.) ♦ *Max makes the rails too messy.*

rain closet *n.* a shower (bath). ♦ *P.U. Willy. You need a trip to the rain closet.*

rain on so/sth Go to rain on so's parade.

rain on so's **parade** AND **rain on** so/sth *in.* to spoil something for someone. ♦ *I hate to rain on your parade, but your plans are all wrong.*

rain pitchforks *tv.* to rain very hard and heavy. ♦ *Every time I go out to rake leaves, it rains pitchforks.*

rainbow *n.* a bowlegged person. (Also a rude term of address.) ♦ *Ask that rainbow if he has to have special trousers made.*

raise a stink (about so/sth**)** AND **make a stink (about** so/sth**)** *tv.* to make a big issue about someone or something. ♦ *I hope you don't plan to make a stink about the problem.* ♦ *If they use that kind of language with me, I'll raise a stink.*

raise Cain [...ken] *tv.* to make a lot of trouble; to raise hell. ♦ *Fred was really raising Cain about the whole matter.*

raise hell 1. *tv.* to make a lot of trouble; to go on a rampage. ♦ *Stop raising hell so much of the time!* **2.** *tv.* to go on a drinking spree and get drunk. ♦ *Let's go out and really raise hell.*

raise hell (with so**)** Go to raise the devil (with so).

raise hell (with sth**)** Go to raise the devil (with sth).

raise the devil (with so**)** AND **raise hell (with** so**)** *tv.* to confront someone and complain or scold. ♦ *I really raised the devil with my brother for being late.* ♦ *She's raising hell again. What's it this time?*

raise the devil (with sth**)** AND **raise hell (with** sth**)** *tv.* to cause trouble with something. ♦ *That idea raises hell with my plan.*

raisin ranch *n.* a retirement community; an old folks home. (Refers to wrinkles.) ♦ *You won't get me into one of those raisin ranches. I like my independence.*

rake on so Go to rag on so.

rake sth **in** *tv.* to take in a lot of something, usually money. ♦ *Our candidate will rake votes in by the thousand.*

rally ['ræli] **1.** *n.* get-together of some kind; a party, usually informal, possibly spontaneous. ♦ *There's a rally over at Tom's tonight.* **2.** *in.* to hold a get-together of some kind; to party. (Collegiate.) ♦ *Let's rally tonight about midnight.*

ralph AND **rolf** [rælf AND rɔlf] *in.* to empty one's stomach; to vomit. (Teens and collegiate. See also cry ruth.) ♦ *She went home and ralphed for an hour.*

ralph sth **up** *tv.* to vomit (something). (Teens and collegiate.) ♦ *The doctor gave him some stuff that made him ralph it up.*

ram sth **down** so's **throat** *tv.* to force something upon someone. (Not literal.) ♦ *Don't try to ram that nonsense down my throat.*

rambo(ize) ['ræmbo(ɑɪz)] *tv.* to (figuratively) annihilate someone or something; to harm someone or something. (Collegiate. From the powerful film character Rambo.) ♦ *The students ramboed the cafeteria, and the cops were called.*

rammy ['ræmi] *mod.* sexually excited or aroused. (Refers to the ram, a symbol of arousal.) ♦ *Fred was looking a little rammy, so I excused myself and left.*

ramrod *tv.* to lead something; to act as the driving force behind something. ♦ *Who is going to ramrod this project?*

ranch 1. *n.* semen. (Alludes to Ranch [salad] dressing. Objectionable if understood.) ♦ *God! There's ranch on the bathroom floor!* **2.** *in.* to ejaculate. (Objectionable if understood.) ♦ *Just looking at her makes me want to ranch.*

randy ['rændi] *mod.* sexually excited or aroused. ♦ *The town is full of randy sailors when the fleet's in.*

rank *tv.* to give someone a hard time; to hassle someone. (Possible from *pull rank* = use rank to dominate someone.) ♦ *Stop ranking me!*

rank and file *n.* the common members of something. ♦ *What will the rank and file think of the proposal?*

rank on so *in.* to attack someone verbally; to gossip about someone. (See also rank.) ♦ *Please stop ranking on my family!*

rank so **(out)** *tv.* to annoy or chastise someone. (See also rank.) ♦ *He really ranks me out. What a pest!*

rap 1. *in.* to talk or chat about something. ♦ *Something wrong? Let's rap about it.* **2.** *n.* a conversation; a chat. ♦ *Let's have a rap sometime.* **3.** *n.* sweet talk; seductive talk; line. ♦ *Don't lay that rap on me! You're not my type.* **4.** *n.* a criminal charge; the blame for something. (Underworld.) ♦ *The cops tried to make the rap stick, but they didn't have enough evidence.*

rap session *n.* an informal conversation session. ♦ *The kids settled down for a long rap session.*

(rap) sheet *n.* a criminal record listing all recorded criminal charges. (See also rap.) ♦ *The sergeant asked if there was a sheet on the prisoner.*

rare bird *n.* an unusual person; a person with rare talents or abilities. ♦ *An inter-esting kind of rare bird is the man who can take long vacations and still make money.*

rare old time *n.* a fine and enjoyable time at a party or something similar. (Folksy.) ♦ *That was a rare old time at Tom's the other night.*

raring to go *mod.* anxious and eager to go. ♦ *Come on, I'm raring to go!*

raspberry ['ræzbɛri] *n.* the Bronx cheer. ♦ *The entire audience gave the performer the raspberry.*

rasty ['ræsti] *mod.* having to do with a harsh-looking young woman. (Collegiate.) ♦ *Who is that rasty dame I saw you with?*

rat 1. *n.* a wretched-acting person. (Also a term of address.) ♦ *You dirty rat, you!* **2.** Go to rat (on so).

rat around *in.* to waste time loafing around; to kick around. (Collegiate.) ♦ *I didn't do anything but rat around all summer.*

rat fink *n.* an informer. (Also a term of address. See also rat.) ♦ *That guy is nothing but a rat fink. A dirty squealer!*

rat (on so**)** *in.* to inform (on someone). ♦ *Bill said he was going to rat on that punk.*

rat out *in.* to quit; to fink out (on so/sth). ♦ *He tried to rat out at the last minute.*

rat race *n.* a dull and repetitive situation; a dull and unrewarding job. (See also daily grind.) ♦ *I am really tired of this rat race—day after day.* ♦ *She dropped out of the rat race and moved to Vermont, where she opened a barber shop.*

rat-bastard *n.* a really wretched or despised person. (Rude and derogatory.) ♦ *Stay away from Albert, he's a real rat-bastard when he's drunk.*

ratchet-mouth AND **motor-mouth** *n.* someone who talks incessantly. (Also a term of address.) ♦ *Tell that ratchet-mouth to shut up!* ♦ *Hey, motor-mouth! Don't you ever stop?*

rathole 1. *n.* a run-down place; a dump or a joint. ♦ *I refuse to live in this rathole any longer.* **2.** *n.* a bottomless pit. (Typically with *throw* and *down* as in the examples.)

♦ *Why do they keep throwing money down that rathole?*

Rats! *exclam.* Oh, damn! ♦ *Rats! I broke a nail!*

the **rats** *n.* the delirium tremens. ♦ *The way he was shaking, I knew he had the rats.*

ratted *mod.* drunk. ♦ *I think you are too ratted to drive.*

rattlebones *n.* a nickname for a very skinny person. (Also a term of address.) ♦ *Hey, rattlebones, come over here a minute.*

rattlebrain *n.* a stupid person. ♦ *Please try not to be such a rattlebrain! Pay attention to what you are doing.*

rattled 1. *mod.* confused; bewildered. ♦ *He tends to get a little rattled at minor things.* **2.** *mod.* tipsy; alcohol intoxicated. ♦ *After an hour of drinking, Bill was more than a little rattled.*

rattle-trap *n.* a rattly (old) car; any rattly vehicle. ♦ *I hear Ted's rattle-trap in the driveway.*

rattling *mod.* excellent. (Collegiate. See also rocking.) ♦ *Her party was really rattling.*

raunch so out [rɑntʃ...] *tv.* to disgust someone. (From raunchy.) ♦ *These dirty socks absolutely raunch me out!*

raunchy AND **raunchie; ronchie** ['rɑntʃi] **1.** *mod.* crude; tasteless; bad. ♦ *He told a very raunchy story at the party.* **2.** *mod.* alcohol intoxicated. ♦ *Those guys were raunchy as hell.* **3.** *mod.* sick; ill. ♦ *After I ate dinner, my stomach felt a little raunchie, so I went home.* **4.** *mod.* untidy; unclean. ♦ *We decided to leave the raunchy movie about halfway through.*

rave *n.* a party; a wild celebration. ♦ *Let's have a little rave next Friday.*

raw 1. *mod.* inexperienced; brand new. ♦ *The raw recruit did as well as could be expected.* **2.** *mod.* vulgar; crude; raucous; untamed. ♦ *I've had enough of your raw humor.* **3.** *mod.* [of alcoholic spirits] undiluted; neat. ♦ *I'll drink it raw—just the way it is now.* **4.** *mod.* [of alcoholic spirits] unaged; fiery and strong. ♦ *My* gosh, this stuff is raw! It'll burn a hole in me.

a **raw deal** *n.* an unfair deal; unfair treatment. ♦ *My last job was a raw deal. I hope this is better.*

rays *n.* sunshine. (Collegiate.) ♦ *I'm going to go out and get some rays today.*

razz [ræz] *tv.* to tease someone. ♦ *I was just razzing you. I didn't mean any harm.*

razzamatazz Go to razzmatazz.

razzle-dazzle ['ræzl'dæzl] *n.* flamboyant publicity; hype. ♦ *After all the razzle-dazzle dies down, we'll see what things are really like.*

razzmatazz AND **razzamatazz** ['ræz(ə)mə'tæz] *n.* deceptive talk; hype. ♦ *Cut out the razzamatazz. How dumb do you think I am?*

reach for the sky 1. Go to aim for the sky. **2.** *in.* (a command) to put one's hands up, as in a robbery. ♦ *The bank teller reached for the sky without having to be told.*

Read my lips! Go to Watch my lips!

Read the fucking FAQ! AND **RTFF; RTF-FAQ** *exclam. & comp. abb.* Simply read the information in the FAQ, Frequently Asked Questions. (Usually objectionable.) ♦ *Don't ask the group to explain everything just for you! RTFF!*

Read the fucking instructions! AND **RTFI** *exclam. & comp. abb.* Simply read the instructions. (Usually objectionable.) ♦ *RTFI! It's really very simple.*

Read the fucking manual! AND **RTFM** *exclam. & comp. abb.* Simply read the manual and stop asking someone else to explain it to you! (Usually objectionable.) ♦ *Why should I write you a how-to book? RTFM!*

reader *n.* a piece of paper with writing on it; a note; a prescription; an IOU. (Underworld.) ♦ *I got a reader for some morphine.*

Ready for this? Go to (Are you) ready for this?

real *mod.* very; really. ♦ *This is a real fine party.*

real bitch *n.* a very difficult or annoying thing or person. (Can refer to male or female.) ♦ *Fred is a true problem. A real bitch.*

real gone *mod.* really cool; mellow and pleasant. (See also **gone**.) ♦ *Man, this music is real gone.*

the **(real) McCoy 1.** *n.* something authentic. ♦ *This is the real McCoy. Nothing else like it.* **2.** *n.* pure drugs or alcohol. ♦ *If it's not the real McCoy, I don't want it.*

ream *so* **out** *tv.* to scold someone severely. ♦ *The coach reamed out the whole team.*

rear (end) *n.* the tail end; the buttocks. (Euphemistic.) ♦ *The dog bit her in the rear end.*

rear-ender AND **back-ender** *n.* an automobile wreck where one car runs into the back of another. (See also **fender-bender**.) ♦ *It wasn't a bad accident, just a rear-ender.* ♦ *The rain caused a couple of "back-enders," but there were no serious accidents.*

red gravy *n.* blood. ♦ *If you're gonna pick your scabs, keep your red gravy and stuff off me!*

red hot 1. *mod.* important; in great demand. ♦ *The stock market is a red hot issue right now.* **2.** *n.* a hot dog; a frankfurter. ♦ *"Get your red hots right here!" shouted the vendor.*

red ink *n.* debt; indebtedness as shown in red ink on a financial statement. ♦ *There is too much red ink in my financial statement.*

red tide *n.* a menstrual period. (Punning on the name of a tidal phenomenon where the water appears reddish owing to the presence of certain kinds of microscopic creatures.) ♦ *Sorry, she's down with the red tide and really prefers to stay home.*

red-hot mama *n.* an exciting woman; a sexually exciting or excited woman. ♦ *I'm no red-hot mama, just a country girl.*

red-letter day *n.* an important day that might well be marked in red on the calendar. ♦ *Today was a red-letter day in our history.*

redneck 1. *n.* a stereotypic southern bigot. (Derogatory. Also a term of address.) ♦ *Look, you stupid redneck, try to understand.* **2.** *mod.* in the manner of a southern bigot. ♦ *I don't follow that kind of redneck thinking.*

redonkulous *mod.* ridiculous. (Many variations.) ♦ *What a redonkulous thing to say!*

reef Go to **reefer**.

reefer ['rifɚ] **1.** *n.* a refrigerator. ♦ *A new reefer costs nearly $1,000!* **2.** AND **reef** *n.* cannabis; a marijuana cigarette. (Drugs. Akin to **greefo**.) ♦ *He had a fat reef in his hand when he was busted.*

ref [rɛf] **1.** *n.* a referee. (Also a term of address.) ♦ *Hey, ref! Get some glasses!* **2.** *tv.* to referee something, such as a game. ♦ *Are you going to ref this one, or am I?*

refi *n.* refinancing. ♦ *I've done three refis in the past two years. I still owe as much as I started with, but my payments are lower.*

regs *n.* regulations. ♦ *There is a list of regs posted on the back of your door.*

reinvent the wheel *tv.* to make unnecessary or redundant preparations. ♦ *You don't need to reinvent the wheel. Read up on what others have done.*

rent(al)s *n.* one's parents. (Teens. See also **(parental) units**. Also a term of address.) ♦ *Hey, rentals, let's go out for dinner.*

rents Go to **rent(al)s**.

rep [rɛp] **1.** *n.* a representative, usually a sales representative. ♦ *Please ask your rep to stop by my office.* **2.** *n.* someone's reputation. ♦ *I've got my own rep to think about.* **3.** *n.* repertory theater. ♦ *Rep is the best place to get experience, but not to make connections.* **4.** *n.* Go to **reps**.

rep out *in.* to do too many repetitions of an exercise and reach exhaustion. ♦ *After forty crunches, he repped out. He's got some work to do.*

repo ['ripo] **1.** *n.* a repossessed car. ♦ *I'd rather have a plain used car than a repo.* **2.** *tv.* to repossess a car. ♦ *Some guy came around and tried to repo my car.*

repo man ['ripo 'mæn] *n.* a man who repossesses cars for a living. ♦ *I'd rather beg than get a job as a repo man.*

reps *n.* repetitions of an exercise. (Bodybuilding.) ♦ *After twenty reps, I think I could just keep going.*

ret [rɛt] *n.* a tobacco cigarette. (Collegiate.) ♦ *Give my buddy a ret, will you?*

retard ['ritɑrd] **1.** *n.* a rude nickname for a retarded person. (Derogatory and unkind.) ♦ *That retard is having a rough time.* **2.** *n.* a stupid person. (Also a term of address.) ♦ *Don't be a retard! Get with it!*

retarded *mod.* bad; defective. ♦ *This old DVD player is so retarded. Time for a new one.*

retread ['ritrɛd] *n.* a burned-out person; a made-over person. ♦ *Chuck is just a retread. He's through.*

rev *mod.* revolting. ♦ *Fix you hair! You are so rev!*

rev sth **up** *tv.* to speed up an engine in short bursts. ♦ *Tom sat at the traffic light revving up his engine.*

reverse gears *tv.* to wretch as a prelude to vomiting; to vomit the stomach contents. ♦ *Beavis is reversing gears and might be going to vomit. You never know with Beavis.*

revved (up) *mod.* excited, perhaps by drugs. ♦ *The kids were all revved up, ready to party.*

rhoid *n.* a bothersome person; a person who is a pain in the ass. (From hemorrhoid.) ♦ *Get away from me, you rhoid!*

rhubarb ['rubɑrb] *n.* a brawl, especially in a baseball game. (Old.) ♦ *There's a noisy rhubarb down on the field.*

rib 1. *n.* a joke; an act of teasing. ♦ *I didn't mean any harm. It was just a little rib.* **2.** *tv.* to tease someone. ♦ *Please don't rib me any more tonight. I've had it.*

rib-tickler *n.* a joke; something very funny. ♦ *That was a real rib-tickler. I'll remember that joke.*

rice-rocket *n.* a Japanese motorcycle; a crotch-rocket from Japan. ♦ *He added a crack-rack to his rice-rocket.*

ricockulous *mod.* ridiculous. (Word play based on dick = cock.) ♦ *What a stupid thing to say! That is ricockulous!*

ride *n.* a car. ♦ *Do you care if I leave my ride parked in your driveway?*

ride shotgun 1. *tv.* to accompany and guard someone or something. (A term derived from the imagery of stagecoaches and their armed guards via Western movies. See also shotgun.) ♦ *I have to take the beer over to the party. Why don't you come along and ride shotgun?* **2.** *tv.* to ride in the passenger seat of a car, next to the driver. ♦ *I want to ride shotgun so I don't have to sit back there with those guys.*

ride the porcelain bus Go to drive the big bus.

ridic *mod.* ridiculous. ♦ *What nonsense! That's so ridic!*

rif [rɪf] **1.** *tv.* to dismiss an employee. (From the euphemism *reduction in force.*) ♦ *They're going to rif John tomorrow.* **2.** *n.* a firing; a dismissal. ♦ *There's a rif in your future.*

riff 1. *n.* a short, repeated line of music played by a particular performer. ♦ *Jim just sat there and forgot his riff.* **2.** *n.* a digression while speaking. (From sense 1.) ♦ *If she didn't make so many riffs while she spoke, we could understand her better.*

riffed 1. *mod.* alcohol or drug intoxicated. ♦ *I can't keep getting riffed every night like this.* **2.** AND **rift** *mod.* fired; released from employment. (From rif, "reduction in force." A dismissal not for cause, but simply to reduce the number of workers.) ♦ *Most of the sales force was rift last week.*

rift Go to riffed.

rig 1. *tv.* to arrange or tamper with the results of something. ♦ *Somebody rigged the contest so no one got first prize.* **2.** *n.* a large truck; an eighteen-wheeler; a large recreational vehicle. ♦ *There were three rigs sitting in the parking lot when we got there.*

right as rain Go to (as) right as rain.

right guy *n.* a good guy; a straight guy. ♦ *Tom is a right guy. No trouble with him.*

right in the kisser *mod.* right in the mouth or face. (See also kisser.) ♦ *Max poked the cop right in the kisser.*

Right on! *exclam.* Exactly!; That is exactly right! ♦ *After the speaker finished, many people in the audience shouted, "Right on!"*

(right) up one's **alley** *mod.* exactly one's kind of thing; exactly what one is best equipped to do. ♦ *It's not exactly up my alley, but I'll try it.*

righteous ['raɪtʃəs] *mod.* good; of good quality. (Originally black.) ♦ *She is a righteous mama.*

righteous collar *n.* a justifiable arrest. (As opposed to a setup or a frame.) ♦ *Spike was taken in, and the gang agreed it was a righteous collar. Mooshoo was caught red-handed.*

ring a bell *tv.* to stir something in someone's memory. ♦ *Yes, that rings a bell. I seem to remember it.*

ring off the hook *in.* [for a telephone] to ring endlessly or constantly. ♦ *The phone was ringing off the hook when I came in.*

ring the bell *tv.* to be just what is needed; to hit the spot. ♦ *A good hot bowl of soup would ring the bell about now.*

ringer *n.* the obvious choice; the one identical to the one you have; the best match; the best match for one's needs; the most likely choice. (See also (dead) ringer (for so).) ♦ *That's the best horse racing today. It's a ringer if I ever saw. one.*

ringer (for so**)** Go to (dead) ringer (for so).

ringtailed snorter *n.* someone or something energetic and powerful. ♦ *Ask that ringtailed snorter to calm down and come over here for a minute.*

rinky-dink ['rɪŋki'dɪŋk] *mod.* cheap; inferior; broken down. ♦ *I sold my rinky-dink old car yesterday.*

riot ['raɪət] *n.* someone or something entertaining or funny. ♦ *Tom was a riot last night.*

rip 1. *n.* a drinking bout. (See also tear.) ♦ *Fred had another rip last night. He's rotten now.* **2.** *n.* the loot from a rip-off. ♦ *Give him some of the rip and tell him to beat it.* **3.** *n.* a theft; a rip-off. ♦ *The crooks pulled a rip on Fourth Street last night.* **4.** *n.* a tear in the flesh of the hand, as in an athletic event where the flesh comes in contact with solid material, such as in gymnastics and weightlifting. ♦ *I keep getting rips from the bar.*

rip on so *in.* to give someone a hard time; to hassle someone. ♦ *Fred was ripping on me, and I heard about it.*

rip snorter *n.* a remarkable person or thing; a hilarious joke. (Folksy.) ♦ *Old Fred is a real rip snorter.*

rip so **off** *tv.* to assault, kill, beat, rob, rape, or cheat someone. ♦ *Man, they ripped me off for three hundred dollars.*

rip sth **off** *tv.* to steal something. ♦ *The crooks ripped off the hubcaps of my car.*

ripe 1. *mod.* alcohol intoxicated. ♦ *Yes, they were ripe all right. Stinking drunk.* **2.** *mod.* foul; smelly. ♦ *Whooey! This place is ripe. What died?* **3.** *mod.* crude; raunchy. ♦ *Your jokes are a bit ripe.*

rip-off 1. *n.* a theft; a deception; an exploitation. (See also rip.) ♦ *What a rip-off! I want my money back.* **2.** *mod.* having to do with theft and deception. ♦ *I consider myself to be rip-off champion of North America.*

(rip-)off artist *n.* a con artist. ♦ *Beware of the rip-off artist who runs that shop.*

ripped 1. *mod.* intoxicated on drugs or alcohol. ♦ *I don't know what I drank, but I'm really ripped.* **2.** *mod.* muscular; having sharply defined muscles. ♦ *I worked and worked to get ripped, but I'm just not made that way.*

ripped (off) Go to ripped (up).

ripped (up) AND **ripped (off)** *mod.* alcohol or drug intoxicated; under the effects of marijuana. ♦ *Why do you have to get ripped up like that?*

Rise and shine! *exclam.* Get up and get going! ♦ *Get up! Rise and shine! It's late.*

ritzy ['rɪtsi] *mod.* elegant; flamboyant. ♦ *That is a real ritzy car.*

rivets ['rɪvəts] *n.* dollars; money. (From copper rivets.) ♦ *You got enough rivets on you for a snack?*

rizzi *n.* a means of transportation; a car. (Streets. Probably from *rizzle* = ride.) ♦ *Sammy's got himself a new rizzi.*

rizzle a wild card word for words beginning with *R*, such as *ride* or *real*. (Streets. Also for other words with initial *R*.) ♦ *Where's my rizzle kizzle?*

roach 1. *n.* a police officer. (Derogatory. From *cockroach*.) ♦ *A roach caught him while he was at work.* **2.** *n.* the butt end of a marijuana cigarette. (Drugs.) ♦ *The cops found a roach on the bathroom floor.* **3.** *n.* an ugly girl or woman. (Derogatory. From *cockroach*.) ♦ *Who was that roach you were with last night?*

roach clip AND **roach pick** *n.* a device to hold a roach and make it smokable. (Drugs.) ♦ *When the cops find a roach clip on you, you've had it.* ♦ *He held the roach on a paper clip "roach pick."*

roach pick Go to roach clip.

roach-coach *n.* a mobile snack truck. (The term was revived in the Persian Gulf War.) ♦ *The roach-coach pulled up in front of the dorm every night about eleven.*

roached *mod.* hungover; exhausted. (Perhaps the notion of being down to the roach sense 2, and therefore, exhausted.) ♦ *I'm roached. I feel lousy.*

road apple *n.* a lump of horse excrement. (See also alley apple.) ♦ *There must be horses around here. I see road apples.*

road hog *n.* someone who takes too much space on a road or highway; someone who seems to run other people off the road. ♦ *Get over! Road hog!*

road pizza *n.* a dead animal on the road. ♦ *A bunch of crows were feasting on road pizza when we drove by.*

roadie AND **roady 1.** AND **roadster** *n.* someone who helps rock groups set up for performances. ♦ *I was a roadster for a while, but I didn't like it.* **2.** AND **roadster** *in.* to help rock groups set up. ♦ *Let's go downtown and roadster tonight. The Red Drips are in town.* **3.** *mod.* eager to travel; eager to get on the road. ♦ *I get a little roady when the weather gets warm.*

road-rash *n.* an injury from contact with the ground, as in motorcycling or biking. ♦ *Shane picked up a bit of road rash when she fell off her bike.*

roadster Go to roadie.

roadtrip *n.* a sudden trip in a car. (Sometimes yelled, **Roadtrip!** to indicate an impending jaunt in an automobile.) ♦ *"Roadtrip!" hollered Ken. "We're gonna go out and get some dames!"*

roady Go to roadie.

roast 1. *tv.* to put on an entertaining program, usually with a dinner, where the guest of honor is teased and insulted. ♦ *They roasted Dave when he retired.* **2.** *n.* an entertaining program where the guest of honor is insulted all in fun. ♦ *It was a wonderful roast. The guest of honor was pleased with the quality of the insults.*

roasted *mod.* alcohol intoxicated. ♦ *He was stewed, roasted, and boiled.*

rob so **blind 1.** *tv.* to steal freely from someone. ♦ *Her maid was robbing her blind.* **2.** *tv.* to overcharge someone. ♦ *Those auto repair shops can rob you blind if you don't watch out.*

rock 1. AND **rock candy** *n.* crack, a crystallized form of cocaine. (Drugs. See also rocks.) ♦ *Some call it rock candy, and some call it crack.* **2.** *n.* a crystallized form of heroin used for smoking. (Drugs.) ♦ *Max is hooked on rock—the kind that you smoke.* ♦ *Powder is everywhere, but you can hardly find rock anymore.* **3.** *n.* a diamond or other gemstone. ♦ *Look at the size of that rock in her ring.* **4.** Go to rocks. **5.** *n.* a baseball; a basketball. ♦ *Michael passed the rock to Scottie, who turned and dropped it in the basket.* **6.** *in.* to be really great. ♦ *The concerts didn't rock, but we had a good time throwing chairs.*

rock bottom 1. *n.* the lowest point or level. ♦ *The value of the goods is at rock bottom right now.* **2.** *mod.* absolute lowest, especially in reference to price. ♦ *I am offering you the rock bottom price.*

rock candy Go to rock.

rocker 1. *n.* a rocking chair. (Not slang.) ♦ *I love to spend a sunny afternoon in my rocker.* **2.** *n.* a rock and roll singer, song, or fan. (See also off one's rocker.) ♦ *Let's listen to a good rocker.*

rockhead *n.* someone who seems to have rocks in the head; a hardheaded or stubborn person. ♦ *What a rockhead! That's a stupid thing to do.*

rocking *mod.* excellent. (Collegiate.) ♦ *We had a rocking time!*

rock-jock *n.* a mountain or rock climber. ♦ *The sides of every mountain are covered with rock-jocks.*

rocks 1. *n.* ice cubes. ♦ *Can I have a few rocks in my drink, please?* **2.** *n.* Xerox Inc. (Securities markets, New York Stock Exchange.) ♦ *When she says, "Buy me a thousand rocks at the market," that means she wants one thousand shares of Xerox at whatever the market price is at the moment.* **3.** *n.* money; a dollar. (Underworld.) ♦ *Twenty rocks for that?* **4.** *n.* the testicles. (See also stones. Usually objectionable.) ♦ *I was afraid I'd get kicked in the rocks, so I stayed back.*

rod 1. *n.* a gun; a revolver. (Underworld.) ♦ *I got a rod in my pocket. Don't move.* **2.** Go to (hot) rod.

rode hard and put away wet *mod.* misused; ill-used. (Alludes to the mistreatment of a horse.) ♦ *Bad day at the office. I was rode hard and put away wet.*

ROF Go to RO(T)F(L).

roger ['rɑdʒɚ] *interj.* okay; That is correct. ♦ *Roger, I'll do it.*

roids *n.* steroids. ♦ *The guy's on roids. He looks like G. I. Joe.*

rolf Go to ralph.

roll 1. *n.* a bankroll; lots of money. ♦ *I earned a roll off that last deal.* **2.** *tv.* to rob a drunkard. ♦ *Those punks can't get much money by rolling drunks.* **3.** *n.* a sustained period of luck or productivity. (See also on a roll.) ♦ *The fantastic roll that this performer is on is truly exciting.* **4.** *in.* to leave, perhaps in a car. ♦ *I can't wait around any longer. Let's roll.*

roll (a set) AND **roll a set of prints.** *tv.* to take a set of fingerprints (from someone). ♦ *Danny asked Muggerman to roll a set of prints from the bum and then throw him in the jug.* ♦ *Take him downstairs and roll a set, Sergeant Tartaglia.*

roll in 1. *in.* to pull in; to drive up; to arrive. ♦ *The car rolled into the parking lot at a high speed.* **2.** Go to turn in.

roller *n.* a police car. ♦ *There are rollers in the next block, driving slow, looking for someone.*

rolling buzz *n.* a long-lasting drug high. (Drugs.) ♦ *That stuff will give you a rolling buzz without putting you to sleep.*

rolling on the floor laughing (my ass off) AND **ROTFL(MAO)** *phr. & comp. abb.* a description of how hard someone is laughing at someone else's comments. (Usually objectionable.) ♦ *ROTFLMAO! Gee, that was funny!*

ronchie Go to raunchy.

roni Go to rony.

rony AND **roni** *n.* pepperoni sausage, as for pizza. ♦ *The geek asked for rony and shrooms, and the counter guy just stared at him.*

rook [rʊk] *tv.* to cheat someone. ♦ *Don't go into that store. They'll rook you.*

rookie AND **rooky** ['rʊki] **1.** *n.* a person new at something; a neophyte, especially a police officer or a ballplayer. ♦ *The rookie tackled the old-time player and earned a lot of cheering and applause.* **2.** *mod.* new; inexperienced. ♦ *Fred is a rookie first baseman for the home team.*

rooky Go to rookie.

room for rent *n.* a person who acts very stupid. (Also a term of address. This implies that one's head is so empty of brains that the space could be rented out.) ♦ *My* *brother is a room for rent if I ever saw one. What a dope!*

rooster ['rustɚ] *n.* the posterior; one's butt end. (Because one *roosts* on it.) ♦ *Don't just sit there on your rooster. Get to work.*

root 1. *n.* a cigarette or a cigar. ♦ *That root you're smoking sure stinks.* **2.** *in.* to eat food like a pig. ♦ *Bart is downstairs rooting now. It won't take that slob long to eat.*

rooting-tooting *mod.* exciting; renown; famous; illustrious. (A vague adjective of praise.) ♦ *We really had a rooting-tooting time last weekend.*

rope so **in 1.** *tv.* to cause someone to get involved in some project. ♦ *She's always trying to rope me into her club.* **2.** Go to take so in.

roscoe ['rasko] *n.* a pistol, especially a revolver. (Underworld.) ♦ *I'm going down there to talk to Harry the Horse, and I'm taking my roscoe.*

rosy *mod.* good; satisfactory. (As a life that is seen through rose-colored glasses.) ♦ *Things are looking rosy now that the economy is improving.*

rot *n.* nonsense. ♦ *Don't give me any more of your rot. Speak straight with me.*

RO(T)F(L) *interj.* rolling on the floor laughing. (Used in electronic mail and computer forum or news group messages. Not pronounced aloud.) ♦ *I was ROTFL when I read your note. That was too much.*

ROTFL(MAO) Go to rolling on the floor laughing (my ass off).

rotgut 1. *n.* strong or inferior liquor, especially whiskey. (Folksy.) ♦ *The old man nearly went blind drinking all that rotgut.* **2.** *mod.* [of liquor] strong or fiery. ♦ *You've got to stop drinking that rotgut liquor and think of your health.* **3.** *n.* weak or otherwise inferior beer. ♦ *She can afford something better, but she drinks nothing but cheap rotgut.*

rotorhead *n.* a helicopter pilot or member of a helicopter crew. (Military. Also a term of address.) ♦ *Radio those rotorheads and tell them to get back to the base, now!*

Rots of ruck! ['ratsə'rək] *exclam.* Lots of luck! (Mocking a Japanese pronunciation.) ♦ *Have a good trip, and rots of ruck!*

rotsee ['ratsi] *n.* ROTC, the Reserve Officers Training Corps. ♦ *I joined rotsee to help pay my way through school.*

rotten 1. *mod.* smelly; disgusting. (Not slang.) ♦ *What is that rotten smell?* **2.** *mod.* alcohol intoxicated. (From sense 1. See also putrid.) ♦ *It takes a case of beer to get Wilbur rotten.* **3.** *mod.* poor or bad. (From sense 1.) ♦ *We have nothing but one rotten problem after another.*

rotten apple *n.* a single bad person or thing. ♦ *There always is a rotten apple to spoil it for the rest of us.*

rotten egg *n.* a bad or despised person; a stinker. ♦ *She sure has turned out to be a rotten egg.*

rotten luck *n.* bad luck. ♦ *Of all the rotten luck!*

rotten to the core *mod.* really bad. (See also rotten apple.) ♦ *That lousy punk is rotten to the core.*

rough and ready *mod.* vigorous and eager. ♦ *After a good night's sleep, I feel rough and ready—I could take on a bear.* ♦ *My friend is the rough and ready type. I'd rather sit and think about things.*

rough and tumble *mod.* disorderly; aggressive. ♦ *George is too rough and tumble for me. He doesn't know how to act around civilized people.*

rough it *tv.* to live for a short period of time in a relatively primitive state. ♦ *We went camping and had to rough it for a week.*

rough so **up** *tv.* to beat someone up; to mistreat someone. ♦ *Am I going to have to rough you up, or will you cooperate?*

rough stuff *n.* unnecessary roughness; physical violence or threats of violence. ♦ *There was too much rough stuff in Friday's game.*

rough time *n.* a hard time; a bad time. ♦ *I didn't mean to give you such a rough time. I'm sorry.*

roughhouse AND **roughneck 1.** *n.* a mean kid; a boisterous child, usually male. ♦

Jimmy! Stop acting like such a roughhouse. **2.** *in.* to be boisterous. ♦ *The boys broke the lamp when they were roughnecking around in the family room.*

roughneck Go to roughhouse.

round file Go to circular file.

round the bend Go to (a)round the bend.

round tripper *n.* a home run in baseball. ♦ *Ted is responsible for four round trippers in Saturday's game.*

roundhouse punch *n.* a punch to the head made by swinging the arm in an arc rather than by a jabbing punch. ♦ *He let him have a roundhouse punch that would have cracked a two-by-four.*

roundup *n.* a collection or summary of news items, such as a weather roundup, news roundup, etc. ♦ *Tune in at eleven for a roundup of the day's news.*

roust [raʊst] **1.** *tv.* [for a police officer] to bother or interfere with someone; to arrest someone. (See also rousted. Underworld.) ♦ *The cops rousted the gang without warning.* **2.** *tv.* to raid someone's residence; to bust a person or place. (Underworld.) ♦ *That bar was rousted last week.* **3.** *n.* a raid or a bust. ♦ *Okay, stand still. This is a roust!*

rousted [ˈraʊstəd] *mod.* arrested. (Underworld.) ♦ *The cops rousted the dealers, but that didn't even slow down the drug trade.*

royal pain *n.* someone or something irritating; a severe annoyance. ♦ *Her questions were a royal pain, but I had to answer them as part of my job.*

RSN *interj.* real soon now. (Used in electronic mail and computer forum or news group messages. Not pronounced aloud.) ♦ *I will post the rest of my trip report RSN.*

RTFF Go to Read the fucking FAQ!

RTFFAQ Go to Read the fucking FAQ!

RTFI Go to Read the fucking instructions!

RTFM Go to Read the fucking manual!

rub so **out** *tv.* to kill someone. (Underworld.) ♦ *The gunman was eager to rub somebody out.*

rub so's **nose in** sth *tv.* to remind someone of something constantly; to make a big issue about someone's mistake. (From the practice of training a puppy by rubbing its nose in the messes it makes.) ♦ *So I made a mistake! I wish you'd stop rubbing my nose in it.*

rubber 1. *n.* automobile tires; the rubber of automobile tires left on the street from spinning tires. ♦ *The rubber on my car is practically ruined.* **2.** Go to rubber (check). **3.** *n.* a condom. ♦ *He always carries a rubber "just in case."*

rubber (check) *n.* a check that bounces; a forged check. (See also bounce.) ♦ *The bank says I wrote a rubber check, but I'm sure there was enough money on deposit.*

rubber sock *n.* a timid person; a passive and compliant person. ♦ *Come on! Stand up for your rights. Don't be such a rubber sock!*

rubberneck 1. *n.* one who stares at something or someone; a tourist. (As if the tourist's neck is stretching to see even farther. See also gander.) ♦ *At noon the sidewalks are crowded with rubbernecks.* **2.** *in.* to stare (at something or someone). ♦ *Traffic is stalled because of all the drivers who are rubbernecking.*

rubbish *n.* nonsense. (Also an exclamation.) ♦ *Rubbish! That's the stupidest thing I've ever heard.*

ruckus [ˈrəkəs] *n.* a commotion; an uproar. ♦ *Quiet, please. Don't raise such a ruckus.*

rude 1. *mod.* undesirable; unpleasant. ♦ *The prof in my history class is a rude dude, for sure.* **2.** *mod.* cool; pleasant; excellent. ♦ *Man, that's a rude bike!*

rug *n.* a wig or toupee. (See also divot.) ♦ *I wear just a little rug to cover up a shiny spot.*

rug rat AND **ankle biter** *n.* a child. ♦ *Hey, you cute little rug rat, come over here.* ♦ *I got three little ankle biters at home.*

rule *in.* to dominate; to be the best. (Slang only in certain contexts. Typical in graffiti.) ♦ *Pizza rules around here.*

ruley *mod.* ideal; excellent. (See also rule.) ♦ *Her idea is ruley! She knows what we ought to do!*

rumble 1. *in.* to fight. ♦ *The gangs are rumbling over on Fourth Street.* **2.** *n.* a fight; a street fight; a gang fight. ♦ *My brother was hurt in a gang rumble.*

rumdum AND **rum-dum** ['rəm'dəm] **1.** *n.* a drunkard; a ruined alcoholic. ♦ *I don't want to end up like a dirty rum-dumb.* **2.** *n.* a stupid person. ♦ *Hey, rumdum, wise up and do what you are told.* **3.** *mod.* alcohol intoxicated. ♦ *The old lady got rumdum on gin.*

rummed (up) *mod.* alcohol intoxicated. ♦ *Sailors like to go into town and get rummed up.*

rummy ['rəmi] **1.** *n.* a drunkard; an alcoholic; an alcoholic hobo. ♦ *Ask that rummy to leave before he throws up.* **2.** *mod.* alcohol intoxicated. ♦ *She's rummy, and she's going to be sick.* **3.** *mod.* habitually confused and inept. ♦ *I get more rummy as I grow older.*

rump 1. *n.* the hindquarters; the buttocks; the posterior. ♦ *He fell on his rump.* **2.** *tv.* to flog someone on the buttocks. ♦ *I'm going to get rumped when my dad gets home.*

rump-ranger *n.* a homosexual male. (Refers to pederasty.) ♦ *A bunch of rump-rangers drifted in just as we drifted out.*

rumpus ['rəmpəs] *n.* a commotion. ♦ *Please don't make such a rumpus.*

rumpus room *n.* a family recreation room. (Old but still heard.) ♦ *If you kids are going to play rough, you'll have to go down to the rumpus room.*

run 1. *n.* a session or period of time spent doing something; a period of time when something happens. ♦ *The market had a good run today.* **2.** *tv.* to transport contraband, alcohol, or drugs. ♦ *Harry the Horse used to run booze during prohibition.* **3.** *n.* an act of transporting contraband. ♦ *Four soldiers were killed during a run.*

run a make on so *tv.* to perform an identity check on someone. (Underworld.) ♦ *We tried to run a make on him and came up with nothing.*

run amok ['rən ə'mək] *in.* to go awry. (From a Malay word meaning to run wild in a violent frenzy.) ♦ *Our plan ran amok.*

run down some lines 1. *in.* to converse (with someone). ♦ *I was running down some lines with Fred when the bell rang.* **2.** *in.* to try to seduce someone; to go through a talk leading to seduction. (See also run one's rhymes.) ♦ *I was just standing there running down some lines with Mary when those guys broke in.*

run it down *tv.* to tell the whole story; to tell the truth. ♦ *I don't care what happened. Run it down. I can take it.*

run off *in.* to have diarrhea. ♦ *Jimmy has been running off since midnight.*

run off at the mouth *in.* to talk too much; to have diarrhea of the mouth. ♦ *Tom runs off at the mouth too much. I wish he would temper his remarks.*

run on all cylinders 1. *in.* to run well and smoothly. ♦ *My plan is now running on all cylinders.* **2.** *in.* to operate sensibly and intelligently. ♦ *Pay attention to what you are doing. Start running on all cylinders.*

run one's rhymes *tv.* to say what you have to say; to give one's speech or make one's plea. (Collegiate.) ♦ *Go run your rhymes with somebody else!*

run out of gas *in.* to lose momentum or interest. ♦ *I hope I don't run out of gas before I finish what I set out to do.*

run scared *in.* to act panicked. ♦ *Don't panic. There is no reason to run scared.*

run so in *tv.* to arrest someone; to take someone to the police station. ♦ *Don't argue with me, or I'll run you in.*

Run that by (me) again. AND **Run that by (me) one more time.** *sent.* Please tell it to me again. ♦ *I can't believe my own ears. Can you run that by again, please?* ♦ *What? Run that by one more time, Fred.*

Run that by (me) one more time. Go to Run that by (me) again.

runaround *n.* a wild-goose chase. (Especially with *give*, as in the examples.) ♦ *The*

IRS gave us the runaround when we asked for a review.

rundown *n.* a summary bringing someone up to date. ♦ *Can you give me a rundown on what's happened since noon?*

runner 1. *n.* a messenger. ♦ *I work as a runner in the financial district.* **2.** *n.* a person who transports contraband. (Underworld.) ♦ *The runners got away, but we have the goods.*

run-of-the-mill *mod.* average; typical. (Referring to the typical quality of a product that comes out of a mill.) ♦ *This stuff is just run-of-the-mill.*

the **runs** *n.* a case of diarrhea. ♦ *I can't believe those cute little hamburgers could give anybody the runs.*

runt *n.* a small person; someone whose growth has been stunted. (Also a rude term of address.) ♦ *He can't play basketball. He's just a runt.*

run-up *n.* a movement upward in the value of one or more securities. (Securities markets.) ♦ *The market's had a good run-up in the past week.*

rush 1. *n.* a quick print of a day's shooting of a film. (Filmmaking. Usually plural.) ♦ *After today's shooting, we'll watch yesterday's rushes.* **2.** *n.* a period of time when fraternities and sororities are permitted to pursue new members. (Collegiate.) ♦ *When does rush start this year?* **3.** *tv.* [for a fraternity or sorority member] to try to persuade someone to join. ♦ *They can't rush anyone except during rush week.* **4.** *tv.* to court or date someone, usually a woman. (From sense 3.) ♦ *He spent some time trying to rush her but had to give up.* **5.** *n.* a burst of energy or good feeling from a drug; the explosive euphoria of some kinds of drugs. (Drugs.) ♦ *What kind of rush does this have?* **6.** *n.* any excitement; any burst of good feeling. (From sense 5.) ♦ *The wonderful ending to the movie gave me a rush.*

rust belt *n.* the industrial north of the U.S. (Patterned on sun belt.) ♦ *The salt they put on the roads in the winter made my car all rusty. I guess that's why they call this area the rust belt.*

rust bucket *n.* a naval destroyer; any ship. (Military.) ♦ *Why don't I ever get assigned to a new ship? It's always some crummy rust bucket!*

rusty-dusty *n.* the posterior; the buttocks. (See also duster.) ♦ *I almost kicked him in the rusty-dusty.*

ruth [ruθ] **1.** *n.* a women's restroom. (See also john.) ♦ *Point me toward the ruth!* **2.** *in.* to empty one's stomach; to vomit. (See also cry ruth; ralph.) ♦ *I just can't stand to ruth!*

S

sack 1. *n.* a bed. ♦ *I was so tired I could hardly find my sack.* **2.** *tv.* to dismiss someone from employment; to fire someone. ♦ *If I do that again, they'll sack me.* **3.** the **sack** *n.* a dismissal. (Always with *the* in this sense.) ♦ *The boss gave them all the sack.* **4.** *tv.* in football, to tackle the quarterback behind the line of scrimmage. ♦ *I tried to sack him, but he was too fast.* **5.** *n.* the completion of a tackle in football. ♦ *Andy made the sack on the ten-yard line.*

sack out *in.* to go to bed or go to sleep. (See also sacked out.) ♦ *It's time for me to sack out.*

sack rat *n.* someone who spends a lot of time in bed; someone who does not ever seem to get enough sleep. ♦ *Tom is such a sack rat. He can't seem to get enough sleep.*

sack time 1. *n.* a period of time spent in bed. ♦ *I need more sack time than most people.* **2.** *n.* time to go to bed. ♦ *Okay, gang, it's sack time. Go home so I can get some sleep!*

sack up Go to nut up.

sacked out *mod.* asleep. ♦ *Here it is ten o'clock, and you are still sacked out!*

sacred mushrooms Go to magic mushrooms.

sad *mod.* poor; undesirable. ♦ *This steak is really sad.*

sad sack *n.* a sad person; a listless or depressed person. ♦ *Tom always looks like such a sad sack.*

saddled with so or sth *mod.* burdened with someone or something. ♦ *I've been saddled with the children all day. Let's go out tonight.*

sail into so AND **light into** so *in.* to beat or scold someone. ♦ *Jimmy's mother really sailed into him for breaking the window.* ♦ *The boss lit into his secretary for losing the contract.*

sail (right) through sth *in.* to get through something easily. ♦ *I sailed right through my homework.*

salt *n.* a sailor. (Especially with *old.*) ♦ *I've sailed a little, but you could hardly call me an old salt.*

salt and pepper 1. *n.* a black and white police car. ♦ *There is a salt and pepper around the corner waiting for speeders.* **2.** *mod.* interracial, including black and white. ♦ *It was sort of a salt and pepper meeting, with representatives from all neighborhoods.*

salt horse *n.* corned or salted beef. ♦ *We made spaghetti sauce with salt horse because that was the only meat we could find.*

saltine *n.* a white person. (A play on a kind of salted white cracker [biscuit]. A *cracker* is a derogatory term for a white person.) ♦ *What are those saltines doing in this neighborhood?*

salty *n.* expensive; [of a price] falsely bid up. ♦ *That price is a little salty. Is that the best you can do?*

Sam *n.* federal agents; federal narcotics agents. (Also a term of address. From Uncle (Sam).) ♦ *Sam is working hard to put an end to all this drug trouble.*

Sam and Dave *n.* the police; police officers. (Black.) ♦ *And there at the door were my old buddies Sam and Dave with a warrant.*

same difference *n.* the same; no difference at all. ♦ *Pink, fuchsia, what does it matter? Same difference.*

same here *phr.* me too; I agree. ♦ MARY: *I think I'll have the broiled halibut.* JANE: *Same here.*

same o(l)' same o(l)' AND **SOSO** ['semo(l) 'semo(l)] *n.* the same old thing. ♦ *I'm getting tired of the same ol' same ol'.*

same old story *n.* an often repeated story or situation. ♦ *It's the same old story. Boy meets girl, girl gets consumption, girl dies.*

San Fran *n.* San Francisco. ♦ *When will you be in San Fran next?*

sand *n.* sugar. ♦ *Do you use sand in your coffee?*

sandbag 1. *tv.* to force someone to do something. ♦ *I don't want to have to sandbag you. Please cooperate.* **2.** *tv.* to deceive someone; to fool someone about one's capabilities. ♦ *Don't let them sandbag you into expecting too little.*

sap 1. *n.* a stupid person. ♦ *That poor sap thinks he can convince them.* **2.** *n.* a blackjack. (Underworld.) ♦ *Bart had a sap in his pocket when they arrested him for possession.*

saphead *n.* a sap. ♦ *Don't be such a saphead, dude.*

Saturday night special *n.* a small, easily obtainable pistol. ♦ *There was another killing last night with a Saturday night special.*

sauce *n.* liquor; any alcoholic beverage. (See also **on the sauce.**) ♦ *Did you bring the sauce? Can't have a good party without lots of sauce.*

sauce parlor *n.* a tavern. ♦ *I wouldn't be caught dead in that sauce parlor.*

sauced *mod.* alcohol intoxicated. ♦ *She went out and got herself sauced.*

savage *mod.* excellent. (Collegiate.) ♦ *Man, Fred is a totally savage guy.*

Save it! *exclam.* Be quiet! ♦ *I don't care what you think you have to say. Save it!*

saved by the bell *mod.* saved by the timely intervention of someone or something.

♦ *I was going to have to do my part, but someone knocked on the door and I didn't have to do it. I was saved by the bell.*

savvy ['sævi] **1.** *tv. & in.* to understand (someone or something). (Adapted from Spanish *sabe, he knows.*) ♦ *Do you savvy?* **2.** *n.* knowledge; know-how. ♦ *I don't have the savvy necessary to do the job.* **3.** *mod.* knowledgeable. ♦ *He is one of the most savvy directors in New York.*

sawbones *n.* a doctor. (Folksy. Referring to someone who amputates limbs.) ♦ *Call the sawbones. This is an emergency.*

sawbuck *n.* a ten-dollar bill. (From the time when the *10* was indicated by the Roman numeral *X* (10), which looks like the crosspiece that supports wood that is being sawed.) ♦ *It cost me a sawbuck to have my car pulled out of the mud.*

sawed *mod.* alcohol intoxicated. (Perhaps an elaboration of **cut.**) ♦ *I got sawed last weekend, and I still have a headache.*

sawed-off *mod.* short of stature. ♦ *Tom called Mike a sawed-off little runt.*

Say cheese! *exclam.* Please smile! (A phrase said by a photographer who is trying to get someone to smile for a photograph.) ♦ *Say cheese for the camera, please.*

say uncle *tv.* to admit defeat; to give up. ♦ *I never say uncle. I just keep right on going.*

Say what? *interrog.* What did you say? ♦ *The old man held his hand to his ear and said, "Say what?"*

Says me! AND **Sez me!** *exclam.* a formulaic answer to **Says who?** ♦ TOM: *Says who?* FRED: *Says me, that's who!* ♦ TOM: *You?* FRED: *You got it, buster. Says me!*

Says who? AND **Sez who?** *interrog.* a formulaic challenge indicating disagreement with someone who has said something. (See also **Says you!**) ♦ TOM: *Says who?* FRED: *Says me, that's who!* ♦ *She drew herself up to her full height, looked him straight in the eye, and said, "Says who?"*

Says you! *exclam.* That's just what you say!; You don't know what you are talking about! ♦ FRED: *You are fat and ugly.*

TOM: *Says you!* ♦ MARY: *People who go around correcting other people were found to be very annoying in a recent survey.* BILL: *Says you!*

say-so *n.* a command; an authorization; permission. ♦ *We can begin as soon as we get the boss's say-so.*

SBD Go to silent but deadly.

scabbed ['skæbd] *mod.* cheated in a drug deal; having been sold bogus or inferior drugs. ♦ *Bart got scabbed by a dealer who got arrested the next day.*

scads [skædz] *n.* lots (of something). ♦ *I have just scads and scads of paper.*

scag Go to skag.

scag jones Go to skag jones.

scale *n.* the regular union rate of pay; union wages. ♦ *We pay scale and not a penny more. I don't care who you think you are!*

scam [skæm] **1.** *n.* a swindle; a hustle. ♦ *I lost a fortune in that railroad scam.* **2.** *tv.* to swindle someone; to deceive someone. ♦ *They were scammed by a sweet-talking southern lady who took all their money.* **3.** *in.* to seek out and pick up young women, said of males. (Collegiate.) ♦ *Bob was out scamming last night and ran into Clare.* **4.** *in.* to copulate. ♦ *All you ever want to do is scam.* **5.** *in.* to fool around and waste time. ♦ *Quit scamming and get busy.*

scammer ['skæmɚ] **1.** *n.* a swindler; a hustler. ♦ *There are a couple of scammers on the street corner. Watch out.* **2.** *n.* a lecher; a fast worker with the opposite sex. ♦ *Bob thinks he's a great scammer, but he's just a wimp.*

scammered *mod.* alcohol intoxicated. ♦ *She is scammered out of her mind.*

scamp [skæmp] *n.* a small child. ♦ *There are three little scamps at the door saying, "Trick or treat!"*

scandal sheet *n.* a tabloid newspaper featuring lurid news. ♦ *I like to read a scandal sheet every now and then.*

scank Go to skank.

scanless Go to skanless.

scare so or sth **up** *tv.* to find someone or something. (As if one were flushing wild game.) ♦ *I have to scare a date up for Friday night.*

scare the hell out of so *tv.* to frighten someone badly. (Use caution with hell.) ♦ *The door blew shut and scared the hell out of me.*

scare the pants off so *tv.* to frighten someone suddenly. ♦ *The piano lid fell and scared the pants off my parents.*

scared shitless *mod.* very frightened. (Potentially offensive. Use caution with shit.) ♦ *He wasn't just frightened. He was scared shitless!*

scared stiff *mod.* frightened; unable to move from fear. ♦ *The poor little kid stood there—scared stiff.* ♦ *I was scared stiff for hours after the accident.*

scarf 1. *tv.* to eat something. ♦ *Andy scarfed the whole pie.* **2.** *in.* to eat. ♦ *I'll be with you as soon as I scarf.* **3.** *n.* food. ♦ *I want some good scarf. This stuff stinks.* **4.** *tv.* to steal or swipe something. ♦ *The kid scarfed a candy bar, and the store owner called the cops.* **5.** *tv.* to discard something. ♦ *Scarf that thing. It's no good.*

scarf out *in.* to overeat. (See also blimp out; pig out, mac out.) ♦ *I scarf out every weekend.*

scarf sth **down** *tv.* to eat something, perhaps in a hurry; to swallow something, perhaps in a hurry. ♦ *Are you going to scarf this whole thing down?*

scary *mod.* [of women] ugly. ♦ *Why do I always end up with a scary woman?*

scat [skæt] **1.** *n.* nonsense syllables sung to music. (Refers to a [primarily black] jazz practice in the jazz era.) ♦ *She used to do scat but moved on to blues.* **2.** *exclam.* Go away! (Usually **Scat!** Often said to a cat to get it to go away.) ♦ *Get out! Scat! Beat it, cat!* **3.** *in.* to leave. ♦ *You guys scat now. I have to go to work.* **4.** *n.* heroin. (Drugs. From an old term for dung. See also shit.) ♦ *Bart is trying to sell scat in the neighborhood again.* **5.** *n.* inferior whiskey. ♦ *You got anything better than that scat, bartender?*

scatterbrain *n.* a forgetful person; someone who is mentally disorganized. ♦ *Aunt Martha is a real scatterbrain. She always forgets where her glasses are.*

scattered *mod.* drug intoxicated; confused by drug use. (Drugs. See also scat.) ♦ *Those poor kids are so scattered, they can't even get themselves to class.*

scene [sin] **1.** *n.* a place; a setting. (See also make the scene.) ♦ *I need a different scene. Life is too hectic here.* **2.** *n.* the drug-use environment; the drug scene. ♦ *The longer you spend in a scene like this, the harder it is to sober up and go straight.* **3.** *n.* one's preference. (See also bag.) ♦ *This nine-to-five stuff just isn't my scene. I quit.*

schicker Go to shicker.

schickered Go to shicker.

schizo ['skɪzo OR 'skɪtso] **1.** *mod.* schizophrenic. ♦ *That gal is sort of schizo, isn't she?* **2.** *n.* a schizophrenic person. ♦ *That guy is an absolute schizo!*

schiz(z) out [skɪz...] *in.* to freak out; to lose mental control. ♦ *I schizzed out during the test. Got an F.*

schlemazel AND **schlemozzle; shlimazl** [ʃlə'mɑzl̩] *n.* an awkward, bumbling person; a loser. (Yiddish.) ♦ *And this poor schlemazel tries to get me to help him paint his fence!*

schlemiel AND **schlemihl; shlemiel** [ʃlə'mil] *n.* a gullible person; a loser. (From Hebrew *Shelumiel* via Yiddish.) ♦ *See if you can get that schlemiel to buy the Brooklyn Bridge.*

schlemihl Go to schlemiel.

schlemozzle Go to schlemazel.

schlep AND **shlep** [ʃlɛp] **1.** *tv.* to drag or carry someone or something. (From German *schleppen* via Yiddish.) ♦ *Am I supposed to schlep this whole thing all the way back to the store?* **2.** *n.* a journey; a distance to travel or carry something. ♦ *It takes about twenty minutes to make the schlep from here to there.* **3.** *n.* a stupid person; a bothersome person. (Literally,

a drag.) ♦ *Ask that shlep to wait in the hall until I am free. I'll sneak out the back way.*

schlepper AND **shlepper** ['ʃlɛpɚ] *n.* an annoying person who always wants a bargain or a favor. (See also schlep.) ♦ *Why am I surrounded by people who want something from me? Is this a schlepper colony or what?*

schlock [ʃlɑk] **1.** *n.* inferior merchandise. (From German *schlacke,* "dregs" via Yiddish.) ♦ *That store has nothing but schlock.* **2.** AND **schlocky** ['ʃlɑki] *mod.* cheap; junky; inferior. ♦ *Schlocky stuff like this I can get from a no overhead mail order.*

schlocky Go to schlock.

schloomp AND **schlump; shlump** [ʃlump OR ʃlʊmp] *n.* a stupid and lazy person. (From German via Yiddish.) ♦ *Tell that schloomp to get busy or get out.*

schlub AND **zhlub** [ʃləb OR ʒləb] *n.* a dull, unpolished person, usually a male. (Yiddish.) ♦ *I spent the whole evening listening to that schlub from New Hampshire.*

schlump Go to schloomp.

schmaltz AND **shmaltz** [ʃmɑlts] *n.* extreme sentimentality; corny sweetness. (From a Yiddish word meaning fat or oil.) ♦ *I didn't like that movie. Too much schmaltz.*

schmaltzy AND **shmaltzy** ['ʃmɑltsi] *mod.* overly sweet and sentimental. (See also schmaltz.) ♦ *This movie is too schmaltzy for me.*

schmegegge AND **schmegeggy** [ʃmə'gegi] **1.** *n.* a stupid person. (Yiddish.) ♦ *Ask the schmegegge standing over by the workbench if he's seen my sky hook.* **2.** *n.* nonsense. ♦ *I've heard enough of your schmegegge. Out!*

schmegeggy Go to schmegegge.

schmendrick AND **shmendrick** ['ʃmɛndrɪk] *n.* a stupid and ineffectual nobody. (Yiddish.) ♦ *Some schmendrick from downstairs asked if you could turn down your stereo.*

schmo AND **shmo; shmoe; schmoe** [ʃmo] *n.* a foolish and naive person, usually a male. (Yiddish. See also Joe Schmo.) ♦

What a schmo! He thinks I caused the problem.

schmoose Go to schmooze.

schmooze AND **shmooze; schmoose** **1.** *in.* to chat; to chew the fat. (From Hebrew *schmuos* via Yiddish.) ✦ *You were schmoozing when you should have been listening.* **2.** *n.* a session of chatting or conversing. ✦ *Come over, and let's have a schmooze before you go.*

schmoozer *n.* someone who chats or converses well. ✦ *Two old schmoozers sat muttering to one another all afternoon by the duck pond.*

schmuck [ʃmək] **1.** *n.* a jerk; a repellent male. (Also a rude term of address. Yiddish.) ✦ *Who is that stupid schmuck over there?* **2.** *n.* a penis. (Yiddish. Usually objectionable.) ✦ *If I hear that joke about a camel's schmuck one more time, I'm going to scream.*

schnockered AND **schnoggered; shnockered; snoggered** ['ʃnakɚd AND 'ʃnagɚd] *mod.* alcohol or drug intoxicated. ✦ *How can anybody be so schnockered on four beers?*

schnoggered Go to schnockered.

schnook AND **schnuck; shnook** [ʃnʊk] *n.* a naive person; a dope. (Yiddish.) ✦ *What's a good-looking dame like her doing with a shnook like him?*

schnorrer ['ʃnorɚ] *n.* a beggar; a person who sponges off of friends and relatives. (Yiddish.) ✦ *Buy your own ciggies if you don't like mine. Shnorrers can't be choosers.*

schnozz AND **schnozzle; schnozzola; shnozz** [ʃnaz AND ʃnaz, ʃna'zolə, ʃnaz] *n.* the nose. (From German *Schnauze* via Yiddish.) ✦ *Look at the schnozz on that guy!*

schnozzle Go to schnozz.

schnozzola Go to schnozz.

schnuck Go to schnook.

school so *tv.* to teach someone something, usually as a demonstration of power. (As in *I'll teach you a thing or two* which sug-gests violence.) ✦ *Am I gonna have to school you in how to act?*

schoolboy Scotch *n.* wine. ✦ *Give me a pint of that schoolboy Scotch.*

schtick AND **shtik** [ʃtɪk] *n.* a routine or act that is the trademark of an entertainer, especially in vaudeville. (Yiddish.) ✦ *His schtick was a trained dog and cat act.*

schtoonk AND **shtoonk** [ʃtʊŋk] *n.* a detestable person. (Yiddish.) ✦ *The schtoonk from downstairs was here to talk to you. I told him you died.*

Schwing! [ʃʌɪŋ] *exclam.* How exciting!; How stimulating!; Wow! (Originally said on seeing an extremely good-looking or sexually attractive girl. The word is onomatopoetic for the imaginary whishing sound of instant arousal. Many users are not aware of the origins. Potentially offensive.) ✦ *Did you see her? Schwing!*

scientific wild ass guess AND **SWAG** *phr. & comp. abb.* a simple guess. (Often objectionable.) ✦ *I don't know at all. That was a SWAG. I always use the SWAG system.*

Sco. 1. *n.* Frisco; San Francisco. ✦ *If you ever get back to Sco, look me up.* **2.** *imperative* Let's go! ✦ *It's late! Sco!*

scoff [skɔf] **1.** *tv. & in.* to eat (something). (See also scarf.) ✦ *She scoffed three hamburgers and a large order of fries.* **2.** *n.* food. ✦ *This scoff is gross!*

scooch [skutʃ] **1.** *in.* to move (oneself), while seated, forward, backward, or sideways by sliding. ✦ *Scooch over here by me.* **2.** *tv.* to push or move something. ✦ *Scooch your chair over where the light is better.*

scoop 1. *n.* a news story gathered by a reporter before any other reporter hears of it. ✦ *I got a great scoop! I was right there when it happened.* **2.** *tv.* to beat someone—such as another reporter—in the race to get a news story first. ✦ *They scooped the other paper on both stories.* **3.** *n.* a general roundup and arrest of criminals; a bust. (Underworld.) ✦ *Bart got picked up in that big drug scoop last month.* **4.** *n.* liquor; a glass of beer. ✦ *A* *little scoop helps pass the time when you're waiting.* **5.** *n.* a folded matchbook cover used to **snort** cocaine or heroin. ♦ *I need a scoop. It's no good without one.* **6.** *tv. & in.* to **snort** cocaine or heroin, using a folded matchbook cover. ♦ *He scooped two lines together.*

scoot 1. *in.* to run or scurry quickly from one place to another. ♦ *I scooted from the bank to the cleaners and then on to the dentist's.* **2.** *n.* a motorcycle. ♦ *Do you wear a brain-bucket on your scoot?*

scooters ['skutɚz] *mod.* crazy; confused. ♦ *It's days like this that make me think I'm scooters.*

the **scoots** *n.* a case of diarrhea. ♦ *Our vacation was ruined by a case of the scoots.*

scope (on) SO *tv. & in.* to evaluate a member of the opposite sex visually. ♦ *He scoped every girl who came in the door.*

scope SO **out** *tv.* to look someone over; to check someone out. ♦ *Dave was scoping out all the girls.*

scorched 1. *mod.* alcohol or drug intoxicated. ♦ *Who wants to go out and get scorched?* **2.** AND **singed** [sɪndʒd] *mod.* having to do with hair burned while smoking marijuana. (Collegiate.) ♦ *If you go to sleep, you'll be singed for sure.*

scorcher 1. *n.* a very hot day. ♦ *This is really a scorcher, isn't it?* **2.** *n.* a caustic remark. ♦ *Bob made a real scorcher about Tom's shoes.*

scorching 1. *mod.* winning at gambling; about to win something big. ♦ *Let me roll again. I'm really scorching.* **2.** *mod.* caustic. ♦ *That remark was really scorching.*

score 1. *in.* to succeed. ♦ *I knew if I kept trying I could score.* **2.** *tv. & in.* to obtain something; to obtain drugs or sex. (Very close to sense 1.) ♦ *Fred is always trying to score with women.* **3.** *n.* the result of a scoring: drugs, loot, winnings, etc. ♦ *The crooks dropped the score as they made their getaway.* **4.** *in.* [for a male] to copulate with a female; [for a female] to copulate with a male. (Usually objectionable.) ♦ *Fred can't think about anything but scoring with Martha.* **5.** *n.* the client of a male

or female prostitute. ♦ *She conked the score over the head and robbed him.* **6.** *n.* a summary; a conclusion; the sum total. (See also **bottom line**.) ♦ *Okay, waiter, what's the score?*

scrag [skræg] **1.** *n.* the neck. (Underworld.) ♦ *The cop grabbed him by the scrag and pushed him along to the squad car.* **2.** *tv.* to kill someone or something. (Originally underworld to *strangle*.) ♦ *The gang decided that somebody was going to have to scrag the witness.*

scraggy ['skrægi] *mod.* bony. ♦ *Who is that scraggy dame?*

scram [skræm] *in.* to exit fast; to get out of a place in a hurry. ♦ *Go on, scram! Get out of here fast!*

scrambled eggs *n.* rank insignia on a military officer's uniform. ♦ *I know his rank is high because of the "scrambled eggs," but I don't know how high.*

scrape the bottom of the barrel *tv.* to utilize the last or only things or people available, even if unsatisfactory. (See also **bottom of the barrel**.) ♦ *They were really scraping the bottom of the barrel when they picked you.*

scratch 1. *n.* money. ♦ *I just don't have the scratch.* **2.** *tv.* to eliminate something from a list; to cancel something. ♦ *We decided to scratch the idea of a new car. The old one will have to do.* **3.** *mod.* impromptu; temporary. (See also **pickup**.) ♦ *We started a scratch game of basketball, but most of the girls had to leave at dinnertime.*

scratch sheet *n.* a daily horse-racing newsletter at the racetrack. ♦ *I picked up a scratch sheet from Lucky Louie and proceeded to lay down my life's saving on a horse named Felicity Anne.*

scream 1. *n.* someone or something very funny. (Usually **a scream**.) ♦ *The joke Tom told was really a scream.* **2.** *n.* ice cream. (Collegiate.) ♦ *How about a nice big dish of scream?*

scream bloody murder *tv.* to scream very loudly; to complain or protest loudly. ♦

She screams bloody murder every time I get near her.

screamer 1. *n.* a newspaper headline. ♦ *Did you see the screamer in the paper today? "The King Died."* **2.** *n.* an exclamation point. (Printing.) ♦ *Clean up this copy. There are too many screamers. Looks like junior high stuff.* **3.** *n.* anything challenging. ♦ *What a horrible assignment I got. A classic screamer.* **4.** *n.* someone or something very exciting or attention getting. ♦ *This guy is a real screamer! Wait'll you meet him.*

screaming fantods AND **(howling) fantods** *n.* extreme anxiety; nervous hysteria. (Old. One might call this vintage literary mock colloquial, since it survives in the works of well-known writers and occasional literary use. The origin is unknown, but the *Oxford English Dictionary* lists *Fantad* with the same meaning, and cautiously suggests that is related to *fantasy* and similar words containing *fan*.) ♦ *The afternoon's excitement has left Lady Waddington with a case of the screaming fantods.* ♦ *The reviewer felt that any slang dictionary that excluded "fantods" was defective.*

screaming-meemie AND **screamie-meemie** *n.* a screaming child or adult. ♦ *Oh, don't be such a screaming-meemie!*

screaming-meemies AND **screaming-meamies** *n.* the willies—a mental breakdown. ♦ *They sent Bart away with the screaming-meemies.*

screeching (drunk) *mod.* alcohol intoxicated; very drunk. ♦ *How can anybody be so screeching drunk on four beers?*

screw 1. *tv. & in.* to copulate [with] someone. (Very old. Usually objectionable.) ♦ *The sailor wanted to screw somebody bad.* **2.** *tv. & in.* to cheat or deceive someone. ♦ *You can count on somebody screwing you at a traveling carnival.* **3.** *n.* an act of copulation. (Usually objectionable.) ♦ *The sailor said he needed a good screw.* **4.** *n.* a person with whom one can copulate. (Usually objectionable.) ♦ *His teeth are crooked and his hands are callused, but he's a good screw.* **5.** *n.* a jailer. (Very old.

Underworld.) ♦ *See if you can get the screw's attention.*

screw around 1. to engage in copulation. ♦ *She wants to talk about their relationship and he only wants to screw around.* **2.** *in.* to waste time. ♦ *John's always screwing around and never does anything on time.*

screw around with *so* or *sth in.* to toy with, fiddle with, or play around with someone or something. ♦ *Andy screwed around with his clock until he broke it.*

screw *so* or *sth* **up** *tv.* to interfere with someone or something; to mess up someone or something. ♦ *Try again and don't screw it up this time.*

screw *so* **out of** *sth tv.* to cheat someone of out something. ♦ *You are trying to screw me out of what is rightfully mine!*

screw *so* **over** *tv.* to give someone a very bad time; to scold someone severely. ♦ *Let's get those kids in here and screw over every one of them. This stuff can't continue.*

screw up 1. *in.* to mess up. ♦ *The waiter screwed up again.* **2.** *n.* a mess; a blunder; utter confusion. (Usually **screw-up**. See also **screwed up**.) ♦ *This is the chef's screw-up, not mine.*

screwage *n.* copulation; acts of copulation; the people and actions of copulation. ♦ *His mind is on nothing but "screwage" and how to get some of it.*

screwball 1. *n.* an eccentric person; a clown or a dunce. (Also a rude term of address.) ♦ *Tom is such a screwball!* **2.** *n.* [in baseball] a (pitched) ball that does not travel in a straight line. ♦ *Jim threw another screwball, but somehow the batter hit it.*

screwed 1. *mod.* copulated with. (Usually objectionable.) ♦ *I got myself good and screwed, and I haven't felt better in months.* **2.** *mod.* cheated. ♦ *Wow, you got screwed on that watch.* **3.** AND **screwed tight** *mod.* alcohol intoxicated. ♦ *She's not just drunk; she's screwed tight.* **4.** *mod.* bested; defeated; cheated. ♦ *I really got screwed at the garage.*

screwed, blued, and tattooed ['skrud 'blud æn tæ'tud] **1.** *mod.* badly mistreated; badly screwed. ♦ *When John bought his wreck of a car, he got screwed, blued, and tattooed.* **2.** *mod.* alcohol intoxicated. ♦ *Who wants to go out and get screwed, blued, and tattooed?*

screwed tight Go to screwed.

screwed up *mod.* ruined; messed up. ♦ *This is a really screwed up schedule. Let's start over again.*

screwy 1. *mod.* crazy. ♦ *I've never heard such a screwy idea.* **2.** *mod.* alcohol intoxicated. ♦ *I've never seen anybody so screwy.*

script(t) *n.* a note; any piece of paper with a written message. (Underworld.) ♦ *Make him sign this script before you let him in on the deal.*

scrog [skrɔg] *tv. & in.* to have sex; to copulate [with] someone. (Usually objectionable.) ♦ *You know what! I think those people over in the corner are scrogging!*

scronched [skrɔntʃt] *mod.* alcohol intoxicated. ♦ *She just sat there and got scronched.*

scrooge [skrudʒ] *n.* a stingy person; a penny-pincher. (From the character in Dickens's *A Christmas Carol.*) ♦ *Ask scrooge over there if you can borrow a quarter to call the cops.*

scrounge (around (for so or sth**))** [skraʊndʒ...] *in.* to look around for someone or something; to seek someone or something in every likely place. ♦ *Ask John to scrounge around for a wrench.*

scrounge so or sth **up** *tv.* to get someone or something somehow. ♦ *I scrounged a doctor up in the middle of the night.*

scrub *tv.* to cancel something. ♦ *We had to scrub the whole plan because of the weather.*

scrud *n.* a serious disease; a sexually transmitted disease. (Military.) ♦ *Poor dumb Charlie can't tell scrud from crotch rot.*

scruff(y) ['skrəf(i)] *mod.* sloppy; unkempt. ♦ *Why don't you clean up this scruff car? It's—like—grody!*

scrump [skrəmp] *tv. & in.* to copulate [with] someone. (Usually objectionable.) ♦ *The movie showed a scene of some woman scrumping her lover.*

scrumptious ['skrəmpʃəs] *mod.* excellent; tasty. ♦ *Who makes the most scrumptious chocolate chip cookies in the world—besides me, that is?*

scrunch [skrəntʃ] *tv.* to crush or crunch. ♦ *I hate crowds. I am afraid people will scrunch me.*

scrunge [skrəndʒ] *n.* nastiness; gunk. ♦ *What is this scrunge on my shoe?*

scrungy ['skrəndʒi] **1.** *mod.* filthy. ♦ *What a scrungy guy. Put him somewhere to soak for a day or two.* **2.** *mod.* inferior; bad. ♦ *I don't need scrungy merchandise like this. I'm going elsewhere.*

scum 1. *n.* a totally worthless and disgusting person. (Rude and derogatory.) ♦ *You scum! Get out of here!* **2.** *n.* low-life in general; disgusting and worthless people. (Rude and derogatory.) ♦ *Fourth Street is where all the scum in town hangs out.* **3.** *n.* semen; seminal fluid. (Usually objectionable.) ♦ *You'd better clean up the scum from the backseat before you take the car home.*

scumbag 1. *n.* a condom; a used condom. (Usually objectionable.) ♦ *I saw a used scumbag in the school parking lot.* **2.** *n.* a totally disgusting person. (Rude and derogatory.) ♦ *Oh, he's a scumbag. I wouldn't be seen dead with him!*

scupper up *in.* to drink liquor, especially beer. ♦ *Tom goes home to scupper up every evening.*

scurvy ['skɚvi] *mod.* repulsive; gross. (Collegiate.) ♦ *That class is scurvy. You'll wish you hadn't taken it.*

scut [skət] *n.* a despicable person. (Teens and collegiate.) ♦ *It's scuts like that who give all us really rad kids a bad name.*

scuttlebutt *n.* news; information; gossip. (The legend of origin is that the scuttlebutt was a butt [= cask, keg] of drinking water located near a scuttle [= hatch]. Sailors gathered there to exchange gossip.) ♦ *What's the scuttlebutt on the steeple clock? Why did it stop?*

scuz(z) [skəz] **1.** *n.* filth. ♦ *What is this scuzz all over the floor?* **2.** *n.* a nasty person; an undesirable person; a scraggly person. ♦ *And this scuzz comes up to me and asks me to dance, and I'm like, "What?"*

scuzz so out *tv.* to nauseate someone. ♦ *It's not nice to scuzz out people like that, especially when you hardly know them.*

scuzzbag AND **scuzzbucket** *n.* a despicable person. (Rude and derogatory.) ♦ *Look, scuzzbucket, we don't want your kind around here.*

scuzzbucket Go to scuzzbag.

scuzzo *n.* a repellent person. ♦ *There's the scuzzo who thinks I like him.*

scuzzy ['skəzi] *mod.* repellent; unkempt. ♦ *His clothes are always so scuzzy. He probably keeps them in a pile in his room.*

sea *n.* cocaine. (Drugs. A spelling-out of C.) ♦ *I never used sea before. I hear there's nothing like it.*

sealed (up) *mod.* settled; secured; cinched. ♦ *The matter was sealed by Monday morning.*

sealed with a kiss AND **SWAK** *mod.* written and sent with love and care. (The initialism is sometimes written on love letters. Also an acronym.) ♦ *I know they are sealed with a kiss, because she says so.*

seam-squirrels *n.* lice. (See also pants rabbits. Contrived.) ♦ *I got an itch. Must be seam-squirrels.*

Search me. *sent.* I don't know. (There is a heavy stress on both words.) ♦ TOM: *How do crickets make that chirping noise?* BILL: *Search me.* ♦ *You can search me. How should I know?*

seat *n.* the buttocks. ♦ *I was so angry. I wanted to kick him in the seat as he left.*

sec [sɛk] **1.** *n.* a second; an instant. (See also tick.) ♦ *I'll be with you in a sec. Keep your pants on!* **2.** AND **secs** *n.* a Seconal barbiturate capsule. (Drugs.) ♦ *I started taking sec in the hospital and just couldn't stop.*

second fiddle *n.* a person in a secondary role; the second best. (Frequently with play.) ♦ *I won't stay around here playing second fiddle for someone half my age and ability!*

second sacker *n.* the second baseman in baseball. ♦ *The second sacker missed the throw, and the runner went on home.*

secs Go to sec.

see *tv.* to equal someone's bet in poker. ♦ *I see your five and raise you ten.*

see a man about a dog *tv.* to leave a place for a mysterious reason, usually to go to the toilet. ♦ *Fred went to see a man about a dog. I hope he remembers to put the seat down.*

see eye to eye *in.* [for two or more people] to agree on something or view something the same way. ♦ *We never seem to see eye to eye.*

See if I care! AND **SIIC** *exclam. & comp. abb.* Go ahead and do it because I don't care. ♦ *Leave early! SIIC!*

see no further than the end of one's **nose** AND **cannot see (any) further than the end of** one's **nose** *in.* to be narrowminded; to lack understanding and perception. ♦ *You don't care about anyone but yourself. You can't see any further than the end of your nose.*

see red *tv.* to be angry. ♦ *When she hung up the phone, I saw red. I've never been so angry in my life.*

see stars *tv.* to be (knocked) unconscious. ♦ *I saw stars for a few seconds, and then someone threw cold water in my face.*

See ya. Go to See you.

See you. AND **See ya.** *interj.* Good-bye. ♦ *See you, old chum. Give me a ring.*

See you in another life. AND **CUIAL** *sent. & comp. abb.* I will see you later. ♦ *Bye. CUIAL.*

See you in church. AND **CUIC.** *sent. & comp. abb.* See you around.; See you where I normally see you. (Has nothing to do with an actual church.) ♦ *Bye. See you in church.*

See you in the funny pages. AND **SYITFP** *sent. & comp. abb.* I will see you around. (See also **See you in church**.) ♦ *Bye, Tom. SYITFP.*

See you later. AND **CUL8R** *sent. & comp. abb.* I will see you later. (See also **L8TR**. Common colloquial. Also said to people one knows one will never see again.) ♦ *Have a great trip, Mary. See you later.* ♦ *Bye. CUL8R.*

See you later, alligator. *interj.* Good-bye. (From the 1930s. Answered with **After while, crocodile**.) ♦ TOM: *Bye.* BILL: *See you later, alligator.* ♦ BILL: *See you later, alligator.* TOM: *After while, crocodile.*

See you, too. AND **CU2** *phr. & comp. abb.* I will see you also. (A reply to *CU*, See you.) ♦ BOB: *CUIAL.* BILL: *CU2.*

seegar ['sigɑr] *n.* a cigar. (Folksy. The stress is on the first syllable.) ♦ *There's nothing like a fine seegar after a nice bowl of hot chili.*

seeing pink elephants AND **seeing pink spiders; seeing snakes** *tv.* alcohol intoxicated; recovering from a drinking bout; having the delirium tremens. ♦ *When I got to the point of seeing pink elephants, I knew that something had to be done.* ♦ *He's screaming something about seeing pink spiders, and he wants a drink.*

seeing pink spiders Go to seeing pink elephants.

seeing snakes Go to seeing pink elephants.

seen better days *tv.* showing signs of wear or exhaustion. (Always a past participle.) ♦ *This coat has seen better days.*

seeyabye ['sijə'baɪ] *interj.* bye. (California.) ♦ *Gotta go now. Seeyabye.*

self-propelled sandbag *n.* a U.S. Marine. (Persian Gulf War.) ♦ *Those guys are just self-propelled sandbags. They are fearless.*

sell a woof ticket AND **sell woof tickets** *tv.* to boast, bluff, or lie. (Originally black. Also spelled wolf. Compare this with buy so's woof ticket.) ♦ *Freddie is out selling woof tickets again.*

sell buicks *tv.* to vomit. ♦ *I hear somebody in the john selling buicks.*

sell so out *tv.* to betray someone. ♦ *How could you sell me out like that?*

sell woof tickets Go to sell a woof ticket.

sellout 1. *n.* the event of selling all of something. (Advertising.) ♦ *Come to our gigantic sellout of all name-brand merchandise!* **2.** *n.* a betrayal. (See also sell so out.) ♦ *Any one of you could have stood up for me. What a sellout!*

send so from pillar to post *tv.* to send someone from place to place; to give someone the runaround. ♦ *Red tape everywhere I went. They sent me from pillar to post until closing time.*

send so or sth up *tv.* to perform a parody of someone or something. (See also send-up.) ♦ *Last week, he sent the president up.*

send so to glory 1. *tv.* to kill someone. ♦ *One shot sent him to glory.* **2.** *tv.* to officiate at the burial services for someone. ♦ *The preacher sent him to glory amidst the sobs of six or seven former fans.*

send so up the river *tv.* to send someone to prison. (Underworld. As done by a judge or indirectly by the police.) ♦ *They tried to send me up the river, but my lip got me off.*

send-up *n.* a parody. ♦ *I enjoy a good send-up, even if it is about me.*

senior moment *n.* a lapse of memory in an older person. ♦ *I had a senior moment and forgot your name. Sorry.*

sense (bud) Go to sinse.

sent 1. *mod.* alcohol or drug intoxicated. ♦ *Two glasses and she's sent.* **2.** *mod.* carried away by mellow music. ♦ *All the musicians were sent. Maybe they were on something.*

serious *mod.* good; profound; excellent. (See also heavy.) ♦ *Man, these tunes are, like, serious.*

serious about so *mod.* in love, or almost in love, with someone. ♦ *I'm afraid I'm getting serious about Bill.*

serve so right *tv.* to be just what someone deserves. ♦ *It would serve you right if you lost your money.*

sesh *n.* a session of drug use or sexual activity. ◆ *They were too weak for another sesh.*

session 1. *n.* a drinking bout. ◆ *He was just sobering up from a session with the bottle.* **2.** *n.* a marijuana-smoking session; time spent on a drug high. (Collegiate.) ◆ *What a fine session that was!*

set 1. *n.* a period of time that a band plays without a break; a thirty-minute jam session. ◆ *We do two sets and then take a twenty-minute break.* **2.** *n.* a party. ◆ *Your set was a totally major bash!*

set of pipes *n.* a very loud voice; a singing voice. ◆ *With a set of pipes like that, she's a winner.*

set of wheels *n.* a car. ◆ *Man, look at that set of wheels that chick has!*

set so **back** *tv.* to cost someone. ◆ *This bracelet set me back plenty.*

set so **up (for** sth**)** *tv.* to set the scene for something to happen to someone. ◆ *His buddies set him up for the gag—which ended up injuring two of them severely.* ◆ *Who set me up for this anyway?*

settle so's **hash** *tv.* to calm someone down, perhaps by threats or by violence. ◆ *If he comes in here, I'll settle his hash.*

setup 1. *n.* a place to live. ◆ *This is a pretty nice setup. What's the rent?* **2.** *n.* a scheme; a plot. (Underworld.) ◆ *I got a good little setup for earning some money.* **3.** *n.* a person who is set up for some swindle; a **mark.** (Underworld.) ◆ *The setup got wise at the last minute.* **4.** *n.* a glass with ice for an alcoholic beverage. (Usually plural.) ◆ *Can we have a couple of setups brought to our room, please?*

seven-seven-three-aitch AND **773H** *n.* hell. (This is based on the printed word *HELL* rotated 180 degrees. Jocular.) ◆ *What the seven-seven-three-aitch is going on around here?*

seven-year itch *n.* a real or imagined longing for other women in a man's seventh year of marriage. ◆ *Looks like Jack has the seven-year itch.*

sew sth **up** *tv.* to finalize something; to conclude something. (See also **sewed up.**) ◆ *Let's sew this up and get out of here.*

sewed up 1. *mod.* completed. ◆ *I've just about got this contract sewed up.* **2.** *mod.* alcohol intoxicated. ◆ *She's not just drunk; she's sewed up.*

sewer hog *n.* a ditch digger; a sewer worker. ◆ *A sewer hog doesn't get a lot of chances to pal around with the gentry, but the pay's plenty good.*

sewermouth *n.* someone who uses vile language constantly. (Also a rude term of address.) ◆ *If you're going to be a sewermouth, I wish you would leave.*

sex goddess *n.* a sexy-looking female movie or television star. ◆ *I wonder what these sex goddesses look like when they get up in the morning.*

sex kitten *n.* a woman with enormous sexual potential. ◆ *He thought he was getting a sex kitten, but she turned out to be just a plain cat.*

sex pot *n.* one who flaunts one's sexuality, usually a woman. ◆ *About 20,000 young sex pots hit Hollywood every year hoping to be discovered.*

sex-machine *n.* a sexually promising person; a person obsessed with sex. ◆ *Heidi looks like such a sex-machine, but she is a real wallflower.*

sexy 1. *mod.* having great sex appeal. ◆ *He's not what I would call sexy, but I suppose it's a matter of taste.* **2.** *mod.* neat; exciting. ◆ *That's a sexy set of wheels.*

Sez me! Go to Says me!

Sez who? Go to Says who?

SF *mod.* alcohol intoxicated. (Initialism. From **shit-faced.**) ◆ *Fred was really SF last night.*

sgo Go to sko.

shack up (with so**) 1.** *in.* to have a one-night stand with someone; to copulate [with] someone. ◆ *He only wanted to shack up with me.* **2.** *in.* to move in with someone temporarily, presumably for sexual purposes. ◆ *They shacked up for* *over a year until her parents found out and stopped sending her money.*

shades *n.* dark glasses. (See also sunshades.) ◆ *Where are my shades? The sun is too bright.*

shaft 1. *n.* a bad deal; unfair treatment. ◆ *He really gave me the shaft.* **2.** *tv.* to do wrong to someone; to harm or cheat someone. (See also shafted.) ◆ *We are going to shaft this guy in a way that he will remember.*

shafted *mod.* beaten; bested; cheated. ◆ *I really got shafted in that deal.*

shag ass (out of somewhere**)** Go to bag ass (out of somewhere).

shag (off) *in.* to depart. ◆ *I gotta shag. It's late.*

shagged *mod.* alcohol intoxicated. ◆ *Nobody is not too shagged to drive—or something like that.*

shagged out *mod.* exhausted. ◆ *What a day! I'm shagged out!*

shag-nasty *mod.* nasty. ◆ *I want out of this shag-nasty mess.*

shake *n.* a milkshake. (Colloquial or Standard English.) ◆ *I'd like a chocolate shake, please.*

shake a leg 1. *tv.* to hurry; to move faster. (Often as a command.) ◆ *Let's shake a leg, you guys. We gotta be there in twenty minutes.* **2.** *tv.* to dance. ◆ *Let's shake a leg. The music's great.*

Shake it (up)! *exclam.* Hurry!; Move faster! ◆ *Get going, chum! Shake it up!*

shake so **down 1.** *tv.* to blackmail someone. (Underworld.) ◆ *The police chief was trying to shake down just about everybody in town.* **2.** *tv.* to put pressure on someone to lend one money. ◆ *We tried to shake them down for a few hundred, but no deal.*

shake the dew off the lily Go to knock the dew off the lily.

shakedown *n.* an act of extortion. (Underworld.) ◆ *Mary was giving Bruno the shakedown, so he tried to put her out of the way.*

shakeout *n.* an event that eliminates the weak or unproductive elements from a system. ◆ *After a shakeout that lasted a month, we went into full production.*

shakes *n.* the delirium tremens. ◆ *I got the shakes again. That's what I get for putting soda water in my whiskey.*

shake-up *n.* a reorganization. ◆ *After a shake-up like the one we've just been through, everybody's a little upset.*

shaky-cam *n.* a camera, used mainly in advertisements and documentaries, that is shaken and moved constantly to create a sense of excitement, urgency, or crisis. ◆ *We can't afford much in the way of costumes for the sequence, so we will use the shaky-cam and shoot it in dim light.*

sham Go to cham.

shammered *mod.* drunk. ◆ *The guys went out and really got shammered.*

sham(m)us ['ʃeməs] *n.* a police officer or a detective. (Probably from Yiddish.) ◆ *One thing that a shamus always knows is when another shamus is following him.*

shammy Go to cham.

shampers Go to champers.

shampoo *n.* champagne. (See also cham; champers; poo.) ◆ *There is nothing like shampoo to liven up a party!*

shank 1. *n.* a knife; a homemade knife. (Possibly named for a bone handle.) ◆ *The mugger pulled a shank on the victim.* **2.** *in.* to dance. (This *shank* refers to a leg bone.) ◆ *They were busy shankin' and didn't hear the gunshots.*

shank it *tv.* to use one's legs to get somewhere; to walk. ◆ *My car needs fixing so I had to shank it to work today.*

shank's mare *n.* foot travel. (Old. Lacking a horse, one uses the legs. This does not refer to a person named shank.) ◆ *You'll find that shank's mare is the quickest way to get across town.*

shape up 1. *in.* to improve; to reform. ◆ *I guess I'd better shape up if I want to stay in school.* **2.** *in.* to assume a final form or structure. ◆ *The game plan for the election was beginning to shape up.*

shape up or ship out *in.* improve or get out. ♦ *I'll tell you one more time. Shape up or ship out!*

shark 1. *n.* a swindler; a confidence operator. (Underworld.) ♦ *The sharks were lined up ten deep to get at the blue-eyed new owner of the bowling alley.* **2.** *n.* a lawyer. (Derogatory.) ♦ *Some shark is trying to squeeze a few grand out of me.*

shark repellent *n.* something that prevents corporate takeovers. (Securities markets.) ♦ *Acme Systems tried again to get its board to approve a shark repellent to keep the Widget cartel from acquiring it.*

sharp 1. *mod.* clever; intelligent. ♦ *She's sharp enough to see right through everything you say.* **2.** *mod.* good-looking; well-dressed. ♦ *That's a sharp set of wheels you got there.*

sharpie *n.* a clever operator; a clever person. ♦ *She's a real sharpie. She'll take you for everything you've got.*

shave *tv.* to reduce or lessen something. ♦ *The coach thought that the other team was shaving points, so he complained the next day.*

shaved *mod.* alcohol intoxicated. ♦ *So what if I'm a bit shaved? I shtill have all my shenses.*

shavetail *n.* a second lieutenant; a noncommissioned officer in the army; any inexperienced person. (Military. From a nickname for an untrained mule that is marked by a shaved tail.) ♦ *Who's the shavetail dancing with the colonel's daughter?*

Shazzam! [ʃəˈzæm] *exclam.* Wow!; Would you believe? (An incantation used by the comic book character Captain Marvel.) ♦ *And there was my ring—Shazzam!—right on the sidewalk!* ♦ *Shazzam! I passed the test!*

sheen [ʃin] *n.* a car. (From *machine*.) ♦ *You have one fine sheen there.*

sheepskin *n.* a high school or college diploma. ♦ *When you get that sheepskin on the wall, you'll feel like it was all worth something.*

Sheesh! [ʃiʃ] *exclam.* Damn!; Shit! (A euphemism for Shit!) ♦ *Sheesh! What a mess!*

sheet Go to (rap) sheet.

sheisty *mod.* unscrupulous in the manner of a shyster lawyer. ♦ *What a sheisty thing to do! Can't trust anybody!*

shekels [ˈʃɛkl̩z] *n.* dollars; money. (From the Hebrew name for a unit of weight.) ♦ *You got a few shekels you can spare?*

shell out (an amount of money) AND **shell** (an amount of money) **out** *tv. & in.* to spend a certain amount of money. ♦ *I'm not going to shell $400 out for that!*

shellac [ʃəˈlæk] *tv.* to beat someone; to outscore someone. (See also shellacked; shellacking.) ♦ *We're gonna shellac those bums Friday night.*

shellacked 1. *mod.* beaten; outscored. ♦ *They were shellacked, and they knew it.* **2.** *mod.* alcohol intoxicated; overcome by booze. ♦ *Ernie was so shellacked he couldn't see.*

shellacking *n.* a beating. ♦ *We gave them a shellacking they'll never forget.*

Sherlock 1. *n.* a term of address for someone who is clever or perceptive. (Often sarcastic. Based on the name of fictional detective. See also No shit, Sherlock!) ♦ *Brilliant deduction, Sherlock. I never would have guessed!* **2.** *n.* one's pal or buddy. (A play on holmes or *Sherlock Holmes*.) ♦ *Come on, Sherlock, let's go!*

shicker [ˈʃɪkɚ] **1.** AND **schicker; schickered** [ˈʃɪkɚd] *mod.* alcohol intoxicated. (From Hebrew *shiqor* via Yiddish.) ♦ *It took her about ten minutes to get schicker and three days to get sober.* **2.** *n.* liquor; beer. ♦ *Fill it up with shicker again.* **3.** *in.* to tipple; to become alcohol intoxicated. ♦ *I'm gonna go out and shicker till I'm silly.*

shield *n.* a police officer's badge. ♦ *The fuzz flashed his shield, and I knew the game was over.*

shill [ʃɪl] **1.** *n.* someone planted in the crowd to urge others to buy something, participate in something, etc. ♦ *The guy's a shill! Don't fall for this setup!* **2.** *in.* to advertise for something; to give a sales pitch for something. ♦ *Four stars of an old television show were there shilling for a major computer firm.*

shindig [ˈʃɪndɪg] *n.* a party; a dance. (Probably from *shindy* = spree, celebration.) ♦ *What a fancy shindig! They even have glass glasses!*

shine so *tv.* to insult someone; to deceive someone. ♦ *Stop shining me. I'm cool, man, ice.*

shined *mod.* alcohol intoxicated, especially by moonshine. ♦ *Tipsy? He's shined from dawn to dusk.*

shiner *n.* a black eye. ♦ *Wow, look at Marty's shiner!*

shit 1. *n.* dung; feces. (Usually objectionable. Colloquial. Objectionable for many people. See the complete list of all entries with shit in the **Index of Hidden Key Words**.) ♦ *Gee! I stepped in some shit!* **2.** *in.* to defecate. (Usually objectionable.) ♦ *This dog needs to shit. Take it for a walk.* **3.** *n.* any trash or unwanted material; junk; clutter. (Usually objectionable.) ♦ *Clean up this shit and don't let this place get so messy.* **4.** *n.* a wretched person; a despised person. (Rude and derogatory.) ♦ *You stupid shit! Look what you did!* **5.** *n.* one's personal belongings. (See also get one's **shit together**. Usually objectionable.) ♦ *I gotta get my shit from the kitchen and get outa here.* **6.** *n.* lies; nonsense. (From bullshit. Usually objectionable.) ♦ *All I ever hear out of you is shit.* **7.** *tv.* to deceive someone; to lie to someone. ♦ *Stop shittin' me, you bastard!* **8.** *n.* drugs, especially heroin or marijuana. (Usually objectionable.) ♦ *You are going to have to get off this shit or you're gonna die.* **9.** *exclam.* a general expression of disgust. (Usually Shit! Usually objectionable.) ♦ *Oh, shit! What a mess!*

shit a brick *tv.* to be very upset; to be extremely angry. (Usually objectionable.) ♦ *I was so mad, I almost shit a brick!*

Shit happens. *interj.* Bad things just happen. (Usually objectionable.) ♦ *Shit happens. There's nothing that can be done about it.*

shit on a shingle *n.* creamed chipped beef on toast. (See also creamed foreskins. Military. Usually objectionable.) ♦ *Oh, no, it's shit on a shingle again tonight.*

shit on so **1.** *in.* to defecate on someone. (Usually objectionable.) ♦ *Watch out! That cow almost shit on you!* **2.** *tv.* to treat someone very badly. (Usually objectionable.) ♦ *The prof shit on the whole class by assigning a paper due Monday morning.*

Shit or get off the pot! *in.* Do something or go away!; Do something or give someone else a chance!; Hurry up! (Usually objectionable.) ♦ *Hurry up with it, Fred! Shit or get off the pot!*

shit out of luck AND **SOL** *phr. & comp. abb.* Completely out of luck. (Usually objectionable.) ♦ *Sorry. U R SOL.*

shit work Go to grunt work.

shit-ass 1. *n.* a disgusting and wretched person. (Rude and derogatory.) ♦ *The guy's a shit-ass. What're you gonna do?* **2.** *mod.* pertaining to someone or something disgusting and wretched. (Usually objectionable.) ♦ *He's nothing but a shit-ass bastard!*

shit-bag 1. *n.* an unpleasant or inept person. (Rude and derogatory.) ♦ *I don't want that shit-bag working for me anymore!* **2.** *n.* a collection of unpleasant problems or annoyances. (Usually objectionable.) ♦ *You can just take your whole shit-bag and bother somebody else with it.*

shitbox *n.* a worthless, despised person. (Usually objectionable.) ♦ *You worthless shitbox! Get out of my sight.*

shitcan 1. *n.* a toilet; an outhouse. (Usually objectionable.) ♦ *I gotta spend some time on the shitcan.* **2.** a trash can. (Military. Usually objectionable.) ♦ *Just throw all this stuff in the shitcan.* **3.** *tv.* to throw something in the garbage can. (Usually objectionable.) ♦ *Who shitcanned my dirty socks?*

shit-faced AND **shitty** *mod.* alcohol intoxicated. (Usually objectionable. See also poopied; SF.) ♦ *I'm shit-faced, and I know it.*

shithead *n.* a stupid and obnoxious person, usually a male. (Rude and derogatory.) ♦ *You stupid shithead! Get out of my life!*

shit-hooks Go to cunt-hooks.

shit-house *n.* an outdoor toilet; an outhouse. (Usually objectionable.) ♦ *Some boys tipped over the shit-house, and I've got no place to go.*

shit-list AND **crap-list** *n.* a list of people who are as worthless as dung; a list of problem people. (The phrase with *crap* is milder. Usually objectionable.) ♦ *From now on you are on my shit-list!*

shitload Go to buttload.

shitrag *n.* toilet paper. (Usually objectionable.) ♦ *I'm outta shitrag in here!*

the **shits** *n.* diarrhea. (Usually objectionable.) ♦ *I can't eat that stuff. It always gives me the shits.*

shitsky ['ʃɪtski] **1.** *n.* dung. (Usually objectionable.) ♦ *Some rude dog has left a little pile of grade-A shitsky on the sidewalk.* **2.** *n.* a despicable person. (Rude and derogatory.) ♦ *With a shitsky like that on your side, who needs enemies?*

shitstick 1. *n.* a wretched and undesirable person. (Rude and derogatory.) ♦ *Why are you such a shitstick all the time?* **2.** *n.* a rod of dung. (Usually objectionable.) ♦ *How would you like a shitstick in your lap?*

shitty 1. *mod.* covered or soiled with dung. (Usually objectionable.) ♦ *I got my shoes all shitty.* **2.** *mod.* lousy; rotten. (Usually objectionable.) ♦ *This has been a real shitty trip for me.* **3.** Go to shit-faced.

shitty end of the stick *n.* the bad side of a bargain; the troublesome part of a transaction. (Usually objectionable.) ♦ *If you don't want to get stuck with the shitty end of the stick, you'd better make your plans carefully.*

shiv AND **chiv** [ʃɪv] **1.** *n.* a knife. (Underworld.) ♦ *Swiftly and silently his shiv found its way up under Rocko's ribs. All for a silly dame.* **2.** *tv.* to stab someone. (Underworld.) ♦ *The boss told Joel Cairo to get Sam one way or the other—shiv him, burn him, clobber him—but get him.*

Shiznits! *exclam.* Shit! ♦ *Oh, shiznits! I broke it.*

shlemiel Go to schlemiel.

shlep Go to schlep.

shlepper Go to schlepper.

shlimazl Go to schlemazel.

shlump Go to schloomp.

shmaltz Go to schmaltz.

shmaltzy Go to schmaltzy.

shmen [ʃmɛn] *n.* freshmen. ♦ *A couple of shmen wandered by—looking sort of lost.* ♦ *The shmen are having a party all to themselves this Friday.*

shmendrick Go to schmendrick.

shmo Go to schmo.

shmoe Go to schmo.

shmooze Go to schmooze.

shnazz Go to snazz.

shnazzy Go to snazzy.

shnockered Go to schnockered.

shnook Go to schnook.

shnozz Go to schnozz.

shocker *n.* something shocking. ♦ *Now, here's a shocker for you!*

shocks *n.* shock absorbers in an automobile. ♦ *How much is a set of shocks for a buggy like this?*

shoe polish *n.* liquor; whiskey; inferior whiskey. ♦ *The old lush would be delighted to get some of your shoe polish.*

shoestring *mod.* low-cost; cheap. (See also on a shoestring.) ♦ *We have nothing but a shoestring budget this year.*

shoo-in ['ʃuɪn] *n.* an easy winner. ♦ *My horse was a shoo-in. It won by a mile.*

shook up Go to (all) shook up.

shoot 1. AND **shoot up** *tv. & in.* to inject drugs, especially heroin. (Drugs.) ♦ *He actually had to leave the meeting to shoot.* **2.** *n.* an injection of heroin. (Drugs. Usually **shoot-up**.) ♦ *The way Ernie was yawning, I knew he needed a shoot-up.* **3.** *tv.* to spike a drink with liquor. ♦ *I'm* *gonna shoot the punch with rum.* **4.** *in.* to begin to tell [something]. ♦ *Okay, shoot. I'm all ears.* **5.** *exclam.* Darn! (Usually **Shoot!** An exclamation or a very mild curse. A substitute if not a euphemism for *shit*.) ♦ *Oh, shoot! I left my shades in the car.*

shoot 'em up 1. *n.* a Western action movie. ♦ *Most films are more sophisticated nowadays than the old shoot 'em ups.* **2.** *mod.* having to do with a Western action film. ♦ *He was a shoot 'em up star in the thirties.*

shoot for the sky Go to aim for the sky.

shoot from the hip *in.* to speak quickly and without thinking. (See also hip-shooter.) ♦ *She has a tendency to shoot from the hip, but that's not really a problem.*

shoot one's **breakfast** Go to shoot one's cookies.

shoot one's **cookies** AND **shoot** one's **breakfast; shoot** one's **supper** *tv.* to empty one's stomach; to vomit. ♦ *I shot my supper, and I was glad to get rid of it.* ♦ *Whoa! I think I'm gonna shoot my cookies!*

shoot one's **mouth off** *tv.* to brag; to tell secrets. ♦ *So you had to go and shoot off your mouth about the bankruptcy proceedings!*

shoot one's **supper** Go to shoot one's cookies.

shoot one's **wad** *tv.* to spend or use everything. ♦ *I can't afford a cab. I shot my wad at the restaurant.*

shoot oneself **in the foot** *tv.* to cause oneself difficulty; to be the author of one's own doom. ♦ *Again, he shot himself in the foot with his open and honest dealings with the press.*

shoot so **down in flames** *tv.* to ruin someone; to bring about someone's downfall. (See also go down in flames.) ♦ *It was a bad idea, okay, but you didn't have to shoot me down in flames.*

shoot so or sth **down** *tv.* to ruin someone or something; to debunk someone or something. (See also shot down.) ♦ *Just as*

I was making the final point, she shot me down with a simple fact I should have remembered.

shoot the breeze *tv.* to chat casually and without purpose. ♦ *We spent the entire afternoon just shooting the breeze.*

shoot the bull AND **shoot the crap; shoot the shit** *tv.* to chat and gossip. (The same as throw the bull.) ♦ *Let's get together sometime and shoot the bull.* ♦ *I don't have time to stand around shooting the crap with these jerks.*

shoot the cat *tv.* to empty one's stomach; to vomit. ♦ *I must have shot the cat a dozen times during the night.*

shoot the crap Go to shoot the bull.

shoot the dozens Go to play the dozens.

shoot the shit Go to shoot the bull.

shoot the works 1. *tv.* to do everything; to use everything; to bet all one's money. ♦ *Don't shoot the works! Save some for a cab.* **2.** *tv.* to empty one's stomach; to vomit. ♦ *Suddenly she turned sort of green, and I knew she was going to shoot the works.*

shoot up Go to shoot.

shoot up (on sth**) 1.** *in.* to inject (a drug). (Drugs. See also shoot.) ♦ *He couldn't wait to get home and shoot up.* **2.** *n.* an injection of narcotics. (Drugs. Usually **shoot-up.**) ♦ *Marlowe watched the dame do a shoot-up on H. and settle down so they could talk.*

shooting iron *n.* a pistol. (Cowboy and folksy.) ♦ *Millard "Shorty" Wilson always carried his shooting iron with him, except for one fateful day back in '92—1892, that is.* ♦ *He pulled out his shooting iron and got down to cleaning it.*

shoot-out 1. *n.* a gunfight. ♦ *There was a big shoot-out at the end of the movie.* **2.** *n.* an argument. ♦ *When the shoot-out was over, the boss—confident she had won—went back into her office.* ♦ *A big public shoot-out like that sours morale a lot.*

short 1. *n.* a small drink of hard liquor or of beer. ♦ *I'll have a short and a pack of cigarettes.* **2.** *mod.* having to do with a single drink of undiluted liquor. ♦ *I'll take mine short, innkeeper.* **3.** *n.* a purchase of drugs that counts or weighs out less than the amount agreed upon. ♦ *You gave me a short. Fix it now, or this thing goes off accidentally in your ear.* **4.** *tv.* to give someone less of something than was agreed upon. ♦ *They shorted us on the last order, so we switched suppliers.* **5.** *n.* a car. (Streets.) ♦ *Man, that's some short you got!* **6.** *n.* the sale of borrowed shares of stock; a short sale. (Securities markets.) ♦ *There is a lot of covering of shorts this week. After that the market is in for a steady decline.* **7.** *tv.* to sell borrowed stock. (Securities markets.) ♦ *The way the deficit is running, I'd short the whole market.*

the **short end of the stick** *n.* the burden, responsibility, etc., for doing something. ♦ *I am the one who plans all this stuff, and when you jerks drop the ball, I'm left holding the short end of the stick.*

short fuse *n.* a quick temper. ♦ *I knew she'd blow. She's got a short fuse.*

short one *n.* a small or quickly drunk drink of liquor, including beer. (Compare this with **tall one**.) ♦ *How about a short one, innkeeper?*

the **shorts** AND **case of the shorts** *n.* the lack of money. ♦ *The shorts always come around at the end of the month.* ♦ *Yo, dog! Loan me a hondo. I got a case of the shorts.*

short-snort *n.* a quick drink of whiskey from a bottle, flask, or jug. ♦ *Jed offered the visitor a short-snort from a jar of shine.*

shot 1. *n.* a try at something. ♦ *Go ahead. Give it another shot.* **2.** *mod.* exhausted; ruined. ♦ *Here's your pen back. It's shot anyway.* **3.** *n.* a rocket launching. ♦ *The shot was canceled because of the weather.* **4.** *n.* a small or quickly drunk drink of liquor, usually whiskey. ♦ *He stopped at every bar on the strip for a quick shot.* **5.** *n.* an injection of drugs. ♦ *Just one shot of that stuff and you're hooked for life.* **6.** *mod.* alcohol intoxicated. ♦ *They are a little noisy, I guess, but after all they are shot—you know, plastered.*

shot down 1. *mod.* demolished; destroyed. ♦ *I felt shot down, even though I was sure* of what I was getting into. **2.** *mod.* rejected by a young woman. ♦ *Tiffany is a cruel chick. I was shot down from day one.*

shot in the arm 1. *n.* a drink of liquor. ♦ *I could use a little shot in the arm.* **2.** *n.* an injection of narcotics. (The same as **bang in the arm**.) ♦ *You might say that I really needed this shot in the arm.* **3.** *n.* a boost or act of encouragement. ♦ *The pep talk was a real shot in the arm for all the guys.*

shot in the dark *n.* a very general attempt; a wild guess. ♦ *It was just a shot in the dark. I had no idea I was exactly correct.*

shot in the neck 1. *n.* a drink of straight whiskey. ♦ *Willy took a little shot in the neck before heading out into the cold.* **2.** *mod.* alcohol intoxicated. ♦ *What's wrong with Harry is that he's shot in the neck every day by supper.*

shot to hell *mod.* ruined; decimated. (An elaboration of **shot**.) ♦ *This thing is shot to hell. Let's get a new one.*

shot to the curb *mod.* without money or a place to live; living in the gutter; down and out. (Alluding to being on the streets.) ♦ *I'm totally out of bills, man. Shot to the curb.*

shot-away Go to **shot-up**.

shotgun 1. *mod.* broad; general. ♦ *A shotgun approach to a problem like this is useless. You must get specific.* **2.** *exclam.* a phrase called out by someone who claims the privilege of riding in a car's passenger seat. (Usually **Shotgun!**) ♦ *Whoever yelled "shotgun" has to sit holding the cake all the way.*

shotgun wedding *n.* a forced wedding, presumably because the bride is pregnant. ♦ *It was a shotgun wedding, but they sure are in love.*

shotty back *n.* the seat in a car behind the shotgun or passenger seat. (See also **ride shotgun** for an explanation.) ♦ *I wanna ride shotty back!*

shot-up 1. AND **shot-away** *mod.* alcohol or drug intoxicated. ♦ *Well, you see, he's shot-up and can't come to the phone.* **2.** *mod.* severely injured by gunshots.

♦ *Tom got himself shot-up in a hunting accident.*

shouldn't happen to a dog *in.* describes something that is so bad that no creature deserves it. ♦ *This cold I got shouldn't happen to a dog.*

shout *n.* an exclamation point. (See also **screamer; shriek**.) ♦ *Put a shout at the end of the line. Make this dull story more sexy.*

shove *tv.* to pass counterfeit money. (Underworld.) ♦ *She got sent up for three years for shoving funny-money.*

show and tell *n.* a session where objects are presented and described. (Essentially a kindergarten or grade school activity.) ♦ *It was a short lecture with lots of show and tell.*

show biz *n.* show business. ♦ *Anybody who can make a living in show biz has to be clever and talented.*

shower ['ʃo wɚ] a large flaccid penis that doesn't get much bigger. (Compare to **grower**.) ♦ *It's a shower, not a grower.*

shower scum *n.* a despised person; despised people. (See also **bathtub scum; pond scum**.) ♦ *Who is the shower scum who put a cigarette butt in my houseplant?*

Showtime! Go to **(It's) showtime!**

shpleef Go to **spliff**.

shrapnel *n.* a few small coins left as a tip. ♦ *He just toked me a few bits of schrapnel!*

shredded *mod.* alcohol intoxicated. (Collegiate.) ♦ *We are all too shredded to drive home. What shall we do?*

shriek *n.* an exclamation point. (Printers. See also **screamer; shout**.) ♦ *Take off that shriek. You use too many of those things.*

shrimp *n.* a small person. ♦ *I'm such a shrimp. I just have short genes.*

shrink *n.* a psychoanalyst or psychotherapist. ♦ *I dropped a bundle on a shrink, but it didn't help me.*

shroom [ʃrum] *in.* to take or eat peyote cactus. (Drugs. See also **shrooms**.) ♦ *They spent all afternoon shrooming.*

shrooms [ʃrumz] **1.** *n.* the tips of the peyote cactus that contain mescaline. (Drugs. From *mushrooms*. Not really a mushroom.) ♦ *I got some shrooms. Ya wanna come over?* **2.** *n.* mushrooms. (From sense 1.) ♦ *Do you want shrooms on your pizza?*

shtik Go to **schtick**.

shtoonk Go to **schtoonk**.

shuck [ʃək] **1.** *n.* an insincere person. ♦ *The guy's a shuck. Don't believe a thing he says!* **2.** *tv. & in.* to kid someone; to tease someone. ♦ *Cool it! I'm just shucking.* **3.** *tv.* to swindle someone; to deceive someone. ♦ *He was going to shuck the mayor, but people were beginning to talk, so he blew town.* **4.** *n.* a hoax. ♦ *How could you fall for that old shuck?* **5.** AND **shuck down** *tv. & in.* to undress oneself; to remove one's clothing. ♦ *He shucked down and showered and was at work in twenty minutes.*

shuck down Go to **shuck**.

Shucks! Go to **(Aw) shucks!**

shuffler *n.* a drunkard; a **tippler**. ♦ *The tavern was full of aged shufflers hoping for a handout.*

shush (up) *in.* to be quiet. ♦ *Shush! I want to hear the weather.*

shut up *in.* to be quiet. ♦ *Shut up and listen!*

Shut your face! AND **Shut your mouth!; Shut your trap!** *exclam.* Shut up!; Be quiet! ♦ *Oh, shut your face! I've heard enough.* ♦ *Shut your trap! All you do is talk.*

Shut your mouth! Go to **Shut your face!**

Shut your trap! Go to **Shut your face!**

shut-eye *n.* sleep. ♦ *I could use about another hour of shut-eye.*

shutout 1. *n.* a game where one team prevents the other from scoring any points at all. ♦ *He was still reveling from last week's shutout.* **2.** *mod.* having to do with a game where one team has no score. ♦ *Another shutout game gave the fans nothing to cheer about this afternoon.*

shutters *n.* the eyelids. ♦ *She blinked those yummy shutters over those bedroom eyes, and my knees turned to mush.*

shwag *n.* marijuana. ♦ *Where can I score some shwag?*

shwench [ʃʍɛntʃ] *n.* a female freshman. (Collegiate. From *fresh* + *wench*.) ♦ *A couple of giggling shwenches showed up to cheer on the team.*

shyster ['ʃɑɪstɚ] *n.* an unethical or unscrupulous lawyer. (Also a rude term of address.) ♦ *Look, you cheap shyster, I paid you to help me, not ruin me!*

Siberian express *n.* an enormous mass of very cold air moving from Siberia, across the North Pole, and down onto North America. ♦ *The country braced itself for a return Friday of the Siberian express with temperatures dropping to twenty below in many areas.*

sick to death (of so or sth**)** *mod.* totally disgusted with someone or something. ♦ *I am sick to death of your constant bickering.*

sick (up) *in.* to empty one's stomach; to vomit. ♦ *I think I'm going to sick up. Isn't there supposed to be a barf bag in one of these seat pockets?*

sicks *n.* nausea; vomiting. ♦ *Oh man, I got the sicks.*

sicky *n.* someone who seems mentally deranged. ♦ *Some sicky drew these obscene pictures on the wall.*

side *n.* a side of a record (recording). (Refers to older vinyl recording.) ♦ *Let's cruise over to Sam's pad and hear some sides.*

sidewalk superintendent 1. *n.* someone who—out of curiosity—watches excavations being dug and buildings being built. ♦ *All day, the lines of sidewalk superintendents oozed by.* **2.** *n.* any critic. ♦ *If another sidewalk superintendent comes in here and tries to tell me how to manage this office, heads will roll.*

sidewalk surfing *n.* skateboarding. ♦ *Bill spent a lot of time sidewalk surfing until the town passed an ordinance against it.*

sidewinder *n.* a sneaky and despicable man. (Western jargon. From the name of the sidewinder rattlesnake.) ♦ *You dirty, lowdown sidewinder! That's too much!*

sidney *n.* the hallucinogenic drug LSD. (Drugs. Also capitalized.) ♦ *Sidney and I have a little business trip planned.*

Siegfried and Roy *n.* [in poker] a pair of queens. (Refers to the three-decade-long Las Vegas show performed by Siegfried Fischbacher and Roy Horn who raised tigers and lions in their home until Roy was bitten by a tiger onstage. See queen.) ♦ *He's holding a Siegfried and Roy.*

sieg-heil so ['sɪɡ'haɪl] *tv.* to show homage to someone; to salute and obey someone. (From German. Use caution with this reminder of Nazi Germany.) ♦ *The guy expects all his underlings to sieg-heil him and worship the ground he walks on.*

signify 1. *in.* to cause trouble for fun; to stir things up. (Black.) ♦ *What are all these cats signifying about anyway?* **2.** *in.* to try to look more important than one really is; to brag; to strut one's stuff. (Black.) ♦ *See that dude signify like somebody important?*

SIIC Go to See if I care!

silent but deadly AND **SBD** *mod.* [pertaining to a release of intestinal gas] soundless but smelling horribly. ♦ *Who floated that SBD air biscuit?*

silk *n.* a Caucasian. (Black.) ♦ *He told his mama that if she doesn't treat him better, he's gonna bring some silk home for dinner and let her see what the neighbors think.*

silked to the bone Go to laid to the bone.

silks *n.* clothing. ♦ *I gotta get some new silks before spring.*

silky *mod.* smooth; unctuous. ♦ *What a silky character. He could talk his way into the heart of some unsuspecting chick.*

silo drippings *n.* alcohol allegedly obtained at the base of a silo containing fermenting corn. ♦ *The old-timer called his moonshine "silo drippings."*

silver *n.* money. ♦ *I have some silver stashed at home if you need it.*

silver bullet AND **magic bullet** *n.* a specific, fail-safe solution to a problem. (From the notion that a bullet made of silver is required to shoot a werewolf.) ♦ *I'm not suggesting that the committee has provided us with a silver bullet, only that their advice was timely and useful.* ♦ *I don't know the answer. I don't have a magic bullet!*

silver goose *n.* a proctoscope. (Medical. See also **goose**.) ♦ *When the nurse brought in the silver goose, the patient nearly fainted.*

simmer (down) **1.** *in.* to reduce one's anger. ♦ *Simmer down, you guys.* **2.** *in.* to get quiet. ♦ *I waited till things began to simmer down, and then I started.*

simoleon [sɪ'moliən] *n.* a dollar. (Underworld.) ♦ *For only one simoleon, you get a ticket to the greatest show on earth.*

Simon Legree ['saɪmən lə'gri] *n.* a very hard taskmaster; a hard boss. (From the name of the slave driver in *Uncle Tom's Cabin.*) ♦ *Ask Simon Legree if I will be able to stop work and go home for breakfast now.*

simp *n.* a simpleton. ♦ *You are such a simp!*

sin *n.* synthetic marijuana. (Drugs. From *synthetic*.) ♦ *Most of this stuff the kids put down good money for is not sin but angel dust.*

sin-bin *n.* a van fitted with bedding as a place for necking and lovemaking. ♦ *Willy said he was saving his money to buy a sin-bin so he could have more fun on dates.*

sing *in.* to inform (on someone). (Underworld.) ♦ *Rocko knew the stoolie would sing. He had to do something to stop her.*

singed Go to **scorched**.

single **1.** *n.* one dollar; a dollar bill. ♦ *I don't have enough singles in the register to get me through the morning.* **2.** *n.* an unmarried person. (Usually plural.) ♦ *I'm holding a little party for singles.*

sink *tv.* to swallow some food or drink. ♦ *Larry stopped at a tavern to sink a short one.*

sink one's **teeth into** sth Go to **get** one's **teeth into** sth.

sinker *n.* a doughnut. ♦ *All our sinkers are brought in fresh on Monday.*

sinse AND **sense (bud)** [sɪnts AND 'sɛnts (bəd)] *n.* seedless marijuana. (Drugs. From Spanish *sinsemilla*, "seedless.") ♦ *Where's the sinse I was saving?* ♦ *Tom only gets high on sense bud.*

sip **1.** *n.* a puff of a marijuana cigarette. (Drugs.) ♦ *He took a big sip and held it so long he almost turned blue.* **2.** *tv. & in.* to take a puff of a marijuana cigarette. ♦ *The alley was populated by a bunch of teeny-boppers sipping away the afternoon.*

sipster *n.* a tippler; a drunkard. ♦ *The old lady is a sipster who says she drinks a little wine to help her arthritis.*

sis [sɪs] *n.* sister. (Also a term of address and a common pet name for one's sister.) ♦ *Come on, sis. We're going to be late.*

sissified ['sɪsɪfaɪd] *mod.* effeminate; sissy-style. ♦ *I'm not comfortable in a sissified place like that.*

sister **1.** *n.* a (female) friend. (Originally underworld. Sometimes a term of address.) ♦ *Come here, sister. I gotta have a word with you.* **2.** *n.* a fellow sorority member. ♦ *One of my sisters let me borrow her car.* **3.** *n.* a fellow feminist. ♦ *We can do this thing, sisters, we can do it!* **4.** Go to **(soul) sister**.

sitch *n.* situation. (Streets.) ♦ *You in one bad sitch, bitch!*

sitcom ['sɪtkam] *n.* a situation comedy as found on television. (See also **kid-vid**.) ♦ *These sitcoms are made for juvenile minds.*

sitting duck *n.* someone who waits unsuspectingly for doom or destiny; an easy target for something bad. ♦ *Get out of the way! You're a sitting duck.*

sitting pretty *mod.* doing very nicely; in a very pleasant and secure position. ♦ *She married a millionaire, and now she's sitting pretty.*

situation *n.* an event, crime, or suspicious happening that warrants investigation or action by the police. (Law enforcement.)

♦ *We have a situation out on 114 Maple Street. See the man.*

six feet under *mod.* dead and buried. ♦ *They put him six feet under two days after he died.*

six-bits *n.* seventy-five cents. (A *bit* is equal to twelve and one-half U.S. cents.) ♦ *Just try one of these things. It's only six-bits.*

sixer *n.* a six-pack beverage container. (Usually refers to beer.) ♦ *Tom showed up with three sixers and a bushel of pretzels, and we all watched the game together.*

six-pack 1. *in.* to while away a specified period of time drinking a six-pack of beer. (See also **Joe Six-pack**.) ♦ *He sat in front of the television and six-packed the entire afternoon.* **2.** *n.* a well-muscled abdomen. ♦ *Tom's gut is a real six-pack. He must work out every day.*

the **sixty-four-dollar question** *n.* the most important question; the question that everyone wants to know the answer to. ♦ *When? Now, that is the sixty-four-dollar question.*

sixty-nine *n.* an act of mutual oral sex. (Based on the interlocking numerals in 69. Usually objectionable.) ♦ *The old lady caught them in the bushes doing a sixty-nine.*

sizzle a wild card word for words beginning with *S*, such as *suck, smoke, sister.* (Streets. Also for other words with initial *S.*) ♦ *Come on, sizzle, time to go.*

sizzled *mod.* alcohol intoxicated. (See also **fried**.) ♦ *I'd like to go out tonight and get sizzled—maybe that would help me forget Tiffany.* ♦ *Harold got himself sizzled and couldn't drive to the dance.*

sizzler *n.* a very hot day. ♦ *What a sizzler! I'm sweating like a horse.*

skag AND **scag** [skæg] **1.** *n.* a rotten thing or person. ♦ *Don't be such a skag. Who do you think you are?* **2.** *n.* a very ugly woman. (Collegiate.) ♦ *What a skag! I wouldn't be seen with her.* **3.** *n.* a tobacco cigarette; a tobacco cigarette butt. (Military.) ♦ *Can I bum a scag off you?* **4.** *in.* to smoke (a tobacco cigarette). ♦ *He stopped scagging for about a week.* **5.** *n.*

heroin, especially poor-quality heroin; any powerful drug. (Drugs.) ♦ *Scag has sent a lot of my friends to the bone orchard.* **6.** *n.* hard liquor. ♦ *The two of them put away a quart of my finest skag.*

skag jones AND **scag jones** *n.* an addiction to heroin. (Drugs. Here *jones* is a "thing" = craving.) ♦ *She has a serious skag jones.*

skagged out *mod.* drug intoxicated; very high. (Drugs. See also **skag**.) ♦ *Bart was rocking back and forth on the top step— skagged out, as usual.* ♦ *He got to the point where being skagged out was more important than eating.*

skank AND **scank** [skæŋk] **1.** *n.* an ugly (young) woman. (Collegiate.) ♦ *What a skank she is! Give her a comb or something.* **2.** *in.* to appear ugly. ♦ *Both sisters skank. Must be hereditary.*

skanky ['skæŋki] *mod.* ugly; repellent, usually said of a woman. (Collegiate.) ♦ *She is so skanky! That grody hairdo doesn't help either.*

skanless AND **scanless** *mod.* scandalous. (Eye-dialect.) ♦ *Who did that? That skanless! Just skanless.*

skat [skæt] *n.* beer. ♦ *You got any pretzels to go with the skat?*

skate 1. *n.* a drinking bout. ♦ *He's off on another three-day skate.* **2.** *n.* a drunkard; a person on a drinking spree. ♦ *A couple of skates celebrating the new year ran into my car.* **3.** *n.* something really easy. ♦ *The test was a skate!* **4.** *in.* to get drunk. ♦ *Let's go out and skate, okay?*

skates *n.* shoes. *It looks like somebody looged on your skates!*

skating *mod.* drug intoxicated. ♦ *He's high all right—I'd say he's skating.* ♦ *He took some wicked pills and is totally skating.*

skedaddle [skə'dædl] *in.* to get out; to leave in a hurry. (Folksy.) ♦ *Well, I'd better skedaddle on home.*

skeet *n.* a blob of nasal mucus. (Collegiate. See also **skeet-shooting**.) ♦ *God, Fred, there's a gross skeet hanging outa your nose!*

skeeter ['skidɚ] *n.* a mosquito. (Folksy.) ♦ *A skeeter bit me on the arm.*

skeet-shooting *n.* the act of blowing one's nose by pinching one nostril and using no tissue or handkerchief. (See also skeet.) ♦ *There is nothing more disgusting than a bunch of college boys belching and skeet-shooting.*

skeevy ['skivi] *mod.* sleazy and disgusting. ♦ *That butterface sure looks skeevy.*

skeezer ['skizɚ] *n.* a weird person; a geek. (Also a term of address.) ♦ *Dave is a nice guy, but sort of a skeezer.*

sketchy *mod.* unsafe; illegal; risky. (Alluding to danger due to lack of knowledge.) ♦ *Why are we going down in the sketchy place on this silly errand?*

skid marks *n.* unclean, brownish marks on one's underpants. ♦ *Just looking at him, you know he's the type who has skid marks and enjoys popping zits.*

skid row *n.* the name for a place populated with ruined alcoholics and other down-and-out people. ♦ *Just because they're on skid row, it doesn't mean they're beyond help.*

skid row bum *n.* a down-and-out person; a low alcoholic beggar. ♦ *Do you want to end up a skid row bum?*

skid-lid *n.* a motorcycle helmet. ♦ *The law has no business telling me I gotta wear a skid-lid.*

skillion ['skɪljən] *n.* an imaginary enormous number. ♦ *I have a skillion reasons why I won't marry you.*

skin 1. *n.* a dollar bill. ♦ *This ticket cost me a couple of skins—and it's not worth it.* ♦ *You got a skin for the tollbooth?* **2.** AND **skinhead** *n.* someone with a shaved or bald head. (Some such persons may also engage in political violence.) ♦ *Who's the skinhead with the earrings?* **3.** *tv.* to cheat or overcharge someone. ♦ *The guy who sold me this car really skinned me.*

skin a goat *tv.* to empty one's stomach; to vomit. (From the bleating sound of the wretching.) ♦ *Was my cooking so bad that everybody had to skin a goat?*

skin flick *n.* a movie featuring nudity. (See also nudie.) ♦ *Max likes skin flicks better than real girls.*

skin game *n.* any swindle. (Underworld.) ♦ *Spike was mixed up in a skin game for a while.*

Skin me! *exclam.* Give me some skin!; Shake my hand! (Originally black.) ♦ *Hey, old buddy. Don't walk on! Skin me!*

skinful *n.* an intoxicating quantity of liquor; enough liquor. (See also have a skinful.) ♦ *She knows enough to stop drinking before she gets a skinful.*

skinhead Go to skin.

skinny Go to (hot) skinny.

skins *n.* drums. (Musicians. The same as hides.) ♦ *Andy can really make the skins talk.*

Skip it! *exclam.* Forget it!; Never mind! ♦ *I won't bother you with my question again. Skip it!*

skip (out) *in.* to leave; to run away without doing something, such as paying a bill. ♦ *Fred skipped out, leaving me with the bill.*

skirt *n.* a woman. ♦ *Some skirt comes up to me and asks where the police station is.*

skivvies ['skɪviz] *n.* underpants; underwear. ♦ *I don't have any clean skivvies!*

sko 1. AND **sgo** ['sko AND 'sgo] *in.* Let's go. (Now considered current slang even though it has been informal colloquial for decades.) ♦ *It's time to hit the road. Sgo.* **2.** *n.* a skanky hoe. ♦ *What a sko, fo sho!*

skosh *mod.* a bit more. ♦ *Move down a skosh so I can sit down.*

skrag [skræg] *tv.* to murder someone. (Underworld.) ♦ *Marlowe wanted to skrag him right then and there.*

skrilla AND **skrill** *n.* money. ♦ *I'm totally outa skrilla, man. Shot to the curb.*

skrungy ['skrʌndʒi] *mod.* disgusting. ♦ *What is this skrungy stuff they are serving here?*

skull-buster AND **skull-popper 1.** *n.* a difficult course in school or college. ♦ *The* *course was a skull-buster, and I had to drop it.* **2.** *n.* a police officer. (Refers to the striking of skulls.) ♦ *Two skull-poppers came up and started asking questions.*

skullduggery ['skəl'dəgɚi] *n.* deceitful doings; dirty work. ♦ *Without skullduggery, politics wouldn't be interesting.*

skulled *mod.* alcohol or drug intoxicated. ♦ *He's too skulled to drive.*

skull-popper Go to skull-buster.

skully *n.* an act of fellatio. (See also **give head**.) ♦ *A bit of skully would have held him for a few days.*

skunk 1. *n.* a mean and hateful person. (See also **polecat; stinker**.) ♦ *Must you be such a skunk in front of my friends?* **2.** *tv.* to outwit someone. ♦ *That fish skunked me. I thought I caught him for sure this time.*

skunk-drunk *mod.* alcohol intoxicated. ♦ *He was skunk-drunk and didn't want to be bothered.*

skunked 1. *mod.* alcohol intoxicated. ♦ *He was so skunked he couldn't find his house.* **2.** *mod.* outwitted; outscored; defeated. ♦ *The home team skunked the visitors for the third year in a row.*

skurf [skɚf] *in.* to skateboard. (From the words *skate* and *surf*.) ♦ *He skurfed from city hall to the post office.*

sky *in.* to travel (to somewhere) in an airplane. ♦ *I decided to sky down to Orlando for the weekend.*

sky hook *n.* an imaginary crane; an imaginary tool. ♦ *I can't get this thing outa here without a sky hook.*

sky rug *n.* a toupee; a man's wig. ♦ *I think he is wearing a sky rug.*

the **sky's the limit** *phr.* there is no upper limit. ♦ *You can do anything you set your mind to, Billy. The sky's the limit.*

sky-pilot *n.* a chaplain. ♦ *The sky-pilot says we can park in the church's lot, if we don't mess anything up or make too much noise.*

slackmaster *n.* someone who slacks off a lot; someone who doesn't work hard

enough or at all. ♦ *He never does his share. Nothing but a slackmaster!*

Slade *n.* a Caddy Escalade. (Streets.) ♦ *That's no ghetto sled, that's a Slade.*

slam 1. *tv.* to criticize someone or something. ♦ *The secretary was slamming the boss in one room, and the boss was slamming the secretary in another.* **2.** *n.* a criticism. ♦ *Harry took another slam at the sales record the sales force had produced for the meeting.* **3.** *tv.* to drink something quickly. ♦ *Bart slammed a couple of beers and left.*

slam a beer Go to pound a beer.

slam dunk 1. *tv. & in.* to force a basketball into the basket from above. (See also **jam**.) ♦ *Wilbur slam dunked another one, raising the score from 108 to 110.* **2.** *n.* an act of making a basket as in sense 1. ♦ *Another slam dunk and Wilbur ties the score again!*

slam some beers Go to pound a beer.

slam-bang *mod.* wild; exciting. ♦ *It was a slam-bang weekend, and I loved every minute of it.*

slammer 1. *n.* a jail. ♦ *I got out of the slammer on Monday and was back in by Wednesday.* **2.** *n.* a slam dunk. ♦ *He really has that slammer perfected!*

slamming *mod.* great. ♦ *We had one slamming time last night.*

slang *tv.* to sell drugs. (May be related to *sling* or one of the very old senses of *slang*.) ♦ *The cops got him for slanging.*

slant *n.* a biased view; a unique perception. (A synonym for **angle**.) ♦ *You can probably give us yet another slant on this problem.*

slap happy *mod.* silly; giddy. ♦ *I get slap happy when I have to stay up this late.*

a **slap in the face** *n.* an insult; a rejection. ♦ *That remark was a real slap in the face.*

slap so on the wrist Go to slap so's wrist.

slap so's wrist AND **slap so on the wrist** *tv.* to administer a minor reprimand. ♦ *The courts only slap them on the wrist and send them back out on the streets.*

slap-dab *mod.* directly; exactly in place. (See also smack (dab) in the middle.) ◆ *I found this pop bottle slap-dab on top of the car! How'd it get there?*

slap-dash *mod.* fast and careless. ◆ *I wish you hadn't done it in such a slap-dash fashion.*

slash *n.* a drink of liquor. ◆ *Just one slash, and I have to be going.*

slaughter Go to murder.

slaughtered *mod.* drunk. ◆ *Garth went out and got himself slaughtered again last night.*

slave away (at sth**)** *in.* to work very hard (doing something). ◆ *I'm slaving away for $7 an hour and have no prospects for the future.*

slave market *n.* a job market where many candidates for jobs come face to face with potential employers. ◆ *I gotta go to the annual slave market this year. We're hiring for a change.*

slay *tv.* to overwhelm someone with one's performance or other excellence. ◆ *These jokes always slay the audience.*

sleaze AND **sleez** [sliz] **1.** *n.* a low and despicable person. ◆ *You'd expect to find a sleaze like that in a sleazoid joint like this.* **2.** *n.* any junk. ◆ *I won't sell sleez like that! I won't even have it in my store.* **3.** *in.* to act low; to be sexually promiscuous. ◆ *She looks like the type who will sleaze and lie to get her own way.*

sleazebag *n.* a repellent person or place. ◆ *I won't go into a sleazebag like that.*

sleazeball *n.* a repellent person. ◆ *Who is that sleazeball with the earring?*

sleaze-bucket *n.* a repellent person, thing, or place. ◆ *Gad, what a sleaze-bucket! Let me out of here!*

sleazo AND **sleazoid** ['slizo(ɪd)] *mod.* low; disreputable; sleazy. ◆ *Let's get out of this sleazo joint.*

sleazoid ['slizoɪd] **1.** *n.* a sleazy person. ◆ *Who was that sleazoid I saw you with last night?* **2.** Go to sleazo.

sleep it off *tv.* to sleep while the effects of drugs or alcohol wear off. ◆ *I'm polluted, I guesh. Have to get home and sleep it off.*

sleeper 1. *n.* a sleeping pill. ◆ *She took a handful of sleepers with a glass of booze, and that was it.* **2.** *n.* someone or something that achieves fame after a period of invisibility. ◆ *The movie "Red Willow" was undoubtedly the sleeper of the year, winning six awards.*

sleepfest *n.* something, such as a dull lecture, that induces a long period of sleep. ◆ *The history lecture today was a real sleepfest.*

sleepwalk *n.* a movement toward something without effort; easy advancement; an easy task. (Something that could be done *in one's sleep.* See also cakewalk; walk.) ◆ *Getting the degree was a sleepwalk. Getting a job was hell.*

sleez Go to sleaze.

slew 1. *in.* to drink to intoxication. ◆ *They must have been slewing for an hour before one got up and left.* **2.** AND **slews** *n.* a lot; lots. ◆ *I have a whole slew of old computer programs at home in a box somewhere.*

slewed AND **slewy; slued; sloughed (up)** [slud AND 'slui, slud…] *mod.* alcohol intoxicated. ◆ *Wallace is too slewed to drive.*

slews Go to slew.

slewy Go to slewed.

slice of the action Go to piece (of the action).

slick 1. *mod.* clever; glib. ◆ *His talk is slick, but his action is zotz.* **2.** *mod.* excellent. ◆ *That is a slick idea.* **3.** *n.* a high-quality magazine printed on slick [coated] paper. ◆ *The slicks are all carrying ads for products and services that couldn't even be mentioned a few years ago.* **4.** *n.* a racing tire. (Auto racing.) ◆ *That set of wheels has slicks. I wonder why.*

slick-chick *n.* an attractive and cute girl. ◆ *Tiffany is a slick-chick. I wonder if she'd go out with me.*

slickum ['slɪkəm] *n.* hair dressing, especially if thick and heavy. ◆ *What kind of* *slickum do you have on your hair—bear grease?* ♦ *His hair was plastered down with slickum, and he looked like something in an old movie.*

slightly rattled 1. *mod.* upset; confused. (See also rattled.) ♦ *Tom was slightly rattled by the trouble at the door.* **2.** *mod.* tipsy; alcohol intoxicated. ♦ *She can be stone blind and still seem only slightly rattled.*

slim *n.* a tobacco cigarette. (The same as straight, as opposed to a marijuana cigarette, which may be thicker.) ♦ *I'll take a slim and a little mist, thanks.*

slime 1. *n.* a worthless person; a low and wretched person. ♦ *What a slime that guy is!* **2.** *n.* degrading matters; corrupt people or situations. ♦ *I don't want to be involved in slime like that.*

slime bag AND **slime bucket; slimebag; slimeball** *n.* a despicable person, usually a male. (See also slime.) ♦ *Gee, a slime bag like that in the same room with me! Yuck!*

slime bucket Go to slime bag.

slimebag Go to slime bag.

slimeball Go to slime bag.

sling the cat *tv.* to empty one's stomach; to vomit. ♦ *Suddenly Ralph left the room to sling the cat, I guess.*

Slip me five! Go to Give me (some) skin!

slip one's **trolley** *tv.* to become a little crazy; to lose one's composure. (See also off one's trolley.) ♦ *I was afraid I would slip my trolley.*

slip so a **Mickey** *tv.* to secretly put a Mickey Finn in someone's alcoholic drink. (This drug either makes the victim pass out or causes immediate diarrhea.) ♦ *Somebody slipped Marlowe a Mickey and sent him into action.*

slip so **five** *tv.* to shake someone's hand. ♦ *Billy slipped me five, and we sat down to discuss old times.*

slip (up) 1. *in.* to make an error. ♦ *Don't slip up and pay this bill twice, please.* **2.** AND **slip(-up)** *n.* an error. ♦ *That was a silly slip-up. I'm sorry.*

slipstick *n.* a slide rule. (Very common a few decades ago, a slide rule is a computing device that allowed the user to compute by positioning moveable scales printed on various sliding parts of the rule.) ♦ *Who carries a slipstick these days?*

slob [slɑb] *n.* a rude, fat, and unpleasant person. ♦ *What a slob! Comb your hair, if you can get a comb through it!*

slob up *in.* to eat. ♦ *Fred stopped slobbing up long enough to change the channel on the TV set.*

slobber *n.* nonsense. (From the term for saliva running out of the mouth.) ♦ *I've heard enough of your slobber. Can it!*

slopped *mod.* alcohol intoxicated. ♦ *I've never seen a senior citizen so inelegantly slopped as was Walter.*

slop(s) *n.* bad beer; inferior liquor. ♦ *Why do we have to drink slops like this? Can't Tom afford to give his guests something decent?*

slosh 1. *n.* beer; liquor. ♦ *How about a glass of slosh?* **2.** *tv. & in.* to drink liquor, including beer; to drink to excess. ♦ *Are you going to slosh gin all night?*

sloshed (to the ears) *mod.* alcohol intoxicated. ♦ *Man, is he sloshed to the ears!*

slots *n.* slots machines. (Usually plural.) ♦ *He won three large just on the slots.*

slough (off) Go to sluff (off).

sloughed (up) Go to slewed.

slow burn *n.* the act of becoming angry very slowly or being resentful for a long period of time. (See also do a slow burn.) ♦ *His lips were pressed together and he was angry but just having a slow burn.*

sludgeball ['slədʒbɑl] *n.* a despicable and repellent person. ♦ *Mike is such a sludgeball! Why do you keep seeing him?*

slued Go to slewed.

sluff (off) AND **slough (off)** *in.* to waste time; to goof off. ♦ *Watch him. He will sluff off if you don't keep after him.*

slug 1. *n.* a drink of liquor; a shot of whiskey. ♦ *Have a slug of this stuff. It will—I'm sorry to say, ma'am—put hair on your* chest. ♦ *A couple more slugs and he was ready to face the huge bull-necked ruffian.* **2.** *n.* a bullet. ♦ *Marlowe sent a couple of slugs into Rocko's chest. Rocko crumpled soundlessly.*

slug it out *tv.* to fight something out; to fight about something figuratively. ♦ *We'll just have to sit down in the conference room and slug it out.*

slugfest 1. *n.* a fight; a festival of slugging. ♦ *They went out in the alley for a real slugfest.* **2.** *n.* a festival of arguing. ♦ *The president emerged from the slugfest with control of the company still hers.*

slugged *mod.* alcohol intoxicated. ♦ *I'm slugged—skunked, you know, corned. And I think I am going to sick up.* ♦ *Ted realized that he was slugged out of his mind, but tried to get the bartender to serve him another drink.*

slummy ['sləmi] *mod.* lousy. ♦ *This place is not slummy!*

slush fund *n.* a fund of money that can be used for various unofficial and discretionary purposes. ♦ *How much is left in the slush fund?*

slush up *in.* to drink liquor; to get drunk. ♦ *They slushed up for a while and went out to look for some chicks.*

slushed (up) *mod.* alcohol intoxicated. ♦ *I hate to come home slushed and wake up everybody. I have to sing, you see.*

sly *mod.* excellent; cool. ♦ *That is really a sly jacket you got there.*

smack (dab) in the middle *mod.* exactly in the middle. (See also **slap-dab.**) ♦ *Not too big and not too small. Just smack in the middle.*

smack the road *tv.* to leave; to hit the road. ♦ *Let's smack the road. I have to get up early.*

smacker 1. *n.* the face. (See also **kisser.**) ♦ *She ought to give that ugly smacker back to the horse before it runs into something.* **2.** *n.* a dollar. (Underworld.) ♦ *You got a couple of smackers for the toll booth?* **3.** *n.* a kiss. ♦ *He planted a smacker square on*

her lips. She kicked him in the shins for his trouble.

small beer *n.* nothing or next to nothing; an insignificant person. (From a very old word for weak or inferior beer.) ♦ *Small beer or not, he's my customer, and I will see that he is taken care of.*

small change *n.* an insignificant person. (Also a rude term of address.) ♦ *The guy you think is small change happens to own this building you seem to be guarding so well.*

small fry 1. *n.* anything or anyone small or unimportant. (*Fry* are juvenile fish.) ♦ *Don't worry about the small fry. You have to please the fat-cats.* **2.** *n.* small children. ♦ *The small fries have eaten and are getting ready for bed.*

small potatoes *n.* something or someone insignificant. ♦ *This contract is small potatoes, but it keeps us in business till we get into the real money.*

small-time *mod.* insignificant; petty. ♦ *Bart was involved in a lot of small-time crime when he was twelve.*

smarmy ['smɑrmi] *mod.* insincere and obsequious. ♦ *He's obnoxious but brazen rather than smarmy.*

smart ass *n.* someone who makes wisecracks and acts cocky. (Usually objectionable.) ♦ *Don't be such a smart ass!*

smart cookie *n.* a clever person. ♦ *She's really a smart cookie if you give her a chance.*

smart guy *n.* a man who acts cocky; a wise guy. ♦ *All right, smart guy, see if you like this one.*

smart money *n.* money belonging to smart or clever people. ♦ *Most of the smart money is going into utility stocks right now.*

smart mouth *n.* someone who makes wisecracks; a cocky person who speaks out of turn. ♦ *Don't be a smart mouth with me!*

smarts *n.* intelligence. ♦ *I got the smarts to do the job. All I need is someone to trust me.*

smarty *n.* a cocky person. (Also a term of address.) ♦ *Well, if you're such a smarty, why aren't you rich?*

smarty-pants *n.* a cocky person; a smart aleck. ♦ *Look, smarty-pants, let's cut the clowning around.*

smash *n.* wine. (Streets. Because it is made from smashed grapes.) ♦ *I got a bottle of smash in my car.*

smashed *mod.* alcohol or drug intoxicated. ♦ *He was so smashed he couldn't stand up.*

smashing *mod.* excellent; really tremendous. ♦ *This whole meal has been smashing.*

smear *tv.* to defeat someone; to outscore someone. ♦ *They said they would smear us, but we smeared them.*

smeared *mod.* alcohol or drug intoxicated. ♦ *I feel sort of smeared. Maybe I should have drunk less.*

smeg 1. *n.* smegma. ♦ *Smeg sounds completely disgusting.* **2.** *n.* a nasty thing, substance, or person. (Also a term of address.) ♦ *Get out of here, you smeg.*

smell a rat *tv.* to suspect that something is wrong. ♦ *Keep everything normal. I don't want her to smell a rat. She has never had a surprise party before.*

smell blood *tv.* to be ready for a fight; to be ready to attack; to be ready to act. (Like sharks, which are sent into a frenzy by the smell of blood.) ♦ *Lefty was surrounded, and you could tell that the guys from the other gang smelled blood.*

smell fishy *in.* to seem suspicious. (See also fishy.) ♦ *Marlowe squinted a bit. Something smells fishy here, he thought.*

smell it up AND **smell the stuff** *tv.* to sniff or snort powdered drugs, usually cocaine. (Drugs.) ♦ *One of those guys shoots it; the other smells it up.* ♦ *The addict put the powder in a narrow row in order to "smell the stuff."*

smell like a rose *in.* to seem innocent. ♦ *I came out of the whole mess smelling like a rose, even though I caused all the trouble.*

smell the stuff Go to smell it up.

smell to (high) heaven 1. *in.* to smell very bad. ♦ *This kitchen smells to high heaven. What besides garlic are you cooking?* **2.** *in.* to give signals that cause suspicion. ♦ *Something's wrong here. Somebody blabbed. This setup smells to high heaven.*

smeller *n.* (one's) nose. ♦ *I think my smeller's gone bad because of my cold.*

smidgen ['smɪdʒn̩] *n.* a tiny bit. ♦ *Oh, come on, more than a smidgen. Just a little?*

smile AND **smiler; smiley** *n.* a drink of liquor; liquor. ♦ *Come over and join me for a smiley.*

Smile when you say that. *sent.* Give some sort of a signal that you are only joking when you say something potentially offensive. ♦ *I told him he'd better smile when he says that, or he's going to get in trouble.*

smiler Go to smile.

Smiley 1. *n.* a circular, smiling yellow face. (The face appears in many forms: stick-on labels, pin-on buttons, hand-drawn, etc. It is possible to re-create the smiling face on any keyboard through the use of the punctuation symbols, as with :) or :-). All computer Smileys and their variants appear sideways. A major variant is the *Unsmiley,* which is basically :(or :-(. The following faces are a sample of the variants that can be seen in computer forum or news group messages and informal typewriter or word processed notes. This type of symbol is called an *emoticon* because it is intended to show *emotion* in what is otherwise a rather cold medium of communication. The typical use is to show that the writer is just joking or writing in good, well-intentioned spirits. Recently, more complex graphics have allowed actual smiley face versions of many of these variants to be inserted into the text. The following Smileys are separated by slashes, and an equal sign separates the actual Smiley from its explanation.) :-] = Squarejaw Smiley / :-o = Singing Smiley; Shocked Smiley; Surprised Smiley / :-(= Sad Smiley / :-) = Happy Smiley / : -=) = Smiley with a Big Mustache / :-)' = Drooling Smiley; Smoking Smiley / :-)8 = Smiley Wearing a Bow Tie / :-D = Big-mouth Smiley / :-# = Smiley with Sealed Lips / :-* = Pursed-lips Smiley; Shocked Smiley / :-s = Twisted-mouth Smiley (after hearing or saying something strange) / :-" = Smiley with Walrus Mustache / :-| = Smiley Making Dull Response; "Have-a-dull-day" Smiley / :-> = Wry-faced Smiley / :-0 = Loud-mouth Smiley; Big-mouth Smiley / :-x = Sealed-lips Smiley / :-Q = Smoking Smiley; Drooling Smiley / :> = Midget Smiley / ;-) = Winking Smiley / (-) = Smiley Needing a Haircut / ":-) Smiley with its Hair Parted in the Middle / +:-) Smiley Priest / *-(= Smiley Cyclops, Poked in the Eye / *:o) Bozo Smiley / <:I = Dunce Smiley / @-) = Cyclops Smiley / @:I = Smiley Wearing a Turban / |-) = Gleeful Smiley / |-| = Sleeping Smiley; Bored Smiley / 0-) = Smiley Wearing a Scuba Mask / 8-) = Smiley in Glasses / 8:-) A Smiley with Glasses on its Forehead / B-) = Smiley Wearing Horn-rim Glasses / o-) = Cyclops Smiley / [:-) = Smiley Happily Listening to a Walkman / [:|] = Robot Smiley; Squarejaw Smiley Listening to a Walkman. **2.** Go to smile.

smoke 1. *n.* a tobacco cigarette; a pipe of tobacco; a cigar. ♦ *I think I'll have a smoke now.* **2.** *n.* the act of smoking anything smokable, including drugs. ♦ *I need a smoke—of anything.* ♦ *I'm going to stop here for a smoke.* **3.** *n.* methyl alcohol; bad liquor; any liquor. ♦ *They call it smoke because when you mix it with water and shake it, it's cloudy.* **4.** *n.* exaggeration; deception. (See also blow smoke; smoke and mirrors.) ♦ *If the smoke is too obvious, they'll just get suspicious.* **5.** *tv.* to annihilate someone; to shoot someone. (Underworld.) ♦ *Rocko tried time and time again to smoke Marlowe, always without success.* **6.** *tv.* to beat someone in a contest; to outrun, outdistance, or outplay someone. ♦ *Jill smoked Dave in the bicycle race.*

smoke and mirrors *n.* a strategy of deception and cover up. ♦ *Her entire report was nothing but smoke and mirrors. Who could believe any of it?*

smoke both ends of the cigar *tv.* to perform male to male fellatio. ♦ *I think they're smoking both ends of the cigar.*

smoke eater *n.* a firefighter. ♦ *A couple of off-duty smoke eaters wandered around the store doing a little shopping.*

smoke like a chimney *in.* to smoke a great deal of tobacco or other smokable substances. ♦ *Somebody who smokes like a chimney in a restaurant ought to be thrown out.*

smoke-filled room *n.* a room where a small group of people make important decisions. (Usually used in reference to political parties.) ♦ *The smoke-filled rooms are still producing the candidates for most offices, even as we approach the year 2000.*

smoke-in *n.* a young people's public gathering of the 1960s where marijuana was smoked in open defiance of the law. ♦ *My uncle was at a smoke-in. He says the reporters were getting kids to pose for shots.*

Smokey (the Bear) *n.* a highway patrol officer; a police officer. (Citizens band radio. See also bear, lady bear.) ♦ *A Smokey was hiding behind a billboard!*

smokin' ['smokən] *mod.* excellent; really hot; overpowering. ♦ *If you wanna hear some smokin' vinyl, just stay tuned.*

smoking gun *n.* the indisputable sign of guilt. ♦ *The chief of staff decided that the admiral should be found with the smoking gun.*

smooch [smutʃ] **1.** *in.* to kiss and neck. ♦ *Too much smooching in a movie ruins it for me.* **2.** *n.* a kiss. ♦ *I like a good smooch from my hubby.*

smooth operator AND **smoothie** *n.* a clever and quiet person, especially in reference to romantic involvement; a seducer. ♦ *He thinks he's such a smooth operator!* ♦ *Clare is an old smoothie till she thinks she's got everything the way she wants. Then you see the real Clare.*

smoothie Go to smooth operator.

smurf [sməf] **1.** *n.* someone who "cleans" ill-gotten money by buying cashier's checks at banks and shifting funds from place to place, often in small transactions. (Underworld. From the name of a type of cartoon character. See also **greenwash, launder**.) ♦ *I think the guy at the first window is a smurf. He's in here twice a week with $9,500 in cash each time.* **2.** *tv. & in.* to shift illicit money from place to place to conceal its origin, often in small transactions. (Underworld.) ♦ *I smurfed a fortune for a famous drug kingpin and got fourteen years up the river—with some very interesting people.*

smurfbrain ['smɚfbren] *n.* a simple-minded person. (A smurf is an innocent little cartoon character.) ♦ *You can be such a smurfbrain!*

smurfed [smɚft] *mod.* having to do with a bank that has been used to launder money. (See also **smurf**.) ♦ *The teller came slowly into the office. "I think we were smurfed," she said.*

snafu [snæ'fu] *n.* an accident; a foul-up. (Acronym. From *situation normal, all fouled (fucked) up*. Also capitalized.) ♦ *What a snafu! All the power went off when you turned on the coffeepot.*

snag 1. *n.* a difficulty. ♦ *There's a little snag in our plan.* **2.** *n.* an ugly (young) woman. ♦ *Who's the snag your brother is running around with?* **3.** AND **SNAG** *n.* a Sensitive New-Age Guy. ♦ *There were only snags and bimbos at the rally, so I left.* **4.** *tv.* to procure, grab, or steal something. ♦ *See if you can snag a couple of good seats while I get the popcorn.*

snail-mail *n.* post office mail; regular mail as opposed to electronic mail. (Refers to the slowness of regular mail in comparison to electronic mail or faxes.) ♦ *There are lots of color pictures in the article, so I will send you the original by snail-mail.*

snake 1. *in.* to scheme; to plot and plan. (Prisons.) ♦ *He spent a lot of time snaking about that job.* **2.** *tv.* to steal something. ♦ *Where did you snake that bike?*

snake eyes *n.* the two in dice, one spot on each die. ♦ *The baby needs shoes, and all I get is snake eyes.*

snake in the grass *n.* a sneaky and despised person. ♦ *How could I ever have trusted that snake in the grass?*

snakebite medicine *n.* inferior whiskey; strong whiskey; homemade whiskey. ♦ *Snakebite medicine is a tremendous protection against snakebites if you can get the snake to drink the stuff before it tries to bite you.*

snap 1. *n.* a snapshot. ♦ *I got some good snaps of the fish you caught.* **2.** *in.* to go crazy. ♦ *His mind snapped, and he's never been right since.* **3.** a **snap** *n.* an easy thing to do. (Always with *a* in this sense.) ♦ *Nothing to it. It's a snap.*

Snap! *exclam.* Wow! ♦ *Snap! Great idea!*

snap course *n.* an easy course (in school). ♦ *I took a snap course in algebra and flunked it.*

Snap it up! *exclam.* Hurry up! ♦ *Come on, snap it up! I don't have all day.*

snap one's **cookies** *tv.* to vomit; to regurgitate. ♦ *Some jerk snapped his cookies on the sidewalk.*

snap out of sth *in.* to recover from something. ♦ *It was an emotional blow, but he'll snap out of it in a while.*

snap sth **up** *tv.* to buy up something. (See also **snapped (up)**.) ♦ *The customers snapped up all the humidifiers on the second day of the cold spell.*

snap to (attention) *in.* to come to attention; to look alert immediately. ♦ *When they realized what was happening, they began to snap to.*

Snap to it! *exclam.* Get busy! ♦ *Snap to it! We've got lots to do.*

snapped (up) 1. *mod.* alcohol intoxicated. ♦ *Pete was snapped up by eight-thirty.* **2.** *mod.* arrested. ♦ *The bacon busted the joint and snapped everybody in sight.*

snapper *n.* a strange person. ♦ *Willy is sort of a snapper, but he's a nice guy.*

snappers *n.* the teeth. (Folksy.) ♦ *I couldn't talk to you on the phone till I got my snappers in.*

snappy 1. *mod.* quick. ♦ *You can get there if you're snappy.* **2.** *mod.* sharp-looking. ♦ *Who's driving that snappy car over there?*

snatch 1. *tv.* to kidnap someone. (Underworld.) ♦ *We're gonna snatch the kid when the baby-sitter comes out to see what happened.* **2.** *n.* a kidnapping. (Underworld.) ♦ *The Bradley snatch had the detectives up all night for weeks.* **3.** *tv.* to grab something; to steal something. ♦ *Snatch me the paper there on the table as you walk by, would you please?* **4.** *n.* a theft. (Underworld.) ♦ *The snatch went off without a hitch except that the safe was empty.* **5.** *n.* women considered as a receptacle for the penis. (Rude and derogatory.) ♦ *The sailor walked around the port, looking for some snatch.*

snatched *mod.* arrested. ♦ *Everybody in the crack house got snatched in the bust.*

snatcher *n.* a police officer; a detective. (Underworld.) ♦ *One of the local snatchers came around to see if the door was locked.*

snaved in [snevd...] *mod.* drug intoxicated. ♦ *By midnight they were so snaved in they couldn't walk.*

snazz AND **shnazz** [snæz AND ʃnæz] *n.* class; glitter and excitement. ♦ *The curtain opened on a dazzling display of snazz and bright lights.*

snazz sth **up** *tv.* to make something classy or exciting. ♦ *Come on, let's try to snazz this up.*

snazzy AND **shnazzy** ['snæzi AND 'ʃnæzi] *mod.* elegant; classy. ♦ *This is a snazzy place all right.*

sneak *n.* a sneak preview of a movie. ♦ *There was a good sneak at the Granada last night.*

sneaks *n.* sneakers. ♦ *She wore red sneaks and a mini.*

sneaky *mod.* unfair and sly. ♦ *Jerry is sneaky. Don't trust him.*

snide remark *n.* a caustic, haughty, or insulting remark. ♦ *You're really quick with the snide remark. Ever say anything nice to anybody?*

sniff *n.* a drink of liquor. (See also snort.) ♦ *I'd like just a sniff of that Scotch.*

snipe *n.* a cigarette or cigar butt. ♦ *Down on skid row, a snipe won't be on the sidewalk for ten seconds.*

snit [snɪt] *n.* a state of resentment. ♦ *Don't work yourself into such a snit.*

snitch [snɪtʃ] **1.** *n.* an informer. ♦ *Who needs a snitch? If he can't keep his mouth shut, he can beat it.* **2.** *in.* to inform (on someone). (Often with *on*.) ♦ *The cops were waiting for us. Who snitched?* **3.** *tv.* to steal something. ♦ *Why don't you snitch the salt from one of the other tables?* **4.** *n.* a theft. (Underworld.) ♦ *The snitch went off without a hitch.*

snitcher ['snɪtʃɚ] *n.* an informer. (Originally underworld.) ♦ *Clare is a snitcher. Watch what you say around her.*

snitzy ['snɪtsi] *mod.* classy; ritzy. ♦ *This is a pretty snitzy place—tablecloths and everything.* ♦ *Tiffany is too snitzy for me.*

snoggered Go to schnockered.

snookered ['snʊkɚd] *mod.* cheated; deceived. ♦ *I was snookered skillfully and quickly. It was almost a pleasure.*

snookums ['snʊkəmz OR 'snukəmz] *n.* a nickname for a child or a lover. (Also a term of address.) ♦ *Now, now, snookums, it's all right.*

snoop 1. *in.* to prowl around looking for something. ♦ *What are you snooping around here for?* **2.** *n.* someone who prowls around looking for something. ♦ *Fred is just a snoop. He went through my desk!*

snoot [snut] *n.* the nose. ♦ *That's one fine zit you got on your snoot.*

snooted ['snudəd] *mod.* alcohol intoxicated. ♦ *He got himself thoroughly snooted.*

snooty *mod.* haughty; conceited. (As if looking down one's nose = snoot, at someone. Alludes also to having one's nose in the air meaning haughtiness.) ♦ *Tiffany can be snooty if she wants to, and she usually wants to.*

snoozamorooed ['snuzəmə'rud] *mod.* alcohol intoxicated. ♦ *The groom went and* *got himself snoozamorooed before the wedding.*

snooze [snuz] **1.** *in.* to sleep; to take a little nap. ♦ *I snoozed a little bit before the party.* **2.** *n.* a little nap. ♦ *Why not go up and take a little snooze?* **3.** *n.* something that is boring enough to put someone to sleep. ♦ *The play was a snooze. I left before it was over.*

snork [snork] *in.* to smoke marijuana or hashish. (Drugs.) ♦ *They snorked until they could snork no more.*

snort 1. *tv. & in.* to sniff (insufflate) a powdered drug, now usually cocaine. (Drugs.) ♦ *Here, snort this.* **2.** *n.* a nasal dose of a drug, usually cocaine. ♦ *I don't want a snort. I'm clean, and I'm going to stay that way.*

snot 1. *n.* nasal mucus. (Crude.) ♦ *He sneezed and got snot all over the newspaper.* **2.** *n.* a nasty person; an obnoxious person. (Rude and derogatory.) ♦ *You needn't be such a snot about it.*

snotnose(d) kid AND **snotnose** *n.* a young child; a relatively young person. (Rude and derogatory.) ♦ *Some little snotnose swiped my wallet.*

snotrag *n.* a handkerchief. (Usually objectionable.) ♦ *Don't you carry a snotrag?*

snotted *mod.* very drunk. ♦ *Wilbur gets totally snotted almost every night.*

snotty AND **snottie** ['snɑdi] **1.** *mod.* nasty with nasal mucus. (Usually objectionable.) ♦ *Don't leave your snotty tissues all over the house!* **2.** *mod.* bitchy; rude. (Usually objectionable.) ♦ *Now, there's no reason to get snottie with me.*

snow 1. *n.* deceitful talk; deception. ♦ *All I heard for an hour was snow. Now, what's the truth?* **2.** *tv.* to attempt to deceive someone. (See also **snowed**.) ♦ *You can try to snow me if you want, but I'm onto your tricks.* **3.** AND **snowball; snowflakes; snow stuff** *n.* a powdered or crystalline narcotic: morphine, heroin, or cocaine. (Now almost always the latter.) ♦ *The price of snow stuff has come down a lot as South America exports more of it.*

snow bunny 1. *n.* someone learning to ski. ♦ *Most of the snow bunnies come here to socialize.* **2.** *n.* a female skier. ♦ *This place is swarming with snow bunnies who have never even seen a ski.* **3.** *n.* a cocaine user. ♦ *How can these suburban snow bunnies afford such big habits?*

snow job *n.* a systematic deception. ♦ *You can generally tell when a student is trying to do a snow job.*

snow stuff Go to **snow**.

snowball 1. *in.* to grow at an increasing rate. (As a snowball rolling down a hill might increase in size.) ♦ *Offers to help with money and prayers began to snowball, and we had to get volunteers to help answer the phones.* **2.** Go to **snow**.

snowball's chance in hell *n.* a very poor chance. (Usually in the negative.) ♦ *She doesn't have a snowball's chance in hell of getting it done on time.*

snowed *mod.* deceived. ♦ *He was one snowed coach. He still doesn't know what really happened.*

snowflakes Go to **snow**.

snozzled ['snɑzl̩d] *mod.* alcohol intoxicated. ♦ *How can anybody be so snozzled on four beers?*

snozzle-wobbles ['snɑzl̩'wɑbl̩z] *n.* a hangover; the delirium tremens. ♦ *Freddy had the snozzle-wobbles this morning. He has no idea what caused it.*

snuff film *n.* a film that records an actual death or killing. ♦ *Some of these snuff films have a loyal following of real sickies.*

snuff it *tv.* to die. ♦ *The cat leapt straight up in the air and snuffed it.*

snuff SO **(out)** *tv.* to kill someone. ♦ *Max really wanted to snuff the eyewitness out, once and for all.*

snuffy ['snəfi] *mod.* alcohol intoxicated. ♦ *Who's the snuffy little guy in the corner booth?*

so *mod.* very. (An intensifier that can appear before prepositional phrases and other selected adjectives that typically are not intensified.) ♦ *I was so toasted that I said, "I'm so out of here!"*

so bad one **can taste it** *mod.* very much, indeed. ♦ *He had to get to Philadelphia so bad he could taste it.*

So gross! *exclam.* How disgusting! (California.) ♦ *He put chocolate syrup on his pie! So gross!*

so last year *n.* outdated. ♦ *That outfit is so last year!*

So long. *interj.* Good-bye. ♦ *It's been good talking to you. So long.*

So much for that. *sent.* That is all for that. (Also in other variants as in the examples.) ♦ *It's gone, ruined, broken—so much for that.* ♦ *He's finished as a friend of mine. So much for him!*

so or sth **from hell** *n.* someone or something very intense, annoying, or challenging. (As if the person or thing were a demon from hell.) ♦ *I just came back from a cruise from hell and have lots of horror stories to tell about the trip.*

so's ass is grass *phr.* Someone has had it.; It is the end for someone. (Usually objectionable.) ♦ *You do that again, and your ass is grass!*

So's your old man! *exclam.* The same to you!; Drop dead! (Indicates basic disagreement or hostility.) ♦ BILL: *You're acting like an idiot!* TOM: *So's your old man!* ♦ *I don't know what you said, but so's your old man!*

(So,) sue me! *tv.* So, if you are so bothered or offended, take me into court and sue me. (A way of saying *There is nothing you can do about it.*) ♦ *You don't like the way I talk? So, sue me!*

soak 1. *in.* to drink heavily; to get drunk. (See also **soaked**.) ♦ *The two old ladies put on their coats and went out to soak.* **2.** *n.* a drinking bout. ♦ *Both guys declined to go out and stayed home and enjoyed a soak in front of the TV.* **3.** *n.* a drunkard. ♦ *Some old soak lay moaning in the gutter.* **4.** *tv.* to overcharge someone; to extort money from someone. ♦ *They soaked me for twenty dollars for the parts, but at least it runs now.*

soak one's **face** *tv.* to drink heavily. ♦ *They're down at the tavern soaking their faces.*

soaked *mod.* alcohol intoxicated. ♦ *All the guys came home soaked.*

soaker *n.* a drunkard; a tippler. ♦ *Uncle Charlie was a soaker, and the family never realized it.*

so-and-so *n.* a euphemistic way of addressing someone with an insulting term of address. (This is usually euphemistic for *son of a bitch.* However, it is also used for good friends, especially male to male, to show affection.) ♦ *This lousy so-and-so tried to take me for 400 bucks.*

soap *n.* a soap opera. ♦ *Soaps are very popular on college campuses these days.*

SOB *n.* a *son of a bitch*; a despised person, usually a male. (Initialism only. Crude. Also a rude and provocative term of address.) ♦ *Tell that SOB to mind his own business.*

sob sister *n.* a weak woman who is prone to crying. ♦ *I had another sob sister in the office today. Went through half a box of tissues.*

sob story *n.* a sad story that is likely to draw tears. ♦ *I've heard nothing but sob stories today. Isn't anybody happy?*

sober as a judge Go to (as) sober as a judge.

sober up *in.* to recover from alcohol or drug intoxication. ♦ *Marlowe had one hour to sober up and get to the station.*

sobersides *n.* a very serious person; a grumpy old man. ♦ *Old sobersides can't manage to laugh at anything.*

sock *tv.* to punch someone or something. ♦ *He socked the door with his fist and began to howl with pain.*

sock hop *n.* a dance party where everyone dances in stocking feet. (From the 1950s.) ♦ *Sock hops were popular in schools that had expensive wooden floors in their gymnasiums.*

Sock it to me! *exclam.* Come on, let me have it! (Refers to bad news.) ♦ *Come on! I can take it. Sock it to me!*

socked *mod.* alcohol intoxicated. ♦ *She got socked out of her mind.*

socked in *mod.* fogged in. ♦ *We couldn't take off because we were socked in.*

sofa spud ['sofə 'spəd] *n.* someone who spends a great deal of time sitting and watching television. (A play on couch potato.) ♦ *Sofa spuds have been getting a lot of attention in the newspapers.*

soft 1. *mod.* alcohol intoxicated. ♦ *After a few hours at the party, it appeared that most people were getting soft.* **2.** *mod.* having to do with nonaddictive drugs. (Compare this with hard.) ♦ *The "soft stuff" just leads to really bad stuff.* **3.** *mod.* stupid. ♦ *The guy's soft in the head. He just can't think straight.*

soft berth *n.* an easy situation; employment at an easy job. ♦ *I hope I can arrange a soft berth for my brother, who just applied for a job here.*

soft core 1. *mod.* referring to a mild type of pornography. ♦ *Now even the soft core stuff is getting harder to find at newsstands.* **2.** *n.* mild pornography. ♦ *They keep some soft core under the counter.*

soft in the head *mod.* stupid; witless. ♦ *George is just soft in the head. He'll never get away with his little plan.*

soft money *n.* easy money; money obtained without much effort. ♦ *There's not even very much soft money around now.*

soft on so *mod.* romantically attracted to someone. ♦ *He looked like he was getting a little soft on Sally.*

soft on so or sth *mod.* too easy on someone or something. ♦ *The judge was viewed as being too soft on pushers.*

soft pedal sth *tv.* to play something down; to de-emphasize something. (Refers to the soft pedal on the piano.) ♦ *Try to soft pedal the problems we have with the cooling system.*

soft sell *n.* a polite attempt to sell something; a very gentle sales pitch. ♦ *Some people won't bother listening to a soft sell. You gotta let them know you believe in what you are selling.*

soft soap 1. *n.* flattering talk; sweet talk. ♦ *I don't mind a little soft soap. It won't affect what I do, though.* **2.** *tv.* to attempt to convince someone (of something) by gentle persuasion. ♦ *Don't try to soft soap her. She's an old battle-ax.*

soft touch 1. *n.* a gentle way of handling someone or something. ♦ *Kelly lacks the kind of soft touch needed for this kind of negotiation.* **2.** *n.* a gullible person; a likely victim of a scheme. ♦ *John is a soft touch for a few bucks.*

soft-core 1. *mod.* [of pornography] less revealing or realistic than real life; not showing genitals. ♦ *They are showing a lot of soft-core stuff on cable and most of the soap operas.* **2.** *mod.* less intense or extreme than hard-core. *She had a soft-core approach to portraying suffering.*

softie AND **softy 1.** *n.* a gentle person; a very agreeable person. ♦ *He shouldn't give you much trouble. He's such a softie.* **2.** *n.* a weakling; a coward. ♦ *He's too much of a softie to fight back.*

software rot *n.* an imaginary disease that causes computer programs to go bad over a long period of time. (Computers.) ♦ *What you have here is not a bug, but just plain old software rot.*

softy Go to softie.

soggy ['sɑgi] *mod.* alcohol intoxicated. ♦ *They weren't sopping wet, just soggy.*

SOL Go to shit out of luck.

sold cober ['sold 'kobɚ] *mod.* sober. (A deliberate spoonerism on cold sober. Similar to jober as a sudge.) ♦ *What do you mean drunk? Why, I'm sold cober.*

sold on so or sth *mod.* convinced of the value of someone or something. ♦ *The crowd was sold on Gary. Nothing he had done or could do would cool their enthusiasm.*

soldier 1. *n.* a liquor bottle; an empty liquor bottle. (See also dead soldier.) ♦ *Toss your soldier into the garbage, please.* **2.** *n.* a whole tobacco cigarette. ♦ *The old man almost fell over trying to pick up the soldier from the sidewalk.*

soldier rag *n.* a cap to cover a hairdo. ♦ *The mugger was wearing a soldier rag and threatened me with a gun.*

solid 1. *mod.* good; great; cool. ♦ *Listen to that solid beat.* **2.** *mod.* consecutive; consecutively. ♦ *Then he "had the flu" for three days solid.*

some pumpkins AND **some punkins** *n.* someone or something great or special. ♦ *That chick is some punkins!*

some punkins Go to some pumpkins.

a **somebody** *n.* an important person. (Compare this with nobody.) ♦ *Aren't you a somebody?*

Somebody died in here! Go to Who died in here?

Something's got to give. *sent.* Things cannot go on like this.; The stalemate will be broken. ♦ *The pressure on me is getting to be too much. Something's got to give.*

son of a bitch 1. *n.* a despicable person, usually a male. (Rude and derogatory. Abbreviated SOB.) ♦ *Tell that son of a bitch to get out of here, but fast.* **2.** *n.* old buddy. (Used between close male companions.) ♦ *Where you been keeping yourself, you son of a bitch?* **3.** *exclam.* Dammit! (Usually objectionable. Usually **Son of a bitch!**) ♦ *Son of a bitch! I didn't even see that car pull out.*

son of a gun 1. *n.* a despicable person, usually a male. (Euphemistic for son of a bitch.) ♦ *If that son of a gun thinks he can boss me around like that, he's got another think coming.* **2.** *n.* old buddy. ♦ *I went to school with this son of a gun! He's my old buddy.* **3.** *exclam.* I am totally surprised!; I am shocked! (Usually **Son of a gun!**) ♦ *The thing just blew up! Son of a gun!*

sop 1. *n.* a drunkard; an alcoholic. ♦ *Give the old sop a buck and tell him to beat it.* **2.** *tv. & in.* to guzzle (liquor). ♦ *You've sopped booze long enough. Go home.*

soph [sɔf] *n.* a sophomore. ♦ *He's just a soph, so he still might grow a little.*

sopping (wet) AND **soppy** *mod.* alcohol intoxicated. (See also wet.) ♦ *After about six beers, Ralph found himself a little soppy.*

soppy Go to sopping (wet).

sore *mod.* angry. ♦ *She is one sore old lady. You should give her teeth back.*

sorehead 1. *n.* a grumpy person. (Also a term of address.) ♦ *She's sort of a sorehead right now. Wait a day or two and then ask her.* **2.** *n.* a poor loser. ♦ *Don't be a sorehead. You knew what you're getting into.*

sorry AND **pathetic** *mod.* pitiful; drawing ridicule or scorn; worthy more of condemnation than pity. (In colloquial use these words are usually used in sarcasm and disgust.) ♦ *You are one sorry bastard!* ♦ *You are a pathetic person and a pathetic example of a quarterback!*

sorry about that AND **sorry 'bout that** *interj.* sorry; whoops. (A gross understatement, said more as a self-deprecating joke than as an apology.) ♦ *When the passenger stepped on my toe, she said, "Sorry about that."*

sorry 'bout that Go to sorry about that.

sorry-ass(ed) 1. *mod.* sad and depressed. (Usually objectionable.) ♦ *Man, old Charlie was about the most sorry-ass dude you ever saw.* **2.** *mod.* worthless; poor quality. (Usually objectionable.) ♦ *How much longer do I have to drive this sorry-ass excuse for an automobile?*

sosh [sɔʃ] *n.* a (young female) socialite. ♦ *Tiffany looks like a sosh, but she's just a working girl.*

so-so 1. *mod.* average; mediocre. ♦ *It was just so-so. Nothing to write home about.* **2.** *mod.* tipsy; alcohol intoxicated. ♦ *They were so-so after a while—in front of the television with all that beer and stuff.* ♦ *He's so-so, but he can still stand up.*

SOSO Go to same o(l)' same o(l)'

sossled Go to sozzled.

(soul) brother *n.* a black person's male, black friend. ♦ *Another brother took a fall last night.*

soul kiss 1. *n.* a kiss where the kissers' tongues interact; a French kiss. ♦ *Yes, a soul kiss sounds silly—till you try it with some-*

body you really like. **2.** *in.* [for two peo-ple] to kiss with interacting tongues. ♦ *The creep had bad breath and wanted to soul kiss!*

(soul) sister *n.* a black person's female, black friend. (See also **sister.**) ♦ *One of the soul sisters dropped by to talk.*

sound off (about sth**) 1.** *in.* to complain about something; to gripe about some-thing. ♦ *You are always sounding off about something that gripes your soul.* **2.** *in.* to speak out of turn about something. ♦ *Who asked you to sound off about this?* **3.** *in.* to announce something. ♦ *Why did you have to go and sound off about the surprise party?*

sounds *n.* music; records. ♦ *I got some new sounds. Ya wanna come over and listen?*

Sounds like a winner! *sent.* It sounds ac-ceptable. ♦ *Sounds like a winner! Let's do it!*

soup *n.* nitroglycerin, a liquid explosive. (Underworld.) ♦ *Lefty was a master with the soup till he blew off his hand.*

Soup's on! *in.* Dinner is ready. ♦ *Time to eat! Soup's on!*

soup sandwich *n.* something impossibly messy or impossible to deal with. ♦ *This whole project is just a soup sandwich. I'll never get it straightened out.*

soup sth **up** *tv.* to increase the power of something. (See also **souped up.**) ♦ *If only I could soup up this computer to run just a little faster.*

souped up *mod.* made more powerful. ♦ *Why do all cars driven by males under the age of twenty have to be souped up?*

soup-strainer *n.* a mustache. ♦ *Jerry had a big bushy soup-strainer that he was very proud of.*

soupy ['supi] *mod.* alcohol intoxicated; drunk and vomiting. ♦ *These young kids tend to get soupy rather than pass out.*

sourpuss ['saʊɚpʊs] *n.* a grouchy or frowning person. (See also **picklepuss.**) ♦ *What a sourpuss! He makes King Kong look sweet.*

souse [saʊs] **1.** *in.* to drink excessively; to go on a drinking bout; to get drunk. (From a word meaning "to soak or pickle." See also **soused.**) ♦ *Let us retire from the table and souse in the parlor.* **2.** *n.* a drinking bout. ♦ *The souse lasted longer than anyone would have thought.* **3.** *n.* a drunkard. ♦ *The best thing you can do for a souse like John is to take away his car keys.*

soused *mod.* alcohol intoxicated. (See also **souse.**) ♦ *All we need right now is a soused bus driver.*

southern-fried *mod.* alcohol intoxicated. (An elaboration of **fried,** referring to *fried chicken.*) ♦ *When Bob came home southern-fried, his wife nearly killed him.*

southpaw *n.* a left-handed person. ♦ *My sister is a southpaw, but I'm not.*

sozzle ['sazl̩] *in.* to drink to excess. (See also **sozzled; sozzler.**) ♦ *The guys are soz-zling over at John's place.*

sozzled AND **sossled; sozzly** ['sazl̩d AND 'sazl̩d, 'sazli] *mod.* alcohol intoxicated. ♦ *She was so sozzly she didn't even know her name, or my name, or anybody's name.*

sozzler ['sazlɚ] *n.* a drunkard. ♦ *The sozzler leaned against the tavern window. I thought he would break it.*

sozzly Go to **sozzled.**

space Go to **space out.**

space cadet 1. *n.* a person who is always silly or giddy. ♦ *Here comes a space cadet who looks like he has more money than he needs.* **2.** *n.* a person who is always high on drugs. ♦ *The space cadets can usually be found sitting on a bench outside the principal's office.*

space out 1. *n.* a giddy person. (Usually **space-out.**) ♦ *Terry is becoming such a space-out!* **2.** AND **space** *in.* to become giddy; to become disoriented. ♦ *She is spacing again. She doesn't even know where she is.*

space so **out** *tv.* to cause someone to be-come giddy. ♦ *The whole business just spaced me out.*

spaced (out) AND **spacy** *mod.* silly; giddy. ♦ *I have such spaced out parents!*

spacy Go to spaced (out).

spam 1. *n.* something disliked, typically, but not necessarily, food. (From the brand name of a canned meat product.) ♦ *I can't eat this "spam." It could be spoiled.* **2.** *n.* one or a series of uninvited email messages advertising money-making schemes, pornography, or sales of any kind. ♦ *If I don't recognize the sender, I assume the message is spam and I delete it.* **3.** *tv.* to clutter or fill someone's email account with spam (sense 2). ♦ *Some jerk is spamming me with an advertisement for dirty pictures.*

spanked *n.* drunk. ♦ *Those gals are spanked. Who served them all that booze?*

spanking new Go to (brand) spanking new.

spare tire 1. *n.* a thickness in the waist; a roll of fat around one's waist. ♦ *The spare tire started when I was twenty-six.* **2.** *n.* an unneeded person; an unproductive person. ♦ *Gary is a spare tire. Send him home.*

sparkler *n.* a diamond; gemstones. ♦ *Look at the sparklers on that old dame.*

spastic *mod.* overly responsive; out of control. ♦ *She can get so spastic when I come in late.*

spaz [spæz] **1.** *n.* a fit or an attack; a strong reaction to a bad or funny situation. ♦ *Take it easy! Don't have a spaz.* **2.** *n.* a total jerk; someone who overreacts to something. (Not used for a congenitally spastic condition.) ♦ *Some spaz is in the other room screaming about a stolen car.*

spaz around *in.* to waste time; to mess around. ♦ *You kids are always spazzing around. Why don't you get a job?*

spaz down *in.* to relax. ♦ *We tried to get the crowd to spaz down, but they were very excited.*

spaz out 1. *in.* to overreact to something; to become overly excited about something. ♦ *I knew you would spaz out! It's not that bad!* **2.** *n.* an emotional display. (Usually **spaz-out.**) ♦ *She threw a hell of a spaz-out.*

Speak it! *exclam.* Say it!; You said it!; That's telling them! ♦ *Speak it, girlfriend! Tell him off!*

speak of the devil *in.* said when someone whose name has just been mentioned appears or is heard from. (Cliché.) ♦ *And speak of the devil, here's Ted now.*

speak so's **language** *tv.* to say something that one agrees with or understands. ♦ *I gotcha. Now you're speaking my language.*

specs [spɛks] *n.* eyeglasses; spectacles. ♦ *I need specs to find where I left my specs.*

speed 1. *n.* methamphetamine; amphetamine in general. (Drugs.) ♦ *Kids think that speed won't get them into trouble.* **2.** *in.* to use methamphetamine; to be high on methamphetamine or amphetamine. (Drugs.) ♦ *Kids who speed think it is a harmless blow-off.*

speed demon 1. *n.* a fast runner; a fast driver. ♦ *Tom is a speed demon. He qualified for the Olympics.* **2.** *n.* a habitual user of methamphetamine. (Drugs.) ♦ *When they are high, most speed demons don't know what they are doing.*

speed freak AND **speedhead** *n.* a drug user who injects methamphetamine; an amphetamine user. (Drugs and general slang.) ♦ *Speed freaks, not heroin addicts, account for a high proportion of drug-related crime.*

speed merchant *n.* someone who does something fast: a runner, pitcher, swimmer, driver, etc. ♦ *What a pitch! That guy is a speed merchant for sure.*

speedball *n.* [in baseball] a fast (pitched) ball. ♦ *The pitcher threw a speedball, and I didn't even see it!*

speeder 1. *n.* a speeding ticket. ♦ *The cop that gave Mary a speeder Wednesday gave her another one Friday.* **2.** *n.* an amphetamine or methamphetamine tablet, capsule, or ampoule. (Drugs. See also **speed.**) ♦ *Somebody dropped some speeders on the floor of the car, and my father spazzed out.* **3.** AND **speedster** *n.* a user of amphetamines or methamphetamine; a person who is hyperactive from amphetamine use. (Drugs.) ♦ *That kid is really hyped up—must be a speeder.* ♦ *The speedsters can seem crazy when they're on a run.*

speedhead Go to speed freak.

speedo 1. *n.* a speedometer. ♦ *I think my speedo is broken. It says we're standing still.* **2.** a tight-fitting swim brief, usually revealing. (From the protected trade name of the swimming suit manufacturer.) ♦ *You can't go out in public wearing that speedo! I can see everything!*

speedster Go to speeder.

spending money *n.* cash, as opposed to money in the bank. ♦ *I'm a little short of spending money at the present. Could I borrow ten dollars?*

spendy *mod.* expensive; pricey. *That brand is a little spendy, but the difference may be worth it.*

spew *in.* to empty one's stomach; to vomit. ♦ *After dinner, I suddenly had the urge to spew.*

spew one's **guts (out) 1.** *tv.* to empty one's stomach; to vomit. ♦ *Fred is spewing his guts out because of that lousy fish you served.* **2.** *tv.* to tell everything that one knows; to confess everything. (Underworld.) ♦ *Lefty was sitting there in the cop-shop spewing his guts out about the bank job.*

spiff *n.* extra money paid to a salesperson to sell certain merchandise aggressively. (See also **push money**.) ♦ *The manufacturer supplied a little spiff that even the store manager didn't know about.*

spiffed out *mod.* nicely dressed up; decked out. ♦ *I like to get all spiffed out every now and then.*

spiffed up *mod.* dressed up, brushed up, and polished up nicely. ♦ *See if you can get yourself a little spiffed up before we get to the front door. We wouldn't want the Wilmington-Thorpes to think you only have one suit.*

spifflicated AND **spificated** ['spɪf(l)əkedəd] *mod.* alcohol intoxicated.

♦ *Mrs. Wilmington-Thorpe drank champagne until she was nearly spifflicated.*

spiffy ['spɪfi] *mod.* excellent. ♦ *This is a real spiffy place you've got here, Sam.*

spificated Go to spifflicated.

spike 1. *n.* a hypodermic needle; a hypodermic syringe and needle; a medicine dropper and a needle. (Drugs.) ♦ *The addict caught some strange disease from a dirty spike.* **2.** *tv.* to add ether or alcohol to beer, originally by injecting it through the cork with a hypodermic needle; to add alcohol to a nonalcoholic drink. (From prohibition times. See also spiked.) ♦ *He spiked the beer with ether, which is a dangerous thing to do.* **3.** *tv.* to puncture an idea. ♦ *I explained the plan, but the boss spiked it immediately.*

spiked 1. *mod.* having to do with a drink with alcohol added; having to do with a punch with an alcoholic content. ♦ *Is the punch spiked? I want some without.* **2.** *mod.* alcohol or drug intoxicated. ♦ *I knew that Mrs. Wilmington-Thorpe was spiked when she belched like a real country thunder-boomer.* **3.** *mod.* having to do with hair that stands up straight. ♦ *His spiked hair wouldn't look so bad if it wasn't orange.*

spill *in.* to confess. (Underworld.) ♦ *The cops tried to get her to spill, but she just sat there.*

spill one's **guts on** so Go to spill one's guts (to so).

spill one's **guts (to so)** AND **spill** one's **guts on** so *tv.* to tell all; to confess; to pour one's heart out to someone. (See also spew one's guts (out).) ♦ *I had to spill my guts to someone about the broken window.*

spill the beans AND **spill the works** *tv.* to give away a secret or a surprise. ♦ *There is a surprise party for Heidi on Wednesday. Please don't spill the beans.* ♦ *Sorry, I didn't mean to spill the works.*

spill the works Go to spill the beans.

spin doctor *n.* someone who provides an interpretation of news or an event in a way that makes the news or event work to the advantage of the entity employing the **spin doctor**. (Usually in political contexts in reference to manipulating the news.) ♦ *Things were going bad for the president, so he got himself a new spin doctor.*

spin one's **wheels** *tv.* to waste time; to remain in a neutral position, neither advancing nor falling back. ♦ *I'm just spinning my wheels in this job. I need more training to get ahead.*

spinach *n.* money. (Because it is green. See also cabbage; lettuce.) ♦ *Look at this! One hundred dollars in good old American spinach!*

spinner *n.* a bullet. ♦ *Harry the Horse's shot sent a spinner into Lefty's gut.*

spit and polish *n.* orderliness; ceremonial precision and orderliness. (Alludes to carefully polishing shoes to a high level of shine.) ♦ *I like spit and polish. It comes from being in the military.*

Spit it out! *exclam.* Say it! ♦ *Say what you have to say and leave. Hurry up! Spit it out!*

spizzerinktum [spɪzɚ'rɪŋktəm] *n.* energy; vitality. ♦ *The kid's got spizzerinktum! I like that.*

spleef Go to spliff.

spliff AND **shpleef; spleef; splim** [splɪf AND ʃplif, splif, splɪm] *n.* marijuana; a marijuana cigarette; hashish. ♦ *They consume an enormous amount of spliff and try to sell it to the tourists.*

splim Go to spliff.

split *in.* to leave. ♦ *Look at the clock. Time to split.*

split a gut 1. *tv.* to laugh very hard. ♦ *He laughed until he nearly split a gut.* **2.** *tv.* to work very hard. ♦ *Don't split a gut for me. I love things that are falling apart.*

split up 1. *in.* to separate. ♦ *The two split up and went their separate ways.* **2.** *n.* an act of separating or breaking up. (Usually **split-up**.) ♦ *Everyone was mentally prepared for the company's split-up.*

splooge AND **spooge 1.** *n.* semen. ♦ *Clean up that splooge before somebody sees it!*

2. *in.* to ejaculate. ♦ *I almost splooged when I saw her bend over.*

splurge *in.* to indulge oneself with much spending or eating. ♦ *I have to splurge every now and then. I deserve it.*

spoil *tv.* to kill someone. ♦ *It was Joel Cairo's job to make sure that nobody got close enough to Mr. Big to spoil him.*

spoiling for a fight *in.* argumentative; asking for a fight. ♦ *They were just spoiling for a fight, and they went outside to settle the matter.*

spokes *n.* lists of jokes, sent from friends via email; joke spam. ♦ *I don't know what's worse, spokes or spam.*

spondulicks AND **spondulics; spondulix** [spɑn'dulɪks] *n.* money. ♦ *How much spondulicks will this set me back?*

spondulics Go to spondulicks.

spondulix Go to spondulicks.

sponge AND **spunge 1.** *in.* to drink heavily. ♦ *She was sponging like there was no tomorrow.* **2.** *n.* a drunkard; a tippler. (See also blotter.) ♦ *She was a sponge, and she wasn't going to do anything about it.* **3.** *n.* a parasitic person. ♦ *Here comes that sponge, Willy. Hide your wallet, pencils, glasses, and any clothes in his size.*

sponge off so *in.* to live off someone; to take advantage of someone by taking food and shelter from them without compensation. ♦ *Go get a job! Stop sponging off me!*

sponged *mod.* thirsty. ♦ *I gotta get a drink, man. I'm sponged!*

spoof [spuf] **1.** *n.* a parody. ♦ *The first act was a spoof of a Congressional investigation.* **2.** *tv.* to make a parody of someone or something. ♦ *The comedian spoofed the executive branch by sitting in a big chair and going to sleep.* **3.** Go to phish.

spoofing AND **carding; phishing 1.** *n.* stealing passwords and personal information on the internet. (See also phish for an explanation.) ♦ *He set up an evil twin for spoofing at the coffee shop.*

spooge Go to splooge.

spook 1. *tv.* to frighten or startle someone or something. (See also **spooked**.) ♦ *Something I did spooked the teller, and she set off the silent alarm.* **2.** *n.* a spy; a CIA (U.S. Central Intelligence Agency) agent. ♦ *I just learned that my uncle had been a spook for years.*

spook factory *n.* the CIA (U.S. Central Intelligence Agency) near Washington, D.C., where spies are said to be trained. ♦ *Tom got a job in the spook factory.*

spooked *mod.* frightened or startled. ♦ *The guy looked sort of spooked. He was sweating and panting like someone had scared him to death.*

spoon 1. *in.* to neck and pet. ♦ *They like to go out and spoon under the stars.* **2.** Go to **cokespoon, (flake) spoon.**

sport *n.* friend; chum. (A term of address.) ♦ *Well, sport, looks like we have a little problem here.*

spot 1. *n.* a small drink of liquor. ♦ *I'll just have a spot, please.* **2.** *n.* a nightclub; a night spot. ♦ *It was a nice little spot, with a combo and a canary.*

spot market *n.* the open market where deals are made on the spot. (Securities markets.) ♦ *Oil reached nearly fifty-five dollars a barrel on the spot market.*

spot of lunch *n.* a small amount of lunch. ♦ *How about a spot of lunch?*

spot so (sth) 1. *tv.* to give an advantage to someone. ♦ *I'll spot you twenty points.* **2.** *tv.* to lend someone something. ♦ *Can you spot me a few bucks?*

sprain one's **ankle** *tv.* to become pregnant. ♦ *From the looks of her, she must have sprained her ankle some months ago.*

spring chicken *n.* a young and naive person, especially a young woman. (Usually in the negative.) ♦ *Well, I may not be a spring chicken, but I got some spizzerinktum left.*

spring for sth AND **bounce for** sth *in.* to treat (someone) by buying something. (See also **pop for** sth.) ♦ *Can you spring for coffee? I've got a case of the shorts.* ♦ *I'm bouncing for pizza. Any takers?*

spring so *tv.* to get someone out of jail on bond or permanently. ♦ *My wife came down and sprung me; otherwise, I'd still be in the slammer.*

sprout *n.* a child. ♦ *A little sprout came up and tried to sell me a ticket to a game.*

sprout wings 1. *tv.* to die and become an angel. ♦ *I'm not ready to sprout wings yet. I've got a few more years.* **2.** *tv.* to be so good as to become an angel. ♦ *The kid is not about to sprout wings, but he probably won't get into jail again.*

spud [spəd] **1.** *n.* a potato. ♦ *Mashed spuds are the best of all.* **2.** *n.* vodka. (Presumed to be made from potatoes.) ♦ *She keeps a big jug of spud in the reefer and drinks it like water.* **3.** *n.* a vodka drunkard. ♦ *That silly spud thinks we can't smell what's on her breath.* **4.** *n.* a short person. (Also a term of address.) ♦ *He can jump pretty high for a spud.*

spunge Go to **sponge.**

spunk [spəŋk] *n.* courage. ♦ *Show some spunk. Get in there and stand up for your rights.*

spunky ['spəŋki] *mod.* gutsy; courageous. ♦ *I like a spunky girl—one who can really dance.* ♦ *The guy's a shrimp, but he's spunky.*

spyware AND **data miner** *n.* a kind of malicious software that gathers private information from a personal computer and sends it to another computer. ♦ *I have a little program that roots out spyware from my computer.* ♦ *It found a data miner lurking among my digital images.*

square 1. *mod.* old-fashioned; law-abiding; stodgy. ♦ *Man, you are really square.* **2.** *n.* a person who behaves properly. ♦ *You are a square if I ever saw one.* **3.** AND **square joint** *n.* a tobacco cigarette, compared to a marijuana cigarette. ♦ *I'll take a reefer. I've heard that square joints will give you cancer.* **4.** *tv.* to settle or to make something right. ♦ *Will twenty bucks square the matter?* **5.** Go to **square (meal).**

square apple Go to **square john.**

square biscuit *n.* a plain, drab, and dull person. ♦ *Old Roger is a square biscuit and acts like a school marm.*

square john AND **square apple** *n.* someone who obeys the rules; a square. ♦ *Fred is a square john. There's no point in worrying about him.* ♦ *I look like a square john, but I'm really quite a devil.*

square john broad *n.* an honest, straightforward woman. (Underworld.) ♦ *We need a square john broad to give this place a look of respectability.*

square joint Go to square.

square (meal) *n.* a good and nutritious meal. (Always with quantifier when **square** is used without *meal*.) ♦ *I need three squares a day—at least.* ♦ *The old soak looks like he could use a square meal.*

square off *in.* to prepare to fight; to prepare to argue or compete. ♦ *They were squaring off, so I asked them if they'd like to step outside.*

square peg (in a round hole) *n.* someone who does not fit in. ♦ *I'm a square peg in a round hole. Maybe I am meant to be eccentric.*

square shooter *n.* an honest person. (See also **straight shooter**.) ♦ *He wouldn't do anything shabby. He's a square shooter.*

square with so *in.* to become honest with someone. ♦ *I want you to square with me. Tell the truth this time.*

squared away *mod.* straightened out. ♦ *I'm not really squared away on this stuff, but I'm beginning to see the light.*

squared up *mod.* no longer taking drugs. (Drugs.) ♦ *Walter is squared up now and spends a lot of time trying to help others.*

squat 1. *in.* to sit (down). ♦ *Come on in and squat for a while.* **2.** *n.* nothing. (See also **diddly-squat**.) ♦ *I earn just a little more than squat, but I am very pleased with my life.*

squawk 1. *in.* to complain. ♦ *Some people squawk because they don't have anything else to do.* **2.** *n.* a complaint. ♦ *Here's another squawk from the lady on the third floor.* **3.** *tv. & in.* to reveal or blab something. ♦ *She squawked the whole business to the fuzz.*

squawk box *n.* a public-address system; a loudspeaker, especially if installed in a box or other housing. ♦ *A raspy voice came over the squawk box announcing the arrival of what we had been waiting for.*

squeaky clean *mod.* very clean. (Like a clean glass that squeaks when one rubs a finger on it.) ♦ *I got this floor squeaky clean. Don't spill anything on it.*

squeal *in.* to inform (someone about something). ♦ *Who squealed to the cops?*

squealer 1. *n.* an informer. (Underworld.) ♦ *Some squealer let the cops know what was going to happen.* **2.** *n.* a pig; a piglet. ♦ *They sent their squealers to market at just the right time.*

squeeze 1. *n.* liquor. (Streets. See also **grape(s)**.) ♦ *Let's stop on the way and get some squeeze.* **2.** *tv.* to put pressure on someone. ♦ *The mob began to squeeze Bart for money.* **3.** *n.* a tight situation; a situation where pressure is felt. ♦ *When the squeeze is over, we'll be able to get squared away.* **4.** *n.* one's lover. (See also **main squeeze**.) ♦ *I'll see if my squeeze wants to go.*

squeeze play *n.* a special play in baseball where there is a runner on third base and the batter bunts. (With an early start the runner may reach home plate.) ♦ *They pulled off that squeeze play like the professionals they are.*

(squeeze-)box *n.* an accordion. (See also **groan box**.) ♦ *My brother plays the squeeze-box—not very well, but who can tell?* ♦ *The band consisted of drums, clarinet, and a box. A real winner.*

squib [skʌɪb] *n.* a notice; a small advertisement. ♦ *There was a squib in the paper about your project.*

squid [skʌɪd] *n.* an earnest student; a collegiate wimp. (Collegiate. Refers to sliminess.) ♦ *This whole campus is populated by squids and nerds.*

squiff [skʌɪf] *n.* a drunkard. (See also **on the squiff**.) ♦ *Is there anything that can be done for a confirmed squiff?*

squiff out *in.* to collapse from drink. ♦ *Hank squiffed out at midnight, right on the dot.*

squiffed AND **squiffy** [skʌɪft AND 'skʌɪfi] *mod.* alcohol intoxicated. ♦ *The hostess was so squiffed she could hardly stand.*

squiffy Go to squiffed.

squiggle ['skʌɪgl̩] *n.* a wiggly mark. ♦ *That squiggle is my signature.*

squirrel 1. *n.* a strange or eccentric person. ♦ *Martin can be such a squirrel.* **2.** *n.* a car engine's horsepower. (Usually plural.) ♦ *I got 440 squirrels and a gaggle of carburetors.*

squirrel out of sth *in.* to wiggle out of something; to manage to extricate oneself from a situation one does not wish to be in. ♦ *He will do anything he can to squirrel out of going to the dance.*

squirrel sth **away** *tv.* to hide something in reserve. ♦ *Here is some food. I squirreled it away in my suitcase.*

squirrel-food *n.* a nut; a loony person. ♦ *The driver of the car—squirrel-food, for sure—just sat there smiling.* ♦ *Some squirrel-food came over and asked for a sky hook.*

squirrelly *mod.* loony. ♦ *Good old squirrelly Tom! Isn't he a wonder?*

squirt 1. *n.* a small person; a young child, especially a young boy. (Also a term of address.) ♦ *Hey, squirt, come over here.* **2.** *n.* beer or champagne. ♦ *How about a nice bubbly glass of squirt?*

the **squirts** *n.* a case of diarrhea. ♦ *He's got the squirts and can't go out.*

squooshy ['skʌʊʃi AND 'skʌʊʃi] *mod.* soft; squishy. ♦ *I like to walk barefooted in squooshy mud.*

stache Go to stash.

stack the deck *tv.* to arrange things secretly for a desired outcome. (From card playing where a cheater may arrange the order of the cards that are to be dealt to the players.) ♦ *The president stacked the deck so I would be appointed head of the finance committee.*

stacked *mod.* having to do with a person with a sexually attractive body, usually a female. ♦ *I like to see stacked dames like that starting to do business in this place.*

stag 1. *mod.* having to do with someone going to a party without a date. (Originally said of a male.) ♦ *A bunch of the guys got together and went stag to the dance.* **2.** *mod.* having to do with a gathering for men only. ♦ *The party is stag, so Tom and I are going together.*

stag line *n.* a line of dateless men at a dance. ♦ *The guys in the stag line looked so forlorn. She suddenly wanted to do something to make them all happy.*

staggers 1. *n.* liquor. ♦ *She poured herself a huge glass of staggers and mumbled something about cough medicine.* **2.** the **staggers** *n.* drunkenness; the delirium tremens. (Always with *the* in this sense.) ♦ *He seems to have a little touch of the staggers.*

stag-party *n.* a party for men only. (Thought to be raunchy.) ♦ *They hired a stripper for the stag-party—you know, the kind that jumps out of a cake.*

stake so/sth **out 1.** *tv.* to position a person so that someone or something can be observed or followed. ♦ *Marlowe staked out the apartment building and watched patiently for an hour.* **2.** *tv.* to position a person to observe someone or something. ♦ *We staked out two men to keep watch.*

stake so **to** sth **1.** *tv.* to lend or give someone money to buy something. ♦ *Stake the man to a meal and a flop, and he'll tell us what we want to know.* **2.** *tv.* to treat someone to something. ♦ *Can I stake you to a drink to celebrate?*

stakeout 1. *n.* a person who is positioned to observe someone or something. (See also **stake** so/sth **out.**) ♦ *The stakeout stuck out like a sore thumb—standing there under the streetlight reading a paper.* ♦ *The stakeout was one of Marlowe's best operatives.* **2.** *n.* a (police) assignment where someone is positioned to observe someone or something. ♦ *The stakeout at the warehouse backfired. They only found cats.*

stale drunk *n.* a long-standing and frequently renewed drunken state. ♦ *Are you on a stale drunk again, or is this the same one?*

stallion *n.* a tall, good-looking woman. ♦ *Dana is really a stallion!*

stamp so **out** *tv.* to get rid of or kill someone. (Fig. on stamp sth out.) ♦ *You just can't stamp somebody out on your own!*

stamping ground AND **stomping ground** *n.* one's favorite or customary location. ♦ *I like to go back and look at my old stamping ground every now and then.*

stand pat (on sth**)** *in.* to stick firmly to one's position or opinions. ♦ *I thought you would stand pat in the absence of new information.*

stand so **up** *tv.* to break a date by not showing up. ♦ *He stood up his date while he played basketball with the guys.*

stand tall *in.* to be brave and proud. ♦ *I can still stand tall. I'm innocent.*

stand there with one's **bare face hanging out** *in.* to stand someplace looking helpless and stupid. ♦ *Say something. Don't just stand there with your bare face hanging out.*

standee *n.* someone who must stand (at some event). ♦ *Can I get in as a standee, or do I have to wait for the next showing?*

stand-in *n.* a substitute; a temporary replacement. ♦ *The audience booed the stand-in. They had paid to hear a star.*

standoffish [stænd'ɔfɪʃ] *mod.* aloof. ♦ *Bob is sort of standoffish until he gets to know you.*

stand-out *n.* an extraordinary thing or person. ♦ *Bob is a real stand-out in our bowling league.*

stanza ['stænzə] *n.* an inning in baseball or some other division of a ball game. ♦ *He's doing better than he was in the last stanza.*

starched AND **starchy** *mod.* alcohol intoxicated. (See also stiff.) ♦ *No, he wasn't quite stiff, but he was starched.*

starchy Go to starched.

stash 1. AND **stache** *n.* a mustache. ♦ *I cut my stash off because it was too much trouble to remember not to cut it off.* **2.** *tv.* to hide something (somewhere). ♦ *Stash this under the chair until I can think of a place to put it.* **3.** *n.* a concealed supply of drugs, especially marijuana; drugs and equipment to use them stored in a secret place. (Drugs.) ♦ *Albert's stash was never located by the fuzz.*

stat [stæt] **1.** *n.* a thermostat. (See also stats.) ♦ *I'm afraid you need a new stat.* **2.** AND **STAT** *mod.* a medical notation meaning "immediately." (From Latin *statim* "immediately.") ♦ *The order is marked stat, so do it now.*

static *n.* complaints. ♦ *I don't expect any static because of the noise. I warned the neighbors about the party.*

stats [stæts] *n.* statistics. ♦ *The stats are expected to show that the trade balance is growing steadily worse.*

stay loose Go to hang loose.

Stay tuned. 1. *sent.* Stay tuned in to this radio or television station. (A formula uttered before a commercial.) ♦ *I'll be right back after these announcements. Stay tuned.* **2.** *sent.* Continue to pay attention to this matter.; Watch for further developments. (From sense 1.) ♦ *Things are developing rapidly in this area. Stay tuned.*

steady *n.* a boyfriend or girlfriend. ♦ *She showed up with Tom, her steady for the past few months.*

a **steal** *n.* a bargain. ♦ *This car wasn't exactly a steal at this price, but it's still a good value.*

steam 1. *tv.* to anger someone. ♦ *The prof steamed the class with the long assignment.* **2.** *in.* to be angry. ♦ *They steamed for a while and then did as they were told.*

steam so's **beam** *tv.* to make someone angry. ♦ *Come on, don't steam your beam. Remember how hard times are now.*

steam so **up 1.** *tv.* to get someone excited. ♦ *The coach can really steam up those guys.* **2.** *tv.* to get someone angry. (See also steamed (up).) ♦ *This whole mess steamed me up but good.*

steam up *in.* to drink heavily; to get drunk. (See also steamed (up).) ♦ *Let's go down to the tavern and steam up, okay?*

steamed (up) 1. *mod.* angry. ♦ *Now, now, don't get so steamed up!* **2.** *mod.* alcohol intoxicated and fighting. ♦ *He was really steamed—and could hardly stand up.* ♦ *By midnight, Larry was too steamed to drive home, and he had to spend the night.*

steamroller *tv.* to force something to be approved; to force something to happen. ♦ *He plans to steamroller this bill through Congress, but it just won't work.*

steamy *mod.* lewd; sensuous; passionate. ♦ *Hank and Bess were having a steamy session on the couch.*

steelo *n.* style. ♦ *What you lack is steelo! Style! Class! You are dull!*

steenth [stintθ] *n.* one *sixteenth,* used in quoting securities prices. (Securities markets. See also teenie.) ♦ *This issue was up only a few steenths for the whole week.*

steep *mod.* [of a price] high; expensive. ♦ *Their prices are pretty steep, but their goods are of high quality.*

stellar ['stɛlɚ] *mod.* excellent; grand. ♦ *Ronald Simpson gave us a stellar characterization of Boris, but the chorus was a disappointment.*

step off the curb *in.* to die. (Alludes to stepping out in front of a vehicle that causes one's death.) ♦ *Ralph almost stepped off the curb during his operation.*

Step on it! *in.* Hurry up! (As if one were pressing down on the gas pedal. Not limited to vehicles, though.) ♦ *We're late. Come on! Step on it!*

step out on so *in.* to betray one's lover by going out with someone else. ♦ *Hank has been stepping out on Bess, and she doesn't know it yet.*

step outside *in.* to leave the present area and go to another place, presumably to fight. ♦ *The two—who had been arguing—stepped outside to settle the matter.* ♦ *Do you want to step outside, smart ass?*

step right up *in.* come forward and do not be bashful. ♦ *Step right up and buy a ticket to the greatest show on earth!*

step up to the plate *phr.* to voluntarily assume responsibility for something. (From baseball, referring to a batter approaching home plate.) ♦ *The company stepped up to the plate and paid for the time and effort I spent repairing the unit.*

stepped on *mod.* having to do with diluted drugs. (Drugs.) ♦ *This stuff is too stepped on. It's sugar, and it won't do.*

stern *n.* the posterior; buttocks. ♦ *The little airplane crashed right into the stern of an enormous lady who didn't even notice.*

stew 1. *n.* a drinking bout. ♦ *These frequent stews must stop. You will ruin your health.* **2.** *n.* a drunkard. ♦ *There are three stews sleeping in the alley.* **3.** Go to stewed (up). **4.** *n.* a stewardess or steward on an airplane. (Although officially replaced by *flight attendat,* this term and *steward(ess)* are still in use.) ♦ *My sister is a stew for a major airline.* **5.** *in.* to fret. ♦ *I spent most of last night stewing about my job.* **6.** *n.* a fretful state. ♦ *Don't work yourself into a stew.*

stew bum *n.* a drunkard; an alcoholic. ♦ *You're going to end up a stew bum if you don't lay off the moonshine.*

stewed to the ears Go to stewed to the gills.

stewed to the gills AND **stewed to the ears** *mod.* alcohol intoxicated. ♦ *When I get stewed to the gills, I usually fall asleep, right then and there.* ♦ *Here's old Charlie—stewed to the ears, as always.*

stewed (up) AND **stew** *mod.* alcohol intoxicated. (See also stew (sense 1).) ♦ *The kid was stewed up and scɑ ed to death of what his parents were going to do to him.*

stick 1. *n.* a baseball bat. (Baseball.) ♦ *He holds the stick up higher than most batters.* **2.** *n.* a pool cue. ♦ *He drew the stick back slowly, sighted again, and gave the cue ball a sharp knock.* **3.** *n.* a golf club. ♦ *These aren't my sticks, and you aren't my caddy. What's going on around here?* **4.** *n.* the lever that controls the horizontal and vertical surfaces of the tail of an aircraft. ♦ *The pilot pulled back on the stick, and the plane did nothing—being that he hadn't even started the engine or anything.* ♦ *You pull back on the stick, which lowers the tail and raises the nose, and up you go.* **5.** *n.* a gearshift lever in a car. (See also **stick shift**.) ♦ *I keep reaching for the stick in a car with automatic.* **6.** *n.* a drunkard. (Possibly from **dipstick, shitstick,** or **swizzle-stick**.) ♦ *Get that stick out of here before he makes a mess.* **7.** *n.* a person's legs. (Always plural.) ♦ *He's got good sticks under him, but he won't use them.* **8. the sticks** *n.* a rural or backwoods area. (Always with *the* in this sense and always plural.) ♦ *You hear a lot about how things are in the sticks. They're worse.*

stick around *in.* to remain nearby. ♦ *I think if you'll stick around, you'll get a seat sooner or later.*

Stick 'em up! Go to **Hands up!**

stick in the mud *n.* a dull and old-fashioned person. ♦ *Don't be such an old stick in the mud.*

stick it to so *tv.* to give someone a problem; to confront someone. ♦ *They stuck it to me about the stopped-up drain.*

stick like shit to a shovel Go to **cling like shit to a shovel.**

stick man *n.* a police patrol officer (who carries a stick). ♦ *The stick man is due here in about three minutes. Hurry.*

stick one's **nose in (where it's not wanted)** Go to **put** one's **nose in (where it's not wanted).**

stick out like a sore thumb *in.* to be very obvious. ♦ *Do you think I would stick out like a sore thumb at the party if I wear this coat?*

stick shift 1. *mod.* having to do with a nonautomatic transmission or a car that has one. ♦ *I prefer a stick shift car—I don't know why.* ♦ *The stick shift models are cheaper—that's why.* ♦ *This one's stick shift.* **2.** *n.* a nonautomatic transmission. ♦ *My husband took the other car and stuck me with the stick shift.*

stick so **with** sth *tv.* to burden someone with something. ♦ *Please don't stick me with the stick shift again.*

sticker shock *n.* the shock at seeing just how much something new, usually an automobile, costs as determined by looking at the price tag or sticker. ♦ *I went to a car dealer today, and I am still suffering from sticker shock.*

sticks Go to **stick.**

sticktoitiveness [stɪk'tuɪtɪvnəs] *n.* tenacity. ♦ *The kid has sticktoitiveness. I like that in a kid.*

stickum ['stɪkəm] **1.** *n.* glue. ♦ *Put some stickum on this paper and paste it up where it can be seen.* **2.** *n.* any thick and sticky substance, especially hair dressing. (See also **slickum**.) ♦ *He uses too much stickum on his hair.*

sticky 1. *mod.* gooey. (Standard English.) ♦ *What is this sticky stuff on my shoe? Oh, no!* **2.** *mod.* chancy; awkward. ♦ *Things began to get a little sticky, and Marlowe began to move toward the door.* **3.** *mod.* sentimental. ♦ *Things were getting a little sticky the more Harriet drank. She tried to kiss me, and I left.* **4.** *mod.* having to do with hot and humid weather. ♦ *I can't take another sticky day like this.*

sticky fingers *n.* a tendency to steal. ♦ *Watch these young kids with sticky fingers who come in here "just looking."*

stiff 1. AND **stiffed** *mod.* alcohol intoxicated; dead drunk. ♦ *She knows how to stop drinking before she gets stiff.* **2.** *n.* a drunkard. ♦ *Some stiff staggered by—belching clouds of some beery smell.* ♦ *The guy's a stiff, and you want to run him for mayor? Even in this town that's going too far.* **3.** *mod.* dead. (Originally underworld.) ♦ *He's stiff. There's nothing that can be done.* **4.** *n.* a corpse. (Underworld.) ♦ *They pulled another stiff out of the river last night. Looks like another mob killing.* **5.** *n.* a fellow worker; a fellow tramp. (Originally hobos.) ♦ *This stiff wants some help finding a flop for the night.* **6.** *tv.* to fail to tip someone who expects it. ♦ *Ya know, you can tell right away when a guy's gonna stiff you—ya* just know. ♦ *I guess I get stiffed two, three times a day.* **7.** *tv.* to cheat someone. ♦ *The clown selling hot dogs stiffed me for about forty cents.*

stiffed Go to stiff.

stiffy an erection. ♦ *He was so tired that a stiffy was out of the question.*

sting 1. *tv.* to cheat or swindle someone; to overcharge someone. ♦ *That street merchant stung me, but good.* **2.** *n.* a well-planned scheme to entrap criminals. ♦ *The sting came off without a hitch.* **3.** *tv.* to entrap and arrest someone. ♦ *"We've been stung!" they hollered.*

sting so **for** sth *tv.* to cheat someone of a particular amount; to make someone pay for something. ♦ *That guy stung me for twenty bucks!*

stinger *n.* the drawback; the catch; the hitch. ♦ *Sounds good, but what's the stinger?*

stink 1. *in.* to be repellent; to be suspicious and poorly planned. (Of schemes and plots.) ♦ *This whole setup stinks.* **2.** *n.* a commotion. (See also raise a stink (about so/sth).) ♦ *The stink you made about money has done no good at all. You're fired.*

stink on ice *in.* to be really rotten, bad, poorly done, or repellent. (So rotten as to reek even when frozen.) ♦ *This show stinks on ice.*

stinker 1. *n.* an unpleasant or wicked person. ♦ *Jerry is a real stinker. Look what he did!* **2.** *n.* a serious problem. ♦ *This whole business is a real stinker.*

stinking 1. Go to stinking (drunk). **2.** *mod.* lousy; rotten. ♦ *That was a mean stinking thing to do. Really stinking!*

stinking (drunk) *mod.* alcohol intoxicated. ♦ *He was really stinking.*

stinking rich *mod.* very rich. ♦ *I'd like to be stinking rich for the rest of my life.*

stinking with sth *mod.* with lots of something. ♦ *Mr. Wilson is just stinking with dough.*

stinkpot 1. *n.* a baby with a dirty diaper. (Also a term of address.) ♦ *Come here, you little stinkpot. I'll fix you.* **2.** *n.* anything smelly. ♦ *Why don't you drive this stinkpot into a service station and get it tuned?* **3.** *n.* a motorboat. (Because the engine smells bad, especially when compared to a sailboat.) ♦ *Those guys in their stinkpots sure make a lot of noise.*

stinky *mod.* bad. ♦ *You have a very stinky attitude. Really stinky.*

stir *n.* prison. (Underworld.) ♦ *I can't stand being in stir!*

stir crazy *mod.* anxious and mentally disturbed from being confined, as in prison. (See also stir.) ♦ *I was going stir crazy in my little room, so I moved to a bigger place.*

a **stitch 1.** *n.* a very funny person. ♦ *Harry is a stitch. What a sense of humor!* **2.** *n.* a sharp pain, usually in the side. ♦ *I got a stitch and had to drop out of the marathon.*

stocking-stuffer *n.* a small gift that is suitable for putting inside a Christmas stocking. ♦ *I got some little stocking-stuffers for the kids.*

stog(ie) ['stogi] *n.* a cigar. ♦ *Then this guy pulls out a big stogie and starts to smoke it right there in the restaurant.*

stoke sth **up** *tv.* to start something, such as an engine. ♦ *Stoke up your motorcycle and let's get going.*

stoked (on so or sth**)** *mod.* excited by someone or something. (See also stokin'.) ♦ *We were stoked on Mary. She is the greatest.*

stoked out *mod.* exhausted. ♦ *I ran all the way and got stoked out.*

stokin' *mod.* excellent; exciting. ♦ *We had a stokin' time at Fred's house.*

stomach *tv.* to tolerate someone or something. (Usually negative.) ♦ *Spike couldn't stomach the opera, and he left after the first ten minutes.*

stomp (on) so *tv. & in.* to beat someone; to misuse someone. ♦ *One team stomped on the other so hard and fast, the scoreboard couldn't keep up.*

stomping ground Go to stamping ground.

stone *mod.* completely; totally. ♦ *This lecture is stone dull.*

stone blind *mod.* heavily alcohol intoxicated. ♦ *Jerry drank the sauce till he was stone blind.*

stone broke *mod.* completely broke. ♦ *I'm sorry, I'm stone broke. Can I send you a check?*

a **stone cold fox** *n.* a very fine and sexy woman. (Streets. See also fox.) ♦ *That dame is a stone cold fox. What's her phone number?*

stone (cold) sober *mod.* absolutely sober. ♦ *I am stone cold sober, or I will be by morning anyway.*

stone dead *mod.* dead; unquestionably dead; long dead. ♦ *The cat was stone dead and stiff as a board by the time we got to him.*

stone fox *n.* an attractive woman; a very sexy woman. ♦ *Who is that stone fox I saw you with last night?*

stone groove *n.* something really cool; a fine party or concert. ♦ *This affair is not what I would call a stone groove. Stone beige, maybe.*

stone sober Go to stone (cold) sober.

stoned (out) *mod.* alcohol or drug intoxicated. ♦ *I have never seen anybody so stoned who could still talk.*

stoned out of one's **gourd** Go to stoned out of one's head.

stoned out of one's **head** AND **stoned out of** one's **gourd** *mod.* under the effects of marijuana. ♦ *Tiffany was stoned out of her head and started giggling.* ♦ *That stuff makes me stoned out of my gourd.*

stoned out of one's **squash** *mod.* alcohol or drug intoxicated. ♦ *Britney will drink a little now and then, but she never gets stoned out of her squash.*

stoned silly *mod.* alcohol or drug intoxicated. ♦ *I hate to get stoned silly in public. At home—ah, that's a different matter.* ♦ *He got stoned silly at the rally, and for all I know he is still there on the floor in the corner.*

stoner *n.* a drug user who is generally stoned (out). ♦ *He's a stoner. He'll never amount to much.*

stones 1. *n.* the testicles. (Also a Standard English euphemism. See also rocks.) ♦ *He got hit in the stones.* **2.** *mod.* courage; bravado. (The same as balls sense 3.) ♦ *Come on, Willy, show some stones!*

stonewall 1. *tv.* to obstruct something or someone. ♦ *And again, the mayor tried to stonewall the investigation.* **2.** *n.* an obstructionist act. ♦ *His answer to the committee was another stonewall that caught them all by surprise.*

stonkered ['stɔŋkɚd] **1.** *mod.* killed. ♦ *The car crashed into him and he was stonkered for sure.* **2.** *mod.* alcohol intoxicated. ♦ *My buddy here is stonkered and needs a ride, and can I have one, too?*

stooge [studʒ] **1.** *n.* someone's pawn; someone controlled or maneuvered by someone else. ♦ *The guy's a stooge for the mob's Mr. Gutman. Ignore him.* **2.** *in.* to work as someone's underling; to serve as someone's pawn. ♦ *You will do what I tell you, and if it's stooging you will do it, and you will smile and say thank you.*

stool (on so**)** *in.* to inform (on someone). (To act as a stool (pigeon).) ♦ *Britney would stool on anybody, even her own mother.*

stool (pigeon) AND **stoolie** ['stul 'pɪdʒən AND 'stuli] *n.* an informer. (Originally underworld.) ♦ *Some stool pigeon spilled the works to the boys in blue.* ♦ *I'm no stoolie!*

stoolie Go to stool (pigeon).

stoop Go to stupe.

stop on a dime *in.* to stop immediately. ♦ *Imagine a bus that could stop on a dime.*

Stop the music! *exclam.* Stop!; Stop whatever is happening! (From an old radio game show called *Stop the Music!*) ♦ *"Stop the music!" hollered the conductor, making a little joke.*

storked *mod.* pregnant. ♦ *She got herself good and storked. Now what?*

story stock *n.* shares in a company that are bought because of an appealing story about the company. ♦ *I never buy a story stock. By the time I hear about it, it's already gone up as much as it ever will.*

Stow it! *exclam.* Shut up! ♦ *Stow it! That is enough of your applesauce.*

stozzled ['stɑzl̩d] *mod.* alcohol intoxicated. ♦ *Marty can drink and drink and never get stozzled or even tipsy.*

str8 *mod.* straight. ♦ *Now tell it to me str8!*

straddle the fence *tv.* to support both sides of an issue. ♦ *The mayor is straddling the fence on this issue, hoping the public will forget it.*

straight 1. *mod.* honest; unembellished. ♦ *Have I ever been anything but straight with you?* **2.** *n.* a tobacco cigarette; a tobacco cigarette butt. (As opposed to a marijuana cigarette. See also slim.) ♦ *No, I want a straight. That spliff makes me sneeze.* **3.** *mod.* having to do with undiluted liquor. ♦ *I'll take mine straight.* **4.** *mod.* relieved and satisfied by a dose of drugs. (Drugs.) ♦ *She will be straight for a few hours, and then the same struggle all over again—all through the night.* **5.** *mod.* off drugs; no longer addicted to drugs. ♦ *I'm straight now, and I'm gonna stay that way.* **6.** *n.* a square person (who does not use drugs, etc.). ♦ *The straights are putting pressure on city hall to clean up this neighborhood.* **7.** *n.* a nonhomosexual; a heterosexual. (Often from the homosexual point of view.) ♦ *Walter invited a few straights to the affair, just to keep things calm.* **8.** *mod.* not homosexual; not having a homosexual orientation. ♦ *He wandered into a straight bar by mistake.* **9.** *mod.* excellent. ♦ *This news is truly straight and I am happy to hear it.* **10.** *mod.* satisfied; having enough food or anything. ♦ *Another beer? No thanks. I'm straight.*

straight arrow *n.* an honest person; a law-abiding citizen. (See also straight shooter.) ♦ *Willy is really a straight arrow at heart—as long as he's not around Max.* ♦ *Max is not a straight arrow. Slime is more like it.*

straight dope *n.* the true information. (See also dope sense 3 = news, information.) ♦ *I want the straight dope. I can take it.*

straight from the horse's mouth *mod.* directly from the source, not just a horse. (As if a racehorse were giving racing tips.) ♦ *This came straight from the horse's mouth. It's Zeerocks Copy in the sixth race.*

straight from the shoulder *mod.* very direct, without attenuation or embellishment. ♦ *Right straight from the shoulder: clean out your desk; you're through.*

straight low *n.* the absolute truth; the true lowdown. (Prisons.) ♦ *Nobody ain't gonna tell no warden the straight low; you can be sure of that.*

straight man *n.* someone who sets up jokes or gags so that someone else can say the punch line. ♦ *I'm tired of being a straight man for a has-been comic.*

straight shooter *n.* an honest person. (See also straight arrow.) ♦ *We need a straight shooter in office who will work for the people rather than some political party.*

straight talk *n.* direct and honest talk. ♦ *If they want straight talk and can handle straight talk, give 'em straight talk.*

straight up 1. *mod.* [of someone] upright and honest. ♦ *A fine guy—really straight up.* ♦ *She is one of the most straight up brokers in town.* **2.** *mod.* without ice; neat. ♦ *I'll have a bourbon, straight up, please.* **3.** *mod.* sunny-side up; having to do with eggs cooked with yellow yolks facing straight up. ♦ *I like my eggs straight up, but the white part has to be cooked solid.*

straighten up and fly right *in.* to get serious and start behaving properly. ♦ *Straighten up and fly right before you get into difficulty.*

straight-faced *mod.* with a serious, unsmiling face. ♦ *He was a very straight-faced prof, but he has a tremendous sense of humor.*

strange bird Go to odd bird.

strap *n.* an athlete, not necessarily male. (From jockstrap.) ♦ *The guy's a strap all right, but he's not dumb.*

strap so **with** so or sth *tv.* to burden someone with someone or something. (Often passive.) ♦ *Don't you try to strap me with your baby brother!*

straphanger *n.* a subway passenger; bus passenger; commuter. ♦ *I didn't think I could get used to being a straphanger.*

strapped 1. *mod.* broke; short of money. ♦ *I'm sorry I can't pay you right now. I'm strapped.* **2.** *mod.* wearing a gun holster. ♦ *Be careful. He's strapped. I see it under his jacket.*

straw 1. *n.* marijuana. (Drugs.) ♦ *He stood right on the corner, selling straw by the handful from a bucket at his feet—and nobody even called the cops.* ♦ *This straw is not the best quality I've seen.* **2.** *n.* papers for rolling marijuana cigarettes. (Drugs.) ♦ *I can't manage the straw with one hand. How do these cowboys do it?*

straw boss *n.* a foreman; anyone who is second in command. ♦ *I don't mind being a straw boss as long as they pay me.*

strawberry *n.* a pimple from drinking excessively. (See also **toddy blossom**.) ♦ *His disability made itself manifest by the occasional strawberry.*

streak 1. *in.* to move rapidly from one place to another. ♦ *The train streaked into the station and came to a stop just inches from the end of the track.* **2.** *in.* to run about in a public place naked. ♦ *This kid was streaking back and forth until the cops caught him.* **3.** *tv.* to grace or ornament a public place or event with a naked run. ♦ *Charles streaked the baseball game, but nobody noticed him.* **4.** *n.* a naked run in a public place. (See also **streaker**.) ♦ *There was a streak at the end of the game, but people were leaving then and didn't see it.* **5.** *n.* an exciting time; a wild party. ♦ *We had a streak at Tom's.*

streaker *n.* someone who runs naked in public places. ♦ *The streaker ran through a glass door and was severely injured.*

the **street 1.** *n.* the real, free world, as opposed to prison. ♦ *The street just isn't the same as stir.* **2.** *n.* Wall Street in New York City. (Usually capitalized.) ♦ *The Street* doesn't seem to believe the policy makers in Washington.

street cred *n.* credibility on the streets. (Streets.) ♦ *If I drove a ride like that, I'd lose my street cred.*

street people *n.* people who live in the streets; homeless people. ♦ *There are a lot of cold street people at this time of the year.*

street pusher *n.* a drug dealer who works at the retail level on the streets. ♦ *It's the street pushers who take the risk and end up doing a few months in the pen.*

street smart *mod.* wise in the ways of urban life; wise in the ways of tough neighborhoods. ♦ *Bess wasn't street smart enough to survive by herself.*

street smarts *n.* the knowledge and ability to survive on the urban street. ♦ *If you don't have street smarts, you won't last long out there.*

street sweeper *n.* a machine gun. ♦ *In my neighborhood, the sound of street sweepers is about as common as the sound of horns honking.*

street time *n.* time not spent in prison. (Underworld.) ♦ *I want out of this place. I need a little street time to renew some old acquaintances.*

street-casting *n.* selecting amateurs to be performers or models. ♦ *I do a lot of street-casting. Almost everybody can act a little.*

streeter *n.* an urban *street person.* ♦ *These streeters have to be bright and clever just to survive.*

stress 1. *in.* to suffer annoyance; to experience stress. ♦ *Clare finds that she is stressing more and more about little things.* **2.** *tv.* to annoy or bother someone. (See also **stressed**.) ♦ *Don't stress Willy! He's had a hard day.*

stressed *mod.* upset; annoyed. ♦ *Come on, man, don't get stressed! It's only a gag.*

stretch 1. *n.* a period of time. (Folksy.) ♦ *Let's talk here for a stretch and then go up and see if dinner's ready.* **2.** *n.* a prison term. ♦ *I was away for a stretch of about seven years.* **3.** *in.* to hang (as with a death sentence). ♦ *You will stretch for this, Lefty!* **4.** *tv.* to cut or dilute a drug. ♦ *Let's stretch this stuff, sell it, and then blow town.* **5.** *n.* a nickname for a tall person, usually male. (Usually **Stretch**.) ♦ *Well, stretch, think you'll go out for basketball this season?*

stretch one's **legs** *tv.* to stand up and perhaps walk about. ♦ *I need to get out of here and stretch my legs for a while.*

(strictly) from hunger *mod.* very strange; acceptable only when nothing else is available. ♦ *The singer was strictly from hunger.*

strike *n.* a dose of drugs. (Drugs. See also hit.) ♦ *Just one strike, Bart, come on, just one. I'll pay you tomorrow, Bart, come on, just one little strike. Anything, Bart. I really hurt, Bart.*

strike it rich *tv.* to become rich suddenly. ♦ *Pete is the kind of guy who wants to strike it rich and live in the lap of luxury for the rest of his life.*

strike out 1. *in.* [for a baseball batter] to be declared out after three strikes. (Baseball.) ♦ *He struck out in the second inning, and manager Willy "Herky" Simpson read him out then.* **2.** *in.* to fail. ♦ *I hear you struck out on that Acme proposal. Better luck next time.*

strike pay dirt Go to hit pay dirt.

stringbean *n.* a thin person. (Also a term of address.) ♦ *Who's the stringbean standing by the punch bowl? Somebody ought to feed him.*

stripper *n.* a striptease artist. ♦ *Strippers from all over assembled here for their fourth annual convention and immediately took off on a sight-seeing tour.*

stroke *tv. & in.* to flatter someone; to soothe and comfort someone. ♦ *She "strokes" everybody to keep them on her side during the bad times.*

strong-arm 1. *tv.* to force someone (to do something). ♦ *Spike tried to strong-arm Frank into cooperating.* **2.** *mod.* forceful; by physical force. ♦ *The strong-arm approach got him nowhere.*

strong-arm man *n.* a bully; a man who is employed to use physical power to force someone to do something. ♦ *Wilbur is Mr. Gutman's strong-arm man.*

strong-arm tactics *n.* tactics based on the use of force. ♦ *Strong-arm tactics are out. The boss says be gentle and don't break anybody.*

strung out 1. AND **strung (up)** *mod.* drug intoxicated and bewildered. (Drugs.) ♦ *Marlon is really strung out lately. What's he shooting now?* **2.** *mod.* badly addicted to heroin; dissipated by heroin. (Drugs.) ♦ *Clare is strung out and can't deny her problem any longer.* **3.** *mod.* depressed; nervous. ♦ *I'm a little strung out—because of the accident, I guess.* **4.** *mod.* in love and disoriented. ♦ *Sam is strung out over Mary.*

strung (up) Go to strung out.

strung-out shape *n.* a tired and exhausted condition. ♦ *They were sort of in strung-out shape, tired and ready for the sack.*

strunk *mod.* stoned and drunk. (Contrived.) ♦ *He's too strunk to stand up.*

strut one's **stuff** *tv.* to walk proudly and show off one's best features or talents. ♦ *Get out there on that stage and strut your stuff!*

stubby *mod.* cool; good-looking. ♦ *Man, you're stubby. Nice kicks!*

stuccoed ['stəkod] *mod.* alcohol intoxicated. (A play on plastered.) ♦ *The guy was too stuccoed to drive and couldn't stand up to walk.*

stuck on so or sth *mod.* enamored with someone or something; obsessed with someone or something. ♦ *Tom is stuck on himself—as conceited as can be.* ♦ *I'm really stuck on this stuff. It's just yummy.*

stuck-up *mod.* conceited. ♦ *Don't be so stuck-up. Unbend a little.*

stud [stəd] **1.** *n.* a male horse used for breeding purposes. (Not slang.) ♦ *Last spring, we rented out all our studs and made some money.* **2.** *n.* a human male viewed as very successful with women.

(Parallel to sense 1.) ♦ *Fred thinks he is a real stud.*

studhammer *n.* a male who is successful sexually with women. ♦ *The guy thinks he is a studhammer, but he is just a jerk.*

studly *mod.* a virile and attractive male. ♦ *I had no idea you were going to bring along such a studly guy!*

stud-muffin *n.* a really good-looking guy; a stud. ♦ *Who's the stud-muffin with Sally?*

study animal *n.* someone who studies hard. (A play on party animal.) ♦ *At the end of the school year every party animal turns into a study animal.*

Stuff a sock in it! AND **Put a sock in it!; Put a cork in it!** *exclam.* Shut up! ♦ *I've heard enough. Stuff a sock in it!* ♦ *Put a sock in it and watch the movie*

stuff one's **face** Go to fill one's face.

stuffed shirt *n.* a dull and stuffy person, usually a male. ♦ *Mr. Wilson is a stuffed shirt, and people would tell him so if he didn't have so much money.*

stum [stəm] **1.** *n.* marijuana. (Drugs.) ♦ *This stum is cashed. Trash it.* **2.** Go to stumbles.

stumblebum *n.* a tramp or bum, especially drunk and stumbling. ♦ *The poor old stumblebum got to the other side of the street the best he could.*

stumble-bumbles Go to stumbles.

stumbles ['stəmblz] **1.** AND **stum** [stəm]; **stumble-bumbles** ['stəmbl'bəmblz] *n.* barbiturates; sedatives; tranquilizers; alcohol. (Drugs.) ♦ *Kelly was shocked to find a handful of stumble-bumbles in his brother's jeans.* **2.** *n.* the inability to stand up and walk straight. ♦ *I guess I have the stumbles today. Not enough sleep, I guess.*

stump 1. *tv.* to confuse or puzzle someone. ♦ *I like to stump people with hard questions.* **2.** *tv.* to visit or tour a place. ♦ *We stumped all of Europe this summer.* **3.** *n.* a visit or tour. ♦ *The old girl is off on another stump.* **4.** Go to stumps.

stumper *n.* a shoe. (Streets. Usually plural.) ♦ *Make those stumpers shine!*

stumps *n.* a person's legs. ♦ *You need good strong stumps to do that kind of climbing.*

stung *mod.* alcohol intoxicated. ♦ *I'm a little stung by the mule, but I can find my way home if you'll just remind me how to open this door.*

stunned *mod.* alcohol intoxicated. ♦ *Kelly was stunned and had to be carried home to recover.*

stunner *n.* a stunningly good-looking woman. ♦ *Did you see that stunner who just came in?*

stunting *mod.* well dressed. ♦ *Mooshoo is iced out and stunting!*

stupe AND **stoop** *n.* a stupid person. (Also a term of address.) ♦ *Look, stoop, just do what you are told.*

stupehead *n.* a stupid person; a blockhead. (Also a term of address. See also stupe.) ♦ *What a stupehead!*

stupid *mod.* drunk. (See also get stupid.) ♦ *These kids are so stupid they can't see straight. They're all going to be sick.*

stupid fresh *mod.* very, very good. (See also fresh; funky fresh.) ♦ *Her looks were stupid fresh. Bonus!*

stupid-ass Go to dumb-ass.

style *in.* to show off; to strut around. (Black. See also strut one's stuff.) ♦ *Why don't you style over here and meet my man?*

stylin(g) *n.* looking good; showing off how good one looks. ♦ *Dave thinks that stylin' is his sole occupation.*

stymie ['staimi] *tv.* to obstruct someone or something. ♦ *He did everything he could to stymie the investigation.*

suave [swɑv] *n.* personal polish and smoothness. ♦ *Man, does that guy ever have suave!*

sub 1. *n.* a substitute. ♦ *I was a sub in the school system for a while.* **2.** *in.* to serve as a temporary replacement. ♦ *I subbed for Mary in a couple of games.* **3.** *n.* a submarine. ♦ *I was aboard a sub for twenty minutes—and that was at Disney World.* **4.** Go to submarine (sense 1). **5.** *n.* a subscription, as to a magazine. ♦ *I got a sub to a computer magazine for my birthday.*

submarine 1. AND **sub; hoagy; torpedo; grinder; poor boy; hero** *n.* a long sandwich containing many different foods. (Sometimes many feet long. It is cut into smaller segments for serving a group. Usually contains sliced meats and cheese, as well as tomatoes and onions. Terms vary depending on where you are in the country.) ♦ *He ordered a submarine, but he couldn't finish it.* **2.** *n.* a large marijuana cigarette. ♦ *Look at the size of that sub!* **3.** *n.* [menstrual] tampon. ♦ *My God! I'm out of submarines!*

suck 1. AND **suction** *n.* liquor; wine; beer; strong drink. ♦ *How about a little glass of suck before we leave?* **2.** AND **suck** sth **up** *tv.* to drink beer or liquor. ♦ *Yeah, I'll suck one up with ya.* **3.** *in.* [for someone or something] to be bad or undesirable. ♦ *This movie sucks!* **4.** AND **suction** *n.* influence. ♦ *He thinks he has suck, but he's just a pain in the neck.*

suck face *tv.* to kiss. (See also swap spits.) ♦ *The kid said he was going out to suck face. It sounds awful.*

suck (some) brew AND **suck (some) suds** *tv.* to drink beer. ♦ *Wanna go suck some brew?* ♦ *Let's go out and suck suds.*

suck (some) suds Go to suck (some) brew.

suck so's **hind tit** AND **kiss** so's **hind tit** *tv.* to be obsequious to someone. (Usually objectionable.) ♦ *What does he want me to do, suck his hind tit or something?*

suck sth **up** Go to suck.

suck up to so *in.* to attempt to gain influence with or favor from someone. ♦ *Don't suck up to me. It won't do any good.*

sucka Go to sucker.

suckabuck *mod.* greedy; exhibiting greed. ♦ *She is such a suckabuck landlady that it makes me want to move.*

sucker 1. AND **sucka** *n.* a dupe; an easy mark. ♦ *See if you can sell that sucker the Brooklyn Bridge.* **2.** *tv.* to trick or victimize someone. ♦ *That crook suckered me. I should have known better.* **3.** *n.* an

annoying person. (Also a rude term of address.) ♦ *I am really sick of that sucker hanging around here.* **4.** *n.* a gadget; a thing. ♦ *Now, you put this little sucker right into this slot.*

sucker for so or sth *n.* someone who is prejudiced in favor of someone or something. ♦ *Ted is a sucker for any dessert with whipped cream on it.*

sucker list *n.* a list of potential dupes; a list of people who might be taken in by deception. ♦ *I'm sure on their sucker list. They are trying to get me to go to a lecture and receive a free clock or something.*

sucker so **into** sth AND **sucker** so **in** *tv.* to deceive someone into some sort of scam or confidence game; to play someone for a fool. ♦ *Surely you don't think you can sucker me into doing something as stupid as that, do you?* ♦ *I'm too smart. You can't sucker me in!*

sucky *mod.* poor; undesirable. ♦ *This is the suckiest movie I ever saw.*

suction Go to suck.

sudden death *mod.* having to do with something short, quick, and decisive. ♦ *The game ended in a sudden death play-off.*

suds 1. *n.* beer. ♦ *How about some suds, Bill?* **2.** *in.* to drink beer. ♦ *How 'bout going out and sudsing for a while?*

suds-swiller *n.* a beer-drinker. ♦ *Ted is a suds-swiller and Bill won't touch the stuff. What strange roommates.*

Sue me! Go to (So,) sue me!

sue the pants off (of) so *tv.* to sue someone for a lot of money. ♦ *If they do it, I'll sue the pants off of them.*

sugar daddy *n.* an older man who takes care of a younger person, especially a young man or woman. ♦ *Mr. Wilson is sort of a sugar daddy to the whole team.*

sugarcoated *mod.* palatable; inoffensive; easy to take. ♦ *Math is so sugarcoated these days. Even I could learn it.*

suit *n.* a businessman or businesswoman; someone who is in charge. ♦ *A couple of* suits checked into a working-class hotel and caused some eyebrows to raise.

summer complaint *n*. diarrhea, especially that experienced in the summer. ♦ *I've got a touch of the summer complaint.*

sun belt *n*. the southern U.S. states, where it is generally warm and sunny. (See also rust belt.) ♦ *I want to retire to the sun belt.*

Sunday best *n*. one's best clothing, which one would wear to church. ♦ *We are in our Sunday best, ready to go.*

Sunday driver *n*. a slow and leisurely driver who appears to be sightseeing and enjoying the view, holding up traffic in the process. (Also a term of address.) ♦ *Move over, you Sunday driver!*

Sunday punch *n*. a very solid and destructive blow; one's best blow. ♦ *Ralph aimed a Sunday punch at Frederick's nose, but he missed and spun about, striking his elbow on the banister.*

sunny-side up *mod*. [of eggs] having yolks facing up and still yellow and hot, but not cooked through; straight up. ♦ *I'll have my eggs sunny-side up, with toast and coffee.*

sunshades *n*. sunglasses. (See also shades.) ♦ *I left my sunshades in the car.*

Sup? Go to (T)sup?

super 1. *mod*. fine; excellent. ♦ *This report is just super!* **2.** *n*. superintendent. ♦ *The super comes by every now and then to check on things.*

super-dooper Go to super-duper.

super-duper AND **super-dooper** *mod*. excellent. ♦ *That's just super-duper. Couldn't have asked for better.*

superfly *mod*. excellent; wonderful. ♦ *I don't care about this superfly gent of yours. If he doesn't have a job, I don't want you seeing him anymore. Ya hear?*

supergrass *n*. high-quality marijuana. ♦ *The cannabis that is the richest in resin is sometimes called "supergrass."*

superjock 1. *n*. an excellent athlete. ♦ *All those superjocks get special meals and tutors to help them pass their classes.* **2.** *n*. a very well built man regardless of athletic ability. ♦ *My boyfriend is a superjock, and does he look good!*

super-strap *n*. an earnest and hardworking student. (As compared to a jock; strap; superjock.) ♦ *I couldn't be a super-strap even if I had the brains. I just don't care that much.*

sure as hell Go to (as) sure as hell.

sure thing *n*. something that is absolutely certain. ♦ *It's a sure thing! You can't lose!*

surefire *mod*. certain; effective; fail-safe. (Alludes to a gun that will always fire.) ♦ *I've got a surefire method for fixing cracks in drywall.*

surf 1. *mod*. wonderful; with it; excellent. (California.) ♦ *This party is, like, surf.* **2.** *in*. to use a remote control to check a large number of TV stations. (See also channel hopping.) ♦ *Don spends almost an hour surfing before he falls asleep in front of the TV.*

surf the net *tv*. to browse through the offerings of the internet. ♦ *He surfs the net for three hours each evening.*

suss SO **out** ['səs...] *tv*. to try to figure someone out. ♦ *I can't seem to suss Tom out. What a strange guy.*

Suzy *n*. a U.S. one-dollar coin bearing a likeness of Susan B. Anthony. ♦ *I've got two Suzies I want to get rid of.*

Suzy Homemaker *n*. a personification of the quintessential female American housewife. (During the 1960s, this was a brand of child-sized kitchen appliances and also a doll of the same name.) ♦ *Well, aren't you just Miss Suzy Homemaker! You're even wearing an apron!*

swacked [swækt] *mod*. alcohol intoxicated. ♦ *He walked straight out of the office and went straight into the bar with the intention of getting swacked.*

SWAG Go to scientific wild ass guess.

SWAK Go to sealed with a kiss.

swallow 1. *n*. a puff of cigarette smoke. ♦ *He took just one swallow and started coughing.* **2.** *tv*. to believe or accept something. (See also eat sth up.) ♦ *Nobody's gonna swallow that nonsense.*

swallow the dictionary *tv.* to acquire an enormous vocabulary. (Usually in the past tense.) ♦ *My uncle says I've swallowed the dictionary. That's because I know so many big words.*

swamped 1. *mod.* very, very busy. ♦ *I can't handle it now. I'm swamped.* **2.** *mod.* alcohol intoxicated. ♦ *Look at him! He's swamped—stoned out of his mind.*

swamper *n.* a helper or assistant, especially an assistant in food service or in trucking. (Very old.) ♦ *This guy and his swamper showed up to deliver the stuff, but neither one of them would touch it.*

swank [swæŋk] **1.** *n.* class; visible quality. ♦ *This place has swank. I like it.* **2.** *n.* swag. ♦ *Where'd he hide the swank?*

swanky ['swæŋki] *mod.* classy; ritzy. ♦ *This place is too swanky. I like to eat where I can pronounce the names of the food.*

swap notes (on so or sth**)** *tv.* to share information on someone or something. ♦ *The mechanics were swapping notes on rude customers they had dealt with in the past month.*

swap spits *tv.* to kiss with someone. ♦ *Tiffany and Wilbur were off somewhere swapping spits, I guess.*

swear like a trooper *in.* to curse and swear with great facility. ♦ *The clerk started swearing like a trooper, and the customer started crying.*

swear on a stack of Bibles *in.* to make a very solemn pledge of one's honesty. (Folksy. Official oaths are sometimes taken with one hand on a Bible. This phrase implies that more Bibles make an even stronger oath.) ♦ *I swear on a stack of Bibles that I was in Atlanta on the night of January sixteenth.*

sweat 1. *tv. & in.* to fret (about something) while waiting for an outcome. ♦ *This whole promotion business really has me sweating.* **2.** *n.* trouble; bother. (See also no sweat.) ♦ *I can handle it. It won't cause me any sweat.*

sweat blood *tv.* to work very hard at something; to endure distress in the process of accomplishing something. (See also piss blood.) ♦ *And here I sweated blood to put you through college, and you treat me like a stranger.*

sweat bullets *tv.* to suffer about something; to be anxious or nervous about something; to sweat blood. ♦ *The kid sat in the waiting room, sweating bullets while the surgeons worked on his brother.*

sweat sock *n.* an athlete; a jock. (Usually plural.) ♦ *I live in a dorm with a bunch of sweat socks. They feed us well, anyway.*

sweat sth **out** *tv.* to wait out something; to fret and worry until the end of something. ♦ *You'll just have to sweat it out. There's no way to hurry it up.*

sweat-shop *n.* a workplace where employees work long hours for low pay in poor conditions. ♦ *The bank manager is unfair! I've been a teller in this sweat-shop for thirteen years, and I've never had a new carpet in my office.*

sweet *mod.* good; profitable; excellent. ♦ *I got involved in a sweet deal having to do with a better job.*

sweet nothings *n.* loving comments; pleasant remarks between lovers. ♦ *They are out on the porch swing whispering sweet nothings in each other's ears.*

sweeten *tv.* to make a bargain or agreement better or more attractive. ♦ *Okay, I'll sweeten the deal. I'll throw in a lighted mirror on the visor.*

sweetener *n.* extra encouragement, usually in the form of money. ♦ *Money makes the best sweetener around.*

sweetheart deal *n.* a deal made between friends so that both may profit well. (Such deals usually involve illegal or unethical practices.) ♦ *Most of the general contractors in town would be out of business if they didn't offer "sweetheart deals" to the politicians.*

swell *mod.* fine; excellent. (Also sarcastic use.) ♦ *Where did you get that swell hat?*

swellelegant ['swɛl'ɛləgənt] *mod.* really fine. (From *swell* and *elegant*.) ♦ *Gee, this place is sure swellelegant!*

swellhead *n.* a conceited person. ♦ *Tom is getting to be such a swellhead.*

swift 1. *mod.* smart and clever. ♦ *Excuse my brother. He's not too swift.* **2.** *mod.* sexually fast or easy, usually said of a woman. ♦ *Britney is swift, they say, but I find her to be a perfect lady.*

swig 1. *n.* a deep drink of liquor; a swallow of liquor. ♦ *She took a swig of rum and leaped into the lagoon.* **2.** *tv.* to drink liquor deeply. ♦ *He nearly swigged the whole bottle before he needed to take a breath.*

swigged AND **swiggled** [swɪgd AND 'swɪgl̩d] *mod.* alcohol intoxicated; tipsy. ♦ *Man, is she ever swigged!*

swiggled Go to swigged.

swill 1. *n.* liquor. ♦ *The swill they serve here is better than you can get elsewhere.* **2.** *n.* a drink of liquor. ♦ *Here, you can have a little swill of mine.* **3.** *tv. & in.* to drink liquor. ♦ *He swilled a whole case of beer yesterday. Isn't he joyful yet?* **4.** *n.* any nasty food or drink. ♦ *Let's go over to the ptomaine-domain and get our evening swill.*

swill-up *n.* a drinking bout. ♦ *There was a swill-up at the frat house last week.*

swimming in sth *in.* having lots of something. ♦ *Right now we are swimming in merchandise. In a month it will be gone.*

swimmingly *mod.* quite nicely. ♦ *I'm having a fine time here. Everything is going along just swimmingly.*

swindle sheet *n.* an expense account record sheet or book. ♦ *I turned in my swindle sheet yesterday, and no one challenged the $400 for new shoes.*

swing 1. *in.* [for a person] to be up to date and modern. ♦ *Tom really swings. Look at those blue suede shoes!* **2.** *in.* [for a party or other event] to be fun or exciting. ♦ *I've never been to a gathering that swings like this one.* **3.** *in.* to be involved in sexual fads, group sex, or the swapping of sexual partners. ♦ *Carol says that Tom, Ted, and Heidi swing. How does she know?* **4.** *tv.* to bring something off; to execute

a deal. ♦ *They want to elect me president of the club. I hope they can swing it.*

swing both ways *in.* to be bisexual. ♦ *Since he swings both ways, he may stand a better chance at finding a date.*

swing into high gear *in.* to begin operating at a fast pace; to increase the rate of activity. ♦ *The chef swings into high gear around eight o'clock in preparation for the theater crowd.*

swing shift *n.* an evening work shift in a factory, usually from midafternoon to midnight. (See also graveyard shift.) ♦ *My brother works the swing shift, so I never get to see him.*

swing with so/sth *in.* to appreciate someone or something. (See also swing.) ♦ *I can really swing with John. He and I are real close.*

swinger 1. *n.* a person who participates in innovative sexual activities. (See also swing.) ♦ *We watched a movie about a swinger, but everything interesting happened in dim blue light.* **2.** *n.* a youthful, socially active, and knowledgeable person. ♦ *Tom is a swinger. Look at those mod shoes.*

swinging *mod.* great. ♦ *The concert was swinging—nothing like it, ever.*

swingman *n.* a drug seller; a drug connection. ♦ *Bart couldn't deliver till he met with his swingman.*

swipe 1. *tv.* to drink liquor rapidly and to excess; to bolt a drink of liquor. ♦ *Fred sat at the bar and swiped two gins and ate an egg.* **2.** *n.* moonshine; inferior liquor. ♦ *I can't stand the swipe they serve here.* **3.** *tv.* to steal something. ♦ *Bart swiped a pack of cigarettes from the counter.* **4.** *n.* a blow or an act of striking someone or something. (See also take a swipe at so/sth.) ♦ *The cat gave the mouse a swipe with its paw.*

swish [swɪʃ] **1.** *mod.* overly fancy; effeminate; displaying effeminacy. ♦ *The lobby of the theater was a little swish, but not offensive.* **2.** *n.* elaborate decoration; effeminacy. ♦ *What this place needs is more swish. Hang some baubles here and there.*

3. *n.* a gay male. (Rude and derogatory.) ♦ *This place is full of swishes. Let's leave.*

switch *n.* a switchblade knife. (The folding pocket knife springs open when a button is pushed.) ♦ *They found a switch in his pocket when they searched him.*

switch off *in.* to become oblivious to everything. ♦ *I want to go home and switch off—just forget this whole day.* ♦ *I have to switch off when I go home.*

switch on 1. *in.* to come alive. ♦ *She saw her child and immediately switched on.* **2.** *in.* to become modern and participate in current fads and events. ♦ *Most kids I know switched on when they went to high school.* **3.** *in.* to get high on drugs; to begin taking LSD or some other hallucinogens. (Drugs. See also turn on; switched on.) ♦ *There was some old man who seemed to get pleasure from getting kids to switch on. Maybe he was a dealer.*

switched on 1. *mod.* alert and up-to-date; with it. ♦ *My brother is switched on and has lots of friends.* **2.** *mod.* excited. ♦ *I am never switched on by raucous music.*

switcheroo ['swɪtʃ⭑'ru] *n.* a reversal; a switching around. ♦ *He pulled a switcheroo on us and showed up at the other door, so we missed getting his autograph.*

switch-hitter 1. *n.* a ballplayer who bats either right-handed or left-handed. (Base-ball.) ♦ *I'm not a switch-hitter. In fact, I can hardly hit the ball at all.* **2.** *n.* a bisexual person. (From sense 1.) ♦ *Bart finally decided he was a switch-hitter and asked Brad for a date since Mary was busy.*

swizzle ['swɪzl̩] **1.** *tv. & in.* to drink (liquor), probably to excess; to tipple. ♦ *Have you been swizzling again?* **2.** *n.* liquor; beer; a drink of an alcoholic beverage. ♦ *What I need is a nice cold swizzle.*

swizzled ['swɪzl̩d] *mod.* alcohol intoxicated. ♦ *Fred went out and got himself swizzled.*

swizzle-stick *n.* a drunkard. (From the name of a short stick used to stir an alcoholic drink.) ♦ *That guy is a swizzle-stick. Don't give him any more.*

swoozled AND **swozzled** ['swuzl̩d AND 'swazl̩d] *mod.* alcohol intoxicated. ♦ *How can anybody be so swoozled on three beers?*

sword swallowing *n.* fellatio. ♦ *The headmaster caught him in an act of sword swallowing.*

swozzled Go to swoozled.

SYITFP Go to See you in the funny pages.

SYSOP ['sɪsap] *n.* system operator, the person who manages a computer system or forum or news group. ♦ *The SYSOP tried to bring order to the news group discussion but failed.*

T

T. *n.* marijuana. (Drugs. From tea.) ♦ *All she thinks about is smoking T. and where she's gonna get more of it.*

T. and A. 1. *n.* an operation to remove one's tonsils and adenoids. (Hospitals.) ♦ *She was scheduled for a T. and A. this morning at six sharp.* **2.** AND **tits and ass** *n.* a display of *tits and ass*, breasts and buttocks. (See also B. and B. Usually objectionable.) ♦ *The magazines featuring tits and ass flourish in their under-the-counter trade.*

tab 1. *n.* a bill (for something). (From *tabulation*. See also chit.) ♦ *Marlowe paid the tab and left quietly.* **2.** *n.* a tablet (of medicine). ♦ *Take a couple of aspirin tabs and call me in the morning.* **3.** *tv.* to identify someone. ♦ *I couldn't quite tab her, but when she started talking I knew right away who she was.*

tabbed *mod.* well-dressed. (Streets.) ♦ *She's really tabbed in some nice threads.*

table-hop *in.* to move from table to table in a restaurant, nightclub, bar, etc. ♦ *They would table-hop—to the great dismay of the waiters.*

tackhead *n.* an overdressed male. (One who looks tacky.) ♦ *Gary is sort of a tackhead when it comes to clothing.*

tacky 1. *mod.* cheap; crude. ♦ *That was a tacky thing to do to her.* **2.** *mod.* alcohol intoxicated. ♦ *Tom was a little tacky, so he gave me his car keys.*

taco stand ['tɑko...] *n.* a lousy place; a tacky place. ♦ *It's time to get out of this taco stand and go somewhere decent.*

tad *n.* a bit; a small bit. ♦ *That's a little more than a tad, but it's all right.*

tag 1. *n.* a name. ♦ *Everybody knows that tag well.* **2.** *n.* euphoria from drug use; a drug rush. ♦ *The tag from this mojo is something to behold.* **3.** *n.* a car license plate or sticker. ♦ *Don't forget to get a new tag for this year.* **4.** *n.* a blow to the body in boxing. ♦ *Wilbur landed another tag to the right shoulder before the gong sounded.* **5.** *tv.* to punch someone in boxing. ♦ *The guy tagged him back right in the gut.* **6.** *tv.* (in baseball) to touch a runner with the baseball. ♦ *Wilbur tagged the runner and fell flat on his face.* **7.** *n.* the coda or ending section of a piece of music. ♦ *Now, I want everybody to slow down and watch me on the tag.* **8.** *tv.* to charge someone with a crime; to identify and arrest a criminal. ♦ *The cop tagged him with the bank caper immediately.* **9.** *tv.* to mark something with spray paint; to paint something with graffiti. ♦ *Our guys tagged the school walls last night.* **10.** *n.* the painted signature of a graffiti artist. ♦ *Jeb puts somebody else's tag on his worst work.*

tagger *n.* a gang member who puts gang signs and themes on things with spray paint. ♦ *Sam is our best tagger. Man, he's an artist.*

tail-end *n.* the back end of something or someone. ♦ *He was at the tail-end of the long line.*

tailgate 1. *tv. & in.* to follow (someone) too closely in a car. ♦ *That guy tailgating me is drunk, I think.* **2.** *in.* to have a tailgate party. ♦ *We planned to tailgate before the game, but it was massively cold.*

tailgate party *n.* a small party held on the folded-down tailgate of a station wagon in a parking lot. (Something that is done before a ball game, concert, etc.) ♦ *They had a tailgate party before the Bears game.*

tailor-made *n.* a machine-made cigarette. (From an expression for something, such as an article of clothing, that is custom made.) ♦ *They used to call these things tailor-made, meaning professionally made, as opposed to homemade.*

tails *n.* a tuxedo with long sections in back. ♦ *Ralph had to rent tails for the evening.*

taint Go to gooch.

take 1. *n.* a section of a film that is pronounced acceptable just after it is shot. ♦ *After seven straight takes the crew demanded a break.* **2.** *n.* the amount of money taken in at some event; the money received for the tickets that have been purchased. ♦ *The take was much larger than we expected.* **3.** *tv.* to cheat or deceive someone. ♦ *When they think you're going to count your change, they won't try to take you.* **4.** *tv.* to defeat someone, as in a fight. ♦ *Max thought he could take the guy, but he wasn't sure.* **5.** *n.* money taken in a theft or illegal scheme. ♦ *Let's spilt up the take now, not later!*

take a bath (on sth**)** *tv.* to have large financial losses on an investment. ♦ *The broker warned me that I might take a bath if I bought this stuff.*

take a beating *tv.* to be beaten, bested, or defeated. ♦ *The candidate took a beating in the runoffs.*

take a break *tv.* to stop working for a rest period. ♦ *Let's take a break here. Be back in five minutes.*

take a chill pill *tv.* to calm down; to relax. (See also chill (out).) ♦ *The police officer told Jim to take a chill pill and answer the questions.*

take a crack at sth **AND have a crack at** sth *tv.* to take a try at something. ♦ *She had a crack at food preparation, but that wasn't for her.* ♦ *Let me have a crack at changing the tire.*

take a crap Go to take a shit.

take a dig at so **AND take a jab at** so *tv.* to insult or needle someone. ♦ *You're always taking digs at people who think they're your friends.* ♦ *Jed took a jab at Tom about the way he was driving.*

take a dirt nap *tv.* to die and be buried. ♦ *I don't want to end up taking a dirt nap during this operation.*

take a dive Go to take a fall.

take a dump Go to take a shit.

take a fall **AND take a dive 1.** *tv.* to fake being knocked out in a boxing match. ♦ *The boxer took a dive in the second round and made everyone suspicious.* **2.** *tv.* to get arrested. (Underworld. See also take the fall.) ♦ *I didn't wanna take a fall, but the cop left me no choice.*

take a flyer (on sth**)** *tv.* to take a chance on something. ♦ *Fred is too wise an investor to take a flyer on some story stock like that.*

take a gander (at so/sth**)** *tv.* to look at someone or something. (See also gander.) ♦ *Wow, take a gander at this chick!*

take a hike **AND take a walk** *tv.* to leave; to beat it. ♦ *I had enough of the boss and the whole place, so I cleaned out my desk and took a walk.* ♦ *Get out! It's time for you to take a walk.*

take a jab at so Go to take a dig at so.

take a leak **AND take a piss; take a squirt** *tv.* to urinate. (Crude. Often objectionable. Usually in reference to a male. *Leak* is the mildest and *piss* is the strongest.) ♦ *I gotta go take a leak. Back in a minute.* ♦ *We stopped at a rest area so old Harry could take a piss.*

take a load off one's **feet** Go to get a load off one's feet.

take a lot of nerve 1. *tv.* to utilize a large reserve of rudeness (to behave so badly). ♦ *That took a lot of nerve! You took my parking place!* **2.** *tv.* to require courage. ♦ *He climbed the mountain with a bruised foot. That took a lot of nerve.*

take a nosedive *tv.* to collapse; to fail. ♦ *The market took a nosedive again today.*

take a page from so's **book** *tv.* to copy or emulate. ♦ *I took a page from Edison's book and began inventing useful little things.*

take a piss Go to take a leak.

take a pop at so *tv.* to punch at someone. ♦ *The drunk took a pop at the cop—which was the wrong thing to do.*

take a powder *tv.* to leave; to leave town. (Underworld.) ♦ *Bruno took a powder and will lie low for a while.*

Take a running jump (in the lake)! *exclam.* Go away!; Get away from me! ♦ *You can just take a running jump in the lake, you creep!*

take a shit AND **take a crap; take a dump; take a squat** *tv.* to defecate. (It is always *taken* not *given*, *done*, or *put*. Shit is the most offensive with the others following in descending order of offense.) ♦ *Hurry up in there! I gotta take a shit.* ♦ *Why didn't you take a squat before we left home?*

take a shot (at sth) *tv.* to try (to do) something. ♦ *I don't think I can do it, but I'll take a shot at it.*

take a squat Go to take a shit.

take a squirt Go to take a leak.

take a swipe at so/sth **1.** *tv.* to hit at someone or something. ♦ *Max took a swipe at the cop by mistake.* **2.** *tv.* to have a try at someone or something. ♦ *I will probably fail, but I'll take a swipe at it.*

take a walk Go to take a hike.

take a whack at so/sth *tv.* to hit at someone or something. ♦ *Jerry got an ax and took a whack at the tree but didn't do much damage.*

take a whack at sth *tv.* to have a try at something. ♦ *Why don't you practice a little while and take a whack at it tomorrow?*

Take care. *tv.* Good-bye, be careful. ♦ *Take care. See you in Philly.*

take care of number one AND **take care of numero uno** *tv.* to take care of oneself. (See also number one; numero uno.) ♦ *Arthur, like everybody else, is most concerned with taking care of number one.*

take care of numero uno Go to take care of number one.

take care of so *tv.* to kill someone. (Underworld.) ♦ *The boss told Spike to take care of Bart.*

take five *tv.* to take a five-minute break. ♦ *She told them to take five, but they turned the five into fifty.*

take it *tv.* to endure something, physically or mentally. (See also take it on the chin.) ♦ *I just can't take it anymore.*

Take it down a thou(sand)! *in.* Cool down!; Calm down!; Quiet down! ♦ *You are wild! Take it down a thou and let's try again to talk this out.*

take it easy 1. *tv.* relax and take care. ♦ *They told me to take it easy for a few days.* **2.** *exclam.* Let up!; Not so hard!; Be gentle! (Usually **Take it easy!**) ♦ *Take it easy; he's just a kid!*

take it on the chin AND **take it on the nose 1.** *tv.* to stand up to something adverse, such as criticism. (*Chin* is more common.) ♦ *They laid some rude chops on him, but he took it on the chin.* **2.** *tv.* to receive the full brunt of something. ♦ *Why do I have to take it on the nose for something I didn't do?*

take it on the lam *tv.* to get out of town; to run away. (Underworld.) ♦ *Bruno knew that the time had come to take it on the lam.*

take it on the nose Go to take it on the chin.

Take it or leave it. *sent.* There are no other choices.; It is this or nothing. ♦ *This is what you get for the money. Take it or leave it.*

take it out on so/sth *tv.* to punish or harm someone or something because one is angry or disturbed about something. ♦ *I'm sorry about your difficulty, but don't take it out on me.*

take it slow *tv.* to go slowly and carefully. ♦ *Just relax and take it slow. You've got a good chance.*

take it through the nose *tv.* to snort cocaine. (Drugs. A play on take it on the nose and take it on the chin.) ♦ *Max liked* *taking it through the nose better than anything, except maybe a shot in the arm.*

take it to the street *tv.* to tell everyone about your problems. (See also on the street.) ♦ *If there's something bothering her, she's gonna take it to the street, first thing.*

take names *tv.* to make a list of wrongdoers. (Often figuratively, as with a schoolteacher, whose major weapon is to take names and send them to the principal.) ♦ *The boss is madder than hell, and he's taking names.*

take off 1. *in.* [for someone] to leave in a hurry. ♦ *I've got to take off—I'm late.* **2.** *in.* [for something] to start selling well. ♦ *The fluffy dog dolls began to take off, and we sold out the lot.* **3.** *n.* an imitation of something; a copy of something. (Usually **take-off.**) ♦ *This robot is capable of producing 200 circuit board take-offs per hour.* **4.** *n.* a parody of someone or something. (Usually with *on.* Usually **take-off.**) ♦ *The comedian did a take-off on the wealthy senator.* **5.** *n.* a robbery. (Underworld. Usually **take-off.**) ♦ *That was some take-off Lefty pulled, huh?*

take on fuel *tv.* to drink alcohol to excess. ♦ *They stopped at the tavern to take on fuel.*

take one's **belt in (a notch)** AND **pull** one's **belt in (a notch)** *tv.* to prepare for lean times; to reduce expenditures. (See also tighten one's belt.) ♦ *It was clear that we would have to bite the bullet and take our belt in a notch.* ♦ *I gotta pull in my belt or get a second job.*

take one's **lumps** *tv.* to accept the result or punishment one deserves. (See also get one's lumps.) ♦ *You've got to learn to take your lumps if you're going to be in politics.*

take pictures *tv.* for a highway patrol officer to use radar. (Citizens band radio.) ♦ *There's a smokey under the bridge taking pictures.*

take some doing *tv.* to require added effort and planning. ♦ *It'll take some doing, but it'll get done.*

take some heat Go to take the heat.

take so **in 1.** AND **rope** so **in** *tv.* to cheat or deceive someone. ♦ *He might try to rope you in. Keep an eye on him and count your change.* **2.** *tv.* to give shelter to someone. ♦ *We took her in and gave her some soup and a place to stay.*

take so **off** *tv.* to kill someone. (Underworld.) ♦ *The mob took the witness off a week before the trial.*

take so/sth **apart 1.** *tv.* to criticize or defame someone or something. ♦ *They really took me apart, but what the hell?* **2.** *tv.* to beat or damage someone or something. ♦ *The mugger really took the old lady apart.*

take so/sth **off** *tv.* to rob someone or something. (Underworld.) ♦ *Weren't you in that bunch that took the bank off in Philly?*

take so/sth **on** *tv.* to accept the task of handling a difficult person or thing. ♦ *I'll take it on if nobody else will do it.*

take so **out 1.** *tv.* to block someone, as in a football game. ♦ *I was supposed to take the left end out, but I was trapped under the center.* **2.** *tv.* to kill someone. (Underworld.) ♦ *The boss told Rocko to take out Marlowe.* **3.** *tv.* to date someone. ♦ *She wanted to take him out for an evening.*

take so **to the cleaners 1.** *tv.* to take all of someone's money. ♦ *The lawyers took the insurance company to the cleaners, but I still didn't get enough to pay for my losses.* **2.** *tv.* to defeat or best someone. ♦ *Look at the height they've got! They'll take us to the cleaners!*

take sth **out** *tv.* to bomb or destroy something. ♦ *The enemy took out one of the tanks, but not the one carrying the medicine.*

take sth **public 1.** *tv.* to make something known to the public. ♦ *You gotta take it public—put it on the street—even when it's none of your business.* ♦ *Don't take it public. You'll just get talked about.* **2.** *tv.* to sell shares in a company to the general public. (Securities markets.) ♦ *We're going to take it public whenever the market looks good.*

take the cure *tv.* to enter into any treatment program or treatment center. (Especially those dealing with drugs and alcohol.) ◆ *I wanted to take the cure, but I just couldn't bring myself to do it.*

take the fall *tv.* to get arrested for a particular crime. (Especially when others are going unpunished for the same crime. See also take a fall.) ◆ *Joel Cairo and Wilbur pulled the job off together, but only Wilbur took the fall.*

take the fifth 1. AND **five it** *tv.* to refuse to testify to a U.S. legislative committee under the protection of the Fifth Amendment to the U.S. Constitution. ◆ *The lawyer just sat there and said, "Five it" after every question.* **2.** *tv.* to decline to answer any questions. ◆ *I'll take the fifth on that one. Ask Fred.*

take the gas pipe Go to take the pipe.

take the heat AND **take some heat** *tv.* to receive criticism (for something); to receive punishment. ◆ *The cops have been taking some heat about the Quincy killing.*

take the heat off so *tv.* to relieve the pressure on someone; to free someone from suspicion, responsibility, a deadline, etc. ◆ *The confession by Rocko took the heat off the cop-shop for a while.*

take the (long) count *tv.* to die. ◆ *The poor cat took the long count at last.*

take the pipe 1. AND **take the gas pipe** *tv.* to commit suicide. (Originally by inhaling gas.) ◆ *The kid was dropping everything in sight and finally took the pipe.* **2.** *tv.* to fail to perform under pressure; to cave in. (From sense 1.) ◆ *Don't take the pipe, man. Stick in there!*

take the piss out of so *tv.* to humble someone; to make someone—usually a male—less cocky, perhaps by violence. (Usually objectionable.) ◆ *You need somebody to take the piss outa you!*

take the pledge *tv.* to promise to abstain from alcohol. ◆ *I'm not ready to take the pledge yet, but I will cut down.*

take the plunge *tv.* to marry someone. ◆ *I'm not ready to take the plunge yet.*

take the rap (for sth**)** *tv.* to take the blame for something. (Originally underworld. See also rap.) ◆ *I didn't want to take the rap for the job, but, after all, I was guilty.*

take the spear (in one's **chest)** *tv.* to accept full blame for something; to accept the full brunt of the punishment for something. ◆ *The admiral got the short straw and had to take the spear in his chest.*

take the starch out of so *tv.* to reduce someone's self-assurance; to reduce someone's conceit. ◆ *I took the starch out of Kelly by telling him where he was headed if he didn't change his ways.*

take the wind out of so's **sails** *tv.* to put a barrier in someone's path; to reduce the effectiveness of someone. ◆ *When the cops showed Bart the evidence, it took the wind out of his sails.*

take things easy 1. *tv.* to live well and comfortably. ◆ *I'll be glad when I can make enough money to take things easy.* **2.** *tv.* to relax temporarily and recuperate. ◆ *The doctor says I'm supposed to take things easy for a while.*

taken AND **had; took 1.** *mod.* cheated; deceived. ◆ *I counted my change, and I knew I was taken.* **2.** *mod.* drug intoxicated; unconscious from drugs. ◆ *The guy in the corner booth was taken and crying in his beer.* **3.** *mod.* dead. ◆ *I'm sorry, your cat is taken—pifted.* ◆ *Your cat's took, lady, tough luck.* **4.** *mod.* already claimed as someone's mate or lover. ◆ *Sorry, Bill, I'm already taken. Sam and I are engaged.*

take-off artist *n.* a thief. (Underworld.) ◆ *A take-off artist known as the Cat is cleaning out closets and jewelry boxes all over town.*

taker *n.* one who accepts an offer; a buyer. ◆ *Are there any takers for this fine, almost new caddy?*

takes two to tango *phr.* requires two people to do certain things. ◆ *There's no such thing as a one-sided argument. It takes two to tango.*

taking care of business *tv.* doing what one is meant to do; coping with life as it is. (Black. See also TCB.) ♦ *Walter is taking care of business. Back in a minute.*

tale of woe *n.* a sad story; a list of personal problems; an excuse for failing to do something. ♦ *I listened to her tale of woe without saying anything.*

talk a blue streak *tv.* to talk fast or a lot. ♦ *Some parrots never talk. Others talk a blue streak whenever it's light.*

talk big *in.* to brag; to make grandiose statements. ♦ *He has some deep need to talk big. He can't do anything.*

talk like a nut *in.* to say stupid things. ♦ *You're talking like a nut! You don't know what you are saying.*

talk on the big white phone *in.* to vomit into a toilet. ♦ *One more beer and I'm gonna have to go talk on the big white phone.*

talk one's **head off** *tv.* to talk endlessly; to argue persuasively or vigorously. ♦ *I talked my head off trying to convince them.*

talk so **ragged** *tv.* to talk to someone too much; to bore someone. ♦ *That was not an interview. She talked me ragged.*

talk so's **ear off** *tv.* to talk to someone endlessly; to bore someone with too much talk. ♦ *Stay away from Mr. Jones. He will talk your ear off if he gets a chance.*

talk through one's **hat** *in.* to say baseless things; to speak carelessly and tell lies. ♦ *You don't know what you are talking about. You're just talking through your hat.*

talk to earl [...ɚl] *in.* to vomit. (Onomatopoetic.) ♦ *I think I hear Pete in the john talking to earl.*

talk to hear one's **own voice** *in.* to talk far more than is necessary; to talk much, in an egotistical manner. ♦ *Am I just talking to hear my own voice, or are you listening to me?*

talk to Herb and Al *in.* to use marijuana and drink alcohol. (See also **herb**. *Al* is alcohol.) ♦ *I've been out talking to Herb and Al—that's where I've been.* ♦ *Let's go talk to Herb and Al while we're waiting.*

talk turkey *tv.* to talk serious business; to talk frankly. ♦ *We've got to sit down and talk turkey—get this thing wrapped up.* ♦ *It's time to talk turkey and quit messing around.*

talk until one **is blue in the face** *in.* to talk until one is exhausted. ♦ *She talked until she was blue in the face but could not change their minds.*

talking head *n.* a television news reader or announcer whose head and neck appear on the screen. (See also **meat puppet**.) ♦ *I've had it with talking heads. I can read the paper and learn as much in twenty minutes.*

tall 1. *mod.* high on drugs; intoxicated with marijuana. (Drugs.) ♦ *When Jerry gets a little tall, he gets overwhelmed with a sense of guilt.* **2.** *mod.* high-quality. ♦ *You're bringing in some tall ideas, man.*

tall in the saddle *mod.* proud. (Often with *sit*.) ♦ *I'll still be tall in the saddle when you are experiencing the results of your folly.*

tall one *n.* a large drink; a long drink. (Compare this with **short one**.) ♦ *She ordered a tall one and sat back to cool off.*

tall order *n.* a request that is difficult to fulfill. ♦ *That's a tall order. Do you think anyone can do it?*

tall timbers *n.* some remote well-forested place; the **boondocks**. ♦ *Oh, Chuck lives out in the tall timbers somewhere. He only has a post office box number.*

tallywhacker *n.* the penis. ♦ *Stop scratching your tallywhacker in public!*

tamp *n.* a tampon. ♦ *You need a tamp, honey?*

tangle with so/sth *in.* to quarrel or fight with someone or something. ♦ *It's like tangling with a grizzly.*

Tango Yankee *phr.* thank you. (NATO Phonetic Alphabet.) ♦ *Tango Yankee for the email.*

tank 1. AND **tank up** *in.* to drink too much beer; to drink to excess. ♦ *Let's go out this Friday and tank a while.* **2.** *n.* a drunkard. (Usually **tank-up**.) ♦ *You're turning into a real tank, Harry.* **3.** *n.* a jail cell for holding drunks. ♦ *One night in the tank was enough to make John take the pledge.* **4.** *tv. & in.* to lose a game deliberately. ♦ *The manager got wind of a plan to tank Friday's game.* **5.** *in.* for something to fail. ♦ *The entire stock market tanked on Friday.*

tank up Go to tank.

tanked 1. AND **tanked up** *mod.* alcohol intoxicated. ♦ *That old codger is really tanked.* **2.** *mod.* defeated; outscored. ♦ *The team was tanked again—20–17.* **3.** *mod.* dead. ♦ *My cat got hit be a truck and is totally tanked.*

tanked up Go to tanked.

tanker *n.* a drinker; a drunkard. ♦ *When I came into the bar, a few tankers were in the back.*

tanky *mod.* alcohol intoxicated. ♦ *He found a way to slow down and keep from getting tanky at parties.*

tanned *mod.* alcohol intoxicated. (Preserved like a tanned hide of an animal.) ♦ *Tom is too tanned to drive. Get him out of that car.*

TANSTAAFL Go to There ain't no such thing as a free lunch.

tap dance like mad *in.* to be busy continuously; to have to move fast to distract someone. ♦ *Any public official knows how to tap dance like mad without getting out of breath or sweating.*

tap out 1. *in.* to lose one's money gambling or in the securities markets. (See also tapped.) ♦ *I'm gonna tap out in about three more rolls—just watch.* ♦ *I really tapped out on that gold-mining stock.* **2.** *in.* to die; to expire. ♦ *Mary was so tired that she thought she was going to tap out.*

tap so **(for** sth**)** *tv.* to select someone for some purpose or position. ♦ *The committee tapped John to run for Congress.*

taped [tept] *mod.* finalized; sealed (up); cinched. (As if one were taping a package.) ♦ *I'll have this deal taped by Thursday. Then we can take it easy.*

tapped [tæpt] **1.** AND **tapped out** *mod.* broke. ♦ *The consumer is just about tapped. Don't expect much buying in that sector.* **2.** AND **tapped out** *mod.* exhausted. ♦ *I need a nap. I'm tapped out.* **3.** AND **tapped out** *mod.* ruined. ♦ *We are tapped. That really did it to us.* **4.** *mod.* arrested. (As if one were tapped on the shoulder by a police officer.) ♦ *I knew I was gonna get tapped eventually, but I just couldn't stop stealing.*

tapped out Go to tapped.

tard *n.* a person who behaves as if retarded. (See also retard. Derogatory and potentially cruel.) ♦ *You tard! Why did you do that?*

taste *n.* a share; a piece (of the action). ♦ *Whatever the deal is, I want a taste.*

taste blood *tv.* to experience something exciting, and perhaps dangerous, for the first time. ♦ *Once you taste blood, you're hooked.*

tat *n.* a tattoo. ♦ *Nice tats!*

tatas *n.* the female breasts. (Often bodacious tatas.) ♦ *Hairball, girlfriend! You'll never get those tatas into that swimmer!*

tater *n.* a potato. (Folksy. The plural, *taters* can refer to individual potatoes or a mass of potatoes as with mashed potatoes.) ♦ *Give me more meat and less taters.*

tawny ['tɔni] *mod.* excellent. ♦ *Who is throwing this tawny party anyway?*

TCB *tv.* taking care of business; doing things that have to be done. (Black. Initialism.) ♦ *He's TCB; that's where he is.*

tchotchke AND **chotchke** *n.* a trinket or ornament. (From Yiddish.) ♦ *Her whole house is filled with tchotchkes and old photographs.*

tea 1. *n.* liquor; alcoholic drink. ♦ *Would you care for more tea?* **2.** *n.* urine. (Usually objectionable.) ♦ *Is that tea on your pants leg?* **3.** *n.* marijuana. (Drugs.) ♦ *Can't you lay off that tea a while?*

tea party 1. *n.* a wild drinking party. (Like the Mad Hatter's party in Lewis Carroll's *Alice in Wonderland*.) ♦ *There was a loud tea party going on in the corner booth when Marlowe came in.* **2.** *n.* something easy; a pleasant and unstressful event. ♦ *The test was a real tea party. No sweat.*

team Xerox *n.* the imaginary source of copied documents, such as term papers. (Implies cheating or plagiarism. *Xerox* is a protected trade name.) ♦ *I got the term paper in on time with the help of team Xerox.*

tear [tɛr] *n.* a wild drinking bout. (See also rip.) ♦ *Sally is off on a tear again.*

tear into a place *in.* to run or rush into a place. ♦ *I tore into the office and answered the phone.*

tear into so *in.* to scold someone severely; to attack someone. ♦ *I was late, and the super tore into me like a mad dog.*

tear into sth *in.* to begin eating food with gusto. ♦ *The family tore into the mountain of food like they hadn't eaten since breakfast—which was true, in fact.* ♦ *Jimmy tore into the turkey leg and cleaned it off in no time.*

tear loose (from so/sth**)** [tɛr…] *in.* to manage to break away from someone or something. ♦ *The quarterback tore loose and ran twenty yards for a first down.*

tear off *in.* to break away; to run away. ♦ *Don't tear off without having some of my pie.*

tear so **a new asshole** AND **tear** so **a new one** to chastise someone severely. (Usually objectionable.) ♦ *The colonel glared at him and threatened to tear him a new asshole.* ♦ *If you don't get it right this time, I'll tear you a new one!*

tear so/sth **apart** *tv.* to criticize someone or something severely. ♦ *I was late, and the boss tore me apart.*

tear so/sth **up** *tv.* to rip someone or something to pieces. ♦ *The two drunks tore the bar up the best they could.*

tear so **up** *tv.* to cause someone much grief. (See also tore (up).) ♦ *The situation really tore up his father.*

tear-jerker ['tɪrdʒɚkɚ] *n.* a very sad story or film. ♦ *I don't care to read a steady diet of tear-jerkers.*

teaser ['tizɚ] **1.** *n.* a (found) cigarette butt. ♦ *The hobo picked up the teaser from the street and put it in a little bag.* **2.** *n.* a brief sample of something, such as a performance. ♦ *The teasers they showed before the film were the best part of the evening.*

techie ['tɛki] **1.** *n.* a student in a technical or engineering college. ♦ *Of course, one groovy guy proves that techies aren't nerds, right?* **2.** *n.* a person with technical skills or knowledge. ♦ *The techies say it should work, theoretically, that is.* **3.** *mod.* having to do with technical people or things. ♦ *I don't like this techie jargon.*

tech-nerd ['tɛknɚd] *n.* a technically oriented, dull person, typically a male computer enthusiast. ♦ *My brother, who is a tech-nerd, spends more than ten hours a day on his computer.*

Technicolor yawn *n.* vomit. (See also throw a Technicolor yawn. Technicolor is a protected trade name.) ♦ *This horrible pizza will bring on a few Technicolor yawns if we serve it.*

tee so **off** *tv.* to make someone angry. (See also teed off.) ♦ *Well, you sure managed to tee off everybody!*

teed off *mod.* angry. ♦ *I was so teed off I could have spit!*

teed (up) *mod.* alcohol or drug intoxicated. ♦ *She was totally teed up by midnight.*

teenie AND **teeny** *n.* a sixteenth. (Securities markets. From six*teen*th. One sixteenth of a point in a stock price. See also steenth.) ♦ *It's going at three and two teenies at the moment.*

teenie-weenie Go to teeny-weeny.

teensy-weensy Go to teeny-weeny.

teeny Go to teenie.

teenybopper ['tinibɑpɚ] *n.* a young teenager, usually a girl. ♦ *The teenyboppers moved around the mall in droves, not buying and not causing any trouble, just being available for anyone who wanted to see them.*

teeny-weeny AND **teenie-weenie; teensy-weensy** ['tini'wini AND 'tintsi'wintsi] *mod.* tiny. ♦ *Could you move just a teenie-weenie bit to the left?*

teepee Go to TP.

tee-tee ['titi] **1.** *in.* to urinate. (Juvenile. Usually objectionable.) ♦ *Jimmy, please go tee-tee before we leave.* **2.** *n.* urine. (Juvenile. Usually objectionable.) ♦ *There's tee-tee on the floor.*

telegraph one's **punches 1.** *tv.* to signal, unintentionally, what blows one is about to strike. (Boxing.) ♦ *Don't telegraph your punches, kid! You'll be flat on your back in twenty seconds.* **2.** *tv.* to signal, unintentionally, one's intentions. ♦ *The mediator telegraphed his punches, and we were prepared with a strong counter argument.*

Tell it like it is! AND **TILII** *exclam. & comp. abb.* a phrase encouraging someone to continue to make whatever points were being made; Speak frankly.; Tell the truth no matter how much it hurts. ♦ *Right on, Fred! TILII!* ♦ *Come on man, tell it like it is!*

Tell me another (one)! *exclam.* Tell me another fairy tale!; That was a lie. Tell me another just as good! ♦ *You a stockbroker? Tell me another one!*

tell shit from Shinola Go to know shit from Shinola.

tell so **what to do with** sth *tv.* to tell someone to do something rude with something. (With the unspoken notion that one should stick it up one's ass.) ♦ *If that's the way he wants to be, you can just tell him what to do with it.*

tell so **where to get off** *tv.* to tell someone when enough is enough; to tell someone off. ♦ *He told me where to get off, so I walked out on him.*

tell the (whole) world *tv.* to spread around private business. ♦ *Well, you don't have to tell the whole world.*

telly ['tɛli] *n.* a television set. (Originally British.) ♦ *What's on the telly tonight?*

temp-tat *n.* a temporary tattoo. (Viewed as wimpy by those bearing real ink.) ♦ *My father nearly croaked until I convinced him they were temp-tats.*

a **ten** *n.* the highest rank on a scale of one to ten. ♦ *On a scale of one to ten, this pizza's a ten.*

ten percenter *n.* an agent who collects 10 percent. ♦ *I've been supporting that ten percenter for years, and he was robbing me blind.*

ten-four AND **10-4** *interj.* okay. (Citizens band radio.) ♦ *Ten-four, old buddy. I will do that.*

tenner *n.* a ten-dollar bill. (See also fiver.) ♦ *For a tenner, the bum led Marlowe to the place where the crate still lay in the alley.*

tennies *n.* tennis shoes; sneakers. ♦ *Let me get my tennies on, and I'll be right with you.*

ten-spot *n.* a ten-dollar bill. ♦ *I slipped him a ten-spot, and suddenly there was a table available.*

TEOTWAWKI Go to the end of the world as we know it.

terps Go to turps.

terrific *mod.* excellent. ♦ *Glad to hear it. That's just terrific.*

TFS Go to three-finger salute.

TGIF 1. *interj.* Thank God it's Friday. (Initialism.) ♦ *Everybody was muttering TGIF by Friday afternoon.* **2.** *n.* a party held on Friday in honor of the end of the workweek. ♦ *Everyone is invited to the TGIF tonight.*

thank you very much *phr.* a (sometimes sarcastic) tag added to a statement for emphasis. (Often used when there is really nothing to thank anyone for.) ♦ *I will manage somehow to find my own way out, thank you very much.*

thanks a bunch *phr.* thanks. ♦ *Thanks a bunch for your help.*

Thanks in advance. AND **TIA** *phr. & comp. abb.* an expression of gratitude given in advance of the hoped-for receipt of an answer to a question. ♦ *I hope you can help me. TIA. Bob.*

that 1. *mod.* a stylistic replacement for *the*. (Especially in citizens band radio jargon and much daily colloquial speech. It is the pervasive overuse of this form that makes it notable as colloquial.) ♦ *Can you tell me where that next rest stop is?* **2.** *mod.* a stylistic modifier of personal and place names and some other nouns that do not normally take modifiers. (Citizens band radio.) ♦ *How do I get to that Kansas City?*

That ain't hay! *exclam.* That's money, not something worthless. ♦ *That car cost $40,000, and that ain't hay!*

That sucks. AND **It sucks.** *in.* That is worthless. ♦ *This meat loaf is terrible. It sucks.*

That tears it! [...tɛrz...] *exclam.* That is too much! ♦ *I thought yesterday's error was bad enough, but that tears it!*

that way 1. *mod.* in love. ♦ *Well, Martha's that way, but Sam's just out for a good time.* **2.** *mod.* alcohol intoxicated. ♦ *I'm sorry, but Fred's that way again and can't drive to work.* **3.** *mod.* homosexual. ♦ *Ken said that you-know-who was acting sort of that way. What a gossip!*

That-a-boy! *exclam.* That is the way to do it! (Said to a boy or man.) ♦ *Come on, Chuck. That-a-boy!*

That'll be the day! *exclam.* That will never happen! ♦ *When he gets his own car—that'll be the day!*

That'll teach so. *sent.* That is what someone deserves. ♦ *That'll teach you to pull out in front of me.*

That's a new one on me. *sent.* That is truly amazing.; I did not know that. ♦ *A talking camera? That's a new one on me.*

That's about the size of it. *sent.* That is the way things are.; That's all there is to tell. ♦ *Well, that's about the size of it. See you tomorrow.*

That's all she wrote. AND **That's what she wrote.** *sent.* That is all of it. ♦ *Here's the last one we have to fix. There, that's all she wrote.*

That's all so **needs.** *sent.* That is too much.; That is the last straw. ♦ *Now the sewer's backing up. That's all I need.*

That's my boy. *sent.* That is my son of whom I am proud.; I'm proud of this young man. ♦ *After the game, Tom's dad said, "That's my boy!"*

That's show business (for you). *sent.* That is the way that life really is. (Also with **biz** and **show biz**.) ♦ *And now the car won't start. That's show business for you.*

That's so suck! *phr.* That's so awful. ♦ *Eat sweet potatoes? That's so suck!*

That's that! *exclam.* That is final!; That is the end of it! ♦ *I said no, and that's that!*

That's the stuff! *exclam.* That is good work! ♦ *Good shot, Willy! That's the stuff!*

That's the ticket! *exclam.* That is exactly what is needed! ♦ *Good! That's the ticket! Now you're cooking with gas.*

That's the way the ball bounces. *sent.* That is life.; That is the random way things happen. ♦ *It's tough, I know, but that's the way the ball bounces.*

That's the way the cookie crumbles. *sent.* That is life.; That is typical of the unequal share of things you are likely to get in life. ♦ *I lost my job. Oh, well. That's the way the cookie crumbles.*

That's the way the mop flops. *sent.* This is the way things happen.; This is typical of a random pattern of events. (Contrived.) ♦ *Sorry to hear about that, but that's the way the mop flops.*

(That's the) way to go! *exclam.* Nicely done! ♦ *That's the way to go! You did it!*

That's what I say. *sent.* I agree with you. ♦ *That's what I say. The way to cut spending is just to do it.*

That's what she wrote. Go to That's all she wrote.

thawed *mod.* alcohol intoxicated. ♦ *Tad is sort of soppy, you might say, thawed.*

the B *n.* the Frizbee. ♦ *Let's go out and play with the B.*

the big one *n.* a serious heart attack, possibly fatal, especially if anticipated or dreaded. ♦ *He survived the big one but kept on smoking.*

the end of the world as we know it AND **TEOTWAWKI** *phr. & comp. abb.* said to emphasize that things change, often a lot.

♦ *Yes, you have to buy the operating system separately. It's TEOTWAWKI.*

The Force *n.* duct (duck) tape. ♦ *She used The Force to hold it all together.*

then and there *mod.* right then. ♦ *Right then and there, he pulled up his shirt and showed everyone the jagged scar.*

There ain't no such thing as a free lunch. AND **TANSTAAFL** *sent. & comp. abb.* Careful, nothing is really free of charge. ♦ *Of course, you have to pay extra for the data file. There ain't no such thing as a free lunch.*

There ought to be a law! AND **TOBAL** *exclam. & comp. abb.* There ought to be a law against what you just did or what I just saw happen. (Uttered when something happens that one does not like.) ♦ *Listen to them talk like that. TOBAL!*

There's no such thing as a stupid question. AND **TNSTAASQ** *sent. & comp. abb.* Go ahead and ask your question without referring to it as stupid. ♦ *There's no such thing as a stupid question. But keep trying, you're getting close.*

There's nobody home. *sent.* There are no brains in someone's head. ♦ *You twit! There's nobody home—that's for sure.*

There will be hell to pay. *sent.* Things will be so bad that one will have to bribe the devil to straighten them out. (Use caution with hell.) ♦ *If I don't get this done on time, there will be hell to pay.*

There you are. *sent.* This is the result.; This is the way things turned out. ♦ *Well, there you are. Another first-class mess.*

There you go. 1. *sent.* Hooray! You did it right! (Usually **There you go!**) ♦ *Good shot, Chuck! There ya go!* **2.** *sent.* That is the way things are, just like I told you.; Isn't this just what you would expect? ♦ *There you go. Isn't that just like a man!* **3.** *sent.* You are doing it again. ♦ *I just told you not to put that junk on the table, and there you go.*

thick 1. *mod.* stupid; thickheaded. ♦ *She's sort of thick, but she means well.* **2.** *mod.* involved (with someone). ♦ *They're thick as can be.* **3.** *mod.* unbelievable. ♦ *This story is too thick for me. I'm cruising outa here.*

thickheaded *mod.* stupid; with more bone than brain in the head. ♦ *He's so thickheaded he can play football without a helmet.*

thick-skinned *mod.* able to withstand much criticism. (Compare this with thinskinned.) ♦ *You gotta be more thickskinned if you want to be a cop.*

thin dime *n.* a dime, thought of as a very small amount of money. (A concept eroded by inflation.) ♦ *For only one thin dime you will receive our exciting catalog of novelties and tricks.*

thing *n.* one's interest; one's bag. ♦ *This isn't exactly my thing, but I'll give it a try.*

thingamajig AND **thingy** [ˈθɪŋəmədʒɪg AND ˈθɪŋi] *n.* a gadget for which the proper name has been forgotten or is unknown. ♦ *Hand me that thingamajig with the copper base, will you?*

thingy Go to thingamajig.

think-box *n.* the skull; the head. ♦ *Use your think-box for something other than to hold your ears apart.*

think-piece *n.* a thoughtful piece of writing in a newspaper or magazine. ♦ *Mr. Wilson's think-piece about the need for more concern for the middle class was not well received.*

think-tank *n.* a place where great minds are assembled to try to think up solutions to problems or to envision the future. ♦ *She spent a few months in a California thinktank, then came back to teach.*

thin-skinned *mod.* sensitive to criticism. (Compare this with thick-skinned.) ♦ *Don't be so thin-skinned. You can't expect everyone to like you.*

third degree *n.* a session of questioning, usually by the police. ♦ *Bart got the third degree, but—being the thoroughbred he is—he was a clam.* ♦ *They gave Spike the third degree, but he refused to say anything.*

third wheel *n.* an extra person; a person who gets in the way. (Such a person is as useful as a third wheel on a bicycle. See also **spare tire**.) ◆ *Well, let's face it. We don't need you. You are a third wheel.*

thirst-aid station *n.* a place to purchase liquor. (Punning on *first-aid station*.) ◆ *Let's stop at the next thirst-aid station and get a snort.*

thirsty soul *n.* a drunkard; a person in need of a drink. ◆ *Yes, I'd call Bill a thirsty soul—he always seems thirsty for booze.* ◆ *There was a long line of thirsty souls waiting for the liquor joint to open.*

This is it! 1. *exclam.* This is exactly what I have been looking for!; I have found it! ◆ *This is it! The world's best pizza!* **2.** *exclam.* This is the crucial moment! ◆ *Get ready, this is it! Jump now!*

This is where I came in. *sent.* This all seems very familiar. ◆ *This is where I came in. It's the same thing all over again.*

thoroughbred *n.* an underworld person who is trustworthy and loyal to the underworld. (Underworld.) ◆ *Bart is an A-1 thoroughbred.*

thou [θaʊ] *n.* one thousand. ◆ *I managed to get a couple of thou from the bank, but I need a little more than that.*

thrash on so *in.* to scold, criticize, or berate someone. ◆ *She's always thrashing on her roommate.*

threads *n.* clothing. ◆ *When'd you get new threads, man?*

three bricks shy of a load *mod.* stupid; dense; shortchanged on intelligence. ◆ *I would never say she was dense. Just three bricks shy of a load.*

three point two Go to **three-two**.

three sheets in the wind AND **three sheets (to the wind); two sheets to the wind** *mod.* alcohol intoxicated and unsteady. (Sheets are the ropes used to manage a ship's sails. It is assumed that if these ropes were blowing in the wind, the ship would be unmanageable.) ◆ *He was three sheets to the wind and didn't pay attention to my warning.*

three sheets (to the wind) Go to **three sheets in the wind**.

three squares *n.* three square meals a day. ◆ *I was glad to get back home to three squares.*

a three-alarm fire AND **a five-alarm fire** *n.* someone or something very exciting. ◆ *Work was a nightmare today. A five-alarm fire with crisis after crisis.*

a three-finger salute AND **TFS** *n. & comp. abb.* The keyboard keys Control, Alternate, Delete pressed at the same time when a program fails under the Windows operating system. (This is a play on one-finger salute, the *digitus impudicus*.) ◆ *I had to give the TFS twice before the program would run.*

three-two AND **three point two** *n.* a weak beer containing 3.2 percent alcohol. (Not found in all states.) ◆ *James likes three point two because he can drink more of it without getting stoned.*

thriller-diller ['θrɪlɚˈdɪlɚ] *n.* something like a movie, book, or television program that is thrilling. (See also **whodunit**.) ◆ *The film was a real thriller-diller. I remember having to force myself to exhale.*

throat *n.* an earnest student; a *cutthroat* student. (Collegiate.) ◆ *Martin is not a throat! He's not that smart.*

throat gag *n.* liquor; strong liquor. ◆ *Pour me another glass of that throat gag, barkeep.*

throg *in.* to drink beer or liquor. (Possibly *throw* + *grog*.) ◆ *the guys were throgging till early beams.*

the **throne** *n.* a toilet; a toilet seat. ◆ *And there was the cat—right on the throne, just staring at me.*

throne room *n.* a restroom; a bathroom. (See also **throne**.) ◆ *Hank is in the throne room, reading, I think.*

through the mill *mod.* abused; well-worn. ◆ *That was some convention. I've really been through the mill.*

throw 1. *n.* a try; a time. ◆ *Have another throw at it, why don't you?* **2.** *tv.* to confuse someone. ◆ *The question really threw me.*

throw a fight *tv.* to lose a boxing match on purpose. (Boxing. Other words can replace *a*.) ♦ *I just know that Wilbur didn't throw that fight.*

throw a fit *tv.* to have a display of bad temper. ♦ *I knew you'd throw a fit when I told you.*

throw a game *tv.* to lose a game on purpose. (See also throw a fight.) ♦ *There's a couple of those guys who would throw a game if they got enough money to do it.*

throw a map *tv.* to empty one's stomach; to vomit. ♦ *Somebody threw a map on the sidewalk.*

throw a punch *tv.* to jab; to punch. ♦ *She tried to throw a punch at me, but I blocked it.*

throw a Technicolor yawn *tv.* to vomit. (See also Technicolor yawn.) ♦ *John stumbled into the living and threw a Technicolor yawn on the new carpet.*

throw down *in.* to eat; to gobble one's food. (The opposite of *throw up* = to vomit.) ♦ *Man, I'm starved. Let's find a hamburger joint and throw down.*

throw in the sponge Go to throw in the towel.

throw in the towel AND **throw in the sponge; toss in the sponge** *tv.* to quit; to give up. (From boxing, where a towel or sponge thrown into the ring indicates that a boxer has given up.) ♦ *The candidate who was exposed by the press as a former pickpocket tossed in the sponge in a tearful press conference.* ♦ *I'm done! I'm tossing in the sponge!*

throw money at sth *tv.* to try to solve a problem by spending money on it. (Often said of the U.S. federal government.) ♦ *This agency has thrown billions at the housing problem, but it has been nothing but a long-term disaster.*

throw one **out on** one's **ear** *tv.* to remove someone from a place forcibly. ♦ *The caretaker caught us and threw us out on our ear.*

throw one's **cookies** Go to toss one's cookies.

throw one's **hat in the ring** *tv.* to indicate that one is to be a contestant or a candidate. ♦ *The con claimed he needed parole so he could throw his hat in the ring for the mayoral election.*

throw one's **voice** *tv.* to empty one's stomach; to vomit. ♦ *Willy's in the john throwing his voice.*

throw one's **weight around** *tv.* to show off one's importance or power; to use one's rank or station to advantage. ♦ *The vice president was throwing his weight around, but that had little effect on anything.*

throw salt on so's **game** *tv.* to mess up someone's plans. ♦ *I don't mean to throw salt on your game, but I don't think you can pull it off.*

throw so **for a loop** *tv.* to confuse or surprise someone. ♦ *Don't let this question throw you for a loop.*

throw sth **back** *tv.* to eat or drink something. ♦ *Jed threw back a quick snort and went on with his complaining.*

throw sth **together** Go to knock sth together.

throw the book at so *tv.* [for the police] to charge someone with everything possible; [for a judge] to find someone guilty of everything possible. (As if one were being charged with violating all the laws in a law book.) ♦ *The judge wanted to throw the book at Joel Cairo, but the prosecutor convinced him to go easy in hope that Cairo would lead them to Mr. Gutman.*

throw the bull AND **throw the crap** *tv.* to chat; to boast. (Use caution with crap.) ♦ *Tom could really throw the bull and sound right as rain.* ♦ *Stop throwing the crap and tell me what you really think!*

throw the crap Go to throw the bull.

throw up one's **toenails** *tv.* to wretch; to vomit a lot. ♦ *It sounded like he was throwing up his toenails.*

throw-away 1. *n.* a flyer or handbill. ♦ *I passed out the throw-aways, but not many people would take them.* **2.** *n.* a comedian's quickly uttered one-line joke. ♦ *He* *tossed off his best throw-away of the evening just as the curtain fell.*

thumb a ride *tv.* to beg a ride; to stand at the side of the street and signal to cars with one's thumb for a ride; to hitchhike. ♦ *I'll thumb a ride to get there if I have to.*

thumber ['θəmɚ] *n.* a beggar; a moocher. (As one who thumbs or begs a ride.) ♦ *Don't be a thumber, Frank. Go buy your own cancer sticks.*

thumbnail sketch *n.* a quick and concise description. (One that could be written on someone's thumbnail.) ♦ *Let me give you a thumbnail sketch of what happened.*

thumbs down 1. *n.* a sign of disapproval. (See also **turn thumbs down (on** so/sth**).**) ♦ *The board gave our proposal a thumbs down.* **2.** *mod.* disapproving; negative. ♦ *It was thumbs down, and I was disappointed.*

thumbs up 1. *n.* a sign of approval. ♦ *It was a thumbs up on the new filtration plant at Thursday's village board meeting.* **2.** *mod.* approving; positive. ♦ *The new filtration plant got a thumbs up decision at the board meeting.*

thunder-boomer *n.* a thunderstorm. ♦ *There will be thunder-boomers in the boonies tonight.*

thunderbox *n.* a portable stereo radio, often played very loudly in public. (See also **boom box**.) ♦ *Someday I'm going to smash one of these thunderboxes!*

thunder-thighs *n.* big or fat thighs. (Cruel. Also a rude term of address.) ♦ *Here, thunder-thighs, let me get you a chair or two.*

TIA Go to **Thanks in advance**.

TIC Go to **tongue in cheek**.

tick *n.* a minute; a second. (See also **sec**.) ♦ *This won't take a tick. Sit tight.*

tick so **off** *tv.* to make someone angry. (See also **ticked (off)**.) ♦ *That really ticks me off!*

ticked (off) *mod.* angry. ♦ *Kelly was so ticked!*

ticker 1. *n.* a heart. ♦ *His ticker finally gave out.* **2.** *n.* a watch. ♦ *My ticker stopped. The battery must be dead.*

ticket 1. *n.* the exact thing; the needed thing. ♦ *This degree will be your ticket to a bright and shining future.* **2.** *n.* a license. ♦ *I showed her my ticket, and she let me off with a warning.*

tickle the ivories *tv.* to play the piano. ♦ *I used to be able to tickle the ivories real nice.*

tickled (pink) *mod.* amused; utterly delighted; pleased. ♦ *I am tickled pink you could come this evening.*

tick-tock ['tɪktɑk] **1.** *n.* a heart. (See also **ticker**.) ♦ *My tick-tock is as strong as an ox's.* **2.** *n.* a watch or clock. (Juvenile.) ♦ *Wind your tick-tock before you forget.*

ticky-tacky ['tɪkitæki] *n.* cheap and shabby material. ♦ *Those houses are just made of ticky-tacky, and they won't even be here in twenty years.*

tiddled *mod.* alcohol intoxicated. ♦ *He had a tendency to get a little tiddled.*

tie it on Go to **tie one on**.

tie on the nosebag Go to **put on the feedbag**.

tie one on AND **lay one on; tie it on** *tv.* to get drunk. ♦ *The boys went out to tie one on.* ♦ *I'm gonna really lay one on tonight.*

tie the knot 1. *tv.* to marry a mate. ♦ *We tied the knot in a little chapel on the Arkansas border.* **2.** *tv.* [for a cleric] to unite a couple in marriage. ♦ *It was hard to find somebody to tie the knot at that hour.*

tied up *mod.* busy. ♦ *I was tied up and couldn't get to the phone.*

tie-in *n.* a connection; a liaison. ♦ *I got a call from Mary—my tie-in with the mayor's office—who says it's all set.*

tiffled ['tɪf!d] *mod.* alcohol intoxicated. ♦ *Harry was too tiffled to drive.*

tiger *n.* a strong and virile man. ♦ *The guy's a tiger. Watch out for him.*

tiger juice Go to **tiger sweat**.

tiger('s) milk Go to tiger sweat.

tiger sweat AND **tiger juice; tiger('s) milk** *n.* bad liquor; strong liquor; any beer or liquor. (Older.) ♦ *This tiger milk would kill a tiger of any age or disposition.* ♦ *Give me some of that tiger juice, will ya?*

tight 1. *mod.* stingy. ♦ *She's really tight with her cash.* **2.** *mod.* alcohol intoxicated. ♦ *Frank was tight and didn't want to drive.* **3.** *mod.* stressful; with little margin for error. ♦ *When the schedule is tight and we are busy as all get out, the telephone won't stop ringing.* **4.** *mod.* cool; super. ♦ *His new car is tight!* **5.** *mod.* close to someone; friendly with someone. ♦ *Those two are really tight. True buds.*

tight as a tick Go to (as) tight as a tick.

tight money *n.* money that is hard to get. ♦ *In these days of tight money, no new expenditures will be approved.*

tight spot *n.* a difficulty. ♦ *Sure, I like helping people out of tight spots as long as it doesn't cost me any money.*

tight wad *n.* a stingy person; a miser. (See also **wad**.) ♦ *There's no need to be such a tight wad.*

tighten one's **belt** *tv.* to prepare for economies. (As if one would not be able to afford enough food to make one's stomach press against one's belt. See also **take** one's **belt in (a notch)**.) ♦ *The entire country will have to tighten its belt.*

TIIC *n.* the idiots in charge. ♦ *I can't give you the answer until I consult with TIIC.*

Tijuana taxi ['tiəwɑnɑ 'tæksi] *n.* a police car. (Citizens band radio.) ♦ *There's a Tijuana taxi back a few cars watching you awful close.*

TILII Go to Tell it like it is!

till hell freezes over *mod.* forever. (Use caution with *hell*.) ♦ *That's all right, boss; I can wait till hell freezes over for your answer.*

till kingdom come *mod.* until the end of the world; forever. ♦ *I'll hate her guts till kingdom come.*

till the fat lady sings AND **when the fat lady sings** *mod.* at the end; a long time from now. (Supposedly from a tale about a child—sitting through an opera—who asks a parent when it will be over. "Not until the fat lady sings" is the answer.) ♦ *Relax. It won't be over till the fat lady sings.* ♦ *This trial will be over when the fat lady sings, and that's all there is to it!*

Time (out)! *exclam.* Stop talking for a minute! (A way of interrupting someone.) ♦ *Just a minute! Time out! I want to speak!*

time to cruise *n.* Time to leave. ♦ *Time to cruise. We're gone.*

tin cow *n.* canned milk. ♦ *This tin cow is okay in coffee or something, but you can't drink it.*

tin dog *n.* a snowmobile (in Alaska). ♦ *Who's out there riding the tin dog?*

tin grin *n.* a smile with a mouth having braces. ♦ *I'll be glad when I get rid of this tin grin.*

tin hat *n.* a soldier's helmet. ♦ *You use your tin hat for everything—washing, hauling water—you name it.*

tingle 1. *n.* a party. ♦ *This tingle is really da bomb.* **2.** *in.* to party. ♦ *Hay, man, let's tingle.*

tinkle 1. *in.* to urinate. (Mostly juvenile use. Usually objectionable.) ♦ *Jimmy, be sure and tinkle before we leave.* **2.** *n.* urine. (Essentially juvenile. Usually objectionable.) ♦ *There's tinkle on the bathroom floor.*

tinklebox *n.* a piano. (See also **joybox**.) ♦ *The tinklebox in the bar seemed to be a bit loud.*

tinseled *mod.* forged or decorated, as with a bad check. (Underworld.) ♦ *He almost got caught kiting tinseled checks.*

tinsel-teeth *n.* a nickname for someone who wears dental braces. (Also a rude nickname.) ♦ *Well, tinsel-teeth, today's the day your braces come off.*

Tinseltown *n.* Hollywood, California. ♦ *She's talented and has her eye on Tinseltown.*

tints *n.* sunglasses. ♦ *I have to get some prescription tints.*

tip one's **hand** *tv.* to reveal what one is going to do; to reveal one's secrets. (From card playing.) ♦ *I didn't tip my hand at all. I left them guessing.*

tip-off *n.* a clue; an indication. ♦ *The tip-off was when the dog started wagging his tail. We knew you were hiding somewhere close.*

tipple 1. *n.* liquor; strong liquor. ♦ *A little more tipple, Tom?* **2.** *tv. & in.* to drink liquor; to sip at a vessel of liquor. ♦ *He's been tippling beer since early morning.* **3.** *n.* a drink of liquor. ♦ *I'll take just a little tipple—for my arthritis, you know.* **4.** *n.* a drinking bout. ♦ *Well, Uncle Harry's off on a tipple again.*

tippler 1. *n.* a tavern keeper. ♦ *John is the best tippler this place has ever seen. Tip me another, John.* **2.** *n.* a drunkard. ♦ *Uncle Ben was a tippler—a harmless one.* ♦ *He started drinking at fifteen and has been a tippler ever since.*

tipply *mod.* alcohol intoxicated. ♦ *Ben is too tipply to drive home.*

tipster *n.* someone who gives special information; an informer. ♦ *We got this from a tipster who has usually proven reliable in the past.*

titless wonder 1. *n.* an oafish or awkward person. (Usually objectionable.) ♦ *That stupid jerk is the classic titless wonder. What a twit!* **2.** *n.* an unsatisfactory thing or situation. ♦ *I've got to take this titless wonder into the shop for an oil change.*

tits *n.* breasts, usually a woman's. (Very old colloquial. Usually objectionable.) ♦ *She's nothing but tits and teeth! Not a brain in her head!*

tits and ass Go to T. and A.

tits up *mod.* upside down; on its or someone's back. (Usually objectionable.) ♦ *Her lousy pie fell tits up onto the kitchen floor.*

tizzle a wild card word for words beginning with *T*, such as *town*. (Streets. Also for other words with initial *T*.) ♦ *I'm ready to blow this tizzle.*

tizzy ['tɪzi] *n.* a state of confusion. (See also **twit**.) ♦ *The kind of tizzy that this place gets into drives me up the wall.*

TJATAW Go to Truth, justice, and the American Way.

TLC *n.* tender loving care. (Initialism.) ♦ *This old car will keep running as long as I give it lots of TLC.*

T-man *n.* a federal narcotics agent; a Treasury agent. (The *T* is from *Treasury*.) ♦ *It's curtains for you, T-man!*

TNSTAASQ Go to There's no such thing as a stupid question.

to back Go to tore back.

to beat the band *mod.* very hard and very fast. ♦ *He's selling computers to beat the band since he started advertising.*

to boot *mod.* in addition. ♦ *She got an F on her term paper and flunked the final to boot.*

to die for *mod.* important or desirable enough to die for; worth dying for. ♦ *This chocolate cake is to die for!*

to go *mod.* packaged to be taken out; packaged to be carried home to eat. ♦ *Do you want it to go, or will you eat it here?*

to hell and gone *mod.* gone; ruined. (Use caution with hell.) ♦ *Fred was to hell and gone before anybody figured out what he had done.*

To hell with that! *exclam.* That's the end of that!; No more of that! (Use caution with hell.) ♦ *I've heard stories like that before, and I don't believe any of them. To hell with that!*

to the max *mod.* maximally. (California. See also **max**.) ♦ *They worked to the max their whole shift.*

to the tune of sth *phr.* for the sum of a specific amount of money. ♦ *You will end up paying to the tune of twenty dollars a month.*

to up (from the flo up) ['to əp frəm ðə 'flo əp] *mod.* tore [torn] up from the floor up = messed up; hungover. (Streets.) ♦ *What's in you? You to up from the flo up!*

toast 1. *n.* a drunkard. ♦ *The old toast stumbled in front of a car.* **2.** *mod.* excellent. ♦ *This stuff is so toast!* **3.** *mod.* burned; done for. ♦ *If you don't get here in twenty minutes, you're toast.*

toasted *mod.* alcohol intoxicated. ♦ *The chick got toasted on two glasses of cheap white wine.*

TOBAL Go to There ought to be a law!

today *mod.* now; immediately. (Sarcastic.) ♦ *I want it done, now—today.* ♦ *Come on. Sam. Move it. Today!*

toddle off *in.* to depart; to walk away. ♦ *She said good-bye and toddled off.*

toddy blossom *n.* a large pimple from too much drinking. (See also strawberry.) ♦ *He was sporting a toddy blossom that would be the envy of any bum on skid row.*

to-do *n.* a commotion. ♦ *They made quite a to-do about the broken window.*

toe jam *n.* a nasty, smelly substance that collects between the toes of unwashed feet. ♦ *Wash your feet, you turkey! I don't want you getting all your toe jam all over the room!*

toe tag *tv.* to kill someone. (Bodies in the morgue are identified by tags on their big toes.) ♦ *Man, you treat me that way one more time and I'm gonna toe tag you!*

together *mod.* organized. ♦ *I'm not together yet. Lemme call you back.*

toilet mouth Go to potty mouth.

toilet water *n.* beer; draft beer. (Alludes to the term for cologne and trips to the toilet after drinking much beer.) ♦ *This toilet water has me running back and forth to the john.*

toke [tok] **1.** *n.* a puff of marijuana smoke. (Drugs.) ♦ *After a big toke, he settled back to drift.* **2.** *tv. & in.* to puff a marijuana cigarette. (Drugs.) ♦ *He sat on a stone to toke one before bean time.* **3.** *n.* a cigarette. ♦ *I left my tokes in my jacket.* **4.** *in.* to smoke crack. (Drugs.) ♦ *They were toking when her mother called on the phone.* **5.** *n.* a token. ♦ *Yeah. Just a little toke of my approval.* **6.** *n.* a tip. ♦ *He left a dollar toke. Wow.* **7.** *tv.* to tip someone; to tip some amount. ♦ *He only toked me a buck.* **8.** *in.* to tip. ♦ *She doesn't toke very well.*

tokus AND **tukkis; tuchus** ['tokəs AND 'tukəs] *n.* the buttocks; the rump. (Yiddish.) ♦ *Look at the tukkis on that fat guy.*

tomato *n.* an attractive girl or woman. ♦ *A good-looking tomato brought me my change.*

tomcat 1. *n.* a sexually active male; a stud. ♦ *Old Fred's getting to be quite a tomcat.* **2.** *in.* [for a man] to prowl around searching for sex. ♦ *Harry was out tomcatting again last night.*

tongue in cheek AND **TIC** *phr. & comp. abb.* a phrase said when the speaker is joking or not being sincere. ♦ *My comment was made TIC. Don't take me seriously.*

tongue loosener Go to tongue oil.

tongue oil AND **tongue loosener** *n.* liquor. ♦ *She had a little too much tongue oil and was telling all about everybody.* ♦ *A little tongue loosener will help to break the ice.*

tongue-tied 1. *mod.* unable to speak from fear or confusion. (Standard English.) ♦ *Why do you get tongue-tied in front of a crowd?* **2.** *mod.* alcohol intoxicated. ♦ *He was tongue-tied and couldn't stand up.*

tonic *n.* liquor. ♦ *Just a bit of tonic. I'm cutting down.*

tons of sth *n.* lots of something. ♦ *We got tons of fried chicken, so help yourself.*

tonsil bath *n.* liquor; a drink of liquor. ♦ *I could use a little tonsil bath about now.*

tonsil hockey 1. *n.* oral sex performed on the penis; fellatio. (Usually objectionable.) ♦ *Give him a good round of tonsil hockey, and you've got a customer for life.* **2.** *n.* French kissing. ♦ *The two kids spent the rest of the evening playing tonsil hockey.*

tonsil paint AND **tonsil varnish** *n.* liquor; whiskey. ♦ *The cowboy had to have his daily dose of tonsil paint before he stuffed his face full of beans and hardtack.* ♦ *This tonsil varnish would take the paint off a barn.*

tonsil varnish Go to tonsil paint.

too much *mod.* overwhelming; excellent. ♦ *It's wonderful. It's just too much!*

too rich for so's **blood 1.** *mod.* too expensive for one's budget. ♦ *Europe is getting too rich for our blood.* **2.** *mod.* too high in fat content for one's diet. ♦ *Most ice cream is too rich for my blood.*

Toodle(-oo). ['tudḷ('u)] *interj.* Good-bye. ♦ *Take it easy. Toodle-oo.*

tooey Go to tooie.

tooie AND **tooey; tuie** *n.* a capsule of Tuinal, a barbiturate. ♦ *The cops saw a few tuies on the sidewalk and made the arrest.*

took Go to taken.

tool 1. *n.* an earnest student. (See also power tool.) ♦ *Of course he's a tool. See the plastic liner in his pocket?* **2.** *n.* a dupe; someone who can be victimized easily. ♦ *They were looking for some tool to drive the getaway car.* **3.** *in.* to speed along (in a car). (See also tool around.) ♦ *We were tooling along at about seventy-five when the cop spotted us.*

tool around *in.* to drive or cruise around. (See also tool.) ♦ *We tooled around for a while and then rented a horror movie.*

toot 1. *n.* a binge; a drinking spree. ♦ *Harry's on a toot again.* **2.** *tv. & in.* to drink copiously. ♦ *She could toot booze from dusk to dawn.* **3.** *n.* an emotional jag of some kind. ♦ *She's on a toot about how nobody loves her anymore.* **4.** *n.* a line or dose of cocaine; cocaine. ♦ *These tootheads get sort of frantic when they can't get a toot.* **5.** *tv. & in.* to snort a portion of cocaine. ♦ *She tooted a couple of lines and came back.*

toot one's **own horn** Go to blow one's own horn.

tooter 1. *n.* a person on a drinking spree. ♦ *The streets belong to the tooters on New Year's Eve.* **2.** *n.* a drunkard. ♦ *Hank offered the tooter a drink, which was gratefully accepted, of course.*

tootle along *in.* to depart. ♦ *I think I'd better tootle along now.*

tootonium ['tu'toniəm] *n.* an imaginary, potent type of cocaine. (Drugs. A play on titanium.) ♦ *He called it tootonium. She called it trouble.*

tootuncommon [tutn̩'kɑmən] *n.* an imaginary, potent type of cocaine; any potent cocaine. (Drugs. A play on *King Tutankhamen.*) ♦ *Bart laughed when the student asked for tootuncommon.*

top 1. *tv.* to surpass someone or something. ♦ *Can you top this one?* **2.** *tv.* to kill someone. ♦ *Spike was gonna top Bart first.* **3.** *n.* the first half of a baseball inning. ♦ *Wilbur hit a nice double-bagger in the top half of the fourth.*

top banana 1. *n.* the lead comedian in a burlesque or vaudeville act. ♦ *The top banana didn't show up for the gig.* **2.** *n.* the boss; the leader or head of something. (See also big cheese; big enchilada.) ♦ *You'll have to ask the top banana. He's out right now.*

top brass *n.* the highest leader(s); the boss(es). (Originally military.) ♦ *You'll have to check it out with the top brass. She'll be home around five.*

top dog *n.* the person in charge or in power; a company officer. ♦ *The reporter tried to get hold of one of the top dogs but couldn't get past the secretary.*

top heavy *mod.* heavy-breasted; buxom. ♦ *Britney gets a little top heavy when she is gaining weight.*

top of the heap *n.* a position superior to everyone else. ♦ *For some reason, Jerry has to be at the top of the heap.*

top story AND **upper story** *n.* the brain. ♦ *I don't think her top story is occupied.* ♦ *A little weak in the upper story, but other than that, a great guy.*

top-drawer *mod.* top-quality. ♦ *I want to hire a young MBA who's top-drawer.*

top-flight *mod.* of the highest caliber. ♦ *We are looking for a top-flight manager for our new division.*

topless *mod.* having to do with someone wearing no clothing above the waist, usually a woman. ♦ *The cops closed down the topless joint on Maple Street.*

topsy-boozy AND **topsy-boosy** ['tɑpsi'buzi] *mod.* alcohol intoxicated. ♦ *She was so topsy-boosy she couldn't stand up.*

topsy-turvy ['tɑpsi'təˑvi] **1.** *mod.* upside down; in disarray. ♦ *He came in and turned everything topsy-turvy.* **2.** *mod.* alcohol intoxicated. ♦ *She was too topsy-turvy to stand up.*

tore back AND **to back** [... 'to 'bæk] torn back = hungover. (Black.) ♦ *Man, was I to back!*

tore down Go to tore (up).

tore (up) AND **torn (up); tore down 1.** *mod.* distraught; emotionally upset. ♦ *Fred's really torn up about the accident.* **2.** *mod.* alcohol or drug intoxicated. ♦ *He wasn't just drunk—he was massively tore up.*

torn (up) Go to tore (up).

tornado juice *n.* whiskey; strong whiskey. ♦ *This "tornado juice" smells like antifreeze.*

torpedo 1. *n.* a drink containing chloral hydrate; a knockout drink. ♦ *Marlowe signaled the bartender to give the stoolie a torpedo.* **2.** Go to submarine sense 1.

torqued [torkt] **1.** *mod.* angry; bent. ♦ *Now, now! Don't get torqued!* **2.** *mod.* drunk. (A play on twisted.) ♦ *Mary gets torqued on just a few drinks.*

toss 1. *in.* to empty one's stomach; to vomit. ♦ *I was afraid I was going to toss.* **2.** *tv.* to throw something away. ♦ *I'll toss this one. It's all scratched.* **3.** *tv.* to search someone. (Underworld.) ♦ *The cops tossed him and found nothing.* **4.** *tv.* to drink some liquor; to take a drink of liquor. ♦ *Toss that drink, and let's get out of here!*

toss in the sponge Go to throw in the towel.

Toss it! *tv.* Throw it away! ♦ *You don't need that hat. Toss it!*

toss off Go to beat off.

toss one's cookies AND **throw one's cookies; toss one's lunch; toss one's tacos** *tv.* to empty one's stomach; to vomit. ♦ *Fred stepped over to the bushes and raucously tossed his tacos.* ♦ *Yuck! He tossed his cookies in the backseat!*

toss one's lunch Go to toss one's cookies.

toss one's tacos Go to toss one's cookies.

toss sth off 1. *tv.* to do something quickly without much time or effort. ♦ *It was no big deal. I tossed it off in thirty minutes.* **2.** *tv.* to drink something quickly. ♦ *He tossed it off and ordered another.* **3.** *tv.* to ignore criticism; to ignore defeat or a setback. ♦ *She just tossed it off like nothing had happened.* **4.** *tv.* to resist or fight off a disease. ♦ *I caught a little cold, but I tossed it off right away.*

toss-up *n.* a matter of chance. (As predictable as the outcome of the toss of a coin.) ♦ *Nobody knew what to do. It was a toss-up.*

totalled 1. *mod.* wrecked; damaged beyond repair. (From *totally wrecked.*) ♦ *The car was totaled. There was nothing that could be saved.* **2.** *mod.* alcohol intoxicated. ♦ *Tom was too totaled to talk.*

totally *mod.* absolutely; completely. (Standard. Achieves slang status through overuse.) ♦ *How totally gross!*

totally awesome *mod.* very, very impressive. ♦ *His motorcycle is totally awesome. It must have cost a fortune.*

totally clueless *mod.* ignorant (of something). (See also cluelessness.) ♦ *Everybody was totally clueless as to what to do.*

tote 1. *n.* someone who abstains from alcohol. (From *total abstainer.*) ♦ *I'm not a tote, but I do have a limit—rather low by your standards.* ♦ *Have a drink, or are you still a tote?* **2.** *n.* a small portion of cannabis. (Drugs.) ♦ *The cops found a tote when they tossed Bart, but that was all.* **3.** *n.* a small pipe for smoking cannabis. (Drugs.) ♦ *Her father found a tote in her room and really hit the ceiling.*

touch 1. *n.* a likely target for begging; someone who is asked for a loan. (See also soft touch.) ♦ *He was just the kind of touch we were looking for, not too bright and not too poor.* **2.** *n.* a request for money (from a beggar); a request for a loan. ♦ *I ignored the touch and walked on* *by.* **3.** *tv.* to ask someone for a loan. ♦ *He touched me for a hundred bucks.* **4.** *n.* a small portion of something to eat or drink. (Folksy.) ♦ *I'll have just a touch. I'm on a diet, you know.* **5.** *tv.* to deal with or handle someone or something. (Usually in the negative.) ♦ *Mr. Wilson is a real pain, and I wouldn't touch his account. Find somebody else to handle it.*

touch a sore point *tv.* to mention something that upsets someone. ♦ *I touched a sore point with Larry when I mentioned taxes.*

touch and go *mod.* chancy. ♦ *It was touch and go for a while, but we are out of the woods now.*

touch base (with so**)** *tv.* to make contact with someone. ♦ *I wanted to touch base with you just in case something had gone wrong.*

touched 1. *mod.* flattered; honored. (Standard English.) ♦ *We were both touched by your thoughtfulness.* **2.** *mod.* alcohol intoxicated. ♦ *She was acting a little touched, but we didn't smell anything on her breath.*

touchy-feely *mod.* very sensitive and empathetic; pretentiously compassionate. ♦ *Marge is so touchy-feely. She worries that anything she says may possibly offend someone.*

tough break *n.* a bit of bad luck. ♦ *You've had a lot of tough breaks lately.*

tough cookie *n.* a tough person. ♦ *There was a tough cookie in here this morning who demanded to see the manager.*

tough cookies Go to **tough luck.**

tough customer *n.* someone who is difficult to deal with. ♦ *Bruno is a tough customer. Just keep away from him.*

tough egg to crack AND **tough nut to crack** *n.* a person or thing that is hard to figure out or hard to deal with. ♦ *She won't talk. She's going to be a tough nut to crack!* ♦ *I wish Jill wasn't such a tough nut to crack.*

tough guy *n.* a tough man; a man who might be part of the underworld. ♦ *He was your typical tough guy—jutting chin,* gruff voice—but he was just our decorator checking up on the drapes. ♦ *So, you want to be a tough guy, huh?*

tough luck AND **tough cookies** *interj.* That is too bad. ♦ *Tough luck, but that's the way the cookie crumbles.* ♦ *Tough cookies, Tom! That's life.*

tough nut to crack Go to **tough egg to crack.**

tough row to hoe *n.* a difficult task to carry out; a heavy set of burdens. ♦ *This is not an easy task. This is a tough row to hoe.*

tough shit AND **TS** *n.* tough luck; too bad. (Usually objectionable.) ♦ *If you really think I did wrong, then tough shit! I don't care.*

tough sth **out** *tv.* to carry on with something despite difficulties or setbacks. ♦ *I think I can tough it out for another month.*

Tough titty! AND **Tough titties!** *exclam.* That's too bad! (Usually objectionable.) ♦ *Tough titty! I told you it wouldn't be easy.*

tourist trap *n.* a place set up to lure tourists in to spend money. (Can be a shop, a town, or a whole country.) ♦ *It looked like a tourist trap, so we didn't even stop the car.*

touron *n.* tourist moron. ♦ *Another touron tried to take a bath in a hot spring this morning.*

townie ['tɑʊni] *n.* a permanent (nonstudent) resident of a college town. ♦ *The townies get upset when we make a lot of noise on Sundays.*

toxic waste dump *n.* a horrible person or place. ♦ *Frank, stop acting like a toxic waste dump and do as you're asked.*

toxicated AND **toxy** ['tɑksəkedəd AND 'tɑksi] *mod.* alcohol intoxicated. ♦ *The boss showed up totally toxicated after lunch and shocked the secretaries.*

toxy Go to **toxicated.**

TP AND **teepee 1.** *n.* toilet paper. (The abbreviation is an initialism.) ♦ *Don't forget to get teepee at the store.* **2.** *tv.* to festoon the trees and shrubbery of a residential yard with toilet paper. (A teenage prank.) ♦ *All the swimmers' houses get teepeed the night before a meet.*

TPT Go to trailer park trash.

track 1. *in.* [for a laser beam, a phonograph stylus, a tape head, etc.] to successfully transfer information to or from a recording medium. ♦ *Something here won't track. Must be the stylus.* **2.** *in.* [for a person] to make sense. (Usually in the negative.) ♦ *She wasn't tracking. There was no sense in trying to talk to her before she came out of it.* **3.** *in.* to coincide; to agree; to jibe. ♦ *These two things don't track. I don't know what's wrong.* **4.** *n.* a musical selection on a recording of some kind. ♦ *The next track is my favorite.*

trad [træd] *mod.* traditional. ♦ *A more trad style might make the grownups more comfortable.*

traf [træf] *n.* a release of intestinal gas. (This is fart spelled backward. Usually objectionable.) ♦ *Who let the traf?*

tragic-magic *n.* heroin. ♦ *This "tragic-magic," which has swept over the land, has taken too many of our youth.*

trailer *mod.* trashy, as in trailer park trash. ♦ *The guy's a loser. Strictly trailer.*

trailer park trash AND **TPT** *n.* trailer park trash. ♦ *My motor home cost more than your house, and you call me TPT?*

trailer trash *n.* the poorest of people who live in run-down house trailers in bad neighborhoods. (Used with singular or plural force. Rude and derogatory.) ♦ *She's just trailer trash. Probably doesn't even own shoes.*

trammeled ['træmḷd] *mod.* alcohol intoxicated. (Collegiate.) ♦ *Jim came home trammeled and was sick on the carpet.*

tranny ['træni] **1.** *n.* an automobile transmission. ♦ *It looks like you get a new tranny, and I get 900 bucks.* **2.** *n.* a transgendered person. ♦ *She said she was a tranny, but nobody could tell.*

trans [trænts] *n.* an automobile. (From transportation.) ♦ *I don't have any trans—I can't get myself anywhere.* ♦ *What are you using for trans these days?*

trap 1. *n.* the mouth. (Crude.) ♦ *Put this in your trap and chew it up.* **2.** *n.* a low place; a dive. ♦ *This trap is a mess. Clean it up!*

traps *n.* the trapezium muscles, considered in pairs. (Bodybuilding.) ♦ *This exercise is really good for your traps.*

trash 1. *tv.* to throw something away. ♦ *Trash this stuff. Nobody will ever use it.* **2.** *n.* a low, worthless person; worthless people. ♦ *Running around with that trash—no wonder he's in trouble.* **3.** *tv.* to vandalize something. ♦ *Somebody trashed the statue with spray paint.* **4.** *tv.* to beat, as in a ball game. ♦ *You trashed us this game, but watch out next season!* **5.** *tv.* to libel someone. ♦ *Who is the chick who was trashing Bart in the newspapers?*

Trash it! *tv.* Throw it away! ♦ *We don't have space for this old chair. Trash it!*

trash mouth *n.* someone who uses obscene language. ♦ *Some "trash mouth" is making everybody mad over in the park.*

trashed *mod.* alcohol or drug intoxicated. (Collegiate.) ♦ *Let's all get trashed and raid the girls' dorm.*

trashy *mod.* cheap; obscene; low; (sexually) promiscuous. ♦ *Cut out the trashy talk, you guys.*

tree *n.* marijuana. ♦ *Grass, tree, bush. It's all pot!*

tree-suit *n.* a wooden coffin. ♦ *You'd better shut up if you don't want to end up wearing a tree-suit.*

trekkie ['trɛki] *n.* a fan of *Star Trek,* the television series and the movies. ♦ *The trekkies seem to have their own language.*

trendy *n.* someone who has to be right in style or first with the latest trend. ♦ *All the trendies are wearing pink and charcoal clothing this month.*

trial balloon *n.* a test of someone's reaction. ♦ *It was just a trial balloon, and it didn't work.*

tribe *n.* a group of friends or relatives. ♦ *When are you and your tribe going to come for a visit?*

trick on so *in.* to deceive someone. ♦ *Mary is always tricking on people and now nobody trusts her.*

tricks of the trade *n.* special skills and knowledge associated with any trade or profession. ♦ *I know a few tricks of the trade that make things easier.*

trigger 1. *n.* a hired gunman. (Underworld.) ♦ *Get your triggers outa here—then we can talk.* **2.** *tv.* to start something; to set something off. ♦ *The noise triggered an avalanche.*

trigger-happy *mod.* eager to fire a gun; eager to shoot someone or something. ♦ *Rocko is sort of trigger-happy. Watch out.*

trip 1. *n.* a prison sentence; a trip up the river. (Underworld.) ♦ *Yeah, me and Lefty both was on a little trip for a few years.* **2.** *n.* a high from a drug. (Drugs.) ♦ *Me and Sid went on a little trip.* **3.** *in.* to experience a high from a drug, especially LSD. ♦ *Don't bother Bart. He's tripping.* **4.** *n.* a bad drug experience. (Drugs.) ♦ *Boy, did I ever have a trip with that stuff!* **5.** *n.* an annoying person or thing. ♦ *She is such a trip.* **6.** *in.* to leave. ♦ *Time to trip. See ya.*

tripe 1. *n.* nonsense. ♦ *That's just tripe. Pay no attention.* **2.** *n.* a bad performance; something worthless. ♦ *I know tripe when I see tripe, and that was tripe.*

triple 1. *n.* a large alcoholic drink containing three measures of hard liquor. ♦ *One triple, but no more. I'm cutting down, remember?* **2.** Go to triple-bagger.

triple whammy [ˈtrɪpl ˈʍæmi] *n.* a powerful treatment; a powerful shock. ♦ *The market crash, the trade figures, and the death of the secretary of defense was a powerful triple whammy in Washington politics this week.*

triple-bagger 1. AND **triple** *n.* a hit in baseball that gets the batter to third base. ♦ *Wilbur connected for another triple-bagger in the fifth.* **2.** *n.* a person whose ugly face is so frightful that three bags are required to conceal it. (Crude. See also double-bagger; coyote-ugly.) ♦ *He's worse than a triple-bagger—if that's possible.*

tripped out *mod.* great; excellent. ♦ *We had a tripped out time in class today. The teacher brought his pet rabbit.*

tris [traɪz] *n.* the triceps. ♦ *I'm working on building up my tris. Been doing lots of pushups.*

trojan horse *n.* a kind of malicious software that arrives at a personal computer embedded in some other software and then introduces routines that can gather personal information or destroy the operationality of the computer. ♦ *The consultant called the intruder a "trojan horse" and said I needed yet another program to get rid of it.*

troll 1. *n.* an ugly person; a grouchy person. ♦ *Gee, that dame is a real troll. What's her problem?* **2.** *n.* an internet user who sends inflammatory or provocative messages designed to elicit negative responses or start a flame-war. (As a fisherman trolls for an unsuspecting fish.) ♦ *Don't answer those silly messages. Some troll is just looking for an argument.* **3.** *n.* a message sent by a troll (sense 2). ♦ *Every time I get a troll, I just delete it.*

troll booth *n.* a (highway) toll booth. ♦ *There's another troll booth up ahead!*

trollkin *n.* a youthful or inexperienced troll (sense 2). ♦ *Some trollkin sent me a message trying to make me angry.*

the **trots** *n.* a case of diarrhea. ♦ *I got the trots and can't go out tonight.*

trotters 1. *n.* pig's feet. ♦ *Pickled trotters are good in the summer.* **2.** *n.* the feet. ♦ *Sit down and give your trotters a rest.*

trounce [traʊnts] *tv.* to beat someone; to outscore someone. (Sports.) ♦ *Western trounced Eastern for the tenth year in a row.*

trouser snake AND **trouser trout** *n.* the penis. ♦ *The doctor was taken aback when young Willard used the term "trouser snake."* ♦ *Stop scratching your trouser trout in public.*

trouser trout Go to trouser snake.

Tru dat. *sent.* That's true.; I agree. ♦ *Tru dat. I know just what you mean.*

trump sth **up** *tv.* to promote or boost something. (See also **trumped up**.) ♦ *They trumped up the movie so much that many people were disappointed when it finally came out.*

trumped up 1. *mod.* heavily promoted; overly praised. ♦ *That movie was so trumped up. I expected to see something much better than it turned out to be.* **2.** *mod.* made up; contrived. ♦ *They put Larry in the slammer on some trumped up charge.*

trumpet spider Go to barking spider.

Trust me! *exclam.* Believe me!; Honestly! ♦ *He actually said it just like Tom told you. Trust me!*

Truth, justice, and the American Way AND **TJATAW** *phr. & comp. abb.* a phrase said in response to impassioned declarations about almost anything. (This phrase was used to introduce the *Superman* radio and television programs.) ♦ *Sure, Mom and apple pie, as well as TJATAW.*

try so **back (again)** *tv.* to call someone back on the telephone (again) later. ♦ *I'll try her back later.*

TS Go to tough shit.

(T)sup? ['(t)səp] *interrog.* What's up?; What is happening?; What have you been doing? ♦ *Hi! Tsup?*

tub of guts Go to tub of lard.

tub of lard AND **tub of guts** *n.* a fat person. (Cruel. Also a rude term of address.) ♦ *Shut up, you stupid tub of lard!* ♦ *Who's that tub of guts who just came in?*

tube 1. *n.* a can of beer. (See also **crack a tube**.) ♦ *Toss me a tube, will ya?* **2.** *n.* the inner curve of a tall wave. (Surfing. See also **tubular**.) ♦ *I'm waiting for the best tube.* **3.** *in.* to fail; to go down the tube(s). (See also **tube it**.) ♦ *The whole plan tubed at the last minute.* **4.** *n.* a television set. ♦ *The tube is in the shop, so I read a book.* **5.** *n.* a cigarette. ♦ *There's a pack of tubes in my jacket.*

tube it *tv.* to fail a test. (See also **tube**.) ♦ *I was afraid I'd tube it, so I studied my head off.*

tube steak 1. *n.* a frankfurter or a wiener. (See also **pimp steak**.) ♦ *I could live on tube steak. Nothing is better!* **2.** AND **tube steak of love** *n.* the penis. ♦ *She laughed so hard when he said "tube steak of love," that he lost interest, so to speak.* ♦ *His tube steak was reminding him that it was time to get up.*

tube steak of love Go to tube steak.

tubed *mod.* alcohol intoxicated. (See also **tube**.) ♦ *They were both tubed and giggling.*

tubular *mod.* excellent. (Surfing and later general youth slang. Having to do with a tube [wave] that is good to surf in.) ♦ *That pizza was totally tubular!*

tuchus Go to tokus.

tude [tud] *n.* a bad *attitude*. ♦ *Hey, you really got a tude, dude.*

tuie Go to tooie.

tukkis Go to tokus.

tunage ['tunɪdʒ] *n.* music; tunes. ♦ *My stereo is down and I'm running a tunage deficit.*

tune in (to sth**)** *in.* to become alert to something. ♦ *She tuned in to the comments about acid rain.*

tune out *in.* to begin to ignore everything. ♦ *The entire class had tuned out, so no one heard the teacher ask the question.*

tune so/sth **out** *tv.* to ignore or disregard someone or something. ♦ *I managed to tune out the constant clamor in the streets.*

tuned *mod.* tipsy; drunk. ♦ *Willy was a little tuned so Sally swiped his car keys.*

tuned in *mod.* aware; up-to-date. ♦ *Jan is tuned in and alert to what is going on around her.*

tunes *n.* a record; a record album; music in general. (See also **tunage**.) ♦ *I got some new tunes. Wanna come over and listen?*

turd 1. *n.* a formed mass of fecal material; a fecal bolus. (Usually objectionable.) ♦

There's a turd floating in the swimming pool! **2.** *n.* a wretched or worthless person. (Rude and derogatory.) ♦ *You stupid turd!*

turd face *n.* a wretched and obnoxious person. (Rude and derogatory.) ♦ *You stupid turd face! Why did you do that?*

turf *n.* (one's) ground or territory. ♦ *When you're on my turf, you do what I say—savvy?* ♦ *This is my turf, and what I say goes.*

turistas [tuˈristɑs] *n.* diarrhea; a case of diarrhea. (From Spanish.) ♦ *Nobody ever died of the turistas—right away, anyway.* ♦ *Turistas can be very unpleasant.*

turkey 1. *n.* a failure; a sham. (Especially a stage production.) ♦ *The turkey at the town theater closed on its first night.* **2.** *n.* a stupid person. ♦ *Who's the turkey who put the scallops in the scalloped potatoes?*

turkey bacon *n.* a (untrained) night watchman; a uniformed but unoffical "police officer;" fake **bacon** = cop. ♦ *The place is guarded by creeky-kneed turkey bacon. I'll distract them while you sneak in.*

turn 1. *in.* to go over to the other side, as with a spy or a criminal turning into an informer. (Underworld.) ♦ *Is there a chance that Bart would turn?* **2.** *tv.* to corrupt someone; to turn someone to a life of crime. ♦ *Pete was trying to turn a young kid.*

turn a trick *tv.* to perform an act of prostitution. (Usually objectionable.) ♦ *She can turn a trick and be on the streets again in six minutes flat.*

turn around AND **turn over** *in.* [for something] to undergo a major, dynamic change. ♦ *When life turned over and things went more smoothly, Frank was happier.*

turn belly up AND **go belly up 1.** *in.* to fail. ♦ *I sort of felt that the whole thing would go belly up, and I was right. (See also belly up.)* ♦ *The computer—on its last legs anyway—turned belly up right in the middle of an important job.* **2.** *in.* to die. (As a fish does when it dies.) ♦ *Every fish in Greg's tank went belly up last night.*

turn in AND **roll in** *in.* to go to bed. ♦ *Well, it's about time to turn in.*

turn on 1. *in.* to become interested or excited. ♦ *She turned on when she heard her name called.* **2.** *in.* to take a drug. (Drugs.) ♦ *He will turn on with anybody at the drop of a hat.* **3.** *n.* someone or something that excites someone. (Usually **turn-on**.) ♦ *David can be a real turn-on when he's in a good mood.*

turn on a dime *in.* to turn sharply; to turn in a small radius. ♦ *A car that will turn on a dime at high speed without turning turtle is what I want.*

turn on the waterworks *in.* to begin to cry. ♦ *His lower lip was quivering, and I knew he was going to turn on the waterworks.*

turn one's **toes up** *tv.* to die. ♦ *The cat turned up its toes right after church. Ah, the power of prayer.*

turn onto so/sth *in.* to become interested in someone or something. ♦ *I tried to get her to turn onto me, but she could only think of John.*

turn over 1. *in.* to get off of drugs. (Like *turn over a new leaf.*) ♦ *There is a clinic on Maple Street that'll help heads turn over.* **2.** Go to turn around.

turn so **off** *tv.* to dull someone's interest in someone or something. ♦ *The preacher set out to turn off the congregation to sin.*

turn so **on** *tv.* to excite or interest someone. (See also turn on.) ♦ *Fast music with a good beat turns me on.*

turn so **out** *tv.* to introduce someone to drugs, prostitution, homosexuality, etc. (Underworld.) ♦ *There are laws against turning out people the way Max was doing.*

turn so's **stomach** *tv.* to nauseate someone. ♦ *That stuff turns my stomach. Do I have to eat it?*

turn so's **water off** *tv.* to deflate someone; to silence someone. ♦ *He said you were stupid, huh? Well, I guess that turns your water off!*

turn so **upside down** *tv.* to upset someone; to confuse someone. ♦ *The events of the week turned us both upside down.*

turn sth **upside down** *tv.* to search a place or thing. ♦ *We turned his place upside down but never found the gun.*

turn tail (and run) *tv.* to flee; to run away in fright. ♦ *I couldn't just turn tail and run, but I wasn't going to fight that monster either.*

turn thumbs down (on so/sth**)** *tv.* to reject someone or something. ♦ *The board turned thumbs down on Rocko's application for parole.*

turn turtle *in.* to turn over, as with a ship. ♦ *The old dog finally turned turtle, and that was the end.*

Turn your caps lock off! AND **TYCLO** *exclam. & comp. abb.* Release you caps lock key! (Submitting a message in all caps is certain to produce one or more negative remarks.) ♦ *TYCLO! I can't read all caps!*

turned off *mod.* uninterested. ♦ *I'm sort of turned off to stuff like that these days. Part of getting older, I guess.*

turned on 1. *mod.* made alert to what is new and exciting. ♦ *I want to hire someone who's really turned on—a real comer.* ♦ *A young, turned on MBA would be just right.* **2.** *mod.* drug intoxicated. (Drugs.) ♦ *Jerry's turned on by noon—every day.* ♦ *The kid over there looks sort of turned on. Let's go talk to him a bit.*

turn-off *n.* something that repels someone. ♦ *The movie was a turn-off. I couldn't stand it.*

turps AND **terps** [tɚps] *n.* liquor. (From turpentine.) ♦ *Don't forget to stop at the comfort station and get the turps.*

turtle heading *n.* popping up and down in an office cubicle, looking at what's going on in the rest of the office. (See also prairie dog.) ♦ *Everybody was turtle heading, trying to see what was happening in Willy's cubicle.*

turtle-neck *n.* the penile foreskin. (A play on the type of collar.) ♦ *He's talking to the*

doctor about getting rid of his little turtle-neck.

tush(y) *n.* the buttocks. (Probably from Yiddish.) ♦ *I fell down right on my tush.*

tux [təks] *n.* a tuxedo. ♦ *Rent your tux well in advance.*

TV dinner *n.* roadkill; a turkey vulture dinner. ♦ *Whoops. I just made a TV dinner out of a squirrel!*

twack *n.* a twelve pack of beer (cans). (Twelve + pack.) ♦ *Let's pick up a couple of twacks for the game.*

tweak [twik] *tv.* to adjust something slightly. ♦ *Tweak the tuner a little and see if you can get that station just a little bit clearer.*

tweased [twizd] *mod.* alcohol intoxicated. ♦ *Jim came in a little tweased last night.*

tweeked [twikt] *mod.* alcohol intoxicated. (Collegiate.) ♦ *They're not really bombed—just tweeked a little.* ♦ *Fred was too tweeked to stand up.*

twenty-four, seven AND **24-7** *mod.* all the time, twenty-four hours a day, seven days a week. ♦ *He's always at home, 24-7!*

twenty-twenty hindsight AND **20/20 hindsight** *n.* an ability to figure out what one should have done after it is too late to do it. ♦ *Everybody has twenty-twenty hindsight!*

twerp Go to twirp.

twiddle one's **thumbs** *tv.* to do nothing; to wait nervously, playing with one's fingers. ♦ *I sat twiddling my thumbs while you were out doing I don't know what all!*

twinkie ['twɪŋki] *n.* a cute, teenage girl. (California.) ♦ *These twinkies ought to be a little more grown up than they seem to be.*

twirp AND **twerp** [twɚp] *n.* an annoying runt of a person. (Also a term of address.) ♦ *Some little twerp threatened to kick me in the shin.*

twist AND **frail** *n.* a girl; a woman. (Underworld. Possibly rhyming slang *twist and twirl = girl* and *frail frame = dame.* Detective novels and movies.) ♦ *This* good-looking twist comes over to the table and asks Lefty if he'd like to dance. ♦ *I'll shoot the frail if you don't hand it over!*

twist in the wind Go to twist (slowly) in the wind.

twist (slowly) in the wind *in.* to suffer the agony of some punishment, powerless to do anything about it, as if one had been hanged. (Figurative only.) ♦ *I'll see you twist in the wind for trying to frustrate this investigation.*

twist so's **arm** *tv.* to pressure someone. ♦ *I had to twist her arm a little, but she agreed.*

twisted 1. *mod.* alcohol intoxicated. ♦ *That chick is really twisted bad.* **2.** *mod.* suffering from drug withdrawal. (Drugs.) ♦ *When you're twisted, your head spins, and you feel like screaming.*

twister 1. *n.* a key. (Underworld.) ♦ *Marlon snatched the jailer's twisters and waited until midnight to try something.* **2.** *n.* a tornado. ♦ *A twister touched down yesterday at an isolated farm seventy miles north of Adamsville.* **3.** *n.* a drunken spree. (See also **bender**.) ♦ *Harry's off on a twister again.*

twit 1. *n.* a nervous or frantic state. ♦ *The twit I was in made me seem sort of silly, I'm afraid.* **2.** *n.* a stupid person. (Also a term of address.) ♦ *What a yuppie twit!*

twity *mod.* giddy; in the manner of a twit sense 2. ♦ *He keeps giving twity answers to the easiest questions!*

two fingers *n.* a measurement of liquor in a glass. ♦ *I'll take two fingers of that tiger milk, John.*

two shakes of a lamb's tail *mod.* quickly; rapidly. ♦ *I'll be there in two shakes of a lamb's tail.*

two sheets to the wind Go to three sheets in the wind.

two umlauts ['tu 'umlɑʊts] *n.* a Löwenbräu (brand) beer. ♦ *Calling a beer "two*

umlauts" is the most contrived bit of slang I have ever heard of.

two-bit *mod.* cheap; small-time. ♦ *Max is just a two-bit pusher. I want Mr. Big.*

two-bits *n.* twenty-five cents; a quarter coin. ♦ *Here's two-bits for your piggy bank.*

two-by-four *mod.* small. ♦ *A two-by-four office with a chair and a desk was where Marlowe hung out.*

twofer ['tufɚ] *n.* an item that is selling two for the price of one. ♦ *Here's a good deal— a twofer—only $7.98.* ♦ *Everything in this store is a twofer. I only want one of these. Do I have to bring a friend who wants one, too?*

two-fisted drinker *n.* a heavy drinker; someone who drinks with both hands. ♦ *The world is filled with guys who aspire to be two-fisted drinkers.*

two-planker *n.* a skier. (From a snowboarder's point of view.) ♦ *A couple of two-plankers zoomed past us and scared us to death.*

two-time *tv.* to deceive one's lover. ♦ *Sam wouldn't two-time Martha. He just wouldn't!*

two-time loser *n.* a confirmed loser. ♦ *Martin is a two-time loser, or at least he looks like one.*

two-timer *n.* one who deceives one's lover. ♦ *Sam just isn't my idea of the typical two-timer.*

two-topper *n.* a restaurant table that will seat two people. (Restaurant jargon.) ♦ *There are two-toppers on each side of the kitchen door.*

two-way street *n.* a reciprocal situation. ♦ *This is a two-way street, you know. You will have to help me someday in return.*

TYCLO Go to Turn your caps lock off!

type *n.* a combining form indicating a specified type of person. (Colloquial.) ♦ *He's a caveman type. You know, sort of hairy and smelly.*

U

ugly as sin Go to (as) ugly as sin.

uke AND **yuke** [juk] **1.** *in.* to empty one's stomach; to vomit. (Collegiate. See also puke.) ♦ *I think somebody yuked in the backseat, Tom.* **2.** *n.* vomit. (Collegiate.) ♦ *Tell me that the stuff in the backseat isn't uke!*

ump [əmp] *n.* an *umpire.* ♦ *The ump was gonna get killed if he didn't open his eyes.*

umpteen ['əmptin] *mod.* many; innumerable. ♦ *There are umpteen ways to do this right. Can you manage to do one of them?*

umpteenth Go to umpty-umpth.

umpty-umpth AND **umpteenth** ['əmpti'əmpθ AND 'əmp'tintθ] *mod.* thousandth, billionth, zillionth, etc. (Represents some very large but indefinite number.) ♦ *This is the umpty-umpth time I've told you to keep your dog out of my yard.*

Uncle nab *n.* a policeman. ♦ *Watch out for Uncle nab. He's been asking about you.*

Uncle (Sam) AND **Uncle Sugar 1.** *n.* the personification of the U.S. ♦ *Uncle Sugar wants a little more of your money this year.* **2.** *n.* a federal agent; federal agents. ♦ *Uncle has some pretty strong ideas about who's in charge of this investigation.*

Uncle Sugar Go to Uncle (Sam).

Uncle Whiskers Go to Mr. Whiskers.

uncool *mod.* square; dull and orthodox. ♦ *This place is uncool. Let's cruise.*

uncut 1. *mod.* unedited; not shortened by editing. ♦ *The uncut version is too long.* **2.** *mod.* not circumcised. ♦ *My brother and I are both uncut.*

under so's **thumb** *mod.* under someone's control. ♦ *You can't keep your kids under your thumb all their lives.*

under the affluence of incohol *mod.* alcohol intoxicated. (A deliberate spoonerism on *under the influence of alcohol.*) ♦ *You are very, very much under the affluence of incohol, as you have so aptly put it.*

under the gun *mod.* under pressure; under scrutiny. ♦ *They've got the boss under the gun to get this thing wound up by Saturday.*

under the table 1. *mod.* alcohol intoxicated. ♦ *Jed was under the table by midnight.* **2.** *mod.* secret; clandestine. (This is hyphenated before a nominal.) ♦ *It was strictly an under-the-table deal.*

under the weather 1. *mod.* ill. ♦ *Whatever I ate for lunch is making me feel a bit under the weather.* **2.** *mod.* alcohol intoxicated. ♦ *Willy's just a tad under the weather.*

under the wire *mod.* at the very last minute. ♦ *I got it in just under the wire.*

under wraps *mod.* (held) in secret. ♦ *We kept it under wraps until after the election.*

underpinnings *n.* the legs. ♦ *He has good underpinnings—ought to be able to run faster.* ♦ *With underpinnings like that, he ought to be able to win the marathon.*

understanding *n.* the feet. (Old. A pun. Always singular.) ♦ *The boy has a good understanding. Majorly big gunboats, in fact.*

underwater basket weaving *n.* an imaginary, very easy high school or college course. ♦ *If I can just find a course in un-*

derwater basket weaving, I'll have an easy semester.

underwhelm *tv. & in.* to fail to impress (someone). ♦ *As we were being under whelmed by a buxom soprano, my thoughts drifted to more pleasant matters.*

undies *n.* underclothing; underpants, especially women's. ♦ *Where are my clean undies?*

unearthly *mod.* weird; terrible. ♦ *There was an unearthly smell coming out of the kitchen.*

unflappable *mod.* not subject to distraction; imperturbable. ♦ *She is totally unflappable.*

ungodly *mod.* horrendous; inconceivable. ♦ *What do you want at this ungodly hour?*

unit ['junət] **1.** *n.* a gadget. ♦ *Now, take one of the red units—put the copper strip in the slot—place the whole thing in this larger unit—and you're done.* ♦ *Hand me that unit on the thingy there.* **2.** *n.* the penis. (Usually objectionable.) ♦ *Why are you always scratching your unit?* **3.** Go to (parental) units.

unk-jay *n.* dope; junk. (Underworld. Pig Latin for junk.) ♦ *The creep deals in unk-jay, you know—narcotics.* ♦ *Stay away from the unk-jay.*

unlax [ən'læks] *in.* to unwind and relax. ♦ *I just can't wait to get home and unlax.*

unload *tv.* to get rid of someone or something. ♦ *We're gonna unload all the cats and dogs during the Christmas rush.*

unobtanium *n.* something highly desirable that cannot be found; a fantastic, perfect metallic substance. (See also obtanium.) ♦ *Of course, his bike is made of unobtanium and should stand up in a volcanic eruption.*

unreal *mod.* unbelievable. ♦ *Your hairdo is so yummy—almost unreal.* ♦ *Who started this unreal argument?*

up 1. *mod.* happy; cheery; not depressed; upbeat. ♦ *I'm up today. Let's celebrate.* **2.** *tv.* to increase something. ♦ *She tried to up the price on me, thinking I wouldn't no-*

tice. **3.** *in.* to take a stimulant drug. ♦ *Ted upped before going in to take the test.*

up a creek Go to up shit creek (without a paddle).

up a storm *mod.* with an enthusiastic spirit. (Note syntax in examples. Usually with *sing, dance, talk, blow, play.*) ♦ *We talked up a storm until past midnight.*

up a tree 1. *mod.* confused; without an answer to a problem; in difficulty. ♦ *This whole business has me up a tree.* **2.** *mod.* alcohol intoxicated. ♦ *My buddy here is up a tree and needs a crash for the night.*

up against it *mod.* having a personal crisis; having a financial crisis. ♦ *This is my bad season. I'm really up against it.*

up an' Adam Go to up and at them.

up an' at 'em Go to up and at them.

up and at them AND **up an' at 'em; up an' Adam** *phr.* to get up and go at people or things; to get active and get busy. (*Adam* is a [purposeful] misunderstanding of *at 'em.*) ♦ *Up and Adam! The sun is shining.*

up close and personal *phr.* intimately; more intimately than one might have wished for. (Colloq. The phrase has been the title of a movie and the name of a television show.) ♦ *When my trunks slipped down, she got to know me a little more up close and personal that we were ready for at that moment.*

up for grabs 1. *mod.* available for anyone; not yet claimed. ♦ *I don't know who will get it. It's up for grabs.* **2.** *mod.* in total chaos. ♦ *When the market crashed, the whole office was up for grabs.*

up for sth *mod.* agreeable to something. ♦ *I'm up for a pizza. Anybody want to chip in?*

up front 1. *mod.* at the beginning; in advance. ♦ *The more you pay up front, the less you'll have to finance.* **2.** *mod.* open; honest; forthcoming. ♦ *I wish the salesman had been more up front about it.* **3.** *mod.* in the forefront; under fire (at the front). ♦ *You guys who are up front are gonna get the most fire.*

up high *n.* a stimulating rather than a depressing drug high. (Drugs. See also up pot.) ♦ *Many of them have to have an up high. They are too close to clinical depression to chance anything else.*

up in arms *mod.* angry; excited. ♦ *The whole town was up in arms about the planned highway.*

up in so's **gold ones** AND **up on** so's **bumper.** *n.* in someone's face. (Alludes to gold teeth.) ♦ *He had his smelly face up in my gold ones, so I clobbered him.* ♦ *Why are you up on my bumper, dawg?*

up in the air (about so/sth**)** *mod.* undecided about someone or something. ♦ *I'm sort of up in the air about whether to marry Mary or not.*

up on so's **bumper** Go to up in so's gold ones.

up one's **alley** Go to (right) up one's alley.

up pot *n.* stimulating marijuana, as opposed to relaxing marijuana. (Drugs. See also up high.) ♦ *I can only handle up pot. Everything else makes me cry.*

up shit creek (without a paddle) AND **up the creek (without a paddle); up a creek** *mod.* in an awkward position with no easy way out. (Usually objectionable.) ♦ *There I was, at Disney World with only a measly $47.54. I was literally up the creek without a paddle.* ♦ *You are up a creek! You got yourself into it, so get yourself out.*

up stakes *tv.* to prepare for leaving and then leave. (*Up* has the force of a verb here. The phrase suggests pulling up tent stakes in preparation for departure.) ♦ *It's that time of the year when I feel like upping stakes and moving to the country.*

up the creek (without a paddle) Go to up shit creek (without a paddle).

up the pole *mod.* alcohol intoxicated. ♦ *You sound a little up the pole. Why don't you call back when you're sober?*

up the river *mod.* in prison. (Underworld.) ♦ *The judge who sent him up the river was indicted for accepting bribery. If Gary had only known sooner!*

up the wall *mod.* in a very bad situation. ♦ *We were all up the wall until the matter was resolved.*

up time *n.* the time when a computer is running. (Compare this with down time.) ♦ *On some systems the down time is longer than the up time.*

up to here *mod.* having as much as one can bear. ♦ *I'm up to here with your excuses!*

up to one's **ears** Go to up to one's eyeballs

up to one's **eyeballs** AND **up to** one's **ears** *mod.* filled up with something. ♦ *We are up to our eyeballs with trouble around here.* ♦ *She's up to her ears in marriage proposals.*

up to one's **knees** *mod.* deep in something, such as paperwork or water. (See also knee-deep in sth.) ♦ *We're up to our knees with orders and getting more all the time.*

up to one's **neck** *mod.* filled up with something. ♦ *I am up to my neck in other people's grief and anguish.*

up to scratch AND **up to snuff** *mod.* satisfactory; up to what is expected. (Colloquial. *Snuff* is related in some way to tobacco. *Scratch* may allude to the starting or finish line in a contest.) ♦ *We felt that the entertainment was not up to scratch.* ♦ *The food was up to snuff, but the hotel staff was not at its usually efficient best.*

up to snuff Go to up to scratch.

Up yours! *exclam.* Go to hell!; Drop dead! (Usually objectionable.) ♦ *I won't do it! Up yours!*

upbeat *mod.* bright and cheery; not negative. (Compare this with downbeat.) ♦ *I'd prefer to open the conference with an upbeat topic.*

upchuck ['əptʃək] **1.** *tv. & in.* to vomit (something). ♦ *Willy upchucked his whole dinner.* **2.** *n.* vomit. ♦ *Is that upchuck on your shoe?*

upholstered [ə'polstɚd] **1.** *mod.* alcohol intoxicated. ♦ *She was a little upholstered, but not seriously impaired.* **2.** Go to (well-)upholstered.

upper story Go to top story.

uppity [ˈəpədi] *mod.* haughty. (Folksy.) ♦ *Why is she so uppity?*

the **upshot (of** sth**)** *n.* the result of something; the outcome of something. ♦ *The upshot of it all was that we don't get the new coffeepot.*

upside *n.* the good side. ♦ *There's not much to look forward to on the upside.*

uptight *mod.* anxious. ♦ *Dave always seems uptight about something.*

the **urge to purge** *n.* the need to throw up. ♦ *Pete felt the urge to purge and ran for the john.*

urp Go to earp.

use [juz] *tv. & in.* to use (drugs); to take drugs habitually. (Drugs and now widely known.) ♦ *I tried to stop using, but I couldn't.*

Use your head! AND **Use your noggin!; Use your noodle!** *exclam.* Think!; Think it through! ♦ *You know the answer. Use your head!* ♦ *Use your noggin', dogg!*

Use your noggin! Go to Use your head!

Use your noodle! Go to Use your head!

user *n.* a drug user; a drug addict. (Drugs.) ♦ *I want to stop being a user, but I can't do it by myself.*

UVs [ˈjuˈviz] *n.* ultraviolet rays from the sun; sunshine. (Initialism.) ♦ *I wanna get some UVs before we go home.*

vac 1. *n.* a vacuum cleaner. ♦ *Bring the vac and clean this place up.* **2.** *tv. & in.* to clean with a vacuum cleaner. ♦ *You are supposed to vac the whole house, not just your room!*

vacation *n.* a prison sentence. (Underworld.) ♦ *It was a three-year vacation, with time off for good behavior.*

vag 1. [veg] *n.* a vagrant person; a person who does not work and who wanders from place to place. ♦ *A couple of vags on the curb were trying to hitch a ride.* **2.** [veg] *mod.* having to do with a charge of vagrancy. ♦ *They booked him on a vag charge and gave him a nice warm place to* **3.** [vædʒ] *n.* vagina. ♦ *She had been suffering from itching in the vag.* **4.** [vædʒ] sexual activity; copulation. ♦ *Wilbur needed some vag.* **5.** [vædʒ] a despised male. (See also **cunt** sense 3.) ♦ *You stupid vag! Ain't you got no brains?*

vals [vælz] *n.* Valium tranquilizers. ♦ *I'm taking vals for this, but the doctor says to get off of them as soon as possible.*

Vamoose! [væ'mus] *exclam.* Beat it!; Go away! (From Spanish.) ♦ *Go on, beat it! Vamoose!*

vanilla 1. *mod.* plain; dull. (See also **beige**.) ♦ *The entire production was sort of vanilla, but it was okay.* **2.** *n.* a Caucasian. ♦ *Some vanilla's on the phone—selling something, I guess.*

varnished *mod.* alcohol intoxicated. (See also **shellacked**.) ♦ *Really varnished, he was. Couldn't see a hole in a ladder.*

varoom Go to **vroom**.

Vatican roulette *n.* the rhythm method of birth control. ♦ *My parents lost at Vatican roulette, and I am the booby prize.*

V-ball *n.* volleyball. (See also **B-ball**.) ♦ *You wanna play some V-ball?*

vblog Go to **videoblog**.

veejay AND **VJ; video jock** *n.* a *video jockey*; a host on a television program that features music videos. (The abbreviation is an initialism. Patterned on **deejay**. See also **disk jockey**.) ♦ *Sally tried out for the veejay job, but she looked too old and stuffy for that kind of work.*

veep [vip] *n.* a vice president. ♦ *The veep is going to preside today.*

veg [vɛdʒ] **1.** *n.* a vegetable. (See also **veggy**.) ♦ *You want a veg with this?* **2.** *n.* a stupid person. ♦ *Where is your brain, you veg?* **3.** Go to **veg (out)**.

veg (out) *in.* to cease working and take it easy; to vegetate. (See also **vegged out**.) ♦ *Someday, I just want to veg out and enjoy life.*

vegetable 1. *mod.* alcohol intoxicated. ♦ *Helen drank till she was totally vegetable.* **2.** *n.* someone who is brain-dead; someone who acts brain-dead; a person almost totally destroyed by drugs. ♦ *Cable TV is turning me into a vegetable.*

vegged out *mod.* debilitated by drugs or alcohol. (Drugs.) ♦ *Ernie is vegged out and has quit his job and everything.*

veggy AND **veggie** ['vɛdʒi] **1.** *n.* a vegetarian. ♦ *We have a lovely salad bar for the veggies among you.* **2.** *n.* a vegetable; a chunk or piece of vegetable. (Usually plural.) ♦ *Do you want any veggies with this?* **3.** *n.* a comatose patient in a hospital. (Medical.) ♦ *Mary's aunt has been a veggie in the hospital for more than a year.* **4.** *n.* someone who is tired or exhausted.

♦ *I want to be a veggy this weekend. I'll just stay at home and relax.*

vent one's **spleen** *tv.* to release one's anger. ♦ *I just feel like I have to vent my spleen at somebody.*

vertical bathtub *n.* a men's urinal. ♦ *When I walked into the room with vertical bathtubs, I knew I was in the wrong place.*

vest 1. *n.* an important businessman or businesswoman. (See also **suit**.) ♦ *Some vest jumped out the window this afternoon.* **2.** *n.* a bullet-proof vest. ♦ *The cop wasn't wearing a vest, and the shot killed him.*

vet 1. *n.* a veterinarian. (Standard English.) ♦ *The vet didn't charge much to look at the turtle.* **2.** *tv.* to give a medical examination to and treat a person (or an animal). ♦ *The doctor vetted me quickly and charged an unbelievable sum for it.* **3.** *n.* a (war) veteran. ♦ *The vets in the hospitals across the land appreciate your kindness.*

vette [vɛt] *n.* a Corvette automobile. ♦ *Vettes aren't as popular as they once were.*

vibes [vaɪbz] *n.* vibrations; atmosphere; feelings. (Usually with *good* or *bad*.) ♦ *I just don't get good vibes about this deal.*

vic [vɪk] **1.** *n.* a victim. (Streets. See also **vivor**.) ♦ *We're all vics, but we all keep going.* **2.** *n.* a convict. ♦ *We try to give the vics a chance at employment where they won't be treated badly.*

vicious ['vɪʃəs] *mod.* great; excellent. ♦ *Man, this burger is really vicious.*

vicked [vɪkt] *mod.* cheated; victimized. (See also **vic**.) ♦ *I feel so vicked when I see where my taxes are spent.*

Vickie *n.* a Crown Victoria police car; the police in a Crown Victoria car. ♦ *Two cops in a Vickie followed the suspect's car.*

vid *n.* a video [tape]. ♦ *I rented some vids for tonight so we can stay in and drink beer.*

video jock Go to **veejay**.

videoblog AND **vblog** *n.* a weblog that includes video. ♦ *With my new videoblog, people can see that I don't look as stupid as I sound.* ♦ *Vblogs aren't just for nerds!*

vim and vigor *n.* energy; enthusiasm; moxie. ♦ *Show more vim and vigor! Let us know you're alive.*

vines *n.* clothing. (Black.) ♦ *Good-looking vines on that guy, right?*

vinyl ['vaɪnl] *n.* phonograph records. ♦ *I got some new vinyl. Come over and listen.*

Viola! Go to **Walla!**

VIP 1. *n.* a very important person. (Initialism.) ♦ *Who's the VIP in the Mercedes?* **2.** *mod.* something reserved for a VIP. (Initialism.) ♦ *My smile and casual manner didn't get me into the VIP lounge.*

visit from Flo [...'flo] *n.* a menstrual period. (See also **Aunt Flo**.) ♦ *I am expecting a visit from Flo, but she seems late.*

visit from the stork *n.* the birth of a baby. ♦ *The last visit from the stork was in March.*

visit the plumbing Go to **check out the plumbing**.

visiting fireman *n.* someone paying a visit to observe one's workplace. ♦ *We have a couple of visiting firemen coming today.*

vital statistics *n.* the measurements of a person's body. ♦ *Her vital statistics must require higher math to work out!*

vivor ['vaɪvɚ] *n.* a survivor; a street person who manages to survive. (Streets. Compare this with **vic**.) ♦ *Harry's a vivor, and I like him.*

viz [vaɪz] *n.* Levis; blue jeans. ♦ *Those viz are too tight for her.*

vizzle a wild card word for words beginning with *V*, such as *very*, *vagina*. (Streets. Also for other words with initial *V*.) ♦ *His thoughts were on her "vizzle" etc.*

VJ Go to **veejay**.

vomatose ['vɑmətos] *mod.* drunk, vomiting, and nearly comatose. (From *vomit* and *comatose*.) ♦ *Claude is completely vomatose. What a party!*

vomity ['vɑmɪdi] *mod.* nasty. (Crude.) ♦ *What is this vomity stuff on my plate?*

vote with one's **feet** *in.* to show one's displeasure by walking out. ♦ *When the au-*

dience votes with its feet, you know you don't have a hit.

vroom AND **varoom** [vrum AND vɑ'rum] **1.** *interj.* the noise of a loud engine. (Onomatopoetic.) ♦ *Vroom, vroom went the engine as Vic gunned it over and over.* **2.** *in.* to move rapidly from place to place; to travel at high speed, making the noise of a loud engine. ♦ *The little boy varoomed down the sidewalk on his tricycle.*

VSA *mod.* vital signs absent: dead. (Hospital jargon.) ♦ *The intern made a note in the chart: VSA, 10:18 A.M.*

vújà day *mod.* described the feeling of never having been in a place before or having never had the current experience before. (A play on *déjà vu.*) ♦ *I was lost! I looked around, and a feeling of vújà day crept over me!*

vurp *in.* to regurgitate = to vomit and burp. ♦ *I just vurped! Tastes awful!*

W

waa-zooed Go to whazood.

WAC Go to What a crock!

wack Go to whack.

wack off Go to beat off.

wacky *mod.* loony; silly and giddy. ♦ *You are about the wackiest guy I ever met.*

wacky-tabbacky ['wækɪtə'bæki] *n.* marijuana. (Collegiate.) ♦ *He gets that silly look in his eye from smoking "wacky-tabbacky."*

wad 1. [wɑd] *n.* a bundle of money; a bankroll. (Originally underworld. See also tight wad.) ♦ *I lost my wad on a rotten horse in the seventh race.* **2.** *n.* a gob of semen. ♦ *He called the wad a cumquat and thought he'd made a joke.*

wag one's **chin** *tv.* to talk or jabber; to chatter aimlessly. ♦ *The two old buzzards sat on the park bench wagging their chins all afternoon.*

wagger Go to wand waver.

wagon *n.* the police wagon. ♦ *I called the wagon. It'll come and get these two thugs in about fifteen minutes.*

wail *in.* to be great. (See also wailing.) ♦ *Things really started to wail about midnight when the band really got going.*

wail on so *in.* to beat someone. (See also whale the tar out of so.) ♦ *Who are those two guys wailing on Sam?*

wailing AND **whaling** *mod.* excellent. (Teens.) ♦ *What a whaling guitar!*

Wala! Go to Walla!

walk 1. *n.* something easy. (Always with *a* in this sense. See also cakewalk; sleepwalk.) ♦ *That game was a walk!* **2.** *in.* to walk out on someone; to quit a job. ♦ *They had a big fight, and he walked.* **3.** *in.*
to walk away from something unharmed. ♦ *It couldn't have been much of an accident. Both drivers walked.* **4.** *in.* to get out of prison; to get off from a criminal charge. (Underworld.) ♦ *They thought they had Spike on a vice rap, but he walked.*

walk heavy *in.* to be important. (Black.) ♦ *Harry's been walking heavy since he graduated.*

walk on eggs AND **walk on thin ice** *in.* to walk very cautiously; to be in a very precarious position. ♦ *I have to remember that I'm walking on eggs when I give this speech.* ♦ *You're walking on thin ice when you criticize a member of that group.*

walk on sunshine *n.* to be really happy. ♦ *I'm in love and I'm walking on sunshine.*

walk on thin ice Go to walk on eggs.

walk soft *in.* to take it easy; to be gentle and humble. ♦ *I try to walk soft and not rock the boat.*

walk tall *in.* to be brave and self-assured. (See also stand tall.) ♦ *I know I can walk tall because I'm innocent.*

walk-in 1. *mod.* having to do with a customer who just comes in off the street. ♦ *We were hoping for more walk-in trade.* **2.** *n.* a customer who walks in off the street. ♦ *We had a couple of walk-ins this morning, but none of the hotel residents came.*

walking dandruff AND **galloping dandruff** *n.* lice. (See also pants rabbits.) ♦ *The bum called his lice "walking dandruff."* ♦ *I don't know anybody with galloping dandruff—I hope.*

walking on rocky socks *mod.* alcohol intoxicated. ♦ *He looks like he's walking on rocky socks.*

walking papers *n.* a notice of being fired, released, divorced, etc. ♦ *I hope I don't get my walking papers today. I need this job.*

walking wounded 1. *n.* soldiers who are injured but still able to walk. (Standard English.) ♦ *Many of the walking wounded helped with the more seriously injured cases.* **2.** *n.* a person who is injured— mentally or physically—and still able to go about daily life. ♦ *The outpatient clinic was filled with the walking wounded.* **3.** *n.* stupid people in general. ♦ *Most of network programming seems to be aimed at the walking wounded of our society.*

walkover *n.* an easy victory; an easy task. (From sports.) ♦ *Learning the computer's operating system was no walkover for me.*

wall job *n.* a car—in the shop for repairs— which is parked against the wall with no repairs done. (The customer is charged anyway.) ♦ *Places like those we surveyed may charge hundreds of dollars for what they call "wall jobs."*

Walla! AND **Wala!; Wallah!; Viola!** [wɑ 'lɑ] ♦ *exclam.* And there you have it! (All versions are misspellings or misunderstandings of the French *Voila!* The *Viola!* is a well-meant spelling error.) ♦ *And walla! There it is. Cooked just right!*

Wallah! Go to Walla!

wallet *n.* a college student's parents and financial source. ♦ *My wallet won't send me another penny this semester.*

wall-eyed *mod.* alcohol intoxicated. ♦ *Who's the wall-eyed guy carrying the ham sandwich?*

wallop ['wɑləp] **1.** *n.* a hard blow. ♦ *She planted a hard wallop on his right shoulder.* **2.** *tv.* to strike someone or something hard. ♦ *The door swung open and walloped me in the back.* **3.** *n.* influence; pull; clout. ♦ *I don't have enough wallop to make that kind of demand.*

wallpaper *n.* worthless checks. (Underworld.) ♦ *The feds followed a trail of wall-*paper from St. Louis to San Francisco and made the pinch.

walls have ears *tv.* Someone may be listening. (Sometimes with *the.*) ♦ *The walls have ears, so be careful about what you say.*

wall-to-wall *mod.* expansive and comprehensive. (From *wall-to-wall carpeting.*) ♦ *Old Tom is wall-to-wall hostility these days. What's wrong?*

waltz *n.* an easy task. ♦ *The job was a waltz. We did it in a day.*

waltz off (with sth) *in.* to take something away easily. ♦ *They just picked the thing up and waltzed off. Nobody asked them any questions.*

waltz through sth *in.* to get through something easily. ♦ *I waltzed through my comps and started on my research in my second year.*

wampum ['wɑmpəm] *n.* money. (From an American Indian word.) ♦ *I don't have enough wampum to swing the deal.*

wana ['wɑnə] *n.* marijuana. (Drugs.) ♦ *How much is this wana, man?*

wand waver AND **wagger** an exhibitionist. ♦ *The cops picked up a wand waver on Main Street.*

wank off Go to beat off.

wanna ['wɑnə OR 'wənə] *phr.* want to. (Eyedialect. Typical spoken English. Used in writing only for effect. Used in the examples of this dictionary.) ♦ *I will if I wanna.*

Wanna make sumpin' of it? Go to Want to make sth of it?

wannabe AND **wanna be** ['wɑnə bi] *n.* someone who wants to be something or someone. (Associated with Madonna, the singer.) ♦ *All these teenyboppers are wannabes, and that's why we can sell this stuff to them at any price.*

Want a piece of me? Go to (You) want a piece of me?

want out *in.* to want to remove oneself from some association or relationship. ♦ *Ted had had as much as he could stand, and he wanted out.*

Want to make sth **of it?** AND **Wanna make sumpin' of it?** *interrog.* Do you want to fight about it? ♦ *So, I'm a little ugly. Wanna make sumpin' of it?*

war chest *n.* a political campaign fund. ♦ *They say the vice president has more than one million dollars in his war chest.*

war paint *n.* a woman's makeup. ♦ *She'll be ready when she gets on her war paint.*

war zone *n.* an area where things get rough; a tough neighborhood. ♦ *Unfortunately our offices are in a war zone, and we have to be on the way home before dark.*

warchalking *n.* making a mark in a location where a wireless interconnection is available. ♦ *Since more and more Wi-Fi hot spots are available, warchaulking has become rare.*

wardrobe malfunction *n.* the failure of a costume to fully cover its wearer as intended. (From an incident on broadcast television where this failure allowed a woman's naked breast to be seen. The term itself was concocted to be an excuse for the incident.) ♦ *Now he spends hours watching TV, hoping for another wardrobe malfunction.*

wardrobing *n.* the practice of buying clothing, wearing it once, and returning it for a refund. ♦ *The company put a stop to wardrobing by making customers mail their returns to a central warehouse.*

warhorse *n.* a tough old thing, person, or idea. ♦ *What time does the old warhorse's train get in, and how long is she staying this time?*

warm body *n.* just anyone who can be counted on to stay alive. ♦ *See if you can get a couple of warm bodies to stand at the door and hand out programs.*

warm so **up** *tv.* to prepare an audience for another—more famous—performer. ♦ *This man Bennett is a superb choice to warm up the audience.*

warmed over *mod.* not very original; rehashed. ♦ *I am not interested in reading warmed-over news on a computer screen.*

warped *mod.* drug intoxicated. (A variant of bent.) ♦ *Too many yellows made Jerry warped as the dickens.*

wart 1. *n.* an annoying person. (Also a rude term of address.) ♦ *Tell the wart to leave, or we will be forced to call Spike, who doesn't care for such persons.* **2.** *n.* a problem or an obstruction in a plan. ♦ *Okay, now we come to the wart. We don't have the money to carry out this plan.*

was had Go to been had.

wash 1. *in.* to be believed. (As if untruth were a stain that will not come out in the wash.) ♦ *That'll never wash! It's totally unbelievable.* **2.** *n.* a drink that follows a previous drink; a chaser. ♦ *Can I have a wash with this, bartender?* **3.** *n.* the almost simultaneous sale and purchase of the same stock, usually to make the stock appear to be trading actively. (Securities markets. The practice is illegal. Tax loss selling must be done in such a way to avoid appearing to be a wash.) ♦ *I sold the stock and couldn't buy it back for thirty days to avoid an illegal wash.* **4.** *n.* a whitewash or covering up (of a problem). ♦ *What the administration presented was not an explanation but a wash.*

wash out 1. *in.* to fail and be removed from something, such as school. (See also washout.) ♦ *I don't want to wash out. It's my whole future.* **2.** *in.* to have a serious wreck; to wipe out. ♦ *The vehicles have a tendency to wash out when cornering.* **3.** *in.* to lose a large amount of money. ♦ *Fred washed out on that stock deal.* **4.** *in.* to slow down or collapse from exhaustion. (See also washed out.) ♦ *The whole play began to wash out during the second act. It was a lost cause by the third.*

wash so **away** *tv.* to kill someone. (Underworld.) ♦ *The mob triggers came by and tried to wash away a druggy type.*

washboard abs *n.* heavily marked abdominal muscles, divided into six equal sections. ♦ *If I work out hard enough I can build those washboard abs.*

washed out *mod.* exhausted; tired. ♦ *I feel too washed out to go to work today.*

washout *n.* a failure; a fiasco. ♦ *The whole project was a washout. A lost cause from beginning to end.*

WASP 1. *n.* a white Anglo-Saxon protestant. (Usually derogatory. Acronym.) ♦ *Would you call Pete a WASP?* **2.** *mod.* having to do with white Anglo-Saxon protestants; waspish. ♦ *What a silly old WASP idea.*

waspish *mod.* in the manner of a WASP. ♦ *She looks sort of "waspish," but she's not.*

Wassup? Go to Wusup?

waste *tv.* to kill someone. (Underworld.) ♦ *The mob's triggers sped by in a car and wasted four pushers.*

wasted 1. *mod.* dead; killed. ♦ *That's silly. We all end up wasted one way or another.* **2.** *mod.* alcohol or drug intoxicated. ♦ *I've never seen a bartender get wasted before.* **3.** *mod.* exhausted. ♦ *I worked two shifts, and I'm totally wasted.*

Watch it! *exclam.* Be careful!; Watch your step!; Careful of what you say! ♦ *You're walking on thin ice. Watch it!*

Watch my lips! AND **Read my lips! 1.** *exclam.* I am going to say something rude to you that I will not say out loud! ♦ *You jerk! Watch my lips!* **2.** *exclam.* Listen very carefully to what I am saying!; If you can't understand what I am saying, then watch the formation of words by my lips. ♦ *Read my lips! Do not ask any more stupid questions!*

Watch your mouth! AND **Watch your tongue!** *exclam.* Pay attention to what you are saying!; Do not say anything rude! ♦ *Hey, don't talk that way! Watch your mouth!* ♦ *Listen, potty-mouth! Watch your tongue!*

Watch your tongue! Go to Watch your mouth!

water one's **cheeks** *tv.* to cry; to shed tears sobbing. ♦ *Poor Billy was watering his cheeks all night because his dog ran away.*

watering hole *n.* a tavern. ♦ *Now this place is one of my favorite watering holes.*

wax 1. *tv.* to beat or defeat someone; to assault someone. ♦ *The muggers waxed the vest and swiped his briefcase.* **2.** *n.* a phonograph recording; a substance onto which a recording is put. (Never singular or plural. The oldest recordings were wax cylinders. The nickname survives.) ♦ *This is one of the finest pieces of music ever put on wax.*

waxed *mod.* alcohol intoxicated. (See also polished (up).) ♦ *Sam got waxed and had to be taken home.*

way 1. *mod.* extremely; totally. ♦ *Oh, this is way gross!* **2.** *interj.* There is too a way!, as an answer to No way! ♦ *A: I won't do it. No way! B: Way! Yes, you will.*

Way! *exclam.* Yes it can!; Yes it does! (The opposite of No way!) ♦ *TOM: It can't be done. No way! BILL: Way! Yes, it can!* ♦ *Way! You will do it and you will like it!*

way down *mod.* very depressed. ♦ *Poor Clare is way down. I think she has something wrong with her.*

the **way it plays** *in.* the way it is; the way things are. ♦ *The world is a rough place, and that's the way it plays.*

way off (base) *mod.* on the wrong track; completely wrong. (See also off base.) ♦ *Sorry. You are way off. You should just give up.*

way out AND **way-out 1.** *mod.* extreme; arcane. ♦ *Some of your ideas are really way out.* **2.** *mod.* heavily alcohol or drug intoxicated. ♦ *That guy is way out—can't even walk.* ♦ *She was so way-out, she was almost unconscious.*

way rad *mod.* quite excellent. (California. See also rad.) ♦ *Oh, Tiff! That's way rad!*

Way to go! Go to (That's the) way to go!

wazoo Go to bazoo.

WBMTTP *interj.* Which brings me to the point. (Initialism. Used in email and computer forum or news group messages. Not pronounced aloud.) ♦ *Of course, you may not like that approach. WBMTTP. You need someone to help you choose the proper method.*

weak sister *n.* a timid person, usually a male. ♦ *Another weak sister and we'll have to quit. We've got to pull together.*

wear *tv.* to tolerate something. (Usually negative.) ♦ *That's no good. I won't wear it.*

wear the pants (in the house) *tv.* to be the boss in the house; to run a household. ♦ *All right, if you have to wear the pants, have it your way.*

wearing (nothing but) a smile *tv.* naked. ♦ *This doll came on stage and within ten minutes she was wearing nothing but a smile.*

weasel 1. *n.* a sneaky person. ♦ *If Fred weren't such a weasel, we could get along better.* **2.** *n.* an earnest student. (Collegiate.) ♦ *Martin is your classic weasel.*

weasel out of *sth in.* to get out of doing something; to wiggle out of a responsibility. ♦ *I know how to weasel out of something like that. You get a headache.*

weblog AND **blog** *n.* a type of online diary that someone makes available to other people on the internet. (A very popular way to communicate one's personal details without any social interaction.) ♦ *John started a weblog so that other people could read about what he eats for breakfast.* ♦ *I deleted my blog, since it was too silly.*

wedgy AND **wedgie** *n.* a situation where one's underpants are drawn up tightly between the buttocks; a melvin. ♦ *Willy skipped up behind Greg and gave him a wedgy.*

weed 1. *n.* tobacco; a cigarette or cigar. ♦ *This weed is gonna be the death of me.* **2.** *n.* marijuana; a marijuana cigarette. (Drugs.) ♦ *This is good weed, man.*

weed-eater Go to weedhead.

weeder *n.* a difficult introductory college course designed to get rid of the weaker students; a course meant to weed out the weaker students. ♦ *Don't get into the morning section of the course. The prof is tough and thinks it's supposed to be a weeder.*

weedhead AND **weed-eater** *n.* a smoker of marijuana. ♦ *The weedheads are taking over this neighborhood.*

weeds *n.* clothing. ♦ *Good-looking weeds you're wearing.*

weekend warrior *n.* a member of the military reserves. ♦ *I wanted to be a weekend warrior and get some of the educational benefits.*

weenie AND **wienie 1.** *n.* a stupid and inept male. ♦ *Tell that stupid weenie to get himself over here and get back to work.* **2.** *n.* the penis. (Usually objectionable.) ♦ *He held his hands over his weenie and ran for the bedroom.* **3.** *n.* an earnest student. ♦ *That weenie keeps getting As and raising the grade scale.*

weeper *n.* a sad movie, novel, television program, etc. ♦ *I can't seem to get enough of these weepers.*

weird out *in.* to become emotionally disturbed or unnerved; to flip (out). (See also weirded out.) ♦ *The day was just gross. I thought I would weird out at noon.*

weirded out *mod.* disturbed or unnerved by drugs or events. ♦ *I was totally weirded out and couldn't control myself.*

weirdo ['wɪrdo] *n.* a strange person. ♦ *She is sure a weirdo lately.*

Welcome to the club. AND **Join the club.; WTTC** *sent. & comp. abb.* The rest of us are in the same situation. ♦ *So you're short of cash? Welcome to the club.* ♦ *You're just like us. Join the club; we've got jackets.*

welk [wɛlk] *phr.* you are welcome. ♦ *"Welk," said Fred, accepting my thanks.*

(Well,) pardon me for living! AND **Excuse me for breathing!; Excuse me for living!** *tv.* I am SOOO sorry! (A very sarcastic response to a rebuke, seeming to regret the apparent offense of even living.) ♦ *A: You are blocking my view. Please move. B: Well, pardon me for living!* ♦ *You say you were here first? Well excuse me for breathing!*

Well, wash my mouth out with soap. AND **WWMMOWS** *sent. & comp. abb.* a request indicating pretend remorse for saying something profane or objectionable. ♦ *So you don't like my advanced vocabulary. WWMMOWS.*

well-fixed AND **well-heeled 1.** *mod.* rich. ◆ *His father died and left him pretty well-fixed.* **2.** AND **well-healed** *mod.* alcohol intoxicated. ◆ *You might say he is well-heeled. You might say he's dead drunk, too.*

well-healed Go to well-fixed.

well-heeled Go to well-fixed.

well-hung AND **hung 1.** *mod.* having large [male] genitals. (Widely known and very old. Usually objectionable.) ◆ *If Tom was as well-hung as he thinks he is, he wouldn't even say anything at all.* **2.** *mod.* having large breasts. (Usually objectionable.) ◆ *She is so hung, she's top heavy.*

well-oiled 1. *mod.* alcohol intoxicated. ◆ *He was well-oiled and couldn't stand up.* **2.** *mod.* talkative. ◆ *She was sure well-oiled. I thought she'd never stop talking.*

(well-)upholstered *mod.* chubby; plump. ◆ *Fortunately, he was upholstered enough that the fall didn't really hurt.*

wenchy AND **whenchy** ['wɛntʃi AND 'ʌwɛntʃi] *mod.* bitchy; snotty. (Collegiate.) ◆ *I really wish you wouldn't be so wenchy with me!*

wep *n.* a weapon. ◆ *Get your wep ready?*

Were you born in a barn? *interrog.* Weren't you trained to close the door by yourself? ◆ *You sure are careless with that door. Were you born in a barn?*

wet 1. *mod.* alcohol intoxicated. ◆ *He's been drinking since noon and is pretty wet.* **2.** *mod.* having to do with an area where is it legal to sell alcohol. (Compare this with dry.) ◆ *Is it wet or dry in this county?* **3.** *mod.* feeble; in the manner of a nerd. ◆ *Tom is totally wet. What a jerk.*

wet blanket *n.* someone who ruins a good time. (In the way that a wet blanket is used to put out a fire.) ◆ *Oh, Martin! Why do you have to be such a wet blanket?*

wet noodle *n.* a dupe; a wimp. ◆ *Don't be such a wet noodle. Don't let them push you around.*

wet one *n.* a cold beer. ◆ *I could sure use a wet one about now.*

wet rag Go to wet sock.

wet sock AND **wet rag** *n.* a wimp; a useless jerk. (See also rubber sock.) ◆ *Don't be such a wet sock! Stand up for your rights!* ◆ *Willard is a wet rag, but he's kind and helpful.*

wetware ['wɛtwɛr] *n.* the human brain. (Compared to computer *hardware* and *software*.) ◆ *This isn't a hardware problem; it's a wetware problem.*

WFM Go to Works for me.

whack AND **wack 1.** *tv.* to strike someone or something. ◆ *Larry reached down and wacked the dog across the snout.* **2.** *n.* a blow or hit (at someone or something). ◆ *She landed a nasty wack on his thigh.* **3.** *n.* a drink of liquor. ◆ *Take a whack of this stuff.* **4.** Go to w(h)acked.

whack off Go to beat off.

w(h)ack so/sth **up** *in.* to damage someone or something. (See also whack sth up.) ◆ *Bob got mad at Greg and whacked him up.*

w(h)ack so **(out)** *tv.* to kill somebody. (Underworld.) ◆ *Willie made another try at whacking Albert out last evening.*

whack sth **off 1.** *tv.* to complete something easily or quickly. ◆ *If you want a pair of these, I can whack them off for you in a few minutes.* **2.** *tv.* to cut or chop something off. ◆ *A tree branch is rubbing against the house. I guess I'll go out and whack that branch off.*

w(h)ack sth **(out)** *tv.* to rob a place; to swindle a business establishment. (Underworld.) ◆ *Did your guys wack the church collection box?*

whack sth **up** *tv.* to chop something up. ◆ *In about an hour, he had whacked the tree up into small logs.*

w(h)acked AND **w(h)ack 1.** *mod.* wild; silly. ◆ *Bill was wacked as always and embarrassed us all.* **2.** Go to w(h)acked (out).

w(h)acked (out) *mod.* alcohol or drug intoxicated. ◆ *Dave was so whacked out he couldn't stand up.*

whale 1. *n.* a very fat person. (Cruel.) ◆ *Britney is getting to be such a whale.* **2.** *n.* a drunkard; a person with an enormous capacity for liquor. ◆ *Arthur is getting to*

be a regular whale. What does he drink?
3. *n.* a high roller in a casino or similar gambling setting. ♦ *We take good care of our whales, comping them with anything they ask for.*

whale into so/sth *in.* to attack someone or something. ♦ *Jimmy's dad really whaled into him.*

whale on *mod.* excellent. (Possibly confused with or in error for **wailing**.) ♦ *We had a whale on time at Bob's house.*

whale the tar out of so *tv.* to spank or beat someone. (Sometimes said to a child.) ♦ *My father threatened to whale the tar out of me.*

whaling Go to **wailing**.

wham-bang [ˈʍæmˈbæŋ] *mod.* boisterous. ♦ *We had a really wham-bang time at your party.*

whang(y)doodle [ˈʍæŋ(i)ˈdud]] **1.** *n.* a gadget. ♦ *Toss me one of the little whangdoodles, would ya?* **2.** *n.* nonsense. ♦ *Now that's enough of your whangdoodle.*

whank off Go to **beat off**.

whankster AND **wankster; whangster; wangster** *n.* a phony gangsta; a bogus, nonblack, ghetto dweller, affecting the language and dress of the streets. (The "w" and "wh" difference is dialectal. Derived from *white + gangster*, although some say *white +* **whanker** = masturbator.) ♦ *He's a phony and a whankster!*

What a crock! AND **WAC** *exclam. & comp. abb.* What a crock of shit!; What a lot of nonsense! ♦ *Y3. WAC!*

What (a) nerve! *exclam.* What insolence!; How rude and presumptuous! ♦ *Did you hear what she said? What nerve!*

What can I do you for? *interrog.* How can I help you?; How can I serve you? ♦ *Now it's your turn. What can I do for you?*

What can I say? *interj.* I'm speechless.; I can't explain.; What more can I say?; What do you want me to say?; I'm speechless. ♦ *So, I dented your car. I'm sorry. What can I say?*

What do you say? 1. *interrog.* Hello, how are you? (Most often [wədəjəˈse].) ♦ *Hi,*

Jim. What do you say? **2.** *interrog.* What is your answer? ♦ *Come on, I need an answer now. What do you say?*

What else is new? *interrog.* But isn't that what you expect?; What you said isn't new, so what is new? ♦ *So, there's not enough money this week. What else is new?*

What gives? *interrog.* What is going on?; What is happening? ♦ *Hey! What gives? Who left this here?*

What in Sam Hill? Go to **What in (the) Sam Hill?**

What (in) the devil? *interrog.* What has happened?; What? (Often with the force of an exclamation.) ♦ *What the devil? Who are you? What are you doing in my room?*

What (in) the fucking hell! *exclam.* an angry and surprised elaboration of *What?* (Taboo. Usually objectionable.) ♦ *What the fucking hell do you think you are doing?*

What (in) the hell? 1. *interrog.* What has happened?; What? ♦ *What the hell happened here?* **2.** *interrog.* What does it matter? (Usually with the force of an exclamation.) ♦ *Don't be such a cheapskate. Get the nice one. What the hell!*

What in (the) Sam Hill? *interrog.* What has happened?; What? (An elaboration of *what. Sam Hill* is **hell.** Often with the force of an exclamation. See examples for variations.) ♦ *What in the Sam Hill do you think you are doing?*

What is it? *interrog.* Hello, what is happening? ♦ *What is it? What's happening?*

What so **said.** *sent.* I agree with what someone just said, although I might not have been able to say it as well or so elegantly. ♦ *What John said. And I agree 100 percent.*

What the deuce? *interrog.* What has happened?; What? (*Deuce* is an old word for devil.) ♦ *What the deuce! Who are you?*

What the devil? Go to **What (in) the devil?**

What the fucking hell! Go to **What (in) the fucking hell!**

What the heck! *exclam.* It doesn't matter! (Often with the force of an exclamation.)

♦ *Oh, what the heck! Come on in. It doesn't matter.*

What the hell? Go to What (in) the hell?

What you see is what you get. 1. *sent.* The product you are looking at is exactly what you get if you buy it. ♦ *What you see is what you get. The ones in the box are just like this one.* **2.** AND **WYSIWYG** [ˈwɪsiwɪg] *phr.* What you see on the screen is what will print on the printer. (Computers. Acronym.) ♦ *I need something that's WYSIWYG. I have no imagination.*

whatchamacallit [ˈmʌtʃəməˈkɑlɪt] *n.* a name for a person or thing whose real name has been forgotten or is being avoided. ♦ *I lost my—you know—my whatchamacallit—my watch!*

whatever *mod.* I don't care; it doesn't matter which choice; whatever you want. ♦ Q: *I have chocolate, vanilla, strawberry, kiwi, and lime. Which do you want?* A: *Oh, whatever.*

whatever floats your boat Go to whatever turns you on.

whatever turns you on AND **whatever floats your boat** *tv.* whatever excites you or interests you. (Main entry was said originally about sexual matters.) ♦ *I can't stand that kind of music, but whatever turns you on.* ♦ *Ketchup on hot dogs! Yuck! But whatever floats your boat.*

What'll it be? *interrog.* What do you want. (Typically said when offering someone drinks. See also What's yours?) ♦ *Okay, Mac, what'll it be?*

What's buzzin' (cousin)? *interrog.* What's happening? ♦ *Hey, chum! What's buzzin' cousin?*

What's coming off? AND **What's going down?** *interrog.* What is happening here?; What is going to happen? (Also a greeting inquiry.) ♦ BILL: *Hey, man! What's coming off?* TOM: *Oh, nothing, just takin' it easy.* ♦ *What's going down, dawg?*

What's cooking? *interrog.* What is happening?; What's about to happen? ♦ *What's cooking? Anything interesting?*

What's eating SO? *interrog.* What is bothering someone? ♦ *What's eating Fred? He's in a rotten humor.*

What's going down? *interrog.* What's happening? ♦ *Hey, man, what's going down?*

What's going on? *interrog.* What is happening here? ♦ *What's all this broken glass? What's going on?*

What's happ(ening)? *interrog.* Hello, what's new? ♦ *Hey, dude! What's happening?*

what's his face AND **what's his name** *n.* someone whose name has been forgotten; someone whose name is being avoided. ♦ *I can't remember what's his face's name either.* ♦ *I remember what's his name's face, but the moniker is lost and gone forever.*

what's his name Go to what's his face.

What's in it for me? AND **WIIFM** *sent. & comp. abb.* What benefit will I get from this activity? ♦ *Sounds like a plan, but WIIFM?*

What's in the bag! *interrog.* Hello, how are you? ♦ *Hey, man! What's in the bag?*

What's it to you? *interrog.* What does it matter to you?; Is it any of your business? ♦ *So I broke my glasses. What's it to you?*

What's new? *interrog.* Hello, how are you?; What has happened since I last saw you? ♦ *Hi, Jim! What's new?*

What's poppin' *interrog.* Hello, what is happening? ♦ *What's poppin'? Anything new?*

What's really good witcha? *interrog.* How are you? ♦ *Mooshoo! What's really good witcha.*

What's shakin' (bacon)? *interrog.* How are you?; What is new? ♦ *What's shakin' bacon? What's going down?*

What's the catch? *interrog.* What is the drawback?; It sounds good. Are there any hidden problems? ♦ *Sounds too good to be true. What's the catch?*

What's the damage? *interrog.* What are the charges?; How much is the bill? ♦ BILL: *That was delicious. Waiter, what's* *the damage?* WAITER: *I'll get the check, sir.*

What's the deal? Go to What's the scam?

What's the dilly? *interrog.* What's going on?; What's the deal? (*Dilly* is a pronunciation of *dealy.*) ♦ *Who's shouting? What's the dilly?*

What's the (good) word? *interrog.* Hello, how are you? ♦ *Haven't seen you in a long time. What's the good word?*

What's the scam? AND **What's the deal?** *interrog.* What is going on around here?; Explain what is happening or what you are doing. ♦ *What's the scam? What's happening, dude?* ♦ *I gave you a twenty, and you give me five back? What's the deal? Where's my other five?*

What's the scoop? *interrog.* What is the news? ♦ *"Hi, you guys!" beamed John's little brother. "What's the scoop?"*

What's up? *interrog.* What is going on?; What is happening? (See also **(T)sup?**; **Wusup?**) ♦ *Haven't seen you in a month of Sundays. What's up?*

What's up doc? *interrog.* What is happening here? ♦ *What's up doc? How're things going?*

What's up, G? *interrog.* Hello, what is up, guy? ♦ *What's up G? How ya living?*

What's with so/sth? *interrog.* What is wrong with someone or something? ♦ *What's with this can opener? It won't turn.*

What's your age? *interrog.* Hello, how are you? ♦ *Yo, Sam! What's your age?*

What's your damage? *interrog.* What's your problem? (Like a *damage report.*) ♦ *You look beat, man. What's your damage?*

What's yours? *interrog.* What (or which) do you want? (Typically said on offering drinks. See also **What'll it be?**) ♦ *"What's yours?" said the bartender.*

whatsis AND **whatsit; whatzit; whazzit** ['ʍətsɪs AND 'ʍətsɪt, 'ʍətsɪt, 'ʍəzɪt] *n.* a name for a person or thing whose real name has been forgotten or is being avoided. ♦ *Put this little whatzit on the top and another on the bottom.*

whatsit Go to whatsis.

whatzit Go to whatsis.

whazood AND **waa-zooed** ['ʍɑ'zud AND 'wɑ'zud] *mod.* alcohol intoxicated. ♦ *Pete was too waa-zooed to stand up.*

whazzit Go to whatsis.

wheel *tv. & in.* to drive a car. ♦ *Let's wheel my heap over to Marty's place.*

wheel and deal *in.* to negotiate, cajole, and connive—aggressively. (See also wheeler-dealer.) ♦ *If you can't wheel and deal, you can't run for elective office.*

wheel estate *n.* a mobile home or RV. ♦ *His wheel estate includes two cars, a motor home, and a couple of bicycles.*

wheel man *n.* the (male) driver of a criminal escape car. (Underworld.) ♦ *Lefty was the wheel man for the bank job.*

wheeler-dealer *n.* someone who bargains aggressively. (See also wheel and deal.) ♦ *Who's the wheeler-dealer who set up this deal?*

wheels *n.* a car; transportation by automobile. ♦ *I'll need a ride. I don't have any wheels.*

wheely AND **wheelie** *n.* an act of rearing up on a bike or motorcycle, balancing on the rear wheel. ♦ *The kid did a wheelie and scared his mother to death.*

when push comes to shove AND **if push comes to shove** *phr.* when things get a little pressed; when the situation gets more active or intense. ♦ *If push comes to shove, the front office can help with some statistics.*

when the eagle flies AND **day the eagle flies** *in.* payday. (The *eagle* is the one found on U.S. currency.) ♦ *I'll pay you back when the eagle flies.* ♦ *I'll find you the day the eagle flies.*

when the fat lady sings Go to till the fat lady sings.

when the shit hits the fan *tv.* when all the expected trouble materializes. (Usually objectionable.) ♦ *When the shit hits the fan, you had better be prepared to support those of us who are involved in this mess.*

♦ *We had one hell of an afternoon around here. Where were you when the shit hit the fan?*

whenchy Go to wenchy.

Where have you been keeping yourself? *interrog.* I haven't seen you in a long time. Where have you been? ♦ *I haven't seen you in a long time. Where you been keeping yourself?*

Where in (the) Sam Hill? *interrog.* Where? (An intensive form of *where. Sam Hill* is hell.) ♦ *Where in Sam Hill did I put my hat?*

Where in the world? *interrog.* Where? (An intensive form of *where.*) ♦ *Where in the world did I put my glasses?*

where it's at *phr.* what one is aiming for; what is needed. (This does not refer to a place.) ♦ *Keep on trying. That's where it's at!*

Where on earth? Go to Where on (God's green) earth?

Where on (God's green) earth? *interrog.* (Exactly) where? (An intensive form of *where.* See examples for variations.) ♦ *Where on God's green earth did you get that ridiculous hat?*

Where's the fire? *interrog.* Why are you going so fast?; What's the hurry? ♦ *Going a little fast there, weren't you? Where's the fire?*

where so **is at** *in.* what mental condition someone is in. ♦ *You said it! I know just where you're at!*

where so **lives** *in.* at one's core; in one's own personal situation. ♦ *That really hits you where you live, doesn't it?*

where so's **head is at** *in.* the state of one's mental well-being. ♦ *As soon as I figure where my head is at, I'll be okay.*

where the action is *in.* where important things are happening. ♦ *I want to be where the action is.*

Where the Sam Hill? Go to Where in (the) Sam Hill?

where the sun don't shine *in.* in a dark place, namely the anus. (Often with *put*

it or *shove it.* Part of the answer to the question *Where shall I put it?* Always with *don't*; never with *doesn't.*) ♦ *For all I care you can shove it where the sun don't shine.*

wherewithal ['ʌɛrwɪθɑl] **1.** *n.* money. ♦ *I don't have the wherewithal to invest in anything like that.* **2.** *n.* motivation; gumption. ♦ *As soon as I get some wherewithal, I'll get a new computer.*

whiffled ['ʌɪfld] *mod.* alcohol intoxicated. ♦ *Jed found himself a mite whiffled, but nobody else knew.*

whiff-sniffer AND **wiff-sniffer** *n.* a prohibitionist; someone always alert for the smell of alcohol on someone's breath. (Prohibition.) ♦ *No wiff-sniffer is going to tell me what to do.*

whigga AND **wigga; whigger; wigger** *n.* a gangsta term for a nonblack who affects the speech, dress, and behavior of the black males of ghetto or streets. (Streets. Derogatory. A blend of *white* + *nigga.*) ♦ *Not bad for a whigga.*

whing-ding AND **wing-ding 1.** *n.* a love affair; a sexual affair. ♦ *Sam and Martha brought their little whing-ding to an end.* **2.** *n.* a gadget. ♦ *I've never seen one of these little wing-dings so banged up.* **3.** AND **whinger** *n.* a wild drinking party; drinking spree. ♦ *Fred had one of the best whing-dings this town has ever seen.*

whinger Go to whing-ding.

whip *n.* an expensive car. (Streets. Possibly from the power or control this car gives its owner.) ♦ *Great new whip, right? It's a Slade, right?*

whip off Go to beat off.

whip one's **wire** Go to beat the dummy.

whip sth **into shape** Go to lick sth into shape.

whip sth **off** *tv.* to finish something quickly, especially food or drink. ♦ *Did you just whip that whole pizza off?*

whip the dummy Go to beat the dummy.

whipped 1. *mod.* exhausted; beat. ♦ *Wow, you look whipped.* **2.** *mod.* alcohol intoxicated. ♦ *She was too whipped to find money to pay her bill.* **3.** *mod.* great. ♦ *The* band was whipped and the food was unbelievable.

whipsaw 1. *tv.* to assault a person; to gang up and beat a person. ♦ *What kind of creeps would whipsaw an old buzzard like that?* **2.** *tv.* [for the stock market] to reduce the capital of investors by frightening them into selling when stock prices are low and encouraging them to buy when prices are high. (Securities markets.) ♦ *A lot of people were whipsawed in the recent market volatility.*

whirlybird *n.* a helicopter. ♦ *See that whirlybird up there? It's timing your speed. Slow down.*

whiskers (man) Go to Mr. Whiskers.

whiskey dick 1. *n.* a penis exhibiting impotence, as from too much alcohol. ♦ *Well, it looks like a case of whiskey dick.* **2.** a limp windsock at an airport. ♦ *There's a whiskey dick over there on the right, so it looks like we can go in.*

whiskey tenor *n.* a strained tenor. ♦ *Four whiskey tenors do not a barbershop quartet make.*

whistle in the dark *in.* to guess aimlessly; to speculate as to a fact. ♦ *She was whistling in the dark. She has no idea of what's going on.*

whistle-blower *n.* someone who calls a halt to something; an informer; an enforcer; a **stool (pigeon)**. ♦ *I don't know who the whistle-blower was, but a good time was really ruined.*

whistler *n.* someone who is a police informer; a **stoolie**. (Underworld. More specialized than **whistle-blower**.) ♦ *Britney turned into a whistler after her last little vacation.*

white elephant *n.* a useless or unwanted object. (From the notion that an extremely valuable gift that requires great expense for its care and protection is an unwanted gift.) ♦ *Take all those white elephants to the flea market.*

white hat *n.* a good guy; a hero. (From Western movies where you could tell the good guys from the bad guys by the color of their hats: white for good, black for

bad.) ♦ *He seems like a white hat, but he's a worm.*

white knuckler 1. *n.* a tense and nervous person. ♦ *You white knucklers are just going to have to relax.* **2.** *n.* a suspenseful event, such as an exciting movie or a rough airplane flight. ♦ *The movie was a real white knuckler.*

white man's disease *n.* the inability to jump in basketball. ♦ *You break your leg, Walter? Or you got a case of white man's disease.*

whitebread *mod.* plain; dull. ♦ *If I wanted a white bread vacation, I'd have gone to the beach.*

white-knuckle 1. *mod.* having to do with an event that creates a lot of tension, especially an airplane flight. ♦ *We came in during the storm on a white-knuckle flight from Chicago.* **2.** *mod.* of a person who is made tense by something such as flying or sailing. ♦ *I'm afraid I'm a white-knuckle sailor, and you'd all be much happier if I stay on dry land.*

whitewash 1. *tv.* to make something look better than it really is; to conceal something bad. ♦ *Now, don't try to whitewash this incident. Open up about it.* **2.** *n.* an act or campaign of covering up something bad. ♦ *They tried to give the scandal the old whitewash, but it didn't work.*

whittled *mod.* alcohol intoxicated; filled with liquor. (See also **cut**.) ♦ *Fred's whittled again and shouldn't drive home.*

whiz 1. *n.* a talented or skilled person. ♦ *She's a real whiz with stats.* **2.** *in.* to urinate. (Usually objectionable.) ♦ *I gotta stop here and whiz.*

whiz kid *n.* a young whiz. ♦ *The boss's new whiz kid doesn't seem to be doing the job very well.*

Who died in here? AND **Somebody died in here!** *sent.* Who or what caused this terrible odor in this bathroom or restroom. (Also with variable syntax.) ♦ *It smells like somebody died in here!* ♦ *Yuck! Who died in here?*

Who (in) the devil? Go to Who (in) the hell?

Who (in) the hell? AND **Who (in) the devil?** *interrog.* Who? (An elaboration of *who*. See examples for variations.) ♦ *Who in the hell was that masked man?* ♦ *Who the devil do you think you are?*

Who's your daddy? *interrog.* Who is your boss? It's me isn't it? (A reminder of who's the boss.) ♦ *Don't waver. Do it! Who's your daddy?*

Who's your friend? *interrog.* Who is that following along behind you? ♦ JOHN: *Hi, Tom. Who's your friend?* TOM: *Oh, this is my little brother, Willie.* JOHN: *Hi, Willie.*

who shot John *n.* moonshine; illicit whiskey. (Prohibition.) ♦ *You know where I can get a little of that who shot John?*

Who the deuce? *interrog.* Who? (An elaboration of *who*. The *deuce* is the devil. See examples for variations.) ♦ *Who the deuce do you think you are?*

Who the devil? Go to Who (in) the hell?

Who the hell? Go to Who (in) the hell?

Whoa! [wo] *exclam.* Stop! (Said to a horse or any person or thing.) ♦ *You've gone about far enough. Whoa!*

whodunit [hu'dənɪt] *n.* a detective story. (See also thriller-diller.) ♦ *I go through about three whodunits a week.*

whole bag of tricks *n.* everything; every possibility. ♦ *Well now. I've used my whole bag of tricks, and we still haven't solved this.*

the **whole ball of wax** *n.* everything; the whole thing. ♦ *Well, that just about ruins the whole ball of wax.*

a **whole bunch** AND **whole bunches** *mod.* a whole lot; very much. (Always with *a* in the singular.) ♦ *I like to spend evenings at home a whole bunch.* ♦ *Tom likes Mary whole bunches, but she thinks he's a dork.*

the **whole enchilada** [...ɛntʃə'ladə] *n.* the whole thing; everything. (From Spanish.) ♦ *Pete wants the whole enchilada.*

the **whole fam damily** [...'fæm 'dæmli] *n.* the entire family. (A deliberate spoonerism for *whole damn family*.) ♦ *The whole fam damily has had this virus. Yuck!*

a **whole new ball game** *n.* a completely different situation; something completely different. ♦ *Now that you're here, it's a whole new ball game.*

the **whole nine yards** *n.* the entire amount; everything. (Origin unknown. It does not matter what substance is being referred to. It means all of it, no matter what it is.) ♦ *For you I'll go the whole nine yards.*

the **whole schmear** [...ʃmɪr] *n.* the entire amount; the entire affair. (Based on Yiddish.) ♦ *I'll take a hamburger with everything on it—the whole schmear.*

the **whole shebang** AND the **whole shooting match** [...ʃə'bæŋ] *n.* the whole affair; everything and everyone. (Folksy.) ♦ *The whole shebang is just about washed up.* ♦ *The boss put an end to the whole shooting match.*

the **whole shooting match** Go to the whole shebang.

the **whole wide world** *n.* everywhere; everywhere and everything. ♦ *I've searched the whole wide world for just the right hat.*

whomp Go to whump.

whoopie cakes *n.* female buttocks. ♦ *You put those whoopie cakes back down in that chair and listen to me!*

whooshed *mod.* alcohol intoxicated. ♦ *Jerry was totally whooshed by midnight.*

whoozis AND **whoozit** ['huzis AND 'huzit] *n.* a name for a person whose real name is forgotten or being avoided. ♦ *I met whoozis—you know, with the big whatsis —today.*

whoozit Go to whoozis.

whopper 1. *n.* something that is of relatively great size. ♦ *It was a whopper of an argument.* **2.** *n.* a very big lie. ♦ *That one's a whopper. I don't believe a word of it.*

whopping (great) *mod.* enormous. ♦ *What a whopping fool he is!*

Whuhap? *interrog.* Hello.; What's new? (Black. A greeting inquiry.) ♦ *Whuhap? Where's the action?*

whump AND **whomp; womp** [ʍəmp AND ʍɑmp, wɑmp] **1.** *tv.* to beat or outscore someone. ♦ *They set out to whump us, and they sure did.* **2.** *n.* the sound made when two flat surfaces fall together. ♦ *I heard the whump when the shed collapsed.*

wicked *mod.* excellent; impressive; cool. (Also in compounds, *wicked smart, wicked cool,* etc.) ♦ *Now this is what I call a wicked guitar.*

wicked bad *mod.* really quite good. (*Bad* has a long history of being used as an intensifier. *Wicked* here is a synonym of the intensifier *bad.*) ♦ *Man, this stuff is wicked bad.*

wicky *mod.* wicked; excellent. ♦ *Whose wicky red convertible is parked in front of the house?*

wide *mod.* drug intoxicated. ♦ *How'd you get so wide, man? What are you on?*

wide open 1. *mod.* as fast as possible; at full throttle. ♦ *I was driving along wide open when I became aware of a flashing red light.* **2.** *mod.* vice-ridden. ♦ *This town is wide open!*

wide place in the road *n.* a very small town. ♦ *The town is little more than a wide place in the road.*

widget ['wɪdʒɪt] **1.** *n.* a gadget. ♦ *Now, try to fit this widget into this slot here.* **2.** *n.* a hypothetical product made by a hypothetical company. ♦ *No, we stopped making widgets last year. Too much foreign competition.*

widow-maker *n.* a dangerous horse; anything dangerous: a gun, strong alcohol, etc. ♦ *I call this stuff widow-maker. It's really strong.*

wiener nose ['winɚ...] *n.* a simpleton. (Also a derogatory term of address.) ♦ *Look, wiener nose, mind your own business.*

wife *n.* a girlfriend. (Collegiate.) ♦ *Me and my wife are going to Fred's this Friday.*

wife-beater *n.* a sleeveless undershirt. (Indicating a low regard for the wearers of the garment. See also boy-beater.) ♦ *He al-*

ways wears wife-beaters with no outer shirt.

wiff-sniffer Go to whiff-sniffer.

wig out 1. *in.* to lose control of oneself; to flip one's wig. (See also wigged (out).) ♦ *I was afraid I would wig out if I stayed any longer.* **2.** *in.* to have a good time at a party, etc. ♦ *We wigged out at John's little get together.*

wigged (out) AND **wiggy 1.** *mod.* alcohol or drug intoxicated. ♦ *The kid got a little wigged and slipped under the table.* **2.** *mod.* having lost control of oneself; having flipped one's wig. ♦ *After she heard the bad news, she was totally wigged out.*

wiggle out of sth *in.* to successfully avoid doing something. ♦ *We wiggled out of the appointment.*

wiggy Go to wigged (out).

WIIFM Go to What's in it for me?

wild *mod.* exciting; eccentric; cool. ♦ *Things are really wild here.*

wild and woolly *mod.* exciting; hairy. ♦ *Things get a little wild and woolly on a Friday evening at Willy's place.*

will do *phr.* I will do it. ♦ *Will do. I'll get right on it.*

willies *n.* a case of fear or anxiety. (See also screaming-meemies.) ♦ *That kind of movie always gives me the willies.*

Wilma ['wɪlmə] *n.* a stupid woman. (From the Flintstones character. Also a term of address.) ♦ *She is such a Wilma! What a twit!*

wimp 1. *mod.* windows, icons, mouse pointer. (Usually **WIMP**. Acronym. Refers to a computer system, such as Macintosh or Microsoft Windows, with an elaborate user interface including resizable windows, clever icons, and a movable mouse. The term implies that such systems are for computer weaklings.) ♦ *I am happier with a computer system that doesn't have all that WIMP stuff.* **2.** *n.* a weak and retiring person; a square. ♦ *What a wimp. People walk all over her.*

wimp out (of sth**)** *in.* to chicken out (of sth); to get out of something, leaving others to carry the burden. ♦ *Come on! Don't wimp out now that there's all this work to be done.*

wimpy *mod.* weak; inept; square. ♦ *You are just a wimpy nerd!*

Win a few, lose a few. *tv.* Sometimes one wins; other times one loses. ♦ *Too bad. Sorry about that. Win a few, lose a few.*

Win some, lose some. AND **WSLS** *phr. & comp. abb.* Sometimes one will succeed, other times, one will fail. ♦ *WSLS. I'm philosophical about it.*

windbag AND **bag of wind** *n.* a talkative person; a braggart. ♦ *Quiet, you windbag!*

windy 1. *mod.* talkative. ♦ *She's so windy! Won't she ever let up?* **2.** *mod.* flatulent; having intestinal gas. ♦ *If you're windy, why don't you take the day off? Do us all a favor.*

wing *in.* to travel by airplane. ♦ *They winged from there to London.*

wing heavy *mod.* alcohol intoxicated. ♦ *From the way he's staggering, I'd say he's more than a little wing heavy.*

wing it *tv.* to improvise; to do something extemporaneously. ♦ *Don't worry. Just go out there and wing it.*

wing-ding Go to whing-ding.

a **wink of sleep** *n.* a bit of sleep; the smallest amount of sleep. (Usually in the negative.) ♦ *I couldn't get a wink of sleep because of the noise.*

winks *n.* some sleep. (See also forty winks.) ♦ *I gotta have some winks. I'm pooped.*

winky Go to blinky.

winner *n.* an excellent person or thing. ♦ *This one is a real winner.*

wino ['waɪno] **1.** *n.* wine. ♦ *How about a little more wino?* **2.** *n.* a wine drunkard. ♦ *I gave the wino some money to help him stop the shakes.*

win-win *n.* [of a situation] winning for both sides; [of a situation] winning for buyer and seller. ♦ *What have you got to lose? It's a win-win situation.*

win-win-win [of a situation] winning for three parties, such as manufacturer, seller, and customer. ♦ *Everybody makes money! It's win-win-win!*

wipe *n.* a murder; a killing. (Underworld. See also wipe out.) ♦ *The victim of the latest mob wipe was hauled out of the river this morning.*

Wipe it off! *exclam.* Wipe that smile off your face! ♦ *Wipe it off! Nothing funny here, soldier.*

wipe out 1. *in.* to crash. ♦ *The car wiped out on the curve.* **2.** *in.* to fall off or away from something, such as a bicycle, skates, a surfboard, a skateboard, etc. ♦ *I wiped out and skinned my knee.* **3.** ['waɪpaʊt] *n.* a wreck. (Usually **wipe-out**.) ♦ *There was a four-car wipe-out on the expressway when I came in this morning.* **4.** *n.* an accident on a bicycle, skates, surfboard, skateboard, etc. (Usually **wipe-out**.) ♦ *I had a nasty wipe-out, but I only bruised my elbow.* **5.** *n.* a loser; someone who is likely to wipe out. (Usually **wipe-out**.) ♦ *The guy's a wipe-out, for sure.*

wipe so out 1. *tv.* to eliminate someone; to kill someone. (Underworld.) ♦ *Max almost wiped Spike out.* **2.** *tv.* to exhaust or tire someone. ♦ *Jogging always wipes me out.* **3.** *tv.* to ruin someone financially. ♦ *The storm ruined the corn crop and wiped out everyone in the county.*

wipe sth out *tv.* to use up all of something. (See also wiped (out).) ♦ *I wiped the cookies out—not all at once, of course.*

wipe the floor up with so Go to mop the floor up with so.

wiped (out) 1. AND **wiped over** *mod.* alcohol or drug intoxicated. ♦ *Oh, man! I'm really wiped.* **2.** *mod.* [of a person or creature] exhausted. ♦ *I'm so wiped out that I just want to go home and go to bed.* **3.** *mod.* broke. ♦ *Medical bills left us totally wiped out.*

wiped over Go to wiped (out).

wire 1. *n.* a spy smuggled into a place. ♦ *Marlon thought Lefty was a wire.* **2.** *tv.* to install electronic eavesdropping equipment. ♦ *Somebody wired the mayor's office.* **3.** Go to (live) wire.

wired 1. *mod.* nervous; extremely alert. ♦ *The guy is pretty wired because of the election.* **2.** AND **wired up** *mod.* alcohol or drug intoxicated. ♦ *Ken was so wired up he couldn't remember his name.*

wired into so/sth *mod.* concerned with someone or something; really involved with someone or something. ♦ *Mary is really wired into classical music.*

wired up Go to wired.

wise guy *n.* a foolish person; a smart aleck. (See also **smart guy**. Also a term of address.) ♦ *Look, wise guy, mind your own business!*

wise to so/sth *mod.* having found out about someone or something. (Underworld.) ♦ *The cops are wise to the plan.*

wise up (to so/sth**)** *in.* to (finally) begin to understand someone or something; to realize and accept the facts about someone or something. (Also as a command.) ♦ *Come on, Sally! Wise up!*

wiseacre *n.* a jerk; a wiseguy. ♦ *We've got ways of dealing with a wiseacre like you!*

wish book *n.* a large, mail-order catalog. ♦ *Where's the wish book? I have to order something.*

wish list *n.* a list of things one wishes to have. ♦ *I put a new car at the top of my wish list.*

wishy-washy ['wɪʃi'waʃi] *mod.* indecisive; insipid; weak. ♦ *Don't be such a wishy-washy wimp.*

with a bang *mod.* in a flamboyant or exciting manner. (Especially with *go out, quit, finish.*) ♦ *The old year went out with a bang.*

with bells on *mod.* ready to go; eager. ♦ *I promise to be there at five in the morning with bells on.*

with flying colors *mod.* flamboyantly; boldly. ♦ *Paul came home with flying colors after the match.*

with it *mod.* up-to-date; contemporary. ♦ *Come on, chum. Get with it.*

with (one's**) eyes (wide) open** *mod.* totally aware of what is going on. ♦ *I went into this with my eyes open.*

within an ace of (doing) sth *mod.* very close to doing something. ♦ *We were within an ace of beating the all-time record.*

within spitting distance *mod.* close by. ♦ *The house you're looking for is within spitting distance, but it's hard to find.*

without a hitch *mod.* with no problem(s). ♦ *Everything went off without a hitch.*

WIYGW Go to Write if you get work.

wizzle a wild card word for words beginning with *W*, such as *weed, wizz, word, wigga.* (Streets. Also for other words with initial *W*.) ♦ *Where can I score some wizzle?*

woefits AND **woofits** ['wofɪts AND 'wufɪts] *n.* a hangover. ♦ *The poor guy is suffering from the woefits.*

wolf *n.* a bold and aggressive male. (See also **fine wolf**.) ♦ *He sees himself as a lady-killer. The chicks see him as an old-fashioned wolf.*

wolf sth **down** *tv.* to gobble something up; to bolt down food or drink. ♦ *Enjoy your food. Don't just wolf it down.*

wombat ['wambæt] *n.* a strange person; a geek. (Collegiate.) ♦ *Who's the wombat in the 1957 Chevy?*

womp Go to whump.

wonder water *n.* steroids. (See also **juice**.) ♦ *Look at the guns on that dude! Must be using wonder water.*

wonk [wɔŋk] **1.** *n.* an earnest student. (Collegiate.) ♦ *Yes, you could call Martin a wonk. In fact, he's the classic wonk.* **2.** *n.* a bureaucrat; a flunky. ♦ *The State Department policy wonks were up all night putting together the report.*

wonky ['wɔŋki] *mod.* studious. (Collegiate.) ♦ *You ought to get a little wonky yourself.*

wood Go to peckerwood.

wood butcher *n.* a carpenter. ◆ *See if you can get a wood butcher to fix this broken panel.*

wood-pussy *n.* a skunk. ◆ *Do I smell the faint perfume of a wood-pussy?*

the **woods are full of** sth *phr.* there are lots and lots of something. ◆ *The woods are full of cheap, compatible computer clones.*

woody 1. *n.* a wooden surfboard; a surfboard. ◆ *Get your woody, and let's get moving.* **2.** *n.* an erection of the penis. ◆ *His morning woody made a little mountain with the sheets on his bed.*

woof [wʊf] **1.** *in.* to boast; to sell a woof ticket; to chatter. (Black.) ◆ *They're just woofing. Ignore them.* **2.** *in.* to vomit. (Onomatopoetic.) ◆ *Somebody woofed on our driveway.*

woof cookies *tv.* to vomit. ◆ *Waldo had to woof cookies in the bushes.*

woofits Go to woefits.

woofled ['wʊfl̩d] *mod.* alcohol intoxicated. ◆ *Good grief, was he woofled!*

woofle-water AND **wozzle-water** *n.* whiskey; liquor. ◆ *Haven't you had just about enough woofle-water?*

woolies *n.* long underwear. ◆ *It's the time of the year for woolies!*

woozy ['wuzi] **1.** *mod.* sleepy; disoriented. ◆ *I'm still sort of woozy. Give me a minute or two to wake up.* **2.** *mod.* alcohol intoxicated. ◆ *I felt a little woozy, but that didn't stop me from having more.*

Word. 1. AND **Word up.** *interj.* Correct.; Right. ◆ *I hear you, man. Word.* **2.** *interj.* Hello. (See also What's the (good) word?) ◆ *Word. What's new?* ◆ *A: Word. B: Word.*

word hole AND **cake hole; pie hole** *n.* the mouth. ◆ *Put this food in your word hole, chew it up, and swallow it.* ◆ *Shut up your pie hole!*

word of mouse *n.* a message spread by email. (Contrived. Refers to a computer mouse. A play on *word of mouth*.) ◆ *A lot of these jokes are spread by word of mouse.*

Word up. Go to Word.

work one's **ass off** Go to work one's tail off.

work one's **buns off** Go to work one's tail off.

work one's **butt off** Go to work one's tail off.

work one's **tail off** AND **work** one's **ass off; work** one's **buns off; work** one's **butt off** *tv.* to work very hard. (Often objectionable.) ◆ *You spend half your life working your butt off—and for what?* ◆ *I worked my buns off to get this done on time!*

work oneself **up** *tv.* to allow oneself to become emotionally upset. ◆ *Todd worked himself up, and I thought he would scream.*

work oneself **(up) into a lather 1.** *tv.* to work very hard and sweat very much. (In the way that a horse works up a lather.) ◆ *Don't work yourself up into a lather. We don't need to finish this today.* **2.** *tv.* to get excited or angry. (An elaboration of work oneself up to sth.) ◆ *Now, now, don't work yourself up into a lather.*

work oneself **up to** sth *tv.* to get oneself mentally ready to do something. ◆ *I spent all morning working myself up to taking the driver's test.*

work so **over 1.** *tv.* to threaten, intimidate, or beat someone. ◆ *Bruno had worked over Terry, and Sam knew that this was no idle threat.* **2.** *tv.* to give someone's body a thorough examination or treatment. ◆ *The doctors worked her over to the tune of $1,500 but couldn't find anything wrong with her.*

workaholic *n.* someone who is obsessed with work. ◆ *Jerry is a workaholic. He can't enjoy a vacation.*

working man's smile Go to plumber's smile.

working stiff *n.* a working man; a man who must work to live. (See also stiff.) ◆ *But does the working stiff really care about all this economic stuff?*

the **works** *n.* the entire amount; everything. ◆ *I'd like my hamburger with onions, pickles, ketchup, mustard—the works.* ◆ *She's getting the works at the beauty shop—cut, wash, dye, and set.*

Works for me. Go to (It) works for me.

The **world is** one's **oyster.** *sent.* one rules the world; one is in charge of everything. ◆ *I feel like the world is my oyster, today.*

world-beater *n.* an aggressive and ambitious person. ◆ *They hired an alleged world-beater to manage the office.*

world-class *mod.* absolutely top rate. ◆ *Now this is a world-class computer. Lots and lots of memory.*

worm *n.* a repellent person, usually a male. ◆ *Gad, you are a worm, Tom.*

worm burner *n.* a fast, but low-rolling ball in golf, baseball, etc. ◆ *Walter sent a worm burner down the third-base line.*

worm-food *n.* a corpse. ◆ *You wanna end up worm-food? Just keep smarting off.*

worms *n.* noodles; spaghetti. ◆ *Let's have worms tonight.*

worms in blood *n.* spaghetti in tomato sauce. ◆ *I'm getting tired of worms in blood every Wednesday.*

worry wart *n.* someone who worries all the time. ◆ *Don't be such a worry wart.*

worship the porcelain god(dess) *tv.* to empty one's stomach; to vomit. (Collegiate.) ◆ *Somebody was in the john worshiping the porcelain god till all hours.*

worst-case scenario *n.* the worst possible future outcome. ◆ *Now, let's look at the worst-case scenario.*

worth one's **salt** *mod.* worth (in productivity) what it costs to keep one. ◆ *You're not worth your salt. Pack up!*

would not be seen dead *phr.* would not do something under any circumstances. ◆ *I wouldn't be seen dead going out with Spike!*

Would you believe? *interrog.* Isn't it amazing? ◆ *Would you believe? A three-cent per hour raise?*

wouldn't touch so/sth **with a ten-foot pole** *tv.* would not get involved with someone or something. ◆ *Forget it. I wouldn't touch it with a ten-foot pole.*

wow 1. *exclam.* an indication of amazement or surprise. (Usually **Wow!**) ◆ *A whole quarter! Wow! Thanks, mister.* **2.** *tv.* to delight or impress someone. ◆ *That ought to wow them right out of their seats.* **3.** *n.* something exciting. ◆ *For a pretty good wow, try the Empire Theater's production of "Mame" this weekend.* **4.** *n.* an exclamation point. ◆ *Almost every sentence you write has a wow at the end of it.*

wozzle-water Go to woofle-water.

wrap one's **car around** sth *tv.* to drive one's car into something at fairly high speed. ◆ *She wrapped her car around a light pole.*

wrap sth **up** *tv.* to finish something; to bring something to a conclusion. ◆ *Well, that about wraps up our little session together.*

wrapped up (in so/sth**)** *mod.* concerned or obsessed with someone or something. ◆ *I'm too wrapped up in my charity work to get a job.*

wrapped up (with so/sth**)** *mod.* busy with someone or something. ◆ *He's wrapped up with a client right now.*

wrecked *mod.* alcohol or drug intoxicated. ◆ *Larry was far too wrecked to drive.*

wrench *n.* a mechanic. (Possibly from *Mr. Goodwrench.*) ◆ *I gotta get my ride in and have a wrench look at the serpentine.*

wrinkle 1. *n.* a new idea; a new aspect of something. ◆ *Here's a clever wrinkle for you. Nobody has ever tried this one.* **2.** *n.* a minor problem. ◆ *A wrinkle has developed in the Wilson proposal.*

wrinkle-rod *n.* the crankshaft of an engine. ◆ *A wrinkle-rod'll set you back about $199, plus installation charges, of course.*

Write if you get work. AND **WIYGW** *sent. & comp. abb.* Good-bye, call me sometime. (A catchphrase, like **See you in church,** said in imitation of what very good friends might say when parting.) ◆ *CU. WIYGW.*

wrong side of the tracks *n.* the poor side of town. ◆ *I'm glad I'm from the wrong side of the tracks. I know what life is really like.*

wrongo ['rɔŋo] **1.** *mod.* wrong. ◆ *Wrongo, wrongo! You lose!* **2.** *n.* an undesirable thing or person; a member of the underworld. ♦ *This whole business is a complete wrongo. Something's fishy.*

WSLS Go to Win some, lose some.

WTTC Go to Welcome to the club.

wuffo *n.* an (imaginary) annoying person who keeps asking why = what for = wuffo. ♦ *I was trying to get here on time, but a wuffo was holding me hostage.*

wuss(y) ['wʊs(i)] *n.* a wimp; a weak person. ♦ *Don't be such a wuss. Stand up for your rights.*

Wusup? AND **Wassup?** *interrog.* What's up? ♦ *Hey, man! Wassup?*

WWMMOWS Go to Well, wash my mouth out with soap.

WYSIWYG Go to What you see is what you get.

X marks the spot. *sent.* This is the exact place! (Cliché.) ♦ *This is where it happened. X marks the spot.*

X'd out 1. *mod.* eliminated; crossed-out. ♦ *But the Babbits are X'd out.* **2.** *mod.* killed. (Underworld.) ♦ *Mr. Big wanted Pete X'd out.*

XMT *tv.* excuse my typing; I am sorry I type so poorly. (Used in email and computer forum or newsgroup messages. Not pronounced aloud.) ♦ *XMT. I have a sore finger and I keep hitting the wrong keys.*

XYZ *tv.* examine your zipper; make sure your fly is zipped up. (Initialism. Said to men when necessary.) ♦ *I say there, Willy, XYZ.*

Y3 Go to yada, yada, yada.

ya *pro.* you. (Eye-dialect. Typical spoken English. Used in writing only for effect. Used in the examples of this dictionary.) ♦ *See ya!*

yack AND **yock; yuck; yuk** [jæk AND jɔk, jək] **1.** *n.* a foolish person. ♦ *Who's the yock wearing the red bandana?* **2.** *n.* idle chatter. ♦ *I've heard enough yack to last me a lifetime.* **3.** Go to yak.

yackety-yak ['jækədi'jæk] *n.* chatter; gossip. ♦ *That's enough yackety-yak. Quiet!*

yada, yada, yada AND **Y3** *phr. & comp. abb.* talk, talk, talk. (See also yatata-yatata.) ♦ *Y3. What utter B.S.*

yahoo ['jɑhu] *n.* a rustic oaf; an uncouth jerk. ♦ *Ask that yahoo to close the door after him.*

yak AND **yack** [jæk] **1.** *in.* to talk. ♦ *Stop yakking for a minute.* **2.** *n.* a chat. ♦ *We had a nice little yack and then left for work.* **3.** *n.* a joke. ♦ *Don't tell that yack again. It's not a winner.* **4.** *n.* a laugh from a joke. ♦ *The audience produced a feeble yak that was mostly from embarrassment.* **5.** *in.* to vomit. (Onomatopoetic.) ♦ *Hank was in the john yakking all night.* **6.** *n.* cognac. (Streets.) ♦ *My man, have some yak.*

yak it up *tv.* to talk incessantly or a lot. ♦ *Why don't you all just yak it up while I get ready to give the talk?*

yakky ['jæki] *mod.* talkative. ♦ *He's a yakky old man, but I like him.*

yank 1. *tv.* to harass someone. (See also yank so around.) ♦ *Stop yanking me!* **2.** *n.* a Yankee; a U.S. soldier. (Usually **Yank.**) ♦ *I don't care if you call me a yank. That's what I am.* **3.** *in.* to vomit. ♦ *Somebody or some animal yanked on the driveway.*

yank one's **strap** Go to beat the dummy.

yank so **around** *tv.* to harass someone; to give someone a hard time. (See also jerk so around.) ♦ *Please stop yanking me around.*

yank so's **chain** AND **pull** so's **chain** *tv.* to harass someone; to give someone a hard time. (As if one were a dog wearing a choker collar, on a leash.) Stop yanking my chain, you twit! ♦ *Do you really think you can just pull my chain whenever you want?*

yank so's **crank** *tv.* to tease a male sexually. ♦ *Don't pay any attention to her. She's just yanking your crank.*

yanked *mod.* arrested. (Underworld.) ♦ *Lefty got himself yanked one too many times.*

yap 1. *n.* the mouth. ♦ *Shut your yap!* **2.** *in.* to chatter; to gossip. ♦ *Did you just come here to yap?* **3.** *n.* nonsense; gibberish. ♦ *That windbag can produce an enormous amount of yap.* **4.** *in.* to empty one's stomach; to vomit. ♦ *Who yapped in the bushes?* **5.** *n.* a naive person; a dupe. ♦ *See if you can get that yap to bring over a left-handed monkey wrench.*

yard *n.* a one-hundred-dollar bill. (Underworld.) ♦ *The guy wanted a yard just to fix a little dent in the fender.*

yard dog *n.* a repellent person; an uncouth person. ♦ *Is that lousy yard dog hanging around the neighborhood again?*

yardbird 1. *n.* a convict. ♦ *Who's the yardbird with the headphones on his noodle?* **2.** *n.* an inept soldier. (Military.) ♦ *How many of you yardbirds would like to go home in one piece?*

yard-sale *n.* the site of a crash involving one or more bikes, skateboards, snowboards, etc., where the debris is spread far and wide. (Looking like a disorganized yard-, garage-, or tag-sale. ♦ *Man, did you see that yard-sale at the last turn?*

yarf *in.* to vomit. ♦ *She yarfed right in her lap!*

yatata-yatata ['jætətə'jætətə] *n.* the sound of chatter or yak. ♦ *He gets on the phone, and it's yatata-yatata for hours.*

yawner *n.* a boring show or performance. ♦ *It was a yawner from the opening curtain straight through to the end.*

yazzihamper ['jæzihæmpɚ] *n.* an obnoxious person. ♦ *You are the most annoying yazzihamper I know!*

Ye gods! *exclam.* Good grief! ♦ *Ye gods! What is this stuff here?*

yea big ['je 'bɪg] *mod.* about so big. (Accompanied by a hand gesture.) ♦ *Oh, it was about yea big.*

yeah ['jæə OR 'jæɔ] *interj.* yes. ♦ LEFTY: *You okay?* BRUNO: *Yeah.* ♦ LEFTY: *Yeah?* BRUNO: *Yeah! I said yeah! Did you hear me say yeah?*

Yeah, right! *exclam.* the ultimate sarcastic response of disbelief. ♦ *Yeah, right! You were just going through my desk looking for a pencil.*

yeaster *n.* a beer drinker. ♦ *A couple of yeasters in the back of the tavern were singing a dirty song.*

Yec(c)h! [jɛk OR jɛtʃ] *exclam.* Horrible!; It's yucky! ♦ *Oh, yech! What's that stuff?*

yegg [jɛg] **1.** *n.* a tramp, thief, or safecracker. (Underworld.) ♦ *See if you can find that yegg we worked with on the bank job. He'll do.* **2.** *n.* an obnoxious male. ♦ *A couple of drunken yeggs were talking a little too loud, so Spike showed them the door.*

yell one's **guts out** Go to yell one's **head off.**

yell one's **head off** AND **yell** one's **guts out 1.** *tv.* to yell loud and long. ♦ *Stop yelling your head off and listen to me.* **2.** *tv.* to complain bitterly and loudly. ♦ *I yell my guts out about tripe when I see tripe!*

Yello. ['jɛ'lo] *interj.* Hello. (Said with any intonation that would be appropriate with *hello.*) ♦ *Yello, Smith residence.*

yellow *mod.* cowardly. ♦ *A: Mooshoo says you're yellow. B: Wanna make something of it?*

yellow-bellied *mod.* cowardly. ♦ *What yellow-bellied skunk ran off with my horse?*

yellow-belly *n.* a coward. ♦ *Tell the yellow-belly to come outside and say that.*

yelper *n.* the whooping (electronic) siren on emergency vehicles. ♦ *The black and white rounded the corner, yelper blasting.*

yench [jɛntʃ] *tv.* to swindle someone; to victimize someone. (Underworld.) ♦ *The flimflam artist yenched a couple of banks and then moved on.*

yenta ['jɛntə] *n.* a gossip, usually a woman. (Regarded as Yiddish.) ♦ *She can be such a yenta when she's got news.*

yep Go to yup.

Yes! *interj.* Absolutely yes! (Always with a special intonation that holds the *y* on a higher pitch and then drops the pitch sharply. The word itself is not slang, but the word with this intonation is part of many slang contexts.) ♦ *Yes! Exactly right!*

YGWYPF Go to You get what you pay for.

YHTBT Go to You had to be there.

yizzle a wild card word for words beginning with *Y*, such as *yes, you, your,* etc. (Streets. Also for other words with initial *Y.*) ♦ *Do I? Yizzle my bizzle.*

YMHMMFSWGAS Go to You must have mistaken me for someone who gives a shit.

YMMD Go to You made my day.

YMMV Go to Your mileage may vary.

Yo! *interj.* Hello!; Attention, please!; Wait a minute! ♦ *Yo, Michael! What's new?*

yo mama *interj.* so you say. (Black.) ♦ *Not enough bread! Yo mama.*

yock AND **yok** [jɔk] **1.** *in.* to laugh loudly. (See also yak.) ♦ *Everybody yocked at the joke and when things calmed down, I announced the mass firings.* **2.** *n.* a loud laugh. ◆ *Sue let out an enormous yock and quickly covered her mouth.* **3.** Go to yack.

yodeling in a canyon *in.* talking aimlessly. ◆ *You are just yodeling in a canyon if you think I really care about it.*

yoink sth *tv.* to steal something. ◆ *He yoinked a bike from the rack.*

yok Go to yock.

yoked [jokt] *mod.* having well-marked abdominal muscles; have heavy muscles. ◆ *That guy is really yoked. I wonder how much he works out.*

yokes *n.* muscles; abdominal muscles. (See also yoked. Also seen as *yolks.* Possibly as if muscular shoulders can be seen as yokes of muscle.) ◆ *Look at the yokes on that broad.*

yola *n.* cocaine. ◆ *Albert spends too much time snorting yola.*

yolk *n.* semen. (Possibly confused with egg white.) ◆ *Clean up that yolk before somebody sees it.*

york [jork] **1.** *in.* to empty one's stomach; to vomit. ◆ *He ate the stuff, then went straight out and yorked.* **2.** *n.* vomit. ◆ *Hey, Jimmy! Come out in the snow and see the frozen york!*

You and what army? Go to You and who else?

You and who else? AND **You and what army?** *interrog.* Who besides you is threatening me? ◆ *You and what army are gonna yank my chain?*

You asked for it! *exclam.* Here it comes, and you deserve it! ◆ *So you want the full treatment? You asked for it!*

You bet. *interj.* Yes.; You can bet on it. ◆ *Can you have two? You bet.*

You bet your boots! *exclam.* You can be absolutely certain! ◆ *Am I happy? You bet your boots!*

You bet your sweet life! *exclam.* You are absolutely correct! ◆ *You bet your sweet life I am glad!*

You bet your sweet patoot(ie)! *exclam.* You can be absolutely certain! (*Patootie* is

the buttocks.) ◆ *I'll be there! You bet your sweet patoot!*

You betcha! [ˈju ˈbɛtʃə] *interj.* Yes!; You can be sure of it! (Literally, You bet, you.) ◆ *Will I be there? You betcha.*

You can say that again! *exclam.* I agree! ◆ *You can say that again! You hit the nail right on the head.*

You can't dance at two weddings. *sent.* You cannot do two things at once. ◆ *Either go to the beach with Fred or stay here with me. You can't dance at two weddings.*

You can't fight city hall. *sent.* You cannot fight a bureaucracy. ◆ *You can't fight city hall. Pay the parking ticket and forget it.*

You can't get there from here. *sent.* Where you want to go is in a very remote location. (Cliché.) ◆ *Adamsville? Sorry, you can't get there from here.*

You can't take it with you. *sent.* You cannot take wealth with you when you die. ◆ *Enjoy it now. You can't take it with you.*

You can't win them all. AND **You can't win 'em all.** *sent.* No one succeeds all the time. (Said when someone fails.) ◆ *Don't fret about it, Tom. You can't win them all.*

You could have knocked me over with a feather. *sent.* I was completely surprised. ◆ *I was shocked. You could have knocked me over with a feather.*

You don't know the half of it. *sent.* Things are far more complicated than you think. ◆ *You don't know the half of it, and I'm too much a lady to tell.*

You eat with that mouth? Go to (Do) you eat with that mouth?

You get what you pay for. AND **YGWYPF** *sent. & comp. abb.* You get whatever value you actually pay for. ◆ *Yup, your machine crashes because it's junk. YGWYPF.*

You got it! 1. *exclam.* I agree to what you asked!; You will get what you want! ◆ *You want a green one? You got it!* **2.** *exclam.* You are right! ◆ *That's the answer. You got it!*

You got that? *interrog.* Do you understand? ♦ *You are not to go into that room! You got that?*

You guys bitchin'? *interrog.* Hello, how are you? ♦ *Tsup? You guys bitchin'?*

You (had) better believe it! *exclam.* It is true without question! ♦ *Yes, this is the best, and you had better believe it!*

You had to be there. AND **YHTBT** *sent. & comp. abb.* You had to be in a place to understand what happened or what was said there. ♦ *Yeah, it was funnier when I heard it. YHTBT.*

You heard the man. *sent.* Do what the man tells you. (See also man.) ♦ *You heard the man. Get over there and stand still.*

You kiss your momma with that mouth? Go to (Do) you eat with that mouth?

You made my day. AND **YMMD** *sent. & comp. abb.* Thanks, you made me happy today. ♦ *You are very kind. YMMD.*

You must have mistaken me for someone who gives a shit. AND **YMHMMFSWGAS** *sent. & comp. abb.* What makes you think I care about what you are saying? (Usually objectionable.) ♦ *So you're unhappy. Why tell me. You must have mistaken me for someone who gives a shit*

(You) want a piece of me? *interrog.* Do you want to fight with me? ♦ *Come on, Wussy. You want a piece of me?*

You want to step outside? *interrog.* Do you intend to start a fight?; Shall we go outside and fight? ♦ *You want to step outside? We can settle this once and for all.*

You wish! Go to (Don't) you wish!

young blood 1. *n.* a newcomer. ♦ *We keep young bloods so busy they never have a chance to look out the window.* **2.** *n.* a young, black male. (Black. See also blood.) ♦ *Tell that young blood to beat it.*

young Turk *n.* a contentious young person who goes against the system. ♦ *The young Turks are acting up again.*

Your guess is as good as mine. *sent.* I don't know either. ♦ *I don't know. Your guess is as good as mine.*

Your mileage may vary. and **YMMV** *sent. & comp. abb.* You may have a different experience or different results. ♦ *It worked for me. Your mileage may vary.*

Your place or mine? *interrog.* Shall we carry on an affair at your dwelling or mine? ♦ *Your place or mine? It doesn't matter.*

You're on your own. AND **YOYO** *sent. & comp. abb.* You will have no help if you continue. ♦ *That's my advice. Ignore it or you're on your own.*

You're the doctor. *sent.* I will do anything you say!; You are in charge! ♦ *Put it over here. Okay, you're the doctor.*

You('re) the man! AND **YTM** *exclam. & comp. abb.* Congratulations!; You've completed the task successfully. (Now often *You da man!*) ♦ *Good job, Fred. You the man.*

yours truly *n.* me, the speaker or writer. ♦ *If it was up to yours truly, there wouldn't be any such problem.*

You've got another think coming. *sent.* You have made an error. Think again. (Especially with *if*. The word *think* is original, although some speakers change this to *thing*.) ♦ *If you think I'm going to let you get away with that, you've got another think coming.*

yoyo AND **yo-yo** ['jojo] **1.** *n.* a fool; an obnoxious person. ♦ *Some yoyo wants to talk to you on the phone.* **2.** *mod.* stupid. ♦ *Ask that yo-yo jerk to move along.* **3.** *in.* to vacillate; to be wishy-washy. ♦ *Stop yoyoing and make up your mind.* **4.** Go to You're on your own.

YTM Go to You('re) the man!

yuck AND **yuk** [jək] **1.** *n.* someone or something disgusting. (Also a term of address.) ♦ *I don't want any of that yuck on my plate!* **2.** *exclam.* Horrible! (Usually **Yuck!**) ♦ *Oh, yuck! Get that horrible thing out of here!* **3.** *n.* a joke. ♦ *Come on! Chill out! It was just a yuck.* **4.** Go to yack.

yucky ['jəki] *mod.* nasty. ♦ *What is this yucky pink stuff on my plate?*

yuk Go to yack; yuck.

yuke Go to uke.

yummy ['jəmi] **1.** *mod.* delicious. ♦ *This stuff is really yummy.* **2.** *mod.* delightful; beautiful. ♦ *Who is that yummy blonde?*

yup AND **yep** [jəp AND jɛp] *interj.* yes. (Colloquial.) ♦ *Yup, I'd say so.*

yuppie AND **yuppy** ['jəpi] **1.** *n.* a young urban professional. ♦ *The yuppies are getting a lot of flack these days.* **2.** *mod.* having to do with yuppies. ♦ *I don't want to drive one of those yuppie cars.*

yuppy Go to yuppie.

yutz [juts] *n.* a fool; a simpleton. ♦ *Don't act like such a yutz!*

Z

za [zɑ] *n.* pizza. (Collegiate.) ♦ *I'm gonna spring for some za.*

zagged *mod.* alcohol intoxicated. ♦ *How can anybody get so zagged on three beers?*

zap 1. *tv.* to shock someone. ♦ *That fake snake zapped me for a minute.* **2.** *tv.* to kill someone. ♦ *The stress from it all nearly zapped him.* **3.** *tv.* to impress someone. ♦ *My big idea really zapped the boss. I may get a raise.* **4.** *tv.* to stun someone with an imaginary ray gun. ♦ *He zapped me with a water gun.* **5.** *exclam.* Wow! (Usually **Zap!**) ♦ *He said, "Zap!" indicating that he really liked the present, I guess.* **6.** *tv.* to defeat someone or a team. ♦ *Fred zapped Britney in the spelling bee.* **7.** *in.* to zip or move to somewhere very fast. ♦ *He's zapping to the drugstore for some aspirin.*

zapped 1. *mod.* tired; exhausted. ♦ *I'm too zapped to go on.* **2.** *mod.* alcohol or drug intoxicated. ♦ *We all got zapped and then went home.*

zappy *mod.* energetic; zippy. ♦ *That music is a little too zappy for me.*

zarf [zɑrf] *n.* an ugly and repellent male. ♦ *That zarf is Martin, and he makes all As, and he helps me with my homework, so just shut up!*

zebra *n.* a referee. (Because of the black-and-white striped shirt.) ♦ *The zebra blew the whistle on almost every play.*

zeek out [zik…] *in.* to lose control of oneself. ♦ *I was in a pretty bad state. I almost zeeked out.*

Zelda ['zɛldə] *n.* a dull and ugly female. (See also **Clyde**.) ♦ *Nobody's gonna call my sister a Zelda and get away with it.*

zeltoids *n.* marijuana. (Possibly named for an imaginary planet.) ♦ *Where can I score some zeltoids?*

zerk [zɚk] *n.* a stupid person; a jerk. ♦ *Don't be a zerk! Do what you're told.*

zerked (out) ['zɚkt…] *mod.* drug intoxicated. ♦ *Gary looked so zerked out, and I thought he was really stoned.*

zerking *mod.* strange; zerk-like. ♦ *Who is that zerking nerd over there?*

zero *n.* an insignificant person; a nobody. ♦ *I want to be more in life than just another zero.*

zhlub Go to **schlub**.

zhlubby ['ʒləbi] *mod.* dull; boorish. (See also **schlub**.) ♦ *I can't sit through this zhlubby thing one more minute.*

ziggy-wiggling *n.* copulation. ♦ *The watchman caught them ziggy-wiggling in the lounge.*

zilch [zɪltʃ] *n.* nothing. ♦ *And what do I get? Zilch, that's what!*

zing 1. *n.* energy; dynamism. ♦ *Put some zing into this dance number. You wanna put the audience to sleep?* **2.** *tv.* to make something penetrate; to shoot or fire something. ♦ *The kid zinged a paper clip into the wall.* **3.** *tv.* to assault someone verbally. ♦ *She zinged him with another clever remark.*

zinger 1. *n.* something nice or fine. ♦ *What a zinger of a hat!* **2.** *n.* a stinging remark. ♦ *She got off another zinger at her brother.*

zings *n.* the delirium tremens. ♦ *The old guy was suffering from the zings.*

zip 1. *n.* nothing. ♦ *There was no mail today. Nothing. Zip.* **2.** *n.* a score or grade of zero. ♦ *Well, you got zip on the last test. Sorry about that.* **3.** *n.* vigor; spunk. ♦ *Put some zip into it. It's too ho-hum.* **4.** *in.* to move to a place fast. ♦ *I'll zip to the office and get a new form.* **5.** *n.* a worthless person; a person who amounts to zero. ♦ *Garth is such a zip. No brains in his head at all.* **6.** *n.* an ounce of a drug. ♦ *How much for a zip of hash.* **7.** *n.* cocaine. ♦ *He's freezing his nose with zip nearly every night.*

zip along *in.* to move along rapidly. ♦ *Days are zipping along, and we're all getting lots done.*

zip gun *n.* a homemade handgun. (Underworld.) ♦ *The kid had a zip gun, so I didn't argue.*

Zip it up! Go to Zip (up) your lip!

Zip (up) your lip! AND **Zip it up!** *exclam.* Be quiet!; Zip up your mouth! ♦ *Shhhh! Zip up your lip!* ♦ *Zip it up and keep it zipped.*

Zip your lip! Go to Zip (up) your lip!

zipped *mod.* drug intoxicated. (Drugs.) ♦ *The kid is too zipped to talk.*

zipper head *n.* a man with his hair parted in the middle. ♦ *Some zipper head behind the counter told me I couldn't come in without a shirt.*

zipper morals *n.* loose morals that lead to the easy unzipping of clothing. ♦ *Ah, youth and its zipper morals!*

zippy ['zɪpi] *mod.* lively; active. ♦ *This is a real zippy number.*

zissified ['zɪsɪfaɪd] *mod.* alcohol intoxicated. ♦ *Two of them got zissified on rum. The rest just got a little wrecked.*

zit [zɪt] *n.* a pimple. ♦ *Don't squeeze your zits on my mirror!*

zit doctor *n.* a dermatologist. ♦ *The zit doctor I went to was a crater-face!*

zit-face Go to crater-face.

zizzle a wild card word for words beginning with Z, such as *Zippo* (lighter). (Streets. Also for other words with initial Z.) ♦ *He held a stogie in his hand, looked at his buddy, and said, "Zizzle?"*

zob [zɑb] *n.* a worthless person; a nobody. ♦ *Another zob came in to try out for the part.*

zod [zɑd] **1.** *n.* any repellent thing or person. (California. General Zod was a villain in the movie *Superman II.*) ♦ *Is this grody zod yours or mine?* **2.** *n.* a studious person. ♦ *Quiet. You don't want to disturb the zods. his courses.*

Zoit! *n.* Wow! ♦ *Zoit, he's ugly!*

zombie ['zambi] **1.** *n.* a weird and frightening person. ♦ *Martin is practically a zombie. Doesn't he ever go out—in the daylight, I mean?* ♦ *Britney's getting to look like a zombie. Is she well?* **2.** *n.* a very stupid person. ♦ *Please ask one of those zombies to stand by the door.* **3.** *n.* a very tired person. ♦ *I feel like such a zombie. Maybe I'm not eating right.*

zoned (out) 1. *mod.* alcohol or drug intoxicated. ♦ *What's the matter with your eyes? Get a little zoned last night?* **2.** *mod.* exhausted. ♦ *After a day like this, I'm really zoned.*

zonk [zɔŋk] **1.** *tv.* to overpower someone or something. ♦ *We zonked the dog with a kick.* **2.** *tv.* to tire someone out. (See also zonked (out).) ♦ *The pills zonked me, but they made my cold better.*

zonk out *in.* to collapse from exhaustion; to go into a stupor from drugs or exhaustion; to go to sleep. ♦ *I'm gonna go home and zonk out.*

zonk SO **out 1.** *tv.* to make someone tired or exhausted. ♦ *All the work zonked him out.* **2.** *tv.* to cause someone to become intoxicated. ♦ *The drug zonked Max out totally.*

zonked (out) AND **zounked (out)** [zɔŋkt... AND zɑʊŋkt...] **1.** *mod.* alcohol or drug intoxicated. ♦ *She's too zonked to drive.* **2.** *mod.* exhausted; asleep. ♦ *She was totally zonked out by the time I got home.*

zonker ['zɔŋkɚ] **1.** *n.* a drunkard. ♦ *The zonker just can't help himself.* **2.** *n.* a marijuana smoker. (Drugs.) ♦ *A lot of these zonkers may take six years to get through high school.*

zoo *n.* a confusing and chaotic place. ♦ *This place is a zoo on Monday mornings.*

zoobang ['zubæŋ] *mod.* alcohol intoxicated. ♦ *Boy howdy! Are you ever zoobang!*

zooed [zud] *mod.* drunk. ♦ *Sam likes to go out and get zooed every weekend.*

zooie AND **zooey** ['zui] *mod.* confusing and chaotic. (See also zoo.) ♦ *I can't get anything done in this zooie place.*

zoom 1. *tv.* to gain entry to someplace without paying. ♦ *Both of them zoomed the circus, and both of them got arrested.* **2.** AND **zoom off** *in.* to have a drug rush. (Drugs.) ♦ *Sam zoomed off and thought he had gone to heaven.* **3.** AND **zoom off** *in.* to depart; to leave in a hurry. ♦ *Time's up. I've gotta zoom.*

zoom in (on so/sth**)** *in.* to focus or concentrate narrowly on someone or something. ♦ *Let's zoom in on the question of salary.*

zoom off Go to zoom.

zoom out *in.* to lose control. ♦ *I nearly zoomed out when I got the news.*

zoom so **out** *tv.* to impress someone. ♦ *Freddie is trying to zoom out Tiffany again.*

zoom up *in.* to drive or pull up to a place. ♦ *A car zoomed up, and seven kids got out.*

zoomies ['zumiz] *n.* members of the U.S. Air Force. (A nickname used by the army.

Persian Gulf War.) ♦ *The zoomies attacked the airfield and damaged a lot of planes.*

zooted ['zudəd] *mod.* alcohol intoxicated. ♦ *Both of them were zooted to the max.*

zootied ['zutid] *mod.* intoxicated with drugs or alcohol. ♦ *Hank seems to be zootied. What's he on?*

zorked ['zorkt] *mod.* alcohol intoxicated. ♦ *She was zorked beyond help.*

zosted *mod.* drunk. (Like toasted.) ♦ *He's so zosted! He can't drive!*

zotz [zɑts] **1.** AND **zot.** [zɑt] *n.* zero; nothing. ♦ *I went out to get the mail, but there was zot.* **2.** *tv.* to kill someone or something. ♦ *Sam threatened to zotz Joel Cairo, but it was just a threat.*

zounked (out) Go to zonked (out).

zowie ['zaʊi] **1.** *n.* energy; sparkle; zest. ♦ *This one sounds better because the drummer has more zowie.* **2.** *exclam.* Wow! (Usually **Zowie!**) ♦ *Zowie! They just pulled Mr. Gutman out of the river.*

zozzled ['zɑzl̩d] *mod.* drunk. ♦ *Dave was too zozzled to drive.*

zuke [zuk] *in.* to vomit. ♦ *The cat zuked on the living room carpet.*

zunked [zəŋkt] *mod.* alcohol or drug intoxicated. ♦ *The party went on and on. When the preacher got himself zunked on the punch, I knew it had reached the end.*

Index of Hidden Key Words

When seeking a particular expression, always look it up first in the body of the dictionary. Consult this index for key words that are not the first word in an entry but are "hidden" within the entry and are therefore not available through a normal alphabetical search. This allows the user to find a phrasal entry by looking up any noninitial key word in the phrase. Slang expressions that consist of only one word are not indexed here. However, index entries containing a hidden key word will include all instances of that key word, even if it is the first word in an entry. Words in **bold face type** are Index entries, and words in sans serif type are entries in the body of the dictionary. Always consult the dictionary first, and then this index.

abs washboard abs
academy laughing academy
ace ace so out ♦ ace boom-boom ♦ ace boon-coon ♦ ace in the hole ♦ ace in(to sth) ♦ ace out ♦ have an ace up one's sleeve ♦ hold all the aces ♦ within an ace of (doing) sth
acre God's acre
across come across (with sth)
act the Dutch act ♦ class act ♦ clean one's act up ♦ get one's act together ♦ get in on the act
action bit of the action ♦ chill so's action ♦ in action ♦ piece (of the action) ♦ slice of the action ♦ where the action is
adam Adam Henry ♦ up an' Adam
adjuster attitude-adjuster
advance Thanks in advance.
affluence under the affluence of incohol
age golden-ager ♦ What's your age?
ahead come out ahead ♦ Go ahead, make my day. ♦ go-ahead ♦ one jump ahead of so/sth ♦ quit while one is ahead
aid thirst-aid station
ain't ain't long enough ♦ If it ain't broke don't fix it. ♦ If it ain't broke, fix it till it is. ♦ That ain't hay! ♦ There ain't no such thing as a free lunch.
air air one's belly ♦ air one's pores ♦ air ball ♦ air biscuit ♦ air guitar ♦ air hose ♦ air kiss ♦ air-bags ♦ bear in the air ♦ come up for air ♦ float an air biscuit ♦ full of hot air ♦ hot air ♦ up in the air (about so/sth)

aitch seven-seven-three-aitch
Al Herb and Al ♦ talk to Herb and Al
alarm a five-alarm fire ♦ a three-alarm fire
Albert Prince Albert
alive Look alive!
alley (right) up one's alley ♦ alley apple ♦ up one's alley
alligator See you later, alligator.
along buzz along ♦ hump (along) ♦ tootle along ♦ zip along
already All right already! ♦ Enough, already!
altar bow to the porcelain altar
American Truth, justice, and the American way.
amok run amok
amount carry (an amount of) weight ♦ pull down an amount of money ♦ shell out (an amount of money)
anchor anchor-clanker ♦ boat anchor
angel angel dust ♦ angel hair ♦ dust of angels
anger the cage of anger
angles know all the angles
animal party animal ♦ study animal
ankle ankle biter ♦ sprain one's ankle
another another peep (out of you) ♦ See you in another life. ♦ Tell me another (one)! ♦ You've got another think coming.
ante penny-ante
ants have ants in one's pants
apart take so/sth apart ♦ tear so/sth apart

ape ape hangers ♦ go ape (over so/sth) ♦ go apeshit over so/sth

applause anal applause

apple the Big Apple ♦ alley apple ♦ apple-polisher ♦ apples to oranges ♦ green apple quickstep ♦ one smart apple ♦ road apple ♦ rotten apple ♦ square apple

arm arm-twister ♦ arm-twisting ♦ bang in the arm ♦ long arm of the law ♦ put the arm on so ♦ shot in the arm ♦ strong-arm ♦ strong-arm man ♦ strong-arm tactics ♦ twist so's arm ♦ up in arms

army army brat ♦ You and what army?

arrow straight arrow

article genuine article

artillery heavy artillery

artist (rip-)off artist ♦ booze artist ♦ bullshit artist ♦ burn artist ♦ castor oil artist ♦ con artist ♦ flimflam artist ♦ hype artist ♦ make-out artist ♦ off artist ♦ take-off artist

artsy artsy (fartsy) ♦ artsy-craftsy

ask Don't ask. ♦ You asked for it!

ass (flat) on one's ass ♦ so's ass is grass ♦ ass is grass, so's ♦ ass out ♦ ass over tit ♦ ass-chewing ♦ ass-kicker ♦ ass-kisser ♦ ass-kissing ♦ ass-licker ♦ ass-licking ♦ ass-wipe ♦ bag ass (out of somewhere) ♦ bare-ass(ed) ♦ barrel ass ♦ barrel ass (out of somewhere) ♦ bust (one's) ass (to do sth) ♦ bust ass (out of somewhere) ♦ bust-ass ♦ candy-ass ♦ candy-ass(ed) ♦ chew so's ass out ♦ Cover your ass. ♦ cut ass (out of somewhere) ♦ drag ass (out of somewhere) ♦ drag ass around ♦ dumb-ass ♦ fat-ass(ed) ♦ flat-ass ♦ get one's ass in gear ♦ Get off my ass! ♦ Get your ass over here! ♦ gripe one's ass ♦ hairy-ass(ed) ♦ half-ass(ed) ♦ haul ass (out of somewhere) ♦ have one's ass in a crack ♦ have one's ass in a sling ♦ have a wild hair up one's ass ♦ horse's ass ♦ hunk of ass ♦ It will be your ass! ♦ jive-ass ♦ kick ass ♦ kick in the ass ♦ kick some ass (around) ♦ kick-ass ♦ kick-ass on so ♦ kiss so's ass ♦ Kiss my ass! ♦ kiss-ass ♦ know one's ass from a hole in the ground ♦ lard ass ♦ not know one's ass from a hole in the ground ♦ on one's ass ♦ pain in the ass ♦ piece of ass ♦ rolling on the floor laughing (my ass off) ♦ scientific wild ass guess ♦ shag ass (out of somewhere) ♦ shit-ass ♦ smart ass ♦ sorry-ass(ed) ♦ stupid-ass ♦ tits and ass ♦ work one's ass off

asshole bouquet of assholes ♦ tear so a new asshole

attack Big Mac attack

attention snap to (attention)

attitude attitude-adjuster ♦ cop an attitude ♦ pull an attitude

avenue avenue tank ♦ Madison Avenue

awesome totally awesome

ax get the ax ♦ give so the ax

babe babe magnet ♦ make drain babies

baby (baby) boomer ♦ The baby needs shoes. ♦ baby bear ♦ baby gangsta ♦ Baby it's cold outside. ♦ baby-kisser ♦ bottle baby ♦ jelly babies ♦ Keep the faith (baby)!

back back number ♦ back room ♦ back room boys ♦ back to square one ♦ back to the salt mines ♦ back up ♦ backed up ♦ back-ender ♦ be right back ♦ been to hell and back ♦ boys in the back room ♦ drunk back ♦ get off so's back ♦ Get off my back! ♦ have a monkey on one's back ♦ have a yellow streak down one's back ♦ juice sth back ♦ kick back ♦ knock sth back ♦ knock back a drink ♦ knock one back ♦ laid back ♦ on the back burner ♦ pin so's ears back ♦ Put it in their back yard! ♦ set so back ♦ shotty back ♦ throw sth back ♦ to back ♦ tore back ♦ try so back (again)

backyard Not in my backyard!

bacon turkey bacon ♦ What's shakin' (bacon)?

bad bad egg ♦ bad hair day ♦ bad news ♦ bad paper ♦ bad rap ♦ bad shit ♦ bad trip ♦ bad-mouth ♦ get in bad (with so) ♦ in a bad way ♦ in bad shape ♦ My bad. ♦ so bad one can taste it ♦ wicked bad

badge lost-and-found badge

bag one's bag ♦ air-bags ♦ bag so ♦ bag ass (out of somewhere) ♦ Bag it! ♦ bag of wind ♦ bag on so ♦ bag some rays ♦ Bag that! ♦ Bag your face! ♦ barf bag ♦ brown bag it ♦ brown-bag ♦ doggy bag ♦ douche bag ♦ half in the bag ♦ in the bag ♦ shit-bag ♦ slime bag ♦ What's in the bag!

bagel catholic bagel

bagger double-bagger ♦ four-bagger ♦ triple-bagger

bail bail (out) ♦ bail on so ♦ bail out on so ♦ jump bail

bait Fish or cut bait.

bake bake the tube steak ♦ half-baked

bald bald-headed hermit ♦ bald-headed mouse

ball a whole new ball game ♦ one's ball and chain ♦ The ball is in so's court. ♦ the whole ball of wax ♦ African golf ball ♦ air ball ♦ B-ball ♦ ball so/sth up ♦ ball of fire ♦ ball off ♦ ball up ♦ ball-breaker ♦ ball-buster ♦ ball-busting ♦ balled up ♦ behind the eight ball ♦

blue balls ♦ break one's balls to do sth ♦ break so's balls ♦ drop the ball ♦ end of the ball game ♦ gopher ball ♦ have a man by the balls ♦ have a ball ♦ have a lot on the ball ♦ on the ball ♦ play ball (with so) ♦ put balls on sth ♦ That's the way the ball bounces. ♦ V-ball

balloon balloon knot ♦ go over like a lead balloon ♦ trial balloon

banana banana hammock ♦ banana oil ♦ banana-head ♦ Cool bananas! ♦ go bananas ♦ top banana

band to beat the band

bandwagon on the bandwagon

bang (bang) dead to rights ♦ 4-banger ♦ bang for the buck ♦ bang in (sick) ♦ bang in the arm ♦ bang-up ♦ gang-bang ♦ get a bang out of so/sth ♦ slam-bang ♦ wham-bang ♦ with a bang

bar behind bars ♦ no holds barred

bare bare-ass(ed) ♦ stand there with one's bare face hanging out

barf barf so out ♦ barf bag ♦ Barf City ♦ barf out ♦ Barf out! ♦ barf-out

bargain more than one bargained for ♦ no bargain

barn can't hit the (broad) side of a barn ♦ Were you born in a barn?

barrel barrel ass ♦ barrel ass (out of somewhere) ♦ barrel fever ♦ barrel of fun ♦ barreled (up) ♦ bottom of the barrel ♦ double-barreled slingshot ♦ loaded to the barrel ♦ scrape the bottom of the barrel

base get to first (base) (with so) ♦ touch base (with so) ♦ way off (base)

bash fag-bashing

basket basket case ♦ dinner basket ♦ underwater basket weaving

bastard rat-bastard

bat batted out ♦ have bats in one's belfry ♦ like a bat out of hell

bath take a bath (on sth) ♦ tonsil bath

bathtub bathtub crank ♦ bathtub scum ♦ vertical bathtub

beach (as) fat as a beached whale ♦ beach bum ♦ beach bunny ♦ fat as a beached whale

beagle legal-beagle

beam (I-)beam ♦ Beam me up, Scotty! ♦ beam up ♦ early beam(s) ♦ on the beam ♦ steam so's beam

bean bean head ♦ bean time ♦ Bean Town ♦ bean-counter ♦ beaned up ♦ Cool beans! ♦ do a bean count ♦ full of beans ♦ not know

beans (about sth) ♦ not worth beans ♦ on the bean ♦ spill the beans

bear baby bear ♦ bear cage ♦ bear in the air ♦ bear trap ♦ lady bear ♦ loaded for bear ♦ mama bear ♦ Smokey (the Bear)

beat beat one's brains out (to do sth) ♦ beat one's gums ♦ beat one's meat ♦ beat so/sth out ♦ beat so's brains out ♦ beat sth out ♦ beat box ♦ Beat it! ♦ beat off ♦ beat the drum for so/sth ♦ beat the dummy ♦ beat the meat ♦ beat the pup ♦ beat the rap ♦ beat the shit out of so ♦ beat up ♦ beats me ♦ boy-beater ♦ egg-beater ♦ take a beating ♦ to beat the band ♦ wife-beater ♦ world-beater

beaver beaver-cleaver ♦ eager-beaver

bed bed of roses ♦ bed-bunny ♦ fall out of bed ♦ make one's bed ♦ musical beds ♦ put so to bed with a shovel ♦ put to bed with a shovel

bedpost between you, me, and the bedpost

beef beef sth up ♦ beef about so/sth ♦ beef-head ♦ beef-hearts ♦ bogus beef ♦ bum beef

beer beer and skittles ♦ beer belly ♦ beer blast ♦ beer bust ♦ beer goggles ♦ beer gut ♦ beer up ♦ hammer a beer ♦ hammer some beers ♦ near-beer ♦ pound a beer ♦ pound some beers ♦ queer-beer ♦ slam a beer ♦ slam some beers ♦ small beer

beeswax mind your own beeswax ♦ none of so's beeswax

beet blow beets

belfry have bats in one's belfry

believe Believe it or not. ♦ Believe you me! ♦ I don't believe this! ♦ Would you believe? ♦ You (had) better believe it!

bell Be there with bells on. ♦ bells and whistles ♦ Hell's bells (and buckets of blood)! ♦ Ma Bell ♦ ring a bell ♦ ring the bell ♦ saved by the bell ♦ with bells on

belly air one's belly ♦ Basra belly ♦ beer belly ♦ belly button ♦ belly fiddle ♦ belly laugh ♦ belly up ♦ belly up (to sth) ♦ Delhi belly ♦ go belly up ♦ turn belly up ♦ yellow-bellied ♦ yellow-belly

bellyaching Quit your bellyaching!

below hit so below the belt

belt belt the grape ♦ hit so below the belt ♦ pull one's belt in (a notch) ♦ rust belt ♦ sun belt ♦ take one's belt in (a notch) ♦ tighten one's belt

bench bench jockey ♦ bench warmer ♦ grab some bench

bend (a)round the bend ♦ bend one's elbow ♦ Bend over, here it comes again. ♦ bend the law ♦ drive so around the bend ♦ elbow-bending ♦ fender-bender ♦ gender-bender ♦ mind-bender ♦ round the bend

berth soft berth

best one's best shot ♦ best bud ♦ best buy ♦ level best ♦ Sunday best

bet bet one's bottom dollar ♦ bet so dollars to doughnuts ♦ You bet your boots! ♦ You bet your sweet life! ♦ You bet your sweet patoot(ie)! ♦ You bet. ♦ You betcha!

better one's better half ♦ better get used to it ♦ Better luck next time. ♦ seen better days ♦ You (had) better believe it!

bible swear on a stack of Bibles

big the Big Apple ♦ the big house ♦ big blue ♦ big board ♦ big brother ♦ big bucks ♦ big cheese ♦ big deal ♦ big Dick ♦ Big Dig ♦ big drink ♦ big drink of water ♦ big enchilada ♦ big fat grin ♦ big fish ♦ big gun ♦ big iron ♦ big jab ♦ big John ♦ big juice ♦ big kahuna ♦ big league ♦ Big Mac attack ♦ big man on campus ♦ big mouth ♦ big name ♦ big noise ♦ big of so ♦ big shot ♦ big stink ♦ big time ♦ big top ♦ big woman on campus ♦ big wheel ♦ big with so ♦ big Zs ♦ big-C. ♦ big-D. ♦ big-H. ♦ big-O. ♦ big-ticket ♦ big-time operator ♦ big-time spender ♦ bite the big one ♦ buy the big one ♦ drive the big bus ♦ go over big ♦ have a (big) head ♦ have a big mouth ♦ in a big way ♦ Like it's such a big deal. ♦ make (it) big ♦ Mr. Big ♦ no big deal ♦ no big whoop ♦ play in the big leagues ♦ talk big ♦ talk on the big white phone ♦ the big one ♦ yea big

biggie no biggie

bike bike boys ♦ On your bike!

bilge drain the bilge

bill (as) phony as a three-dollar bill ♦ (as) queer as a three-dollar bill ♦ bill and coo ♦ pay the water bill ♦ phony as a three-dollar bill ♦ queer as a three-dollar bill

bin loony bin ♦ sin-bin

bird bird watcher ♦ bird-dog ♦ birds of a feather ♦ boo-bird ♦ early bird ♦ flip so the bird ♦ for the birds ♦ ghetto bird ♦ odd bird ♦ on the bird ♦ rare bird ♦ strange bird

biscuit air biscuit ♦ float an air biscuit ♦ gorilla biscuits ♦ mystic biscuit ♦ square biscuit

bit a bit much ♦ bit of the action ♦ bit-bucket ♦ four-bits ♦ naughty bits ♦ six-bits ♦ two-bit ♦ two-bits

bitch bitch so off ♦ bitch sth up ♦ bitch box ♦ bitch of a so/sth ♦ bitch out ♦ bitch session ♦

bitch slammer ♦ bitch tits ♦ bull bitch ♦ bush bitch ♦ Life's a bitch, then you die. ♦ pitch a bitch ♦ real bitch ♦ son of a bitch ♦ You guys bitchin'?

bitchcakes go bitchcakes

bite ankle biter ♦ bite on so ♦ bite the big one ♦ bite the bullet ♦ bite the dust ♦ Bite the ice! ♦ I'll bite. ♦ monkey bite ♦ put the bite on so

bitsy itsy-bitsy

bitty itty-bitty

biz show biz

bizarro mondo bizarro

black black and blue ♦ black and white ♦ black eye ♦ black-collar workers ♦ early black ♦ in the black ♦ little black book

blah the blahs ♦ blah-blah

blanket blanket drill ♦ wet blanket

blast (ghetto) blaster ♦ beer blast ♦ blast off (for somewhere) ♦ full blast

blazes Go to blazes!

bleed bleed so dry ♦ bleed so white ♦ bleed for so ♦ on the bleeding edge

blimp blimp out ♦ Have a blimp!

blind blind drunk ♦ half-blind ♦ male blindness ♦ rob so blind ♦ stone blind

bling bling-bling

blink on the blink

bliss bliss so out ♦ bliss ninny ♦ bliss out ♦ blissed (out)

blitz blitz so out ♦ blitzed (out)

block been around (the block) ♦ cock-blocking ♦ knock so's block off ♦ on the chopping block

blond blond moment ♦ blood (brother) ♦ blood and guts ♦ cold blood ♦ Hell's bells (and buckets of blood)! ♦ in one's blood ♦ in cold blood ♦ piss blood ♦ smell blood ♦ sweat blood ♦ taste blood ♦ too rich for so's blood ♦ worms in blood ♦ young blood

bloody abso-bloody-lutely ♦ scream bloody murder

blooey go blooey

blossom toddy blossom

blow (Go) blow it out your ear! ♦ blow (one's) cookies ♦ blow (one's) lunch ♦ blow one's cool ♦ blow one's cork ♦ blow one's doughnuts ♦ blow one's fuse ♦ blow one's groceries ♦ blow one's lid ♦ blow one's lines ♦ blow one's own horn ♦ blow one's stack ♦ blow one's top ♦ blow so/sth off ♦ blow so's brains out ♦ blow so's cover ♦ blow so's doors off ♦ blow so's mind ♦ blow so away ♦ blow so out ♦ blow so out of the water ♦ blow so to sth ♦ blow sth ♦

blow sth wide open ♦ blow a fuse ♦ blow a gasket ♦ blow a hype ♦ blow a snot rocket ♦ blow beets ♦ blow chow ♦ blow chunks ♦ blow cold ♦ blow grits ♦ blow in ♦ Blow it out your ear! ♦ blow jive ♦ blow job ♦ blow lunch ♦ blow off ♦ blow off (some) steam ♦ Blow on it! ♦ blow smoke ♦ blow snot rockets ♦ blow the joint ♦ blow the lid off sth ♦ blow town ♦ blow up ♦ blow Zs ♦ blow-out ♦ blowed (away) ♦ Joe Blow ♦ land a blow ♦ low blow ♦ mind-blower ♦ mow, blow, and go ♦ whistle-blower

blown blown (out) ♦ blown (up) ♦ blown away

blowout have a blowout

blue big blue ♦ black and blue ♦ blue and white ♦ blue around the gills ♦ blue balls ♦ blue boys ♦ blue chip ♦ blue coats ♦ blue devils ♦ blue flu ♦ blue funk ♦ blue in the face ♦ blue screen of death ♦ blue suit ♦ blue-eyed ♦ boys in blue ♦ burn with a low blue flame ♦ in a blue funk ♦ little boy blue ♦ men in blue ♦ once in a blue moon ♦ screwed, blued, and tattooed ♦ talk a blue streak ♦ talk until one is blue in the face

blunt phat blunt

board big board ♦ boogie-board ♦ draft board

boat boat anchor ♦ just off the boat ♦ miss the boat ♦ whatever floats your boat

bob been bobbing for fries

bod odd-bod

body body count ♦ body shake ♦ Over my dead body! ♦ warm body

boil boil the ocean ♦ boiling (mad) ♦ pot boiler

bolt bolt-on ♦ bucket of bolts ♦ nuts and bolts

bomb the bomb ♦ bomb (out) ♦ bomb out (of sth) ♦ bombed (out) ♦ da bomb ♦ love bombs

bombshell drop a bomb(shell)

bond junk bond

bone bone factory ♦ bone out ♦ crazy bone ♦ have a bone on ♦ jump so's bones ♦ knuckle bones ♦ laid to the bone ♦ silked to the bone

boner pull a boner

bong bonged (out) ♦ do some bongs

bonkers drive so bonkers

boo boo-bird ♦ boo-boo ♦ make a boo-boo

boogie boogie down (to somewhere) ♦ boogie-board

book book (on) out ♦ crack a book ♦ hit the books ♦ little black book ♦ make book on sth

♦ pound the books ♦ take a page from so's book ♦ throw the book at so ♦ wish book

boom (baby) boomer ♦ ace boom-boom ♦ boom box ♦ boom sticks ♦ thunder-boomer

boon ace boon-coon

boot boot so out ♦ fuck-me boots ♦ Jesus boots ♦ knock boots ♦ to boot ♦ You bet your boots!

booth troll booth

booty booty call ♦ booty check ♦ booty-cheddar ♦ ghetto booty

booze booze artist ♦ booze it (up) ♦ booze up ♦ hit the booze

boozy boozy-woozy ♦ topsy-boozy

bop drop a bop

born natural-born ♦ Were you born in a barn?

bosom bosom chums ♦ bosom friends

boss boss dick ♦ boss lady ♦ boss man ♦ straw boss

both both sheets in the wind ♦ can't find one's butt with both hands (in broad daylight) ♦ It cuts both ways. ♦ smoke both ends of the cigar ♦ swing both ways

bottle bottle baby ♦ brown bottle flu ♦ chief cook and bottle washer ♦ crack open a bottle ♦ head cook and bottle washer ♦ hit the bottle

bottom one's bottom dollar ♦ the bottom line ♦ bet one's bottom dollar ♦ bottom fishing ♦ bottom of the barrel ♦ bottom of the heap ♦ bottom out ♦ Bottoms up. ♦ from the bottom of my heart ♦ rock bottom ♦ scrape the bottom of the barrel

bounce bounce sth off (of) so ♦ bounce for sth ♦ deadcat bounce ♦ That's the way the ball bounces.

bow bow to the porcelain altar ♦ bow-wow

bowels Don't get your bowels in an uproar! ♦ get one's bowels in an uproar

bowl party bowl

box (ghetto) box ♦ (squeeze-)box ♦ beat box ♦ bitch box ♦ boom box ♦ box so in ♦ box on the table ♦ boxed (up) ♦ boxed in ♦ doc(s)-in-a-box ♦ eternity-box ♦ fuse box ♦ go home in a box ♦ groan box ♦ idea box ♦ idiot box ♦ knowledge-box ♦ squawk box ♦ think-box

boy back room boys ♦ bike boys ♦ blue boys ♦ Boy howdy! ♦ boy-beater ♦ boys in blue ♦ boys in the back room ♦ but-boy ♦ fair-haired boy ♦ good old boy ♦ little boy blue ♦ little boys' room ♦ Oh, boy! ♦ poor boy ♦ That's my boy. ♦ That-a-boy!

brain BB brain ♦ beat one's brains out (to do sth) ♦ beat so's brains out ♦ blow so's brains out ♦ brack-brain ♦ brain bucket ♦ brain-burned ♦ brain-dead ♦ brain-drain ♦ brain-fried ♦ brain-teaser ♦ brain-twister ♦ feather brain ♦ fuck-brained ♦ get brain ♦ have one's brain on a leash ♦ have sth on the brain ♦ have shit for brains ♦ no-brainer

brand (brand) spanking new ♦ no brand cigarette ♦ off-brand cigarette

brass brass so off ♦ brass hat ♦ brass tacks ♦ top brass

brat army brat

bread bread and butter ♦ heavy bread ♦ long bread

break ball-breaker ♦ bio break ♦ break one's balls to do sth ♦ break so's balls ♦ Break a leg! ♦ Break it up! ♦ break out ♦ break the ice ♦ cut so a break ♦ cut so a break ♦ Gimme a break! ♦ Give me a break! ♦ take a break ♦ tough break

breakfast breakfast of champions ♦ donkey's breakfast ♦ Mexican breakfast ♦ shoot one's breakfast

breath Excuse me for breathing! ♦ mouth-breather

breeze fan the breeze ♦ shoot the breeze

brew brew-ha ♦ brew-out ♦ brews brothers ♦ home-brew ♦ quaff a brew ♦ suck (some) brew

brick built like a brick shithouse ♦ drop a brick ♦ hit the bricks ♦ like a ton of bricks ♦ one brick shy of a load ♦ shit a brick ♦ three bricks shy of a load

bring bring so down ♦ bring so on ♦ bring sth up ♦ bring-down ♦ Earp slop, bring the mop.

broad can't find one's butt with both hands (in broad daylight) ♦ can't hit the (broad) side of a barn ♦ square john broad

broke dead broke ♦ flat broke ♦ go for broke ♦ If it ain't broke don't fix it. ♦ If it ain't broke, fix it till it is. ♦ stone broke

brother (soul) brother ♦ big brother ♦ blood (brother) ♦ brews brothers

brow no-brow

brown brown so off ♦ brown bag it ♦ brown bottle flu ♦ brown hole ♦ brown out ♦ brown-bag ♦ brown-nose ♦ brown-noser ♦ browned (off) ♦ code brown

bruise cruising for a bruising

brushoff give so the brushoff

bubble bubble water ♦ half a bubble off plumb

buck bang for the buck ♦ big bucks ♦ buck for sth ♦ buck up ♦ fast buck ♦ pass the buck ♦ quick buck

bucket bit-bucket ♦ brain bucket ♦ bucket of bolts ♦ gash bucket ♦ Hell's bells (and buckets of blood)! ♦ kick the bucket ♦ rust bucket ♦ sleaze-bucket ♦ slime bucket

bud best bud ♦ sense (bud)

buddy buddy up (with so) ♦ buddy up to so ♦ buddy-buddy ♦ buddy-buddy ♦ fuck buddy ♦ good buddy

budget budget crunch ♦ budget dust ♦ budget squeeze

buff in the buff

buffalo double buffalo

bug bug nut ♦ Bug off! ♦ bug out ♦ bug-fucker ♦ crank bugs

buick sell buicks

built built like a brick shithouse ♦ jerry-built

bulb dim bulb ♦ light bulb

bulge battle of the bulge

bull bull bitch ♦ bull session ♦ bull-dagger ♦ bull-pucky ♦ company bull ♦ full of bull ♦ hit the bull's-eye ♦ hung like a bull ♦ shoot the bull ♦ throw the bull

bullet bite the bullet ♦ bullet-stopper ♦ faster than a speeding bullet ♦ magic bullet ♦ silver bullet ♦ sweat bullets

bullshit bullshit artist ♦ knowledge in, bullshit out

bum beach bum ♦ bum so out ♦ bum sth (off so) ♦ bum about so/sth ♦ bum around ♦ bum beef ♦ bum check ♦ bum out ♦ bum rap ♦ bum steer ♦ bum trip ♦ bum's rush ♦ bummed (out) ♦ Hey, bum! ♦ skid row bum ♦ stew bum

bumbles stumble-bumbles

bump bump so off ♦ Bump that! ♦ bump uglies ♦ bumping fuzzies ♦ Let's bump this place!

bumper bumper sticker ♦ fanny-bumper ♦ Get off my bumper! ♦ up on so's bumper

bun work one's buns off

bunch a whole bunch ♦ bunch of fives ♦ bunch-punch ♦ thanks a bunch

bundle bundle from heaven ♦ bundle of joy ♦ bundle of nerves ♦ drop a bundle (on so) ♦ drop a bundle (on sth) ♦ lose a bundle ♦ make a bundle

bunny beach bunny ♦ bed-bunny ♦ blouse bunnies ♦ cuddle bunny ♦ dumb bunny ♦ fuck bunny ♦ puck bunny ♦ snow bunny

burger burger-flipper ♦ flipping burgers

burn bra-burner ♦ brain-burned ♦ burn so down ♦ burn so up ♦ burn artist ♦ burn rubber ♦ burn with a low blue flame ♦ burned out ♦ burned up ♦ burnt out ♦ crash

cause lost cause
ceiling hit the ceiling
central Grand Central Station
chain one's ball and chain ♦ chain(-smoke) ♦ chain-smoker ♦ pull so's chain ♦ yank so's chain
champion breakfast of champions
chance fat chance ♦ not a chance ♦ snowball's chance in hell
change and change ♦ change the channel ♦ chump change ♦ go through the changes ♦ small change
channel change the channel ♦ channel hopping ♦ channel surfer ♦ channel surfing ♦ channel zapping
Charlie Alpha Charlie ♦ Charlie Foxtrot ♦ Charlie Irvine ♦ good-time Charley
chase ambulance chaser ♦ chase the dragon ♦ cut to the chase ♦ Go chase your tail! ♦ Go chase yourself!
chassis classy-chassis
chauvinist male chauvinist pig
cheap all over so like a cheap suit ♦ cheap shot ♦ dirt cheap ♦ el cheapo
check booty check ♦ bum check ♦ cash in (one's) checks ♦ check sth out ♦ check out the plumbing ♦ check that ♦ check your six ♦ cut a check ♦ gravity check ♦ hot check ♦ rubber (check)
checkout the eternal checkout
cheddar booty-cheddar
cheek tongue in cheek ♦ water one's cheeks
cheer Bronx cheer
cheese big cheese ♦ cheese so off ♦ Cheese it (the cops)! ♦ cheese-eater ♦ cheesed off ♦ chew the cheese ♦ cock-cheese ♦ crotch-cheese ♦ cut the cheese ♦ Say cheese!
cherry desert cherry
chest flat-chested ♦ take the spear (in one's chest) ♦ war chest
chew ass-chewing ♦ chew so's ass out ♦ chew so out ♦ chew sth over ♦ chew face ♦ chew the cheese ♦ chew the fat ♦ chew the rag
chick chick magnet ♦ chick-flick ♦ slick-chick
chicken chicken feed ♦ chicken out (of sth) ♦ chicken powder ♦ chicken shit ♦ chicken-hearted ♦ choke the chicken ♦ for chicken feed ♦ spring chicken
chill chill (out) ♦ chill so's action ♦ take a chill pill ♦ living chilly
chimney smoke like a chimney
chin take it on the chin ♦ wag one's chin
ching Ka-ching!

chip blue chip ♦ cash in (one's) chips ♦ cow chips ♦ in the chips
chocks pull chocks
chop chop-shop ♦ chopped liver ♦ on the chopping block
chow blow chow ♦ chow sth down ♦ chow down ♦ chow hound
Christmas cancel so's Christmas ♦ Christmas tree
chuck chuck sth down ♦ chuck a dummy ♦ chuck it in ♦ chuck up
chump chump change ♦ off one's chump
chums bosom chums
chunk blow chunks ♦ chunk so
church church key ♦ See you in church.
chute go down the chute ♦ poop chute
cigar Close, but no cigar. ♦ smoke both ends of the cigar
cigarette cigarette with no name ♦ no brand cigarette ♦ no name cigarette ♦ off-brand cigarette
cinch dead cinch ♦ have sth cinched
circle circle-jerk ♦ circling (the drain)
citizen Joe Citizen
city Barf City ♦ cement city ♦ fat city ♦ Headstone City ♦ Marble City ♦ You can't fight city hall.
clamp put the clamps on so/sth
clanker anchor-clanker
clap golf-clap
class class act ♦ world-class
clean clean one's act up ♦ clean so out ♦ clean sweep ♦ clean up (on sth) ♦ cleaned out ♦ come clean (with so) (about sth) ♦ keep one's nose clean ♦ squeaky clean ♦ take so to the cleaners
clear (as) clear as mud ♦ (as) clear as vodka ♦ clear as mud ♦ clear as vodka ♦ clear out ♦ clear sailing
cleaver beaver-cleaver
climb climb the wall(s) ♦ Go climb a tree!
clip clip so's wings ♦ clip a butt ♦ clip joint ♦ roach clip
clock clock in ♦ clock watcher
close (as) close as stink on shit ♦ close as stink on shit ♦ close call ♦ close combat sock ♦ close shave ♦ Close, but no cigar. ♦ up close and personal
closet come out of the closet ♦ rain closet
club Join the club. ♦ Welcome to the club.
cluck dumb cluck
clueless totally clueless
coach roach-coach
coast left coast

coat blue coats

cober sold cober

cobra crotch-cobra

cock cock-blocking ♦ cock-cheese ♦ go off half-cocked ♦ half-cocked ♦ horse cock ♦ knock sth into a cocked hat

code code brown ♦ code yellow

coffee coffee and ♦ coffee in, coffee out ♦ cold coffee

coffin coffin nail ♦ coffin tack ♦ coffin varnish ♦ coffin-dodger

coin do some fine coin ♦ hard coin

cold a cold piece of work ♦ a stone cold fox ♦ Baby it's cold outside. ♦ blow cold ♦ cold blood ♦ cold call ♦ cold coffee ♦ cold feet ♦ cold fish ♦ cold sober ♦ cold turkey ♦ freezing cold ♦ get one's nose cold ♦ in a cold sweat ♦ in cold blood ♦ in cold storage ♦ kick cold (turkey) ♦ leave so cold ♦ out cold ♦ pour cold water on sth ♦ stone (cold) sober

collar black-collar workers ♦ dog collar ♦ hot under the collar ♦ righteous collar

collected cool, calm, and collected

college Graystone College ♦ Joe College

color off color ♦ with flying colors

combat close combat sock

come Bend over, here it comes again. ♦ come across (with sth) ♦ come clean (with so) (about sth) ♦ come down ♦ come down hard ♦ come down hard on so ♦ Come off it! ♦ come on ♦ come on like gangbusters ♦ come on strong ♦ come on to so ♦ come out ahead ♦ come out in the wash ♦ come out of the closet ♦ come out on top ♦ come up for air ♦ come-hither look ♦ coming out of one's ears ♦ if push comes to shove ♦ Johnnie-come-lately ♦ know where so is coming from ♦ This is where I came in. ♦ till kingdom come ♦ What's coming off? ♦ when push comes to shove ♦ You've got another think coming.

comedy Cut the comedy!

commando go commando

commerce chamber of commerce

company company bull ♦ company man

complaint summer complaint

compos non compos ♦ non compos poopoo

con con artist ♦ con job ♦ con man ♦ put a con on so

conk conk off ♦ conk out ♦ conk-buster

connect connect (with so) ♦ connect (with sth)

coo bill and coo ♦ coo-coo

cook chief cook and bottle washer ♦ cooked up ♦ cooking with gas ♦ head cook and bottle washer ♦ What's cooking?

cookie blow (one's) cookies ♦ cookie pusher ♦ drop one's cookies ♦ shoot one's cookies ♦ smart cookie ♦ snap one's cookies ♦ That's the way the cookie crumbles. ♦ throw one's cookies ♦ toss one's cookies ♦ tough cookie ♦ tough cookies ♦ woof cookies

cool blow one's cool ♦ cool so out ♦ Cool bananas! ♦ Cool beans! ♦ cool cat ♦ cool down ♦ Cool it! ♦ cool off ♦ cool out ♦ cool, calm, and collected ♦ cooled out ♦ keep one's cool ♦ keep cool ♦ lose one's cool ♦ play it cool

coon ace boon-coon

coop fly the coop

cop Cheese it (the cops)! ♦ cop a drag ♦ cop a fix ♦ cop a head ♦ cop a heel ♦ cop a plea ♦ cop a squat ♦ cop a tube ♦ cop an attitude ♦ cop onto sth ♦ cop out ♦ cop some Zs ♦ cop-shop

core hard-core ♦ rotten to the core ♦ soft core ♦ soft-core

cork blow one's cork ♦ corked (up) ♦ liquid cork ♦ pop one's cork ♦ Put a cork in it!

corn can of corn ♦ corn squabble

corner cut corners

cotton cotton-picking ♦ in tall cotton

couch casting couch ♦ couch potato ♦ couch-doctor ♦ couch-turkey

cough cough sth up ♦ Cough it up!

count bean-counter ♦ body count ♦ comma-counter ♦ do a bean count ♦ down for the count ♦ take the (long) count

courage Dutch courage

course snap course

court The ball is in so's court.

cousin What's buzzin' (cousin)?

cover blow so's cover ♦ Cover your ass. ♦ cover-up

cow cash cow ♦ cow chips ♦ cow flop ♦ cow juice ♦ cow plop ♦ cow-doots ♦ Don't have a cow! ♦ Holy cow! ♦ tin cow

cowboy drugstore cowboy

crack crack so up ♦ crack a book ♦ crack a tube ♦ crack house ♦ crack open a bottle ♦ crack some suds ♦ crack up ♦ crack-rack ♦ cracked up to be ♦ dirty crack ♦ Get cracking! ♦ have one's ass in a crack ♦ have a crack at sth ♦ take a crack at sth ♦ tough egg to crack ♦ tough nut to crack

craftsy artsy-craftsy

crank bathtub crank ◆ crank sth out ◆ crank sth up ◆ crank bugs ◆ yank so's crank

crap crap out ◆ crap-list ◆ crapped (out) ◆ crapper dick ◆ Cut the crap! ◆ shoot the crap ◆ take a crap ◆ throw the crap

crash crash and burn ◆ crash cart

crazy crazy bone ◆ like crazy ◆ stir crazy

cream cream (in) one's pants ◆ cream one's jeans ◆ cream puff ◆ creamed foreskins

cred street cred

creek God willing and the creek don't rise ◆ up a creek ◆ up shit creek (without a paddle) ◆ up the creek (without a paddle)

creep the creeps ◆ creep dive ◆ creep joint ◆ creeping-crud ◆ Jeepers(-creepers)!

cricket not cricket

critter crispy-critter

crock crock (of shit) ◆ crock so/sth up ◆ half-crocked ◆ What a crock!

crocodile After while(, crocodile).

cross cross so (up) ◆ cross up so ◆ cross-eyed (drunk) ◆ double cross ◆ double-crosser ◆ nail so to a cross ◆ nail Jell-O to a cross

crotch crotch rocketeer ◆ crotch-cheese ◆ crotch-cobra ◆ crotch-monkey ◆ crotch-pheasant ◆ crotch-rocket ◆ crotch-rot

crow eat crow

crud creeping-crud

cruise cruising for a bruising ◆ time to cruise

crumb crum sth up ◆ crumb sth up ◆ crumb-cruncher ◆ crumb-crusher

crumble That's the way the cookie crumbles.

crunch budget crunch ◆ crumb-cruncher ◆ number crunching ◆ number-cruncher

crush crumb-crusher

crutch p-crutch

cry cry hughie ◆ cry ralph ◆ cry ruth ◆ crying drunk ◆ crying towel ◆ crying weed

cunt cunt fart ◆ cunt hound ◆ cunt-hooks

curb shot to the curb ◆ step off the curb

cure Dutch cure ◆ take the cure

curl (just) curl up and die ◆ curl up and die

customer tough customer

cut able to cut sth ◆ cut (up) ◆ cut one's losses ◆ cut one's own throat ◆ cut one's wolf loose ◆ cut so a break ◆ cut so a break ◆ cut so in (on sth) ◆ cut a check ◆ cut a deal ◆ cut a fart ◆ cut a muffin ◆ cut and run ◆ cut ass (out of somewhere) ◆ cut corners ◆ cut loose ◆ cut no ice (with so) ◆ cut one ◆ cut out ◆ cut some Zs ◆ cut the cheese ◆ Cut the comedy! ◆ Cut the crap! ◆ cut the dust ◆ cut the mustard ◆ cut to the chase ◆ cut up (about so/sth) ◆ cut-

rate ◆ Fish or cut bait. ◆ It cuts both ways. ◆ It cuts two ways. ◆ piss-cutter ◆ cutie pie

cylinder run on all cylinders

dab slap-dab ◆ smack (dab) in the middle

daddy daddy (of them all) ◆ mack daddy ◆ sugar daddy ◆ Who's your daddy?

dagger bull-dagger

daily daily dozen ◆ daily grind

daisy (as) fresh as a daisy ◆ fresh as a daisy ◆ pushing up daisies

damage hail damage ◆ What's the damage? ◆ What's your damage?

damn Damn straight! ◆ Damned if I know. ◆ not worth a damn

damper put a damper on sth

dance erotic dancer ◆ grave-dancer ◆ lap dancer ◆ lap dancing ◆ pole dancer ◆ pole dancing ◆ tap dance like mad ◆ You can't dance at two weddings.

dandruff galloping dandruff ◆ walking dandruff

dandy fine and dandy

dangle dingle(-dangle)

dark dark horse ◆ shot in the dark ◆ whistle in the dark

dash slap-dash

date heavy date

Dave Sam and Dave

dawg my dawg

day bad hair day ◆ day one ◆ day person ◆ day the eagle flies ◆ day the eagle shits ◆ day-tripper ◆ Go ahead, make my day. ◆ Have a nice day. ◆ if one's a day ◆ Make my day! ◆ red-letter day ◆ seen better days ◆ That'll be the day! ◆ vújà day ◆ You made my day.

daylight can't find one's butt with both hands (in broad daylight)

dazzle razzle-dazzle

DC AC-DC

dead (bang) dead to rights ◆ (dead) ringer (for so) ◆ brain-dead ◆ dead and gone ◆ dead broke ◆ dead cinch ◆ dead drunk ◆ dead duck ◆ dead easy ◆ dead from the neck up ◆ dead horse ◆ dead in the water ◆ dead issue ◆ dead letter ◆ dead man ◆ dead marine ◆ dead on ◆ dead one ◆ dead president ◆ dead soldier ◆ dead to rights ◆ dead to the world ◆ dead-catty ◆ dead-end kid ◆ Drop dead! ◆ drop-dead ◆ drop-dead gorgeous ◆ drop-dead list ◆ have so dead to rights ◆ knock so dead ◆ Over my dead body! ◆ stone dead ◆ would not be seen dead

deadly deadly (dull) ◆ silent but deadly

deal a raw deal ♦ big deal ♦ cut a deal ♦ deal stock ♦ deal with so ♦ dirty deal ♦ done deal ♦ Good deal! ♦ Here's the deal. ♦ Like it's such a big deal. ♦ no big deal ♦ sweetheart deal ♦ What's the deal? ♦ wheel and deal ♦ wheeler-dealer

death blue screen of death ♦ death on so/sth ♦ death on sth ♦ kiss of death ♦ like death warmed over ♦ nickel and dime so (to death) ♦ sick to death (of so/sth) ♦ sudden death

deck double-decker ♦ hit the deck ♦ play with a full deck ♦ stack the deck

deep deep pockets ♦ deep six ♦ go off the deep end ♦ in deep ♦ in deep doo-doo ♦ knee-deep in sth ♦ knee-deep navy

degree third degree

demon speed demon

department headache department

deuce deuce-deuce ♦ double-deuces ♦ What the deuce? ♦ Who the deuce?

devil a devil of a time ♦ the devil's own time ♦ blue devils ♦ for the devil of it ♦ full of the devil ♦ Go to the devil! ♦ play the devil with so/sth ♦ raise the devil (with so) ♦ raise the devil (with sth) ♦ speak of the devil ♦ What (in) the devil? ♦ What the devil? ♦ Who (in) the devil? ♦ Who the devil?

dew (mountain) dew ♦ dog-dew ♦ knock the dew off the lily ♦ shake the dew off the lily

diarrhea diarrhea of the jawbone ♦ diarrhea of the mouth

dice no dice

dick big Dick ♦ boss dick ♦ crapper dick ♦ dick around ♦ dick for ♦ dick smack ♦ dick-sucker ♦ dicky-licker ♦ whiskey dick

dictionary swallow the dictionary

diddle diddle sth out of so ♦ diddle with sth

diddly diddly-shit ♦ diddly-squat

die (just) curl up and die ♦ curl up and die ♦ die of throat trouble ♦ die on so ♦ do or die ♦ fixing to die ♦ Life's a bitch, then you die. ♦ Somebody died in here! ♦ to die for ♦ Who died in here?

difference same difference ♦ different strokes for different folks

dig Big Dig ♦ Dig up! ♦ give so a dig ♦ take a dig at so

digger gold digger ♦ hole digger

diggety Hot diggety (dog)!

digits double digits

diller killer-diller ♦ thriller-diller

dilly What's the dilly

dime dime store ♦ dime-dropper ♦ drop a dime ♦ get off the dime ♦ nickel and dime so (to death) ♦ stop on a dime ♦ thin dime ♦ turn on a dime

ding ding-a-ling ♦ ding-dong ♦ dinged out ♦ whing-ding ♦ wing-ding

dink dink so off ♦ rinky-dink

dinner dinner basket ♦ TV dinner

diploma federal diploma

dipper double-dipper ♦ fanny-dipper

dirt dirt cheap ♦ dish the dirt ♦ do so dirt ♦ hit pay dirt ♦ strike pay dirt ♦ take a dirt nap

dirty the (dirty) dozens ♦ dirty crack ♦ dirty deal ♦ dirty dog ♦ dirty joke ♦ dirty laundry ♦ dirty linen ♦ dirty look ♦ dirty old man ♦ dirty pool ♦ dirty word ♦ dirty work ♦ dirty-minded ♦ dirty-mouth ♦ quick-and-dirty

discount five-finger discount

disease foot-in-mouth disease ♦ white man's disease

dish dish sth out ♦ dish the dirt

dishrag (limp) dishrag

dishwater (as) dull as dishwater ♦ dull as dishwater

dismount involuntary dismount

distance put some distance between so and so/sth ♦ within spitting distance

dive creep dive ♦ dive a muff ♦ gin dive ♦ take a dive

divide great divide

dixie not just whistling Dixie

Doakes Joe Doakes

doc doc(s)-in-a-box ♦ What's up doc?

doctor couch-doctor ♦ dome-doctor ♦ horse doctor ♦ just what the doctor ordered ♦ spin doctor ♦ You're the doctor. ♦ zit doctor

dodge coffin-dodger ♦ get out of Dodge

dodo dumb-dodo

doe John Doe

dog (It's) not my dog. ♦ bird-dog ♦ cats and dogs ♦ dirty dog ♦ dog and pony show ♦ dog collar ♦ dog meat ♦ dog's mother ♦ dog-dew ♦ dog-do ♦ dog-doo ♦ dog-eat-dog ♦ dog-fashion ♦ dog-log ♦ dog-style ♦ dog-ways ♦ doggy bag ♦ Fuck a dog! ♦ Hong Kong dog ♦ Hot diggety (dog)! ♦ Hot dog! ♦ lucky dog ♦ my dog ♦ Not my dog. ♦ prairie dog ♦ put on the dog ♦ see a man about a dog ♦ shouldn't happen to a dog ♦ tin dog ♦ top dog ♦ yard dog

doggo lie doggo

doll Barbie doll

dollar (as) phony as a three-dollar bill ♦ (as) queer as a three-dollar bill ♦ one's bottom dollar ♦ the sixty-four-dollar question ♦ adobe dollar ♦ bet one's bottom dollar ♦ bet so dollars to doughnuts ♦ like a million (dollars) ♦ phony as a three-dollar bill ♦ queer as a three-dollar bill

domain ptomaine-domain

dome chrome-dome ♦ dome-doctor ♦ double-dome ♦ marble dome

dong ding-dong

donkey donkey's breakfast ♦ donkey's years

doo doo-doo ♦ in deep doo-doo

doodly (doodly-)squat ♦ doodly-shit

dooper super-dooper

door blow so's doors off ♦ house of many doors

doots cow-doots

dope do dope ♦ dope sth out ♦ dope fiend ♦ dope up ♦ inside dope ♦ straight dope

dora dumb Dora

dory hunky-dory

dose go through so like a dose of (the) salts

double double buffalo ♦ double cross ♦ double digits ♦ double nickels ♦ double saw(buck) ♦ double six ♦ double take ♦ double whammy ♦ double-bagger ♦ double-barreled slingshot ♦ double-crosser ♦ double-decker ♦ double-deuces ♦ double-dipper ♦ double-dome ♦ double-gaited ♦ double-trouble ♦ H-E-double-toothpicks ♦ on the double

doughnut bet so dollars to doughnuts ♦ blow one's doughnuts ♦ lose one's doughnuts

downhill go downhill

dozen the (dirty) dozens ♦ daily dozen ♦ long dozen ♦ play the dozens ♦ shoot the dozens

drabs in dribs and drabs

draft draft board ♦ feel a draft

drag a drag (on so) ♦ a drag (on sth) ♦ cop a drag ♦ drag ass (out of somewhere) ♦ drag ass around ♦ dragged out ♦ draggin'-wagon ♦ in drag ♦ knockdown drag-out fight ♦ knuckle-dragger ♦ Look (at) what the cat dragged in! ♦ main drag

dragon chase the dragon ♦ drain the dragon

drain brain-drain ♦ circling (the drain) ♦ down the drain ♦ drain the bilge ♦ drain the dragon ♦ make drain babies

draw Do I have to draw (you) a picture? ♦ luck of the draw

drawer droopy-drawers ♦ top-drawer

dress dressed to kill ♦ dressed to the nines ♦ dressed to the teeth

dribs in dribs and drabs

drift (Do you) get my drift? ♦ Get my drift?

drill blanket drill

drink the drink ♦ big drink ♦ big drink of water ♦ do the drink thing ♦ Drink up! ♦ get down to some serious drinking ♦ knock back a drink ♦ two-fisted drinker

drippings silo drippings

drive backseat driver ♦ drive so around the bend ♦ drive so bonkers ♦ drive so nuts ♦ drive so up the wall ♦ drive the big bus ♦ drive the porcelain bus ♦ Fuck it, shit happens, drive on. ♦ in the driver's seat ♦ Sunday driver

drool drool (all) over so/sth ♦ drool-proof

drop dime-dropper ♦ drop one's cookies ♦ drop one's teeth ♦ drop so ♦ drop so/sth like a hot potato ♦ drop so some knowledge ♦ drop a bomb(shell) ♦ drop a bop ♦ drop a brick ♦ drop a bundle (on so) ♦ drop a bundle (on sth) ♦ drop a dime ♦ Drop dead! ♦ Drop it! ♦ drop out ♦ drop the ball ♦ Drop you! ♦ drop-dead ♦ drop-dead gorgeous ♦ drop-dead list ♦ get the drop on so ♦ pill-dropper

drug do drugs ♦ do the drug thing ♦ drug lord ♦ drug out ♦ head drug

drum beat the drum for so/sth

drunk blind drunk ♦ commode-hugging drunk ♦ country drunk ♦ cross-eyed (drunk) ♦ crying drunk ♦ dead drunk ♦ drunk back ♦ drunk tank ♦ falling-down drunk ♦ funky-drunk ♦ glazed (drunk) ♦ howling (drunk) ♦ punch-drunk ♦ screeching (drunk) ♦ skunk-drunk ♦ stale drunk ♦ stinking (drunk)

dry bleed so dry ♦ Dry up! ♦ dry-as-dust ♦ high and dry

duck dead duck ♦ duck-butt ♦ duck-squeezer ♦ Fuck a duck! ♦ lame duck ♦ Lord love a duck! ♦ milk a duck ♦ mud duck ♦ sitting duck

duddy fuddy-duddy

dude dude (oneself) up ♦ dude up ♦ duded up

dues pay one's dues ♦ pay one's dues (to society)

duke duke so out ♦ duke it out

dull (as) dull as dishwater ♦ deadly (dull) ♦ dull as dishwater ♦ dull roar

dumb dum-dum ♦ dumb bunny ♦ dumb cluck ♦ dumb Dora ♦ dumb ox ♦ dumb-ass ♦ dumb-dodo ♦ dumb-dumb ♦ dumb-dumb

dummy beat the dummy ♦ chuck a dummy ♦ dummy up ♦ My mama didn't raise no dummy. ♦ whip the dummy

dump do a dump on so/sth ♦ dump one's load ♦ dump all over so/sth ♦ Dump it. ♦ dump on so ♦ dump on so/sth ♦ dumped on ♦ Let's dump. ♦ take a dump ♦ toxic waste dump

dunk slam dunk

duo dynamic duo

duper super-duper

dust angel dust ♦ bite the dust ♦ budget dust ♦ corral dust ♦ cut the dust ♦ dry-as-dust ♦ dust so's pants ♦ dust so off ♦ dust of angels ♦ dust-up ♦ ear-duster ♦ heaven dust ♦ joy dust ♦ kiss the dust

dusty dusty butt ♦ rusty-dusty

dutch the Dutch act ♦ Dutch courage ♦ Dutch cure ♦ go Dutch ♦ in Dutch

duty rack duty

eager eager-beaver ♦ day the eagle flies ♦ day the eagle shits ♦ eagle freak ♦ eagle-eye ♦ legal-eagle ♦ when the eagle flies

ear (Go) blow it out your ear! ♦ Blow it out your ear! ♦ coming out of one's ears ♦ ear candy ♦ ear hustle ♦ ear hustler ♦ ear hustling ♦ ear-duster ♦ I'm all ears. ♦ mickey mouse ears ♦ pin so's ears back ♦ pound one's ear ♦ sloshed (to the ears) ♦ stewed to the ears ♦ talk so's ear off ♦ throw one out on one's ear ♦ up to one's ears ♦ walls have ears

earful give so an earful

earl call earl ♦ talk to earl

early early beam(s) ♦ early bird ♦ early black

earth earth pads ♦ Earth to so. ♦ no earthly reason ♦ Where on (God's green) earth? ♦ Where on earth?

easy dead easy ♦ Easy does it. ♦ easy make ♦ easy mark ♦ easy money ♦ easy street ♦ on easy street ♦ take it easy ♦ take things easy

eat (Do) you eat with that mouth? ♦ dog-eat-dog ♦ eat one's gun ♦ eat one's hat ♦ eat one's heart out ♦ eat so's lunch ♦ eat sth up ♦ eat at the Y ♦ eat crow ♦ eat face ♦ Eat me! ♦ Eat my shorts! ♦ eat nails ♦ Eat shit! ♦ eat up ♦ What's eating so? ♦ You eat with that mouth?

eater cheese-eater ♦ smoke eater ♦ weed-eater

eco eco freak ♦ eco nut

edgar J. Edgar (Hoover)

edge have an edge on ♦ moist around the edges ♦ on the bleeding edge

edition bulldog edition

egg bad egg ♦ egg-beater ♦ egg-sucker ♦ Go fry an egg! ♦ goose egg ♦ have egg on one's face ♦ lay an egg ♦ nest egg ♦ rotten egg ♦ scrambled eggs ♦ tough egg to crack ♦ walk on eggs

ego ego trip ♦ ego tripper

Egypt butt-fucking Egypt

eight the eighty-eight ♦ behind the eight ball

eighty the eighty-eight ♦ eighty-six

elbow bend one's elbow ♦ elbow-bending ♦ elbow-grease ♦ lift one's elbow

elegant piss elegant ♦ swellelegant

elephant pink elephants ♦ seeing pink elephants ♦ white elephant

else What else is new? ♦ You and who else?

enamel pray to the enamel god

enchilada the whole enchilada ♦ big enchilada

end the end ♦ the short end of the stick ♦ at loose ends ♦ back-ender ♦ business end (of sth) ♦ cannot see (any) further than the end of (one's) nose ♦ dead-end kid ♦ end of the ball game ♦ go off the deep end ♦ know which end is up ♦ no end of sth ♦ pointy end ♦ rear (end) ♦ rear-ender ♦ see no further than the end of one's nose ♦ shitty end of the stick ♦ smoke both ends of the cigar ♦ tail-end ♦ the end of the world as we know it

enemy meals rejected by the enemy

enough ain't long enough ♦ Enough, already! ♦ not enough room to swing a cat

estate wheel estate

Ethiopians meals rejected by Ethiopians

even even-Steven ♦ evened out

everything Everything's going to be okay. ♦ everything but the kitchen sink ♦ everything from A to Z ♦ everything from soup to nuts ♦ Hold everything!

excuse Excuse me for breathing! ♦ Excuse me for living! ♦ Excuse my French.

expedition fishing expedition

express Siberian express

expression if you'll pardon the expression

eye bedroom eyes ♦ black eye ♦ blue-eyed ♦ bright-eyed and bushy-tailed ♦ cross-eyed (drunk) ♦ eagle-eye ♦ eye candy ♦ eye-in-the-sky ♦ eye-opener ♦ eye-popper ♦ four-eyes ♦ get some shut-eye ♦ glass(y)-eyed ♦ goggle-eyed ♦ goo-goo eyes ♦ googly-eyed ♦ Here's mud in your eye. ♦ hit the bull's-eye ♦ one-eyed pants mouse ♦ pie-eyed ♦ pigeon-eyed ♦ pop-eyed ♦ private eye ♦ see eye to eye ♦ see eye to eye ♦ shut-eye ♦ snake eyes ♦ wall-eyed ♦ with (one's) eyes (wide) open

eyeball eyeball to eyeball ♦ get an eyeball on so/sth ♦ up to one's eyeballs

face (face) fungus ♦ a slap in the face ♦ Bag your face! ♦ blue in the face ♦ butter face ♦ chew face ♦ crater-face ♦ eat face ♦ face card ♦ face man ♦ face the music ♦ face time ♦ face to face ♦ face-off ♦ feed one's face ♦ fill one's face ♦ frog face ♦ fungus-face ♦ fuzz-face ♦ get face ♦ get in so's face ♦ Get out of my face! ♦ have egg on one's face ♦ in so's face ♦ in-your-face ♦ mace so's face ♦ mess so's face up ♦ pizza-face ♦ powder one's face ♦ put a smile on so's face ♦ rack face ♦ shit-faced ♦ Shut your face! ♦ soak one's face ♦ stand there with one's bare face hanging out ♦ straight-faced ♦ stuff one's face ♦ suck face ♦ talk until one is blue in the face ♦ turd face ♦ what's his face ♦ zit-face

fact as a matter of fact ♦ facts of life

factor fudge factor

factory bone factory ♦ gargle factory ♦ glue factory ♦ nut factory ♦ piss factory ♦ spook factory

fade do a fade

fag fag so out ♦ fag-bashing ♦ fag-busting ♦ fagged out

fair fair shake ♦ fair-haired boy ♦ fair-weather ♦ No fair!

fairy airy-fairy ♦ fairy tale

faith Keep the faith (baby)!

faithful one of the faithful

fake fake so out ♦ fake it ♦ fake off ♦ fake on so ♦ fake the funk

fall fall guy ♦ fall off the wagon ♦ fall out ♦ fall out of bed ♦ falling-down drunk ♦ falling-out ♦ take a fall ♦ take the fall

familiar in a familiar way

family the whole fam damily ♦ family jewels ♦ in a family way ♦ in the family way

fan fan the breeze ♦ hit the fan ♦ when the shit hits the fan

fancy fancy footwork ♦ Fancy that! ♦ fancy-schmancy

fanny fanny-bumper ♦ fanny-dipper

fantods (howling) fantods ♦ screaming fantods

fAQ Read the fucking FAQ!

far far gone ♦ far out

farm buy the farm ♦ funny farm

fart boring old fart ♦ cunt fart ♦ cut a fart ♦ fart around ♦ fart hole ♦ fart off ♦ fart sack ♦ fiddle-fart ♦ let a fart ♦ monkey-fart ♦ pussy fart

fartsy artsy (fartsy)

fashion dog-fashion

fast fast buck ♦ fast footwork ♦ fast one ♦ faster than a speeding bullet ♦ Get one's tail somewhere fast! ♦ get nowhere fast ♦ play fast and loose (with so/sth) ♦ pull a fast one

fat (as) fat as a beached whale ♦ big fat grin ♦ chew the fat ♦ fat as a beached whale ♦ fat chance ♦ fat city ♦ fat lip ♦ fat skrill ♦ fat-

ass(ed) ♦ fat-cat ♦ till the fat lady sings ♦ when the fat lady sings

fax junk fax

fear I'm shaking (in fear).

feather birds of a feather ♦ feather brain ♦ in fine feather ♦ leather or feather ♦ You could have knocked me over with a feather.

federal Don't make a federal case out of it! ♦ federal diploma ♦ federal jug ♦ make a federal case out of sth

feed chicken feed ♦ feed one's face ♦ for chicken feed

feedbag put on the feedbag

feel feel so ♦ feel so up ♦ feel a draft ♦ feel groovy ♦ feeling no pain ♦ touchy-feely

feet cold feet ♦ get a load off one's feet ♦ patter of tiny feet ♦ six feet under ♦ take a load off one's feet ♦ vote with one's feet

fence fence hanger ♦ go for the fences ♦ straddle the fence

fever barrel fever

few a few ticks ♦ hang a few on ♦ Win a few, lose a few.

fiddle belly fiddle ♦ fiddle-fart ♦ second fiddle

field field grounders ♦ out in left field ♦ out of left field

fiend dope fiend

fifth fifth wheel ♦ take the fifth

fig moldy fig

fight fish-fight ♦ knockdown drag-out fight ♦ spoiling for a fight ♦ throw a fight ♦ You can't fight city hall.

figure Go figure. ♦ key figure

file circular file ♦ file thirteen ♦ rank and file ♦ round file

fill fill one's face ♦ fill so full of lead ♦ fill or kill ♦ fill-mill ♦ filling station ♦ smoke-filled room

film snuff film

filter bozo filter

filthy filthy lucre ♦ filthy rich

find can't find one's butt with both hands (in broad daylight)

fine do some fine coin ♦ fine and dandy ♦ fine wolf ♦ finer than frog hair ♦ in fine feather ♦ New York's finest

finger a three finger salute ♦ finger so as so ♦ finger wave ♦ five-finger discount ♦ give so the finger ♦ one finger salute ♦ put the finger on so ♦ sticky fingers ♦ two fingers

finish Mickey finished

fink fink (on so) ♦ fink out (on so/sth) ♦ rat fink

Finn Mickey (Finn)

fire a five-alarm fire ♦ a three-alarm fire ♦ ball of fire ♦ fire so up ♦ fire sth up ♦ fire a line ♦

fire away ♦ fire up ♦ fired up ♦ on fire ♦ play with fire ♦ Where's the fire?

fireman visiting fireman

first the firstest with the mostest ♦ get to first (base) (with so)

fish big fish ♦ bottom fishing ♦ cold fish ♦ Fish or cut bait. ♦ fish story ♦ fish tale ♦ fish-fight ♦ fish-kiss ♦ fishing expedition ♦ queer fish ♦ smell fishy

fist hand over fist ♦ two-fisted drinker

fit conniption (fit) ♦ have a shit-fit ♦ If the shoe fits, wear it. ♦ throw a fit

five a five-alarm fire ♦ bunch of fives ♦ five it ♦ five-finger discount ♦ five-oh ♦ give so five ♦ Give me five! ♦ hang five ♦ high five ♦ low five ♦ nine-to-five ♦ slip so five ♦ Slip me five! ♦ take five

fix cop a fix ♦ fix-up ♦ fixed up ♦ fixing to die ♦ get a fix ♦ If it ain't broke don't fix it. ♦ If it ain't broke, fix it till it is. ♦ quick fix ♦ well-fixed

flake (flake) spoon ♦ flake (out) ♦ flake down ♦ flaked out ♦ joy flakes

flame burn with a low blue flame ♦ flame-war ♦ go down in flames ♦ old flame ♦ shoot so down in flames

flash flash on so ♦ flash on sth ♦ flash the hash ♦ in a flash

flat (flat) on one's ass ♦ flat broke ♦ flat out ♦ flat-ass ♦ flat-chested ♦ flat-hatting ♦ granny flat ♦ in nothing flat

flesh flesh-presser ♦ press (the) flesh

flick chick-flick ♦ skin flick

flight top-flight

fling fling up ♦ fling-wing

flip burger-flipper ♦ flip (out) ♦ flip one's lid ♦ flip one's wig ♦ flip so off ♦ flip so out ♦ flip so the bird ♦ flip over so/sth ♦ flip side ♦ flip the script ♦ flip-flop ♦ flipping burgers

flo Aunt Flo ♦ to up (from the flo up) ♦ visit from Flo

float float an air biscuit ♦ whatever floats your boat

flooey go flooey

floor mop the floor up with so ♦ rolling on the floor laughing (my ass off) ♦ wipe the floor up with so

flop cow flop ♦ flip-flop ♦ flopper-stopper ♦ That's the way the mop flops.

floss butt floss

flow cash flow ♦ go with the flow

flower hearts and flowers

flu blue flu ♦ brown bottle flu

flub flub (up) ♦ flub sth up ♦ flub the dub

fluid embalming fluid

flusher four-flusher

fly day the eagle flies ♦ fly kites ♦ fly light ♦ fly mink ♦ fly the coop ♦ fly trap ♦ fly-by-night ♦ flying-fuck ♦ Go fly a kite! ♦ I've got to fly. ♦ I('ve) gotta fly. ♦ on the fly ♦ straighten up and fly right ♦ when the eagle flies ♦ with flying colors

flyer take a flyer (on sth)

Flynn in like Flynn

fog the foggiest (idea)

fogey old fogey

fold folding money ♦ folding stuff ♦ green folding ♦ Hold some, fold some.

folks different strokes for different folks

food junk food ♦ rabbit food ♦ squirrel-food ♦ worm-food

fool play so for a fool

foot foot it ♦ foot-in-mouth disease ♦ have one foot in the grave ♦ My foot! ♦ shoot oneself in the foot ♦ wouldn't touch so/sth with a ten-foot pole

footwork fancy footwork ♦ fast footwork

force The Force

foreskins creamed foreskins

forget Forget it! ♦ Forget you!

fork fork sth over ♦ Fork you!

form in rare form

fort hold the fort

foul foul mouth ♦ foul up ♦ fouled up

found lost-and-found badge

foundry nut-foundry

four the sixty-four-dollar question ♦ four sheets (to the wind) ♦ four sheets in the wind ♦ four wheels ♦ four-bagger ♦ four-bits ♦ four-eyes ♦ four-flusher ♦ four-oh-four ♦ four-one-one ♦ four-topper ♦ ten-four ♦ twenty-four, seven ♦ two-by-four

fox a stone cold fox ♦ fox trap ♦ stone fox

foxtrot Charlie Foxtrot

fran San Fran

freak eagle freak ♦ eco freak ♦ freak (out) ♦ freaked (out) ♦ freak so out ♦ freak mommy ♦ fuck-freak ♦ garbage freak ♦ juice freak ♦ kick freak ♦ pill freak ♦ speed freak

free for free ♦ free lunch ♦ free ride ♦ free show ♦ free trip ♦ free-wheeling ♦ There ain't no such thing as a free lunch.

freeballing go freeball(ing)

freeze freeze so out ♦ freezer burn ♦ freezing cold ♦ play freeze-out ♦ put the freeze on so ♦ till hell freezes over

french Excuse my French. ♦ French kiss ♦ french-fried-fuck ♦ Pardon my French.

gate ♦ give so the go-by ♦ give so the nod ♦ give so the raspberry ♦ give so the shaft ♦ give so the slip ♦ give so up ♦ give a fuck (about so/sth) ♦ give a shit (about so/sth) ♦ give head ♦ Give it a rest! ♦ give it the gun ♦ Give it up! ♦ Give me (some) skin! ♦ Give me a break! ♦ Give me a rest! ♦ Give me five! ♦ Like I really give a shit! ♦ Something's got to give. ♦ What gives? ♦ You must have mistaken me for someone who gives a shit.

glad glad rags ♦ glad-hand ♦ glad-hander

glass glass gun ♦ glass(y)-eyed

glaze glazed (drunk) ♦ glazed (over)

glory morning glory ♦ send so to glory

gloss lip gloss

glove hand-in-glove

glow glow worm ♦ have a glow on

goat get so's goat ♦ skin a goat

god God willing and the creek don't rise ♦ God's acre ♦ has more money than God ♦ kiss the porcelain god ♦ pray to the enamel god ♦ pray to the porcelain god ♦ Where on (God's green) earth? ♦ Ye gods!

goddess hug the porcelain god(dess) ♦ sex goddess ♦ worship the porcelain god(dess)

goggle beer goggles ♦ goggle-eyed

goiter German goiter ♦ Milwaukee goiter

gold Columbian (gold) ♦ gold digger ♦ up in so's gold ones

golden golden handcuffs ♦ golden parachute ♦ golden-ager

golf African golf ball ♦ golf-clap

golly Good golly, Miss Molly!

goober goober-grabber ♦ goober-grease

gooch on the gooch

good (Good) gravy! ♦ (good) looker ♦ get (out) while the gettin(g)'s good ♦ get (out) while the goin's good ♦ get the goods on so ♦ give so a (good) talking to ♦ give so a (good) working over ♦ good and sth ♦ good buddy ♦ Good call! ♦ Good deal! ♦ Good golly, Miss Molly! ♦ Good heavens! ♦ good Joe ♦ good old boy ♦ good trip ♦ good-for-nothing ♦ good-time Charley ♦ good-time it ♦ good-time man ♦ good-to-go ♦ Have a good one. ♦ have good vibes ♦ if one knows what's good for one ♦ Johnny-be-good ♦ kiss sth good-bye ♦ no-good ♦ onto a good thing ♦ What's really good witcha? ♦ What's the (good) word? ♦ Your guess is as good as mine.

gooder do-gooder

goodie oldie but goodie

goodnik no-goodnik

goof goof sth up ♦ goof around ♦ goof off ♦ goof on so ♦ goof up ♦ goof-proof ♦ goofed (up)

goon goon squad ♦ goon-platoon

goose gone goose ♦ goose egg ♦ silver goose

gorgeous drop-dead gorgeous

gorilla gorilla biscuits ♦ gorilla juice ♦ gorilla pills

gourd stoned out of one's gourd

grab goober-grabber ♦ grab some bench ♦ How does that grab you? ♦ up for grabs

grade grade-grubber ♦ grade-grubbing

grape African grape ♦ belt the grape ♦ grape shot ♦ grape smugglers ♦ grapes of wrath ♦ in the grip of the grape

grass so's ass is grass ♦ ass is grass, so's ♦ grass party ♦ snake in the grass

grasshopper knee-high to a grasshopper

grave grave-dancer ♦ have one foot in the grave

gravy (Good) gravy! ♦ gravy train ♦ have gravy on one's grits ♦ red gravy

grease elbow-grease ♦ goober-grease ♦ grease so's palm ♦ grease monkey ♦ grease the skids ♦ greased lightning ♦ greasy spoon

great the great unwashed ♦ go great guns ♦ great divide ♦ no great shakes ♦ whopping (great)

green go green on so ♦ green apple quickstep ♦ green around the gills ♦ green folding ♦ green light ♦ green paper ♦ green stamps ♦ green stuff ♦ long green ♦ Where on (God's green) earth?

grin big fat grin ♦ tin grin

grind daily grind

grip in the grip of the grape ♦ key grip ♦ lose one's grip

gripe gripe one's ass ♦ gripe one's butt ♦ gripe one's soul

grits blow grits ♦ have gravy on one's grits

gritty get down to the nitty-gritty ♦ nitty-gritty

groceries blow one's groceries

grod King Grod

groove get in the groove ♦ groove on so/sth ♦ in the groove ♦ stone groove

groovy feel groovy

gross gross so out ♦ gross-out ♦ So gross!

ground field grounders ♦ ground-pounder ♦ know one's ass from a hole in the ground ♦ not know one's ass from a hole in the ground ♦ stamping ground ♦ stomping ground

grow not grow on trees

the head ♦ stoned out of one's head ♦ talk one's head off ♦ talking head ♦ turtle heading ♦ Use your head! ♦ where so's head is at ♦ yell one's head off ♦ zipper head

headache headache department ♦ headache house ♦ headache man

healed well-healed

heap bottom of the heap ♦ in a heap ♦ junk heap ♦ top of the heap

hear I hear what you are saying. ♦ I hear you. ♦ talk to hear one's own voice

heard You heard the man.

heart beef-hearts ♦ chicken-hearted ♦ eat one's heart out ♦ from the bottom of my heart ♦ heart-to-heart (talk) ♦ hearts and flowers

hearty party hearty

heat If you can't stand the heat, keep out of the kitchen. ♦ put the heat on so ♦ take some heat ♦ take the heat ♦ take the heat off so

heave old heave-ho

heaven bundle from heaven ♦ Good heavens! ♦ heaven dust ♦ pig heaven ♦ smell to (high) heaven

heavy carrying a (heavy) load ♦ heavy artillery ♦ heavy bread ♦ heavy date ♦ heavy hash ♦ heavy into so/sth ♦ heavy joint ♦ heavy money ♦ heavy scene ♦ heavy soul ♦ heavy-handed ♦ lay a (heavy) trip on so ♦ top heavy ♦ walk heavy ♦ wing heavy

heck for the heck of it ♦ What the heck!

heel cop a heel ♦ well-heeled

heil sieg-heil so

hell (as) sure as hell ♦ so/sth from hell ♦ been to hell and back ♦ for the hell of it ♦ from hell, so/sth ♦ give so hell ♦ hell around ♦ hell of a so/sth ♦ hell of a mess ♦ hell of a note ♦ hell raiser ♦ Hell's bells (and buckets of blood)! ♦ hell-on-wheels ♦ like a bat out of hell ♦ Like hell! ♦ play hell with so/sth ♦ quicker than hell ♦ raise hell ♦ raise hell (with so) ♦ raise hell (with sth) ♦ scare the hell out of so ♦ shot to hell ♦ snowball's chance in hell ♦ sure as hell ♦ There will be hell to pay. ♦ till hell freezes over ♦ to hell and gone ♦ To hell with that! ♦ What (in) the fucking hell! ♦ What (in) the hell? ♦ What the fucking hell! ♦ What the hell? ♦ Who (in) the hell? ♦ Who the hell?

help pitch in (and help)

hen hen fruit ♦ hen party

Henry Adam Henry

herb Herb and Al ♦ talk to Herb and Al

hermit bald-headed hermit

hey But, hey ♦ Hey, bum!

hide nail so('s hide) to the wall ♦ play hide the sausage

high going high ♦ high and dry ♦ high five ♦ high mucky-muck ♦ high on sth ♦ high roller ♦ high sign ♦ high ups ♦ high, wide, and handsome ♦ high-maintenance ♦ high-res ♦ higher ups ♦ hold one's high ♦ knee-high to a grasshopper ♦ on one's high horse ♦ smell to (high) heaven ♦ swing into high gear ♦ up high

hike take a hike

hill The Hill ♦ go over the hill ♦ over the hill ♦ What in (the) Sam Hill? ♦ What in Sam Hill? ♦ Where in (the) Sam Hill? ♦ Where the Sam Hill?

hind kiss so's hind tit ♦ suck so's hind tit

hindsight 20/20 hindsight ♦ twenty-twenty hindsight

hip hip-shooter ♦ hit me on the hip ♦ joined at the hip ♦ shoot from the hip

history ancient history ♦ I'm history.

hit can't hit the (broad) side of a barn ♦ hit so (up) for sth ♦ hit so below the belt ♦ hit so with sth ♦ hit by the stupid stick ♦ hit by the ugly stick ♦ hit it with so ♦ hit list ♦ hit man ♦ hit me again ♦ hit me on the hip ♦ Hit me. ♦ hit on so ♦ hit on sth ♦ hit pay dirt ♦ hit the books ♦ hit the booze ♦ hit the bottle ♦ hit the bricks ♦ hit the bull's-eye ♦ hit the ceiling ♦ hit the deck ♦ hit the fan ♦ hit the hay ♦ hit the jackpot ♦ hit the panic button ♦ hit the pavement ♦ hit the road ♦ hit the roof ♦ hit the sack ♦ hit the skids ♦ hit the spot ♦ hit the trail ♦ hit under the wing ♦ nose hit ♦ pinch hitter ♦ power hitter ♦ switch-hitter ♦ when the shit hits the fan

hitch without a hitch

hither come-hither look

hock hock a luggie ♦ in hock

hockey hockey-whore ♦ horse hockey ♦ play tonsil hockey ♦ tonsil hockey

hoe tough row to hoe

hog call hogs ♦ hog cadillac ♦ hog-wild ♦ road hog ♦ sewer hog

hold hold one's high ♦ hold one's horses ♦ hold one's liquor ♦ hold all the aces ♦ Hold everything! ♦ Hold it! ♦ Hold some, fold some. ♦ hold the fort ♦ Hold the phone! ♦ hold water ♦ lose one's hold ♦ no holds barred ♦ A-hole ♦ ace in the hole ♦ brown hole ♦ cake hole ♦ fart hole ♦ hole digger ♦ hole in the wall ♦ hole up ♦ in the hole ♦ know one's ass from a hole in the ground ♦ nineteenth hole ♦ not know one's ass from a

jeans cream one's jeans

jeebies heebie-jeebies

jerk circle-jerk ♦ jerk so around ♦ jerk so over ♦ jerk around ♦ jerk off ♦ knee-jerk ♦ tear-jerker

jewel family jewels

jiffy in a jiff(y)

jive blow jive ♦ jive talk ♦ jive turkey ♦ jive-ass ♦ pull jive

job an inside job ♦ blow job ♦ con job ♦ do a job on so/sth ♦ do a snow job on so ♦ hand job ♦ head-job ♦ hum job ♦ land a job ♦ nose job ♦ pull a job ♦ put-up job ♦ snow job ♦ wall job

jober (as) jober as a sudge ♦ jober as a sudge

jock rock-jock ♦ video jock

jockey bench jockey ♦ desk jockey ♦ disc jockey ♦ disk jockey

joe good Joe ♦ holy Joe ♦ Joe Blow ♦ Joe Citizen ♦ Joe College ♦ Joe Doakes ♦ Joe Schmo ♦ Joe Six-pack ♦ quality Joe

john big John ♦ Dear John letter ♦ John Doe ♦ John Hancock ♦ John(ny) Law ♦ Johnnie-come-lately ♦ Johnny-be-good ♦ square john ♦ square john broad ♦ who shot John

join Join the club. ♦ joined at the hip

joint blow the joint ♦ case the joint ♦ clip joint ♦ creep joint ♦ get one's nose out of joint ♦ heavy joint ♦ juice joint ♦ put so's nose out of joint ♦ square joint

joke dirty joke

jones scag jones ♦ skag jones

josé No way, José!

joy bundle of joy ♦ joy dust ♦ joy flakes ♦ joy juice ♦ joy ride ♦ joy water

judge (as) sober as a judge ♦ sober as a judge

jug federal jug ♦ jug up ♦ jug wine ♦ jugged (up)

juice big juice ♦ BO juice ♦ cactus juice ♦ cow juice ♦ gorilla juice ♦ happy juice ♦ idiot juice ♦ joy juice ♦ juice sth back ♦ juice sth up ♦ juice freak ♦ juice house ♦ juice joint ♦ juice racket ♦ juice up ♦ jungle juice ♦ juniper juice ♦ moo juice ♦ on the juice ♦ tiger juice ♦ tornado juice

jump Go jump in the lake! ♦ jump (street) ♦ jump so's bones ♦ jump bail ♦ jump smooth ♦ jump the gun ♦ jump-start ♦ jump-start so ♦ one jump ahead of so/sth ♦ puddle jumper ♦ Take a running jump (in the lake)!

jungle asphalt jungle ♦ jungle juice ♦ jungle mouth

junk junk bond ♦ junk fax ♦ junk food ♦ junk heap ♦ Junk it! ♦ junk squad ♦ junk tank ♦ on the junk

just (just) curl up and die ♦ just off the boat ♦ just the ticket ♦ just what the doctor ordered ♦ not just whistling Dixie

justice Truth, justice, and the American way.

kahuna big kahuna

keen peachy (keen)

keep for keeps ♦ If you can't stand the heat, keep out of the kitchen. ♦ keep one's cool ♦ keep one's head right ♦ keep one's nose clean ♦ keep cool ♦ Keep in touch. ♦ Keep it real! ♦ Keep on trucking. ♦ Keep out of this! ♦ Keep the faith (baby)! ♦ Keep your hands to yourself. ♦ Keep your nose out of my business! ♦ Keep your pants on! ♦ Keep your shirt on! ♦ play for keeps ♦ Where have you been keeping yourself?

key church key ♦ key figure ♦ key grip ♦ keyed (up) ♦ keyed up to the roof ♦ low-key

kibosh put the kibosh on sth

kick ass-kicker ♦ butt-kicker ♦ for kicks ♦ get one's kicks (from so/sth) ♦ get a kick out of so/sth ♦ kick (off) ♦ kick around ♦ kick ass ♦ kick back ♦ kick butt ♦ kick cold (turkey) ♦ kick down with sth ♦ kick freak ♦ kick in the (seat of the) pants ♦ kick in the ass ♦ kick in the butt ♦ kick in the guts ♦ kick in the rear ♦ kick in the teeth ♦ kick in the wrist ♦ kick it ♦ kick party ♦ kick some ass (around) ♦ kick some butt ♦ kick the bucket ♦ kick the habit ♦ kick the shit out of so ♦ kick up a storm ♦ kick-ass ♦ kick-ass on so

kid dead-end kid ♦ I kid you not. ♦ I'm not kidding. ♦ kid stuff ♦ kid-vid ♦ No kidding! ♦ punk kid ♦ snotnose(d) kid ♦ whiz kid

kill dressed to kill ♦ fill or kill ♦ I could tell you but then I'd have to kill you. ♦ kill for sth ♦ killed (off) ♦ killer weed ♦ killer-diller ♦ lady-killer ♦ make a killing

kilter out of kilter

kimono open (up) one's kimono

king Cash is king. ♦ King Grod ♦ King Kong pills ♦ King Kong specials

kingdom till kingdom come

kiss (Do) you kiss your momma with that mouth? ♦ air kiss ♦ ass-kisser ♦ ass-kissing ♦ baby-kisser ♦ fish-kiss ♦ French kiss ♦ kiss so/sth off ♦ kiss so's ass ♦ kiss so's hind tit ♦ kiss sth good-bye ♦ kiss sth off ♦ Kiss my ass! ♦ kiss of death ♦ kiss off ♦ kiss the dust ♦ kiss the porcelain god ♦ kiss up to so ♦ kiss-ass ♦ right in the kisser ♦ sealed with a kiss ♦ soul kiss ♦ You kiss your momma with that mouth?

kitchen everything but the kitchen sink ♦ If you can't stand the heat, keep out of the kitchen.

kite fly kites ♦ Go fly a kite!

kitten have kittens ♦ sex kitten

knee knee-deep in sth ♦ knee-deep navy ♦ knee-high to a grasshopper ♦ knee-jerk ♦ knee-mail ♦ up to one's knees

knife long knife

knob get one's knob polished

knock knock so's block off ♦ knock so's socks off ♦ knock so dead ♦ knock so off ♦ knock so out ♦ knock so some skin ♦ knock so up ♦ knock sth back ♦ knock sth down ♦ knock sth into a cocked hat ♦ knock sth off ♦ knock sth out ♦ knock sth together ♦ knock around ♦ knock back a drink ♦ knock boots ♦ Knock it off! ♦ knock off (work) ♦ knock one back ♦ knock one back ♦ knock one over ♦ knock one over ♦ knock over sth ♦ knock some heads together ♦ knock the dew off the lily ♦ knock the habit ♦ knock the shit out of so ♦ knocked in ♦ knocked out ♦ knocked up ♦ You could have knocked me over with a feather. ♦ knockdown drag-out fight

knot balloon knot ♦ tie the knot

know Damned if I know. ♦ Don't I know it! ♦ for all I know ♦ if one knows what's good for one ♦ in the know ♦ know one's ass from a hole in the ground ♦ know all the angles ♦ know from sth ♦ know shit from Shinola ♦ know the score ♦ know what's what ♦ know where so is coming from ♦ know where it's at ♦ know which end is up ♦ know-how ♦ know-it-all ♦ like, you know ♦ not know beans (about sth) ♦ not know from nothing ♦ not know one's ass from a hole in the ground ♦ not know shit about sth ♦ not know shit from shinola ♦ the end of the world as we know it ♦ You don't know the half of it.

knowledge drop so some knowledge ♦ knowledge in, bullshit out ♦ knowledge-box

knuckle knuckle bones ♦ knuckle down (to sth) ♦ knuckle sandwich ♦ knuckle under (to so/sth) ♦ knuckle-dragger ♦ white knuckler ♦ white-knuckle

kong Hong Kong dog ♦ King Kong pills ♦ King Kong specials

kush purple kush

lady boss lady ♦ foxy lady ♦ ladies' room ♦ lady bear ♦ Lady Snow ♦ lady-killer ♦ old lady

♦ till the fat lady sings ♦ when the fat lady sings

lake Go jump in the lake! ♦ Take a running jump (in the lake)!

lam on the lam ♦ take it on the lam

lamb two shakes of a lamb's tail

lamppost between you, me, and the lamppost

land land a blow ♦ land a job

lane Mammary Lane

language speak so's language

lap lap dancer ♦ lap dancing ♦ Make a lap!

lard lard ass ♦ tub of lard

large Living large.

last last roundup ♦ last straw ♦ on one's last legs ♦ so last year

lately Johnnie-come-lately

later Catch you later. ♦ Later, gator. ♦ See you later, alligator. ♦ See you later.

lather work oneself (up) into a lather

latrine latrine lips ♦ latrine rumor ♦ latrine wireless

laugh belly laugh ♦ Don't make me laugh! ♦ horse laugh ♦ laugh at the carpet ♦ laughing academy ♦ laughing soup ♦ laughing water ♦ liquid laugh ♦ rolling on the floor laughing (my ass off)

laundry dirty laundry

lavender lay so out in lavender

law the law ♦ bend the law ♦ John(ny) Law ♦ long arm of the law ♦ There Ought to be a law!

lawn mow one's lawn ♦ mow the lawn

lay laid back ♦ laid out ♦ laid to the bone ♦ lay (some) rubber ♦ lay so out ♦ lay so out in lavender ♦ lay sth on so ♦ lay sth out ♦ lay a (heavy) trip on so ♦ lay a guilt trip on so ♦ lay an egg ♦ lay down ♦ lay it on the line ♦ lay off (so/sth) ♦ lay one on ♦ lay some sweet lines on so

lead fill so full of lead ♦ Get the lead out! ♦ go over like a lead balloon ♦ have lead in one's pencil ♦ lead poisoning

league big league ♦ play in the big leagues

leak take a leak

leash have one's brain on a leash ♦ on a tight leash

leave leave so cold ♦ make like a tree and leave ♦ Take it or leave it.

left hang a left ♦ left coast ♦ left-handed monkey wrench ♦ out in left field ♦ out of left field

leg Break a leg! ♦ have a leg up on so ♦ leg work ♦ on one's last legs ♦ peg-leg ♦ pull so's leg ♦ shake a leg ♦ stretch one's legs

legal legal-beagle ♦ legal-eagle

legged loop-legged

legree Simon Legree

less I could(n't) care less.

let let a fart ♦ Let her rip! ♦ let it all hang out ♦ Let it roll! ♦ let off (some) steam ♦ let one ♦ Let's bump this place! ♦ Let's do lunch (sometime). ♦ Let's do the lunch thing. ♦ Let's dump. ♦ Let's have it! ♦ let sth ride

letter dead letter ♦ Dear John letter ♦ red-letter day

level level one's locks ♦ level best ♦ level the locks ♦ level with so ♦ on the level

lick a lick and a promise ♦ ass-licker ♦ dicky-licker ♦ lick sth into shape

licking ass-licking

licorice licorice pizza ♦ licorice stick

lid blow one's lid ♦ blow the lid off sth ♦ flip one's lid ♦ lid poppers ♦ lid proppers ♦ skid-lid

lie lie doggo ♦ lie like a rug ♦ No lie! ♦ pack of lies

life facts of life ♦ Get a life! ♦ Life's a bitch, then you die. ♦ low-life ♦ See you in another life. ♦ You bet your sweet life!

lift lift one's elbow ♦ lift-up

light fly light ♦ green light ♦ idiot light ♦ light bulb ♦ light into so ♦ light stuff ♦ lights out ♦ once over lightly ♦ out like a light ♦ punch so's lights out

lightning greased lightning ♦ lightning rod

lily knock the dew off the lily ♦ lily-livered ♦ shake the dew off the lily

limit the sky's the limit ♦ go the limit

line the bottom line ♦ blow one's lines ♦ do a line ♦ fire a line ♦ go down the line ♦ hook, line, and sinker ♦ lay it on the line ♦ lay some sweet lines on so ♦ line one's own pocket(s) ♦ out of line ♦ put some sweet lines on so ♦ run down some lines ♦ stag line

linen dirty linen

lip Button your lip! ♦ fat lip ♦ get lip ♦ in a lip lock ♦ latrine lips ♦ lip gloss ♦ Read my lips! ♦ Watch my lips! ♦ Zip (up) your lip! ♦ Zip your lip!

liquid liquid cork ♦ liquid laugh ♦ liquid lunch

liquor hard liquor ♦ hold one's liquor

list crap-list ♦ drop-dead list ♦ hit list ♦ shit-list ♦ sucker list ♦ wish list

listen I'm listening. ♦ listen up

lit half-lit ♦ lit up

little (little) pinkie ♦ have a little visitor ♦ little black book ♦ little boy blue ♦ little boys' room ♦ little girls' room ♦ little shit

live (live) wire ♦ (Well,) pardon me for living! ♦ all the way live ♦ Excuse me for living! ♦ how the other half lives ♦ How ya living? ♦ living chilly ♦ Living large. ♦ Pardon me for living! ♦ where so lives

liver chopped liver ♦ lily-livered

load carrying a (heavy) load ♦ dump one's load ♦ get a load of sth or so ♦ get a load off one's feet ♦ get a load off one's mind ♦ have a load on ♦ loaded for bear ♦ loaded to the barrel ♦ loaded to the gills ♦ one brick shy of a load ♦ take a load off one's feet ♦ three bricks shy of a load

lock goldie locks ♦ in a lip lock ♦ level one's locks ♦ level the locks ♦ locked down ♦ Turn your caps lock off!

loco plumb loco

log dog-log

long ain't long enough ♦ long arm of the law ♦ long bread ♦ long dozen ♦ long green ♦ long knife ♦ long shot ♦ long story short ♦ Long time no see. ♦ long-tall-Sally ♦ So long. ♦ take the (long) count

look (good) looker ♦ a look-see ♦ be on the look out ♦ come-hither look ♦ dirty look ♦ Here's looking at you. ♦ Look (at) what the cat dragged in! ♦ look after number one ♦ Look alive! ♦ Look who's talking!

loop fruit loop ♦ loop-legged ♦ throw so for a loop

loose at loose ends ♦ cut one's wolf loose ♦ cut loose ♦ hang loose ♦ have a loose screw ♦ have a screw loose ♦ loose cannon ♦ play fast and loose (with so/sth) ♦ stay loose ♦ tear loose (from so/sth) ♦ tongue loosener

lord drug lord ♦ Lord love a duck!

lose lose (all) one's marbles ♦ lose one's cool ♦ lose one's doughnuts ♦ lose one's grip ♦ lose one's hold ♦ lose one's lunch ♦ lose one's shirt ♦ lose a bundle ♦ lose it ♦ two-time loser ♦ Win a few, lose a few. ♦ Win some, lose some.

loss cut one's losses

lost Get lost! ♦ lost cause ♦ lost in the sauce ♦ lost-and-found badge

lot have a lot on the ball ♦ Lots of luck! ♦ take a lot of nerve

lotion motion-lotion

louie hang a louie

love (I) love it! ♦ (love) handles ♦ For the love of Mike! ♦ Lord love a duck! ♦ love bombs ♦ Love it! ♦ Love you! ♦ love-in ♦ puppy love ♦ tube steak of love

low the down low ♦ burn with a low blue flame ♦ low blow ♦ low five ♦ low rent ♦ low-key ♦ low-life ♦ low-res ♦ straight low

luck Better luck next time. ♦ Lots of luck! ♦ luck of the draw ♦ luck out ♦ lucky dog ♦ out of luck ♦ rotten luck ♦ shit out of luck ♦ tough luck

lucre filthy lucre

luggie hock a luggie

lump get one's lumps ♦ Like it or lump it! ♦ Lump it! ♦ take one's lumps

lunch blow (one's) lunch ♦ blow lunch ♦ eat so's lunch ♦ free lunch ♦ launch (one's lunch) ♦ Let's do lunch (sometime). ♦ Let's do the lunch thing. ♦ liquid lunch ♦ lose one's lunch ♦ out to lunch ♦ spot of lunch ♦ There ain't no such thing as a free lunch. ♦ toss one's lunch

lunger nose-lunger

mac Big Mac attack ♦ mac out

macarena cellular Macarena

machine sex-machine

mack mack daddy ♦ mack on so

mackerel Holy mackerel!

mad boiling (mad) ♦ get mad (at sth) ♦ hopping mad ♦ like mad ♦ mad money ♦ tap dance like mad

made have it made ♦ have it made in the shade ♦ tailor-made ♦ You made my day.

magazine girlie magazine

magic magic bullet ♦ magic mushrooms ♦ tragic-magic

magnet babe magnet ♦ chick magnet ♦ nerd magnet

mail knee-mail ♦ snail-mail ♦ main drag ♦ main squeeze ♦ main stash

maintenance high-maintenance

make Don't make a federal case out of it! ♦ Don't make me laugh! ♦ easy make ♦ Go ahead, make my day. ♦ It don't make (me) no nevermind. ♦ make (it) big ♦ make one's bed ♦ make oneself scarce ♦ make so ♦ make a boo-boo ♦ make a bundle ♦ make a federal case out of sth ♦ make a killing ♦ Make a lap! ♦ make a mountain ♦ make a pig of oneself ♦ make a pile ♦ make a score ♦ make a stink (about so/sth) ♦ make book on sth ♦ make drain babies ♦ make for somewhere ♦ make hamburger out of so/sth ♦ make it ♦ make it hot for so ♦ Make it snappy! ♦ make like so/sth ♦ make like a tree and leave ♦ make mincemeat out of so/sth ♦ Make my day! ♦ Make no mistake (about it)! ♦ make out ♦

make the scene ♦ make tracks ♦ make waves ♦ make with the sth ♦ make-out artist ♦ on the make ♦ put the make on so ♦ run a make on so ♦ Wanna make sumpin' of it? ♦ Want to make something of it? ♦ widow-maker

male male blindness ♦ male chauvinist pig

malfunction wardrobe malfunction

mama mama bear ♦ My mama didn't raise no dummy. ♦ red-hot mama ♦ yo mama

mambo mattress mambo

man the man ♦ big man on campus ♦ boss man ♦ candy man ♦ company man ♦ con man ♦ dead man ♦ dirty old man ♦ face man ♦ front man ♦ fuzz man ♦ G-man ♦ good-time man ♦ have a man by the balls ♦ headache man ♦ hit man ♦ my man ♦ old man ♦ one-man show ♦ point man ♦ repo man ♦ see a man about a dog ♦ So's your old man! ♦ stick man ♦ straight man ♦ strong-arm man ♦ T-man ♦ wheel man ♦ whiskers (man) ♦ white man's disease ♦ working man's smile ♦ You heard the man. ♦ You('re) the man!

mania merger-mania

manual Read the fucking manual!

map throw a map

marble have all one's marbles ♦ lose (all) one's marbles ♦ Marble City ♦ marble dome ♦ marble orchard

mare shank's mare

marine dead marine ♦ marine (recruit) ♦ marine officer

mark easy mark ♦ mark time ♦ skid marks ♦ X marks the spot.

market slave market ♦ spot market

Mary Mary J. ♦ Mary Jane

mash mish-mash

match the whole shooting match ♦ pissing-match

mate label mate

matter as a matter of fact

max grody to the max ♦ max out ♦ maxed out ♦ to the max

maximus dorkus maximus

maybe I don't mean maybe!

McCoy the (real) McCoy

meal meals rejected by Ethiopians ♦ meals rejected by the enemy ♦ square (meal)

mean a mean sth ♦ I don't mean maybe! ♦ lean and mean ♦ mean business

meat all (that) meat and no potatoes ♦ all meat and no potatoes ♦ beat one's meat ♦ beat the meat ♦ buzzard meat ♦ dog meat ♦ meat puppet ♦ meat wagon ♦ meat whistle ♦ mystery meat ♦ pound one's meat

medicine snakebite medicine ♦ off one's meds

meemie screaming-meemie ♦ screaming-meemies

meet nice meeting you

melvin give so a melvin

mental go mental ♦ mental giant ♦ mental midget

merchant speed merchant

mess hell of a mess ♦ mess so's face up ♦ mess so over ♦ mess so up ♦ mess about (with so) ♦ mess about (with sth) ♦ mess around (with so) ♦ mess around (with sth) ♦ messed up ♦ mess up ♦ mess with so/sth

message Get the message?

metal put the pedal to the metal

mickey Mickey (Finn) ♦ Mickey D's ♦ Mickey finished ♦ mickey mouse ♦ mickey mouse ears ♦ mickey mouse habit ♦ slip so a Mickey

middle middle of nowhere ♦ smack (dab) in the middle

midget mental midget

mike For the love of Mike!

mileage Your mileage may vary.

milk milk a duck ♦ tiger('s) milk

mill fill-mill ♦ gin mill ♦ run-of-the-mill ♦ through the mill

million like a million (dollars)

mincemeat make mincemeat out of so/sth

mind blow so's mind ♦ dirty-minded ♦ fuck so's mind (up) ♦ get a load off one's mind ♦ have one's mind in the gutter ♦ mind your own beeswax ♦ mind-bender ♦ mind-blower ♦ never mind ♦ one-track mind ♦ out of sight, out of mind

mine back to the salt mines ♦ data miner ♦ Your guess is as good as mine. ♦ Your place or mine?

mink fly mink

minute in a New York minute

mirror done by mirrors ♦ done with mirrors ♦ smoke and mirrors

miss Good golly, Miss Molly! ♦ miss the boat

missile morning missile

mistake Make no mistake (about it)! ♦ You must have mistaken me for someone who gives a shit.

mix mix it up (with so) ♦ mixed (up)

mobile nerd mobile

mode in one's sth mode

mojo on the mojo

moley Holy moley!

molly Good golly, Miss Molly! ♦ Molly whop so

moment blond moment ♦ senior moment

momma (Do) you kiss your momma with that mouth? ♦ You kiss your momma with that mouth?

mommy freak mommy

money shell out (an amount of money) ♦ easy money ♦ folding money ♦ front money ♦ funny money ♦ has more money than God ♦ heavy money ♦ hush money ♦ mad money ♦ money from home ♦ money grubber ♦ money talks ♦ on the money ♦ pull down an amount of money ♦ push money ♦ Put your money where your mouth is! ♦ smart money ♦ soft money ♦ spending money ♦ throw money at sth ♦ tight money

monkey crotch-monkey ♦ grease monkey ♦ have a monkey on one's back ♦ left-handed monkey wrench ♦ monkey around (with so) ♦ monkey around (with sth) ♦ monkey bite ♦ monkey business ♦ monkey swill ♦ monkey talk ♦ monkey wagon ♦ monkey wards ♦ monkey with so/sth ♦ monkey-fart ♦ powder monkey

monster meth monster ♦ monster weed

moo déjà moo ♦ moo juice

moon once in a blue moon

mop Earp slop, bring the mop. ♦ mop the floor up with so ♦ mopping-up operation ♦ That's the way the mop flops.

morals zipper morals

morning the morning after (the night before) ♦ morning glory ♦ morning missile

moss house moss

most the firstest with the mostest ♦ the most

mother dog's mother ♦ mother nature('s)

motor get so's motor running ♦ motor-mouth ♦ motorized rice

mountain (mountain) dew ♦ make a mountain

mounty county-mounty

mouse bald-headed mouse ♦ mickey mouse ♦ mickey mouse ears ♦ mickey mouse habit ♦ mouse potato ♦ one-eyed pants mouse ♦ word of mouse

mouth (Do) you eat with that mouth? ♦ (Do) you kiss your momma with that mouth? ♦ a mouth ♦ a mouth full of South ♦ bad-mouth ♦ big mouth ♦ diarrhea of the mouth ♦ dirty-mouth ♦ foot-in-mouth disease ♦ foul mouth ♦ garbage mouth ♦ have a big mouth ♦ jungle mouth ♦ motor-mouth ♦ mouth off ♦ mouth-breather ♦ poor-mouth ♦ potty mouth ♦ Put your money where your mouth is! ♦ ratchet-mouth ♦ run off at the mouth ♦ shoot one's

mouth off ♦ Shut your mouth! ♦ smart
mouth ♦ straight from the horse's mouth ♦
toilet mouth ♦ trash mouth ♦ Watch your
mouth! ♦ Well, wash my mouth out with
soap. ♦ You eat with that mouth? ♦ You kiss
your momma with that mouth?

move bust a move ♦ move on so ♦ put the
moves on so ♦ movers and shakers

mow mow one's lawn ♦ mow the lawn ♦ mow,
blow, and go

Mr. Mr. Big ♦ Mr. Hawkins ♦ Mr. Nice Guy ♦
Mr. Right ♦ Mr. Whiskers

muchachos adios muchachos

muck high mucky-muck ♦ muck sth up ♦ high
mucky-muck

mud (as) clear as mud ♦ clear as mud ♦
Here's mud in your eye. ♦ mud duck ♦ stick
in the mud

muff dive a muff

muffin cut a muffin ♦ meadow muffin ♦
stud-muffin

munch butt-munch ♦ munch out

murder scream bloody murder

Murphy Mrs. Murphy

mushrooms magic mushrooms ♦ sacred
mushrooms

music elevator music ♦ face the music ♦
musical beds ♦ Stop the music!

must a must (do) ♦ You must have mistaken
me for someone who gives a shit.

mustard cut the mustard

nab Uncle nab

nail coffin nail ♦ eat nails ♦ nail so to a cross
♦ nail so('s hide) to the wall ♦ nail Jell-O to a
cross ♦ nail Jell-O to a tree ♦ nail Jell-O to
the wall ♦ nail-em-and-jail-em

naked butt naked ♦ get naked ♦ naked truth

name the name of the game ♦ big name ♦
cigarette with no name ♦ Name your poison.
♦ no name cigarette ♦ take names ♦ what's
his name

nap take a dirt nap

narkied get narkied

nasty shag-nasty

natch on the natch

nature call of nature ♦ mother nature('s) ♦
nature stop ♦ nature's call

navy knee-deep navy

neck dead from the neck up ♦ get it in the
neck ♦ neck and neck ♦ pain in the neck ♦
shot in the neck ♦ turtle-neck ♦ up to one's
neck

need The baby needs shoes. ♦ That's all so
needs.

needle needle candy ♦ on the needle

Nellie nervous Nellie

nerd nerd magnet ♦ nerd mobile ♦ nerd pack
♦ tech-nerd

nerve bundle of nerves ♦ Of all the nerve! ♦
take a lot of nerve ♦ What (a) nerve!

nest empty-nesters ♦ nest egg

net net result ♦ surf the net

nevermind It don't make (me) no
nevermind.

new (brand) spanking new ♦ a whole new
ball game ♦ bad news ♦ in a New York
minute ♦ New York's finest ♦ spanking new ♦
tear so a new asshole ♦ That's a new one on
me. ♦ What else is new? ♦ What's new?

next Better luck next time.

nice Have a nice day. ♦ Have a nice one. ♦
Mr. Nice Guy ♦ nice meeting you ♦ nice
talking to you

nick full of Old Nick

nickel double nickels ♦ nickel and dime so (to
death) ♦ not worth a plugged nickel

night the morning after (the night before) ♦
fly-by-night ♦ night person ♦ one-night stand
♦ Saturday night special

nighter all-nighter

nine the whole nine yards ♦ dressed to the
nines ♦ nine-to-five ♦ sixty-nine

ninny bliss ninny

nit nit-picker ♦ nit-picking

nitty get down to the nitty-gritty ♦ nitty-
gritty

nizzle Fo shizzle, ma nizzle!

nobody a nobody ♦ like nobody's business ♦
There's nobody home.

nod get the nod ♦ give so the nod ♦ nodded
out

noggin Use your noggin!

noise big noise

non non compos ♦ non compos poopoo

noodle Use your noodle! ♦ wet noodle

nose brown-nose ♦ brown-noser ♦ cannot see
(any) further than the end of (one's) nose ♦
get one's nose cold ♦ get one's nose out of
joint ♦ Get your nose out of my business! ♦
hard-nosed ♦ have one's nose wide open ♦
keep one's nose clean ♦ Keep your nose out
of my business! ♦ nose (candy) ♦ nose habit
♦ nose hit ♦ nose job ♦ nose-burner ♦ nose-
lunger ♦ nose-warmer ♦ on the nose ♦
powder one's nose ♦ put one's nose in (where
it's not wanted) rub so's nose in sth ♦ see no
further than the end of one's nose ♦ stick one's
nose in (where it's not wanted) ♦ take it on

the nose ♦ take it through the nose ♦ wiener nose

nosebag put on the nosebag ♦ tie on the nosebag

nosedive take a nosedive

not the have-nots

notch pull one's belt in (a notch) ♦ take one's belt in (a notch)

note C-note ♦ century note ♦ hell of a note ♦ swap notes (on so/sth)

nothing abbreviated piece of nothing ♦ good-for-nothing ♦ in nothing flat ♦ not know from nothing ♦ Nothing doing! ♦ Nothing to it! ♦ nothing to sneeze at ♦ nothing to write home about ♦ nothing upstairs ♦ wearing (nothing but) a smile ♦ sweet nothings

now Bye-bye, for now. ♦ Ciao, for now. ♦ get one's tail somewhere now! ♦ now generation ♦ Now what? ♦ Now you're talking!

nowhere get nowhere fast ♦ middle of nowhere

nuke No nukes! ♦ nuke oneself ♦ Nuke it!

number A number 1 ♦ back number ♦ do a number on so ♦ do a number on sth ♦ have the wrong number ♦ hot number ♦ look after number one ♦ number crunching ♦ number one ♦ number two ♦ number-cruncher ♦ take care of number one

nut bug nut ♦ bust (one's) nuts to do sth ♦ bust a nut ♦ drive so nuts ♦ eco nut ♦ everything from soup to nuts ♦ fuck nut ♦ get one's nuts off ♦ nut factory ♦ nut up ♦ nut-foundry ♦ nuts and bolts ♦ Nuts to you! ♦ off one's nut ♦ talk like a nut ♦ tough nut to crack

nutty (as) nutty as a fruitcake ♦ nutty as a fruitcake

ocean boil the ocean

odd odd bird ♦ odd-bod ♦ odds-on

officer marine officer

oil banana oil ♦ castor oil artist ♦ idiot oil ♦ oil it ♦ palm-oil ♦ tongue oil ♦ well-oiled

okay Everything's going to be okay.

old the old one-two ♦ boring old fart ♦ dirty old man ♦ fucking old person ♦ full of Old Nick ♦ good old boy ♦ old flame ♦ old fogey ♦ old girl ♦ old hand (at sth) ♦ old hat ♦ old heave-ho ♦ old lady ♦ old man ♦ old school ♦ old skool ♦ old soldier ♦ old woman ♦ old-timer ♦ oldie but goodie ♦ rare old time ♦ same o(l)' same o(l)' ♦ same old story ♦ So's your old man!

once the once-over ♦ if I've told you once, I've told you a thousand times ♦ once in a blue moon ♦ once over lightly

one the old one-two ♦ back to square one ♦ bite the big one ♦ bust so one ♦ buy the big one ♦ cut one ♦ day one ♦ dead one ♦ fast one ♦ four-one-one ♦ frosty one ♦ hang one on ♦ Have a good one. ♦ Have a nice one. ♦ have one foot in the grave ♦ hoist one ♦ knock one back ♦ knock one back ♦ knock one over ♦ lay one on ♦ let one ♦ look after number one ♦ number one ♦ on the one hand ♦ one and one ♦ one brick shy of a load ♦ one finger salute ♦ one for the road ♦ one jump ahead of so/sth ♦ one of the faithful ♦ one smart apple ♦ one too many ♦ one-eyed pants mouse ♦ one-horse town ♦ one-man show ♦ one-night stand ♦ one-track mind ♦ paste so one ♦ pull a fast one ♦ quick one ♦ Run that by (me) one more time. ♦ short one ♦ take care of number one ♦ tall one ♦ Tell me another (one)! ♦ That's a new one on me. ♦ the big one ♦ tie one on ♦ wet one ♦ up in so's gold ones

open blow sth wide open ♦ bust so wide open ♦ bust sth wide open ♦ crack open a bottle ♦ eye-opener ♦ have one's nose wide open ♦ open (up) one's kimono ♦ wide open ♦ with (one's) eyes (wide) open

opera horse opera

operation mopping-up operation

operator big-time operator ♦ smooth operator

option All options stink.

oranges apples to oranges

orbit go into orbit ♦ in orbit

orchard marble orchard

order just what the doctor ordered ♦ tall order

other how the other half lives

ought There ought to be a law!

outie I'm outie.

outs the ins and outs ♦ on the outs (with so)

outside Baby it's cold outside. ♦ step outside ♦ You want to step outside?

overboard go overboard

own the devil's own time ♦ blow one's own horn ♦ cut one's own throat ♦ do one's (own) thing ♦ for sale by owner ♦ line one's own pocket(s) ♦ mind your own beeswax ♦ on one's own hook ♦ talk to hear one's own voice ♦ toot one's own horn ♦ You're on your own.

ox dumb ox

oyster The world is one's oyster.

ozone in the ozone

pace at a snail's pace

pack Joe Six-pack ♦ nerd pack ♦ pack of lies ♦ packing a gun ♦ six-pack

pad earth pads ♦ pad down (somewhere) ♦ pad out ♦ pussy pad

paddle up shit creek (without a paddle) ♦ up the creek (without a paddle)

page on the same page ♦ See you in the funny pages. ♦ take a page from so's book

pain feeling no pain ♦ give so a pain ♦ pain in the ass ♦ pain in the butt ♦ pain in the neck ♦ pain in the rear ♦ royal pain

paint Do I have to paint (you) a picture? ♦ paint remover ♦ paint the town (red) ♦ tonsil paint ♦ war paint

palace gin palace ♦ ice palace ♦ ptomaine-palace

palm grease so's palm ♦ palm so/sth off (on so) ♦ palm sth off on so ♦ palm-oil ♦ palm-presser

pamby namby-pamby

panic hit the panic button ♦ press the panic button ♦ push the panic button

panky hanky-panky

pants cream (in) one's pants ♦ dust so's pants ♦ get in(to) so's pants ♦ have ants in one's pants ♦ have hot pants (for so) ♦ Keep your pants on! ♦ kick in the (seat of the) pants ♦ one-eyed pants mouse ♦ pants rabbits ♦ scare the pants off so ♦ smarty-pants ♦ sue the pants off (of) so ♦ wear the pants (in the house)

paper bad paper ♦ go peddle your papers ♦ green paper ♦ hot paper ♦ paper over sth ♦ paper-hanger ♦ paper-pusher ♦ walking papers

parachute golden parachute

parade rain on so's parade

pardon (Well,) pardon me for living! ♦ if you'll pardon the expression ♦ Pardon me for living! ♦ Pardon my French.

park park it (somewhere) ♦ park the pink Plymouth ♦ trailer park trash

parker nosy parker

parlor sauce parlor

party grass party ♦ hen party ♦ keg party ♦ kick party ♦ party animal ♦ party bowl ♦ party down ♦ party hearty ♦ Party on! ♦ party-pooper ♦ petting-party ♦ pot party ♦ stag-party ♦ tailgate party ♦ tea party

pass gas-passer ♦ pass for sth ♦ pass go ♦ pass the buck

paste get pasted ♦ paste so one ♦ paste sth on so

pat stand pat (on sth)

patootie You bet your sweet patoot(ie)!

patrol bush patrol

pavement hit the pavement

pay hit pay dirt ♦ pay one's dues ♦ pay one's dues (to society) ♦ pay a call ♦ pay the water bill ♦ strike pay dirt ♦ There will be hell to pay. ♦ You get what you pay for.

peanut for peanuts ♦ peanut head

peas (as) alike as (two) peas in a pod ♦ alike as (two) peas in a pod

pedal put the pedal to the metal ♦ soft pedal sth

peddle go peddle your papers ♦ pill-peddler

peep another peep (out of you)

peeve pet peeve

peg peg so ♦ peg out ♦ peg-leg ♦ square peg (in a round hole)

pencil have lead in one's pencil ♦ pencil-pusher

penny penny-ante ♦ penny-pincher ♦ pretty penny

people people processor ♦ street people

pep pep pill ♦ pep talk ♦ pepped (up)

pepper pepper-upper ♦ salt and pepper

percenter ten percenter

period honeymoon (period)

person day person ♦ fucking old person ♦ night person

personal up close and personal

pet pet peeve ♦ petting-party

Pete For Pete's sake!

peter Peter Jay ♦ peter out

phat phat blunt ♦ phat-phree

pheasant crotch-pheasant

phone Hold the phone! ♦ talk on the big white phone

phony (as) phony as a three-dollar bill ♦ phony as a three-dollar bill

phree phat-phree

pick cotton-picking ♦ nit-picker ♦ nit-picking ♦ pick up on sth ♦ pick-me-up ♦ roach pick

picture Do I have to draw (you) a picture? ♦ Do I have to paint (you) a picture? ♦ Get the picture? ♦ out of the picture ♦ take pictures

pie cutie pie ♦ pie hole ♦ pie in the sky ♦ pie-eyed

piece (You) want a piece of me? ♦ a cold piece of work ♦ abbreviated piece of nothing ♦ piece (of the action) ♦ piece of ass ♦ piece of cake ♦ piece of snatch ♦ piece of tail ♦ think-piece ♦ Want a piece of me?

pifky mifky-pifky (in the bushes)

pig bush pig ♦ make a pig of oneself ♦ male chauvinist pig ♦ pig heaven ♦ pig out

pigeon clay pigeon ♦ pigeon-eyed ♦ stool (pigeon)

pile make a pile ♦ pile of shit

pill go-pills ♦ gorilla pills ♦ happy pills ♦ idiot pills ♦ King Kong pills ♦ on the pill ♦ pep pill ♦ pill freak ♦ pill-dropper ♦ pill-peddler ♦ pill-popper ♦ pill-pusher ♦ pill-roller ♦ poison pill ♦ take a chill pill

pillar send so from pillar to post

pilot sky-pilot

pimp popcorn pimp

pincher penny-pincher

pink (as) gay as pink ink ♦ gay as pink ink ♦ in the pink ♦ park the pink Plymouth ♦ pink elephants ♦ pink slip ♦ pink spiders ♦ pink-slipped ♦ seeing pink elephants ♦ seeing pink spiders ♦ tickled (pink)

pinkie (little) pinkie

pipe hash pipe ♦ pipe down ♦ Put that in your pipe and smoke it! ♦ set of pipes ♦ take the gas pipe ♦ take the pipe

pipeline in the pipeline

piss piss so off ♦ piss sth away ♦ piss around ♦ piss blood ♦ piss elegant ♦ piss factory ♦ piss in the wind ♦ piss off ♦ piss on so/sth ♦ Piss on it! ♦ piss quiz ♦ piss-cutter ♦ piss-poor ♦ piss-whiz ♦ pissed (off) (at so/sth) ♦ pissed off about so/sth ♦ pissing-match ♦ take a piss ♦ take the piss out of so

pit bottomless pit ♦ passion-pit ♦ pit stop

pitch pitch (the) woo ♦ pitch a bitch ♦ pitch a tent ♦ pitch in (and help) ♦ Pitch it

pitchforks rain pitchforks

pity For pity's sake!

pizza licorice pizza ♦ pizza-face ♦ pizza-puss ♦ road pizza

place bust out (of some place) ♦ between a rock and a hard place ♦ Let's bump this place! ♦ tear into a place ♦ wide place in the road ♦ Your place or mine?

plan game plan

planker two-planker

plaster plastered to the wall ♦ pleasantly plastered

plate step up to the plate

platoon goon-platoon

play the way it plays ♦ grandstand play ♦ in play ♦ play so for a fool ♦ play around (with so) ♦ play ball (with so) ♦ play fast and loose (with so/sth) ♦ play for keeps ♦ play freeze-out ♦ play hardball (with so) ♦ play hell with so/sth ♦ play hide the sausage ♦ play hooky ♦ play in the big leagues ♦ play it cool ♦ play the devil with so/sth ♦ play the dozens ♦ play

tonsil hockey ♦ play with a full deck ♦ play with fire ♦ squeeze play

plea cop a plea

pledge take the pledge

plop cow plop

plow plowed (under) ♦ plowing water

plug not worth a plugged nickel ♦ plug-ugly ♦ plugged in ♦ pull the plug (on so/sth)

plumb half a bubble off plumb ♦ plumb loco

plumbing check out the plumbing ♦ visit the plumbing

plunge take the plunge

Plymouth park the pink Plymouth

pocket deep pockets ♦ line one's own pocket(s) ♦ out of pocket ♦ pocket of time ♦ pocket pool ♦ pocket-rocket

pod (as) alike as (two) peas in a pod ♦ alike as (two) peas in a pod

point And your point is? ♦ brownie points ♦ point man ♦ three point two ♦ touch a sore point

pointy pointy end ♦ pointy-head

poison lead poisoning ♦ Name your poison. ♦ poison pill

pole half up the pole ♦ pole dancer ♦ pole dancing ♦ up the pole ♦ wouldn't touch so/sth with a ten-foot pole

polish apple-polisher ♦ get one's knob polished ♦ polished (up) ♦ shoe polish ♦ spit and polish

pony baloney pony ♦ dog and pony show

poo icky-poo ♦ poo-poo

pooh poo(h)-poo(h)

pool dirty pool ♦ pocket pool ♦ pool-hopping

poop party-pooper ♦ poop chute ♦ poop out ♦ poop sheet ♦ pooped (out) ♦ pooper-scooper

poopoo non compos poopoo

poor piss-poor ♦ poor boy ♦ poor-mouth

pop jab pop ♦ pop (some) tops ♦ pop one's cork ♦ pop for sth ♦ pop off ♦ pop the question ♦ pop wine ♦ pop-eyed ♦ take a pop at so ♦ What's poppin'

popper eye-popper ♦ lid poppers ♦ pill-popper ♦ skull-popper

porcelain bow to the porcelain altar ♦ drive the porcelain bus ♦ hug the porcelain god(dess) ♦ kiss the porcelain god ♦ pray to the porcelain god ♦ ride the porcelain bus ♦ worship the porcelain god(dess)

pores air one's pores

pork pork hammer ♦ pork out

poser mod poser

posilutely absotively (posilutely)

post send so from pillar to post

postal go postal

pot pot boiler ♦ pot hound ♦ pot party ♦ pot sniffer ♦ sex pot ♦ Shit or get off the pot! ♦ up pot

potato all (that) meat and no potatoes ♦ all meat and no potatoes ♦ couch potato ♦ drop so/sth like a hot potato ♦ hot potato ♦ mouse potato ♦ potato soup ♦ small potatoes

pound give one one's pounds ♦ gravel-pounder ♦ ground-pounder ♦ pound one's ear ♦ pound one's meat ♦ pound so's head in ♦ pound sth out ♦ pound a beer ♦ pound some beers ♦ pound the books

powder chicken powder ♦ powder one's nose ♦ powder monkey ♦ powder one's face ♦ powder room ♦ powder up ♦ powdered (up) ♦ take a powder

power power hitter ♦ power tool

pray pray to the enamel god ♦ pray to the porcelain god

president dead president ♦ President Wilson

press flesh-presser ♦ palm-presser ♦ press (the) flesh ♦ press the panic button

pretty pretty penny ♦ sitting pretty

primo (el) primo

problem No problem

processor people processor

program get with the program

promise a lick and a promise

proof drool-proof ♦ goof-proof

propell self-propelled sandbag

propper lid proppers

prowl on the prowl ♦ owl-prowl

prune full of prunes

psych psych so out ♦ psych so up ♦ psych out ♦ psyched (out) ♦ psyched (up)

ptomaine ptomaine-domain ♦ ptomaine-palace

public go public ♦ take sth public

pucky bull-pucky

pud pull one's pud

puff cream puff

puke the pukes ♦ puke hole

pull pull one's belt in (a notch) ♦ pull one's pud ♦ pull one's punches ♦ pull one's wire ♦ pull oneself off ♦ pull so's chain ♦ pull so's leg ♦ pull sth off ♦ pull a boner ♦ pull a fast one ♦ pull a job ♦ pull an attitude ♦ pull chocks ♦ pull down an amount of money ♦ pull jive ♦ pull out all the stops ♦ pull the plug (on so/sth)

pump pump (so) up ♦ pump (some) iron ♦ pump sth up ♦ pump iron ♦ pump ship ♦ pump up ♦ pumped (up)

pumpkin some pumpkins ♦ some punkins

punch bunch-punch ♦ get one's ticket punched ♦ pull one's punches ♦ punch so's lights out ♦ punch so out ♦ punch-drunk ♦ rabbit punch ♦ roundhouse punch ♦ Sunday punch ♦ telegraph one's punches ♦ throw a punch

punk plastic punk ♦ punk kid ♦ punk out

pup beat the pup

puppet fuck puppet ♦ meat puppet ♦ puppy love

purge the urge to purge

purpose accidentally-on-purpose

push cookie pusher ♦ if push comes to shove ♦ paper-pusher ♦ pencil-pusher ♦ pill-pusher ♦ push money ♦ push the panic button ♦ pushing up daisies ♦ street pusher ♦ when push comes to shove

puss glamour puss ♦ pizza-puss

pussy pussy fart ♦ pussy pad ♦ pussy-whipped ♦ wood-pussy

put put the clamps on so/sth ♦ put one's nose in (where it's not wanted) ♦ put oneself straight ♦ put so/sth out of the way ♦ put so's nose out of joint ♦ put so away ♦ put so on ♦ put so out of the way ♦ put so to bed with a shovel ♦ put so up ♦ put sth away ♦ put sth on the street ♦ put a con on so ♦ Put a cork in it! ♦ put a damper on sth ♦ put a smile on so's face ♦ Put a sock in it! ♦ put balls on sth ♦ Put it in their back yard! ♦ put on the dog ♦ put on the feedbag ♦ put on the nosebag ♦ put on the ritz ♦ put some distance between so and so/sth ♦ put some sweet lines on so ♦ Put that in your pipe and smoke it! ♦ put the arm on so ♦ put the bite on so ♦ put the finger on so ♦ put the freeze on so ♦ put the heat on so ♦ put the kibosh on sth ♦ put the make on so ♦ put the moves on so ♦ put the pedal to the metal ♦ put the screws on so ♦ put the skids under so/sth ♦ put the squeeze on so ♦ put them together for so ♦ put to bed with a shovel ♦ put to it ♦ put too much on it ♦ Put up or shut up! ♦ put your hands together for so ♦ Put your money where your mouth is! ♦ put-down ♦ put-up job ♦ rode hard and put away wet

putt putt-putt

queen ice queen

queer (as) queer as a three-dollar bill ♦ queer as a three-dollar bill ♦ queer fish ♦ queer for sth ♦ queer-beer

question the sixty-four-dollar question ♦ pop the question ♦ There's no such thing as a stupid question.

quick quick buck ♦ quick fix ♦ quick one ♦ quick-and-dirty ♦ quicker than hell

quickstep green apple quickstep

quit quit while one is ahead ♦ Quit your bellyaching!

quiz piss quiz

quote cuff quote ♦ quote, unquote

rabbit pants rabbits ♦ rabbit food ♦ rabbit punch

race rat race

rack crack-rack ♦ rack (out) ♦ rack sth up ♦ rack duty ♦ rack face ♦ rack time ♦ rack up ♦ racked (up)

racket juice racket

rad way rad

rag chew the rag ♦ glad rags ♦ on the rag ♦ rag on so ♦ rag out ♦ soldier rag ♦ talk so ragged ♦ wet rag

rain (as) right as rain ♦ rain closet ♦ rain on so/sth ♦ rain on so's parade ♦ rain pitchforks ♦ right as rain

raise My mama didn't raise no dummy. ♦ raise a stink (about so/sth) ♦ raise Cain ♦ raise hell ♦ raise hell (with so) ♦ raise hell (with sth) ♦ raise the devil (with so) ♦ raise the devil (with sth) ♦ hell raiser

rake rake sth in ♦ rake on so

ralph call ralph ♦ cry ralph ♦ hang a ralph ♦ ralph sth up

ranch raisin ranch

ranger rump-ranger

rank rank so (out) ♦ rank and file ♦ rank on so

rap (rap) sheet ♦ bad rap ♦ beat the rap ♦ bum rap ♦ rap session ♦ take the rap (for sth)

rare in rare form ♦ rare bird ♦ rare old time ♦ raring to go

rash road-rash

raspberry give so the raspberry

rat frat-rat ♦ hood rat ♦ rat (on so) ♦ rat around ♦ rat fink ♦ rat out ♦ rat race ♦ rat-bastard ♦ rug rat ♦ sack rat ♦ smell a rat ♦ the rats

rate cut-rate

rattle rattle-trap ♦ slightly rattled

ray bag some rays ♦ catch some rays

reaction gut reaction (to sth)

read Read my lips! ♦ Read the fucking FAQ! ♦ Read the fucking instructions! ♦ Read the fucking manual!

ready (Are you) ready for this? ♦ Ready for this? ♦ rough and ready

real 4 real ♦ the (real) McCoy ♦ for real ♦ Get real! ♦ Keep it real! ♦ real bitch ♦ real gone

really Like I really give a shit! ♦ What's really good witcha?

rear get off one's rear ♦ kick in the rear ♦ pain in the rear ♦ rear (end) ♦ rear-ender

reason no earthly reason

recruit marine (recruit)

red cam (red) ♦ paint the town (red) ♦ red gravy ♦ red hot ♦ red ink ♦ red tide ♦ red-hot mama ♦ red-letter day ♦ see red

reject meals rejected by Ethiopians ♦ meals rejected by the enemy

remark snide remark

remember can't remember a fucking thing ♦ can't remember shit

remover paint remover

rent low rent ♦ room for rent

repellent shark repellent

requisition moonlight requisition

rest Give it a rest! ♦ Give me a rest!

result net result

rev rev sth up ♦ revved (up)

revenge Montezuma's revenge

rhyme run one's rhymes

rice as the white on rice ♦ like the white on rice ♦ motorized rice ♦ rice-rocket

rich filthy rich ♦ stinking rich ♦ strike it rich ♦ too rich for so's blood

ride free ride ♦ joy ride ♦ let sth ride ♦ ride shotgun ♦ ride the porcelain bus ♦ thumb a ride

right (as) right as rain ♦ (bang) dead to rights ♦ (right) up one's alley ♦ all right ♦ All right already! ♦ Am I right? ♦ be right back ♦ dead to rights ♦ get right ♦ gets one right here ♦ hang a right ♦ have so dead to rights ♦ keep one's head right ♦ Mr. Right ♦ right as rain ♦ right guy ♦ right in the kisser ♦ Right on! ♦ sail (right) through sth ♦ serve so right ♦ step right up ♦ straighten up and fly right ♦ Yeah, right!

rilla on the rilla

ring pudding ring ♦ ring a bell ♦ ring off the hook ♦ ring the bell ♦ throw one's hat in the ring

ringer (dead) ringer (for so) ♦ ringer (for so)

rinso go Rinso

shinola know shit from Shinola ♦ No Shinola! ♦ not know shit from shinola ♦ tell shit from Shinola

ship pump ship ♦ shape up or ship out

shirt Been there, done that (got the T-shirt). ♦ Keep your shirt on! ♦ lose one's shirt ♦ stuffed shirt

shit (as) close as stink on shit ♦ the shits ♦ bad shit ♦ beat the shit out of so ♦ can't remember shit ♦ chicken shit ♦ cling like shit to a shovel ♦ close as stink on shit ♦ crock (of shit) ♦ day the eagle shits ♦ diddly-shit ♦ doodly-shit ♦ Eat shit! ♦ Fuck it, shit happens, drive on. ♦ fuck-shit ♦ full of shit ♦ get one's shit together ♦ give a shit (about so/sth) ♦ have a shit-fit ♦ have shit for brains ♦ hot shit ♦ jack-shit ♦ kick the shit out of so ♦ knock the shit out of so ♦ know shit from Shinola ♦ Like I really give a shit! ♦ little shit ♦ No shit! ♦ No shit, Sherlock! ♦ not know shit about sth ♦ not know shit from shinola ♦ pile of shit ♦ shit a brick ♦ Shit happens. ♦ shit on so ♦ shit on a shingle ♦ Shit or get off the pot! ♦ shit out of luck ♦ shit work ♦ shit-ass ♦ shit-bag ♦ shit-faced ♦ shit-hooks ♦ shit-house ♦ shit-list ♦ shitty end of the stick ♦ shoot the shit ♦ stick like shit to a shovel ♦ take a shit ♦ tell shit from Shinola ♦ tough shit ♦ up shit creek (without a paddle) ♦ when the shit hits the fan ♦ You must have mistaken me for someone who gives a shit.

shithouse built like a brick shithouse

shitless scared shitless

shitload metric shitload

shizzle fo shizzle ♦ Fo shizzle, ma nizzle! ♦ full of shizzle

shock sticker shock

shoe The baby needs shoes. ♦ goody two-shoes ♦ gym shoe ♦ If the shoe fits, wear it. ♦ shoe polish

shoestring on a shoestring

shook (all) shook up ♦ shook up

shoot the whole shooting match ♦ hip-shooter ♦ shoot one's breakfast ♦ shoot one's cookies ♦ shoot one's mouth off ♦ shoot one's supper ♦ shoot one's wad ♦ shoot oneself in the foot ♦ shoot so/sth down ♦ shoot so down in flames ♦ shoot for the sky ♦ shoot from the hip ♦ shoot the breeze ♦ shoot the bull ♦ shoot the cat ♦ shoot the crap ♦ shoot the dozens ♦ shoot the shit ♦ shoot the works ♦ shoot up ♦ shoot up (on sth) ♦ shoot-out ♦ shooting iron ♦ skeet-shooting ♦ square shooter ♦ straight shooter

shop chop-shop ♦ cop-shop ♦ happy shop ♦ hook shop ♦ sweat-shop

short the short end of the stick ♦ the shorts ♦ case of the shorts ♦ Eat my shorts! ♦ have so by the short hairs ♦ have a short fuse ♦ long story short ♦ short fuse ♦ short one ♦ short-snort

shot one's best shot ♦ big shot ♦ call (all) the shots ♦ cheap shot ♦ grape shot ♦ long shot ♦ mug shot ♦ parting shot ♦ shot down ♦ shot in the arm ♦ shot in the dark ♦ shot in the neck ♦ shot to hell ♦ shot to the curb ♦ shot-away ♦ shot-up ♦ take a shot (at sth) ♦ who shot John

shotgun call shotgun ♦ ride shotgun ♦ shotgun wedding

shoulder straight from the shoulder

shove if push comes to shove ♦ when push comes to shove

shovel cling like shit to a shovel ♦ put so to bed with a shovel ♦ put to bed with a shovel ♦ stick like shit to a shovel

show all show and no go ♦ dog and pony show ♦ free show ♦ get the show on the road ♦ girlie show ♦ no show ♦ one-man show ♦ show and tell ♦ show biz ♦ That's show business (for you).

showtime (It's) showtime!

shuck (Aw) shucks! ♦ shuck down

shut get some shut-eye ♦ Put up or shut up! ♦ shut up ♦ Shut your face! ♦ Shut your mouth! ♦ Shut your trap! ♦ shut-eye

shy one brick shy of a load ♦ three bricks shy of a load

sick bang in (sick) ♦ sick (up) ♦ sick to death (of so/sth)

side can't hit the (broad) side of a barn ♦ flip side ♦ on the safe side ♦ on the side ♦ sunny-side up ♦ wrong side of the tracks

sidewalk sidewalk superintendent ♦ sidewalk surfing

sierra Bravo Sierra

sight out of sight ♦ out of sight, out of mind

sign high sign ♦ Nebraska sign ♦ O-sign ♦ Q-sign

silly stoned silly

silver silver bullet ♦ silver goose

simple pure and simple

sin (as) ugly as sin ♦ sin-bin ♦ ugly as sin

sing till the fat lady sings ♦ when the fat lady sings

sink everything but the kitchen sink ♦ hook, line, and sinker ♦ sink one's teeth into sth

sister (soul) sister ♦ sob sister ♦ weak sister

sit sitting duck ♦ sitting pretty

situation no-win situation

six check your six ♦ deep six ♦ double six ♦ eighty-six ♦ Joe Six-pack ♦ on your six ♦ six feet under ♦ six-bits ♦ six-pack

sixty the sixty-four-dollar question ♦ sixty-nine

size That's about the size of it.

skag skag jones ♦ skagged out

sketch thumbnail sketch

skid grease the skids ♦ hit the skids ♦ on the skids ♦ put the skids under so/sth ♦ skid marks ♦ skid row ♦ skid row bum ♦ skid-lid

skillet home skillet

skin Give me (some) skin! ♦ knock so some skin ♦ skin a goat ♦ skin flick ♦ skin game ♦ Skin me! ♦ thick-skinned ♦ thin-skinned

skinful have a skinful

skinny (hot) skinny

skip skip (out) ♦ Skip it!

skittles beer and skittles

skool old skool

skrill fat skrill

skull out of one's skull ♦ skull-buster ♦ skull-popper

sky the sky's the limit ♦ aim for the sky ♦ eye-in-the-sky ♦ pie in the sky ♦ reach for the sky ♦ shoot for the sky ♦ sky hook ♦ sky rug ♦ sky-pilot

slam bitch slammer ♦ slam a beer ♦ slam dunk ♦ slam some beers ♦ slam-bang

slap a slap in the face ♦ slap so's wrist ♦ slap so on the wrist ♦ slap happy ♦ slap-dab ♦ slap-dash

slave slave away (at sth) ♦ slave market

sled ghetto sled

sleep a wink of sleep ♦ beauty sleep ♦ sleep it off

sleeve have an ace up one's sleeve

slice frog slicing ♦ It's been a slice! ♦ slice of the action

slim iceberg slim

slime slime bag ♦ slime bucket

sling hash-slinger ♦ have one's ass in a sling ♦ ink slinger ♦ sling the cat

slingshot double-barreled slingshot

slip give so the slip ♦ pink slip ♦ slip (up) ♦ slip one's trolley ♦ slip so a Mickey ♦ slip so five ♦ Slip me five!

slop Earp slop, bring the mop.

slough slough (off) ♦ sloughed (up)

slow do a slow burn ♦ slow burn ♦ take it slow ♦ twist (slowly) in the wind

sly on the sly

smack dick smack ♦ smack (dab) in the middle ♦ smack the road

small small beer ♦ small change ♦ small fry ♦ small potatoes ♦ small-time

smart get smart (with so) ♦ one smart apple ♦ smart ass ♦ smart cookie ♦ smart guy ♦ smart money ♦ smart mouth ♦ smarty-pants ♦ street smart ♦ street smarts

smell I smell you. ♦ smell a rat ♦ smell blood ♦ smell fishy ♦ smell it up ♦ smell like a rose ♦ smell the stuff ♦ smell to (high) heaven

smile plumber's smile ♦ put a smile on so's face ♦ Smile when you say that. ♦ wearing (nothing but) a smile ♦ working man's smile

smoke blow smoke ♦ chain(-smoke) ♦ chain-smoker ♦ Put that in your pipe and smoke it! ♦ smoke and mirrors ♦ smoke both ends of the cigar ♦ smoke eater ♦ smoke like a chimney ♦ smoke-filled room ♦ smoke-in ♦ Smokey (the Bear) ♦ smoking gun

smooth jump smooth ♦ smooth operator

smuggler grape smugglers

snail at a snail's gallop ♦ at a snail's pace ♦ snail-mail

snake seeing snakes ♦ snake eyes ♦ snake in the grass ♦ trouser snake

snap Make it snappy! ♦ snap one's cookies ♦ snap sth up ♦ snap course ♦ Snap it up! ♦ snap out of sth ♦ snap to (attention) ♦ Snap to it! ♦ snapped (up)

snatch piece of snatch

sneeze nothing to sneeze at

sniffer pot sniffer ♦ whiff-sniffer ♦ wiff-sniffer

snit in a snit

snort ringtailed snorter ♦ rip snorter ♦ short-snort

snot blow a snot rocket ♦ blow snot rockets

snow do a snow job on so ♦ have snow on the roof ♦ Lady Snow ♦ snow bunny ♦ snow job ♦ snow stuff

snuff snuff so (out) ♦ snuff film ♦ snuff it ♦ up to snuff

soak Go soak your head! ♦ Go soak yourself! ♦ soak one's face

soap no soap ♦ soft soap ♦ Well, wash my mouth out with soap.

sob sob sister ♦ sob story

sober (as) sober as a judge ♦ cold sober ♦ sober as a judge ♦ sober up ♦ stone (cold) sober ♦ stone sober

society pay one's dues (to society)

sock close combat sock ♦ knock so's socks off ♦ Put a sock in it! ♦ rubber sock ♦ sock hop ♦

Sock it to me! ♦ socked in ♦ Stuff a sock in it! ♦ sweat sock ♦ walking on rocky socks ♦ wet sock

soft soft berth ♦ soft core ♦ soft in the head ♦ soft money ♦ soft on so ♦ soft on so/sth ♦ soft pedal sth ♦ soft sell ♦ soft soap ♦ soft touch ♦ soft-core ♦ walk soft

sold sold cober ♦ sold on so/sth

soldier dead soldier ♦ old soldier ♦ soldier rag

son son of a bitch ♦ son of a gun

sore stick out like a sore thumb ♦ touch a sore point

sorry sorry 'bout that ♦ sorry about that ♦ sorry-ass(ed)

soul (soul) brother ♦ (soul) sister ♦ gripe one's soul ♦ heavy soul ♦ soul kiss ♦ thirsty soul

sound sound off (about sth) ♦ Sounds like a winner!

soup alphabet soup ♦ cat-soup ♦ everything from soup to nuts ♦ in the soup ♦ laughing soup ♦ potato soup ♦ soup sth up ♦ soup sandwich ♦ Soup's on! ♦ soup-strainer ♦ souped up

sour go sour

south a mouth full of South ♦ go South ♦ head South ♦ southern-fried

space space so out ♦ space cadet ♦ space out ♦ spaced (out)

spade in spades

spank (brand) spanking new ♦ spanking new

spaz have a spaz ♦ spaz around ♦ spaz down ♦ spaz out

speak speak so's language ♦ Speak it! ♦ speak of the devil

spear take the spear (in one's chest)

special King Kong specials ♦ Saturday night special

speed faster than a speeding bullet ♦ speed demon ♦ speed freak ♦ speed merchant

spend big-time spender ♦ spending money

spider barking spider ♦ pink spiders ♦ seeing pink spiders ♦ trumpet spider

spiff spiffed out ♦ spiffed up

spill spill one's guts (to so) ♦ spill one's guts on so ♦ spill the beans ♦ spill the works

spin spin one's wheels ♦ spin doctor

spit spit and polish ♦ Spit it out! ♦ swap spits ♦ within spitting distance

spleen vent one's spleen

split I've got to split. ♦ lickety-split ♦ split a gut ♦ split up

sponge sponge off so ♦ throw in the sponge ♦ toss in the sponge

spoon (flake) spoon ♦ greasy spoon

spot C-spot ♦ hit the spot ♦ spot so (sth) ♦ spot market ♦ spot of lunch ♦ ten-spot ♦ tight spot ♦ X marks the spot.

spring spring so ♦ spring chicken ♦ spring for sth

sprung half-sprung

spud sofa spud

spun get spun

squabble corn squabble

squad goon squad ♦ junk squad

square back to square one ♦ Be there or be square. ♦ square (meal) ♦ square apple ♦ square biscuit ♦ square john ♦ square john broad ♦ square joint ♦ square off ♦ square peg (in a round hole) ♦ square shooter ♦ square with so ♦ squared away ♦ squared up ♦ three squares

squash stoned out of one's squash

squat (doodly-)squat ♦ cop a squat ♦ diddly-squat ♦ take a squat

squeak narrow squeak ♦ squeaky clean

squeeze (squeeze-)box ♦ budget squeeze ♦ main squeeze ♦ put the squeeze on so ♦ squeeze play ♦ duck-squeezer

squiff on the squiff ♦ squiff out

squirrel seam-squirrels ♦ squirrel sth away ♦ squirrel out of sth ♦ squirrel-food

squirt the squirts ♦ take a squirt

stack blow one's stack ♦ stack the deck ♦ swear on a stack of Bibles

stag stag line ♦ stag-party

stage honeymoon stage

stake stake so/sth out ♦ stake so to sth ♦ up stakes

stamp green stamps ♦ stamp so out ♦ stamping ground

stand If you can't stand the heat, keep out of the kitchen. ♦ one-night stand ♦ stand so up ♦ stand pat (on sth) ♦ stand tall ♦ stand there with one's bare face hanging out ♦ stand-in ♦ stand-out ♦ taco stand

star see stars

starch take the starch out of so

start jump-start ♦ jump-start so

stash main stash

station comfort station ♦ filling station ♦ fuzz station ♦ Grand Central Station ♦ thirst-aid station

statistic vital statistics

stay stay loose ♦ Stay tuned.

steak bake the tube steak ♦ pimp steak ♦ tube steak ♦ tube steak of love

steam blow off (some) steam ♦ let off (some) steam ♦ steam so's beam ♦ steam so up ♦ steam up ♦ steamed (up)

steer bum steer

step Aztec two-step ♦ step off the curb ♦ Step on it! ♦ step out on so ♦ step outside ♦ step right up ♦ step up to the plate ♦ stepped on ♦ You want to step outside?

steven even-Steven

stew half-stewed ♦ stew bum ♦ stewed (up) ♦ stewed to the ears ♦ stewed to the gills

stick the short end of the stick ♦ boom sticks ♦ bumper sticker ♦ cancer stick ♦ carry the stick ♦ get on the stick ♦ hit by the stupid stick ♦ hit by the ugly stick ♦ licorice stick ♦ shitty end of the stick ♦ Stick 'em up! ♦ stick one's nose in (where it's not wanted) ♦ stick so with sth ♦ stick around ♦ stick in the mud ♦ stick it to so ♦ stick like shit to a shovel ♦ stick man ♦ stick out like a sore thumb ♦ stick shift ♦ sticker shock ♦ sticky fingers ♦ swizzle-stick

stiff scared stiff ♦ working stiff

stink (as) close as stink on shit ♦ All options stink. ♦ big stink ♦ close as stink on shit ♦ holy stink ♦ like stink ♦ make a stink (about so/sth) ♦ raise a stink (about so/sth) ♦ stink on ice ♦ stinking (drunk) ♦ stinking rich ♦ stinking with sth

stock deal stock ♦ stocking-stuffer ♦ story stock

stoke stoke sth up ♦ stoked (on so/sth) ♦ stoked out

stomach turn so's stomach

stomp stomp (on) so ♦ stomping ground

stone a stone cold fox ♦ stone (cold) sober ♦ stone blind ♦ stone broke ♦ stone dead ♦ stone fox ♦ stone groove ♦ stone sober ♦ stoned (out) ♦ stoned out of one's gourd ♦ stoned out of one's head ♦ stoned out of one's squash ♦ stoned silly

stool stool (on so) ♦ stool (pigeon)

stop bullet-stopper ♦ flopper-stopper ♦ nature stop ♦ pit stop ♦ pull out all the stops ♦ stop on a dime ♦ Stop the music!

storage in cold storage

store candy store ♦ dime store ♦ leeky store

stork visit from the stork

storm kick up a storm ♦ up a storm

story bedtime story ♦ fish story ♦ long story short ♦ same old story ♦ sob story ♦ story stock ♦ top story ♦ upper story

straight Damn straight! ♦ get straight ♦ go straight ♦ put oneself straight ♦ straight arrow

♦ straight dope ♦ straight from the horse's mouth ♦ straight from the shoulder ♦ straight low ♦ straight man ♦ straight shooter ♦ straight talk ♦ straight up ♦ straight-faced ♦ straighten up and fly right

strainer soup-strainer

strap strap so with so/sth ♦ super-strap ♦ yank one's strap

straw last straw ♦ straw boss

streak have a yellow streak down one's back ♦ talk a blue streak

street the street ♦ easy street ♦ jump (street) ♦ on easy street ♦ on the street ♦ put sth on the street ♦ street cred ♦ street people ♦ street pusher ♦ street smart ♦ street smarts ♦ street sweeper ♦ street time ♦ street-casting ♦ take it to the street ♦ two-way street

stress no stress

stretch in the (home) stretch ♦ stretch one's legs

strike strike it rich ♦ strike out ♦ strike pay dirt

stroke different strokes for different folks

strong come on strong ♦ strong-arm ♦ strong-arm man ♦ strong-arm tactics

strung strung (up) ♦ strung out ♦ strung-out shape

stuck stuck on so/sth ♦ stuck-up

stuff and stuff like that (there) ♦ fluff-stuff ♦ folding stuff ♦ get one's stuff together ♦ green stuff ♦ hot stuff ♦ kid stuff ♦ light stuff ♦ rough stuff ♦ smell the stuff ♦ snow stuff ♦ stocking-stuffer ♦ strut one's stuff ♦ stuff one's face ♦ Stuff a sock in it! ♦ stuffed shirt ♦ That's the stuff!

stupid get stupid ♦ hit by the stupid stick ♦ stupid fresh ♦ stupid-ass ♦ There's no such thing as a stupid question.

style dog-style

suck dick-sucker ♦ egg-sucker ♦ It sucks. ♦ suck (some) brew ♦ suck (some) suds ♦ suck so's hind tit ♦ suck sth up ♦ suck face ♦ suck up to so ♦ sucker so into sth ♦ sucker for so/sth ♦ sucker list ♦ That sucks. ♦ That's so suck!

sudge (as) jober as a sudge ♦ jober as a sudge

suds bust (some) suds ♦ crack some suds ♦ in the suds ♦ suck (some) suds ♦ suds-swiller

sue (So,) sue me! ♦ Sue me! ♦ sue the pants off (of) so

sugar sugar daddy ♦ Uncle Sugar

suit all over so like a cheap suit ♦ blue suit ♦ tree-suit

sun sun belt ♦ where the sun don't shine

sunday Sunday best ♦ Sunday driver ♦ Sunday punch

sunshine walk on sunshine

super super-dooper ♦ super-duper ♦ super-strap

superintendent sidewalk superintendent

supper shoot one's supper

sure (as) sure as hell ♦ for sure ♦ I am so sure! ♦ sure as hell ♦ sure thing

surf channel surfer ♦ channel surfing ♦ sidewalk surfing ♦ surf the net

swallow hard to swallow ♦ swallow the dictionary ♦ sword swallowing

swap swap notes (on so/sth) ♦ swap spits

swear swear like a trooper ♦ swear on a stack of Bibles

sweat Don't sweat it! ♦ in a cold sweat ♦ no sweat ♦ sweat sth out ♦ sweat blood ♦ sweat bullets ♦ sweat sock ♦ sweat-shop ♦ tiger sweat

sweep clean sweep ♦ street sweeper

sweet fresh and sweet ♦ lay some sweet lines on so ♦ put some sweet lines on so ♦ sweet nothings ♦ You bet your sweet life! ♦ You bet your sweet patoot(ie)!

swill monkey swill ♦ swill-up ♦ suds-swiller

swing not enough room to swing a cat ♦ swing both ways ♦ swing into high gear ♦ swing shift ♦ swing with so/sth

swipe take a swipe at so/sth

switch asleep at the switch ♦ switch off ♦ switch on ♦ switch-hitter ♦ switched on

sync out of sync

system All systems are go.

table box on the table ♦ table-hop ♦ under the table

tack brass tacks ♦ coffin tack ♦ ticky-tacky

taco taco stand ♦ toss one's tacos

tactic strong-arm tactics

tag toe tag

tail bright-eyed and bushy-tailed ♦ fuzzy (tail) ♦ Get one's tail somewhere fast! ♦ get one's tail somewhere immediately! ♦ get one's tail somewhere now! ♦ Get off my tail! ♦ Go chase your tail! ♦ have a tiger by the tail ♦ hunk of tail ♦ on so's tail ♦ piece of tail ♦ tail-end ♦ turn tail (and run) ♦ two shakes of a lamb's tail ♦ work one's tail off

take double take ♦ have what it takes ♦ on the take ♦ take one's belt in (a notch) ♦ take one's lumps ♦ take so/sth apart ♦ take so/sth off ♦ take so/sth on ♦ take so in ♦ take so off ♦ take so out ♦ take so to the cleaners ♦ take sth out ♦ take sth public ♦ take a bath (on sth) ♦ take a beating ♦ take a break ♦ take a chill pill ♦ take a crack at sth ♦ take a crap ♦ take a dig at so ♦ take a dirt nap ♦ take a dive ♦ take a dump ♦ take a fall ♦ take a flyer (on sth) ♦ take a gander (at so/sth) ♦ take a hike ♦ take a jab at so ♦ take a leak ♦ take a load off one's feet ♦ take a lot of nerve ♦ take a nosedive ♦ take a page from so's book ♦ take a piss ♦ take a pop at so ♦ take a powder ♦ Take a running jump (in the lake)! ♦ take a shit ♦ take a shot (at sth) ♦ take a squat ♦ take a squirt ♦ take a swipe at so/sth ♦ take a walk ♦ take a whack at so/sth ♦ take a whack at sth ♦ take care of so ♦ take care of number one ♦ take care of numero uno ♦ Take care. ♦ take five ♦ take it ♦ Take it down a thou(sand)! ♦ take it easy ♦ take it on the chin ♦ take it on the lam ♦ take it on the nose ♦ Take it or leave it. ♦ take it out on so/sth ♦ take it slow ♦ take it through the nose ♦ take it to the street ♦ take names ♦ take off ♦ take on fuel ♦ take pictures ♦ take some doing ♦ take some heat ♦ take the (long) count ♦ take the cure ♦ take the fall ♦ take the fifth ♦ take the gas pipe ♦ take the heat ♦ take the heat off so ♦ take the pipe ♦ take the piss out of so ♦ take the pledge ♦ take the plunge ♦ take the rap (for sth) ♦ take the spear (in one's chest) ♦ take the starch out of so ♦ take the wind out of so's sails ♦ take things easy ♦ take-off artist ♦ takes two to tango ♦ taking care of business ♦ You can't take it with you.

tale fairy tale ♦ fish tale ♦ tale of woe

talk give so a (good) talking to ♦ heart-to-heart (talk) ♦ jive talk ♦ Look who's talking! ♦ money talks ♦ monkey talk ♦ nice talking to you ♦ Now you're talking! ♦ pep talk ♦ straight talk ♦ talk one's head off ♦ talk so's ear off ♦ talk so ragged ♦ talk a blue streak ♦ talk big ♦ talk like a nut ♦ talk on the big white phone ♦ talk through one's hat ♦ talk to earl ♦ talk to hear one's own voice ♦ talk to Herb and Al ♦ talk turkey ♦ talk until one is blue in the face ♦ talking head

tall in tall cotton ♦ long-tall-Sally ♦ stand tall ♦ tall in the saddle ♦ tall one ♦ tall order ♦ tall timbers ♦ walk tall

tango takes two to tango ♦ Tango Yankee

tank avenue tank ♦ drunk tank ♦ junk tank ♦ on a tank ♦ on the tank ♦ tank up ♦ tanked up ♦ think-tank

tap on tap ♦ tap so (for sth) ♦ tap dance like mad ♦ tap out ♦ tapped out

tar whale the tar out of so

target on-target

task on task

taste so bad one can taste it ♦ taste blood

tat temp-tat

tatas bodacious tatas

tattoo screwed, blued, and tattooed

taxi Tijuana taxi

tea cup of tea ♦ tea party

teach That'll teach so.

tear tear so/sth apart ♦ tear so/sth up ♦ tear so a new asshole ♦ tear so up ♦ tear into so ♦ tear into sth ♦ tear into a place ♦ tear loose (from so/sth) ♦ tear off ♦ tear-jerker ♦ That tears it!

tease brain-teaser

Technicolor Technicolor yawn ♦ throw a Technicolor yawn

tee tee so off ♦ tee-tee ♦ teed (up) ♦ teed off

teeth dressed to the teeth ♦ drop one's teeth ♦ get one's teeth into sth ♦ kick in the teeth ♦ sink one's teeth into sth ♦ tinsel-teeth

tell Do tell. ♦ I could tell you but then I'd have to kill you. ♦ show and tell ♦ tell so what to do with sth ♦ tell so where to get off ♦ Tell it like it is! ♦ Tell me another (one)! ♦ tell shit from Shinola ♦ tell the (whole) world

ten a ten ♦ hang ten ♦ ten percenter ♦ ten-four ♦ ten-spot ♦ wouldn't touch so/sth with a ten-foot pole

tenda my tenda

tenor whiskey tenor

tent pitch a tent

terror holy terror

thank thank you very much ♦ thanks a bunch ♦ Thanks in advance.

thigh thunder-thighs

thin thin dime ♦ thin-skinned ♦ walk on thin ice

thing the in thing to do ♦ can't remember a fucking thing ♦ do one's (own) thing ♦ do the drink thing ♦ do the drug thing ♦ girl thing ♦ guy thing ♦ Let's do the lunch thing. ♦ onto a good thing ♦ sure thing ♦ take things easy ♦ There ain't no such thing as a free lunch. ♦ There's no such thing as a stupid question.

think think-box ♦ think-piece ♦ think-tank ♦ You've got another think coming.

third third degree ♦ third wheel

thirst thirst-aid station ♦ thirsty soul

thirteen file thirteen

thong butt thong

thou holier-than-thou

thousand if I've told you once, I've told you a thousand times ♦ Take it down a thou(sand)!

three (as) phony as a three-dollar bill ♦ (as) queer as a three-dollar bill ♦ a three finger salute ♦ a three-alarm fire ♦ phony as a three-dollar bill ♦ queer as a three-dollar bill ♦ seven-seven-three-aitch ♦ three bricks shy of a load ♦ three point two ♦ three sheets (to the wind) ♦ three sheets in the wind ♦ three squares ♦ three-two

throat cut one's own throat ♦ die of throat trouble ♦ ram sth down so's throat ♦ throat gag

throne the throne ♦ hug the throne ♦ on the throne ♦ throne room

throw throw one's cookies ♦ throw one's hat in the ring ♦ throw one's voice ♦ throw one's weight around ♦ throw one out on one's ear ♦ throw so for a loop ♦ throw sth back ♦ throw sth together ♦ throw a fight ♦ throw a fit ♦ throw a game ♦ throw a map ♦ throw a punch ♦ throw a Technicolor yawn ♦ throw down ♦ throw in the sponge ♦ throw in the towel ♦ throw money at sth ♦ throw salt on so's game ♦ throw the book at so ♦ throw the bull ♦ throw the crap ♦ throw up one's toenails ♦ throw-away

thumb stick out like a sore thumb ♦ thumb a ride ♦ thumbs down ♦ thumbs up ♦ turn thumbs down (on so/sth) ♦ twiddle one's thumbs ♦ under so's thumb

thunder thunder-boomer ♦ thunder-thighs

tick (as) tight as a tick ♦ a few ticks ♦ tick so off ♦ tick-tock ♦ ticked (off) ♦ tight as a tick

ticket big-ticket ♦ buy so's woof ticket ♦ get one's ticket punched ♦ just the ticket ♦ sell a woof ticket ♦ sell woof tickets ♦ That's the ticket!

tickle rib-tickler ♦ tickle the ivories ♦ tickled (pink)

tide red tide

tie tie it on ♦ tie on the nosebag ♦ tie one on ♦ tie the knot ♦ tie-in ♦ tied up ♦ tongue-tied

tiger have a tiger by the tail ♦ tiger juice ♦ tiger sweat ♦ tiger('s) milk ♦ (as) tight as a tick ♦ on a tight leash ♦ screwed tight ♦ tight as a tick ♦ tight money ♦ tight spot ♦ tight wad ♦ tighten one's belt

till If it ain't broke, fix it till it is. ♦ till hell freezes over ♦ till kingdom come ♦ till the fat lady sings

timber tall timbers

time doss down (for some time) ♦ a devil of a time ♦ the devil's own time ♦ bean time ♦ Better luck next time. ♦ big time ♦ big-time operator ♦ big-time spender ♦ do time ♦ down time ♦ face time ♦ game time ♦ good-time Charley ♦ good-time it ♦ good-time man ♦ hard time ♦ have a whale of a time ♦ if I've told you once, I've told you a thousand times ♦ Long time no see. ♦ mark time ♦ old-timer ♦ pocket of time ♦ rack time ♦ rare old time ♦ rough time ♦ Run that by (me) one more time. ♦ sack time ♦ small-time ♦ street time ♦ Time (out)! ♦ time to cruise ♦ two-time ♦ two-time loser ♦ two-timer ♦ up time

tin tin cow ♦ tin dog ♦ tin grin ♦ tin hat

tiny patter of tiny feet

tip tip one's hand ♦ tip-off

tire spare tire

tit ass over tit ♦ bitch tits ♦ go tits up ♦ kiss so's hind tit ♦ suck so's hind tit ♦ tits and ass ♦ tits up ♦ Tough titty!

titanic go Titanic

tizzy in a tizzy

toe camel toes ♦ toe jam ♦ toe tag ♦ turn one's toes up

toehold get a toehold

toenail throw up one's toenails ♦ get one's act together ♦ get one's head together ♦ get one's shit together ♦ get one's stuff together ♦ get it (all) together ♦ have it all together ♦ knock sth together ♦ knock some heads together ♦ put them together for so ♦ put your hands together for so ♦ throw sth together

toilet toilet mouth ♦ toilet water

toke harsh toke

told if I've told you once, I've told you a thousand times

tomorrow like there was no tomorrow

ton like a ton of bricks ♦ tons of sth

tongue tongue in cheek ♦ tongue loosener ♦ tongue oil ♦ tongue-tied ♦ Watch your tongue!

tonsil play tonsil hockey ♦ tonsil bath ♦ tonsil hockey ♦ tonsil paint ♦ tonsil varnish

tool garden tool ♦ power tool ♦ tool around ♦ rooting-tooting

toothpicks H-E-double-toothpicks

top big top ♦ blow one's top ♦ come out on top ♦ four-topper ♦ pop (some) tops ♦ top banana ♦ top brass ♦ top dog ♦ top heavy ♦ top of the heap ♦ top story ♦ top-drawer ♦ top-flight ♦ two-topper

topsy topsy-boozy ♦ topsy-turvy

tore tore (up) ♦ tore back ♦ tore down ♦ torn (up)

toss toss one's cookies ♦ toss one's lunch ♦ toss one's tacos ♦ toss sth off ♦ toss in the sponge ♦ Toss it! ♦ toss off ♦ toss-up

totally totally awesome ♦ totally clueless

totsy hotsy-totsy

touch Keep in touch. ♦ soft touch ♦ touch a sore point ♦ touch and go ♦ touch base (with so) ♦ touchy-feely ♦ wouldn't touch so/sth with a ten-foot pole

tough hang tough (on sth) ♦ tough sth out ♦ tough break ♦ tough cookie ♦ tough cookies ♦ tough customer ♦ tough egg to crack ♦ tough guy ♦ tough luck ♦ tough nut to crack ♦ tough row to hoe ♦ tough shit ♦ Tough titty!

towel crying towel ♦ throw in the towel

tower ivory tower

town A-town ♦ Bean Town ♦ blow town ♦ Chi(town) ♦ Get out of town! ♦ go to town ♦ one-horse town ♦ paint the town (red)

track make tracks ♦ off the track ♦ one-track mind ♦ railroad tracks ♦ wrong side of the tracks

trade tricks of the trade

trail hit the trail

trailer trailer park trash ♦ trailer trash

train gravy train

transfer celestial transfer

trap bear trap ♦ fly trap ♦ fox trap ♦ rattle-trap ♦ Shut your trap! ♦ tourist trap

trash Cash is trash. ♦ trailer park trash ♦ trailer trash ♦ Trash it! ♦ trash mouth

tree Christmas tree ♦ Go climb a tree! ♦ make like a tree and leave ♦ nail Jell-O to a tree ♦ not grow on trees ♦ tree-suit ♦ up a tree

trick a hat trick ♦ do the trick ♦ How's tricks? ♦ trick on so ♦ tricks of the trade ♦ turn a trick ♦ whole bag of tricks

trip bad trip ♦ bum trip ♦ day-tripper ♦ down trip ♦ ego trip ♦ ego tripper ♦ free trip ♦ good trip ♦ head trip ♦ lay a (heavy) trip on so ♦ lay a guilt trip on so ♦ round tripper ♦ tripped out

triple triple whammy ♦ triple-bagger

trolley off one's trolley ♦ slip one's trolley

trooper swear like a trooper

trot the trots ♦ backdoor trot(s)

trouble die of throat trouble ♦ double-trouble ♦ for (all) one's trouble

trouser trouser snake ♦ trouser trout

trout trouser trout

truck Keep on trucking.

true yours truly

trump trump sth up ♦ trumped up

truth gospel (truth) ◆ naked truth ◆ Truth, justice, and the American way.

tub tub of guts ◆ tub of lard

tube bake the tube steak ◆ boob-tube ◆ cop a tube ◆ crack a tube ◆ go down the tube(s) ◆ in the tube ◆ tube it ◆ tube steak ◆ tube steak of love

tuck nip and tuck

tumble rough and tumble

tune Stay tuned. ◆ to the tune of sth ◆ tune so/sth out ◆ tune in (to sth) ◆ tune out ◆ tuned in

turd ghost turd ◆ turd face

turk young Turk

turkey cold turkey ◆ couch-turkey ◆ jive turkey ◆ kick cold (turkey) ◆ talk turkey ◆ turkey bacon

turn done to a turn ◆ turn one's toes up ◆ turn so's stomach ◆ turn so's water off ◆ turn so off ◆ turn so on ◆ turn so out ◆ turn so upside down ◆ turn sth upside down ◆ turn a trick ◆ turn around ◆ turn belly up ◆ turn in ◆ turn on ◆ turn on a dime ◆ turn on the waterworks ◆ turn onto so/sth ◆ turn over ◆ turn tail (and run) ◆ turn thumbs down (on so/sth) ◆ turn turtle ◆ Turn your caps lock off! ◆ turn-off ◆ turned off ◆ turned on ◆ whatever turns you on

turtle turn turtle ◆ turtle heading ◆ turtle-neck

turvy topsy-turvy

twenty twenty-four, seven ◆ twenty-twenty hindsight

twin evil twin

twist arm-twister ◆ arm-twisting ◆ brain-twister ◆ twist (slowly) in the wind ◆ twist so's arm ◆ twist in the wind

twit in a twit

twitter in a twitter

two (as) alike as (two) peas in a pod ◆ the old one-two ◆ alike as (two) peas in a pod ◆ Aztec two-step ◆ goody two-shoes ◆ It cuts two ways. ◆ number two ◆ takes two to tango ◆ three point two ◆ three-two ◆ two fingers ◆ two shakes of a lamb's tail ◆ two sheets to the wind ◆ two umlauts ◆ two-bit ◆ two-bits ◆ two-by-four ◆ two-fisted drinker ◆ two-planker ◆ two-time ◆ two-time loser ◆ two-timer ◆ two-topper ◆ two-way street ◆ You can't dance at two weddings.

twosome gruesome-twosome

ugly (as) ugly as sin ◆ bump uglies ◆ butt-ugly ◆ coyote-ugly ◆ hit by the ugly stick ◆ plug-ugly ◆ pug-ugly ◆ ugly as sin

umlauts two umlauts

uncle say uncle ◆ Uncle (Sam) ◆ Uncle nab ◆ Uncle Sugar ◆ Uncle Whiskers

underground go underground

underworld hero (of the underworld)

unit (parental) units

unquote quote, unquote

until talk until one is blue in the face

upholstered (well-)upholstered

upper pepper-upper ◆ upper story

uproar Don't get your bowels in an uproar! ◆ get one's bowels in an uproar

ups high ups ◆ higher ups ◆ jack-ups

upshot the upshot (of sth)

upside turn so upside down ◆ turn sth upside down

upstairs nothing upstairs

urge the urge to purge

use better get used to it ◆ Use your head! ◆ Use your noggin! ◆ Use your noodle!

variety Heinz 57 (variety)

varnish coffin varnish ◆ tonsil varnish

vary Your mileage may vary.

veg veg (out) ◆ vegged out

verse chapter and verse

very thank you very much

vibes have good vibes

vid kid-vid

vigor vim and vigor

visit have a little visitor ◆ visit from Flo ◆ visit from the stork ◆ visit the plumbing ◆ visiting fireman

vodka (as) clear as vodka ◆ clear as vodka

voice talk to hear one's own voice ◆ throw one's voice

vulture culture-vulture

wack wack off ◆ wacky-tabbacky

wad shoot one's wad ◆ tight wad

wagon draggin'-wagon ◆ fall off the wagon ◆ honey wagon ◆ meat wagon ◆ monkey wagon ◆ off the wagon ◆ on the wagon ◆ paddy wagon

wait hurry up and wait

walk take a walk ◆ walk heavy ◆ walk on eggs ◆ walk on sunshine ◆ walk on thin ice ◆ walk soft ◆ walk tall ◆ walk-in ◆ walking dandruff ◆ walking on rocky socks ◆ walking papers ◆ walking wounded

wall climb the wall(s) ◆ drive so up the wall ◆ go over the wall ◆ hole in the wall ◆ nail so('s hide) to the wall ◆ nail Jell-O to the wall ◆ off-the-wall ◆ plastered to the wall ◆ up the wall ◆ wall job ◆ wall-eyed ◆ wall-to-wall ◆ walls have ears

waltz waltz off (with sth) ♦ waltz through sth

want (You) want a piece of me? ♦ put one's nose in (where it's not wanted) ♦ stick one's nose in (where it's not wanted) ♦ Wanna make sumpin' of it? ♦ Want a piece of me? ♦ want out ♦ Want to make something of it? ♦ You want to step outside?

war flame-war ♦ war chest ♦ war paint ♦ war zone

ward monkey wards

warm bench warmer ♦ like death warmed over ♦ nose-warmer ♦ warm so up ♦ warm body ♦ warmed over

warpath on the warpath

warrior weekend warrior

wart worry wart

wash the great unwashed ♦ chief cook and bottle washer ♦ come out in the wash ♦ head cook and bottle washer ♦ wash so away ♦ wash out ♦ washed out ♦ Well, wash my mouth out with soap. ♦ wishy-washy

waste caucasian waste ♦ toxic waste dump

watch bird watcher ♦ clock watcher ♦ on so's watch ♦ Watch it! ♦ Watch my lips! ♦ Watch your mouth! ♦ Watch your tongue!

water big drink of water ♦ blow so out of the water ♦ bubble water ♦ dead in the water ♦ foo-foo water ♦ hold water ♦ joy water ♦ laughing water ♦ pay the water bill ♦ plowing water ♦ pour cold water on sth ♦ toilet water ♦ turn so's water off ♦ water one's cheeks ♦ watering hole ♦ wonder water ♦ woofle-water ♦ wozzle-water

waterworks turn on the waterworks

wave finger wave ♦ make waves

wavelength on the same wavelength

waver wand waver

wax the whole ball of wax

way (That's the) way to go! ♦ the way it plays ♦ all the way ♦ all the way live ♦ dog-ways ♦ go all the way ♦ in a bad way ♦ in a big way ♦ in a familiar way ♦ in a family way ♦ in the family way ♦ It cuts both ways. ♦ It cuts two ways. ♦ No way! ♦ No way, José! ♦ only way to go ♦ out of the way ♦ put so/sth out of the way ♦ put so out of the way ♦ swing both ways ♦ that way ♦ That's the way the ball bounces. ♦ That's the way the cookie crumbles. ♦ That's the way the mop flops. ♦ Truth, justice, and the American way. ♦ two-way street ♦ way down ♦ way off (base) ♦ way out ♦ way rad ♦ Way to go!

wear If the shoe fits, wear it. ♦ wear the pants (in the house) ♦ wearing (nothing but) a smile

weather fair-weather ♦ under the weather

weave underwater basket weaving

wedding shotgun wedding ♦ You can't dance at two weddings.

wedgie atomic wedgie

weed crying weed ♦ killer weed ♦ monster weed ♦ weed-eater

weight carry (an amount of) weight ♦ throw one's weight around

weird weird out ♦ weirded out

west go West

wet all wet ♦ rode hard and put away wet ♦ sopping (wet) ♦ wet blanket ♦ wet noodle ♦ wet one ♦ wet rag ♦ wet sock

whack out of w(h)ack ♦ take a whack at so/sth ♦ take a whack at sth ♦ w(h)ack so/sth up ♦ w(h)ack so (out) ♦ w(h)ack sth (out) ♦ whack sth off ♦ whack sth up ♦ whack off ♦ w(h)acked (out)

whale (as) fat as a beached whale ♦ fat as a beached whale ♦ have a whale of a time ♦ whale into so/sth ♦ whale on ♦ whale the tar out of so

wham double whammy ♦ triple whammy ♦ wham-bang

wheel big wheel ♦ eighteen-wheeler ♦ fifth wheel ♦ four wheels ♦ free-wheeling ♦ hell-on-wheels ♦ reinvent the wheel ♦ set of wheels ♦ spin one's wheels ♦ third wheel ♦ wheel and deal ♦ wheel estate ♦ wheel man ♦ wheeler-dealer

while After while(, crocodile).

whip pussy-whipped ♦ whip one's wire ♦ whip sth into shape ♦ whip sth off ♦ whip off ♦ whip the dummy

whisker Mr. Whiskers ♦ Uncle Whiskers ♦ whiskers (man)

whiskey whiskey dick ♦ whiskey tenor

whistle meat whistle ♦ not just whistling Dixie ♦ whistle in the dark ♦ whistle-blower ♦ bells and whistles

white as the white on rice ♦ black and white ♦ bleed so white ♦ blue and white ♦ like the white on rice ♦ talk on the big white phone ♦ white elephant ♦ white hat ♦ white knuckler ♦ white man's disease ♦ white-knuckle

whiz piss-whiz ♦ whiz kid

whole a whole bunch ♦ a whole new ball game ♦ the whole ball of wax ♦ the whole enchilada ♦ the whole fam damily ♦ the whole nine yards ♦ the whole schmear ♦ the whole shebang ♦ the whole shooting match ♦ the whole wide world ♦ tell the (whole) world ♦ whole bag of tricks

whoop no big whoop ♦ whoopie cakes

whop Molly whop so ♦ whopping (great)

whore hockey-whore

wide the whole wide world ♦ blow sth wide open ♦ bust so wide open ♦ bust sth wide open ♦ have one's nose wide open ♦ high, wide, and handsome ♦ wide open ♦ wide place in the road ♦ with (one's) eyes (wide) open

wig flip one's wig ♦ wig out ♦ wigged (out)

wiggle Get a wiggle on! ♦ wiggle out of sth ♦ ziggy-wiggling

wild have a wild hair up one's ass ♦ hog-wild ♦ scientific wild ass guess ♦ wild and woolly

will God willing and the creek don't rise ♦ heads will roll ♦ It will be your ass! ♦ There will be hell to pay. ♦ will do

win can't win (th)em all ♦ no-win situation ♦ Sounds like a winner! ♦ Win a few, lose a few. ♦ Win some, lose some. ♦ win-win ♦ win-win-win ♦ You can't win them all.

wind bag of wind ♦ both sheets in the wind ♦ four sheets (to the wind) ♦ four sheets in the wind ♦ piss in the wind ♦ take the wind out of so's sails ♦ three sheets (to the wind) ♦ three sheets in the wind ♦ twist (slowly) in the wind ♦ twist in the wind ♦ two sheets to the wind

window bay window ♦ out the window

wine jug wine ♦ pop wine

wing clip so's wings ♦ fling-wing ♦ get one's wings ♦ hit under the wing ♦ sprout wings ♦ wing heavy ♦ wing it ♦ wing-ding

wink a wink of sleep ♦ forty winks

wipe ass-wipe ♦ butt-wipe ♦ wipe so out ♦ wipe sth out ♦ Wipe it off! ♦ wipe out ♦ wipe the floor up with so ♦ wiped (out) ♦ wiped over

wire (live) wire ♦ down to the wire ♦ hot wire ♦ on the wires ♦ pull one's wire ♦ under the wire ♦ whip one's wire ♦ wired into so/sth ♦ wired up

wireless latrine wireless

wise wise guy ♦ wise to so/sth ♦ wise up (to so/sth)

wish (Don't) you wish! ♦ wish book ♦ wish list ♦ wishy-washy ♦ You wish!

witcha What's really good witcha?

wobbles snozzle-wobbles

woe tale of woe

wolf cut one's wolf loose ♦ fine wolf ♦ lone wolf ♦ wolf sth down

woman old woman

wonder gutless wonder ♦ titless wonder ♦ wonder water

woo pitch (the) woo

wood the woods are full of sth ♦ out of the woods ♦ wood butcher ♦ wood-pussy

woof buy so's woof ticket ♦ sell a woof ticket ♦ sell woof tickets ♦ woof cookies

woolly wild and woolly

woozy boozy-woozy

word dirty word ♦ F-word ♦ What's the (good) word? ♦ word hole ♦ word of mouse ♦ Word up.

work (It) works for me. ♦ a cold piece of work ♦ the works ♦ black-collar workers ♦ dirty work ♦ give so a (good) working over ♦ grunt work ♦ knock off (work) ♦ leg work ♦ shit work ♦ shoot the works ♦ spill the works ♦ work one's ass off ♦ work one's buns off ♦ work one's butt off ♦ work one's tail off ♦ work oneself (up) into a lather ♦ work oneself up ♦ work oneself up to sth ♦ work so over ♦ working man's smile ♦ working stiff ♦ Works for me. ♦ Write if you get work.

world the whole wide world ♦ The world is one's oyster. ♦ dead to the world ♦ out of this world ♦ tell the (whole) world ♦ the end of the world as we know it ♦ Where in the world? ♦ world-beater ♦ world-class

worm can of worms ♦ glow worm ♦ worm burner ♦ worm-food ♦ worms in blood

worry Not to worry. ♦ worry wart

worth not worth a damn ♦ not worth a plugged nickel ♦ not worth beans ♦ worth one's salt

wound walking wounded

wrap under wraps ♦ wrap one's car around sth ♦ wrap sth up ♦ wrapped up (in so/sth) ♦ wrapped up (with so/sth)

wrath grapes of wrath

wrench left-handed monkey wrench

wrinkle penis wrinkle ♦ wrinkle-rod

wrist kick in the wrist ♦ slap so's wrist ♦ slap so on the wrist

write nothing to write home about ♦ Write if you get work.

wrong have the wrong number ♦ wrong side of the tracks

wrote That's all she wrote. ♦ That's what she wrote.

xerox team Xerox

yak yackety-yak ♦ yak it up

Thematic Index

Look up a Standard English expression in this index to locate a slang or colloquial expression with the same or approximately the same meaning. Words in **bold face type** are Index entries, and words in sans serif type are entries in the body of the dictionary. The user should go to the dictionary entry to find the complete meaning of the slang expression and the usage restrictions relevant to it. The index uses internal cross-referencing indicated by *Try* and *Try also* to lead the user to appropriate slang and colloquial expressions.

abandon bail on so ♦ bail out on so ♦ ditch
abandoned high and dry
abbreviations alphabet soup
abdominal muscles abs ♦ six-pack ♦ yokes (Try also **tight abdominal muscles.**)
ability Try **survival ability.**
able able to cut sth
abortion hoovering
about it bout it
about to bousta
above board on the up-and-up
absent AWOL
absent minded lunching ♦ out to lunch (Try also **memory failure.**)
absent minded person scatterbrain
absolutely Fucking-A! ♦ Make no mistake (about it)! ♦ totally (Try also **yes.**)
absorb cost eat
absorber Try **shock absorbers.**
abstainer dry ♦ tote
abstention Try **promise abstention.**
abundance Try **in abundance ♦ lots.**
abuse (v) fuck so over ♦ give so the finger ♦ give so the shaft ♦ stomp (on) so
abused been had ♦ chewed ♦ dumped on ♦ rode hard and put away wet ♦ through the mill
academia ivory tower
accelerate put the pedal to the metal (Try also **increase speed.**)
accelerator hammer
accent Try **southern accent.**
accept bite the bullet ♦ go with it ♦ go with the flow ♦ knuckle under (to so/sth) ♦ Like it or lump it! ♦ swallow ♦ Take it or leave it.
accept blame take the spear (in one's chest)

accept invitation I'm there!
accept loss kiss sth good-bye
accept punishment take one's lumps
accept task take so/sth on
acceptable cricket ♦ down with sth ♦ koshe ♦ kosher ♦ okay (Try also **make acceptable.**)
acceptable filming take
acceptance Try **force acceptance.**
accepted Try **be accepted.**
accessories (all) loaded
accident fender-bender ♦ snafu ♦ wipe out ♦ yard-sale (Try also **fecal accident ♦ hit and run accident ♦ urinary accident.**)
accidentally accidentally-on-purpose
accompany comp ♦ ride shotgun
accomplish easily waltz through sth
accordion (squeeze-)box ♦ groan box
accost buttonhole
accountant bean-counter ♦ number-cruncher
accumulate clock ♦ rack sth up
ache Try **testicle ache.**
achieve ace in(to sth) ♦ make it (Try also **late achiever.**)
achieve results have sth cinched
achieve speed make
achieved in the bag
acne scar crater
acquainted Try **get acquainted.**
acquire by scheming fanigle ♦ finagle
acrimonious blood and guts
acronyms alphabet soup
act dog and pony show ♦ number ♦ schtick (Try also **perform act of prostitution ♦ one person act ♦ over act.**)
act first break the ice
act important throw one's weight around

act like make like so/sth (Try also **copy (v).**)

act tough bogart

act vigorous have lead in one's pencil

act without knowledge go off half-cocked

acting stupid bojangling

action Try **take permanent action ♦ widely effective action.**

active up an' Adam ♦ up an' at 'em ♦ up and at them (Try also **socially active person.**)

activity Try **illegal activity ♦ past activity ♦ reduce activity ♦ sexual activity.**

actor Try **bad actor.**

actual 4 real

actually as a matter of fact

add alcohol lace ♦ shoot ♦ spike

add drug lace

add up notch

added bolt-on added (Try also **alcohol added.**)

addict cokeaholic ♦ dope fiend ♦ hog ♦ hook ♦ hype ♦ jabber ♦ junkie ♦ mojo ♦ moocher ♦ speed demon ♦ speed freak ♦ speedhead (Try also **computer addict ♦ pill addict.**)

addicted have a monkey on one's back ♦ hooked (on sth) ♦ on the junk ♦ on the mojo ♦ pushed ♦ strung out (Try also **internet addicted person ♦ become addicted ♦ cocaine addicted ♦ get addicted ♦ heroin addicted.**)

addiction habit ♦ jones ♦ monkey ♦ scag jones ♦ skag jones (Try also **heroin addiction.**)

addictive hard

addictive drug jock(e)y

additional on the side

additionally and stuff like that (there)

address addy ♦ eddress (Try also **email address.**)

address book little black book

adenoids Try **tonsils and adenoids.**

adjust slightly tweak

admission pass duck ♦ in

admit Try **confess.**

admit defeat say uncle

adult Try **middle-aged adult.**

adulterate hocus ♦ lace ♦ shoot ♦ spike

advance (various) Try **in advance ♦ pay in advance ♦ sexual advance ♦ make advances.**

advantage Try **get advantage ♦ give advantage ♦ have advantage.**

advertise shill

advertisement squib (Try also **free advertisement.**)

advertising Madison Avenue

advertising agency flackery

advice Try **false advice.**

advise (v) maven ♦ mavin

advisor bench jockey ♦ guru ♦ maven ♦ mavin

affair Try **love affair ♦ sexual affair.**

affect gets one right here

affection love bombs

afraid Try **frightened.**

African American Try **black person.**

again There you go. (Try also **try again with a hope of success ♦ call again ♦ taking drugs again ♦ tell again ♦ think again.**)

against anti

against nuclear No nukes!

age Try **check age.**

agency Try **advertising agency.**

agent ten percenter (Try also **FBI agent ♦ federal agent ♦ narcotics agent ♦ PR agent ♦ prostitute's agent.**)

aggravated ag

aggressive Try **be aggressive.**

aggressive man wolf

aggressively like gangbusters

agree bury the hatchet ♦ jibe ♦ same here ♦ see eye to eye ♦ That's what I say. ♦ Tru dat. ♦ What so said. ♦ will do ♦ You can say that again!

agreeable (I) love it! ♦ up for sth (Try also **say something agreeable.**)

agreement And how!

agressive ballsy ♦ fresh ♦ pushy ♦ rough and tumble

agriculture aggie

ahead of one jump ahead of so/sth (Try also **go ahead.**)

aid failure grease the skids

aid success grease the skids

aim gun get the drop on so

air Try **cool air.**

Air Force zoomies

airplane bird ♦ gashawk (Try also **small airplane.**)

airplane control joystick ♦ stick

airport Try **fogged in (airport).**

Alabama nickname bamma

alcohol Try **behave well (alcohol) ♦ marijuana and alcohol ♦ undiluted (alcohol).**

alcohol added loaded ♦ spiked

alcohol effect buzz ♦ lift

alcoholic content hard

alcoholic tremors Try **delirium tremens.**

ale berpwater

aleck Try **smart aleck.**

alert (n) Heads up!

alert (mod) fresh as a daisy ♦ jazzed (up) ♦ perky ♦ savvy ♦ turned on ♦ wired ♦ wired up (Try also **be alert ♦ become alert ♦ look alert.**)

alerted onto so/sth

alike (as) alike as (two) peas in a pod ♦ alike as (two) peas in a pod

alimony Try **common-law alimony.**

alive with crawling with so/sth

all Try **lasting all night ♦ study all night ♦ work out all right ♦ working all night ♦ accessories (all) ♦ bet all ♦ consume all ♦ eat all ♦ risk all ♦ selling all ♦ that is all ♦ use all.**)

all right aight

all that stuff all that jazz

alligator Try **later, alligator.**

allowances Try **make allowances.**

alone on the shelf ♦ on one's own hook (Try also **leave alone ♦ men alone.**)

aloof biggity ♦ hincty ♦ on one's high horse ♦ standoffish ♦ uppity

already attached (person) taken

alteration Try **nose alteration.**

altered jazzed (up)

alternate Try **control alternate delete.**

always 24-7 ♦ twenty-four, seven

am not ain't

amateur homegrown

amateur casting street-casting

amateur radio operator ham

amaze blow so away (Try also **express amazement.**)

amazed pie-eyed

amazing That's a new one on me. ♦ Would you believe?

ambitious person ball of fire ♦ fireball ♦ world-beater ♦ hungry ♦ on the make

ambulance meat wagon

amendment Try **take fifth amendment.**

American Try **American housewife ♦ American Indian as white ♦ Asian American as white.**

American housewife Suzy Homemaker

American Indian as white apple

ammunition ammo

amount pinch (Try also **earn some amount ♦ force to pay amount ♦ insignificant amount ♦ no less than some amount ♦ small amount.**)

amount of liquor finger ♦ two fingers

amphetamine amps ♦ bathtub crank ♦ blue ♦ chicken powder ♦ go-pills ♦ gorilla biscuits ♦ gorilla pills ♦ jelly babies ♦ jug ♦ leapers ♦ lid poppers ♦ lid proppers ♦ pepper-upper ♦ speed ♦ speeder ♦ speedster (Try also **use amphetamine.**)

amphetamine user speeder ♦ speedster

anal poke cob ♦ cornhole

analysis Try **qualitative analysis.**

analyst Try **market analyst.**

android droid

anesthetist gas-passer

anger (n) conniption (fit) (Try also **burst of anger ♦ express anger ♦ release anger.**)

anger (v) bitch so off ♦ brass so off ♦ brown so off ♦ burn so up ♦ chap ♦ cheese so off ♦ dink so off ♦ frost ♦ piss so off ♦ PO ♦ slow burn ♦ steam ♦ steam so's beam ♦ steam so up ♦ tee so off ♦ tick so off (Try also **easy to anger.**)

angry amped ♦ bent ♦ bent out of shape ♦ boiled ♦ boiling (mad) ♦ brassed (off) ♦ browned (off) ♦ burned ♦ burned up ♦ chapped ♦ cheesed off ♦ fenced ♦ flexed out of shape ♦ frosted (over) ♦ hacked (off) ♦ hopping mad ♦ hot ♦ hot under the collar ♦ huffy ♦ jacked (out) ♦ loaded for bear ♦ miffed ♦ on the warpath ♦ pee'd off ♦ pissed ♦ pissed (off) (at so/sth) ♦ pissed off about so/sth ♦ POed ♦ sore ♦ steam ♦ steamed (up) ♦ teed off ♦ ticked (off) ♦ torqued ♦ up in arms (Try also **be angry ♦ get angry.**)

angry internet messages flamage

announcer Try **television announcer ♦ TV announcer.**

annoy bug ♦ chap ♦ get on so's case ♦ get to so ♦ get so's goat ♦ give so a pain ♦ give so hell ♦ gripe one's ass ♦ gripe one's butt ♦ gripe one's soul ♦ hack ♦ jack so around ♦ jerk so around ♦ jerk so over ♦ mess with so/sth ♦ monkey around (with so) ♦ monkey with so/sth ♦ nark ♦ needle ♦ play hell with so/sth ♦ play the devil with so/sth ♦ pull so's chain ♦ rake on so ♦ rank ♦ rank so (out) ♦ roust ♦ stress ♦ yank so's chain ♦ yank so around

annoyance gig ♦ pet peeve ♦ PITA ♦ royal pain (Try also **mention annoyance.**)

annoyed chapped ♦ hacked (off) ♦ hung ♦ jacked ♦ jacked (out) ♦ jacked up ♦ jammed ♦ narked ♦ stressed

annoying in so's face ♦ (Try also **stop annoying.**)

annoying fax junk fax

annoying person drag ♦ holy terror ♦ jack ♦ loser ♦ nark ♦ nudnik ♦ pain ♦ pain in the ass ♦ pain in the butt ♦ pain in the neck ♦ pain in the rear ♦ real bitch ♦ rhoid ♦ schlepper ♦ shlepper ♦ sucker ♦ trip ♦ twirp ♦ wart ♦ wuffo ♦ so/sth from hell

annoying thing pain ♦ pain in the ass ♦ pain in the butt ♦ pain in the neck ♦ pain in the rear ♦ so/sth from hell

another Try **serve me another drink.**

answer Try **refuse to answer ♦ request answer ♦ what is answer.**

anti-intellectual (n) lowbrow

anus asshole ♦ balloon knot ♦ barking spider ♦ bazoo ♦ brown hole ♦ bunghole ♦ butthole ♦ cornhole ♦ keester ♦ keyster ♦ kiester ♦ trumpet spider ♦ wazoo ♦ (Try also **poke in anus ♦ poke anus.**)

anxiety heebie-jeebies ♦ willies ♦ the creeps ♦ (Try also **freeze with anxiety ♦ release anxiety.**)

anxious dragged ♦ jumpy ♦ keyed (up) ♦ uptight ♦ (Try also **be anxious ♦ get anxious.**)

Anyone here? Hello?

anything diddly-shit

apart Try **fall apart ♦ rip apart.**

apartment granny flat

appeal Try **give appeal ♦ sex appeal.**

appealing stock story stock ♦ jazzy

appear Try **morning face appearance ♦ not appear.**

appear publicly come out of the closet

applaud put them together for so ♦ put your hands together for so (Try also **quiet applause.**)

appointment Try **avoid appointment.**

appreciate dig ♦ eat sth up ♦ grok ♦ groove on so/sth ♦ swing with so/sth

approach (n) Try **gentle approach.**

approach (v) belly up (to sth) ♦ push

approval Try **force approval.**

approval sign thumbs up

arbitrageur arb

arcane far out

are not ain't

Are you there? Hello?

area areous (Try also **primitive area ♦ remote area ♦ rural area ♦ urban area.**)

argument big stink ♦ blow off ♦ donnybrook ♦ flap ♦ line ♦ shoot-out ♦ slugfest

argumentative spoiling for a fight

armpits pits

around Try **mess around ♦ play around ♦ strut around ♦ walk around ♦ wander around.**

arouse bring so on ♦ get so's motor running (Try also **sexual arousal ♦ sexually aroused.**)

arousing hot

arrest (n) bust ♦ collar ♦ cop ♦ fall ♦ pickup ♦ pinch (Try also **fair arrest (n) ♦ prior arrest.**)

arrest (v) bust ♦ collar ♦ cop ♦ flag ♦ gaffle ♦ glom ♦ gotcha ♦ nab ♦ nail ♦ nick ♦ pinch ♦ put the arm on so ♦ run so in ♦ tag ♦ sting

arrested bagged ♦ batted ♦ batted out ♦ busted ♦ clouted ♦ collared ♦ copped ♦ dropped ♦ fall ♦ flagged ♦ gaffled ♦ glommed ♦ glued ♦ guzzled ♦ jacked ♦ jacked up ♦ jammed ♦ knocked in ♦ nabbed ♦ nailed ♦ nicked ♦ pinched ♦ pinned ♦ popped ♦ rousted ♦ snapped (up) ♦ snatched ♦ take a fall ♦ tapped ♦ yanked (Try also **get arrested.**)

arrive blow in ♦ roll in (Try also **early arrival ♦ record arrival ♦ see the arrival.**)

artist black-collar workers (Try also **striptease artist.**)

artistic artsy (fartsy)

art(s) Try **exhibition (art) by one person ♦ fine arts.**

arts exploiter culture-vulture

arts supporter culture-vulture

Asian dink ♦ gooner (Try also **East Asian.**)

Asian American as white banana

aside Try **set aside.**

asleep dead to the world ♦ flaked ♦ sacked out ♦ zounked (out) (Try also **fall asleep.**)

aspire aim for the sky ♦ go for the fences ♦ shoot for the sky

ass Try **tits and ass.**

assassin gun ♦ hit man ♦ long knife (Try also **paid assassin.**)

assassinate frag

assassination hit

assault (v) rip so off

assemble knock sth together ♦ throw sth together

assertive bodacious (Try also **make assertive ♦ begin assertively.**)

assign work internally insource

assistant grunt ♦ second fiddle

assume responsibility step up to the plate

asterisk gear

astounding PFM

asylum booby hatch ✦ funny farm ✦ funny-farm ✦ laughing academy ✦ loony bin ✦ nut factory ✦ nut-foundry ✦ nuthatch ✦ nuthouse ✦ nuttery

at limit maxed out

at one's best in rare form

at risk in the tube

at the last moment under the wire

AT&T Ma Bell

athlete baller ✦ ballhead ✦ jock ✦ jockstrap ✦ jockstrapper ✦ strap ✦ superjock ✦ sweat sock

athlete supporter jock

Atlanta, GA AA-town

Atlantic Ocean big drink

attached Try **already attached (person).**

attack (n) blitz ✦ blow ✦ flame ✦ the old one-two (Try **gang attack ✦ heart attack ✦ nervous attack.**)

attack (v) blast ✦ bust on so/sth ✦ flame ✦ jump ✦ mace so's face ✦ mug ✦ rank on so ✦ tear into so ✦ whale into so/sth

attacker mugger

attain hit

attempt (n) go ✦ one's best shot

attempt a cover up tap dance like mad

attend Be there or be square. ✦ Be there with bells on. ✦ make the scene

attend uninvited crash

attending without date (male or female) stag

attention snap to (attention) (Try also **attract attention ✦ come to attention.**)

attentive on the ball

attitude cop an attitude ✦ tude (Try also **bad attitude.**)

attract attention signify

attracted to soft on so

attraction Try **tourist attraction ✦ dullard attractor.**

attractive Try **sexually attractive man ✦ sexually attractive.**

attractive investment play ✦ package

attune get in the groove

auction block block

audacious bodacious

audience Try **beg audience for laughter ✦ prepare audience.**

Australia down under

authentic thing McCoy ✦ the (real) McCoy

authority big kahuna

automatic knee-jerk

available off-the-shelf ✦ up for grabs (Try also **immediately available.**)

available money cash flow

average middlebrow ✦ run-of-the-mill ✦ so-so (Try also **law of averages.**)

average male college student Joe College

average man joe ✦ Joe Blow ✦ Joe Citizen ✦ Joe Doakes ✦ John Doe

avoid drop so/sth like a hot potato ✦ duck ✦ wiggle out of sth (Try also **vacation avoidance.**)

avoid appointment play hooky

avoid school play hooky

avoid work goldbrick

awake bright-eyed and bushy-tailed

aware of onto so/sth ✦ hep ✦ hip ✦ tuned in ✦ with (one's) eyes (wide) open

away Try **far away place ✦ sleep away liquor ✦ go away ✦ right away ✦ run away ✦ speed away ✦ walk away.**

away from desk out of pocket

awful That's so suck!

awkward backassed ✦ sticky (Try also **in awkward situation.**)

awkward person lommix ✦ lummox ✦ lummux ✦ schlemazel ✦ schlemozzle ✦ titless wonder

awkwardly built jerry-built

AWOL Try **go AWOL.**

baby bundle from heaven ✦ bundle of joy (Try also **dirty baby ✦ premature baby.**)

bachelor ba(t)ch (it) ✦ bach (it)

back end tail-end

back muscles lats

back seat shotty back

back talk fat lip ✦ jive ✦ lip

background music ear candy ✦ elevator music

backward backassed ✦ Podunk

backward town one-horse town ✦ Podunk

bad bum ✦ dank ✦ dook ✦ harsh ✦ heinous ✦ ill ✦ illin' ✦ It sucks. ✦ janky ✦ lousy ✦ lowdown ✦ no-good ✦ nowhere ✦ pathetic ✦ phat-phree ✦ shitty ✦ slummy ✦ sorry ✦ stinking ✦ stinky ✦ That sucks. (Try also **have bad experience ✦ in bad situation ✦ reject bad check ✦ sold bad drugs ✦ spending bad checks ✦ write bad check ✦ be bad ✦ smell badly ✦ speak badly.**)

bad actor ham

bad attitude tude

bad bargain shitty end of the stick

bad beer belch ✦ piss ✦ queer-beer ✦ jungle mouth

bad check bad paper ✦ bum check ✦ hot check ✦ hot paper ✦ kite ✦ rubber

be anxious have ants in one's pants ♦ piss blood ♦ sweat bullets
be bad suck
be believed wash
be boss wear the pants (in the house)
be brave nut up ♦ sack up ♦ stand tall
be buddies with pal around (with so)
be busy tap dance like mad
be calm keep cool
be cautious pussyfoot (around)
be certain bet one's bottom dollar
be chosen get the nod
be cowardly have a yellow streak down one's back
be crazy have a loose screw ♦ have bats in one's belfry ♦ have rocks in one's head
be deceived bite
be defeated take a beating
be dejected have one's ass in a sling
be drunk burn with a low blue flame ♦ have a buzz on ♦ have a glow on ♦ have a load on ♦ have a skinful ♦ have an edge on ♦ have one's brain on a leash
be embarrassed have egg on one's face
be excellent wail
be exciting swing
be foolish have rocks in one's head
be friends with pal around (with so)
be fun swing
be gentle take it easy ♦ walk soft
be giddy space
be good enough (It) works for me. ♦ Works for me.
be greedy line one's own pocket(s)
be happy walk on sunshine
be haughty pull an attitude
be heavy walk heavy
be homeless carry the stick
be honest with square with so
be humble walk soft
be ideal ring the bell
be in love have one's nose wide open
be in trouble have one's ass in a sling
be informed know shit from Shinola ♦ know the score ♦ know what's what ♦ know where it's at ♦ know which end is up
be intelligent know shit from Shinola
be jealous eat one's heart out
be knowledgeable know one's ass from a hole in the ground
be lucky luck out
be mentally sound have all one's marbles
be near death have one foot in the grave
be nervous have ants in one's pants

be obnoxious suck
be obsequious suck so's hind tit
be obsessed have sth on the brain
be obvious stick out like a sore thumb
be of sound mind have it all together
be panicked run scared
be poorly executed stink
be proud walk tall
Be quiet! Try **Shut up!**
be realistic Get real!
be repellent stink ♦ stink on ice ♦ suck
be right hit the bull's-eye ♦ hit the jackpot ♦ hit the spot
be risky play with fire
be rotten stink on ice
be rough roughhouse ♦ roughneck
be sent home dead go home in a box
be serious Keep it real! ♦ mean business
be silly clown around
be stupid have shit for brains
be surprised have kittens
be tipsy have a buzz on ♦ have a glow on
be trapped have one's ass in a crack
be unfair hit so below the belt
be up-to-date swing
be wealthy have gravy on one's grits
be wrong have the wrong number ♦ miss the boat
be yourself let it all hang out
beach regular beach bum ♦ beach bunny
beam Try **on a radio beam (aviation).**
beard (face) fungus
beard and mustache pudding ring
bearded man fungus-face ♦ fuzz-face
beat Try **good beat ♦ music with beat.**
beat (v) beat the shit out of so ♦ beat so's brains out ♦ bust so up ♦ bust so wide open ♦ chunk so ♦ cream ♦ done over ♦ dust so off ♦ give so a (good) working over ♦ jack so up ♦ kick the shit out of so ♦ knock the shit out of so ♦ light into so ♦ make hamburger out of so/sth ♦ make mincemeat out of so/sth ♦ mess so's face up ♦ mess so over ♦ mess so up ♦ Molly whop so ♦ mop the floor up with so ♦ murder ♦ pin so's ears back ♦ pound so's head in ♦ rip so off ♦ sail into so ♦ settle so's hash ♦ shellac ♦ slaughter ♦ smoke ♦ stomp (on) so ♦ take ♦ trash ♦ trounce ♦ wail on so ♦ wax ♦ whale into so/sth ♦ whale the tar out of so ♦ whipped ♦ whipsaw ♦ whomp ♦ whump ♦ wipe the floor up with so ♦ womp ♦ work so over
beat generation person longhair

beat up bank on so ♦ eat so's lunch ♦ rough so up

beaten basted ♦ creamed ♦ done to a turn ♦ knocked up ♦ shafted ♦ shellacked

beating pasting ♦ shellacking

beautiful yummy

beautiful face glamour puss

become addicted graduate

become alert tune in (to sth)

become euphoric (drugs) switch on ♦ bliss out

become giddy space out

become good sprout wings

become honest go straight

become known to public (news) break

become legitimate jump smooth

become oblivious switch off

become punk punk out

bed fart sack ♦ rack ♦ sack (Try also **cheap bed ♦ get out of bed ♦ go to bed ♦ time in bed.**)

bed down pad down (somewhere)

bedtime lights out ♦ sack time

beef Try **corned beef ♦ salted beef.**

beep (n) feep ♦ feep

beer belch ♦ berps ♦ berpwater ♦ brew ♦ brew-ha ♦ brewski ♦ brewsky ♦ brewster ♦ bud ♦ burps ♦ cold blood ♦ cold coffee ♦ drafty ♦ foam ♦ frosty ♦ frosty one ♦ froth ♦ greenie ♦ gusto ♦ honey ♦ hop ♦ joy juice ♦ near-beer ♦ plug ♦ skat ♦ slop(s) ♦ slosh ♦ squirt ♦ suds ♦ tube ♦ twack ♦ two umlauts ♦ wet one (Try also **bad beer ♦ can of beer ♦ draft beer ♦ drink beer ♦ homemade beer ♦ keg of beer ♦ open beer ♦ weak beer.**)

beer belly beer gut ♦ German goiter ♦ keg ♦ Milwaukee goiter

beer drinker belcher ♦ brewster ♦ budhead ♦ suds-swiller ♦ yeaster

beer drinkers (male) brews brothers

beer drinking device beerbong

beer opener church key

beer party beer blast ♦ beer bust ♦ brew-out ♦ keg party ♦ kegger

beer truck honey wagon

beg mooch

beg audience for laughter milk

beg from bum sth (off so) ♦ cadge sth from so

beggar mooch ♦ moocher ♦ schnorrer ♦ thumber

begging target touch

begin get it on

begin assertively come on like gangbusters ♦ come on strong

begin telling shoot

beginner Try **computer beginner.**

beginner's drug kid stuff

beginning git-go ♦ jump (street)

beginning skier snow bunny

behave well (alcohol) hold one's liquor

behave well (drugs) hold one's high

behaved Try **well-behaved person.**

behind (score) down

being played in play

being purchased in play

being questioned on the hot seat

being risk free on the safe side

being sick illin'

belch (n) burp ♦ grunt

believe BION ♦ buy ♦ eat sth up ♦ swallow ♦ You (had) better believe it! (Try also **be believed.**)

believe me Believe you me! ♦ Trust me!

belittle dis(s) ♦ dis(s) (on so) ♦ poo(h)-poo(h)

belligerent blood and guts ♦ low-life

belly bay window ♦ beer gut ♦ breadbasket ♦ dinner basket ♦ gut ♦ guts ♦ labonza (Try also **pork belly futures ♦ beer belly ♦ big belly.**)

benched player bench warmer (Try also **go to bench.**)

benefit Try **what is benefit.**

benefit (employment) perk

benefits benies

Benzedrine benny ♦ benz

berate go off on so ♦ zing

berserk Try **go berserk.**

besides you You and what army? ♦ You and who else?

best (el) primo ♦ A-1 ♦ A-OK ♦ ace ♦ berries ♦ da bomb ♦ daddy (of them all) ♦ level best ♦ number one ♦ numero uno ♦ primo ♦ rule ♦ world-class ♦ A number 1 ♦ a ten ♦ the most (Try also **at one's best ♦ second best.**)

best clothing Sunday best

best man Mr. Right

best situation win-win-win

best way only way to go

bested screwed ♦ shafted

bet ante (Try also **high-bet gambler ♦ make bet ♦ match bet ♦ place bet ♦ take bets.**)

bet all shoot the works

bet value bet so dollars to doughnuts

betray double cross ♦ give so up ♦ sell so out ♦ step out on so
betrayal double cross ♦ sellout
betrayed burned
betrayer double-crosser
better def (Try also **make deal better.**)
beverages drinkage
beware of listeners walls have ears
bewildered pixilated ♦ punch-drunk ♦ punchy
biceps bi ♦ guns ♦ pythons
bicycle bike
bicycle lifting wheely
bid up salty
big bigass ♦ honking (Try also **this big.**)
big belly beer belly ♦ potbelly
big car ark ♦ boat ♦ hog ♦ hog cadillac
big casino spender whale
big feet battleships
big one whopper
big shoe(s) boat ♦ clodhopper ♦ battleships ♦ gunboats
big wave tube
biggest (grand)daddy (of them all)
bigot redneck
big-time big league
bikini (male) banana hammock
bilabial trill give so the raspberry ♦ raspberry
bill bad news ♦ damage ♦ tab (Try also **fifty-dollar-bill ♦ five-dollar bill ♦ large twenty-dollar bill ♦ one-dollar bill ♦ one-hundred-dollar bill ♦ put on bill ♦ ten-dollar bill ♦ twenty-dollar bill.**)
biology class frog slicing
biplane Try **fly (in biplane).**
bird dung birdturd
birth visit from the stork
birth control pill pill ♦ Vatican roulette
bisexual AC-DC ♦ bi ♦ heteroflexible ♦ swing both ways
bisexual person bi ♦ combo ♦ switch-hitter
bit (n) tad (Try also **tiny bit ♦ eat bits.**)
bitch beotch ♦ biatch ♦ bizatch ♦ biznitch ♦ bizzle ♦ dog's mother
bitchy wenchy ♦ whenchy
bite Try **love bite.**
black as white oreo
black buddy blood ♦ blood (brother) ♦ bluh ♦ brother ♦ bruva ♦ (soul) brother
black dates white grayhound
black eye shiner
black friend (female) (soul) sister
black man young blood

black person nicca ♦ nigga ♦ nizzle (Try also **black as white ♦ black buddy ♦ black dates white ♦ black friend (female) ♦ black man.**)
blackjack sap
blackmail (v) shake so down
blame the short end of the stick (Try also **accept blame ♦ take blame.**)
blame else pass the buck ♦ frame ♦ hang sth on so
blatant out-and-out
blatant homosexual flamer
blemish Try **moral blemish.**
blob Try **fecal blob.**
block (n) Try **auction block.**
block (v) put the clamps on so/sth
blood red gravy
blow (n) belt ♦ biff ♦ kick in the guts ♦ knuckle sandwich ♦ swipe (Try also **final blow ♦ hard blow ♦ hard punch (blow) ♦ mucus blow ♦ unfair blow ♦ withstand blows ♦ nose blowing.**)
blues the blahs
bluff (v) sell a woof ticket ♦ sell woof tickets
blunder (n) flub (up) ♦ foul up ♦ goof ♦ screw up
blunder (v) chunk ♦ flub (up) ♦ foul up ♦ goof ♦ slip (up)
BMW beema ♦ beemer
board Try **above board ♦ Federal Reserve Board.**
board plane hop
board train hop
boast (v) sell a woof ticket ♦ sell woof tickets ♦ throw the bull ♦ throw the crap ♦ woof
boat Try **fresh off the boat.**
body bod ♦ carcass (Try also **strange bodied person ♦ dead bodies ♦ expose private body parts ♦ woman's body.**)
body cavity search booty check
body odor BO
bodybuilder muscleman
bodyguard enforcer
bogus bogue ♦ phony as a three-dollar bill ♦ pseudo
bohemian beat ♦ boheme
boisterous hog-wild ♦ wham-bang
boisterous child roughhouse ♦ roughneck
boldly with flying colors
bomb (v) take sth out
bond Try **risky bond.**
bong (n) bizzle

bonus golden handcuffs ♦ golden parachute ♦ spiff (Try also **executive bonus.**)

bony scraggy

boo (v) hoot

booing person boo-bird

book Try **thrilling book or movie** ♦ **address book.**

bookmaker bookie

boorish zhlubby

booth Try **toll booth.**

booze (n) hootch (Try also **superior booze.**)

bore (n) nudnik ♦ talk so's ear off ♦ talk so ragged

bored at loose ends ♦ burned out

boring jeff ♦ beige ♦ dead

boring event big drink of water ♦ drag ♦ snooze ♦ yawner

borrow bum sth (off so) ♦ cadge sth from so (Try also **sale of borrowed stock** ♦ **sell borrowed stock** ♦ **live by borrowing.**)

borrower schnorrer

boss (female) boss lady

boss (male) boss man

boss (n) big cheese ♦ big enchilada ♦ big fish ♦ big kahuna ♦ big wheel ♦ bigwig ♦ face card ♦ head cook and bottle washer ♦ high mucky-muck ♦ honcho ♦ key figure ♦ kingpin ♦ main squeeze ♦ Mr. Big ♦ old man ♦ Simon Legree ♦ suit (Try also **be boss** ♦ **crime boss** ♦ **who is boss** ♦ **you are the boss.**)

boss (v) honcho

bosses and managers high ups ♦ higher ups

bossy on one's high horse

bossy person backseat driver

Boston, MA Bean Town

Boston tunnel Big Dig

both nostrils one and one

bother (n) sweat (Try also **no bother.**)

bother (v) mess with so/sth ♦ monkey around (with so) ♦ monkey with so/sth ♦ needle ♦ rag on so ♦ rake on so ♦ stress

bottle Try **empty bottle** ♦ **open bottle.**

bottomed Try **fat-bottomed person.**

bottomless pit rathole

bounce checks fly kites

bow of ship pointy end

bowels Try **empty bowels.**

bowels emptied cleaned out

bowl bizzle

bowlegged person rainbow

boxer palooka ♦ paluka

boy or man guy (Try also **man or boy** ♦ **small boy.**)

boyfriend BF ♦ crush ♦ main squeeze ♦ squeeze ♦ steady

braces Try **dental braces** ♦ **smile with braces.**

braces wearer tinsel-teeth

brag blow one's own horn ♦ gas ♦ shoot one's mouth off ♦ talk big

braggart bag of wind ♦ blowhard ♦ crock (of shit) ♦ gasbag ♦ loose cannon ♦ windbag

brain idea box ♦ mind ♦ wetware

brain damaged (drugs) brain-burned ♦ brain-fried

brassiere double-barreled slingshot ♦ flopper-stopper

brave Try **be brave** ♦ **walk brave.**

break (n) Try **take a break** ♦ **toilet break.**

break dancer breaker

break date stand so up

break down conk out ♦ crack ♦ crack up

break in crack

break out bust out (of some place)

break wind Try **fart (v).**

breaking of wind Try **fart (n).**

breast apple ♦ boob ♦ booby ♦ can ♦ jug ♦ murphy (Try also **flat breasted** ♦ **false breasts** ♦ **with large breasts.**)

breasts balloons ♦ bawangos ♦ bazoom(s) ♦ bazoongies ♦ bezongas ♦ blouse bunnies ♦ bodacious tatas ♦ boobage ♦ boosiasm(s) ♦ cones ♦ dairies ♦ doughboys ♦ garbanzos ♦ honkers ♦ hooters ♦ knockers ♦ melons ♦ naughty bits ♦ rack ♦ rackage ♦ tatas ♦ tits (Try also **flat breasted** ♦ **false breasts** ♦ **with large breasts.**)

breasts (male) bitch tits

breed Try **mixed breed dog** ♦ **horse for breeding (male).**

bribe (n) kick back ♦ drugola ♦ fix ♦ palm-oil ♦ payola ♦ plugola ♦ push money ♦ spiff (Try also **taking bribes.**)

bribe (v) fix ♦ grease ♦ grease so's palm

bribe to informer hush money

bribed fixed

briefs Try **swimming briefs.**

British citizen limejuicer ♦ limey

broad or wide shotgun

broadcast error blooper

broke (flat) on one's ass ♦ ass out ♦ behind the eight ball ♦ case of the shorts ♦ cleaned out ♦ dead broke ♦ flat broke ♦ in the hole ♦ on the rocks ♦ on one's ass ♦ piss-poor ♦ shot to the curb ♦ stone broke ♦ strapped ♦ tapped ♦ tapped out ♦ wiped (out) (Try also **go broke** ♦ **make someone broke.**)

broken on the fritz ♦ out of kilter
broken English FOBlish
brothel call house ♦ fuck-house ♦ fuckery ♦ hook shop
brothel keeper madam
browse Web surf the net
bruised black and blue
bucket Try **refuse bucket ♦ urinal bucket.**
buckskin buck
buddy Try **black buddy ♦ friend.**
budgeted on a shoestring
Budweiser beer bud
build muscles get some yokes on
built Try **well-built man ♦ awkwardly built ♦ well built.**
bull dung bull-pucky
bullet slug ♦ spinner
bullet-proof vest vest
bullshit shit
bully gazoony ♦ muscleman ♦ strong-arm man
bum (n) skid row bum
bumbler duffer ♦ schlemazel ♦ schlemozzle (Try also **land of bumblers.**)
bumper banger
bumpkin gaffer ♦ hayseed ♦ yahoo
bungled foozlified
burden stick so with sth ♦ strap so with so/sth ♦ a drag (on so)
burdened saddled with so/sth ♦ up to here ♦ up to one's ears ♦ up to one's eyeballs ♦ up to one's knees ♦ up to one's neck
bureaucrat paper-pusher ♦ pencil-pusher ♦ wonk
burial Try **prepare for burial.**
burial at sea deep six
buried put to bed with a shovel ♦ six feet under
burned (hair) scorched ♦ singed
burned out person retread
burp vurp
burst of anger conniption (fit)
burst of drug euphoria rush
burst of energy rush
bury put so to bed with a shovel ♦ send so to glory
bus avenue tank ♦ double-decker
bus passenger straphanger
business beeswax ♦ biz ♦ brass tacks (Try also **mind your own business ♦ none of your business ♦ not your business ♦ show business ♦ talk business ♦ tend to own business.**)
business person pinstriper ♦ suit ♦ vest

busy biz ♦ swamped ♦ tied up ♦ wrapped up (with so/sth) (Try also **be busy ♦ get busy.**)
busy place Grand Central Station
busybody eagle-eye
but But, hey
butt Try **buttocks ♦ cigar butt ♦ cigarette butt ♦ look for butts.**
butter lube (Try also **peanut butter.**)
buttocks ass ♦ BA ♦ backside ♦ behind ♦ boody ♦ bootie ♦ booty ♦ bottom ♦ bucket ♦ buns ♦ butt ♦ caboose ♦ cakes ♦ can ♦ differential ♦ duck-butt ♦ duff ♦ duster ♦ dusty butt ♦ fanny ♦ gazoo ♦ ghetto booty ♦ heinie ♦ keester ♦ keyster ♦ kiester ♦ labonza ♦ moon ♦ pooper ♦ prat(t) ♦ rear (end) ♦ rooster ♦ rump ♦ rusty-dusty ♦ seat ♦ stern ♦ tuchus ♦ tukkis ♦ tush(y) ♦ whoopie cakes (Try also **large buttocked person ♦ well buttocked ♦ crack (buttocks) ♦ fall on buttocks ♦ fat buttocks ♦ flog buttocks ♦ show buttocks.**)
buttocks crack Try **gluteal cleft.**
buttocks gap Try **gluteal cleft.**
buy (v) snap sth up (Try also **legal to buy liquor ♦ money to buy silence.**)
buy and sell churn
buy drugs dope up ♦ get a fix ♦ get a gift ♦ make a score
buyer taker
buzzer Try **signal with buzzer ♦ wanted by police.**
bytes Try **four bytes.**
cache Try **contraband cache.**
Cadillac caddy ♦ Slade
cafeteria ptomaine-domain ♦ ptomaine-palace
call (n) Try **fake telephone call ♦ phone call ♦ telephone call.**
call (v) buzz
call a stranger cold call
call again try so back (again)
call for luck God willing and the creek don't rise ♦ The baby needs shoes.
call in sick bang in (sick)
call my pager hit me on the hip
calm cool so out ♦ cool, calm, and collected ♦ cooled out ♦ laid back (Try also **be calm ♦ remain calm ♦ wait calmly.**)
calm down chill (out) ♦ cool down ♦ Cool it! ♦ cool off ♦ cool out ♦ Don't get your bowels in an uproar! ♦ Don't have a cow! ♦ Don't make a federal case out of it! ♦ Easy does it. ♦ get one's act together ♦ mellow out

◆ settle so's hash ◆ simmer (down) ◆ Take it down a thou(sand)! ◆ take it easy

calmed down defrosted

camera Try **conceal microphone or camera ◆ moving camera ◆ overhead camera.**

campaign fund war chest

campuses campi

can Try **trash can.**

can of beer brewster ◆ chill ◆ chilly ◆ jug ◆ popper ◆ tube

cancel scratch ◆ scrub (Try also **fill or cancel stock order.**)

cancel out hang up

cancel that check that

cancer big-C.

canned milk tin cow

cannot always succeed You can't win them all.

cannot do it no can do ◆ no dice ◆ no go ◆ no-no

canvas shoes sneaks

capable lean and mean

capable person dynamite

capsule cap (Try also **make capsule.**)

capture bag ◆ get one's hooks into so

capture passwords card ◆ phish ◆ spoof

car (hot) rod ◆ babe magnet ◆ buggy ◆ can ◆ chick magnet ◆ cruiser ◆ crutch ◆ four wheels ◆ fox trap ◆ load ◆ ride ◆ rizzi ◆ rizzle ◆ set of wheels ◆ sheen ◆ short ◆ trans ◆ wheels ◆ whip (Try also **junky car ◆ police car lights ◆ start car without key ◆ big car ◆ family car ◆ fast car ◆ gaudy car ◆ good car ◆ old car ◆ police car ◆ repossessed car ◆ start car ◆ wreck car.**)

car crash back-ender

car (specific) goat

carbohydrates carb(o)s

carburetor carb

card Try **credit card ◆ cue card ◆ deal card(s) to me ◆ queen in cards ◆ two of cards.**

care don't give a hoot ◆ don't give a rip ◆ give a fuck (about so/sth) ◆ give a shit (about so/sth) ◆ I could(n't) care less. ◆ Like I care. ◆ Like I really give a shit! ◆ LIRGAS ◆ See if I care! ◆ SIIC ◆ TLC ◆ YMHMMFSWGAS (Try also **take care of the home ◆ requiring care.**)

care for self look after number one ◆ take care of number one ◆ take care of numero uno

carefree high, wide, and handsome

careful Watch it! (Try also **look carefully.**)

careless quick-and-dirty ◆ slap-dash ◆ a lick and a promise (Try also **do carelessly ◆ speak carelessly.**)

caressing Try **no caressing.**

carpenter chips ◆ wood butcher

carrier Try **contraband carrier ◆ drug carrier.**

carry schlep ◆ shlep

carry drugs hold

carry lunch brown bag it ◆ brown-bag

carrying contraband hot

carrying drugs heeled

carrying gun packing a gun

case line (Try also **make one's case.**)

cash (n) bank ◆ bankroll ◆ spending money (Try also **keep cash ◆ paid in cash ◆ reduce cash.**)

cash register sound Ching! ◆ Ka-ching!

casino Try **big casino spender.**

casting Try **amateur casting.**

castrate pet fix

castrated fixed

casual cazh ◆ lah-di-dah

casualties body count

catalog wish book

catch red-handed have so dead to rights

catch sight get an eyeball on so/sth

catsup blood ◆ cat-soup

Caucasian Try **white person.**

cause Try **hopeless cause.**

cause grief tear so up

cause lovers to separate bust so up

cause much laughter fracture

cause of death kiss of death

cause of end kiss of death

cause of panic freaker

cause of software error software rot

cause trouble raise the devil (with sth) ◆ signify

caustic remark snide remark

cautious Try **be cautious ◆ walk cautiously.**

cavity Try **body cavity search.**

CB radio intruder breaker

celebrate ball ◆ bash ◆ gas ◆ have a ball ◆ paint the town (red) ◆ partay ◆ party down ◆ party hearty ◆ rage

celebrity celeb

cell Try **jail cell.**

cellulite hail damage

cemetery bone factory ◆ boneyard ◆ cement city ◆ God's acre ◆ Headstone City ◆ Marble City ◆ marble orchard

cents Try **fifty cents ◆ seventy-five cents.**

certain sure as hell ♦ surefire (Try also **be certain.**)

certainly jolly-well

certainty dead cinch ♦ sure thing

C-grade hook

chair Try **bad seat or chair** ♦ **die in chair** ♦ **electric chair** ♦ **rocking chair.**

challenge (n) last straw ♦ screamer

challenge (v) buy so's woof ticket ♦ call ♦ call so out ♦ front

champagne berpwater ♦ bubble water ♦ bubbles ♦ bubbly ♦ cham ♦ chammy ♦ champers ♦ grape(s) ♦ laughing soup ♦ laughing water ♦ Minnehaha ♦ poo ♦ sham ♦ shammy ♦ shampers ♦ shampoo ♦ squirt

champagne drinker bubblehead

champion champ

chance (n) crapshoot ♦ toss-up (Try also **fair chance** ♦ **no chance** ♦ **poor chance** ♦ **take a chance.**)

chance (v) ace in(to sth)

chance results luck of the draw

chancy dicey ♦ sticky ♦ touch and go

change Try **endure change** ♦ **undergo change** ♦ **channel changer** ♦ **mental changes** ♦ **channel changing.**

change tables table-hop

change topics change the channel

channel Try **search channels.**

channel changer channel surfer

channel changing channel hopping ♦ channel surfing ♦ channel zapping

chaotic up for grabs ♦ zooie

chaotic place zoo

chaplain holy Joe ♦ padre ♦ sky-pilot

character Try **sales character.**

charge (n) Try **criminal charge** ♦ **false criminal charge** ♦ **get free of criminal charge** ♦ **person in charge** ♦ **take charge** ♦ **while one is in charge.**

charge (v) beat (Try also **keep charging.**)

charge with crime paste sth on so ♦ tag ♦ throw the book at so

charges damage ♦ tab

charisma mojo

chase (n) runaround

chaser Try **woman chaser.**

chastise rank so (out) ♦ tear so a new asshole

chat (n) jaw ♦ yak

chat (v) chew the fat ♦ chew the rag ♦ fan the breeze ♦ jaw ♦ rap ♦ schmoose ♦ schmooze ♦ shmooze ♦ shoot the breeze ♦ shoot the bull ♦ shoot the crap ♦ shoot the shit ♦ throw the bull ♦ throw the crap

chat session schmooze

chatter (n) blab ♦ chinmusic ♦ chitchat ♦ gab ♦ gibber-gabber ♦ jabber ♦ yack ♦ yackety-yak ♦ yap ♦ yatata-yatata

chatter (v) beak ♦ chitchat ♦ gab ♦ jabber ♦ run off at the mouth ♦ wag one's chin ♦ yack ♦ yak it up ♦ yap

chatterer flapjaw ♦ magpie ♦ schmoozer

cheap budget ♦ cheesy ♦ cut-rate ♦ dirt cheap ♦ low rent ♦ penny-ante ♦ rinky-dink ♦ schlock ♦ schlocky ♦ shoestring ♦ tacky ♦ ticky-tacky ♦ trashy ♦ two-bit

cheap bed flop

cheap hotel fleabag ♦ flophouse

cheap merchandise cheapie ♦ sleaze

cheap person cheapskate

cheap place taco stand

cheapest bottom of the barrel ♦ bottom of the heap ♦ el cheapo (Try also **seeking cheapest.**)

cheat (v) bamboozle ♦ bend the law ♦ blow so/sth off ♦ burn ♦ clip ♦ con ♦ dick ♦ diddle ♦ diddle sth out of so ♦ do so in ♦ euchre ♦ fleece ♦ flimflam ♦ fuck so over ♦ fudge ♦ futz ♦ give so the shaft ♦ hook ♦ hose ♦ make a score ♦ phutz ♦ rip so off ♦ rook ♦ screw ♦ screw so out of sth ♦ skin ♦ stack the deck ♦ stiff ♦ sting ♦ sting so for sth ♦ take ♦ take so in

cheated been had ♦ burned ♦ clipped ♦ had ♦ hooked (on sth) ♦ scabbed ♦ screwed ♦ shafted ♦ taken ♦ vicked ♦ was had

cheater burn artist ♦ clip joint ♦ con artist ♦ con man ♦ flimflam artist ♦ four-flusher ♦ team Xerox

check (n) chit (Try also **bad check passer** ♦ **ID check (v)** ♦ **bad check** ♦ **forged check** ♦ **reject bad check** ♦ **return check** ♦ **write bad check** ♦ **write check** ♦ **bounce checks** ♦ **spending bad checks** ♦ **worthless checks.**)

check age card ♦ ID

check identity run a make on so

check out scope so out

check zipper XYZ

cheery bright-eyed and bushy-tailed

Chicago, IL Chi(town)

child ankle biter ♦ army brat ♦ bohunk ♦ crumb-cruncher ♦ crumb-crusher ♦ deduction ♦ expense ♦ patter of tiny feet ♦ rug rat ♦ scamp ♦ small fry ♦ snotnose(d) ♦ kid ♦ sprout ♦ squirt (Try also **bad child** ♦

boisterous child ♦ impish child ♦ playful child ♦ small child ♦ children's television.)

children patter of tiny feet

children's television kid-vid

chill chizzle ♦ freeze so out

chip fleabite

chocolate lover chocoholic

choice different strokes for different folks (Try also **food choice ♦ no choice ♦ limit choices.**)

choose give so the nod ♦ leather or feather ♦ Name your poison. ♦ tap so (for sth) ♦ What'll it be? ♦ What's yours?

choosy picky

chop off whack sth off

chop up whack sth up

chosen Try **be chosen.**

chuckle (n) buzz

CIA spook factory

cigar cig ♦ hemp ♦ puffer ♦ root ♦ seegar ♦ stog(ie) ♦ weed

cigar butt old soldier ♦ snipe

cigarette blower ♦ burn ♦ butt ♦ cancer stick ♦ choker ♦ cig ♦ ciggy ♦ coffin nail ♦ coffin tack ♦ fag ♦ jigger ♦ maggot ♦ nail ♦ OP's ♦ pimpstick ♦ ret ♦ root ♦ tailor-made ♦ tube ♦ weed (Try also **marijuana cigarette (with drugs) ♦ marijuana cigarette stub ♦ crush cigarette ♦ fat marijuana cigarette ♦ light marijuana cigarette ♦ marijuana cigarette ♦ tobacco cigarette ♦ smuggling cigarettes.**)

cigarette and coffee Mexican breakfast

cigarette butt butt ♦ corpse ♦ dead soldier ♦ doofer ♦ dufer ♦ dummy ♦ snipe ♦ teaser

cigarette pack deck

cigarette papers straw

circumcised clipped ♦ cut

circus big top

city asphalt jungle

civil servant civil serpent

civilian clothes civvies

claim dibs on sth

claim front seat call shotgun

clarinet licorice stick

class (n) snazz (Try also **biology class ♦ middle class.**)

classical music lover longhair

classy snazzy ♦ snitzy ♦ swanky

clean (mod) squeaky clean

clean marijuana manicure

clear sky clear as vodka

cleavage Gland Canyon ♦ Mammary Lane

cleft Try **gluteal cleft ♦ underpants in cleft ♦ vulval cleft.**

cleric holy Joe ♦ padre

clerical collar dog collar

clerk paper-pusher ♦ pencil-pusher

clever sharp ♦ slick ♦ swift

clever person one smart apple ♦ sharpie ♦ Sherlock ♦ smart cookie ♦ smooth operator ♦ smoothie

climax capper

climber Try **mountain climber ♦ rock climber.**

clincher capper

cling cling like shit to a shovel ♦ stick like shit to a shovel

clitoris clit

clock tick-tock

close (mod) close as stink on shit ♦ Close, but no cigar. ♦ hand-in-glove ♦ joined at the hip ♦ like the white on rice ♦ on so's tail ♦ up in so's gold ones ♦ up on so's bumper ♦ within an ace of (doing) sth ♦ within spitting distance (Try also **follow closely.**)

close (mod) friend homeboy ♦ homegirl

close door Were you born in a barn? ♦ fold

cloth Try **head cloth.**

clothes Try **civilian clothes ♦ person obsessed with clothes.**

clothes swapping wardrobing

clothing duds ♦ fronts ♦ glad rags ♦ outfit ♦ rag ♦ silks ♦ threads ♦ vines ♦ weeds

clown bimbo ♦ bozo

clue giveaway ♦ tip-off

clumsy half-ass(ed) ♦ ham-handed

clumsy person klotz ♦ klutz

Coast Guard knee-deep navy

coastal dweller coaster

cocaine blow ♦ brick ♦ cane ♦ Charles ♦ flake ♦ heaven dust ♦ hooter ♦ hubbas ♦ ice ♦ icicles ♦ incentive ♦ initiative ♦ joy dust ♦ joy flakes ♦ Lady Snow ♦ leaf ♦ line ♦ moonrock ♦ nose (candy) ♦ sea ♦ snow stuff ♦ snowball ♦ snowflakes ♦ yola ♦ zip (Try also **take cocaine ♦ use cocaine.**)

cocaine addicted candied ♦ flaky ♦ nose habit

cocaine crystal user crackhead

cocaine crystals crack ♦ crystal ♦ hubbas ♦ rock ♦ rock candy ♦ snow

cocaine device (flake) spoon ♦ cokespoon ♦ scoop

cocaine dose snort

cocaine house crack house

cocaine lines rails

cocaine user blower ♦ C-head ♦ cokeaholic ♦ cokehead ♦ horner ♦ jerker ♦ snow bunny

cocky person smart ass ♦ smart guy ♦ smart mouth ♦ smarty ♦ smarty-pants

coddling Try requiring coddling.

code Try bad computer code.

coffee brew ♦ java ♦ joe ♦ box (Try also cigarette and coffee.)

coffee and doughnut coffee and

coffee without milk black

coffin eternity-box ♦ tree-suit

cognac yak

cohorts BOF

coin Try one-dollar coin ♦ quarter (coin).

coincide track

coincidence coincidink

coins shekels ♦ shrapnel

cold airish ♦ Baby it's cold outside. ♦ baltic ♦ burrnips ♦ freezing cold ♦ nipply ♦ Siberian express

cold hearted person iceberg ♦ iceberg slim

cold weather BICO

cold woman ice queen

collapse Try stock price collapse (n).

collar Try clerical collar.

collection Try news collection.

college Try average male college student ♦ ordinary male college student ♦ technical college student ♦ typical male college student.

cologne foo-foo water

comatose person veggy

comb hair level the locks ♦ level one's locks ♦ mow the lawn ♦ mow one's lawn

combination combo

come Try when the time comes ♦ more trouble is coming.

come forward step right up

come here Get your ass over here!

come to attention snap to (attention)

comedy Try situation comedy.

comfort (n) crying towel

comfort (v) stroke

comfortable down with sth

comfortable living easy street

commanding officer old man

comment on departure parting shot

commit crime pull a job

commit suicide eat one's gun ♦ go off the deep end ♦ take the gas pipe ♦ take the pipe

common man joe ♦ Joe Blow ♦ Joe Citizen ♦ Joe Doakes ♦ John Doe

common people grassroots ♦ the great unwashed

common-law alimony palimony

commotion hoo-ha ♦ ruckus ♦ rumpus ♦ stink

communicate touch base (with so)

communist pinko

commuter straphanger

company outfit

comparison A2O ♦ apples to oranges

compassionate touchy-feely

competent able to cut sth ♦ on the ball (Try also look competent.)

competition dog-eat-dog (Try also pointless competition.)

competitive skill game ♦ big league

complain beef ♦ beef about so/sth ♦ bitch ♦ bitch out ♦ front off about sth ♦ gritch ♦ grouse ♦ kick ♦ kvetch ♦ make a stink (about so/sth) ♦ pitch a bitch ♦ poor-mouth ♦ quetch ♦ scream bloody murder ♦ sound off (about sth) ♦ squawk ♦ yell one's guts out ♦ yell one's head off

complainer gritch ♦ kvetch

complaining bitchy

complaint another peep (out of you) ♦ beef ♦ bitch ♦ flack ♦ flak ♦ guff♦ kick ♦ squawk ♦ static (Try also false complaint.)

complaint session bitch session

complete (mod) from A to Z ♦ out-and-out

complete easily sail (right) through sth ♦ pass go ♦ whack sth off

completed cinched ♦ sewed up

completed deal done deal

completely full sesh ♦ hook, line, and sinker ♦ stone ♦ totally

compliant easy

complicated You don't know the half of it.

comprehensive wall-to-wall

computation number crunching

computer iron (Try also bad computer code ♦ human computer user ♦ refuse computer data ♦ steal computer data ♦ when computer operates ♦ large computer ♦ start computer ♦ useless computer.)

computer addict mouse potato

computer application app

computer beginner muggle

computer crash barf ♦ blue screen of death ♦ BSOD

computer invader hacker

computer key hotkey

computer lover tech-nerd

computer parts hardware

473

bones ♦ lay ♦ make it ♦ park the pink
Plymouth ♦ play hide the sausage ♦ poke
♦ pork ♦ pound ♦ scam ♦ score ♦ screw ♦
screw around ♦ scrog ♦ scrump ♦ shack up
(with so)

copulated with been had ♦ laid ♦ layed ♦
porked ♦ screwed

copulation bang ♦ biggie ♦ bumping fuzzies ♦
bunch-punch ♦ fast one ♦ flying-fuck ♦ fuck ♦
honey fuck ♦ horizontal hula ♦ hump ♦ hunk
of ass ♦ hunk of tail ♦ lay ♦ mattress mambo
♦ mifky-pifky (in the bushes) ♦ nookie ♦
nooky ♦ piece of ass ♦ piece of snatch ♦
piece of tail ♦ screwage ♦ vag ♦ ziggy-
wiggling (Try also **quick copulation** ♦ **serial
copulation.**)

copulation in public love-in

copulator fucker

copy (n) dub ♦ dupe ♦ take off

copy (v) bite ♦ bite on so ♦ dub ♦ dupe ♦
knock sth off ♦ take a page from so's book

copycat biter

corned beef salt horse

corny cornball

corpse dog meat ♦ landowner ♦ stiff ♦ worm-
food

correct Party on! ♦ right as rain ♦ You bet
your boots! ♦ You bet your sweet life!

correct thing just the ticket ♦ just what the
doctor ordered

corrupt someone turn

corruption slime

Corvette vette

cost (n) ante (Try also **absorb cost** ♦ **split
cost.**)

cost (v) set so back

cough hack

cough up hawk

count Try **people count.**

counterfeit queer (Try also **spend
counterfeit money** ♦ **pass counterfeit** ♦
sell counterfeit.)

counterfeit money funny-money

couple Try **serious couple** ♦ **young couple.**)

couple in love hot item

courage backbone ♦ balls ♦ chones ♦ grit ♦
guts ♦ spunk ♦ stones (Try also **get courage**
♦ **require courage.**)

courageous ballsy ♦ gutsy ♦ nervy ♦ spunky

course weeder (Try also **difficult course** ♦
easy course ♦ **imaginary course** ♦ **off
course** ♦ **on course** ♦ **pass course** ♦
psychology course.)

court rush

cousin cuz

cover Try **attempt a cover up** ♦ **hair cover.**

cover distance make

cover up (n) whitewash

cover up (v) tap dance like mad ♦
whitewash

covered with crawling with so/sth

cow dung cow chips ♦ cow flop ♦ cow plop ♦
cow-doots ♦ meadow muffin

coward (limp) dishrag ♦ candy-ass ♦ chicken
♦ fraidy cat ♦ yellow-belly

cowardly candy-ass ♦ candy-ass(ed) ♦
chicken shit ♦ chicken-hearted ♦ lily-livered ♦
yellow ♦ yellow-bellied (Try also **be
cowardly.**)

crack (buttocks) Try **gluteal cleft.**

crack device blinky ♦ winky

crack houses abandominiums

crafts lover artsy-craftsy

crankshaft wrinkle-rod

crash (n) beef ♦ fender-bender ♦ rear-ender ♦
wipe out ♦ yard-sale (Try also **car crash** ♦
computer crash ♦ **market crash.**)

crash (v) crack up ♦ gronk (out) ♦ beef ♦ biff
♦ bomb (out)

crashed down

crave drool (all) over so/sth ♦ feen for sth ♦
hurt for so/sth ♦ jones

craving hurting ♦ jones (Try also **hamburger
craving.**)

crazy (a)round the bend ♦ balmy ♦ bananas ♦
bats ♦ batty ♦ bonkers ♦ bonzo ♦ cockeyed ♦
coo-coo ♦ cracked ♦ crackers ♦ crunk ♦
cuckoo ♦ daffy ♦ dippy ♦ gaga ♦ gonzo ♦ half
a bubble off plumb ♦ haywire ♦ loco ♦ loony
♦ meshuga ♦ non compos ♦ not all there ♦
nuts ♦ nutz ♦ off the hook ♦ off one's chump
♦ off one's meds ♦ off one's nut ♦ out in left
field ♦ plumb loco ♦ potty ♦ round the bend
♦ scooters ♦ screwy ♦ squirrelly (Try also **be
crazy** ♦ **drive crazy** ♦ **go crazy.**)

crazy person crazy ♦ loony ♦ nutcase ♦
nutter ♦ psycho ♦ sicky ♦ squirrel-food

create disturbance kick up a storm

create ideas brainstorm

credibility cred ♦ street cred

credit card plastic

credits brownie points

crime caper ♦ situation (Try also **charge with
crime** ♦ **commit crime** ♦ **insider's crime.**)

crime boss kingpin ♦ pin

crime syndicate mob

criminal perp (Try also **false criminal charge
♦ get free of criminal charge ♦ loyal
criminal.**)
criminal charge beef ♦ rap
criminal driver wheel man
criminal record (rap) sheet
criminal roundup scoop
crisis crunch
critic nit-picker ♦ sidewalk superintendent
critical picky
criticism kicker ♦ nit-picking ♦ potshot ♦ slam
(Try also **easy criticism ♦ hold back
criticism ♦ ignore criticism ♦ impervious
to criticism ♦ receive criticism ♦ suffer
criticism ♦ unjustified criticism ♦
withstand criticism.**)
criticism draw (n) lightning rod
criticize bag on so ♦ bash ♦ dish ♦ do a dump
on so/sth ♦ dog ♦ dump all over so/sth ♦ get
down on so ♦ knock ♦ lay a (heavy) trip on
so ♦ lay so out in lavender ♦ rag on so ♦ rake
on so ♦ slam ♦ take so/sth apart ♦ tear so/sth
apart ♦ thrash on so
crook big juice (Try also **trustworthy crook.**)
crosshatch Try **number sign.**
crowd (n) fanny-bumper
crowded bumping ♦ not enough room to
swing a cat
crowded place hellhole
Crown Victoria (car) Vickie
crucial moment This is it!
crude gross ♦ raunchy ♦ raw ♦ ripe ♦ ronchie
crude man animal ♦ beast ♦ greaser
cruel dog-eat-dog ♦ in cold blood
crunch (v) scrunch
crush (v) scrunch
crush cigarette clip a butt
crushed bashed
cry (v) turn on the waterworks ♦ water one's
cheeks
crying woman sob sister
crystal Try **cocaine crystal user ♦ cocaine
crystals ♦ heroin crystals.**)
cubes Try **ice cubes.**
cuddle grouse ♦ neck
cue card idiot card
cull stock Hold some, fold some.
culling shakeout
culture Try **drug culture.**
cumulative cum
cunnilinguist (male) cocksucker
cunnilingus Try **perform cunnilingus.**
cure fix (Try also **diarrhea cure.**)
current in (Try also **technologically current.**)

current thinking where so's head is at
curse (v) swear like a trooper
curses Try **damn and similar curses and
expressions.**
curvaceous woman built like a brick
shithouse
customer walk-in (Try also **prostitute's
customer ♦ reward a customer.**)
cute person cutie
cute thing cutie
Dairy Queen DQ
Dallas, TX big-D.
damage (v) crock so/sth up ♦ take so/sth apart
♦ w(h)ack so/sth up ♦ whack so/sth up
damaged hurt (Try also **brain damaged
(drugs).**)
damn and similar curses and expressions
Drat! ♦ flipping ♦ fricking ♦ frigging ♦ Fuck a
dog! ♦ Fuck a duck! ♦ Fuck it (all)! ♦ fucking
♦ greldge ♦ hell ♦ Hell's bells (and buckets of
blood)! ♦ nerts ♦ nurts ♦ phooey ♦ piffle ♦
Piss on it! ♦ Rats! ♦ Sheesh! ♦ shit ♦ Shiznits!
♦ Shoot! ♦ Shucks! ♦ son of a bitch ♦ son of
a gun ♦ That tears it!
damned blasted ♦ ding-dong ♦ doggone(d) ♦
freaking ♦ jiggered
dance (n) hop ♦ shindig (Try also **erotic
dance ♦ break dancer.**)
dance (v) boogie ♦ get down ♦ get it on ♦
shake a leg ♦ shank
dancer erotic dancer ♦ hoofer ♦ lap dancer ♦
pole dancer
danger Behind you!
dangerous sketchy
dangerous end business end (of sth)
dangerous horse widow-maker
dangerous situation situation
daring nervy
darn (Aw) shucks! ♦ Shucks!
data Try **lost data container ♦ refuse
computer data ♦ steal computer data.**)
date (n) calendar ♦ heavy date up-to-date
person ♦ be up-to-date ♦ break date ♦ forget
date ♦ important date ♦ out of date ♦
provided with date.)
date (v) take so out (Try also **black dates
white.**)
dawn candlelight
day Try **bad day ♦ first day ♦ hot day ♦
important day ♦ work day.**
daytime drama soap
dead belly up ♦ blown ♦ blown away ♦ boxed
♦ cold ♦ crapped (out) ♦ crumped (out) ♦
dead and gone ♦ DOA ♦ done for ♦ feeling

seeing snakes ♦ shakes ♦ snozzle-wobbles ♦ staggers ♦ zings ♦ the rats

deltoids delts

demand money put the arm on so ♦ put the bite on so

Democrat demo

demolish knock sth into a cocked hat

demolished shot down

demonstrate demo ♦ show and tell

demonstrate power kick ass ♦ kick butt ♦ kick some ass (around) ♦ knock some heads together

demonstration dem ♦ demo

den of thieves crib

denigrate piss on so/sth

dent ding

dental braces railroad tracks ♦ tin grin

deodorant BO juice ♦ pit stop

depart Try **leave.**

departure Try **comment on departure.**

departure of intellectuals brain-drain

depress bring so down

depressant down

depressed blue ♦ bum about so/sth ♦ bummed (out) ♦ bumming ♦ down ♦ drag ass around ♦ drug ♦ drug out ♦ in a blue funk ♦ sorry-ass(ed) ♦ strung out ♦ way down

depressed person sad sack

depression blue devils ♦ blue funk ♦ funk ♦ the blahs

dermatologist zit doctor

describe show and tell

description Try **concise description.**

deserved Try **get what is deserved.**

desire Try **have desire.**

desire (n) jones

desire (v) feen for sth ♦ hurt for so/sth ♦ jones

desirous have the hots (for so) ♦ hurting ♦ queer for sth

desk Try **desk worker ♦ away from desk.**

desk worker desk jockey

despair (n) bummage ♦ pits

despicable cocksucking ♦ gweebo ♦ lowdown ♦ motherfucking ♦ rotten to the core ♦ shit-ass

despicable person (usually male) grunch ♦ grunge ♦ motherfucker ♦ schtoonk ♦ scut ♦ scuz(z) ♦ scuzzbag ♦ scuzzbucket ♦ shithead ♦ shitsky ♦ sidewinder ♦ sleaz ♦ sleaze ♦ slime ♦ slime bag ♦ slime bucket ♦ slimebag ♦ slimeball ♦ sludgeball ♦ smeg ♦ son of a bitch ♦ son of a gun ♦ turd ♦ turd face

despised pukey ♦ pukoid ♦ scurvy ♦ skanky ♦ stinky

despised man butt-munch ♦ hodad ♦ hodaddy ♦ King Grod ♦ louse ♦ penis wrinkle ♦ schmuck ♦ vag ♦ zarf

despised person (usually male) bad egg ♦ bad news ♦ bad trip ♦ Barf City ♦ barf-out ♦ bathtub scum ♦ butt ♦ fuckface ♦ hole ♦ horse's ass ♦ ick ♦ jackal ♦ little shit ♦ louse ♦ low rent ♦ low-life ♦ maggot ♦ mutant ♦ rat-bastard ♦ rotten egg ♦ schtoonk ♦ scuzzo ♦ scuzzy ♦ shit ♦ shitbox ♦ shower scum ♦ shtoonk ♦ sleaze-bucket ♦ sleazebag ♦ sleazeball ♦ sludgeball ♦ SOB ♦ turd ♦ turd face ♦ worm ♦ yard dog ♦ zod

despised place Barf City

despised thing Barf City ♦ barf-out ♦ turn-off ♦ zod

despite efforts for (all) one's trouble

destroy blow ♦ blow so out of the water ♦ bust sth up ♦ chain(saw) ♦ do a job on so/sth ♦ do a number on sth ♦ nuke ♦ rambo(ize) ♦ take sth out

destroyed blooey ♦ fragged ♦ shot down ♦ shot to hell

destroyed by drugs vegged out

destroyer Try **pleasure destroyer.**

destruction blow up ♦ death on so/sth

details chapter and verse ♦ the ins and outs

detain buttonhole

detective dick ♦ fuzz ♦ gumshoe ♦ private eye ♦ sham(m)us ♦ snatcher

detector Try **liquor detector.**

determining factor clincher

Detroit, MI Motown

device Try **beer drinking device ♦ cocaine device ♦ crack device ♦ defective device ♦ hashish device ♦ marijuana device ♦ install spy devices.**

devil deuce ♦ dickens

devilish full of Old Nick ♦ full of the devil

devilish person holy terror

devious person jackal

devotee Try **enthusiast.**

diamond ice ♦ rock ♦ sparkler (Try also **wearing diamonds.**)

diarrhea Aztec two-step ♦ backdoor trot(s) ♦ Basra belly ♦ Delhi belly ♦ green apple quickstep ♦ Hong Kong dog ♦ Montezuma's revenge ♦ movies ♦ turistas ♦ the runs ♦ the scoots ♦ the shits ♦ the squirts ♦ the trots (Try also **have diarrhea.**)

diarrhea cure liquid cork

diary blog ♦ vblog ♦ videoblog ♦ weblog (Try also **using diary online.**)

dice bones ♦ cube ♦ ivories ♦ knuckle bones

dice score big Dick ♦ snake eyes

dictator big brother

die bag ♦ beam up ♦ bite the big one ♦ bite the dust ♦ box on the table ♦ buy it ♦ buy the big one ♦ buy the farm ♦ cash in (one's) checks ♦ cash in (one's) chips ♦ cool ♦ croak ♦ curl up and die ♦ die on so ♦ flatline ♦ fry ♦ get one's ticket punched ♦ go belly up ♦ go tits up ♦ go West ♦ kick (off) ♦ kick the bucket ♦ kiss off ♦ kiss the dust ♦ off ♦ pop off ♦ snuff it ♦ sprout wings ♦ step off the curb ♦ take a dirt nap ♦ take the (long) count ♦ tap out ♦ turn belly up

die in chair burn

difference diff (Try also **no difference.**)

different needs different strokes for different folks

difficult ball-breaker ♦ ball-buster ♦ ball-busting ♦ hairy ♦ hell (Try also **too difficult to understand ♦ make difficult ♦ in difficulty.**)

difficult course skull-buster ♦ skull-popper

difficult experience hard time

difficult person bitch ♦ handful ♦ tough customer ♦ tough egg to crack ♦ tough nut to crack ♦ a cold piece of work

difficult problem tough egg to crack

difficult request tall order

difficult task ball-breaker ♦ ball-buster ♦ bitch ♦ tough row to hoe

difficult thing handful ♦ tough nut to crack

difficult time a devil of a time ♦ the devil's own time

difficulty motherfucker ♦ snag ♦ tight spot

digitus impudicus bird ♦ finger wave ♦ flip so off ♦ flip so out ♦ flip so the bird ♦ give so the finger ♦ OFS ♦ one-finger salute

digression riff

dilemma between a rock and a hard place ♦ catch-22

dilute drugs (v) stretch

diluted (drugs) choked ♦ stepped on

dime thin dime

dimming of lights brown out

diner beanery ♦ greasy spoon ♦ hash-house

dinner where one is insulted roast

dinnertime bean time ♦ Soup's on!

diploma sheepskin

direct (mod) straight from the horse's mouth ♦ straight from the shoulder

direct person hip-shooter

direct talk straight talk

direction Try **from surprising direction.**

dirt dreck

dirty grungy

dirty baby stinkpot

disagreement falling-out

disappointed burned

disappointment anticipointment ♦ come down

disapproval sign thumbs down

disaster cluster fuck

disbelief I don't believe this!

discard 86 ♦ chuck ♦ deep six ♦ ditch ♦ Dump it. ♦ eighty-six ♦ Junk it! ♦ kiss so/sth off ♦ Nuke it! ♦ Pitch it ♦ scarf ♦ shitcan ♦ toss ♦ Toss it! ♦ trash ♦ Trash it!

discounted on the street

discourage bum so out ♦ bummed (out) ♦ turned off

discover hit on sth ♦ hit pay dirt ♦ strike pay dirt

discretionary fund slush fund

discussion heart-to-heart (talk)

disease Try **fight off disease ♦ resist disease ♦ sexually transmitted disease.**

disgust (v) gross so out ♦ raunch so out ♦ barf so out

disgusted cheesed off ♦ sick to death (of so/sth)

disgusting person heap ♦ pisshead ♦ scum ♦ scumbag ♦ sleazoid ♦ yuck ♦ yuk ♦ gross-out ♦ heap ♦ groaty ♦ grody ♦ grody to the max ♦ gross ♦ gross-out ♦ icky-poo ♦ rotten ♦ shit-ass ♦ skeevy ♦ skrungy ♦ So gross!

dishes Try **wash dishes.**

dishonest bent ♦ fly-by-night

disinterest Try **show disinterest.**

disliked person gym shoe

dismiss pink slip ♦ sack ♦ tell so what to do with sth ♦ tell so where to get off

dismissal notice pink slip ♦ brushoff ♦ kiss off ♦ old heave-ho ♦ rif ♦ sack ♦ walking papers

disorder Try **stumbling disorder.**

disorient blitz so out ♦ freak so out ♦ fuck so's mind (up)

disoriented freaked (out) ♦ haywire ♦ strung out

display Try **muscular display (male) ♦ female display ♦ woman on display.**

display temper throw a fit

disputing on the outs (with so)

disreputable sleazo

disrespect dis(s) ♦ dis(s) (on so)

drive up zoom up

driver Try **criminal driver ♦ fast driver ♦ motorcycle driver ♦ reckless driver ♦ ride next to driver ♦ slow driver ♦ speeder (driver) ♦ taxi driver.**

drop Try **fall.**

drop down hit the deck

drug (n) barb ♦ benny ♦ gyve ♦ head drug ♦ headfucker ♦ hit ♦ idiot juice ♦ idiotic ♦ jock(e)y ♦ jolt ♦ leaf ♦ narc ♦ narco ♦ narky ♦ noise ♦ sacred mushrooms ♦ snort ♦ speed (Try also **bad drug experience ♦ burst of drug euphoria ♦ get drug intoxicated ♦ good drug experience ♦ help drug user ♦ inhale drug fumes ♦ obtain drug dose ♦ replay of a drug high ♦ add drug ♦ addictive drug ♦ beginner's drug ♦ glue (as a drug) ♦ inhaled drug ♦ inject drug ♦ pill (drug) ♦ powdered drug ♦ powerful drug ♦ unaffected by drug ♦ taking drugs again ♦ bad drugs ♦ become euphoric (drugs) ♦ behave well (drugs) ♦ brain damaged (drugs) ♦ buy drugs ♦ carry drugs ♦ carrying drugs ♦ conceal drugs ♦ destroyed by drugs ♦ diluted (drugs) ♦ emergency drugs ♦ fake drugs ♦ free of drugs ♦ get off drugs ♦ go back to drugs ♦ hide (drugs) ♦ injecting drugs ♦ marijuana cigarette (with drugs) ♦ needing drugs ♦ off drugs ♦ plant drugs ♦ possess drugs ♦ pure drugs ♦ quit drugs ♦ ruined by drugs ♦ sell drugs ♦ selling drugs ♦ sold bad drugs ♦ transport drugs ♦ use drugs ♦ using drugs ♦ dilute drugs (v).**)

drug (v) slip so a Mickey

drug carrier mule

drug culture scene

drug dealer bagman ♦ candy man ♦ connection ♦ courier ♦ drug lord ♦ good-time man ♦ junkie ♦ man ♦ mother ♦ pusher ♦ street pusher ♦ swingman

drug dose bindle ♦ bop ♦ charge ♦ check ♦ fix ♦ snort ♦ jolt ♦ strike

drug euphoria tag ♦ trip

drug free clean ♦ on the natch ♦ straight

drug injection bang ♦ belt ♦ shot ♦ shot in the arm

drug injector hit man ♦ hyper ♦ jabber

drug intoxicated amped ♦ backed up ♦ baked ♦ beaned up ♦ belted ♦ bent ♦ bent out of shape ♦ blind(ed) ♦ blissed (out) ♦ blitzed (out) ♦ blixed ♦ blocked ♦ blowed (away) ♦ blown (out) ♦ blown away ♦ bombed (out) ♦ boxed (up) ♦ charged (up) ♦ cooked ♦ crisp ♦ destroyed ♦ dopey ♦ edged ♦ enhanced ♦ faded ♦ far out ♦ feel groovy ♦ fixed ♦ flaked out ♦ foxy ♦ fried ♦ funked out ♦ gassed (up) ♦ GBed ♦ girked ♦ gone ♦ gonged ♦ goofed (up) ♦ groovy ♦ high ♦ horsed ♦ hurt ♦ hyped (up) ♦ in orbit ♦ in the ozone ♦ jacked ♦ jacked up ♦ jazzed (up) ♦ keyed (up) ♦ keyed up to the roof ♦ killed (off) ♦ knocked out ♦ KOed ♦ laid ♦ laid back ♦ laid out ♦ layed ♦ loaded ♦ mellow ♦ messed up ♦ monolithic ♦ numbed out ♦ off ♦ oiled ♦ ossified ♦ out ♦ out of it ♦ out of sight ♦ out of this world ♦ over the hump ♦ overamped ♦ perking ♦ perma-fried ♦ phased ♦ phazed ♦ phumfed ♦ plowed (under) ♦ plugged in ♦ polluted ♦ popped ♦ primed ♦ psyched (out) ♦ racked (up) ♦ riffed ♦ ripped ♦ ripped (off) ♦ ripped (up) ♦ scattered ♦ schnockered ♦ schnoggered ♦ scorched ♦ sent ♦ shot-up ♦ skagged out ♦ skating ♦ skulled ♦ smashed ♦ smeared ♦ snaved in ♦ spiked ♦ stoned (out) ♦ stoned out of one's gourd ♦ stoned out of one's head ♦ stoned out of one's squash ♦ stoned silly ♦ strung (up) ♦ strung out ♦ taken ♦ teed (up) ♦ trashed ♦ turned on ♦ w(h)acked ♦ w(h)acked (out) ♦ warped ♦ way out ♦ wide ♦ wigged (out) ♦ wiggy ♦ wiped over ♦ wired ♦ wired up ♦ wrecked ♦ zerked (out) ♦ zipped ♦ zoned (out) ♦ zonked (out) ♦ zootied ♦ zounked (out) ♦ zunked

drug intoxicated and drunk strunk

drug panic freak (out)

drug party kick party

drug rush bang ♦ belt ♦ blast ♦ call ♦ jag ♦ jolt ♦ kick ♦ lift ♦ lift-up ♦ org ♦ tag

drug transporter carrier ♦ courier ♦ mule

drug user bean head ♦ blower ♦ dope fiend ♦ druggie ♦ drughead ♦ garbage freak ♦ garbagehead ♦ grasser ♦ grasshead ♦ grasshopper ♦ guru ♦ hammerhead ♦ head ♦ hippy ♦ hophead ♦ horner ♦ huffer ♦ hyper ♦ jerker ♦ kick freak ♦ kite ♦ loady ♦ stoner ♦ user

drug-sniffing dog pot hound ♦ pot sniffer

drums hides ♦ skins

drumsticks boom sticks

drunk activated ♦ alkied (up) ♦ annihilated ♦ antifreezed ♦ aped ♦ apeshit ♦ bagged ♦ baked ♦ balmed ♦ balmy ♦ bamboozled ♦ banjaxed ♦ barreled (up) ♦ bashed ♦ basted ♦ bats ♦ batted ♦ battered ♦ batty ♦ belly up ♦ belted ♦ bent ♦ bent out of shape ♦ bewottled ♦ binged ♦ bladdered ♦ blimped ♦

blind drunk ✦ blind(ed) ✦ blissed (out) ✦ blitzed (out) ✦ blocked ✦ blooey ✦ blotto ✦ blowed (away) ✦ blown (out) ✦ blown (up) ✦ blown away ✦ blue ✦ blue around the gills ✦ bobo ✦ boiled ✦ bombed (out) ✦ bonkers ✦ boozed ✦ boozy-woozy ✦ both sheets in the wind ✦ boxed (up) ✦ brewed ✦ bruised ✦ bunked ✦ busted ✦ buzzing ✦ canned ✦ carrying a (heavy) load ✦ chucked ✦ clear ✦ clobbered ✦ cocked ✦ comboozelated ✦ commode-hugging drunk ✦ cooked ✦ corked (up) ✦ corky ✦ corned ✦ country drunk ✦ crashed ✦ creamed ✦ crocked ✦ cross-eyed (drunk) ✦ crumped (out) ✦ crunk ✦ crying drunk ✦ cut ✦ damaged ✦ dead drunk ✦ dead to the world ✦ dinged out ✦ dipsy ✦ discombobulated ✦ discomboobulated ✦ down ✦ drunk back ✦ edged ✦ electrified ✦ elevated ✦ eliminated ✦ embalmed ✦ faced ✦ faded ✦ falling-down drunk ✦ far gone ✦ far out ✦ feel groovy ✦ feeling no pain ✦ feshnushkied ✦ fitshaced ✦ fixed ✦ flaked ✦ flaked out ✦ flako ✦ flaky ✦ flash ✦ flooey ✦ floored ✦ folded ✦ foozlified ✦ four sheets (to the wind) ✦ four sheets in the wind ✦ foxy ✦ fractured ✦ fried ✦ funked out ✦ funky-drunk ✦ fuzzed ✦ fuzzled ✦ fuzzy ✦ gargler ✦ gassed (up) ✦ giffed ✦ glad ✦ glass(y)-eyed ✦ glazed (drunk) ✦ glazed (over) ✦ glued ✦ goggle-eyed ✦ gone ✦ goofy ✦ googly-eyed ✦ gooned ✦ grape shot ✦ greased ✦ groggified ✦ groggy ✦ guzzled ✦ half in the bag ✦ half up the pole ✦ half-baked ✦ half-blind ✦ half-canned ✦ half-cocked ✦ half-crocked ✦ half-lit ✦ half-sprung ✦ half-stewed ✦ half-under ✦ hammered ✦ happy ✦ hard up ✦ heeled ✦ heister ✦ hepped (up) ✦ high ✦ hit under the wing ✦ honked ✦ honkers ✦ hooched (up) ✦ hooted ✦ hootered ✦ horizontal ✦ hot ✦ howling (drunk) ✦ illuminated ✦ impaired ✦ in a bad way ✦ in a heap ✦ in orbit ✦ in rare form ✦ in the bag ✦ in the grip of the grape ✦ in the gun ✦ in the ozone ✦ in the pink ✦ in the suds ✦ inside out ✦ jagged ✦ jambled ✦ jammed ✦ jazzed (up) ✦ jiggered ✦ jingled ✦ jolly ✦ jugged (up) ✦ juicy ✦ jungled ✦ Kentucky fried ✦ keyed (up) ✦ keyed up to the roof ✦ killed (off) ✦ kited ✦ knocked out ✦ knocked up ✦ KOed ✦ laid ✦ laid back ✦ laid out ✦ laid to the bone ✦ lathered ✦ layed ✦ lifted ✦ light ✦ liquefied ✦ lit ✦ lit up ✦ loaded ✦ loaded for bear ✦ loaded to the barrel ✦ loaded to the gills ✦ loony ✦ loop-legged ✦ looped ✦ loopy ✦ loose ✦ lost in the sauce ✦

lubricated ✦ maggot(t)y ✦ mashed ✦ maxed out ✦ mellow ✦ messed up ✦ Mickey finished ✦ milled ✦ mixed (up) ✦ moist around the edges ✦ moonlit ✦ mopped ✦ moppy ✦ muddled (up) ✦ muggy ✦ nipped ✦ non compos ✦ non compos poopoo ✦ obliterated ✦ off ✦ oiled ✦ on the blink ✦ on the fritz ✦ on the sauce ✦ ossified ✦ Otis ✦ out ✦ out cold ✦ out like a light ✦ out of it ✦ out of sight ✦ out of the way ✦ out of one's skull ✦ overserved ✦ packaged ✦ pafisticated ✦ paid ✦ parboiled ✦ pee'd ✦ peonied ✦ pepped (up) ✦ perked (up) ✦ perking ✦ perma-fried ✦ petrified ✦ phfft ✦ pickled ✦ pie-eyed ✦ piff(l)icated ✦ piffed ✦ piffled ✦ pigeon-eyed ✦ pilfered ✦ pinked ✦ pipped (up) ✦ pissed ✦ pixilated ✦ pixolated ✦ plastered ✦ plastered to the wall ✦ pleasantly plastered ✦ plonked (up) ✦ plootered ✦ plotzed ✦ plowed (under) ✦ polished (up) ✦ polluted ✦ pooped (out) ✦ poopied ✦ pop-eyed ✦ popped ✦ potted ✦ powdered (up) ✦ preserved ✦ primed ✦ psyched (out) ✦ puggled ✦ pummelled ✦ pushed ✦ put to bed with a shovel ✦ putrid ✦ quartzed ✦ queer ✦ queered ✦ racked (up) ✦ ratted ✦ rattled ✦ raunchy ✦ riffed ✦ ripe ✦ ripped ✦ ripped (off) ✦ ripped (up) ✦ roasted ✦ rotten ✦ rumdum ✦ rummed (up) ✦ rummy ✦ sauced ✦ sawed ✦ scammered ✦ schicker ✦ schickered ✦ schnockered ✦ schnoggered ✦ scorched ✦ screeching (drunk) ✦ screwed ✦ screwed tight ✦ screwy ✦ scronched ✦ seeing pink elephants ✦ sent ✦ sewed up ✦ SF ✦ shagged ✦ shammered ✦ shaved ✦ shellacked ✦ shicker ✦ shined ✦ shit-faced ✦ shitty ✦ shnockered ✦ shot ✦ shot in the neck ✦ shot-away ✦ shot-up ✦ shredded ✦ sizzled ✦ skulled ✦ skunk-drunk ✦ skunked ✦ slaughtered ✦ slewed ✦ slewy ✦ slightly rattled ✦ slopped ✦ sloshed (to the ears) ✦ sloughed (up) ✦ slued ✦ slugged ✦ slushed (up) ✦ smashed ✦ smeared ✦ snapped (up) ✦ snoggered ✦ snooted ✦ snoozamorooed ✦ snotted ✦ snozzled ✦ snuffy ✦ so-so ✦ soaked ✦ socked ✦ soft ✦ soggy ✦ sopping (wet) ✦ soppy ✦ sossled ✦ soupy ✦ soused ✦ southern-fried ✦ sozzled ✦ sozzly ✦ spanked ✦ spifflicated ✦ spificated ✦ spiked ✦ squiffed ✦ squiffy ✦ stale drunk ✦ starched ✦ starchy ✦ steamed (up) ✦ stew ✦ stewed (up) ✦ stewed to the ears ✦ stewed to the gills ✦ stiff ✦ stiffed ✦ stinking ✦ stinking (drunk) ✦ stone blind ✦ stoned (out) ✦ stoned out of one's squash ✦ stoned silly ✦ stonkered ✦

stozzled ♦ stuccoed ♦ stung ♦ stunned ♦ stupid ♦ swacked ♦ swamped ♦ swigged ♦ swiggled ♦ swizzled ♦ swoozled ♦ swozzled ♦ tacky ♦ tanked ♦ tanked up ♦ tanky ♦ tanned ♦ teed (up) ♦ that way ♦ thawed ♦ three sheets (to the wind) ♦ three sheets in the wind ♦ tiddled ♦ tiffled ♦ tight ♦ tight as a tick ♦ tipply ♦ tore (up) ♦ tore down ♦ torn (up) ♦ torqued ♦ totalled ♦ touched ♦ toxicated ♦ toxy ♦ trammeled ♦ trashed ♦ tubed ♦ tuned ♦ tweased ♦ tweeked ♦ twisted ♦ two sheets to the wind ♦ under the affluence of incohol ♦ under the table ♦ under the weather ♦ up the pole ♦ upholstered ♦ varnished ♦ vegetable ♦ vomatose ♦ w(h)acked ♦ w(h)acked (out) ♦ waa-zooed ♦ walking on rocky socks ♦ wall-eyed ♦ waxed ♦ way out ♦ well-fixed ♦ well-oiled ♦ wet ♦ whack ♦ whazood ♦ whiffled ♦ whittled ♦ whooshed ♦ wigged (out) ♦ wiggy ♦ wing heavy ♦ wiped (out) ♦ wiped over ♦ wired ♦ wired up ♦ woofled ♦ woozy ♦ wrecked ♦ zagged ♦ zissified ♦ zoned (out) ♦ zonked (out) ♦ zonker ♦ zoobang ♦ zooed ♦ zooted ♦ zootied ♦ zorked ♦ zosted ♦ zounked (out) ♦ zozzled ♦ zunked (Try also **be drunk ♦ drug intoxicated and drunk ♦ get drunk ♦ make drunk.**)

drunk (n) belt ♦ coffin nail ♦ double ♦ drinkypoo ♦ drop ♦ fast one ♦ finger ♦ gee ♦ geezer ♦ glug ♦ guzzle ♦ hit ♦ hooter ♦ jigger ♦ jollop ♦ jolt ♦ kick in the wrist ♦ load ♦ mouthwash ♦ nip ♦ one for the road ♦ pick-me-up ♦ pickup ♦ pull ♦ quencher ♦ short ♦ short one ♦ short-snort ♦ shot ♦ shot in the arm ♦ shot in the neck ♦ sniff ♦ spot ♦ swig ♦ swill ♦ tall one ♦ tipple ♦ touch ♦ wack ♦ whack

drunkard alchy ♦ alkie ♦ alky ♦ barfly ♦ barrel ♦ bat ♦ belcher ♦ bender ♦ blotter ♦ booze artist ♦ bottle ♦ bottle baby ♦ brewster ♦ Christmas tree ♦ crock ♦ dip ♦ dipso ♦ falling-down drunk ♦ ginhead ♦ glow worm ♦ groghound ♦ guzzle-guts ♦ guzzler ♦ hammerhead ♦ hellbender ♦ hooch head ♦ hooch hound ♦ hoocher ♦ hootcher ♦ hophead ♦ horner ♦ jagster ♦ jerker ♦ jingler ♦ job ♦ jugger ♦ juice freak ♦ juicehead ♦ juicer ♦ lapper ♦ loady ♦ lush ♦ mooner ♦ mop ♦ oilhead ♦ one of the faithful ♦ Otis ♦ pickler ♦ pisshead ♦ plonko ♦ rumdum ♦ rummy ♦ shuffler ♦ sipster ♦ skate ♦ skid row bum ♦ soak ♦ soaker ♦ sop ♦ souse ♦ sozzler

♦ sponge ♦ spud ♦ spunge ♦ squiff ♦ stew ♦ stew bum ♦ stiff ♦ stumblebum ♦ suds-swiller ♦ swizzle-stick ♦ tank ♦ tanker ♦ thirsty soul ♦ tippler ♦ two-fisted drinker ♦ whale ♦ wino ♦ yeaster

drunkard street skid row

drunken tremors Try **delirium tremens.**

drunkenness barrel fever ♦ glow ♦ staggers

dual-handed batter switch-hitter

dubious fishy

duct tape The Force

dull blah ♦ dead ♦ deadly (dull) ♦ deadpan ♦ dull as dishwater ♦ ho-hum ♦ ill ♦ illin' ♦ L7 ♦ nowhere ♦ punk ♦ uncool ♦ vanilla ♦ whitebread ♦ zhlubby

dull job rat race

dull lecture sleepfest ♦ snooze ♦ yawner

dull man hard off

dull person cube ♦ dim bulb ♦ dull person big drink of water ♦ boring old fart ♦ dumb-dumb ♦ jeff ♦ L7 ♦ laine ♦ lame ♦ lane ♦ mossback ♦ neb(bish) ♦ nerd ♦ newt ♦ schlub ♦ square biscuit ♦ stick in the mud ♦ stuffed shirt ♦ tech-nerd ♦ wimp ♦ zhlub

dull place dullsville

dull thing dullsville

dull woman Zelda

dullard attractor nerd magnet

dung caca ♦ cack ♦ crap ♦ do ♦ doo ♦ doo-doo ♦ dreck ♦ hockey ♦ hocky ♦ horse ♦ horse hockey ♦ horseshit ♦ kaka ♦ mess ♦ poo ♦ poop ♦ road apple ♦ shit ♦ shitsky ♦ shitstick (Try also **bird dung ♦ bull dung ♦ cow dung ♦ dog dung ♦ horse dung ♦ soiled with dung.**)

dung lifter pooper-scooper

dungy crappy ♦ shitty

dupe Try **victim.**

duplicate (mod) (dead) ringer (for SO) ♦ ringer

duplicate (v) dub

dusk candlelight ♦ early black

dweller Try **coastal dweller.**

dwelling crib ♦ digs ♦ layout ♦ setup

dying circling (the drain) ♦ fixing to die ♦ FTD ♦ in the O-zone

dynamite user powder monkey

eager hungry ♦ raring to go ♦ rough and ready ♦ with bells on

eager person eager-beaver

eager shooter trigger-happy

ear Try **large eared person.**

early the firstest with the mostest (Try also **newspaper early edition ♦ start early.**)

empty bottle corpse ♦ dead man ♦ dead marine ♦ dead on ♦ dead one ♦ dead soldier ♦ dummy ♦ em ♦ empty ♦ marine (recruit) ♦ marine officer ♦ MT ♦ old soldier ♦ soldier

empty bowels clean so out

empty talk noise

emulate take a page from so's book

emulating other people on the bandwagon

enamored of hooked (on so/sth) ♦ stuck on so/sth

encounter brush

encouragement kick in the (seat of the) pants ♦ kick in the ass ♦ kick in the butt ♦ kick in the rear ♦ kick in the teeth ♦ pep talk ♦ shot in the arm ♦ sweetener ♦ That-a-boy!

end (n) end of the ball game ♦ kibosh ♦ TEOTWAWKI ♦ That's that! ♦ the end of the world as we know it (Try also **back end ♦ cause of end ♦ dangerous end ♦ music end ♦ penis end ♦ ring endlessly ♦ talk endlessly.**)

end (v) kibosh ♦ kill ♦ pour cold water on sth ♦ pull the plug (on so/sth) ♦ put the kibosh on sth

endure change go through the changes ♦ hack it ♦ hang in there ♦ If you can't stand the heat, keep out of the kitchen. ♦ sweat blood ♦ sweat sth out ♦ take it ♦ take it on the chin ♦ take it on the nose ♦ tough sth out

energetic bright-eyed and bushy-tailed ♦ kicky ♦ peppy ♦ perky ♦ zappy

energetic person (live) wire ♦ ball of fire ♦ fireball ♦ go-getter ♦ hotshot

energy (ma)hoska ♦ bounce ♦ juice ♦ moxie ♦ oomph ♦ spizzerinktum ♦ zing ♦ zip ♦ zowie (Try also **burst of energy ♦ lacking energy.**)

engine 4-banger (Try also **race engine ♦ rev engine ♦ run engine ♦ run well (engine).**)

engine noise varoom

engine power pickup

English Try **broken English ♦ foreign English.**

enjoy oneself ball ♦ get it on ♦ get naked ♦ get one's rocks off (on sth) ♦ get off (on sth) ♦ go great guns

enlargement Try **photographic enlargement.**

enormous moby ♦ whopping (great)

enormous number bazillion ♦ jillion ♦ skillion

enough bellyful (Try also **be good enough ♦ having enough.**)

entertainment Try **recorded entertainment ♦ trivial entertainment.**

enthusiasm rah-rah ♦ vim and vigor

enthusiast bug ♦ addict ♦ nut

enthusiastic high on sth ♦ bananas ♦ fired up ♦ gung-ho ♦ on fire

entice get to so

entrap sting

entrapment sting

environmentalist duck-squeezer ♦ eagle freak ♦ eco freak ♦ eco nut

erection boner ♦ chub(by) ♦ fucker ♦ hard-on ♦ joystick ♦ morning glory ♦ morning missile ♦ President Wilson ♦ stiffy ♦ woody (Try also **get erection ♦ have erection.**)

erotic dance lap dancing ♦ pole dancing

err blow one's lines ♦ flub (up) ♦ fluff ♦ make a boo-boo ♦ mess up ♦ miss the boat ♦ pull a boner ♦ slip (up)

error 404 ♦ baddy ♦ blooper ♦ boner ♦ boo-boo ♦ clinker ♦ flub (up) ♦ fluff ♦ foozle ♦ howler ♦ slip (up) ♦ snafu (Try also **broadcast error ♦ cause of software error ♦ make error ♦ margin of error.**)

escape (n) getaway (Try also **narrow escape ♦ prison escape.**)

escape (v) barrel ass (out of somewhere) ♦ blow the joint ♦ blow town ♦ bolt ♦ book (on) out ♦ break out ♦ bug out ♦ bust ass (out of somewhere) ♦ bust out (of some place) ♦ cut and run ♦ cut ass (out of somewhere) ♦ cut out ♦ drag ass (out of somewhere) ♦ fly the coop ♦ get (out) while the gettin(g)'s good ♦ get (out) while the goin's good ♦ get out of Dodge ♦ give so the slip ♦ go over the hill ♦ go over the wall ♦ go South ♦ jet ♦ put some distance between so and so/sth ♦ scram ♦ shag ass (out of somewhere) ♦ skip (out) ♦ take it on the lam ♦ take off ♦ tear loose (from so/sth) ♦ tear off ♦ turn tail (and run) ♦ zoom

escape punishment beat the rap

escape responsibility buckpasser ♦ weasel out of sth

escaped over the hill

essence guts ♦ nitty-gritty

estimate cuff quote

euphoria going high ♦ high ♦ joy ride ♦ kick ♦ lift ♦ rolling buzz (Try also **burst of drug euphoria ♦ drug euphoria ♦ experience euphoria ♦ nondepressing euphoria ♦ become euphoric (drugs) ♦ make euphoric.**)

euphoric blissed (out) ♦ in orbit ♦ nodded out

euphoric event love-in

euphoric person space cadet

evade chicken out (of sth) ♦ crap out ♦ ditch ♦ duck ♦ goldbrick ♦ wiggle out of sth

evaluate case the joint ♦ case so/sth out

evaluate person scope (on) so

even even-Steven ♦ neck and neck ♦ nip and tuck

evening dim

evening shift swing shift

event big deal ♦ big noise ♦ caper ♦ goings-on ♦ happening ♦ haps (Try also **boring event ♦ euphoric event ♦ exciting event ♦ expired event ♦ frenetic event ♦ important event ♦ owl watching event ♦ prepare event ♦ suspenseful event ♦ suspicious event ♦ unimportant event ♦ unstressful event.**)

everyone the whole fam damily ♦ the whole shebang ♦ the whole shooting match

everything all the way ♦ everything but the kitchen sink ♦ everything from a to z ♦ everything from soup to nuts ♦ kit and caboodle ♦ whole bag of tricks ♦ the whole ball of wax ♦ the whole enchilada ♦ the whole nine yards ♦ the whole schmear ♦ the whole shebang ♦ the whole shooting match ♦ the works

everywhere out the gazoo ♦ the whole wide world

evidence ammo ♦ ammunition ♦ giveaway (Try also **find evidence ♦ leave evidence.**)

evil poison (Try also **speaker of evil.**)

exact need (n) ticket

exactly slap-dab

exactly right on-target ♦ on the bean ♦ on the button ♦ on the money

exaggerate make a federal case out of sth ♦ put too much on it ♦ raise a stink (about so/sth)

exaggerated trumped up

exaggeration hype ♦ lip gloss ♦ smoke (Try also **no exaggeration.**)

examination going over ♦ a look-see (Try also **give medical examination ♦ preliminary examination.**)

examine check sth out ♦ work so over

example Try **excellent example.**

excellent awesome ♦ bad ♦ bang-up ♦ beautiful ♦ bitchen ♦ bitchin' ♦ bogus ♦ Bonus! ♦ boss ♦ brutal ♦ bumping ♦ bust-ass ♦ butter ♦ chillin' ♦ cold ♦ cool ♦ Cool bananas! ♦ Cool beans! ♦ cosmic ♦ crack ♦ crackerjack ♦ cranking ♦ crazy ♦ dank ♦ deathly ♦ diesel ♦ dope ♦ dude ♦ dudical ♦ dynamite ♦ evil ♦ fat ♦ fierce ♦ fine and dandy ♦ froody ♦ funky-fresh ♦ gear ♦ ghetto ♦ (g)narly ♦ (Good) gravy! ♦ golden ♦ gone ♦ gravycakes ♦ heavy ♦ hellacious ♦ hotsy-totsy ♦ hype ♦ ice ♦ ill ♦ illin' ♦ jamming ♦ kick-ass ♦ kicken ♦ kickin' ♦ major ♦ marvy ♦ massive ♦ mean ♦ narly ♦ neat ♦ neato (canito) ♦ organic ♦ peachy (keen) ♦ phat ♦ primo ♦ rad ♦ radical ♦ rattling ♦ rocking ♦ rude ♦ ruley ♦ savage ♦ scrumptious ♦ serious ♦ slamming ♦ slick ♦ sly ♦ smashing ♦ smokin' ♦ spiffy ♦ stellar ♦ stokin' ♦ straight ♦ super ♦ super-dooper ♦ super-duper ♦ superfly ♦ surf ♦ sweet ♦ swell ♦ swellelegant ♦ swinging ♦ tawny ♦ terrific ♦ tight ♦ tripped out ♦ tubular ♦ vicious ♦ wailing ♦ way rad ♦ whale on ♦ whaling ♦ whipped ♦ wicked ♦ wicked bad ♦ wicky ♦ YMMD (Try also **be excellent.**)

excellent example honey of a sth ♦ a mean sth

excellent person beaut ♦ darb ♦ humdinger ♦ hummer ♦ killer-diller ♦ peach ♦ piss-cutter ♦ piss-whiz ♦ pisser ♦ some pumpkins ♦ some punkins ♦ winner

excellent thing daisy ♦ darb ♦ dilly ♦ doosie ♦ doozie ♦ doozy ♦ humdinger ♦ hummer ♦ killer-diller ♦ peach ♦ pisser ♦ some pumpkins ♦ some punkins ♦ winner ♦ zinger

excess Try **emotional excess.**

excite fire so up ♦ get so's motor running ♦ get so going ♦ pump (so) up ♦ steam so up ♦ turn so on (Try also **get excited ♦ be exciting ♦ make exciting.**)

excited amped ♦ apeshit ♦ charged (up) ♦ crunk ♦ fired up ♦ have a wild hair up one's ass ♦ high on sth ♦ hopped up ♦ hyped (up) ♦ hyper ♦ in orbit ♦ jacked ♦ jacked up ♦ on fire ♦ psyched (out) ♦ pumped (up) ♦ revved (up) ♦ stoked (on so/sth) ♦ switched on ♦ turned on ♦ up in arms

excited person hyper ♦ (all) shook up

excitement action ♦ bang ♦ bang for the buck ♦ pizzazz ♦ rush ♦ shnazz ♦ shnazzy ♦ snazz ♦ fireworks

exciting all the way live ♦ banging ♦ blockbuster ♦ kicky ♦ knockout ♦ out of this world ♦ sexy ♦ slam-bang ♦ wild ♦ wild and woolly ♦ with a bang

exciting event stone groove ♦ streak

exciting music hot number

exciting person or thing panic ♦ riot ♦ screamer ♦ turn on ♦ a five-alarm fire ♦ a three-alarm fire

exclamation point screamer ♦ shout ♦ shriek ♦ wow

exclamations Try **wow.**

excuse (n) cop out

excuse me Pardon me for living! ♦ PMJI

execute burn ♦ fry

execute a deal swing

executed Try **be poorly executed.**

executive exec

executive bonus golden handcuffs ♦ golden parachute

exemplary one one

exercise daily dozen (Try also **over exercise.**)

exhaust (v) do so in ♦ wipe so out ♦ zonk so out ♦ fag so out (Try also **sexually exhausted.**)

exhausted condition strung-out shape ♦ nag ♦ veggy ♦ (flat) on one's ass ♦ beat ♦ blue in the face ♦ bonged (out) ♦ bushed ♦ cashed ♦ clanked ♦ creased ♦ dragged out ♦ fagged out ♦ flaked out ♦ freaked (out) ♦ fucked out ♦ hacked ♦ knocked out ♦ maxed out ♦ on one's ass ♦ pooped (out) ♦ puggled ♦ roached ♦ shagged out ♦ shot ♦ stoked out ♦ tapped ♦ washed out ♦ wasted ♦ whipped ♦ zapped ♦ zoned (out) ♦ zonked (out) ♦ zounked (out) (Try also **talk to exhaustion.**)

exhibition (art) by one person one-man show

exhibitionist (male) flasher ♦ wagger ♦ wand waver

exit to fight step outside ♦ You want to step outside?

expectations Try **great expectations.**

expected the in thing to do

expel bust so out of somewhere

expenditures Try **reduce expenditures.**

expense report swindle sheet

expensive big-ticket ♦ out of sight ♦ pric(e)y ♦ salty ♦ spendy ♦ steep

experience Try **bad drug experience ♦ bad experience ♦ difficult experience ♦ ego experience ♦ good drug experience ♦ have bad experience ♦ sexually experienced.**

experience euphoria trip

experience first time taste blood

experience in urban life street smart

experienced Been there, done that (got the T-shirt).

experienced person graduate ♦ old hand (at sth)

experienced sexually been around (the block)

expert maven ♦ mavin

expired cashed ♦ phfft

expired event dead horse ♦ dead issue ♦ dead letter

expired person/thing buzzard meat ♦ gone goose ♦ goner

expiring on one's last legs

explain Go figure.

explain plan lay sth out

explanation (hot) skinny (Try also **find explanation.**)

exploit (v) hit so below the belt

exploiter Try **arts exploiter.**

exploration fishing expedition

expose blow the lid off sth ♦ blow so's cover ♦ blow sth wide open ♦ bust sth wide open ♦ drop a brick ♦ get the goods on so ♦ go public ♦ spill the beans ♦ spill the works ♦ big mouth ♦ tip one's hand

expose private body parts flash ♦ gaucho

express amazement eat one's hat

express anger Try **release anger.**

extended luck roll

extort bleed ♦ bleed so dry ♦ bleed so white ♦ shake so down

extortion shakedown

extra icing on the cake ♦ on the side

extra gadgets bells and whistles

extra person third wheel

extramarital on the side

extraordinary killer

extraordinary person stand-out ♦ a lulu

extraordinary thing killer ♦ stand-out

extravagantly in spades

extreme (g)narly ♦ far gone ♦ hard-core

extremely way out

extricate oneself squirrel out of sth

eyeglasses specs

eyelid lid ♦ shutters

eyes blinkers ♦ brights ♦ lamps ♦ lights ♦ peepers (Try also **black eye ♦ sharp eye ♦ seductive eyes.**)

fabricated story bedtime story ♦ fairy tale

fabulous fab ♦ Fantabulous!

face map ♦ mug ♦ mush ♦ pan ♦ puss ♦ smacker (Try also **morning face appearance ♦ beautiful face ♦ in the face ♦ plain face ♦ sour face ♦ pimple faced person ♦ scar-faced person ♦ pimple faced.**)

face lift lift

face to face eyeball to eyeball ◆ F2F

facial hair (male) (face) fungus ◆ fungus ◆ pudding ring ◆ soup-strainer ◆ stache ◆ stash

facing face to face

facts Try **information.** (Try also **tell facts.**)

fad the rage (Try also **merging fad.**)

fail bite the dust ◆ bomb (out) ◆ bomb out (of sth) ◆ crash and burn ◆ drop the ball ◆ fizzle ◆ flag ◆ flub the dub ◆ fold ◆ go belly up ◆ go down in flames ◆ go down the chute ◆ go down the tube(s) ◆ go haywire ◆ go over like a lead balloon ◆ go Rinso ◆ go Titanic ◆ gronk (out) ◆ lay an egg ◆ strike out ◆ take a nosedive ◆ tank ◆ tube ◆ turn belly up ◆ wash out

fail test tube it

fail to convince cut no ice (with so)

fail to impress underwhelm

fail to tip stiff

failed basketball shot air ball ◆ brick

failing grade flag

fail-safe Try **foolproof.**

failure bomb ◆ brick ◆ bust ◆ dead duck ◆ dud ◆ fizzle ◆ flop ◆ fuck-up ◆ goose egg ◆ turkey ◆ washout (Try also **aid failure ◆ memory failure ◆ social failure.**)

fair arrest (n) righteous collar

fair chance fair shake

fake bogue ◆ bogus ◆ faulty ◆ phony ◆ phony as a three-dollar bill ◆ plastic ◆ pseudo ◆ queer as a three-dollar bill

fake doctor quack ◆ bolus ◆ bones ◆ butch ◆ castor oil artist ◆ croaker ◆ doc(s)-in-a-box ◆ horse doctor ◆ medico ◆ pill-peddler ◆ pill-pusher ◆ pill-roller ◆ sawbones

fake drugs betty

fake gangster whankster ◆ whigga

fake knockout take a dive ◆ take a fall

fake person mod poser ◆ phony ◆ poser ◆ pseudo

fake stylishness plastic punk

fake telephone call phony

fake thing phony

fall (n) gravity check ◆ involuntary dismount ◆ nosedive ◆ prattfall

fall (v) fall out of bed ◆ go South ◆ head South ◆ kiss the dust

fall and rise whipsaw

fall apart go blooey ◆ go flooey ◆ go tits up

fall asleep conk off ◆ conk out ◆ flake (out)

fall down hit the deck

fall in love go off the deep end

fall off something wipe out

fall on buttocks prattfall

falling baseball can of corn

false As if! ◆ bogus ◆ bolt-on ◆ bullshit ◆ crank

false advice bum steer

false breasts falsies

false complaint bogus beef

false criminal charge bad rap ◆ bogus beef ◆ bum beef ◆ bum rap

false information bum steer

false surfer hodad ◆ hodaddy

falsify hocus

familiar Try **seems familiar.**

family car nerd mobile

famous big name ◆ hot

famous person big name

fan addict ◆ bug ◆ nut (Try also **Star Trek Fan.**)

fancy fancy-schmancy ◆ swish

fancy clothing glad rags

fantastic person lollapalooza

far away place Bumfuck ◆ Bumblefuck ◆ butt-fucking Egypt

farmer hayseed

fart (n) air biscuit ◆ anal applause ◆ backfire ◆ beef ◆ beef-hearts ◆ bender ◆ cheezer ◆ float an air biscuit ◆ SBD ◆ silent but deadly ◆ traf

fart (v) beef ◆ cut a fart ◆ cut a muffin ◆ cut one ◆ cut the cheese ◆ cut the mustard ◆ let a fart ◆ let one ◆ poot

fart (vaginal) Try **vaginal fart.**

fashion Try **out of fashion.**

fashionable happening ◆ in ◆ mod ◆ the in thing to do ◆ the rage

fast death on sth ◆ faster than a speeding bullet ◆ like a bat out of hell ◆ like crazy ◆ like mad ◆ like nobody's business ◆ like stink ◆ on the double ◆ pronto ◆ quicker than hell (Try also **go fast ◆ go there fast ◆ recover too fast ◆ talk fast ◆ very fast.**)

fast car (hot) rod ◆ rod

fast drink quick one ◆ quickie

fast driver speed demon ◆ speed merchant

fast person hell-on-wheels

fast pitch in baseball speedball

fast profit quick buck

fast runner speed demon ◆ speed merchant

fast talker motor-mouth ◆ ratchet-mouth

fast thing greased lightning

fast thinking fancy footwork

fast vehicle hell-on-wheels

fastcar draggin'-wagon

faster Try **make faster.**

fast-food cook burger-flipper

fat (love) handles ♦ (well-)upholstered ♦ all (that) meat and no potatoes ♦ all meat and no potatoes ♦ battle of the bulge ♦ chunky ♦ fat as a beached whale ♦ fugly ♦ padded ♦ porky ♦ spare tire ♦ upholstered (Try also **waist fat.**)

fat buttocks lard ass

fat marijuana cigarette phat blunt

fat person blimp ♦ blubber gut(s) ♦ chub ♦ chubbo ♦ chunk ♦ crisco ♦ fatso ♦ fatty ♦ gutbucket ♦ oinker ♦ pig ♦ porker ♦ slob ♦ tub of guts ♦ tub of lard ♦ whale

fat rolls handles

fat thighs thunder-thighs

fat woman chank ♦ cow

fat-bottomed person lard ass

father old man

fatigues fattygews

fatness battle of the bulge ♦ fat city

fatty food junk food

fault My bad.

faulty bum

favored odds-on

favored person (male) fair-haired boy

favorite place stamping ground

fax Try **annoying fax.**

FBI feebee ♦ feeby ♦ J. Edgar (Hoover)

FBI agent G-man

fear heebie-jeebies

fear of Iraq Iraqnophobia

fearful Try **frightened.**

fecal accident code brown

fecal blob dingleberry

feces doodle ♦ duky ♦ turd

federal agent fed ♦ Mr. Whiskers ♦ Sam ♦ T-man ♦ Uncle (Sam) ♦ Uncle Sugar ♦ Uncle Whiskers ♦ whiskers (man)

Federal Reserve Board fed

feeble gweebo ♦ wet

feel Try **make someone feel guilty ♦ oily feeling ♦ trapped feeling ♦ have good feelings about.**

feel mellow feel groovy

feel rejection feel a draft

feel sexually diddle ♦ feel so up ♦ paw

feeling well in the pink

feet crunchers ♦ trotters ♦ understanding (Try also **foot ♦ big feet ♦ pig's feet ♦ thousand feet.**)

fellatio B.J. ♦ bejeer ♦ blow job ♦ head-job ♦ hum job ♦ skully ♦ sword swallowing (Try also **perform fellatio ♦ receive fellatio ♦ reciprocal fellatio.**)

fellatio performer cocksucker ♦ dick-sucker ♦ dicky-licker

fellator (male) dick-sucker ♦ dicky-licker

fellow fella

fellow hobo stiff

fellow worker stiff

felonious big time

female Try **black friend (female) ♦ boss (female) ♦ fight (female) ♦ freshman (female) ♦ friend (female) ♦ genitals (female) ♦ important student (female) ♦ movie (female) ♦ nudity (female) ♦ perform oral sex (female) ♦ police officer (female) ♦ prison (female) ♦ restroom (female) ♦ skier (female) ♦ threat (female) ♦ threatening (female).**

female display cheesecake

female interest girl thing

feminine lacy

feminist bra-burner ♦ sister

festered festy

festoon (v) TP ♦ teepee

fiddle with diddle with sth ♦ fuck around with so ♦ mess about (with sth) ♦ mess around (with sth) ♦ monkey around (with sth)

fifth Try **take fifth amendment.**

fifty cents four-bits

fifty-dollar bill nifty

fifty-five miles per hour double buffalo ♦ double nickels

fight (female) fish-fight

fight (n) corn squabble ♦ donnybrook ♦ dust-up ♦ fish-fight ♦ knockdown drag-out fight ♦ rhubarb ♦ rumble ♦ slugfest (Try also **second in fight ♦ suspect a fight.**)

fight (v) duke it out ♦ mix it up (with so) ♦ slug it out ♦ tangle with so/sth (Try also **want to fight (various) ♦ exit to fight ♦ prepare to fight.**)

fight off disease toss sth off

figure out dope sth out ♦ suss so out

fill or cancel stock order fill or kill

film portion clip

filming Try **acceptable filming.**

filter Try **email filter.**

final blow last straw ♦ the end

final comment parting shot

final operation mopping-up operation

final total net result ♦ score ♦ the bottom line

finalize sew sth up

finalized done and done ♦ taped

finance (v) bankroll

financial Try **student's financial source.**

financial success killing

financially independent on easy street ♦ have gravy on one's grits

financier angel ♦ backer

find hit pay dirt ♦ scare so/sth up ♦ strike pay dirt

find employment land a job

find evidence get the goods on so

find explanation hit pay dirt ♦ strike pay dirt

find perfect wave cop a tube

fine finer than frog hair

fine arts farts

finger, the Try **digitus impudicus.**

fingerprints Try **take fingerprints.**

finger(s) cunt-hooks ♦ shit hooks (Try also **little finger ♦ smallest finger ♦ the finger.**)

finish wrap sth up

finish quickly whip sth off

finished blooey ♦ crapped (out) ♦ deaded ♦ down ♦ phfft ♦ sealed (up) ♦ The jig is up. (Try also **nearly finished.**)

fire Try **under fire.**

fire (v) can ♦ give so the ax ♦ pink slip ♦ rif ♦ sack (Try also **get fired.**)

fired pink-slipped ♦ riffed ♦ rift (Try also **get fired.**)

firefighter smoke eater

first the firstest with the mostest (Try also **experience first time ♦ act first ♦ speak first.**)

first day day one

first drink constitutional

first person to leave party-pooper

first response nibble

first thing on the one hand

fist bunch of fives

fists dukes

fit (n) spaz

five-dollar bill fin ♦ finn ♦ fiver

fix quick fix

fix (n) kludge ♦ kluge

fix (v) kludge ♦ kluge ♦ lick sth into shape ♦ whip sth into shape

flak hype artist

flamboyant pimpish ♦ ritzy ♦ with flying colors

flash of light blip

flask Try **liquor flask.**

flat breasted flat-chested

flatter brown-nose ♦ kiss up to so ♦ kiss so's ass ♦ kiss so's hind tit ♦ stroke ♦ suck up to so

flattered touched

flatterer apple-polisher ♦ ass-kisser ♦ ass-licker ♦ brownie ♦ brown-nose ♦ brown-noser ♦ cocksucker ♦ cookie pusher ♦ egg-sucker ♦ grade-grubber

flattering ass-kissing ♦ ass-licking ♦ grade-grubbing ♦ hoovering

flattery malark(e)y ♦ soft soap

flatware artillery

flavored bagel catholic bagel

flaw Try **computer program flaw.**

flee barrel ass (out of somewhere) ♦ blow the joint ♦ blow town ♦ bolt ♦ book (on) out ♦ break out ♦ bug out ♦ bust ass (out of somewhere) ♦ bust out (of some place) ♦ cut and run ♦ cut ass (out of somewhere) ♦ cut out ♦ drag ass (out of somewhere) ♦ fly the coop ♦ get (out) while the gettin(g)'s good ♦ get (out) while the goin's good ♦ get out of Dodge ♦ give so the slip ♦ go over the hill ♦ go over the wall ♦ go South ♦ jet ♦ make tracks ♦ put some distance between so and so/sth ♦ scram ♦ shag ass (out of somewhere) ♦ skip (out) ♦ take it on the lam ♦ take off ♦ tear off ♦ turn tail (and run) ♦ zoom

fleeing police on the lam ♦ on the run

flesh Try **tear in flesh.**

flex muscle pump sth up

flight Try **remove from flight.**

flirt (v) play around (with so)

flirt with hit on so

flog buttocks rump

floor plan layout

flunky wonk

fly (in biplane) barnstorm

fly (in plane) sky ♦ wing

flyer (paper) throw-away

flying low flat-hatting

focus (v) zoom in (on so/sth)

focus on one thing You can't dance at two weddings.

focused on task ♦ unflappable

fogged in (airport) socked in

foist off palm so/sth off (on so)

follow Try **drink to follow a drink ♦ band follower ♦ hockey player follower ♦ rock group follower ♦ who is following.**

follow closely cling like shit to a shovel ♦ dog ♦ on so's tail ♦ stick like shit to a shovel ♦ tailgate

follow rules get with the program

fondle grovel (Try also **self-fondling.**)

food chow ♦ chuck ♦ grindage ♦ grub ♦ scarf ♦ three squares ♦ blob ♦ bozo ♦ bubblehead ♦

clown ♦ dorkus maximus ♦ fizzle ♦ gazizzey ♦ gazob ♦ gleep ♦ gump ♦ helium head ♦ horse's ass ♦ lamebrain ♦ yutz (Try also **fast-food cook ♦ sloppy food (n) ♦ bad food ♦ fatty food ♦ nasty food ♦ serve food.**)

food bag from restaurant doggy bag

food choice leather or feather

food craving munchies

food hobbyist foodie

fool Try **treat like a fool ♦ be foolish.**

foolish jive-ass ♦ klutzy ♦ lamebrain ♦ lamebrained ♦ lardhead ♦ McFly ♦ meatheaded

foolish person schmo ♦ shmo ♦ shmoe ♦ yack

foolproof drool-proof ♦ goof-proof ♦ surefire

foolproof (v) goof-proof

foot dog ♦ hock (Try also **feet ♦ travel on foot.**)

foot travel (various) foot it ♦ hoof it ♦ shank's mare

football pigskin ♦ pill

for a thrill for kicks

for fun for kicks

for men only stag

for no good reason for the devil of it ♦ for the heck of it ♦ for the hell of it

for sale for sale by owner

for sure fer shur ♦ fo shizzle ♦ fo sho ♦ fosho

for very little for chicken feed ♦ for peanuts

force (n) strong-arm tactics

force (v) steamroller ♦ strong-arm

force acceptance ram sth down so's throat

force approval steamroller

force basketball jam ♦ slam dunk

force to pay amount sting so for sth

forced exit the gate

forced wedding shotgun wedding

forceful heavy-handed ♦ strong-arm

foreign English FOBlish

foreign money funny money

foreman straw boss

foreskin helmet ♦ turtle-neck

forever for keeps ♦ till hell freezes over ♦ till kingdom come

forfeit bail jump bail

forged jazzed (up) ♦ tinseled

forged check bum check ♦ paper ♦ rubber (check)

forget date stand so up

forget it Bag that! Bump that! ♦ Drop it! ♦ Fuck it! ♦ Fuck it, shit happens, drive on. ♦ never mind ♦ Skip it!

forgetful Try **absent minded ♦ memory failure.**

forgotten Try **name forgotten.**

form Try **take form.**

former important person has-been

former lover or spouse ex

fortitude backbone

forty-four pistol fo-fo

forum(s) Try **silent forum reader ♦ read forums without responding.**

foul ripe

found out The jig is up.

found something good onto a good thing ♦ This is it!

four Try **table for four.**

four bytes nybble

frank straight from the shoulder

frank speaker hip-shooter

frankfurter tube steak

frankly Try **speak frankly ♦ talk frankly.**

frantic in a twit

fraternity frat

fraternity member frat-rat

freak phreak

free for free (Try also **get free of criminal charge ♦ being risk free ♦ debt free ♦ drug free ♦ gun free ♦ not free ♦ rob freely.**)

free advertisement plug

free from worry out of the woods

free of drugs Try **drug free.**

free spender big-time spender

free thing free lunch ♦ freebee ♦ freebie

freely no holds barred

freeze with anxiety choke ♦ clutch (up)

frenetic event gangbusters

fresh off the boat FOB

freshman frosh ♦ shmen

freshman (female) shwench

fret stew ♦ sweat

fretful state stew

friend ace ♦ ace boom-boom ♦ ace boon-coon ♦ amigo ♦ baby ♦ best bud ♦ BF ♦ bitch ♦ bizatch ♦ bucko ♦ cat ♦ chum ♦ cuddie ♦ dawg ♦ dizzle ♦ dog ♦ dogg ♦ dognutz ♦ dude ♦ fella ♦ fucker ♦ good buddy ♦ good Joe ♦ good old boy ♦ goombah ♦ holmes ♦ home skillet ♦ homeboy ♦ homegirl ♦ homes ♦ homeslice ♦ homey ♦ homie ♦ hoser ♦ Mac(k) ♦ man ♦ Mr. Nice Guy ♦ my dawg ♦ my dog ♦ my dogg ♦ my man ♦ pal ♦ palsy-walsy ♦ pard ♦ Sherlock ♦ son of a bitch ♦ son of a gun ♦ sport (Try also **be friends with ♦ black friend (female) ♦ close (mod)**

friend ♦ group of friends ♦ overly friendly person ♦ get friendly ♦ overly friendly.)
friend (female) girlfriend ♦ sister
friendly buddy-buddy ♦ chummy ♦ down (with so) ♦ pally (with so) ♦ tight
frighten chill ♦ scare the hell out of so ♦ scare the pants off so ♦ spook
frightened I'm shaking (in fear). ♦ in a cold sweat ♦ scared shitless ♦ scared stiff ♦ spooked ♦ white-knuckle
frightening creepy
Frisbee friz ♦ the B
from a satellite on the bird
from surprising direction out of left field
from the start from (the) git-go
from the street walk-in
front Try **claim front seat.**
front teeth grill
frown dirty look
frozen yogurt froyo
fuck F-word ♦ fizzle (Try also **copulate.**)
fuck you Drop you! ♦ Fork you!
fucking effing ♦ freaking ♦ fricking ♦ frigging ♦ funking
fuel motion-lotion
full jampacked ♦ up to one's eyeballs
full effect double whammy
full of lies full of shit
full of nonsense full of beans ♦ full of bull ♦ full of hot air ♦ full of it ♦ full of prunes ♦ full of shit
full of shit full of shizzle
full throttle wide open
fully equipped loaded.
fun Try **be fun ♦ for fun ♦ much fun ♦ person who is fun.**
fund Try **campaign fund ♦ discretionary fund.**
fundamental bedrock
fund-raiser (person) can-shaker
funny joke scream
funny person card ♦ corker ♦ panic ♦ scream ♦ a stitch
funny thing howl ♦ scream
fussy hincty
future(s) Try **decide one's future ♦ worst future ♦ orange juice futures ♦ pork belly futures ♦ soybean futures.**
gabby diarrhea of the jawbone ♦ diarrhea of the mouth
gadget dingbat ♦ dingus ♦ doodad ♦ doohickey ♦ doojigger ♦ doowacky ♦ fakus ♦ gazinkus ♦ gazunkus ♦ geegaw ♦ gewgaw ♦ gizmo ♦ goofus ♦ googaw ♦ jigger ♦ jobber ♦

jobby ♦ johnson ♦ motherfucker ♦ puppy ♦ sucker ♦ thingamajig ♦ thingy ♦ unit ♦ whang(y)doodle ♦ whatchamacallit ♦ whatsis ♦ whatsit ♦ whatzit ♦ whazzit ♦ whing-ding ♦ widget ♦ wing-ding (Try also **extra gadgets.**)
gain respect get face
gall crust
gamble (n) crapshoot
gambler high roller ♦ hustler ♦ whale (Try also **high-bet gambler ♦ risk-taking gambler.**)
game Try **no score game ♦ remove from game.**
game control joystick
game segment stanza
gang goon squad ♦ posse
gang attack gang-bang
gang member gangbanger
gang rape gang-bang ♦ gang-shag
gang up crowd
gangster gizzle (Try also **fake gangster ♦ white gangster.**)
gangster woman doxy
gap Try **buttocks gap.**
garment Try **midlength garment ♦ ugly garment.**
gas Try **having gas ♦ release of intestinal gas ♦ releasing gas.**
gasoline motion-lotion
gather rally
gather possessions get one's shit together ♦ get one's stuff together
gathering party ♦ rally
gathering place hotbed of sth
gaudy Hollywood
gaudy car pimpmobile
gay Try **homosexual ♦ homosexual (man) ♦ lesbian.**
gay oriented camp
gay sensor gaydar
gearshift lever stick
gemstone sparkler
generation Try **beat generation person.**
genes Try **in one's genes.**
genitals (female) beaver ♦ boody ♦ box ♦ cunt ♦ gash ♦ mizzle ♦ nookie ♦ nooky ♦ pussy (Try also **vagina ♦ vulva.**)
genitals (in general) meat ♦ naughty bits
genitals (male) box ♦ junk (Try also **penis ♦ scrotum ♦ testicles ♦ with large genitals (male).**)
genius mental giant
gentile goy

gentle Try **be gentle ✦ persuade gently.**
gentle approach soft touch
gentle man snag
gentle selling job soft sell
genuine for real
get bag ✦ score
get a share chisel in (on so/sth)
get acquainted get with so
get addicted get narkied
get advantage get the drop on so
get angry blow a hype ✦ blow ✦ blow a fuse
    ✦ blow a gasket ✦ blow up ✦ blow one's cool
    ✦ blow one's cork ✦ blow one's fuse ✦ blow
    one's lid ✦ blow one's stack ✦ blow one's top ✦
    flash on so ✦ get one's bowels in an uproar ✦
    go off the deep end ✦ have kittens ✦ hit the
    ceiling ✦ hit the roof ✦ kick up a storm ✦
    lose it ✦ lose one's cool ✦ pop off ✦ pop one's
    cork ✦ work oneself (up) into a lather
get anxious get one's bowels in an uproar
get arrested drop ✦ go down ✦ take the fall
get as much as possible go the limit
get busy get hot ✦ get on the stick ✦ knuckle
    down (to sth) ✦ Snap to it!
get courage nut up ✦ sack up
get drug intoxicated cop a head ✦ get
    pasted
get drunk booze up ✦ cop a head ✦ cut one's
    wolf loose ✦ fuzz ✦ fuzzle ✦ gas ✦ gas up ✦
    get a can on ✦ get down to some serious
    drinking ✦ get pasted ✦ get spun ✦ get stupid
    ✦ get there ✦ hang one on ✦ hit the booze ✦
    hit the bottle ✦ lay one on ✦ paint the town
    (red) ✦ powder up ✦ puff ✦ rack up ✦ raise
    hell ✦ shicker ✦ skate ✦ slew ✦ slush up ✦
    soak ✦ steam up ✦ tie it on ✦ tie one on
get erection get it on ✦ get it up ✦ make a
    tent ✦ pitch a tent
get excited crunk ✦ flip over so/sth ✦ get it up
    ✦ get one's bowels in an uproar ✦ go ape
    (over so/sth) ✦ go apeshit over so/sth ✦ go
    bananas ✦ go into orbit ✦ pump up ✦ switch
    on ✦ work oneself (up) into a lather
get fired get the ax ✦ get the sack
get free of criminal charge beat
get friendly buddy up to so ✦ come on to so
    ✦ cozy up (to so)
get hired land a job
get hold of get one's hooks into so ✦ get one's
    hooks into sth
get hysterical have a spaz
get interested turn on ✦ turn onto so/sth
get intimate get to first (base) (with so)
get into trouble get in bad (with so)

get involved get in on the act ✦ get into sth
get lucky get hot
get modern switch on
get money clean so out
get moving get off the dime
get naked air one's pores
get new members rush
get off drugs go straight
get organized get it (all) together ✦ get on
    the stick ✦ get one's act together ✦ get one's
    ass in gear ✦ get one's head together ✦ get
    one's shit together ✦ get one's stuff together
get out of bed hit the deck
get pleasure from get off (on sth) ✦ get one's
    kicks (from so/sth)
get pregnant sprain one's ankle
get punishment get it in the neck ✦ get one's
    lumps
get quiet clam up ✦ dummy up ✦ hush sth up
    ✦ pipe down ✦ simmer (down)
get ready work oneself up to sth
get rich strike it rich
get rid of give so the brushoff ✦ give so the
    gate ✦ stamp so out ✦ unload
get serious Cut the comedy! ✦ straighten up
    and fly right
get sober sober up
get thrill get a bang out of so/sth ✦ get a buzz
    out of so/sth ✦ get a kick out of so/sth
get through easily waltz through sth
get to the point get down to the nitty-gritty
    ✦ get to point
get up hit the deck ✦ Rise and shine!
get upset work oneself up
get value You get what you pay for.
get what is deserved That'll teach so. ✦
    serve so right
giddy balmy ✦ dingy ✦ ditsy ✦ ditzy ✦ dizzy ✦
    flaky ✦ half a bubble off plumb ✦ in a twitter
    ✦ lunching ✦ not all there ✦ nutty ✦ off one's
    rocker ✦ OTL ✦ out to lunch ✦ pixolated ✦
    slap happy ✦ spaced (out) ✦ spacy ✦ twity ✦
    wacky (Try also **be giddy ✦ become giddy ✦
    make giddy.**)
giddy person bliss ninny ✦ ditz ✦ ditzo ✦
    flake ✦ scatterbrain ✦ space cadet ✦ space
    out
giddy woman Barbie doll ✦ dumb Dora ✦
    gidget
gift handout (Try also **small gift.**)
giggle (n) gig
gimmick angle
gin juniper juice

girl chick ♦ twist (Try also **teenage girl ♦ steal girlfriend.**)

girlfriend bitch ♦ bizatch ♦ crush ♦ main squeeze ♦ moose ♦ old lady ♦ squeeze ♦ steady ♦ wife

give come across (with sth) ♦ Cough it up! ♦ cough sth up ♦ fork sth over ♦ kick down with sth ♦ make with the sth ♦ palm so/sth off (on so)

give advantage spot so (sth)

give appeal jazz so/sth up

give hard time rank

give in knuckle under (to so/sth) ♦ You can't fight city hall.

give information drop so some knowledge

give me gimme

give medical examination vet

give up chuck it in ♦ Come off it! ♦ Get off it! ♦ lay down ♦ say uncle

glamorous glam ♦ glitzy ♦ Hollywood

glamour glitz ♦ pizzazz

glance at blix

glance (n) the once-over ♦ once over lightly

glass containing ice setup

glasses wearer four-eyes

glitter shnazz ♦ shnazzy ♦ snazz

glue stickum

glue (as a drug) gunk

glue sniffer gluer ♦ gluey ♦ huffer

gluteal cleft crack ♦ plumber's smile ♦ working man's smile

glutted jammed up

glutton foodaholic ♦ pig

go ahead Make my day!

go away (Go) blow it out your ear! ♦ (So,) sue me! ♦ Bag it! ♦ Bug off! ♦ Butt out! ♦ Drop dead! ♦ Dry up! ♦ Forget you! ♦ Get away! ♦ Get lost! ♦ Get off my ass! ♦ Get off my back! ♦ Get off my bumper! ♦ Get off my tail! ♦ get off one's rear ♦ get off so's back ♦ get off so's case ♦ Get out of here! ♦ Get out of my face! ♦ Get out of town! ♦ Get your nose out of my business! ♦ Gimme a break! ♦ GMAB ♦ Go chase your tail! ♦ Go chase yourself! ♦ Go climb a tree! ♦ Go fly a kite! ♦ Go fry an egg! ♦ Go fuck yourself! ♦ Go jump in the lake! ♦ go peddle your papers ♦ Go soak your head! ♦ Go soak yourself! ♦ Go to your room! ♦ Lump it! ♦ Nuts to you! ♦ On your bike! ♦ piss off ♦ scat ♦ skedaddle ♦ So's your old man! ♦ Sue me! ♦ take a hike ♦ Take a running jump (in the lake)! ♦ take a walk ♦ Up yours! ♦ Vamoose!

go AWOL go over the hill

go back to drugs kick back

go berserk go postal

go broke lose one's shirt

go crazy flip ♦ flip (out) ♦ flip one's lid ♦ flip one's wig ♦ go bananas ♦ go bitchcakes ♦ go haywire ♦ go mental ♦ go postal ♦ go zonkers ♦ lose (all) one's marbles ♦ nut up ♦ run amok ♦ slip one's trolley ♦ snap

go fast go great guns

go out (baseball) strike out

go out on strike hit the bricks ♦ hit the pavement

go out without underpants go commando ♦ freeball ♦ go freeball(ing)

go public hit the fan

go slowly take it slow

go there fast Get one's tail somewhere fast! ♦ get one's tail somewhere immediately! ♦ get one's tail somewhere now!

go to bed hit the hay ♦ hit the sack ♦ pad out ♦ rack (out) ♦ roll in ♦ sack out ♦ turn in

go to bench grab some bench

Go to hell! Bite the ice! ♦ Blow it out your ear! ♦ Eat me! ♦ Eat my shorts! ♦ Eat shit! ♦ Go to blazes! ♦ Go to the devil! ♦ Go to! ♦ Kiss my ass! ♦ Up yours!

go to powder room powder one's face ♦ powder one's nose

go to the toilet check out the plumbing ♦ pay a call ♦ potty ♦ visit the plumbing

goal Try **basketball goal (net) ♦ set goal.**

gobble binge ♦ chow sth down ♦ chuck ♦ dog ♦ down ♦ eat sth up ♦ garbage sth down ♦ root ♦ scarf sth down ♦ scoff ♦ stuff one's face ♦ tear into sth ♦ throw down ♦ wolf sth down

going to gonna

golf club stick

golfer Try **poor golfer.**

gone casper ♦ dead and gone ♦ down the drain ♦ out of the picture ♦ out the window

gonorrhea clap

good all right ♦ butter ♦ decent ♦ diesel ♦ ducky ♦ fine and dandy ♦ funky-fresh ♦ gravy ♦ hi-res ♦ high-res ♦ like a million (dollars) ♦ nifty ♦ on it ♦ righteous ♦ rosy ♦ solid ♦ stellar ♦ stupid fresh ♦ wicked bad (Try also **be good enough ♦ for no good reason ♦ have good feelings about ♦ have good time ♦ in good spirits ♦ become good ♦ found something good ♦ look good ♦ old and good.**)

good beat bumping

good car cream puff

good condition A number 1 ♦ A-OK

good decision Good call!

good drug experience good trip

good film scene take.

good guy right guy ♦ white hat

good looking banging ♦ blazing ♦ drop-dead gorgeous ♦ fresh ♦ mint ♦ on fire ♦ sharp ♦ stacked ♦ studly

good looking man babe magnet ♦ baldwin ♦ Barney ♦ beauhunk ♦ chick magnet ♦ face man ♦ fine wolf ♦ stud-muffin ♦ studhammer

good looking person (good) looker ♦ eye-popper ♦ hottie ♦ knockout ♦ looker

good looking woman babe ♦ betty ♦ cupcake ♦ dish ♦ doll ♦ fly mink ♦ fox ♦ foxy lady ♦ freak mommy ♦ pigeon ♦ quail ♦ sex goddess ♦ slick-chick ♦ stallion ♦ stunner

Good luck! Break a leg! ♦ Lots of luck! ♦ Rots of ruck!

good magazine slick

good meal square (meal)

good person goody two-shoes ♦ hell of a so/sth ♦ mensch

good result hit

good side upside

good time good trip ♦ rare old time ♦ riot

good-bye letter Dear John letter

good-bye (various) adios muchachos ♦ After while(, crocodile). ♦ BBFN ♦ BCNU ♦ Bye-bye, for now. ♦ C4N ♦ Catch you later. ♦ chow ♦ ciao ♦ Ciao, for now. ♦ CU ♦ CU2 ♦ CUIAL ♦ CUL8R ♦ Geronimo! ♦ Have a good one. ♦ Have a nice day. ♦ Have a nice one. ♦ I'm gone. ♦ I'm history. ♦ It's been a slice! ♦ It's been. ♦ Keep in touch. ♦ L8R ♦ L8R G8R ♦ Later, gator. ♦ Later. ♦ Laters. ♦ nice meeting you ♦ nice talking to you ♦ See ya. ♦ See you in another life. ♦ See you in church. ♦ See you in the funny pages. ♦ See you later, alligator. ♦ See you later. ♦ See you, too. ♦ See you. ♦ seeyabye ♦ So long. ♦ SYITFP ♦ Take care. ♦ WIYGW ♦ Write if you get work.

good-looking from distance monet

goods Try **stolen goods.**

gooey squooshy ♦ sticky

gooey stuff gook

goose honker

gossip (n) gab ♦ dirt ♦ earful ♦ flapjaw ♦ gibber-gabber ♦ scuttlebutt ♦ skinny ♦ yackety-yak

gossip (v) gab ♦ beak ♦ chew the fat ♦ chew the rag ♦ dish the dirt ♦ fan the breeze ♦ give so an earful ♦ shoot the breeze ♦ shoot the bull ♦ shoot the crap ♦ shoot the shit

gossip about rank on so

gossip party gabfest ♦ hen party

gossip source grapevine ♦ latrine wireless

gossip spreader big mouth

gossiper cat ♦ big mouth ♦ ear-duster ♦ ear hustler ♦ flapjaw ♦ yenta

gossiping place latrine wireless

got you gotcha

grab filch sth (from so/sth) ♦ snatch

grade Try **earn a C grade ♦ failing grade ♦ passing grade.**

graffiti signature tag

grant sex easily chippy around

grasp surfboard hang five ♦ hang ten

gratis for free

grave deep six

gravy goozlum

gray Try **have gray hair.**

great awesome ♦ bitchin' ♦ bold ♦ Fantabulous! ♦ far out ♦ gravycakes ♦ hotshot ♦ live ♦ neat ♦ neato (canito) ♦ solid ♦ swinging ♦ whipped

great expectations The world is one's oyster.

great performance grandstand play

greatly mongo

greedy suckabuck (Try also **be greedy.**)

greens rabbit food (Try also **salad greens.**)

greet give one one's pounds ♦ glad-hand ♦ high five ♦ Yello.

greet me hit me again ♦ Hit me.

greetings Try **hello (various greetings).**

grief Try **cause grief.**

grieve eat one's heart out

grin BFG ♦ BG ♦ big fat grin ♦ G ♦ GBG

gross base ♦ gee

grouch (n) meany

group Try **rock group follower ♦ want to leave group.**

group lunch brown-bag

group of friends tribe

group of things for sale package

group rape bunch-punch ♦ cluster fuck

group sex group-grope

gruff crusty

grumpy person crank ♦ sorehead ♦ sourpuss ♦ troll

guess long shot ♦ scientific wild ass guess ♦ shot in the dark ♦ SWAG (Try also **wild guess.**)

guess wildly whistle in the dark

guest Try **uninvited guest.**

guilt Try **place guilt.**

guilty (bang) dead to rights ♦ dead to rights (Try also **looking for guilty person ♦ make**

someone feel guilty ♦ plead guilty ♦ sign of guilty ♦ you are as guilty.)

guitar belly fiddle (Try also **pantomime guitar.**)

gullible just off the boat

gullible person clay pigeon ♦ schlemiel ♦ schlemihl ♦ shlemiel ♦ soft touch

gummy goopy

gun burner ♦ cannon ♦ chunk ♦ deuce-deuce ♦ equalizer ♦ gat ♦ glock ♦ hardware ♦ heat ♦ heater ♦ iron ♦ persuader ♦ piece ♦ rod ♦ roscoe ♦ Saturday night special ♦ shooting iron ♦ wep ♦ widow-maker ♦ zip gun (Try also **aim gun ♦ carrying gun ♦ machine gun ♦ hired gunman.**)

gun free clean

gunfight shoot-out

gunman gun

guns artillery

gutsy spunky

guy cat ♦ G ♦ joker (Try also **good guy ♦ tough guy.**)

gym shoes tennies ♦ sneaks

gynecologist gynie

hackysack Try **play hackysack.**

hair mop (Try also **facial hair (male) ♦ burned (hair) ♦ comb hair ♦ have gray hair ♦ have white hair ♦ pubic hair.**)

hair cover doorag ♦ soldier rag (Try also **flag.**)

hair dressing slickum

haircut type gumby ♦ mullet

hairdo Afro ♦ do ♦ doo ♦ gumby ♦ helmet ♦ mop ♦ mullet ♦ zipper head

half halvsies (Try also **second half.**)

hallucinations crank bugs ♦ horrors ♦ pink elephants ♦ pink spiders (Try also **delirium tremens.**)

hamburger burger ♦ hamburg

hamburger craving Big Mac attack

hand slap high five ♦ low five

handbill throw-away

handcuffs bracelets ♦ cuffs ♦ nippers

handkerchief blower ♦ hanky ♦ snotrag

handle bars ape hangers

hand(s) cunt-hooks ♦ grabbers ♦ hooks ♦ meathooks ♦ mitt ♦ paw ♦ shit hooks ♦ shithooks (Try also **hide in hand ♦ dual handed batter ♦ left-handed person ♦ catch redhanded ♦ raise hands ♦ shake hands ♦ slap hands.**)

hands up reach for the sky ♦ Stick 'em up!

hang die of throat trouble

hang with a noose stretch

hangover barrel fever ♦ bighead ♦ blue flu ♦ bottleache ♦ brown bottle flu ♦ head ♦ woefits ♦ woofits ♦ a mouth ♦ the morning after (the night before) (Try also **have a hangover.**)

happen come down ♦ go down (Try also **make happen ♦ never happen ♦ soon to happen ♦ high-quality happening ♦ what is happening.**)

happy high, wide, and handsome ♦ up ♦ upbeat (Try also **be happy ♦ make happy.**)

happy person happy camper

harass bullyrag ♦ fuck so around ♦ pull so's chain ♦ yank ♦ yank so's chain ♦ yank so around

hard Try **give hard time ♦ laugh hard ♦ rain hard ♦ study hard ♦ studying hard ♦ try hard ♦ work hard.**

hard blow wallop

hard punch (blow) Sunday punch

hard to get money tight money

hard work dirty work ♦ grunt work ♦ shit work

harm (v) bite ♦ do a number on so ♦ do so dirt ♦ mess so over ♦ rambo(ize) ♦ shaft (Try also **abuse, wish to harm.**)

harm oneself cut one's own throat ♦ shoot oneself in the foot ♦ backfire (on so)

harmed Try **abused.**

harming homosexuals fag-bashing ♦ fag-busting

harsh-looking rasty

hashish clay ♦ hash ♦ heesh

hashish device hash cannon ♦ hash pipe

hashish user hash-head

hashish using place hash-house

hassle jack so around ♦ jerk so around ♦ jerk so over ♦ rank ♦ rip on so ♦ screw so over

hat brim ♦ lid

hatchet man long knife

hate very much hate so's guts

haughty biggity ♦ dicty ♦ hincty ♦ huffy ♦ on one's high horse ♦ snooty ♦ standoffish ♦ uppity (Try also **be haughty.**)

have a hangover have a (big) head

have a problem in a jam

have advantage have a leg up on so ♦ hold all the aces

have bad experience bum out

have desire have an itch for sth

have diarrhea run off

have erection have a bone on ♦ have a hard-on ♦ have lead in one's pencil

have good feelings about have good vibes

have good time have a whale of a time
have gray hair have snow on the roof
have intelligence have what it takes
have lunch Let's do lunch (sometime). ♦ Let's do the lunch thing.
have menses have a little visitor
have money have what it takes
have orgasm come ♦ cum
have proof have so dead to rights
have skill have game ♦ have what it takes
have something settled have sth cinched
have spirit have game
have succeeded have it made ♦ have it made in the shade
have temper tantrum have a shit-fit
have trick in reserve have an ace up one's sleeve
have trouble have a run-in (with so/sth)
have white hair have snow on the roof
having enough straight
having gas windy
having lots swimming in sth ♦ knee-deep in sth ♦ stinking with sth
having money flush
HBO BO
head attic ♦ bean ♦ biscuit ♦ block ♦ can ♦ conk ♦ dome ♦ fuse box ♦ gourd ♦ knowledge-box ♦ konk ♦ mind ♦ noodle ♦ nut ♦ potato ♦ think-box ♦ upper story (Try also **shaved head person ♦ bald head ♦ hit on head ♦ strike head.**)
head cloth flag
head laborer key grip
headache pain bighead ♦ head
headline screamer
hear catch sth
heart pump ♦ tick-tock ♦ ticker (Try also **cold hearted person.**)
heart attack the big one
heartless hardboiled ♦ dog-eat-dog
heavens blue
heavily like a ton of bricks
heavy Try **be heavy.**
heavy eater chow hound
heavy smoker coffin-dodger ♦ chain-smoker
heck of a hecka
heel Try **raised heel.**
held in reserve on ice
helicopter bear in the air ♦ chopper ♦ egg-beater ♦ eye-in-the-sky ♦ fling-wing ♦ ghetto bird ♦ whirlybird (Try also **police helicopter.**)
helicopter pilot rotorhead

hell 773H ♦ blazes ♦ H-E-double-toothpicks ♦ hizzle ♦ seven-seven-three-aitch (Try also **Go to hell!**)
hell of a hella ♦ helluva so/sth
hello (various greetings) Earth to so. ♦ Getting any? ♦ Hey! ♦ Hey, bum! ♦ How goes it? ♦ How ya living? ♦ How's tricks? ♦ How('re) they hanging? ♦ howdy ♦ Long time no see. ♦ Que pasa? ♦ Skin me! ♦ Sup? ♦ Tsup? ♦ Wassup? ♦ What can I do you for? ♦ What do you say? ♦ What's in the bag! ♦ What's new? ♦ What's really good witcha? ♦ What's shakin' (bacon)? ♦ What's the (good) word? ♦ What's the scam? ♦ What's the scoop? ♦ What's up, G? ♦ What's up? ♦ What's your age? ♦ Where have you been keeping yourself? ♦ Whuhap? ♦ Word up. ♦ Word. ♦ Wusup? ♦ Yello. ♦ Yo! ♦ You guys bitchin'?
helmet brain bucket ♦ hardhat ♦ skid-lid ♦ tin hat
help give so five ♦ pitch in (and help)
help drug user bring so down
helper do-gooder ♦ gofer ♦ gopher ♦ grunt ♦ roadie ♦ swamper
helpless Try **look helpless.**
helpless person (limp) dishrag
here X marks the spot.
here is scheme Here's the deal.
hero white hat
heroin big-H. ♦ gulf ♦ H. ♦ hazel ♦ heavy soul ♦ hero (of the underworld) ♦ horse ♦ horseradish ♦ junk ♦ load ♦ moonrock ♦ noise ♦ overjolt ♦ scag ♦ scat ♦ skag ♦ tragic-magic (Try also **taking heroin ♦ use heroin.**)
heroin addicted horsed ♦ on the horse ♦ strung out
heroin addiction skag jones ♦ scag jones
heroin crystals rock
herpes Try **person with herpes.**
herpes infected herped up
heterosexual breeder ♦ straight
hick bamma
hidden doggo
hide (v) hole up ♦ squirrel sth away
hide drugs stash
hide in hand palm
hideaway getaway
hideous hiddy ♦ hidi
high Try **replay of a drug high.**
high on marijuana on the beam
high quality blue chip
high roller whale

high seats nosebleed seats
high-bet gambler high roller ♦ whale
high-class class
high-pressure selling hard sell
high-quality happening class act
highway police bear ♦ county-mounty ♦ Smokey (the Bear)
hillbilly bamma
hindsight twenty-twenty hindsight
hippie longhair
hips hams
hired Try **get hired.**
hired gunman trigger
hit (n) Try **two base hit.**
hit (v) Try **strike.**
hit a ball connect (with sth)
hit-and-run accident bam and scram
hit home run homer
hit on head crown
hitchhike hook it ♦ thumb a ride
HIV positive poz
hoax shuck
hobby thing
hobbyist Try **food hobbyist.**
hobo bagman ♦ gook ♦ stumblebum ♦ yegg (Try also **fellow hobo.**)
hockey player follower hockey-whore ♦ puck bunny
hold Try **get hold of.**
hold back criticism pull one's punches
hold back punches pull one's punches
hold still freeze
Hollywood Tinseltown
holster Try **wearing holster.**
home Try **dwelling.** (Try also **be sent home dead** ♦ **hit home run** ♦ **leave home** ♦ **retirement home** ♦ **take care of the home.**)
home plate plate
home run in baseball four-bagger ♦ gopher ball ♦ homer ♦ round tripper
homeless shot to the curb
homeless people street people
homemade beer home-brew ♦ homespun
homemade liquor bathtub gin ♦ home-brew ♦ homespun ♦ jungle juice ♦ moonshine
homosexual blade ♦ fruity ♦ gay as pink ink ♦ guppy ♦ homo ♦ queer ♦ queer as a three-dollar bill ♦ queer-beer ♦ that way (Try also **blatant homosexual** ♦ **reveal someone's homosexuality** ♦ **harming homosexuals** ♦ **threatening homosexuals.**)

homosexual man fag ♦ faggot ♦ fairy ♦ flamer ♦ fruit ♦ fruitcake ♦ fruiter ♦ queen ♦ queer ♦ queer-beer ♦ rump-ranger ♦ swish
homosexuality revealed outed
honest legit ♦ No lie! ♦ on the level ♦ straight ♦ straight up ♦ up front (Try also **above board** ♦ **be honest with** ♦ **become honest.**)
honest person square ♦ square apple ♦ square john ♦ square shooter ♦ straight arrow ♦ straight shooter
honest talk straight talk
honest woman square john broad
honestly str8 (Try also **speak honestly.**)
honored touched
hoodlum ape ♦ punk
hope Try **try again with a hope of success** ♦ **no hope.**
hope for reward pie in the sky
hopeless mess
hopeless cause lost cause
hopeless youth dead-end kid
hopping Try **bar hopping.**
horrible heinous ♦ like death warmed over ♦ lousy ♦ ungodly
horse hay burner ♦ hay head ♦ nag (Try also **dangerous horse.**)
horse dung horse ♦ horse hockey ♦ horseshit ♦ road apple
horse for breeding (male) stud
horse power horses
horsepower squirrels
hospital bone factory
hot day scorcher ♦ sizzler
hot dog pimp steak ♦ red hot
hot place hellhole
hotel Try **cheap hotel.**
house (n) hizzle ♦ hut (Try also **cocaine house** ♦ **crack houses.**)
house (v) put so up
housewife Try **American housewife.**
how much What's the damage?
huge honking ♦ humongous ♦ humungous ♦ mongo
Huh! Chuch!
human computer user liveware
humble (v) take the piss out of so ♦ take the starch out of so (Try also **be humble.**)
humid sticky
humiliate burn so down ♦ rag on so ♦ rake on so
humiliated burned
humility Try **show humility.**
humor Try **overdrawn (humor).**

hundred hundo (Try also **one-hundred-dollar bill ♦ one-hundred dollars.**)

hunger chuckers ♦ chucks ♦ the hungries ♦ munchies

hungover bigheaded ♦ hung ♦ roached ♦ tore back ♦ to up (from the flo up)

hungry hungarian ♦ peckish

hungry person bottomless pit

hurry bag ass (out of somewhere) ♦ barrel ass ♦ Get a wiggle on! ♦ Get cracking! ♦ Get the lead out! ♦ get with it ♦ Giddy up! ♦ hump (along) ♦ hump it (to somewhere) ♦ hurry up and wait ♦ hustle ♦ jet ♦ Look alive! ♦ Make it snappy! ♦ shake a leg ♦ Shake it (up)! ♦ Shit or get off the pot! ♦ Snap it up! ♦ Step on it! ♦ varoom ♦ zap

hurt boo-boo

husband hubby ♦ old man ♦ one's better half

hymen cherry

hype (n) flack ♦ flak ♦ hoopla ♦ razzamatazz ♦ razzle-dazzle ♦ razzmatazz

hype (v) boost ♦ flog ♦ plug ♦ push ♦ trump sth up

hyped glorified ♦ trumped up

hypodermic needle spike

hypodermic syringe banger ♦ glass gun ♦ hype

hypothetical product widget

hysterical Try **get hysterical.**

I am not stupid My mama didn't raise no dummy.

I am right I am so sure!

I see IC

I understand I hear what you are saying.

IBM (I-)beam ♦ big blue

ice Try **glass containing ice ♦ without ice.**

ice cream geedunk ♦ scream

ice cubes rocks

ID check (v) card

idea brainchild ♦ brainstorm (Try also **new idea ♦ poor idea ♦ present idea ♦ ruin idea ♦ suggest idea ♦ try idea.**)

ideal Try **be ideal ♦ create ideas ♦ person with ideas.**

identical (as) alike as (two) peas in a pod ♦ alike as (two) peas in a pod

identical one ringer

identified nailed

identify finger ♦ finger so as so ♦ ID ♦ make ♦ make so ♦ nail ♦ put the finger on so ♦ tab ♦ proofed

identity Try **check identity.**

idiot Try **moron.**

idler mooner

ignorant not know beans (about sth) ♦ not know from nothing ♦ not know one's ass from a hole in the ground ♦ not know shit about sth ♦ not know shit from shinola ♦ not tell shit from shinola ♦ totally clueless

ignore blow so/sth off ♦ fan ♦ freeze ♦ freeze so out ♦ give so the brushoff ♦ give so the go-by ♦ ice ♦ kiss sth off ♦ let sth ride ♦ put the chill on so ♦ put the freeze on so ♦ tune out ♦ tune so/sth out ♦ wouldn't touch so/sth with a ten-foot pole (Try also **stop ignoring me.**)

ignore criticism toss sth off

ignored OOSOOM ♦ out of sight, out of mind

ignored person chopped liver

ill on the blink ♦ raunchy ♦ under the weather (Try also **speak ill.**)

ill-behaved illin'

illegal bootleg ♦ dirty ♦ fishy

illegal activity action

illicit Try **make illicit liquor ♦ maker of illicit liquor ♦ sell illicit liquor ♦ traffic in illicit liquor.**

illicit liquor jake ♦ (mountain) dew ♦ moonlight

illness pip

ill-tempered on the rag

imaginary course underwater basket weaving

imaginary socks air hose

imaginary tool sky hook ♦ left-handed monkey wrench

imagine Fancy that!

imitate make like so/sth

immediately in a flash ♦ in a jiff(y) ♦ in nothing flat ♦ pronto ♦ stat

immediately available on tap

immigrant bohunk

immobile dead in the water

impede put the clamps on so/sth

imperceptive cannot see (any) further than the end of (one's) nose

impervious to criticism thick-skinned

impish child dickens

important big name ♦ big time ♦ heavyweight ♦ red hot (Try also **former important person ♦ very important person ♦ act important ♦ look important ♦ not important ♦ overly important.**)

important date heavy date

important day red-letter day

important event big noise ♦ biggie

important person big gun ♦ big kahuna ♦ big name ♦ big noise ♦ big shot ♦ big wheel

◆ biggie ◆ bigwig ◆ BMOC ◆ dynamite ◆ face card ◆ heavy artillery ◆ heavyweight ◆ high mucky-muck ◆ hotshot ◆ key figure ◆ a somebody
important points nitty-gritty
important question the sixty-four-dollar question
important student (female) BWOC
important student (male) big man on campus
impotent penis whiskey dick
impress blow so's mind ◆ slay ◆ wow ◆ zap ◆ zoom so out (Try also **fail to impress.**)
impressed blown away
impressive totally awesome
impressive person the bomb
impressive thing beaut ◆ hell-on-wheels ◆ the bomb
imprison put so away ◆ send so up the river
improbable off-the-wall
impromptu scratch
improve clean one's act up ◆ lick sth into shape ◆ shape up ◆ shape up or ship out ◆ whip sth into shape
improved Try **altered.**
improvise punt ◆ wing it
impudence fat lip ◆ jive ◆ lip
impudent fresh
impudent person smart ass ◆ smart guy ◆ smart mouth ◆ smarty ◆ smarty-pants
in in like Flynn
in a wave in the tube
in abundance out the gazoo
in advance one jump ahead of so/sth ◆ up front
in awkward situation up a creek ◆ up shit creek (without a paddle) ◆ up the creek (without a paddle)
in bad situation up the wall
in control hold all the aces ◆ in the catbird seat ◆ in the driver's seat
in debt in deep ◆ in the hole
in difficulty up a tree
in good spirits in fine feather
in jail away ◆ behind bars ◆ boxed (up) ◆ locked down
in last term lame duck
in love strung out ◆ that way
in love with serious about so
in middle smack (dab) in the middle
in one's genes in one's blood
in one's situation where so lives ◆ in prison away ◆ behind bars ◆ up the river
in process in the hopper ◆ in the pipeline

in reserve on ice
in secret under wraps
in small portions in dribs and drabs
in style trendy
in the face right in the kisser
in trouble behind the eight ball ◆ in a jam ◆ in deep doo-doo ◆ in Dutch ◆ in the soup ◆ jammed ◆ jammed up ◆ put to it ◆ up against it
inability to jump white man's disease
inactive down for the count
inadequate ain't long enough ◆ laine ◆ lame ◆ lane ◆ piddling
inappropriate not cricket ◆ out of line
inattentive asleep at the switch
inborn in one's blood
incisive on-target
incompetent can't find one's butt with both hands (in broad daylight)
incomprehensible Greek to so
inconsequential lightweight ◆ nothing to sneeze at ◆ nothing to write home about
increase (n) hike ◆ pickup ◆ run-up
increase (v) hike ◆ snowball ◆ up
increase power soup sth up
increase speed swing into high gear
indecisive wishy-washy
independent You're on your own. (Try also **financially independent.**)
Indian Try **American Indian as white.**
indication tip-off
indulge oneself splurge
industrial states rust belt
industrious ball-busting
ineffectual can't hit the (broad) side of a barn ◆ doormat ◆ drippy ◆ half-ass(ed) ◆ not know one's ass from a hole in the ground
ineffectual man dickwad ◆ dickweed ◆ limpdick ◆ nimrod ◆ numbnuts ◆ pussycat ◆ weenie
ineffectual person burnout ◆ dishrag ◆ dode ◆ doofus ◆ duffis ◆ mope ◆ neb(bish) ◆ nerd ◆ nurd ◆ puppy ◆ rubber sock ◆ schmendrick ◆ schnook ◆ schnuck ◆ shit-bag ◆ wet noodle ◆ wet rag ◆ wet sock ◆ wimp ◆ wuss(y)
inefficient clunky ◆ kludgy
inept laine ◆ lame ◆ lane ◆ wimpy
inept person fish ◆ laine ◆ lame ◆ lane ◆ loser
inept soldier yardbird
inexperienced raw ◆ rookie ◆ rooky
inexperienced man shavetail
infatuation puppy love

inferior crumbum ♦ crumby ♦ crummy ♦ punk ♦ rinky-dink ♦ rotten ♦ scrungy

inferior liquor Try **bad liquor.**

inferior merchandise schlock

influence (n) juice ♦ suck ♦ suction ♦ wallop (Try also **lose influence ♦ seek influence.**)

influential carry (an amount of) weight

inform clue so in ♦ drop a dime ♦ fink ♦ fink (on so) ♦ hip ♦ nark ♦ rat ♦ rat (on so) ♦ sing ♦ snitch ♦ spew one's guts (out) ♦ spill one's guts (to so) ♦ spill one's guts on so ♦ squeal ♦ stool (on so)

information (hot) skinny ♦ 411 ♦ ammo ♦ ammunition ♦ four-one-one ♦ lowdown ♦ poop ♦ scuttlebutt ♦ skinny ♦ straight dope ♦ the down low (Try also **false information ♦ give information ♦ piece of information ♦ privileged information ♦ seek information ♦ share information.**)

information sheet handout ♦ poop sheet ♦ throw-away

informed hep ♦ hip

informer burn artist ♦ canary ♦ cheese-eater ♦ dime-dropper ♦ finger ♦ fink ♦ nark ♦ pigeon ♦ rat fink ♦ snitch ♦ snitcher ♦ squealer ♦ stool (pigeon) ♦ stoolie ♦ tipster ♦ whistle-blower ♦ whistler (Try also **bribe to informer.**)

inhale drug fumes chase the dragon

inhaled drug nose (candy)

inject drug bang ♦ jab pop ♦ shoot ♦ shoot up (on sth) ♦ get narkied ♦ shoot up

injecting drugs on the needle

injection bang in the arm ♦ big jab ♦ hype (Try also **drug injection ♦ lethal injection ♦ scars (injection).**)

injector Try **drug injector.**

injured in a bad way ♦ in bad shape ♦ shot-up

injured person walking about walking wounded

injury boo-boo

inner workings guts ♦ nuts and bolts

inning Try **baseball inning.**

innocent blue-eyed (Try also **seem innocent.**)

innocent man quality Joe

innocent of lawbreaking clean

inoffensive sugarcoated

inoperative down ♦ on the fritz ♦ out of kilter ♦ out of w(h)ack

insane bonkers

inseparable (as) close as stink on shit ♦ close as stink on shit ♦ hand-in-glove ♦ joined at the hip ♦ like the white on rice

insider in

insider's crime an inside job

insignia Try **military insignia.**

insignificant jerkwater ♦ small-time

insignificant amount small change ♦ small potatoes

insignificant thing small potatoes

insincere fair-weather ♦ jive ♦ smarmy

insincere person shuck

insipid beige ♦ wishy-washy

inspection Try **rectal inspection.**

inspiration lift

install spy devices wire

instant (n) flash ♦ jiffy ♦ sec ♦ tick

instant meals (military) MRE

instantly cold ♦ cold turkey ♦ in a New York minute

institute Try **research institute.**

instruction (touching equipment) hands-on

instrument Try **musical instrument ♦ play an instrument ♦ leave surgical instruments in patient.**

insult (n) blow off ♦ dirty crack ♦ dozens ♦ put-down ♦ a slap in the face ♦ the (dirty) dozens ♦ zinger (Try also **trade insults ♦ war of insults.**)

insult (v) chop ♦ ding ♦ give so a dig ♦ give so the finger ♦ put-down ♦ shine so ♦ take a dig at so ♦ take a jab at so (Try also **dinner where one is insulted.**)

insulter dirty-mouth ♦ flamer

insulting remark scorching ♦ snide remark

intellectual (mod) highbrow

intellectual (n) conehead ♦ pointy-head ♦ double-dome ♦ egghead (Try also **anti-intellectual (n) ♦ departure of intellectuals.**)

intelligence smarts (Try also **have intelligence.**)

intelligent sharp (Try also **be intelligent.**)

intense bad ♦ deep (Try also **reduce intensity.**)

interest (v) turn so on

interest (various) Try **female interest ♦ lose interest ♦ male interest ♦ ruin interest ♦ special interest ♦ get interested ♦ persons sharing interests.**)

interfere mess with so/sth ♦ put one's nose in (where it's not wanted) ♦ screw so/sth up ♦ stick one's nose in (where it's not wanted)

interfering cock-blocking
internally Try **assign work internally.**
internet addicted person internut
internet message flamage
interracial salt and pepper
interrupter buttinsky
intestinal Try **release of intestinal gas ♦ release intestinal gas.**
intestines gut ♦ guts
intimate (as) close as stink on shit ♦ up close and personal (Try also **get intimate.**)
intimidate work so over
intoxicated Try **drug intoxicated and drunk ♦ marijuana intoxicated person ♦ drug intoxicated ♦ get drug intoxicated ♦ marijuana intoxicated.**)
intrigue click (with so)
intrigued ate up with so/sth
introduce oneself break the ice
invent hit on sth
invest Try **people who invest well ♦ attractive investment.**
invisible socks air hose
invitation come on (Try also **accept invitation.**)
involve rope so in
involved in deep ♦ thick (Try also **get involved.**)
involved with wired into so/sth
inward navel innie ♦ insy
IOU chit ♦ marker ♦ reader
Iraq Try **fear of Iraq.**
irritable bitchy ♦ cranky ♦ gritchy
irritate Try **annoy.**
irritated Try **annoyed.**
irritation Try **skin irritation.**
isolated location middle of nowhere
items Try **needed items.**
jabber Try **chatter.**
Jack Daniels JD
Jaguar (car) jag
jail brig ♦ calaboose ♦ can ♦ clink ♦ cooler ♦ Graybar Hotel ♦ Graystone College ♦ hoosegow ♦ joint ♦ jug ♦ junk tank ♦ pokey ♦ poky ♦ slammer (Try also **out of jail.**)
jail cell drunk tank ♦ pokey ♦ poky ♦ tank
jail sentence bit (Try also **prison sentence.**)
jailer fuzz ♦ screw
jam (n) bind
January jan
Japanese motorcycle rice-rocket
jargon gobbledygook
jealous Try **be jealous.**
jealous person playa hata

jelly sandals jellies
jerk A-hole ♦ Adam Henry ♦ AH ♦ asshat ♦ asshole ♦ baboon ♦ bean head ♦ beef-head ♦ bird ♦ bozo ♦ durge ♦ Joe Schmo ♦ Joe Six-pack ♦ jork ♦ quimp ♦ schmuck ♦ zerk
jerk underpants up give so a melvin
Jesus Jeez!
jettison deep six (Try also **discard.**)
jewelry bling-bling (Try also **see jewelry.**)
jewelry store ice palace
jewels ice
jitters heebie-jeebies ♦ the creeps
job gig ♦ racket (Try also **dull job ♦ easy job ♦ gentle selling job ♦ musician's job ♦ observation job ♦ quit a job ♦ work second job.**)
job market slave market
jockey Try **video jockey.**
join contest throw one's hat in the ring
join us Welcome to the club.
joint jizzle
joke (n) pisser ♦ yak ♦ crack ♦ gag ♦ gas ♦ gasser ♦ hoot ♦ howl ♦ killer ♦ rib ♦ rib-tickler ♦ rip snorter ♦ yuck ♦ yuk (Try also **funny joke ♦ obscene joke ♦ quick joke ♦ email jokes.**)
joke helper straight man
journey schlep ♦ shlep
jugular vein jug
juice Try **orange juice futures.**
jump Try **inability to jump.**
junk abbreviated piece of nothing ♦ crap ♦ crud ♦ dreck ♦ POS ♦ schlock ♦ shit ♦ sleaz ♦ sleaze ♦ unk-jay
junk email spam
junky crappy ♦ schlock ♦ schlocky
junky car ark ♦ heap
junkyard boneyard
just in time saved by the bell
juvenile (mod) juvie
juvenile (n) juvie ♦ punk kid
juvenile delinquent baby gangsta ♦ busta ♦ JD ♦ punk ♦ punk kid
keep Try **brothel keeper ♦ thing worth keeping.**
keep cash Cash is king.
keep charging nickel and dime so (to death)
keep doing Keep on trucking.
keep listening Stay tuned.
keep out Keep out of this! ♦ Keep your nose out of my business!
keep quiet clam up ♦ dummy up ♦ hush sth up ♦ pipe down ♦ simmer (down)
keep stocks Hold some, fold some.

keepable keepage ♦ keeper
keg of beer kegger ♦ keggers
kept things keepage
ketamine K.
ketchup cat-soup
key kizzle ♦ twister (Try also **computer key ♦ shortcut key ♦ start car without key ♦ piano keys.**)
kid busta ♦ josh (Try also **not kidding.**)
kidnap snatch
kidnapping snatch
kill kill for sth ♦ blot so out ♦ blow so's brains out ♦ blow so away ♦ blow so out ♦ bump so off ♦ cack ♦ cancel so's Christmas ♦ cancel so out of sth ♦ cap ♦ chill ♦ clip ♦ croak ♦ deaded ♦ deal with so ♦ deep six ♦ dispose of so ♦ do so in ♦ drop ♦ erase ♦ fill so full of lead ♦ ghost so ♦ give so the business ♦ hit ♦ hose so down ♦ hush so up ♦ ice ♦ kack ♦ kak ♦ kevork ♦ kiss so/sth off ♦ kizzle ♦ knock so off ♦ liquidate ♦ off ♦ OJ so ♦ put so away ♦ put so out of the way ♦ put so to bed with a shovel ♦ rip so off ♦ rub so out ♦ scrag ♦ send so to glory ♦ skrag ♦ smoke ♦ snuff so (out) ♦ spoil ♦ stamp so out ♦ take care of so ♦ take so off ♦ take so out ♦ w(h)ack so (out) ♦ wash so away ♦ waste ♦ wipe so out ♦ zap ♦ zotz
killed blown ♦ blown away ♦ eliminated ♦ offed ♦ out of the way ♦ outed ♦ piffed ♦ wasted
killer iceman
killing (n) wipe
kilo K. ♦ kee ♦ key ♦ ki ♦ kizzle
kind Try **speak kindly.**
kind man Mr. Nice Guy
kind of person type
kiss (n) fish-kiss ♦ lip ♦ air kiss ♦ monkey bite ♦ smacker ♦ smooch (Try also **deep kiss ♦ thrown kiss ♦ tongue kiss.**)
kiss (v) bill and coo ♦ chew face ♦ fish-kiss ♦ get lip ♦ lip ♦ mack on so ♦ maw ♦ neck ♦ smooch ♦ suck face ♦ swap spits
kiss deeply eat face ♦ French ♦ play tonsil hockey ♦ soul kiss
kissing in a lip lock (Try also **need kissing.**)
kleptomaniac klepto
knees dukes ♦ prayerbones
knick-knack chotchke
knife blade ♦ chiv ♦ shank ♦ shiv ♦ switch ♦ wep
knock down deck ♦ drop so ♦ flatten ♦ lay so out

knock out duke so out ♦ kayo ♦ KO ♦ punch so's lights out ♦ punch so out ♦ put so away
knock out drops Mickey (Finn) ♦ micky
knocked down floored ♦ laid out
knocked out KOed
knockout KO (Try also **fake knockout.**)
knockout drink torpedo
know get with so (Try also **not know.**)
know about know from sth
know schemes know all the angles
know the real world know the score ♦ know what's what ♦ know where it's at ♦ know which end is up
know what is what know all the angles ♦ know shit from Shinola ♦ know the score ♦ know what's what ♦ know where it's at ♦ know which end is up
knowledge know-how ♦ LOK ♦ savvy (Try also **act without knowledge ♦ lack knowledge ♦ be knowledgeable.**)
knowledgeable down with the haps ♦ fly ♦ hep ♦ hip ♦ in the know ♦ on the ball ♦ onto so/sth ♦ savvy ♦ tuned in ♦ wise to so/sth ♦ with (one's) eyes (wide) open
known Try **become known to public (news) ♦ widely known.**
knows everything know-it-all
laborer boomer ♦ hole digger (Try also **head laborer.**)
lack knowledge not know one's ass from a hole in the ground
lack of money the shorts
lacking energy all show and no go
lad lizzle
lady Try **old lady.**
lady's man drugstore cowboy ♦ mack daddy
lame gimpy
lame person gimp
land of bumblers Bumblefuck ♦ Bumfuck
language lingo
large honking ♦ mega (Try also **with large breasts ♦ with large genitals (male) ♦ with large penis.**)
large buttocked person bigass ♦ lard ass
large computer big iron ♦ number-cruncher
large drink (n) double ♦ triple
large eared person dumbo
large one whopper
large twenty-dollar bill bigface
largest portion lion's share
last Try **at the last moment ♦ in last term ♦ person in last term of office.**
last dollar one's bottom dollar
last minute down to the wire

last word parting shot
lasting all night all-nighter
late JCL ♦ Johnnie-come-lately
late achiever sleeper
late passenger no show
later, alligator L8R G8R ♦ L8R
latissimus dorsi lats
laugh (n) belly laugh ♦ hoot ♦ horse laugh ♦ yock ♦ yok
laugh (v) crack up ♦ lay an egg ♦ split a gut ♦ yock ♦ yok (Try also **make laugh.**)
laugh hard have kittens ♦ howl
laughing LOL ♦ RO(T)F(L) ♦ ROF ♦ rolling on the floor laughing (my ass off) ♦ ROTFL(MAO)
laughter Try **beg audience for laughter ♦ cause much laughter ♦ recorded laughter.**
launch Try **rocket launch.**
launder money greenwash
laundered (money) smurfed
launderer Try **money launderer.**
law long arm of the law (Try also **common-law alimony.**)
law of averages the avs
lawbreaking Try **innocent of lawbreaking.**
lawn service mow, blow, and go
lawyer ambulance chaser ♦ chaser ♦ fixer ♦ legal-beagle ♦ legal-eagle ♦ lip ♦ mouth(piece) ♦ shark ♦ shyster
lazy person couch potato ♦ couch-turkey ♦ goldbrick ♦ goldbricker ♦ lazybones ♦ piker ♦ schloomp ♦ schlump ♦ slackmaster ♦ sofa spud
lead (v) quarterback
leader ass-kicker ♦ big cheese ♦ big enchilada ♦ big fish ♦ big gun ♦ big wheel ♦ butt-kicker ♦ front runner ♦ gun ♦ Mr. Big (Try also **talk show leader.**)
learn words swallow the dictionary
learner's permit pink slip
leave (various) Are we away? ♦ bag ass (out of somewhere) ♦ Bag your face! ♦ bail (out) ♦ bail on so ♦ ball ♦ barrel ass (out of somewhere) ♦ Beat it! ♦ blast off (for somewhere) ♦ blow ♦ blow the joint ♦ blow town ♦ bolt ♦ bone out ♦ boogie ♦ book (on) out ♦ bounce ♦ break out ♦ bug out ♦ bust a move ♦ bust ass (out of somewhere) ♦ buzz along ♦ clear out ♦ cop a heel ♦ cruise ♦ cut ass (out of somewhere) ♦ cut out ♦ do a fade ♦ drag ass (out of somewhere) ♦ dust ♦ fade ♦ fall out ♦ fuck off ♦ get (out) while the gettin(g)'s good ♦ get (out) while the goin's good ♦ get on one's horse ♦ get out of

Dodge ♦ haul ass (out of somewhere) ♦ hit the trail ♦ I'm out of here. ♦ I'm outa here. ♦ I'm outie. ♦ I've got to fly. ♦ I've got to split. ♦ I('ve) gotta fly. ♦ jam ♦ jet ♦ Let's bump this place! ♦ Let's dump. ♦ make like a tree and leave ♦ make tracks ♦ make oneself scarce ♦ motor ♦ peace out ♦ piss off ♦ pop off ♦ pull chocks ♦ roll ♦ scat ♦ scram ♦ shag (off) ♦ shag ass (out of somewhere) ♦ skedaddle ♦ skip (out) ♦ smack the road ♦ split ♦ take a hike ♦ take a powder ♦ take a walk ♦ take it on the lam ♦ take off ♦ tear off ♦ vote with one's feet ♦ zoom ♦ zoom off (Try also **want to leave group ♦ first person to leave ♦ prepare to leave ♦ time to leave.**)
leave alone If it ain't broke don't fix it. ♦ If it ain't broke, fix it till it is.
leave evidence plant sth on so
leave for make for somewhere
leave home cut loose
leave prison walk
leave school drop out
leave surgical instruments in patient bury the hatchet
leave unaffected leave so cold
lecher cunt hound ♦ dirty old man ♦ make-out artist ♦ scammer ♦ stud
lecture Try **dull lecture.**
lecture (v) give so a (good) talking to
leer perve on so
left Try **turn left.**
left-handed person southpaw
legal legit
legal to buy liquor wet
legitimate legit ♦ on the up-and-up (Try also **become legitimate.**)
leg(s) chevrolegs ♦ gams ♦ hams ♦ pin ♦ stick ♦ stump ♦ stumps ♦ underpinnings (Try also **person with wooden leg.**)
lend spot so (sth)
lend money stake so to sth
lesbian bull-dagger ♦ bulldiker ♦ bulldyker ♦ dike ♦ dikey ♦ dyke ♦ dykey
less Try **no less than some amount ♦ provide less than ordered.**
lessen shave
let me lemme
let us go Sco. ♦ sgo ♦ sko
lethal injection big jab
letter Try **good-bye letter.**
lever Try **gearshift lever.**
Levis viz
lewd dirty-minded ♦ raunchy ♦ steamy
Lexus (car) Lex

liar bullshit artist ♦ bullshitter ♦ crock (of shit) ♦ fibber
libel (v) trash
liberation Try **woman's liberation supporter.**
lice bosom chums ♦ bosom friends ♦ crab ♦ crotch-monkey ♦ crotch-pheasant ♦ galloping dandruff ♦ pants rabbits ♦ seam-squirrels ♦ walking dandruff
license ticket
license plate tag
license sticker tag
lie (n) bedtime story ♦ bull ♦ bullshit ♦ crock ♦ crock (of shit) ♦ fairy tale ♦ fib ♦ fish story ♦ fish tale ♦ lip gloss ♦ lollapalooza ♦ pack of lies ♦ pile of shit ♦ whopper (Try also **full of lies.**)
lie (v) bullshit ♦ fake on so ♦ fib ♦ flip the script ♦ front ♦ hand so sth ♦ lie like a rug ♦ sell a woof ticket ♦ sell woof tickets ♦ talk through one's hat ♦ Tell me another (one)!
life Try **experience in urban life ♦ that is life.**
lifeless deadpan ♦ dry-as-dust
lifetime prisoner lifer
lifetime soldier lifer
lift weights pump (some) iron ♦ pump iron
light (n) Try **douse light ♦ flash of light ♦ signal light ♦ turn off light ♦ dimming of lights ♦ police car lights.**
light (v) fire sth up
light marijuana cigarette fire up
lighter lizzle ♦ zizzle
lightly Try **punish lightly.**
like AI ♦ lizzle
likely winner front runner
limit Try **at limit ♦ reach limit.**
limit choices box so in
limp windsock whiskey dick
line Try **music line ♦ punch line ♦ cocaine lines.**
lint ghost turd ♦ house moss
liquor (mountain) dew ♦ alchy ♦ alkie ♦ alky ♦ ammunition ♦ antifreeze ♦ beast ♦ belted ♦ bent ♦ berps ♦ blotto ♦ booze ♦ bottle ♦ breakfast of champions ♦ coffin varnish ♦ conk-buster ♦ dew ♦ drinkage ♦ drinkies ♦ drinkypoo ♦ Dutch courage ♦ embalming fluid ♦ evidence ♦ eye-opener ♦ eyewash ♦ firewater ♦ gargle ♦ gas ♦ giggle goo ♦ greased lightning ♦ grog ♦ happy juice ♦ hard liquor ♦ hardware ♦ headache ♦ hootch ♦ idiot oil ♦ joy juice ♦ joy water ♦ juice ♦ jungle juice ♦ juniper juice ♦ kong ♦ konk-buster ♦ laughing soup ♦ laughing water ♦ light stuff ♦ liquid lunch ♦ load ♦ lubrication ♦ lush ♦ meth ♦ Minnehaha ♦ monkey swill ♦ moonlight ♦ moonshine ♦ muddler ♦ painkiller ♦ plonk ♦ pluck ♦ plug ♦ poison ♦ potato soup ♦ Q. ♦ rotgut ♦ sauce ♦ shicker ♦ shoe polish ♦ silo drippings ♦ skag ♦ skinful ♦ slop(s) ♦ slosh ♦ smoke ♦ snakebite medicine ♦ spud ♦ squeeze ♦ staggers ♦ suck ♦ suds ♦ swill ♦ swizzle ♦ tea ♦ terps ♦ throat gag ♦ tiger juice ♦ tiger sweat ♦ tiger('s) milk ♦ tipple ♦ tornado juice ♦ turps ♦ who shot John ♦ widow-maker ♦ woofle-water ♦ wozzle-water ♦ yak (Try also **amount of liquor ♦ bad liquor ♦ homemade liquor ♦ illicit liquor ♦ inferior liquor ♦ legal to buy liquor ♦ make illegal liquor ♦ maker of illegal liquor ♦ sell illicit liquor ♦ sleep away liquor ♦ traffic in illicit liquor ♦ unaged (liquor).**)
liquor detector whiff-sniffer ♦ wiff-sniffer
liquor flask micky ♦ mickey
liquor store candy store ♦ comfort station ♦ filling station ♦ guzzlery ♦ happy shop ♦ headache department ♦ headache house ♦ juice house ♦ leeky store ♦ LIQ ♦ oasis ♦ thirst-aid station
list Try **make list of offenders.**
list of banned people blacklist
list of things wanted wish list
list of victims hit list ♦ sucker list
list of worthless people drop-dead list (Try also **bad people list.**)
listen Dig up! ♦ listen up ♦ Read my lips! ♦ Watch my lips! (Try also **beware of listeners ♦ keep listening.**)
listen to music boom
listener I'm all ears. ♦ I'm listening. ♦ radioland
literature lit
little Try **for very little.**
little finger pinkie ♦ pinky
live by borrowing sponge off so
live mellow cruise
live primitively rough it
live well take things easy
livelihood bread and butter
lively zippy
living Try **comfortable living.**
living dead person zombie
living together LT
loaded (bases in baseball) drunk
loafing place getaway ♦ hangout
loan Try **request for loan ♦ request loan.**

local homegrown
local resident local yokel
local theater nabe
location Try **isolated location.**
loiter hang (around)
lonely hard up
loner (male) lone wolf
long distance schlep ♦ shlep
long story megillah
long time donkey's years ♦ till the fat lady sings ♦ when the fat lady sings
long tuxedo tails
look (n) gander (Try also **seductive look.**)
look alert snap to (attention)
look at get a load of sth or so ♦ glom ♦ lamp ♦ take a gander (at so/sth)
look carefully eyeball
look competent play it cool
look for butts field grounders
look good stylin(g)
look helpless stand there with one's bare face hanging out
look important signify
look sharp(ly) Look alive!
look stupid stand there with one's bare face hanging out
look ugly scank ♦ skank
looking for guilty person blame shifting
looking suburban burbed out
loose morals zipper morals
loose pants droopy-drawers
loose woman bed-bunny ♦ benda ♦ bender ♦ best buy ♦ bim ♦ bimbo ♦ FB ♦ floozie ♦ glutz ♦ hobeast
loot (n) boodle ♦ haul ♦ swank ♦ take
loot (v) rip ♦ score
lose can't win (th)em all ♦ crap out
lose control flip (out) ♦ lose it ♦ lose one's cool ♦ lose one's grip ♦ lose one's hold ♦ schiz(z) out ♦ wig out ♦ zeek out ♦ zoom out
lose deliberately tank ♦ throw a fight ♦ throw a game
lose everything lose one's shirt
lose influence fade
lose interest run out of gas
lose momentum run out of gas
lose money lose a bundle ♦ take a bath (on sth) ♦ tap out ♦ wash out
lose power fade
lose temper pop off
loss Try **accept loss ♦ URL loss ♦ stop losses.**

lost Try **deliberately lost (contest) ♦ time lost.**
lost data container bit-bucket
lost time down time
lots all that and then some ♦ a whole bunch ♦ buttload ♦ gob ♦ heap ♦ heaps ♦ jillion ♦ kilobucks ♦ metric shitload ♦ no end of sth ♦ oodles ♦ scads ♦ shitload ♦ slew ♦ slews ♦ the woods are full of sth (Try also **spend a lot ♦ having lots ♦ talk lots.**)
loud banging (Try also **speak loudly.**)
loud talker loudmouth
loudspeaker bitch box ♦ squawk box
love (n) Try **in love with ♦ be in love ♦ couple in love ♦ fall in love ♦ in love ♦ with love.**
love (v) heart
love affair whing-ding ♦ wing-ding
love bite hickey
lover dreamboat ♦ squeeze (Try also **former lover or spouse ♦ chocolate lover ♦ classical music lover ♦ computer lover ♦ crafts lover ♦ nature lover ♦ old lover ♦ party lover ♦ woman lover ♦ cause lovers to separate ♦ search for lovers.**)
low Try **flying low.**
low quality bottom of the barrel ♦ bottom of the heap
low tavern creep dive ♦ creep joint ♦ joint ♦ juice joint ♦ puke hole ♦ trap
lower price knock sth off
lowest point rock bottom
lowest price rock bottom
lowest quality bottom of the barrel ♦ bottom of the heap
loyal criminal champ ♦ thoroughbred
LSD acid ♦ blotter ♦ cube ♦ mickey mouse ♦ sid ♦ sidney
LSD user C-head ♦ guru
luck Try **bad luck ♦ call for luck ♦ extended luck ♦ Good luck! ♦ you will need luck ♦ be lucky ♦ get lucky.**
lucky hot
lucky person lucky dog
lucky success narrow squeak
lump goose egg
lunch spot of lunch (Try also **bag lunch ♦ carry lunch ♦ group lunch ♦ have lunch.**)
lungs air-bags
lurid newspaper scandal sheet
luxury bed of roses
lyrics Try **suggestive lyrics.**
machine Try **start machine.**
machine gun street sweeper

meeting room smoke-filled room
megabyte moby
mellow cool ♦ crunk ♦ downbeat ♦ frosty ♦ ghetto ♦ gone ♦ groovy ♦ kewl ♦ real gone ♦ sent (Try also **feel mellow ♦ live mellow.**)
mellow person cool cat
member(s) rank and file (Try also **fraternity member ♦ gang member ♦ get new members.**)
memorized down
memory Try **memory failure ♦ past memory ♦ recall a memory ♦ sudden memory.**
memory failure blond moment ♦ can't remember a fucking thing ♦ can't remember shit ♦ CRAFT ♦ CRS ♦ senior moment
men alone stag line
men-only party stag-party
menses Aunt Flo ♦ flow ♦ monthlies ♦ on the rag ♦ red tide ♦ visit from Flo ♦ the curse (Try also **have menses.**)
mental changes changes
mental state in one's sth mode
mentally Try **be mentally sound.**
mention bring sth up
mention annoyance touch a sore point
mention someone speak of the devil
Mercedes Benz auto benz
merchandise Try **bad merchandise ♦ cheap merchandise ♦ inferior merchandise ♦ straw merchandise.**
merging fad merger-mania
merits brownie points
mescaline mesc
mess Try **bad mess ♦ terrible mess.**
mess (n) can of worms ♦ fuck-up ♦ gobbledygook ♦ hell of a mess ♦ holy stink ♦ mell of a hess ♦ screw up ♦ soup sandwich
mess around clown around ♦ effing around ♦ fuck around ♦ fuck around with so ♦ spaz around
mess up (various) ball up ♦ ball so/sth up ♦ bitch sth up ♦ crum sth up ♦ crumb sthup ♦ flub (up) ♦ flub sth up ♦ foozle ♦ fuck up ♦ fuck so/sth up ♦ fuck sth up ♦ futz sth up ♦ goof up ♦ goof sth up ♦ jack sth up ♦ louse sth up ♦ muck sth up ♦ mung ♦ mung sth up ♦ screw up ♦ screw so/sth up ♦ throw salt on so's game
mess with fuck with sth
message Try **provocative message sender ♦ email message ♦ internet message ♦ send provocative message ♦ angry internet messages.**

messed up confuckulated ♦ fouled up ♦ fucked up ♦ goofed (up) ♦ janky ♦ screwed up
messenger runner
messy mungy
methadone meth
methamphetamine crystal ♦ meth ♦ speeder ♦ speedster (Try also **use methamphetamine.**)
methamphetamine user meth monster ♦ speed demon ♦ speed freak ♦ speedhead
microphone Try **conceal microphone or camera.**
microwave (n) nuker
microwave (v) nuke
middle Try **in middle.**
middle class buzhie
middle-aged adult (baby) boomer ♦ boomer
midlength garment midi
mild soft core
mild pornography soft core
mile low-key
military Try **instant meals (military).**
military dog tag lost-and-found badge
military insignia scrambled eggs
milk (n) cow juice ♦ moo juice (Try also **canned milk ♦ coffee without milk.**)
milkshake shake
million mil
mind attic (Try also **be of sound mind ♦ obsessed mind ♦ speak mind ♦ absent minded person ♦ absent minded ♦ narrow minded.**)
mind your own business MYOB.
miniature mini
minimal dime store ♦ pissing
minimalistic funky ♦ phunky
miniskirt mini
minor problem no big deal ♦ no big whoop ♦ no biggie
minute(s) a few ticks (Try also **last minute.**)
misadjusted haywire ♦ on the blink ♦ on the fritz ♦ out of w(h)ack
misbehaving illin'
mischief monkeyshines
misconduct Try **sexual misconduct.**
miser penny-pincher ♦ piker ♦ scrooge ♦ tight wad
miserly tight
misfit goon-platoon ♦ square peg (in a round hole)
missionary position mish
mistake Try **remind of mistake.**

MRE meals rejected by Ethiopians ♦ meals rejected by the enemy

much fun barrel of fun

much money big bucks ♦ budget dust ♦ bundle ♦ fat skrill ♦ hard coin ♦ heavy bread ♦ heavy money ♦ megabucks ♦ mint ♦ package ♦ pile ♦ pretty penny ♦ roll

mucousy snotty

mucus booger ♦ boogie ♦ nose-lunger ♦ snot

mucus blow blow a snot rocket ♦ blow snot rockets ♦ skeet-shooting

murder (n) wipe

murder mystery whodunit

muscles abs ♦ cuts ♦ guns ♦ lats ♦ pythons ♦ quads ♦ traps ♦ yokes (Try also **flex muscle ♦ abdominal muscles ♦ back muscles ♦ build muscles ♦ pectoral muscles ♦ tight abdominal muscles.**)

muscular buff(ed) ♦ cut ♦ cut (up) ♦ ripped ♦ yoked

muscular display (male) beefcake

muscular man beef ♦ beefcake

mushrooms shrooms

music sounds ♦ tunage ♦ tunes (Try also **classical music lover.**)

music end tag

music line riff

music ranking charts

music session set

music style bop ♦ funk ♦ gutbucket ♦ punk

music with beat bumping

musical instrument axe

musical score chart

musician longhair

musician's job gig

mustache soup-strainer ♦ stache ♦ stash (Try also **beard and mustache.**)

mustache and beard pudding ring

muster Try **pass muster.**

muster strength get mad (at sth)

mutual masturbation circle-jerk

mystery Try **murder mystery.**

nag noodge ♦ nudge

nagger nudge

naive person schnook ♦ schnuck ♦ shnook

naked bare-ass(ed) ♦ butt naked ♦ in the buff ♦ laid to the bone ♦ silked to the bone ♦ wearing (nothing but) a smile (Try also **get naked ♦ run naked.**)

naked run streak

naked runner streaker

name handle ♦ moniker ♦ tag

name forgotten what's his face ♦ what's his name

nap forty winks (Try also **take nap.**)

napkin Try **sanitary napkin.**

narcotic (mod) narc ♦ narco

narcotics agent narc ♦ narco

narrow escape close call ♦ close shave

narrow minded see no further than the end of one's nose

nasal mucus skeet

nastiness crud ♦ scuz(z)

nasty cruddie ♦ cruddy ♦ gungy ♦ icky ♦ scrungy ♦ shag-nasty ♦ snotty ♦ vomity ♦ yucky

nasty food swill

nasty substance creeping-crud ♦ greldge ♦ gronk ♦ grunch ♦ grunge ♦ gunk ♦ ick ♦ scrunge ♦ smeg ♦ yuck ♦ yuk

native American Try **American Indian as white.**

naturally natch

naturally talented natural-born

nature lover crunchy

nausea sicks ♦ the pukes ♦ the urge to purge

nauseate nause so out ♦ scuzz so out ♦ turn so's stomach

nauseated pukish

navel belly button (Try also **inward navel ♦ outward navel.**)

near Try **be near death ♦ near death ♦ remain nearby.**

near death in the O-zone

nearly finished in the (home) stretch

neck (n) scrag

neck (v) mack on so ♦ make out ♦ mash ♦ maw ♦ park ♦ pitch (the) woo ♦ spoon

necking petting-party

necking place passion-pit

necking session bush patrol

necktie choker

need Try **exact need (n) ♦ you will need luck ♦ what is needed ♦ different needs.**

needed items outfit

needing drugs hard up

needing kissing kissyface

needle Try **hypodermic needle.**

needs vary different strokes for different folks

negative negatory ♦ thumbs down

neglect blow so/sth off

negotiation brass tacks

neighborhood nabe (Try also **tough neighborhood.**)

nerd peanut head

nerve crust ♦ grit

nervous antsy ♦ at loose ends ♦ clutched ♦ jumpy ♦ keyed (up) ♦ nervy ♦ strung out ♦ wired ♦ wired up (Try also **be nervous.**)

nervous attack screaming-meemies ♦ spaz

nervous person bundle of nerves ♦ nervous Nellie ♦ white knuckler

nervous state twit

nervous wreck basket case

nervously Try **wait nervously.**

net Try **basketball goal (net).**

never happen That'll be the day!

new (brand) spanking new ♦ raw ♦ spanking new (Try also **get new members.**)

new idea wrinkle

new person newbie ♦ noob ♦ oldbie ♦ rookie ♦ rooky ♦ young blood

new situation a whole new ball game

new soldier desert cherry

new to place vújà day

New York, NY the Big Apple

New York Stock Exchange big board

news dope ♦ scuttlebutt ♦ the down low (Try also **win news race ♦ bad news ♦ become known to public (news) ♦ disturbing news ♦ early news ♦ shocking news.**)

news collection roundup

news reader meat puppet ♦ talking head

news twister spin doctor

newspaper rag (Try also **lurid newspaper ♦ tabloid newspaper.**)

newspaper early edition bulldog edition

next Try **ride next to driver.**

nice big of so ♦ choice ♦ namby-pamby

nice man right guy

nice person carebear

nicely swimmingly

nicotine nick

night dim (Try also **one-night romance ♦ lasting all night ♦ spend the night ♦ study all night ♦ working all night.**)

night shift graveyard shift

nightclub nitery ♦ spot

nightstick attitude-adjuster

night-working person night person

nipple(s) bean ♦ bullets

nitroglycerin soup

no 86 ♦ My foot! ♦ naw ♦ negatory ♦ nix ♦ no dice ♦ no go ♦ no sale ♦ no soap ♦ No way! ♦ No way, José! ♦ nope ♦ not a chance ♦ Nothing doing! ♦ nuts ♦ nutz ♦ Over my dead body!

no bother no stress

no caressing Keep your hands to yourself.

no chance fat chance

no choice luck of the draw

no difference same difference

no exaggeration No shit!

no hope no-win situation

no less than some amount cool

no reason no earthly reason

no route You can't get there from here.

no score game shutout

nobody chopped liver

noise peep ♦ racket (Try also **engine noise.**)

nonaddictive soft

nonautomatic transmission stick shift

nondepressing euphoria up high

nondepressing marijuana up pot

nondrinker Try **abstainer.**

none not all that

none of your business nunya

nonfunctional haywire ♦ on the blink ♦ out of w(h)ack

nonintellectual person lowbrow ♦ lowbrow

nonproductive workers deadwood

nonsense applesauce ♦ baloney ♦ banana oil ♦ beans ♦ birdseed ♦ bologna ♦ booty-cheddar ♦ Bravo Sierra ♦ BS ♦ bull ♦ bull-pucky ♦ bullshit ♦ buncombe ♦ bunkum ♦ corral dust ♦ crap ♦ crock ♦ crock (of shit) ♦ déjà moo ♦ eyewash ♦ fadoodle ♦ falderal ♦ flamdoodle ♦ flapdoodle ♦ flimflam ♦ fluff ♦ folderol ♦ fooey ♦ fudge ♦ fun and games ♦ garbage ♦ gas ♦ gobbledygook ♦ gubbish ♦ guff ♦ hogwash ♦ hokum ♦ hoo-ha ♦ hooey ♦ Horsefeathers! ♦ horseshit ♦ hot air ♦ jive ♦ kafooster ♦ malark(e)y ♦ mickey mouse ♦ moonshine ♦ mush ♦ noise ♦ nurts ♦ phedinkus ♦ phooey ♦ piffle ♦ poo ♦ poppycock ♦ rot ♦ rubbish ♦ scat ♦ schmegegge ♦ schmegeggy ♦ shit ♦ slobber ♦ tripe ♦ whang(y)doodle ♦ What a crock! ♦ yap (Try also **full of nonsense ♦ stop your nonsense.**)

noodles worms

noose Try **hang with a noose.**

normalized evened out

nose beak ♦ beezer ♦ honker ♦ hooter ♦ horn ♦ schnozz ♦ schnozzle ♦ schnozzola ♦ shnozz ♦ smeller ♦ snoot

nose alteration nose job

nose blowing skeet-shooting

nostrils Try **both nostrils.**

nosy person nosy parker

not appear no show

not drinking on the wagon

not free There ain't no such thing as a free lunch.

not important Don't make a federal case out of it! ♦ Like it's such a big deal.

not kidding I don't mean maybe! ♦ I kid you not. ♦ No shit! ♦ No shit, Sherlock!

not know Damned if I know. ♦ Search me. ♦ Your guess is as good as mine. ♦ Keep your hands to yourself.

not matter It don't make (me) no nevermind.

not my problem (It's) not my dog. ♦ Not my dog.

not obligated off the hook

not so Like hell! ♦ Not!

not teasing No kidding!

not worry Don't sweat it! ♦ Everything's going to be okay. ♦ Not to worry.

not your business none of so's beeswax ♦ What's it to you?

note bookmark ♦ script(t) (Try also **bank note.**)

nothing (doodly-)squat ♦ beans ♦ chicken shit ♦ dick ♦ diddly-squat ♦ doodly-shit ♦ french-fried-fuck ♦ jack ♦ jack-shit ♦ nada ♦ nix ♦ squat ♦ zilch ♦ zip ♦ zotz

notice Try **dismissal notice** ♦ **take notice.**

novice cherry

nuclear Try **against nuclear.**

nuclear weapon nuke

nudity Try **movie with nudity.**

nudity (female) B. and B. girlie magazine ♦ girlie show ♦ T. and A.

numb feeling no pain

number Try **enormous number.**

number one numero uno

number sign mesh ♦ pigpen

nuts nerts ♦ nurts

oath Try **take oath.**

object Try **unwanted object.**

objector (various) but-boy ♦ NIMBY ♦ Not in my backyard!

obligated Try **not obligated.**

oblivious Try **become oblivious.**

obnoxious birdturd ♦ obno(c) ♦ pukey ♦ pukoid ♦ shit-ass ♦ skanky ♦ snotty (Try also **be obnoxious.**)

obnoxious man animal ♦ bug-fucker ♦ butt-munch ♦ choad ♦ cunt ♦ dick-sucker ♦ fag ♦ heel ♦ male chauvinist pig ♦ MCP ♦ neanderthal ♦ pecker ♦ peckerhead ♦ prick ♦ putz ♦ sidewinder

obnoxious person ass-wipe ♦ birdturd ♦ bitch of a so/sth ♦ blivit ♦ BM ♦ boody ♦ bouquet of assholes ♦ bummer ♦ butt ♦ butt-wipe ♦ butthead ♦ cabbagehead ♦ crud

♦ crumb ♦ crumbum ♦ cull ♦ dingbat ♦ dipshit ♦ dipstick ♦ douche bag ♦ drag ♦ fart ♦ fart hole ♦ fuck-shit ♦ fuckhead ♦ furball ♦ gagger ♦ geek ♦ geekazoid ♦ gug ♦ hairball ♦ headache ♦ headache department ♦ ick ♦ jack ♦ maggot ♦ megabitch ♦ pisshead ♦ pond scum ♦ poohead ♦ poophead ♦ puke ♦ quimp ♦ rat ♦ rotten egg ♦ schtoonk ♦ scuzzo ♦ shit ♦ shit-ass ♦ shit-bag ♦ shitbox ♦ shithead ♦ shitsky ♦ shower scum ♦ shtoonk ♦ sleaz ♦ sleaze ♦ slob ♦ smeg ♦ snot ♦ toxic waste dump ♦ turd ♦ turd face ♦ turkey ♦ yard dog ♦ yazzihamper ♦ yoyo ♦ so/sth from hell

obnoxious place toxic waste dump

obnoxious thing bitch of a so/sth ♦ boody ♦ bouquet of assholes ♦ bummer ♦ gagger ♦ toxic waste dump ♦ so/sth from hell

obnoxious woman bitch ♦ bush bitch ♦ bush pig ♦ megabitch

obscene blue ♦ dirty ♦ dirty-minded ♦ graphic ♦ trashy (Try also **user of obscene vocabulary** ♦ **think obscenely.**)

obscene joke dirty joke

obscene talker dirty-mouth ♦ four mouth ♦ garbage mouth ♦ latrine lips ♦ trash mouth

obscenity dirty word

obsequious smarmy (Try also **be obsequious.**)

observation job stakeout

observe catch sth

observer stakeout

obsessed happy ♦ have a wild hair up one's ass ♦ heavy into so/sth ♦ stuck on so/sth ♦ wrapped up (in so/sth) (Try also **person obsessed with clothes** ♦ **person obsessed with work** ♦ **sexually obsessed person** ♦ **be obsessed** ♦ **sexually obsessed.**)

obsessed mind one-track mind

obsession bug

obsessive worker workaholic

obsolete person pip

obstruct stonewall ♦ stymie

obstruction stonewall

obtain bag ♦ score

obtain drug dose cop a fix

obtainable obtanium

obvious ob ♦ out-and-out (Try also **be obvious.**)

occasion Try **make special occasion.**

ocean big drink

October ak ♦ ok

odd looking man gunzel-butt

odor GAPO (Try also **bad odor** ♦ **body odor.**)

off course off the track

off drugs squared up ♦ straight

offend put so's nose out of joint

offenders Try **make list of offenders.**

offense Try **take offense.**

offer Try **reject offer.**

office Try **mall doctor's office.**

officer big gun ♦ brass ♦ brass hat ♦ occifer (Try also **commanding officer ♦ police officer ♦ private police officer ♦ restroom police officer.**)

oily feeling mungy

okay 10-4 ♦ abso-bloody-lutely ♦ absotively (positulely) ♦ all right ♦ All right already! ♦ Anytime. ♦ cas ♦ check ♦ down ♦ ducky ♦ fresh ♦ Good deal! ♦ high sign ♦ hunky-dory ♦ I'll bite. ♦ jake ♦ NBD ♦ NBT ♦ no big deal ♦ no big whoop ♦ no biggie ♦ No problem ♦ no stress ♦ no sweat ♦ not too shabby ♦ NP ♦ oak(s) ♦ OIC ♦ OK ♦ okey-dokey ♦ roger ♦ Sounds like a winner! ♦ ten-four ♦ WFM ♦ whatever ♦ whatever floats your boat ♦ whatever turns you on ♦ Works for me. ♦ yeah ♦ Yeah, right. ♦ yep ♦ Yes! ♦ You bet your sweet patoot(ie)! ♦ You bet. ♦ You betcha! ♦ You got it! ♦ yup (Try also **turn out okay ♦ yes.**)

old Try **same old thing ♦ too old.**

old and good oldie but goodie

old car beater ♦ bucket ♦ bucket of bolts ♦ clunker ♦ crate ♦ flivver ♦ gas-guzzler ♦ ghetto sled ♦ heap ♦ junk heap ♦ rattle-trap

old clothing grubbers ♦ grubbies

old lady bluehair ♦ old girl

old lover old flame

old man buzzard ♦ geezer ♦ old-timer ♦ pops

old person boring old fart ♦ FOP ♦ fucking old person ♦ geri ♦ GERK ♦ golden-ager ♦ old-timer

oldest (grand)daddy (of them all) ♦ daddy (of them all)

old-fashioned dead from the neck up ♦ square

old-fashioned man old fogey

old-fashioned person back number ♦ buzzard meat ♦ fossil ♦ fud ♦ fuddy-duddy ♦ granddad ♦ moldy fig ♦ mossback ♦ old fogey ♦ square ♦ stick in the mud

old-fashioned thing old hat

on a radio beam (aviation) on the beam

on back tits up

on course on the beam

on the toilet on the throne

on time on the nose

on Wall Street on the street

one dollar ace ♦ smacker

one-dollar bill eagle ♦ greenback ♦ single ♦ skin

one-dollar coin Suzy

one-hundred-dollar bill Benjamin ♦ C-note ♦ C-spot ♦ century note ♦ domino ♦ yard

one hundred dollars bird ♦ C.

one-night romance one-night stand

one-person act one-man show

oneself number one ♦ numero uno

online Try **seek passwords online ♦ seek secrets online ♦ using diary online.**

open beer crack a tube ♦ pop (some) tops

open bottle crack open a bottle

open market spot market

open windows play freeze-out

opener Try **beer opener.**

opera Try **soap opera.**

operate sensibly play with a full deck ♦ run on all cylinders

operates Try **when computer operates.**

operating in business

operation Try **final operation.**

operative long knife

operator Try **amateur radio operator ♦ systems operator.**

opinion IM(H)O ♦ IYHO (Try also **retain opinion.**)

opium big-O.

opportunity break

opposite side flip side

opposition anti

optimist good-time Charley

options All options stink.

oral sex French (Try also **perform oral sex (female).**)

orange juice futures juice ♦ OJ

ordain call (all) the shots

order Try **fill or cancel stock order ♦ provide less than ordered.**

orderliness spit and polish

ordinary male college student Joe College

ordinary man joe ♦ Joe Blow ♦ Joe Citizen ♦ Joe Doakes ♦ John Doe

organization org

organized Try **get organized.**

organizers movers and shakers

orgasm Try **have orgasm.**

orient (v) Try **understand someone's orientation ♦ gay oriented.**

ornament tchotchke

other people how the other half lives

otherwise OTOH

ounce zip

out of outa

out of control out of pocket ♦ spastic ♦ wigged (out)

out of date groovy ♦ so last year

out of fashion camp ♦ out

out of jail fresh and sweet

out of square out of kilter

outboard motor egg-beater

outburst blow up

outcry hoopla

outhouse library ♦ privy ♦ shit-house ♦ shitcan

outscore cream ♦ dust ♦ murder ♦ paste ♦ shellac ♦ slaughter ♦ smear ♦ take so to the cleaners ♦ trounce ♦ wax ♦ whomp ♦ whump ♦ zap

outscored creamed ♦ done over ♦ done to a turn ♦ screwed, blued, and tattooed ♦ shellacked ♦ skunked ♦ tanked ♦ pasting

outsmart pull a fast one

outstanding bold

outward navel outsy ♦ outy

outwit eat so's lunch ♦ skunk

over act camp it up

over exercise rep out

overabundance coming out of one's ears ♦ out the gazoo

overbearing big shot ♦ bigass

overblown glorified

overcharge rob so blind ♦ skin ♦ soak

overdo go overboard

overdo effeminacy camp it up

overdone effeminacy campy

overdose (n) OD ♦ overjolt (Try also **take overdose.**)

overdose (v) OD

overdrawn (humor) corny

overdressed man tackhead

overeat blimp out ♦ mac out ♦ make a pig of oneself ♦ oink out ♦ pig out ♦ pork out ♦ scarf out

overeater pig

overhead camera eye-in-the-sky

overly friendly palsy-walsy

overly friendly person backslapper ♦ flesh-presser ♦ glad-hander ♦ palm-presser

overly important big shot ♦ have a man by the balls

overpower zonk

overreact blow a hype ♦ spaz out

overreacting person spaz

overspend throw money at sth

overwhelm blow so's mind ♦ blow so away ♦ kick-ass on so ♦ knock so's socks off ♦ murder ♦ shellac ♦ slaughter ♦ slay

overwhelmed blown away ♦ knocked out ♦ psyched (out)

owe Try **pay someone money owed.**

owl watching event owl-prowl

own Try **mind your own business ♦ tend to own business.**

owning ownage

PA system bitch box

pacifier passy

pack bindle (Try also **cigarette pack.**)

pager beeper (Try also **call my pager.**)

paid assassin hired gun

paid in cash out of pocket

pain (n) a stitch (Try also **headache pain ♦ testicle ache.**)

paint Try **mark with paint ♦ spray painter.**

pair of people dynamic duo

pajamas PJs

pal bucko ♦ chum ♦ cuddie ♦ homes ♦ homeslice ♦ homey ♦ homie

panic (n) Try **cause of panic ♦ drug panic.**

panic (v) choke ♦ freak (out) ♦ hit the panic button ♦ press the panic button ♦ psych out ♦ psych so out ♦ push the panic button ♦ weird out

panicked weirded out (Try also **be panicked.**)

panicked person freak (out) ♦ freaker

pantomime guitar air guitar

pants Try **loose pants.**

paper reader ♦ script(t) (Try also **flyer (paper) ♦ toilet paper ♦ cigarette papers.**)

paper money dead president ♦ federal diploma ♦ folding money ♦ folding stuff ♦ green ♦ green folding ♦ green paper ♦ green stuff

paranoid person noid

parasitic spunge

parasitic person freeloader ♦ sponge

pardon my vocabulary Excuse my French. ♦ if you'll pardon the expression ♦ Pardon my French.

parent breeder ♦ fossil

parents (parental) units ♦ empty-nesters ♦ folks ♦ rent(al)s ♦ rents

parody (n) send-up ♦ spoof ♦ take off

parody (v) send so/sth up ♦ spoof

partial to sucker for so/sth

participate Be there or be square. ♦ Be there with bells on. ♦ play in the big leagues

particular dicty ♦ hincty

partner párd (Try also **sex partner ♦ swap sex partners.**)

parts Try **computer parts ♦ expose private body parts ♦ peek at private parts.**

party (n) bash ♦ blast ♦ blow ♦ blow-out ♦ boogie ♦ brew-out ♦ do ♦ set ♦ shindig ♦ sock hop ♦ TGIF ♦ tingle (Try also **beer party ♦ drug party ♦ gossip party ♦ marijuana party ♦ men-only party ♦ wild party.**)

party (v) ball ♦ bash ♦ gas ♦ have a ball ♦ paint the town (red) ♦ partay ♦ party down ♦ party hearty ♦ rage

party behind vehicle tailgate party

party lover party animal

party ruiner party-pooper ♦ wet blanket

pass Try **admission pass.**

pass counterfeit palm sth off on so

pass course cruise

pass muster hold water

pass out crash ♦ flake (out) ♦ gouch off ♦ squiff out

passenger PAX (Try also **bus passenger ♦ late passenger ♦ subway passenger.**)

passenger seat shotgun

passer Try **bad check passer.**

passing grade pass

passionate steamy

passwords Try **seek passwords online ♦ capture passwords.**

past activity ancient history

past memory flashback

patch (n) kludge

patter jive talk

pause (v) come up for air

pawn (v) hock

pawn (person) stooge

pawned in hock

pawnshop hockshop

pay (n) Try **union pay.**

pay (v) shell out (an amount of money) (Try also **force to pay amount.**)

pay in advance front

pay rate scale

pay someone money owed cash so out

payday day the eagle flies ♦ day the eagle shits ♦ when the eagle flies

PCP angel dust ♦ angel hair ♦ DOA ♦ dust of angels ♦ flake ♦ hog ♦ killer weed

peace supporter dove

peanut butter goober-grease

peanut picker goober-grabber

pectoral muscles pecks ♦ pecs ♦ pects

pedantic person comma-counter

pee pizzle

peek (v) prairie dog

peek at private parts free show

peeking turtle heading

penis bald-headed hermit ♦ bald-headed mouse ♦ baloney pony ♦ Barney ♦ beaver-cleaver ♦ bug-fucker ♦ choad ♦ cock ♦ crotch-cobra ♦ dick ♦ ding-dong ♦ dingle(-dangle) ♦ dingus ♦ dingy ♦ dink ♦ dipstick ♦ doje ♦ dong ♦ doodle ♦ dork ♦ dragon ♦ dummy ♦ fucker ♦ grower ♦ hose ♦ jimmy johnson ♦ joint ♦ joystick ♦ manhood ♦ meat ♦ meat puppet ♦ meat whistle ♦ one-eyed pants mouse ♦ oscar ♦ pecker ♦ peter ♦ pocket-rocket ♦ pork hammer ♦ prick ♦ pud ♦ putz ♦ schmuck ♦ shower ♦ tallywhacker ♦ trouser snake ♦ trouser trout ♦ tube steak ♦ tube steak of love ♦ unit ♦ weenie (Try also **with large penis ♦ small-penised man.**)

penis end dickhead ♦ helmet ♦ peckerhead

penitentiary pen

Pennsylvania Pennsy

people peep (Try also **bad people list ♦ common people ♦ emulating other people ♦ homeless people ♦ list of banned people ♦ list of worthless people ♦ other people ♦ pair of people ♦ poor people ♦ rich people ♦ two people ♦ useless people ♦ worthless white people ♦ young people.**)

people count (n) body count

people who invest well smart money

pep bounce

pepperoni roni ♦ rony

per Try **fifty-five miles per hour ♦ per piece.**

per piece pop ♦ a copy

perception Try **unique perception.**

perfect solution magic bullet ♦ silver bullet

perfect substance unobtanium

perfect thing just the ticket ♦ just what the doctor ordered

perform barnstorm ♦ gig

perform act of prostitution turn a trick

perform cunnilingus eat at the Y

perform fellatio blow ♦ hoover

perform oral sex (female) dive a muff ♦ eat ♦ French ♦ give head ♦ go down on so

perform well kill ♦ knock so dead

performance blockbuster ♦ number (Try also **bad performance ♦ great performance ♦ single performance ♦ successful performance ♦ series of performances.**)

perineum choad ♦ gooch ♦ grundle ♦ taint

period Try **recruitment period ♦ rest period ♦ time period.**

period of time pocket of time ♦ stretch

permanent Try **take permanent action.**

permission go-ahead ♦ green light ♦ OK ♦ say-so

permit Try **learner's permit.**

perpetrator perp

perplex discombobulate

perplexed buffaloed ♦ discombobulated ♦ discomboobulated

persevere hang in there

person ass ♦ bod ♦ number ♦ warm body (Try also **despicable person (usually male) ♦ despised person (usually male) ♦ exciting person or thing ♦ favored person (male) ♦ first person to leave ♦ injured person walking about ♦ one person act ♦ absent minded person ♦ already attached (person) ♦ ambitious person ♦ annoying person ♦ awkward person ♦ bad person ♦ beat generation person ♦ bisexual person ♦ black person ♦ booing person ♦ bossy person ♦ bowlegged person ♦ burned out person ♦ business person ♦ capable person ♦ cheap person ♦ clever person ♦ clumsy person ♦ cocky person ♦ cold hearted person ♦ comatose person ♦ conceited person ♦ contentious person ♦ crazy person ♦ cute person ♦ dead person ♦ deceitful person ♦ depressed person ♦ devilish person ♦ devious person ♦ difficult person ♦ direct person ♦ disgusting person ♦ disliked person ♦ dull person ♦ eager person ♦ eccentric person ♦ energetic person ♦ euphoric person ♦ evaluate person ♦ excellent person ♦ excited person ♦ exhibition (art) by one person ♦ experienced person ♦ expired person ♦ extra person ♦ extraordinary person ♦ fake person ♦ famous person ♦ fantastic person ♦ fast person ♦ fat person ♦ fat-bottomed person ♦ foolish person ♦ former important person ♦ fund-raiser (person) ♦ funny person ♦ giddy person ♦ good looking person ♦ good person ♦ grumpy person ♦ gullible person ♦ happy person ♦ helpless person ♦ honest person ♦ hungry person ♦ ignored person ♦ important person ♦ impressive person ♦ impudent person ♦ ineffectual person ♦ inept person ♦ insincere person ♦ internet addicted person ♦ jealous person ♦ kind of person ♦ lame person ♦ large buttocked person ♦ large eared person ♦ lazy person ♦ left-handed person ♦ living dead person ♦ looking for guilty person ♦ lucky person ♦ marijuana intoxicated person ♦ mellow person ♦ mobile injured person ♦ naive person ♦ nervous person ♦ new person ♦ nice person ♦ night-working person ♦ nonintellectual person ♦ nosy person ♦ obnoxious person ♦ obsolete person ♦ old person ♦ old-fashioned person ♦ overly friendly person ♦ overreacting person ♦ panicked person ♦ paranoid person ♦ parasitic person ♦ pawn (person) ♦ pedantic person ♦ pimple faced person ♦ pious person ♦ powerful person ♦ predatory person ♦ quick-tempered person ♦ radical person ♦ remarkable person ♦ respected street person ♦ retarded person ♦ rhythm person ♦ rich person ♦ rough person ♦ rowdy person ♦ rural person ♦ sad person ♦ scar-faced person ♦ schizophrenic person ♦ screaming person ♦ serious person ♦ servile person ♦ setup person ♦ sexually obsessed person ♦ sexually willing person ♦ sexy person ♦ shaved head person ♦ short person ♦ silent person ♦ silly person ♦ skilled person ♦ sloppy person ♦ small person ♦ smart person ♦ sneaky person ♦ socially active person ♦ spineless person ♦ stingy person ♦ strange bodied person ♦ strange person ♦ strict person ♦ stubborn person ♦ stuffy person ♦ stunning person ♦ stupid person ♦ successful person ♦ superior person ♦ talented person ♦ talk to wrong person ♦ talkative person ♦ tall person ♦ thin person ♦ time spent in person ♦ timid person ♦ tired person ♦ tough person ♦ transgendered person ♦ troublesome person ♦ ugly person ♦ undecided person ♦ undesirable person ♦ unemotional person ♦ unnamed person ♦ unneeded person ♦ unpleasant person ♦ unresponsive person ♦ unsuccessful person ♦ unusual person ♦ up-to-date person ♦ upright (person) ♦ very important person ♦ weak person ♦ wealthy person ♦ weird person ♦ well-behaved person ♦ white person ♦ witless person ♦ worthless person ♦ young person.)**

person in charge brains ♦ chief ♦ chief cook and bottle washer ♦ high mucky-muck

person in last term of office lame duck

person obsessed with clothes clotheshorse

person obsessed with work workaholic

person of streets streeter

person of the past history
person showing promise comer
person who is fun barrel of fun
person who withdrew drop out
person with herpes herpie
person with ideas brainchild
person with problem hard case
person with wooden leg peg-leg
personal polish suave
persons sharing interests birds of a feather
perspective Try **unique perspective.**
persuade jaw ♦ jaw(bone) ♦ twist SO's arm
persuade gently soft soap
persuader arm-twister
persuasion arm-twisting
Peso adobe dollar
pester nag
pet grovel (Try also **castrate pet ♦ spay pet.**)
peyote cactus (buttons) ♦ mystic biscuit ♦ sacred mushrooms ♦ shrooms (Try also **use peyote.**)
phase Try **early phase.**
Philadelphia, PA Philly
phlegm lunger
phone call buzz
phone number digits
phonograph recording vinyl ♦ wax
phony glorified ♦ hokey ♦ Hollywood ♦ plastic ♦ queer as a three-dollar bill
photo mug shot
photographic enlargement blow up
physical work leg work
piano box ♦ joybox ♦ tinklebox ♦ the eighty-eight (Try also **play piano.**)
piano keys ivories
pick up women scam
picker Try **peanut picker.**
pickpocket dip ♦ dipper
picture piccie ♦ pix (Try also **tiny picture.**)
piece Try **per piece.**
piece of information bit
pig squealer
pig's feet trotters
pill Try **birth control pill ♦ sleeping pill.**
pill addict pill freak ♦ pill-dropper ♦ pill-popper ♦ pillhead ♦ popper
pill (drug) bop
pilot flyboy (Try also **helicopter pilot.**)
pimp iceberg slim ♦ mack (Try also **small-time pimp.**)
pimple goob ♦ goober ♦ goophead ♦ guber ♦ hickey ♦ pip ♦ strawberry ♦ zit
pimple faced pizza-face ♦ pizza-puss

pimple faced person crater-face ♦ zit-face
pious Try **more pious.**
pious person holy Joe
pipe Try **short tobacco pipe.**
piss pizzle (Try also **urinate.**)
pistol Try **gun ♦ forty-four pistol.**
pit Try **bottomless pit.**
pitch Try **fast pitch in baseball ♦ twisting pitch.**
pizza za
place Try **bad place ♦ busy place ♦ chaotic place ♦ cheap place ♦ crowded place ♦ despised place ♦ dull place ♦ far away place ♦ favorite place ♦ gathering place ♦ gossiping place ♦ hashish using place ♦ hot place ♦ loafing place ♦ necking place ♦ new to place ♦ obnoxious place ♦ remote place ♦ run-down place ♦ sleeping place ♦ study a place ♦ unpleasant place ♦ send many places.**
place bet get down
place guilt dump on SO
plain generic ♦ vanilla ♦ whitebread
plain face deadpan
plain woman Mary Jane
plan play (Try also **explain plan ♦ floor plan ♦ present plan ♦ suggest plan ♦ poorly planned ♦ reveal plans.**)
plane Try **board plane ♦ fly (in plane).**
plant drugs flake
plate Try **home plate ♦ license plate.**
play (v) gig
play (various) Try **baseball play ♦ being played ♦ hockey player follower ♦ ball player ♦ benched player ♦ pool player ♦ record player ♦ sexual player.**
play an instrument blow
play around horse around
play ball ball
play hackysack hack
play music beat sth out ♦ boom
play piano pound sth out ♦ tickle the ivories
play with screw around with SO/sth
play with sexually fomp ♦ mess about (with SO) ♦ mess around (with SO)
playful child monkey
playing time set
plead guilty cop a plea ♦ cop out
pleasant in the groove
pleasant thing groove
Please! Puh-leez!
please (v) get to SO
please yourself do one's (own) thing
pleased grooved

pleasure Try **get pleasure from.**
pleasure destroyer buzzkill ♦ killjoy
pledge swear on a stack of Bibles
plot (n) hustle ♦ setup
plot (v) fanigle ♦ finagle ♦ snake
point Try **bargaining point ♦ exclamation point ♦ get to the point ♦ lowest point ♦ make point ♦ reach lowest point ♦ pointless competition ♦ important points.**
point out finger ♦ finger so as so
point scorer point man
pointless competition pissing-match
poke anus goose ♦ brown hole
poke in anus cob ♦ cornhole ♦ goose
police 5-O ♦ arm ♦ baby bear ♦ bacon ♦ bear ♦ big John ♦ bike boys ♦ black and white ♦ blue ♦ blue and white ♦ blue boys ♦ blue coats ♦ boys in blue ♦ bust ♦ Ervine ♦ five-oh ♦ fur ♦ fuzz ♦ goon squad ♦ heat ♦ J. Edgar (Hoover) ♦ jake ♦ junk squad ♦ lard ♦ long arm of the law ♦ man ♦ men in blue ♦ metros ♦ nail-em-and-jail-em ♦ nailer ♦ popo ♦ pork ♦ the law (Try also **private police officer ♦ restroom police officer ♦ fleeing police ♦ highway police ♦ rookie (police) ♦ wanted by police.**)
police car black and white ♦ blue and white ♦ light ♦ p-crutch ♦ pigmobile ♦ roller ♦ salt and pepper ♦ Tijuana taxi
police car lights mickey mouse ears
police helicopter bear in the air
police officer blisterfoot ♦ blue suit ♦ boss dick ♦ bull ♦ Charlie Irvine ♦ cop ♦ copper ♦ Ervine ♦ flatfoot ♦ flatty ♦ fuzz man ♦ fuzzy (tail) ♦ gimpy ♦ gumshoe ♦ hog ♦ Irv ♦ Irvine ♦ jake ♦ John(ny) Law ♦ Johnny-be-good ♦ Kojak ♦ mallet ♦ mickey mouse ♦ nab ♦ nabber ♦ occifer ♦ oink ♦ ossifer ♦ paddy ♦ penny ♦ Peter Jay ♦ pig ♦ pounder ♦ roach ♦ Sam and Dave ♦ sham(m)us ♦ skull-buster ♦ Smokey (the Bear) ♦ snatcher ♦ stick man ♦ Uncle nab ♦ the man
police officer (female) goldie locks ♦ lady bear ♦ mama bear
police officer (male) headache man ♦ little boy blue
police officer (New York) New York's finest
police station bear cage ♦ blotter ♦ cop-shop ♦ fuzz station ♦ pig heaven
police van paddy wagon ♦ wagon
politician baby-kisser ♦ backslapper ♦ flesh-presser ♦ glad-hander ♦ palm-presser ♦ pol
ponytail piece
pool cue stick

pool player hustler
pooled money pot
pools Try **visiting various pools.**
poor lo-res ♦ low-res (Try also **make poor progress ♦ be poorly executed.**)
poor chance fat chance
poor district wrong side of the tracks
poor golfer duffer
poor idea the foggiest (idea)
poor people the have-nots
poor quality cold ♦ piss-poor ♦ sorry-ass(ed)
poor shot can't hit the (broad) side of a barn
poorly planned half-baked
popular pop
popular music pop
pork belly futures bellies
pornographic graphic ♦ hard-core
pornography Try **mild pornography.**
portable stereo thunderbox
portable urinal duck
portion largest portion ♦ marijuana portion ♦ recording portion ♦ video portion ♦ in small portions ♦ (Try also **missionary position ♦ stick to position.**)
positive pository ♦ thumbs up ♦ up ♦ upbeat (Try also **HIV positive.**)
possess get one's hooks into so
possess drugs carry ♦ hold
possessions crud ♦ jonx ♦ junk ♦ shit (Try also **gather possessions.**)
postponed on the shelf
potato murphy ♦ spud ♦ tater
powdered drug dust
power juice ♦ oof (Try also **control power ♦ demonstrate power ♦ engine power ♦ horse power ♦ increase power ♦ lose power ♦ money is power ♦ show power ♦ made more powerful ♦ make more powerful.**)
powerful brutal ♦ bust-ass ♦ dynamite ♦ heavyweight ♦ kick-ass
powerful drug Cadillac ♦ dynamite
powerful person big gun ♦ heavyweight ♦ high mucky-muck ♦ ringtailed snorter
powerful punch roundhouse punch
powerful shock triple whammy
powerful thing Cadillac ♦ greased lightning ♦ heavy artillery ♦ ringtailed snorter
powerful treatment triple whammy
PR agent flack ♦ flak
praise boost ♦ hand it to so
prayer knee-mail
predatory person barracuda

propeller people processor
proper respect props
propose marriage pop the question
proposition (v) mack on so
prostitute call-girl ♦ garden tool ♦ gook ♦ ho ♦ hoe ♦ hooker ♦ hustler ♦ pro ♦ prosty
prostitute's agent pimp
prostitute's customer john ♦ score
prostitute's route ho stro
prostitution Try **perform act of prostitution.**
protect Cover your ass. ♦ hold the fort ♦ look after number one
protector Try **shirt protector.**
protector (various) nard guard ♦ nerd pack
proud tall in the saddle (Try also **be proud ♦ walk proudly.**)
proven (bang) dead to rights
provide less than ordered short
provided with date fixed up
provocative Try **send provocative message.**
provocative message sender troll ♦ trollkin
provoke get in so's face
prowl (n) snoop
prowler snoop
psychiatrist couch-doctor
psychoanalyst couch-doctor ♦ dome-doctor ♦ guru ♦ nutpick ♦ shrink
psychologist dome-doctor
psychology course nuts and bolts
pubic hair bush
public Try **become known to public (news) ♦ copulation in public ♦ go public ♦ appear publicly.**
publicity hype
publicize hype ♦ take sth public
puff (n) drag ♦ sip ♦ a drag (on sth) (Try also **take puff.**)
puff (v) swallow
punch (n) swipe (Try also **hard punch (blow) ♦ powerful punch ♦ small punch ♦ hold back punches ♦ signal punches.**)
punch (v) boff ♦ brick ♦ bust so one ♦ sock ♦ tag ♦ take a pop at so ♦ take a swipe at so/sth ♦ take a whack at so/sth ♦ throw a punch ♦ the old one-two
punch line button
punish nail so to a cross ♦ nail so('s hide) to the wall ♦ tear so a new asshole
punish lightly slap so's wrist ♦ slap so on the wrist
punishment heads will roll (Try also **accept punishment ♦ escape punishment ♦ get punishment.**)

punk baby gangsta ♦ BG ♦ busta (Try also **become punk.**)
purchase (n) buy (Try also **sale and purchase.**)
pure drugs the (real) McCoy
purge (v) go through so like a dose of (the) salts
put on bill cuff
puzzle (n) brain-teaser ♦ brain-twister
puzzle (v) stump
Quaalude lude
quadriceps quads
qualitative analysis qual
quality swank (Try also **high-quality happening ♦ high quality ♦ low quality ♦ lowest quality ♦ poor quality.**)
quantitative quant
quarrel (v) mix it up (with so) ♦ tangle with so/sth
quart Q.
quarter (coin) two-bits
queen in cards girl
question qizzle ♦ the sixty-four-dollar question (Try also **easy question ♦ important question ♦ stupid question ♦ being questioned.**)
questioning third degree
questions FAQ
quick Try **temper (quick) ♦ do quickly ♦ drink quickly ♦ finish quickly ♦ speak quickly ♦ write quickly.**
quick copulation quickie ♦ quick one
quick joke throw-away
quickly once over lightly ♦ PDQ ♦ quick-and-dirty ♦ snappy ♦ sudden death ♦ two shakes of a lamb's tail
quick-tempered person hot head
quiet Try **make quiet (v) ♦ Be quiet! ♦ get quiet ♦ keep quiet ♦ win news race.**
quiet applause golf-clap
quit chuck it in ♦ conk out ♦ cop out ♦ die on so ♦ Give it up! ♦ Give me a rest! ♦ go South ♦ hang it up ♦ knock off (work) ♦ poop out ♦ rat out ♦ throw in the sponge ♦ throw in the towel ♦ toss in the sponge
quit a job ankle ♦ walk
quit drugs catch up ♦ kick ♦ kick cold (turkey) ♦ kick the habit ♦ knock the habit ♦ turn over
quit trying lay down
quit with success quit while one is ahead
quits easily quitter
quoting quote, unquote
race (v) drag

race engine gun
racing form scratch sheet
racing tire slick
racketeer bagman
radar Try use radar.
radical person rad
radio Try amateur radio operator ♦ CB radio intruder ♦ on a radio beam (aviation).
raid (n) bust ♦ roust
raid (v) bust ♦ roust
raid refrigerator pillage
raided crashed
rain hard rain pitchforks
raise hands Hands up!
raise price gazumph ♦ jack sth up
raise volume crank sth up
raised heel lift
rampage (v) hell around
random luck of the draw
rank Try reduce rank ♦ music ranking.
rape (n) Try gang rape ♦ group rape ♦ serial rape.
rape (v) rip so off
rapidly Try travel rapidly.
rarely once in a blue moon
raspberry bird ♦ Bronx cheer
rate Try pay rate.
rate of speed clip
rave about go on (and on) about so/sth
reach (v) hit
reach limit max out
reach lowest point bottom out
react with surprise drop one's teeth
reaction gut reaction (to sth)
reaction test trial balloon
read Read the fucking FAQ! ♦ Read the fucking instructions! ♦ Read the fucking manual! ♦ RTFF ♦ RTFFAQ ♦ RTFI ♦ RTFM (Try also news reader ♦ silent forum reader.)
read forums without responding lurk
ready (various) (a)bout it ♦ (Are you) ready for this? ♦ All systems are go. ♦ fresh as a daisy ♦ good-to-go ♦ lean and mean ♦ psyched (up) ♦ pumped (up) ♦ Ready for this? (Try also get ready.)
real 4 real ♦ rizzle (Try also know the real world.)
real thing genuine article
real world jungle ♦ the street
realistic Try be realistic.
reality inducer bring-down
realize wise up (to so/sth)
rear Try motorcycle seat (rear).
reason Try for no good reason ♦ no reason.

rebuke lay so out in lavender (Try also receive rebuke.)
recall (v) flash on sth
recall a memory ring a bell
receive criticism take some heat ♦ take the heat
receive fellatio get brain
receive much money rake sth in
receive rebuke face the music ♦ take some heat ♦ take the heat
reciprocal fellatio sixty-nine ♦ smoke both ends of the cigar
reciprocal situation two-way street
reckless driver fender-bender ♦ road hog
reckless man cowboy
record Try criminal record ♦ vinyl record ♦ phonograph recording.
record a win notch
record arrival clock in
record player box
recorded entertainment canned
recorded laughter canned
recorded music sounds ♦ tunage ♦ tunes
recording portion cut ♦ side ♦ platter ♦ track
recover come down ♦ snap out of sth
recover too fast come down hard
recreation R. & R.
recreation room rumpus room
recreational vehicle rig ♦ wheel estate
recruit head hunt
recruiter headhunter
recruitment period rush
rectal inspection booty check
rectum poop chute
red Try catch red-handed.
reduce shave
reduce activity put a damper on sth
reduce cash Cash is trash.
reduce conceit take the piss out of so ♦ take the starch out of so ♦ take the wind out of so's sails
reduce expenditures take one's belt in (a notch) ♦ tighten one's belt
reduce intensity put a damper on sth
reduce rank bust
referee (n) ref ♦ zebra
referee (v) ref
refinancing refi
refined highbrow
reform (v) clean one's act up ♦ shape up ♦ shape up or ship out
refresh hit the bull's-eye ♦ hit the spot
refrigerator fridge ♦ reefer (Try also raid refrigerator.)

refuse bucket gash bucket ♦ gutbucket
refuse computer data choke
refuse to answer take the fifth
refuse to speak clam up
register Try **cash register sound.**
regular Try **bar regular ♦ beach regular.**
regulations regs
reject (v) chill ♦ turn thumbs down (on so/sth)
reject bad check bounce
reject offer Don't make me laugh!
rejected faced ♦ shot down
rejection a slap in the face (Try also **feel rejection.**)
relatives tribe
relax Blow on it! ♦ chill ♦ chill (out) ♦ chiz ♦ Easy does it. ♦ gel ♦ get a load off one's feet ♦ get naked ♦ get one's act together ♦ Give me a break! ♦ hang loose ♦ hang with so ♦ kick back ♦ kick it ♦ let it all hang out ♦ mellow out ♦ modulate ♦ spaz down ♦ stay loose ♦ take a chill pill ♦ Take it down a thou(sand)! ♦ take it easy ♦ take things easy ♦ unlax
relaxed cool ♦ chillaxin' ♦ mellow ♦ laid back
relaxing maxin'
release anger blow off (some) steam ♦ let off (some) steam ♦ vent one's spleen
release anxiety climb the wall(s)
release intestinal gas Try **fart (v).**
release of intestinal gas Try **fart (n).**
releasing gas windy
relieve scrutiny take the heat off so
remain calm keep one's cool
remain nearby stick around
remain united Keep the faith (baby)!
remain unrecognized lie doggo
remark Try **caustic remark ♦ insulting remark ♦ sweet remarks.**
remarkable person pisser ♦ rip snorter
remarkable thing pisser
remind prod
remind of mistake rub so's nose in sth
reminder prod
remote area the sticks
remote place tall timbers
removal old heave-ho
remove boot ♦ boot so out ♦ lift ♦ put so/sth out of the way ♦ throw one out on one's ear
remove clothing air one's pores ♦ peel ♦ shuck
remove from flight bump
remove from game bench

remove from prison bust so out of somewhere ♦ spring so
reorganization shake-up
repeated warmed over
repeated story same old story
repellent Try **be repellent.**
repertory rep
repetition rep
replacement pinch-hitter ♦ stand-in ♦ sub
replay of a drug high free trip
replay of the past flashback
reply tentatively nibble
reporter hack ♦ ink slinger ♦ newshound
report(s) credenzaware (Try also **expense report.**)
repossess repo
repossessed car repo
repossessor repo man
representative front man ♦ rep
reproduction facts of life
repulsive scurvy
reputation rep
request (n) Try **difficult request.**
request (v) hit so (up) for sth
request answer pump
request for loan touch
request loan touch
require courage take a lot of nerve
require effort take some doing
requires two takes two to tango
requiring care high-maintenance
requiring coddling high-maintenance
research institute think-tank
resentment snit
reserve (n) Try **have trick in reserve ♦ held in reserve ♦ in reserve ♦ talent in reserve.**
reserve (v) squirrel sth away
reserve soldier weekend warrior
reserved talent ace in the hole
reserved territory turf
resident Try **local resident ♦ town resident.**
resist buck
resist disease toss sth off
respect (n) Try **gain respect ♦ proper respect.**
respectable front
respected street person playa
respond Try **read forums without responding.**
response Try **first response.**
responsibility Try **assume responsibility ♦ escape responsibility ♦ take responsibility.**
rest (n) R. & R. (Try also **move with the rest.**)

rest (v) take a break ♦ take five
rest period breather
restaurant Try **food bag from restaurant ♦ McDonald's restaurant.**
restless antsy
restore lick sth into shape ♦ whip sth into shape
restored evened out
restrain clip so's wings
restroom comfort station ♦ crapper ♦ gab room ♦ head ♦ john ♦ loo ♦ throne room
restroom (female) jane ♦ ladies' room ♦ little girls' room ♦ powder room ♦ ruth
restroom (male) little boys' room
restroom police officer crapper dick
result(s) net result ♦ Your mileage may vary. ♦ the bottom line ♦ the upshot (of sth) ♦ fallout (Try also **good result ♦ achieve results ♦ chance results ♦ suffer results.**)
resume drinking fall off the wagon
resuscitate bag ♦ bag so
retain opinion stand pat (on sth)
retard tard
retarded mental
retarded person mental
retch gag
retirement home raisin ranch
retreat bug out ♦ curl up and die
retribution payback
return back to square one
return check bounce
return empty deadhead
return to work back to the salt mines
return trip flip side ♦ flip-flop
rev engine goose ♦ gun
reveal blow so's cover ♦ drop a brick ♦ open (up) one's kimono ♦ squawk (Try also **homosexuality revealed.**)
reveal plans tip one's hand
reveal secrets Try **expose.**
reveal someone's homosexuality out
revelation bomb ♦ bomb(shell)
revenue haul ♦ take
reversal flip-flop ♦ switcheroo
reverse flip the script ♦ flip-flop
revolting rev
reward comp ♦ pie in the sky ♦ plum (Try also **hope for reward.**)
reward a customer comp
rhythm beat
rhythm person beat box
rich Try **get rich.**
rich people the haves
rich person deep pockets ♦ fat-cat

rid Try **get rid of.**
ride (n) lift (Try also **death ride ♦ rough ride ♦ motorcycle rider.**)
ride next to driver ride shotgun
ridiculous cockamamie ♦ crackbrained ♦ redonkulous ♦ ricockulous ♦ ridic
right Try **all right ♦ be right ♦ exactly right ♦ I am right ♦ make right ♦ turn right ♦ work out all right.**
right (various) on the reezie ♦ Party on! ♦ Right on! ♦ Word.
right away in a flash ♦ in a jiff(y)
right task (right) up one's alley ♦ up one's alley
right way That-a-boy!
ring endlessly ring off the hook
rip apart tear so/sth up
rise Try **fall and rise.**
risk Try **being risk free ♦ at risk ♦ be risky.**
risk all go for broke ♦ shoot the works
risk-taking gambler high roller
risky sketchy
risky bond junk bond
road Try **rough road.**
roadkill road pizza ♦ TV dinner
rob burn ♦ fleece ♦ futz ♦ hit ♦ knock over sth ♦ make a score ♦ mug ♦ pull a job ♦ rip so off ♦ roll ♦ take so/sth off ♦ w(h)ack sth (out)
rob freely rob so blind
robber kiper ♦ mugger ♦ yegg
robbery heist ♦ hit ♦ job ♦ rip ♦ take off
robot droid
rock climber rock-jock
rock group follower groupie
rock singer rocker
rocket launch shot
rocking chair rocker
role bit
roll Try **high roller ♦ fat rolls.**
rolling ball worm burner
romance mush (Try also **one-night romance ♦ start romance.**)
rookie (police) baby bear
room Try **go to powder room ♦ meeting room ♦ recreation room ♦ share a room.**
roommate bunkie
ROTC rotsee
rotten lousy ♦ lowdown ♦ shitty ♦ stinking (Try also **be rotten.**)
rough Try **be rough.**
rough person diamond in the rough
rough ride kidney-buster
rough road kidney-buster
roundup Try **criminal roundup.**

route beat (Try also **no route ♦ prostitute's route.**)

routine schtick

row Try **three in a row.**

rowdy person heller

RSVP Try **accept invitation.**

rub Try **scalp rubbing.**

rude base ♦ drop-dead ♦ harsh ♦ snotty

rudeness Watch your mouth! ♦ Watch your tongue!

ruin (v) blow ♦ wipe so out ♦ blow sth ♦ crum sth up ♦ do a job on so/sth ♦ do a number on sth ♦ frig ♦ muck sth up ♦ mung ♦ put the skids under so/sth ♦ shoot so/sth down ♦ shoot so down in flames (Try also **veins ruined ♦ party ruiner.**)

ruin idea spike

ruin interest turn so off

ruined by drugs burnout ♦ banjaxed ♦ beat ♦ burnt out ♦ fouled up ♦ on the rocks ♦ screwed up ♦ shot ♦ shot to hell ♦ tapped

rule (various) do's and don'ts (Try also **slide rule ♦ follow rules.**)

rumor (hot) skinny ♦ furphy ♦ latrine rumor ♦ latrino(gram) ♦ lowdown ♦ scuttlebutt

run scoot (Try also **hit-and-run accident ♦ home run in baseball ♦ hit home run ♦ naked run ♦ fast runner ♦ naked runner ♦ touch baseball runner.**)

run away Cheese it (the cops)! ♦ hoof it ♦ turn tail (and run)

run engine give it the gun ♦ rev sth up

run naked streak

run smoothly run on all cylinders

run well run on all cylinders

run well (engine) purr (like a cat)

run-down place rathole

running hoofing

rural cornfed ♦ jerkwater ♦ Podunk

rural area boonies ♦ sticks ♦ the sticks

rural bigot redneck

rural person bamma

rush Try **drug rush.**

rush in tear into a place

rush through town barnstorm

sad in a blue funk ♦ sorry-ass(ed)

sad movie tear-jerker ♦ weeper

sad person sad sack

sad story sob story ♦ tale of woe ♦ tear-jerker

safecracker yegg

sailor anchor-clanker ♦ salt

salad rabbit food

salad greens grass

sale Try **for sale ♦ group of things for sale.**

sale and purchase wash

sale of borrowed stock short

sales character pitchcharacter

saloon dive ♦ draft board ♦ dump ♦ fill-mill ♦ gargle factory ♦ gin dive ♦ gin mill ♦ gin palace ♦ groggery ♦ gutbucket ♦ guzzery ♦ guzzlery ♦ piss factory

salted beef salt horse

salute TFS ♦ three finger salute

same old thing same o(l) same o(l)' ♦ SOSO ♦ What else is new?

same understanding on the same page ♦ on the same wavelength

sample (n) teaser ♦ touch

San Francisco Frisco ♦ San Fran ♦ Sco.

sandals Jesus boots (Try also **jelly sandals.**)

sandwich dagwood (sandwich) ♦ double-decker (Try also **sub sandwich.**)

sanitary napkin rag

sanitary tampon tamp

sarcasm LABTYD ♦ Life's a bitch, then you die.

sass lip

satellite Try **from a satellite.**

satisfaction jollies

satisfactory copasetic ♦ ducky ♦ hunky-dory ♦ oak(s) ♦ rosy ♦ up to scratch ♦ up to snuff

satisfied straight

satisfy do the trick

satisfying bang-up ♦ hi-res ♦ high-res

sausage horse cock

saved saved by the bell

saved money nest egg

savvy (a)bout it ♦ hep

saxophone Try **baritone saxophone.**

say go (Try also **so you say ♦ who says.**)

say it Speak it! ♦ Spit it out!

say one's speech run one's rhymes

say something agreeable speak so's language

say something understandable speak so's language

saying like

scalp rubbing noogie

scandal big stink ♦ dirty laundry ♦ dirty linen ♦ flap

scandalous scanless ♦ skanless

scar Try **acne scar.**

scar-faced person crater-face

scars (injection) railroad tracks

scarse not grow on trees

scheme (n) game plan ♦ hustle ♦ angle ♦ layout ♦ setup (Try also **confidence scheme ♦ here is scheme ♦ know schemes.**)

scheme (v) snake ♦ fanigle ♦ finagle ♦ frame (Try also **acquire by scheming.**)

schizophrenic schizo

schizophrenic person schizo

school Try **prep school student ♦ avoid school ♦ leave school.**

scold (v) chew so's ass out ♦ chew so out ♦ climb ♦ come down hard on so ♦ dish sth out ♦ dump on so ♦ give so a (good) talking to ♦ give so a (good) working over ♦ give so an earful ♦ give so hell ♦ give so the business ♦ lay so out ♦ lay so out in lavender ♦ light into so ♦ nail so to a cross ♦ nail so('s hide) to the wall ♦ pin so's ears back ♦ raise hell (with so) ♦ raise hell (with sth) ♦ raise the devil (with so) ♦ ream so out ♦ sail into so ♦ screw so over ♦ tear into so ♦ tear so a new asshole ♦ thrash on so

scolded dumped on

scolding Alpha Charlie ♦ ass-chewing ♦ earful

score (n) Try **no score game ♦ behind (score) ♦ dice score ♦ musical score ♦ zero score ♦ point scorer.**

score (v) notch

score of zero zip

scoreless shutout

scotch whiskey (mountain) dew

scrape (n) road-rash

scream scream bloody murder

screaming person screaming-meemie

scrotum nutsack

scrutiny Try **vulnerable to scrutiny.**

scurry scoot

sea Try **burial at sea.**

seal (v) clinch

sealed SWAK

search Try **body cavity search.**

search (n) body shake ♦ fishing expedition

search channels surf ♦ google ♦ surf the net

search everywhere turn sth upside down

search for gun for so

search for lovers bush patrol

seat Try **bad seat or chair ♦ motorcycle seat (rear) ♦ back seat ♦ claim front seat ♦ passenger seat ♦ balcony seats ♦ high seats.**

second sec ♦ tick (Try also **work second job.**)

second baseman second sacker

second best second fiddle

second half bottom

second in fight back

seconds a few ticks

secret back room ♦ closet ♦ hush-hush ♦ I could tell you but then I'd have to kill you. ♦ under the table (Try also **in secret ♦ tell secret ♦ work in secret ♦ seek secrets online ♦ reveal secrets.**)

secretion Try **vaginal secretion.**

secretly hush-hush ♦ on the DL ♦ on the QT ♦ on the sly

section of tire debris alligator ♦ gator

secured cinched

sedate (v) gork

sedated gorked (out)

seduce dialog ♦ hustle ♦ move on so ♦ put the make on so ♦ put the moves on so ♦ run down some lines

seducer hustler ♦ make-out artist ♦ smooth operator ♦ smoothie ♦ stud ♦ studhammer

seductive all over so like a cheap suit

seductive eyes bedroom eyes

seductive look come-hither look

see catch sth (Try also **sight worth seeing.**)

see jewelry freezer burn

see the arrival Look (at) what the cat dragged in!

see there Viola! ♦ Wala! ♦ Walla! ♦ Wallah!

seek ping so ♦ scare so/sth up ♦ scrounge (around (for so/sth)) ♦ scrounge so/sth up (Try also **money seeker.**)

seek influence suck up to so

seek information pump

seek out scrounge (around (for so/sth)) ♦ scrounge so/sth up

seek passwords online phish

seek secrets online phish

seek sex cruise ♦ on the prowl

seek women scam

seeking cheapest bottom fishing

seeking trouble cruising for a bruising

seem innocent smell like a rose

seem suspicious smell fishy ♦ smell to (high) heaven

seems familiar This is where I came in.

segment Try **game segment.**

select tap so (for sth)

self Try **care for self.**

self-assured unflappable

self-defeating piss in the wind

self-fondling pocket pool

self-important bigass

sell Try **buy and sell ♦ gentle selling job ♦ high-pressure selling ♦ something that sells well.**

sell borrowed stock short

sell counterfeit bootleg

sell drugs grind ♦ make a score ♦ push ♦ slang

sell illicit liquor moonlight

sell shares go public ♦ take sth public

sell well take off

selling all sellout

selling drugs in action ♦ on the street

selling well hot

semen chism ♦ come ♦ cream ♦ cum ♦ fuck ♦ gism ♦ gizzum ♦ gubb ♦ jism ♦ jizz ♦ jizzum ♦ ranch ♦ scum ♦ splooge ♦ spooge ♦ wad ♦ yolk

semiconscious half-under

send many places send so from pillar to post

send provocative message troll

send voluminous email spam

sense Try **make sense.**

senseless Fuckheaded

sensibly Try **operate sensibly.**

sensitive touchy-feely

sensor Try **gay sensor.**

sensuous steamy

sentence Try **jail sentence ♦ prison sentence ♦ serve sentence.**

sentiment hearts and flowers ♦ shmaltz

sentimental corny ♦ schmaltzy ♦ shmaltzy ♦ sticky

sentimentality schmaltz

separate (v) bust up ♦ split up (Try also **cause lovers to separate.**)

serial copulation fuckathon ♦ gang-bang

serial rape gang-bang ♦ gang-shag

series of performances run

serious hard-core ♦ heavy ♦ intense ♦ major ♦ mega ♦ straight-faced (Try also **be serious ♦ get serious.**)

serious couple hot item

serious person sobersides

serious problem hot potato

serious situation heavy scene

serious talk heart-to-heart (talk)

servant Try **civil servant.**

serve pay one's dues

serve food dish sth out

serve me another drink hit me again ♦ Hit me.

serve sentence do time ♦ pay one's dues (to society)

serve well do

service Try **lawn service ♦ telephone service.**

servile kiss-ass

servile person kiss-ass

session run ♦ sesh (Try also **chat session ♦ complaint session ♦ conversation session ♦ marijuana session ♦ music session ♦ necking session.**)

set aside on the back burner

set down plop

set goal go for the fences

set of problems can of worms

set out make for somewhere

setback blow

setting scene

settle clinch

settle something square

settled cinch ♦ cinched ♦ iced ♦ out of the woods ♦ sealed (up) ♦ squared away ♦ taped (Try also **have something settled.**)

setup person roadie ♦ roadster ♦ roady

seventy-five cents six-bits

severe major

sewage wagon honey cart ♦ honey wagon

sewer worker sewer hog

sex Try **grant sex easily ♦ perform oral sex (female) ♦ swap sex partners ♦ group sex ♦ man as sex ♦ oral sex ♦ seek sex ♦ woman as sex.**

sex appeal mojo ♦ oomph

sex drive mojo

sex partner fuck buddy ♦ fuck puppet ♦ pickup ♦ piece of ass ♦ piece of snatch ♦ piece of tail ♦ screw ♦ sex-machine

sexual activity action

sexual advance pass

sexual affair whing-ding ♦ wing-ding

sexual arousal booty call

sexual misconduct hanky-panky

sexual player swinger

sexual promiscuity musical beds

sexual signal fuck-me boots

sexual urge booty call

sexually Try **experienced sexually ♦ feel sexually ♦ play with sexually.**

sexually aroused have hot pants (for so) ♦ have the hots (for so) ♦ horny ♦ humpy ♦ rammy ♦ randy

sexually attractive stacked

sexually attractive man hunk

sexually easy boinkable ♦ swift

sexually exhausted fucked out

sexually experienced been around (the block)

sexually obsessed fuck-brained

sexually obsessed person fuck-freak

sexually transmitted disease scrud

sexually unconventional kink ◆ kinky

sexually willing fuckable

sexually willing person easy make ◆ fuck ◆ hump

sexy fat ◆ foxy ◆ hot ◆ on fire (Try also **make sexy.**)

sexy person hottie

sexy woman hot number ◆ red-hot mama ◆ sex kitten ◆ sex pot ◆ stone fox ◆ a stone cold fox

shabby not too shabby ◆ ticky-tacky

shake hands Give me (some) skin! ◆ Give me five! ◆ knock so some skin ◆ press (the) flesh ◆ Slip me five! ◆ slip so five

shakedown body shake

shakes the jitters

shapely woman brickhouse

share (n) bit of the action ◆ cut ◆ piece (of the action) ◆ slice of the action ◆ taste (Try also **get a share ◆ sell shares.**)

share (v) cut so in (on sth) ◆ divvy ◆ divvy sth up (Try also **persons sharing interests.**)

share a room buddy up (with so)

share information swap notes (on so/sth)

share of profits action

sharp eye eagle-eye

sharply Try **look sharp(ly) ◆ turn sharply.**

shaved head person skin

sheet Try **information sheet.**

sheet music chart ◆ map

shift Try **evening shift ◆ night shift.**

shift money smurf

ship Try **bow of ship ◆ steel ship.**

shirker piker

shirt Try **sleeveless shirt.**

shirt protector nerd pack

shit Try **defecate ◆ full of shit.**

shock (n) bomb ◆ bomb(shell) (Try also **powerful shock ◆ price shock.**)

shock (v) drop a bomb(shell) ◆ drop a brick ◆ freak so out ◆ zap

shock absorbers shocks

shocked freaked (out) ◆ You could have knocked me over with a feather.

shocking news dynamite ◆ shocker

shoe stumper

shoes earth pads ◆ ends ◆ kicks ◆ skates (Try also **big shoe(s) ◆ canvas shoes ◆ gym shoes ◆ tennis shoes.**)

shoot blast ◆ blow so's brains out ◆ blow so out ◆ burn ◆ ding ◆ fill so full of lead ◆ smoke ◆ zing (Try also **eager shooter.**)

shoot oneself eat one's gun

shooting lead poisoning

shop bodega (Try also **tiny shop.**)

shoplift boost

shoplifter booster ◆ klepto

shoplifter of meat cattle-rustler

shoplifting five-finger discount

short knee-high to a grasshopper ◆ sawed-off (Try also **story shortened.**)

short person duck-butt ◆ dusty butt ◆ spud

short time jiffy

short tobacco pipe nose-warmer

short workday banker's hours

shortcut Try **take shortcuts.**

shortcut key hotkey

shot Try **failed basketball shot ◆ poor shot.**

shot up Stow it!

show dog and pony show (Try also **talk show leader ◆ person showing promise.**)

show anger Try **be angry.**

show business show biz

show buttocks hang a BA (at so) ◆ moon

show disinterest blow cold

show humility eat crow

show off (pro)file ◆ ego trip ◆ ego tripper ◆ file ◆ grandstand ◆ hotdog ◆ style

show power throw one's weight around

showerbath rain closet

shut up Bag it! ◆ Button your lip! ◆ Can it! ◆ Dry up! ◆ Give it a rest! ◆ Put a cork in it! ◆ Put a sock in it! ◆ Put up or shut up! ◆ Quit your bellyaching! ◆ Knock it off! ◆ shush (up) ◆ shut up ◆ Shut your face! ◆ Shut your mouth! ◆ Shut your trap! ◆ Stuff a sock in it!

sick blue around the gills ◆ down with sth ◆ green around the gills ◆ raunchy (Try also **being sick ◆ call in sick.**)

sickness blue flu

side Try **good side ◆ opposite side ◆ support both sides ◆ swap sides ◆ two sides.**

sight Try **catch sight.**

sight worth looking at eye candy

sight worth seeing eyeful

sign Try **approval sign ◆ dead sign ◆ death sign ◆ disapproval sign ◆ number sign.**

sign of guilty smoking gun

signal (n) high sign (Try also **sexual signal.**)

signal (v) give so the nod ◆ telegraph one's punches

signal light idiot light

signal punches telegraph one's punches

signal with buzzer buzz

signature John Hancock (Try also **graffiti signature.**)

signed done and done

silence (n) Try **money to buy silence.**

silence (v) turn so's water off
silent forum reader lurker
silent person clam
silliness funny business ♦ monkey business
silly dingy ♦ fruity ♦ goofy ♦ in a twitter ♦ nutty ♦ nutty as a fruitcake ♦ off one's rocker ♦ slap happy ♦ w(h)acked ♦ wacky ♦ whack
silly person bozo ♦ flake ♦ fruitcake ♦ gidget ♦ gonzo ♦ goose ♦ space cadet ♦ twit
silverware Try **flatware.**
similar (as) alike as (two) peas in a pod ♦ alike as (two) peas in a pod (Try also **damn and similar curses and expressions.**)
similarly and stuff like that (there)
simpleton simp
sincere in there
sincerely from the bottom of my heart
singer canary (Try also **rock singer.**)
single performance one-night stand
sink (v) go titanic
siren yelper
sister sis ♦ sizzle (Try also **sorority sister.**)
sit cop a squat
sit down Make a lap! ♦ park it (somewhere) ♦ plop ♦ squat ♦ take a load off one's feet
situation Try **best situation ♦ dangerous situation ♦ emotional situation ♦ in awkward situation ♦ in bad situation ♦ in one's situation ♦ new situation ♦ reciprocal situation ♦ serious situation ♦ understand situation ♦ winning situation.**
situation comedy sitcom ♦ sitch
six-pack sixer
sixteenth steenth ♦ teenie ♦ teeny
skateboard boogie-board ♦ skurf
skateboarding sidewalk surfing
skier two-planker (Try also **beginning skier.**)
skier (female) snow bunny
skill Try **competitive skill ♦ have skill ♦ special skills.**
skilled person hell of a so/sth ♦ hell-on-wheels
skin (n) hide (Try also **bare skin.**)
skin irritation creeping-crud ♦ crotch-rot ♦ gunge
skip (v) ditch
skip eating fly light
skull headbone
skunk wood-pussy
sky Try **clear sky.**
slang jive talk
slap (n) backhander (Try also **hand slap.**)
slap hands give so five ♦ high five ♦ knock so some skin ♦ hit me again ♦ Hit me.

sleazy skeevy ♦ sleazo
sleep (n) beauty sleep ♦ big Zs ♦ blanket drill ♦ forty winks ♦ rack duty ♦ shut-eye ♦ rack time ♦ a wink of sleep
sleep (v) blow Zs ♦ catch some Zs ♦ cop some Zs ♦ crash ♦ cut some Zs ♦ doss down (for some time) ♦ flack (out) ♦ flake (out) ♦ flake down ♦ get some shut-eye ♦ kip ♦ pad out ♦ pound one's ear ♦ rack (out) ♦ sack out ♦ snooze ♦ zonk out ♦ zonked (out)
sleep away liquor sleep it off
sleeper Try **constant sleeper.**
sleeping out like a light
sleeping pill sleeper
sleeping place crash
sleepy dopey ♦ woozy
sleeveless shirt boy-beater
sleeveless undershirt wife-beater
slide rule slipstick
slightly Try **adjust slightly.**
slop (v) glop ♦ goup
sloppy kludgy ♦ scruff(y)
sloppy food (n) gobbledygook ♦ glop ♦ goop
sloppy person grod ♦ grub
sloppy speaker mushmouth
sloppy woman groddess
slow at a snail's gallop ♦ at a snail's pace ♦ pokey ♦ poky
slow driver Sunday driver
slowly Try **go slowly ♦ move slowly.**
sly sneaky
small dinky ♦ mini ♦ piddling ♦ two-by-four (Try also **in small portions.**)
small airplane puddle jumper
small amount tad
small bathroom powder room
small boy pipsqueak
small child squirt
small drink short one
small gift stocking-stuffer
small man pipsqueak
small person munchkin ♦ a nobody ♦ runt ♦ shrimp ♦ squirt ♦ small beer ♦ small fry ♦ small potatoes ♦ twerp
small punch rabbit punch
small sum birdseed ♦ chicken feed ♦ chump change ♦ peanuts
small toilet potty
small town one-horse town ♦ Podunk ♦ wide place in the road
small vehicle putt-putt
smallest finger (little) pinkie
small-penised man bug-fucker
small-time two-bit

small-time pimp popcorn pimp
smart swift
smart aleck wise guy ♦ wiseacre
smart person head ♦ pistol
smegma cock-cheese ♦ crotch-cheese ♦ smeg
smell Try **terrible smell ♦ what is smell ♦ smelly thing.**
smell badly smell to (high) heaven
smelly foxy ♦ funky ♦ grungy ♦ phunky ♦ ripe
smelly thing stinkpot
smile (v) cheese ♦ Say cheese!
smile with braces tin grin
smiling cheesing (Try also **stop smiling.**)
smoke (n) Try **swallow of smoke.**
smoke (v) burn ♦ cop a drag ♦ funk ♦ pull ♦ sizzle ♦ skag
smoke marijuana blaze ♦ blow ♦ blow jive ♦ blow smoke ♦ bong ♦ burn ♦ hotbox ♦ snork
smoke much chain(-smoke) ♦ smoke like a chimney
smoker chain-smoker (Try also **heavy smoker ♦ marijuana smoker.**)
smoking smoke
smooth silky (Try also **run smoothly.**)
smuggle plant sth on so
smuggling cigarettes buttlegging
smutty off color
snack (n) nosh ♦ pick-me-up ♦ pickup
snack (v) nosh
snack on nosh on sth
snack truck roach-coach
snacker nosher
snacks munchies
snapshot snap
sneak in zoom
sneak preview sneak
sneakers sneaks ♦ tennies
sneaky cagey ♦ dirty
sneaky deeds dirty work
sneaky person dirty dog ♦ snake in the grass ♦ weasel
sniff Try **glue sniffer ♦ drug-sniffing dog.**
sniper angel
snobbish biggity ♦ dicty ♦ hincty
snore call hogs
snow (n) fluff-stuff
snow (v) dump on so/sth
snowed on dumped on
snowmobile tin dog
snuff dip
so there Put that in your pipe and smoke it!
so what AIIC ♦ lah-di-dah
so you say Says you!
soap opera soap

sober clean ♦ cold sober ♦ dry ♦ jober as a sudge ♦ sober as a judge ♦ sold cober ♦ stone (cold) sober ♦ stone sober (Try also **get sober.**)
sober up get right
social failure loser ♦ two-time loser ♦ geekazoid ♦ geke ♦ mutant ♦ quimp
socialite sosh
socially active person swinger
sock boff ♦ bonk ♦ bust so one
socks Try **imaginary socks.**
soft cushy ♦ squooshy
software Try **cause of software error ♦ bad software.**
soil Try **underpants soil.**
soiled with dung shitty
sold bad drugs scabbed
sold in barrel on tap
sold on hooked (on so/sth)
soldier blisterfoot ♦ crunchie ♦ dogface ♦ gravel-pounder ♦ ground-pounder ♦ grunt (Try also **inept soldier ♦ lifetime soldier ♦ new soldier ♦ reserve soldier ♦ U.S. soldier.**)
solo break ♦ riff
solution Try **perfect solution.**
solvent in the black
something one must do must (do) ♦ must
something that sells well hot item
soon RSN ♦ two shakes of a lamb's tail (Try also **very soon.**)
soon to happen on tap
soothe stroke
sophomore soph
sorority sister sister
sorry Excuse me for breathing! ♦ Excuse me for living! ♦ sorry 'bout that ♦ sorry about that ♦ Well, wash my mouth out with soap.
sound Try **be of sound mind ♦ be mentally sound ♦ cash register sound.**
soup goozlum
sour face picklepuss
source bottomless pit (Try also **gossip source ♦ money source ♦ student's financial source ♦ trouble source.**)
southern accent a mouth full of South
soybean futures beans
spank dust so's pants ♦ whale the tar out of so
sparkling bling-bling
spay pet fix
spayed fixed

speak Let's have it! ♦ Sock it to me! (Try also **refuse to speak ♦ frank speaker ♦ sloppy speaker ♦ unclear speaker.**)

speak badly bad-mouth

speak carelessly talk through one's hat

speak first break the ice

speak frankly lay it on the line ♦ pop off ♦ Tell it like it is.

speak honestly level with so

speak ill poor-mouth

speak kindly lay some sweet lines on so ♦ put some sweet lines on so

speak loudly have a big mouth

speak mind get a load off one's mind

speak out about sound off (about sth)

speak quickly shoot from the hip

speak truly level with so

speaker of evil bad-mouth

special Try **make special occasion.**

special interest thing

special skills tricks of the trade

specialist artist

speech Try **distorted speech ♦ say one's speech.**

speed (n) Try **achieve speed ♦ increase speed ♦ rate of speed ♦ top speed.**

speed (v) barrel ♦ barrel ass ♦ buzz along ♦ cruise ♦ zip along

speed away lay (some) rubber

speed trap bear trap

speeder (driver) leadfoot

speeding ticket speeder ♦ speedster

speedometer speedo

spend (v) blow ♦ drop a bundle (on sth) ♦ lay sth out ♦ shell out (an amount of money) (Try also **big casino spender ♦ free spender ♦ time spent in person.**)

spend a lot drop a bundle (on so)

spend counterfeit money shove

spend everything shoot one's wad

spend the night crash

spend time hang

spending bad checks paperhanging

spike Try **market spike.**

spin wheels burn rubber

spineless person (limp) dishrag

spirit moxie (Try also **have spirit ♦ in good spirits.**)

spit (v) hock a luggie ♦ hork

split cost go Dutch

spoil queer ♦ rain on so/sth ♦ rain on so's parade

sponge on freeload

sponsor sugar daddy

spontaneous pickup

spouse Try **former lover or spouse.**

spray painter tagger

spree Try **drinking spree.**

spy (n) plant ♦ snoop ♦ spook ♦ wire (Try also **install spy devices.**)

spy (v) snoop

spy on stake so/sth out

square Try **out of square.**

squelch chill so's action ♦ kibosh ♦ put the kibosh on sth

stab jack so up ♦ joog ♦ OJ so ♦ shiv

stall bogard ♦ bogart

stalled dead in the water

standing viewer standee

Star Trek Fan trekkie

stare (v) do a bean count ♦ rubberneck ♦ crank sth up ♦ fire away ♦ fire sth up ♦ get the show on the road ♦ get one's teeth into sth ♦ jump-start so ♦ Let her rip! ♦ Let it roll! ♦ sink one's teeth into sth ♦ stoke sth up

start jump-start (Try also **computer start ♦ from the start ♦ time to start.**)

start (n) jump (street)

start car jump-start

start car without key hot wire

start computer boot

start early jump the gun

start machine stoke sth up

start over reinvent the wheel

start romance get sth going (with so)

start something trigger

start traveling hit the road

start walking hit the bricks ♦ hit the pavement

startle knock so's socks off

startled spooked

state Try **fretful state ♦ mental state ♦ nervous state ♦ industrial states.**

station Try **police station.**

statistics stats

stay out of trouble keep one's nose clean

steal bamboozle ♦ boost ♦ cop ♦ doink ♦ filch sth (from so/sth) ♦ gack sth ♦ gaffle ♦ gank sth ♦ glom ♦ heist ♦ hook ♦ jack ♦ kipe ♦ knock over sth ♦ liberate ♦ lift ♦ nick ♦ nip ♦ pinch ♦ rip sth off ♦ scarf ♦ snake ♦ snatch ♦ snitch ♦ swipe ♦ yoink sth

steal computer data hack

steal easily waltz off (with sth)

steal girlfriend bird-dog

steel ship rust bucket

stereo (ghetto) blaster ♦ (ghetto) box ♦ blaster ♦ boom box ♦ box (Try also **portable stereo.**)

stern hard-nosed

steroids abolic ♦ gorilla juice ♦ roids ♦ wonder water

steward stew

stewardess stew

stick (v) cling like shit to a shovel

stick to position hang tough (on sth)

sticker Try **license sticker.**

sticky gucky

sticky substance goo ♦ goozlum ♦ guck ♦ stickum

still Try **hold still.**

stimulant pep pill

stimulate jack so up

stimulated hyped (up)

stimulating jazzy

stingy mingy ♦ tight

stingy person money grubber ♦ scrooge ♦ tight wad

stock Try **fill or cancel stock order** ♦ **New York Stock Exchange** ♦ **appealing stock** ♦ **cull stock** ♦ **McDonald's stock** ♦ **sale of borrowed stock** ♦ **sell borrowed stock** ♦ **keep stocks.**

stock price collapse (n) crater ♦ conk out ♦ flack (out) ♦ fold ♦ take a nosedive ♦ wash out ♦ zonk out

stockbroker guru

stolen hot

stolen goods loot

stolen money loot

stomach basket ♦ bazoo ♦ breadbasket ♦ dinner basket ♦ gutbucket ♦ labonza ♦ wazoo

stomachache bellyache

stop (v) Break it up! ♦ Come off it! ♦ Enough, already! ♦ Hold it! ♦ hold one's horses ♦ kill ♦ nix ♦ Quit your bellyaching! ♦ stop on a dime ♦ Stop the music! ♦ Time (out)! ♦ Whoa! ♦ Hold everything!

stop annoying get off so's back ♦ lay off (so/sth)

stop ignoring me Hello?

stop losses cut one's losses

stop smiling Wipe it off!

stop without tapering off cold turkey

stop working take a break ♦ veg (out)

stop your nonsense Cut the crap!

store bodega (Try also **jewelry store** ♦ **liquor store.**)

story bedtime story ♦ fairy tale ♦ line (Try also **fabricated story** ♦ **long story** ♦ **repeated story** ♦ **sad story.**)

story shortened long story short

stout chunky

straight str8

straightened out squared away

strained tenor whiskey tenor

strange (strictly) from hunger ♦ crackpot ♦ freaky ♦ from hunger ♦ funky ♦ JDLR ♦ kinky ♦ kookish ♦ off-the-wall ♦ phunky ♦ zerking

strange meat mystery meat

strange person crank ♦ fink ♦ fruit ♦ glick ♦ guff ♦ kink ♦ kook ♦ nut ♦ odd bird ♦ odd-bod ♦ queer fish ♦ queer-beer ♦ snapper ♦ weirdo

strange-bodied person odd-bod

stranger Try **call a stranger.**

straw merchandise donkey's breakfast

stray Try **urge to stray.**

street Try **respected street person** ♦ **drunkard street** ♦ **from the street** ♦ **main street** ♦ **on Wall Street** ♦ **Wall Street** ♦ **person of streets.**

strength (ma)hoska (Try also **muster strength.**)

strengthen beef sth up

stress Try **suffer stress.**

stressful tight

strict person hardliner

strife blood and guts

strike (n) wack ♦ wallop ♦ whack (Try also **go out on strike.**)

strike (v) belt ♦ biff ♦ bonk ♦ bop ♦ brick ♦ bust so one ♦ clunk ♦ coldcock ♦ knock so's block off ♦ land a blow ♦ paste ♦ paste so one ♦ paste sth on so ♦ pop ♦ punch so's lights out ♦ punch so out ♦ sock ♦ take a whack at so/sth ♦ throw a punch ♦ wack ♦ wallop ♦ whack

strike head bean ♦ brain

striptease artist stripper

stroll Try **whore stroll.**

strong man caveman ♦ husky ♦ knuckle-dragger ♦ powerhouse ♦ tiger

strongly full blast

struck in testicles racked

strut around style

stub Try **marijuana cigarette stub.**

stubborn bonehead ♦ boneheaded ♦ bullheaded ♦ hardheaded ♦ pigheaded

stubborn person hard head ♦ pighead ♦ rockhead

student Try **earnest student domain ♦ important student (female) ♦ important student (male) ♦ average male college student ♦ earnest student ♦ ordinary male college student ♦ prep school student ♦ technical college student ♦ typical male college student.**

student's financial source wallet

study crack a book ♦ hit the books ♦ pound the books

study a place case the joint

study all night oil it

study hard geek out ♦ powerstudy

studying hard grade-grubbing

stuff crud ♦ jonx ♦ junk ♦ shit (Try also **all that stuff ♦ gooey stuff.**)

stuffy person stuffed shirt

stumbling disorder stumble-bumbles ♦ stumbles

stun zap

stunning drop-dead

stunning person knockout

stunning thing knockout

stunt caper

stupid airheaded ♦ birdbrain ♦ birdbrained ♦ birdturd ♦ birdy ♦ boneheaded ♦ brain-dead ♦ can't find one's butt with both hands (in broad daylight) ♦ clucky ♦ cornball ♦ crackbrained ♦ dead from the neck up ♦ dizzy ♦ dopey ♦ dorky ♦ dumb-ass ♦ dumbshit ♦ dumbski ♦ fatheaded ♦ flatheaded ♦ fuck-brained ♦ Fuckheaded ♦ hit by the stupid stick ♦ klutzy ♦ McFly ♦ meatheaded ♦ mess ♦ nothing upstairs ♦ nutty ♦ nutty as a fruitcake ♦ one brick shy of a load ♦ pigheaded ♦ soft ♦ soft in the head ♦ stupid-ass ♦ thick ♦ thickheaded ♦ three bricks shy of a load ♦ yoyo (Try also **acting stupid ♦ be stupid ♦ I am not stupid ♦ look stupid.**)

stupid man clod ♦ dick ♦ dick smack ♦ dickhead ♦ dildo ♦ helmet ♦ jake ♦ Joe Schmo ♦ Joe Six-pack ♦ knuckle-dragger ♦ lug ♦ musclehead ♦ neanderthal ♦ palooka ♦ paluka ♦ pecker ♦ peckerhead ♦ prick ♦ weenie

stupid person A-hole ♦ abbreviated piece of nothing ♦ ace ♦ Adam Henry ♦ AH ♦ airbrain ♦ airhead ♦ ass-wipe ♦ asshat ♦ asshole ♦ baboon ♦ banana-head ♦ Barney ♦ BB brain ♦ bean head ♦ beef-head ♦ beetlebrain ♦ birdbrain ♦ blob ♦ block ♦ blockhead ♦ bohunk ♦ bonehead ♦ boob ♦ bozo ♦ bubblehead ♦ butthead ♦ cabbagehead ♦

cheesehead ♦ choad ♦ chowderhead ♦ chump ♦ chumphead ♦ clod ♦ clodhopper ♦ clown ♦ cluck ♦ cluckhead ♦ clunkhead ♦ Clyde ♦ conehead ♦ cornball ♦ crackbrain ♦ deadhead ♦ deadneck ♦ dick ♦ dick for ♦ dick smack ♦ dickhead ♦ dickwad ♦ dickweed ♦ dildo ♦ dim bulb ♦ dimwit ♦ ding-a-ling ♦ ding-dong ♦ dingbat ♦ dinghead ♦ dingleberry ♦ dip ♦ diphead ♦ dipshit ♦ dipstick ♦ dipwad ♦ dode ♦ doofus ♦ dope ♦ dorf ♦ dork ♦ dorkmeier ♦ dorkmunder ♦ dorkus maximus ♦ dough head ♦ drip ♦ droid ♦ droob ♦ drube ♦ duffer ♦ duffis ♦ dum-dum ♦ dumb bunny ♦ dumb cluck ♦ dumb ox ♦ dumb-ass ♦ dumb-dodo ♦ dumb-dumb ♦ dumbbell ♦ dumbhead ♦ dumbo ♦ dumbshit ♦ dumbski ♦ dummy ♦ durge ♦ dweeb ♦ fathead ♦ feather brain ♦ feeb ♦ fish ♦ flathead ♦ frog face ♦ fruit loop ♦ fruitcake ♦ fuck nut ♦ fuckhead ♦ gazizzey ♦ gazob ♦ geke ♦ gleep ♦ glick ♦ gomer ♦ gonzo ♦ goob ♦ goober ♦ goobrain ♦ goof ♦ goofball ♦ goofer ♦ goofus ♦ gook ♦ goomer ♦ goon ♦ goopus ♦ goose ♦ gork ♦ guff ♦ gumbyhead ♦ gump ♦ hamburger ♦ hammerhead ♦ hayseed ♦ helium head ♦ helmet ♦ honyock ♦ horse's ass ♦ hoser ♦ jack-shit ♦ jel ♦ jerk ♦ jive turkey ♦ Joe Schmo ♦ Joe Six-pack ♦ jork ♦ jughead ♦ klotz ♦ kluck ♦ klutz ♦ knothead ♦ knuckle-dragger ♦ knucklehead ♦ lardhead ♦ little shit ♦ lommix ♦ lorg ♦ lug ♦ lughead ♦ lummox ♦ lummux ♦ lump ♦ lumpus ♦ marble dome ♦ McFly ♦ meathead ♦ megadork ♦ mental ♦ mental midget ♦ mouth-breather ♦ mushhead ♦ newt ♦ nimrod ♦ nitwit ♦ no-brow ♦ numbnuts ♦ nurd ♦ nutcake ♦ palooka ♦ paluka ♦ peanut head ♦ pecker ♦ pighead ♦ potatohead ♦ puddinghead ♦ puttyhead ♦ putz ♦ quimp ♦ rattlebrain ♦ retard ♦ room for rent ♦ rumdum ♦ sap ♦ saphead ♦ schlemazel ♦ schlemozzle ♦ schlep ♦ schloomp ♦ schlump ♦ schmegegge ♦ schmegeggy ♦ schmendrick ♦ shithead ♦ smurfbrain ♦ stoop ♦ stupe ♦ stupehead ♦ stupid-ass ♦ tard ♦ titless wonder ♦ turkey ♦ twit ♦ veg ♦ wiener nose ♦ yack ♦ yahoo ♦ yap ♦ yutz ♦ zerk ♦ zombie

stupid question There's no such thing as a stupid question.

stupid tourist touron

stupid woman Wilma

stupidity (various) cluelessness ♦ krudzu ♦ There's nobody home. (Try also **talk stupidity.**)

style steelo (Try also **in style ♦ music style ♦ fake stylishness.**)

stylish fly

sub sandwich grinder ♦ hero ♦ hoagy ♦ poor boy ♦ sub ♦ submarine ♦ torpedo

submarine sub

subscription Try **magazine subscription.**

subservient kiss-ass

substance Try **nasty substance ♦ perfect substance ♦ sticky substance.**

substitute (n) pinch hitter ♦ stand-in ♦ sub

substitute (v) sub

substitution switcheroo

suburb burb

suburban Try **looking suburban.**

subway passenger straphanger

succeed ace in(to sth) ♦ ace out ♦ make (it) big ♦ score (Try also **cannot always succeed ♦ have succeeded.**)

succeeded in like Flynn

succeeding on a roll

success boffo ♦ hit ♦ Win a few, lose a few. ♦ Win some, lose some. (Try also **aid success ♦ be a success ♦ financial success ♦ lucky success ♦ quit with success ♦ try again with a hope of success.**)

successful big time ♦ boffo ♦ heavyweight ♦ in tall cotton

successful man lady-killer

successful performance blockbuster

successful person big-time operator ♦ heavyweight

suck sizzle

sucker sucka

sudden memory flash

suddenly out of left field

sue sue the pants off (of) so

suffer Try **you will suffer.**

suffer criticism thin-skinned

suffer results twist (slowly) in the wind ♦ twist in the wind

suffer stress stress

suffered been to hell and back

suffering bumming

suffering withdrawal twisted

sugar sand

suggest idea hit so with sth

suggest plan hit so with sth

suggestive lyrics leerics

suicide Dutch cure ♦ the Dutch act (Try also **commit suicide.**)

suitcase keester ♦ keyster ♦ kiester

sum Try **small sum.**

summary rundown ♦ score

sunbathe bag some rays ♦ catch some rays

sunburned baked ♦ fried

sunglasses cheaters ♦ shades ♦ sunshades ♦ tints

sunny zone sun belt

sunshine rays ♦ UVs

super awesome

superintendent super

superior (g)narly ♦ holier-than-thou ♦ mint

superior booze the (real) McCoy

superior person hot stuff

superiors high ups ♦ higher ups

supervisor honcho

support beat the drum for so/sth ♦ boost ♦ get behind so/sth ♦ get behind sth ♦ hype

support both sides straddle the fence

supporter backer ♦ booster (Try also **arts supporter ♦ athlete supporter ♦ peace supporter ♦ woman's liberation supporter.**)

supporter of war hawk

supposed cracked up to be

sure yeah ♦ Yeah, right. ♦ yo mama (Try also **for sure.**)

surfboard boogie-board ♦ woody (Try also **grasp surfboard.**)

surfer Try **false surfer.**

surgical Try **leave surgical instruments in patient.**

surpass blow so's doors off

surprise blindside ♦ bomb ♦ bomb(shell) ♦ double take ♦ drop a bomb(shell) ♦ drop a brick ♦ eye-opener ♦ eye-popper ♦ hell of a note ♦ knock so's socks off ♦ knock so out ♦ throw so for a loop (Try also **react with surprise ♦ be surprised ♦ from surprising direction.**)

surprised floored

survival ability street smarts

survive scrutiny hold water

survived been to hell and back

survivor vivor ♦ warhorse

suspect (v) smell a rat

suspect a fight smell blood

suspects lineup

suspenseful event white knuckler

suspicious event situation

swallow (n) pull

swallow (v) chug ♦ hook sth down ♦ pop ♦ scarf sth down ♦ sink

swallow of smoke poke

swap sex partners swing

swap sides turn

swapping Try **clothes swapping.**

swear swear like a trooper
sweatshirt hoodie
sweet remarks sweet nothings
sweetheart angel ♦ babycakes ♦ honeybunch ♦ honeycakes ♦ HTH ♦ my tenda ♦ snookums ♦ squeeze ♦ steady
swimmer fanny-dipper
swimming briefs grape smugglers ♦ speedo
swindle (n) dodge ♦ scam ♦ skin game
swindle (v) dupe ♦ futz ♦ phutz ♦ put a con on so ♦ scam ♦ shuck ♦ sting ♦ yench
swindler hustler ♦ scammer ♦ shark
sympathize bleed for so
syndicate Try **crime syndicate.**
synthetic marijuana sin
syringe Try **hypodermic syringe.**
syrup goozlum
systems operator SYSOP
table for four four-topper
table for two deuce ♦ two-topper
tables Try **change tables.**
tablet tab
tabloid newspaper scandal sheet
tackle sack
tactics Try **unfair tactics.**
tactless heavy-handed
tag Try **military dog tag.**
tailgater bumper sticker
take nick (Try also **risk-taking gambler.**)
take a break take five
take a chance take a flyer (on sth)
take a try have a crack at sth
take bets make book on sth
take blame take the rap (for sth)
take care of the home hold the fort
take charge kick some ass (around) ♦ kick some butt
take cocaine get one's nose cold ♦ snort
take fifth amendment five it
take fingerprints roll (a set)
take form shape up
take nap snooze
take notice pick up on sth
take oath swear on a stack of Bibles
take offense get one's nose out of joint
take overdose overjolt
take permanent action play for keeps
take puff sip ♦ toke
take responsibility step up to the plate
take shortcuts cut corners
takeover preventer poison pill ♦ shark repellent
taking bribes on the take
taking contraceptive on the pill

taking drugs again off the wagon
taking heroin on the horse
talent Try **reserved talent ♦ naturally talented.**
talent in reserve ace in the hole
talented person natural ♦ whiz
talented youth whiz kid
talk (n) chinmusic ♦ chitchat ♦ fat lip ♦ yada, yada, yada (Try also **back talk ♦ direct talk ♦ empty talk ♦ honest talk ♦ serious talk.**)
talk (v) blab ♦ chitchat ♦ fan the breeze ♦ rap ♦ wag one's chin ♦ yak
talk about chew sth over
talk back get smart (with so) ♦ mouth off
talk business talk turkey
talk down jaw so down
talk endlessly talk to hear one's own voice ♦ talk one's head off ♦ talk so's ear off ♦ talk so ragged
talk fast talk a blue streak
talk frankly talk turkey
talk in vain beat one's gums
talk lots yak it up
talk show leader gabmeister
talk stupidity talk like a nut
talk to exhaustion talk until one is blue in the face
talk to wrong person have the wrong number
talk too much talk to hear one's own voice ♦ talk until one is blue in the face ♦ talk so's ear off ♦ talk so ragged
talkative well-oiled ♦ windbag ♦ windy ♦ yakky
talkative person loose cannon
talkativeness foot-in-mouth disease
talker bag of wind ♦ big mouth ♦ magpie (Try also **fast talker ♦ loud talker ♦ obscene talker.**)
talking yodeling in a canyon
tall person big drink of water ♦ stretch
tall woman long-tall-Sally ♦ stallion
tamper with mess about (with sth) ♦ mess around (with sth) ♦ monkey around (with sth) ♦ monkey with so/sth ♦ rig
tampon rag ♦ submarine ♦ tamp (Try also **sanitary tampon.**)
tan oneself nuke oneself
tantrum Try **have temper tantrum.**
tape Try **duct tape.**
taper Try **stop without tapering off.**
target Try **begging target ♦ easy target.**
task Try **accept task ♦ difficult task ♦ easy task ♦ right task.**

tasteless raunchy

tasty nummy ♦ scrumptious

tattle fink (on so)

tattoo ink ♦ paint ♦ tat ♦ temp-tat (Try also temporary tattoo.)

tavern fill-mill ♦ joint ♦ juice joint ♦ piss factory ♦ puke hole ♦ sauce parlor ♦ watering hole (Try also low tavern.)

taxi hack

taxi driver hacker

tea brew

teach school so

tear in flesh rip

tease (v) joke ♦ rib ♦ yank so's crank ♦ bag on so ♦ joke ♦ josh ♦ play around (with so) ♦ pull so's leg ♦ razz ♦ shuck (Try also not teasing.)

technical techie

technical college student techie

technician techie

technologically current on the bleeding edge

teenage girl twinkie

teenager Try young teenager.

teeth biters ♦ China ♦ choppers ♦ crockery ♦ ivories ♦ snappers (Try also front teeth.)

telephone (n) Ameche ♦ horn (Try also using the telephone.)

telephone (v) give so a buzz

telephone call jingle (Try also fake telephone call.)

telephone service POTS

television Try children's television.

television announcer talking head

tell give (out) with sth

tell again Run that by (me) again. ♦ Run that by (me) one more time.

tell everyone put sth on the street ♦ take it to the street ♦ take sth public ♦ tell the (whole) world

tell facts run it down

tell secret blab ♦ blabbermouth

tell troubles get it out

tell truth fack ♦ I'm not kidding. ♦ run it down ♦ Tell it like it is.

telling Try begin telling.

temper Try have temper tantrum ♦ display temper ♦ lose temper ♦ quick-tempered person.

temper (quick) short fuse

temporary scratch

temporary tattoo temp-tat

tenacity sticktoitiveness

tend to own business mind your own beeswax

ten-dollar bill sawbuck ♦ ten-spot ♦ tenner

tennis shoes tennies

tenor Try strained tenor.

tentatively Try reply tentatively.

tequila cactus juice

term Try in last term ♦ person in last term of office ♦ prison term.

terminate pour cold water on sth ♦ pull the plug (on so/sth)

termination kibosh

terrible hellacious ♦ unearthly ♦ ungodly

terrible mess hell of a mess

terrible smell Somebody died in here! ♦ Who died in here?

territory turf (Try also reserved territory.)

test Try fail test ♦ reaction test ♦ urine test.

testicle ache blue balls

testicles balls ♦ chones ♦ chooms ♦ cojones ♦ crystals ♦ family jewels ♦ knockers ♦ nads ♦ nards ♦ nuggets ♦ nuts ♦ nutz ♦ rocks ♦ stones

testimony Try withhold testimony.

thank you Tango Yankee ♦ thank you very much ♦ thanks a bunch ♦ Thanks in advance. ♦ TIA ♦ You made my day.

that is all So much for that. ♦ That's about the size of it. ♦ That's all she wrote. ♦ That's that! ♦ That's what she wrote.

that is life That's show business (for you). ♦ That's the way the ball bounces. ♦ That's the way the cookie crumbles. ♦ That's the way the mop flops.

the that

the finger Try digitus impudicus.

theater Try local theater.

theft cop ♦ heist ♦ job ♦ moonlight requisition ♦ rip ♦ rip-off ♦ snatch ♦ snitch ♦ take off

theft prone sticky fingers

then then and there

thermostat stat

thief (rip-)off artist ♦ biter ♦ kiper ♦ klepto ♦ off artist ♦ take-off artist ♦ yegg (Try also den of thieves.)

thighs Try fat thighs.

thin person beanpole ♦ bones ♦ rattlebones ♦ stringbean

thing dingus ♦ johnson ♦ jones ♦ number ♦ puppy

thing of the past history

thing worth keeping keeper

think Use your head! ♦ Use your noggin! ♦ Use your noodle! (Try also **current thinking** ♦ **fast thinking.**)

think about chew sth over

think again You've got another think coming.

think obscenely have one's mind in the gutter

think up hit on sth

thirsty sponged

thirteen long dozen

this big yea big

thong butt floss ♦ butt thong

thought Try **without thought.**

thousand K. ♦ thou

thousand dollars gee ♦ grand ♦ large

thousand feet angel

threat boogieman ♦ if one knows what's good for one ♦ It will be your ass!

threat (female) ball-breaker ♦ ball-buster

threat (male) boogieman

threaten crowd ♦ fuck with so ♦ put the heat on so ♦ put the screws on so ♦ put the squeeze on so ♦ settle so's hash ♦ work so over

threatening (female) ball-busting

threatening homosexuals fag-bashing ♦ fag-busting

three bases in baseball triple ♦ triple-bagger

three in a row a hat trick

thrill (n) bang ♦ belt ♦ blast ♦ boot ♦ buzz ♦ jollies (Try also **for a thrill** ♦ **get thrill.**)

thrilled psyched (out)

thrilling book or movie thriller-diller

throttle Try **full throttle.**

throw Try **baseball throw.**

throw a contest fix

thrown kiss air kiss

thug ape ♦ bruiser ♦ enforcer ♦ goon ♦ husky ♦ mug ♦ muscleman ♦ strong-arm man ♦ tough guy

thugs goon squad

thunderstorm thunder-boomer

thwart cross up so ♦ cross so (up)

ticket duck ♦ in (Try also **speeding ticket.**)

tight tight as a tick

tight abdominal muscles six-pack ♦ washboard abs

time (n) throw (Try also **small-time pimp** ♦ **when the time comes** ♦ **bad time** ♦ **difficult time** ♦ **easy time** ♦ **experience first time** ♦ **give hard time** ♦ **good time** ♦ **have good time** ♦ **just in time** ♦ **long time**

♦ **lost time** ♦ **on time** ♦ **period of time** ♦ **playing time** ♦ **short time** ♦ **spend time** ♦ **waste of time** ♦ **waste time** ♦ **work time.**)

time in bed rack duty ♦ rack time ♦ sack time

time lost down time

time out of prison street time

time period stretch

time spent in person face time

time to leave time to cruise

time to start (It's) showtime! ♦ Showtime!

time waster blow off ♦ goof off ♦ piddler

timid man pipsqueak ♦ pussycat

timid person rubber sock ♦ weak sister

timidity cold feet

tiny incy-wincy ♦ itsy-bitsy ♦ itty-bitty ♦ teenie-weenie ♦ teensy-weensy ♦ teeny-weeny

tiny bit smidgen

tiny picture piccie

tiny shop hole in the wall

tip (n) palm-oil

tipsiness glow ♦ jingle

tipsy activated ♦ balmy ♦ bewottled ♦ bonkers ♦ corkscrewed (up) ♦ elevated ♦ half up the pole ♦ half-canned ♦ half-sprung ♦ half-under ♦ happy ♦ jolly ♦ pinked ♦ pixilated ♦ pleasantly plastered ♦ rattled ♦ slightly rattled ♦ so-so ♦ swigged ♦ swiggled

tipsy stage edge

tirade mouthful

tire out zonk

tired burned out ♦ cashed ♦ dead ♦ groggy ♦ zapped

tired person zombie

tire(s) rubber (Try also **section of tire debris** ♦ **racing tire.**)

tits and ass B. and B. T. and A.

toast Try **drinking toast.**

tobacco dip ♦ dust ♦ jack ♦ plug ♦ weed (Try also **short tobacco pipe.**)

tobacco cigarette joint ♦ pill ♦ skag ♦ slim ♦ smoke ♦ soldier ♦ square ♦ square joint ♦ straight

together Try **living together.**

toilet bank ♦ biffy ♦ can ♦ chamber of commerce ♦ crapper ♦ flusher ♦ growler ♦ gutbucket ♦ head ♦ jake ♦ john ♦ joint ♦ loo ♦ pot ♦ puke hole ♦ shitcan ♦ the throne (Try also **go to the toilet** ♦ **on the toilet** ♦ **small toilet.**)

toilet break bio break ♦ pit stop ♦ see a man about a dog ♦ nature stop

537

toilet paper ammunition ♦ ass-wipe ♦ butt-wipe ♦ shitrag ♦ teepee ♦ TP

toilet urge nature's call

told you before if I've told you once, I've told you a thousand times

tolerant easy

tolerate stomach ♦ wear

toll booth troll booth

tomorrow mañana

tongue licker

tongue kiss soul kiss

tonsils and adenoids T. and A.

too difficult to understand over one's head

too many drinks one too many

too much bellyful ♦ overkill ♦ That's all so needs. ♦ a bit much

too old over the hill

tool Try **imaginary tool.**

top speed flat out

topics Try **change topics.**

topsy-turvy ass over tit

tornado twister

total Try **final total.**

totally flat out ♦ flat-ass ♦ hook, line, and sinker ♦ massively ♦ mondo ♦ so ♦ way

touch paw

touch baseball runner tag

tough badass ♦ hardboiled (Try also **act tough.**)

tough guy badass

tough man bruiser

tough neighborhood war zone

tough person baddy ♦ tough cookie ♦ warhorse

toupee divot ♦ rug ♦ sky rug

tour stump

tourist day-tripper ♦ rubberneck (Try also **stupid tourist.**)

tourist attraction tourist trap

town burg ♦ tizzle (Try **backward town ♦ rush through town ♦ small town.**)

town resident townie

trade insults play the dozens ♦ shoot the dozens

traditional trad

traffic in illicit liquor moonshine

train Try **board train.**

tranquilizer mickey ♦ happy pills

transgendered person tranny

transmission tranny (Try also **nonautomatic transmission.**)

transmitted Try **sexually transmitted disease.**

transport contraband run

transport drugs carry

transportation four wheels ♦ trans

transporter Try **drug transporter.**

trap Try **speed trap.**

trapesius traps

trapped feeling stir crazy

trash can circular file ♦ file thirteen ♦ shitcan

trashy trailer

travel boogie down (to somewhere) ♦ hump it (to somewhere) (Try also **foot travel (various) ♦ wealthy travelers ♦ start traveling.**)

travel on foot shank's mare

travel rapidly streak

traveling on the road

treat blow so to sth

treat like a fool play so for a fool

treat someone blow so to sth ♦ pass for sth ♦ pop for sth ♦ stake so to sth ♦ bounce for sth ♦ spring for sth

treat unfairly play fast and loose (with so/sth)

treatment Try **get treatment ♦ powerful treatment ♦ unfair treatment.**

tremors the jitters (Try also **alcoholic tremors ♦ drunken tremors.**)

trendy happening

triceps TRIs

trick fast one ♦ monkeyshines (Try also **have trick in reserve.**)

trill Try **bilabial trill.**

trinket tchtchotchke

trip (n) roadtrip (Try also **return trip.**)

trivial kitschy ♦ mickey mouse ♦ penny-ante

trivial entertainment kitsch

trombone bone

trouble (n) big stink ♦ fireworks ♦ hell ♦ holy stink ♦ jam ♦ sweat (Try also **more trouble is coming ♦ be in trouble ♦ cause trouble ♦ get into trouble ♦ have trouble ♦ in trouble ♦ make trouble ♦ seeking trouble ♦ stay out of trouble ♦ when there is trouble ♦ tell troubles.**)

trouble maker hell raiser ♦ heller

trouble source headache department

troublesome double-trouble

troublesome person holy terror

truck eighteen-wheeler ♦ rig (Try also **beer truck ♦ snack truck.**)

true Now you're talking! ♦ on the gooch ♦ on the reezie ♦ on the rilla

truly Try **speak truly.**

trunk keester ♦ keyster ♦ kiester

trustworthy crook thoroughbred

truth Don't I know it! ✦ facts of life ✦ gospel (truth) ✦ inside dope ✦ mouthful ✦ naked truth ✦ not just whistling Dixie ✦ straight dope ✦ straight low (Try also **tell truth.**)

try (n) crack ✦ go ✦ shot ✦ shot in the dark ✦ throw ✦ one's best shot (Try also **take a try.**)

try (v) Go for it! ✦ go for the fences ✦ take a crack at sth ✦ take a shot (at sth) ✦ take a swipe at so/sth ✦ take a whack at sth (Try also **quit trying.**)

try again with a hope of success Better luck next time.

try hard bust (one's) ass (to do sth) ✦ bust (one's) butt to do sth ✦ bust (one's) nuts to do sth ✦ bust a gut (to do sth) ✦ bust a nut ✦ do or die

try idea bounce sth off (of) so

tumor boogie ✦ guber

tunnel Try **Boston tunnel.**

turn (n) The ball is in so's court.

turn (v) Try **make U turn.**

turn against go green on so

turn left hang a left ✦ hang a louie

turn off light kill

turn on juice sth up

turn out okay pan out

turn over turn turtle

turn right hang a ralph ✦ hang a right

turn sharply turn on a dime

tuxedo tux (Try also **long tuxedo.**)

TV boob-tube ✦ idiot box ✦ telly ✦ tube

TV announcer meat puppet

twenty Try **large twenty-dollar bill.**

twenty-dollar bill bigface ✦ double ✦ double saw(buck) ✦ dub

twenty-two double-deuces

twice Try **profit twice.**

twister Try **news twister.**

twisting pitch screwball

two Try **requires two ✦ table for two ✦ twenty two.**

two base hit double-bagger

two dollars deuce

two for the price of one twofer

two of cards deuce

two people gruesome-twosome

two sides It cuts both ways. ✦ It cuts two ways.

two things gruesome-twosome

two years in prison deuce

type (n) Try **haircut type.**

type (v) beat sth out ✦ pound sth out

typical run-of-the-mill

typical male college student Joe College

typical man Joe Doakes

ugly been bobbing for fries ✦ bugly ✦ butt-ugly ✦ coyote-ugly ✦ fugly ✦ hiddy ✦ hidi ✦ hit by the ugly stick ✦ hurt ✦ hurting ✦ nay ✦ plug-ugly ✦ pug-ugly ✦ scary ✦ skanky ✦ ugly as sin (Try also **look ugly.**)

ugly garment rag

ugly man cromagnon ✦ zarf

ugly person beast ✦ bowser ✦ double-bagger ✦ mud duck ✦ pug-ugly ✦ triple-bagger ✦ troll

ugly woman bag ✦ bear ✦ bow-wow ✦ bush bitch ✦ bush pig ✦ butter face ✦ chank ✦ cow ✦ dog ✦ douche bag ✦ hellpig ✦ roach ✦ scank ✦ skag ✦ skank ✦ sko ✦ Zelda

umpire (n) ump

unaffected Try **leave unaffected.**

unaffected by drug burned out

unaged (liquor) raw

unattractive man Barney ✦ melvin

unauthorized bootleg

unaware clueless ✦ totally clueless

unbelievable hard to swallow ✦ thick ✦ unreal

uncertain iffy

uncircumcised uncut

unclean grubby

unclear clear as mud

unclear speaker mushmouth

unconscious coo-coo ✦ gone ✦ gone under ✦ out cold ✦ out like a light (Try also **vomiting and unconscious.**)

uncontrolled free-wheeling

unconventional Try **sexually unconventional.**

uncoordinated out of sync

undecided in a dither ✦ up in the air (about so/sth)

undecided person fence hanger

undependable fly-by-night

under control on a tight leash ✦ under so's thumb

under fire up front

under pressure under the gun

under scrutiny under the gun

undercover hush-hush

undergo change turn around ✦ turn over

underling gofer ✦ gopher ✦ grunt ✦ roadie ✦ stooge ✦ swamper

underpants beeveedees ✦ pissovers ✦ skivvies ✦ undies (Try also **jerk underpants up ✦ go out without underpants.**)

underpants in cleft atomic wedgie ✦ melvin ✦ wedgy

underpants (male) BVDs

underpants soil skid marks
undersexed man hard off
undershirt Try **sleeveless undershirt.**
understand capish ♦ cop onto sth ♦ dig ♦ (Do you) get my drift? ♦ Do I have to draw (you) a picture? ♦ Do I have to paint (you) a picture? ♦ feel so ♦ get it ♦ Get my drift? ♦ Get the message? ♦ Get the picture? ♦ gotcha ♦ grok ♦ I've been there. ♦ savvy ♦ wise up (to so/sth) ♦ You got that? (Try also **I understand ♦ too difficult to understand ♦ say something understandable ♦ same understanding.**)
understand motivation know where so is coming from
understand situation make the scene
understand someone's orientation know where so is coming from
understand you I smell you.
understandable clear as vodka
undertake get one's teeth into sth ♦ sink one's teeth into sth
underwear woolies
undeserved shouldn't happen to a dog
undesirable beasty ♦ for the birds ♦ grotty ♦ laine ♦ lame ♦ lane ♦ sad ♦ sucky
undesirable person no bargain ♦ no great shakes ♦ scuz(z) ♦ shitstick
undesirable thing no bargain ♦ no great shakes
undiluted clear ♦ naked ♦ raw ♦ short ♦ straight ♦ straight up
undiluted (alcohol) koshe ♦ kosher
undress shuck ♦ shuck down
unedited uncut
unembellished straight
unemotional person iceberg
unemployed at loose ends
uneventful dead
unfair heavy-handed ♦ No fair! ♦ not cricket ♦ sneaky (Try also **be unfair ♦ treat unfairly.**)
unfair blow low blow
unfair deal dirty deal
unfair tactics dirty pool
unfair treatment shaft ♦ a raw deal
unfashionable geek-chic ♦ low rent
unimportant dead
unimportant event blip
uninterested turned off
uninvited Try **attend uninvited.**
uninvited email spam
uninvited guest crasher
union pay scale
unique perception slant

unique perspective angle
unit crack
united Try **remain united.**
unjustified criticism bad rap
unkempt funky ♦ grubby ♦ phunky ♦ scruff(y) ♦ scuzzy
unknown (various) beats me ♦ dark horse ♦ four-oh-four ♦ gork
unlimited the sky's the limit
unlucky out of luck ♦ shit out of luck ♦ SOL
unmanageable out of pocket
unnamed person whatchamacallit ♦ whatsis ♦ whoozis ♦ whoozit
unneeded person fifth wheel ♦ spare tire
unoriginal warmed over
unorthodox not cricket
unplanned pickup
unpleasant bummer ♦ lo-res ♦ low-res ♦ rude
unpleasant person harsh toke ♦ slob ♦ stinker
unpleasant place hellhole
unpleasant thing harsh toke
unprepared half-cocked
unquestionably hands down
unrealistic out of it
unrecognized Try **remain unrecognized.**
unreliable flaky
unresponsive person cold fish
unrestricted no holds barred
unscrupulous sheisty
unseated viewer standee
unsmiling straight-faced
unsocial on the shelf
unstable punch-drunk ♦ punchy
unstressful event tea party
unsuccessful person hacker ♦ loser ♦ sucker
unsupported high and dry
unsympathetic hard-nosed
untipped stiffed
untroubled mellow
ununderstandable clear as mud ♦ over one's head
unusual person rare bird
unwanted object white elephant
unwelcome email meatloaf
up-and-about in action
upfront money Try **advance money.**
upright (person) straight up
uproar ruckus
upset (mod) (all) shook up ♦ cut up (about so/sth) ♦ illin' ♦ in a twit ♦ jacked ♦ jacked up ♦ jammed ♦ shook up ♦ slightly rattled ♦ tore (up) ♦ tore down ♦ torn (up) (Try also **get upset.**)

upset oneself work oneself up

upside down (various) tits up ♦ turn so upside down ♦ turn sth upside down

up-to-date hip ♦ switched on ♦ tuned in ♦ with it

up-to-date person swinger

urban Try **experience in urban life** ♦ **young urban professional.**

urban area asphalt jungle

urge (n) bug (Try also **sexual urge** ♦ **toilet urge** ♦ **urinary urge.**)

urge to stray seven-year itch

urgently in a big way ♦ like there was no tomorrow

urinal Try **portable urinal.**

urinal bucket gash bucket ♦ gutbucket

urinal (male) pisser ♦ vertical bathtub

urinary accident code yellow

urinary urge call of nature

urinate drain the dragon ♦ knock the dew off the lily ♦ pay the water bill ♦ piddle ♦ piss ♦ piss on so/sth ♦ pump ship ♦ shake the dew off the lily ♦ take a leak ♦ tee-tee ♦ tinkle ♦ whiz

urinate on do a number on sth

urination number one

urine piddle ♦ piss ♦ tea ♦ tee-tee ♦ tinkle

urine test piss quiz

URL loss linkrot

U.S. soldier yank

use all shoot one's wad ♦ wipe sth out

use amphetamine speed

use cocaine do a line ♦ go down the line ♦ powder one's nose ♦ scoop ♦ smell it up ♦ smell the stuff ♦ take it through the nose

use drugs binge ♦ do ♦ do dope ♦ do drugs ♦ do the drug thing ♦ dope up ♦ drop ♦ drop a bop ♦ drug ♦ fire a line ♦ fix ♦ get a fix ♦ get a gift ♦ get narkied ♦ get off (on sth) ♦ get straight ♦ get stupid ♦ get one's wings ♦ go down the line ♦ goof ♦ horn ♦ party ♦ put oneself straight ♦ use ♦ zoom

use everything pull out all the stops

use heroin goof

use marijuana talk to Herb and Al

use methamphetamine speed

use peyote shroom

use radar take pictures

use something make with the sth

useless dead

useless computer boat anchor

useless people deadwood

user Try **amphetamine user** ♦ **cocaine crystal user** ♦ **cocaine user** ♦ **drug user** ♦

dynamite user ♦ **hashish user** ♦ **help drug user** ♦ **human computer user** ♦ **LSD user** ♦ **methamphetamine user.**

user of obscene vocabulary potty mouth ♦ sewermouth

using diary online blogging

using drugs on the street ♦ plugged in

using marijuana on the beam

using the telephone on the wires

usury juice racket

utilize everything go the limit

utter go

vacation getaway

vacation avoidance presenteeism

vacillate yoyo

vacuum (n) vac

vacuum (v) vac

vagina cocksocket ♦ cooch ♦ cunt ♦ pussy ♦ vag ♦ vizzle

vaginal fart cunt fart ♦ pussy fart

vaginal secretion cream

vagrancy vag

vagrant bum ♦ vag

vague word fuzzword

vain Try **talk in vain.**

Valium blue ♦ vals

value bang for the buck ♦ That ain't hay! ♦ YGWYPF (Try also **bet value** ♦ **decrease in value** ♦ **get value.**)

van sin-bin (Try also **police van.**)

vandalize trash

variety package

vegetable veg ♦ veggy

vegetarian veggy

vegetate veg (out)

vehicle Try **fast vehicle** ♦ **party behind vehicle (n)** ♦ **party behind vehicle (v)** ♦ **recreational vehicle** ♦ **small vehicle.**

vein Try **jugular vein.**

veins ruined burned out

Velcro cros

very majorly ♦ massively ♦ mucho ♦ pretty ♦ so ♦ vizzle

very fast lickety-split

very important person VIP

very much good and sth ♦ in a big way ♦ like crazy ♦ mondo ♦ so bad one can taste it

very soon in a New York minute

very well like nobody's business

vessel pot

vest Try **bullet-proof vest** ♦ **wearing vest.**

veteran vet

veterinarian vet

vibrations vibes

vice Try **convert to vice.**
vice president veep
victim dupe ♦ easy mark ♦ fall guy ♦ john ♦ mark ♦ patsy ♦ pigeon ♦ setup ♦ soft touch ♦ sucker ♦ vic (Try also **list of victims.**)
victimize sucker ♦ yench
victimized vicked
victor grave-dancer
video vid
video jockey veejay ♦ video jock ♦ VJ
video portion clip
viewer Try **standing viewer ♦ unseated viewer.**
vigor zip
vigorous go-go ♦ kick-ass ♦ peppy ♦ rough and ready (Try also **act vigorous ♦ active.**)
village burg
villain heavy ♦ tough guy
vintage old skool
vinyl record licorice pizza
violence rough stuff
violent graphic
virile butch ♦ hairy-ass(ed) ♦ macho ♦ studly
virile man caveman ♦ hustler ♦ macho ♦ tiger
vision Try **deceptive vision.**
visiting various pools pool-hopping
visitor visiting fireman
vitality spizzerinktum
vivacious (live) wire
vocabulary lingo (Try also **pardon my vocabulary ♦ user of obscene vocabulary.**)
vodka potato soup ♦ spud
voice set of pipes
Volkswagen beetle
volleyball V-ball
volume Try **raise volume.**
voluminous Try **send voluminous email.**
volunteer (v) pitch in (and help) ♦ step up to the plate
vomit (n) barf ♦ cheese ♦ earp ♦ hurl ♦ liquid laugh ♦ lung-butter ♦ puke ♦ Technicolor yawn ♦ uke ♦ upchuck ♦ urp ♦ york ♦ yuke
vomit (v) air one's belly ♦ barf ♦ bison ♦ blow (one's) cookies ♦ blow (one's) lunch ♦ blow beets ♦ blow chow ♦ blow chunks ♦ blow grits ♦ blow lunch ♦ blow one's doughnuts ♦ blow one's groceries ♦ boag ♦ boff ♦ boot ♦ bring sth up ♦ buick ♦ cack ♦ call earl ♦ call hughie ♦ call ralph ♦ call ruth ♦ cat ♦ cheese ♦ chew the cheese ♦ chuck ♦ chuck a dummy ♦ chuck up ♦ chunk ♦ cry hughie ♦ cry ralph ♦ cry ruth ♦ drain the bilge ♦ drive the big bus ♦ drive the porcelain bus ♦ drop one's cookies ♦ duke ♦ dump ♦ dump one's load ♦ earl ♦ earp ♦ fetch up ♦ flash the hash ♦ fling up ♦ heave ♦ honk ♦ hork ♦ hug the porcelain god(dess) ♦ hug the throne ♦ hughie ♦ hurl ♦ kack ♦ kak ♦ kiss the porcelain god ♦ laugh at the carpet ♦ launch (one's lunch) ♦ lose it ♦ lose one's doughnuts ♦ lose one's lunch ♦ pray to the enamel god ♦ pray to the porcelain god ♦ puke ♦ pump ship ♦ ralph ♦ ralph sth up ♦ reverse gears ♦ ride the porcelain bus ♦ rolf ♦ ruth ♦ sell buicks ♦ shoot the cat ♦ shoot the works ♦ shoot one's breakfast ♦ shoot one's cookies ♦ shoot one's supper ♦ sick (up) ♦ skin a goat ♦ sling the cat ♦ snap one's cookies ♦ spew ♦ spew one's guts (out) ♦ talk on the big white phone ♦ talk to earl ♦ throw a map ♦ throw a Technicolor yawn ♦ throw up one's toenails ♦ throw one's cookies ♦ throw one's voice ♦ toss ♦ toss one's cookies ♦ toss one's lunch ♦ toss one's tacos ♦ uke ♦ upchuck ♦ urp ♦ vurp ♦ woof ♦ woof cookies ♦ worship the porcelain god(dess) ♦ yak ♦ yank ♦ yap ♦ yarf ♦ york ♦ yuke ♦ zuke
vomit bag barf bag
vomiting and unconscious vomatose
vote against blackball
vulgar gross ♦ raw
vulnerable on the chopping block
vulnerable to scrutiny on the hot seat
vulva camel toes ♦ cunt
vulval cleft crack
wagon Try **sewage wagon.**
waist fat (love) handles ♦ spare tire
wait Hold the phone! ♦ hold one's horses ♦ marinate ♦ mark time
wait calmly Keep your pants on! ♦ Keep your shirt on!
wait nervously twiddle one's thumbs
waiter hash-slinger
waiting doggo
waitress hash-slinger
walk foot it ♦ hoof it
walk about stretch one's legs
walk around galumph (around)
walk away walk
walk brave stand tall
walk cautiously walk on eggs ♦ walk on thin ice
walk out walk
walk proudly strut one's stuff
walk somewhere ankle ♦ shank it
walking hoofing (Try also **injured person walking about ♦ start walking.**)
Wall Street the street

wander around bum around ♦ kick around ♦ knock around

want to wanna

want to be wannabe

want to fight (various) Oh, yeah? ♦ Wanna make sumpin' of it? ♦ Want to make something of it? ♦ (You) want a piece of me? ♦ Want a piece of me?

want to leave group want out

wanted Try **list of things wanted.**

wanted by police hot

war Try **supporter of war.**

war of insults flame-war

warning Behind you! ♦ check your six ♦ Heads up! ♦ on your six

wash dishes bust (some) suds

waste (v) blow sth ♦ piss sth away (Try also **time waster.**)

waste effort boil the ocean ♦ milk a duck ♦ nail Jell-O to a cross ♦ nail Jell-O to a tree ♦ nail Jell-O to the wall ♦ piss in the wind ♦ plowing water

waste of time circle-jerk ♦ fun and games

waste time beat off ♦ blow off ♦ dick around ♦ dork off ♦ fake off ♦ fart around ♦ fart off ♦ fiddle-fart ♦ fuck off ♦ futz around ♦ goof around ♦ goof off ♦ hack around ♦ hang (around) ♦ horse around ♦ jack around ♦ jerk around ♦ kick around ♦ knock around ♦ mark time ♦ mess about (with so) ♦ mess around (with so) ♦ monkey-fart ♦ piddle ♦ piddle (around) ♦ piss around ♦ play around (with so) ♦ putz around ♦ rat around ♦ scam ♦ screw around ♦ slough (off) ♦ sluff (off) ♦ spaz around ♦ spin one's wheels

wastebasket circular file ♦ file thirteen ♦ shitcan

wasted down the drain ♦ out the window

watch stake so/sth out ♦ (Try also **construction watcher ♦ woman watcher ♦ owl watching event.**)

watch (n) tick-tock ♦ ticker

watch for be on the look out ♦ BOLO

water the drink

watermelon African golf ball ♦ African grape

wave Try **big wave ♦ find perfect wave ♦ in a wave.**

waver flip-flop

way Try **best way ♦ right way.**

way it is the name of the game ♦ the way it plays

weak drippy ♦ namby-pamby ♦ wimpy (Try also **elimination of weak element.**)

weak beer three point two ♦ three-two

weak man limpdick ♦ milquetoast

weak person dishrag ♦ doormat ♦ gutless wonder ♦ puppy ♦ wuss(y)

weakling cream puff

wealth fat city ♦ You can't take it with you.

wealthy filthy rich ♦ flush ♦ has more money than God ♦ in the chips ♦ loaded ♦ lousy with so/sth ♦ stinking rich ♦ well-fixed ♦ well-heeled (Try also **be wealthy.**)

wealthy person fat-cat ♦ filthy rich ♦ moneybags

wealthy travelers jet-set(ters)

weapon wep (Try also **nuclear weapon.**)

wear Try **braces wearer ♦ glasses wearer ♦ man wearing women's clothing.**

wear out peter out ♦ poop out

wearing diamonds iced out ♦ living chilly

wearing holster strapped

wearing vest goosed

weather Try **cold weather.**

Web Try **browse Web ♦ World Wide Web.**

wedding Try **forced wedding.**

weed wizzle

weights Try **lift weights.**

weird kinky ♦ mondo bizarro ♦ unearthly

weird person crackpot ♦ creep ♦ skeezer

welcome Welcome to the club. ♦ welk ♦ WTTC

welcome thing money from home

well like a million (dollars)

well built built like a brick shithouse

well buttocked fat-ass(ed)

well cooked done to a turn

well done (That's the) way to go! ♦ That's the stuff! ♦ That's the ticket! ♦ That-a-boy! ♦ There you go. ♦ Way to go! ♦ You('re) the man!

well worn through the mill

well-behaved person square

well-built man superjock

well-dressed clean ♦ dap ♦ dressed to kill ♦ dressed to the nines ♦ dressed to the teeth ♦ fitted ♦ g'ed up ♦ gussied up ♦ in fine feather ♦ laid out ♦ sharp ♦ snappy ♦ stunting ♦ tabbed

well-supplied fat

west coast left coast

Western movie horse opera ♦ oater ♦ shoot 'em up

what (various) How does that grab you? ♦ Say what? ♦ What (in) the devil? ♦ What (in) the fucking hell! ♦ What (in) the hell? ♦ What in (the) Sam Hill? ♦ What in Sam Hill? ♦ What the deuce? ♦ What the devil? ♦ What the fucking hell! ♦ What the heck! ♦ What the hell?

what else? or what?

what is answer What do you say?

what is benefit What's in it for me? ♦ WIIFM

what is happening What gives? ♦ What is it? ♦ What's buzzin' (cousin)? ♦ What's coming off? ♦ What's cooking? ♦ What's going down? ♦ What's going on? ♦ What's happ(ening)? ♦ What's poppin' ♦ What's the deal? ♦ What's the dilly ♦ What's the scam? ♦ What's up doc? ♦ What's up, G? ♦ What's up?

what is needed where it's at

what is problem What's your damage?

what is smell Somebody died in here! ♦ Who died in here?

what is wrong Now what? ♦ What's eating so? ♦ What's with so/sth?

wheels Try **spin wheels.**

when computer operates up time

when the time comes if push comes to shove

when there is trouble when the shit hits the fan

where (various) Where in (the) Sam Hill? ♦ Where in the world? ♦ Where on (God's green) earth? ♦ Where on earth? ♦ where the action is ♦ Where the Sam Hill? ♦ Where's the fire? ♦ Your place or mine?

while in motion on the fly

while moving on the run

while one is in charge on so's watch

whip (v) fishtail

whiskers (face) fungus ♦ fungus

whiskey dew ♦ firewater (Try also **scotch whiskey.**)

white Try **have white hair ♦ worthless white people ♦ American Indian as white ♦ Asian American as white ♦ black as white ♦ black dates white.**

white gangster whankster

white man Charles ♦ chuck ♦ honk ♦ honky ♦ hunky ♦ jeff ♦ junk

white person blanco ♦ peckerwood ♦ pig ♦ saltine ♦ silk ♦ vanilla ♦ WASP ♦ whigga ♦ wood (Try also **American Indian as white ♦ Asian American as white ♦ black as white ♦ black dates white ♦ white gangster ♦ white man ♦ white-like ♦ worthless white people.**)

white-like waspish

who Who (in) the devil? ♦ Who (in) the hell? ♦ Who the deuce? ♦ Who the devil? ♦ Who the hell?

who is boss Who's your daddy?

who is following Who's your friend?

who says Says me! ♦ Says who? ♦ Sez me! ♦ Sez who?

whore garden tool ♦ ho ♦ hoe

whore stroll ho stro

wicked poison ♦ wicky

wide Try **broad or wide.**

widely effective action clean sweep

widely known on the street

wiener tube steak

wife old lady ♦ old woman ♦ one's ball and chain ♦ one's better half

WiFi Try **marking WiFi.**

wig rug ♦ sky rug

wiggle out squirrel out of sth

wiggly mark squiggle

wild frantic ♦ hairy-ass(ed) ♦ hellacious ♦ hog-wild ♦ slam-bang

wild guess long shot ♦ shot in the dark ♦ SWAG

wild party freak (out) ♦ rave

wildly Try **guess wildly.**

willing Try **sexually willing person ♦ sexually willing.**

willingness game

win ace out ♦ beat so/sth out ♦ come out on top ♦ hit the jackpot

win news race scoop

wind hawk ♦ Mr. Hawkins (Try also **break wind ♦ breaking of wind.**)

windows Try **open windows.**

windsock Try **limp windsock.**

wine berries ♦ grape(s) ♦ grapes of wrath ♦ ink ♦ jug wine ♦ juice ♦ mickey ♦ plonk ♦ pluck ♦ plug ♦ pop wine ♦ schoolboy Scotch ♦ smash ♦ wino (Try also **drink wine.**)

winner ass-kicker ♦ butt-kicker (Try also **easy winner ♦ likely winner.**)

winning situation win-win ♦ win-win-win

Wisconsinite cheesehead

wish Try **you wish.**

wish to harm have a hard-on for so

wishful airy-fairy

with large breasts well-hung

with large genitals (male) hung ♦ hung like a bull ♦ well-hung

with large penis well-hung

with love sealed with a kiss

withdraw back up ♦ bail (out) ♦ drop out ♦ fink out (on so/sth) ♦ hang up ♦ punk out ♦ rat out ♦ wimp out (of sth) (Try also **suffering withdrawal ♦ person who withdrew.**)

withhold testimony take the fifth
without condom bareback
without ice on the rocks ♦ straight up
without problems without a hitch
without thought knee-jerk
withstand blows take it on the chin ♦ take it on the nose
withstand criticism take it on the chin ♦ take it on the nose
witless soft in the head
witless person twit
woman ankle ♦ betty ♦ bird ♦ broad ♦ chick ♦ chickster ♦ dudette ♦ girl ♦ mink ♦ number ♦ pussycat ♦ quail ♦ skirt ♦ twist (Try also **cold woman ♦ crying woman ♦ curvaceous woman ♦ dull woman ♦ fat woman ♦ gangster woman ♦ giddy woman ♦ good looking woman ♦ honest woman ♦ loose woman ♦ masculine woman ♦ obnoxious woman ♦ plain woman ♦ pregnant woman ♦ sexy woman ♦ shapely woman ♦ sloppy woman ♦ stupid woman ♦ tall woman ♦ ugly woman ♦ man wearing women's clothing ♦ pick up women ♦ seek women.**)
woman as sex ass ♦ beaver ♦ bush ♦ cooch ♦ crack ♦ cunt ♦ fuck buddy ♦ fuck puppet ♦ grouse ♦ hunk of ass ♦ hunk of tail ♦ lay ♦ meat ♦ nookie ♦ nooky ♦ piece ♦ piece of ass ♦ piece of snatch ♦ piece of tail ♦ pussy ♦ snatch
woman chaser big-time operator
woman lover cuddle bunny
woman on display cheesecake
woman watcher bird watcher
woman's body chassis ♦ classy-chassis
woman's liberation supporter libber
wonderful out of this world
wooden Try **person with wooden leg.**
word wizzle (Try also **last word ♦ vague word ♦ learn words.**)
work bread and butter ♦ daily grind ♦ elbow-grease (Try also **assign work internally ♦ avoid work ♦ hard work ♦ person obsessed with work ♦ physical work ♦ return to work ♦ short workday ♦ desk worker ♦ fellow worker ♦ obsessive worker ♦ sewer worker ♦ nonproductive workers ♦ night-working person ♦ stop working ♦ inner workings ♦ bad workplace.**)
work day nine-to-five
work hard break one's balls to do sth ♦ break so's balls ♦ beat one's brains out (to do sth) ♦ beat so's brains out ♦ piss blood ♦ slave away (at sth) ♦ split a gut ♦ sweat blood ♦ work one's ass off ♦ work one's buns off ♦ work one's butt off ♦ work one's tail off ♦ work oneself (up) into a lather
work in secret go underground
work into something get a toehold
work out pan out
work out all right come out in the wash
work second job moonlight
work time game time
work toward buck for sth
worker hardhat
working all night all-nighter
working man working stiff
world Try **know the real world ♦ real world.**
World Wide Web dub-dub-dub ♦ dubya-dubya-dubya
worn beat up ♦ seen better days (Try also **well worn.**)
worn out beat ♦ crapped (out)
worrier worry wart
worry (n) Try **free from worry.**
worry (v) eat ♦ eat one's heart out ♦ stew ♦ sweat ♦ sweat bullets ♦ sweat sth out (Try also **not worry.**)
worst future worst-case scenario
worth Try **sight worth looking at ♦ sight worth seeing ♦ thing worth keeping.**
worthless chicken shit ♦ cotton-picking ♦ diddly-shit ♦ good-for-nothing ♦ gronk ♦ motherfucking ♦ no-good ♦ not worth a damn ♦ not worth a plugged nickel ♦ not worth beans ♦ pissant ♦ pissing ♦ sorry-ass(ed) (Try also **list of worthless people ♦ worthless white people.**)
worthless checks wallpaper
worthless man bug-fucker ♦ cocksucker ♦ numbnuts ♦ pond scum
worthless matter dust
worthless person blob ♦ chopped liver ♦ clinker ♦ clunker ♦ cookie pusher ♦ dirt ♦ dirtbag ♦ good-for-nothing ♦ jack-shit ♦ jerk ♦ lightweight ♦ little shit ♦ lost cause ♦ low rent ♦ no-good ♦ no-goodnik ♦ pile of shit ♦ pissant ♦ trash ♦ turd ♦ turd face ♦ wipe out ♦ zero ♦ zip ♦ zob
worthless thing boat anchor ♦ clunker ♦ dog ♦ flying-fuck ♦ lost cause ♦ piece ♦ pile of shit
worthless white people caucasian waste
would not do would not be seen dead
wow (various exclamations) Boy howdy! ♦ Boy! ♦ cool ♦ gee ♦ Good golly, Miss Molly! ♦ Good heavens! ♦ gravy ♦ hairball ♦ Hell's

bells (and buckets of blood)! ♦ Holy cow! ♦ Holy mackerel! ♦ Holy moley! ♦ Hot diggety (dog)! ♦ Hot dog! ♦ Hot ziggety! ♦ ick ♦ If that don't fuck all! ♦ Jeepers(-creepers)! ♦ Lord love a duck! ♦ man ♦ neat ♦ neato (canito) ♦ Of all the nerve! ♦ Oh, boy! ♦ Schwing! ♦ Shazzam! ♦ Snap! ♦ son of a gun ♦ What (a) nerve! ♦ wow ♦ Ye gods! ♦ zap ♦ Zoit! ♦ zowie

wreck (n) crack up ♦ wipe out (Try also **nervous wreck.**)

wreck (v) fuck sth up ♦ wash out ♦ rack sth up

wreck car wrap one's car around sth

wrecked banjaxed ♦ totalled

wrestler grunt

write bad check bounce ♦ kite

write check cut a check

write program hack

write quickly knock sth out

writer hack ♦ ink slinger

wrong 404 ♦ all wet ♦ faulty ♦ way off (base) ♦ wrongo ♦ You've got another think coming. (Try also **talk to wrong person ♦ be wrong ♦ what is wrong.**)

WWW dub-dub-dub ♦ dubya-dubya-dubya

Xerox, Inc. rocks

year double six

yell yell one's guts out ♦ yell one's head off

yes Bingo! ♦ cas ♦ Damn straight! ♦ Fucking A! ♦ hoo-ah ♦ okey-dokey ♦ pository ♦ ten-four ♦ way ♦ Way! ♦ yeah ♦ Yeah, right. ♦ yep ♦ Yes! ♦ yizzle ♦ You bet your sweet patoot(ie)! ♦ You bet. ♦ You betcha! (Try also **okay.**)

yes man company man

yogurt Try **frozen yogurt.**

you ya ♦ yizzle

you are as guilty Look who's talking!

you are great Love you!

you are the boss You're the doctor.

you get it You asked for it!

you will need luck Lots of luck!

you will suffer It's your funeral!

you wish (Don't) you wish!

young couple dink

young man blade

young people now generation

young person spring chicken

young teenager teenybopper

young urban professional yuppie ♦ yuppy

youth juvie ♦ punk ♦ punk kid (Try also **hopeless youth ♦ talented youth.**)

yummy nummy

zero zotz

zero score goose egg

zest zowie

zipper Try **check zipper.**

Zippo zizzle

zone Try **sunny zone.**